Mathematics

CBSE Class 10

Focused Theory | Practice Exercises | Sample Papers & Boards Papers

Recommended by Teachers
Trusted by Toppers

Mathematics

CBSE Class 10

Focused Theory | Practice Exercises | Sample Papers & Boards Papers

Author
Er. Prem Kumar

Co-authors
Jitender Gupta, Brijesh Dwivedi

arihant
SUCCESS AND NOTHING LESS

ARIHANT PRAKASHAN

(School Division Series)

卐 *ADMINISTRATIVE & PRODUCTION OFFICES*

Regd. Office

'Ramchhaya' 4577/15, Agarwal Road, Darya Ganj, New Delhi -110002
Tele: 011- 47630600, 43518550; Fax: 011- 23280316

卐 *Head Office*

Kalindi, TP Nagar, Meerut (UP) - 250002, Tel: 0121-7156203, 7156204

卐 *SALES & SUPPORT OFFICES*

Agra, Ahmedabad, Bengaluru, Bareilly, Chennai, Delhi, Guwahati, Hyderabad, Jaipur, Jhansi, Kolkata, Lucknow, Nagpur & Pune.

PO No. : TXT-59-T064340-04-25

Published By Arihant Publications (India) Ltd.

For further information about the books published by Arihant, log on to www.arihantbooks.com or e-mail at info@arihantbooks.com

Follow us on 

卐 *PRICE* ₹ 515.00

PRODUCTION TEAM

Publishing Managers	*Cover Designer*	*Inner Designer*
Mahendra Singh Rawat & Keshav Mohan	Salman Shaikh	Ankit Tyagi
Project Head	*Page Layouting*	*Proof Reader*
Ashwani	Mayank Saini	Mukul Kaushik

Index *cum* Study Planner

One Book- Endless Features

to Help you Succeed

Chapter Intro

A quick information about the coverage of the chapter to explain students about what they are going to study.

CHAPTER 1

Real Numbers

In the earlier classes, we initiated the study of real numbers. Here, we continue our discussion on real numbers and study some properties of real numbers. We begin with very important properties of positive integers namely the fundamental theorem of arithmetic.

TOPIC 01 Fundamental Theorem of Arithmetic

Factors of a Number

If a number divides another number exactly (without leaving any remainder), then the number which divides, is called a **factor** of the number that has been divided.
e.g. 1, 2, 3, 6, 12 are the factors of 24.

Factor Tree

A chain of factors which is represented in the form of a tree, called **factor tree.**

e.g. Factors of 24 by factor tree are given as

Thus, factors of 24 as a product of powers of prime

$$= 2 \times 2 \times 2 \times 3 = 2^3 \times 3$$

On dividing 1365 by 3, we get the quotient 455.

On dividing 455 by 5, we get the quotient 91 and on dividing 91 by 7, we get the quotient 13.

Hence, the complete factor tree, obtained by joining all the above trees, is

Thus, 4095 as a product of primes $= 3 \times 3 \times 5 \times 7 \times 13$

Complete Theory

Each chapter has Complete, Easy to Understand and Simplified theory covering latest syllabus and rationalized NCERT Textbook.

Example 2. Explain why $(7 \times 11 \times 13 + 2 \times 11)$ is not a prime number? CBSE 2024 (Basic)

Sol. Simplify the given expression

$$7 \times 11 \times 13 + 2 \times 11 = 1001 + 22 = 1023$$

Prime factorisation of $1023 = 3 \times 11 \times 31$

Thus, 1023 is divisible by 3, 11 and 31.

Since, a prime number is a natural number greater than 1 that has no positive divisors other than 1 and itself. Therefore, 1023 is not a prime number as it has other divisor other than 1 and itself.

Hence, $(7 \times 11 \times 13 + 2 \times 11)$ is not a prime number.

Solved Examples

Solved Examples have been solved in step-by-step manner, so that students can learn the problem solving process completely.

Try These 1.1

1. Complete the following factor tree by finding the unknown variables.

(i) (ii)

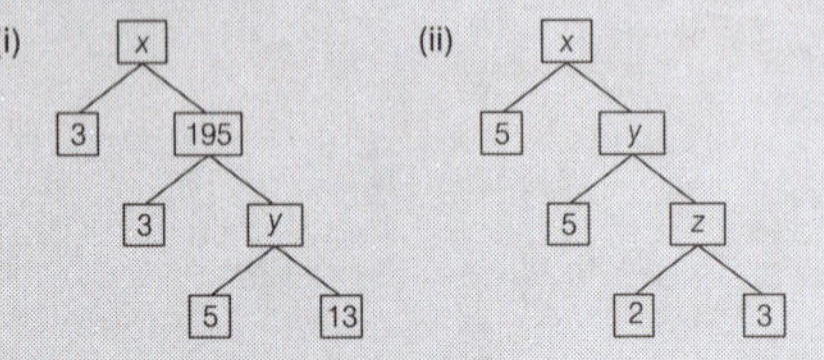

2. Factorise the following numbers through the factor tree.

(i) 420	(ii) 468
(iii) 308	(iv) 528
(v) 9072	(vi) 19530

Try These

A set of Questions given after topic end, helps students to remain connected with topic while studying. They can instantly assess themselves for their understanding.

One Book- Endless Features

to Help you Succeed

Illustrative Figures

To make the concepts completely visible, illustrative diagrams have been given at various place.

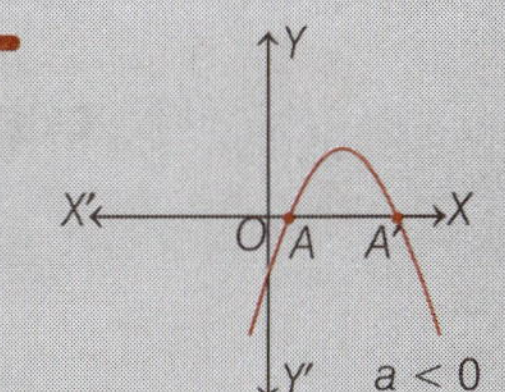

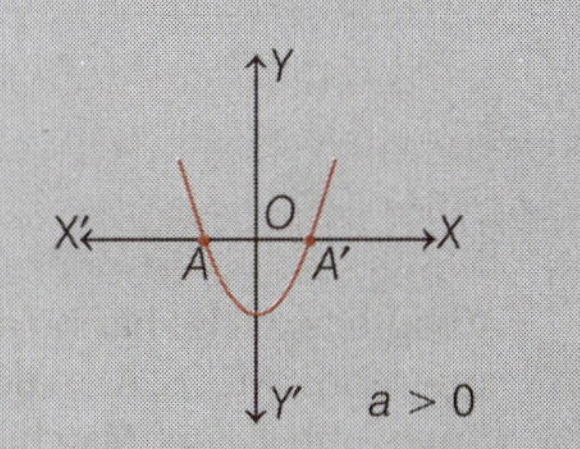

13. $p(x) = ax^2 - 8x + 3$, where a is a non-zero real number. One zero of $p(x)$ is 3 times the other zero.

(i) Find the value of a. Show your work.

(ii) What is the shape of the graph of $p(x)$? Give a reason for your answer. **Competency Based Question**

17. If the zeroes of the cubic polynomial $x^3 - 6x^2 + 3x + 10$ are of the form $a, a + b$ and $a + 2b$ for some real numbers a and b, then find the values of a and b. **NCERT Exemplar**

18. Can the quadratic polynomial $x^2 + kx + k$ have equal zeroes for some odd integer $k > 1$? **NCERT Exemplar**

NCERT Exemplar

Each chapter has selected problems from NCERT Exemplar, the best problem books for School/Board Exams.

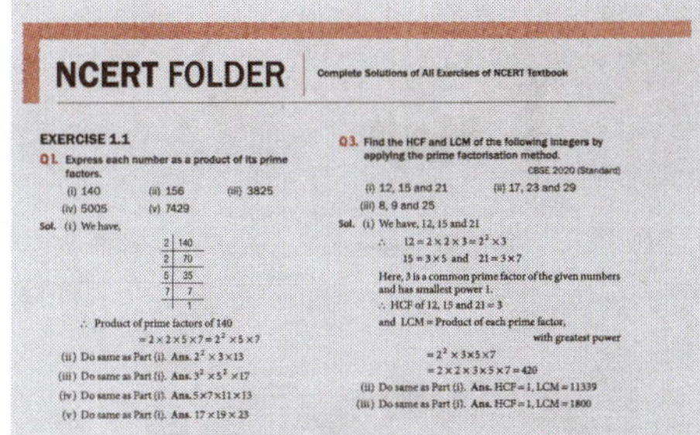

NCERT FOLDER | Complete Solutions of All Exercises of NCERT Textbook

EXERCISE 1.1

Q1. Express each number as a product of its prime factors.

(i) 140 (ii) 156 (iii) 3825 (iv) 5005 (v) 7429

Sol. (i) We have,

2	140
2	70
5	35
7	7
	1

$\therefore$ Product of prime factors of 140

$= 2 \times 2 \times 5 \times 7 = 2^2 \times 5 \times 7$

(ii) Do same as Part (i). **Ans.** $2^2 \times 3 \times 13$

(iii) Do same as Part (i). **Ans.** $3^2 \times 5^2 \times 17$

(iv) Do same as Part (i). **Ans.** $5 \times 7 \times 11 \times 13$

(v) Do same as Part (i). **Ans.** $17 \times 19 \times 23$

Q3. Find the HCF and LCM of the following integers by applying the prime factorisation method. CBSE 2020 (Standard)

(i) 12, 15 and 21 (ii) 17, 23 and 29 (iii) 8, 9 and 25

Sol. (i) We have, 12, 15 and 21

$\therefore$ $12 = 2 \times 2 \times 3 = 2^2 \times 3$

$15 = 3 \times 5$ and $21 = 3 \times 7$

Here, 3 is a common prime factor of the given numbers and has smallest power 1.

$\therefore$ HCF of 12, 15 and 21 = 3

and LCM = Product of each prime factor, with greatest power

$= 2^2 \times 3 \times 5 \times 7$

$= 2 \times 2 \times 3 \times 5 \times 7 = 420$

(ii) Do same as Part (i). **Ans.** HCF = 1, LCM = 11339

(iii) Do same as Part (i). **Ans.** HCF = 1, LCM = 1800

NCERT Folder

Complete explanations of all the questions of NCERT Exercises.

13. $p(x) = ax^2 - 8x + 3$, where a is a non-zero re

One zero of $p(x)$ is 3 times the other zero.

(i) Find the value of a. Show your work.

(ii) What is the shape of the graph of $p(x)$? Give a reason for your answer. **Competency Based Question**

17. If the zeroes of the cubic polynomial $x^3 - 6x^2 + 3x + 10$ are of the form $a, a + b$ and $a + 2b$ for some real numbers a and b, then find the values of a and b. **NCERT Exemplar**

18. Can the quadratic polynomial $x^2 + kx + k$ have equal zeroes for some odd integer $k > 1$? **NCERT Exemplar**

Competency based Questions

Each chapter has sufficient number of Competency based Questions of all types.

One Book- Endless Features

to Help you Succeed

Chapter exercise having all types of questions; MCQs, Assertion-Reason, True-False, Fillers, Matching, Case based, VSA, SA, LA.

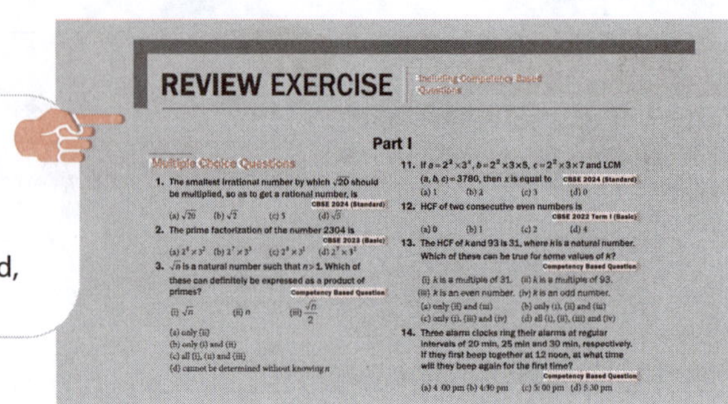

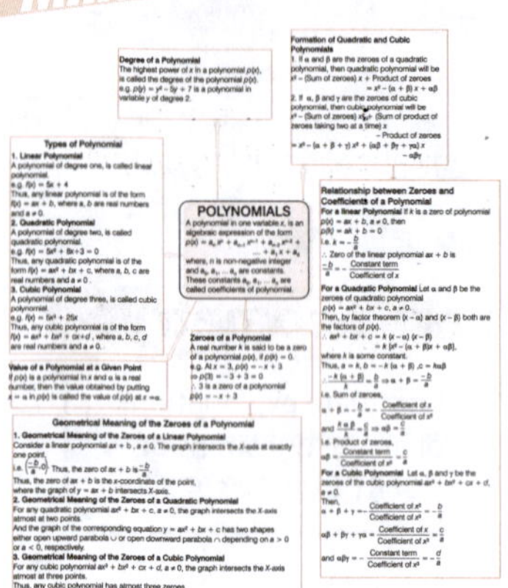

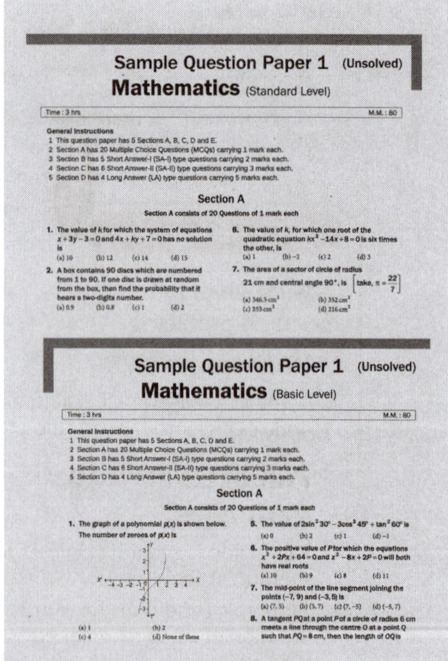

Mind Map

A quick revision visual tool for the complete chapter.

Sample Question Papers

There are 2 Sample Question Papers (2 Basic Level and 2 Standard Level) at the end. All these Sample Questions Papers are exactly prepared on the latest syllabus & pattern of examination.

Latest Course *Structure*

Time: 3 Hrs | Total Marks : 80

Units	Unit Name	Marks
I	Number Systems	06
II	Algebra	20
III	Coordinate Geometry	06
IV	Geometry	15
V	Trigonometry	12
VI	Mensuration	10
VII	Statistics & Probability	11
	Total	**80**

UNIT I : Number Systems

1. Real Numbers

Fundamental Theorem of Arithmetic - statements after reviewing work done earlier and after illustrating and motivating through examples, Proofs of irrationality of $\sqrt{2}$, $\sqrt{3}$, $\sqrt{5}$.

UNIT II : Algebra

1. Polynomials

Zeros of a polynomial. Relationship between zeros and coefficients of quadratic polynomials.

2. Pair of Linear Equations in Two Variables

Pair of linear equations in two variables and graphical method of their solution, consistency/inconsistency.

Algebraic conditions for number of solutions. Solution of a pair of linear equations in two variables algebraically - by substitution, by elimination. Simple situational problems.

3. Quadratic Equations

Standard form of a quadratic equation $ax^2 + bx + c = 0$, $(a ^1 0)$. Solutions of quadratic equations (only real roots) by factorization, and by using quadratic formula. Relationship between discriminant and nature of roots.

Situational problems based on quadratic equations related to day-to-day activities to be incorporated.

4. Arithmetic Progressions

Motivation for studying Arithmetic Progression Derivation of the *n*th term and sum of the first *n* terms of AP and their application in solving daily life problems.

UNIT III : Coordinate Geometry

1. Coordinate Geometry

Review : Concepts of coordinate geometry, graphs of linear equations. Distance formula. Section formula (internal division).

UNIT IV : Geometry

1. Triangles

Definitions, examples, counter examples of similar triangles.

I. (Prove) If a line is drawn parallel to one side of a triangle to intersect the other two sides in distinct points, the other two sides are divided in the same ratio.

II. (Motivate) If a line divides two sides of a triangle in the same ratio, then the line is parallel to the third side.

III. (Motivate) If in two triangles, the corresponding angles are equal, their corresponding sides are proportional and the triangles are similar.

IV. (Motivate) If the corresponding sides of two triangles are proportional, their corresponding angles are equal and the two triangles are similar.

V. (Motivate) If one angle of a triangle is equal to one angle of another triangle and the sides including these angles are proportional, two triangles are similar.

2. Circles

Tangents to a circle at point of contact.

I. (Prove) The tangent at any point of a circle is perpendicular to the radius through the point of contact.

II. (Prove) The lengths of tangents drawn from an external point to circle are equal.

UNIT V : Trigonometry

1. Introduction to Trigonometry

Trigonometric ratios of an acute angle of a right angled triangle. Proof of their existence (well-defined); motivate the ratios, whichever are defined at 0° and 90°. Values of the trigonometric ratios of 30°, 45° and 60°. Relationships between the ratios.

2. Trigonometric Identities

Proof and applications of the identity $\sin^2 A + \cos^2 A = 1$. Only simple identities to be given.

3. Heights and Distances : Angle of Elevation, Angle of Depression

Simple problems on heights and distances. Problems should not involve more than two right triangles. Angles of elevation/depression should be only 30°, 45° and 60°.

UNIT VI : Mensuration

1. Areas Related to Circles

Area of sectors and segments of a circle. Problems based on areas and perimeter /circumference of the above solid plane figures. (In calculating area of segment of a circle, problems should be restricted to central angle of 60°, 90° and 120° only.

2. Surface Areas and Volumes

I. Surface areas and volumes of combinations of any two of the following: cubes, cuboids, spheres, hemispheres and right circular cylinders/cones.

UNIT VII : Statistics and Probability

1. Statistics

Mean, median and mode of grouped data (bimodal situation to be avoided).

2. Probability

Classical definition of probability. Simple problems on finding the probability of an event.

CHAPTER 1

Real Numbers

In the earlier classes, we initiated the study of real numbers. Here, we will continue our discussion on real numbers and study some properties of real numbers. We begin with very important properties of positive integers namely the fundamental theorem of arithmetic.

TOPIC 01 Fundamental Theorem of Arithmetic

Factors of a Number

If a number divides another number exactly (without leaving any remainder), then the number which divides, is called a **factor** of the number that has been divided.
e.g. 1, 2, 3, 6, 12 are the factors of 24.

Factor Tree

A chain of factors which is represented in the form of a tree, called **factor tree.**

e.g. Factors of 24 by factor tree are given as

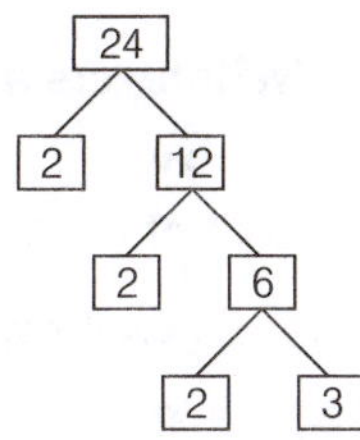

Thus, factors of 24 as a product of powers of prime

$$=2\times2\times2\times3=2^3\times3$$

Example 1. **Factorise the number 4095 using factor tree.**

Sol. On dividing 4095 by 3, we get the quotient 1365.

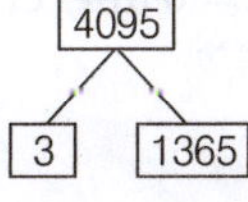

On dividing 1365 by 3, we get the quotient 455.

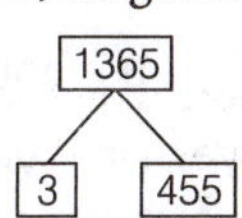

On dividing 455 by 5, we get the quotient 91 and on dividing 91 by 7, we get the quotient 13.

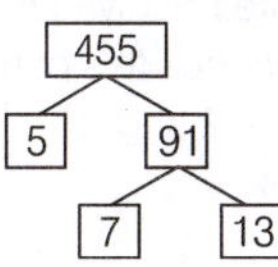

Hence, the complete factor tree, obtained by joining all the above trees, is

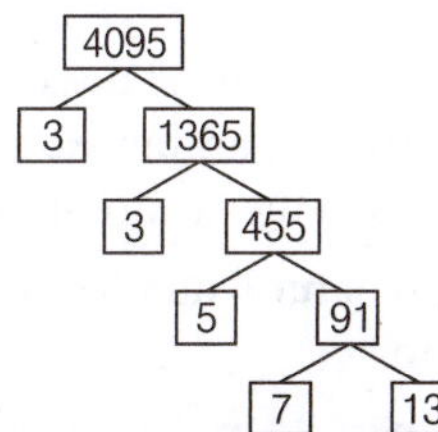

Thus, 4095 as a product of primes $=3\times3\times5\times7\times13$

Fundamental Theorem of Arithmetic

According to the fundamental theorem of arithmetic, every composite number can be written (factorised) as the product of primes and this factorisation is unique, apart from the order in which the prime factors occur.

$\therefore$ Composite number = Product of prime numbers

e.g. 230 can be written as $2 \times 5 \times 23$ or $23 \times 5 \times 2$, where 2, 5 and 23 are prime numbers.

2	230
5	115
23	23
	1

These factors of 230 can be found by division method or by factor tree method.

Note it The prime factorisation of a natural number is unique, except for the order of its factors.

e.g. 12 is equal to the product of the prime numbers 2, 2 and 3 together i.e. $12 = 2 \times 2 \times 3$, which is same as $3 \times 2 \times 2$ or $2 \times 3 \times 2$. We would probably write it as $12 = 2^2 \times 3$ which is still a unique combination (2, 2 and 3).

Example 2. **Explain why $(7 \times 11 \times 13 + 2 \times 11)$ is not a prime number?** CBSE 2024 (Basic)

Sol. Simplify the given expression

$$7 \times 11 \times 13 + 2 \times 11 = 1001 + 22 = 1023$$

Prime factorisation of $1023 = 3 \times 11 \times 31$

Thus, 1023 is divisible by 3, 11 and 31.

Since, a prime number is a natural number greater than 1 that has no positive divisors other than 1 and itself. Therefore, 1023 is not a prime number as it has other divisor other than 1 and itself.

Hence, $(7 \times 11 \times 13 + 2 \times 11)$ is not a prime number.

Example 3. **Check whether 4^n, where n is a natural number, can end with the digit 0 for any natural number n.**

If a number ends with the digit 0, then it will be divisible by both 2 and 5. So, here first, write the given number as the product of prime factors and then check this prime factorisation contains 2 and 5 or not. If it contains 2 and 5 both, then given number ends with the digit 0, otherwise not.

Sol. Given, n is a natural number. If a number were to end with 0, then it would be divisible by both 2 and 5.

We have, $4^n = (2 \times 2)^n = 2^{2n}$

Thus, prime factorisation of 4^n does not contain 5 and the Fundamental theorem of arithmetic guarantees that there are no other primes in the factorisation of 4^n.

Hence, there is no natural number n for which 4^n ends with the digit zero.

HCF and LCM By Prime Factorisation Method

The method of finding HCF and LCM of two or more positive numbers using the Fundamental theorem of arithmetic is called **prime factorisation method.**

In this method, we first express the given two or more numbers as the product of prime factors separately.

Then,

(i) HCF (Highest Common Factor) of two or more numbers is the product of the smallest power of each common prime factor involved in the numbers.

If there is no common prime factor, then HCF of given numbers is 1.

(ii) LCM (Least Common Multiple) of two or more numbers is the smallest number which is divisible by all the given numbers.

LCM of two or more numbers is the product of the greatest power of each prime factor involved in the numbers.

Example 4. **Find the HCF and LCM of 72 and 120.** CBSE 2023 (Standard)

Sol. Prime factorisation of 72 and 120 are

$$72 = 2 \times 2 \times 2 \times 3 \times 3$$
$$120 = 2 \times 2 \times 2 \times 3 \times 5$$

So, HCF $(72, 120) = 2 \times 2 \times 2 \times 3 = 24$

and LCM $(72, 120) = 2 \times 2 \times 2 \times 3 \times 3 \times 5 = 360$

Example 5. **Write the HCF of the smallest composite number and the smallest prime number.**

Sol. Smallest composite number $= 4 = 2 \times 2 = 2^2$

and smallest prime number $= 2 = 2^1$

$\therefore$ HCF $(4, 2) = 2^1 = 2$

[since, HCF is the product of the smallest power of each common prime factor involved in the numbers]

Example 6. **Using prime factorisation, find the HCF of 180, 140 and 210.**

Sol. Prime factorisation of 180, 140 and 210 are as follows

$$180 = 2 \times 2 \times 3 \times 3 \times 5$$
$$140 = 2 \times 2 \times 5 \times 7$$
$$210 = 2 \times 3 \times 5 \times 7$$

HCF of 180, 140 and $210 = 2 \times 5 = 10$

Example 7. **Two positive integers a and b can be written as $a = x^3y^2$ and $b = xy^3$. If x and y are the prime numbers, then find the LCM of (a, b).** CBSE 2019

Sol. Given, $a = x^3y^2 = x \times x \times x \times y \times y$, $b = xy^3 = x \times y \times y \times y$

$\therefore$ LCM $(a, b) = x^3 \times y^3 = x^3y^3$

Example 8. **The length, breadth and height of a room are 8 m 25 cm, 6 m 75 cm and 4 m 50 cm, respectively. Find the length of the longest rod that can measure the three dimensions of the room exactly.**

Sol. Given, length of the room = 8m25 cm

= 825 cm [$\because$ 1m = 100 cm]

Breadth of the room = 6 m 75 cm = 675 cm

and height of the room = 4 m 50 cm = 450 cm

Clearly, the length of the longest rod (in cm) is the HCF of 825, 675 and 450.

Using prime factorisation, we get

$$825 = 3 \times 5^2 \times 11$$
$$675 = 3^3 \times 5^2$$
and $$450 = 2 \times 3^2 \times 5^2$$

Now, HCF (825, 675, 450) = Product of the smallest power of each common prime factor

$$= 3 \times 5^2 = 75$$

Hence, the required length of the longest rod is 75 cm.

Relation between Numbers and their HCF and LCM

For any two positive integers a and b, the relation between these numbers and their HCF and LCM is

$$\text{HCF}(a, b) \times \text{LCM}(a, b) = a \times b$$

$$\Rightarrow \quad \text{HCF}(a, b) = \frac{a \times b}{\text{LCM}(a, b)}$$

or $$\text{LCM}(a, b) = \frac{a \times b}{\text{HCF}(a, b)}$$

Note it The product of three numbers is not equal to the product of their HCF and LCM.

Example 9. If HCF of two numbers is 2 and their product is 120, then find their LCM.

Sol. Let the two numbers be a and b.

Given, $\text{HCF}(a, b) = 2$ and product $(a \times b) = 120$

We know that

$\text{HCF}(a, b) \times \text{LCM}(a, b) =$ Product of a and b

$$\therefore \quad 2 \times \text{LCM}(a, b) = 120$$

$$\Rightarrow \quad \text{LCM}(a, b) = \frac{120}{2} = 60$$

Hence, the required LCM is 60.

Example 10. If the HCF of 35 and 45 is 5, LCM of 35 and 45 is $63 \times a$, then find the value of a.

Sol. We know that

HCF × LCM = Product of two numbers

$$\Rightarrow \quad 5 \times 63 \times a = 35 \times 45$$

$$\Rightarrow \quad a = \frac{35 \times 45}{5 \times 63} = 5$$

Example 11. The HCF of two numbers a and b is 5 and their LCM is 200. Find the product of a and b. CBSE 2019

Sol. Given, $\text{HCF}(a, b) = 5$ and $\text{LCM}(a, b) = 200$

$\because$ HCF × LCM = Product of two numbers

$$\Rightarrow \quad 5 \times 200 = ab$$

$$\Rightarrow \quad ab = 1000$$

Try These 1.1

1. **Complete the following factor tree by finding the unknown variables.**

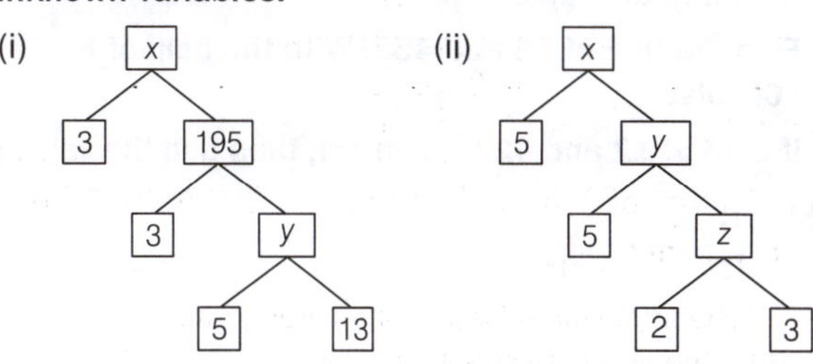

2. **Factorise the following numbers through the factor tree.**
   (i) 420 (ii) 468
   (iii) 308 (iv) 528
   (v) 9072 (vi) 19530
3. **Explain whether the following numbers are prime or composite numbers.**
   (i) $7 \times 11 \times 26 + 13$
   (ii) $(3 \times 5 \times 13 \times 46) + 23$
   (iii) $2 \times 3 \times 3 \times 5 + 5$
   (iv) $6 \times 5 \times 4 \times 3 \times 2 \times 1 + 10$
   (v) $7 \times 11 \times 13 + 5$
4. **Check whether 12^n can end with the digit 0 or 5, for any natural number n.** NCERT Exemplar
5. **Express each of the following integers as a product of its prime factors**
   (i) 945 (ii) 204 (iii) 660 (iv) 7325
   (v) 99792 (vi) 874944 (vii) 3825
6. **Find the HCF and LCM of 260 and 910 by prime factorisation method.** CBSE 2024 (Basic)
7. **Using prime factorisation, find HCF and LCM of 96 and 120.** CBSE 2023 (Standard)
8. **Find the LCM and HCF of the following integers by applying the prime factorisation method**
   (i) 40, 36, 126 (ii) 84, 90, 120
   (iii) 24, 15, 36 (iv) 60, 84, 108
9. **If two positive integers p and q can be expressed as $p = ab^2$ and $q = a^3b$; where a, b being prime numbers, find the LCM (p, q).**
10. **Find the greatest possible length which can be used to measure exactly the length 7 m, 3 m 85 cm and 12 m 95 cm.**
11. **Find the least number that is divisible by all the numbers from 1 to 10 (both inclusive).** NCERT Exemplar
12. **A circular field has a circumference of 360 km. Three cyclists start together and can cycle 48, 60 and 72 km in a day around the field. When will they meet again?**
13. **If the LCM of 26 and 91 is 182, then find their HCF.**
14. **If the HCF of 150 and 100 is 50, then find the LCM of 150 and 100.**

15. **The HCF of two numbers is 113 and their LCM is 56952. If one number is 904, then find the other number.**

16. **If HCF (253, 440) = 11 and LCM (253, 440) = 253 × *R*, then find the value of *R*.**

17. **Find the HCF of 26 and 455. With the help of HCF, find LCM also.**

18. **If LCM of 12 and 42 is 10*m* + 4, then find the value of *m*.**

Answers

1. (i) **Hint** $x=3\times195=585$ and $y=5\times13=65$

(ii) Do same as Part (i) **Ans.** $x=150, y=30, z=6$

2. **Hint** Do same as Example 1.

Ans. (i) $420=2^2\times3\times5\times7$

(ii) $468=2^2\times3^2\times13$

(iii) $308=2^2\times7\times11$

(iv) $528=2^4\times3\times11$

(v) $9072=2^4\times3^4\times7$

(vi) $19530=2\times3^2\times5\times7\times31$

3. (i) **Hint** Do same as Example 2. **Ans.** Composite number.

(ii) **Hint** Do same as Example 2. **Ans.** Composite number.

(iii) **Hint** Do same as Example 2. **Ans.** Composite number.

(iv) **Hint** Do same as Example 2. **Ans.** Composite number.

(v) **Hint** We have, $7\times11\times13+5=1001+5=1006$

Now, prime factorisation of $1006=2\times503$

Since, it has a factor other than 1 and itself.

So, it is a composite number.

4. **Hint** Do same as Example 3. **Ans.** No

5. (i) **Hint** Factorisation of 945 is

3	945
3	315
3	105
5	35
7	7
	1

Hence, $945=3^3\times5\times7$. (Product of its prime factors)

(ii) **Hint** Do same as Part (i). **Ans.** $2^2\times3\times17$

(iii) **Hint** Do same as Part (i). **Ans.** $2^2\times3\times5\times11$

(iv) **Hint** Do same as Part (i). **Ans.** $5^2\times293$

(v) **Hint** Do same as Part (i). **Ans.** $2^4\times3^4\times7\times11$

(vi) **Hint** Do same as Part (i). **Ans.** $2^6\times3^2\times7^2\times31$

(vii) **Hint** Do same as Part (i). **Ans.** $3^2\times5^2\times17$

6. **Hint** Do same as Example 5. **Ans.** HCF = 130 and LCM = 1820

7. **Hint** Do same as Example 5.

Ans. HCF (96,120) = 24 and LCM (96, 120) = 480

8. (i) **Hint** Do same as Example 6. **Ans.** LCM = 2520, HCF = 2

(ii) **Hint** Do same as Example 6. **Ans.** LCM = 2520, HCF = 6

(iii) **Hint** Do same as Example 6. **Ans.** LCM = 360, HCF = 3

(iv) **Hint.** Do same as Example 6. **Ans.** LCM = 3780, HCF = 12

9. **Hint** Do same as Example 7.

Ans. LCM $(p, q)=a^3b^2$

10. **Hint** Do same as Example 8. **Ans.** 35 cm

11. **Hint** Factors of numbers from 1 to 10 are

$1=1$

$2=1\times2$

$3=1\times3$

$4=1\times2\times2$

$5=1\times5$

$6=1\times2\times3$

$7=1\times7$

$8=1\times2\times2\times2$

$9=1\times3\times3$

$10=1\times2\times5$

∴ Least number that is divisible by all numbers from 1 to 10.

= LCM of numbers from 1 to 10

$=2\times2\times2\times3\times3\times5\times7$ **Ans.** 2520

12. **Hint** Cyclist 1 can cover 48 km in 1 day

∴ For covering 360 km $=\frac{360}{48}=7.5$ days $=7.5\times24=180$ h

Cyclist 2 can cover 60 km in 1 day

∴ For covering 360 km $=\frac{360}{60}=6$ days $=6\times24=144$ h

Cyclist 3 can cover 72 km in 1 day

∴ For covering 360 km $=\frac{360}{72}=5$ days $=5\times24=120$ h

Now, the cyclist will meet after = LCM (180,144,120)

Ans. 30 days

13. **Hint** HCF (26, 91) $=\frac{26\times91}{\text{LCM }(26, 91)}$

$=\frac{26\times91}{182}$

Ans. 13

14. **Hint** LCM (150, 100) $=\frac{150\times100}{\text{HCF }(150, 100)}$

$=\frac{150\times100}{50}$

Ans. 300

15. **Hint** Let another number be x.

∴ $\text{HCF}=\frac{x\times904}{\text{LCM}} \Rightarrow 113=\frac{x\times904}{56952}$

Ans. 7119

16. **Hint** Do same as Example 10.

Ans. $R=40$

17. **Hint** First, do same as Example 5.

We get, HCF (26, 455) = 13

Now, LCM (26, 455) $=\frac{26\times455}{\text{HCF}(26, 455)}$

Ans. HCF (26, 455) = 13 and LCM (26, 455) = 910.

18. **Hint** Given, LCM (12, 42) $=10m+4 \Rightarrow 84=10m+4$

Ans. $m=8$

TOPIC 02 Revisiting Irrational Numbers

Irrational Numbers

A number that cannot be expressed in the form $\frac{p}{q}$, where p, q are integers and $q \neq 0$, is called an irrational number.

e.g. $\sqrt{2}, \sqrt{3}, \sqrt{15}, \pi, -\frac{\sqrt{2}}{\sqrt{3}}$, 0.1011011101111,..., etc.

In this section, we will prove that $\sqrt{2}$, $\sqrt{3}$ and in general $\sqrt{p}$ is irrational, where p is prime.

Note it A pair of integers having HCF 1, are called coprime integers. e.g. (1, 3), (−2, 5), (6, 35), etc are coprime integers.

Theorem 1 Let p be a prime number and a be a positive integer. If p divides a^2, then p divides a.

Given Let p be a prime number and a be a positive integer, such that p divides a^2.

To prove p divides a.

Proof We know that every positive integer can be expressed as the product of primes.

So, let $a = p_1 \cdot p_2 \cdot ... \cdot p_n$, where $p_1, p_2, ..., p_n$ are primes, not necessarily all distinct.

Then, $a^2 = (p_1 \cdot p_2 \cdot ... \cdot p_n)(p_1 \cdot p_2 \cdot ... \cdot p_n)$

$\Rightarrow$ $a^2 = (p_1^2 \cdot p_2^2 \cdot ... \cdot p_n^2)$

Now, since p divides a^2.

$\Rightarrow$ p is a prime factor of a^2

$\Rightarrow$ p is one of $p_1, p_2, ..., p_n$.

[since, using fundamental theorem of arithmetic, the only prime factors of a^2 are $p_1, p_2, ..., p_n$.]

$\Rightarrow$ p divides a. $[\because a = p_1 \cdot p_2 \cdot ... \cdot p_n]$

Hence proved.

Theorem 2 $\sqrt{2}$ is irrational.

CBSE 2023 (Standard), 19, 10, 09, 08

Proof Let us assume that $\sqrt{2}$ be rational.

Then, it will be of the form $\frac{a}{b}$, where a, b are integers and $b \neq 0$.

Again, let a and b have no common factor other than 1.

$\therefore$ $\sqrt{2} = \frac{a}{b}$, where a and b are coprime integers.

On squaring both sides, we get

$$2 = \frac{a^2}{b^2}$$

$\Rightarrow$ $2b^2 = a^2$ ...(i)

$\Rightarrow$ 2 divides a^2

$\Rightarrow$ 2 divides a [from Theorem 1]

Then, a can be written as $2m$, where m is an integer.

On putting $a = 2m$ in Eq. (i), we get

$$2b^2 = (2m)^2 \Rightarrow 2b^2 = 4m^2 \Rightarrow b^2 = 2m^2$$

So, 2 divides $b^2 \Rightarrow$ 2 divides b [from Theorem 1]

Thus, 2 is a common factor of a and b.

But this contradicts the fact that a and b have no common factor other than 1. The contradiction arises by assuming that $\sqrt{2}$ is rational.

Hence, $\sqrt{2}$ is irrational. **Hence proved.**

Method of Finding Irrationality of Numbers

To prove the irrationality of the numbers, we use the method of contradiction which can be understood from the following examples.

Example 1. **Prove that $\sqrt{3}$ is an irrational number.**

CBSE 2023 (Standard), 2020 (Basic); CBSE Sample Paper 2023 (Basic)

Sol. Let us assume that $\sqrt{3}$ is a rational number. Then, there exist positive integers a and b such that

$\sqrt{3} = \frac{a}{b}$, where a and b are coprime.

Now, $\sqrt{3} = \frac{a}{b} \Rightarrow 3 = \frac{a^2}{b^2} \Rightarrow 3b^2 = a^2$

$\Rightarrow$ 3 divides $a^2 \Rightarrow$ 3 divides a

So, 3 is a factor of a. ...(i)

$\Rightarrow$ $a = 3c$ for some integer c.

$\Rightarrow$ $a^2 = 9c^2 \Rightarrow 3b^2 = 9c^2$ $[\because a^2 = 3b^2]$

$\Rightarrow$ $b^2 = 3c^2 \Rightarrow$ 3 divides $b^2 \Rightarrow$ 3 divides b

So, 3 is a factor of b. ...(ii)

From Eqs. (i) and (ii), we observe that a and b have atleast 3 as a common factor. But this contradicts the fact that a and b are coprime. This means that our assumption is not correct.

Hence, $\sqrt{3}$ is an irrational number. **Hence proved.**

Example 2. **Show that $3\sqrt{2}$ is an irrational number.**

Here, we will prove it by contradiction i.e. assume that $3\sqrt{2}$ is a rational and then show that our assumption is wrong.

Sol. Let us assume that $3\sqrt{2}$ be a rational number. Then, it will be of the form $\frac{p}{q}$, where p, q are coprime integers and $q \neq 0$.

Now, $\frac{p}{q} = 3\sqrt{2} \Rightarrow \frac{p}{3q} = \sqrt{2}$ ...(i)

Since, p is an integer and $3q$ is also an integer $(3q \neq 0)$.

So, $\frac{p}{3q}$ is a rational number.

$\therefore \sqrt{2}$ is a rational number.

But this contradicts the fact that $\sqrt{2}$ is an irrational number.

Therefore, our assumption is wrong.

Hence, $3\sqrt{2}$ is an irrational number. **Hence proved.**

Example 3. **Show that $5-\sqrt{3}$ is irrational.**

Sol. Let us assume that $5-\sqrt{3}$ is rational number. Then, it will be of the form $\frac{p}{q}$, where p, q are coprime integers and $q \neq 0$.

Now, $5-\sqrt{3} = \frac{p}{q}$

On rearranging, we get

$$5 - \frac{p}{q} = \sqrt{3}$$

Since, 5 and $\frac{p}{q}$ are rational. So, their difference will be rational.

$\therefore \sqrt{3}$ is rational.

But we know that $\sqrt{3}$ is irrational.

So, this contradicts the fact that $\sqrt{3}$ is irrational.

Therefore, our assumption is wrong.

Hence, $5-\sqrt{3}$ is irrational. **Hence proved.**

Example 4. **Prove that $3-2\sqrt{5}$ is an irrational number, given that $\sqrt{5}$ is an irrational number.**

CBSE 2023 (Basic), 2019

Sol. Let us assume that $3-2\sqrt{5}$ is a rational number, so it can be expressed in the form $\frac{p}{q}$, where p and q are coprimes and $q \neq 0$.

$$\therefore \quad 3-2\sqrt{5} = \frac{p}{q}$$

$$\Rightarrow \quad 3 - \frac{p}{q} = 2\sqrt{5}$$

$$\Rightarrow \quad \frac{3q-p}{2q} = \sqrt{5}$$

Since, $3q-p$ is an integer and $2q$ is also an integer $(2q \neq 0)$.

So, $\frac{3q-p}{2q}$ is a rational number.

Therefore, $\sqrt{5}$ is a rational number.

But it is given that $\sqrt{5}$ is irrational. So, it contradicts our assumption.

$\Rightarrow$ Our assumption of $3-2\sqrt{5}$ is rational is incorrect.

$\therefore$ $3-2\sqrt{5}$ is an irrational number. **Hence proved.**

Try These 1.2

1. **Prove that each of the following is irrational number.**
   (i) $3\sqrt{7}$
   (ii) $\frac{2\sqrt{3}}{5}$
   (iii) $5-\sqrt{2}$
2. **Prove that $2\sqrt{3}+\sqrt{5}$ is an irrational number.**
3. **Prove that $-7-2\sqrt{3}$ is an irrational number, given that $\sqrt{3}$ is an irrational number.** CBSE 2024 (Basic)
4. **Prove that $5-2\sqrt{3}$ is an irrational number. It is given that $\sqrt{3}$ is an irrational number.** CBSE 2024 (Standard)

Answers

1. (i) **Hint** Do same as Example 2.
   (ii) **Hint** Do same as Example 2.
   (iii) **Hint** Do same as Example 3.
2. Let us assume that $2\sqrt{3}+\sqrt{5}$ is rational. Then, it will be of the form $\frac{a}{b}$, where a and b are coprime integers and $b \neq 0$.

   Now, $2\sqrt{3}+\sqrt{5} = \frac{a}{b} \Rightarrow 2\sqrt{3} = \frac{a}{b} - \sqrt{5}$

   On squaring both sides, we get

   $$12 = \left(\frac{a}{b} - \sqrt{5}\right)^2$$

   $$\Rightarrow \quad 12 = \frac{a^2}{b^2} + 5 - 2\sqrt{5}\frac{a}{b}$$

   $$\Rightarrow \quad 2\sqrt{5}\frac{a}{b} = \frac{a^2}{b^2} - 7$$

   $$\Rightarrow \quad \sqrt{5} = \frac{a^2-7b^2}{2ab}$$

   Now, $\frac{a^2-7b^2}{2ab}$ is rational. $[\because a, b$ are integers and $b \neq 0]$

   $\therefore \sqrt{5}$ is a rational number, which is a contradiction to the fact that $\sqrt{5}$ is irrational.

   So, our assumption is wrong.

   Hence, $2\sqrt{3}+\sqrt{5}$ is irrational.
3. **Hint** Do same as Example 4.
4. **Hint** Do same as Example 4.

NCERT FOLDER

Complete Solutions of All Exercises of NCERT Textbook

EXERCISE 1.1

Q1. Express each number as a product of its prime factors.

(i) 140 (ii) 156 (iii) 3825
(iv) 5005 (v) 7429

Sol. (i) We have,

2	140
2	70
5	35
7	7
	1

$\therefore$ Product of prime factors of 140

$= 2 \times 2 \times 5 \times 7 = 2^2 \times 5 \times 7$

(ii) Do same as Part (i). **Ans.** $2^2 \times 3 \times 13$

(iii) Do same as Part (i). **Ans.** $3^2 \times 5^2 \times 17$

(iv) Do same as Part (i). **Ans.** $5 \times 7 \times 11 \times 13$

(v) Do same as Part (i). **Ans.** $17 \times 19 \times 23$

Q2. Find the LCM and HCF of the following pairs of integers and verify that

LCM × HCF = Product of the two numbers.

(i) 26 and 91 (ii) 510 and 92 (iii) 336 and 54

Sol. (i) We have, 26 and 91

2	26
13	13
	1

7	91
13	13
	1

$\therefore$ Prime factors of $26 = 2 \times 13$

and prime factors of $91 = 7 \times 13$

Now, LCM of 26 and $91 = 2 \times 7 \times 13 = 182$

and HCF of 26 and 91 = 13

For verification

$\text{LCM} \times \text{HCF} = 182 \times 13 = 2366$

and product of two numbers $= 26 \times 91 = 2366$

Thus, LCM × HCF = Product of two numbers

Hence verified.

(ii) Do same as Part (i). **Ans.** LCM = 23460, HCF = 2

(iii) Do same as Part (i). **Ans.** LCM = 3024, HCF = 6

Q3. Find the HCF and LCM of the following integers by applying the prime factorisation method.

CBSE 2020 (Standard)

(i) 12, 15 and 21 (ii) 17, 23 and 29
(iii) 8, 9 and 25

Sol. (i) We have, 12, 15 and 21

$\therefore \quad 12 = 2 \times 2 \times 3 = 2^2 \times 3$

$15 = 3 \times 5$ and $21 = 3 \times 7$

Here, 3 is a common prime factor of the given numbers and has smallest power 1.

$\therefore$ HCF of 12, 15 and 21 = 3

and LCM = Product of each prime factor with greatest power

$= 2^2 \times 3 \times 5 \times 7$

$= 2 \times 2 \times 3 \times 5 \times 7 = 420$

(ii) Do same as Part (i). **Ans.** HCF = 1, LCM = 11339

(iii) Do same as Part (i). **Ans.** HCF = 1, LCM = 1800

Q4. Given that HCF (306, 657) = 9, find LCM (306, 657).

Sol. Given, HCF of 306 and 657 = 9

We know that

LCM × HCF = Product of two numbers

$\Rightarrow \quad \text{LCM} \times 9 = 306 \times 657$

$\Rightarrow \quad \text{LCM} = \dfrac{306 \times 657}{9} = 34 \times 657 = 22338$

$\therefore$ LCM of 306 and 657 = 22338

Q5. Check whether 6^n can end with the digit 0 for any natural number n. CBSE 2023, 12, 11, 10 (Standard)

Sol. Do same as Example 3 of Topic 1. **Ans.** No.

Q6. Explain, why $(7 \times 11 \times 13) + 13$ and $(7 \times 6 \times 5 \times 4 \times 3 \times 2 \times 1) + 5$ are composite numbers?

Sol. We have, $(7 \times 11 \times 13) + 13 = 1001 + 13 = 1014$

$\Rightarrow \quad 1014 = 2 \times 3 \times 13 \times 13$

We know that a number is called a composite number, if it has atleast one factor other than 1 and the number itself.

Here, 1014 is the product of more than two prime numbers i.e. 2, 3 and 13.

So, it is a composite number.

Now, $(7 \times 6 \times 5 \times 4 \times 3 \times 2 \times 1) + 5 = 5040 + 5 = 5045$

$\Rightarrow \quad 5045 = 5 \times 1009$

Thus, it is the product of prime factors 5 and 1009.

Hence, it is also a composite number.

Q7. There is a circular path around a sports field. Sonia takes 18 minutes to drive one round of the field, while Ravi takes 12 minutes for the same. Suppose they both start at the same point and at the same time and go in the same direction. After how many minutes will they meet again at the starting point?

Sol. Time taken by Sonia to drive one round of the field $= 18$ minutes

Time taken by Ravi to drive one round of the field $= 12$ minutes

The LCM of 18 and 12 gives the exact number of minutes after which they will meet at the starting point again.

Now, $18 = 2 \times 3 \times 3 = 2 \times 3^2$

and $12 = 2 \times 2 \times 3 = 2^2 \times 3$

$\therefore$ LCM of 18 and 12 $= 2^2 \times 3^2 = 2 \times 2 \times 3 \times 3 = 36$

Hence, Sonia and Ravi will meet again at the starting point after 36 minutes.

EXERCISE 1.2

Q1. Prove that $\sqrt{5}$ is an irrational number.

CBSE 2025 (Standard) CBSE 2024 (Basic) Compartment 2020 (Standard), 19, 15

Sol. Do same as Example 1 of Topic 2.

Q2. Prove that $3 + 2\sqrt{5}$ is irrational.

Sol. Do same as Example 3 of Topic 2.

Q3. Prove that the following are irrationals.

(i) $\dfrac{1}{\sqrt{2}}$ (ii) $7\sqrt{5}$ (iii) $6 + \sqrt{2}$

Sol. (i) Let us assume that $\dfrac{1}{\sqrt{2}}$ is rational.

Then, it will be of the form $\dfrac{p}{q}$, where p, q are coprime integers and $q \neq 0$.

Now, $\dfrac{1}{\sqrt{2}} = \dfrac{p}{q}$

$\Rightarrow \quad \dfrac{1 \times \sqrt{2}}{\sqrt{2} \times \sqrt{2}} = \dfrac{p}{q}$

$\Rightarrow \quad \dfrac{\sqrt{2}}{2} = \dfrac{p}{q}$

$\Rightarrow \quad \sqrt{2} = \dfrac{2p}{q}$

Since, p, q are integers and $q \neq 0$, therefore $\dfrac{2p}{q}$ is rational. This implies that $\sqrt{2}$ is rational.

But this contradicts the fact that $\sqrt{2}$ is irrational.

This shows that our assumption is wrong.

So, we conclude that $\dfrac{1}{\sqrt{2}}$ is an irrational.

Hence proved.

(ii) Do same as Part (i).

(iii) Do same as Example 3 of Topic 2.

REVIEW EXERCISE

Including Competency Based Questions

Part I

Multiple Choice Questions

1. The prime factorization of the number 2304 is **CBSE 2023 (Basic)**

(a) $2^8 \times 3^2$ (b) $2^7 \times 3^3$ (c) $2^8 \times 3^1$ (d) $2^7 \times 3^2$

2. $\sqrt{n}$ is a natural number such that $n > 1$. Which of these can definitely be expressed as a product of primes? **Competency Based Question**

(i) $\sqrt{n}$ (ii) n (iii) $\frac{\sqrt{n}}{2}$

(a) only (ii)
(b) only (i) and (ii)
(c) all (i), (ii) and (iii)
(d) cannot be determined without knowing n

3. If n is a natural number, then $2(5^n + 6^n)$ always ends with **CBSE 2022 (Standard)**

(a) 1 (b) 4 (c) 3 (d) 2

4. If n is a natural number, then 8^n cannot end with digit **CBSE 2025 (Standard)**

(a) 4 (b) 2 (c) 0 (d) 6

5. If a and b are two coprime numbers, then a^3 and b^3 are

(a) coprime (b) not coprime
(c) even (d) odd

6. The LCM of smallest two-digit number and smallest composite number is **CBSE 2023 (Standard)**

(a) 12 (b) 4 (c) 20 (d) 40

7. HCF of $(3^3 \times 5^2 \times 2)$, $(3^2 \times 5^3 \times 2^2)$ and $(3^4 \times 5 \times 2^3)$ is **CBSE Sample Paper 2025 (Basic)**

(a) 450 (b) 90 (c) 180 (d) 630

8. HCF (132, 77) is **CBSE 2024 (Basic)**

(a) 11 (b) 77 (c) 22 (d) 44

9. If $a = 2^2 \times 3^x$, $b = 2^2 \times 3 \times 5$, $c = 2^2 \times 3 \times 7$ and LCM $(a, b, c) = 3780$, then x is equal to **CBSE 2024 (Standard)**

(a) 1 (b) 2 (c) 3 (d) 0

10. If $a = 2^7 \cdot 3^{10}$ and $b = 2^3 \cdot 3^7$, then HCF (a, b) is **CBSE 2024 (Basic) Compartment**

(a) $2^7 \cdot 3^{10}$ (b) $2^{10} \cdot 3^{17}$ (c) $2^3 \cdot 3^7$ (d) $2^7 \cdot 3^7$

11. The HCF of k and 93 is 31, where k is a natural number. Which of these can be true for some values of k? **Competency Based Question**

(i) k is a multiple of 31. (ii) k is a multiple of 93.
(iii) k is an even number. (iv) k is an odd number.

(a) only (ii) and (iii) (b) only (i), (ii) and (iii)
(c) only (i), (iii) and (iv) (d) all (i), (ii), (iii) and (iv)

12. Three alarm clocks ring their alarms at regular intervals of 20 min, 25 min and 30 min, respectively. If they first beep together at 12 noon, at what time will they beep again for the first time? **Competency Based Question**

(a) 4 :00 pm (b) 4:30 pm (c) 5: 00 pm (d) 5:30 pm

13. The LCM of two numbers is 2400. Which of the following cannot be their HCF? **CBSE 2022 (Standard)**

(a) 300 (b) 400 (c) 500 (d) 600

14. If two positive integers p and q can be expressed as $p = 18a^2b^4$ and $q = 20a^3b^2$, where a and b are prime numbers, then LCM (p, q) is **CBSE 2024 (Standard)**

(a) $2a^2b^2$ (b) $180a^2b^2$ (c) $12a^2b^2$ (d) $180a^3b^4$

15. The (HCF $\times$ LCM) for the numbers 50 and 20 is **CBSE 2022 Term I (Basic)**

(a) 1000 (b) 50 (c) 100 (d) 500

16. If HCF (420, 189) = 21, then LCM (420, 189) is **CBSE Sample Paper 2025 (Basic)**

(a) 420 (b) 1890 (c) 3780 (d) 3680

17. Given HCF (2520, 6600) = 40 and LCM (2520, 6600) $= 252 \times k$, then the value of k is **CBSE 2024 (Standard)**

(a) 1650 (b) 1600 (c) 165 (d) 1625

18. HCF of two numbers is 27 and their LCM is 162. If one of the number is 54, then the other number is **CBSE 2022 (Standard)**

(a) 36 (b) 35 (c) 9 (d) 81

19. The smallest irrational number by which $\sqrt{20}$ should be multiplied, so as to get a rational number, is **CBSE 2024 (Standard)**

(a) $\sqrt{20}$ (b) $\sqrt{2}$ (c) 5 (d) $\sqrt{5}$

20. A pair of irrational numbers whose product is a rational number is **CBSE 2024 (Standard)**

(a) $(\sqrt{16}, \sqrt{4})$ (b) $(\sqrt{5}, \sqrt{2})$
(c) $(\sqrt{3}, \sqrt{27})$ (d) $(\sqrt{36}, \sqrt{2})$

Assertion-Reason Type Questions

21. **Assertion** The number 5^n cannot end with the digit 0, where n is a natural number. CBSE 2023 (Standard)

Reason Prime factorisation of 5 has only two factors 1 and 5.

(a) Both Assertion and Reason are correct and Reason is the correct explanation of Assertion.
(b) Both Assertion and Reason are correct but Reason is not the correct explanation of Assertion.
(c) Assertion is correct but Reason is incorrect.
(d) Assertion is incorrect but Reason is correct.

22. **Assertion** $(a+\sqrt{b})\cdot(a-\sqrt{b})$ is a rational number, where a and b are positive integers. CBSE 2025 (Basic)

Reason Product of two irrationals is always rational.

(a) Both Assertion and Reason are correct and Reason is the correct explanation of Assertion.
(b) Both Assertion and Reason are correct but Reason is not the correct explanation of Assertion.
(c) Assertion is correct but Reason is incorrect.
(d) Assertion is incorrect but Reason is correct.

23. **Assertion** The HCF of two numbers is 5 and their product is 150. Then, their LCM is 40.

Reason For any two positive integers a and b, HCF $(a, b) \times$ LCM $(a, b) = a \times b$

CBSE Sample Paper 2023 (Basic)

(a) Both Assertion and Reason are correct and Reason is the correct explanation of Assertion.
(b) Both Assertion and Reason are correct but Reason is not the correct explanation of Assertion.
(c) Assertion is correct but Reason is incorrect.
(d) Assertion is incorrect but Reason is correct.

24. **Assertion** $2+\sqrt{2}$ is an irrational number.

Reason The sum of a non-zero rational number and an irrational number is always an irrational number.

CBSE 2024 (Basic) Compartment

(a) Both Assertion and Reason are correct and Reason is the correct explanation of Assertion.
(b) Both Assertion and Reason are correct but Reason is not the correct explanation of Assertion.
(c) Assertion is correct but Reason is incorrect.
(d) Assertion is incorrect but Reason is correct.

25. **Assertion** $\sqrt{2}(5-\sqrt{2})$ is an irrational number.

Reason Product of two irrational numbers is always irrational. CBSE 2024 (Basic)

(a) Both Assertion and Reason are correct and Reason is the correct explanation of Assertion.
(b) Both Assertion and Reason are correct but Reason is not the correct explanation of Assertion.
(c) Assertion is correct but Reason is incorrect.
(d) Assertion is incorrect but Reason is correct.

26. **Assertion** 2 is a rational number.

Reason The square roots of all positive integers are irrationals.

(a) Both Assertion and Reason are correct and Reason is the correct explanation of Assertion.
(b) Both Assertion and Reason are correct but Reason is not the correct explanation of Assertion.
(c) Assertion is correct but Reason is incorrect.
(d) Assertion is incorrect but Reason is correct.

Case Study Based Questions

27. Teaching Mathematics through activities is a powerful approach that enhances students' understanding and engagement. Keeping this in mind, Ms. Mukta planned a prime number game for class 5 students. She announces the number 2 in her class and asked the first student to multiply it by a prime number and then pass it to second student. Second student also multiplied it by a prime number and passed it to third student. In this way, by multiplying to a prime number, the last student got 173250.

Now, Mukta asked some questions as given below to the students. CBSE 2024

(i) What is the least prime number used by students ?

(ii) (a) How many students are in the class ?

Or

(b) What is the highest prime number used by students ?

(iii) Which prime number has been used maximum times ?

Part II

Very Short Answer Type Questions

1. Find the HCF and LCM of 480 and 720 using the prime factorisation method. CBSE Sample Paper 2025 (Standard)

2. For what value of n, $2^n \times 5^n$ ends with 5?

3. Find the greatest three-digit number which is divisible by 18, 24 and 36. CBSE 2023 (Standard)

4. The traffic lights at three different road crossings change after every 48 s, 72 s and 108 s, respectively. If they change simultaneously at 7 am, at what time will they change together next. CBSE 2023 (Standard)

5. Prove that $6-4\sqrt{5}$ is an irrational number, given that $\sqrt{5}$ is an irrational number. CBSE 2024 (Basic)

Short Answer Type Questions

6. Check whether 15^n can end with digit zero for any natural number n.

7. $(n^2 + 3n - 4)$ can be expressed as a product of only 2 prime factors where n is a natural number. Find the value(s) of n for which the given expression is an even composite number. Show your work and give valid reasons. **Competency Based Question**

8. The sum of two numbers is 528 and their HCF is 33, then find the number of pairs satisfying the above condition.

9. The HCF of 85 and 238 is expressible in the form $85m - 238$. Find the value of m. **CBSE Sample Paper 2025 (Standard)**

10. Find the least number that is divisible by all the numbers from 1 to 5 (both inclusive).

11. In a teacher's workshop, the number of teachers teaching French, Hindi and English are 48, 80 and 144, respectively. Find the minimum number of rooms required if in each room the same number of teachers are seated and all of them are of the same subject. **CBSE 2024 (Standard)**

12. The numbers 525 and 3000 are both divisible by 3, 5, 15, 25 and 75. What is the HCF of 525 and 3000? Justify your answer. **NCERT Exemplar**

13. Ravi and Shikha drive around a circular sports field. Ravi takes 16 min to complete one round, while Shikha completes the round in 20 min. If both start at the same point, at the same time and go in the same direction, then after how much time will they meet at the starting point? **Competency Based Question**

14. Find HCF and LCM of 404 and 96 and verify that HCF $\times$ LCM $=$ Product of the two given numbers. **CBSE 2018**

15. Prove that $2 + \sqrt{5}$ is an irrational number.

16. Given that $\sqrt{2}$ is irrational, prove that $(5 + 3\sqrt{2})$ is an irrational number. **CBSE 2018**

Long Answer Type Questions

17. Grow More plantations have two rectangular fields of the same width but different lengths. They are required to plant 84 trees in the smaller field and 231 trees in the larger field. In both fields, the trees will be planted in the same number of rows but in different numbers of columns.

(i) What is the most number of rows that can be planted in this arrangement? Show your work.

(ii) If the trees are planted in the number of rows obtained in part (i), how many columns will each field have? **Competency Based Question**

18. Prove that if a, b, c and d are positive rationals such that, $a + \sqrt{b} = c + \sqrt{d}$, then either $a = c$ and $b = d$ or b and d are squares of rationals.

19. Let a, b, c and p be the rational numbers such that p is not a perfect cube if $a + bp^{1/3} + cp^{2/3} = 0$, then prove that $a = b = c$. **Competency Based Question**

20. Prove that $(\sqrt{p} + \sqrt{q})$ is irrational, where p and q are primes. **NCERT Exemplar**

21. If $\sqrt{ab}$ is an irrational number, then prove that $(\sqrt{a} + \sqrt{b})$ is an irrational number.

HINTS & SOLUTIONS

Part I

1. (a) **Hint** Do same as Question 1 of NCERT Folder Exercise 1.1.

2. (a) **Hint** Here, $\sqrt{n}$ is a natural number, then possible value of n could be 4, 9, 16, 25, 36, … .

Considering $n = 4$

(i) $\sqrt{n} = \sqrt{4} = 2$, which is a prime number.

(ii) $n = 4 = 2 \times 2$, which is the product of two prime numbers.

(iii) $\frac{\sqrt{n}}{2} = \frac{\sqrt{4}}{2} = 1$, not a prime number.

3. (d) Since, 5^n and 6^n always ends with 5 and 6, respectively.

Thus, $2\,(5^n + 6^n) = 2(5 + 6) = 22$, is always ends with 2.

4. (c) **Hint** Do same as Example 3 of Topic 1.

5. (a) Since, a and b are coprimes, then a^3 and b^3 are also coprimes.

6. (c) **Hint** We know that

Smallest two-digit number $= 10 = 2 \times 5$

and smallest composite number $= 4 = 2 \times 2$

7. (b) We have, $(3^3 \times 5^2 \times 2)$, $(3^2 \times 5^3 \times 2^2)$ and $(3^4 \times 5 \times 2^3)$.

We know that

HCF = Product of smallest power of each common prime factor in the numbers.

$\therefore$ HCF $= 3^2 \times 5 \times 2 = 90$

8. (a) **Hint** Do same as Example 5 of Topic 1.

9. (c) Given, $a = 2^2 \times 3^x = 2^2 \times 3^1 \times 3^{x-1}$

$$b = 2^2 \times 3 \times 5 \text{ and } c = 2^2 \times 3 \times 7$$

Here, LCM $(a, b, c) = 2^2 \times 3 \times 3^{x-1} \times 5 \times 7$ ...(i)

and given that LCM $(a, b, c) = 3780$ ...(ii)

Thus, from Eqs. (i) and (ii), we get

$$2^2 \times 3 \times 3^{x-1} \times 5 \times 7 = 3780$$

$$\Rightarrow \quad 3^{x-1} = \frac{3780}{2^2 \times 3 \times 5 \times 7}$$

$$\Rightarrow \quad 3^{x-1} = 9 \Rightarrow 3^{x-1} = 3^2$$

On comparing the exponents of 3, we get

$$x - 1 = 2 \Rightarrow x = 3$$

10. (c) Given, $a = 2^7 \cdot 3^{10}, b = 2^3 \cdot 3^7$

$\therefore$ HCF of $2^7 \cdot 3^{10}$ and $2^3 \cdot 3^7$ is $2^3 \cdot 3^7$.

11. (c) **Hint** HCF is the highest common factor between two numbers.

If HCF of k and 93 is 31, then k is a multiple of 31.

k can be an even or an odd number.

12. (c) **Hint** LCM of 20, 25 and 30 = 300

300 min $= \frac{300}{60} = 5$ h. Clocks ring at 5:00 pm again.

13. (c) **Hint** $2400 = 2 \times 2 \times 2 \times 2 \times 2 \times 3 \times 5 \times 5$

In the given option, only 500 is not a factor of 2400.

$$500 = 2 \times 2 \times 5 \times 5 \times 5$$

14. (d) **Hint** Do same as Example 7 of Topic 1.

15. (a) **Hint** HCF $\times$ LCM = Product of two numbers

16. (c) Given, HCF (420, 189) = 21

Let LCM of 420 and 189 be x.

We know that LCM $\times$ HCF = Ist number $\times$ IInd number

$$\Rightarrow \quad x \times 21 = 420 \times 189$$

$$\therefore \quad x = \frac{420 \times 189}{21} = 3780$$

17. (a) Given, HCF (2520, 6600) = 40

LCM (2520, 6600) = $252 \times k$

We know that LCM $(a, b) \times$ HCF $(a, b) = a \times b$

$\Rightarrow$ LCM (2520, 6600) $\times$ HCF (2520, 6600) $= 2520 \times 6600$

$$\Rightarrow \quad 252 \times k \times 40 = 2520 \times 6600$$

$$\Rightarrow \quad k = \frac{2520 \times 6600}{252 \times 40} = 1650$$

$$\therefore \quad k = 1650$$

18. (d) **Hint** Do same as Example 10 of Topic 1.

19. (d) We have,

$$\sqrt{20} = 2\sqrt{5}$$

From the given options, if we multiply $\sqrt{20}$ i.e. $2\sqrt{5}$ by $\sqrt{5}$, we will get a rational number.

20. (c) **Hint** We know that product of two irrational numbers can be rational or irrational.

Using the given options

(a) $\sqrt{16} \times \sqrt{4} = 4 \times 2 = 8$, rational

(b) $\sqrt{5} \times \sqrt{2} = \sqrt{10}$, irrational

(c) $\sqrt{3} \times \sqrt{27} = \sqrt{81} = 9$, rational

(d) $\sqrt{36} \times \sqrt{2} = \sqrt{72}$, irrational

Here, from option (a), we get rational number but $\sqrt{16}$ and $\sqrt{4}$ are not irrational numbers.

21. (a) **Hint** Do same as Example 3 of Topic 1.

Prime factorisation of $5 = 1 \times 5$

$\therefore$ Assertion and Reason are correct and Reason is the correct explanation of Assertion.

22. (c) **Assertion** $(a + \sqrt{b})(a - \sqrt{b})$

$$= (a)^2 - (\sqrt{b})^2$$

$$= a^2 - b$$

Since, a and b are integers, a^2 is also an integer.

The difference between two integers (a^2 and b) is also an integer.

Therefore, $a^2 - b$ is an integer, and all integers are rational.

Reason The product of two irrationals is not always rational.

e.g. $\sqrt{2} \cdot \sqrt{3} = \sqrt{6}$ which is irrational.

However, $\sqrt{2} \cdot \sqrt{2} = 2$ which is rational.

Therefore, Reason is false.

Hence, Assertion is true, but Reason is false.

23. (d) We know that

HCF $(a, b) \times$ LCM $(a, b) = a \times b$

$$\Rightarrow \quad 5 \times \text{LCM}(a, b) = 150$$

$$\Rightarrow \quad \text{LCM}(a, b) = \frac{150}{5} = 30$$

$\therefore$ Assertion is incorrect but Reason is correct.

24. (a) Since, 2 is a rational number and $\sqrt{2}$ is an irrational number.

$\therefore$ Their sum $2 + \sqrt{2}$ is an irrational number.

Hence, Assertion and Reason both are correct and Reason is the correct explanation of Assertion.

25. (c) **Assertion** (A) Simplifying the expression

$\sqrt{2}(5 - \sqrt{2}) = 5\sqrt{2} - (\sqrt{2})^2 = 5\sqrt{2} - 2$

It is known that $\sqrt{2}$ is an irrational number and multiplying an irrational number by a rational number (here, 5) results in an irrational number. Subtracting a rational number (2) from an irrational number still gives us an irrational number.

Thus, $\sqrt{2}(5-\sqrt{2})$ is an irrational number.

Hence, Assertion (A) is true.

Reason (R) It is known that $\sqrt{2}$ is an irrational number. Product of $\sqrt{2}$ and $\sqrt{2}$ is equal to 2, which is a rational number.

Therefore, product of two irrational numbers is always an irrational number is false.

Hence, Reason (R) is false.

26. (c) $\because \sqrt{4} = \pm 2$, which is not an irrational number.

$\therefore$ Assertion is correct but Reason is incorrect.

27. (i) Prime factorisation of $173250 = 2 \times 3^2 \times 5^3 \times 7 \times 11$.

So, the least prime number used by students = 2

(ii) (a) Number of students = Number of prime numbers used by the students $= 2+3+1+1 = 7$

(b) Highest prime number used by students = 11

(iii) Prime number 5 has been used 3 times.

$\therefore$ Prime number used maximum times = 5

Part II

1. Prime factorisation of 480 and 720

$$480 = 2^5 \times 3 \times 5$$

$$720 = 2^4 \times 3^2 \times 5$$

LCM $(480, 720) = 2^5 \times 3^2 \times 5 = 1440$

HCF $(480, 720) = 2^4 \times 3 \times 5 = 240$

2. Hint If $n = 1$, then $2^n \times 5^n = 2 \times 5 = 10$

If $n = 2$, then $2^n \times 5^n = 2^2 \times 5^2 = (2 \times 5)^2 = 10^2 = 100$ and so on.

Thus, for any value of n, we get that $2^n \times 5^n$ ends with zero (always). So, for no value of n, $2^n \times 5^n$ ends with 5.

3. Hint LCM $(18, 24, 36) = 2^3 \times 3^2 = 72$

So, the greatest three-digit number divisible by 18, 24 and 36 is the highest multiple of 72 which is less than 1000.

$$13 \times 72 = 936$$

$$14 \times 72 = 1008$$

Hence, the greatest three-digit number divisible by 18, 24 and 36 is 936.

4. Hint LCM of 48, 72 and $108 = 2 \times 2 \times 2 \times 2 \times 3 \times 3 \times 3$
$= 432$

Therefore, after 432 s, they will change simultaneously.

We know that $60 \text{ s} = 1 \text{ min}$

$$\Rightarrow \quad 1 \text{ s} = \frac{1}{60} \text{ min}$$

$$\Rightarrow \quad 432 \text{ s} = \frac{432}{60} \text{ min} = 7 \text{ min } 12 \text{ sec}$$

Hence, the lights change together at 7 : 07 : 12 am.

5. Do same as Example 4 of Topic 2.

6. Hint Do same as Example 3 of Topic 1. **Ans.** No

7. Factorising
$$n^2 + 3n - 4 = n^2 + 4n - n - 4 = n(n+4) - 1(n+4) = (n-1)(n+4)$$

For $n^2 + 3n - 4$ to be even, one of the factor of $n^2 + 3n - 4$ must be 2.

Hence, $n - 1 = 2$

$n = 3$

8. Hint Let the required number be $33x$ and $33y$.

Then, $33x + 33y = 528$

$\Rightarrow \quad x + y = 16$

Now, coprimes with sum 16 are (1, 15), (3, 13), (5, 11), (7, 9).

$\therefore$ Required numbers are $(33 \times 1, 33 \times 15)$, $(33 \times 3, 33 \times 13)$, $(33 \times 5, 33 \times 11)$ and $(33 \times 7, 33 \times 9)$.

The number of such pairs is 4.

9. Prime factorisation of 85 and 238

$$85 = 5 \times 17$$

$$238 = 2 \times 7 \times 17$$

$$\text{HCF} = (85, 238) = 17$$

So, $\quad 17 = 85 \times m - 238$ [given]

$\Rightarrow \quad 85m = 255$

$\therefore \quad m = 3$

10. Hint Required number = LCM (1, 2, 3, 4, 5). **Ans.** 60

11. Hint HCF of 48, 80 and $144 = 2^4 = 16$

$\therefore$ Required number of rooms $= \dfrac{48 + 80 + 144}{16}$ **Ans.** 17

12. Hint Here, $525 = 3 \times 5 \times 5 \times 7$

and $3000 = 3 \times 5 \times 5 \times 2 \times 2 \times 2 \times 5 = 3 \times 5 \times 5 \times 5 \times 2^3$

Thus, highest common factor among these is $3 \times 5 \times 5$.

Ans. 75

13. Hint Do same as Question 7 of NCERT Folder Exercise 1.1. **Ans.** 80 min

14. Hint Do same as Question 2 of NCERT Folder Exercise 1.1.

Ans. HCF = 4 and LCM = 9696

15. Hint Do same as Example 3 of Topic 2.

16. Hint Do same as Example 4 of Topic 2.

17. Hint

(i) HCF of 84 and 231 = 21

Number of rows in each field = 21

(ii) Number of columns in smaller field $= \dfrac{84}{21} = 4$

Number of columns in larger field $= \dfrac{231}{21} = 11$

18. Given, $a+\sqrt{b}=c+\sqrt{d}$

If $a=c$, then $\sqrt{b}=\sqrt{d} \Rightarrow b=d$ [squaring both sides]

If $a \neq c$, then there exists a positive rational number x such that $a=c+x$.

Now, $a+\sqrt{b}=c+\sqrt{d}$

$\Rightarrow c+x+\sqrt{b}=c+\sqrt{d}$ [$\because a=c+x$]

$\Rightarrow x+\sqrt{b}=\sqrt{d}$ ...(i)

$\Rightarrow (x+\sqrt{b})^2=(\sqrt{d})^2$ [squaring both sides]

$\Rightarrow x^2+b+2x\sqrt{b}=d$

$\Rightarrow 2x\sqrt{b}=d-b-x^2$

$$\Rightarrow \sqrt{b}=\frac{d-b-x^2}{2x}$$

Since, d, x and b are rational numbers and $x>0$.

So, $\frac{d-b-x^2}{2x}$ is a rational number.

$\Rightarrow \sqrt{b}$ is a rational number.

$\Rightarrow$ b is the square of a rational number.

From Eq. (i), $\sqrt{d}=x+\sqrt{b}$

$\Rightarrow \sqrt{d}$ is a rational number.

$\Rightarrow$ d is the square of a rational number.

Hence, either $a=c$ and $b=d$ or b and d are the squares of rationals. **Hence proved.**

19. We have, $a+bp^{1/3}+cp^{2/3}=0$ ...(i)

On multiplying both sides by $p^{1/3}$, we get

$ap^{1/3}+bp^{2/3}+cp=0$ ...(ii)

On multiplying Eq. (i) by b and Eq. (ii) by c and subtracting, we get

$(ab+b^2p^{1/3}+bcp^{2/3})-(acp^{1/3}+bcp^{2/3}+c^2p)=0$

$\Rightarrow (b^2-ac)p^{1/3}+ab-c^2p=0$

$\Rightarrow b^2-ac=0$ and $ab-c^2p=0$ [$\because p^{1/3}$ is irrational]

$\Rightarrow b^2=ac$ and $ab=c^2p$

$\Rightarrow a^2(ac)=c^4p^2$ [putting $b^2=ac$ in $a^2b^2=c^4p^2$]

$\Rightarrow a^3c-c^4p^2=0$

$\Rightarrow (a^3-c^3p^2)c=0$

$\Rightarrow a^3=p^2c^3$ or $c=0$

$$\Rightarrow p^2=\frac{a^3}{c^3}$$

$$\Rightarrow (p^2)^{1/3}=\left(\frac{a^3}{c^3}\right)^{1/3}=\frac{a}{c}$$

$$\Rightarrow (p^{1/3})^2=\frac{a}{c}$$

This is not possible as $p^{1/3}$ is irrational and $\frac{a}{c}$ is rational.

$\therefore a^3-p^2c^3 \neq 0$,

Hence, $c=0$.

On putting $c=0$ in $b^2-ac=0$, we get

$b=0$

$\therefore b=0, c=0$, then $a=0$

Hence, $a=b=c=0$ **Hence proved.**

20. Let us suppose that $\sqrt{p}+\sqrt{q}$ is a rational number and let $\sqrt{p}+\sqrt{q}=a$, where a is rational.

Therefore, $\sqrt{q}=a-\sqrt{p}$

On squaring both sides, we get

$q=a^2+p-2a\sqrt{p}$ [$\because (a-b)^2=a^2+b^2-2ab$]

$$\Rightarrow \sqrt{p}=\frac{a^2+p-q}{2a}$$

Since, p and q are primes and a is a rational number, so $\frac{a^2+p-q}{2a}$ is rational.

Therefore, $\sqrt{p}$ is a rational number.

But this contradicts the fact that $\sqrt{p}$ is irrational number as p is prime.

So, our assumption was incorrect.

Hence, $\sqrt{p}+\sqrt{q}$ is irrational. **Hence proved.**

21. Let $(\sqrt{a}+\sqrt{b})$ be a rational number.

Then, $\sqrt{a}+\sqrt{b}=r$

where, a, b and r are rational.

$\Rightarrow (\sqrt{a}+\sqrt{b})^2=r^2$ [squaring both sides]

$\Rightarrow a+b+2\sqrt{ab}=r^2$ [$\because (A+B)^2=A^2+B^2+2AB$]

$\Rightarrow 2\sqrt{ab}=r^2-a-b$

$$\Rightarrow \sqrt{ab}=\frac{r^2-a-b}{2}$$

Since, r, a and b are rational numbers.

$\Rightarrow \frac{r^2-(a+b)}{2}$ is rational number.

$\Rightarrow \sqrt{ab}$ is a rational.

This is contrary, because $\sqrt{ab}$ is an irrational number.

So our assumption is worng.

Hence, $(\sqrt{a}+\sqrt{b})$ is an irrational number.

Hence proved.

REAL NUMBERS

Relation between Two Numbers and their HCF and LCM

HCF $(a, b) \times$ LCM $(a, b) = a \times b$

e.g. If HCF = 2 and LCM = 4, then

Product of numbers $= 2 \times 4 = 8$

Theorems

1. Let P be a prime number and a be a positive integer. If P divides a^2, then P divides a.
2. $\sqrt{2}$ is irrational.

Coprime Integers

A pair of integers having HCF 1.

e.g. (1, 3)

Fundamental Theorem of Arithmetic

Every composite number can be written as product of primes and this factorisation is unique, apart from the order in which the prime factors occur.

e.g. 230 can be written as $230 = 2 \times 5 \times 23$

Prime Factorization Method

Expressing the given numbers as the product of its prime factors.

HCF of two or more numbers

Product of smallest power of each common prime factor of numbers.

e.g.

HCF (2, 4) = 2

$2 = 2 \times 1$

$4 = 2 \times 2$

LCM of two or more numbers

Product of greatest power of each prime factor of the numbers

e.g.

LCM of (4, 2) = 4

Factor Tree

A chain of factors which is represented in the form of a tree.

e.g. Factors of 12 by factor tree are given below as

12 → 6, 2; 6 → 3, 2

Rational Numbers

A number that can be expressed as $\frac{p}{q}$, where p and q are integers and $q \neq 0$.

Irrational Numbers

A number that can't be expressed in the form $\frac{p}{q}$, where p and q are integers and $q \neq 0$.

e.g. $\sqrt{2}$, $\sqrt{5}$, 0.101101110.......

Polynomials

CHAPTER 2

In this chapter, we will study the geometrical meaning of the zeroes of a polynomial, relationship between zeroes and coefficients of a polynomial, formation of quadratic and cubic polynomial.

TOPIC 01 Polynomials and Their Related Terms

Polynomials

A polynomial in one variable x, is an algebraic expression of the form

$$p(x) = a_n x^n + a_{n-1} x^{n-1} + a_{n-2} x^{n-2} + \dots + a_2 x^2 + a_1 x + a_0$$

where, n is a non-negative integer and $a_0, a_1, a_2, \dots, a_n$ are constants (real numbers).

The constants $a_0, a_1, a_2, \dots, a_n$ are also known as coefficients of polynomial.

Degree of a Polynomial

The highest power of x in a polynomial $p(x)$, is called the degree of the polynomial $p(x)$.

e.g. (i) $p(x) = 5x + 1/3$ is a polynomial in variable x of degree 1 (since, the highest power of x is 1).

(ii) $q(y) = 3y^2 - \frac{5}{2}y + 7$ is a polynomial in variable y of degree 2 (since, the highest power of y is 2).

Example 1. Write the degree of the following polynomials.

(i) $7q^6 + 4q^2 + \frac{3}{2}q^4 + q - 8$

(ii) $x^3 - 3$

Arrange the terms of given polynomial in descending powers and take highest power of the variable as degree.

Sol. (i) In the polynomial $7q^6 + \frac{3}{2}q^4 + 4q^2 + q - 8$, the highest power of the variable q is 6.
Hence, the degree of the polynomial is 6.

(ii) In the polynomial $x^3 - 3$, the highest power of the variable x is 3. Hence, the degree of the polynomial is 3.

Note it Expressions like $\frac{1}{x+2}$, $\sqrt{x+2}$, $\frac{1}{x^2+x+2}$, etc are not polynomials.

Types of Polynomials

1. **Linear Polynomial** A polynomial of degree one, is called linear polynomial.
   e.g. (i) $f(x) = 3x + 5$ (ii) $g(y) = \sqrt{7}y - 1$
   Generally, any linear polynomial in variable x with real coefficients is of the form $f(x) = ax + b$, where a, b are real numbers and $a \neq 0$.
2. **Quadratic Polynomial** A polynomial of degree two, is called quadratic polynomial.
   e.g. (i) $f(x) = 5x^2 + 3x - \frac{7}{5}$ (ii) $f(x) = 7x^2 - 5x$
   Generally, any quadratic polynomial in variable x with real coefficients is of the form $f(x) = ax^2 + bx + c$, where a, b, c are real numbers and $a \neq 0$.
3. **Cubic Polynomial** A polynomial of degree three, is called cubic polynomial.
   e.g. (i) $f(x) = 8x^3$ (ii) $f(x) = 9x^3 + 5x^2$

Generally, any cubic polynomial in variable x with real coefficients is of the form $f(x) = ax^3 + bx^2 + cx + d$, where a, b, c, d are real numbers and $a \neq 0$.

Example 2. **Identify the type of the polynomials given below (on the basis of degree).**

(i) $3x^2 + 4x + c$ (ii) $3y^3 - 4y^2 + 2y$

(iii) $6y + 5$ (iv) $\sqrt{3}y^2 - \frac{3}{4}y + 7$

(v) $3 - \sqrt{2}x^3 + \frac{2}{7}x - 4x^2$

Sol. (i) Here, the highest power of x in the given polynomial is 2, so it is a quadratic polynomial.

(ii) Here, the highest power of y in the given polynomial is 3, so it is a cubic polynomial.

(iii) Here, the highest power of y in the given polynomial is 1, so it is a linear polynomial.

(iv) Here, the highest power of y in the given polynomial is 2, so it is a quadratic polynomial.

(v) Here, the highest power of x in the given polynomial is 3, so it is a cubic polynomial.

Value of a Polynomial at a Given Point

If $p(x)$ is a polynomial in x and α is a real number, then the value obtained by putting $x = \alpha$ in $p(x)$, is called the value of $p(x)$ at $x = \alpha$.

e.g. If $p(x) = 5x^2 - 4x + 2$, then its value at $x = 2$ is

$$p(2) = 5(2)^2 - 4(2) + 2 = 5(4) - 8 + 2 = 20 - 8 + 2 = 14$$

Thus, the value of $p(x)$ at $x = 2$ is 14.

Zero of a Polynomial

A real number k is said to be a zero of a polynomial $p(x)$, if $p(k) = 0$.

e.g. In the given polynomial $p(x) = 5x + 7$, if we put $x = -7/5$, then $p\left(\frac{-7}{5}\right) = 5 \times \left(\frac{-7}{5}\right) + 7 = 0$

i.e. at $x = \frac{-7}{5}$, $p(x) = 0$.

Therefore, $\frac{-7}{5}$ is a zero of a polynomial $p(x) = 5x + 7$.

Note it Every quadratic polynomial can have atmost two zeroes. However, there exist some quadratic polynomials, which do not have any real zero. e.g. $x^2 + x + 1$.

Example 3. **If $p(x) = ax + b$, then find the zero of $p(x)$.**

Sol. Given, $p(x) = ax + b$

For zero of $p(x)$, put $p(x) = 0$

$\Rightarrow$ $ax + b = 0$

$\Rightarrow$ $x = -b/a$

So, the zero of $p(x)$ is $-b/a$.

Example 4. **If 2 is a zero of polynomial $p(x) = 4x^2 + 2x - 5a$, then find the value of a.**

If k is a zero of a polynomial $p(x)$, then it will satisfy the polynomial, $p(x)$ i.e. $p(k) = 0$. Simplify it to get the value of a.

Sol. Given polynomial is $p(x) = 4x^2 + 2x - 5a$.

Since, 2 is a zero of polynomial.

$\therefore$ $p(2) = 0 \Rightarrow 4(2)^2 + 2(2) - 5a = 0$ [putting $x = 2$]

$\Rightarrow$ $16 + 4 - 5a = 0$

$\Rightarrow$ $5a = 20$

$\therefore$ $a = \frac{20}{5} = 4$

Example 5. **Find the value of a if $x + a$ is a factor (zero) of the polynomial $2x^2 + 2ax + 5x + 10$.**

Sol. Let $p(x) = 2x^2 + 2ax + 5x + 10$

Since, $x + a$ is a factor of $p(x)$.

Therefore, $p(-a) = 0$ [$\because x + a = 0 \Rightarrow x = -a$]

$\Rightarrow$ $2(-a)^2 + 2a(-a) + 5(-a) + 10 = 0$

$\Rightarrow$ $2a^2 - 2a^2 - 5a + 10 = 0$

$\Rightarrow$ $5a = 10$

$\Rightarrow$ $a = 2$

Example 6. **If zeroes of the polynomial $x^2 + (a + 1)x + b$ are 2 and -3, then find the value of $(a + b)$.** NCERT Exemplar

Sol. Given, 2 and -3 are the zeroes of $x^2 + (a + 1)x + b$.

$\therefore$ On putting $x = 2$, we get

$(2)^2 + (a + 1)2 + b = 0$

$\Rightarrow$ $4 + 2a + 2 + b = 0$

$\Rightarrow$ $2a + b = -6$ ...(i)

Again, on putting $x = -3$, we get

$(-3)^2 + (a + 1)(-3) + b = 0$

$\Rightarrow$ $9 - 3a - 3 + b = 0$

$\Rightarrow$ $-3a + b = -6$ ...(ii)

On subtracting Eq. (ii) from Eq. (i), we get

$5a = 0$

$\Rightarrow$ $a = 0$

On putting $a = 0$ in Eq. (ii), we get

$-3(0) + b = -6$

$\Rightarrow$ $0 + b = -6 \Rightarrow b = -6$

Now, $a + b = 0 - 6 = -6$

Hence, the value of $(a + b)$ is -6.

Geometrical Meaning of the Zeroes of a Polynomial

We know that a real number k is a zero of the polynomial $p(x)$, if $p(k) = 0$. To understand zeroes of a polynomial geometrically, first we will see the geometrical representations of linear and quadratic polynomials and then the geometrical meaning of their zeroes.

Geometrical Meaning of the Zero of a Linear Polynomial

Consider a linear polynomial $ax + b$, $a \neq 0$. We know that the graph of $y = ax + b$ is a straight line, which intersects the X-axis at exactly one point, namely $\left(\frac{-b}{a}, 0\right)$.

Also, we know that the zero of $ax + b$ is $-\frac{b}{a}$.

Thus, **the zero of $ax + b$ is the x-coordinate of the point, where the graph of $y = ax + b$ intersects X-axis.**

Example 7. **Represent the linear polynomial $2x + 3$ on the graph paper and find the zero.**

Sol. Let $y = 2x + 3$.

To draw its graph, we need two or more than two values of y corresponding to the different values of x.

For this consider the following table

x	-2	0	2
y	-1	3	7

Now, plot the points $A(-2, -1)$, $B(0, 3)$ and $C(2, 7)$ on the graph paper with suitable scale and join them to obtain the graph of the given polynomial. Thus, we get the graph of $y = 2x + 3$, which is a straight line and it intersects the X-axis in the middle of $x = -1$ and $x = -2$ i.e. at the point $\left(\frac{-3}{2}, 0\right)$. Since, the zero of the linear polynomial $ax + b$ is the x-coordinate of the point, where the graph of $y = ax + b$ intersects the X-axis.

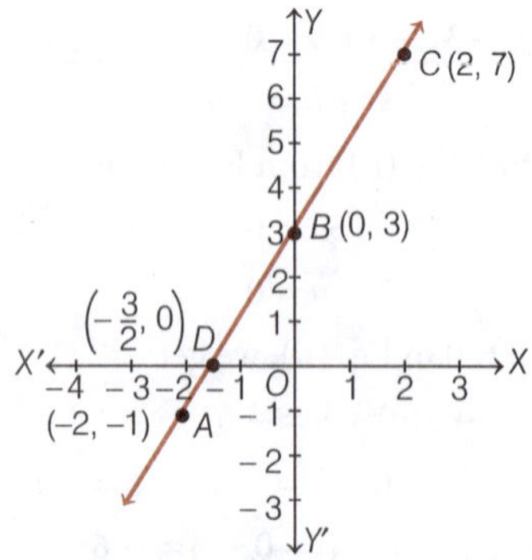

$\therefore$ The zero of $2x + 3$ is $-\frac{3}{2}$.

Geometrical Meaning of the Zeroes of a Quadratic Polynomial

For any quadratic polynomial $ax^2 + bx + c$, $a \neq 0$, the graph of the corresponding equation $y = ax^2 + bx + c$ has one of the two shapes (which are known as parabola) either open downwards like or open upwards like depending on whether $a > 0$ or $a < 0$ i.e. if $a > 0$, then shape of $y = ax^2 + bx + c$ is like and if $a < 0$, then shape of $y = ax^2 + bx + c$ is like .

Now, as per the observation about the shape of the graph of $y = ax^2 + bx + c$, the following three cases arise:

Case I If the graph intersects the X-axis at two points A and A', then the x-coordinate of A and A' are the two zeroes of the quadratic polynomial $ax^2 + bx + c$.

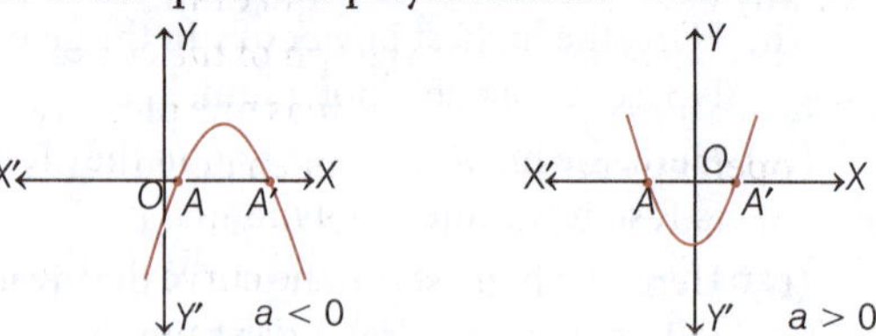

Case II If the graph intersects or touches X-axis at exactly one point, then the two points A and A' (of Case I) coincide. Here, only one intersecting point A is obtained and x-coordinate of A is the only zero for the quadratic polynomial $ax^2 + bx + c$.

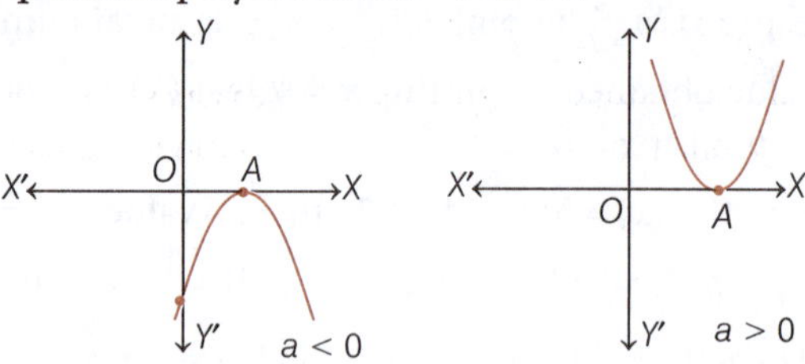

Case III If the graph is either completely above X-axis or completely below X-axis i.e. it does not intersect X-axis at any point. Then, the quadratic polynomial $ax^2 + bx + c$ has no zero.

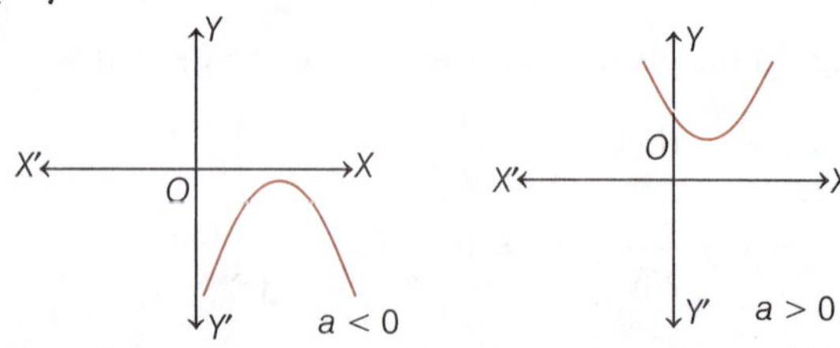

Thus, geometrically we see that a quadratic polynomial can have either two distinct zeroes or two equal zeroes (i.e. one zero) or no zero. From this, we can say that a polynomial of degree 2 has atmost two zeroes.

In general, **the zeroes of a polynomial $p(x)$ are precisely the x-coordinates of the points, where the graph of $y = p(x)$ intersects the X-axis.**

Note it A linear polynomial can have atmost 1 zero and a quadratic polynomial can have atmost 2 zeroes.

Example 8. **Which of the following is not the graph of a quadratic polynomial?** NCERT Exemplar

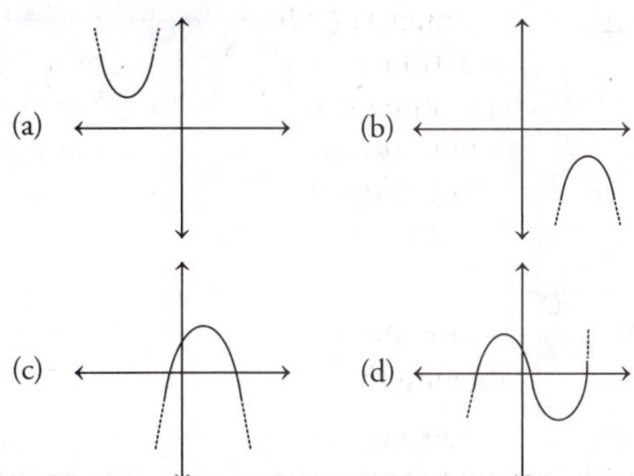

Sol. (d) We know that for any quadratic polynomial $ax^2+bx+c, a \neq 0$, the graph of the corresponding equation $y=ax^2+bx+c$ has one of the two shapes either open upwards like $\cup$ or open downwards like $\cap$ depending on whether $a>0$ or $a<0$. So, option (d) cannot be possible. Also, the curve of a quadratic polynomial crosses the X-axis atmost at two points, but in option (d) the curve crosses the X-axis at three points, so it does not represent the quadratic polynomial.

Example 9. **Represent the quadratic polynomial x^2-4x-5 on the graph paper and find the zeroes.**

Sol. Let $y=x^2-4x-5$.

To draw its graph, we need the values of y corresponding to different values of x. For this consider, the following table:

x	-2	-1	0	1	2	3	4	5
y	7	0	-5	-8	-9	-8	-5	0

Now, plot all these points on the graph paper and join them. Thus, we get the graph of x^2-4x-5, which is a parabola open upwards and it intersects the X-axis at two points whose x-coordinates are -1 and 5.

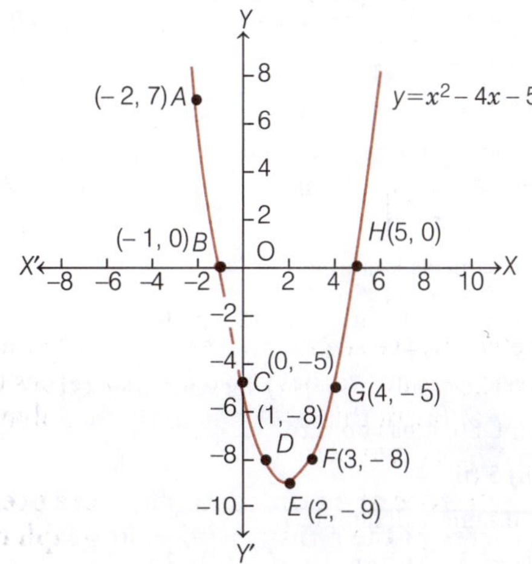

Hence, -1 and 5 are zeroes of the given quadratic polynomial.

Geometrical Meaning of the Zeroes of a Cubic Polynomial

Consider the cubic polynomial $x^3-9x=0$. Make a graph of $y=x^3-9x$.

Let us list the few values of y corresponding to the few values for x as shown below.

x	0	-1	-2	-3	1	2	3
y	0	8	10	0	-8	-10	0

Thus, the graph of $y=x^3-9x$ looks like one given in below figure.

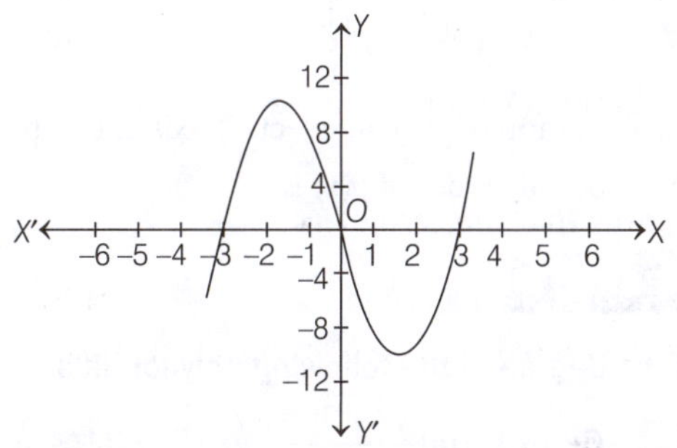

In above table, we see that -3, 0 and 3 are the zeroes of the cubic polynomial x^3-9x. In fact, -3, 0 and 3 are the only x-coordinates where the graph of $y=x^3-9x$ intersects the X-axis.

Thus, any polynomial, of degree 3 can have atmost three zeroes.

Note it In general, given a polynomial $p(x)$ of degree n, the graph of $y=p(x)$ intersects the X-axis atmost at n points. Therefore, a polynomial $p(x)$ of degree n has atmost n zeroes.

Example 10. **Represent the cubic polynomial x^3-4x on the graph paper and find the zeroes.**

Sol. Let $y=x^3-4x$

To draw its graph, we need some values of y corresponding to some different values of x.

For this consider the following table :

x	-2	-1	0	1	2
y	0	3	0	-3	0

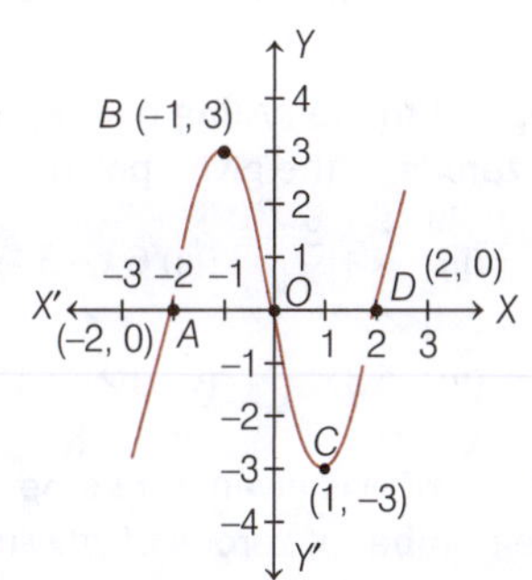

Now, plot these points on graph paper and join them. Thus, we get the graph of $y = x^3 - 4x$. It intersects the X-axis at three points whose x-coordinates are -2, 0 and 2.

Hence, the zeroes of the cubic polynomial $x^3 - 4x$ are -2, 0 and 2.

Example 11. In the given figure, the graph of a polynomial $p(x)$ is shown. Find the number of zeroes of $p(x)$.

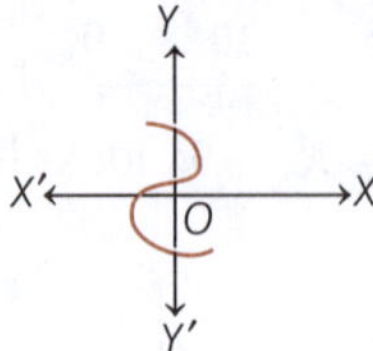

Sol. Here, the graph of $p(x)$ intersects X-axis at one point only.

$\therefore$ Number of zeroes of $p(x)$ is 1.

Try These 2.1

1. Find the degree of the following polynomials:

   (i) $7y^5 + 6y^2 - 1$ (ii) $\dfrac{y^4 + 3y^2 + y}{y}$

   (iii) $3x^2 + 7x + 2$ (iv) $\dfrac{t^8 - 3t^7 + 2t^5 - 6t^2}{t^2}$

   (v) $-x + 1$ (vi) $-10x^2 + 10x$

2. Identify the type of the polynomials given below:

   (i) $f(p) = 3 - p^2 + \sqrt{7}p$ (ii) $q(x) = \dfrac{\sqrt{2}}{5}x^3 + 1$

   (iii) $r(x) = 3x + 4$ (iv) $p(z) = \sqrt{5}z + 2\sqrt{2}$

   (v) $r(t) = \dfrac{-t + 3t^2 - 4t^3}{t}$

3. For what value of k, 3 is a zero of the polynomial $2x^2 + x + k$?

4. If 2 is a zero of polynomial $f(x) = ax^2 - 3(a-1)x - 1$, then find the value of a.

5. If 2 and 3 are zeroes of polynomial $3x^2 - 2kx + 2m$, then find the values of k and m.

6. Find the zeroes of the polynomial $x^2 + 4x - 12$.

   CBSE 2023 (Basic)

7. What is the geometrical meaning of the zeroes of a polynomial?

8. Draw the graph of the following linear polynomials and also find the zeroes of the given polynomials.

   (i) $x + 5$ (ii) $-x + \dfrac{3}{2}$ (iii) $6x - 3$

   (iv) $-\dfrac{7}{2}x + 7$ (v) $-13x$ (vi) $12x - 12$

9. The graph of $y = p(x)$ is given, for some polynomials $p(x)$. Find the number of zeroes of $p(x)$ in each case.

(i) 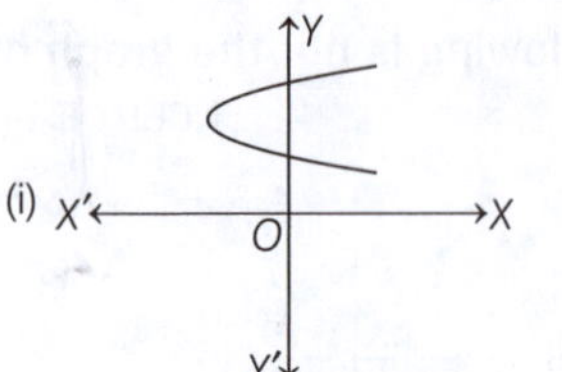

(ii) 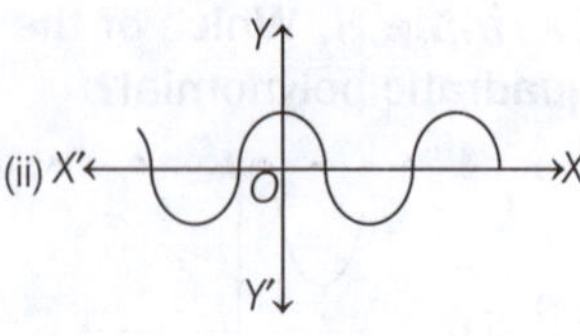

(iii) 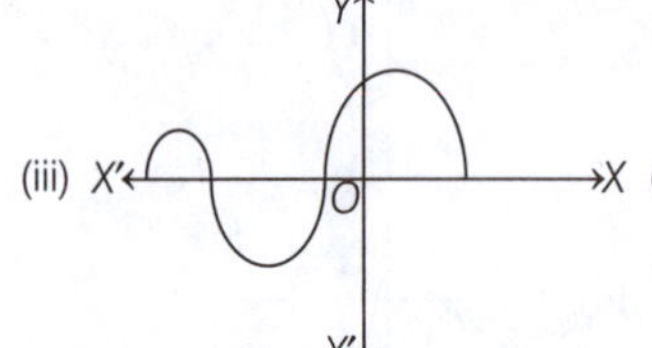

(iv) 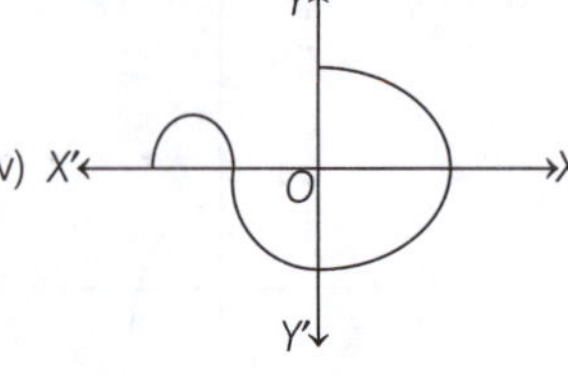

10. Represent the following quadratic polynomials on the graph and also find the zeroes of these polynomials.

    (i) $-x^2 + x + 6$ (ii) $x^2 - 6x + 9$

    (iii) $y^2 - 4$ (iv) $3z^2 - z$

    (v) $6x^2 - 7x + 2$ (vi) $-2x^2 + 5x + 7$

Answers

1. (i) 5 (ii) 3 (iii) 2 (iv) 6 (v) 1 (vi) 2
2. (i) Quadratic polynomial (ii) Cubic polynomial (iii) Linear polynomial (iv) Linear polynomial (v) Quadratic polynomial
3. **Hint** $2(3)^2 + 3 + k = 0$

   Ans. $k = -21$
4. **Hint** $f(2) = 0 \Rightarrow a(2)^2 - 3(a-1)2 - 1 = 0$

   Ans. $a = \dfrac{5}{2}$
5. **Hint** $f(2) = 0$ and $f(3) = 0 \Rightarrow 2k - m = 6$ and $6k - 2m = 27$ and solve both equations.

   Ans. $m = 9$ and $k = \dfrac{15}{2}$
6. **Hint** Let $p(x) = x^2 + 4x - 12$

   On putting $p(x) = 0 \Rightarrow x^2 + 4x - 12 = 0$

   $\Rightarrow \quad x^2 + 6x - 2x - 12 = 0 \Rightarrow x(x+6) - 2(x+6) = 0$

   $\Rightarrow \quad (x+6)(x-2) = 0 \Rightarrow x = -6$ and $x = 2$

   So, the zeroes are -6 and 2.
7. Geometrically, the zeroes of a polynomial $f(x)$ are the x-coordinates of the points, where the graph of $y = f(x)$ intersects the X-axis.
8. **Hint** Do same as Example 7.

   Ans. (i) -5 (ii) $\dfrac{3}{2}$ (iii) $\dfrac{1}{2}$ (iv) 2 (v) 0 (vi) 1
9. (i) **Hint** The graph of $y = p(x)$ does not intersect the X-axis at any point. So, it has no zero.

   Ans. (ii) 5 (iii) 4 (iv) 3
10. **Hint** Do same as Example 9.

    Ans. (i) $-2, 3$ (ii) 3, 3 (iii) $-2, 2$

    (iv) 0, 1/3 (v) $\dfrac{1}{2}, \dfrac{2}{3}$ (vi) $-1, \dfrac{7}{2}$

TOPIC 02 Relationship between Zeroes and Coefficients of a Polynomial, Formation of Quadratic and Cubic Polynomials

Relationship between Zeroes and Coefficients of a Polynomial

For a Linear Polynomial

We know that if k is a zero of polynomial $p(x) = ax + b$, $a \neq 0$, then $p(k) = ak + b = 0$

i.e. $k = -b/a$

Thus, zero of the linear polynomial $ax + b$ is

$$\frac{-b}{a} = \frac{-\text{ Constant term}}{\text{Coefficient of } x}$$

For a Quadratic Polynomial

In general, let α and β be the zeroes of the quadratic polynomial $p(x) = ax^2 + bx + c, a \neq 0$, then by factor theorem $(x - \alpha)$ and $(x - \beta)$ both are the factors of $p(x)$.

Therefore, $ax^2 + bx + c = k(x - \alpha)(x - \beta)$

$$= k[x^2 - (\alpha + \beta)x + \alpha\beta]$$

where, k is some constant.

$$\Rightarrow \quad ax^2 + bx + c = kx^2 - k(\alpha + \beta)x + k\alpha\beta$$

On comparing the coefficients of x^2, x and constant term from both sides, we get

$$a = k, b = -k(\alpha + \beta) \text{ and } c = k\alpha\beta$$

Now, $\dfrac{-k(\alpha + \beta)}{k} = \dfrac{b}{a} \Rightarrow \alpha + \beta = -\dfrac{b}{a}$

i.e. Sum of zeroes, $\alpha + \beta = \dfrac{-\text{ Coefficient of } x}{\text{Coefficient of } x^2} = -\dfrac{b}{a}$

and $\dfrac{k\alpha\beta}{k} = \dfrac{c}{a} \Rightarrow \alpha\beta = \dfrac{c}{a}$

i.e. Product of zeroes, $\alpha\beta = \dfrac{\text{Constant term}}{\text{Coefficient of } x^2} = \dfrac{c}{a}$

For a Cubic Polynomial

In general, let α, β and γ be the zeroes of the cubic polynomial $ax^3 + bx^2 + cx + d, a \neq 0$, then

$$\alpha + \beta + \gamma = \frac{-\text{ Coefficient of } x^2}{\text{Coefficient of } x^3} = \frac{-b}{a},$$

$$\alpha\beta + \beta\gamma + \gamma\alpha = \frac{\text{Coefficient of } x}{\text{Coefficient of } x^3} = \frac{c}{a}$$

and $$\alpha\beta\gamma = \frac{-\text{ Constant term}}{\text{Coefficient of } x^3} = \frac{-d}{a}$$

Example 1. Find the zeroes of the polynomial $2x^2 + 7x + 5$ and verify the relationship between its zeroes and coefficients. CBSE 2025 (Basic)

Sol. Let $f(x) = 2x^2 + 7x + 5 = 2x^2 + 2x + 5x + 5$

$$= 2x(x + 1) + 5(x + 1) = (x + 1)(2x + 5)$$

On putting $f(x) = 0$, we get

$$(x + 1)(2x + 5) = 0$$

$\Rightarrow x + 1 = 0$ or $2x + 5 = 0$

$\Rightarrow \quad x = -1$ or $x = \dfrac{-5}{2}$

Thus, the zeroes of given polynomial are

$$\alpha = -1 \text{ and } \beta = \frac{-5}{2}$$

Verification

Here, the sum of zeroes,

$$\alpha + \beta = -1 + \left(-\frac{5}{2}\right) = \frac{-7}{2} = \frac{-\text{ Coefficient of } x}{\text{Coefficient of } x^2}$$

and product of zeroes $= -1 \times \left(\dfrac{-5}{2}\right) = \dfrac{5}{2} = \dfrac{\text{Constant term}}{\text{Coefficient of } x^2}$

So, the relationship between the zeroes and the coefficients is verified.

Example 2. If α and β are zeroes of the polynomial $x^2 - p(x+1) + c$ such that $(\alpha + 1)(\beta + 1) = 0$, then find the value of c.

Sol. Given, α and β are the zeroes of polynomial $x^2 - p(x + 1) + c$ which can be written as $x^2 - px + c - p$.

So, sum of zeroes, $\alpha + \beta = p$ ...(i)

$$\left[\because \text{Sum of zeroes} = \frac{-\text{ Coefficient of } x}{\text{Coefficient of } x^2}\right]$$

and product of zeroes, $\alpha\beta = c - p$ ...(ii)

$$\left[\because \text{Product of zeroes} = \frac{\text{Constant term}}{\text{Coefficient of } x^2}\right]$$

Also, $(\alpha + 1)(\beta + 1) = 0$ [given]

$\Rightarrow \quad \alpha\beta + (\alpha + \beta) + 1 = 0$

$\Rightarrow \quad c - p + p + 1 = 0$ [from Eqs. (i) and (ii)]

$\Rightarrow \quad c = -1$

Example 3. α, β **are zeroes of the polynomial** $3x^2 - 8x + k$**. Find the value of** k**, if** $\alpha^2 + \beta^2 = \frac{40}{9}$.

CBSE 2025 (Basic)

Sol. Given, α and β are zeroes of the polynomial $3x^2 - 8x + k$ and $\alpha^2 + \beta^2 = \frac{40}{9}$.

$$\therefore \alpha + \beta = \frac{-\text{Coefficient of } x}{\text{Coefficient of } x^2} = \frac{-(-8)}{3} = \frac{8}{3}$$

$$\text{and } \alpha\beta = \frac{\text{Constant term}}{\text{Coefficient of } x^2} = \frac{k}{3}$$

Now, $\alpha + \beta = \frac{8}{3}$

$\Rightarrow (\alpha + \beta)^2 = \left(\frac{8}{3}\right)^2$ [squaring both sides]

$\Rightarrow \alpha^2 + \beta^2 + 2\alpha\beta = \frac{64}{9}$

$\Rightarrow \frac{40}{9} + 2 \times \frac{k}{3} = \frac{64}{9} \Rightarrow \frac{2k}{3} = \frac{64}{9} - \frac{40}{9} = \frac{24}{9}$

$\Rightarrow k = \frac{24}{9} \times \frac{3}{2} \Rightarrow k = 4$

Example 4. $g(x) = px^2 + qx + 152$ **is a polynomial, where** p **and** q **are real numbers. The zeroes of** $g(x)$ **are distinct prime numbers. Find the**

(i) zeroes of $g(x)$**.** **(ii) values of** p **and** q**.**

Show your work and give valid reasons. CBSE QB

Sol. (i) Given, $g(x) = px^2 + qx + 152$

Where, p and q are real numbers.

Then, product of zeroes $= \frac{152}{p} = \frac{2^3 \times 19}{p}$ ...(i)

Also, given that zeroes of $g(x)$ are prime numbers, so possible zeroes of $g(x)$ from Eq. (i) are 2 and 19 (since, both are prime numbers).

(ii) We have, $g(x) = px^2 + qx + 152$

Since, the zeroes are 2 and 19.

$\therefore$ From Eq. (i),

$$2 \times 19 = \frac{2^3 \times 19}{p}$$

$\Rightarrow p = \frac{2^3 \times 19}{2 \times 19} = 2^2 = 4$

Now, sum of zeroes $= \frac{-q}{p} \Rightarrow 2 + 19 = \frac{-q}{4}$

$\therefore q = -(21 \times 4) = -84$

Hence, $p = 4$ and $q = -84$

Example 5. **If one zero of the polynomial** $2x^2 - 5x - (2k+1)$ **is twice the other, then find both the zeroes of the polynomial and the value of** k**.**

Sol. Let α and 2α be the zeroes of the polynomial $2x^2 - 5x - (2k+1)$.

Then, $\alpha + 2\alpha = \frac{5}{2}$ $\left[\because \text{Sum of zeroes} = \frac{-\text{Coefficient of } x}{\text{Coefficient of } x^2}\right]$

$\Rightarrow 3\alpha = \frac{5}{2} \Rightarrow \alpha = \frac{5}{6}$

$\therefore 2\alpha = 2 \times \frac{5}{6} = \frac{5}{3}$

So, the zeroes of the polynomial are $\frac{5}{6}$ and $\frac{5}{3}$.

Now, $\alpha \times 2\alpha = \frac{-2k-1}{2}$

$\left[\because \text{Product of zeroes} = \frac{\text{Constant term}}{\text{Coefficient of } x^2}\right]$

$\therefore \frac{5}{6} \times \frac{5}{3} = \frac{-2k-1}{2} \Rightarrow \frac{25}{18} = \frac{-2k-1}{2}$

$\Rightarrow 25 = 9(-2k-1) \Rightarrow 25 = -18k - 9$

$\Rightarrow 18k = -9 - 25 \Rightarrow 18k = -34$

$\Rightarrow k = \frac{-34}{18} = \frac{-17}{9}$

Example 6. **Find the zeroes of the polynomial** $f(x) = x^3 - 5x^2 - 2x + 24$**, if it is given that the product of its two zeroes is 12.**

Sol. Given polynomial is $f(x) = x^3 - 5x^2 - 2x + 24$.

On comparing with $ax^3 + bx^2 + cx + d$, we get

$$a = 1, b = -5, c = -2 \text{ and } d = 24$$

Let α, β and γ be the zeroes of polynomial $f(x)$, such that $\alpha\beta = 12$.

Then, $\alpha + \beta + \gamma = \frac{-b}{a} = \frac{-(-5)}{1} = 5$ ...(i)

$\alpha\beta + \beta\gamma + \gamma\alpha = \frac{c}{a} = \frac{-2}{1} = -2$ ...(ii)

and $\alpha\beta\gamma = \frac{-d}{a} = \frac{-24}{1} = -24$ ...(iii)

On putting $\alpha\beta = 12$ in Eq. (iii), we get

$$12\gamma = -24 \Rightarrow \gamma = \frac{-24}{12} = -2$$

From Eq. (i), we get $\alpha + \beta - 2 = 5$ [put $\gamma = -2$]

$\Rightarrow \alpha + \beta = 7$

$\therefore \alpha = 7 - \beta$ ...(iv)

Now, $\alpha\beta = 12$

$\Rightarrow (7 - \beta)\beta = 12$ [put $\alpha = 7 - \beta$]

$\Rightarrow 7\beta - \beta^2 = 12$

$\Rightarrow \beta^2 - 7\beta + 12 = 0$

$\Rightarrow \quad \beta^2 - 3\beta - 4\beta + 12 = 0$

[by splitting the middle term]

$\Rightarrow \quad \beta(\beta - 3) - 4(\beta - 3) = 0 \Rightarrow (\beta - 4)(\beta - 3) = 0$

$\Rightarrow \quad \beta = 4$ or 3

When $\beta = 4$, then from Eq. (iv), $\alpha = 7 - 4 = 3$

When $\beta = 3$, then from Eq. (iv), $\alpha = 7 - 3 = 4$

Hence, the zeroes of given polynomial are 3, 4 and – 2.

Formation of Quadratic and Cubic Polynomials

(i) If α and β are the zeroes of a quadratic polynomial, then quadratic polynomial will be

x^2 – (Sum of zeroes) x + Product of zeroes

i.e. $\quad x^2 - (\alpha + \beta)x + \alpha\beta$

where, sum of zeroes $= \alpha + \beta$

and product of zeroes $= \alpha\beta$.

(ii) If α, β and γ are the zeroes of cubic polynomial, then cubic polynomial will be

x^3 – (Sum of zeroes) x^2 + (Sum of the product of zeroes taking two at a time) x – Product of zeroes

i.e. $x^3 - (\alpha + \beta + \gamma)x^2 + (\alpha\beta + \beta\gamma + \gamma\alpha)x - \alpha\beta\gamma$

where, sum of zeroes $= \alpha + \beta + \gamma$, sum of the product of two zeroes taken at a time $= \alpha\beta + \beta\gamma + \gamma\alpha$ and product of zeroes $= \alpha\beta\gamma$.

Example 7. Find a quadratic polynomial whose zeroes are 6 and – 3. CBSE 2023 (Standard)

Sol. Let $\alpha = 6$ and $\beta = -3$

$\therefore \quad \alpha + \beta = 6 + (-3) = 3$

and $\quad \alpha\beta = 6 \times (-3) = -18$

So, quadratic polynomial is given by

$x^2 - (\alpha + \beta)x + \alpha\beta = x^2 - 3x - 18$

Example 8. Find a quadratic polynomial each of whose zeroes is respectively twice the zeroes of the polynomial $2x^2 - 5x + 2$. CBSE 2024 (Basic) Compartment

Sol. Let α and β be the zeroes of the given equation $2x^2 - 5x + 2$.

Then, sum of zeroes $= \alpha + \beta = \dfrac{5}{2}$

and product of zeroes $= \alpha\beta = 1$

$\therefore \quad 2\alpha + 2\beta = 2(\alpha + \beta) = 2 \times \dfrac{5}{2} = 5$

and $\quad (2\alpha)(2\beta) = 4(\alpha\beta) = 4$

So, the required polynomial whose zeroes are 2α and 2β is $x^2 - 5x + 4$.

Example 9. If α and β are zeroes of a quadratic polynomial $x^2 - 5$, then form a quadratic polynomial whose zeroes are $1 + \alpha$ and $1 + \beta$.

Sol. Let $p(x) = x^2 - 5$

For finding the zeroes of $p(x)$, put $p(x) = 0$

$\therefore \quad x^2 - 5 = 0 \Rightarrow x = \pm\sqrt{5}$

Let $\quad \alpha = \sqrt{5}$ and $\beta = -\sqrt{5}$

Now, $1 + \alpha = 1 + \sqrt{5}$ and $1 + \beta = 1 - \sqrt{5}$

Thus, $1 + \sqrt{5}$ and $1 - \sqrt{5}$ are the zeroes of new quadratic polynomial.

$\because$ The quadratic polynomial is given by

x^2 – (Sum of zeroes)x + Product of zeroes

$\therefore$ Required polynomial

$= x^2 - [1 + \sqrt{5} + 1 - \sqrt{5}]x + (1 + \sqrt{5})(1 - \sqrt{5})$

$= x^2 - 2x - 4$

Example 10. Find the cubic polynomial whose three zeroes are 3, –1 and –1/3.

Sol. Let the zeroes of cubic polynomial be

$\alpha = 3, \ \beta = -1$ and $\gamma = -1/3$

Then, $\quad \alpha + \beta + \gamma = 3 + (-1) + (-1/3) = 2 - 1/3 = 5/3$,

$\alpha\beta + \beta\gamma + \gamma\alpha = (3)(-1) + (-1)(-1/3) + (-1/3)(3)$

$= -3 + 1/3 - 1 = -11/3$

and $\quad \alpha\beta\gamma = (3)(-1)(-1/3) = 1$

Now, required cubic polynomial

$= x^3 - (\alpha + \beta + \gamma)x^2 + (\alpha\beta + \beta\gamma + \gamma\alpha)x - \alpha\beta\gamma$

$= x^3 - \left(\dfrac{5}{3}\right)x^2 + \left(\dfrac{-11}{3}\right)x - 1 = \dfrac{3x^3 - 5x^2 - 11x - 3}{3}$

We can consider $3x^3 - 5x^2 - 11x - 3$ as required cubic polynomial because it will also satisfy the given condition.

Try These 2.2

1. **Find the zeroes of the following quadratic polynomial and verify the relationship between the zeroes and the coefficients of the polynomial.**

   (i) $5x^2 - 8x - 4$ (ii) $x^2 - 20x + 91$
   (iii) $x^2 - (\sqrt{2} + 1)x + \sqrt{2}$ (iv) $a(x^2 + 1) - x(a^2 + 1)$
   (v) $2\sqrt{3}x^2 - 5x + \sqrt{3}$

2. **If zeroes α and β of a polynomial $x^2 - 7x + k$ are such that $\alpha - \beta = 1$, then find the value of k.**
3. **If α and β are the zeroes of the polynomial $2y^2 + 7y + 5$, then find the value of $\alpha + \beta + \alpha\beta$.**
4. **If α and β are the zeroes of the quadratic polynomial $f(x) = 3x^2 - 5x - 2$, then evaluate $\alpha^3 + \beta^3$.**
5. **If α and β are the zeroes of $4x^2 + 3x + 7$, then find the value of $\dfrac{1}{\alpha} + \dfrac{1}{\beta}$.**

6. If one zero of the polynomial $(a^2+4)x^2+9x+4a$ is the reciprocal of the other, find the value of a.

7. If one zero of the polynomial $3x^2-8x+2k+1$ is seven times the other, then find the zeroes and the value of k.

8. If α and β are zeroes of the quadratic polynomial $p(x)=6x^2+x-1$, then find the value of $\frac{\alpha}{\beta}+\frac{\beta}{\alpha}+2\left(\frac{1}{\alpha}+\frac{1}{\beta}\right)+3\alpha\beta$.

9. If one of the zeroes of the cubic polynomial x^3+ax^2+bx+c is -1, then find the product of the other two zeroes.

10. Two zeroes of cubic polynomial ax^3+3x^2-bx-6 are -1 and -2. Find the third zero and values of a and b.

11. If the sum and difference of zeroes of quadratic polynomial are -3 and -10, respectively, then find the difference of the squares of zeroes.

12. Find a quadratic polynomial, the sum and product of whose zeroes are respectively

(i) 0 and $-\sqrt{2}$ (ii) $2+\sqrt{3}$ and $2-\sqrt{3}$

(iii) $2\sqrt{5}$ and $-\sqrt{5}$ (iv) $\frac{3}{2}$ and $-\frac{1}{2}$

(v) $\frac{1}{4}$ and $\frac{1}{4}$

13. If sum and product of zeroes of quadratic polynomial are, respectively 8 and 12, then find their zeroes.

14. Find the quadratic polynomial whose zeroes are $2\sqrt{7}$ and $-5\sqrt{7}$.

15. Find the quadratic polynomial whose zeroes are 2 and -6, respectively. Verify the relation between the coefficients and zeroes of the polynomial.

16. How many polynomials will have their zeroes as -2 and 5?

17. If α and β are the zeroes of the quadratic polynomial $f(x)=x^2+x-2$, then find a polynomial whose zeroes are $2\alpha+1$ and $2\beta+1$.

18. If α and β are the zeroes of the quadratic polynomial $f(x)=x^2-3x-2$, find a polynomial whose zeroes are

(i) $\frac{2\alpha}{\beta}$ and $\frac{2\beta}{\alpha}$

(ii) $(2\alpha+3\beta)$ and $(3\alpha+2\beta)$

(iii) $\frac{\alpha^2}{\beta}$ and $\frac{\beta^2}{\alpha}$

(iv) $\frac{1}{2\alpha+\beta}$ and $\frac{1}{2\beta+\alpha}$

19. Write the cubic polynomial whose zeroes are $\frac{2+\sqrt{5}}{2}, \frac{2-\sqrt{5}}{2}$ and 4.

Answers

1. **Hint** Do same as Example 1.
Ans. (i) $-\frac{2}{5}, 2$ (ii) 13, 7 (iii) $\sqrt{2}$, 1 (iv) $a, \frac{1}{a}$ (v) $\frac{1}{\sqrt{3}}, \frac{\sqrt{3}}{2}$

2. **Hint** Do same as Example 2.
Ans. $k=\alpha\beta=12$.

3. **Hint** $\alpha+\beta+\alpha\beta=-\frac{7}{2}+\frac{5}{2}$ **Ans.** -1

4. **Hint** $\alpha^3+\beta^3=(\alpha+\beta)^3-3\alpha\beta(\alpha+\beta)$ **Ans.** $\frac{215}{27}$

5. **Hint** $\frac{1}{\alpha}+\frac{1}{\beta}=\frac{\alpha+\beta}{\alpha\beta}=-\frac{3/4}{7/4}$ **Ans.** $-\frac{3}{7}$

6. **Hint** Let α and $\frac{1}{\alpha}$ be the zeroes of the given polynomial.

$\therefore \quad \alpha\cdot\frac{1}{\alpha}=\frac{4a}{a^2+4} \Rightarrow 1=\frac{4a}{a^2+4}$

$\Rightarrow a^2+4=4a \Rightarrow (a-2)^2=0$ **Ans.** $a=2$

7. **Hint** Do same as Example 5. **Ans.** $k=\frac{2}{3}$

8. **Hint** $\frac{\alpha}{\beta}+\frac{\beta}{\alpha}+2\left(\frac{1}{\alpha}+\frac{1}{\beta}\right)+3\alpha\beta=\frac{\alpha^2+\beta^2}{\alpha\beta}+2\left(\frac{\alpha+\beta}{\alpha\beta}\right)+3\alpha\beta$

Ans. $-\frac{2}{3}$

9. **Hint** Let the other two zeroes be α and β.
Then, we have $\alpha\beta(-1)=-c \Rightarrow \alpha\beta=c$

10. **Hint** Let $f(x)=ax^3+3x^2-bx-6$.
Since, -1 and -2 are zeroes of $f(x)$.
$\therefore$ Put $f(-1)=0$ and $f(-2)=0$
$\Rightarrow \quad a-b=-3$ and $4a-b=3 \Rightarrow a=2$ and $b=5$
Now, let the third zero be α. Then, we have

$$\alpha(-1)(-2)=\frac{6}{a}$$

Ans. $a=2, b=5$ and $\alpha=\frac{3}{2}$

11. **Hint** We have, $\alpha+\beta=-3$
and $\alpha-\beta=-10$ [assuming $\alpha<\beta$]
$\therefore \quad \alpha=-\frac{13}{2}$ and $\beta=\frac{7}{2}$ **Ans.** $\alpha^2-\beta^2=30$.

12. **Hint** Quadratic polynomial with α and β being its roots is
x^2- (Sum of roots) x + Products of roots $=0$
Ans. (i) $x^2-\sqrt{2}$ (ii) $x^2-(2+\sqrt{3})x+(2-\sqrt{3})$
(iii) $x^2-2\sqrt{5}x-\sqrt{5}$ (iv) $2x^2-3x-1$ (v) $4x^2-x+1$

13. **Hint** For finding zeroes, put
$x^2-8x+12=0 \Rightarrow (x-6)(x-2)=0 \Rightarrow x=2, 6$
Ans. Zeroes are 2 and 6.

14. **Hint** Do same as Example 7.
Ans. $x^2+3\sqrt{7}x-70$

15. Hint Let $\alpha = 2$ and $\beta = -6$.

Then, required polynomial is given by

$$x^2 - (\alpha + \beta)x + \alpha\beta = x^2 + 4x - 12$$

Also, here sum of zeroes $= \alpha + \beta = -4 = -\dfrac{\text{Coefficient of } x}{\text{Coefficient of } x^2}$

and product of zeroes $= \alpha\beta = -12 = \dfrac{\text{Constant term}}{\text{Coefficient of } x^2}$

Ans. The required polynomial is $x^2 + 4x - 12$ and the relationship between zeroes and coefficients is verified.

16. Hint Polynomials, which have their zeroes as α and β, are given by $k[x^2 - (\alpha + \beta)x + \alpha\beta]$, where k is non-zero constant.

Ans. There are infinite polynomials which have their zeroes as -2 and 5.

17. Hint Do same as Example 9. **Ans.** $x^2 - 9$

18. Hint We have, $\alpha + \beta = 3$ and $\alpha\beta = -2$.

Now, required polynomial is given by

(i) $x^2 - \left(\dfrac{2\alpha}{\beta} + \dfrac{2\beta}{\alpha}\right)x + \left(\dfrac{2\alpha}{\beta}\right)\cdot\left(\dfrac{2\beta}{\alpha}\right)$

$$= x^2 - 2\left(\frac{\alpha^2 + \beta^2}{\alpha\beta}\right)x + 4 = x^2 - 2\left(\frac{(\alpha + \beta)^2 - 2\alpha\beta}{\alpha\beta}\right)x + 4$$

Ans. $x^2 + 13x + 4$

(ii) **Hint** $x^2 - (2\alpha + 3\beta + 3\alpha + 2\beta)x + (2\alpha + 3\beta)(3\alpha + 2\beta)$

$$= x^2 - (5\alpha + 5\beta)x + (6\alpha^2 + 4\alpha\beta + 9\alpha\beta + 6\beta^2)$$

$$= x^2 - 5(\alpha + \beta)\, x + [6(\alpha^2 + \beta^2) + 13\alpha\beta]$$

Ans. $x^2 - 15x + 52$

(iii) **Hint** $\left[x^2 - \left(\dfrac{\alpha^2}{\beta} + \dfrac{\beta^2}{\alpha}\right)x + \left(\dfrac{\alpha^2}{\beta}\right)\left(\dfrac{\beta^2}{\alpha}\right)\right]$

$$= \left[x^2 - \left(\frac{\alpha^3 + \beta^3}{\alpha\beta}\right)x + \alpha\beta\right]$$

$$= x^2 - \left[\frac{(\alpha + \beta)\{(\alpha + \beta)^2 - 3\alpha\beta\}}{\alpha\beta}\right]x + \alpha\beta$$

Ans. $\dfrac{1}{2}(2x^2 + 45x - 4)$

(iv) **Hint** Do same as Part (iii).

Ans. $x^2 - \dfrac{9}{16}x + \dfrac{1}{16}$

19. Hint Do same as Example 10.

Ans. $4x^3 - 24x^2 + 31x + 4$

NCERT FOLDER

Complete Solutions of All Exercises of NCERT Textbook

EXERCISE 2.1

Q1. The graphs of $y = p(x)$ are given below, for some polynomials $p(x)$. Find the number of zeroes of $p(x)$ in each case.

(i) 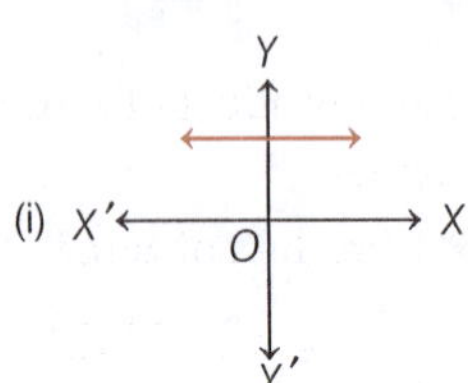

(ii) 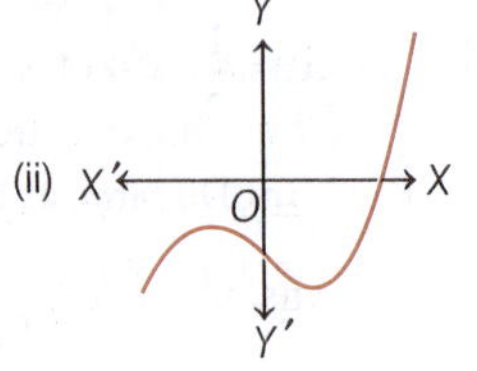

(iii) 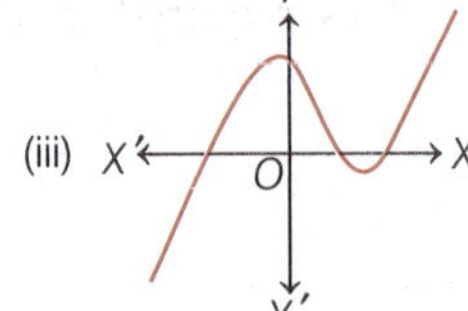

(iv) 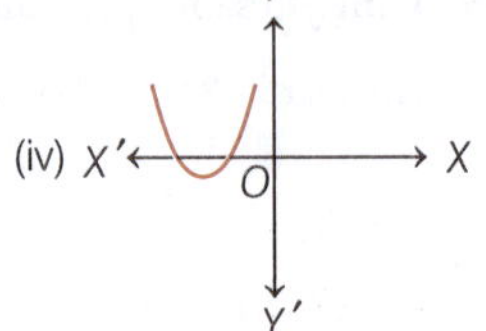

(v) 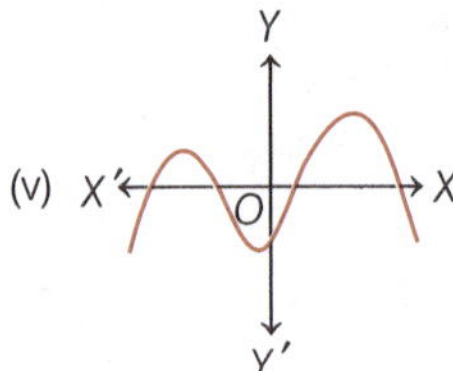

(vi) 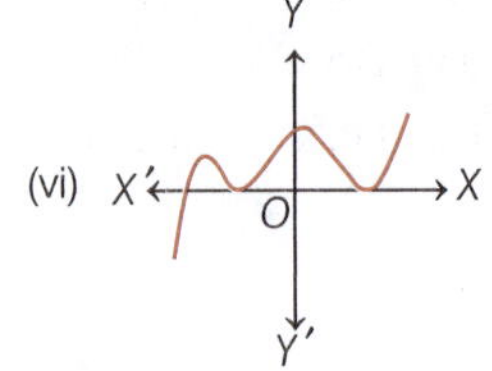

The number of points at which the graph of $p(x)$ intersects the X-axis, gives the number of zeroes and their x-coordinate, give the zeroes.

Sol. (i) Here, the graph of $y = p(x)$ does not intersect the X-axis, so $p(x)$ has no zero.

(ii) The number of zeroes is one, as the graph of $y = p(x)$ intersects the X-axis at one point only.

(iii) The number of zeroes is three, as the graph of $y = p(x)$ intersects the X-axis at three points.

(iv) The number of zeroes is two, as the graph of $y = p(x)$ intersects the X-axis at two points.

(v) The number of zeroes is four, as the graph of $y = p(x)$ intersects the X-axis at four points.

(vi) The number of zeroes is three, as the graph of $y = p(x)$ intersects the X-axis at three points.

Exercise 2.2

Q2. Find the zeroes of the following quadratic polynomials and verify the relationship between the zeroes and its coefficients. CBSE 2020 (Basic)

(i) $x^2 - 2x - 8$ (ii) $4s^2 - 4s + 1$

(iii) $6x^2 - 3 - 7x$ (iv) $4u^2 + 8u$

(v) $t^2 - 15$ (vi) $3x^2 - x - 4$

First, factorise the given polynomial and then put each factor equal to zero to find the required zeroes and then for verification, show that

$$\text{Sum of zeroes} = -\frac{\text{Coefficient of } x}{\text{Coefficient of } x^2}$$

and $$\text{product of zeroes} = \frac{\text{Constant term}}{\text{Coefficient of } x^2}$$

Sol. (i) Let $p(x) = x^2 - 2x - 8$

$= x^2 - 4x + 2x - 8$ [by splitting the middle term]

$= x(x-4) + 2(x-4) = (x+2)(x-4)$

To find zeroes, put $p(x) = 0$

$\Rightarrow x - 4 = 0$ or $x + 2 = 0 \Rightarrow x = 4$ or $x = -2$

Hence, zeroes of the given polynomial are -2 and 4.

Verification

Here, sum of the zeroes $= -2 + 4 = 2 = -(-2/1)$

$$= -\frac{\text{Coefficient of } x}{\text{Coefficient of } x^2}$$

and product of the zeroes $= -2 \times 4 = -8 = -8/1$

$$= \frac{\text{Constant term}}{\text{Coefficient of } x^2}$$

So, the relationship between the zeroes and its coefficients is verified.

(ii) Do same as Part (i). **Ans.** $\frac{1}{2}$ and $\frac{1}{2}$

(iii) Do same as Part (i). **Ans.** $\frac{-1}{3}$ and $\frac{3}{2}$

(iv) Let $p(u) = 4u^2 + 8u = 4u(u+2)$

To find zeroes, put $p(u) = 0$

$\Rightarrow \quad 4u(u+2) = 0$

$\Rightarrow \quad u = 0$ or $u + 2 = 0$ $\quad [\because 4 \neq 0]$

$\Rightarrow \quad u = 0$ or $u = -2$

Hence, zeroes of the given polynonial are 0 and -2.

Verification

Here, sum of zeroes $= 0-2=-2=-(8/4)$

$$= -\frac{\text{Coefficient of } u}{\text{Coefficient of } u^2}$$

and product of zeroes

$$= 0\times -2 = 0 = (0/4) = \frac{\text{Constant term}}{\text{Coefficient of } u^2}$$

so, the relationship between the zeroes and its coefficients is verified.

(v) Let $p(t) = t^2 - 15 = t^2 - (\sqrt{15})^2$

$= (t-\sqrt{15})(t+\sqrt{15})$ $[\because a^2 - b^2 = (a-b)(a+b)]$

To find zeroes, put $p(t) = 0$

$\Rightarrow$ $(t-\sqrt{15})(t+\sqrt{15}) = 0$

$\Rightarrow t-\sqrt{15} = 0$ or $t+\sqrt{15} = 0$

$\Rightarrow$ $t = \sqrt{15}$ or $t = -\sqrt{15}$

Hence, zeroes of the given polynomial are $-\sqrt{15}$ and $\sqrt{15}$.

Verification

Hence, sum of zeroes $= -\sqrt{15}+\sqrt{15} = 0 = -(0/1)$

$$= -\frac{\text{Coefficient of } t}{\text{Coefficient of } t^2}$$

and product of zeroes $= -\sqrt{15}\times\sqrt{15}$

$$= -15 = \frac{-15}{1}$$

$$= \frac{\text{Constant term}}{\text{Coefficient of } t^2}$$

So, the relationship between the zeroes and its coefficients is verified.

(vi) Do same as Part (i). **Ans.** -1 and $4/3$

Q2. **Find a quadratic polynomial each with the given numbers as sum and product of its zeroes, respectively.**

(i) $\frac{1}{4}, -1$ (ii) $\sqrt{2}, \frac{1}{3}$

(iii) $0, \sqrt{5}$ (iv) 1, 1

(v) $-\frac{1}{4}, \frac{1}{4}$ (vi) 4, 1

Put the sum and product of zeroes, in x^2- (Sum of zeroes) x + Product of zeroes, to get the required quadratic polynomial.

Sol. (i) Given, sum of zeroes $= 1/4$ and product of zeroes $= -1$

Then, the quadratic polynomial

$= x^2 - (\text{Sum of zeroes})x + \text{Product of zeroes}$

$$= x^2 - \left(\frac{1}{4}\right)x - 1 = x^2 - \frac{x}{4} - 1 = \frac{4x^2-x-4}{4}$$

We can consider $4x^2-x-4$ as required quadratic polynomial because it will also satisfy the given conditions.

(ii) Do same as Part (i). **Ans.** $3x^2-3\sqrt{2}x+1$

(iii) Do same as Part (i). **Ans.** $x^2+\sqrt{5}$

(iv) Do same as Part (i). **Ans.** x^2-x+1

(v) Do same as Part (i). **Ans.** $4x^2+x+1$

(vi) Do same as Part (i). **Ans.** x^2-4x+1

REVIEW EXERCISE

Including Competency Based Questions

Part I

Multiple Choice Questions

1. If one zero of the polynomial $kx^2 + 3x + k$ is 2, then the value of k is **CBSE 2023 (Basic)**

(a) $-\frac{6}{5}$ (b) $\frac{6}{5}$ (c) $\frac{5}{6}$ (d) $-\frac{5}{6}$

2. What should be added from the polynomial $x^2 - 5x + 4$, so that 3 is the zero of the resulting polynomial? **CBSE 2024 (Standard)**

(a) 1 (b) 2 (c) 4 (d) 5

3. The zeroes of the quadratic polynomial $16x^2 - 9$ are **CBSE 2023 (Basic)**

(a) $\frac{3}{4}, \frac{3}{4}$ (b) $-\frac{3}{4}, \frac{3}{4}$

(c) $\frac{9}{16}, \frac{9}{16}$ (d) $-\frac{3}{4}, -\frac{3}{4}$

4. Zeroes of a quadratic polynomial $x^2 - 5x + 6$ are

(a) $-5, 1$ (b) $5, 1$

(c) $2, 3$ (d) $-2, -3$

5. If $x - 1$ is a factor of the polynomial $p(x) = x^3 + ax^2 + 2b$ and $a + b = 4$, then **Competency Based Question**

(a) $a = 5$ and $b = -1$ (b) $a = 9$ and $b = -5$

(c) $a = 7$ and $b = -3$ (d) $a = 3$ and $b = 1$

6. In the given graph, the polynomial $p(x)$ is shown. Number of zeroes of $p(x)$ is **CBSE 2025 (Basic)**

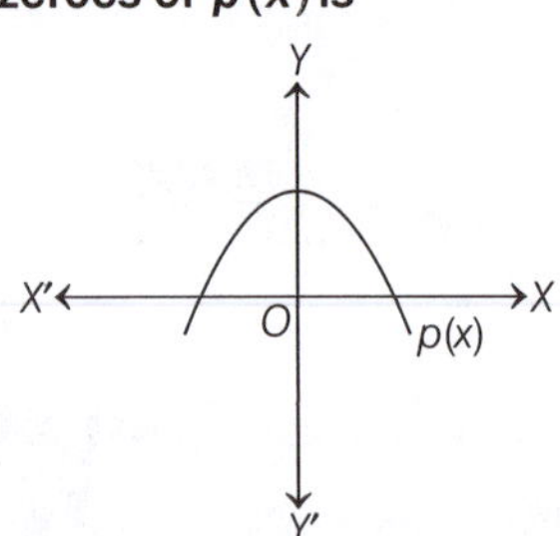

(a) 3 (b) 2 (c) 1 (d) 4

7. The graph of a quadratic polynomial $p(x)$ passes through the points (– 6, 0), (0, – 30), (4, – 20) and (6, 0). The zeroes of the polynomial are **CBSE Sample Paper 2025 (Standard)**

(a) –6, 0 (b) 4, 6

(c) –30, –20 (d) –6, 6

8. The given linear polynomial $y = f(x)$ has **CBSE 2023 (Standard)**

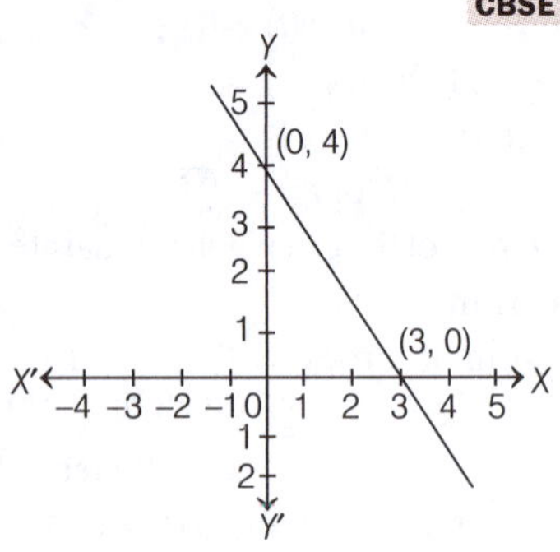

(a) 2 zeroes (b) 1 zero and the zero is 3

(c) 1 zero and the zero is 4 (d) no zero

9. If the sum of zeroes of the polynomial $p(x) = 2x^2 - k\sqrt{2}x + 1$ is $\sqrt{2}$, then the value of k is **CBSE 2024 (Standard)**

(a) $\sqrt{2}$ (b) 2 (c) $2\sqrt{2}$ (d) $\frac{1}{2}$

10. If the zeroes of the quadratic polynomial $x^2 + (a+1)x + b$ are 2 and – 3, then **CBSE 2023 (Standard); 2022 (Basic)**

(a) $a = -7, b = -1$ (b) $a = 5, b = -1$

(c) $a = 2, b = -6$ (d) $a = 0, b = -6$

11. If α and β are the zeroes of the polynomial $x^2 - 1$, then the value of $\alpha + \beta$ is **CBSE 2023 (Standard)**

(a) 2 (b) 1 (c) – 1 (d) 0

12. If α, β are the zeroes of the quadratic polynomial $p(x) = x^2 - (k+6)x + 2(2k-1)$, then the value of k, if $\alpha + \beta = \frac{1}{2}\alpha\beta$, is

(a) –7 (b) 7 (c) –3 (d) 3

13. For what value of k, the product of zeroes of the polynomial $kx^2 - 4x - 7$ is 2? **CBSE 2024 (Basic)**

(a) $-\frac{1}{14}$ (b) $-\frac{7}{2}$ (c) $\frac{7}{2}$ (d) $-\frac{2}{7}$

14. The zeroes of a polynomial $x^2 + px + q$ are twice the zeroes of the polynomial $4x^2 - 5x - 6$. The value of p is **CBSE 2024 (Standard)**

(a) $-\frac{5}{2}$ (b) $\frac{5}{2}$ (c) –5 (d) 10

15. **If one of the zeroes of the cubic polynomial $ax^3 + bx^2 + cx + d$ is zero, then product of other two zeroes is** **NCERT Exemplar**

(a) $\frac{-c}{a}$ (b) $\frac{c}{a}$ (c) 0 (d) $\frac{-b}{a}$

16. **If one of the zeroes of the cubic polynomial $x^3 + ax^2 + bx + c$ is –1, then the product of the other two zeroes is**

(a) $b-a+1$ (b) $b-a-1$ (c) $a-b+1$ (d) $a-b-1$

17. **A quadratic polynomial whose zeroes are $\frac{2}{5}$ and $\frac{-1}{5}$ is** **CBSE Sample Paper 2025 (Basic)**

(a) $25x^2+5x-2$ (b) $5x^2-2x+1$
(c) $5x^2+2x-1$ (d) $25x^2-5x-2$

18. **The number of quadratic polynomial having zeroes – 5 and – 3 is**

(a) 1 (b) 2 (c) 3 (d) more than 3

19. **The number of polynomials having zeroes – 3 and 5 is**

(a) only one (b) infinite
(c) exactly two (d) atmost two

20. **A quadratic polynomial having zeroes $-\sqrt{\frac{5}{2}}$ and $\sqrt{\frac{5}{2}}$ is** **CBSE Sample Paper 2025 (Standard)**

(a) $x^2-5\sqrt{2}x+1$ (b) $8x^2-20$
(c) $15x^2-6$ (d) $x^2-2\sqrt{5}x-1$

21. **If a cubic polynomial with the sum of its zeroes, sum of the products of its zeroes taken two at a time and product of its zeroes are 0, –7 and –6 respectively, then the cubic polynomial is** **Competency Based Question**

(a) x^3+7x-6 (b) x^3+7x+6
(c) x^3-7x-6 (d) x^3-7x+6

Assertion-Reason Type Questions

22. **Assertion** Zeroes of a polynomial $P(x) = x^2-2x-3$ are –1 and 3.

Reason The graph of polynomial $P(x) = x^2-2x-3$ intersects X-axis at (–1, 0) and (3, 0). **CBSE 2024 (Basic)**

(a) Both Assertion and Reason are correct and Reason is the correct explanation of Assertion.
(b) Both Assertion and Reason are correct but Reason is not the correct explanation of Assertion.
(c) Assertion is correct but Reason is incorrect.
(d) Assertion is incorrect but Reason is correct.

23. **Assertion** If the graph of a polynomial intersects the X-axis at exactly two points, then the number of zeroes of that polynomial is 2.

Reason The number of zeroes of a polynomial is equal to the number of points where the graph of the polynomial intersects X-axis. **CBSE 2024 (Standard) Compartment**

(a) Both Assertion and Reason are correct and Reason is the correct explanation of Assertion.
(b) Both Assertion and Reason are correct but Reason is not the correct explanation of Assertion.
(c) Assertion is correct but Reason is incorrect.
(d) Assertion is incorrect but Reason is correct.

24. **Assertion** If the zeroes of polynomial $x^3-12x^2+3x+10$ are $(a-d)$, a and $(a+d)$, then value of a is 4.

Reason If α, β and γ are the zeroes of $p(x) = ax^3+bx^2+cx+d$, $a \neq 0$, then $\alpha\beta\gamma = \frac{-d}{a}$.

(a) Both Assertion and Reason are correct and Reason is the correct explanation of Assertion.
(b) Both Assertion and Reason are correct but Reason is not the correct explanation of Assertion.
(c) Assertion is correct but Reason is incorrect.
(d) Assertion is incorrect but Reason is correct.

25. **Assertion** If 3 and 4 are the zeroes of a quadratic polynomial, then polynomial is $x^2-7x+12$.

Reason If α, β are the zeroes of a quadratic polynomial, then quadratic polynomial is $x^2-(\alpha+\beta)x+\alpha\beta$.

(a) Both Assertion and Reason are correct and Reason is the correct explanation of Assertion.
(b) Both Assertion and Reason are correct but Reason is not the correct explanation of Assertion.
(c) Assertion is correct but Reason is incorrect.
(d) Assertion is incorrect but Reason is correct.

Case Study Based Questions

26. In a pool at an aquarium, a dolphin jumps out of the water travelling at 20 cm/s. Its height above water level after t s is given by $p(t) = 20t - 16t^2$.

On the basis of above information, answer the following questions. **CBSE 2023 (Standard)**

(i) Find zeroes of polynomial $p(t) = 20t - 16t^2$.

(ii) Which of the following types of graph represents $p(t)$?

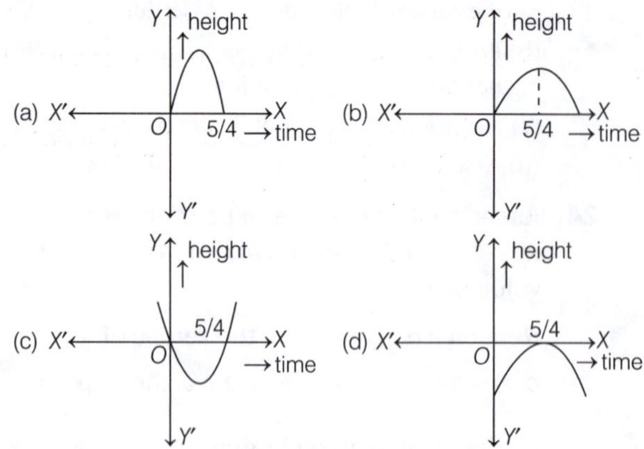

(iii) (a) What would be the value of h at $t = \frac{3}{2}$? Interpret the result.

Or (b) How much distance has the dolphin covered before hitting the water level again?

27. Rainbow is an arch of colours that is visible in the sky after rain or when water droplets are present in the atmosphere. The colours of the rainbow are generally, red, orange, yellow, green, blue, indigo and violet. Each colour of the rainbow makes a parabola. We know that any quadratic polynomial $p(x) = ax^2 + bx + c, (a \neq 0)$ represents a parabola on the graph paper.

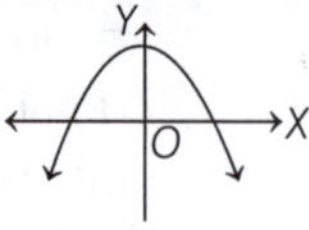

CBSE 2023 (Basic)

Based on the above information, answer the following questions.

(i) The graph of a rainbow $y = f(x)$ is shown in the figure. Write the number of zeroes of the curve.

(ii) If the graph of a rainbow does not intersect the X-axis but intersects Y-axis at one point, then how many zeroes will it have?

(iii) (a) If a rainbow is represented by the quadratic polynomial $p(x) = x^2 + (a+1)x + b$, whose zeroes are 2 and -3, find the values of a and b.

Or (b) The polynomial $x^2 - 2x - (7p + 3)$ represents a rainbow. If -4 is a zero of it, then find the value of p.

28. Amit designs a flower vase using a graph of polynomial equations. Equation of the curve l is given in the graph.

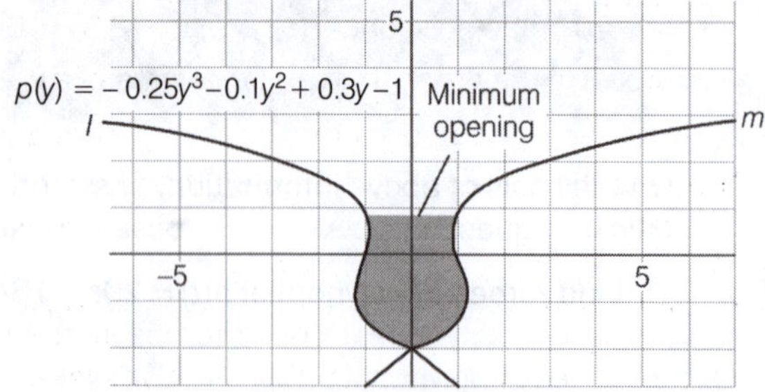

Based on the above information, answer the following questions.

(i) Sara looks at the graphical model and makes an observation, "The zero of the polynomial is at the origin." Is she correct? If not, then what are the coordinates of the zero of the polynomial?

(ii) The curve m is a mirror image of $p(y)$ on the Y-axis. Find the polynomial represents curve m.

(iii) (a) Sara changes the coefficient of y^3 in the polynomials for the curves l and m. How does it affect the shape of the flower pot?

Or

(b) Amit wants to decrease the minimum opening of the flower pot. Which term of the polynomials for the curves l and m should he change?

29. The below pictures are few natural examples of parabolic shape which is represented by a quadratic polynomial. A parabolic arch is an arch in the shape of a parabola.

In structures, their curve represents an efficient method of load and so can be found in bridges and in architecture in a variety of forms.

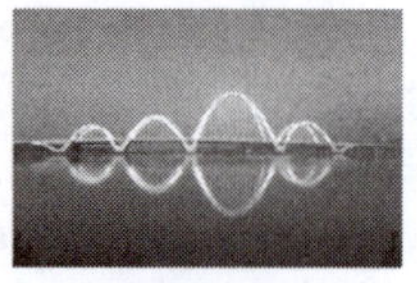

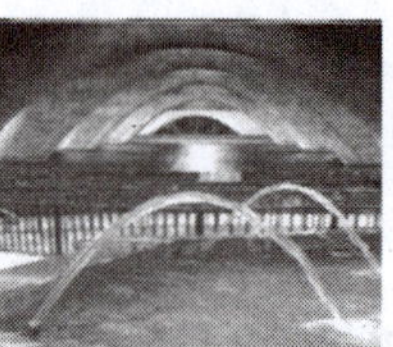

On the basis of above information, answer the following questions.

(i) Jaya says the graphical shape of quadratic polynomial $P(x) = ax^2 + bx + c, a \neq 0$ is open downward parabola like $\cap$ if $a < 0$. Is Jaya right? Explain.

(ii) If α and $\frac{1}{\alpha}$ are the zeroes of the quadratic polynomial $2x^2 - x + 8k$, then find the value of k.

(iii) (a) Is the graph of $x^2 + 1 = 0$ intersect X-axis at two distinct points?

Or

(b) If the sum of the zeroes is $-p$ and the product of two zeroes is $-\frac{1}{p}$, then find the quadratic polynomial.

30. Two friends Reena and Romi during their summer vacations went to Manali. They decided to go for trekking. While trekking, they observes that the trekking path is in the shape of parabola.

The mathematical representation of the track is shown in the graph.

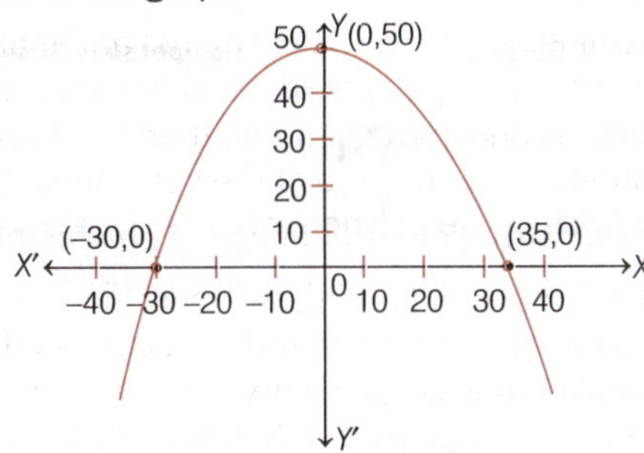

Based on the above information, anwer the following questions.

(i) Find the zeroes of the polynomial whose graph is given.

(ii) What will be the expression of the given polynomial $P(x)$?

(iii) For what value of x, the value of the polynomial $P(x) = x^2 - 5x - 1050$ is -750?

Part II

Very Short Answer Type Questions

1. Find the degree of the polynomial $\dfrac{-t^9 + 4t^6 + 7t^5}{t^5}$.

2. For what value of k, -2 is a zero of the polynomial $3x^2 + 4x + 2k$?

3. Is the following statement True or False? Justify your answer. 'If the zeroes of a quadratic polynomial $ax^2 + bx + c$ are both negative, then a, b and c all have the same sign.' **NCERT Exemplar**

4. If the zeroes of the quadratic polynomial $ax^2 + bx + c$, where $c \neq 0$, are equal, then show that c and a have same sign. **NCERT Exemplar**

5. The graphs of $y = p(x)$, where $p(x)$ is a polynomial in x are given. Find the number of zeroes of $p(x)$ in each case. For each case, also state whether $p(x)$ is linear or quadratic. **Competency Based Question**

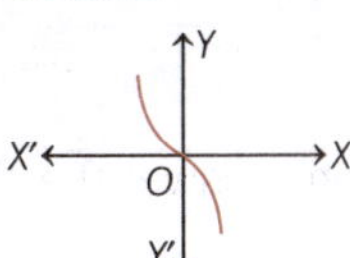

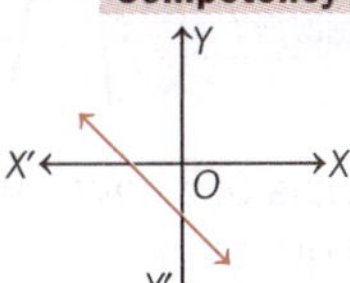

6. Two polynomials are shown in the graph below.

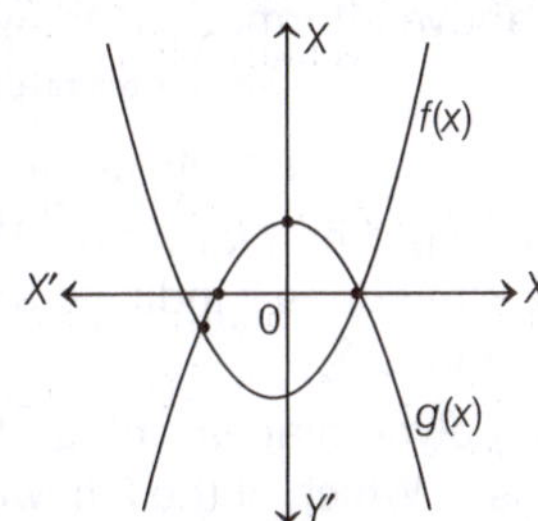

Find the number of zeroes that are common to both the polynomials. Explain your answer. **Competency Based Question**

7. If one zero of $2x^2 - 3x + k$ is reciprocal to the other, then find the value of k.

8. If α and β are zeroes of a polynomial $6x^2 - 5x + 1$, then form a quadratic polynomial whose zeroes are α^2 and β^2. **CBSE Sample Paper 2025 (Standard)**

9. Sum of zeroes of the polynomial $3x^2 - 10x + 13$ is 5. Aryan at once said, 'it is false'. Do you agree with Aryan? Justify. **Competency Based Question**

Short Answer Type Questions

10. Write whether the following expressions are polynomials or not. Give reasons for your answer. **CBSE 2018**

(i) $x^3 + \dfrac{1}{x^2} + \dfrac{1}{x} + 1$ (ii) $x^2 + x + 3$

(iii) $y^{-1/2} - 3y + 2$ (iv) $\sqrt{2}y^3 + \sqrt{3}y$

11. If $(x + a)$ is a factor of two polynomials $x^2 + px + q$ and $x^2 + mx + n$, then prove that $a = \dfrac{n - q}{m - p}$.

12. Use the relationship between the zeroes and coefficients of a polynomial to find the value of k. Show your steps. Write a quadratic polynomial whose sum of zeroes is less than that of the polynomial shown in the graph above. **Competency Based Question**

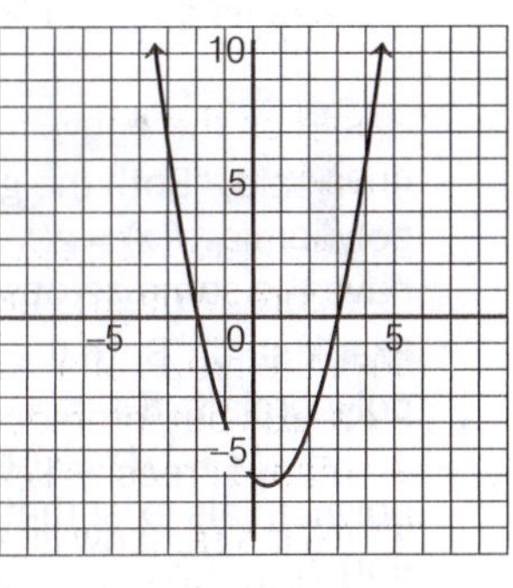

13. $p(x) = ax^2 - 8x + 3$, where a is a non-zero real number. One zero of $p(x)$ is 3 times the other zero.

(i) Find the value of a. Show your work.

(ii) What is the shape of the graph of $p(x)$? Give a reason for your answer. **Competency Based Question**

14. If one zero of the polynomial $(a^2 + 9)x^2 + 13x + 6a$ is reciprocal of the other, then find the value of a.

15. If the zeroes of the polynomial $x^2 + px + q$ are double in value to the zeroes of $2x^2 - 5x - 3$, then find the values of p and q.

16. Find the zeroes of the polynomial $r(x) = 4x^2 + 3x - 1$. Hence, write a polynomial whose zeroes are reciprocal of the zeroes of polynomial $r(x)$. **CBSE 2025 (Standard)**

17. Can the quadratic polynomial $x^2 + kx + k$ have equal zeroes for some odd integer $k > 1$? **NCERT Exemplar**

18. If the sum of the zeroes of the polynomial $p(x) = (a+1)x^2 + (2a+3)x + (3a+4)$ is -1, then find the product of its zeroes. **Competency Based Question**

19. Find the zeroes of the following polynomial by factorisation method and verify the relations between the zeroes and their coefficients

(i) $7y^2 - \frac{11}{3}y - \frac{2}{3}$

(ii) $\sqrt{3}x^2 + 10x + 7\sqrt{3}$

(iii) $4\sqrt{3}x^2 + 5x - 2\sqrt{3}$

20. A class consists of a group of 18 average students and 7 best students of the class. Write a quadratic polynomials whose zeroes are equal to number of average students and number of best students. **Competency Based Question**

21. Shown below are the graphs of two cubic polynomial, $f(x)$ and $g(x)$. Both polynomials have the zeroes -1, 0 and 1. **Competency Based Question**

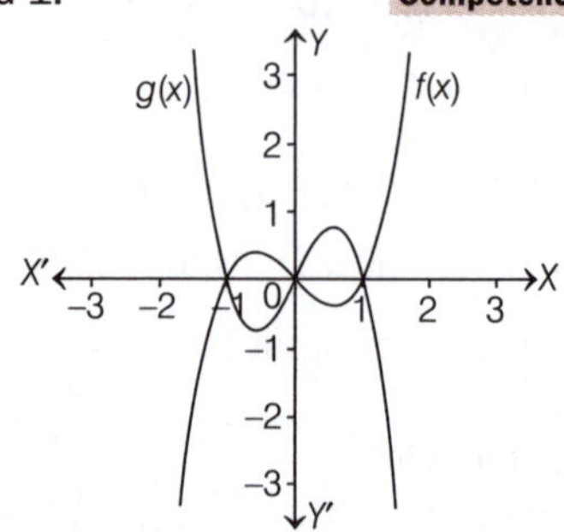

Anya said, "Both the graphs represent the same polynomial, $f(x) = g(x) = (x+1)(x-0)(x-1)$ as they have the same zeroes".

Pranit said, "Both the graphs represent two different polynomials, $f(x) = (x+1)(x-0)(x-1)$ and $g(x) = -(x+1)(x-0)(x-1)$ and only two such polynomials exist that can have the zeroes (-1), 0 and 1."

Aadar said, "Both the graphs represents two different polynomials and infinitely many such polynomials exist that have the zeroes -1, 0 and 1."

Who is right? Justify your answer.

22. If the zeroes of the cubic polynomial $x^3 - 6x^2 + 3x + 10$ are of the form a, $a+b$ and $a+2b$ for some real numbers a and b, then find the values of a and b. **NCERT Exemplar**

23. A polynomial is given by $q(x) = x^3 - 2x^2 - 9x + k$, where k is a constant.

The sum of two zeroes of $q(x)$ is zero.

Using the relationship between the zeroes and coefficients of a polynomial, find the

(i) zeroes of $q(x)$.

(ii) value of k.

Show your steps. **Competency Based Question**

Long Answer Type Questions

24. If the zeroes of the polynomial $ax^2 + bx + b = 0$ are in the ratio $m : n$, then find the value of $\sqrt{\frac{m}{n}} + \sqrt{\frac{n}{m}}$.

25. If α and β are the zeroes of the quadratic polynomial $f(x) = px^2 + qx + r$, then evaluate $\frac{1}{p\alpha + q} + \frac{1}{p\beta + q}$.

26. If α and β are the zeroes of the quadratic polynomial $p(s) = 3s^2 - 6s + 4$, then find the value of $\frac{\alpha}{\beta} + \frac{\beta}{\alpha} + 2\left(\frac{1}{\alpha} + \frac{1}{\beta}\right) + 3\alpha\beta$.

27. If α and β are the zeroes of the quadratic polynomial $f(x) = x^2 - px + q$, then prove that $\frac{\alpha^2}{\beta^2} + \frac{\beta^2}{\alpha^2} = \frac{p^4}{q^2} - \frac{4p^2}{q} + 2$

28. A graph of a cubic polynomial is plotted on a graph paper.

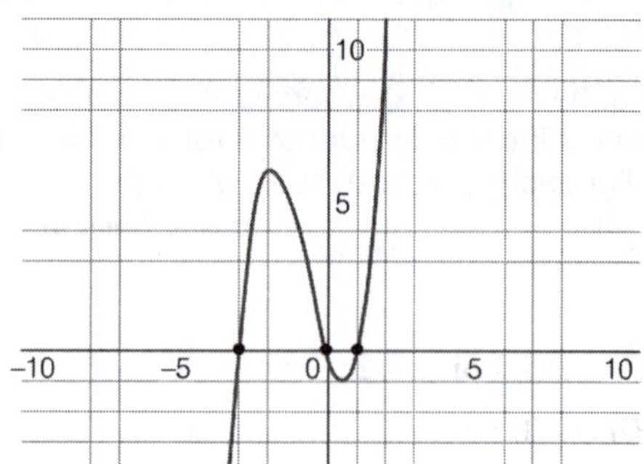

Based on the above information, answer the following questions. **Competency Based Question**

(i) What is the sum of the roots of the polynomial?

(ii) The graph of a polynomial shows it is extended on both sides. What does it indicate about the values of the y-coordinate?

(iii) A quadratic polynomial has integral roots. The sum of its roots is 7. Which of the following cannot be the constant term of the polynomial?

(a) 6 (b) 10 (c) 12 (d) 14

(iv) A polynomial is given by $p(x) = x^3 - 2x^2 + \frac{3}{4}x$.

For what values of x is the polynomial $p(x) = 0$?

29. Find the cubic polynomial whose three zeroes are -3, 0 and 3. Is 5 a zero of polynomial $5x^2 - 10$.

HINTS & SOLUTIONS

1. (a) Let $f(x) = kx^2 + 3x + k$

Since, 2 is a zero of $f(x)$.

$\therefore \quad f(2) = 0 \Rightarrow k(2)^2 + 3(2) + k = 0$

$\Rightarrow \quad 4k + 6 + k = 0 \Rightarrow 5k = -6$

$\Rightarrow \quad k = \frac{-6}{5}$

2. (b) Let $P(x) = x^2 - 5x + 4$

$\therefore \quad P(3) = 3^2 - 5 \times 3 + 4$

$= 9 - 15 + 4 = -2$

Since, -2 is the remainder.

Therefore, 2 must be added to $P(x)$, so that 3 will be a zero of the polynomial.

3. (b) Let $p(x) = 16x^2 - 9$

To find zeroes of $p(x)$, put $p(x) = 0$

$\therefore \; 16x^2 - 9 = 0 \Rightarrow 16x^2 = 9$

$\Rightarrow \quad x^2 = \frac{9}{16} \Rightarrow x = \pm \frac{3}{4}$

So, the zeroes are $\frac{3}{4}$ and $\frac{-3}{4}$.

4. (c) Let $f(x) = x^2 - 5x + 6$

By splitting the middle term, we get

$f(x) = x^2 - 3x - 2x + 6 = x(x-3) - 2(x-3)$

$\Rightarrow \quad f(x) = (x-3)(x-2)$

On putting $f(x) = 0$, we get

$x - 3 = 0$ or $x - 2 = 0$

$\Rightarrow \quad x = 3$ or $x = 2$

5. (b) **Hint** $p(1) = 0$

$\because \quad p(x) = x^3 + ax^2 + 2b$

$\therefore \quad p(1) = 1 + a + 2b = 0$

$\Rightarrow \quad a + 2b = -1 \quad$ ...(i)

Also given, $a + b = 4 \quad$ ...(ii)

On solving Eqs. (i) and (ii), we get

$a = 9$ and $b = -5$

6. (b) In the given figure, the graph of a polynomial $p(x)$ cuts X-axis at two distinct points.

Hence, there are only two zeroes of the polynomial $p(x)$.

7. (d) Given graph of a quadratic polynomial $p(x)$ passes through the points $(-6, 0)$, $(0, -30)$, $(4, -20)$ and $(6, 0)$.

We know that the zero of a polynomial is the x-coordinate of the point, where the graph of a polynomial intersects X-axis. Here, the polynomial $p(x)$ intersects the X-axis at the points $(-6, 0)$ and $(6, 0)$. Thus, the zeroes of the polynomial are -6 and 6.

8. (b) Since, the given polynomial $y = f(x)$ intersect the X-axis at point $(3, 0)$ only. So, the polynomial has 1 zero and the zero is 3.

9. (b) Given, $p(x) = 2x^2 - k\sqrt{2}x + 1$ and sum of zeroes of polynomial $= \sqrt{2}$

$\therefore$ Sum of zeroes $= \frac{k\sqrt{2}}{2}$

$\Rightarrow \quad \frac{k\sqrt{2}}{2} = \sqrt{2} \Rightarrow k = 2$

10. (d) Let $\alpha = 2$ and $\beta = -3$

Then, the quadratic polynomial will be

$x^2 - (\alpha + \beta)x + \alpha\beta = x^2 - (2-3)x + 2(-3)$

$= x^2 - (-1)x - 6 = x^2 + x - 6$

On comparing this polynomial with $x^2 + (a+1)x + b$, we get

$a + 1 = 1$ and $b = -6$

$\Rightarrow \quad a = 0$ and $b = -6$

11. (d) Let $p(x) = x^2 - 1$

Put $p(x) = 0 \Rightarrow x^2 - 1 = 0$

$\Rightarrow \quad x^2 = 1 \Rightarrow x = \pm 1$

So, the zeroes are 1 and -1.

Let $\alpha = 1$ and $\beta = -1$

$\Rightarrow \quad (\alpha + \beta) = 1 + (-1) = 0$

12. (b) **Hint** Given that $p(x) = x^2 - (k+6)x + 2(2k-1)$

$\therefore \quad \alpha + \beta = k + 6$ and $\alpha\beta = 2(2k-1)$

$\because \quad \alpha + \beta = \frac{1}{2}\alpha\beta$

$\therefore \quad k + 6 = \frac{1}{2}[2\,(2k+1)]$

13. (b) Given polynomial is $kx^2 - 4x - 7$

and product of zeroes, $\alpha\beta = 2$

$\therefore \quad 2 = -\frac{7}{k} \Rightarrow k = \frac{-7}{2}$

14. (a) Given polynomials are $x^2 + px + q \quad$ ...(i)

and $\quad 4x^2 - 5x - 6 \quad$ ...(ii)

Zeroes of polynomial $4x^2 - 5x - 6$ are $x = 2, \frac{-3}{4}$

Therefore, by given condition, zeroes of polynomial $x^2 + px + q$ are 4 and $\frac{-3}{2}$.

$\therefore$ Sum of zeroes $= \frac{-p}{1} \Rightarrow 4 - \frac{3}{2} = \frac{-p}{1}$

$\Rightarrow \quad \frac{5}{2} = \frac{-p}{1} \Rightarrow p = \frac{-5}{2}$

15. (b) Let $p(x) = ax^3 + bx^2 + cx + d$

Given that one of the zeroes of the cubic polynomial $p(x)$ is zero.

Let α, β and γ be the zeroes of cubic polynomial $p(x)$, where $\alpha = 0$.

We know that

sum of product of two zeroes at a time $= \frac{c}{a}$

$$\Rightarrow \quad \alpha\beta + \beta\gamma + \gamma\alpha = \frac{c}{a}$$

$$\Rightarrow \quad 0 \times \beta + \beta\gamma + \gamma \times 0 = \frac{c}{a}$$

$[\because \alpha = 0, \text{ given}]$

$$\Rightarrow \quad 0 + \beta\gamma + 0 = \frac{c}{a} \Rightarrow \beta\gamma = \frac{c}{a}$$

Hence, product of other two zeroes is $\frac{c}{a}$.

16. (a) Let $p(x) = x^3 + ax^2 + bx + c$

Let α, β and γ be the zeroes of the given cubic polynomial $p(x)$.

Here, $\alpha = -1$ [given]

$\therefore \quad p(-1) = 0$

$\Rightarrow \quad (-1)^3 + a(-1)^2 + b(-1) + c = 0$

$\Rightarrow \quad -1 + a - b + c = 0$

$\Rightarrow \quad c = 1 - a + b \quad \ldots(\text{i})$

We know that

product of all zeroes $= \frac{-\text{Constant term}}{\text{Coefficient of } x^3} = -\frac{c}{1}$

$\alpha\beta\gamma = -c$

$\Rightarrow \quad (-1)\beta\gamma = -c \quad [\because \alpha = -1]$

$\Rightarrow \quad \beta\gamma = c$

$\Rightarrow \quad \beta\gamma = 1 - a + b$ [from Eq. (i)]

Hence, product of the other two zeroes is $1 - a + b$.

17. (d) Given zeroes of polynomial are $\frac{2}{5}$ and $-\frac{1}{5}$.

Let $\alpha = \frac{2}{5}$ and $\beta = -\frac{1}{5}$

$\therefore$ Sum of zeroes $= \alpha + \beta = \frac{2}{5} - \frac{1}{5} = \frac{1}{5}$

Product of zeroes $= \alpha\beta = \frac{2}{5} \times \left(-\frac{1}{5}\right) = -\frac{2}{25}$

$\therefore$ Required quadratic polynomial

$$= x^2 - (\alpha + \beta)x + \alpha\beta$$

$$= x^2 - \frac{1}{5}x + \left(-\frac{2}{25}\right) = \frac{25x^2 - 5x - 2}{25}$$

We can consider $25x^2 - 5x - 2$ as required quadratic polynomial because it will also satisfy the given condition.

18. (d) Let $\alpha = -5$ and $\beta = -3$

Then, the quadratic polynomial will be

$$k(x^2 - (\alpha + \beta)x + \alpha\beta)$$

Here, $\alpha + \beta = -5 + (-3) = -8$

and $\alpha\beta = (-5)(-3) = 15$

$\therefore$ The quadratic polynomial, is

$k[x^2 - (-8)x + 15] = (x^2 + 8x + 15)k$

Hence, more than 3 quadratic polynomials having zeroes -5 and -3 are possible.

19. (b) Given zeroes, -3 and 5.

Let $\alpha = -3$ and $\beta = 5$

We know that if α and β are zeroes of a quadratic polynomial, then quadratic polynomial is

$$k[x^2 - (\alpha + \beta)x + \alpha\beta], k \in R$$

$\therefore \quad k[x^2 - (-3 + 5)x + (-3)(5)] = k(x^2 - 2x - 15)$

Since, k is non-zero constant, so there will be infinite polynomials with zeroes -3 and 5.

20. (b) Given zeroes of polynomial are $-\sqrt{\frac{5}{2}}$ and $\sqrt{\frac{5}{2}}$.

$\therefore$ Sum of zeroes $= -\sqrt{\frac{5}{2}} + \sqrt{\frac{5}{2}} = 0$

and product of zeroes $= -\sqrt{\frac{5}{2}} \cdot \sqrt{\frac{5}{2}} = -\frac{5}{2}$

A quadratic polynomial with two zeroes is given by $k(x^2 - (\alpha + \beta)x + \alpha\beta)$.

$\therefore k\left(x^2 - (0)x + \left(\frac{-5}{2}\right)\right) = k\left(x^2 - \frac{5}{2}\right)$

For $k = 8$, the quadratic polynomial is

$8\left(x^2 - \frac{5}{2}\right) = 8x^2 - 20$

21. (d) Let α, β and γ be the zeroes of the required polynomial.

According to given condition,

$$\alpha + \beta + \gamma = 0,$$

$$\alpha\beta + \beta\gamma + \alpha\gamma = -7 \text{ and } \alpha\beta\gamma = -6$$

$\therefore$ Required cubic polynomial is

$k[x^3 - (\alpha + \beta + \gamma)x^2 + (\alpha\beta + \beta\gamma + \gamma\alpha)x - \alpha\beta\gamma]$, where k is non-zero constant

$k[x^3 - (0)x^2 + (-7)x - (-6)]$

$\Rightarrow \quad x^3 - 7x + 6$ [consider, $k = 1$]

22. (a) **Hint** For the polynomial $P(x) = x^2 - 2x - 3$,

$$P(x) = x^2 - 3x + x - 3 \Rightarrow P(x) = (x - 3)(x + 1)$$

So, the zeroes are 3 and -1.

Also, the graph of given polynomial intersects X-axis at points $(3, 0)$ and $(-1, 0)$.

23. (a) Both Assertion and Reason are true and Reason is the correct explanation of Assertion.

24. (b) **Hint** Sum of zeroes $= (a-d)+a+(a+d) = \frac{-b}{a}$

$\Rightarrow \quad 3a = 12$

$\Rightarrow \quad a = 4$

Reason is also correct but not a correct explanation of Assertion.

25. (a) Given, $\alpha = 3$ and $\beta = 4$

Then, quadratic polynomial is

$x^2 - (\alpha+\beta)x + \alpha\beta = 0$

$\Rightarrow \quad x^2 - 7x + 12 = 0$

26. (i) Given, $p(t) = 20t - 16t^2$

For zeroes, $\quad p(t) = 0$

$\Rightarrow \quad 20t - 16t^2 = 0$

$\Rightarrow \quad 4t(5-4t) = 0$

$\Rightarrow \quad 4t = 0$ or $5 - 4t = 0$

$\Rightarrow \quad t = 0, t = \frac{5}{4}$

$\therefore$ Zeroes of $p(t)$ are 0 and $\frac{5}{4}$.

(ii) (a) Because 0 and $\frac{5}{4}$ are zeroes of polynomial and $p(t)$ is increasing when time is increasing after some time. Thus, graph of given polynomial is open downward graph.

(iii) (a) At $t = \frac{3}{2}$, $p\left(\frac{3}{2}\right) = 20 \times \frac{3}{2} - 16 \times \left(\frac{3}{2}\right)^2$

$= 30 - 36 = -6$

$\Rightarrow$ Height $= 6$ cm

'– ve' denotes graph is below the X-axis.

Or

(b) $\therefore$ Distance = Speed $\times$ Time $= 20 \times \frac{5}{4} = 25$ cm

27. (i) Since, the curve intersects X-axis at 2 points.

$\therefore$ Number of zeroes of curve = 2

(ii) If the graph of rainbow does not intersect X-axis, then curve has not real zeroes.

$\therefore$ Number of zeroes = 0

(iii) (a) Given, $p(x) = x^2 + (a+1)x + b$

Since, 2 and -3 are zeroes of $p(x)$.

$\therefore \quad p(2) = 0$

$\Rightarrow \quad 2^2 + (a+1)2 + b = 0$

$\Rightarrow \quad 4 + 2a + 2 + b = 0$

$\Rightarrow \quad 2a + b = -6 \quad$ ...(i)

and $\quad p(-3) = 0$

$\Rightarrow (-3)^2 + (a+1)(-3) + b = 0$

$\Rightarrow \quad 9 - 3a - 3 + b = 0$

$\Rightarrow \quad -3a + b = -6$

$\Rightarrow \quad 3a - b = 6 \quad$ ...(ii)

On adding Eqs. (i) and (ii), we get

$5a = 0 \Rightarrow a = 0$

From Eq. (i), $\quad b = -6$

Hence, $\quad a = 0$ and $b = -6$

Or (b) Let $f(x) = x^2 - 2x - (7p+3)$

Since, -4 is a zero of $f(x)$.

$\therefore \quad f(-4) = 0$

$\Rightarrow \quad (-4)^2 - 2(-4) - (7p+3) = 0$

$\Rightarrow \quad 16 + 8 - 7p - 3 = 0$

$\Rightarrow \quad -7p + 21 = 0 \Rightarrow p = 3$

28. (i) No, Sara is wrong, because the graph intersects the Y-axis at -2.

$\therefore$ The zero of the polynomial is -2 and its coordinates are $(0, -2)$.

(ii) (c) Curve m is represented by the equation,

$p(y) = 0.25y^3 + 0.1y^2 - 0.3y + 1$

(iii) (a) If Sara changes the coefficient of y^3 in the polynomial for the curves l and m. Then, the shape of given polynomial will change and it will make some different shapes that can be anything.

Or (b) If Amit wants to decrease the minimum opening of the flower pot, then he needs to change the points where polynomial cuts the X-axis and change points on X-axis where curve l and m intersect.

29. (i) **Hint** The graph for the quadratic polynomial

$P(x) = ax^2 + bx + c, a \neq 0$

has one of the two shapes (which known as parabola) either open downwards like $\cap$ or open upwards like $\cup$ depending on whether $a > 0$ or $a < 0$.

If $a > 0$, then the shape is like $\cup$

and if $a < 0$, then the shape is like $\cap$.

(ii) Given, α and $\frac{1}{\alpha}$ are the zeroes of quadratic polynomial $2x^2 - x + 8k$.

Now, product of zeroes, $\alpha \times \frac{1}{\alpha} = \frac{\text{Constant term}}{\text{Coefficient of } x^2}$

$\Rightarrow \quad 1 = \frac{8k}{2} \Rightarrow k = \frac{2}{8} = \frac{1}{4}$

(iii) (a) Given equation is $x^2 + 1 = 0$.

$x^2 = -1$

It gives imaginary roots.

Hence, it neither touches nor intersects X-axis.

Ans. No

Or

(b) Given, sum of roots $= -p$

and product of roots $= -\frac{1}{p}$

$\therefore$ Quadratic polynomial

$$= k[x^2 - (\text{Sum of roots})\, x + \text{Product of roots}]$$

$$= k\left[x^2 - (-p)x + \left(-\frac{1}{p}\right)\right] = k\left(x^2 + px - \frac{1}{p}\right)$$

30. (i) The graph intersect the X-axis at two points $(-30, 0)$ and $(35, 0)$.

i.e. $x = -30, x = 35$

So, $-30, 35$ are the zeroes of polynomial.

(ii) Polynomial $P(x) = x^2 - (\text{Sum of zeroes})\, x + \text{Product of zeroes}$

$$= x^2 - (-30 + 35)\,x + (-30)(35)$$
$$= x^2 - 5x - 1050$$

(iii) We have, $P(x) = x^2 - 5x - 1050$

Now, $-750 = x^2 - 5x - 1050$

$\Rightarrow x^2 - 5x - 300 = 0$

$\Rightarrow x^2 + 15x - 20x - 300 = 0$

$\Rightarrow x(x + 15) - 20(x + 15) = 0$

$\Rightarrow (x + 15)(x - 20) = 0$

$\Rightarrow x = -15$ or $x = 20$

Part II

1. Hint $-\frac{t^9}{t^5} + 4\frac{t^6}{t^5} + 7\frac{t^5}{t^5}$. **Ans.** 4

2. Hint Let $p(x) = 3x^2 + 4x + 2k$.

$\therefore$ $p(-2) = 0$. **Ans.** $k = -2$

3. True, since $-\frac{b}{a} =$ sum of the zeroes < 0, so $\frac{b}{a} > 0$. Also, the product of the zeroes $= \frac{c}{a} > 0$.

$\therefore$ a, b and c all have same sign.

4. Hint Let α and α be the same zeroes of the given polynomial $ax^2 + bx + c$. Then, we have

$$\alpha \cdot \alpha = \frac{c}{a} \Rightarrow \alpha^2 = \frac{c}{a} \Rightarrow \frac{c}{a} > 0$$

[$\because \alpha^2$ is always positive]

$\Rightarrow c$ and a have same sign.

5. (i) The graph intersects X-axis at one point only. So, the number of zeroes is 1. The polynomial is neither linear nor quadratic. Since, given curve is not a straight line and not a parabola.

(ii) **Hint** Do same as Part (i).

Ans. 1; linear

6. Parabola $f(x)$ intersects the X-axis at one point and parabola $g(x)$ intersects the X-axis at two points.

But, the two polynomials intersect the X-axis at one common point only.

$\therefore$ The number of zeroes that are common to both the polynomials is 1.

7. Hint Let α and $\frac{1}{\alpha}$ be the two zeroes of the given polynomial. Then, $\alpha \times \frac{1}{\alpha} = \frac{\text{Constant term}}{\text{Coefficient of } x^2}$ **Ans.** $k = 2$

8. Given, α and β are zeroes of a polynomial $6x^2 - 5x + 1$.

So, $\alpha + \beta = \frac{5}{6}$ and $\alpha\beta = \frac{1}{6}$

Now, $(\alpha + \beta)^2 = \left(\frac{5}{6}\right)^2$

$\Rightarrow \alpha^2 + \beta^2 + 2\alpha\beta = \left(\frac{5}{6}\right)^2$

$\Rightarrow \alpha^2 + \beta^2 = \left(\frac{5}{6}\right)^2 - 2\left(\frac{1}{6}\right) = \frac{13}{36}$

And $\alpha^2\beta^2 = \left(\frac{1}{6}\right)^2 = \frac{1}{36}$

We know that quadratic polynomial whose zeroes are P and Q is given by $x^2 - (P + Q)x + PQ$.

Required polynomial is $x^2 - (\alpha^2 + \beta^2)x + \alpha^2\beta^2$

$$= x^2 - \frac{13}{36}x + \frac{1}{36} \text{ or } 36x^2 - 13x + 1$$

Hence, required polynomial is $36x^2 - 13x + 1$.

9. Hint, Sum of zeroes $= \frac{-(-10)}{3} = \frac{10}{3}$

$\therefore$ Aryan is right.

10. (i) No, because powers of any polynomial is always positive integer.

(ii) Yes, because it satisfies the definition of polynomial.

(iii) No, because powers of any polynomial can not be negative integer.

(iv) Yes, because it satisfies the condition of polynomial.

11. Hint If $x + a$ is a factor of $x^2 + px + q$ and $x^2 + mx + n$, then $(-a)^2 + p(-a) + q = (-a)^2 + m(-a) + n$ [$\because x = -a$]

12. The parabola intersects the X-axis on -2 and 3.

$\therefore$ The zeroes of the given polynomial are -2 and 3.

Sum of the zeroes $= 3 + (-2) = 3 - 2 = 1$

Now, write a quadratic polynomial whose sum of zeroes is less than 1. e.g. $x^2 + 3x + 2 = 0$

The zeroes are -2 and -1.

$\therefore$ Sum of zeroes $= -2 - 1 = -3 < 1$

13. (i) Let the zeroes of $p(x)$ be α and β and $\alpha = 3\beta$.

Sum of zeroes $= \alpha + \beta = \dfrac{-(-8)}{a}$

$\Rightarrow \quad 3\beta + \beta = \dfrac{8}{a} \Rightarrow \beta = \dfrac{2}{a}$ ...(i)

Product of zeroes $= \alpha\beta = \dfrac{3}{a} \Rightarrow \beta^2 = \dfrac{1}{a}$ ...(ii)

From Eqs. (i) and (ii), we get

$a = 4$

(ii) Since, $a = 4 > 0$,

$\therefore$ The graph of $p(x)$ is an open upward parabola.

14. Hint Let α and $\dfrac{1}{\alpha}$ be two zeroes of the given polynomial, which are reciprocal of each other.

$\therefore$ Product of zeroes,

$\alpha \times \dfrac{1}{\alpha} = \dfrac{\text{Constant term}}{\text{Coefficient of } x^2} \Rightarrow 1 = \dfrac{6a}{a^2+9}$ **Ans.** $a = 3$

15. Hint Let α and β be the zeroes of $2x^2 - 5x - 3$

$\therefore$ 2α and 2β be the zeroes of $x^2 + px + q$

Ans. $p = -5, q = -6$

16. Hint Given, $r(x) = 4x^2 + 3x - 1$

For zeroes, put $r(x) = 0$

$\Rightarrow \quad 4x^2 + 3x - 1 = 0$

$\Rightarrow \quad x = -1, \dfrac{1}{4}$

Reciprocals of -1 and $\dfrac{1}{4}$ are -1 and 4.

Sum of roots, $S = -1 + 4 = 3$

Product of roots, $p = (-1)(4) = -4$

$\therefore$ Required polynomial is

$P(x) = k(x^2 - Sx + p)$

Ans. $P(x) = k(x^2 - 3x - 4)$

17. Hint Let given polynomial be $p(x) = x^2 + kx + k$.

Let the quadratic polynomial have equal zeroes say α and α.

Then, $\quad \alpha + \alpha = -\dfrac{b}{a} = \dfrac{-k}{1}$

$\Rightarrow \quad \alpha = -k/2$

and $\quad \alpha \cdot \alpha = \dfrac{c}{a} = \dfrac{k}{1} \Rightarrow \alpha^2 = k$

$\therefore \quad \left(-\dfrac{k}{2}\right)^2 = k \quad \left[\because \alpha = \dfrac{-k}{2}\right]$

Ans. The given statement is false because equal roots are possible only when k is even.

18. Hint Sum of zeroes $= \dfrac{-\text{Coefficient of } x}{\text{Coefficient of } x^2}$

$\Rightarrow \quad -1 = \dfrac{-(2a+3)}{a+1}$

Ans. -2

19. Hint Do same as Example 1 of Topic 2.

Ans. (i) $\dfrac{2}{3}, -\dfrac{1}{7}$ (ii) $-\sqrt{3}, \dfrac{-7}{\sqrt{3}}$ (iii) $\dfrac{-2}{\sqrt{3}}, \dfrac{3}{4\sqrt{3}}$

20. Hint Sum of zeroes $= 18 + 7 = 25$

Product of zeroes $= 18 \times 7 = 126$

$\therefore$ Required polynomials $= x^2 -$ (Sum of zeroes)x + Product of zeroes

$= x^2 - 25x + 126$

21. Aadar is right and gives a justification. For example, the factorised form of a cubic polynomial with the zeroes -1, 0 and 1 can be written as $k(x+1)(x-0)(x-1)$, where k is an integer.

22. Hint Given, $a, a+b, a+2b$ are zeroes of $x^3 - 6x^2 + 3x + 10$, thus we know that

$a + a + b + a + 2b = 6$

$\Rightarrow \quad a + b = 2$

$a(a+b) + (a+b)(a+2b) + a(a+2b) = 3$

$\Rightarrow \quad ab = \dfrac{-5-a^2}{2}$

$a(a+b)(a+2b) = -10$

$\therefore \quad a = 5, -1$

When $a = 5$, then $b = -3$

When $a = -1$, then $b = 2$

23. (i) Assume the values of zeroes of $q(x)$ as $(-\alpha)$, α and β. Write the sum of zeroes as

$-\alpha + \alpha + \beta = 2 \Rightarrow \beta = 2$

Write the equation for the sum of the products of zeroes taken two at a time as:

$(-\alpha \times \alpha) + \alpha\beta + (-\alpha)\beta = -9$

$\Rightarrow \quad -\alpha^2 - \alpha\beta + \beta\alpha = -9$

$\Rightarrow \quad \alpha^2 = 9 \Rightarrow \alpha = \pm 3$

Thus, 3 zeroes of $q(x)$ are (-3), 3 and 2.

(ii) Product of zeroes of given polynomial is

$(-\alpha)(\alpha)\beta = -k$

$\Rightarrow \quad (-3)(3)(2) = -k \Rightarrow -18 = -k$

$\therefore \quad k = 18$

24. Hint Let the zeroes of the given polynomial $ax^2 + bx + b$ be $m\alpha$ and $n\alpha$.

$\therefore$ Sum of zeroes,

$m\alpha + n\alpha = \dfrac{-\text{Coefficient of } x}{\text{Coefficient of } x^2} = \dfrac{-b}{a}$

and product of zeroes,

$$m\alpha \times n\alpha = \frac{\text{Constant term}}{\text{Coefficient of } x^2} = \frac{b}{a}$$

Ans. $-\sqrt{\dfrac{b}{a}}$

25. Hint Sum of zeroes,

$$\alpha+\beta = \frac{-\text{Coefficient of } x}{\text{Coefficient of } x^2} = \frac{-q}{p}$$

and product of zeroes, $\alpha\beta = \dfrac{\text{Constant term}}{\text{Coefficient of } x^2} = \dfrac{r}{p}$

Now, $\dfrac{1}{p\alpha+q} + \dfrac{1}{p\beta+q} = \dfrac{p(\alpha+\beta)+2q}{p^2\alpha\beta + pq(\alpha+\beta)+q^2}$

Ans. $\dfrac{q}{pr}$

26. Hint $\alpha+\beta = \dfrac{-\text{Coefficient of } s}{\text{Coefficient of } s^2} = \dfrac{-(-6)}{3} = \dfrac{6}{3} = 2$

and $\quad \alpha\beta = \dfrac{\text{Constant term}}{\text{Coefficient of } s^2} = \dfrac{4}{3}$

Now, $\dfrac{\alpha}{\beta} + \dfrac{\beta}{\alpha} + 2\left(\dfrac{1}{\alpha}+\dfrac{1}{\beta}\right) + 3\alpha\beta$

$$= \frac{(\alpha+\beta)^2 - 2\alpha\beta}{\alpha\beta} + 2\left(\frac{\alpha+\beta}{\alpha\beta}\right) + 3\alpha\beta$$

$$= \frac{(2)^2 - 2(4/3)}{4/3} + 2\left(\frac{2}{4/3}\right) + 3\times\frac{4}{3}$$

Ans. 8

27. Hint Sum of zeroes, $\alpha+\beta = \dfrac{-(-p)}{1} = p$

and product of zeroes, $\alpha\beta = \dfrac{q}{1} = q$

Now, LHS $= \dfrac{\alpha^2}{\beta^2} + \dfrac{\beta^2}{\alpha^2}$

$$= \frac{[(\alpha+\beta)^2 - 2\alpha\beta]^2 - 2(\alpha\beta)^2}{(\alpha\beta)^2}$$

On substituting $\alpha+\beta = p$ and $\alpha\beta = q$, we get

$$\text{LHS} = \frac{p^4}{q^2} - \frac{4p^2}{q} + 2$$

28. (i) The roots of the polynomial are -3, 0 and 1.

$\therefore$ Sum of the roots $= -3+0+1 = -2$.

(ii) Since, the graph of a polynomial is extended on both sides, this means, y-coordinates have both negative and positive values.

(iii) (d) Since, the sum of roots $= 7$

Let α and β be the roots of quadratic polynomial.

$\therefore \quad \alpha+\beta = 7 = \dfrac{-b}{a}$

$\Rightarrow \quad \beta = 7-\alpha$ and $a = 1$

Also, $\quad \alpha\beta = \dfrac{c}{a} = \dfrac{c}{1} \quad [\because a = 1]$

$\Rightarrow \quad \alpha\beta = c \Rightarrow \alpha(7-\alpha) = c$

$\Rightarrow \quad 7\alpha - \alpha^2 = c \Rightarrow \alpha^2 - 7\alpha + c = 0$

Thus, the possible cases of roots for which the sum of roots is 7 are (1, 6), (3, 4), (2, 5)

and $1\times 6 = 6, 3\times 4 = 12, 2\times 5 = 10$

But 14 cannot be possible.

$\therefore$ 14 cannot be the constant term of the given polynomial.

(iv) $p(x) = x^3 - 2x^2 + \dfrac{3}{4}x$

For $p(x) = 0$

$\Rightarrow \quad x^3 - 2x^2 + \dfrac{3}{4}x = 0$

$\Rightarrow \quad 4x^3 - 8x^2 + 3x = 0$

$\Rightarrow \quad x(4x^2 - 8x + 3) = 0$

$\Rightarrow \quad x = 0$ or $4x^2 - 8x + 3 = 0$

$\Rightarrow \quad x = 0$ or $4x^2 - 6x - 2x + 3 = 0$

$\Rightarrow x = 0$ or $2x(2x-3) - 1(2x-3) = 0$

$\Rightarrow \quad x = 0$ or $(2x-3)(2x-1) = 0$

$\Rightarrow \quad x = 0$ or $x = \dfrac{1}{2}$ or $x = \dfrac{3}{2}$

$\therefore$ The values of x are 0, $\dfrac{1}{2}$ and $\dfrac{3}{2}$.

29. Hint Let the zeroes of cubic polynomial be α, β and γ and $\alpha = -3$, $\beta = 0$ and $\gamma = 3$

Now, we have,

$\alpha+\beta+\gamma = -3+0+3 = 0$

$\alpha\beta+\beta\gamma+\gamma\alpha = (-3)(0) + (0)(3) + (3)(-3)$

$= -9$

and $\quad \alpha\beta\gamma = (-3)(0)(3) = 0$

Now, required cubic polynomial

$= x^3 - (\alpha+\beta+\gamma)x^2 + (\alpha\beta+\beta\gamma+\alpha\gamma)x - \alpha\beta\gamma$

$= x^3 - 9x$

Thus, the required cubic polynomial is $x^3 - 9x$.

Now, let $P(x) = 5x^2 - 10$

At $x = 5$, we have

$P(5) = 5(5^2) - 10$

$= 125 - 10$

$= 115 \neq 0$

Thus, 5 is not a zero of polynomial $5x^2 - 10$.

POLYNOMIALS

A polynomial in one variable x, is an algebraic expression of the form $p(x) = a_n x^n + a_{n-1} x^{n-1} + a_{n-2} x^{n-2} + \dots + a_1 x + a_0$

where, n is non-negative integer and $a_0, a_1, \dots a_n$ are constants. These constants $a_0, a_1, \dots a_n$ are called coefficients of polynomial.

Degree of a Polynomial

The highest power of x in a polynomial $p(x)$, is called the degree of the polynomial $p(x)$. e.g. $p(y) = y^2 - 5y + 7$ is a polynomial in variable y of degree 2.

Formation of Quadratic and Cubic Polynomials

1. If α and β are the zeroes of a quadratic polynomial, then quadratic polynomial will be

x^2 – (Sum of zeroes) x + Product of zeroes $= x^2 - (\alpha + \beta) x + \alpha\beta$

2. If α, β and γ are the zeroes of cubic polynomial, then cubic polynomial will be

x^3 – (Sum of zeroes) x^2 + (Sum of product of zeroes taking two at a time) x – Product of zeroes

$= x^3 - (\alpha + \beta + \gamma) x^2 + (\alpha\beta + \beta\gamma + \gamma\alpha) x - \alpha\beta\gamma$

Types of Polynomial

1. Linear Polynomial

A polynomial of degree one, is called linear polynomial.

e.g. $f(x) = 5x + 4$

Thus, any linear polynomial is of the form $f(x) = ax + b$, where a, b are real numbers and $a \neq 0$.

2. Quadratic Polynomial

A polynomial of degree two, is called quadratic polynomial.

e.g. $f(x) = 5x^2 + 8x + 3 = 0$

Thus, any quadratic polynomial is of the form $f(x) = ax^2 + bx + c$, where a, b, c are real numbers and $a \neq 0$.

3. Cubic Polynomial

A polynomial of degree three, is called cubic polynomial.

e.g. $f(x) = 5x^3 + 25x$

Thus, any cubic polynomial is of the form $f(x) = ax^3 + bx^2 + cx + d$, where a, b, c, d are real numbers and $a \neq 0$.

Value of a Polynomial at a Given Point

If $p(x)$ is a polynomial in x and α is a real number, then the value obtained by putting $x = \alpha$ in $p(x)$ is called the value of $p(x)$ at $x = \alpha$.

Zeroes of a Polynomial

A real number k is said to be a zero of a polynomial $p(x)$, if $p(k) = 0$.

e.g. At $x = 3$, $p(x) = -x + 3$

$\Rightarrow p(3) = -3 + 3 = 0$

$\therefore$ 3 is a zero of a polynomial $p(x) = -x + 3$

Relationship between Zeroes and Coefficients of a Polynomial

For a linear Polynomial If k is a zero of polynomial $p(x) = ax + b, a \neq 0$, then

$p(k) = ak + b = 0$

i.e. $k = -\frac{b}{a}$

$\therefore$ Zero of the linear polynomial $ax + b$ is

$$\frac{-b}{a} = -\frac{\text{Constant term}}{\text{Coefficient of } x}$$

For a Quadratic Polynomial Let α and β be the zeroes of quadratic polynomial $p(x) = ax^2 + bx + c, a \neq 0$.

Then, by factor theorem $(x - \alpha)$ and $(x - \beta)$ both are the factors of $p(x)$.

$\therefore ax^2 + bx + c = k(x - \alpha)(x - \beta)$
$= k[x^2 - (\alpha + \beta)x + \alpha\beta]$,

where k is some constant.

Thus, $a = k, b = -k(\alpha + \beta), c = k\alpha\beta$

$\therefore \frac{-k(\alpha + \beta)}{k} = \frac{b}{a} \Rightarrow \alpha + \beta = \frac{-b}{a}$

i.e. Sum of zeroes,

$$\alpha + \beta = -\frac{b}{a} = -\frac{\text{Coefficient of } x}{\text{Coefficient of } x^2}$$

and $\frac{k\alpha\beta}{k} = \frac{c}{a} \Rightarrow \alpha\beta = \frac{c}{a}$

i.e. Product of zeroes,

$$\alpha\beta = \frac{\text{Constant term}}{\text{Coefficient of } x^2} = \frac{c}{a}$$

For a Cubic Polynomial Let α, β and γ be the zeroes of the cubic polynomial $ax^3 + bx^2 + cx + d$, $a \neq 0$.

Then,

$$\alpha + \beta + \gamma = -\frac{\text{Coefficient of } x^2}{\text{Coefficient of } x^3} = -\frac{b}{a}$$

$$\alpha\beta + \beta\gamma + \gamma\alpha = \frac{\text{Coefficient of } x}{\text{Coefficient of } x^3} = \frac{c}{a}$$

$$\text{and } \alpha\beta\gamma = -\frac{\text{Constant term}}{\text{Coefficient of } x^3} = -\frac{d}{a}$$

Geometrical Meaning of the Zeroes of a Polynomial

1. Geometrical Meaning of the Zeroes of a Linear Polynomial

Consider a linear polynomial $ax + b$, $a \neq 0$. The graph intersects the X-axis at exactly one point,

i.e. $\left(\frac{-b}{a}, 0\right)$. Thus, the zero of $ax + b$ is $\frac{-b}{a}$.

Thus, the zero of $ax + b$ is the x-coordinate of the point, where the graph of $y = ax + b$ intersects X-axis.

2. Geometrical Meaning of the Zeroes of a Quadratic Polynomial

For any quadratic polynomial $ax^2 + bx + c$, $a \neq 0$, the graph intersects the X-axis atmost at two points.

And the graph of the corresponding equation $y = ax^2 + bx + c$ has two shapes either open upward parabola $\cup$ or open downward parabola $\cap$ depending on $a > 0$ or $a < 0$, respectively.

3. Geometrical Meaning of the Zeroes of a Cubic Polynomial

For any cubic polynomial $ax^3 + bx^2 + cx + d$, $a \neq 0$, the graph intersects the X-axis atmost at three points.

Thus, any cubic polynomial has atmost three zeroes.

Pair of Linear Equations in Two Variables

In earlier classes, we initiated the study of linear equations, where we studied about linear equations in one and two variable(s) and their graphs. In this chapter, we shall study about pair of linear equations in two variables, various methods of solving them and related word problems.

TOPIC 01 Pair of Linear Equations in Two Variables

Linear Equation in Two Variables

A linear equation in two variables (unknowns), say x and y is usually represented in the following form:

$ax + by + c = 0$, where $a \neq 0, b \neq 0$; a, b and c are real numbers.

e.g. $3x - y + 7 = 0$ and $7x + y = 3$

are linear equations in two variables x and y.

Pair of Linear Equations in Two Variables

Two linear equations in the same two variables, say x and y, are called pair of linear equations in two variables.

The general form of pair of linear equations in two variables x and y is $a_1 x + b_1 y + c_1 = 0$ and $a_2 x + b_2 y + c_2 = 0$, where $a_1, b_1, c_1, a_2, b_2, c_2$ are all real numbers such that $a_1, b_1 \neq 0$ and $a_2, b_2 \neq 0$.

Sometimes we call a pair of linear equations in two variables as system of linear equations in two variables.

Solution of a Pair of Linear Equations in Two Variables

Any pair of values of x and y which satisfies both the equations, $a_1x + b_1y + c_1 = 0$ and $a_2x + b_2y + c_2 = 0$, is called a solution of a given pair of linear equations.

A pair of linear equations in two variables can be solved by two methods namely graphical method and algebraic method.

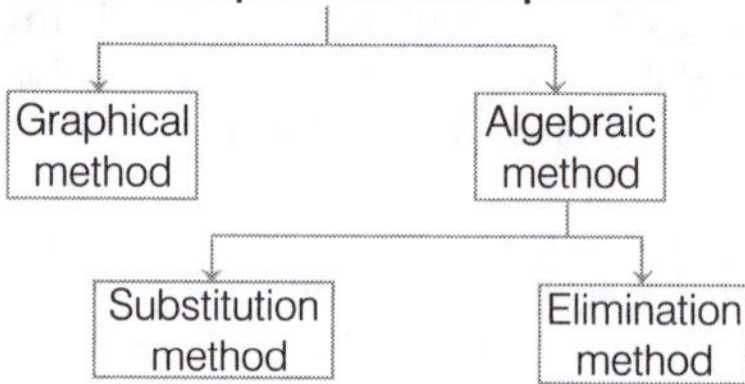

Graphical Method

Let us consider a pair of linear equations in two variables, $a_1x + b_1y + c_1 = 0$ and $a_2x + b_2y + c_2 = 0$.

To find the solution graphically, first draw the graph of both equations on the same graph paper with same scale of representation.

Then, proceed as follows:

(i) **If the graph of system of linear equations will represent two intersecting lines,** then coordinates of point of intersection say (a, b) is the solution of the pair of linear equations. In this case, there will be only one point of intersection. So, the given system of equations will have **unique solution** and such pair of linear equations, is called **consistent** pair of linear equations.

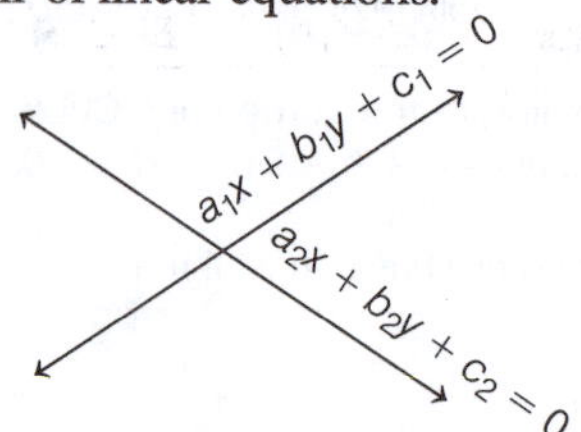

(ii) **If the graph of system of linear equations will represent two parallel lines,** there is **no point** of intersection and consequently there is no pair of values of x and y which satisfy both equations. Thus, given system of equations have **no solution.** Such pair of linear equations, is called **inconsistent** pair of linear equations.

$$a_1x + b_1y + c_1 = 0$$

$$a_2x + b_2y + c_2 = 0$$

(iii) **If the graph of system of linear equations will represent coincident or overlapping lines,** there are infinitely many **common points**. Thus, given system of equations have **infinitely many solutions.** Such pair of linear equations is called **dependent pair** of linear equations. Dependent pair of linear equations is always **consistent.**

Example 1. **Solve graphically**

$$2x - 3y + 13 = 0, 3x - 2y + 12 = 0$$

CBSE 2020 (Basic)

Sol. We have, $2x - 3y + 13 = 0$ ...(i)

and $3x - 2y + 12 = 0$ ...(ii)

Now, $2x = 3y - 13 \Rightarrow x = \dfrac{3y - 13}{2}$

When $y = 1$, we have

$$x = \frac{3 \times 1 - 13}{2} = -5$$

When $y = 3$, we have

$$x = \frac{3 \times 3 - 13}{2} = \frac{-4}{2} = -2$$

Table for $2x - 3y + 13 = 0$ is

x	-5	-2
y	1	3
Points	$A(-5, 1)$	$B(-2, 3)$

Now, $3x - 2y + 12 = 0 \Rightarrow 3x = 2y - 12 \Rightarrow x = \dfrac{2y - 12}{3}$

When $y = 0$, we have

$$x = \frac{2 \times 0 - 12}{3} = \frac{-12}{3} = -4$$

When $y = 3$, we have

$$x = \frac{2 \times 3 - 12}{3} = \frac{-6}{3} = -2$$

Table for $3x - 2y + 12 = 0$ is

x	-4	-2
y	0	3
Points	$C(-4, 0)$	$B(-2, 3)$

Clearly, lines (i) and (ii) interesect each other at point $B(-2, 3)$.

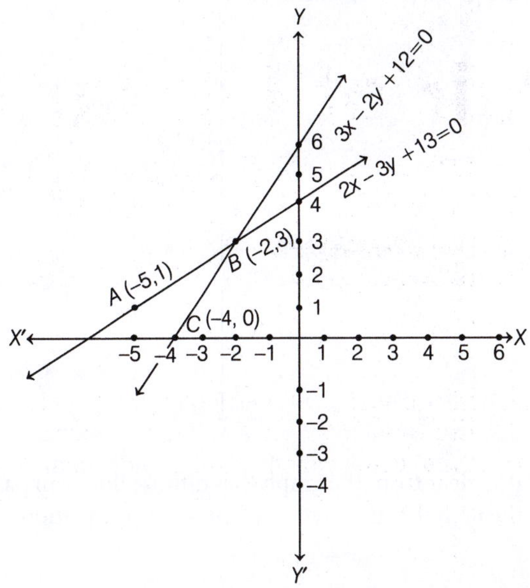

Hence, $x = -2$, $y = 3$ is the solution of the given system of equations.

Example 2. **Write an equation of a line passing through the point representing solution of the pair of linear equations $x + y = 2$ and $2x - y = 1$. How many such lines can we find?**

NCERT Exemplar

Sol. Given, pair of linear equations is

$x + y - 2 = 0$ ...(i)

and $2x - y - 1 = 0$ ...(ii)

Now, table for $x + y - 2 = 0$ or $y = 2 - x$ is

x	0	2
$y = 2 - x$	2	0
Points	A (0, 2)	B (2, 0)

Plot the points A (0, 2) and B (2, 0) and join them to get the straight line AB.

Table for $2x - y - 1 = 0$ or $y = 2x - 1$ is

x	0	2
$y = 2x - 1$	-1	3
Points	C (0, –1)	D (2, 3)

Plot the points C (0, – 1) and D (2, 3) and join them to get the straight line CD.

The lines AB and CD intersect at $E(1, 1)$. So, the solution of the given pair of linear equations is $(1, 1)$.

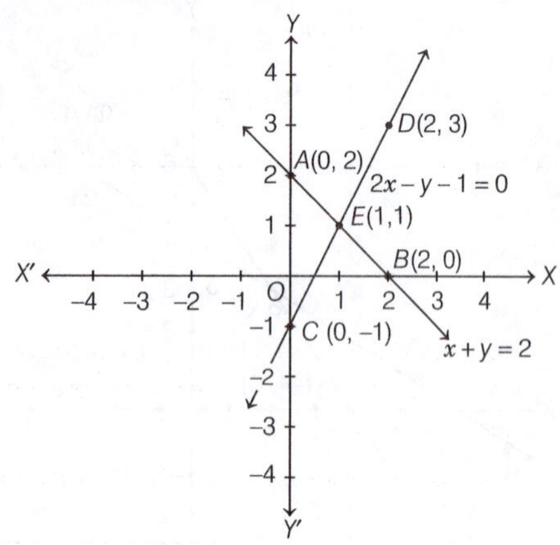

It is clear from the graph that infinite lines can pass through the intersection point of linear equations

$$x + y = 2 \text{ and } 2x - y = 1$$

i.e. point $E(1, 1)$ satisfies many linear equations such as $y = x$, $2x + y = 3$, $x + 2y = 3$ and so on.

Example 3. **Solve graphically the pair of linear equations $3x - 4y + 3 = 0$ and $3x + 4y - 21 = 0$. Find the coordinates of the vertices of triangular region formed by these lines and X-axis. Also, calculate the area of this triangle.**

Sol. Given, the pair of linear equations is

$$3x - 4y + 3 = 0 \quad \text{...(i)}$$

and $$3x + 4y - 21 = 0 \quad \text{...(ii)}$$

Table for $3x - 4y + 3 = 0$ or $y = \dfrac{3x + 3}{4}$ is

x	3	−1
$y = \dfrac{3x+3}{4}$	3	0
Points	$A(3, 3)$	$B(-1, 0)$

Plot the points $A(3, 3)$ and $B(-1, 0)$ on the graph paper and join them to get the straight line AB.

Now, table for $3x + 4y - 21 = 0$ or $y = \dfrac{21 - 3x}{4}$ is

x	3	7
$y = \dfrac{21-3x}{4}$	3	0
Points	$A(3, 3)$	$C(7, 0)$

Plot the points $A(3, 3)$ and $C(7, 0)$ on same graph paper and join them to get the straight line AC.

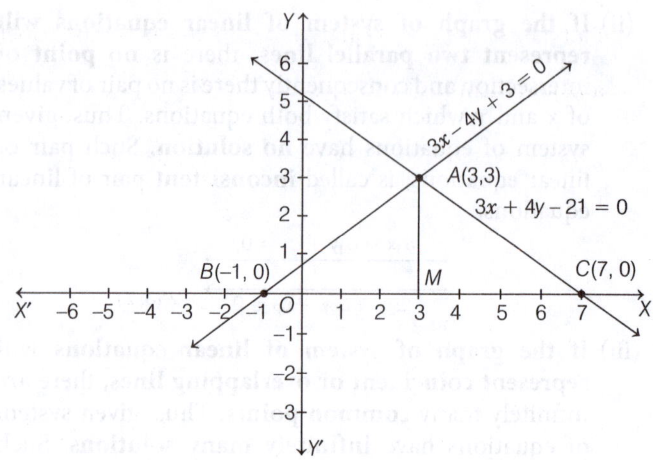

The lines AB and AC intersect each other at point $A(3, 3)$. So, the solution of the given pair of linear equations is $(3, 3)$. The coordinates of the vertices of ΔABC are $A(3, 3)$, $B(-1, 0)$ and $C(7, 0)$.

$\therefore$ Area of $\Delta ABC = \dfrac{1}{2} \times AM \times BC = \dfrac{1}{2} \times 3 \times 8 = 12$ sq units

Example 4. **Show graphically that the following pair of equations is inconsistent (i.e. has no solution).**

$3x - 4y - 1 = 0$ and $2x - \dfrac{8}{3}y + 5 = 0$

Sol. Given, pair of equations is $3x - 4y - 1 = 0$

and $$2x - \frac{8}{3}y + 5 = 0$$

Now, let us find atleast two solutions of each of the above equations, as shown in the following tables.

Table for equation $3x - 4y - 1 = 0$ or $y = \dfrac{3x - 1}{4}$ is

x	3	−1
$y = \dfrac{3x-1}{4}$	2	−1
Points	$A(3, 2)$	$B(-1, -1)$

Plot the points $A(3, 2)$ and $B(-1, -1)$ on a graph paper and join them to get the line AB.

Table for equation $2x - \dfrac{8}{3}y + 5 = 0$ or $y = \dfrac{6x + 15}{8}$ is

x	$\dfrac{3}{2}$	$\dfrac{-5}{2}$
$y = \dfrac{6x+15}{8}$	3	0
Points	$C\left(\dfrac{3}{2}, 3\right)$	$D\left(\dfrac{-5}{2}, 0\right)$

Plot the points $C\left(\frac{3}{2}, 3\right)$ and $D\left(-\frac{5}{2}, 0\right)$ on same graph paper and join them to get the line CD.

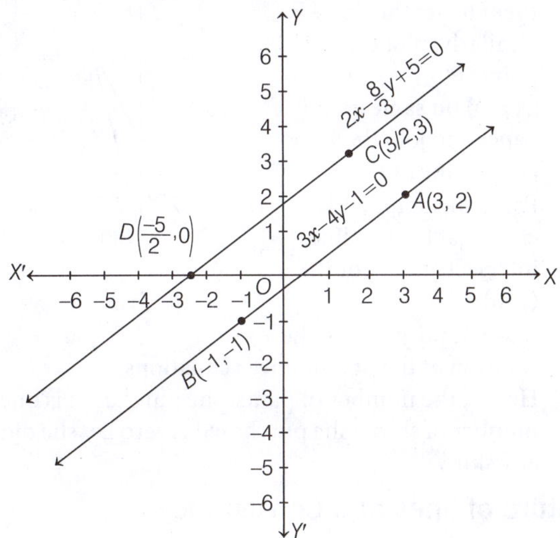

From the graph, it is clear that lines represented by the equations $3x - 4y - 1 = 0$ and $2x - \frac{8}{3}y + 5 = 0$ are **parallel**.

So, the two lines have no common point. Hence, the given pair of equations is inconsistent. **Hence proved.**

Example 5. **Show graphically that system of equations $x + 2y = 5$, $3x + 6y = 15$ has infinitely many solutions.**

System of linear equations has infinitely many solutions, if the graph of the equations represents **coincident lines**.

Sol. Given, pair of equations is $x + 2y = 5$ and $3x + 6y = 15$

Now, let us find atleast two solutions of each of the above equations, as shown in the following tables.

Table for $x + 2y = 5$ or $y = \frac{5 - x}{2}$ is

x	5	3
$y=\frac{5-x}{2}$	0	1
Points	$A(5, 0)$	$B(3, 1)$

Plot the points $A(5, 0)$ and $B(3, 1)$ on graph paper and join them to get the line AB.

Table for $3x + 6y = 15$ or $y = \frac{15 - 3x}{6}$ is

x	1	-1
$y=\frac{15-3x}{6}$	2	3
Points	$C(1, 2)$	$D(-1, 3)$

Plot the points $C(1, 2)$ and $D(-1, 3)$ on same graph paper and join them to get the line CD.

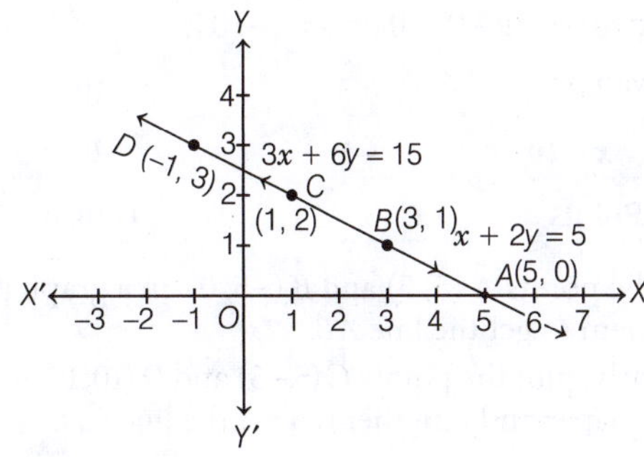

From the graph it is clear that lines represented by the equations $x + 2y = 5$ and $3x + 6y = 15$ are coincident to each other.

So, the system of equations have infinitely many solutions.

Example 6. **Form a pair of linear equations in two variables using the following information and solve it graphically. 5 yr ago, Sagar was twice as old as Tiru. 10 yr later, Sagar's age will be 10 yr more than Tiru's age. Find their present ages.**

Sol. Let the present age of Sagar be x yr and the age of Tiru be y yr.

5 yr ago, Sagar's age $= (x - 5)$ yr

and Tiru's age $= (y - 5)$ yr

According to the given condition,

$$(x - 5) = 2(y - 5)$$
$$\Rightarrow \quad x - 5 = 2y - 10$$
$$\Rightarrow \quad x - 2y + 5 = 0$$

After 10 yr, Sagar's age $= (x + 10)$ yr

and Tiru's age $= (y + 10)$ yr

According to the given condition,

$$x + 10 = (y + 10) + 10$$
$$\Rightarrow \quad x + 10 = y + 20$$
$$\Rightarrow \quad x - y - 10 = 0$$

Thus, we get the following pair of linear equations

$$x - 2y + 5 = 0 \quad \text{...(i)}$$
$$\text{and} \quad x - y - 10 = 0 \quad \text{...(ii)}$$

Now, let us draw the graphs of Eqs. (i) and (ii), by finding at least two solutions of each of the above equations.

The solutions of the equations are given in the following tables.

Table for $x - 2y + 5 = 0$ or $y = \frac{x + 5}{2}$ is

x	5	-5
$y=\frac{x+5}{2}$	5	0
Points	$A(5, 5)$	$B(-5, 0)$

Table for $x-y-10=0$ or $y=x-10$ is

x	5	10
$y=x-10$	-5	0
Points	$C(5,-5)$	$D(10,0)$

Plot the points A (5, 5) and B (–5, 0) on a graph paper and join them to get the line AB.
Similarly, plot the points C (5,–5) and D (10, 0) on the same graph paper and join them to get the line CD.

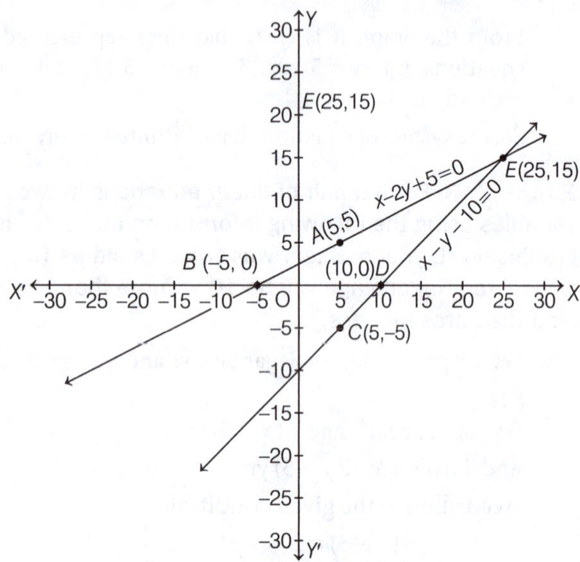

It is clear from the graph that, lines AB and CD intersect each other at point E (25, 15).
So, $x=25$ and $y=15$ is the required solution.
Hence, Sagar's present age = 25 yr
and Tiru's present age = 15 yr

Example 7. **Champa went to a 'Sale' to purchase some pants and skirts. When her friends asked her, how many of each she had bought, she answered, 'The number of skirts is two less than twice the number of pants purchased. Also, the number of skirts is four less than four times the number of pants purchased'. Help her friends to find out how many pants and skirts, had Champa bought?**

Sol. Let number of pants be x and number of skirts be y. Then,

Condition I Number of skirts = 2 × Number of pants – 2

$\Rightarrow \quad y=2x-2 \quad \ldots$(i)

Condition II Number of skirts = 4 × Number of pants – 4

$\Rightarrow \quad y=4x-4 \quad \ldots$(ii)

Now, let us find atleast two solutions of each of the above equations, as shown in the following tables.

Table for $y=2x-2$

x	2	0
$y=2x-2$	2	-2
Points	$A(2,2)$	$B(0,-2)$

Table for $y=4x-4$

x	0	1
$y=4x-4$	-4	0
Points	$P(0,-4)$	$Q(1,0)$

Now, plot the points $A(2, 2)$ and $B(0, -2)$ on a graph paper and join them to get the line AB. Similarly, plot the points $P(0, -4)$ and $Q(1, 0)$ on same graph paper and join them to get the line PQ. From the graph, it is clear that the two lines intersect at the point (1, 0).

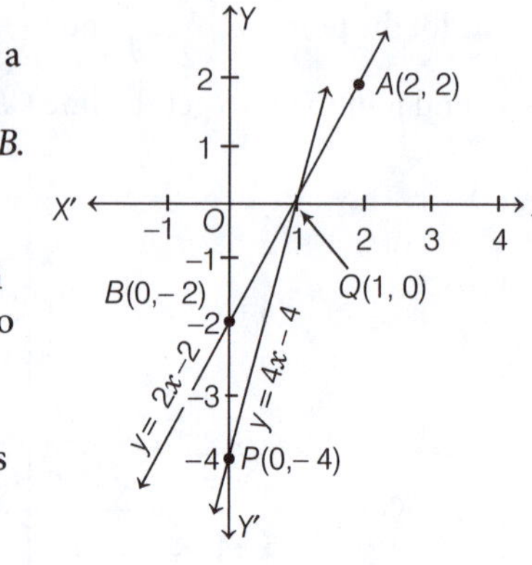

$\therefore x=1$ and $y=0$ is the solution of the pair of linear equations.
Hence, the number of pants, she purchased is one and the number of skirts, she purchased is zero i.e. she did not buy any skirt.

Nature of lines and Consistency

The nature of lines and consistency corresponding to linear equations $a_1x+b_1y+c_1=0$ and $a_2x+b_2y+c_2=0$, is shown in the table given below:

Compare the ratios	Graphical representation	Algebraic interpretation	Consistency
$\frac{a_1}{a_2} \neq \frac{b_1}{b_2}$	Intersecting lines	Exactly one solution (unique)	System is consistent
$\frac{a_1}{a_2} = \frac{b_1}{b_2} = \frac{c_1}{c_2}$	Coincident lines	Infinitely many solutions	System is consistent (dependent)
$\frac{a_1}{a_2} = \frac{b_1}{b_2} \neq \frac{c_1}{c_2}$	Parallel lines	No solution	System is inconsistent

Each of the cases in the table can be understood with the help of following example.

Example 8. **On comparing the ratios $\frac{a_1}{a_2}, \frac{b_1}{b_2}, \frac{c_1}{c_2}$ and without drawing them, find out whether the lines representing the following pairs of linear equations intersect at a point or are parallel or coincide.**

(i) $3x-5y+8=0, 7x+6y-9=0$
(ii) $4x+3y-7=0, 12x+9y=21$
(iii) $x-2y+5=0, 8y-4x+20=0$

Sol. (i) The given pair of linear equations is

$$3x-5y+8=0$$

and $$7x+6y-9=0$$

On comparing the given equations with standard form of pair of linear equations i.e. $a_1x+b_1y+c_1=0$ and $a_2x+b_2y+c_2=0$, we get

$$a_1=3,\ b_1=-5,\ c_1=8$$

and $$a_2=7,\ b_2=6,\ c_2=-9$$

Here, $\frac{a_1}{a_2} = \frac{3}{7}$ and $\frac{b_1}{b_2} = \frac{-5}{6}$

$\because \frac{a_1}{a_2} \neq \frac{b_1}{b_2}$

$\therefore$ The lines representing the given pair of linear equations will intersect at a point.

(ii) The given pair of linear equations is

$$4x + 3y - 7 = 0$$

and $$12x + 9y - 21 = 0$$

On comparing the above equations with standard form of pair of linear equations, we get

$$a_1 = 4, b_1 = 3, c_1 = -7$$

and $$a_2 = 12, b_2 = 9, c_2 = -21$$

Now, $\frac{a_1}{a_2} = \frac{4}{12} = \frac{1}{3}, \frac{b_1}{b_2} = \frac{3}{9} = \frac{1}{3}$

and $\frac{c_1}{c_2} = \frac{-7}{-21} = \frac{1}{3}$

$\because \frac{a_1}{a_2} = \frac{b_1}{b_2} = \frac{c_1}{c_2}$

$\therefore$ The lines representing the given pair of linear equations will coincide.

(iii) The given pair of linear equations is

$$x - 2y + 5 = 0 \text{ and } -4x + 8y + 20 = 0$$

On comparing the above equations with standard form of pair of linear equations, we get

$$a_1 = 1, b_1 = -2, c_1 = 5$$

and $$a_2 = -4, b_2 = 8, c_2 = 20$$

Now, $\frac{a_1}{a_2} = -\frac{1}{4}, \frac{b_1}{b_2} = \frac{-2}{8} = -\frac{1}{4}$ and $\frac{c_1}{c_2} = \frac{5}{20} = \frac{1}{4}$

$\because \frac{a_1}{a_2} = \frac{b_1}{b_2} \neq \frac{c_1}{c_2}$

$\therefore$ The lines representing the given pair of linear equations are parallel.

Example 9. Find out which pair of linear equations are consistent/inconsistent.

(i) $4x - 5y - 12 = 0, 10y + 20 = 8x$

(ii) $3x + 2y = 8, 6x - 4y = 9$ [CBSE Sample Paper 2023 (Basic)]

Sol. (i) The given pair of linear equations is

$$4x - 5y - 12 = 0 \text{ and } -8x + 10y + 20 = 0$$

On comparing with standard form of pair of linear equations, we get

$$a_1 = 4, b_1 = -5, c_1 = -12$$

and $$a_2 = -8, b_2 = 10, c_2 = 20$$

Here, $\frac{a_1}{a_2} = \frac{4}{-8} = -\frac{1}{2}, \frac{b_1}{b_2} = \frac{-5}{10} = -\frac{1}{2}$

and $\frac{c_1}{c_2} = -\frac{12}{20} = -\frac{3}{5}$

$\because \frac{a_1}{a_2} = \frac{b_1}{b_2} \neq \frac{c_1}{c_2}$

$\therefore$ The given pair of linear equations is inconsistent.

(ii) Given, pair of linear equations is

$$3x + 2y = 8$$

$\Rightarrow$ $$3x + 2y - 8 = 0$$

and $$6x - 4y = 9$$

$\Rightarrow$ $$6x - 4y - 9 = 0$$

On comparing with standard form of pair of linear equations, we get

$$a_1 = 3, b_1 = 2, c_1 = -8$$

and $$a_2 = 6, b_2 = -4, c_2 = -9$$

Here, $\frac{a_1}{a_2} = \frac{3}{6} = \frac{1}{2}$

and $\frac{b_1}{b_2} = \frac{2}{-4} = \frac{-1}{2}$

$\because \frac{a_1}{a_2} \neq \frac{b_1}{b_2}$

$\therefore$ The given pair of linear equations is consistent.

Example 10. If the lines given by $2x + ky = 1$ and $3x - 5y = 7$ has unique solution, then find the value of k.

Sol. The given equations can be rewritten as $2x+ky-1 = 0$ and $3x-5y-7 = 0$.

On comparing with $a_1x+b_1y+c_1 = 0$ and $a_2x+b_2y+c_2 = 0$, we get

$$a_1 = 2, b_1 = k, c_1 = -1 \text{ and } a_2 = 3, b_2 = -5, c_2 = -7$$

For unique solution, $\frac{a_1}{a_2} \neq \frac{b_1}{b_2} \Rightarrow \frac{2}{3} \neq \frac{k}{-5} \Rightarrow k \neq \frac{-10}{3}$

Thus, given lines have a unique solution for all real values of k, except $\frac{-10}{3}$.

Example 11. Find the value of k for which the system of equations $kx - 5y = 2$; $6x + 2y = 7$ has no solution.

Sol. Given, pair of linear equations is

$$kx - 5y - 2 = 0 \text{ and } 6x + 2y - 7 = 0$$

On comparing with standard form of pair of linear equations, we get

$$a_1 = k, b_1 = -5, c_1 = -2 \text{ and } a_2 = 6, b_2 = 2, c_2 = -7$$

For no solution, $\frac{a_1}{a_2} = \frac{b_1}{b_2} \neq \frac{c_1}{c_2}$

$\Rightarrow$ $$\frac{k}{6} = \frac{-5}{2} \neq \frac{-2}{-7}$$

$\Rightarrow$ $$\frac{k}{6} = -\frac{5}{2}$$

$\Rightarrow$ $$k = -15$$

Example 12. **For what value of k, does the system of linear equations**

$$2x+3y=7 \text{ and } (k-1)x+(k+2)y=3k$$

have infinite number of solutions? CBSE 2019

Sol. Given, system of linear equations

$$2x+3y=7 \text{ and } (k-1)x+(k+2)y=3k$$

On comparing the above equations with standard form of pair of linear equations, we get

$$a_1=2, b_1=3, c_1=-7$$

and $\quad a_2=k-1, b_2=k+2, c_2=-3k$

For infinitely many solutions,

$$\frac{a_1}{a_2}=\frac{b_1}{b_2}=\frac{c_1}{c_2}$$

$$\therefore \quad \frac{2}{k-1}=\frac{3}{k+2}=\frac{-7}{-3k}$$

Consider $\frac{2}{k-1}=\frac{7}{3k}$ and $\frac{3}{k+2}=\frac{7}{3k}$

$\Rightarrow \quad 6k=7k-7$

and $\quad 9k=7k+14$

$\Rightarrow \quad k=7$ and $2k=14$

$\Rightarrow \quad k=7$ and $k=7$

$\therefore \quad k=7$

Example 13. **For what value of p, will the following system of linear equations represent parallel lines?**

$$-x+py=1 \text{ and } px-y=1$$ NCERT Exemplar

Sol. Given, pair of equations is

$$-x+py-1=0 \quad \ldots\text{(i)}$$

and $\quad px-y-1=0 \quad \ldots$(ii)

On comparing the given equations with standard form i.e. $a_1x+b_1y+c_1=0$ and $a_2x+b_2y+c_2=0$, we get

$$a_1=-1, b_1=p, c_1=-1$$

and $\quad a_2=p, b_2=-1, c_2=-1$

For parallel lines, $\frac{a_1}{a_2}=\frac{b_1}{b_2}\neq\frac{c_1}{c_2}$

$$\Rightarrow \quad \underset{\text{I}}{\frac{-1}{p}}=\underset{\text{II}}{\frac{p}{-1}}\neq\underset{\text{III}}{\frac{-1}{-1}} \quad \ldots\text{(iii)}$$

On taking I and II terms, we get

$$\frac{-1}{p}=\frac{p}{-1}$$

$\Rightarrow \quad p^2=1$

$\Rightarrow \quad p=\pm 1$

Since, $p=-1$ does not satisfy the last two terms of Eq. (iii).

$\therefore \ p=1$ is the required value.

Hence, for $p=1$, the given system of equations will represent parallel lines.

Try These 3.1

1. **Solve the following pair of linear equations by graphical method**

   $2x+y=9$ and $x-2y=2$ CBSE 2025 (Basic)

2. **Solve graphically, the pair of linear equations $x-y=-1$ and $2x+y-10=0$. Also, find the vertices of the triangle formed by these lines and X-axis and shade the triangular region.**

3. **Solve the following system of linear equations graphically $x+2y=6$ and $3x-2y=2$**

   Also, write the coordinates of the vertices of the triangle formed by these lines and Y-axis.

   CBSE 2024 (Basic) Compartment

4. **Solve the following pairs of linear equations graphically and find the vertices of the triangle formed by these lines and Y-axis.**

   $x-y+1=0, 3x+2y-12=0$

5. **Check graphically, whether the pair of linear equations $4x-y-8=0$ and $2x-3y+6=0$ is consistent. Also, find the vertices of the triangle formed by these lines with the X-axis.**

6. **Graphically, find whether the following pair of equations has no solution, unique solution or infinitely many solutions.**

   $15x-30y+1=0,\ 3x-\frac{24}{4}y+\frac{1}{5}=0$

7. **Check graphically, whether the following pair of linear equations is consistent. If yes, solve it graphically.**

   $2x-y=0,\ x+y=0$

8. **Two straight paths are represented by the lines $7x-5y=3$ and $21x-15y=5$. Check whether the paths cross each other.**

9. **A pair of linear equations is shown below.**

   $(k-1)x+y=k+1$

   $(k^2-1)x+(k+1)y=1-k^2$

   If $k>1$, then how many solutions does this pair of equations have? CBSE QB

Directions (Q.Nos. 10-13) Form the pair of linear equations in the following problems and find their solutions graphically.

10. **4 chairs and 3 tables cost ₹ 210 and 5 chairs and 2 tables cost ₹ 175. Find the cost of one chair and one table separately.**

11. **The cost of 4 pens and 4 pencil boxes is ₹ 100. Three times the cost of a pen is ₹ 15 more than the cost of a pencil box. Find the cost of a pen and a pencil box.**

12. **2 years ago, Salim was thrice as old as his daughter and 6 years later, he will be 4 yr older than twice her age. How old are they now?** NCERT Exemplar

13. Two numbers are in the ratio 5 : 6. If 8 is subtracted from each of the numbers, the ratio becomes 4 : 5. Find the numbers.

14. On comparing the ratios $\frac{a_1}{a_2}$, $\frac{b_1}{b_2}$ and $\frac{c_1}{c_2}$, find out whether the following pairs of linear equations are consistent or inconsistent?

(i) $\frac{4}{3}x + 2y = 8$ and $2x + 3y = 12$

(ii) $4x - y = 4$ and $3x + 2y = 14$

(iii) $3x - 5y = 11$ and $6x - 10y = 7$

(iv) $6x - 3y = 12$ and $2x - y = 4$

(v) $6x + 5y = 11$ and $9x + \frac{15}{2}y = 21$

15. On comparing the ratios $\frac{a_1}{a_2}$, $\frac{b_1}{b_2}$ and $\frac{c_1}{c_2}$, find out whether the lines representing the following pairs of linear equations intersect at a point or are parallel or coincide?

(i) $2x + 3y = 3$ and $x - 2y = 2$

(ii) $4x - 2y = 10$ and $6x - 3y = 12$

(iii) $3x - 4y - 1 = 0$ and $2x - \frac{8}{3}y + 5 = 0$

(iv) $x - 3y - 7 = 0$ and $3x - 9y = 21$

(v) $-3x + 4y = 5$ and $\frac{9}{2}x - 6y + \frac{15}{2} = 0$

16. Find the value of k for which the following system of equations has a unique solution.

(i) $kx + 2y = 5, 3x + y = 1$

(ii) $x - 3y = 5, 5x + ky = 10$

(iii) $kx + 2y = 4, 8x + ky = 11$

(iv) $4x - 5y = k, 2x - 3y = 12$

(v) $2x - 3y = k, 3x - 2y = 6$

17. Find the value of k for which the following system of equations has no solution.

(i) $4x + 5y = 17, kx + 15y = 33$

(ii) $2x + ky = 8, x + y = 6$

(iii) $kx + 2y = 5, 8x + ky = 20$

(iv) $3x + y = 1, (2k - 1)x + (k - 1)y = (2k + 1)$

(v) $3x - y - 5 = 0, 6x - 2y + k = 0$

18. Find the value of k for which the following system of equations has infinitely many solutions.

(i) $4x + 7y = 10;\ (k + 2)x + 21y = 3k$

(ii) $x + 2y + 7 = 0, 2x + ky + 14 = 0$

(iii) $2x + (k - 2)y = k;\ 6x + (2k - 1)y = 2k + 5$

(iv) $2x + 3y = 2;\ (k + 2)x + (2k + 1)y = 2(k - 1)$

(v) $x + (k + 1)y = 5, (k + 1)x + 9y = (8k - 1)$

19. Find the values of p and q for which the following system of equations has infinitely many solutions.

(i) $(2p - 1)x + 3y = 5;\ 3x + (q - 1)y = 2$

(ii) $2x + 3y = 7; (p + q + 1)x + (p + 2q + 2)y = 4(p + q) + 1$

(iii) $2x + 3y = 7, (p + q)x + (2p - q)y = 21$

20. Find the value of k, for which system of equations $kx + 3y = 3$ and $12x + ky = 6$ represent parallel lines.

21. For what value of k, the pair of linear equations $x + 2y = 3, 5x + ky + 7 = 0$ represents

(i) intersecting lines

(ii) parallel lines

(iii) Is there any value of k for which the given equations represents coincident lines?

22. Given the linear equation $5x + 8y - 20 = 0$, write another linear equation in two variables such that the geometrical representation of the pair so formed is

(i) intersecting lines (ii) parallel lines

(iii) coincident lines

Answers

1. **Hint** Do same as Example 1. **Ans.** $x = 4, y = 1$
2. **Hint** Do same as Example 3.
 Ans. $x = 3, y = 4$; Vertices of triangle are (3, 4), (–1, 0) and (5, 0).
3. **Hint** Do same as Example 3.
 Ans. $x = 2, y = 2$
 Vertices of triangle are (2, 2), (0, 3) and (0, –1).
4. **Hint** Do same as Example 3.
 Ans. $x = 2, y = 3$; The vertices of the triangle formed by these lines and Y-axis are (0, 6), (0,1) and (2, 3).
5. **Hint** Do same as Example 3.
 Ans. Yes, The vertices of triangle formed by these lines with X-axis are (–3, 0), (2, 0) and (3, 4).
6. **Hint** The graph of given equations represents coincident lines. Hence, the given pair of equations has infinitely many solutions.
7. **Hint** The graph of given linear equations intersect each other at origin. So, the given pair of linear equations is consistent.
 Ans. $x = 0, y = 0$
8. **Hint** Two straight paths are parallel to each other. Hence, they do not cross each other.
9. Given pair of linear equations are $(k-1)x + y = k+1$
 and $(k^2 - 1)x + (k+1)y = 1 - k^2$
 Here, $a_1 = k - 1, b_1 = 1, c_1 = k + 1$
 and $a_2 = k^2 - 1, b_2 = k + 1, c_2 = 1 - k^2$
 $$\therefore \frac{a_1}{a_2} = \frac{k-1}{k^2-1} = \frac{k-1}{(k+1)(k-1)} = \frac{1}{k+1}$$
 $$\frac{b_1}{b_2} = \frac{1}{k+1} \text{ and } \frac{c_1}{c_2} = \frac{k+1}{1-k^2} = \frac{k+1}{(1-k)(1+k)} = \frac{1}{1-k}$$
 If $k > 1$, then $\frac{1}{k+1} = \frac{1}{k+1} \neq \frac{1}{1-k}$ i.e. $\frac{a_1}{a_2} = \frac{b_1}{b_2} \neq \frac{c_1}{c_2}$.
 Hence, given pair of linear equation has no solution.
10. **Hint** Let cost of one chair be ₹ x and cost of one table be ₹ y,
 then $4x + 3y = 210$ ...(i)
 and $5x + 2y = 175$ ...(ii)

Draw graphs of above equation and find the coordinates of intersecting point.

Ans. Cost of one chair = ₹ 15, Cost of one table = ₹ 50

11. Hint Do same as Question 10.

Ans. Cost of one pen = ₹ 10, Cost of one pencil box = ₹ 15

12. Hint Do same as Example 6.

Salim's age = 38 yr, Daughter's age = 14 yr

13. Hint Let the two numbers be x and y, then

$$\frac{x}{y}=\frac{5}{6} \Rightarrow y=\frac{6x}{5} \quad ...(i)$$

Also, $$\frac{x-8}{y-8}=\frac{4}{5} \Rightarrow 5x-4y=8 \quad ...(ii)$$

Draw graphs of Eqs. (i) and (ii) to get the required numbers.

Ans. 40 and 48.

14. (i) **Hint** On comparing the given equations with standard form of pair of linear equations, we get

$a_1=\frac{4}{3}, b_1=2, c_1=-8$ and $a_2=2, b_2=3, c_2=-12$

Now, $\frac{a_1}{a_2}=\frac{2}{3}, \frac{b_1}{b_2}=\frac{2}{3}$ and $\frac{c_1}{c_2}=\frac{2}{3}$; $\therefore \frac{a_1}{a_2}=\frac{b_1}{b_2}=\frac{c_1}{c_2}$

Hence, given equations is consistent.

(ii) **Hint** Do same as Part (i). **Ans.** Consistent.

(iii) **Hint** Do same as Part (i). **Ans.** Inconsistent.

(iv) **Hint** Do same as Part (i). **Ans.** Consistent.

(v) **Hint** Do same as Part (i). **Ans.** Inconsistent.

15. Hint Do same as Example 8.

Ans. (i) Intersecting lines (ii) Parallel lines

(iii) Parallel lines (iv) Coincident lines

(v) Coincident lines

16. (i) **Hint** For unique solution,

$$\frac{a_1}{a_2} \neq \frac{b_1}{b_2} \Rightarrow \frac{k}{3} \neq \frac{2}{1} \Rightarrow k \neq 6$$

(ii) **Hint** Do same as Part (i). **Ans.** $k \neq -15$

(iii) **Hint** Do same as Part (i). **Ans.** $k \neq \pm 4$

(iv) **Hint** For unique solution, $\frac{a_1}{a_2} \neq \frac{b_1}{b_2} \Rightarrow \frac{4}{2} \neq \frac{-5}{-3}$

which is true for any real values of k.

(v) **Hint** Do same as Part (iv). **Ans.** For all real values k.

17. (i) **Hint** For no solution, $\frac{a_1}{a_2}=\frac{b_1}{b_2} \neq \frac{c_1}{c_2}$

$$\Rightarrow \frac{4}{k}=\frac{5}{15} \neq \frac{-17}{-33} \Rightarrow \frac{4}{k}=\frac{5}{15} \Rightarrow k=12$$

(ii) **Hint** Do same as Part (i). **Ans.** $k=2$

(iii) **Hint** Do same as Part (i). **Ans.** $k=\pm 4$

(iv) **Hint** Do same as Part (i). **Ans.** $k=2$

(v) **Hint** Do same as Part (i). **Ans.** $k \neq -10$

18. (i) **Hint** For infinitely many solutions, $\frac{a_1}{a_2}=\frac{b_1}{b_2}=\frac{c_1}{c_2}$

$$\Rightarrow \frac{4}{k+2}=\frac{7}{21}=\frac{-10}{-3k} \Rightarrow \frac{4}{k+2}=\frac{7}{21} \Rightarrow k=10$$

(ii) **Hint** Do same as Part (i). **Ans.** $k=4$

(iii) **Hint** Do same as Part (i). **Ans.** $k=5$

(iv) **Hint** Do same as Part (i). **Ans.** $k=4$

(v) **Hint** Do same as Part (i). **Ans.** $k=2$

19. (i) **Hint** For infinitely many solutions, $\frac{a_1}{a_2}=\frac{b_1}{b_2}=\frac{c_1}{c_2}$

$$\Rightarrow \frac{2p-1}{3}=\frac{3}{q-1}=\frac{-5}{-2}$$ **Ans.** $p=\frac{17}{4}, q=\frac{11}{5}$

(ii) **Hint** Do same as Part (i). **Ans.** $p=3, q=2$

(iii) **Hint** Do same as Part (i). **Ans.** $p=5, q=1$

20. Hint For parallel lines, $\frac{a_1}{a_2}=\frac{b_1}{b_2} \neq \frac{c_1}{c_2}$

Ans. $k=-6$

21. Hint (i) For intersecting lines, $\frac{a_1}{a_2} \neq \frac{b_1}{b_2}$

(ii) For parallel lines, $\frac{a_1}{a_2}=\frac{b_1}{b_2} \neq \frac{c_1}{c_2}$

(iii) For coincident lines, $\frac{a_1}{a_2}=\frac{b_1}{b_2}=\frac{c_1}{c_2}$

Ans. (i) $k \neq 10$ (ii) $k=10$

(iii) There is no value of k for which given system has infinitely many solutions i.e. represent coincident lines.

22. (i) **Hint** Given linear equation is $5x+8y-20=0$ ...(i)

For intersecting lines, $\frac{a_1}{a_2} \neq \frac{b_1}{b_2}$

Here, $a_1=5, b_1=8$

Any line intersecting with Eq. (i) may be taken as

$$a_2x+b_2y+c_2=0, \text{ where } \frac{5}{a_2} \neq \frac{8}{b_2}$$

Ans. $8x+5y-25=0$ or $8x+5y-15=0$

(ii) For parallel line, $\frac{a_1}{a_2}=\frac{b_1}{b_2} \neq \frac{c_1}{c_2}$

$$\therefore \frac{5}{a_2}=\frac{8}{b_2} \neq \frac{-20}{c_2}$$

Ans. $10x+16y+15=0$ or $5x+8y-15=0$

(iii) **Hint** Any line coincident to Eq. (i) may be taken as

$a_2x+b_2+c_2=0$

where, $\frac{5}{a_2}=\frac{8}{b_2}=\frac{-20}{c_2}$

Ans. $10x+16y-40=0$ or $15x+24y-60=0$

TOPIC 02 Algebraic Methods for Solving a Pair of Linear Equations

The graphical method is suitable for integer solutions but it cannot be suitable for non-integer solutions, since it may not be as accurate as we need. So, there are several algebraic methods, which can also be used for solving a pair of linear equations. Some of the algebraic methods for solving a pair of linear equations are:

(i) Substitution Method

(ii) Elimination Method

Substitution Method

In this method, value of one variable can be found out in terms of other variable from one of the given equation and this value is substituted in other equation, then we get an equation in one variable, which can be solved easily.

To understand the substitution method more clearly, we use following steps :

Step I Consider the linear equations

$$a_1x+b_1y+c_1=0 \quad \text{...(i)}$$
$$a_2x+b_2y+c_2=0 \quad \text{...(ii)}$$

Step II Choose any one of the equation say Eq. (i), find the value of one variable, say y in terms of other variable i.e. x.

Step III Substitute this value of y in the Eq. (ii) and reduce it to an equation in one variable i.e. in terms of x, which can be solved.

Step IV Substitute the value of x obtained in Step III in the equation used in Step II to obtain the value of the other variable i.e. y.

Example 1. Solve the following system of equations $x+8y=19$ and $2x+11y=28$, by substitution method and verify it.

Sol. Given, equations are

$$x+8y=19 \quad \text{...(i)}$$

and $$2x+11y=28 \quad \text{...(ii)}$$

From Eq. (i), $$x=19-8y \quad \text{...(iii)}$$

On substituting $x=19-8y$ in Eq. (ii), we get

$$2(19-8y)+11y=28$$
$$\Rightarrow \quad 38-16y+11y=28$$
$$\Rightarrow \quad 5y=38-28=10$$
$$\Rightarrow \quad y=\frac{10}{5}=2$$

Now, on putting $y=2$ in Eq. (iii), we get

$$x=19-8\times 2$$
$$\Rightarrow \quad x=19-16=3$$

Thus, $x=3$ and $y=2$ is the required solution.

Verification

On putting $x=3$ and $y=2$ in Eqs. (i) and (ii) respectively, we get

From Eq. (i), LHS $=x+8y=3+8(2)=3+16=19=$ RHS

From Eq. (ii), LHS $=2x+11y=2(3)+11(2)$
$=6+22=28=$ RHS

Hence, the solution $x=3, y=2$ is verified.

Example 2. Solve the following system of linear equations

$$ax+by-a+b=0$$

and $$bx-ay-a-b=0.$$

Sol. The given system can be rewritten as

$$ax+by=a-b \quad \text{...(i)}$$

and $$bx-ay=a+b \quad \text{...(ii)}$$

From Eq. (i), we get

$$by=a-b-ax$$
$$\Rightarrow \quad y=\frac{a-b-ax}{b} \quad \text{...(iii)}$$

On substituting the value of y in Eq. (ii), we get

$$bx-a\left[\frac{a-b-ax}{b}\right]=a+b$$
$$\Rightarrow \quad b^2x-a(a-b-ax)=b(a+b)$$

[multiplying both sides by b]

$$\Rightarrow \quad b^2x-a^2+ab+a^2x=ab+b^2$$
$$\Rightarrow (b^2+a^2)x=ab+b^2+a^2-ab \Rightarrow x=\frac{a^2+b^2}{a^2+b^2}=1$$

On substituting $x=1$ in Eq. (iii), we get

$$y=\frac{a-b-a}{b} \Rightarrow y=\frac{-b}{b}=-1$$

Hence, solution of the given system of linear equations is $x=1$ and $y=-1$.

Example 3. Romila went to a stationary shop and purchased 2 pencils and 3 erasers for ₹ 9. Her friend Sonali saw the new variety of pencils and erasers with Romila and she also bought 4 pencils and 6 erasers of the same kind for ₹18. Find the cost of each pencil and each eraser.

Sol. Let cost of one pencil be ₹ x and cost of one eraser be ₹ y.

Then, according to given conditions, we get the following equations $$2x+3y=9 \quad \text{...(i)}$$

and $$4x+6y=18 \quad \text{...(ii)}$$

From Eq. (i), we get

$$x=\frac{9-3y}{2}$$

On substituting the value of x in Eq. (ii), we get

$$4\left(\frac{9-3y}{2}\right)+6y=18$$

$\Rightarrow 2(9-3y)+6y=18 \Rightarrow 18-6y+6y=18 \Rightarrow 18=18$

This equation has no variable but this is true for all values of y. [$\because$ LHS = RHS]

Thus, we do not get a specific value of y as a solution and so we cannot obtain a specific value of x.

Hence, Eqs. (i) and (ii) have infinitely many solutions and we cannot find a unique cost of pencil and an eraser.

Note it This situation has arisen, because both the given equations $2x+3y=9$ and $4x+6y=18$ [i.e. $2(2x+3y)=2\times 9$] are the same.

Example 4. **A fraction becomes $\frac{1}{3}$ when 1 is subtracted from the numerator. It becomes $\frac{1}{4}$ when 8 is added to the denominator. Find the fraction.** CBSE 2023 (Standard)

Sol. Let the numerator be x and the denominator be y.

So, the fraction $=\frac{x}{y}$

According to the question,

Condition I

$$\frac{x-1}{y}=\frac{1}{3} \Rightarrow 3(x-1)=y$$

$\Rightarrow \quad 3x-3=y \Rightarrow 3x-y-3=0 \quad \ldots(i)$

Condition II

$$\frac{x}{y+8}=\frac{1}{4} \Rightarrow 4x=y+8$$

$\Rightarrow \quad 4x-y=8 \Rightarrow y=4x-8 \quad \ldots(ii)$

On substituting the value of y in Eq. (i), we get

$$3x-(4x-8)-3=0$$

$\Rightarrow \quad 3x-4x+8-3=0 \Rightarrow x=5$

Now, on substituting the value of x in Eq. (ii), we get

$$y=4(5)-8=20-8=12$$

Hence, the fraction $\frac{x}{y}$ is $\frac{5}{12}$.

Try These 3.2

1. **Find the solution of the following system of equations by substitution method.**
   (i) $x+y=8, 2x-3y=1$
   (ii) $3x+2y=10, 12x+8y=30$
   (iii) $2x-7y=11, 6x-21y=33$
   (iv) $\sqrt{2}x+\sqrt{5}y=0, \sqrt{6}x+\sqrt{15}y=0$
   (v) $3x-y=3, 9x-3y=9$

2. **Solve the following pair of linear equations by substitution method.**
   (i) $\frac{3x-4y}{2}=10, \frac{3x+2y}{4}=2$
   (ii) $y=\frac{2}{3}x+6, 2y-4x=20$
   (iii) $3x-\frac{y+7}{11}=8, 2y+\frac{x+11}{7}=10$
   (iv) $1.1x+1.5y+2.3=0, 0.7x-0.2y=2$
   (v) $0.2x+0.3y=1.3, 0.4x+0.5y=2.3$
   (vi) $\sqrt{7}x+\sqrt{11}y=0, \sqrt{3}x-\sqrt{5}y=0$
   (vii) $7(y+3)-2(x+2)=14, 4(y-2)+3(x-3)=2$

3. **Solve for x and y by substitution method**
   (i) $x+y=a-b, ax-by=a^2+b^2$
   (ii) $\frac{x}{a}+\frac{y}{b}=2, ax-by=a^2-b^2$
   (iii) $\frac{bx}{a}-\frac{ay}{b}+a+b=0, bx-ay+2ab=0$
   (iv) $2(ax-by)+a+4b=0, 2(bx+ay)+(b-4a)=0$
   (v) $2\left(\frac{x}{a}\right)+\frac{y}{b}=2, \frac{x}{a}-\frac{y}{b}=4$

4. (i) Solve $2x-3y=13$ and $7x-2y=20$ and hence find the value of m for which $y=mx+7$.
   (ii) Solve $5x+4y=10$ and $3x-2y+16=0$ and hence find the value of m for which $y=mx+3$.

Directions (Q. Nos. 5-7) Form the pair of linear equations for the following problems and find their solutions by substitution method.

5. **A man has ₹ 100 in ₹ 1 coins and 50 paise coins. All the 50 paise coins are worth as much as all the ₹ 1 coins. How many coins of each he has?**

6. **In ΔABC, $\angle C=5\angle B=3(\angle A+\angle B)$, find all angles of ΔABC.**

7. **The perimeter of rectangular lawn is 54 m. It is reduced in size, so that length is $\frac{3}{5}$th and breadth is $\frac{3}{4}$th of the original dimensions. The perimeter of the reduced rectangle is 36 m. What were the original dimensions of the lawn?**

Answers

1. (i) **Hint** Given, equations are $x+y=8 \quad \ldots(i)$
   and $\quad 2x-3y=1 \quad \ldots(ii)$
   From Eq. (i), $y=8-x$
   Then, from Eq. (ii), $2x-3(8-x)=1$
   $\Rightarrow \quad 5x=25$
   $\Rightarrow \quad x=5$
   $\therefore \quad y=8-5=3$
   Hence, $x=5, y=3$

(ii) **Hint** Given, equations are $3x+2y=10$ ...(i)

and $12x+8y=30$ ...(ii)

From Eq. (i), $y=\frac{10-3x}{2}$

Then, from Eq. (ii), $12x+8\left(\frac{10-3x}{2}\right)=30$

$\Rightarrow 12x+40-12x=30 \Rightarrow 40=30$

Since, this equality is false, therefore no solution exist.

(iii) **Hint** Given equations are $2x-7y=11$ ...(i)

and $6x-21y=33$ ...(ii)

From Eq. (i), $y=\frac{2x-11}{7}$

Then, from Eq. (ii), $6x-21\left(\frac{2x-11}{7}\right)=33$

$\Rightarrow 6x-6x+33=33 \Rightarrow 33=33$

This equality is true for all values of x, therefore given pair of equations have infinitely many solutions.

(iv) **Hint** Do same as Part (iii).
Ans. Infinitely many solutions.

(v) **Hint** Do same as Part (iii).
Ans. Infintely many solutions.

2. (i) **Hint** Given equations are

$\frac{3x-4y}{2}=10 \Rightarrow 3x-4y=20$

and $\frac{3x+2y}{4}=2 \Rightarrow 3x+2y=8$

Now, do same as Q.1 (ii). **Ans.** $x=4, y=-2$

(ii) **Hint** Given equations are $y=\frac{2}{3}x+6$

$\Rightarrow -2x+3y=18$ and $-4x+2y=20$

Now, do same as Q. 1 (ii).

Ans. $x=-3, y=4$

(iii) **Hint** Given equations are

$3x-\frac{y+7}{11}=8 \Rightarrow y=33x-95$

and $2y+\frac{x+11}{7}=10 \Rightarrow 14y+x=59$

Now, do same as Q.1 (ii). **Ans.** $x=3, y=4$

(iv) **Hint** Multiplying the given equations by 10, we get

$11x+15y+23=0$

and $7x-2y=20$

Now, do same as Q.1 (ii) **Ans.** $x=2, y=-3$

(v) **Hint** Do same as Part (iv) **Ans.** $x=2, y=3$

(vi) **Hint** Given equations are $\sqrt{7}x+\sqrt{11}y=0$ ...(i)

and $\sqrt{3}x-\sqrt{5}y=0$ ...(ii)

From Eqs. (ii), $y=\frac{\sqrt{3}x}{\sqrt{5}}$

Then, from Eq. (i), $\sqrt{7}x+\sqrt{11}\times\frac{\sqrt{3}}{\sqrt{5}}x=0 \Rightarrow x=0$

$\therefore y=\sqrt{\frac{3}{5}}\times 0=0$

Hence, $x=0, y=0$

(vii) **Hint** First rewrite the given equations as

$2x-7y-3=0$ and $3x+4y-19=0$

Then, do same as Q.1 (ii) **Ans.** $x=5, y=1$

3. (i) Given equations are

$x+y=a-b \Rightarrow y=a-b-x$ ...(i)

and $ax-by=a^2+b^2$ ...(ii)

On putting $y=a-b-x$ in Eq. (ii), we get

$ax-b(a-b-x)=a^2+b^2$

$\Rightarrow (a+b)x=a^2+b^2+ab-b^2$

$\Rightarrow x=\frac{a(a+b)}{(a+b)}=a$

$\therefore y=a-b-a=-b$

Hence, $x=a, y=-b$

(ii) **Hint** Do same as Part (i). **Ans.** $x=a, y=b$

(iii) **Hint** Do same as Part (i). **Ans.** $x=-a, y=b$

(iv) **Hint** Do same as Part (i). **Ans.** $x=-\frac{1}{2}, y=2$

(v) **Hint** Do same as Part (i) **Ans.** $x=2a, y=-2b$

4. **Hint** First, solve the given equations similar to question 1 to get the values of x and y and then put these values in $y=mx+7$ and $y=mx+3$ to get required values of m.

(i) **Ans.** $x=2, y=-3, m=-5$

(ii) **Ans.** $x=-2, y=5, m=-1$

5. Let the number of ₹ 1 and 50 paise coins be x and y, respectively. Then, $x+\frac{1}{2}y=100$ ...(i)

and $x=\frac{1}{2}y$ ...(ii)

Then, from Eq. (i),

$\frac{1}{2}y+\frac{1}{2}y=100 \Rightarrow y=100$

$\therefore$ From Eq. (ii), $x=\frac{1}{2}\times 100=50$

Hence, ₹ 1 coins $=50$, 50 paise coins $=100$

6. **Hint** Let $\angle A$ and $\angle B$ be x and y, respectively.

Then, $\angle C=5\angle B=3(\angle A+\angle B)$

$\Rightarrow \angle C=5y$ and $\angle C=3(x+y)$

$\Rightarrow 5y=3(x+y)$

$\Rightarrow 2y-3x=0$ ...(i)

Also, $\angle A+\angle B+\angle C=180° \Rightarrow x+y+5y=180°$

$\Rightarrow x+6y=180°$ ...(ii)

Now, solve Eqs. (i) and (ii) to find $\angle A$ and $\angle B$.

Hence, find $\angle C$.

Ans. $\angle A=18°, \angle B=27°, \angle C=135°$

7. **Hint** Let the original length and breadth of the lawn be x m and y m, respectively.

Then, $2(x+y)=54 \Rightarrow x+y=27$

and $2\left(\frac{3}{5}x+\frac{3}{4}y\right)=36 \Rightarrow 4x+5y=120$

Now, do same as Q. 1 (i).

Ans. Length $=15$ m, Breadth $=12$ m

TOPIC 03 Elimination Method

In this method, one variable out of the two variables is eliminated by making the coefficients of that variable equal in both the equations.

After eliminating that variable, the left equation is an equation in one variable, which can be solved easily.

Value of one variable obtained in this way can be substituted in any one of the two given equations to find the value of other variable. This method can be understood with the help of following Steps:

Step I Consider the equation

$$a_1x+b_1y+c_1=0 \quad \ldots(i)$$
$$a_2x+b_2y+c_2=0 \quad \ldots(ii)$$

Step II First multiply both the equations by some suitable non-zero constants to makes the coefficient of the variable to be numerically equal.

Step III Add or subtract the one equation from the other, so that one variable gets eliminated.

Step IV Solve the equation in one variable x (or y), so obtained to get its value.

Step V Substitute this value x (or y) in either of the original equation to get the value of other variable.

Example 1. **Solve the following pair of linear equations $41x+53y=135$ and $53x+41y=147$.**

Sol. Given, pair of linear equations is

$$41x+53y=135 \quad \ldots(i)$$

and $$53x+41y=147 \quad \ldots(ii)$$

On adding Eqs. (i) and (ii), we get

$$94x+94y=282$$

$\Rightarrow$ $x+y=3$ [dividing both sides by 94] ...(iii)

On subtracting Eq. (i) from Eq. (ii), we get

$$12x-12y=12$$

$\Rightarrow$ $x-y=1$ [dividing both sides by 12] ...(iv)

Now, adding Eqs. (iii) and (iv), we get

$$2x=4$$

$\Rightarrow$ $x=2$

On substituting $x=2$ in Eq. (iii), we get

$$y=3-2=1$$

Hence, $x=2$ and $y=1$ is the required solution.

Note it In the above question, coefficient of x and y look alike, therefore for easy calculation we can use the above process.

Example 2. **Use elimination method to find all possible solutions of the following pair of linear equations**

(i) $2x+3y=8, 4x+6y=7$

(ii) $ax+by-a+b=0, bx-ay-a-b=0$

Sol. (i) Given, pair of linear equations is

$$2x+3y=8 \quad \ldots(i)$$

and $$4x+6y=7 \quad \ldots(ii)$$

On multiplying Eq. (i) by 2, to make the coefficients of x equal, we get

$$4x+6y=16 \quad \ldots(iii)$$

On subtracting Eq. (ii) from Eq. (iii), we get

$$(4x-4x)+(6y-6y)=16-7$$

$\Rightarrow$ $0=9$

which is a false equation involving no variable.

So, the given pair of linear equations has no solution i.e. this pair of linear equations is inconsistent.

(ii) Given, pair of linear equations is

$$ax+by=a-b \quad \ldots(i)$$

and $$bx-ay=a+b \quad \ldots(ii)$$

On multiplying Eq. (i) by a and Eq. (ii) by b and adding them, we get

$$a^2x+aby+b^2x-aby=a^2-ab+ba+b^2$$

$$\Rightarrow \quad (a^2+b^2)x=(a^2+b^2) \Rightarrow x=\frac{a^2+b^2}{a^2+b^2}=1$$

On putting $x=1$ in Eq. (i), we get

$$a+by=a-b \Rightarrow y=-\frac{b}{b}=-1$$

Hence, $x=1$ and $y=-1$, which is the required unique solution.

Example 3. **Sabina went to a bank ATM to withdraw ₹ 2000. She received ₹ 50 and ₹ 100 notes only. If Sabina got 25 notes in all, how many notes of ₹ 50 and ₹ 100 did she receive?** CBSE 2023 (Basic)

Sol. Let number of ₹ 50 notes Sabina received be x and number of ₹ 100 notes be y.

According to the question,

Total money withdrawn = ₹ 2000

$\Rightarrow$ $50x+100y=2000$

$\Rightarrow$ $x+2y=40$ ...(i)

and total number of notes = 25

$\Rightarrow$ $x+y=25$ ...(ii)

On subtracting Eq. (ii) from Eq. (i), we get

$$y=15$$

From Eq. (ii), $x=25-15=10$

$\therefore$ Number of ₹ 50 notes = 10

Number of ₹ 100 notes = 15

Example 4. **The sum of the digits of a 2-digit number is 9. Also, nine times this number is twice the number obtained by reversing the order of the digits. Find the number.** CBSE 2024 (Basic)

Sol. Let the number be $10x+y$.

Given, $x+y=9$ ...(i)

According to the question,

$$9(10x+y)=2(10y+x)$$

$\Rightarrow$ $90x+9y=20y+2x$

$\Rightarrow$ $88x-11y=0$

$\Rightarrow$ $8x-y=0$ ...(ii)

On adding Eqs. (i) and (ii), we get

$$9x=9$$

$\Rightarrow$ $x=1$

On substituting $x=1$ in Eq. (i), we get

$$1+y=9$$

$$y=8$$

The number is $10x+y=10\times1+8=18$

Therefore, $x=1$ and $y=8$ are the required digits and the number is 18.

Example 5. **The ratio of incomes of two persons is 9 : 7 and the ratio of their expenditures is 4 : 3. If each of them manages to save ₹ 2000 per month. To find their monthly incomes, form a pair of linear equations from the above data and solve them by elimination method. Also, verify the solution.**

Sol. Given, ratio of incomes = 9 : 7

and ratio of their expenditures = 4 : 3

Saving of each person = ₹ 2000

Let incomes of two persons be $9x, 7x$ and their expenditures be $4y, 3y$.

Then, linear equations so formed are

$9x-4y=2000$ ...(i)

and $7x-3y=2000$ ...(ii)

We make the coefficients of x numerically equal in both equations.

On multiplying Eq.(i) by 7 and Eq. (ii) by 9, we get

$63x-28y=14000$ ...(iii)

and $63x-27y=18000$ ...(iv)

On subtracting Eq. (iv) from Eq. (iii), we get

$$-28y+27y=14000-18000$$

$\Rightarrow$ $-y=-4000$

$\Rightarrow$ $y=4000$

On putting $y=4000$ in Eq. (i), we get

$$9x-4\times4000=2000$$

$\Rightarrow$ $9x=2000+16000$

$\Rightarrow$ $x=\dfrac{18000}{9}=2000$

Thus, monthly income of both persons are 9(2000) and 7(2000) i.e. ₹ 18000 and ₹ 14000, respectively.

Verification

On putting $x=2000$ and $y=4000$ in Eqs. (i) and (ii) respectively, we get

From Eq. (i), LHS $=9x-4y=9(2000)-4(4000)$
$=18000-16000$
$=2000=$ RHS

From Eq. (ii), LHS $=7x-3y=7(2000)-3(4000)$
$=14000-12000$
$=2000=$ RHS

Hence, the solution is verified.

Example 6. **Two people are 16 km apart on a straight road. They start walking at the same time. If they walk towards each other with different speeds, they will meet in 2 h. Had they walked in the same direction with same speeds as before, they would have met in 8 h. Find their walking speeds.** CBSE 2023 (Standard)

Sol. Let the walking speed of Ist person be x km/h and of IInd person be y km/h.

It is given that if they walk towards each other, they will meet in 2 h.

$\Rightarrow$ Distance covered by Ist person in 2h

+ Distance covered by IInd person in 2h = 16 km

$$16=(x+y)\times2$$

$\Rightarrow$ $16=2x+2y$ [$\because$ Distance = Speed $\times$ Time]

$\Rightarrow$ $x+y=8$ ...(i)

Now, it is also given that if they walk in the same direction, then they will meet in 8 h.

$\Rightarrow$ Distance covered by Ist person in 8 h

= Distance covered by IInd person in 8 h + 16 km

$\Rightarrow$ $8x=8y+16$

$\Rightarrow$ $8(x-y)=16$

$\Rightarrow$ $x-y=2$ ...(ii)

On adding Eqs. (i) and (ii), we get

$$2x=10$$

$\Rightarrow$ $x=5$

From Eq. (ii),

$$5-y=2$$

$\Rightarrow$ $y=3$

Hence, walking speeds of both persons are 5 km/h and 3 km/h, respectively.

Try These 3.3

1. **Solve the following pair of equations by using elimination method.**
   (i) $8x+5y=11, x+y=4$
   (ii) $x-y=3, 3x-2y=10$
   (iii) $4x-3y=8, 6x-y=\frac{29}{3}$
   (iv) $11x+15y+23=0, 7x-2y-20=0$
   (v) $3x-2y=5, 2x-5y=4$
   (vi) $x-2y=3, 3x-3y=5$
   (vii) $0.4x+0.3y=1.7, 0.7x-0.2y=0.8$
   (viii) $\frac{x}{4}+\frac{y}{3}=-\frac{1}{12}, \frac{x}{2}-\frac{5}{4}y=\frac{7}{4}$
   (ix) $\frac{x}{3}+\frac{y}{3}=14, \frac{5x}{6}-\frac{y}{3}+7=0$
   (x) $\frac{x}{10}+\frac{y}{5}+1=15, \frac{x}{8}+\frac{y}{6}=15$

2. **Solve the following pair of linear equations by elimination method.**
   (i) $ax+by=c, a^2x+b^2y=c^2$
   (ii) $(a+b)x+(a-b)y=2ab, (a+b)x-(a-b)y=ab$
   (iii) $\frac{bx}{a}+\frac{ay}{b}=a^2+b^2, x+y=2ab,$
   (iv) $5ax+6by=28; 3ax+4by=18$
   (v) $\frac{ax}{b}-\frac{by}{a}=a+b; ax-by=2ab$

3. **Solve the following pair of linear equations by elimination method.**
   (i) $62x+43y=167, 43x+62y=148$
   CBSE 2024 (Standard) Compartment
   (ii) $117x+231y=579, 231x+117y=465$
   (iii) $217x+131y=913, 131x+217y=827$
   (iv) $41x-17y=99, 17x-41y=75$
   (v) $23x-29y=98, 29x-23y=110$

4. **Find the solution of the pair of equations $\frac{x}{10}+\frac{y}{5}-1=0$ and $\frac{x}{8}+\frac{y}{6}=15$ and find λ, if $y=\lambda x+5$.** NCERT Exemplar

Directions (Q. Nos. 5-8) Form the pair of linear equation in the following problems and find their solutions (if they exist) by the elimination method.

5. **5 yr ago, Amit was thrice as old as Baljeet. 10 yr hence, Amit shall be twice as old as Baljeet. What are their present ages?** CBSE 2023 (Standard)

6. **Sheena went to a bank to withdraw ₹ 1000 and asked the cashier to give her ₹ 100 and ₹ 50 notes only. She got 14 notes in all. Find how many notes of ₹ 100 and ₹ 50 she received?**

7. **The sum of the digits of a two-digit number is 12. Seven times the number is equal to four times the number obtained by reversing the order of the digits. Find the number.** CBSE 2024 (Standard) Compartment

8. **The area of a rectangle gets reduced by 80 sq units, if its length is reduced by 5 units and the breadth is increased by 2 units. If we increase the length by 10 units and decrease the breadth by 5 units, then the area is increased by 50 sq units. Find the length and the breadth of the rectangle.**

Answers

1. (i) Given, pair of linear equations is $8x+5y=11$ ...(i)

and $x+y=4$ ...(ii)

On multiplying Eq. (ii) by 8 and then subtracting from Eq. (i), we get $-3y=-21 \Rightarrow y=7$

On putting $y=7$ in Eq. (ii), we get

$$x=4-7=-3$$

Hence, $x=-3, y=7$

(ii) **Hint** Do same as Part (i). **Ans.** $x=4, y=1$

(iii) **Hint** Do same as Part (i). **Ans.** $x=\frac{3}{2}, y=-\frac{2}{3}$

(iv) **Hint** Do same as Part (i). **Ans.** $x=2, y=-3$

(v) **Hint** Do same as Part (i). **Ans.** $x=\frac{17}{11}, y=\frac{-2}{11}$

(vi) **Hint** Do same as Part (i). **Ans.** $x=\frac{1}{3}, y=\frac{-4}{3}$

(vii) Given, pair of linear equations is $0.4x+0.3y=1.7$ ...(i)

and $0.7x-0.2y=0.8$ ...(ii)

On multiplying Eq. (i) by 20 and Eq. (ii) by 30 and then adding both equations, we get

$$29x=58 \Rightarrow x=2$$

On putting $x=2$ in Eq. (ii), we get

$$0.7\times2-0.8=0.2y \Rightarrow y=3$$

Hence, $x=2$ and $y=3$

(viii) Given, pair of linear equations is

$$\frac{x}{4}+\frac{y}{3}=-\frac{1}{12}$$

$\Rightarrow$ $3x+4y=-1$ ...(i)

and $\frac{x}{2}-\frac{5}{4}y=\frac{7}{4} \Rightarrow 2x-5y=7$ ...(ii)

Now, do same as Part (i).

Ans. $x=1, y=-1$

(ix) **Hint** Do same as Part (viii).

Ans. $x=6, y=36$

(x) **Hint** Do same as Part (viii).

Ans. $x=80, y=30$

2. (i) Given pair of linear equation is

$ax+by=c$ ...(i)

$a^2x+b^2y=c^2$ ...(ii)

On multiplying Eq. (i) by a and then subtracting from Eq. (ii), we get

$$b^2y - aby = c^2 - ca$$

$$\Rightarrow \quad by(b-a) = c(c-a) \Rightarrow y = \frac{c(c-a)}{b(b-a)}$$

On putting this value of y in Eq. (i), we get

$$ax = c - \frac{bc(c-a)}{b(b-a)} = \frac{cb - ac - c^2 + ac}{(b-a)}$$

$$\Rightarrow \quad x = \frac{c(b-c)}{a(b-a)}$$

Hence, $x = \dfrac{c(b-c)}{a(b-a)}, y = \dfrac{c(c-a)}{b(b-a)}$.

(ii) **Hint** Do same as Part (i).

Ans. $x = \dfrac{3ab}{2(a+b)}, y = \dfrac{ab}{2(a-b)}$

(iii) **Hint** Do same as Part (i). **Ans.** $x = ab, y = ab$

(iv) **Hint** Do same as Part (i). **Ans.** $x = \dfrac{2}{a}, y = \dfrac{3}{b}$

(v) **Hint** Do same as Part (i). **Ans.** $x = b, y = -a$

3. Hint Do same as Example 1.

Ans.

(i) $x = 2, y = 1$

(ii) $x = 1, y = 2$

(iii) $x = 3, y = 2$

(iv) $x = 2, y = -1$

(v) $x = 3, y = -1$

4. Hint By solving both equations as in Question 1 (viii), find the values of x and y and then put these values in $y = \lambda x + 5$ to get required value of λ.

Ans. $x = 340, y = -165, \lambda = -\dfrac{1}{2}$

5. Let present age of Amit be x yr and present age of Baljeet be y yr.

5 yr ago,

Age of Amit $= x - 5$

Age of Baljeet $= y - 5$

According to the question,

$$x - 5 = 3(y - 5)$$

$$\Rightarrow \quad x - 5 = 3y - 15$$

$$\Rightarrow \quad x - 3y = -10 \quad \ldots\text{(i)}$$

After 10 yr,

Age of Amit $= x + 10$

Age of Baljeet $= y + 10$

According to the question,

$$x + 10 = 2(y + 10)$$

$$\Rightarrow \quad x + 10 = 2y + 20$$

$$\Rightarrow \quad x - 2y = 10 \quad \ldots\text{(ii)}$$

On subtracting Eq. (ii) from Eq. (i), we get

$$-y = -20 \Rightarrow y = 20$$

On substituting the value of y in Eq. (ii), we get

$$x - 2(20) = 10$$

$$\Rightarrow \quad x - 40 = 10$$

$$\Rightarrow \quad x = 50$$

Hence, present age of Amit = 50 yr

and present age of Baljeet = 20 yr

6. Hint Let the number of ₹ 100 and ₹ 50 notes be x and y, respectively. Then, according to the question,

$$x + y = 14 \text{ and } 100x + 50y = 1000$$

Now, do same as Question 1 (i) to solve for x and y.

Ans. ₹ 100 notes = 6 and ₹ 50 notes = 8

7. Hint Do same as Example 4.

Ans. The required two-digit number is 48.

8. Hint Let x and y be length and breadth of rectangle.

Then, its area $= xy$

According to the question,

$$(x-5)(y+2) = xy - 80 \Rightarrow 2x - 5y = -70$$

$$(x+10)(y-5) = xy + 50 \Rightarrow -5x + 10y = 100$$

Now, do same as Question 1 (i) to solve for x and y.

Ans. Length = 40 units, breadth = 30 units

NCERT FOLDER

Complete Solutions of All Exercises of NCERT Textbook

EXERCISE 3.1

Q1. Form the pair of linear equations in the following problems and find their solutions graphically.

(i) 10 students of Class X took part in a Mathematics quiz. If the number of girls is 4 more than the number of boys, then find the number of boys and girls who took part in the quiz.

(ii) 5 pencils and 7 pens together cost ₹ 50, whereas 7 pencils and 5 pens together cost ₹ 46. Find the cost of one pencil and that of one pen.

Sol. (i) Let the number of boys be x and the number of girls be y.

Then, according to the question, $x + y = 10$

Also, number of girls = 4 + Number of boys

$$y = x + 4$$

Thus, we get the following pair of linear equations

$$x + y = 10 \quad \ldots(i)$$

and

$$y = x + 4 \quad \ldots(ii)$$

$\therefore$ Table for linear equation $x + y = 10$ or $y = 10 - x$ is

x	0	8	3
$y = 10 - x$	10	2	7
Points	$A(0, 10)$	$B(8, 2)$	$C(3, 7)$

Plot the points A, B and C and join them to get the line ACB.

Table for linear equation $y = x + 4$ is

x	0	1	6
$y = x + 4$	4	5	10
Points	$D(0, 4)$	$E(1, 5)$	$F(6, 10)$

Plot the points D, E and F and join them to get the line DEF.

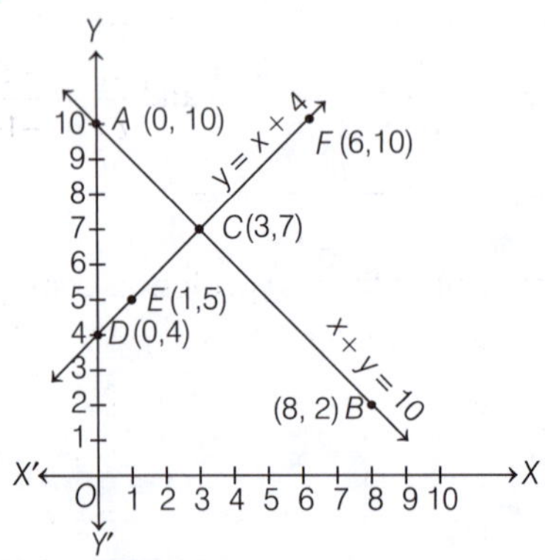

The two lines AB and DF intersect at the point $C(3, 7)$.

So, $x = 3$ and $y = 7$ is the required solution of the pair of linear equations.

Hence, the required number of boys is 3 and girls is 7.

(ii) Let the cost of one pencil be ₹ x and the cost of one pen be ₹ y. Then, according to the question,

Cost of 5 pencils and 7 pens = ₹ 50

$$\therefore \quad 5x + 7y = 50$$

and cost of 7 pencils and 5 pens = ₹ 46

$$\therefore \quad 7x + 5y = 46$$

Thus, we get the following pair of linear equations

$$5x + 7y = 50 \quad \ldots(i)$$

and

$$7x + 5y = 46 \quad \ldots(ii)$$

Table for linear equation $5x + 7y = 50$ or $y = \frac{50 - 5x}{7}$ is

x	10	3
$y = \frac{50 - 5x}{7}$	0	5
Points	$A(10, 0)$	$B(3, 5)$

Table for linear equation $7x + 5y = 46$ or $y = \frac{46 - 7x}{5}$ is

x	8	3
$y = \frac{46 - 7x}{5}$	-2	5
Points	$C(8, -2)$	$B(3, 5)$

Plot the points A, B and C on graph paper and join them to get the lines AB and BC, respectively.

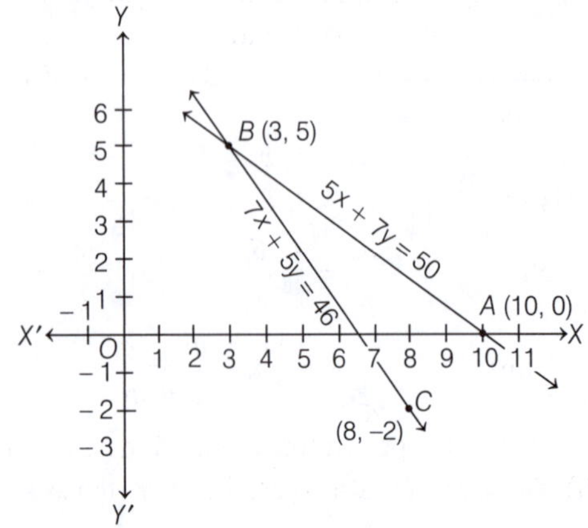

The two lines AB and BC intersect at the point $B(3, 5)$. So, $x = 3$ and $y = 5$ is the required solution. Hence, the cost of one pencil is ₹ 3 and the cost of one pen is ₹ 5.

Q2. On comparing the ratios $\frac{a_1}{a_2}$, $\frac{b_1}{b_2}$ and $\frac{c_1}{c_2}$, find out whether the lines representing the following pairs of linear equations intersect at a point, are parallel or coincident:

(i) $5x-4y+8=0$; $7x+6y-9=0$

(ii) $9x+3y+12=0$; $18x+6y+24=0$

(iii) $6x-3y+10=0$; $2x-y+9=0$

Sol. (i) The given pair of linear equations is

$$5x-4y+8=0 \quad ...(i)$$

and $$7x+6y-9=0 \quad ...(ii)$$

On comparing with standard form of pair of linear equations, we get

$$a_1=5,\ b_1=-4,\ c_1=8$$

and $$a_2=7,\ b_2=6, c_2=-9$$

Here, $\frac{5}{7} \neq \frac{-4}{6}$ i.e. $\frac{a_1}{a_2} \neq \frac{b_1}{b_2}$

So, the lines representing the given pair of linear equations will intersect at a point.

(ii) Do same as Part (i). **Ans.** Coincident lines

(iii) Do same as Part (i). **Ans.** Parallel lines

Q3. On comparing the ratios $\frac{a_1}{a_2}$, $\frac{b_1}{b_2}$ and $\frac{c_1}{c_2}$, find out whether the following pairs of linear equations are consistent or inconsistent.

(i) $3x+2y=5$; $2x-3y=7$

(ii) $2x-3y=8$; $4x-6y=9$

(iii) $\frac{3}{2}x+\frac{5}{3}y=7$; $9x-10y=14$

(iv) $5x-3y=11$; $-10x+6y=-22$

(v) $\frac{4}{3}x+2y=8$; $2x+3y=12$

Sol. (i) The given equations can be rewritten as

$$3x+2y-5=0 \text{ and } 2x-3y-7=0$$

On comparing with standard form of pair of linear equations, we get

$$a_1=3,\ b_1=2,\ c_1=-5$$

and $$a_2=2,\ b_2=-3,\ c_2=-7$$

Now, $\frac{a_1}{a_2}=\frac{3}{2}$, $\frac{b_1}{b_2}=-\frac{2}{3}$ and $\frac{c_1}{c_2}=\frac{5}{7}$

Thus, $\frac{3}{2} \neq -\frac{2}{3}$ i.e. $\frac{a_1}{a_2} \neq \frac{b_1}{b_2}$

Hence, the pair of linear equations is consistent.

(ii) The given equations can be rewritten as

$$2x-3y-8=0 \text{ and } 4x-6y-9=0$$

On comparing with standard form of pair of linear equations, we get

$$a_1=2,\ b_1=-3,\ c_1=-8$$

and $$a_2=4,\ b_2=-6,\ c_2=-9$$

Now, $\frac{a_1}{a_2}=\frac{2}{4}=\frac{1}{2}$, $\frac{b_1}{b_2}=\frac{-3}{-6}=\frac{1}{2}$ and $\frac{c_1}{c_2}=\frac{-8}{-9}=\frac{8}{9}$

Thus, $\frac{1}{2}=\frac{1}{2} \neq \frac{8}{9}$ i.e. $\frac{a_1}{a_2}=\frac{b_1}{b_2} \neq \frac{c_1}{c_2}$

Hence, the pair of linear equations is inconsistent.

(iii) Do same as Part (i). **Ans.** Consistent

(iv) The given equations can be rewritten as

$$5x-3y-11=0 \text{ and } -10x+6y+22=0$$

On comparing with standard form of pair of linear equations, we get

$$a_1=5, b_1=-3, c_1=-11$$

and $$a_2=-10,\ b_2=6,\ c_2=22$$

Now, $\frac{a_1}{a_2}=\frac{5}{-10}=-\frac{1}{2}$, $\frac{b_1}{b_2}=\frac{-3}{6}=-\frac{1}{2}$

and $\frac{c_1}{c_2}=\frac{-11}{22}=-\frac{1}{2}$

Thus, $-\frac{1}{2}=-\frac{1}{2}=-\frac{1}{2}$ i.e. $\frac{a_1}{a_2}=\frac{b_1}{b_2}=\frac{c_1}{c_2}$

Hence, the pair of linear equations is consistent (or dependent).

(v) Do same as Part (iv). **Ans.** Consistent (or dependent)

Q4. Which of the following pairs of linear equations are consistent/inconsistent? If consistent, obtain the solution graphically:

(i) $x+y=5$; $2x+2y=10$

(ii) $x-y=8$; $3x-3y=16$

(iii) $2x+y-6=0$; $4x-2y-4=0$

(iv) $2x-2y-2=0$; $4x-4y-5=0$

Sol. (i) Given, pair of linear equations is

$$x+y=5 \Rightarrow x+y-5=0 \quad ...(i)$$

and $$2x+2y=10 \Rightarrow 2x+2y-10=0 \quad ...(ii)$$

On comparing with standard form of pair of linear equations, we get

$$a_1=1,\ b_1=1,\ c_1=-5$$

and $$a_2=2,\ b_2=2,\ c_2=-10$$

Here, $\frac{a_1}{a_2}=\frac{1}{2}$, $\frac{b_1}{b_2}=\frac{1}{2}$ and $\frac{c_1}{c_2}=\frac{-5}{-10}=\frac{1}{2}$

Thus, $\frac{a_1}{a_2}=\frac{b_1}{b_2}=\frac{c_1}{c_2}=\frac{1}{2}$

So, the pair of linear equations is consistent.

Now, table for $x+y=5$ or $y=5-x$ is ...(iii)

x	0	5	2
$y=5-x$	5	0	3
Points	$A(0,5)$	$B(5,0)$	$C(2,3)$

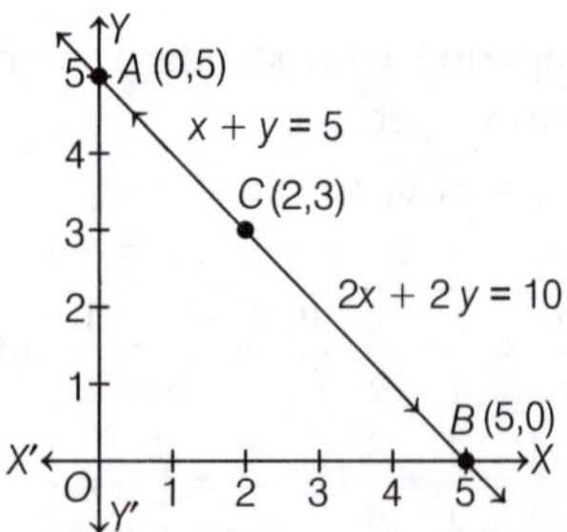

Here, Eq. (ii) is same as Eq. (i) because on dividing Eq. (ii) by 2 on both sides, it becomes same as Eq (i). Therefore, table for both equations is same.

On plotting and joining these points on graph paper, we observe that the lines are coincident, so pair of linear equations have infinitely many solutions and hence consistent. All the points lying on the line ACB satisfy the given pair of linear equations.

(ii) Given, pair of linear equations is

$$x-y=8 \Rightarrow x-y-8=0 \quad \text{...(i)}$$

and $$3x-3y=16 \Rightarrow 3x-3y-16=0 \quad \text{...(ii)}$$

On comparing with standard form of pair of linear equations, we get

$$a_1=1,\ b_1=-1,\ c_1=-8$$

and $$a_2=3,\ b_2=-3,\ c_2=-16$$

Here, $$\frac{a_1}{a_2}=\frac{1}{3},\ \frac{b_1}{b_2}=\frac{1}{3} \text{ and } \frac{c_1}{c_2}=\frac{-8}{-16}=\frac{1}{2}$$

Thus, $$\frac{1}{3}=\frac{1}{3}\neq\frac{1}{2} \text{ i.e. } \frac{a_1}{a_2}=\frac{b_1}{b_2}\neq\frac{c_1}{c_2}$$

So, the pair of linear equations is inconsistent.

(iii) Given, pair of linear equations is

$$2x+y-6=0 \quad \text{...(i)}$$

and $$4x-2y-4=0 \quad \text{...(ii)}$$

On comparing with standard form of pair of linear equations, we get

$$a_1=2, b_1=1, c_1=-6$$

and $$a_2=4, b_2=-2,\ c_2=-4$$

Here, $$\frac{a_1}{a_2}=\frac{2}{4}=\frac{1}{2},\ \frac{b_1}{b_2}=-\frac{1}{2} \text{ and } \frac{c_1}{c_2}=\frac{-6}{-4}=\frac{3}{2}$$

Thus, $$\frac{1}{2}\neq-\frac{1}{2} \text{ i.e. } \frac{a_1}{a_2}\neq\frac{b_1}{b_2}.$$

Hence, the given pair of linear equations is consistent. Now, on plotting the graph similar to Q. 1 (i), we get the following graph.

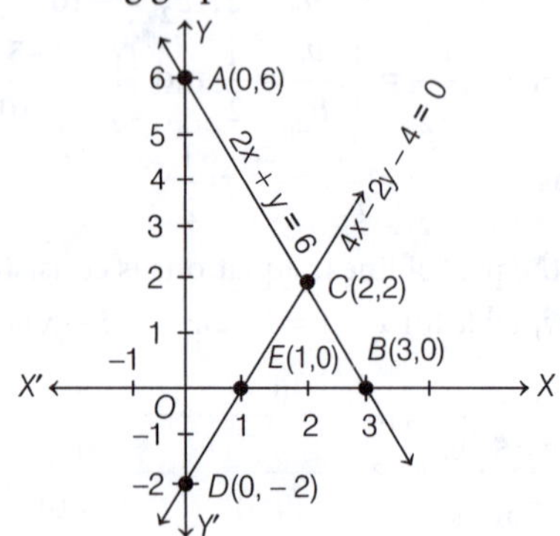

The lines AB and DE intersect at point C (2, 2).
Hence, the unique solution is $x=2$, $y=2$.

(iv) Do same as Part (ii). **Ans.** Inconsistent

Q5. Half of the perimeter of a rectangular garden, whose length is 4 m more than its width, is 36 m. Find the dimensions of the garden.

Perimeter of a rectangular garden = 2 (length + width).
Use this relation to make a pair of linear equations and plot them on graph paper, then intersection point gives the required dimensions.

Sol. Let the length of the garden be x m and its width be y m.
Then, perimeter of the rectangular garden

$$=2\,(\text{length} + \text{width}) = 2(x+y)$$

Therefore, half of the perimeter $=(x+y)$ m

But given that half of the perimeter = 36 m

$$\therefore \quad (x+y)=36 \quad \text{...(i)}$$

Also, length of garden = 4 + width of garden

$$x=y+4 \Rightarrow x-y=4 \quad \text{...(ii)}$$

Table for $x+y=36$ or $y=36-x$ is

x	20	24
$y=36-x$	16	12
Points	$A(20,16)$	$B(24,12)$

Plot the points A (20, 16) and B (24, 12) and join them to get straight line AB.

Table for $x-y=4$ or $y=x-4$ is

x	10	16
$y=x-4$	6	12
Points	$C(10,6)$	$D(16,12)$

Plot the points C(10, 6) and D(16, 12) and join them to get straight line CD. The two lines intersect at point A (20, 16) as shown in the following graph.

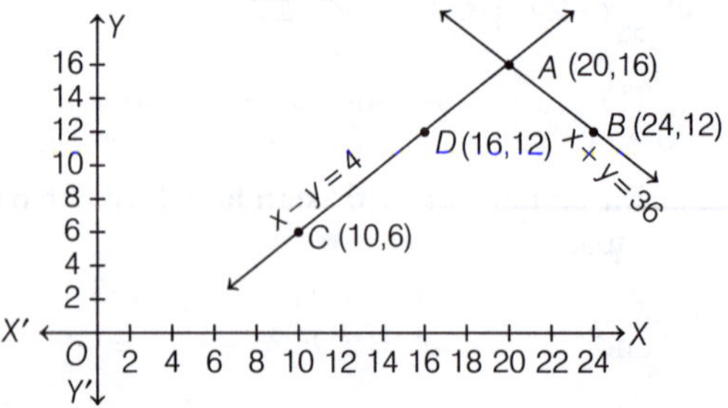

Hence, length of rectangular garden is 20 m and width is 16 m.

Q6. Given the linear equation $2x+3y-8=0$, write another linear equation in two variables such that the geometrical representation of the pair so formed is:

(i) intersecting lines (ii) parallel lines

(iii) coincident lines

Sol. Given, linear equation is

$$2x + 3y - 8 = 0 \quad \text{...(i)}$$

(i) For intersecting lines, $\frac{a_1}{a_2} \neq \frac{b_1}{b_2}$

Here, $a_1 = 2, b_1 = 3, c_1 = -8$.

Any line intersecting with Eq. (i) may be taken as

$a_2x + b_2y + c_2 = 0$, where $\frac{2}{a_2} \neq \frac{3}{b_2}$ or $2b_2 \neq 3a_2$

$\therefore$ $3x+2y-9=0$ or $3x+2y-7=0$ is intersect to given line.

(ii) For parallel lines, $\frac{a_1}{a_2} = \frac{b_1}{b_2} \neq \frac{c_1}{c_2}$.

Here, $a_1 = 2, b_1 = 3, c_1 = -8$

$\therefore$ Any line parallel to Eq. (i) may be taken as

$a_2x + b_2y + c_2 = 0$, where $\frac{2}{a_2} = \frac{3}{b_2} \neq \frac{-8}{c_2}$

$\therefore$ $6x+9y+7=0$ or $2x+3y-12=0$ is parallel to given line.

(iii) For coincident lines, $\frac{a_1}{a_2} = \frac{b_1}{b_2} = \frac{c_1}{c_2}$

Any line coincident to Eq. (i) may be taken as

$a_2x + b_2y + c_2 = 0$, where $\frac{2}{a_2} = \frac{3}{b_2} = \frac{-8}{c_2}$.

$\therefore$ $4x+6y-16=0$ or $6x+9y-24=0$ coincides with the given line.

Q7. Draw the graphs of the equations $x - y + 1 = 0$ and $3x + 2y - 12 = 0$. Determine the coordinates of the vertices of the triangle formed by these lines and the *X*-axis and shade the triangular region.

Sol. Given, pair of linear equations is $x - y + 1 = 0$ and $3x + 2y - 12 = 0$.

Table for $x - y + 1 = 0$ or $y = x + 1$ is

x	0	4	-1
$y = x + 1$	1	5	0
Points	$A(0,1)$	$B(4,5)$	$C(-1,0)$

Plot the points $A(0,1), B(4,5), C(-1,0)$ and join them to get a line *CB*.

Table for $3x+2y-12=0$ or $y = \frac{12-3x}{2}$ is

x	0	2	4
$y = \frac{12-3x}{2}$	6	3	0
Points	$D(0,6)$	$E(2,3)$	$F(4,0)$

Plot the points $D(0,6), E(2,3), F(4,0)$ and join them to get a line *DF*.

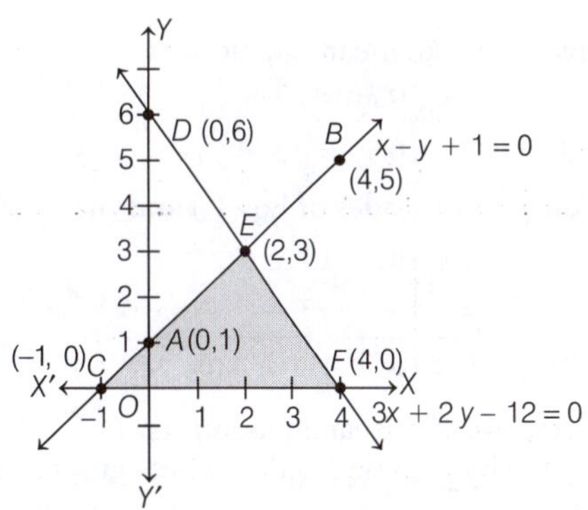

Clearly, the two lines intersect each other at the point $E(2, 3)$. Hence, $x = 2$ and $y = 3$ is the solution of the given pair of equations. The line *DE* cuts *X*-axis at the point $F(4, 0)$ and the line *AB* cuts *X*-axis at the point $C(-1, 0)$. Hence, the coordinates of the vertices of the ΔEFC are $E(2, 3), F(4, 0)$ and $C(-1, 0)$.

EXERCISE 3.2

Q1. Solve the following pairs of linear equations by the substitution method.

(i) $x + y = 14$; $x - y = 4$

(ii) $s - t = 3$; $\frac{s}{3} + \frac{t}{2} = 6$

(iii) $3x - y = 3$; $9x - 3y = 9$

(iv) $0.2x + 0.3y = 1.3$; $0.4x + 0.5y = 2.3$

(v) $\sqrt{2}x + \sqrt{3}y = 0$; $\sqrt{3}x - \sqrt{8}y = 0$

(vi) $\frac{3x}{2} - \frac{5y}{3} = -2$; $\frac{x}{3} + \frac{y}{2} = \frac{13}{6}$

Sol. (i) Given, pair of linear equations is

$$x + y = 14 \quad \text{...(i)}$$

and $\quad x - y = 4 \Rightarrow y = x - 4 \quad \text{...(ii)}$

On substituting the value of y from Eq. (ii) in Eq. (i), we get $\quad x + x - 4 = 14$

$\Rightarrow \quad 2x = 18$

$\Rightarrow \quad x = 9$

On substituting $x = 9$ in Eq. (ii), we get

$$y = 9 - 4 = 5 \Rightarrow y = 5$$

Hence, $x = 9$ and $y = 5$.

(ii) Do same as Part (i). **Ans.** $s = 9, t = 6$

(iii) Given, pair of linear equations is

$$3x - y = 3 \Rightarrow y = 3x - 3 \quad \text{...(i)}$$

and $\quad 9x - 3y = 9 \quad \text{...(ii)}$

On substituting the value of y from Eq. (i) in Eq. (ii), we get

$$9x - 3(3x - 3) = 9$$

$\Rightarrow \quad 9 = 9$

This equation has no variable but it is true for all values of x. So, this pair of linear equations has infinitely many solutions.

(iv) Given, pair of linear equations is

$$0.2x+0.3y=1.3 \quad \ldots(i)$$

and $$0.4x+0.5y=2.3 \quad \ldots(ii)$$

Multiply both sides of Eqs. (i) and (ii) by 10, we get

$$2x+3y=13 \quad \ldots(iii)$$

and $$4x+5y=23 \quad \ldots(iv)$$

Now, proceed as Part (i). **Ans.** $x=2, y=3$

(v) Given, pair of linear equations is

$$\sqrt{2}x+\sqrt{3}y=0 \quad \ldots(i)$$

and $$\sqrt{3}x-\sqrt{8}y=0$$

$$\Rightarrow \quad y=\frac{\sqrt{3}x}{\sqrt{8}} \quad \ldots(ii)$$

On substituting the value of y in Eq. (i), we get

$$\sqrt{2}x+\sqrt{3}\times\left(\frac{\sqrt{3}x}{\sqrt{8}}\right)=0$$

$$\Rightarrow \quad \sqrt{2}x+\frac{3x}{\sqrt{8}}=0$$

$$\Rightarrow \quad \sqrt{2}\times\sqrt{8}x+3x=0$$

$$\Rightarrow \quad 4x+3x=0 \quad [\because \sqrt{2}\times\sqrt{8}=\sqrt{16}=4]$$

$$\Rightarrow \quad 7x=0 \Rightarrow x=0$$

On substituting $x=0$ in Eq. (ii), we get

$$y=\frac{\sqrt{3}\times 0}{\sqrt{8}}=0 \Rightarrow y=0$$

Hence, $x=0$ and $y=0$.

(vi) Given, pair of linear equations is

$$\frac{3x}{2}-\frac{5y}{3}=-2$$

$$\Rightarrow \quad \frac{9x-10y}{6}=-2 \quad \text{[taking LCM]}$$

$$\Rightarrow \quad 9x-10y=-12 \quad \ldots(i)$$

and $$\frac{x}{3}+\frac{y}{2}=\frac{13}{6}$$

$$\Rightarrow \quad \frac{2x+3y}{6}=\frac{13}{6}$$

$$\Rightarrow \quad 2x+3y=13 \quad \ldots(ii)$$

Now, proceed as Part (i). **Ans.** $x=2, y=3$

Q2. Solve $2x+3y=11$ and $2x-4y=-24$ and hence find the value of m for which $y=mx+3$.

Firstly, find the values of x and y from given equations and then put the values of x and y in $y=mx+3$, to get the value of m.

Sol. Given, pair of linear equations is

$$2x+3y=11 \quad \ldots(i)$$

and $$2x-4y=-24 \quad \ldots(ii)$$

From Eq. (ii), we have

$$4y=2x+24$$

$$\Rightarrow \quad y=\frac{2x+24}{4}$$

$$\Rightarrow \quad y=\frac{x+12}{2} \quad \ldots(iii)$$

On substituting the value of y from Eq. (iii) in Eq. (i), we get

$$2x+3\left(\frac{x+12}{2}\right)=11$$

$$\Rightarrow \quad 4x+3(x+12)=11\times 2$$

$$\Rightarrow \quad 4x+3x+36=22 \Rightarrow 7x=22-36$$

$$\Rightarrow \quad 7x=-14 \Rightarrow x=-2$$

On substituting $x=-2$ in Eq. (iii), we get

$$y=\frac{-2+12}{2} \Rightarrow y=\frac{10}{2} \Rightarrow y=5$$

On substituting $x=-2$ and $y=5$ in the equation $y=mx+3$, we get

$$5=m\times(-2)+3$$

$$\Rightarrow \quad 5=-2m+3$$

$$\Rightarrow \quad 2m=3-5=-2$$

$$\Rightarrow \quad m=-1$$

Q3. Form the pair of linear equations for the following problems and find their solutions by substitution method.

(i) The difference between two numbers is 26 and one number is three times the other. Find them.

(ii) The larger of two supplementary angles exceeds the smaller by 18°. Find them.

(iii) The coach of a cricket team buys 7 bats and 6 balls for ₹ 3800. Later, she buys 3 bats and 5 balls for ₹ 1750. Find the cost of each bat and each ball.

(iv) The taxi charges in a city consist of a fixed charge together with the charge for the distance covered. For a distance of 10 km, the charge paid is ₹ 105 and for a journey of 15 km, the charge paid is ₹ 155. What are the fixed charges and the charge per km? How much does a person have to pay for travelling a distance of 25 km?

(v) A fraction becomes 9/11, if 2 is added to both the numerator and the denominator. If 3 is added to both the numerator and the denominator, it becomes 5/6. Find the fraction.

(vi) Five years hence, the age of Jacob will be three times that of his son. Five years ago, Jacob's age was seven times that of his son. What are their present ages?

Sol. (i) Let the two numbers be x and y $(x>y)$.

According to the question,

$$x-y=26 \quad \ldots(i)$$

and $$x=3y \quad \ldots(ii)$$

On substituting the value of x from Eq. (ii) in Eq. (i), we get
$$3y-y=26$$
$\Rightarrow$ $2y=26$

$\Rightarrow$ $y=13$

On substituting $y=13$ in Eq. (ii), we get
$$x=3\times13$$
$\Rightarrow$ $x=39$

Hence, the two numbers are 39 and 13.

(ii) Let the supplementary angles be x and $y(x>y)$.

Then, $x+y=180°$ ...(i)

Now, according to the question,

$x-y=18°$ ...(ii)

From Eq. (ii), we have

$y=x-18°$ ...(iii)

On substituting the value of y from Eq. (iii) in Eq. (i), we get
$$x+x-18°=180°$$
$\Rightarrow$ $2x=198°$

$\Rightarrow$ $x=99°$

On substituting $x=99°$ in Eq. (iii), we get
$$y=99°-18°$$
$\Rightarrow$ $y=81°$

Hence, the required angles are 99° and 81°.

(iii) Let cost of one bat be ₹ x and cost of one ball be ₹ y.

According to the question,

Cost of 7 bats and 6 balls = ₹3800

i.e. $7x+6y=3800$ ...(i)

Cost of 3 bats and 5 balls = ₹1750

i.e. $3x+5y=1750$ ...(ii)

Now, solve the Eqs. (i) and (ii) similar to Question 1(i).

Then, $x=500$ and $y=50$.

Hence, cost of one bat is ₹500 and cost of one ball is ₹ 50.

(iv) Let fixed charge be ₹ x and charge per kilometre be ₹ y.

According to the question,

$x+10y=105$ ...(i)

and $x+15y=155$ ...(ii)

On solving Eqs. (i) and (ii) similar to Question 1 (i), we get
$$x=5 \text{ and } y=10$$
Hence, fixed charge is ₹5 and charge per kilometre is ₹ 10.

Now, amount to be paid for travelling 25 km
$$= \text{Fixed charge} + ₹\ 10\times25$$
$$= ₹\,5 + ₹250 = ₹\ 255$$
Hence, the amount paid by the person for travelling 25 km is ₹ 255.

(v) Let x/y be the fraction.

Condition I When 2 is added to both numerator and denominator, then
$$\text{New fraction} = \frac{x+2}{y+2}$$
According to the question,
$$\frac{x+2}{y+2}=\frac{9}{11}$$
$\Rightarrow$ $11\times(x+2)=9\times(y+2)$

$\Rightarrow$ $11x+22=9y+18$

$\Rightarrow$ $11x-9y+4=0$ ...(i)

Condition II When 3 is added to both numerator and denominator, then
$$\text{New fraction} = \frac{x+3}{y+3}$$
According to the question,
$$\frac{x+3}{y+3}=\frac{5}{6}$$
$\Rightarrow$ $6\times(x+3)=5\times(y+3)$

$\Rightarrow$ $6x+18=5y+15$

$\Rightarrow$ $6x-5y+3=0$ ...(ii)

Now, from Eq. (ii), we have

$5y=6x+3 \Rightarrow y=\dfrac{6x+3}{5}$ ...(iii)

On substituting the value of y from Eq. (iii) in Eq. (i), we get
$$11x-9\times\left(\frac{6x+3}{5}\right)+4=0$$
$\Rightarrow$ $55x-9\times(6x+3)+20=0$ [multiplying by 5]

$\Rightarrow$ $55x-54x-27+20=0$

$\Rightarrow$ $x=7$

On putting $x=7$ in Eq. (iii), we get
$$y=\frac{6\times7+3}{5} \Rightarrow y=\frac{45}{5}=9$$
Hence, the required fraction is $\frac{7}{9}$.

(vi) Let x (in years) be the present age of Jacob's son and y (in years) be the present age of Jacob.

After 5 yr, Jacob's son age = $(x+5)$ yr

and Jacob's age = $(y+5)$ yr

According to the question,
$$(y+5)=3(x+5) \Rightarrow y+5=3x+15$$
$\Rightarrow$ $3x-y+10=0$ ...(i)

5 yr ago, Jacob's son age = $(x-5)$ yr

and Jacob's age = $(y-5)$ yr

According to the question,
$$(y-5)=7(x-5)$$
$\Rightarrow$ $7x-y-30=0$ ...(ii)

From Eq. (i), we have

$y=3x+10$ ...(iii)

On substituting $y=3x+10$ in Eq. (ii), we get
$$7x-(3x+10)-30=0 \Rightarrow 4x-40=0 \Rightarrow x=10$$
On putting $x=10$ in Eq. (iii), we get
$$y=3\times10+10 \Rightarrow y=40$$
Hence, the present ages of Jacob and his son are respectively, 40 yr and 10 yr.

EXERCISE 3.3

Q1. Solve the following pair of linear equations by the elimination method and the substitution method.

(i) $x+y=5$ and $2x-3y=4$

(ii) $3x+4y=10$ and $2x-2y=2$

(iii) $3x-5y-4=0$ and $9x=2y+7$

(iv) $\frac{x}{2}+\frac{2y}{3}=-1$ and $x-\frac{y}{3}=3$

Sol. (i) **By elimination method**

Given, $x+y=5$ ...(i)

and $2x-3y=4$ ...(ii)

On multiplying Eq. (i) by 3 and Eq. (ii) by 1 and then adding them, we get

$$3(x+y)+1(2x-3y)=3\times5+1\times4$$

$\Rightarrow$ $3x+3y+2x-3y=15+4$

$\Rightarrow$ $5x=19 \Rightarrow x=\frac{19}{5}$

On putting $x=\frac{19}{5}$ in Eq. (i), we get

$$\frac{19}{5}+y=5 \Rightarrow y=5-\frac{19}{5}$$

$\Rightarrow$ $y=\frac{25-19}{5} \Rightarrow y=\frac{6}{5}$

Hence, $x=\frac{19}{5}$ and $y=\frac{6}{5}$.

By substitution method

Given, $x+y=5$ ...(i)

and $2x-3y=4$ ...(ii)

From Eq. (i), we have $y=5-x$ ...(iii)

On putting the value of y from Eq. (iii) in Eq. (ii), we get

$$2x-3(5-x)=4 \Rightarrow 2x-15+3x=4$$

$\Rightarrow$ $5x=19$

$\Rightarrow$ $x=\frac{19}{5}$

On putting $x=\frac{19}{5}$ in Eq. (iii), we get

$$y=5-\frac{19}{5} \Rightarrow y=\frac{6}{5}$$

Hence, $x=\frac{19}{5}$ and $y=\frac{6}{5}$.

(ii) Do same as Part (i). **Ans.** $x=2$ and $y=1$

(iii) Do same as Part (i). **Ans.** $x=\frac{9}{13}$ and $y=-\frac{5}{13}$

(iv) **By elimination method**

Given, $\frac{x}{2}+\frac{2y}{3}=-1$ ...(i)

and $x-\frac{y}{3}=3$ ...(ii)

On multiplying Eq. (i) by 1 and Eq. (ii) by 2, we get

$\frac{x}{2}+\frac{2y}{3}=-1$ ...(iii)

and $2x-\frac{2y}{3}=6$ ...(iv)

On adding Eqs. (iii) and (iv), we get

$$\frac{x}{2}+2x=-1+6 \Rightarrow \frac{5}{2}x=5 \Rightarrow x=2$$

On putting $x=2$ in Eq. (ii), we get

$$2-\frac{y}{3}=3 \Rightarrow \frac{-y}{3}=1$$

$\Rightarrow$ $y=-3$

Hence, $x=2$ and $y=-3$.

By substitution method

Given, $\frac{x}{2}+\frac{2y}{3}=-1$ ...(i)

and $x-\frac{y}{3}=3$ ...(ii)

From Eq. (ii), we have

$\frac{y}{3}=x-3 \Rightarrow y=3(x-3)$ ...(iii)

On substituting $y=3(x-3)$ in Eq. (i), we get

$$\frac{x}{2}+\frac{2}{3}\times3(x-3)=-1$$

$\Rightarrow$ $\frac{x}{2}+2(x-3)=-1$

$\Rightarrow$ $x+4(x-3)=-2$ [multiplying both sides by 2]

$\Rightarrow$ $5x-12=-2$

$\Rightarrow$ $5x=10 \Rightarrow x=2$

On substituting $x=2$ in Eq. (iii), we get

$$y=3(2-3)=-3$$

Hence, $x=2$ and $y=-3$.

Q2. Form the pair of linear equations in the following problems and find their solutions (if they exist) by the elimination method.

(i) If we add 1 to the numerator and subtract 1 from the denominator, a fraction reduces to 1. It becomes 1/2 if we only add 1 to the denominator. What is the fraction?

(ii) Five years ago, Nuri was thrice as old as Sonu. Ten years later, Nuri will be twice as old as Sonu. How old are Nuri and Sonu?

(iii) The sum of the digits of a two-digit number is 9. Also, nine times this number is twice the number obtained by reversing the order of the digits. Find the number.

(iv) Meena went to a bank to withdraw ₹ 2000. She asked the cashier to give her ₹ 50 and ₹ 100 notes only. Meena got 25 notes in all. Find how many notes of ₹ 50 and ₹ 100 she received?

(v) A lending library has a fixed charge for the first three days and an additional charge for each day thereafter. Saritha paid ₹ 27 for a book kept for seven days, while Susy paid ₹ 21 for the book she kept for five days. Find the fixed charge and the charge for each extra day.

Sol. (i) Let the fraction be x/y.

According to the Condition I,

$$\frac{x+1}{y-1}=1$$

$\Rightarrow \quad x+1=y-1 \Rightarrow x-y=-2 \quad$ ...(i)

According to the Condition II,

$$\frac{x}{y+1}=\frac{1}{2}$$

$\Rightarrow \quad 2x=y+1 \Rightarrow 2x-y=1 \quad$ ...(ii)

On subtracting Eq. (i) from Eq. (ii), we get

$(2x-y)-(x-y)=1+2 \Rightarrow x=3$

On putting $x=3$ in Eq. (i), we get

$3-y=-2 \Rightarrow y=5$

Hence, the required fraction is $\frac{3}{5}$.

(ii) Let the present age of Nuri be x yr and the present age of Sonu be y yr.

5 yr ago, Nuri's age $=(x-5)$ yr

and Sonu's age $=(y-5)$ yr

According to the question, $x-5=3(y-5)$

$\Rightarrow \quad x-3y=-10 \quad$ ...(i)

After 10 yr, Nuri's age $=(x+10)$ yr

and Sonu's age $=(y+10)$ yr

According to the question,

$x+10=2(y+10) \Rightarrow x-2y=10 \quad$ ...(ii)

On subtracting Eq. (i) from Eq. (ii), we get

$(x-2y)-(x-3y)=10+10 \Rightarrow -2y+3y=20 \Rightarrow y=20$

On substituting $y=20$ in Eq. (ii), we get

$x-2\times20=10 \Rightarrow x=50$

Therefore, present age of Nuri is 50 yr and present age of Sonu is 20 yr.

(iii) Let x be the digit at unit place and y be the digit at tens place of the two-digit number.

Then, two-digit number $=x+10y$

According to the question, $x+y=9 \quad$ ...(i)

When we reverse the order of the digits, new two-digit number $=y+10x$.

According to the question,

$9\times(x+10y)=2\times(y+10x)$

$\Rightarrow \quad 9x+90y=2y+20x$

$\Rightarrow \quad 88y=11x$

$\Rightarrow \quad x=8y$

or $\quad x-8y=0 \quad$ ...(ii)

On subtracting Eq. (ii) from Eq. (i), we get

$(x+y)-(x-8y)=9-0 \Rightarrow 8y+y=9$

$\Rightarrow \quad 9y=9 \Rightarrow y=1$

On putting $y=1$ in Eq. (ii), we get

$x=8\times1 \Rightarrow x=8$

Hence, the required two-digit number is

$x+10y=8+10\times1=18$

(iv) Let number of ₹ 50 notes be x and number of ₹ 100 notes be y.

According to the question,

$x+y=25 \quad$ ...(i)

and $50\times x+100\times y=2000$

$\Rightarrow \quad x+2y=40$ [dividing both sides by 50] ...(ii)

On subtracting Eq. (i) from Eq. (ii), we get

$(x+2y)-(x+y)=40-25 \Rightarrow y=15$

On putting $y=15$ in Eq. (i), we get

$x+15=25 \Rightarrow x=10$

Hence, the number of ₹ 50 notes is 10 and number of ₹100 notes is 15.

(v) Let the fixed charges for the first three days be ₹ x and the additional charge per day be ₹ y.

According to the question,

Amount paid by Saritha for 7 days = ₹ 27

i.e. $\quad x+4\times y=27 \Rightarrow x+4y=27 \quad$ ...(i)

[since, ₹ $4y$ are to be paid for 4 extra days]

Amount paid by Susy for 5 days = ₹ 21

i.e. $\quad x+2y=21 \quad$ ...(ii)

[since, ₹ $2y$ are to be paid for 2 extra days]

On subtracting Eq. (ii) from Eq. (i), we get

$2y=27-21$

$\Rightarrow \quad 2y=6 \Rightarrow y=3$

On putting $y=3$ in Eq. (i), we get

$x+4\times3=27$

$\Rightarrow \quad x=27-12 \Rightarrow x=15$

Hence, the fixed charge for first three days is ₹ 15 and additional charge for each extra day is ₹ 3.

REVIEW EXERCISE

Including Competency Based Questions

Part I

Multiple Choice Questions

1. **The lines represented by linear equations $x = a$ and $y = b\ (a \neq b)$ are** CBSE 2024 (Basic)

(a) intersecting at (a, b) (b) intersecting at (b, a)
(c) parallel (d) coincident

2. **The system of linear equations represented by the lines l and m is** CBSE Sample Paper 2025 (Basic)

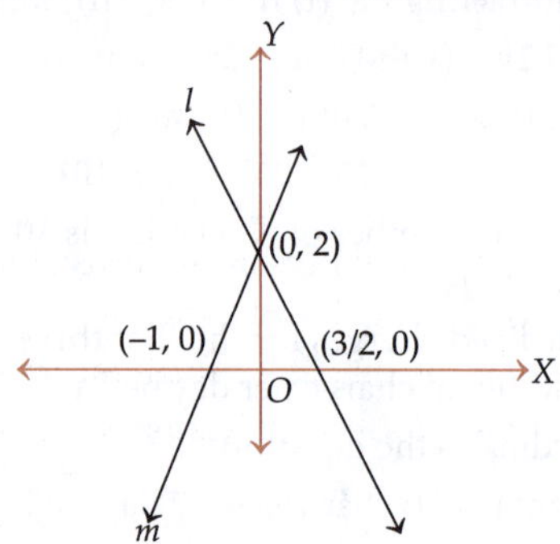

(a) consistent with unique solution
(b) inconsistent
(c) consistent with three solutions
(d) consistent with many solutions

3. **The pair of linear equations $2x + 1 = 0$ and $3y - 5 = 0$ has** CBSE 2025 (Standard)

(a) unique solution
(b) two solutions
(c) no solution
(d) infinitely many solutions

4. **Which of the following pair of equations are inconsistent?**

(a) $3x - y = 9,\ x - \frac{y}{3} = 3$
(b) $4x + 3y = 24,\ -2x + 3y = 6$
(c) $5x - y = 10,\ 10x - 2y = 20$
(d) $-2x + y = 3,\ -4x + 2y = 10$

5. **A system of linear equations is given by**

$$a_1x + b_1y = c_1$$
$$a_2x + b_2y = c_2, \text{ where } \frac{a_1}{a_2} = \frac{b_1}{b_2}$$

$(a_1, a_2, b_1, b_2 \neq 0)$. CBSE 2024 Compartment (Basic)

Where of the following statements is true?

(a) The given system has a unique solution.
(b) The given system has no solution.
(c) The given system has infinite number of solutions.
(d) The given system has no solution or has infinite number of solutions.

6. **The pair of equations $ax + 2y = 9$ and $3x + by = 18$ represent parallel lines, where a, b are integers, if** CBSE 2023 (Standard)

(a) $a = b$ (b) $3a = 2b$
(c) $2a = 3b$ (d) $ab = 6$

7. **The value of k for which the system of equations $3x - ky = 7$ and $6x + 10y = 3$ is inconsistent, is** CBSE Sample Paper 2025 (Standard)

(a) -10 (b) -5 (c) 5 (d) 7

8. **The value of k for which the pair of linear equations $5x + 2y - 7 = 0$ and $2x + ky + 1 = 0$ do not have a solution, is** CBSE 2024 (Basic)

(a) 5 (b) $\frac{4}{5}$ (c) $\frac{5}{4}$ (d) $\frac{5}{2}$

9. **Two lines are given to be parallel. The equation of one of the lines is $3x - 2y = 5$. The equation of the second line can be** CBSE 2022 (Standard)

(a) $9x + 8y = 7$ (b) $-12x - 8y = 7$
(c) $-12x + 8y = 7$ (d) $12x + 8y = 7$

10. **The value of k for which the system of equations $3x - 7y = 1$ and $kx + 14y = 6$ is inconsistent, is** CBSE 2025 (Basic)

(a) -6 (b) $\frac{2}{3}$ (c) 6 (d) $\frac{-3}{2}$

11. **3 chairs and 1 table cost ₹ 900; whereas 5 chairs and 3 tables cost ₹ 2100. If the cost of 1 chair is ₹ x and the cost of 1 table is ₹ y, then the situation can be represented algebraically as** Competency Based Question

(a) $3x + y = 900,\ 3x + 5y = 2100$
(b) $x + 3y = 900,\ 3x + 5y = 2100$
(c) $3x + y = 900,\ 5x + 3y = 2100$
(d) $x + 3y = 900,\ 5x + 3y = 2100$

12. **The solution of the pair of equations $x + y = a + b$ and $ax - by = a^2 - b^2$ is** CBSE 2023 (Standard)

(a) $x = b, y = a$ (b) $x = -a, y = b$
(c) $x = a, y = b$ (d) $x = a, y = -b$

13. **The values of x and y satisfying the two equations $32x + 33y = 34$ and $33x + 32y = 31$ respectively, are** **Competency Based Question**

(a) -1 and 2 (b) -1 and 4 (c) 1 and -2 (d) -1 and -4

14. **The ratio of a two-digit number and the sum of its digits is 7 : 1. How many such two-digit numbers are possible?** **Competency Based Question**

(a) 1 (b) 4 (c) 9 (d) infinitely many

Assertion-Reason Type Questions

15. **Assertion** The graphical representation of $x + 2y - 4 = 0$ and $2x + 4y - 12 = 0$ will be a pair of parallel lines.

Reason Let $a_1x + b_1y + c_1 = 0$ and $a_2x + b_2y + c_2 = 0$ be two linear equations and if $\frac{a_1}{a_2} = \frac{b_1}{b_2} \neq \frac{c_1}{c_2}$, then the pair of equations represent parallel lines and they have no solution.

(a) Both Assertion and Reason are correct and Reason is the correct explanation of Assertion.
(b) Both Assertion and Reason are correct but Reason is not the correct explanation of Assertion.
(c) Assertion is correct but Reason is incorrect.
(d) Assertion is incorrect but Reason is correct.

16. **Assertion** The graphical representation of $2x + y = 6$ and $2x - y + 2 = 0$ will be a pair of parallel lines.

Reason When $k = 1$, then linear equations $5x + ky = 4$ and $15x + 3y = 12$ have infinitely many solutions.

(a) Both Assertion and Reason are correct and Reason is the correct explanation of Assertion.
(b) Both Assertion and Reason are correct but Reason is not the correct explanation of Assertion.
(c) Assertion is correct but Reason is incorrect.
(d) Assertion is incorrect but Reason is correct.

17. **Assertion** The graph of the linear equations $3x + 2y = 12$ and $5x - 4y = 10$ gives a pair of intersecting lines.

Reason The graph of linear equations $a_1x + b_1y + c_1 = 0$ and $a_2x + b_2y + c_2 = 0$ gives a pair of intersecting lines if $\frac{a_1}{a_2} \neq \frac{b_1}{b_2}$.

(a) Both Assertion and Reason are correct and Reason is the correct explanation of Assertion.
(b) Both Assertion and Reason are correct but Reason is not the correct explanation of Assertion.
(c) Assertion is correct but Reason is incorrect.
(d) Assertion is incorrect but Reason is correct.

18. **Assertion** The value of k for which the system of equations $kx - y = 2, 6x - 2y = 3$ has a unique solution is 3.

Reason The system of linear equations $a_1x + b_1y + c_1 = 0$ and $a_2x + b_2y + c_2 = 0$ has a unique solutions, if $\frac{a_1}{a_2} \neq \frac{b_1}{b_2}$.

(a) Both Assertion and Reason are correct and Reason is the correct explanation of Assertion.
(b) Both Assertion and Reason are correct but Reason is not the correct explanation of Assertion.
(c) Assertion is correct but Reason is incorrect.
(d) Assertion is incorrect but Reason is correct.

19. **Assertion** Pair of linear equations $9x + 3y + 12 = 0$ and $18x + 6y + 24 = 0$ has infinitely many solutions.

Reason Pair of linear equations $a_1x + b_1y + c_1 = 0$ and $a_2x + b_2y + c_2 = 0$ have infinitely many solutions, if $\frac{a_1}{a_2} = \frac{b_1}{b_2} = \frac{c_1}{c_2}$.

(a) Both Assertion and Reason are correct and Reason is the correct explanation of Assertion.
(b) Both Assertion and Reason are correct but Reason is not the correct explanation of Assertion.
(c) Assertion is correct but Reason is incorrect.
(d) Assertion is incorrect but Reason is correct.

Case Study Based Questions

20. Lokesh is a production manager in Mumbai, hires a taxi everyday to go to his office. The taxi charges in Mumbai consists of a fixed charges together with the charges or the distance covered. His office is at a distance of 10 km from his home. For a distance of 10 km to his office. Lokesh paid ₹ 105. While coming back home, he took another route. He covered a distance of 15 km and the charges paid by him were ₹ 155. **CBSE 2023 (Basic)**

Based on the above information, answer the following questions.

(i) What are the fixed charges?
(ii) What are the charges per km?

(iii) If fixed charges are ₹ 20 and charges per km are ₹ 10, then how much Lokesh have to pay for travelling a distance of 10 km?

Or Find the total amount paid by Lokesh for travelling 10 km from home to office and 25 km from office to home. (Fixed charges and charges per km are same as in parts (i) and (ii)).

21. Tickets for a play can be booked online as well as purchased from the theatre. A 10% discount is available on online ticket purchase. Simran likes to watch plays. She purchased the ticket online for a play. The ticket and food cost her ₹ 600. The cost of food was one-third the cost of the ticket.

Based on the above information, answer the following questions.

(i) Represent the relation between the cost of the ticket and the cost of food for Simran algebraically. Also, represent the relation between the cost of the ticket and the cost of food for Simran and money spent algebraically.

(ii) Simran purchased the ticket for a musical play from the theatre.How much can she spend on food in ₹ 600?

Or

In the theatre canteen, two packets of popcorn and a mango drink cost ₹ 330. One packet of popcorn and two mango drinks cost ₹ 300. What is the cost of the packet of popcorn?

(iii) A group of friends went to watch a play. Some of them purchased tickets online and some bought them at the theatre. If two more had purchased online tickets the total ticket price would be ₹ 100 less. Is this true for any group greater than 2? Why?

22. Rohit usually goes to a dry fruit shop with his mother. He observes the following two situations.

On Ist day The cost of 2 kg of almonds and 3 kg of raisins was ₹ 1400.

On 2nd day The cost of 3 kg of almonds and 5 kg of raisins was ₹ 2150.

Denoting the cost of 1 kg of almonds by ₹ x and cost of 1 kg of raisins by ₹ y, answer the following questions.

(i) Represent algebraically the situation of day-1 and day-2.

(ii) Find the cost of 1 kg almonds and 1 kg of raisins.

(iii) Find the cost of 1.5 kg almonds and 2.5 kg of raisins.

Or

Find the cost of 5 kg almonds and 0.5 kg of raisins.

23. A coaching institute conducts Mathematics classes in two batches I and II and fee for rich and poor children are different. In batch I there are 20 poor and 5 rich children, whereas in batch II, there are 5 poor and 25 rich children. The total monthly collection of fees from batch I is ₹ 9000 and from batch II is ₹ 26000. Assume that each poor child pays ₹ x per month and each rich child pays ₹ y per month. **CBSE 2023 (Standard)**

Based on the above information, answer the following questions.

(i) Represents the information given above in terms of x and y.

(ii) Find the monthly fee paid by a poor child.

Or Find the difference in the monthly fee paid by a poor child and a rich child.

(iii) If there are 10 poor and 20 rich children in batch II, what is the total monthly collection of fees from batch II?

24. Amit is planning to buy a house and the layout is given below. The design and the measurement has been made such that areas of two bedrooms and kitchen together is 95 m^2. **CBSE Question Bank**

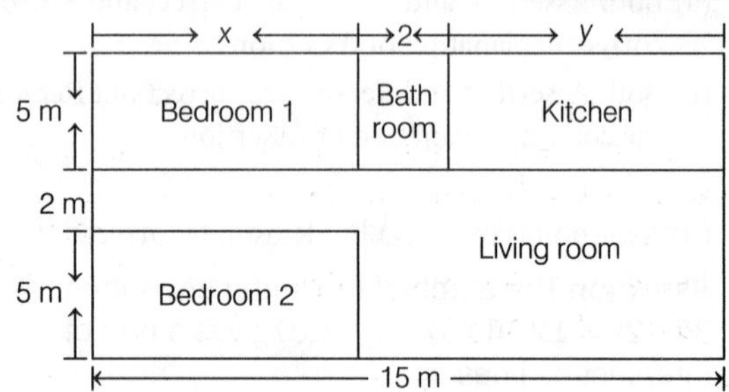

Based on the above information, answer the following questions:

(i) Form the pair of linear equations in two variables from this situation.

(ii) Find the area of each bedroom and kitchen in the layout.

Or

Find the area of living room in the layout.

(iii) Find the cost of laying tiles in kitchen at the rate of ₹ 50 per m^2.

Part II

Very Short Answer Type Questions

Directions (Q.Nos 1-3) Without drawing them, find out whether the line, representing the following pairs of linear equations intersect at a point or parallel or coincide.

1. $5x-4y+8=0; 7x+6y-9=0$

2. $6x-3y+10=0; 2x-y+9=0$

3. $9x+3y+12=0;\ 18x+6y+24=0$

Directions (Q. Nos. 4-5) Given below is a pair of linear equations.

$$4x+y=8 \text{ and } 4x-2y=16$$

Based on the above information, answer the following questions. **Competency Based Question**

4. Is the given pair of equations consistent? Justify your answer.

5. Does $x=3$ and $y=-3$ satisfy the pair of linear equations? Justify your answer.

6. Find the number of solutions of the pair of equations $x+2y+5=0, -3x-6y+1=0$

7. For what values of p does the pair of equations $4x+py+8=0$ and $2x+2y+2=0$ has unique solutions? **CBSE Sample Paper 2022 Term I (Basic)**

8. What should be the value of λ, for the given equations to have infinitely many solutions?
$5x+\lambda y=4$ and $15x+3y=12$

9. For what value of k, the pair of linear equations $3x+y=3$ and $6x+ky=8$ does not have a solution.

10. If $2x+y=13$ and $4x-y=17$, then find the value of $(x-y)$. **CBSE 2024 (Standard)**

11. If $x=a, y=b$ is the solution of the equations $x-y=2$ and $x+y=4$, then find the values of a and b. **NCERT Exemplar**

12. In the given figure, $ABCD$ is parallelogram. Find the values of x and y.

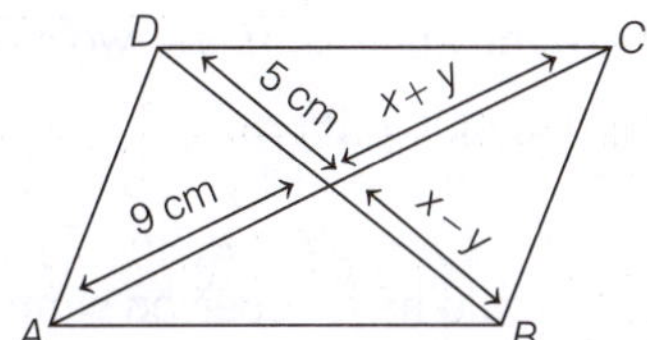

Short Answer Type Questions

13. Solve the following pairs of linear equations in two variables graphically.

$$x+3y=6, 2x-3y=12$$

Identify the shape resulting from the intersection of the pair of equations with the Y-axis and write its vertex coordinates.

14. Draw the graph of the pair of linear equations $x-y+2=0$ and $4x-y-4=0$. Calculate the area of the triangle formed by the lines so drawn and the X-axis. **NCERT Exemplar**

15. Solve graphically, the pair of equations $2x+y=6$ and $2x-y+2=0$. Find the ratio of the areas of the two triangles formed by the lines representing these equations with X-axis and the lines with Y-axis.

16. Determine algebraically, the vertices of the triangle formed by the lines **NCERT Exemplar**

(i) $3x-y=3, 2x-3y=2$ and $x+2y=8$

(ii) $5x-y=5, 6x+y=17$ and $x+2y=1$

17. Equation $2x=5y+4$ is given. Write another linear equation, so that the lines represented by the pair are

(i) intersecting (ii) coincident

(iii) parallel **Competency Based Question**

18. Two straight paths are represented by the lines $7x-5y=3$ and $14x-10y=5$. Check whether the paths cross each other. **Competency Based Question**

19. Determine the values of a and b, for which the following pairs of linear equations has infinitely many solutions

$$3x-(a+1)y=2b-1 \text{ and } 5x+(1-2a)y=3b$$

20. For which value(s) of λ, does the pair of linear equations $\lambda x+y=\lambda^2$ and $x+\lambda y=1$ have

(i) no solution? (ii) infinitely many solutions?

(iii) a unique solution? **NCERT Exemplar**

21. Given below are two lines such that $l_1 \parallel l_2$.

$l_1: 2x+2y+2=0$

$l_2: 3x+3y-3=0$

(i) Using comparison of ratios of coefficients, write the equation of a line l_3 in two variables, such that it intersects l_1 at exactly one point.

(ii) Find the point of intersection of l_2 and l_3. Show your steps.

22. Show that the following system of equations has unique solution.

$$3x+5y=12, 5x+3y=4$$

Also, find the solution of the given system of equations. **NCERT Exemplar**

Directions (Q.Nos 23-28) Solve the following pair of equations by substitution method.

23. $\frac{3}{2}x-y=\frac{1}{4}; x+\frac{1}{2}y=1$

24. $3x+y=4; 2(y-5)=-5x$

25. $1.4x+3.9y=6.4; 0.2x-1.3y=1.2$

26. $0.1x-0.2y=2;\ x+y=17$

27. $\frac{x}{a}+\frac{y}{b}=a+b; \frac{x}{a^2}+\frac{y}{b^2}=2, a, b \neq 0$ **NCERT Exemplar**

28. $ax+by=1;\ bx+ay=\frac{2ab}{a^2+b^2}$

29. Solve $x+2y=6, 2x+y=6$ and hence find the value of p for which $y=px+2$. **CBSE 2024 (Basic) Compartment**

30. Two chairs and three tables cost ₹ 5650 whereas three chairs and two tables cost ₹ 7100. Find the cost of a chair and a table separately. **NCERT Exemplar**

Directions (Q.Nos 31-35) Solve the following pair of equations by elimination method.

31. $3x-4y=11; 7x-5y=4$

32. $2x+3y-5=0; 3x-2y-14=0$

33. $3x+2y=7; 2x-5y+8=0$

34. $0.5x+0.2y=1.6; 0.9x-0.3y=0.9$

35. $\frac{x}{7}+\frac{y}{3}=5; \frac{x}{7}-\frac{y}{9}=1$

36. Sum of two numbers is 105 and their difference is 45. Find the numbers. **CBSE 2024 (Standard)**

37. 16 yr ago, at the time of marriage, Ajay was 5 yr elder to his wife. The present ages of the wife and Ajay are in the ratio 8 : 9. Find their ages at the time of their marriage. **CBSE 2024 (Basic) Compartment**

38. Father's age is 3 times the sum of ages of his two children. After 5 yr, his age will be twice the sum of ages of the two children. Find the age of father. **Competency Based Question**

39. Find a, if the line $3x+ay=8$ passes through the intersection of lines represented by equations $3x-2y=10$ and $5x+y=8$. **Competency Based Question**

40. There are some students in the two examination halls A and B. To make the number of students equal in each hall, 10 students are sent from A to B.

But if 20 students are sent from B to A, the number of students in A becomes double the number of students in B. Find the number of students in the two halls. **NCERT Exemplar**

41. If the angles of a triangle are x, y and $40°$ and the difference between the two angles x and y is $30°$, then find the values of x and y. **NCERT Exemplar**

42. A company has a locker in which valuable documents are kept. The passcode is a four-digit number of the form $xyyx$. The Chief Executive Officer (CEO) and the Vice President (VP) of the company have each been given one clue.

On solving both clues, the passcode that opens the locker can be found.

CEO's clue : When twice the ones digit is subtracted from the tens digit, the result is 1.

VP's clue : Three more than the tens digit is thrice the ones digit.

Find the passcode that opens the locker. Show your work. **Competency Based Question**

43. In figure, $ABCD$ is a rectangle. Find the value of x and y. **CBSE 2018**

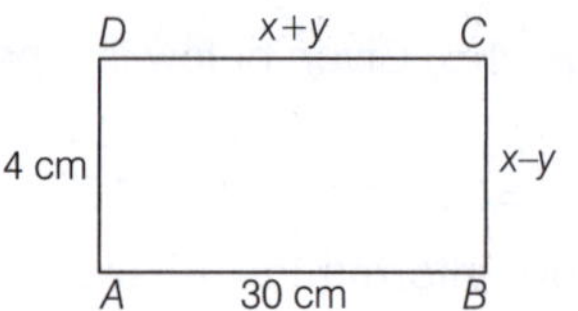

Long Answer Type Questions

44. The equations of the lines l_1, l_2 and l_3 are given by $5x+3y=2p, 35x+21y=pq$ and $100x+4qy=240$ respectively, where p and q are real numbers.

(i) For what values of p and q does the line l_3 coincide with l_1? Show your steps.

(ii) For the values of p and q found in question (i), are the lines l_1 and l_2 parallel? Justify your answer. **CBSE QB**

45. Solve the following system of linear equations $7x-2y=5$ and $8x+7y=15$ and verify your answer. **CBSE 2024 (Standard)**

46. The sum of a two-digit number and the number obtained by reversing the order of its digits is 99. If ten's digit is 3 more than the unit's digit, then find the number. **CBSE Sample Paper 2025 (Basic)**

47. Places A and B are 180 km apart on a highway. One car starts from A and another from B at the same time. If the car travels in the same direction at different speeds, they meet in 9 h. If they travel towards each other with the same speeds as before, they meet in an hour. What are the speeds of the two cars?

48. Nidhi received simple interest of ₹ 1200 when invested ₹ x at 6% p.a. and ₹ y at 5% p.a. for 1 year. Had she invested ₹ x at 3% p.a. and ₹ y at 8% p.a. for that year, she would have received simple interest of ₹ 1260. Find the values of x and y. **CBSE 2025 (Basic)**

49. Ananya had red, blue and yellow marbles in the ratio 4 : 5 : 3. She gave all her red marbles and some blue marbles to Neha. The ratio of the number of blue marbles and yellow marbles left with Ananya was 7 : 9.

If Ananya gave 20 marbles to Neha, then how many of them are red marbles? Show your work. **Competency Based Question**

HINTS & SOLUTIONS

Part I

1. (a) Given equations are $x = a$ and $y = b (a \neq b)$.

The graph of $x = a$ is a line parallel to Y-axis and $y = b$ is a line parallel to X-axis.

$\therefore$ The angle between them is 90° i.e. they intersect each other and the solution is (a, b).

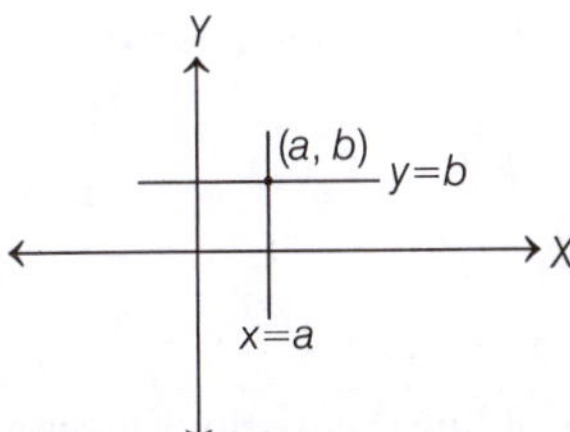

Hence, the point of intersection is (a, b).

2. (a) It is clear from the given figure that line l and line m are intersect at point (0, 2). So, the system of linear equations is consistent with unique solution.

3. (a) Given, pair of equations is

$$2x + 1 = 0$$

and $$3y - 5 = 0$$

On comparing the given equation with standard form of pair of linear equation

i.e. $a_1x + b_1y + c_1 = 0$ and $a_2x + b_2y + c_2 = 0$, we get

$$a_1 = 2, b_1 = 0, c_1 = 1$$

and $$a_2 = 0, b_2 = 3, c_2 = -5$$

Here, $\frac{a_1}{a_2} = \frac{2}{0} = \infty$ and $\frac{b_1}{b_2} = \frac{0}{3} = 0$

$\because \frac{a_1}{a_2} \neq \frac{b_1}{b_2}$

$\therefore$ The system of given equations has unique solution.

4. (d) **Hint** On comparing the above equations with standard form of pair of linear equations

$a_1x+b_1y+c_1 = 0$ and $a_2x+b_2y+c_2 = 0$, we get

(a) Consistent (b) Consistent

(c) Consistent (d) Inconsistent

5. (d) As we know that

if pair of linear equations is parallel i.e. no solution, then

$$\frac{a_1}{a_2} = \frac{b_1}{b_2} \neq \frac{c_1}{c_2}$$

and if pair of linear equations is coincide i.e. infinite number of solutions, then

$$\frac{a_1}{a_2} = \frac{b_1}{b_2} = \frac{c_1}{c_2}$$

Hence, given pair of linear equations has no solution or has infinite number of solutions.

6. (d) Given equations are to be parallel, if

$$\frac{a}{3} = \frac{2}{b} \neq \frac{-9}{-18},$$

Taking $\frac{a}{3} = \frac{2}{b} \Rightarrow ab = 6$

7. (b) We know that the system of equations $a_1x + b_1y + c_1 = 0$ and $a_2x + b_2y + c_2 = 0$ is inconsistent if

$$\frac{a_1}{a_2} = \frac{b_1}{b_2} \neq \frac{c_1}{c_2}$$

So, $\frac{3}{6} = \frac{-k}{10} \neq \frac{7}{3} \Rightarrow -k = \frac{3 \times 10}{6}$

$\therefore \quad k = -5$

8. (b) $\because$ The given system of equations have no solution.

$\therefore \quad \frac{a_1}{a_2} = \frac{b_1}{b_2} \neq \frac{c_1}{c_2} \Rightarrow \frac{5}{2} = \frac{2}{k} \neq \frac{-7}{1} \Rightarrow k = \frac{4}{5}$

9. (c) **Hint** Condition for two lines to be parallel,

$$\frac{a_1}{a_2} = \frac{b_1}{b_2} \neq \frac{c_1}{c_2}$$

10. (a) The system of equations is inconsistent if

$$\frac{a_1}{a_2} = \frac{b_1}{b_2} \neq \frac{c_1}{c_2}$$

Now, $3x - 7y - 1 = 0$ and $kx + 14y - 6 = 0$

$$a_1 = 3, b_1 = -7, c_1 = -1$$

$$a_2 = k, b_2 = 14, c_2 = -6$$

$\therefore \quad \frac{3}{k} = \frac{-7}{14} \neq \frac{-1}{-6}$

$\Rightarrow \quad 14 \times 3 = -7k \Rightarrow -7k = 42$

$\Rightarrow \quad k = -\frac{42}{7} \Rightarrow k = -6$

11. (c) Given, cost of 1 chair = ₹ x

$\therefore$ Cost of 3 chairs = ₹ $3x$

and cost of 5 chairs = ₹ $5x$

Also given, cost of 1 table = ₹y

$\therefore$ Cost of 3 tables = ₹ $3y$

So, the given situation can be represented as

$$3x + y = 900 \text{ and } 5x + 3y = 2100$$

12. (c) Given equations, $x + y = a + b$ ... (i)

$$ax - by = a^2 - b^2 \quad \text{... (ii)}$$

On multiplying Eq. (i) by b, we get

$$bx + by = ab + b^2 \quad \text{... (iii)}$$

On adding Eqs. (ii) and (iii), we get

$$ax + bx = a^2 + ab$$

$\Rightarrow$ $(a + b)x = a(a + b) \Rightarrow x = a$

From Eq. (i), $a + y = a + b \Rightarrow y = b$

13. (a) **Hint** Given equations are

$$32x + 33y = 34 \quad \text{...(i)}$$

$$33x + 32y = 31 \quad \text{...(ii)}$$

On solving Eqs. (i) and (ii), we get

$$x = -1 \text{ and } y = 2$$

14. (b) Let ones digit of the number be x and tens digit of the number be y.

$\therefore$ Two-digit number $= 10y + x$

According to the question, $\frac{10y + x}{x + y} = \frac{7}{1} \Rightarrow \frac{x}{y} = \frac{1}{2}$

$\therefore$ Possible two-digit numbers are 21, 42, 63, 84.

15. (b) $l_1 : x + 2y - 4 = 0$ and $l_2 : 2x + 4y - 12 = 0$

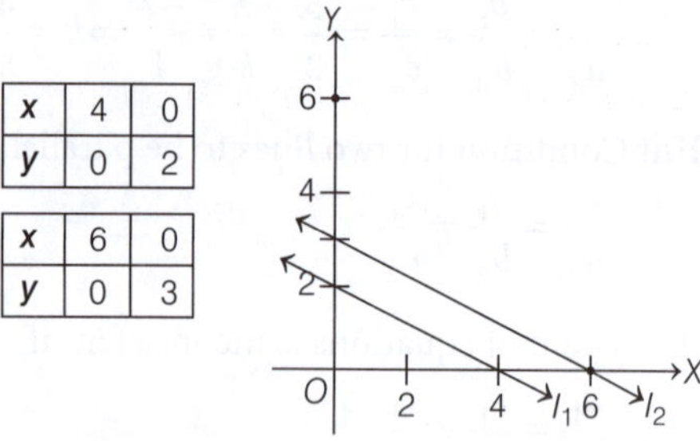

So, the lines l_1 and l_2 are parallel to each other.

Both Assertion (A) and Reason (R) are correct and Reason (R) is not the correct explanation of Assertion (A).

16. (d) **Assertion** We have, $l_1 : 2x + y - 6 = 0$;

$l_2 : 2x - y + 2 = 0, l_1 : y = 6 - 2x; l_2 : y = 2x + 2$

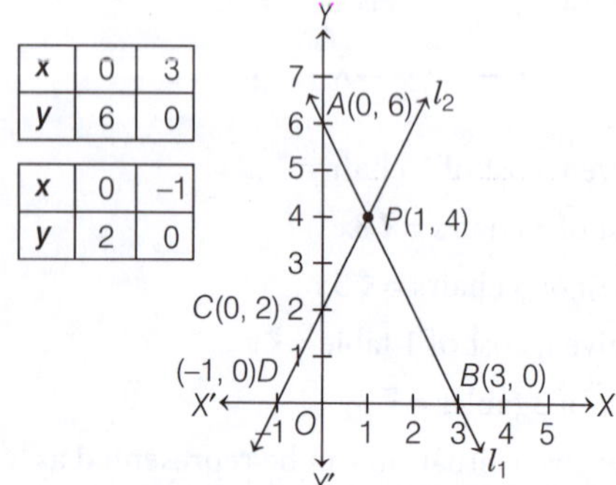

From graph, it is clear that the given lines are not parallel lines.

Reason The linear equations $5x + ky - 4 = 0$ and $15x + 3y - 12 = 0$ have infinitely many solutions.

$$\therefore \quad \frac{5}{15} = \frac{k}{3} = \frac{-4}{-12} \Rightarrow \frac{1}{3} = \frac{k}{3} = \frac{1}{3} \Rightarrow k = 1$$

$\therefore$ Assertion (A) is incorrect but Reason (R) is correct.

17. (a) We have, $3x + 2y - 12 = 0$ and $5x - 4y - 10 = 0$

On comparing with standard form of pair of linear equations, we get

$$a_1 = 3, b_1 = 2 \text{ and } c_1 = -12$$

and $a_2 = 5, b_2 = -4$ and $c_2 = -10$

Now, $\frac{a_1}{a_2} = \frac{3}{5}, \frac{b_1}{b_2} = \frac{2}{-4} = \frac{-1}{2}$ and $\frac{c_1}{c_2} = \frac{-12}{-10} = \frac{6}{5}$

$\because \quad \frac{a_1}{a_2} \neq \frac{b_1}{b_2}$

$\therefore$ Given pair of linear equations gives a pair of intersecting lines.

$\therefore$ Assertion is true and Reason is also true and Reason is correct explanation of Assertion.

18. (d) Given, system of linear equations has a unique solution, if

$$\frac{k}{6} \neq \frac{-1}{-2} \Rightarrow \frac{k}{6} \neq \frac{1}{2} \Rightarrow k \neq 3$$

So, Assertion (A) is incorrect and Reason (R) is correct.

19. (a) From the given equations, we have

$$\frac{9}{18} = \frac{3}{6} = \frac{12}{24} \Rightarrow \frac{1}{2} = \frac{1}{2} = \frac{1}{2} \text{ i.e. } \frac{a_1}{a_2} = \frac{b_1}{b_2} = \frac{c_1}{c_2}$$

Both Assertion (A) and Reason (R) are correct and Reason (R) is the correct explanation of Assertion (A).

20. **Hint** Do same as Question 3 (iv) of NCERT folder Exercise 3.2.

Ans. (i) ₹ 5, (ii) ₹ 10, (iii) ₹ 120

Or

Fixed charges = ₹5

and Charges per km = ₹ 10

Total distance travelled = 10 + 25 = 35 km

Total amount paid = 5 + 10(35) = ₹ 355

21. (i) Let the cost of a ticket be ₹ x and the cost of food be ₹ y.

Given, the cost of food is one-third of the cost of the ticket.

$$y = \frac{1}{3}x \Rightarrow x = 3y \quad \text{...(i)}$$

Also, the ticket and food cost her ₹ 600

$\Rightarrow \quad x + y = 600$ ...(ii)

(ii) Substituting $x = 3y$ from Eq. (i) in Eq. (ii),

$$3y + y = 600$$

$\Rightarrow \quad 4y = 600 \Rightarrow y = 150$

From Eq. (i),

$x = 3y \Rightarrow x = 3\times 150 = 450$

Let the cost of ticket without discount = ₹ z

$\because \quad z = 450 + z\times\frac{10}{100} \Rightarrow z =$ ₹ 500

So, she spends ₹ (600 – 500) = ₹ 100 on food in ₹ 600

Or

Hint Do same as Example 3 of Topic 2. **Ans.** ₹ 120

(iii) It is true for any group because the difference of ₹ 100 depends on online and offline tickets and not on the group size.

22. (i) Situation-I : $2x+3y=1400$ ...(i)

And situation-II : $3x+5y=2150$ ...(ii)

(ii) On multiplying Eq. (i) by 3 and Eq. (ii) by 2 and then subtract Eq. (i) from Eq. (ii), we get

$(6x+10y)-(6x+9y) = 4300-4200$

$\Rightarrow \quad y = 100$

On substituting $y = 100$ in Eq. (i), we get

$2x = 1400 - 300 \Rightarrow x = 550$

Therefore, cost of 1 kg almonds is ₹ 550 and cost of 1 kg raisins is ₹100.

(iii) Cost of 1.5 kg almonds and 2.5 kg of raisins

$= 1.5x + 2.5y$

$= 1.5\times 550 + 2.5\times 100$

$= 825 + 250 =$ ₹ 1075

Or

Cost of 5 kg almonds and 0.5 kg of raisins

$= 5x + 0.5y$

$= 5\times 550 + 0.5\times 100$

$= 2750 + 50$

$=$ ₹ 2800

23. (i) For batch I, $20x + 5y = 9000$ ...(i)

For batch II, $5x + 25y = 26000$ ...(ii)

(ii) **Hint** Solve the above Eqs. (i) and (ii).

Ans. $x = 200$

Or

On substituting $x = 200$ in Eq. (i), we get

$y = 1000$

$\therefore$ Difference in the monthly fee paid by a poor child and a rich child $= y - x =$ ₹ 800

(iii) **Hint** Total monthly collection of fees, if there are 10 poor and 20 rich children $= 10x + 20y$

Put the value of $x = 200$ and $y = 1000$.

Ans. ₹ 22000

24. (i) From the given figure,

we see that area of two bedrooms $= 2(5x) = 10x \text{ m}^2$

$\therefore$ Area of kitchen $= 5\times y = 5y \text{ m}^2$

According to the question,

Area of the two bedrooms and area of kitchen $= 95 \text{ m}^2$

$\therefore \quad 10x + 5y = 95$

$\Rightarrow \quad 2x + y = 19$ [dividing both sides by 5] ...(i)

Also, length of the home = 15 m

$\therefore \quad x + 2 + y = 15$

$\Rightarrow \quad x + y = 13$ ...(ii)

Hence, pair of linear equations is

$2x + y = 19$ and $x + y = 13$

(ii) On solving Eqs. (i) and (ii), we get

$x = 6$ and $y = 7$

$\therefore$ Area of each bedroom $= 5\times x = 5\times 6 = 30 \text{ m}^2$

and area of kitchen $= 5\times y = 5\times 7 = 35 \text{ m}^2$

Or $\therefore$ Area of living room

$= 15\times(5+2) -$ Area of bedroom 2

$= 15\times 7 - 5\times 6$

$= 105 - 30 = 75 \text{ m}^2$

(iii) Since, area of kitchen $= 5\times y = 5\times 7 = 35 \text{ m}^2$

But it is also given, the cost of laying tiles in kitchen at the rate of ₹ 50 per m^2.

$\therefore$ Total cost of laying tiles in the kitchen $= 35\times 50$

$=$ ₹ 1750

Part II

1. **Hint** Do same as Example 8 of Topic 1.
   Ans. Intersect at a point.
2. **Hint** Do same as Example 8 of Topic 1.
   Ans. Parallel lines
3. **Hint** Do same as Example 8 of Topic 1.
   Ans. Coincident lines
4. **Hint** Do same as Example 9 of Topic 1.
   Ans. Consistent.
5. Putting $x = 3$ and $y = -3$ in Eqs. (i) and (ii).
   LHS of Eq. (i), $4(3) - 3 = 12 - 3 = 9 \neq 8$ (RHS)
   LHS of Eq. (ii), $4(3) - 2(-3) = 12 + 6 = 18 \neq 16$ (RHS)
   So, the points $x = 3$ and $y = -4$ do not satisfy the given equations.
6. **Hint** Here, $\frac{a_1}{a_2} = \frac{b_1}{b_2} \neq \frac{c_1}{c_2}$.
   So, the pair of equations have no solution. **Ans.** 0
7. **Hint** Do same as Example 10 of Topic 1. **Ans.** $p \neq 4$

8. Hint Here, $\frac{a_1}{a_2}=\frac{5}{15}=\frac{1}{3}, \frac{b_1}{b_2}=\frac{\lambda}{3}$ and $\frac{c_1}{c_2}=\frac{-4}{-12}=\frac{1}{3}$

For infinitely many solutions,

$$\frac{a_1}{a_2}=\frac{b_1}{b_2}=\frac{c_1}{c_2} \Rightarrow \frac{1}{3}=\frac{\lambda}{3}=\frac{1}{3}$$ **Ans.** $\lambda = 1$

9. Hint Do same as Example 11 of Topic 1. **Ans.** $k = 2$.

10. Hint Solve both the given equations. So, we get $x = 5$ and $y = 3$

Ans. $x - y = 2$

11. Hint The values a and b will satisfy given equations.

Thus, we have

$$a - b = 2 \quad \text{...(i)}$$

and $$a + b = 4 \quad \text{...(ii)}$$

Now, solving Eqs. (i) and (ii) to find a and b.

Ans. $a = 3, b = 1$

12. Hint We know that diagonals of a parallelogram bisect each other.

$\therefore$ $$x + y = 9 \quad \text{... (i)}$$

and $$x - y = 5 \quad \text{... (ii)}$$

Now, solving Eqs. (i) and (ii) to find x and y.

Ans. $x = 7, y = 2$

13. Given, $x + 3y = 6$

and $2x - 3y = 12$

Table for $x + 3y = 6$

x	0	6
y	2	0

Line $x + 3y = 6$ intersects the X-axis at (6, 0) and Y-axis at (0, 2).

Table for $2x - 3y = 12$

x	0	6
y	–4	0

Line $2x - 3y = 12$ intersects the coordinate axis at (0, –4) and (6, 0).

The graph is shown below.

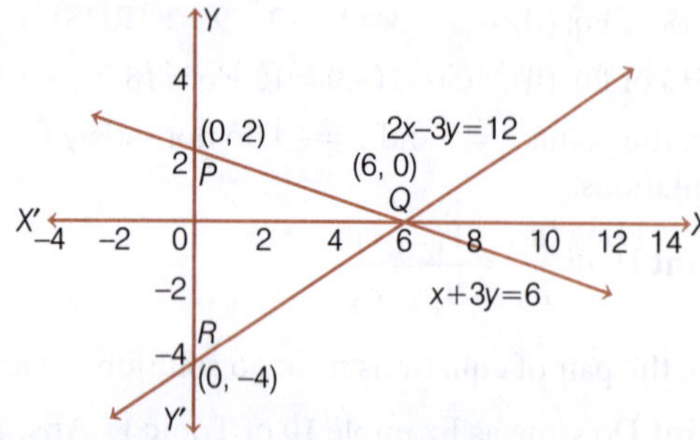

From the graph, both the lines intersect at (6, 0).

Hence, $x = 6$ and $y = 0$

Also, the vertices of triangle PQR are (0, 2), (6, 0) and (0, –4).

14. Hint Do same as Example 3 of Topic 1.

Ans. 6 sq units

15. Hint We plot the given pair of equations as follows:

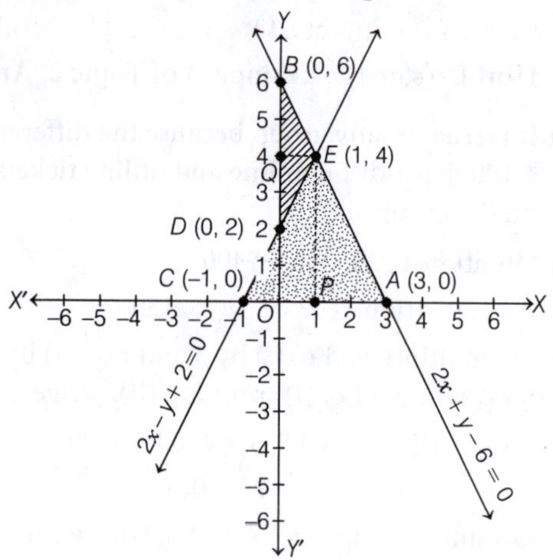

Then, area of $\Delta ACE = \frac{1}{2} \times AC \times PE$

$$= \frac{1}{2} \times 4 \times 4 = 8 \text{ sq units}$$

and area of $\Delta BDE = \frac{1}{2} \times BD \times QE = \frac{1}{2} \times 4 \times 1$

$$= 2 \text{ sq units}$$ **Ans.** 4 : 1

16. (i) **Hint** Given, equation of lines are

$$3x - y = 3 \quad \text{...(i)}$$

$$2x - 3y = 2 \quad \text{...(ii)}$$

and $$x + 2y = 8 \quad \text{...(iii)}$$

Let lines (i), (ii) and (iii) represent the sides of ΔABC, say AB, BC and CA, respectively.

Now, solve Eqs. (i), (ii) and (iii) and then Eqs. (i) and (iii) to find coordinates of points A, B, C, respectively.

Ans. $A(1, 0), B(2, 3)$ and $C(4, 2)$

(ii) Do same as Part (i). **Ans.** (1, 0), (3, –1) and (2, 5)

17. Hint Do same as Question 6 of NCERT Folder Exercise. 3.1.

Ans. (i) $5x - 2y + 8 = 0$ (ii) $4x - 10y - 8 = 0$

(iii) $2x - 5y + 10 = 0$

18. Hint Here, $\frac{a_1}{a_2}=\frac{7}{14}=\frac{1}{2}, \frac{b_1}{b_2}=\frac{-5}{-10}=\frac{1}{2}$ and $\frac{c_1}{c_2}=\frac{3}{5}$

Thus, for the given equations, we have

$$\frac{a_1}{a_2}=\frac{b_1}{b_2} \neq \frac{c_1}{c_2}$$

So, we conclude that the two paths are parallel to each other. **Ans.** No

19. **Hint** Here, $a_1 = 3,\ b_1 = -(a+1),\ c_1 = -(2b-1)$

and $a_2 = 5,\ b_2 = 1-2a,\ c_2 = -3b$

For infinitely many solutions, we must have

$$\underset{\text{I}}{\frac{3}{5}} = \underset{\text{II}}{\frac{-(a+1)}{1-2a}} = \underset{\text{III}}{\frac{2b-1}{3b}}$$

Now, take two terms at a time i.e. I and II, I and III and solve them. **Ans.** $a = 8, b = 5$

20. **Hint** Here, $a_1 = \lambda,\ b_1 = 1, c_1 = -\lambda^2$

and $a_2 = 1,\ b_2 = \lambda, c_2 = -1$

(i) For no solution, we must have $\frac{a_1}{a_2} = \frac{b_1}{b_2} \neq \frac{c_1}{c_2}$

$\Rightarrow \quad \frac{\lambda}{1} = \frac{1}{\lambda} \neq \frac{\lambda^2}{1}$ **Ans.** $\lambda = -1$

(ii) For infinitely many solutions, we must have

$$\frac{a_1}{a_2} = \frac{b_1}{b_2} = \frac{c_1}{c_2} \Rightarrow \underset{\text{I}}{\frac{\lambda}{1}} = \underset{\text{II}}{\frac{1}{\lambda}} = \underset{\text{III}}{\frac{\lambda^2}{1}}$$ **Ans.** $\lambda = 1$

(iii) For a unique solution, we must have

$\frac{a_1}{a_2} \neq \frac{b_1}{b_2} \Rightarrow \frac{\lambda}{1} \neq \frac{1}{\lambda} \Rightarrow \lambda^2 \neq 1$ **Ans.** $\lambda \neq \pm 1$

21. (i) Let the equation of a line l_3 is $x+2y-5=0$

it intersect l_1: $2x+2y+2=0$ at exactly one point, if

$$\frac{a_1}{a_2} \neq \frac{b_1}{b_2} \Rightarrow \frac{2}{1} \neq \frac{2}{2}$$

$\therefore\ x+2y-5=0$ is intersect to given line l_1.

(ii) **Hint** We have, $l_2: 3x+3y-3=0$ ...(i)

and $l_3: x+2y-5=0$ ...(ii)

Multiply Eq. (i) by 2 and Eq. (ii) by 3 after that solve both to find the values of x and y.

Ans. $(-3, 4)$

22. **Hint** Compare the ratios $\frac{a_1}{a_2}, \frac{b_1}{b_2}, \frac{c_1}{c_2}$ and then find the solution by algebraic method.

Ans. $x = -1, y = 3$

23. **Hint** Do same as Question 1 of NCERT Folder Exercise 3.2. **Ans.** $x = \frac{9}{14}, y = \frac{5}{7}$

24. **Hint** Do same as Question 1 of NCERT Folder Exercise 3.2. **Ans.** $x = -2, y = 10$

25. **Hint** Do same as Question 1 of NCERT Folder Exercise 3.2. **Ans.** $x = 5, y = -\frac{2}{13}$

26. **Hint** Do same as Question 1 of NCERT Folder Exercise 3.2. **Ans.** $x = 18, y = -1$

27. **Hint** Do same as Question 3 (i) of Topic 2 Exercise 3.2. **Ans.** $x = a^2, y = b^2$

28. **Hint** Do same as Question 3 (i) of Topic 2 Exercise 3.2. **Ans.** $x = \frac{a}{a^2+b^2}, y = \frac{b}{a^2+b^2}$

29. Given pair of linear equations is

$x + 2y = 6$ ...(i)

and $2x + y = 6$ ...(ii)

From Eq. (ii), we get

$y = 6 - 2x$ ...(iii)

On substituting the value of y from Eq. (iii) in Eq. (i), we get

$x + 2(6-2x) = 6$

$\Rightarrow \quad x + 12 - 4x = 6 \Rightarrow x = 2$

On substituting $x = 2$ in Eq. (iii), we get

$y = 6 - 2 \times 2 = 2$

On substituting $x = 2$ and $y = 2$ in equation $y = px + 2$, we get

$2 = p(2) + 2$

$\Rightarrow \quad p = 0$

30. **Hint** Do same as Example 3 of Topic 2.

Ans. Cost of one chair = ₹ 2000 and cost of one table = ₹ 550

31. **Hint** Do same as Question 1 of NCERT Folder Exercise 3.3. **Ans.** $x = -3, y = -5$

32. **Hint** Do same as Question 1 of NCERT Folder Exercise 3.3. **Ans.** $x = 4, y = -1$

33. **Hint** Do same as Question 1 of NCERT Folder Exercise 3.3. **Ans.** $x = 1, y = 2$

34. **Hint** First multiply the pair of equations on both sides by 10 and then do same as Question 1 of NCERT Folder Exercise 3.3. **Ans.** $x = 2, y = 3$

35. **Hint** Do same as Question 1 of NCERT Folder Exercise 3.3. **Ans.** $x = 14, y = 9$

36. Given, sum of two numbers is 105 and their difference is 45.

Let the two numbers be x and y. $(x > y)$

$\therefore \quad x + y = 105$ ...(i)

and $x - y = 45$ ...(ii)

On adding Eqs. (i) and (ii), we get

$2x = 150 \Rightarrow x = 75$

On putting the value of x in Eq. (i), we get

$75 + y = 105 \Rightarrow y = 30$

Hence, the numbers are 75 and 30.

37. Let age of Ajay at the time of his marriage be x years and the age of his wife at that time be y years.

According to Ist condition

$$x = y + 5 \Rightarrow x - y - 5 = 0 \quad \text{...(i)}$$

And according to II condition,

$$\frac{y+16}{x+16} = \frac{8}{9}$$

$\Rightarrow \quad 9y + 144 = 8x + 128$

$\Rightarrow \quad 8x - 9y - 16 = 0 \quad$ ...(ii)

On solving Eqs. (i) and (ii), we get

$$x = 29 \text{ and } y = 24$$

38. Hint Let father's age be x yr and sum of ages of his two children be y yr.

For condition I $x = 3y$ ...(i)

For condition II After 5 yr, age of father $= (x+5)$ yr

After 5 yr, sum of ages of two children $= (y+10)$ yr

$\Rightarrow \quad x + 5 = 2(y+10) \quad$ ...(ii)

Now, solve Eqs. (i) and (ii) to find x. **Ans.** 45 yr

39. Hint Points of intersection of lines represented by

$$3x - 2y = 10 \quad \text{...(i)}$$

and $\quad 5x + y = 8 \quad$ ...(ii)

is the common solution of this system of equations.

On solving this system of equations, we get the point of intersection of the lines (i) and (ii) is $(2, -2)$.

Now, the line $3x + ay = 8$ passes through the point $(2, -2)$.

So, this point will satisfy the equation $3x + ay = 8$.

$\therefore (3 \times 2) + [(-2) \times a] = 8$ **Ans.** $a = -1$

40. Hint Let the number of students in halls A and B be x and y, respectively.

According to the question,

$$x - 10 = y + 10 \Rightarrow x - y = 20 \quad \text{...(i)}$$

and $(x + 20) = 2(y - 20) \Rightarrow x - 2y = -60$ ...(ii)

Solve Eqs. (i) and (ii) to find x and y. **Ans.** 100, 80

41. Hint We have, $x + y + 40° = 180°$

[$\because$ sum of all the angles of a triangle is 180°]

$\Rightarrow \quad x + y = 140° \quad$ ...(i)

Also, $\quad x - y = 30° \quad$ ...(ii)

Solve Eqs. (i) and (ii) to find x and y. **Ans.** 85°, 55°

42. Hint Given, the ones digit is x and the tens digit is y.

According to CEO's clue,

$$y - 2x = 1 \quad \text{...(i)}$$

According to VP's clue,

$$y + 3 = 3x \quad \text{...(ii)}$$

Now, solve Eqs. (i) and (ii).

Ans. Required passcode is 4994.

43. Hint We know that opposite sides of a rectangle are equal.

$\therefore \quad x + y = 30 \quad$ ...(i)

and $\quad x - y = 14 \quad$ ...(ii)

On solving Eqs. (i) and (ii), we get

Ans. $x = 22$ cm and $y = 8$ cm.

44. (i) Given equations of lines are

$$l_1 : 5x + 3y = 2p; \; l_2 : 35x + 21y = pq$$

and $\quad l_3 : 100x + 4qy = 240$

line $a_1 = 5, b_1 = 3, c_1 = 2p, a_2 = 35, b_2 = 21, c_2 = pq$

and $a_3 = 100, b_3 = 4q, c_3 = 240$

Lines l_3 and l_1 are coincide.

So, $\frac{a_3}{a_1} = \frac{b_3}{b_1} = \frac{c_3}{c_1} \Rightarrow \underset{\text{I}}{\frac{100}{5}} = \underset{\text{II}}{\frac{4q}{3}} = \underset{\text{III}}{\frac{240}{2p}}$

On taking first two terms, we get

$$\frac{100}{5} = \frac{4q}{3} \Rightarrow q = \frac{20 \times 3}{4}$$

$\therefore \quad q = 15$

On taking I and III terms, we get

$$\frac{100}{5} = \frac{240}{2p} \Rightarrow 20 = \frac{240}{2p} \Rightarrow p = \frac{240}{2 \times 20} = 6$$

Hence, $p = 6$ and $q = 15$.

(ii) On putting the values of p and q in l_1 and l_2, we get

$$5x + 3y = 2(6),$$

$\Rightarrow \quad 5x + 3y = 12$ and $35x + 21y = 6 \times 15$

$\Rightarrow \quad 35x + 21y = 90$

Here, $\frac{a_1}{a_2} = \frac{5}{35} = \frac{1}{7}, \frac{b_1}{b_2} = \frac{3}{21} = \frac{1}{7}$ and $\frac{c_1}{c_2} = \frac{12}{90} = \frac{4}{30}$

Thus, $\frac{a_1}{a_2} = \frac{b_1}{b_2} \neq \frac{c_1}{c_2}$

Hence, the lines l_1 and l_2 are parallel.

45. Hint Do same as example-1 of topic-2

Ans. $x = 1$ and $y = 1$

46. Let the two-digit number be $10x + y$.

Then, according to question,

$$(10x + y) + (10y + x) = 99$$

$\Rightarrow \quad 11x + 11y = 99 \Rightarrow 11(x + y) = 99$

$\Rightarrow \quad x + y = \frac{99}{11} = 9 \Rightarrow x + y = 9 \quad$ ...(i)

Also, according to II given condition,

$$x = 3 + y \Rightarrow x - y = 3 \quad \text{...(ii)}$$

On solving Eqs. (i) and (ii), we get

$$x = 6 \text{ and } y = 3$$

Therefore, the required number $= 10 \times 6 + 3 = 60 + 3 = 63$

47. Let car I starts from A with speed x km/hr and car II starts from B with speed y km/hr.

Case I When cars are moving in the same direction.

Distance covered by car I in 9 h $= 9x$

Distance covered by car II in 9 h $= 9y$

Therefore, $9(x - y) = 180$ [assume, $x > y$]

$\Rightarrow \quad x - y = 20$ ...(i)

Case II When cars are moving in opposite directions.

Distance covered by car I in 1 h $= x$

Distance covered by car II in 1 h $= y$

Therefore, $x + y = 180$ ...(ii)

Now, on adding Eqs. (i) and (ii), we get

$$2x = 200 \Rightarrow x = 100$$

$\therefore \quad y = 180 - 100 = 80$

Hence, the speeds of the two cars are 100 km/hr and 80 km/hr.

48. Nidhi received ₹ 1200 when invested ₹ x at 6% p.a. and ₹ y at 5% p.a. for 1 year.

We know that

$$\text{Simple interest} = \frac{P \times R \times T}{100}$$

The total interest is the sum of the simple interest from x and y.

$\therefore \quad 1200 = \frac{x \times 6 \times 1}{100} + \frac{y \times 5 \times 1}{100}$

$\Rightarrow \quad 1200 = \frac{6x}{100} + \frac{5y}{100}$

$\Rightarrow \quad 6x + 5y = 120000$ ...(i)

Similarly, for second condition, we have

$$1260 = \frac{x \times 3 \times 1}{100} + \frac{y \times 8 \times 1}{100}$$

$\Rightarrow \quad 1260 = \frac{3x}{100} + \frac{8y}{100}$

$\Rightarrow \quad 3x + 8y = 126000$ ...(ii)

On multiplying Eq. (ii) by 2, we get

$6x + 16y = 252000$ ...(iii)

On subtracting Eq. (i) from Eq. (iii), we get

$$(6x + 16y) - (6x + 5y) = 252000 - 120000$$

$\Rightarrow \quad 11y = 132000$

$\Rightarrow \quad y = 12000$

On substituting $y = 12000$ in Eq. (i), we get

$$6x + 5 \times 12000 = 120000$$

$\Rightarrow \quad 6x = 120000 - 60000$

$\Rightarrow \quad 6x = 60000$

$\Rightarrow \quad x = 10000$

Hence, the values of x and y are 10000 and 12000, respectively.

49. Ananya had $4x$ red, $5x$ blue and $3x$ yellow marbles.

Let number of blue marbles given to Neha be y.

According to question,

$$4x + y = 20 \text{ and } \frac{5x - y}{3x} = \frac{7}{9}$$

Ans. Number of red marbles = 12

PAIR OF LINEAR EQUATIONS IN TWO VARIABLES

Two linear equations in the same two variables, say x and y, are called pair of linear equations in two variables. The general form of pair of linear equations in two variables x and y is $a_1 x + b_1 y + c_1 = 0$ and $a_2 x + b_2 y + c_2 = 0$, where $a_1, b_1, c_1, a_2, b_2, c_2$ are all real numbers.

Solution of Pair of Linear Equations in Two Variables

Any pair of values of x and y which satisfies both the equations, $a_1 x + b_1 y + c_1 = 0$ and $a_2 x + b_2 y + c_2 = 0$ is called a solution of a given pair of linear equation.
e.g. $x = 2$ and $y = 3$ is the solution of pair of linear equations $2x + 3y - 13 = 0$ and $4x - 5y + 7 = 0$.

Graphical Method

Let us consider a pair of linear equations in two variables, $a_1 x + b_1 y + c_1 = 0$ and $a_2 x + b_2 y + c_2 = 0$.

To find the solution graphically, first draw the graph of both equations on the same graph paper with same scale of representation.
Then,
(i) If the lines intersect at a point, the pair of equations is consistent and the point of intersection gives the unique solution of the equations.
(ii) If the lines are parallel, then there is no solution. The pair of linear equations is inconsistent.
(iii) If the lines coincide, then there are infinitely many solutions. The pair of equations is consistent. Each point on the line is a solution.

Nature of lines and Consistency

The nature of line sand consistency to linear equations $a_1 x + b_1 y + c_1 = 0$ and $a_2 x + b_2 y + c_2 = 0$, is shown in the table given below:

Compare the ratios	Graphical representation	Algebraic interpretation	Consistency
$\frac{a_1}{a_2} \neq \frac{b_1}{b_2}$	intersecting lines	Exactly one solution(unique)	System is consistent
$\frac{a_1}{a_2} = \frac{b_1}{b_2} = \frac{c_1}{c_1}$	Coincident lines	Infinity many solution	System is consistent (dependent)
$\frac{a_1}{a_2} = \frac{b_1}{b_2} \neq \frac{c_1}{c_1}$	Parallel lines	No solution	System is inconsistent

Algebraic Methods

Algebraic method is also suitable for non-integer solutions. Different algebraic methods for solving pair of linear equations are given below.

(i) Substitution Method

In this method, value of one variable can be found out in terms of other variable from one of the given equations and this value is substituted in other equation, then we get an equation in one variable, which can be solved easily.
e.g. Solve $x + y = 3$ and $x + 2y = 5$

Sol. $x + y = 3$ .....(i)
and $x + 2y = 5$ ..... (ii)
On substituting $x = 3 - y$ from Eq. (i) in Eq. (ii), we get
$3 - y + 2y = 5 \Rightarrow y = 5 - 3 = 2$
$\therefore x = 1$

(ii) Elimination Method

In this method, one variable out of the two variables is eliminated by making the coefficients of that variable equal in both the equations.
After eliminating that variable, the left equation is an equation in one variable, which can be solved easily.
e.g. Solve $x + 2y = 6$ and $x + y = 5$

Sol. $x + 2y = 6$ ....(i)
and $x + y = 5$ .... (ii)
On multiplying by 2 in Eq. (ii) on both sides, we get
$2x + 2y = 10$ ... (iii)
On subtracting Eq. (i) from Eq. (iii), we get $x = 4$
Now, on putting $x = 4$, we get $y = 1$

CHAPTER 4

Quadratic Equations

In this chapter, we will study quadratic equation and various ways of finding their roots along with their applications, based on daily life situations.

TOPIC 01 Quadratic Equation and Its Solution

Quadratic Equation

An equation of the form $ax^2 + bx + c = 0$, is called quadratic equation in variable x, where a, b and c are real numbers and $a \neq 0$.

e.g. $2x^2 + x - 100 = 0$, $-x^2 + 1 + 300x = 0$ are quadratic equations.

The form $ax^2 + bx + c = 0, a \neq 0$ is called the **standard form** of a quadratic equation.

To express a quadratic equation in its standard form, write the terms of given equation in the descending order of their degrees.

e.g. $3x^2 + x + 2 = 0$, $x^2 - 2x + 6 = 0$, are in standard form whereas, $x^2 - 3 + 4x = 0$, $x + x^2 + 8 = 0$ are not in their standard form.

Method to Check Whether a Given Equation is Quadratic or Not

To check whether a given equation is quadratic or not, first write the given equation in its simplest form and then compare the equation with the standard form of a quadratic equation i.e. $ax^2 + bx + c = 0, a \neq 0$.

If the given equation follows the standard form of quadratic equation ($ax^2 + bx + c = 0, a \neq 0$), then it is a quadratic equation otherwise not.

Example 1. **Check whether the following are quadratic equations or not.**

(i) $(x-1)(x+2) = (x-3)(x+1)$ (ii) $(x+2)^2 = 4(x+3)$

Sol. (i) Given, $(x-1)(x+2) = (x-3)(x+1)$ ... (i)

Here, in LHS $(x-1)$ and $(x+2)$ are in product and in RHS $(x-3)$ and $(x+1)$ are also in product.

So, first we simplify their product.

LHS $= (x-1)(x+2) = x^2 + 2x - x - 2 = x^2 + x - 2$

RHS $= (x-3)(x+1) = x^2 + x - 3x - 3 = x^2 - 2x - 3$

On substituting these values in Eq. (i), we get

$$x^2 + x - 2 = x^2 - 2x - 3$$

$$\Rightarrow \quad x^2 - x^2 + x + 2x - 2 + 3 = 0 \Rightarrow 3x + 1 = 0$$

It is not of the form $ax^2 + bx + c = 0, a \neq 0$.

[$\because a = 0$ and it is an equation of degree 1]

Hence, the given equation does not represent a quadratic equation.

Note it In the above example, the given equation appears to be a quadratic equation, but it is not a quadratic equation. So, simplify the given equation before deciding whether it is quadratic or not.

(ii) Given, $(x+2)^2 = 4(x+3)$ ...(i)

Here, term $(x+2)$ has power 2. So, first expand it.

LHS $= (x+2)^2 = x^2 + 4 + 4x$

[$\because (a+b)^2 = a^2 + b^2 + 2ab$]

On substituting this value in Eq. (i), we get

$$x^2 + 4 + 4x = 4x + 12$$

$$\Rightarrow \quad x^2 + 4x - 4x + 4 - 12 = 0$$

$$\Rightarrow \quad x^2 - 8 = 0 \text{ or } x^2 + 0x - 8 = 0$$

It is of the form $ax^2 + bx + c = 0, a \neq 0$.

Hence, the given equation represents a quadratic equation.

Solutions or Roots of a Quadratic Equation

All the values of variable which satisfy the given quadratic equation, are called roots or zeroes or solutions of given quadratic equation.

In other words, a real number α is said to be a root or zero or solution of a quadratic equation $ax^2 + bx + c = 0, a \neq 0$, if $a(\alpha)^2 + b(\alpha) + c = 0$.

Any quadratic equation can have atmost two roots.

Method to Check Whether the Given Value is a Solution of the Given Quadratic Equation or Not

Let $p(x) = 0$ be the given quadratic equation and $x = \alpha$ be the given value of x.

To check whether $x = \alpha$ is a solution of the given equation or not, use the following steps.

Step I Write the given equation in the form, $p(x) = 0$ (if not given in this form).

Step II Now, put $x = \alpha$ in $p(x)$. If $p(\alpha) = 0$, then $x = \alpha$ is the solution of given equation, otherwise not.

Example 2. **Determine whether $x = \frac{-1}{2}, x = \frac{1}{3}$ are the solutions of the given equation $6x^2 - x - 2 = 0$, or not.**

Sol. Let $p(x) = 6x^2 - x - 2$ ...(i)

On putting $x = \frac{-1}{2}$ in Eq. (i), we get

$$p\left(\frac{-1}{2}\right) = 6\left(\frac{-1}{2}\right)^2 - \left(\frac{-1}{2}\right) - 2$$

$$= \frac{6}{4} + \frac{1}{2} - 2 = \frac{6 + 2 - 8}{4} = \frac{8 - 8}{4} = 0$$

$$\Rightarrow \quad p\left(\frac{-1}{2}\right) = 0$$

So, $x = \frac{-1}{2}$ is a solution of the given equation.

Now, on putting $x = \frac{1}{3}$ in Eq. (i), we get

$$p\left(\frac{1}{3}\right) = 6\left(\frac{1}{3}\right)^2 - \left(\frac{1}{3}\right) - 2$$

$$= 6 \times \frac{1}{9} - \frac{1}{3} - 2 = \frac{6}{9} - \frac{1}{3} - 2 = \frac{6 - 3 - 18}{9} = \frac{-15}{9}$$

$$\Rightarrow p\left(\frac{1}{3}\right) \neq 0$$

So, $x = \frac{1}{3}$ is not a solution of the given equation.

Method to Determine An Unknown Constant Involved in a Quadratic Equation when its Solution or Root is Given

Sometimes, given quadratic equation involves an unknown constant and its solution or root is given. Then, to find the value of unknown constant, we put the value of root or solution in given quadratic equation and simplify it to get the required unknown constant.

Example 3. **In each of the following equations, determine the value of k for which the given value is a solution of the equation.**

(i) $kx^2 + 2x - 3 = 0, x = 2$ CBSE 2019

(ii) $x^2 + 2ax - k = 0, x = -a$

Sol. (i) We have, $kx^2 + 2x - 3 = 0$

Here, k is unknown. Since, $x = 2$ is a solution of given equation, so it will satisfy the given equation.

On putting $x = 2$ in the given equation, we get

$$k(2)^2 + 2(2) - 3 = 0$$

$$\Rightarrow \quad 4k + 4 - 3 = 0$$

$$\Rightarrow \quad 4k + 1 = 0 \Rightarrow k = \frac{-1}{4}$$

(ii) We have, $x^2 + 2ax - k = 0$

Here, k is unknown. Since, $x = -a$ is a solution of given equation, so it will satisfy the given equation.

On putting $x = -a$ in the given equation, we get

$$(-a)^2 + 2a(-a) - k = 0 \Rightarrow a^2 - 2a^2 - k = 0$$

$$\Rightarrow \quad -a^2 - k = 0 \Rightarrow k = -a^2$$

Example 4. **If $x = 2$ and $x = 3$ are roots of the equation $3x^2 - 2ax + 2b = 0$, then find the value of a and b.**

Sol. Given, $3x^2 - 2ax + 2b = 0$ ...(i)

Here, a and b are unknown constants. Since, $x = 2$ and $x = 3$ are the solutions of given equation, so it will satisfy the given equation.

On putting $x = 2$ and $x = 3$ one-by-one, in Eq. (i), we get

$$3(2)^2 - 2a \times (2) + 2b = 0 \Rightarrow 3 \times 4 - 4a + 2b = 0$$

$$\Rightarrow \quad 12 - 4a + 2b = 0 \Rightarrow -2(2a - b - 6) = 0$$

$$\Rightarrow \quad 2a - b = 6 \quad [\because -2 \neq 0] \quad \text{...(ii)}$$

and $\quad 3(3)^2 - 2a \times 3 + 2b = 0$

$$\Rightarrow \quad 27 - 6a + 2b = 0 \Rightarrow 6a - 2b = 27 \quad \text{...(iii)}$$

On multiplying Eq. (ii) by 2 and then subtract it from Eq. (iii), we get

$$6a - 2b - 4a + 2b = 27 - 12 \Rightarrow 2a = 15 \Rightarrow a = \frac{15}{2}$$

On substituting $a = \frac{15}{2}$ in Eq. (ii), we get $2 \times \frac{15}{2} - b = 6$

$$\Rightarrow 15 - b = 6 \Rightarrow b = 15 - 6 = 9 \Rightarrow b = 9$$

Hence, the required values of a and b are 15/2 and 9, respectively.

Try These 4.1

1. Check whether the following equations are quadratic or not.

(i) $x+\frac{3}{x}=x^2$ (ii) $2x^2-5x=x^2-2x+3$

(iii) $x^2-\frac{1}{x^2}=5$ (iv) $x^2-3x-\sqrt{x}+4=0$

(v) $x(2x+3)=x+2$ (vi) $(x-2)^2+1=2x-3$

(vii) $y(8y+5)=y^2+3$

(viii) $y(2y+15)=2(y^2+y+8)$

(ix) $(x+2)(x-2)=(x+3)(x+4)$

(x) $(2x-1)^2-4x^2+5=0$

(xi) $\frac{16}{x}-1=\frac{15}{x+1}$

(xii) $\frac{1}{(x-1)(x-2)}+\frac{1}{(x-2)(x-3)}=\frac{2}{3}$

2. Is $\sqrt{2}x^2+7x+5\sqrt{2}=0$ a quadratic equation? If yes, then give reason.

**3. One of the roots of the quadratic equation $ax^2+4x+a=0$ is 2.
Find the value of a. Show your work.** CBSE QB

4. Show that $x=-3$ is a solution of equation $x^2+6x+9=0$.

5. In each of the following equations, determine whether the given values are a solution of the given equations or not.

(i) $x^2-x+1=0$; $x=1, x=-1$

(ii) $x^2+\sqrt{2}x-4=0$; $x=\sqrt{2}, x=-2\sqrt{2}$

(iii) $2x^2-x+9=x^2+4x+3$; $x=2, x=3$

(iv) $\sqrt{5}x^2-8x+3\sqrt{5}=0$; $x=\sqrt{5}, x=\frac{3}{\sqrt{5}}$

(v) $\frac{2x}{x-3}+\frac{1}{2x+3}+\frac{3x+9}{(x-3)(2x+3)}$; $x=3,-1$

(vi) $\frac{4}{x}-3=\frac{5}{2x+3}$; $x=1, x=-2$

(vii) $\sqrt{x+4}=x-1$; $x=3,1$

(viii) $x^2+(\sqrt{5}+1)x+\sqrt{5}=0$; $x=1,-\sqrt{5}$

6. Find the value of k for which the roots of the equation $3x^2-10x+k=0$ are reciprocal of each other. CBSE 2019

7. In each of the following equations, find the value of unknown constant(s) for which the given value (s) is (are) solution of the equations.

(i) $x^2-k^2=0$, $x=0.3$

(ii) $3x^2+2ax-3=0$; $x=\frac{-1}{2}$

(iii) $7x^2+kx-3=0$; $x=\frac{2}{3}$

(iv) $kx^2+\sqrt{2}x-4=0$; $x=\sqrt{2}$

(v) $ax^2+bx+1=0$; $x=1, x=2$

(vi) $5x^2+px+q=0$; $x=-2, x=-\frac{1}{5}$

(vii) $ax^2+bx-6=0$; $x=\frac{3}{4}, x=-2$

(viii) $kx^2+tx+1=0$; $x=0.2, x=0.1$

Answers

1. **Hint** Do same as Example 1.

Ans. (i) No (ii) Yes (iii) No (iv) No (v) Yes (vi) Yes (vii) Yes (viii) No (ix) No (x) No (xi) Yes (xii) Yes

2. **Ans.** Yes, because its degree is 2.

3. Given, quadratic equation

$$ax^2+4x+a=0$$

Since, 2 is a root of the given quadratic equation.

Therefore,

$$a\times(2)^2+4\times2+a=0$$

$\Rightarrow$ $4a+8+a=0 \Rightarrow 5a=-8$

$\therefore$ $a=\frac{-8}{5}$

4. **Hint** Do same as Example 2. **Ans.** Yes

5. **Hint** Do same as Example 2.

Ans.

(i) Both 1 and -1 are not the solutions of the given equation.

(ii) Both $\sqrt{2}$ and $-2\sqrt{2}$ are the solutions of the given equation.

(iii) Both 2 and 3 are the solutions of the given equation.

(iv) Both $\sqrt{5}$ and $\frac{3}{\sqrt{5}}$ are the solutions of the given equation.

(v) Only -1 is the solution of the given equation.

(vi) Both -2 and 1 are the solutions of the given equation.

(vii) Both 1 and 3 are not the solutions of the given equation.

(viii) Only $-\sqrt{5}$ is the solution of the given equation.

6. **Hint** Let one root be α, so other will be $\frac{1}{\alpha}$.

Now, $\alpha\times\frac{1}{\alpha}=\frac{k}{3}$ $\left[\because \text{product of roots}=\frac{c}{a}\right]$

$\Rightarrow$ $1=k/3 \Rightarrow k=3$

7. (i) **Hint** Do same as Example 3. **Ans.** $k=-0.3$ or 0.3

(ii) **Hint** Do same as Example 3. **Ans.** $a=-\frac{9}{4}$

(iii) **Hint** Do same as Example 3. **Ans.** $k=-\frac{1}{6}$

(iv) **Hint** Do same as Example 3. **Ans.** $k=1$

(v) **Hint** Do same as Example 4. **Ans.** $a=\frac{1}{2}, b=-\frac{3}{2}$

(vi) **Hint** Do same as Example 4. **Ans.** $p=11, q=2$

(vii) **Hint** Do same as Example 4. **Ans.** $a=4, b=5$

(viii) **Hint** Do same as Example 4. **Ans.** $k=50, t=-15$

TOPIC 02 Solution of a Quadratic Equation by Factorisation

A quadratic equation can be solved using two methods; by factorisation and by quadratic formula. Here, in this topic, we will discuss the solution of quadratic equation by factorisation.

To find the solution of a quadratic equation by factorisation method, we use the following steps.

Step I Write the given equation in standard form i.e. $ax^2+bx+c=0$ (if not given in standard form) and find the value of a, b and c.

Step II Find the product of a and c and write it as a sum of its two factor such that sum is equal to b.
i.e. write $ac = p \times q$ and $p+q=b$
where, p and q are factors of ac.

Step III Put the value of b obtained from Step II in given equation and write it LHS as product of two linear factors.

Step IV Now, equate each factor to zero to get desired roots of given quadratic equation.

Example 1. **Solve the following quadratic equation by factorisation method.**

(i) $x^2-14x+24=0$ **(ii)** $x^2-8x-20=0$

(iii) $4\sqrt{3}x^2+5x-2\sqrt{3}=0$

Sol. (i) The given quadratic equation is $x^2-14x+24=0$.

On comparing with standard form of quadratic equation i.e. $ax^2+bx+c=0$, we get

$$a=1, b=-14 \text{ and } c=24$$

Here, $ac = 1\times 24 = 24$. So, factors are -12 and -2.

$\Rightarrow \quad x^2-(12+2)x+24=0 \Rightarrow x^2-12x-2x+24=0$

$\Rightarrow \quad x(x-12)-2(x-12)=0 \Rightarrow (x-2)(x-12)=0$

$\Rightarrow \quad (x-2)=0$ or $(x-12)=0 \Rightarrow x=2$ or $x=12$

Hence, the roots of the equation $x^2-14x+24$ are 2 and 12.

(ii) Given quadratic equation is $x^2-8x-20=0$, which is already in its standard form.

On comparing it with $ax^2+bx+c=0$, we get

$$a=1, b=-8 \text{ and } c=-20$$

where, $\quad ac = 1\times(-20) = -20$

Here, ac has –ve sign,

So, let $p=-10$ and $q=2$ as $p\times q=-20$ and $p+q=-8$

$\therefore \quad x^2-8x-20=0 \Rightarrow x^2-10x+2x-20=0$

$\Rightarrow \quad x(x-10)+2(x-10)=0 \Rightarrow (x-10)(x+2)=0$

Now, put $x-10=0$ or $x+2=0 \Rightarrow x=10$ or $x=-2$

Thus, 10 and -2 are the required roots of a given quadratic equation.

(iii) Given, $4\sqrt{3}x^2+5x-2\sqrt{3}=0$.

On comparing with standard form of quadratic equation $ax^2+bx+c=0$, we get

$$a=4\sqrt{3},\ b=5 \text{ and } c=-2\sqrt{3}$$

Here, $ac = 4\sqrt{3}\times(-2\sqrt{3}) = -24$

Then, the factors are 8 and -3.

$\Rightarrow \quad 4\sqrt{3}x^2+(8-3)x-2\sqrt{3}=0$

$\Rightarrow \quad 4\sqrt{3}x^2+8x-3x-2\sqrt{3}=0$

$\Rightarrow \quad 4x(\sqrt{3}x+2)-\sqrt{3}(\sqrt{3}x+2)=0$

$\Rightarrow \quad (4x-\sqrt{3})(\sqrt{3}x+2)=0$

$\Rightarrow \quad 4x-\sqrt{3}=0$

or $\quad \sqrt{3}x+2=0$

$\Rightarrow \quad x=\dfrac{\sqrt{3}}{4}$

or $\quad x=\dfrac{-2}{\sqrt{3}}$

Hence, the roots of equation $4\sqrt{3}x^2+5x-2\sqrt{3}=0$ are $\dfrac{\sqrt{3}}{4}$ and $\dfrac{-2}{\sqrt{3}}$.

Example 2. **Using factorisation, solve the following quadratic equation** $\dfrac{x-1}{x-2}+\dfrac{x-3}{x-4}=3\dfrac{1}{3}$.

Sol. Given, $\quad \dfrac{x-1}{x-2}+\dfrac{x-3}{x-4}=3\dfrac{1}{3}$

$\Rightarrow \quad \dfrac{(x-1)(x-4)+(x-3)(x-2)}{(x-2)(x-4)}=\dfrac{10}{3}$

$\Rightarrow \quad \dfrac{x^2-4x-x+4+x^2-2x-3x+6}{x^2-4x-2x+8}=\dfrac{10}{3}$

$\Rightarrow \quad \dfrac{2x^2-10x+10}{x^2-6x+8}=\dfrac{10}{3}$

$\Rightarrow \quad \dfrac{2[x^2-5x+5]}{x^2-6x+8}=\dfrac{10}{3}$

$\Rightarrow \quad 3(x^2-5x+5)=5(x^2-6x+8)$

[dividing both sides by 2 and cross-multiplying]

$\Rightarrow \quad 3x^2-15x+15=5x^2-30x+40$

$\Rightarrow \quad 5x^2-30x+40-3x^2+15x-15=0$

$\Rightarrow \quad 2x^2-15x+25=0$

$\Rightarrow \quad 2x^2-10x-5x+25=0$ [by factorisation]

$\Rightarrow \quad 2x(x-5)-5(x-5)=0 \Rightarrow (x-5)(2x-5)=0$

$\Rightarrow \quad x-5=0$ or $2x-5=0 \Rightarrow x=5$ or $x=\dfrac{5}{2}$

Hence, the roots of the given quadratic equation are 5 and $\dfrac{5}{2}$.

Try These 4.2

Directions (Q.Nos. 1-25) Solve each of the following equations by factorisation.

1. $t^2+3t-10=0$
2. $x^2-10x+21=0$
3. $8x^2-22x-21=0$
4. $15y^2=41y-14$
5. $6x^2+40=31x$
6. $21x^2-2x+\frac{1}{21}=0$
7. $3x^2+2\sqrt{5}x-5=0$
8. $x^2-(\sqrt{2}+1)x+\sqrt{2}=0$
9. $\sqrt{3}x^2+9x+6\sqrt{3}=0$
10. $4\sqrt{5}x^2+3x-2\sqrt{5}=0$
11. $\sqrt{3}x^2-2\sqrt{2}x-2\sqrt{3}=0$
12. $5x+\frac{1}{x}=6;\ x\neq 0$
13. $\frac{1}{x-3}-\frac{1}{x+5}=\frac{1}{6};\ x\neq 3,-5$
14. $\frac{2x}{x-3}+\frac{1}{2x+3}+\frac{3x+9}{(x-3)(2x+3)}=0,\ x\neq 3,-\frac{3}{2}$
15. $\frac{x+1}{x-1}-\frac{x-1}{x+1}=\frac{5}{6};\ x\neq -1,1$
16. $\frac{2x}{x-4}+\frac{2x-5}{x-3}=\frac{25}{3};\ x\neq 4,3$
17. $\frac{x+3}{x+2}=\frac{3x-7}{2x-3}$
18. $\frac{p}{x-q}+\frac{q}{x-p}=2;\ x\neq p,q$
19. $2\left(\frac{x+2}{2x-3}\right)-9\left(\frac{2x-3}{x+2}\right)=3$
20. $2\left(\frac{2x-1}{x+3}\right)-3\left(\frac{x+3}{2x-1}\right)=5$
21. $\frac{21}{x^2}-\frac{29}{x}-10=0;\ x\neq 0$
22. $\frac{2}{x^2}-\frac{5}{x}+2=0$
23. $x^2+5x-(a^2+a-6)=0$
24. $4x^2-4a^2x+(a^4-b^4)=0$
25. $6a^2x^2-7abx-3b^2=0,\ a\neq 0$

Answers

1. **Hint** Do same as Example 1 (i). **Ans.** $-5, 2$
2. **Hint** Do same as Example 1 (i). **Ans.** $3, 7$
3. **Hint** Do same as Example 1 (i). **Ans.** $\frac{7}{2}, \frac{-3}{4}$
4. **Hint** Do same as Example 1 (i). **Ans.** $\frac{7}{3}, \frac{2}{5}$
5. **Hint** Do same as Example 1 (i). **Ans.** $\frac{8}{3}, \frac{5}{2}$
6. **Hint** Multiply the equation with 21, to eliminate the denominator. Then, refer Example 1. **Ans.** $\frac{1}{21}, \frac{1}{21}$
7. **Hint** $ac=-15$, take factors as $3\sqrt{5}$ and $-\sqrt{5}$. **Ans.** $-\sqrt{5}, \frac{\sqrt{5}}{3}$
8. **Hint** Simplify and take common. **Ans.** $\sqrt{2}, 1$
9. **Hint** $ac=(\sqrt{3})(6\sqrt{3})=18$, take factors such that their sum should be 9 and product is 18. **Ans.** $-\sqrt{3}, -2\sqrt{3}$
10. **Hint** Do same as Example 1 (iii). **Ans.** $\frac{-2}{\sqrt{5}}, \frac{\sqrt{5}}{4}$
11. **Hint** Do same as Example 1 (iii). **Ans.** $-\frac{\sqrt{2}}{\sqrt{3}}, \sqrt{6}$
12. **Hint** Multiply the equation by x, then the required equation will be $5x^2-6x+1=0$. **Ans.** $1, \frac{1}{5}$
13. **Hint** Take LCM and cross multiply, to form a quadratic equation. Required equation will be $x^2+2x-63=0$. **Ans.** $-9, 7$
14. **Hint** Do same as Example 2. **Ans.** -1
15. **Hint** Do same as Example 2. **Ans.** $5, \frac{-1}{5}$
16. **Hint** Do same as Example 2. **Ans.** $6, \frac{40}{13}$
17. **Hint** Cross multiply and simplify, the required equation will be $x^2-4x-5=0$. **Ans.** $5, -1$
18. **Hint** Do same as Question 13, required equation will be $2x^2-3x(p+q)+(p+q)^2=0$. **Ans.** $p+q, \frac{p+q}{2}$
19. **Hint** Let $\frac{x+2}{2x-3}=y$, then
$2y-\frac{9}{y}=3 \Rightarrow 2y^2-3y-9=0 \Rightarrow y=3$ or $2y=-3$
Now, $y=3 \Rightarrow \frac{x+2}{2x-3}=3 \Rightarrow x=\frac{11}{5}$
and $2y=-3 \Rightarrow \frac{2(x+2)}{2x-3}=-3 \Rightarrow x=\frac{5}{8}$ **Ans.** $\frac{11}{5}, \frac{5}{8}$
20. **Hint** Do same as Question 19. **Ans.** $\frac{-1}{5}, -10$
21. **Hint** Multiply the equation by $-x^2$, required equation will be $10x^2+29x-21=0$. **Ans.** $\frac{-7}{2}, \frac{3}{5}$
22. **Hint** Do same as Question 21. **Ans.** $2, \frac{1}{2}$
23. **Hint** First factorise, $a^2+a-6=(a-2)(a+3)$, then factorise $x^2+5x-(a-2)(a+3)=0$ **Ans.** $-(a+3), (a-2)$
24. **Hint** First factorise, $a^4-b^4=(a^2-b^2)(a^2+b^2)$, then factorize $4x^2-4a^2x+(a^2-b^2)(a^2+b^2)=0$. **Ans.** $\frac{a^2-b^2}{2}, \frac{a^2+b^2}{2}$
25. **Hint** Do same as Question 24. **Ans.** $-\frac{b}{3a}, \frac{3b}{2a}$

TOPIC 03 Solution of a Quadratic Equation by Quadratic Formula

In the last topic, we learnt to solve quadratic equation by factorisation method. This method for solving quadratic equation is not suited to solve all quadratic equations. Therefore, we will learn one more method of solving quadratic equations, which is known as **quadratic formula**. This formula is stated as if $b^2 - 4ac \geq 0$, then the roots of the quadratic equation $ax^2 + bx + c = 0, a \neq 0$ are given by

$$x = \frac{-b \pm \sqrt{b^2 - 4ac}}{2a} \text{ or } x = \frac{-b \pm \sqrt{D}}{2a}$$

where, $D = b^2 - 4ac$ is known as **discriminant**. This result is known as **quadratic formula** or **Sridharacharya formula**.

Example 1. **Solve $12x^2 + 5x - 3 = 0$ by quadratic formula.**

Sol. Given quadratic equation is $12x^2 + 5x - 3 = 0$.

On comparing the given equation with $ax^2 + bx + c = 0$, we get $a = 12, b = 5$ and $c = -3$

On substituting the values of $a = 12, b = 5$ and $c = -3$ in quadratic formula,

$$x = \frac{-b \pm \sqrt{b^2 - 4ac}}{2a}, \text{ we get}$$

$$x = \frac{-5 \pm \sqrt{(5)^2 - 4 \times 12 \times (-3)}}{2 \times 12}$$

$$\Rightarrow \quad x = \frac{-5 \pm \sqrt{25 + 144}}{24} = \frac{-5 \pm \sqrt{169}}{24} = \frac{-5 \pm 13}{24}$$

Now, $x = \frac{-5 + 13}{24} = \frac{8}{24} = \frac{1}{3}$ [taking +ve sign]

Or $x = \frac{-5 - 13}{24} = -\frac{18}{24} = -\frac{3}{4}$ [taking –ve sign]

Hence, the roots of the given equation are $\frac{1}{3}$ and $-\frac{3}{4}$.

Example 2. **Using the quadratic formula, solve the quadratic equation.**

$$\sqrt{3}x^2 + 10x + 7\sqrt{3} = 0$$ CBSE 2025 (Basic)

Sol. The given equation is $\sqrt{3}x^2 + 10x + 7\sqrt{3} = 0$.

On comparing with $ax^2 + bx + c = 0$, we get

$$a = \sqrt{3}, b = 10 \text{ and } c = 7\sqrt{3}$$

On substituting the values of a, b and c in the quadratic formula,

$$x = \frac{-b \pm \sqrt{b^2 - 4ac}}{2a} = \frac{-10 \pm \sqrt{(10)^2 - 4 \times \sqrt{3} \times 7\sqrt{3}}}{2 \times \sqrt{3}}$$

$$= \frac{-10 \pm \sqrt{100 - 84}}{2\sqrt{3}} = \frac{-10 \pm \sqrt{16}}{2\sqrt{3}} = \frac{-10 \pm 4}{2\sqrt{3}}$$

$$\Rightarrow \quad x = \frac{-10 + 4}{2\sqrt{3}} \text{ or } x = \frac{-10 - 4}{2\sqrt{3}}$$

$$\Rightarrow \quad x = \frac{-6}{2\sqrt{3}} \text{ or } x = \frac{-14}{2\sqrt{3}}$$

$$\Rightarrow \quad x = -\sqrt{3} \text{ or } x = \frac{-7}{\sqrt{3}}$$

Hence, $-\sqrt{3}$ and $\frac{-7}{\sqrt{3}}$ are the required solutions of the given equation.

Relationship between Discriminant and Nature of Roots

The nature of roots depends upon the value of the discriminant D. Since, D can be zero, positive or negative, so three cases may arise.

Case I **When $D = 0$** i.e. $b^2 - 4ac = 0$.

If $D = b^2 - 4ac = 0$, then $x = \frac{-b \pm 0}{2a}$

$$\Rightarrow \quad x = -\frac{b}{2a}, -\frac{b}{2a}$$

So, the quadratic equation has **two equal real roots** or repeated roots or coincident roots.

Case II **When $D > 0$** i.e. $b^2 - 4ac > 0$.

If $D = b^2 - 4ac > 0$, then $x = \frac{-b + \sqrt{D}}{2a}$ and $\frac{-b - \sqrt{D}}{2a}$

So, the quadratic equation has **two distinct real roots.**

Case III **When $D < 0$** i.e. $b^2 - 4ac < 0$.

If $D = b^2 - 4ac < 0$, then $\sqrt{D}$ can not be evaluated as there is no real number whose square root is $b^2 - 4ac$.

So, the quadratic equation has **no real roots** or **imaginary roots** or we can say that roots of the quadratic equation does not exist.

These all three cases can be explained using the flow chart.

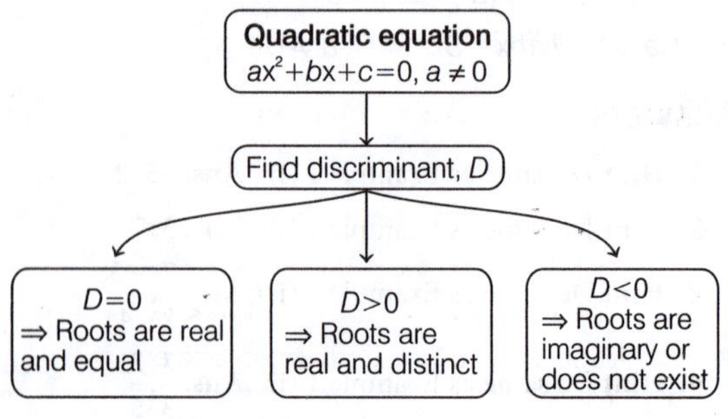

Example 3. **Find the discriminant of the quadratic equation $x^2 - 4x + 1 = 0$.**

Sol. Given quadratic equation is $x^2 - 4x + 1 = 0$.

On comparing with $ax^2 + bx + c = 0$, we get

$$a = 1, b = -4 \text{ and } c = 1$$

Now, discriminant $(D) = \sqrt{b^2 - 4ac} = \sqrt{(-4)^2 - 4 \times 1 \times 1}$

$$= \sqrt{16-4} = \sqrt{12} = \sqrt{2 \times 2 \times 3} = 2\sqrt{3}$$

Example 4. **Find the nature of roots of the following quadratic equations. If the real roots exist, then also find the roots.**

(i) $4x^2 + 12x + 9 = 0$ **(ii) $3x^2 + 5x - 7 = 0$**

(iii) $7y^2 - 4y + 5 = 0$

Sol. (i) Given quadratic equation is $4x^2 + 12x + 9 = 0$

On comparing with $ax^2 + bx + c = 0$, we get

$$a = 4, b = 12 \text{ and } c = 9$$

Now, $D = b^2 - 4ac = (12)^2 - 4(4)(9) = 144 - 144 = 0$

Since, $D = 0$, so given quadratic equation has two equal and real roots which are given by

$$x = \frac{-b \pm \sqrt{D}}{2a} = \frac{-12 \pm 0}{2(4)} = \frac{-12 \pm 0}{8}$$

$$\Rightarrow \quad x = \frac{-12+0}{8} \text{ or } x = \frac{-12-0}{8}$$

$$\Rightarrow \quad x = -\frac{3}{2} \text{ or } x = -\frac{3}{2}$$

Hence, the roots are $\frac{-3}{2}$ and $-\frac{3}{2}$.

(ii) Given quadratic equation is $3x^2 + 5x - 7 = 0$

On comparing with $ax^2 + bx + c = 0$, we get

$$a = 3, b = 5 \text{ and } c = -7$$

Now, $D = b^2 - 4ac = (5)^2 - 4(3)(-7)$

$$= 25 + 84 = 109$$

Since, $D > 0$, so given quadratic equation has two distinct real roots which are given by

$$x = \frac{-b \pm \sqrt{D}}{2a} = \frac{-5 \pm \sqrt{109}}{2(3)}$$

$$\Rightarrow \quad x = \frac{-5 + \sqrt{109}}{6} \quad \text{[taking +ve sign]}$$

$$\text{or} \quad x = \frac{-5 - \sqrt{109}}{6} \quad \text{[taking −ve sign]}$$

Hence, the roots are $\frac{-5 + \sqrt{109}}{6}$ and $\frac{-5 - \sqrt{109}}{6}$.

(iii) Given quadratic equation is $7y^2 - 4y + 5 = 0$

On comparing with $ay^2 + by + c = 0$, we get

$$a = 7, b = -4 \text{ and } c = 5$$

Now, $D = b^2 - 4ac = (-4)^2 - 4(7)(5)$

$$= 16 - 140 = -124 < 0$$

Since, $D < 0$, so given quadratic equation has no real roots.

Method to Determine The Value of Unknown when Nature of Roots is Given

If nature of roots of a quadratic equation is given and quadratic equation involves an unknown, then to find the value of unknown, first we find the value of discriminant in terms of unknown. After that use the given condition i.e. $D > 0$ or $D = 0$ or $D < 0$ and simplify it.

Note it

- $x^2 - a^2 > 0 \Rightarrow x < -a$ or $x > a$
- $x^2 - a^2 \geq 0 \Rightarrow x \leq -a$ or $x \geq a$
- $x^2 - a^2 < 0 \Rightarrow -a < x < a$
- $x^2 - a^2 \leq 0 \Rightarrow -a \leq x \leq a$
- $(x-a)(x-b) > 0$ and $a < b \Rightarrow x < a$ or $x > b$
- $(x-a)(x-b) \geq 0$ and $a < b \Rightarrow x \leq a$ or $x \geq b$
- $(x-a)(x-b) < 0$ and $a < b \Rightarrow a < x < b$
- $(x-a)(x-b) \leq 0$ and $a < b \Rightarrow a \leq x \leq b$

Example 5. **Find the value of k for which the roots of the quadratic equation $5x^2 - 10x + k = 0$ are real and equal.** CBSE 2023 (Basic)

Sol. Given quadratic equation is $5x^2 - 10x + k = 0$

On comparing with $ax^2 + bx + c = 0$, we get

$$a = 5, b = -10 \text{ and } c = k$$

Since, the roots are real and equal.

$$\therefore \quad D = b^2 - 4ac = 0 \Rightarrow (-10)^2 - 4(5)(k) = 0$$

$$\Rightarrow \quad 100 - 20k = 0 \Rightarrow k = 5$$

Example 6. **For what values of k, the roots of the equation $x^2 + 4x + k = 0$ are real?** CBSE 2019

Sol. Given quadratic equation is $x^2 + 4x + k = 0$

On comparing with $ax^2 + bx + c = 0$, we get

$$a = 1, b = 4 \text{ and } c = k$$

Now, $D = b^2 - 4ac = (4)^2 - 4 \times 1 \times k = 16 - 4k$

Since, roots of given equation are real.

$$\therefore \quad D \geq 0 \Rightarrow 16 - 4k \geq 0$$

$$\Rightarrow \quad 4 - k \geq 0 \Rightarrow 4 \geq k \text{ or } k \leq 4$$

Example 7. **Find the values of k for which the equation $9x^2 + 3kx + 4 = 0$ has real roots.**

Sol. Given quadratic equation is $9x^2 + 3kx + 4 = 0$

On comparing with $ax^2 + bx + c = 0$, we get

$$a = 9, b = 3k \text{ and } c = 4$$

Now, $D = b^2 - 4ac = (3k)^2 - 4(9)(4) = 9k^2 - 144$

Since, roots of given equation are real.

$$\therefore \quad D \geq 0$$

$$\Rightarrow \quad 9k^2 - 144 \geq 0 \Rightarrow 9(k^2 - 16) \geq 0$$

$$\therefore \quad k^2 - 16 \geq 0 \quad [\because 9 \neq 0]$$

$$\Rightarrow \quad k^2 - (4)^2 \geq 0$$

$$\Rightarrow \quad (k-4)(k+4) \geq 0 \quad [\because a^2 - b^2 = (a-b)(a+b)]$$

$$\Rightarrow \quad k \leq -4 \text{ or } k \geq 4 \Rightarrow -4 \geq k \geq 4$$

Try These 4.3

Directions (Q.Nos. 1-4) Find the roots of the following quadratic equations by applying the quadratic formula :

1. $\frac{14}{x+3} - 1 = \frac{5}{x+1}; x \neq -3, -1$
2. $abx^2 + (b^2 - ac)x - bc = 0, a, b \neq 0$
3. $3a^2x^2 + 8abx + 4b^2 = 0, a \neq 0$
4. $\frac{1}{2}x^2 - \sqrt{11}x + 1 = 0$
5. **Write the discriminant of the following**
   (i) $3x^2 - 4x + 7 = 0$
   (ii) $\sqrt{3}x^2 - 2\sqrt{2}x - 2\sqrt{3} = 0$
   (iii) $2x^2 + 3x + m = 0$
   (iv) $x^2 + x + 7 = 0$
   (v) $(4x-3)^2 + 20x = 11$
   (vi) $4a^2x^2 + 8abx + 4b^2 = 0$
   (vii) $1 = \frac{13x}{12x^2 + 3}$
   (viii) $(3x+1)^2 + (x-2)^2 = 50$
6. **If the discriminant of the equation $5x^2 - sx + 4 = 0$ is 1, then find the value of s.**
7. **Determine the nature of the roots of the following quadratic equations.**
   (i) $4x^2 - 2x = 3$
   (ii) $3\sqrt{3}x^2 + 10x + \sqrt{3} = 0$
   (iii) $3x^2 - 2\sqrt{15}x + 5 = 0$
   (iv) $(x+3)(x-1) = 3\left(x - \frac{1}{3}\right)$
   (v) $4x^2 - 4a^2x + a^4 - b^4 = 0$ CBSE 2025 (Basic)
8. **Find the value of k for which following equation has real and equal roots**
   (i) $3x^2 + kx + 3 = 0$ CBSE 2019
   (ii) $x^2 - (2k+1)x + k^2 = 0$
   (iii) $kx^2 - 2\sqrt{5}x + 4 = 0$
   (iv) $x^2 - 2x(1 + 3k) + 7(3 + 2k) = 0$
9. **Determine the value(s) of m for which the equation $x^2 + m(4x + m - 1) + 2 = 0$ has real roots.**
10. **For what value(s) of n, the equation $(n + 3)x^2 - (5 - n)x + 1 = 0$ has coincident roots?**
11. **If roots of the equation $(c^2 - ab)x^2 - 2(a^2 - bc)x + b^2 - ac = 0$ are equal, then prove that either $a = 0$ or $a^3 + b^3 + c^3 = 3abc$.**
12. **For which condition, the quadratic equation $(a^2 + b^2)x^2 - 2(ac + bd)x + (c^2 + d^2) = 0$ has equal roots.**

Answers

1. **Hint** First simplify the given equation, then do same as Example 1. **Ans.** 1, 4
2. **Hint** Do same as Example 1. **Ans.** $\frac{c}{b}, \frac{-b}{a}$
3. **Hint** Do same as Example 1. **Ans.** $\frac{-2b}{a}, \frac{-2b}{3a}$
4. **Hint** Do same as Example 2. **Ans.** $-3 + \sqrt{11}, 3 + \sqrt{11}$
5. **Hint** Compare with standard quadratic equation $ax^2 + bx + c = 0; a \neq 0$, to obtain the value of $D = b^2 - 4ac$.
   Ans. (i) -68 (ii) 32 (iii) $9 - 8m$ (iv) -27 (v) 144 (vi) 0 (vii) 25 (viii) 1804
6. **Hint** $b^2 - 4ac = 1$
   $\Rightarrow \quad s^2 - 80 = 1 \Rightarrow s^2 = 81$
   Ans. $s = -9$ or $s = 9$
7. **Hint** Do same as Example 4. **Ans.** (i) Real and distinct. (ii) Real and distinct. (iii) Real and equal. (iv) Real and distinct. (v) Real and distinct
8. **Hint** For real and equal roots, we take $D (= b^2 - 4ac) = 0$
   Ans. (i) $k = \pm 6$ (ii) $k = \frac{-1}{4}$
   (iii) $k = \frac{5}{4}$ (iv) $k = 2$ or $\frac{-10}{9}$
9. **Hint** $x^2 + m(4x + m - 1) + 2 = 0$
   $\Rightarrow x^2 + 4mx + (m^2 - m + 2) = 0.$
   Now, for real roots $D \geq 0$
   Ans. $m \leq -1$ or $m \geq \frac{2}{3}$
10. **Hint** Coincident roots means equal roots i.e $D = 0$.
    Ans. 1 or 13
11. **Hint** For equal roots, $D = 0$.
12. **Hint** Compare given equation with $Ax^2 + Bx + C = 0$ and apply $D = B^2 - 4AC = 0$.
    Ans. $ad = bc$

TOPIC 04 Word Problems and Their Solutions

Many real life situation can be expressed as quadratic equations. The solution of such quadratic equations gives us the solution(s) to the problem.

Method to Solve Word Problems

To solve such problems, working steps are given below.

Step I First, consider the first quantity as a variable (say x) and then find the other quantities in terms of x by using the given condition.

Step II According to the given condition, write the equation in the quantities which is obtained from Step I.

Step III Simplify the equation obtained in Step II to get quadratic equation.

Step IV Now, simplify the quadratic equation by any one of the methods i.e. factorisation and quadratic formula to obtain the value(s) of variable x.

Step V Further check whether the value(s) of variable x, satisfies the given condition or not.

Step VI Find the values of the quantities. Also, find the values of other information, if asked in the question.

Different Types of Word Problems

Here, we will discuss various types of word problems under different types and analyse, how to represent them as a quadratic equation.

Type I Word Problems Based on Numbers

Example 1. **The sum of the squares of three consecutive natural numbers is 110. Determine the numbers.**

Sol. Let three consecutive natural numbers be $x, x+1$ and $x+2$.

According to the question,

$$x^2+(x+1)^2+(x+2)^2=110$$

$$\Rightarrow \quad x^2+x^2+2x+1+x^2+4x+4=110 \quad [\because (a+b)^2=a^2+2ab+b^2]$$

$$\Rightarrow \quad 3x^2+6x+5=110$$

$$\Rightarrow \quad 3x^2+6x-105=0$$

$$\Rightarrow \quad 3(x^2+2x-35)=0$$

$$\Rightarrow \quad x^2+2x-35=0 \quad [\because 3\neq 0]$$

which is the required quadratic equation.

Now, by factorisation, we get

$$x^2+7x-5x-35=0$$

$$\Rightarrow \quad x(x+7)-5(x+7)=0$$

$$\Rightarrow \quad (x+7)(x-5)=0$$

$$\Rightarrow \quad x+7=0 \text{ or } x-5=0$$

$$\Rightarrow \quad x=-7 \text{ or } x=5$$

But $x\neq -7$ because x is natural number.

$\therefore x=5$

Hence, the three consecutive natural numbers are $5, 5+1$ and $5+2$ i.e. 5, 6 and 7.

Example 2. **Divide 16 into two parts such that twice the square of the greater part, exceeds the square of the smaller part by 164.** CBSE 2023 (Basic)

Sol. Let the larger and smaller parts be x and y, respectively.

According to the question,

$$x+y=16 \quad \ldots(\text{i})$$

and
$$2x^2=y^2+164 \quad \ldots(\text{ii})$$

From Eq. (i), we get

$$x=16-y \quad \ldots(\text{iii})$$

From Eqs. (ii) and (iii), we get

$$2(16-y)^2=y^2+164$$

$$\Rightarrow \quad 2(256-32y+y^2)=y^2+164$$

$$\Rightarrow \quad 512-64y+2y^2=y^2+164$$

$$\Rightarrow \quad y^2-64y+348=0$$

$$\Rightarrow \quad y^2-(58+6)y+348=0$$

$$\Rightarrow \quad y^2-58y-6y+348=0$$

$$\Rightarrow \quad (y-58)(y-6)=0$$

$$\Rightarrow \quad y-58=0 \text{ or } y-6=0 \Rightarrow y=6 \quad [\because y<16]$$

On putting the value of y in Eq. (iii), we get

$$x=16-6=10$$

Hence, the two natural numbers are 6 and 10.

Example 3. **"John and Janvi together have 35 marbles. Both of them lost 5 marbles each and the product of the number of marbles they now have is 150. Find out how many marbles they had to start with?**

Sol. Given, John and Janvi together have 35 marbles.

Let John had x marbles.

Then, number of marbles Janvi had $=35-x$

$\because$ Both of them lost 5 marbles each.

$\therefore$ The number of marbles John had $=x-5$

and the number of marbles Janvi had $=35-x-5=30-x$

Now, product of the number of marbles $=150$

$$\therefore \quad (x-5)(30-x)=150$$

$$\Rightarrow \quad 30x-x^2-150+5x=150$$

$$\Rightarrow \quad -x^2+35x-150-150=0$$

$$\Rightarrow \quad -x^2+35x-300=0$$

$$\Rightarrow \quad x^2-35x+300=0 \quad [\text{multiplying by } (-1)]$$

which is a quadratic equation.

Now, by factorisation method, we get

$$x^2 - 20x - 15x + 300 = 0$$

$\Rightarrow \quad x(x-20) - 15(x-20) = 0$

$\Rightarrow \quad (x-20)(x-15) = 0$

$\Rightarrow \quad x = 20 \text{ or } x = 15$

When John has 20 marbles, then Janvi has $= 35 - 20 = 15$ marbles

When John has 15 marbles, then Janvi has $= 35 - 15 = 20$ marbles

Type II Word Problems Based on Age

Example 4. 1 yr ago, a man was 8 times as old as his son. Now, his age is equal to the square of his son's age. Find their present ages.

Sol. Let present age of his son be x yr.

1 yr ago, his son's age $= (x-1)$ yr

1 yr ago, man's age $= 8(x-1)$ yr $= (8x-8)$ yr

Present age of man $= (8x-8+1)$ yr $= (8x-7)$ yr

According to the question,

$$8x - 7 = x^2 \Rightarrow x^2 - 8x + 7 = 0$$

which is a quadratic equation.

Now, $\quad x^2 - 7x - x + 7 = 0$ [by factorisation]

$\Rightarrow \quad x(x-7) - 1(x-7) = 0$

$\Rightarrow \quad (x-7)(x-1) = 0$

$\Rightarrow \quad x - 7 = 0 \text{ or } x - 1 = 0$

$\Rightarrow \quad x = 7 \text{ or } x = 1$

But $x = 1$ is not possible because if $x = 1$, then present age of the son and father are same. So, $x = 7$.

Hence, the present age of his son $= 7$ yr and present age of man $= 8 \times 7 - 7 = 49$ yr.

Example 5. The sum of the reciprocals of Varun's age (in years) 3 yr ago and 5 yr from now is $\frac{1}{3}$. Find his present age. CBSE 2023 (Basic)

Sol. Let the present age of Varun be x yr.

Varun's age 3 yr ago $= (x-3)$ yr

Varun's age 5 yr from now $= (x+5)$ yr

According to the question,

$$\frac{1}{x-3} + \frac{1}{x+5} = \frac{1}{3} \Rightarrow \frac{x+5+x-3}{(x-3)(x+5)} = \frac{1}{3}$$

$\Rightarrow \quad 3(2x+2) = x^2 + 2x - 15$

$\Rightarrow \quad 6x + 6 = x^2 + 2x - 15$

$\Rightarrow \quad x^2 - 4x - 21 = 0$

$\Rightarrow \quad (x-7)(x+3) = 0$ [by factorisation]

$\Rightarrow \quad x = 7$ [$\because x = -3$ not possible]

$\therefore$ Varun's present age $= 7$ yr

Type III Word Problems Based on Time, Distance and Speed

Example 6. A train travels at a certain average speed for a distance of 54 km and then travels a distance of 63 km at an average speed of 6 km/h more than the first speed. If it takes 3h to complete the journey, what was its first average speed? CBSE 2023 (Standard)

Sol. Let the first average speed of train be x km/h.

Time taken by train to cover 54 km with first average speed $= \frac{54}{x}$ h

Time taken by train to cover 63 km with increased speed $= \frac{63}{x+6}$ h

According to the question,

$$\frac{54}{x} + \frac{63}{x+6} = 3$$

$\Rightarrow \quad 54(x+6) + 63x = 3x(x+6)$

$\Rightarrow \quad 18(x+6) + 21x = x(x+6)$

$\Rightarrow \quad 18x + 108 + 21x = x^2 + 6x$

$\Rightarrow \quad x^2 - 33x - 108 = 0$

$\Rightarrow \quad x = \frac{33 \pm \sqrt{1089 + 432}}{2} = \frac{33 \pm 39}{2}$

$\Rightarrow \quad x = \frac{33+39}{2} \text{ or } x = \frac{33-39}{2}$

$x = 36 \text{ or } x = -3$

Since, speed can't be negative

Hence, first average speed is 36 km/h.

Example 7. A motor boat whose speed is 18 km/h in still water takes 1 h more to go 24 km upstream, than to return to the same point. Find the speed of the stream and total time of the journey. CBSE 2023 (Basic)

Sol. Given, the speed of the boat in still water = 18 km/h.

Let the speed of the stream be x km/h.

Speed of the boat for upstream = Speed of boat in still water − Speed of the stream

$\therefore$ Speed of the boat for upstream $= (18 - x)$ km/h

Speed of the boat for downstream = Speed of boat in still water + Speed of the stream

$\therefore$ Speed of the boat for downstream $= (18 + x)$ km/h

Time for upstream journey = Time for downstream journey + 1h

$$\therefore \frac{\text{Distance covered in upstream}}{\text{Speed of the boat for upstream}} = \frac{\text{Distance covered in downstream}}{\text{Speed of the boat for downstream}} + 1\text{h}$$

$$\Rightarrow \quad \frac{24 \text{ km}}{(18-x) \text{ km/h}} = \frac{24 \text{ km}}{(18+x) \text{ km/h}} + 1 \text{ h}$$

$$\Rightarrow \frac{24}{18-x} - \frac{24}{18+x} = 1 \Rightarrow \frac{24(2x)}{(18-x)(18+x)} = 1$$

$$\Rightarrow \quad 48x = 324 - x^2$$

$$\Rightarrow \quad x^2 + 48x - 324 = 0$$

$$\Rightarrow \quad x^2 + 54x - 6x - 324 = 0$$

$$\Rightarrow \quad x(x+54) - 6(x+54) = 0$$

$$\Rightarrow \quad (x+54)(x-6) = 0$$

$$\Rightarrow \quad x = -54 \text{ or } x = 6$$

$\therefore$ $x = 6$ [$\because$ speed of the stream cannot be negative]

Thus, the speed of stream is 6 km/h.

Time for upstream journey $= \frac{24}{18-x} = \frac{24}{18-6} = \frac{24}{12} = 2$ h

Time for downstream journey $= \frac{24}{18+x} = \frac{24}{18+6} = \frac{24}{24}$

$= 1$ h

Hence, total time of the journey is 3 h.

Type IV Word Problems Based on Time and Work

Example 8. **Two pipes together can fill a tank in $\frac{15}{8}$ h. The pipe with larger diameter takes 2 h less than the pipe with smaller diameter to fill the tank separately. Find the time in which each pipe can fill the tank separately.** CBSE 2023 (Standard)

Sol. Let the tap with smaller diameter fills the tank alone in x h.

Let the tap with larger diameter fills the tank alone in $(x-2)$ h.

In 1 h, the tap with smaller diameter can fill $\frac{1}{x}$ part of the tank.

In 1 h, the tap with larger diameter can fill $\frac{1}{x-2}$ part of the tank.

The tank is filled up in $\frac{15}{8}$ h.

Thus in 1 h, the tap fill $\frac{8}{15}$ part of the tank.

$$\therefore \quad \frac{1}{x} + \frac{1}{x-2} = \frac{8}{15}$$

$$\Rightarrow \quad 15(x-2+x) = 8x(x-2)$$

$$\Rightarrow \quad 15(2x-2) = 8x^2 - 16x$$

$$\Rightarrow \quad 30x - 30 = 8x^2 - 16x$$

$$\Rightarrow \quad 8x^2 - 46x + 30 = 0$$

$$\Rightarrow \quad 4x^2 - 23x + 15 = 0$$

By quadratic formula, we get

$$x = \frac{23 \pm \sqrt{529-240}}{8} = \frac{23 \pm 17}{8}$$

$$\Rightarrow \quad x = \frac{40}{8} = 5$$

$$\text{or} \quad x = \frac{6}{8} = \frac{3}{4}$$

If $x = 5, x - 2 = 5 - 2 = 3$

If $x = \frac{3}{4}, x - 2 = \frac{3}{4} - 2 = \frac{3-8}{4} = -\frac{5}{4}$, not possible as time cannot be '– ve'.

Hence, the tap with smaller diameter fills that tank alone in 5 h and the tap with larger diameter fills the tank alone in 3 h.

Type V Word Problems Based on Geometry

Example 9. **The altitude of a right angled triangle is 7 cm less than its base. If its hypotenuse is 17 cm long, then**

(i) represent the above information in the form of a quadratic equation.

(ii) find the length of the sides of the triangle.

CBSE 2024 (Basic)

Sol. Let base of triangle $= x$ cm

Then, its altitude $= (x-7)$ cm

Hypotenuse of triangle $= 17$ cm [given]

(i) By Pythagoras theorem, we have

$$P^2 + B^2 = H^2$$

$$\Rightarrow \quad (x-7)^2 + x^2 = (17)^2$$

$$\Rightarrow \quad x^2 - 14x + 49 + x^2 = 289$$

[$\because (a-b)^2 = a^2 - 2ab + b^2$]

$$\Rightarrow 2x^2 - 14x + 49 - 289 = 0$$

$$\Rightarrow \quad x^2 - 7x - 120 = 0,$$

which is the required quadratic equation.

(ii) We have, $x^2 - 7x - 120 = 0$

By spliting the middle term, we get

$$x^2 - 15x + 8x - 120 = 0$$

$$\Rightarrow x(x-15) + 8(x-15) = 0$$

$$\Rightarrow \quad (x-15)(x+8) = 0$$

$$\Rightarrow \quad x - 15 = 0 \text{ or } x + 8 = 0$$

$$\Rightarrow \quad x = 15 \text{ or } x = -8$$

But the sides of triangle cannot be negative.

$$\therefore \quad x = 15 \text{ cm}$$

Thus, base of triangle $= x = 15$ cm

and altitude of triangle $= (x-7)$

$= (15-7)$ cm

$= 8$ cm

Type VI Word Problems Based on Mensuration

Example 10. A circular garden has a concentric circular fountain area with centre O. The distance between the circumference of the fountain and that of the garden is 5 m as shown in the figure below. The height of the fountain OP is 5 times the radius of the fountain.

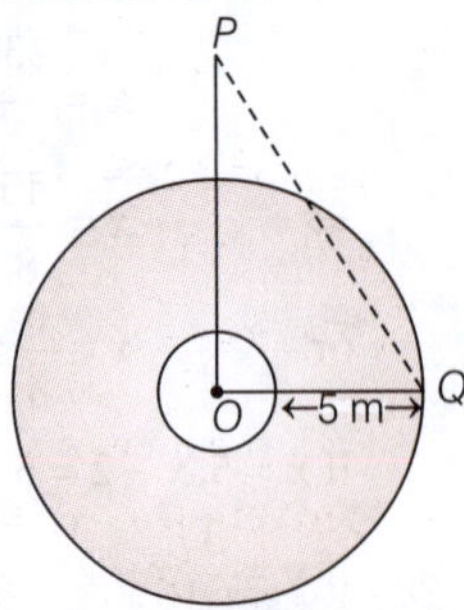

Find the radius of the fountain if the shortest distance between the top of the fountain and the circumference of the garden is 17 m. Show your work.

CBSE QB

Sol. Let the radius of fountain be r metres.

$\therefore OP = 5r$ m and $OQ = (r+5)$ m

In figure, ΔOPQ is a right angled triangle because height of fountain is always perpendicular to the radius of circular fountain area.

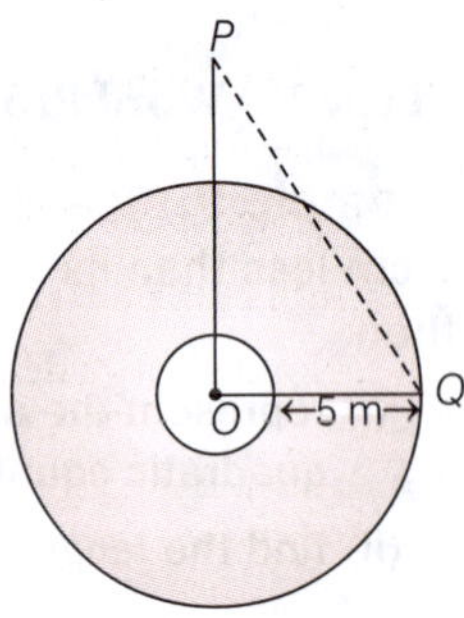

$\therefore$ In ΔOPQ, we have

$$PQ^2 = (OP)^2 + (OQ)^2 \quad \text{[by Pythagoras theorem]}$$

$$\Rightarrow (17)^2 = (5r)^2 + (r+5)^2 \quad [\because PQ = 17 \text{ m given}]$$

$$\Rightarrow 289 = 25r^2 + r^2 + 25 + 10r$$

$$\Rightarrow 26r^2 + 10r - 264 = 0$$

$$\Rightarrow 13r^2 + 5r - 132 = 0$$

Now, using quadratic formula, we get

$$r = \frac{-5 \pm \sqrt{25 + 4 \times 13 \times 132}}{26}$$

$$\Rightarrow r = \frac{-5 \pm \sqrt{6889}}{26} \Rightarrow r = 3 \text{ or } \frac{-44}{13}$$

$$\Rightarrow r = 3 \quad [\because r \text{ cannot be negative}]$$

Hence, the radius of the fountain is 3 m.

Type VII Word Problems Based on Cost Price and Selling Price

Example 11. A dealer sells a toy for ₹ 24 and gains as much per cent as the cost price of the toy. Find the cost price of the toy.

> Here, we have to find out the cost price (CP) of the toy.
> So, we assume it ₹ x and use the formulae,
> $\text{Gain} = \frac{\text{Gain \%} \times \text{CP}}{100}$ and SP = CP + Gain

Sol. Let the cost price (CP) of the toy be ₹ x.

Then, gain % = Cost price [given]

$\therefore$ Gain % $= x$

$$\therefore \quad \text{Gain} = ₹\left(\frac{\text{Gain \%} \times \text{CP}}{100}\right)$$

$$\Rightarrow \quad \text{Gain} = ₹\left(\frac{x \times x}{100}\right) = ₹\left(\frac{x^2}{100}\right)$$

Now, SP = CP + Gain

$$\therefore \quad 24 = x + \frac{x^2}{100} \Rightarrow 24 = \frac{100x + x^2}{100} \quad [\because \text{SP} = ₹\ 24]$$

$$\Rightarrow 2400 = 100x + x^2 \Rightarrow x^2 + 100x - 2400 = 0$$

$$\Rightarrow x^2 + 100x - 2400 = 0$$

$$\Rightarrow x^2 + 120x - 20x - 2400 = 0$$

$$\Rightarrow x(x+120) - 20(x+120) = 0 \Rightarrow (x+120)(x-20) = 0$$

$$\Rightarrow x = 20 \text{ or } x = -120$$

$$\therefore x = 20, -120$$

But cost price cannot be negative.

$$\therefore x = 20$$

Hence, the cost price of the toy is ₹ 20.

Try These 4.4

1. If two numbers differ by 2 and their product is 360, then find the numbers.
2. If the product of two consecutive natural numbers is 210, then determine the numbers.
3. The sum of two numbers is 15. If the sum of their reciprocals is $\frac{3}{10}$, find the two numbers. CBSE 2023 (Standard)
4. Two numbers differ by 3 and their product is 504. Find the numbers.
5. If the product of two consecutive odd numbers is 143, then find the numbers.
6. A two-digit number is such that the product of its digit is 35. When 18 is added to the number, the digits interchange their places. Find the number.
7. Divide 29 into two parts, so that the sum of the squares of the parts is 425.
8. The denominator of a fraction is 3 more than its numerator. The sum of the fraction and its reciprocal is $\frac{29}{10}$. Find the fraction.
9. 27 yr hence, Sanjay's age will be square of what it was 29 yr ago. Find his present age.
10. Some students planned a picnic. The total budget for food was ₹ 2000. But 5 students failed to attend the picnic and thus the cost of food for each member increased by ₹ 20. How many students attended the picnic and how much did each student pay for the food?
11. A shopkeeper buys a number of books for ₹ 1800. If he had bought 15 more books for the same amount, then each book would have cost him ₹ 20 less. Find how many books he bought initially. CBSE 2024 (Standard) Compartment

12. **In a flight of 600 km, an aircraft was slowed down due to bad weather. Its average speed for the trip was reduced by 200 km/h and the time of flight increased by 30 min. Find the duration of the flight.**

13. **Two pipes together can fill a bucket in 6/5 h. The larger pipe takes 1 h less than the smaller pipe to fill the bucket separately. Find the time in which each pipe can fill the bucket separately.**

14. **The perimeter of a right angled triangle is 70 units and its hypotenuse is 29 units we would like to find the length of the other sides.**

15. **A rectangular field is 20 m long and 14 m wide. There is a path of equal width all around it, having an area of 111 sq m. Find the width of the path.**

16. **The area of a right angled triangle is 480 cm^2. If the base of the triangle is 8 cm more than twice the height (altitude) of the triangle, then find the sides of the triangle.**

17. **Gaurav saved a certain amount of money in May. He saved ₹ 3540 in the month of June. He noticed that his total savings in May and June is equal to the square of his savings in May.**
Express this situation in the form of a quadratic equation and find Gaurav's savings in May. Show your work.

CBSE QB

Answers

1. **Hint** $x(x-2)=360$. **Ans.** 18, 20 or –20, –18
2. **Hint** $x(x+1)=210$. **Ans.** 14 and 15
3. **Hint** Let x and y be two numbers.
   According to the question,
   $$x+y=15 \quad \ldots(i)$$
   and $$\frac{1}{x}+\frac{1}{y}=\frac{3}{10} \Rightarrow \frac{x+y}{xy}=\frac{3}{10}$$
   $$\Rightarrow \frac{15}{xy}=\frac{3}{10} \quad \text{[using Eq. (i)]}$$
   $$\Rightarrow xy=50 \Rightarrow x=\frac{50}{y}$$
   On substituting $x=\frac{50}{y}$ in Eq. (i), we get
   $$\frac{50}{y}+y=15$$
   $$\Rightarrow 50+y^2=15y$$
   $$\Rightarrow y^2-15y+50=0.$$ **Ans.** 10 and 5.
4. **Hint** Do same as Question 1. **Ans.** 21, 24 or –24, –21
5. **Hint** The two consecutive odd numbers be x and $x+2$.
   Ans. 11 and 13 or –13 and –11.
6. Let tens digit be x and the unit digits be y.
   Then, $xy=35 \quad \ldots(i)$
   Now, $(10x+y)+18=10y+x$
   $$\Rightarrow 9y-9x=18$$
   $$\Rightarrow y-x=2 \quad \ldots(ii)$$
   From Eqs. (i) and (ii), we get
   $$\frac{35}{x}-x=2 \quad \left[\because y=\frac{35}{x}\right]$$
   $$\therefore x^2+2x-35=0$$
   Then, $x=5$
   $$\therefore y=\frac{35}{5}=7$$
   Thus, the number is $10x+y$ i.e. $10(5)+7=57$
7. **Hint** $x^2+(29-x)^2=425$. **Ans.** 16, 13
8. **Hint** Numerator $=x$, then denominator $=x+3$
   $$\frac{x}{x+3}+\frac{x+3}{x}=\frac{29}{10}$$
   $$\Rightarrow x^2+3x-10=0$$ **Ans.** $\frac{2}{5}$
9. **Hint** Let Sanjay's present age be x.
   Sanjay's age, 27 yr hence $=(x+27)$,
   29 yr ago $=(x-29)$. **Ans.** 37 yr
10. **Hint** Let the total number of students be x.
    $\therefore$ Number of students attending the picnic $=x-5$
    Then, $\frac{2000}{x-5}=\frac{2000}{x}+20 \Rightarrow x^2-5x-500=0$ **Ans.** 20, ₹ 100
11. **Hint** Let the number of books he bought $=x$
    and cost of each book = ₹ y
    $$\therefore xy=1800 \text{ and } (x+15)(y-20)=1800$$
    $$\Rightarrow (x+15)\left(\frac{1800}{x}-20\right)-1800=0$$ **Ans.** 30.
12. **Hint** $\frac{600}{x}-\frac{600}{x+1/2}=200 \Rightarrow 2x^2+x-3=0$. **Ans.** 1 h
13. **Hint** Do same as Example 8. **Ans.** 3h, 2h
14. **Hint** Let one side be x, then other side $=70-(29+x)=41-x$.
    Now, $x^2+(41-x)^2=(29)^2$ solve it. **Ans.** 20 units and 21 units.
15. **Hint** $\therefore$ Area of path = (Area of the field including the path) – (Area of the field excluding the path) **Ans.** 1.5 m
16. **Hint** Let the height be x m. Then, base $=8+2x$.
    $\therefore$ Area of right angle triangle $=\frac{1}{2}\times$ Base $\times$ Height
    Ans. 20 cm, 48 cm and 52 cm
17. Let Gaurav save money in May = ₹x
    and in June = ₹ 3540
    According to given condition,
    $$x+3540=x^2 \Rightarrow x^2-x-3540=0$$
    This is the required quadratic equation.
    Solving for x,
    $$x^2-60x+59x-3540=0$$
    $$\Rightarrow x(x-60)+59(x-60)=0 \Rightarrow (x-60)(x+59)=0$$
    $\therefore x=60$ or -59.
    Since, x cannot be negative.
    $$\therefore x=60$$
    Hence, Gaurav saves ₹ 60 in May.

NCERT FOLDER

Complete Solutions of All Exercises of NCERT Textbook

EXERCISE 4.1

Q1. Check whether the following are quadratic equations

(i) $(x+1)^2 = 2(x-3)$

(ii) $x^2 - 2x = (-2)(3-x)$

(iii) $(x-2)(x+1) = (x-1)(x+3)$

(iv) $(x-3)(2x+1) = x(x+5)$

(v) $(2x-1)(x-3) = (x+5)(x-1)$

(vi) $x^2 + 3x + 1 = (x-2)^2$

(vii) $(x+2)^3 = 2x(x^2-1)$

(viii) $x^3 - 4x^2 - x + 1 = (x-2)^3$

Sol. (i) Do same as Example 1 (ii) of Topic 1.

Ans. It is a quadratic equation.

(ii) Given equation is $x^2 - 2x = (-2)(3-x)$

$\Rightarrow \quad x^2 - 2x = -6 + 2x$

$\Rightarrow \quad x^2 - 2x - 2x + 6 = 0$

$\Rightarrow \quad x^2 - 4x + 6 = 0$

which is of the form $ax^2 + bx + c = 0, a \neq 0$.

$\therefore$ It is a quadratic equation.

(iii) Do same as Example 1 (i) of Topic 1.

Ans. It is not a quadratic equation.

(iv) Do same as Example 1 (i) of Topic 1.

Ans. It is a quadratic equation.

(v) Do same as Example 1 (i) of Topic 1.

Ans. It is a quadratic equation.

(vi) Given equation is $x^2 + 3x + 1 = (x-2)^2$

$\Rightarrow \quad x^2 + 3x + 1 = x^2 + 4 - 4x$

$[\because (a-b)^2 = a^2 + b^2 - 2ab]$

$\Rightarrow \quad x^2 + 3x + 1 - x^2 - 4 + 4x = 0$

$\Rightarrow \quad 7x - 3 = 0$

which is not of the form $ax^2 + bx + c = 0$, since here $a = 0$.

$\therefore$ It is not a quadratic equation.

(vii) Given equation is $(x+2)^3 = 2x(x^2-1)$

$\Rightarrow \quad x^3 + 8 + 3x^2(2) + 3x(2)^2 = 2x^3 - 2x$

$[\because (a+b)^3 = a^3 + b^3 + 3a^2b + 3ab^2]$

$\Rightarrow \quad x^3 + 8 + 6x^2 + 12x = 2x^3 - 2x$

$\Rightarrow x^3 + 8 + 6x^2 + 12x - 2x^3 + 2x = 0$

$\Rightarrow \quad -x^3 + 6x^2 + 14x + 8 = 0,$

which is not of the form $ax^2 + bx + c = 0$, because it has cubic term i.e. x^3.

$\therefore$ It is not a quadratic equation.

(viii) Given equation is $x^3 - 4x^2 - x + 1 = (x-2)^3$

$\Rightarrow x^3 - 4x^2 - x + 1 = x^3 - 3(x^2)2 + 3x(2)^2 - (2)^3$

$[\because (a-b)^3 = a^3 - 3a^2b + 3ab^2 - b^3]$

$\Rightarrow \quad x^3 - 4x^2 - x + 1 = x^3 - 6x^2 + 12x - 8$

$\Rightarrow \quad x^3 - 4x^2 - x + 1 - x^3 + 6x^2 - 12x + 8 = 0$

$\Rightarrow \quad 2x^2 - 13x + 9 = 0$

which is of the form $ax^2 + bx + c = 0, a \neq 0$

$\therefore$ It is a quadratic equation.

Note it In part (viii), the given equation appears to be a cubic equation and not a quadratic equation but it turns out to be a quadratic equation. So, we have to simplify the given equation before deciding whether it is quadratic equation or not.

Q2. Represent the following situations in the form of quadratic equations.

(i) The area of a rectangular plot is 528 m^2. The length of the plot (in metres) is one more than twice its breadth. We need to find the length and breadth of the plot.

(ii) The product of two consecutive positive integers is 306. We need to find the integers. CBSE 2020 (Basic)

(iii) Rohan's mother is 26 years older than him. The product of their ages (in years) 3 years from now will be 360. We would like to find Rohan's present age.

(iv) A train travels a distance of 480 km at a uniform speed. If the speed had been 8 km/h less, then it would have taken 3 h more to cover the same distance. We need to find the speed of the train.

Sol. (i) Let the breadth of the plot be x m.

Then, the length of the plot be $(2x+1)$ m. [by given condition]

$\therefore$ Area of the rectangular plot = Length $\times$ Breadth

$\therefore \quad 528 = (2x+1)x \quad$ [given]

$\Rightarrow \quad 528 = 2x^2 + x$

$\Rightarrow \quad 2x^2 + x - 528 = 0$

which is the required quadratic equation.

(ii) Let the two consecutive positive integers be x and $x+1$. Then, according to the question,

$$x(x+1) = 306 \Rightarrow x^2 + x = 306$$

$$\Rightarrow \quad x^2 + x - 306 = 0$$

which is the required quadratic equation.

(iii) Let the present age of Rohan be x yr.

Then, his mother's present age $= (x+26)$ yr

[by given condition]

After 3 yr, Rohan's age $= (x+3)$ yr

And Rohan's mother's age $= [(x+26)+3]$ yr $= (x+29)$ yr

According to the question,

$$(x+3)(x+29) = 360$$

$$\Rightarrow \quad x^2 + 29x + 3x + 87 = 360$$

$$\Rightarrow \quad x^2 + 32x - 273 = 0,$$

which is the required quadratic equation.

(iv) Let the speed of the train be x km/h.

Distance travelled by the train = 480 km

Therefore, time taken for travelling 480 km

$$= \frac{480}{x} \text{ h} \quad \left[\because \text{Time} = \frac{\text{Distance}}{\text{Speed}}\right]$$

If the speed had been 8 km/h less i.e. $(x-8)$ km/h, then

Time taken for travelling 480 km $= \frac{480}{x-8}$ h

According to the question,

$$\frac{480}{x-8} = 3 + \frac{480}{x}$$

$$\Rightarrow \quad \frac{480}{x-8} - \frac{480}{x} = 3$$

$$\Rightarrow \quad \frac{480x - 480(x-8)}{x(x-8)} = 3$$

$$\Rightarrow \quad 480x - 480x + 3840 = 3x(x-8)$$

$$\Rightarrow \quad 3840 = 3x^2 - 24x$$

$$\Rightarrow \quad 3x^2 - 24x - 3840 = 0$$

$$\Rightarrow \quad x^2 - 8x - 1280 = 0$$

[$\because$ dividing by 3 both sides]

which is the required quadratic equation.

EXERCISE 4.2

Q1. Find the roots of the following quadratic equations by factorisation:

(i) $x^2 - 3x - 10 = 0$

(ii) $2x^2 + x - 6 = 0$

(iii) $\sqrt{2}\,x^2 + 7x + 5\sqrt{2} = 0$

(iv) $2x^2 - x + \frac{1}{8} = 0$

(v) $100x^2 - 20x + 1 = 0$

Sol. (i) Do same as Example 1 (i) of Topic 2. **Ans.** – 2 and 5

(ii) Given equation is $2x^2 + x - 6 = 0$

$$\Rightarrow \quad 2x^2 + 4x - 3x - 6 = 0$$

[$\because 4 \times (-3) = -12$ and $4 - 3 = 1$]

$$\Rightarrow \quad 2x(x+2) - 3(x+2) = 0$$

$$\Rightarrow \quad (x+2)(2x-3) = 0$$

$$\Rightarrow \quad x+2 = 0 \text{ or } 2x-3 = 0$$

$$\Rightarrow \quad x = -2 \text{ or } x = \frac{3}{2}$$

Hence, the roots of the equation $2x^2 + x - 6 = 0$ are -2 and $\frac{3}{2}$.

(iii) Given equation is $\sqrt{2}x^2 + 7x + 5\sqrt{2} = 0$

$$\Rightarrow \quad \sqrt{2}x^2 + 5x + 2x + 5\sqrt{2} = 0$$

$\left[\because 5 \times 2 = 10 \text{ and } 5 + 2 = 7\right]$

$$\Rightarrow \quad x(\sqrt{2}x + 5) + \sqrt{2}(\sqrt{2}x + 5) = 0$$

$$\Rightarrow \quad (\sqrt{2}x + 5)(x + \sqrt{2}) = 0$$

$$\Rightarrow \quad \sqrt{2}x + 5 = 0 \text{ or } x + \sqrt{2} = 0$$

$$\Rightarrow \quad x = \frac{-5}{\sqrt{2}} \text{ or } x = -\sqrt{2}$$

Hence, the roots of the equation $\sqrt{2}x^2 + 7x + 5\sqrt{2} = 0$ are $\frac{-5}{\sqrt{2}}$ and $-\sqrt{2}$.

(iv) Do same as Example 1 (i) of Topic 2. **Ans.** $\frac{1}{4}$ and $\frac{1}{4}$

(v) Do same as Example 1 (i) of Topic 2. **Ans.** $\frac{1}{10}$ and $\frac{1}{10}$

Q2. Solve the following quadratic equations:

(i) $x^2 - 45x + 324 = 0$ (ii) $x^2 - 55x + 750 = 0$

Sol. (i) Given equation is $x^2 - 45x + 324 = 0$

$$\Rightarrow \quad x^2 - 36x - 9x + 324 = 0$$

[$\because (-36) \times (-9) = 324$ and $-36 - 9 = -45$]

$$\Rightarrow \quad x(x-36) - 9(x-36) = 0$$

$$\Rightarrow \quad (x-36)(x-9) = 0$$

$$\Rightarrow \quad x - 36 = 0 \text{ or } x - 9 = 0$$

$$\Rightarrow \quad x = 36 \text{ or } x = 9$$

Hence, the roots of the equation $x^2 - 45x + 324 = 0$ are 9 and 36.

(ii) Do same as Part (i).

Ans. 25 and 30

Q3. Find two numbers whose sum is 27 and product is 182.

Sol. Let one number be x.

Then, another number be $27 - x$.

[$\because$ sum of two numbers = 27]

According to the question,

Product of these two numbers = 182

$\therefore \quad x(27-x) = 182$

$\Rightarrow \quad 27x - x^2 = 182$

$\Rightarrow \quad x^2 - 27x + 182 = 0$

$\Rightarrow \quad x^2 - 14x - 13x + 182 = 0$

$[\because (-14) \times (-13) = 182 \text{ and } -14-13 = -27]$

$\Rightarrow \quad x(x-14) - 13(x-14) = 0$

$\Rightarrow \quad (x-14)(x-13) = 0$

$\Rightarrow \quad x - 14 = 0 \text{ or } x - 13 = 0$

$\Rightarrow \quad x = 14 \text{ or } x = 13$

If $x = 14$, then $27 - x = 27 - 14 = 13$

and if $x = 13$, then $27 - x = 27 - 13 = 14$

Hence, in both cases the numbers are 13 and 14.

Q4. Find two consecutive positive integers, sum of whose squares is 365.

Sol. Do same as Example 1 of Topic 4. **Ans.** 13 and 14

Q5. The altitude of a right angled triangle is 7 cm less than its base. If the hypotenuse is 13 cm long, then find the other two sides.

Sol. Do same as Example 9 of Topic 4.

Base of the triangle cannot be negative, so neglect $x = -5$

Therefore, we get $x = 12$

Hence, the base of the triangle = 12 cm

and altitude of the triangle = 12 – 7 = 5 cm

Q6. A cottage industry produces a certain number of pottery articles in a day. It was observed on a particular day that the cost of production of each article (in ₹) was 3 more than twice the number of articles produced on that day. If the total cost of production on that day was ₹ 90, then find the number of articles produced and the cost of each article.

Sol. Let the number of pottery articles produced on a particular day be x.

Then, cost of production of each article = ₹ $(2x+3)$

[by given condition]

So, the total cost of production

= Number of pottery articles

× Cost of production of each article

= ₹ $x(2x+3)$

According to the question,

$x(2x+3) = 90$

$\Rightarrow \quad 2x^2 + 3x = 90$

$\Rightarrow \quad 2x^2 + 3x - 90 = 0$

$\Rightarrow \quad 2x^2 + 15x - 12x - 90 = 0$

$[\because 15 \times (-12) = -180 \text{ and } 15 - 12 = 3]$

$\Rightarrow \quad x(2x+15) - 6(2x+15) = 0$

$\Rightarrow \quad (2x+15)(x-6) = 0$

$\Rightarrow \quad 2x + 15 = 0 \text{ or } x - 6 = 0$

$\Rightarrow \quad x = -\frac{15}{2} \text{ or } x = 6$

But x cannot be negative, as number of pottery articles should be positive.

$\therefore \quad x = 6$

Hence, the number of articles produced = 6

and the cost of each article = 2 × 6 + 3 = ₹ 15.

EXERCISE 4.3

Q1. Find the nature of the roots of the following quadratic equations. If the real roots exist, then find them.

(i) $2x^2 - 3x + 5 = 0$ **(ii)** $3x^2 - 4\sqrt{3}x + 4 = 0$

(iii) $2x^2 - 6x + 3 = 0$ CBSE 2025 (Basic)

Sol. Do same as Example 4 of Topic 3.

Ans.

(i) No real roots

(ii) Equal roots; $\frac{2}{\sqrt{3}}$ and $\frac{2}{\sqrt{3}}$.

(iii) Distinct real roots; $\frac{3+\sqrt{3}}{2}$ and $\frac{3-\sqrt{3}}{2}$.

Q2. Find the values of k for each of the following quadratic equations, so that they have two equal roots.

(i) $2x^2 + kx + 3 = 0$ **(ii)** $kx(x-2) + 6 = 0$

Sol. (i) Do same as Example 5 of Topic 3. **Ans.** $k = \pm 2\sqrt{6}$

(ii) Do same as Example 5 of Topic 3. **Ans.** $k = 6$

Q3. Is it possible to design a rectangular mango grove whose length is twice its breadth and the area is 800 m^2? If so, then find its length and breadth.

Sol. Let breadth of a rectangular mango grove be x m.

Then, length of a rectangular mango grove = $2x$ m

According to the question,

Area of rectangular mango grove = 800 m^2

$\Rightarrow \quad 2x(x) = 800 \quad [\because \text{Area} = \text{Length} \times \text{Breadth}]$

$\Rightarrow \quad 2x^2 = 800 \Rightarrow x^2 = 400$

$\Rightarrow \quad x = \pm 20$

But, $x = -20$ is not possible because breadth can never be negative. So, $x = 20$.

Thus, length = $2x$ = 40 m and breadth = 20 m.

Q4. Is the following situation possible? If so, then determine their present ages. The sum of the ages of two friends is 20 years. Four years ago, the product of their ages (in years) was 48.

Sol. Let the age of one of two friends be x yr.

Then, age of other friend $= (20 - x)$ yr

[$\because$ the sum of the ages of two friends is 20 yr]

4 yr ago, age of one of two friends $= (x - 4)$ yr

and age of the other friend $= (20 - x - 4)$ yr $= (16 - x)$ yr

According to the question,

$$(x - 4)(16 - x) = 48$$

$$\Rightarrow \quad 16x - x^2 - 64 + 4x = 48$$

$$\Rightarrow \quad x^2 - 20x + 112 = 0$$

On comparing with $ax^2 + bx + c = 0$, we get

$$a = 1, b = -20 \text{ and } c = 112$$

Now, discriminant, $D = b^2 - 4ac$

$$= (-20)^2 - 4 \times 1 \times 112$$

$$= 400 - 448$$

$$= -48 < 0$$

which implies that the real roots are not possible because this condition represents imaginary roots. So, the solution does not exist and hence given situation is not possible.

Q5. Is it possible to design a rectangular park of perimeter 80 m and area 400 m^2? If so, then find its length and breadth.

Sol. Let the breadth of the park be x m.

Given, perimeter of a rectangular park = 80 m

$$\Rightarrow \quad 2\,(\text{Length} + \text{Breadth}) = 80 \text{ m}$$

$$\Rightarrow \quad \text{Length} + \text{Breadth} = 40 \text{ m}$$

$$\Rightarrow \quad \text{Length} = (40 - x) \text{ m}$$

Now, area of a rectangular park = Length $\times$ Breadth

$$= (40 - x)x \text{ m}^2$$

But according to the question, area of the rectangular park is 400 m^2.

$$\therefore \quad (40 - x)\,x = 400$$

$$\Rightarrow \quad x^2 - 40x + 400 = 0$$

$$\Rightarrow \quad x^2 - 2x \times 20 + (20)^2 = 0$$

$$\Rightarrow \quad (x - 20)^2 = 0 \quad [\because a^2 - 2ab + b^2 = (a - b)^2]$$

$$\Rightarrow \quad x = 20$$

Thus, breadth of the park = 20 m

and length of the park = 40 − 20 = 20 m

Hence, it is possible to design the rectangular park having perimeter 80 m and area 400 m^2.

Note it The park will be square in shape with side length 20 m, because here, length and breadth are equal.

REVIEW EXERCISE

Including Competency Based Questions

Part I

Multiple Choice Questions

1. Which of these is a quadratic equation having one of its roots as zero? Competency Based Question

(i) $x^3 + x^2 = 0$ (ii) $x^2 - 2x = 0$ (iii) $x^2 - 9 = 0$

(a) Only (i) (b) Only (ii)
(c) Only (i) and (ii) (d) Only (ii) and (iii)

2. If one root of the quadratic equation $x^2 - 4x + 3 = 0$ is 1, then the other root is CBSE 2024 (Basic) Compartment

(a) 4 (b) -4 (c) 3 (d) -3

3. If $x = 5$ is a solution of the quadratic equation $2x^2 + (k-1)x + 10 = 0$, then the value of k is CBSE 2024 (Standard) Compartment

(a) 11 (b) -11 (c) 13 (d) -13

4. The roots of the quadratic equation $x^2 + x - 1 = 0$ are CBSE Sample Paper 2025 (Standard)

(a) irrational and distinct (b) not real
(c) rational and distinct (d) real and equal

5. If the quadratic equation $ax^2 + bx + c = 0$ has two real and equal roots, then 'c' is equal to CBSE 2023 (Standard)

(a) $\frac{-b}{2a}$ (b) $\frac{b}{2a}$ (c) $\frac{-b^2}{4a}$ (d) $\frac{b^2}{4a}$

6. Which of the following quadratic equations has real and equal roots? CBSE 2025 (Standard)

(a) $(x+1)^2 = 2x + 1$ (b) $x^2 + x = 0$
(c) $x^2 - 4 = 0$ (d) $x^2 + x + 1 = 0$

7. The roots of quadratic equation $3x^2 - 4\sqrt{3}x + 4 = 0$ are CBSE Sample Paper 2025 (Basic)

(a) not real (b) real and equal
(c) rational and distinct (d) irrational and distinct

8. The values of k for which the roots of quadratic equation $x^2 + 6x + k = 0$ are real, is

(a) $k \geq 6$ (b) $k \leq 6$ (c) $k \geq -6$ (d) $k \leq -6$

9. If the roots of quadratic equation $4x^2 - 5x + k = 0$ are real and equal, then the value of k is CBSE 2024 (Basic)

(a) $\frac{5}{4}$ (b) $\frac{25}{16}$ (c) $\frac{-5}{4}$ (d) $\frac{-25}{16}$

10. The sum of the squares of three consecutive integers is 770, then the smallest positive integer is Competency Based Question

(a) 10 (b) 15 (c) 17 (d) 8

11. A line segment AB is 8 cm in length. AB is produced to P such that $BP^2 = AB \cdot AP$. Then, the length of BP is NCERT Exemplar

(a) $5(\sqrt{5} + 1)$ (b) $\sqrt{5} + 1$
(c) $4(\sqrt{5} + 1)$ (d) $\sqrt{3} + 1$

Assertion-Reason Type Questions

12. Assertion The roots of $2x^2 + 7x - 15$ is -5 and $\frac{3}{2}$.

Reason Roots of the quadratic equation $ax^2 + bx + c = 0, a \neq 0$ are given by

$$x = \frac{-b \pm \sqrt{b^2 - 4ac}}{2a}$$

(a) Both Assertion and Reason are correct and Reason is the correct explanation of Assertion.
(b) Both Assertion and Reason are correct but Reason is not the correct explanation of Assertion.
(c) Assertion is correct but Reason is incorrect.
(d) Assertion is incorrect but Reason is correct.

13. Assertion If $5 + \sqrt{7}$ is a root of a quadratic equation with rational coefficients, then its other root is $5 - \sqrt{7}$.

Reason Surd roots of a quadratic equation with rational coefficients occur in conjugate pairs. CBSE 2023 (Standard)

(a) Both Assertion and Reason are correct and Reason is the correct explanation of Assertion.
(b) Both Assertion and Reason are correct but Reason is not the correct explanation of Assertion.
(c) Assertion is correct but Reason is incorrect.
(d) Assertion is incorrect but Reason is correct.

14. Assertion The equation $x^2 + x + 4 = 0$ has equal roots.

Reason Quadratic equation $ax^2 + bx + c = 0, a \neq 0$ has equal roots if $b^2 - 4ac = 0$.

(a) Both Assertion and Reason are correct and Reason is the correct explanation of Assertion.
(b) Both Assertion and Reason are correct but Reason is not the correct explanation of Assertion.
(c) Assertion is correct but Reason is incorrect.
(d) Assertion is incorrect but Reason is correct.

15. **Assertion** $x^2 + 4kx + 25 = 0$ has no real roots if $\frac{-5}{2} < k < \frac{5}{2}$.

Reason Quadratic equation $ax^2 + bx + c = 0$, $a \neq 0$ has real roots, if $b^2 - 4ac \geq 0$.

(a) Both Assertion and Reason are correct and Reason is the correct explanation of Assertion.
(b) Both Assertion and Reason are correct but Reason is not the correct explanation of Assertion.
(c) Assertion is correct but Reason is incorrect.
(d) Assertion is incorrect but Reason is correct.

16. **Assertion** If the equation $y^2 + 4my + n = 0$ has equal roots, then $m^2 = \frac{n}{4}$.

Reason If the quadratic equation $ax^2 + bx + c = 0$, $a \neq 0$ has $b^2 - 4ac = 0$, then $x = \frac{-b}{2a}, \frac{-b}{2a}$.

(a) Both Assertion and Reason are correct and Reason is the correct explanation of Assertion.
(b) Both Assertion and Reason are correct but Reason is not the correct explanation of Assertion.
(c) Assertion is correct but Reason is incorrect.
(d) Assertion is incorrect but Reason is correct.

Case Study Based Questions

17. Raj and Ajay are very close friends. Both the families decide to go to Ranikhet by their own cars. Raj's car travels at a speed of x km/h while Ajay's car travels 5 km/h faster than Raj's car. Raj took 4 h more than Ajay to complete the journey of 400 km.

CBSE Question Bank

(i) What will be the distance covered by Ajay's car in 2 h?
(ii) Find the quadratic equation describe the speed of Raj's car.
(iii) (a) What is the speed of Raj's car?

Or

(b) How much time took Ajay to travel 400 km?

18. The speed of a motorboat is 20 km/h. For covering the distance of 15 km the boat took 1 h more for upstream than downstream. **CBSE Question Bank**

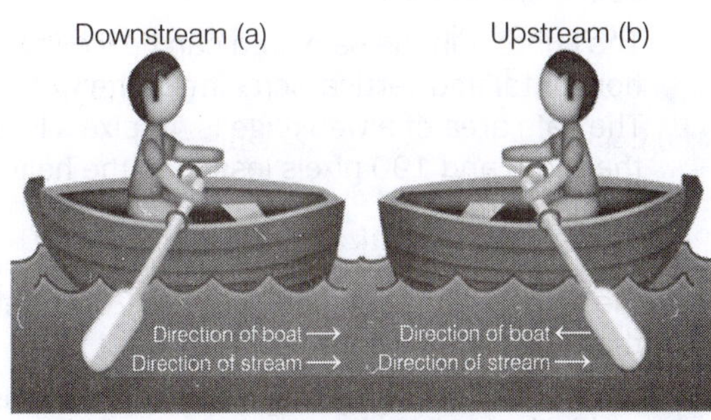

(i) Let speed of the stream be x km/h, find the speed of the motorboat in upstream.
(ii) What is the relation between speed distance and time?
(iii) (a) What is the quadratic equation for the speed of the stream?

Or

(b) What is the speed of stream?

19. Digital images consist of pixels. A pixel can be considered as the smallest unit on a display screen in a mobile or a computer. The number of pixels, their size and colours depend on the display screen and its graphic card. Display screens are rectangular in shape and their size is defined as the length of the diagonal.

Amit is designing a web page for a display on a screen whose size is 1000 pixels. The width of the screen is 800 pixels.

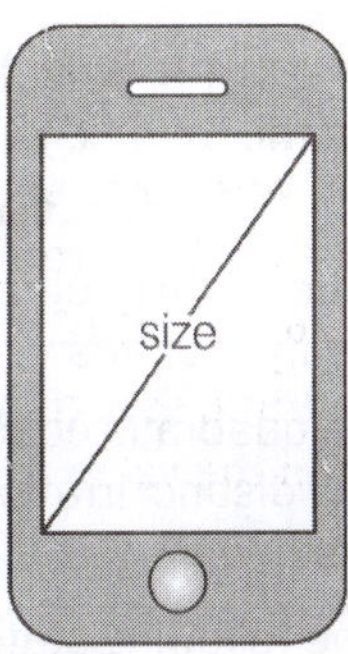

Based on the above information, answer the following questions.

(i) Find the height (h) of the screen.

(ii) The size of a screen display can be measured in inches also. Is it possible to have a screen of size 13 inches where the width is 7 inches more than height? Give an example to justify.

(iii) The size of a screen is an important factor in designing a web page. The page can be opened on different screen sizes but during the initial designing stage, one screen area is considered as the safe area.

The content in the safe area can be viewed without horizontal and vertical scrolling of the web page. The safe area of a web page is 40 pixels less than the width and 190 pixels less than the height of the display screen.

Find the expression represents the safe area for the screen whose screen height is 200 pixels less than the screen width (w).

20. Vitthal went on a long cycling round trip from his home to a nearby hill and back. The journey to the hill started with a 40 km flat road and then a 25 km uphill slope.

While going uphill, his average speed reduced by 10 km/h compared to the flat road leading to an extra half-hour of travel time.

However, he maintained the same average speed on the flat road in both directions.

Based on the above information, answer the following questions.

(i) Find the time taken by Vitthal to reach the end of 65 km stretch in the uphill direction.

(ii) If he took $2\frac{1}{2}$ h to reach home from the hill, find his average speed on the slope while descending. Show your work.

21. Under a relief scheme, ₹ n^2 was distributed among n number of people. The first beneficiary received ₹ 1 plus $\frac{1}{n+1}$ of the remaining amount. The second beneficiary received ₹ 2 plus $\frac{1}{n+1}$ of the remaining amount. The third beneficiary received ₹ 3 plus $\frac{1}{n+1}$ of the remaining amount. The distribution is done in the same pattern for all the beneficiaries.

Based on the above information, answer the following questions.

(i) Find the expression represents money received by the first beneficiary.

(ii) Who will get the maximum amount?

(iii) Is the distribution of the relief fund fair? Justify your answer.

Part II

Very Short Answer Type Questions

1. If $x = 3$ is one root of the quadratic equation $x^2 - 2kx - 6 = 0$, then find the value of k.

2. Does there exist a quadratic equation whose coefficients are rational but both of its roots are irrational? Justify your answer. **NCERT Exemplar**

3. Find value of the roots of quadratic equation $x^2 - x - 6 = 0$. **CBSE 2020 (Basic)**

4. $(2x+1)^3 = 8x(x^2+1)+3$. Write the zeroes of the above equation in the form (x, y). Show your steps. **Competency Based Question**

5. A quadratic equation with integral coefficients has integral roots. Justify your answer.

6. Does there exist a quadratic equation whose coefficients are all distinct irrationals but both the roots are rationals? Why? **NCERT Exemplar**

7. Check whether the following statement is true or false. Justify your answer. 'Every quadratic equation has atleast one real root.'

Directions (Q. Nos. 8 and 9) What is the nature of roots of the following quadratic equation?

8. $5x^2 - 2x - 3 = 0$

9. $2x^2 - \sqrt{5}x + 1 = 0$ **NCERT Exemplar**

10. Find the discriminant of quadratic equation $\sqrt{5}x^2 - 7x + 2\sqrt{5} = 0$.

11. If the discriminant of the equation $kx^2 - 3\sqrt{2}x + 4\sqrt{2} = 0$ is 14, then find the value of k.

12. For what values of k, the equation $9x^2 + 6kx + 4 = 0$ has equal roots? **CBSE Sample Paper 2021 Term I (Standard)**

13. Find the value of m so that the quadratic equation $mx(5x-6) + 9 = 0$ has two equal roots.

14. If a number is added to twice its square, then the resultant is 21. Write the quadratic representation of this situation. **Competency Based Question**

Short Answer Type Questions

15. Which of the following is not a quadratic equation? NCERT Exemplar

(i) $(\sqrt{2}x+\sqrt{3})^2 = 3x^2 - 5x$

(ii) $(x^2 + 2x)^2 = x^4 + 3 + 4x^2$

16. If $\frac{1}{2}$ is a root of the equation $x^2 + kx - \frac{5}{4} = 0$, then find the value of k. NCERT Exemplar

17. Find the value of p, when $px^2 + (\sqrt{3} - \sqrt{2})x - 1 = 0$ and $x = \frac{1}{\sqrt{3}}$ is one root of this equation.

18. Find the solution(s) of the following equation.

$(y-1)(y-3)\left(\frac{1}{y-3} + \frac{2y}{y-1}\right) = 2$ and $y \neq 1, 3$.

Show your steps and give valid reasons. Competency Based Question

Directions (Q.Nos. 19 and 20) Solve for x.

19. $\sqrt{6x+7} - (2x-7) = 0$

20. $\sqrt{2x+9} + x = 13$

21. Find the roots of the equation

$ax^2 + a = a^2x + x$

22. Solve for x, $\frac{1}{a+b+x} = \frac{1}{a} + \frac{1}{b} + \frac{1}{x}$, where $a, b, x \neq 0$ and $a + b + x \neq 0$. CBSE 2019

23. $3(3)^{2m} + 11(3)^m = 4$

Use the substitution $3^m = x$ to solve for m. Show your steps. Competency Based Question

24. Find the roots of the quadratic equation

$a^2b^2x^2 + b^2x - a^2x - 1 = 0$

25. Solve for x, $\frac{16}{x} - 1 = \frac{15}{x+1}$; $x \neq 0, -1$

26. Find the numerical difference of the roots of equation $x^2 - 7x - 18 = 0$.

27. Solve the following quadratic equation for x.

$4\sqrt{3}x^2 + 5x - 2\sqrt{3} = 0$

28. Show that $(x^2 + 1)^2 - x^2 = 0$ has no real roots.

29. For what value(s) of a quadratic equation $30ax^2 - 6x + 1 = 0$ has no real roots?

CBSE Sample Paper 2021 Term I (Standard)

30. Find the least positive value of k for which $x^2 + kx + 16 = 0$ has real roots.

31. If the roots of the equation $x^2 + 2cx + ab = 0$ are real and unequal, then prove that the equation $x^2 - 2(a+b)x + a^2 + b^2 + 2c^2 = 0$ has no real roots. Competency Based Question

32. Find the quadratic equation, if

$x = \sqrt{5 + \sqrt{5 + \sqrt{5 + \ldots\infty}}}$ and x is a real number.

Competency Based Question

33. Find the value of k for which the quadratic equation $2x^2 - kx + k = 0$ has equal roots. NCERT Exemplar

34. A survey carried by the school social club for the student come by car in school. $\frac{x-9}{2}$ cars carry one student, $\sqrt{x}$ cars carry two students, $\frac{x}{7}$ cars carry three students and $\frac{\sqrt{x}}{7}$ cars carry four students, if the total number of students are 59, then find the total number of cars used by 59 students. Competency Based Question

35. Arpit was asked to represent the following statements in the form of a quadratic equation.

'The sum of the squares of two positive integers is 225. The square of the larger number is 16 times the smaller number.'

If Arpit wrote the equation correctly, then what could he have written? Competency Based Question

36. In a cricket match, Harbhajan took three wickets less than twice the number of wickets taken by Zaheer. The product of the numbers of wickets taken by these two is 20. Represent the above situation in the form of a quadratic equation.

37. At t min past 2 pm, the time needed by the minute hand of a clock to show 3 pm was found to be 3 min less than $\frac{t^2}{4}$ min. Find t.

NCERT Exemplar

38. The product of two consecutive positive integers is 306. Find the integers. CBSE 2020 (Basic)

39. Find two consecutive odd positive integers, sum of whose squares is 290.

CBSE Sample Paper 2021 Term I (Basic)

40. Find two consecutive odd natural numbers, sum of whose squares is 130.

CBSE Sample Paper 2025 (Standard)

41. The sum of two numbers is 18 and the sum of their reciprocals is $\frac{9}{40}$. Find the numbers.

42. Three consecutive natural numbers are such that the square of the middle number exceeds the difference of the squares of other two by 60. Find the numbers.

Competency Based Question

43. The difference of two numbers is 4. If the difference of their reciprocals is $\frac{4}{21}$, then find the two numbers.

44. The sum of the squares of three positive numbers that are consecutive multiples of 5 is 725. Find the three numbers.

45. Two students of a class X while solving a quadratic equation, committed the following mistakes.

One of them made a mistakes in the constant term and get the root as 6 and 8.

Another one committed an error in the coefficient of x and he got the roots as 3 and 14. But in the mean time, they realised that they are wrong and they managed to get it right jointly. Find the quadratic equation. **Competency Based Question**

46. If Nidhi were 7 years younger than what she actually is, then the square of her age (in years) would be 1 more than 5 times her actual age. What is her present age? **CBSE 2024 (Standard) Compartment**

47. A plane left 30 min late than its scheduled time and in order to reach the destination 1500 km away in time, it had to increase its speed by 100 km/h from the usual speed. Find its usual speed.

48. While boarding the plane, few passengers are slipped from the stairs and got hurt. The pilot took the passenger in the emergency clinic at the airport for treatment. Due to this, the plane got delayed by half an hour. To reach the destination 1500 km away in time, so that the passengers could catch the connecting flight, the speed of the plane was increased by 250 km/h than the usual speed. Find the usual speed of the plane. **Competency Based Question**

49. A and B are centres of two circles of radii 9 cm and 2 cm respectively, and $AB = 17$ cm. C is the centre of a circle of radius x cm, which touches the above circles externally. Given that $\angle ACB = 90°$, write an equation in x and solve it for x.

Long Answer Type Questions

50. Solve for x,

$$\frac{1}{x+1} + \frac{2}{x+2} = \frac{4}{x+4}, x \neq -1, -2, -4$$

51. Solve for x,

$$\frac{x-4}{x-5} + \frac{x-6}{x-7} = \frac{10}{3}, x \neq 5, 7$$

52. Find the roots of $5^{(x+1)} + 5^{(2-x)} = 5^3 + 1$ by factorisation method.

53. Solve $x = \cfrac{1}{2 - \cfrac{1}{2 - \cfrac{1}{2-x}}}$; $x \neq 2$.

54. If one root of the quadratic equation $3x^2 + px + 4 = 0$ is $\frac{2}{3}$, then find the value of p and the other root of the equation. **CBSE Sample Paper 2021 Term I (Standard)**

55. Find the roots of the quadratic equation $3x^2 - 7x - 6 = 0$.

56. If $x = -2$ is a root of the equation $3x^2 + 7x + p = 0$, then find the values of k, so that the roots of the equation $x^2 + k(4x + k - 1) + p = 0$ are equal.

57. If $x = -5$ is a root of the quadratic equation $2x^2 + px - 15 = 0$ and the quadratic equation $p(x^2 + x) + k = 0$ has equal roots, then find the value of k. **Competency Based Question**

58. If the roots of the equation $(a-b)x^2 + (b-c)x + (c-a) = 0$ are equal, then prove that $2a = b + c$.

59. If the equation $(1 + m^2)x^2 + (2mc)x + (c^2 - a^2) = 0$ has equal roots, then prove that $c^2 = a^2(1 + m^2)$.

60. The angry Arjun carried some arrows for fighting with Bheeshm. With half the arrows, he cut down the arrows thrown by Bheeshm on him and with six other arrows he killed the charioteer of Bheeshm. With one arrow each he knocked down respectively the rath, flag and bow of Bheeshm. Finally, with one more than four times the square root of arrows he laid Bheeshm unconcious on an arrow-bed. Find the total number of arrows Arjun had. **Competency Based Question**

61. If Ritu were younger by 5 yr than what she really is, then the square of her age would have been 11 more than 5 times her present age. What is her present age?

62. A piece of cloth costs ₹ 200. If the piece was 5 m more longer and each metre of cloth costs ₹ 2 less, the cost of the piece would have remained unchanged. How long is the piece and what is the original rate per metre?

63. Two pipes running together can fill a cistern in $11\frac{1}{9}$ min. If one pipe takes 5 min more than the other to fill it, then find the time in which each pipe would fill the cistern.

64. A motor boat whose speed is 18 km/hr in still water takes 1 hr more to go 24 km upstream than to return downstream to the same spot. Find the speed of the stream. **CBSE 2018**

65. There is a square field whose side is 44 m. A square flower bed is prepared in its centre leaving a gravel path all round the flower bed. The total cost of laying the flower bed and gravelling the path at ₹ 2.75 and ₹ 1.50 per m^2 respectively, is ₹ 4904. Find the width of gravel path. **Competency Based Question**

66. A quilt maker has a rectangular quilt measuring 12 units by 8 units. He wants to add a border to it as shown in the figure below. He has 64 sq units of fabric for the border. **Competency Based Question**

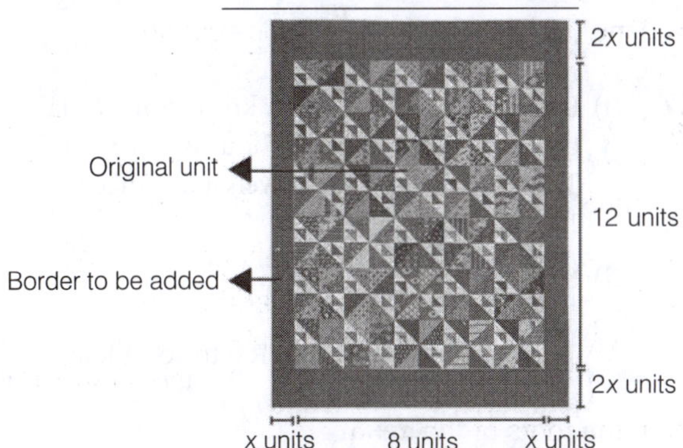

Note The figure is not to scale.

(i) If x and $2x$ are the widths of the border as shown, frame a quadratic equation using the total area enclosed by the new quilt (with the border).

(ii) Find the measures of the new quilt (with the border).

Show your work along with valid reasons.

67. ₹ 6500 were divided equally among a certain number of persons. If there had been 15 more persons, each would have got ₹ 30 less, then find the original number of persons. **Competency Based Question**

68. A shopkeeper buys a number of books for ₹ 1200. If he had bought 10 more books for the same amount, each book would have cost him ₹ 20 less, then how many books did he buy?

69. A factory kept increasing its output by the same percentage every year. Find the percentage, if it is known that the output doubles in the last two years.

Hints & SOLUTIONS

Part I

1. (c) **Hint**

(i) $x^2(x+1)=0 \Rightarrow x=0$ or $x=-1$

(ii) $x^2-2x=0 \Rightarrow x(x-2)=0$

$\Rightarrow \quad x=0$ or $x=2$

(iii) $x^2-9=0 \Rightarrow x=\pm 3$

∴ Quadratic equations (i) and (ii) have one of its roots as zero.

2. (c) Given, $x^2-4x+3=0$

$\Rightarrow \quad x^2-3x-x+3=0$

$\Rightarrow \quad x(x-3)-1(x-3)=0$

$\Rightarrow \quad (x-1)(x-3)=0$

$\Rightarrow \quad x=1$ or $x=3$

Thus, other root of the given equation is 3.

3. (b) Given equation is $2x^2+(k-1)x+10=0$

On putting $x=5$ in above equation, we get

$2(5)^2+(k-1)5+10=0$

$\Rightarrow \quad 50+5k+5=0$

$\Rightarrow \quad 5k=-55$

$\Rightarrow \quad k=-11$

4. (a) Given quadratic equation is $x^2+x-1=0$.

On comparing with standard quadratic equation $ax^2+bx+c=0$, we get

$a=1, b=1$ and $c=-1$

Now, $D=b^2-4ac=(1)^2-4(1)(-1)=1+4=5>0$

Using quadratic formula,

$$x=\frac{-b\pm\sqrt{D}}{2a} \Rightarrow x=\frac{-1\pm\sqrt{5}}{2}$$

Thus, the roots of the quadratic equation are irrational and distinct.

5. (d) Given, $ax^2+bx+c=0$

Since, the given equation has two real and equal roots.

Discriminant, $D=0 \Rightarrow b^2-4ac=0$

$$\Rightarrow \quad c=\frac{b^2}{4a}$$

6. (a) We have, $(x+1)^2=2x+1$

$\Rightarrow \quad x^2+1+2x=2x+1$

$\Rightarrow \quad x^2=0 \quad \ldots$(i)

On comparing Eq. (i) with $ax^2+bx+c=0$, we get

$a=1, b=0, c=0$

∴ Discriminant, $D=b^2-4ac=0-4\times1\times0=0$

So, this equation has real and equal roots.

7. (b) Given quadratic equation is

$3x^2-4\sqrt{3}x+4=0 \quad \ldots$(i)

On comparing Eq. (i) with standard quadratic equation $ax^2+bx+c=0$, we get

$a=3, b=-4\sqrt{3}$ and $c=4$

Here, $D=b^2-4ac=(-4\sqrt{3})^2-4\times3\times4=48-48=0$

i.e. discriminant D is zero.

Therefore, the roots will be real and equal.

8. (b) **Hint** Do same as Example 6 of Topic 3.

9. (b) We know that the quadratic equation has real and equal roots, if its discriminant is equal to zero

i.e. $b^2 - 4ac = 0$

Given quadratic equation is $4x^2 - 5x + k = 0$.

Here, $a = 4, b = -5$ and $c = k$

So, $b^2 - 4ac = 0 \Rightarrow (-5)^2 - 4 \times 4 \times k = 0$

$\Rightarrow 25 - 16k = 0 \Rightarrow k = \frac{25}{16}$

Hence, the values of k is $\frac{25}{16}$.

10. (b) **Hint** Do same as Example 1 of Topic 4.

11. (c) Let BP be x cm.

Then, $AP = AB + BP = (8 + x)$ cm.

8 cm x cm
A B P

Now, $BP^2 = AB \cdot AP \Rightarrow x^2 = 8 \cdot (8 + x)$

$\Rightarrow x^2 - 8x - 64 = 0$

$\therefore x = \frac{-(-8) \pm \sqrt{(-8)^2 - 4 \cdot 1 \cdot (-64)}}{2}$

or $x = \frac{8 \pm \sqrt{64 \times 5}}{2} = \frac{8 \pm 8\sqrt{5}}{2} = 4 \pm 4\sqrt{5}$

But the length of BP cannot be negative.

So, $x = (4 + 4\sqrt{5})$ cm $= 4(\sqrt{5} + 1)$ cm

12. (a) **Hint** We know, for quadratic equation $ax^2 + bx + c = 0$,

by quadratic formula, $x = \frac{-b \pm \sqrt{b^2 - 4ac}}{2a}$

13. (a) Let $ax^2 + bx + c = 0$ be the quadratic equation. Then, roots of this equation are given by

$$x = \frac{-b \pm \sqrt{b^2 - 4ac}}{2a}$$

$$\Rightarrow x = -\frac{b}{2a} \pm \frac{\sqrt{b^2 - 4ac}}{2a}$$

This shows that irrational roots can exist only as conjugate pairs.

14. (d) **Hint** For equal roots,

$$D = b^2 - 4ac = 0$$

15. (b) Since, $x^2 + 4kx + 25 = 0$ has no real roots.

$\therefore (4k)^2 - 4 \times 1 \times 25 < 0$

$\Rightarrow 16k^2 - 100 < 0$

$\Rightarrow 4k^2 < 25$

$\Rightarrow k^2 < \frac{25}{4} \Rightarrow \frac{-5}{2} < k < \frac{5}{2}$

16. (a) Since, $y^2 + 4my + n = 0$ has equal roots.

$\therefore (4m)^2 - 4 \times 1 \times n = 0$

$\Rightarrow 16m^2 = 4n$

$\Rightarrow 4m^2 = n$

$\Rightarrow m^2 = \frac{n}{4}$

17. (i) Let speed of Raj's car is x km/h. Since, Ajay's car travels a distance in one hour is $(x + 5)$ km. Therefore, Ajay's car travels a distance two hours is $2(x + 5)$ km.

(ii) **Hint** $\because$ Time $= \frac{\text{Distance}}{\text{Speed}}$

Time taken by Ajay and Raj to complete the 400 km journey, $t_1 = \frac{400}{x+5}$ h and $t_2 = \frac{400}{x}$ h

According to the question,

$t_2 = t_1 + 4$

$\therefore \frac{400}{x} = \frac{400}{x+5} + 4$

(iii) (a) **Hint** Solve the equation obtained in part (ii) by quadratic formula.

Ans. 20 km/h

Or (b) To travel 400 km, time taken by Ajay

$$t_1 = \frac{400}{(x+5)} = \frac{400}{20+5} = \frac{400}{25} = 16 \text{ h}$$

18. (i) Since, the speed of stream be x km/h and speed of motorboat is 20 km/h. Therefore, the speed of motorboat in upstream will be $(20 - x)$ km/h.

(ii) The relation between speed, distance and time is

$$\text{Speed} = \frac{\text{Distance}}{\text{Time}}$$

(iii) (a) Here, distance = 15 km

Speed of motorboat in downstream

$= (20 + x)$ km/h

and speed of motorboat in upstream

$= (20 - x)$ km/h

Time taken by motorboat in downstream and upstream are $t_1 = \frac{15}{20 + x}$ h and $t_2 = \frac{15}{20 - x}$ h.

According to the question,

$t_2 = 1 + t_1$

Now, put the value of t_1 and t_2 in above equation and simplify it.

Ans. $x^2 + 30x - 400 = 0$

Or (b) **Hint** Solve quadratic equation

$x^2 + 30x - 400 = 0$

Ans. 10 km/h.

19. (i) Given, size $(AC) = 1000$ pixels

and width $(AB) = 800$ pixels

Let the height of screen be h pixels.

Using Pythagoras theorem in ΔABC, we get

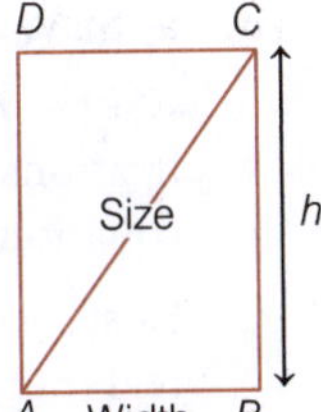

$$AC^2 = AB^2 + BC^2$$

$$\Rightarrow \quad (1000)^2 = (800)^2 + h^2$$

$$\Rightarrow \quad h^2 = 360000$$

$$\Rightarrow \quad h = \pm 600$$

$$h = 600 \text{ pixels}$$

[$\because$ height cannot be negative]

(ii) Let height of the screen be h inch.

Given, size $(AC) = 13$ inch, width $(AB) = (h+7)$ inch

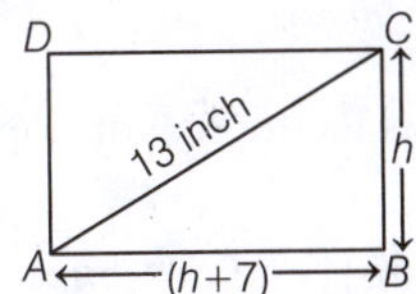

Using Pythagoras theorem in ΔABC, we get

$$AC^2 = AB^2 + BC^2$$

$$\Rightarrow \quad (13)^2 = (h+7)^2 + h^2$$

$$\Rightarrow \quad 169 = h^2 + 49 + 14h + h^2$$

$$\Rightarrow \quad 2h^2 + 14h - 120 = 0$$

$$\Rightarrow \quad h^2 + 7h - 60 = 0$$

$$\Rightarrow \quad h^2 + 12h - 5h - 60 = 0$$

$$\Rightarrow \quad h(h+12) - 5(h+12) = 0$$

$$\Rightarrow \quad (h+12)(h-5) = 0$$

$$\Rightarrow \quad h = -12 \text{ or } h = 5$$

But h cannot be negative.

$$\therefore \quad h = 5$$

Yes, it is possible to have a screen of size 13 inches, where width is 7 inches more than height.

i.e. width = 12 inches, height = 5 inches.

(iii) Given, height (h) is 200 pixels less than screen width (w).

$$\therefore \quad h = w - 200 \qquad \dots\text{(i)}$$

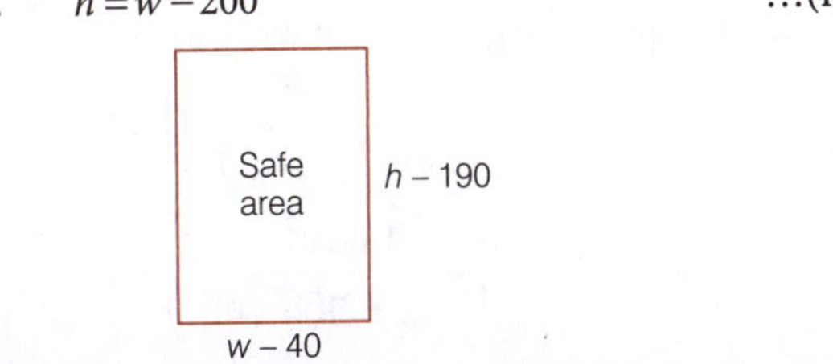

Also, safe area is 40 pixels less than the width and 190 pixels less than the height of the display screen.

$$\therefore \quad \text{Area} = \text{Length} \times \text{Breadth}$$

$$= (h - 190) \times (w - 40)$$

$$= (w - 200 - 190) \times (w - 40) \quad \text{[using Eq. (i)]}$$

$$= (w - 390)(w - 40)$$

$$= w^2 - 40w - 390w + 15600$$

$$\Rightarrow \quad \text{Area} = w^2 - 430w + 15600$$

20. (i) Let speed of Vitthal on the flat road be x km/h and time taken to cover it be t hr.

$\therefore$ Using formula, Distance = Speed × Time

$$\Rightarrow \quad 40 = x \times t \qquad \dots\text{(i)}$$

Now, speed of Vitthal on uphill = $(x - 10)$ km/h

and time taken to cover it = $\left(t + \frac{1}{2}\right)$ h.

$\therefore$ Using again, Distance = Speed × Time

$$25 = (x - 10) \times \left(t + \frac{1}{2}\right) \qquad \dots\text{(ii)}$$

$$\Rightarrow \quad 25 = xt + \frac{x}{2} - 10t - 5$$

$$\Rightarrow \quad 30 = 40 + \frac{x}{2} - 10 \times \frac{40}{x} \qquad \text{[using Eq. (i)]}$$

$$\Rightarrow \quad -10 = \frac{x}{2} - \frac{400}{x} \Rightarrow -10 = \frac{x^2 - 800}{2x}$$

$$\Rightarrow \quad x^2 + 20x - 800 = 0$$

$$\Rightarrow \quad x^2 + 40x - 20x - 800 = 0$$

$$\Rightarrow \quad x(x + 40) - 20(x + 40) = 0$$

$$\Rightarrow \quad (x + 40)(x - 20) = 0$$

$$\Rightarrow \quad x = -40, 20$$

$$\therefore \quad x = 20 \text{ km/h} \qquad [\because x \neq -40 \text{ km/h}]$$

From Eq. (i),

$$t = \frac{40}{x} = \frac{40}{20} = 2 \text{ h}$$

$\therefore$ Time taken by Vitthal to reach the end of 65 km in the uphill direction $= 2 + 2\frac{1}{2} = 4\frac{1}{2}$ h

(ii) While returning home,

time taken by Vitthal on flat road = 2 h

[as he maintained the same average speed on the flat road in both the directions]

$\therefore$ Time taken by him on the slope

$$= 2\frac{1}{2} - 2 = \frac{1}{2} \text{ h}$$

Hence, his average speed on the slope while descending $= \frac{25}{1/2} = 50$ km/h

21. (i) First beneficiary got ₹ $1 + \left(\frac{1}{n+1}\right)$ of the remaining amount.

Total amount = ₹ n^2

Remaining amount = ₹ $(n^2 - 1)$

Money received by first beneficiary

$$= 1 + \left(\frac{1}{n+1}\right)(n^2 - 1)$$

$$= 1 + \frac{(n+1)(n-1)}{n+1} = n$$

(ii) Amount received by second beneficiary

$$= 2 + \frac{1}{n+1}\{n^2 - n - 2\}$$

$$= 2 + \frac{1}{n+1}(n+1)(n-2) = 2 + n - 2 = n$$

Amount received by third beneficiary

$$= 3 + \frac{1}{n+1}(n^2 - 2n - 3)$$

$$= 3 + \frac{(n+1)(n-3)}{n+1} = 3 + n - 3 = n$$

Similarly, all other beneficiaries will also get the same amount n.

(iii) Yes, distribution is fair as every person gets an equal amount alongwith valid mathematical reasoning.

Part II

1. **Hint** Do same as Example 3 of Topic 1. **Ans.** $k = \frac{1}{2}$

2. **Hint** Yes, consider the quadratic equation $2x^2 + x - 4 = 0$, which have rational coefficients.

   The roots of the given quadratic equation are $\frac{-1+\sqrt{33}}{4}$ and $\frac{-1-\sqrt{33}}{4}$, which are irrational.

3. **Hint** Do same as Example 1 (ii) of Topic 2.
   Ans. 3, – 2.

4. Simplifies the given equation as

   $$8x^3 + 12x^2 + 6x + 1 = 8x^3 + 8x + 3$$

   Simplifies the above equation by combining like terms and taking out common factors as

   $$6x^2 - x - 1 = 0$$

   Factorises the above equation as

   $$(3x + 1)(2x - 1) = 0$$

   Writes the zeroes of the above equation in the form (x, y) as

   $$\left(-\frac{1}{3}, 0\right) \text{and} \left(\frac{1}{2}, 0\right)$$

5. **Hint** A quadratic equation with integral coefficients may not have integral roots. Consider the quadratic equation $4x^2 - 8x + 3 = 0$, which have integral coefficients. The roots of the given quadratic equation are $\frac{1}{2}$ and $\frac{3}{2}$, which are not integers.

6. **Hint** Yes, consider the quadratic equation $\sqrt{3}x^2 - 7\sqrt{3}x + 12\sqrt{3} = 0$, which have distinct irrationals coefficients. The roots of this quadratic equation are 3 and 4, which are rational.

7. False, e.g. The quadratic equation, $x^2 + 4 = 0$, has no real roots.

8. **Hint** Do same as Example 4 of Topic 3. **Ans.** Roots of the given quadratic equation are real and distinct.

9. **Hint** Do same as Example 4 of Topic 3.

   Ans. No real roots i.e. the imaginary roots.

10. **Hint** Do same as Example 3 of Topic 3. **Ans.** 9

11. **Hint** Do same as Question 6 of Try these 4.3.

    Ans. $k = \frac{1}{4\sqrt{2}}$

12. **Hint** Do same as Example 5 of Topic 3. **Ans.** 2, –2

13. Given equation,

    $$mx(5x - 6) + 9 = 0 \Rightarrow 5mx^2 - 6mx + 9 = 0$$

    Comparing equation with $ax^2 + bx + c = 0$, we get

    $$a = 5m, b = -6m, c = 9$$

    According to the question, equation has equal roots

    $\therefore \quad D = b^2 - 4ac = 0$

    $\Rightarrow \quad (-6m)^2 - 4 \times 5m \times 9 = 0$

    $\Rightarrow \quad 36m^2 - 180m = 0 \Rightarrow 36m(m - 5) = 0$

    Thus, $m = 0$ and $m = 5$

    $m = 0$ [not possible, the equation would not be a quadratic equation]

    $\therefore$ Correct answer is $m = 5$.

14. **Hint** Let the number be x.

    $\therefore \; 2x^2 + x = 21$ **Ans.** $2x^2 + x - 21 = 0$

15. **Hint** Do same as Example 1 of Topic 1.

    (i) It is a quadratic equation.

    (ii) Not a quadratic equation.

16. **Hint** Do same as Example 3 of Topic 1. **Ans.** $k = 2$

17. **Hint** Do same as Example 3 of Topic 1. **Ans.** $p = \sqrt{6}$

18. Simplifies the given equation, we get

    $$(y-1)(y-3)\left(\frac{y - 1 + 2y(y-3)}{(y-3)(y-1)}\right) = 2$$

    $$\Rightarrow (y-1)(y-3)\left(\frac{y - 1 + 2y^2 - 6y}{(y-3)(y-1)}\right) = 2$$

    $\Rightarrow \quad 2y^2 - 5y - 1 = 2$

    $\Rightarrow \quad 2y^2 - 5y - 3 = 0$

    Factorises the above equation as $(y - 3)(2y + 1) = 0$

    Concludes that the solution of the original equation is

    $$y = \frac{-1}{2} \text{ as } y \neq 3$$

19. Hint $(\sqrt{6x+7})^2 = (2x-7)^2$

$\Rightarrow 2x^2 - 17x + 21 = 0$

Now, do same as Example 1 of Topic 2. **Ans.** $\frac{3}{2}, 7$

20. Hint Do same as Question 19. **Ans.** 8, 20

21. Hint $ax^2 + a = a^2x + x$

$\Rightarrow ax^2 - a^2x - x + a = 0$ **Ans.** $a, 1/a$

22. We have, $\frac{1}{a+b+x} = \frac{1}{a} + \frac{1}{b} + \frac{1}{x}$

$\Rightarrow \quad \frac{1}{a} + \frac{1}{b} = \frac{1}{a+b+x} - \frac{1}{x}$

$\Rightarrow \quad \frac{a+b}{ab} = \frac{x-a-b-x}{(a+b+x)x}$

$\Rightarrow \quad \frac{1}{ab} = \frac{-1}{(a+b+x)x}$

$\Rightarrow \quad ax + bx + x^2 = -ab$

$\Rightarrow \quad x^2 + ax + bx + ab = 0$

$\Rightarrow \quad (x+a)(x+b) = 0$

$\Rightarrow \quad x + a = 0$ or $x + b = 0$

$\Rightarrow \quad x = -a$ or $x = -b$

Hence, $x = -a$ or $-b$.

23. Given, $3(3)^{2m} + 11(3)^m = 4$

Substitute $3^m = x$ and write the given equation as :

$$3x^2 + 11x - 4 = 0$$

Simplifies the above equation as :

$$(3x-1)(x+4) = 0$$

Finds the roots of the above equation as $\frac{1}{3}$ and -4.

$\Rightarrow \quad 3^m = x = \frac{1}{3}$

$\Rightarrow \quad 3^m = 3^{-1}$

$\Rightarrow \quad m = -1$

and $3^m = x = -4$, which is not possible as 3 to any variable power cannot result in a negative number.

24. Hint $a^2b^2x^2 + b^2x - a^2x - 1 = 0$

$\Rightarrow \quad b^2x(a^2x+1) - 1(a^2x+1) = 0$

$\Rightarrow \quad b^2x - 1 = 0$ or $a^2x + 1 = 0$

Ans. $-\frac{1}{a^2}, \frac{1}{b^2}$

25. Hint $\frac{16}{x} - 1 = \frac{15}{x+1}$

$\Rightarrow \quad \frac{16}{x} - \frac{15}{x+1} = 1 \Rightarrow \frac{16(x+1) - 15x}{x(x+1)} = 1$

$\Rightarrow \quad 16x + 16 - 15x = x^2 + x$

$\Rightarrow \quad x^2 = 16 \Rightarrow x = \pm 4$

Hence, the roots are 4 and -4.

26. Hint Do same as Example 1 of Topic 3.

Required numerical difference of the roots

$$= 9 - (-2) = 11$$

Ans. 11

27. Hint Do same as Example 2 of Topic 3.

Ans. $\frac{\sqrt{3}}{4}$ and $-\frac{2}{\sqrt{3}}$

28. Hint First simplify the given equation, then prove that

$$D = b^2 - 4ac < 0$$

29. Given, $30ax^2 - 6x + 1 = 0$

Comparing equation with $Ax^2 + Bx + C = 0$

$$A = 30a, B = -6 \text{ and } C = 1$$

For no real roots, $D < 0$

$B^2 - 4AC < 0$

$\Rightarrow \quad 36 - 120a < 0 \Rightarrow 120a > 36$

$\Rightarrow \quad a > \frac{3}{10}$

30. Hint Do same as Example 6 of Topic 3.

Ans. Least positive value of k is 8.

31. Given, $x^2 + 2cx + ab = 0$ ...(i)

and $x^2 - 2(a+b)x + a^2 + b^2 + 2c^2 = 0$ ...(ii)

Let D_1 and D_2 be the discriminants of Eqs. (i) and (ii), respectively. Then,

$D_1 = (2c)^2 - 4 \times 1 \times ab$

and $D_2 = \{-2(a+b)\}^2 - 4 \times 1 \times (a^2 + b^2 + 2c^2)$

$= -8(c^2 - ab)$

Since, the roots of Eq. (i) are real and unequal.

$\therefore \quad D_1 > 0$

$\Rightarrow \quad 4(c^2 - ab) > 0$

$\Rightarrow \quad -4(c^2 - ab) < 0 \quad [\because A > 0 \Rightarrow -A < 0]$

$\Rightarrow \quad -8(c^2 - ab) < 0$

$\Rightarrow \quad D_2 < 0$

Hence, the roots of Eq. (ii) are not real. **Hence proved.**

32. Hint Given, $x = \sqrt{5 + \sqrt{5 + \sqrt{5 + \ldots \infty}}}$

Then, $\quad x = \sqrt{5+x} \Rightarrow x^2 = (\sqrt{5+x})^2$

Ans. $x^2 - x - 5 = 0$

33. Hint Do same as Example 5 of Topic 3.

Ans. $k = 0, 8$

34. Hint According to the statement of the question, we have

$$\frac{x-9}{2}+2\sqrt{x}+3\times\frac{x}{7}+4\times\frac{\sqrt{x}}{7}=59$$

$\Rightarrow\quad 7x-63+28\sqrt{x}+6x+8\sqrt{x}=826$

$\Rightarrow\quad 13x+36\sqrt{x}=826+63$

$\Rightarrow\quad 13x+36\sqrt{x}-889=0$

Solve it and find the value of x.

The total number of cars

$=\left(\frac{x-9}{2}\right)+(\sqrt{x})+\left(\frac{x}{7}\right)+\left(\frac{\sqrt{x}}{7}\right)$ **Ans.** 35.

35. Let the one positive integer be x and other be $y\ (y>x)$.

According to given condition,

$y^2=16x$ ...(i)

Now, the sum of squares of two positive integers is 225.

$\therefore\quad x^2+y^2=225$

$\Rightarrow\quad x^2+16x=225$ [using Eqs. (i)]

$\Rightarrow x^2+16x-225=0$

$\therefore\ x^2+16x-225=0$, where x is the smaller number.

36. Hint Let the number of wickets taken by Zaheer in a cricket match be x, then number of wickets taken by Harbhajan $=2x-3$

Ans. $2x^2-3x-20=0$

37. Hint The time between 2 pm to 3 pm

$=1\text{h}=60$ min

Given that at t min past 2 pm, the time needed by the minute hand of a clock to show 3 pm was found to be 3 min less than $\frac{t^2}{4}$ min.

$\therefore\ t+\left(\frac{t^2}{4}-3\right)=60$ **Ans.** 14 min

38. Hint Let the two consecutive positive integers be x and $(x+1)$.

Then, according to the question, $x\times(x+1)=306$

Solve it and take only +ve value of x. **Ans.** 17 and 18.

39. Let the first odd integer be x.

Then, second odd integer $=x+2$

Also, given that

Sum of squares of both the numbers $=290$

$x^2+(x+2)^2=290$

$\Rightarrow\quad x^2+2x+2=145\Rightarrow x^2+2x-143=0$

Now, solve it by using quadratic formula and neglect – ve value of x.

Ans. First odd integer = 11 and second odd integer = 13

40. Hint Do same as Example 1 of Topic 4.

Ans. 7 and 9.

41. Let the two numbers be x and $18-x$.

According to the question,

$$\frac{1}{x}+\frac{1}{18-x}=\frac{9}{40}\Rightarrow\frac{18-x+x}{x(18-x)}=\frac{9}{40}$$

$\Rightarrow\quad 18\times40=9x(18-x)$

$\Rightarrow\quad x^2-18x+80=0$

$\Rightarrow\quad (x-10)(x-8)=0$

$\Rightarrow\quad x=10, 8$

So, $18-x=8, 10$

Hence, the two numbers are 8 and 10.

42. Hint Let three consecutive natural numbers be $x, x+1, x+2$.

Then, $(x+1)^2=60+[(x+2)^2-x^2]$

Ans. 9, 10, 11

43. Hint Let the first number be x.

Then, second number $=x+4$

[$\because$ difference of two numbers $=4$]

According to the question,

$$\frac{1}{x}-\frac{1}{x+4}=\frac{4}{21}$$

Ans. $-7, -3$ or 3, 7

44. Hint Let the first number be $5x$,

second number $=5x+5$

and third number $=(5x+5)+5=(5x+10)$

According to the questions,

$(5x)^2+(5x+5)^2+(5x+10)^2=725$

Now, simplify and solve it.

Ans. 10, 15 and 20.

45. Hint When mistake was committed by first one in writing constant term. So, coefficient of x was written correctly and he got roots as 6 and 8.

$\therefore$ Sum of roots $=6+8=14$

The other person did mistake in writing coefficient of x. So, constant term was written correctly and he got roots as 3 and 14.

$\therefore$ Product of roots $=3\times14=42$

$\therefore$ Required quadratic equation $=x^2-14x+42=0$

46. Hint Do same as example 4 of Topic 4. **Ans.** 16 yr

47. Hint Do same as Example 6 of Topic 4. **Ans.** 500 km/h

48. Hint Let the original speed of the plane be x km/h.

$\therefore$ Time taken to travel 1500 km at x km/h $=\frac{1500}{x}$ h

Now, speed of the plane = $(x+250)$ km/h

$\therefore$ Time taken to travel 1500 km at $(x+250)$ km/h

$$=\frac{1500}{x+250}\text{ h}$$

As per given statement of the question, we have

$$\frac{1500}{x}-\frac{1500}{x+250}=\frac{30}{60}$$

Now, solve it and reject – ve value, because speed cannot be negative. **Ans.** 750 km/h.

49. Hint According to the question,

$BC^2+AC^2=AB^2$ [by Pythagoras theorem]

$\Rightarrow (x+2)^2+(x+9)^2=17^2$ [$\because AB=17$ cm]

$\Rightarrow \quad x^2+11x-102=0,$

which is the required equation.

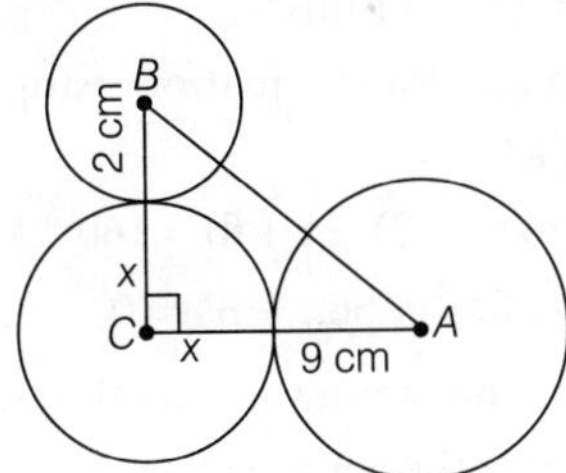

Ans. 6 cm

50. Hint Do same as Example 2 of Topic 2.

Ans. $2\pm2\sqrt{3}$

51. Hint Do same as Example 2 of Topic 2.

Ans. $\frac{11}{2}, 8$

52. Hint $5^x\cdot5+\frac{5^2}{5^x}=126$

Let $5^x=y$, then $5y+\frac{5^2}{y}=126$

$\Rightarrow \quad y=\frac{1}{5}, 25$

$\Rightarrow 5^x=5^{-1}, 5^x=5^2$ [put $y=5^x$]

On comparing the powers, we get

$$x=-1, 2$$

Hence, the required roots of the given equation are – 1 and 2.

53. We have,

$$x=\cfrac{1}{2-\cfrac{1}{2-\cfrac{1}{2-x}}}=\cfrac{1}{2-\cfrac{1}{\cfrac{2(2-x)-1}{2-x}}}$$

$$\Rightarrow \quad x=\cfrac{1}{2-\cfrac{2-x}{4-2x-1}}=\cfrac{1}{2-\cfrac{2-x}{3-2x}}$$

$$\Rightarrow \quad x=\cfrac{1}{\cfrac{2(3-2x)-(2-x)}{3-2x}}$$

$$\Rightarrow \quad x=\frac{3-2x}{2(3-2x)-(2-x)}$$

$$\Rightarrow \quad x=\frac{3-2x}{6-4x-2+x} \Rightarrow x=\frac{3-2x}{4-3x}$$

$\Rightarrow \quad x(4-3x)=3-2x$

$\Rightarrow \quad 4x-3x^2=3-2x$

$\Rightarrow \quad 4x-3x^2-3+2x=0$

$\Rightarrow \quad 3x^2-6x+3=0$

$\Rightarrow \quad x^2-2x+1=0$ [dividing both sides by 3]

$\Rightarrow \quad (x-1)^2=0$ [$\because (a-b)^2=a^2-2ab+b^2$]

$\therefore \quad x=1$

54. Hint Given, $3x^2+px+4=0$ and one root is $\frac{2}{3}$.

On putting $x=\frac{2}{3}$ in given equation, we get

$$3\left(\frac{2}{3}\right)^2+p\left(\frac{2}{3}\right)+4=0$$

$$\Rightarrow \quad \frac{4}{3}+\frac{2p}{3}+4=0$$

$$\Rightarrow \quad p=-8$$

On putting the value of p in given equation, we get

$$3x^2-8x+4=0$$

Solve it and find the roots.

Ans. $p=-8$ and other root = 2

55. Hint Do same as Example 1 of Topic 3.

Ans. $x=3, \frac{-2}{3}$.

56. Hint $3(-2)^2+7(-2)+p=0 \Rightarrow p=2$

Now, $x^2+k(4x+k-1)+p=0$

$\Rightarrow \quad x^2+k(4x+k-1)+2=0$

Apply, $D=b^2-4ac=0$

Ans. $k=-1$ or $k=\frac{2}{3}$

57. Hint $2(-5)^2+p\times(-5)-15=0$

$\Rightarrow \quad p=7$

Now, $p(x^2+x)+k=0$

$\Rightarrow \quad 7(x^2+x)+k=0$

Apply, $D=b^2-4ac=0$

Ans. $p=7, k=\frac{7}{4}$

58. Hint Discriminant, $D=B^2-4AC=0$

$\Rightarrow \quad (b-c)^2-4(a-b)(c-a)=0$

59. Hint On comparing the given equation with $Ax^2 + Bx + C = 0$, we get

$$A = (1 + m^2), B = 2mc$$

and $$C = (c^2 - a^2)$$

Since, the given equation has equal roots.

$\therefore$ Discriminant, $D = 0$

$\Rightarrow$ $B^2 - 4AC = 0$

$\Rightarrow$ $(2mc)^2 - 4(1 + m^2)(c^2 - a^2) = 0$

Simplify it and prove that $c^2 = a^2(1 + m^2)$

60. Hint Suppose that Arjun had x arrows.

According to question,

Number of arrows used to cut down arrows of Bheeshm

$$= \frac{x}{2},$$

Number of arrows used to kill the charioteer = 6,

Number of other arrows used = 3

And remaining arrows $= 4\sqrt{x} + 1$ that used to laid Bheeshm unconcious on arrow bed.

$$\therefore \quad \frac{x}{2} + 6 + 3 + 4\sqrt{x} + 1 = x$$

Put $\sqrt{x} = y$ and solve it. **Ans.** 100.

61. Hint Do same as Example 4 of Topic 4.

Ans. 14 yr

62. Hint Let the length of piece be x m.

Then, rate = ₹ $\frac{200}{x}$ per m

Now, new length $= (x + 5)$ m

Since, the cost remains same.

$\therefore$ New rate = ₹ $\frac{200}{x + 5}$ per m

Then, $\frac{200}{x + 5} = \frac{200}{x} - 2$

Ans. 20 m, ₹ 10

63. Hint Do same as Example 8 of Topic 4.

Ans. 20 min; 25 min

64. Hint Let the speed of stream be x km/h.

$\therefore$ Speed of upstream $= (18 - x)$ km/h

and speed of downstream $= (18 + x)$ km/h

According to the question, we get

$$\frac{24}{18 - x} - \frac{24}{18 + x} = 1$$

Now, solve it.

Ans. Speed of stream = 6 km/h

65. Hint Let the width of the gravel path be x m. Then, each side of the square flower bed is $(44 - 2x)$ m.

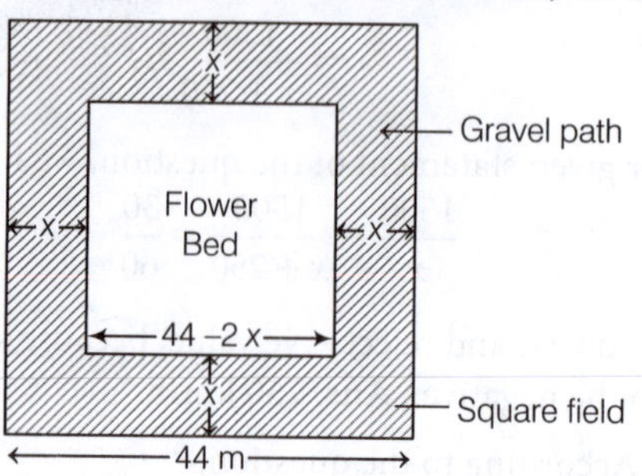

Ans. 2m

66. (i) **Hint** Finds the area of the original quilt as $12 \times 8 = 96$ sq units

Finds the area of the quilt with the border as $96 + 64 = 160$ sq units

Frames a quadratic equation using the total area of the quilt as :

$$(4x + 12)(2x + 8) = 160$$

$$\Rightarrow \quad 8x^2 + 56x - 64 = 0$$

(ii) **Hint** Solve the quadratic equation obtained in part (i) and finds the roots as (-8) and 1.

Mentions that $x \neq (-8)$ as length cannot be negative.

Concludes that the value of x is 1 unit.

Ans. 16 units, 10 units.

67. Hint Let the original number of persons be x.

Then, share of each person = ₹ $\frac{6500}{x}$

If the number of persons is increased by 15.

The, new share of each person = ₹ $\frac{6500}{x + 15}$

$$\therefore \quad \frac{6500}{x + 15} = \frac{6500}{x} - 30$$ **Ans.** 50

68. Hint Do same as Question 67. **Ans.** 20

69. Hint Let P be the initial production (2 yr ago) and the increase in production every year be x %. Then, production at the end of first year

$$= P + \frac{Px}{100} = P\left(1 + \frac{x}{100}\right)$$

Production at the end of second year

$$= P\left(1 + \frac{x}{100}\right) + \frac{xP}{100}\left[\left(1 + \frac{x}{100}\right)\right]$$

$$= P\left(1 + \frac{x}{100}\right)\left(1 + \frac{x}{100}\right) = P\left(1 + \frac{x}{100}\right)^2$$

Since, production doubles in the last 2 yr.

$$\therefore \; P\left(1 + \frac{x}{100}\right)^2 = 2P \Rightarrow \left(1 + \frac{x}{100}\right)^2 = 2$$ **Ans.** 41.4%

QUADRATIC EQUATIONS

An equation of the form $ax^2 + bx + c = 0$ is called quadratic equation in variable x, where a, b and c are real numbers and $a \neq 0$.
e.g. $3x^2 + 5x + 2 = 0$
The form $ax^2 + bx + c = 0, a \neq 0$ is called the standard form of a quadratic equation.

Method to Check Whether a Given Equation is Quadratic or Not

First write the given equation in its simplest form and then compare the equation with the standard form of a quadratic equation
i.e. $ax^2 + bx + c = 0, a \neq 0$.

Solutions or Roots of a Quadratic Equation

1. Method to check the given value is a solution of given quadratic equation or not Put the value of $x = \alpha$ in the given quadratic equation.
If $P(\alpha) = 0$, then $x = \alpha$ is the solution of given equation, otherwise not.

2. Method to determine an unknown constant involved in a quadratic equation when its solution or root is given
To find the value of unknown constant, put the value of root or solution in given quadratic equation and simplify it to get the required unknown constant.

Solution of a Quadratic Equation by Quadratic Formula

The quadratic formula for the quadratic equation $ax^2 + bx + c = 0, a \neq 0$ is

$$x = \frac{-b \pm \sqrt{b^2 - 4ac}}{2a}$$

$$x = \frac{-b \pm \sqrt{D}}{2a}$$

where, $D = b^2 - 4ac = 0$ is known as discriminant.

Relationship Between Discriminant and Nature of Roots

The nature of roots depends upon the value of the discriminant D.

Case I When $D = 0$ i.e. $b^2 - 4ac = 0$,
then $x = \frac{-b \pm 0}{2a} \Rightarrow x = \frac{-b}{2a}, \frac{-b}{2a}$
So, it has two equal and real roots or repeated roots.

Case II When $D > 0$ i.e. $b^2 - 4ac > 0$,
then $x = \frac{-b \pm \sqrt{D}}{2a}$
So, it has two distinct real roots.

Case III When $D < 0$, $b^2 - 4ac < 0$. Since, $\sqrt{D}$ cannot be evaluated for $D < 0$, so there is no real roots or it has imaginary roots.

Solution of a Quadratic Equation by Factorisation

To find the solution of quadratic equation $ax^2 + bx + c = 0$ using factorisation method, first find the product of a and c and write it as a sum of its two factors such that sum is equal to b.
i.e. $ac = p \times q$ and $p + q = b$
where, p and q are factors of ac.
Then, put the value of b obtained from above in given equation and write it LHS as product of two linear factors. Then, equate each factor to zero to get desired roots of given quadratic equation.

Word Problems and Their Solutions

To solve such problems, first consider the one quantity as a variable (say x) and find the other quantity in terms of x using the given condition.
Then, according to the given condition, write the equation in the quantities which is obtained above. Then, simplify it to get the quadratic equation.
Now, to solve the quadratic equation use any method i.e. factorisation or quadratic formula to obtain the value of variable x.

CHAPTER 5

Arithmetic Progressions (AP)

In this chapter, we will study the sequence (list of numbers) in which succeeding terms are obtained by adding a fixed number to the preceding terms. We will find the formulae to find the value of any term and the sum of terms for this sequence.

Sequence (List of Numbers)

A list of numbers arranged in a definite order according to some definite rule, is called a sequence.

e.g.

(i) 1, 2, 3, 4, 5, 6, ...

In this sequence each number is 1 more than the number preceding it, except first number.

(ii) 2, 4, 8, 16, ...

In this sequence, each number is obtained on multiplying the preceding number by 2, except first number.

The various numbers occurring in a sequence are called its **terms**.

Consider, a sequence $a_1, a_2, a_3, a_4 ...$

Here, a_1 is called first term, a_2 is called second term and so on. Its *n*th term is denoted by a_n, which is also known as the general term of sequence.

A sequence is said to be finite or infinite accordingly it has a finite or infinite number of terms.

Progression

Those sequences whose terms always follow certain patterns are called progressions.

e.g.

(i) The sequence 3, 5, 7, 9 ... is a progression, as each term can be found by adding 2 to the term preceding it.

(ii) The sequence 3, 10, 18, 21, 35 ... . is not a progression as its terms are not following any certain pattern.

Note it All progressions are sequences but all sequences need not be progressions.

In this chapter, we will study about one of the progression, ***arithmetic progression****.*

TOPIC 01 Introduction to Arithmetic Progressions

Arithmetic Progressions

An Arithmetic Progression (AP) is a list of numbers in which each term is obtained by adding a fixed number to the preceding term except the first term.

This fixed number is called the common difference (d) of the AP. It can be positive, negative or zero.

In other words, a list of numbers $a_1, a_2, a_3, ..., a_n$ is called an arithmetic progression (AP), if there exists a constant number d (called common difference) such that

$$a_2 - a_1 = d$$
$$a_3 - a_2 = d$$
$$a_4 - a_3 = d$$
$$\vdots$$
$$a_n - a_{n-1} = d \text{ and so on.}$$

Each of the numbers in this list is called a **term**.

In general, $a, a+d, a+2d, a+3d, \ldots$ represent an arithmetic progression, where a is the **first term** and d is the **common difference**. This is called general form of an AP.

If number of terms in an AP is finite, then it is called a **finite AP,** otherwise it is called an **infinite AP**. Such APs do not have a last term.

Note it If the common difference of an AP is zero i.e. $d = 0$, then each term of the AP will be same as the first term of the AP.

Example 1. Find the common difference of the following AP's.

(i) $3, -2, -7, -12, ...$

(ii) 11, 11, 11, 11, ...

(iii) $5\frac{1}{2}, 9\frac{1}{2}, 13\frac{1}{2}, 17\frac{1}{2}, ...$

(iv) $\sqrt{3}, \sqrt{12}, \sqrt{27}, \sqrt{48}, ...$ CBSE 2019

Sol. (i) Given, AP is $3, -2, -7, -12, ...$

Here, $a_1 = 3,\ a_2 = -2,\ a_3 = -7,\ a_4 = -12$ and so on.

$\therefore$ Common difference $(d) = a_2 - a_1 = -2 - 3 = -5$

(ii) Given, AP is 11, 11, 11, 11, ...

Here, $a_1 = 11, a_2 = 11, a_3 = 11, a_4 = 11$ and so on.

$\therefore$ Common difference $(d) = a_2 - a_1 = 11 - 11 = 0$

(iii) Given, AP is $5\frac{1}{2}, 9\frac{1}{2}, 13\frac{1}{2}, 17\frac{1}{2}, ...$

Here, $a_1 = 5\frac{1}{2},\ a_2 = 9\frac{1}{2},\ a_3 = 13\frac{1}{2},\ a_4 = 17\frac{1}{2}$ and so on.

$\therefore$ Common difference $(d) = a_2 - a_1 = 9\frac{1}{2} - 5\frac{1}{2}$

$= \frac{19}{2} - \frac{11}{2} = \frac{8}{2} = 4$

(iv) Given, AP is $\sqrt{3}, \sqrt{12}, \sqrt{27}, \sqrt{48} \ldots$

Here, $a_1 = \sqrt{3}, a_2 = \sqrt{12} = 2\sqrt{3}, a_3 = \sqrt{27} = 3\sqrt{3}$

and $a_4 = \sqrt{48} = 4\sqrt{3}$ and so on.

$\therefore$ Common difference $(d) = a_2 - a_1 = 2\sqrt{3} - \sqrt{3} = \sqrt{3}$

Method to Check an AP When a List of Numbers is Given

Sometimes, a list of numbers or sequence is given and we have to check that this sequence is an AP or not. For this, we find the differences of consecutive terms. If these differences are same, then given list of numbers or sequence is an AP, otherwise not.

Example 2. Examine that the list of numbers 13, 10, 7, 4,... form an AP. If it forms an AP, then write the next two terms.

Sol. Here, we have $a_2 - a_1 = 10 - 13 = -3$,

$a_3 - a_2 = 7 - 10 = -3$,

$a_4 - a_3 = 4 - 7 = -3$ and so on

Since, difference of any two consecutive terms is same, so the given list of numbers form an AP.

Now, the next two terms are $4 + (-3) = 1$ and $1 + (-3) = -2$.

Example 3. Examine that the list of numbers obtained from following situation, will be in the form of an AP. "Amount left with Sandeep (in ₹) out of the total amount of ₹12000 which he had in the beginning, when he spends ₹500 in the beginning of every month."

Sol. Given, in the beginning Sandeep had = ₹ 12000

Also, in the beginning of every month, he spend = ₹ 500

So, in the beginning of 1st month, he had amount, $t_1 =$ ₹ 12000

In the beginning of 2nd month, he had amount,

$t_2 = 12000 - 500 =$ ₹ 11500

In the beginning of 3rd month, he had amount,

$t_3 = 11500 - 500 =$ ₹ 11000

In the beginning of 4th month, he had amount,

$t_4 = 11000 - 500 =$ ₹ 10500 and so on.

Now, the list of amounts is 12000, 11500, 11000, 10500, ...

Here, $t_2 - t_1 = t_3 - t_2 = t_4 - t_3 = -500$

i.e. $t_{k+1} - t_k$ is same everytime.

So, the above list of numbers forms an AP.

Method to Write an AP When First Term and Common Difference are Given

To write an AP, the minimum information required is to know the first term a and the common difference d of the arithmetic progression. Then, we put the values of a and d in $a, a+d, a+2d, a+3d, \ldots$ to get the required AP.

Example 4. **Write an AP having 4 as the first term and −3 as the common difference.**

Sol. Given, first term $(a) = 4$ and common difference $(d) = -3$

On putting the values of a and d in general form $a, a+d, a+2d, a+3d, \ldots$, we get

$$4, 4-3, 4+2(-3), 4+3(-3), \ldots$$

$$4, 1, 4-6, 4-9, \text{ or } 4, 1, -2, -5, \ldots$$

which is the required AP.

Try These 5.1

1. **Which of the following form an AP? Justify your answer.**
   (i) 1, 1, 2, 2, 3, 3, ... NCERT Exemplar
   (ii) $5, 2, -1, -4, -7, \ldots$
   (iii) 0.3, 0.33, 0.333, ...
   (iv) $4, 4+\sqrt{2}, 4+2\sqrt{2}, 4+3\sqrt{2}, \ldots$
2. **Write the common difference of the given AP** $\sqrt{3}, 2\sqrt{3}, 3\sqrt{3}, \ldots$
3. **Write the first term and common difference of the following APs**
   (i) 5, 8, 11, 14, ... (ii) $\frac{1}{4}, \frac{5}{4}, \frac{9}{4}, \frac{13}{4}, \ldots$
4. **Find the common difference and the next two terms of the following APs**
   (i) 6, 12, 18,.... . (ii) 5, 13, 21, 29, ...
5. **Find the first four terms of an AP, whose first term a and the common difference d are given as follows**
   (i) $a = -2, d = -2$ (ii) $a = -1, d = 4$
6. **Examine that the list of numbers 7, 13, 19, 25, ... forms an AP. If they form an AP, then write the next two terms.**
7. **Which of the following are APs? If they form an AP, find the common difference d and write three more terms.**
   (i) 4, 8, 12, 16, ... (ii) $1^2, 2^2, 3^2, 4^2, \ldots$
8. **Write next three terms of the given AP**
   $(a+b), (a+1)+b, (a+1)+(b+1), \ldots$ NCERT Exemplar
9. **Examine that the list of numbers obtained from the following situation, will be in the form of an AP or not.**
   (i) 'The amount of money in the account every year, when ₹ 100 is deposited at compound interest at 4% per annum'.
   (ii) The cost of digging a well after every metre of digging when it cost ₹ 300 for the first metre and rises by ₹ 65 for each subsequent metre.

Answers

1. (i) No (ii) Yes (iii) No (iv) Yes
2. $\sqrt{3}$
3. (i) 5, 3 (ii) $\frac{1}{4}, 1$
4. (i) $d = 6$, The next two terms are 24 and 30.
   (ii) $d = 8$, The next two terms are 37 and 45.
5. (i) $-2, -4, -6$ and -8 (ii) $-1, 3, 7, 11$
6. Yes; 31, 37
7. (i) $a_1 = a = 4, a_2 = 8, a_3 = 12$
   So, $a_2 - a_1 = 8 - 4 = 4$
   and $a_3 - a_2 = 12 - 8 = 4$
   Since, $a_2 - a_1 = a_3 - a_2$
   So, the given list of numbers forms an AP.
   Here, $a = 4$ and $d = 4$
   So, next three terms are
   $$a_5 = a + 4d = 4 + 4 \times 4 = 20$$
   $$a_6 = a + 5d = 4 + 5 \times 4 = 24$$
   $$a_7 = a + 6d = 4 + 6 \times 4 = 28$$
   (ii) $a_1 = 1^2 = 1, a_2 = 2^2 = 4, a_3 = 3^2 = 9$
   $\therefore a_2 - a_1 = 4 - 1 = 3, a_3 - a_2 = 9 - 4 = 5$
   Since, $a_2 - a_1 \neq a_3 - a_2$
   $\therefore$ The given list of numbers does not form an AP.
8. $(a+2)+(b+1), (a+2)+(b+2), (a+3)+(b+2)$
9. (i) No (ii) Yes, consecutive terms differ by same numbers.

TOPIC 02 *n*th Term of an AP

If the first term of an AP is a and its common difference is d, then its nth term is given by the formula

$$a_n = a + (n-1)d$$

The n term of an AP is also called its **general term**.

If there are n terms in an AP, then nth term is known as last term of an AP and it is denoted by l, which is given by the formula

$$l = a + (n-1)d$$

where, a is first term and d is common difference.

Example 1. **Find the 20th term of the AP : 7, 3, −1, −5 ....**

Sol. Given, AP is $7, 3, -1, -5, \ldots$.

Here, $a = 7$ and $d = 3 - 7 = -4$

Since, nth term, $a_n = a + (n-1)d$

On putting $n = 20$, we get

$$a_{20} = a + (20-1)d = 7 + 19(-4)$$
$$= 7 - 19 \times 4 = 7 - 76 = -69$$

Hence, 20th term of given sequence is -69.

Types of Problems Based on *n*th Term of an AP

Type I Problems Based on Finding n, when nth Term or Last Term of an AP are Given

In this type of problems, an AP with last term is given or AP containing n terms is given (or nth term of an AP is given) and we have to find the value of n.

Example 2. **How many terms are there in the AP 3, 6, 9, 12, ..., 111?**

Sol. Given, AP is 3, 6, 9, 12, ..., 111.

Here, $a = 3$ and $d = 6 - 3 = 3$

Let there be n terms in the given AP.

Then, $n\text{th term} = 111$

$\Rightarrow \quad a + (n-1)d = 111 \quad [\because a_n = a + (n-1)d]$

$\Rightarrow \quad 3 + (n-1) \times 3 = 111$

$\Rightarrow \quad 3(1 + n - 1) = 111$

$\Rightarrow \quad n = \dfrac{111}{3} \Rightarrow n = 37$

Hence, the given AP contains 37 terms.

Example 3. **Which term of the AP 21, 18, 15,... is –81? Also, is any term 0? Give reason.** CBSE 2024 (Basic)

Sol. Given, AP is 21, 18, 15,... .

Here, $a = 21$ and $d = 18 - 21 = -3$

Let nth term of given AP be -81.

Then, $a_n = -81$

$\Rightarrow \quad a + (n-1)d = -81 \quad [\because a_n = a + (n-1)d)]$

On putting the values of a and d, we get

$21 + (n-1)(-3) = -81$

$\Rightarrow \quad 21 - 3n + 3 = -81$

$\Rightarrow \quad 24 - 3n = -81$

$\Rightarrow \quad -3n = -81 - 24 = -105$

$\Rightarrow \quad n = \dfrac{-105}{-3} = 35$

Hence, 35th term of given AP is -81.

Now, we want to know that if there is any n for which $a_n = 0$.

If such any n is there, then we have

$21 + (n-1)(-3) = 0 \Rightarrow 3(n-1) = 21$

$\Rightarrow \quad n - 1 = 7 \Rightarrow n = 8$

$\Rightarrow$ So, eighth term is 0.

Example 4. **Check whether 200 is a term of the list of numbers 7, 11, 15, 19, ...**

Sol. Given, list of numbers 7, 11, 15, 19, ...

Here, $11 - 7 = 15 - 11 = 19 - 15... = 4$

So, it an AP with first term, $a = 7$

and common difference, $d = 4$

Let 200 be a term, say the nth term of this AP.

We know that $a_n = a + (n-1)d$

$\therefore \quad 200 = 7 + (n-1)(4)$

$\Rightarrow \quad 193 = (n-1)(4)$

$\Rightarrow \quad n - 1 = \dfrac{193}{4} \Rightarrow n = \dfrac{197}{4} = 49\dfrac{1}{4}$

But the number of terms cannot be a fraction.

$\therefore$ 200 is not a term of the given AP.

Example 5. **Which term of the AP 3, 15, 27, 39,... will be 120 more than its 21st term?** CBSE 2019

Sol. Given, AP is 3, 15, 27, 39, ...

Here, $a = 3$ and $d = (15 - 3) = 12$

$\therefore$ 21st term is given by

$T_{21} = a + (21-1)d = a + 20d = 3 + 20 \times 12 = 243$

Required term $= (243 + 120) = 363$

Let it be nth term.

Then, $T_n = 363 \quad [\because T_n \text{ means } n\text{th term}]$

$\Rightarrow \quad a + (n-1)d = 363$

$\Rightarrow \quad 3 + (n-1) \times 12 = 363$

$\Rightarrow \quad 12n = 372 \Rightarrow n = 31$

Hence, 31st term is the required term.

Type II Problems Based on Finding the AP or nth Term or Both, when its Two Terms are Given

In this type of problems, two terms (or relation between two terms of an AP) is given and we have to find the AP and nth term of AP.

Example 6. **Determine the AP whose 3rd term is 5 and the 7th term is 9.** CBSE 2024 (Standard)

Sol. We have,

$a_3 = a + (3-1)\,d = a + 2d = 5 \quad \text{... (i)}$

$a_7 = a + (7-1)\,d = a + 6d = 9 \quad \text{... (ii)}$

From Eqs. (i) and (ii), we get

$a = 3$ and $d = 1$

Hence, the required AP is 3, 4, 5, 6, ...

Example 7. **If pth term of an AP is q and qth term is p, then prove that its nth term is $(p + q - n)$.** CBSE 2023 (Standard)

Sol. Given, pth term of AP $= q$

qth term of AP $= p$

To prove, nth term of AP $= p + q - n$

Let a be the first term and d be the common difference of the AP. Since, pth term is q.

$a_p = q \Rightarrow a + (p-1)d = q \quad \text{...(i)}$

Similarly, qth term is p.

$a_q = p \Rightarrow a + (q-1)d = p \quad \text{...(ii)}$

On subtracting Eq. (ii) from Eq. (i), we get

$$(p-1-q+1)d = q-p$$

$$\Rightarrow \quad (p-q)d = q-p \Rightarrow d = -1$$

From Eq. (i), $a+(p-1)(-1) = q$

$$\Rightarrow \quad a-p+1 = q \Rightarrow a = p+q-1$$

$\therefore$ nth term, $a_n = a+(n-1)d$

$$= p+q-1+(n-1)(-1)$$

$$= p+q-1-n+1$$

$$= p+q-n$$

Hence proved.

Type III Word Problems

In this type of problems, first we write the AP or list of numbers (sequence) with the help of given information and then find the required value.

Example 8. **How many two-digit numbers are divisible by 7?** CBSE 2019

Sol. Two-digit numbers are 10, 11, 12, 13, 14, 15,..., 97, 98, 99 in which only 14, 21, 28,..., 98 are divisible by 7.

Here, $21-14 = 28-21 ... = 7$.

So, this list of numbers forms an AP, whose first term (a) = 14 and common difference (d) = 7.

Let there be n terms in the above sequence, such that $a_n = 98$

$$\Rightarrow \quad a+(n-1)d = 98 \quad [\because a_n = a+(n-1)d]$$

$$\Rightarrow \quad 14+(n-1)7 = 98$$

$$\Rightarrow \quad 14+7n-7 = 98$$

$$\Rightarrow \quad 7n = 91$$

$$\Rightarrow \quad n = \frac{91}{7} = 13$$

Hence, there are 13 two-digit numbers divisible by 7.

Example 9. **A sum of ₹ 2000 is invested at 7% simple interest per year. Calculate the interest at the end of each year. Do these interest form an AP? If so, then find the interest at the end of 20th year making use of this fact.**

Sol. Given, initial money P = ₹ 2000

Rate of interest, $R = 7\%$ per year; Time, $T = 1, 2, 3, 4,...$

We know that simple interest is given by the following formula

$$\text{SI} = \frac{PRT}{100}$$

$$\therefore \text{ SI at the end of 1st year} = \frac{2000 \times 7 \times 1}{100} = ₹\ 140$$

$$\text{SI at the end of 2nd year} = \frac{2000 \times 7 \times 2}{100} = ₹\ 280$$

$$\text{SI at the end of 3rd year} = \frac{2000 \times 7 \times 3}{100} = ₹\ 420$$

Thus, the required list of numbers is 140, 280, 420,... .

Here, $280-140 = 420-280... = 140$

So, above list of numbers forms an AP, whose first term (a) = 140 and common difference (d) = 140.

Now, SI at the end of 20th year will be equal to 20th term of the above AP.

$$\therefore a_{20} = a+(20-1)d$$

$$= 140+19\times 140 = 140+2660 = 2800$$

Hence, the interest at the end of 20th year will be ₹ 2800.

nth Term from the End of an AP

Let a be the first term, d be the common difference and l be the last term of an AP, then nth term from the end can be found by the formula

$$n\text{th term from the end} = l-(n-1)d$$

Example 10. **Determine the 10th term from the end of the AP 4, 9, 14, ..., 254.**

Sol. Given, AP is 4, 9, 14,..., 254.

Here, l = last term = 254

d = common difference = $9-4 = 5$

$\therefore$ 10th term from the end $= l-(10-1)d = l-9d$

$$= 254-9\times 5 = 254-45 = 209$$

Alternate Method

On reversing the given AP, new AP is 254, ..., 14, 9, 4.

Here, first term (a) = 254

and common difference (d) = -5

Now, 10th term of new AP = a_{10}

$$= 254+(10-1)(-5)$$

$$= 254-9\times 5 = 209$$

Hence, 10th term from the end of given AP is 209.

Try These 5.2

1. **Find 11th term of AP $-5, -5/2, 0, 5/2, ...$** NCERT Exemplar
2. **Fill in the blanks in the following table, given that a is the first term, d is the common difference and a_n is the nth term of the AP.**

	a	d	n	a_n
(i)	5	4	5	
(ii)	3	...	15	31
(iii)	...	-3	11	10
(iv)	10	5	...	25

3. **For what value of n, are the nth terms of two APs 30, 27, 24,... and 6, 11, 16,... equal?**

4. If in an AP, $a=15$, $d=-3$ and $a_n=0$, then find the value of n. CBSE 2019

5. If $d=-4$, $n=7$ and $a_n=4$, then find the value of the first term. NCERT Exemplar

6. The first term of an AP is 5, common difference is 3 and the last term is 80. Find the number of terms.

7. Check if 0 is a term of the AP 31, 28, 25, ...

8. Find p, if the given value of x is the pth term of the following AP 25, 50, 75, 100, ... ; $x=1000$

9. The 11th term of an AP is 80 and the 16th term is 110. Find the 31st term.

10. What will be the value of a_8-a_4 for the following AP 4, 9, 14, ... 254?

11. Which term of AP 3, 8, 13, 18, ... will be 130 more than its 31st term?

12. Two APs have the same common difference. The difference between their 50th terms is 200, what is the difference between their 500th terms?

13. In a flower bed, there are 43 rose plants in the first row, 41 in the second, 39 in the third and so on. There are 11 rose plants in the last row. How many rows are there in the flower bed?

14. A man starts repaying a loan as first instalment of ₹ 100. If he increases the instalment by ₹ 5 every month, then what amount he will pay in the 30th instalment?

15. How many numbers lie between 10 and 300, which divided by 4 leave a remainder 3 ?

16. A sum of ₹ 5000 is invested at 8% simple interest per annum. Calculate the interest at the end of each year. Do these interests form an AP? Find the interest at the end of 30th year.

17. The taxi fare after each kilometre, when the fare is ₹ 15 for the first kilometre and ₹ 8 for each additional kilometre, does not form an AP as the total fare (in ₹) after each kilometre is 15, 8, 8 ,8, ... Is the statement true? Give reason. NCERT Exemplar

18. Find the 6th term from the end of the AP 17, 14, 11, ... (– 40).

19. In an AP, if $a=10$, $d=5$ and $n=100$, then find the value of a_{100} and also find the 50th term from the end.

Answers

1. Do same as Example 1. **Ans.** 20

2. **Hint** Use the general term formula, $a_n=a+(n-1)\,d$
   (i) $a=5, d=4, n=5, a_n=?$
   So, $a_n=5+(5-1)\times 4=21$
   (ii) $a=3, n=15, a_n=31, d=?$
   So, $31=3+(15-1)\,d \Rightarrow d=2$
   (iii) $a=?, d=-3, n=11, a_n=10$
   So, $10=a+(11-1)(-3) \Rightarrow a=40$
   (iv) $a=10, d=5, n=?, a_n=25$
   So, $25=10+(n-1)5 \Rightarrow n=4$

3. **Hint** For the AP 30, 27, 24, ...
   $$a_1=30,\ d_1=27-30=-3$$
   So, $a_n=a_1+(n-1)d_1=30+(n-1)(-3)$ ... (i)
   Now, for the AP, 6, 11, 16, ...
   $$b_1=6,\ d_2=11-6=5$$
   So, $b_n=b_1+(n-1)d_2=6+(n-1)\,5$ ... (ii)
   Now, to find the value of n for which the nth terms of two AP's are equal, we have
   $$a_n=b_n$$
   Ans. 4

4. **Hint** $a_n=a+(n-1)\,d$ **Ans.** 6

5. **Hint** $a_n=a+(n-1)d$ **Ans.** 28

6. **Hint** Solve as Example 2. **Ans.** 26

7. Solve as Example 4. **Ans.** No

8. **Hint** Here, $a_p=1000$ **Ans.** 40

9. Solve as Example 6 and find a_{31}. **Ans.** 200

10. **Hint** First find a_8, a_4 and then find a_8-a_4. **Ans.** 20

11. Solve as Example 5. **Ans.** 57th

12. Let the common difference of both APs be d.
    The first AP be $a_1, a_2, \ldots, a_n$
    and the second AP be $b_1, b_2, \ldots, b_n$.
    Now, $a_{50}-b_{50}=200$
    $\Rightarrow [a_1+(50-1)\,d]-[b_1+(50-1)\,d]=200$
    $\Rightarrow \quad a_1+49d-b_1-49d=200$
    $\Rightarrow \quad a_1-b_1=200$ ... (i)
    Now, consider $a_{500}-b_{500}=[a_1+(500-1)\,d]$
    $-[b_1+(500-1)\,d]$
    $=a_1+499d-b_1-499d$
    $=a_1-b_1$
    $=200$ [From Eq. (i)]
    Thus, difference between the 500th terms of two APs is 200.

13. **Hint** First term $a=43$, common difference $d=-2$, $a_n=11$
    Ans. 17

14. **Hint** $a=100$, $d=5$ **Ans.** ₹ 245

15. **Hint** The required numbers are 11,15,19, ..., 299.
    Ans. 73

16. Solve as Example 9. **Ans.** 400, 800, 1200, ...; Yes, ₹ 12000

17. **Hint** The total fare (in ₹) after each kilometre is 15, 23, 31, 39, ... **Ans.** Yes

18. **Hint** 6th term from the end $=l-(6-1)\,d$
    Ans. –25

19. **Hint** $a_n=a+(n-1)\,d$
    Then, $a_{100}=a+99d$
    and then same as Example 10.
    Ans. 505, 260

TOPIC 03 Sum of First *n* Terms of an AP

If first term of an AP is a and its common difference is d, then the sum of its first n terms S_n, is given by the formula

$$S_n = \frac{n}{2}[2a + (n-1)d]$$

This formula can also be written as

$$S_n = \frac{n}{2}[a + a_n]$$

where, a_n = nth term of the AP

If l is the last term of an AP of n terms, then $a_n = l$ and the sum of all the terms is given by this formula

$$S_n = \frac{n}{2}[a + l]$$

Example 1. **Find the sum of the first 20 terms of the AP** $-\frac{29}{3}, -9, -\frac{25}{3}, -\frac{23}{3}, \ldots\ldots$ CBSE 2023 (Basic)

Sol. Given, AP is $-\frac{29}{3}, -9, -\frac{25}{3}, -\frac{23}{2}, \ldots$ 20 terms

$$a = -\frac{29}{3}, d = -9 + \frac{29}{3} = \frac{-27+29}{3} = \frac{2}{3}$$

$$n = 20$$

$$S_n = \frac{n}{2}[2a + (n-1)d]$$

$$\Rightarrow S_{20} = \frac{20}{2}\left[2\left(-\frac{29}{3}\right) + (19)\frac{2}{3}\right] = 20\left[-\frac{29}{3} + \frac{19}{3}\right]$$

$$= 20 \times \left(-\frac{10}{3}\right) = -\frac{200}{3}$$

Example 2. **The ratio of the 11th term to the 18th term of an AP is 2 : 3. Find the ratio of the 5th term to the 21st term. Also, find the ratio of the sum of first 5 terms to the sum of first 21 terms.** CBSE 2023 (Standard)

Sol. Given, $\frac{a_{11}}{a_{18}} = \frac{2}{3}$

$$\Rightarrow \frac{a+10d}{a+17d} = \frac{2}{3} \quad [\because a_n = a + (n-1)d]$$

$$\Rightarrow 3a + 30d = 2a + 34d$$

$$a = 4d \quad \ldots\text{(i)}$$

$$\therefore \frac{a_5}{a_{21}} = \frac{a+4d}{a+20d} = \frac{2a}{a+5a} \quad [\text{using Eq. (i)}]$$

$$= \frac{2a}{6a} = \frac{1}{3}$$

$$\therefore a_5 : a_{21} = 1 : 3$$

Now, $\frac{S_5}{S_{21}} = \frac{\frac{5}{2}(2a+4d)}{\frac{21}{2}(2a+20d)}$ $\left[\because S_n = \frac{n}{2}[2a + (n-1)d]\right]$

$$= \frac{5(2a+a)}{21(2a+5a)} = \frac{5}{21} \times \frac{3}{7} = \frac{5}{49} \quad [\text{using Eq. (i)}]$$

$$\therefore S_5 : S_{21} = 5 : 49$$

Example 3. **Find the sum of the first 17 terms of an AP, whose 4th and 9th terms are − 15 and − 30 respectively.**

Sol. Here, $a_4 = -15$ and $a_9 = -30$

As $a_n = a + (n-1)d$

$$\therefore \quad a_4 = a + (4-1)d = -15 \Rightarrow a + 3d = -15 \quad \ldots\text{(i)}$$

and $a_9 = a + (9-1)d = -30 \Rightarrow a + 8d = -30 \quad \ldots$(ii)

From Eqs. (i) and (ii), we get

$$a = -6, d = -3$$

So, $S_{17} = \frac{17}{2}[2 \times (-6) + (17-1)(-3)]$

$$\left[\because S_n = \frac{n}{2}[2a + (n-1)d]\right]$$

$$= \frac{17}{2}[-12 - 48] = -510$$

$$\therefore \quad S_{17} = -510$$

Example 4. **Find the sum of first 20 terms of an AP, whose *n*th term is given by $a_n = 5 + 2n$. Can 52 be a term of this AP?** CBSE 2025 (Basic)

Sol. We have, $a_n = 5 + 2n$

$$\therefore \quad a_1 = 5 + 2 \times 1 = 7$$

$$a_2 = 5 + 2 \times 2 = 5 + 4 = 9$$

$$a_3 = 5 + 2 \times 3 = 5 + 6 = 11$$

$$\vdots \quad \vdots \quad \vdots \quad \vdots$$

So, the list of numbers become 7, 9, 11, ...

Here, $d = 9 - 7 = 11 - 9 = 2$ and so on.

So, it forms an AP with common difference, $d = 2$

To find S_{20}, we have $n = 20$, $a = 7$ and $d = 2$

$$\therefore \quad S_{20} = \frac{20}{2}[2 \times 7 + (20-1) \times 2] \quad \left[\because S_n = \frac{n}{2}[2a + (n-1)d]\right]$$

$$= 10[14 + 38] = 10 \times 52 = 520$$

So, the sum of first 20 terms of the AP is 520.

Now, we want to know that if there is any n for which

$$a_n = 52$$

If such any n is there, then we have

$$7 + (n-1)2 = 52 \Rightarrow 2(n-1) = 45$$

$$\Rightarrow \quad n - 1 = \frac{45}{2} \Rightarrow n = \frac{45}{2} + 1 = \frac{47}{2} = 23.5$$

Hence, 52 is not the term of given AP as 23.5 is not a natural number.

Different Types of Problems Based on the Sum of n Terms of an AP

Type I Problems Based on Finding the Sum of First m Terms, When Sum of First p Terms and q Terms are Given

In this type of problems, we form two equations in a and d with the help of given information and solve them to get a and d. Then, find the sum of required number of terms.

Example 5. **If the sum of first 6 terms of an AP is 36 and that of the first 16 terms is 256, then find the sum of first 10 terms.** CBSE 2023 (Standard)

Sol. Given, $S_6 = 36$

$$\Rightarrow \quad \frac{6}{2}[2a + (6-1)d] = 36 \qquad \left[\because S_n = \frac{n}{2}[2a + (n-1)d]\right]$$

$$\Rightarrow \quad 3(2a + 5d) = 36$$

$$\Rightarrow \quad 2a + 5d = 12 \qquad \ldots\text{(i)}$$

Also, $S_{16} = 256$

$$\Rightarrow \quad \frac{16}{2}[2a + (16-1)d] = 256$$

$$\Rightarrow \quad 8(2a + 15d) = 256$$

$$\Rightarrow \quad 2a + 15d = 32 \qquad \ldots\text{(ii)}$$

On subtracting Eq. (i) from Eq. (ii), we get

$$10d = 20$$

$$\Rightarrow \quad d = 2$$

On putting $d = 2$ in Eq. (i), we get

$$2a = 12 - 5(2) = 2$$

$$\Rightarrow \quad a = 1$$

$$\therefore \quad S_{10} = \frac{10}{2}[2(1) + (10-1)2]$$

$$= 5(2 + 18) = 100$$

Hence, the sum of first 10 terms is 100.

Type II Problems Based on Finding the Number of Terms, When Sum of Terms and AP are Given

In this type of problems, we first find a and d and then assume that number of terms is n. After that we use the formula of sum of first n terms to calculate n.

Example 6. **How many terms of the AP $20, 19\frac{1}{3}, 18\frac{2}{3}, \ldots$ must be taken, so that their sum is 300?**

Sol. Given, AP is $20, 19\frac{1}{3}, 18\frac{2}{3}, \ldots$.

Here, $a = 20$ and $d = 19\frac{1}{3} - 20 = \frac{58}{3} - 20 = \frac{58-60}{3} = \frac{-2}{3}$

Let n terms of given AP be required to get sum 300.

We know that

$$S_n = \frac{n}{2}[2a + (n-1)d]$$

$$\Rightarrow \quad 300 = \frac{n}{2}\left[2(20) + (n-1)\left(\frac{-2}{3}\right)\right]$$

$$[\because a = 20 \text{ and } d = -2/3]$$

$$\Rightarrow \quad 600 = n\left[40 - \frac{2}{3}n + \frac{2}{3}\right]$$

$$\Rightarrow \quad 600 = \frac{1}{3}[120n - 2n^2 + 2n]$$

$$\Rightarrow \quad 600 \times 3 = 122n - 2n^2$$

$$\Rightarrow \quad 1800 + 2n^2 - 122n = 0$$

$$\Rightarrow \quad 2[n^2 - 61n + 900] = 0$$

$$\Rightarrow \quad n^2 - 61n + 900 = 0$$

$$\Rightarrow \quad n^2 - 36n - 25n + 900 = 0$$

$$\Rightarrow \quad n(n-36) - 25(n-36) = 0$$

$$\Rightarrow \quad (n-36)(n-25) = 0$$

$$\Rightarrow \quad n = 36 \text{ or } 25$$

Since, a is positive and d is negative, so both values of n are possible.

Hence, the sum of 25 terms of given AP

= Sum of 36 terms of given AP = 300

Note it If a is positive and d is negative, then we get two values of n because some terms will be positive and some others negative, and will cancel out each other.

Type III Problem Based on Finding the th Term, When the Sum of First n Terms is Given

If S_n and S_{n-1} is the sum of first n and $(n-1)$ terms of an AP, then its nth term a_n is given by

$$a_n = S_n - S_{n-1}$$

Example 7. **If in an AP, $a = 2$ and $S_{10} = 335$, then find its 10th term.**

Sol. In a given AP, first term, $a = 2$

and sum of first 10 terms, $S_{10} = 335$

Since, $S_n = \frac{n}{2}[2a + (n-1)d]$

$$\therefore \quad S_{10} = \frac{10}{2}[2 \times 2 + (10-1)d]$$

$$\Rightarrow \quad 335 = 5[4 + 9d] \Rightarrow 4 + 9d = 67$$

$$\Rightarrow \quad 9d = 63$$

$$\Rightarrow \quad d = \frac{63}{9} = 7$$

$\therefore$ Common difference, $d = 7$

Also, nth term $a_n = a + (n-1)d$

$$\therefore \quad a_{10} = a + (10-1)d$$

$$= a + 9d$$

$$= 2 + 9 \times 7$$

$$= 2 + 63 = 65$$

Hence, the 10th term is 65.

Example 8. **If S_n is the sum of first n terms of an AP given by $S_n = 3n^2 - 4n$, then find the nth term.** CBSE 2019

Sol. Given, $S_n = 3n^2 - 4n$ ...(i)

On replacing n by $(n-1)$ in Eq. (i), we get

$$S_{n-1} = 3(n-1)^2 - 4(n-1)$$

nth term of the AP, $a_n = S_n - S_{n-1}$

$\therefore \quad a_n = (3n^2 - 4n) - [3(n-1)^2 - 4(n-1)]$

$\Rightarrow \quad a_n = 3[n^2 - (n-1)^2] - 4[n - (n-1)]$

$\Rightarrow \quad a_n = 3[n^2 - n^2 + 2n - 1] - 4[n - n + 1]$

$\Rightarrow \quad a_n = 3(2n-1) - 4$

$\Rightarrow \quad a_n = 6n - 3 - 4 \Rightarrow a_n = 6n - 7$

Thus, the nth term of the AP $= 6n - 7$.

Example 9. **If the sum of first n terms of an AP is n^2, then find its 10th term.** CBSE 2019

Sol. Given, $S_n = n^2$

We know that

$$T_n = S_n - S_{n-1} = n^2 - (n-1)^2 = n^2 - n^2 + 2n - 1$$

$\Rightarrow \quad T_n = 2n - 1$

Now, 10th term $= T_{10} = 2 \times 10 - 1 = 20 - 1 = 19$

Example 10. **Find the sum of the first 100 positive integers.**

Sol. Let $S = 1 + 2 + 3 + \ldots + 100$

Here, $a = 1$ and the last term l is 100.

$\therefore \quad S_n = \frac{n}{2}(a + l)$

$\Rightarrow S_{100} = \frac{100(1+100)}{2} = \frac{100 \times 101}{2} = 50 \times 101 = 5050$

Note it The sum of first n positive integers is given by $S_n = \frac{n(n+1)}{2}$

Type IV Word Problems

Example 11. **Find the sum of integers between 100 and 200 which are (i) divisible by 9 (ii) not divisible by 9.** CBSE 2023 (Standard)

Sol. (i) The integers between 100 and 200 divisible by 9 are 108, 117, 126, ..., 198.

$\therefore$ Required sum $= 108 + 117 + 126 + \ldots + 198$

Here, first term, $a = 108$

Common difference, $d = 9$

Last term, $l = 198$

$\therefore l = a_n = a + (n-1)d = 198$

$\Rightarrow \quad 108 + (n-1)9 = 198 \Rightarrow (n-1)9 = 90$

$\Rightarrow \quad n - 1 = 10 \Rightarrow n = 11$

Sum of n terms, $S_n = \frac{n}{2}[a + l]$

$\Rightarrow \quad S_{11} = \frac{11}{2}[108 + 198] = \frac{11}{2} \times 306 = 1683$

(ii) Numbers between 100 and 200 are 101, 102, 103 ... 199.

$\therefore$ Total number of terms, $n = 99$

First term, $a = 101$ and last term, $l = 199$

$\therefore \quad S_{99} = \frac{99}{2}[101 + 199] = \frac{99}{2} \times 300 = 14850$

So, the sum of integers between 100 and 200 which are not divisible by 9 $= 14850 - 1683 = 13167$

Example 12. **A man repays a loan of ₹ 3250 by ₹ 20 in the first month and then increases the payment by ₹ 15 every month. How long will it take him to clear the loan?**

Sol. Given, total amount of loan = ₹ 3250

Amount paid in first month = ₹ 20

and amount increase every month = ₹ 15

Clearly, the amounts of repayment form an AP with first term, $(a) = 20$ and common difference, $(d) = 15$

Let the loan be cleared in n months.

Then, $S_n = 3250$

$\Rightarrow \quad \frac{n}{2}[2a + (n-1)d] = 3250$

$\Rightarrow \quad \frac{n}{2}[2(20) + (n-1)15] = 3250$

$\Rightarrow \quad n[40 + 15n - 15] = 3250 \times 2$

$\Rightarrow \quad 25n + 15n^2 = 6500$

$\Rightarrow \quad 3n^2 + 5n - 1300 = 0$ [dividing both sides by 5]

$\Rightarrow 3n^2 + 65n - 60n - 1300 = 0$

$\Rightarrow n(3n + 65) - 20(3n + 65) = 0 \Rightarrow (n - 20)(3n + 65) = 0$

$\Rightarrow \quad n = 20$ or $n = \frac{-65}{3}$

Since, n should be a positive integer, so neglect $n = \frac{-65}{3}$.

$\therefore n = 20$

Hence, the loan is cleared in 20 months.

Example 13. **Kanika got her pocket money on Jan 1st, 2008. She puts ₹ 1 on day 1, ₹ 2 on day 2, ₹ 3 on day 3 and continued doing so till the end of the month, from her pocket money into her piggy bank. She also spent ₹ 204 of her pocket money and found that at the end of the month she still had ₹ 100 with her. How much was her pocket money for the month?** NCERT Exemplar

Sol. Let her pocket money be ₹x.

Now, she puts ₹1 on day 1, ₹2 on day 2, ₹3 on day 3 and so on till the end of the month, from this money into her piggy bank.

Clearly, the amounts that she puts every day of the month, form an AP, in which number of terms is 31, first term $(a) = 1$ and common difference $(d) = 2 - 1 = 1$.

Now, sum of first 31 terms, $(S_{31}) = \frac{31}{2}[2 \times 1 + (31-1) \times 1]$

$$\left[\because \text{sum of } n \text{ terms, } (S_n) = \frac{n}{2}[2a + (n-1)d]\right]$$

$$= \frac{31}{2}(2 + 30) = \frac{31 \times 32}{2} = 31 \times 16 = 496$$

So, Kanika puts ₹496 till the end of the month from her pocket money into her piggy bank.

Also, she spent ₹204 of her pocket money and found that at the end of the month, she still has ₹100 with her.

According to the above condition, we have

$$(x - 496) - 204 = 100$$

$$\Rightarrow \quad x - 700 = 100 \Rightarrow x = ₹\,800$$

Hence, ₹ 800 was her pocket money for the month.

Try These 5.3

1. Find the sum of the following APs
   (i) 50, 46, 42, ... to 10 terms
   (ii) 10, 15, 20, ... to 20 terms
2. Find the sum of the first 20 terms of the AP
   8, 12.5, 17, 21.5, ...
3. Find the sum of the following APs
   (i) $7 + 10 + 13 + \ldots + 94$ (ii) $35 + 32 + 29 + \ldots + 17$
4. Find the sum of first 15 multiples of 4.
5. Find the sum of even positive integers between 1 and 200.
6. Find the sum of all even numbers between 101 and 999.
7. Find the sum of first 25 terms of an AP whose nth term is given by $a_n = 7 + 3n$.
8. The sum of first n terms of an AP is represented by $S_n = 6n - n^2$. Find the common difference.
   CBSE Sample Paper 2025 (Basic)
9. Find the sum of first 21 terms of an AP whose 2nd term is 8 and 4th term is 4.
10. If sum of first 6 terms of an AP is 30 and that of the first 21 terms is 420, then find the sum of first 10 terms.
    CBSE 2024 (Standard)
11. Find the common difference of an AP whose first term is 8, last term is 65 and the sum of all its terms is 730.
    CBSE 2023 (Standard)
12. If the sum of first p terms of an AP is q and the sum of first q terms is p, then find the sum of first $(p+q)$ terms.
13. Find the number of terms of the AP 64,60,56,..., so that their sum is 544.
14. The first term of an AP is 10 and common difference is 4, find the number of terms if its sum is 1344.
15. If S_n is the sum of the first n terms of an AP given by $S_n = 2n^2 + 5n$, then find its nth term. CBSE 2019
16. If the sum of first n terms of an AP is given by $S_n = 3n^2 + n$, then find the nth term of the AP. Also, find the AP. NCERT Exemplar
17. In an AP,
    (i) Given $a = 7$, $d = -5$, $a_n = -28$, find n, a_{30} and S_n.
    (ii) Given $a = 4$, $d = 6$, $S_n = 310$, find n and a_n.
18. 228 logs are to be stacked in a store in the following manner: 30 logs in the bottom, 28 in the next row, then 26 and so on, in how many rows can these 228 logs be stacked? How many logs are there in the last row?
19. Yasmeen saves ₹ 32 during the first month, ₹ 36 in the second month and ₹ 40 in the third month. If she continues to save in this manner, then in how many months will she save ₹ 2000? NCERT Exemplar
20. The ages of the students in a class are in AP, whose common difference is 4 months. If the youngest student is 8 yr old and the sum of the ages of all the students is 168 yr, then find the number of students in the class.
21. Prove that the sum of later half of $2n$ terms of an AP is equal to one-third of the sum of the first $3n$ terms.
22. The sum of first six terms of an arithmetic progression is 42. The ratio of its 10th term to its 30th term is 1 : 3. Calculate the first and the 13th term of the AP.
23. A man arranges to pay off a debt of ₹ 3600 by 40 annual installments which are in AP. When 30 of the installments are paid, he dies leaving one-third of the debt unpaid. Find the value of the 8th installment.
24. Priya is preparing for the Bicycle marathon. Her racing bicycle has a device to calculate the number of kilometres she cycled. She decides to increase the distance she cycles everyday by a fixed number of kilometres.
    (i) On the first day Priya cycled 8 km. In 10 days she cycled a total of 170 km. How many kilometres did she cycle on the 3rd day?
    (ii) Priya plans to go on a cycle tour from Bangalore to Mangalore covering 425 km. She travels 20 km on day 1 and increases the distance covered each day by 5 km. In how many days will she reach her destination? Competency Based Question

Answers

1. **Hint** Solve as Example 1.
   (i) 320 (ii) 1150
2. **Hint** Solve as Example 1. **Ans.** 1015
3. (i) Here, $a = 7$, $d = 10 - 7 = 3$, $a_n = 94$

   Since, $a_n = a + (n-1)\,d$

   $$94 = 7 + (n-1)3$$

   $$\Rightarrow (n-1) = \frac{94-7}{3} = \frac{87}{3} = 29 \Rightarrow n = 30$$

   Now, $S_n = \frac{n}{2}[2a + (n-1)\,d]$

   $$S_{30} = \frac{30}{2}[2(7) + (30-1)3] = 15[14 + 29 \times 3] = 1515$$

   (ii) $a = 35$, $d = 32 - 35 = -3$, $a_n = 17$

   $\therefore \quad a_n = a + (n-1)d$

   $$17 = 35 + (n-1)(-3)$$

   $\therefore \quad n = 7$

   Now, $S_7 = \frac{7}{2}[2(35) + 6(-3)] = 182$

4. Hint Multiples of 4 are 4, 8, 12, 16, 20, ... which forms an AP with $a=4$ and $d=4$. Now, find S_{15}. **Ans.** 480

5. Hint Even integer between 1 and 200 are 2, 4, 6, 8, ... 198, which forms an AP with $a=2$ and $d=2$.

Now, let $a_n=198 \Rightarrow n=99$. After this, find S_{99}. **Ans.** 9900

6. Hint Given, $a=102$, $d=2$, $l=998$

$\because\ l=a+(n-1)d \Rightarrow 998=102+(n-1)(2) \Rightarrow n=449$

Now, $S_n=\frac{n}{2}(a+l)=\frac{449}{2}(102+998)$ **Ans.** 246950

7. Hint Solve as Example 4. **Ans.** 1150

8. Given, the sum of first n terms of an AP is

$$S_n=6n-n^2 \quad \text{...(i)}$$

On putting $n=1$ in Eq. (i), we get

$$S_1=6\times1-(1)^2=a=6-1=5 \Rightarrow a=5$$

Now, on putting $n=2$ in Eq. (i), we get

$$S_2=6\times2-(2)^2=12-4=8$$

$$\therefore \quad 2a+d=8 \quad \text{...(ii)}$$

Now, on putting the value $a=5$ in Eq. (ii), we get

$$2\times5+d=8 \Rightarrow d=8-10 \Rightarrow d=-2$$

Hence, common difference of the AP is -2.

9. Hint Solve as Example 3. **Ans.** -210

10. Hint Solve as Example 5. **Ans.** 90

11. Let a be the first term and d be the common difference of AP.

Given, $a=8$, $a_n=l=65$, $S_n=730$

$$S_n=\frac{n}{2}(a+l)$$

$$\Rightarrow \quad 730=\frac{n}{2}(8+65)$$

$$\Rightarrow \quad 730\times2=73n \Rightarrow n=\frac{730\times2}{73}=20$$

General term, $a_n=a+(n-1)d$

$$\Rightarrow \quad 65=8+(20-1)d \Rightarrow 19d=57 \Rightarrow d=3$$

Hence, the common difference is 3.

12. Hint We have, $S_p=q$ and $S_q=p$.

On subtracting, we get

$$2a+(p+q-1)d=-2.$$

Now, $S_{p+q}=\frac{p+q}{2}[2a+(p+q-1)d]=\left(\frac{p+q}{2}\right)(-2)=-(p+q)$

Ans. $-(p+q)$

13. Hint Solve as Example 6. **Ans.** 16, 17

14. Here $a=10$, $d=4$, $S_n=1344$

As, $S_n=\frac{n}{2}[2a+(n-1)d]$

$$\Rightarrow 1344=\frac{n}{2}[20+(n-1)4]$$

$$\Rightarrow 2688=n[20+4n-4]$$

$$\Rightarrow 4n^2+16n-2688=0 \Rightarrow n^2+4n-672=0$$

$$\Rightarrow \quad n=24,-28$$

Since, $n=-28$ cannot be possible

$$\therefore \quad n=24$$

15. Hint Solve as Example 8. **Ans.** $3+4n$

16. Hint Solve as Example 8. **Ans.** $6n-2$; 4,10,16,...

17. (i) **Hint** $a_n=a+(n-1)d$

$$-28=7+(n-1)(-5)$$

$$\therefore \quad n=8$$

$$S_8=\frac{8}{2}[2(7)+7\times(-5)]=-84$$

$$a_{30}=a+29d=7+29(-5)=-138$$

(ii) Here $a=4$, $d=6$, $S_n=310$

$$S_n=\frac{n}{2}[8+(n-1)6]=310$$

$$\therefore \quad n=10$$

$$a_{10}=a+9d=4+9(6)=58$$

18. Hint Solve as Example 12. **Ans.** $n=12$ and $l=8$

19. Hint Solve as Example 12. **Ans.** 25 months

20. Number of students in the class $=16$

21. Hint To prove $S_{2n}-S_n=\frac{1}{3}S_{3n}$

22. Hint Given, $S_6=42$ and $\frac{a_{10}}{a_{30}}=\frac{1}{3}$. This implies $a=d$.

Ans. $a_1=2$ and $a_{13}=26$

23. Hint Let the amount of instalments be $a, a+d, a+2d, \ldots\ldots$

Then, according to given condition, we have

$$S_{40}=3600 \text{ and } S_{30}=3600-\frac{1}{3}\times3600=2400$$

$\Rightarrow 2a+39d=180$ and $2a+29d=160$

Now, find a and d, and then find a_8. **Ans.** $a_8=$ ₹65

24. (i) Let a be the first term and d be the common difference.

So, $a=8$ km, $S_n=170$ where $n=10$

Since, $S_n=\frac{n}{2}[2a+(n-1)d]$

$$\Rightarrow \quad S_{10}=\frac{10}{2}[2\times8+(10-1)d]=170 \Rightarrow 5[16+9d]=170$$

$$\Rightarrow \quad 9d=18 \Rightarrow d=2$$

$$\therefore \quad a_3=a+2d=8+2\times2=12$$

Thus, she cycled 12 km distance on 3rd day.

(ii) $a=20$, $d=5$, $S_n=425$

$$\therefore \quad S_n=\frac{n}{2}[2a+(n-1)d]$$

$$\Rightarrow \quad 425=\frac{n}{2}[2(20)+(n-1)5]$$

$$\Rightarrow \quad 850=n[40+5n-5]$$

$$\Rightarrow n^2+7n-170=0$$

$$\therefore\ n=-17 \text{ or } n=10$$

Since, number of terms cannot be negative.

$\therefore n=10$

NCERT FOLDER

Complete Solutions of All Exercises of NCERT Textbook

EXERCISE 5.1

Q1. In which of the following situations, does the list of numbers involved make an arithmetic progression and why?

(i) The taxi fare after each kilometre when the fare is ₹ 15 for the first kilometre and ₹ 8 for each additional kilometre.

(ii) The amount of air present in a cylinder when a vacuum pump removes 1/4 of the air remaining in the cylinder at a time.

(iii) The cost of digging a well after every metre of digging, when it costs ₹ 150 for the first metre and rises by ₹ 50 for each subsequent metre.

(iv) The amount of money in the account every year, when ₹ 10000 is deposited at compound interest at 8% per annum.

Sol. (i) According to the question, the fare for journey of 1 km, 2 km, 3 km, 4 km, ... are ₹ 15, ₹ (15 + 8), ₹ (15 + 2 × 8), ₹ (15 + 3 × 8) and so on i.e. 15, 23, 31, 39, ...

Here, each term is obtained by adding 8 to the preceding term except first term. So, it forms an AP.

(ii) Let the amount of air present in the cylinder be y units.

According to the question,

Remaining air in the cylinder after using vacuum pump first time $= y - \frac{y}{4} = \frac{3y}{4}$

Remaining air in the cylinder after using vacuum pump second time

$$= \frac{3y}{4} - \frac{1}{4} \times \frac{3y}{4} = \frac{12y - 3y}{16} = \frac{9y}{16} \text{ and so on.}$$

Thus, the list of numbers is $y, \frac{3y}{4}, \frac{9y}{16}, \ldots$

Here, $\frac{3y}{4} - y = -\frac{y}{4}$ $[\because a_2 - a_1]$

and $\frac{9y}{16} - \frac{3y}{4} = \frac{9y - 12y}{16} = -\frac{3y}{16}$ $[\because a_3 - a_2]$

Since, $\frac{3y}{4} - y \neq \frac{9y}{16} - \frac{3y}{4}$

i.e. difference between any two consecutive terms is not same. Hence, it does not form an AP.

(iii) According to the question, the cost of digging for the first metre, second metre, third metre,... are respectively ₹ 150, ₹ (150 + 50), ₹ (150 + 2 × 50), ... and so on.

Thus, the list of numbers is 150, 200, 250, ...

Here, each term is obtained by adding ₹ 50 to the preceding term except first term. So, it forms an AP.

(iv) We know that amount, $A = P\left(1 + \frac{R}{100}\right)^T$.

Here, $P =$ ₹ 10000, $R = 8\%$ per annum and $T = 1, 2, 3, \ldots$

Now, amount in 1st year $= 10000\left(1 + \frac{8}{100}\right)^1$

$$= 10000 \times \frac{108}{100}$$

$$= ₹\ 10800$$

Amount in 2nd year $= 10000\left(1 + \frac{8}{100}\right)^2$

$$= \frac{10000 \times 108 \times 108}{100 \times 100}$$

$$= ₹\ 11664 \text{ and so on.}$$

Thus, the list of numbers is 10000, 10800, 11664, ...

Here, $10800 - 10000 = 800$

and $11664 - 10800 = 864$

i.e. the common difference is not same.

Hence, it does not form an AP.

Q2. Write first four terms of the AP, when the first term a and the common difference d are given as follows

(i) $a = 10, d = 10$ (ii) $a = -2, d = 0$

(iii) $a = 4, d = -3$ (iv) $a = -1, d = \frac{1}{2}$

(v) $a = -1.25, d = -0.25$

Sol. (i) Given, $a = 10$ and $d = 10$

We know that $a, a + d, a + 2d, a + 3d, \ldots$ are in AP.

Here, $a = 10$

$a + d = 10 + 10 = 20$

$a + 2d = 10 + 2 \times 10 = 30$

and $a + 3d = 10 + 3 \times 10 = 40$

Thus, the first four terms of the AP are 10, 20, 30 and 40.

(ii) Do same as Part (i). **Ans.** −2, −2, −2 and −2.

(iii) Do same as Part (i). **Ans.** 4, 1, −2 and −5.

(iv) Do same as Part (i). **Ans.** $-1, -\frac{1}{2}, 0$ and $\frac{1}{2}$.

(v) Given, $a = -1.25$ and $d = -0.25$

We know that $a, a+d, a+2d, a+3d, \ldots$ are in AP.

Here, $a = -1.25$

$a+d = -1.5 - 0.25 = -1.50$

$a+2d = -1.25 + 2(-0.25) = -1.75$

and $a+3d = -1.25 + 3(-0.25) = -2.00$

Thus, the first four terms of the AP are $-1.25, -1.50, -1.75$ and -2.00.

Q3. For the following AP's, write the first term and the common difference

(i) 3, 1, –1, –3, ... (ii) – 5, – 1, 3, 7, ...

(iii) $\frac{1}{3}, \frac{5}{3}, \frac{9}{3}, \frac{13}{3}, \ldots$ (iv) 0.6, 1.7, 2.8, 3.9, ...

Sol. (i) First term $(a) = 3$

and common difference (d) = 2nd term – 1st term

$= 1 - 3 = -2$

(ii) Do same as Part (i). **Ans.** $a = -5, d = 4$

(iii) Do same as Part (i). **Ans.** $a = \frac{1}{3}, d = \frac{4}{3}$

(iv) Do same as Part (i). **Ans.** $a = 0.6, d = 1.1$

Q4. Which of the following are AP's? If they form an AP, then find the common difference d and write three more terms.

(i) 2, 4, 8, 16, ...

(ii) $2, \frac{5}{2}, 3, \frac{7}{2}, \ldots$

(iii) – 1. 2, – 3.2, – 5.2, – 7.2, ...

(iv) $-10, -6, -2, 2, \ldots$

(v) $3, 3+\sqrt{2}, 3+2\sqrt{2}, 3+3\sqrt{2}, \ldots$

(vi) 0.2, 0.22, 0.222, 0.2222, ...

(vii) $0, -4, -8, -12, \ldots$

(viii) $-\frac{1}{2}, -\frac{1}{2}, -\frac{1}{2}, -\frac{1}{2}, \ldots$

(ix) $1, 3, 9, 27, \ldots$

(x) $a, 2a, 3a, 4a, \ldots$

(xi) $a, a^2, a^3, a^4, \ldots$

(xii) $\sqrt{2}, \sqrt{8}, \sqrt{18}, \sqrt{32}, \ldots$

(xiii) $\sqrt{3}, \sqrt{6}, \sqrt{9}, \sqrt{12}, \ldots$

(xiv) $1^2, 3^2, 5^2, 7^2, \ldots$

(xv) $1^2, 5^2, 7^2, 73, \ldots$

Sol. (i) Here, we have

$a_2 - a_1 = 4 - 2 = 2$, and $a_3 - a_2 = 8 - 4 = 4$

Since, $a_2 - a_1 \neq a_3 - a_2$

Therefore, the given list of numbers does not form an AP.

(ii) Here, we have

$a_2 - a_1 = \frac{5}{2} - 2 = \frac{5-4}{2} = \frac{1}{2}$,

$a_3 - a_2 = 3 - \frac{5}{2} = \frac{6-5}{2} = \frac{1}{2}$,

$a_4 - a_3 = \frac{7}{2} - 3 = \frac{7-6}{2} = \frac{1}{2}$ and so on.

Since, the difference of any two consecutive terms is same. Therefore, the given list of numbers forms an AP and its common difference (d) is $\frac{1}{2}$.

Now, next three terms of this AP are,

$a_5 = a_4 + d = \frac{7}{2} + \frac{1}{2}$

$[\because a_5 = a + 4d = a + 3d + d = a_4 + d]$

$= \frac{7+1}{2} = \frac{8}{2} = 4$

$a_6 = a_5 + d = 4 + \frac{1}{2} = \frac{9}{2}$

and $a_7 = a_6 + d = \frac{9}{2} + \frac{1}{2} = \frac{9+1}{2} = \frac{10}{2} = 5$

(iii) Here, we have

$a_2 - a_1 = -3.2 - (-1.2) = -3.2 + 1.2 = -2$

$a_3 - a_2 = -5.2 - (-3.2) = -5.2 + 3.2 = -2$,

$a_4 - a_3 = -7.2 - (-5.2) = -7.2 + 5.2 = -2$

and so on.

Since, the difference of any two consecutive terms is same. Therefore, the given list of numbers forms an AP and its common difference (d) is -2.

Now, next three terms of this AP are,

$a_5 = a_4 + d = -7.2 + (-2) = -9.2$

$a_6 = a_5 + d = -9.2 + (-2) = -11.2$

and $a_7 = a_6 + d = -11.2 + (-2) = -13.2$

(iv) Do same as Part (iii).

Ans. Yes, $d = 4$ and next three terms are 6, 10, 14.

(v) Here, we have

$a_2 - a_1 = 3 + \sqrt{2} - 3 = \sqrt{2}$,

$a_3 - a_2 = 3 + 2\sqrt{2} - (3 + \sqrt{2}) = \sqrt{2}$,

$a_4 - a_3 = 3 + 3\sqrt{2} - (3 + 2\sqrt{2}) = \sqrt{2}$ and so on.

Since, the difference of any two consecutive terms is same. Therefore, the given list of numbers forms an AP and its common difference (d) is $\sqrt{2}$.

Now, next three terms of this AP are,

$a_5 = a_4 + d = 3 + 3\sqrt{2} + \sqrt{2} = 3 + 4\sqrt{2}$

$a_6 = a_5 + d = 3 + 4\sqrt{2} + \sqrt{2} = 3 + 5\sqrt{2}$

and $a_7 = a_6 + d = 3 + 5\sqrt{2} + \sqrt{2} = 3 + 6\sqrt{2}$

(vi) Here, we have $a_2 - a_1 = 0.22 - 0.2 = 0.02$

and $a_3 - a_2 = 0.222 - 0.22 = 0.002$

Since, $a_2 - a_1 \neq a_3 - a_2$, therefore the given list of numbers does not form an AP.

(vii) Do same as Part (i).

Ans. Yes, $d = -4$ and next three terms are $-16, -20, -24$.

(viii) Here, we have

$$a_2 - a_1 = -\frac{1}{2} - \left(-\frac{1}{2}\right) = -\frac{1}{2} + \frac{1}{2} = 0,$$
$$a_3 - a_2 = -\frac{1}{2} - \left(-\frac{1}{2}\right) = -\frac{1}{2} + \frac{1}{2} = 0,$$
$$a_4 - a_3 = -\frac{1}{2} - \left(-\frac{1}{2}\right) = -\frac{1}{2} + \frac{1}{2} = 0$$

and so on.

Since, the difference of any two consecutive terms is same. Therefore, the given list of numbers forms an AP and its common difference (d) is 0.

Now, next three terms of this AP are

$$a_5 = a_4 + d = -\frac{1}{2} + 0 = -\frac{1}{2}$$
$$a_6 = a_5 + d = -\frac{1}{2} + 0 = -\frac{1}{2}$$
and $a_7 = a_6 + d = -\frac{1}{2} + 0 = -\frac{1}{2}$

(ix) Do same as Part (i).

Ans. Not an AP.

(x) Here, we have

$$a_2 - a_1 = 2a - a = a,$$
$$a_3 - a_2 = 3a - 2a = a,$$
$a_4 - a_3 = 4a - 3a = a$ and so on.

Since, the difference of any two consecutive terms is same. Therefore, the given list of numbers forms an AP and its common difference (d) is a.

Now, next three terms of this AP are,

$$a_5 = a_4 + d = 4a + a = 5a$$
$$a_6 = a_5 + d = 5a + a = 6a$$
and $a_7 = a_6 + d = 6a + a = 7a$

(xi) Here, we have

$$a_2 - a_1 = a^2 - a = a(a - 1),$$
and $a_3 - a_2 = a^3 - a^2 = a^2(a - 1)$

Since, $a_2 - a_1 \neq a_3 - a_2$

Therefore, the given list of numbers does not form an AP.

(xii) Here, we have

$$a_2 - a_1 = \sqrt{8} - \sqrt{2} = 2\sqrt{2} - \sqrt{2} = \sqrt{2},$$
$$a_3 - a_2 = \sqrt{18} - \sqrt{8} = 3\sqrt{2} - 2\sqrt{2} = \sqrt{2},$$
$a_4 - a_3 = \sqrt{32} - \sqrt{18} = 4\sqrt{2} - 3\sqrt{2} = \sqrt{2}$ and so on.

Since, the difference of any two consecutive terms is same. Therefore, the given list of numbers forms an AP and its common difference (d) is $\sqrt{2}$.

Now, next three terms of this AP are,

$$a_5 = a_4 + d = 4\sqrt{2} + \sqrt{2} = 5\sqrt{2} = \sqrt{50}$$
$$a_6 = a_5 + d = 5\sqrt{2} + \sqrt{2} = 6\sqrt{2} = \sqrt{72}$$
and $a_7 = a_6 + d = 6\sqrt{2} + \sqrt{2} = 7\sqrt{2} = \sqrt{98}$

(xiii) Here, we have

$$a_2 - a_1 = \sqrt{6} - \sqrt{3} = \sqrt{3 \times 2} - \sqrt{3} = \sqrt{3}(\sqrt{2} - 1)$$
and $a_3 - a_2 = \sqrt{9} - \sqrt{6}$
$$= 3 - \sqrt{3 \times 2} = \sqrt{3}(\sqrt{3} - \sqrt{2})$$

Since, $a_2 - a_1 \neq a_3 - a_2$

Therefore, the given list of numbers does not form an AP.

(xiv) Here, we have $a_2 - a_1 = 3^2 - 1^2 = 9 - 1 = 8$

and $a_3 - a_2 = 5^2 - 3^2 = 25 - 9 = 16$

Since, $a_2 - a_1 \neq a_3 - a_2$

Therefore, the given list of numbers does not form an AP.

(xv) Here, we have $a_2 - a_1 = 5^2 - 1^2 = 25 - 1 = 24,$

$$a_3 - a_2 = 7^2 - 5^2 = 49 - 25 = 24,$$
and $a_4 - a_3 = 73 - 7^2 = 73 - 49 = 24$ and so on.

Since, the difference of any two consecutive terms is same. Therefore, the given list of numbers forms an AP and its common difference (d) is 24.

Now, next three terms of this AP are,

$$a_5 = a_4 + d = 73 + 24 = 97$$
$$a_6 = a_5 + d = 97 + 24 = 121$$
and $a_7 = a_6 + d = 121 + 24 = 145$

EXERCISE 5.2

Q1. Fill in the blanks in the following table, given that a is the first term, d the common difference and a_n the nth term of the AP.

	a	d	n	a_n
(i)	7	3	8	...
(ii)	−18	...	10	0
(iii)	...	−3	18	−5
(iv)	−18.9	2.5	...	3.6
(v)	3.5	0	105	...

Sol. (i) Here, $a = 7, d = 3$ and $n = 8$

The nth term of an AP is $a_n = a + (n - 1)d$

$$\therefore \quad a_8 = 7 + (8 - 1)3 = 7 + 7 \times 3 = 28$$

(ii) Here, $a = -18$, $n = 10$ and $a_n = 0$

We know that the nth term of an AP is

$$a_n = a + (n - 1)d$$

On putting the given values, we get

$$0 = -18 + (10 - 1)d$$
$$\Rightarrow \quad 18 = 9d$$
$$\Rightarrow \quad d = \frac{18}{9} = 2$$

(iii) Here, $n = 18$, $d = -3$ and $a_n = -5$

We know that the nth term of an AP is

$$a_n = a + (n-1)d$$

On putting the given values, we get

$$-5 = a + (18-1)(-3)$$

$$\Rightarrow \quad a = -5 + 51 = 46$$

(iv) Here, $a = -18.9$, $d = 2.5$ and $a_n = 3.6$

We know that the nth term of an AP is

$$a_n = a + (n-1)d$$

On putting the given values, we get

$$3.6 = -18.9 + (n-1)2.5$$

$$\Rightarrow 3.6 + 18.9 = (n-1)2.5$$

$$\Rightarrow \quad n - 1 = 9 \Rightarrow n = 9 + 1 = 10$$

(v) Do same as part (i) **Ans.** $a_n = 3.5$

Q2. Choose the correct choice in the following and justify.

(i) 30th term of the AP 10, 7, 4, ... is

(a) 97 (b) 77 (c) -77 (d) -87

(ii) 11th term of the AP : $-3, -\frac{1}{2}, 2, \ldots$ is

(a) 28 (b) 22 (c) -38 (d) $-48\frac{1}{2}$

Sol. (i) (c) Here, first term $(a) = 10$,

and common difference $(d) = 7 - 10 = -3$

We know that the nth term of an AP is

$$a_n = a + (n-1)d$$

$$\therefore \quad a_{30} = 10 + (30-1)(-3) = -77$$

(ii) (b) Do same as part (i) **Ans.** $a_{11} = 22$

Q3. In the following APs, find the missing terms of the boxes.

(i) 2, □, 26 (ii) □, 13, □, 3

(iii) 5, □, □, $9\frac{1}{2}$ (iv) -4, □, □, □, □, 6

(v) □, 38, □, □, □, -22

Sol. (i) We know that $a, a+d, a+2d, \ldots$ is the general form of an AP. We have, $a = 2$ and $a + 2d = 26$

$$\Rightarrow \quad 2 + 2d = 26 \qquad [\because a = 2]$$

$$\Rightarrow \quad 2d = 26 - 2 = 24$$

$$\Rightarrow \quad d = \frac{24}{2} = 12$$

Hence, the missing term $= a + d = 2 + 12 = 14$

(ii) We know that $a, a+d, a+2d, a+3d, \ldots$ is the general form of an AP.

$\therefore$ We have, $\quad a + d = 13 \quad \ldots$(i)

and $\quad a + 3d = 3 \quad \ldots$(ii)

On subtracting Eq. (i) from Eq. (ii), we get

$$2d = -10$$

$$\Rightarrow \quad d = -5$$

On putting $d = -5$ in Eq. (ii), we get

$$a + 3(-5) = 3$$

$$\Rightarrow \quad a = 18$$

Hence, the missing terms are $a = 18$ and

$$a + 2d = 18 + 2(-5) = 18 - 10 = 8$$

(iii) We know that $a, a+d, a+2d, a+3d, \ldots$ is the general form of an AP.

$\therefore$ We have, $\quad a = 5 \quad \ldots$(i)

and $\quad a + 3d = 9\frac{1}{2} = \frac{19}{2} \quad \ldots$(ii)

On subtracting Eq. (i) from Eq. (ii), we get

$$3d = \frac{19}{2} - 5 = \frac{19-10}{2} = \frac{9}{2}$$

$$\Rightarrow \quad 3d = \frac{9}{2}$$

$$\Rightarrow \quad d = \frac{1}{3} \times \frac{9}{2} = \frac{3}{2}$$

Hence, the missing terms are

$$a + d = 5 + \frac{3}{2} = \frac{10+3}{2} = \frac{13}{2} = 6\frac{1}{2}$$

and $\quad a + 2d = 5 + 2 \times \frac{3}{2} = 5 + 3 = 8$

(iv) Do same as part (iii) **Ans.** $-2, 0, 2, 4$

(v) Do same as part (ii) **Ans.** 53, 23, 8, -7

Q4. Which term of the AP : 3, 8, 13, 18, ... is 78?

Sol. Do same as Example 3 of Topic 2.

Ans. 16th term is 78.

Q5. Find the number of terms in each of the following APs :

(i) 7, 13, 19, ..., 205 (ii) 18, $15\frac{1}{2}$, 13, ..., -47

Sol. Do same as Example 2 of Topic 2.

Ans. (i) 34 terms (ii) 27 terms

Q6. Check whether -150 is a term of the AP : 11, 8, 5, 2, ...

Sol. Here, $a = 11$ and $d = 8 - 11 = -3$

Assume that, -150 be the nth term of the given AP.

We know that the nth term of an AP is

$$a_n = a + (n-1)d$$

$$\Rightarrow \quad -150 = 11 + (n-1)(-3)$$

$$\Rightarrow \quad n - 1 = \frac{161}{3}$$

$$\Rightarrow \quad n = \frac{161}{3} + 1 = \frac{164}{3}$$

But n should be a positive integer.

So, -150 is not a term of the given AP.

Q7. Find the 31st term of an AP, whose 11th term is 38 and the 16th term is 73.

Sol. Let a be the first term and d be the common difference of given AP.

We know that the nth term of an AP is $a_n = a + (n-1)d$

$\therefore$ 11th term, $a_{11} = a + 10d = 38$ ...(i) $[\because a_{11} = 38, \text{given}]$

and 16th term, $a_{16} = a + 15d = 73$ ...(ii) $[\because a_{16} = 73, \text{given}]$

On subtracting Eq. (i) from Eq. (ii), we get

$$5d = 35 \Rightarrow d = \frac{35}{5} = 7$$

On putting the value of d in Eq. (i), we get

$$a + 10 \times 7 = 38 \Rightarrow a = 38 - 70 = -32$$

Now, 31st term, $a_{31} = a + 30d$

$$= -32 + 30 \times 7 = -32 + 210 = 178$$

Q8. An AP consists of 50 terms of which 3rd term is 12 and the last term is 106. Find the 29th term.

Sol. Let a be the first term and d be the common difference of given AP.

Now, as the nth term of an AP is $a_n = a + (n-1)d$

$\therefore$ $a_3 = a + 2d = 12$ $[\because a_3 = 12, \text{given}]$ ...(i)

and $a_{50} = a + 49d = 106$ ...(ii) $[\because a_{50} = 106, \text{given}]$

On subtracting Eq. (i) from Eq. (ii), we get

$$47d = 94$$

$$\Rightarrow d = \frac{94}{47} = 2$$

On putting the value of d in Eq. (i), we get

$$a + 2 \times 2 = 12 \Rightarrow a = 12 - 4 = 8$$

Now, 29th term, $a_{29} = a + (29-1)d$

$$= 8 + 28 \times 2 = 8 + 56 = 64$$

Q9. If the 3rd and 9th terms of an AP are 4 and –8 respectively, then which term of this AP is zero?

Sol. Let a be the first term and d be the common difference of given AP.

$\because$ The nth term of an AP is $a_n = a + (n-1)d$

$\therefore$ $a_3 = a + 2d = 4$ $[\because a_3 = 4, \text{given}]$ ...(i)

and $a_9 = a + 8d = -8$ $[\because a_9 = -8, \text{given}]$ ...(ii)

On subtracting Eq. (i) from Eq. (ii), we get

$$6d = -12$$

$$\Rightarrow d = \frac{-12}{6} = -2$$

On putting the value of d in Eq. (i), we get

$$a + 2 \times (-2) = 4 \Rightarrow a - 4 = 4 \Rightarrow a = 4 + 4 = 8$$

Let the nth term of this AP be zero,

i.e. $a_n = 0$

$\Rightarrow a + (n-1)d = 0$

$\Rightarrow 8 + (n-1)(-2) = 0$ $[\because a = 8, d = -2]$

$\Rightarrow n - 1 = \frac{-8}{-2} = 4$

$\Rightarrow n = 4 + 1 = 5$

Hence, 5th term of this AP is zero.

Q10. The 17th term of an AP exceeds its 10th term by 7. Find the common difference. CBSE 2019

Sol. Let a be the first term and d be the common difference of given AP.

Now, according to the question, $a_{17} = a_{10} + 7$

$\Rightarrow a_{17} - a_{10} = 7$

$\Rightarrow [a + (17-1)d] - [a + (10-1)d] = 7$ $[\because a_n = a + (n-1)d]$

$\Rightarrow (a + 16d) - (a + 9d) = 7$

$\Rightarrow 7d = 7$

$\Rightarrow d = 1$

Hence, the common difference of this AP is 1.

Q11. Which term of the AP : 3, 15, 27, 39, ... will be 132 more than its 54th term?

Sol. Do same as Example 5 of Topic 2.

Ans. 65th term is 132 more than the 54th term of this AP.

Q12. Two AP's have the same common difference. The difference between their 100th terms is 100. What is the difference between their 1000th terms?

Sol. Let the two APs be $a_1, a_2, a_3, \ldots, a_n \ldots$ and $b_1, b_2, b_3, \ldots, b_n \ldots$.

Also, let d be the same common difference of two APs.

Then, the nth term of first AP is

$$a_n = a_1 + (n-1)d$$

and the nth term of second AP is

$$b_n = b_1 + (n-1)d$$

Now, $a_n - b_n = [a_1 + (n-1)d] - [b_1 + (n-1)d]$

$\Rightarrow a_n - b_n = a_1 - b_1, \forall n \in N$

$\therefore a_{100} - b_{100} = a_1 - b_1 = 100$ [given]

So, $a_{1000} - b_{1000} = a_1 - b_1$

$\Rightarrow a_{1000} - b_{1000} = 100$ $[\because a_1 - b_1 = 100]$

Hence, the difference between their 1000th terms is also 100 for all $n \in N$.

Q13. How many three-digit numbers are divisible by 7?

Sol. We know that 105 is the first and 994 is the last three-digit numbers divisible by 7. Thus, we have to determine the number of terms in the list 105, 112, 119, ..., 994.

Clearly, the successive difference of the terms is same.

So, above list of numbers forms an AP, with first term $(a) = 105$

and common difference $(d) = 112 - 105 = 7$

Let there be n terms in the AP.

Then, nth term $= 994$

$\Rightarrow \quad 105 + (n-1)7 = 994 \quad [\because a_n = a + (n-1)d]$

$\Rightarrow \quad 7(n-1) = 994 - 105$

$\Rightarrow \quad 7(n-1) = 889$

$\Rightarrow \quad n = 127 + 1 = 128$

Hence, there are 128 numbers of three-digit which are divisible by 7.

Q 14. How many multiples of 4 lie between 10 and 250?

Sol. We know that 12 is the first integer between 10 and 250, which is a multiple of 4. Also, when we divide 250 by 4, the remainder is 2. Therefore, $250 - 2 = 248$ is the greatest integer divisible by 4 and lying between 10 and 250.

Thus, we have to find the number of terms in an AP, whose first term $(a) = 12$, last term $(l) = 248$ and common difference $(d) = 4$.

Let the nth term of this AP be $a_n = 248$

Then, $\quad 12 + (n-1)4 = 248 \quad [\because a_n = a + (n-1)d]$

$\Rightarrow \quad 4(n-1) = 248 - 12$

$\Rightarrow \quad 4(n-1) = 236 \Rightarrow n = 59 + 1 = 60$

Hence, there are 60 multiples of 4 lying between 10 and 250.

Q 15. For what value of n, the nth terms of two AP's : 63, 65, 67, ... and 3, 10, 17,... are equal?

Sol. Given, APs are 63, 65, 67, ... and 3, 10, 17, ...

Here, first term of first AP $(a_1) = 63$

common difference of first AP $(d_1) = 65 - 63 = 2$

first term of second AP $(a_2) = 3$

and common difference of second AP $(d_2) = 10 - 3 = 7$

According to the question, nth term of both AP's are equal.

$\therefore \quad 63 + (n-1)2 = 3 + (n-1)7 \quad [\because a_n = a + (n-1)d]$

$\Rightarrow \quad 7(n-1) - 2(n-1) = 63 - 3$

$\Rightarrow \quad (n-1)(7-2) = 60$

$\Rightarrow \quad (n-1) = \frac{60}{5} = 12$

$\Rightarrow \quad n = 12 + 1 = 13$

Hence, the 13th term of the two given AP's are equal.

Q 16. Determine the AP whose 3rd term is 16 and the 7th term exceeds the 5th term by 12.

Sol. Let a be the first term and d be the common difference of given AP.

Given that the third term of the AP is

$a_3 = 16$

$\Rightarrow \quad a + 2d = 16 \quad [\because a_n = a + (n-1)d]$ ...(i)

Also, it is given that

7th term of an AP = 12 + 5th term of an AP i.e.

$a_7 = 12 + a_5$

$\Rightarrow \quad a_7 - a_5 = 12$

$\Rightarrow \quad (a + 6d) - (a + 4d) = 12$

$\Rightarrow \quad 2d = 12 \Rightarrow d = 6$

On putting $d = 6$ in Eq. (i), we get

$a + 2 \times 6 = 16$

$\Rightarrow \quad a = 16 - 12 = 4$

We know that general form of an AP is

$a, a+d, a+2d, a+3d, \dots$.

Then, the required AP is

$4, 4+6, 4+2\times 6, 4+3\times 6, \dots$, i.e. 4, 10, 16, 22, ...

Q 17. Find the 20th term from the last term of the AP : 3, 8, 13, ... ,253.

Sol. Do same as Example 10 of Topic 2. **Ans.** 158

Q 18. The sum of the 4th and 8th terms of an AP is 24 and the sum of the 6th and 10th terms is 44. Find the first three terms of the AP.

Sol. Let a be the first term and d be the common difference of given AP.

Given, $\quad a_4 + a_8 = 24$

$\therefore \quad (a + 3d) + (a + 7d) = 24 \quad [\because a_n = a + (n-1)d]$

$\Rightarrow \quad a + 5d = 12$ ...(i)

[dividing both sides by 2]

and $\quad a_6 + a_{10} = 44$

$\Rightarrow \quad (a + 5d) + (a + 9d) = 44$

$\Rightarrow \quad 2a + 14d = 44$

$\Rightarrow \quad a + 7d = 22$ ...(ii)

[dividing both sides by 2]

On subtracting Eq. (i) from Eq. (ii), we get

$2d = 10 \Rightarrow d = 5$

On putting $d = 5$ in Eq. (i), we get

$a + 25 = 12 \Rightarrow a = -13$

Hence, the first three terms are

$a, (a + d)$ and $(a + 2d)$

i.e. $\; -13, (-13 + 5)$ and $(-13 + 2 \times 5)$

i.e. $\; -13, -8$ and -3.

Q 19. Subba Rao started work in 1995 at an annual salary of ₹ 5000 and received an increment of ₹ 200 each year. In which year, did his income reach ₹ 7000?

Sol. The annual salary received by Subba Rao in the years 1995, 1996, 1997, ... are ₹ 5000, ₹ 5200, ₹ 5400, ... , respectively.

Here, the list of numbers 5000, 5200, 5400, ..., forms an AP with first term $(a) = 5000$ and common difference $(d) = 200$.

Let nth term of this AP be $a_n = 7000$

$\Rightarrow \quad 7000 = a + (n-1)d \quad [\because a_n = a + (n-1)d]$

$\Rightarrow \quad 7000 = 5000 + (n-1)(200)$

$\Rightarrow \quad 200(n-1) = 7000 - 5000 = 2000$

$\Rightarrow \quad n - 1 = \frac{2000}{200} = 10 \Rightarrow n = 10 + 1 = 11$

Thus, in 11th year of his service (2006), Subba Rao received an annual salary of ₹ 7000.

Q 20. Ramkali saved ₹ 5 in the first week of a year and then increased her weekly savings by ₹ 1.75. If in the *n*th week, her weekly savings becomes ₹ 20.75, find *n*.

Sol. Ramkali's savings in the subsequent weeks are respectively ₹ 5, ₹ 5 + ₹ 1.75, ₹ 5 + 2 × ₹ 1.75, ₹ 5 + 3 × ₹ 1.75, ...

i.e. ₹ 5, ₹ 6.75, ₹ 8.50, ₹ 10.25,...

Clearly, Ramkali's savings forms an AP with first term $(a) = 5$ and common difference $(d) = 1.75$

Thus, in nth week, her savings will be ₹ $5 + (n-1) \times 1.75$

$\Rightarrow \quad 5 + (n-1) \times 1.75 = 20.75$

[$\because$ in the nth week saving amount = ₹ 20.75]

$\Rightarrow \quad (n-1) \times 1.75 = 20.75 - 5 = 15.75$

$\Rightarrow \quad n - 1 = \frac{15.75}{1.75} = 9$

$\Rightarrow \quad n = 9 + 1 = 10$

EXERCISE 5.3

Q 1. Find the sum of the following APs

(i) 2, 7, 12, ..., to 10 terms

(ii) $-37, -33, -29, \ldots$, to 12 terms

(iii) 0.6, 1.7, 2.8, ..., to 100 terms

(iv) $\frac{1}{15}, \frac{1}{12}, \frac{1}{10}, \ldots$, to 11 terms

Sol. (i) Given, AP is 2, 7, 12, ..., to 10 terms.

Here, $a = 2, d = 7 - 2 = 5$ and $n = 10$

$\because$ Sum of first n terms of an AP,

$$S_n = \frac{n}{2}[2a + (n-1)d]$$

$\therefore$ On putting $a = 2, d = 5$ and $n = 10$, we get

$$S_{10} = \frac{10}{2}[2 \times 2 + (10-1)5]$$

$$= 5(4 + 9 \times 5) = 5(4 + 45) = 5 \times 49 = 245$$

(ii) Given, AP is $-37, -33, -29, \ldots$ to 12 terms.

Here, $a = -37$,

$d = -33 - (-37) = -33 + 37 = 4$ and $n = 12$

Do same as Part (i). **Ans.** -180

(iii) Given, AP is 0.6, 1.7, 2.8, ... to 100 terms.

Here, $a = 0.6, d = 1.7 - 0.6 = 1.1$ and $n = 100$

Do same as Part (i). **Ans.** 5505

(iv) Given, AP is $\frac{1}{15}, \frac{1}{12}, \frac{1}{10}, \ldots$ to 11 terms.

Here, $a = \frac{1}{15}$, $d = \frac{1}{12} - \frac{1}{15} = \frac{5-4}{60} = \frac{1}{60}$ and $n = 11$

Do same as Part (i). **Ans.** $\frac{33}{20}$

Q 2. Find the sums given below

(i) $7 + 10\frac{1}{2} + 14 + \ldots + 84$

(ii) $34 + 32 + 30 + \ldots + 10$

(iii) $-5 + (-8) + (-11) + \ldots + (-230)$

Sol. (i) The given numbers are $7, 10\frac{1}{2}, 14, \ldots 84$

$\because 10\frac{1}{2} - 7 = 14 - 10\frac{1}{2} = \ldots = \frac{7}{2}$

$\therefore$ The given numbers forms an AP.

Here, first term, $a = 7$,

common difference, $d = 10\frac{1}{2} - 7 = 3\frac{1}{2} = \frac{7}{2}$

and last term, $l = a_n = 84$

$\because \quad a_n = a + (n-1)d$

$\therefore \quad 84 = 7 + (n-1)\frac{7}{2} \quad \left[\because a = 7 \text{ and } d = \frac{7}{2}\right]$

$\Rightarrow \quad n - 1 = 22 \Rightarrow n = 23$

$\because$ Sum of n terms of an AP, $S_n = \frac{n}{2}(a + l)$

$\therefore$ Sum of 23 terms $(S_{23}) = \frac{23}{2}(7 + 84) = \frac{23}{2} \times 91$

$$= \frac{2093}{2} = 1046\frac{1}{2}$$

(ii) Do same as Part (i). **Ans.** 286

(iii) Do same as Part (i). **Ans.** -8930

Q 3. In an AP

(i) given $a = 5, d = 3, a_n = 50$, find n and S_n.

(ii) given $a = 7, a_{13} = 35$, find d and S_{13}.

(iii) given $a_{12} = 37, d = 3$, find a and S_{12}.

(iv) given $a_3 = 15, S_{10} = 125$, find d and a_{10}.

(v) given $d = 5, S_9 = 75$, find a and a_9.

(vi) given $a = 2, d = 8, S_n = 90$, find n and a_n.

(vii) given $a = 8, a_n = 62, S_n = 210$, find n and d.

(viii) given $a_n = 4, d = 2, S_n = -14$, find n and a.

(ix) given $a = 3, n = 8, S = 192$, find d.

(x) given $l = 28, S = 144$, and there are total 9 terms. Find a.

Sol. (i) Here, $a=5,\ d=3$ and $a_n=50$

$\because$ $a_n=a+(n-1)d$

$\therefore$ $5+(n-1)3=50$

$\Rightarrow$ $(n-1)=\frac{45}{3}=15 \Rightarrow n=15+1=16$

On putting $n=16, a=5$ and $l=a_n=50$ in $S_n=\frac{n}{2}(a+l)$, we get

$$S_{16}=\frac{16}{2}(5+50)=8\times 55=440$$

Hence, $n=16$ and $S_n=440$.

(ii) Here, $a=7$ and $a_{13}=35$

$\because$ $a_{13}=35$

$\therefore$ $a+12d=35$ $[\because a_n=a+(n-1)d]$

$\Rightarrow$ $7+12d=35$ $[\because a=7]$

$\Rightarrow$ $d=\frac{28}{12}=\frac{7}{3}$

On putting $n=13, a=7$ and $l=a_{13}=35$ in $S_n=\frac{n}{2}(a+l)$, we get

$$S_{13}=\frac{13}{2}(7+35)=\frac{13}{2}\times 42=13\times 21=273$$

Hence, $d=\frac{7}{3}$ and $S_{13}=273$

(iii) Here, $a_{12}=37$ and $d=3$

Then, $a_{12}=37$

$\Rightarrow$ $a+11d=37$ $[\because a_n=a+(n-1)d]$

$\Rightarrow$ $a+11(3)=37$ $[\because d=3]$

$\Rightarrow$ $a=37-33=4$

On putting $n=12, a=4$ and $l=a_{12}=37$ in $S_n=\frac{n}{2}(a+l)$, we get

$$S_{12}=\frac{12}{2}(4+37)=6\times 41=246$$

Hence, $a=4$ and $S_{12}=246$.

(iv) Here, $a_3=15$ and $S_{10}=125$

$\because$ $a_3=15$

$\therefore a+2d=15$ ...(i)

$[\because a_n=a+(n-1)d]$

Also, $S_{10}=125$

$\therefore$ $\frac{10}{2}[2a+(10-1)d]=125$ $\left[\because S_n=\frac{n}{2}\{2a+(n-1)d\}\right]$

$\Rightarrow$ $2a+9d=25$ [dividing by 5] ...(ii)

On multiplying Eq. (i) by 2 and then subtracting Eq. (ii) from it, we get

$2(a+2d)-(2a+9d)=2\times 15-25$

$\Rightarrow$ $4d-9d=30-25 \Rightarrow -5d=5$

$\Rightarrow$ $d=-\frac{5}{5}=-1$

Now, $a_{10}=a+9d$

$=(a+2d)+7d$

$=15+7(-1)$ [from Eq. (i)]

$=15-7=8$

Hence, $d=-1$ and $a_{10}=8$.

(v) Here, $d=5$ and $S_9=75$

$\because$ $S_9=75$

$\therefore$ $\frac{9}{2}[2a+(9-1)5]=75$

$\left[\because S_n=\frac{n}{2}\{2a+(n-1)d\}\right]$

$\Rightarrow$ $\frac{9}{2}(2a+40)=75$

$\Rightarrow$ $9a+180=75$

$\Rightarrow$ $a=\frac{-105}{9}=\frac{-35}{3}$

Now, $a_9=a+8d=\frac{-35}{3}+8\times 5$

$[\because a_n=a+(n-1)d]$

$=\frac{-35+120}{3}=\frac{85}{3}$

Hence, $a=\frac{-35}{3}$ and $a_9=\frac{85}{3}$.

(vi) Here, $a=2, d=8$ and $S_n=90$

$\because$ $S_n=90$

$\therefore$ $\frac{n}{2}[2\times 2+(n-1)8]=90$ $\left[\because S_n=\frac{n}{2}\{2a+(n-1)d\}\right]$

$\Rightarrow$ $\frac{n}{2}(4+8n-8)=90$

$\Rightarrow$ $\frac{n}{2}(8n-4)=90$

$\Rightarrow$ $n(4n-2)=90$

$\Rightarrow$ $4n^2-2n-90=0$

$\Rightarrow$ $2n^2-n-45=0$

$\Rightarrow$ $(n-5)(2n+9)=0$

$\Rightarrow$ $n=5$ or $\frac{-9}{2}$

Since, n cannot be negative.

$\therefore$ $n=5$

Now, $a_5=2+(5-1)8$

$[\because a_n=a+(n-1)d, a=2$ and $d=8]$

$=2+32=34$

Hence, $n=5$ and $a_n=34$.

(vii) Here, $a=8, a_n=62$ and $S_n=210$

$\because$ $S_n=210$

$\therefore$ $\frac{n}{2}(a+a_n)=210$ $\left[\because S_n=\frac{n}{2}(a+a_n)\right]$

$\Rightarrow \quad \frac{n}{2}(8+62)=210 \quad [\because a=8 \text{ and } a_n=62]$

$\Rightarrow \quad n=210\times\frac{2}{70}=3\times 2=6$

Thus, $a_n = 62$

$\Rightarrow \quad a_6 = 62$

$\Rightarrow \quad a+5d=62 \quad [\because a_n = a+(n-1)d]$

$\Rightarrow \quad 8+5d=62 \quad [\because a=8]$

$\Rightarrow \quad 5d=62-8=54$

$\Rightarrow \quad d=\frac{54}{5}$

Hence, $d=\frac{54}{5}$ and $n=6$.

(viii) Here, $a_n = 4, d=2$ and $S_n = -14$

$\because \quad a_n = 4$

$\therefore \quad a+(n-1)2=4 \quad [\because a_n = a+(n-1)d]$

$\Rightarrow \quad a=4-2(n-1) \quad \ldots(i)$

Also, $S_n = -14$

$\therefore \quad \frac{n}{2}(a+a_n)=-14 \quad \left[\because S_n=\frac{n}{2}(a+a_n)\right]$

$\Rightarrow \quad n(a+4)=-28 \quad [\because a_n=4]$

$\Rightarrow \quad n[4-2(n-1)+4]=-28 \quad$ [from Eq. (i)]

$\Rightarrow \quad n(4-2n+2+4)=-28$

$\Rightarrow \quad n(-n+5)=-14$ [dividing both sides by 2]

$\Rightarrow \quad -n^2+5n=-14$

$\Rightarrow \quad n^2-5n-14=0$

$\Rightarrow \quad (n-7)(n+2)=0$ [by factorisation method]

$\Rightarrow \quad n=7$ or $n=-2$

Since, n cannot be negative.

$\therefore \quad n=7$

On putting $n=7$ in Eq. (i), we get

$a=4-2(7-1)=4-2\times 6=4-12=-8$

Hence, $n=7$ and $a=-8$.

(ix) Here, $a=3, n=8$ and $S=192$

$\because \quad S=\frac{n}{2}[2a+(n-1)d]$

$\therefore \quad 192=\frac{8}{2}[2\times 3+(8-1)d]$

$\Rightarrow \quad 192=4(6+7d)$

$\Rightarrow \quad 48=6+7d$ [dividing both sides by 4]

$\Rightarrow \quad d=\frac{42}{7}=6$

Hence, $d=6$

(x) Here, $l=28, S=144$ and $n=9$

$\because \quad S=144$

$\therefore \quad \frac{n}{2}(a+l)=144 \quad \left[\because S=\frac{n}{2}(\text{first term}+\text{last term})\right]$

$\Rightarrow \quad \frac{9}{2}(a+28)=144 \Rightarrow a+28=32$

Hence, $a=4$

Q4. How many terms of the AP : 9, 17, 25, ... must be taken to give a sum of 636?

Sol. Do same as Example 6 of Topic 3.

Ans. The sum of 12 terms is 636.

Q5. The first term of an AP is 5, the last term is 45 and the sum is 400. Find the number of terms and the common difference.

Sol. Let n be the number of terms in the given AP and d be the common difference.

Given, first term $(a)=5$, last term $(l)=45$ and sum of n terms $(S_n)=400$.

$\because \quad S_n=\frac{n}{2}(a+l)$

$\Rightarrow \quad 400=\frac{n}{2}(5+45)$

$\Rightarrow \quad n=\frac{400\times 2}{50}=8\times 2=16$

Now, $l=45$

$\Rightarrow \quad a+(n-1)d=45 \quad [\because l=a_n=a+(n-1)d]$

$\Rightarrow \quad 5+(16-1)d=45 \quad [\because a=5, n=16]$

$\Rightarrow \quad d=\frac{40}{15}=\frac{8}{3}$

$\therefore$ The number of terms is 16 and the common difference is $\frac{8}{3}$.

Q6. The first and the last terms of an AP are 17 and 350 respectively. If the common difference is 9, then how many terms are there and what is their sum?

Sol. Given, first term, $a=17$, last term, $l=350$ and common difference, $d=9$.

Let there are n terms in the given AP. Then, $l=a_n=350$

$\Rightarrow \quad a+(n-1)d=350 \quad [\because a_n=a+(n-1)d]$

$\Rightarrow \quad 17+(n-1)9=350 \quad [\because a=17 \text{ and } d=9]$

$\Rightarrow \quad n-1=\frac{333}{9}=37$

$\Rightarrow \quad n=37+1=38$

On putting $a=17$, $l=350$ and $n=38$ in $S_n=\frac{n}{2}(a+l)$, we get

$S_{38}=\frac{38}{2}(17+350)=19(367)=6973$

Hence, there are 38 terms in the AP having their sum 6973.

Q7. Find the sum of first 22 terms of an AP, in which $d = 7$ and 22nd term is 149.

Sol. Given, $d = 7$ and $a_{22} = 149$

$\because \quad a_n = a + (n-1)d$

$\therefore \quad a + (22-1)d = 149$

$\Rightarrow \quad a + 21 \times 7 = 149$

$\Rightarrow \quad a = 149 - 147 = 2$

On putting $a = 2, n = 22$ and $d = 7$ in

$S_n = \frac{n}{2}[2a + (n-1)d]$, we get

$S_{22} = \frac{22}{2}[2 \times 2 + (22-1)7]$

$= 11(4 + 21 \times 7) = 11(4 + 147) = 11 \times 151 = 1661$

Hence, the sum of first 22 terms is 1661.

Q8. Find the sum of first 51 terms of an AP whose second and third terms are 14 and 18 respectively.

Sol. Given, second term, $a_2 = 14$ and third term, $a_3 = 18$

$\because \quad a_n = a + (n-1)d$

We have, $\quad a + d = 14 \quad$ ...(i)

and $\quad a + 2d = 18 \quad$ ...(ii)

On subtracting Eq. (i) from Eq. (ii), we get

$d = 4$

On putting $d = 4$ in Eq. (i), we get

$a + 4 = 14$

$\Rightarrow \quad a = 14 - 4 = 10$

$\because$ Sum of first n terms, $S_n = \frac{n}{2}[2a + (n-1)d]$

$\therefore$ Sum of first 51 terms, $S_{51} = \frac{51}{2}[2 \times 10 + (51-1) \times 4]$

$[\because a = 10 \text{ and } d = 4]$

$= \frac{51}{2}[20 + 50 \times 4] = \frac{51}{2}(20 + 200) = \frac{51}{2} \times 220$

$= 51 \times 110 = 5610$

Q9. If the sum of first 7 terms of an AP is 49 and that of 17 terms is 289, then find the sum of first n terms.

Sol. Given, $S_7 = 49$ and $S_{17} = 289$.

Let a be the first term and d be the common difference of given AP. Then,

$S_7 = 49$

$\Rightarrow \quad \frac{7}{2}[2a + 6d] = 49 \Rightarrow a + 3d = 7 \quad$ ...(i)

and $\quad S_{17} = 289$

$\Rightarrow \quad \frac{17}{2}[2a + 16d] = 289$

$\Rightarrow \quad a + 8d = 17 \quad$ ...(ii)

On subtracting Eq. (i) from Eq. (ii), we get

$5d = 10 \Rightarrow d = 2$

On substituting $d = 2$ in Eq. (i), we get

$a + 6 = 7 \Rightarrow a = 1$

Now, $S_n = \frac{n}{2}[2a + (n-1)d] = \frac{n}{2}[2 + (n-1)2]$

$= n[1 + n - 1] = n^2$

Q10. Show that $a_1, a_2, \ldots, a_n, \ldots$ form an AP, where a_n is defined as below :

(i) $a_n = 3 + 4n$ (ii) $a_n = 9 - 5n$

Also, find the sum of the first 15 terms in each case.

Sol. (i) Given, $a_n = 3 + 4n$

Clearly, $a_{n+1} - a_n = 3 + 4(n+1) - (3 + 4n)$

$= 3 + 4n + 4 - 3 - 4n = 4$, which is independent of n.

So, given sequences forms an AP with

first term $(a) = a_1 = 3 + 4 = 7$ and

common difference $(d) = a_2 - a_1 = 11 - 7 = 4$.

$\because$ Sum of n terms, $S_n = \frac{n}{2}[2a + (n-1)d]$

$\therefore \quad S_{15} = \frac{15}{2}[2 \times 7 + (15-1)4]$

$= \frac{15}{2} \times 70 = 15 \times 35 = 525$

(ii) Do same as Part (i). **Ans.** -465

Q11. If the sum of the first n terms of an AP is $4n - n^2$, then what is the first term (i.e. S_1)? What is the sum of first two terms? What is the second term? Similarly, find the 3rd, the 10th and the nth terms.

Sol. Given, the sum of first n terms,

$S_n = 4n - n^2 \quad$ ...(i)

On putting $n = 1$ in Eq. (i), we get

$S_1 = 4 \times 1 - 1^2 = 4 - 1 = 3$

Thus, first term $= 3$

On putting $n = 2$ in Eq. (i), we get

$S_2 = 4 \times 2 - 2^2 = 8 - 4 = 4$

Thus, sum of first two terms $= 4$

$\because$ The nth term of an AP, $a_n = S_n - S_{n-1}$

$\therefore$ Second term $= S_2 - S_1 = 4 - 3 = 1$

On putting $n = 3$ in Eq. (i), we get

$S_3 = 4 \times 3 - 3^2 = 12 - 9 = 3$

$\therefore$ Third term $= S_3 - S_2 = 3 - 4 = -1$

On putting $n = 9$ in Eq. (i), we get

$S_9 = 4 \times 9 - 9^2 = 36 - 81 = -45$

Again, on putting $n = 10$ in Eq. (i), we get

$S_{10} = 4 \times 10 - 10^2 = 40 - 100 = -60$

$\therefore$ 10th term $= S_{10} - S_9$

$= -60 - (-45) = -60 + 45 = -15$

Now, on replacing n by $n-1$ in Eq. (i), we get

$$S_{n-1} = 4(n-1) - (n-1)^2$$
$$= 4n - 4 - n^2 + 2n - 1 = -n^2 + 6n - 5$$

$\therefore$ nth term $= S_n - S_{n-1}$

$$= 4n - n^2 - (-n^2 + 6n - 5)$$
$$= 4n - n^2 + n^2 - 6n + 5 = 5 - 2n$$

Q 12. Find the sum of the first 40 positive integers divisible by 6.

Sol. The first 40 positive integers divisible by 6 are 6, 12, 18, ..., 240. Clearly, these numbers forms an AP with first term, $a = 6$, common difference, $d = 6$ and last term, $l = 240$.

$\because$ Sum of n terms, $S_n = \frac{n}{2}[a + l]$

$\therefore$ Sum of first 40 terms,

$$S_{40} = \frac{40}{2}[6 + 240] = 20 \times 246 = 4920$$

Hence, the sum of first 40 positive integers divisible by 6 is 4920.

Q 13. Find the sum of the first 15 multiples of 8.

Sol. The first 15 multiples of 8 are

$8 \times 1, 8 \times 2, 8 \times 3, ..., 8 \times 15$

i.e. 8, 16, 24, ..., 120 which are in AP.

Here, first term $(a) = 8$, last term $(l) = 120$ and number of terms $(n) = 15$.

$\because$ Sum of n terms, $S_n = \frac{n}{2}(a + l)$

$\therefore$ Sum of 15 terms, $S_{15} = \frac{15}{2}(8 + 120) = \frac{15}{2} \times 128$

$= 15 \times 64 = 960$

Hence, the sum of first 15 multiples of 8 is 960.

Q 14. Find the sum of the odd numbers between 0 and 50.

Sol. The odd numbers between 0 and 50 are 1, 3, 5,..., 49 which form an AP.

Here, first term $(a) = 1$, last term $(l) = 49$ and common difference $(d) = 3 - 1 = 2$.

Let there be n numbers in the AP.

Then, nth term $(a_n) = a + (n-1)d = l$

$\Rightarrow$ $1 + (n-1)(2) = 49$

$\Rightarrow$ $n - 1 = 24 \Rightarrow n = 25$

Now, sum of n terms, $S_n = \frac{n}{2}(a + l)$

$\therefore$ Sum of 25 terms, $S_{25} = \frac{25}{2}(1 + 49) = \frac{25}{2} \times 50$

$= 25 \times 25 = 625$

Q 15. A contract on construction job specifies a penalty for delay of completion beyond a certain date as follows: ₹ 200 for the first day, ₹ 250 for the second day, ₹ 300 for the third day etc. The penalty for each succeeding day being ₹ 50 more than for the preceding day. How much money the contractor has to pay as penalty, if he has delayed the work by 30 days?

Sol. Given, the penalty for each succeeding day is ₹ 50 more than the preceding day, therefore the penalties for the first day, the second day, the third day etc., will form an AP.

Here, $a = 200, d = 250 - 200 = 50$ and $n = 30$.

Clearly, the money required by the contractor to pay as penalty, if he delayed the work by 30 days, will be S_{30}.

We know that

$$S_n = \frac{n}{2}[2a + (n-1)d]$$

$\therefore$ $S_{30} = \frac{30}{2}[2 \times 200 + (30 - 1) 50]$

$= 15(400 + 1450) = 15 \times 1850 = 27750$

Hence, the contractor has to pay ₹ 27750, if he delayed the work.

Q 16. A sum of ₹ 700 is to be used to give seven cash prizes to students of a school for their overall academic performance. If each prize is ₹ 20 less than its preceding prize, then find the value of each of the prizes.

Sol. Here, ₹ 700 is to be used to give 7 cash prizes.

Let the value of first prize be ₹ a. Then, value of second prize ₹ $(a - 20)$, value of third prize be ₹ $[(a - 20) - 20]$ and so on.

Thus, we get an AP whose first term is a and common difference is -20.

Since, $S_7 = 700$

$\therefore$ $\frac{7}{2}[2a + (7-1)(-20)] = 700$ $\left[\because S_n = \frac{n}{2}\{2a + (n-1)d\}\right]$

$\Rightarrow$ $2a - 120 = 200$

$\Rightarrow$ $2a = 320$

$\Rightarrow$ $a = \frac{320}{2} = 160$

Hence, value of 1st prize = ₹ 160

Value of 2nd prize = ₹160 – ₹20 = ₹ 140

Value of 3rd prize = ₹140 – ₹20 = ₹ 120

Value of 4th prize = ₹120 – ₹20 = ₹ 100

Value of 5th prize = ₹100 – ₹20 = ₹ 80

Value of 6th prize = ₹80 – ₹20 = ₹ 60

and value of 7th prize = ₹60 – ₹20 = ₹ 40

Q 17. **In a school, students thought of planting trees in and around the school to reduce air pollution. It was decided that the number of trees, that each section of each class will plant, will be the same as the class, in which they are studying, e.g. section of class I will plant 1 tree, a section of class II will plant 2 trees and so on till class XII. There are three sections of each class. How many trees will be planted by the students?**

Sol. According to the question, there are three sections of each class, so the number of trees that are planted by students of class I, class II, class III,... and class XII, are respectively, $1 \times 3, 2 \times 3, 3 \times 3, \ldots$ and 12×3.

Thus, we get the following list of numbers, 3, 6, 9, ..., 36

Clearly, it forms an AP.

Here, the first term, $a = 3$

common difference, $d = 6 - 3 = 3$ and the last term, $l = 36$

Let the last term of this AP be its nth term.

Then, $a_n = a + (n - 1)d = l$

$\Rightarrow \quad 3 + (n - 1)(3) = 36 \Rightarrow (n - 1)3 = 33$

$\Rightarrow \quad n - 1 = 11 \Rightarrow n = 12$

Hence, the number of the trees planted by the students

$= $ Sum of 12 terms of above AP

$= \frac{12}{2}(3 + 36) \quad \left[\because S_n = \frac{n}{2}(a + l)\right]$

$= 6 \times 39 = 234$

Q 18. **A spiral is made up of successive semi-circles, with centres alternately at A and B, starting with centre at A, of radii 0.5 cm, 1.0 cm, 1.5 cm, 2.0 cm, ... as shown in below figure. What is the total length of such a spiral made up of thirteen consecutive semi-circles? [Take $\pi = 22/7$]**

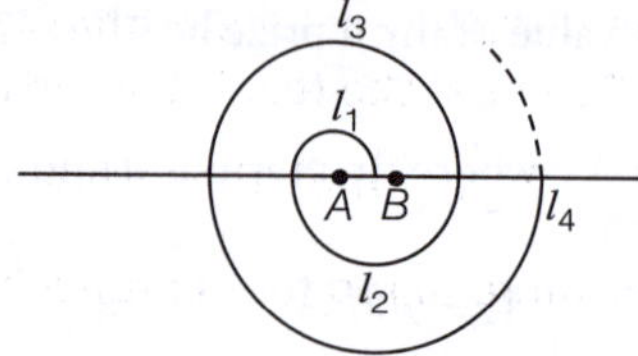

[**Hint** Length of successive semi-circles are $l_1, l_2, l_3, l_4, \ldots$ with centres at $A, B, A, B, \ldots$, respectively.]

Sol. Length of spiral made up of thirteen consecutive semi circles

$= (\pi \times 0.5 + \pi \times 1.0 + \pi \times 1.5 + \pi \times 2.0 + \ldots + \pi \times 6.5)$

[$\because$ circumference of semi-circle $= \pi r$, where, r is radius of circle]

$= 0.5\pi[1 + 2 + 3 + 4 + \ldots + 13]$

$= \pi \times 0.5 \times \frac{13}{2}[2 \times 1 + (13 - 1) \times 1]$

[$\because$ the numbers 1, 2, 3, ..., 13, forms an AP with $a = 1$, $d = 2 - 1 = 1$. Also, $S_n = \frac{n}{2}\{2a + (n - 1)d\}$]

$= \frac{22}{7} \times \frac{5}{10} \times \frac{13}{2} \times 14 = 143$ cm

Q 19. **200 logs are stacked in the following manner : 20 logs in the bottom row, 19 in the next row, 18 in the row next to it and so on (see below figure). In how many rows are the 200 logs placed and how many logs are in the top row?**

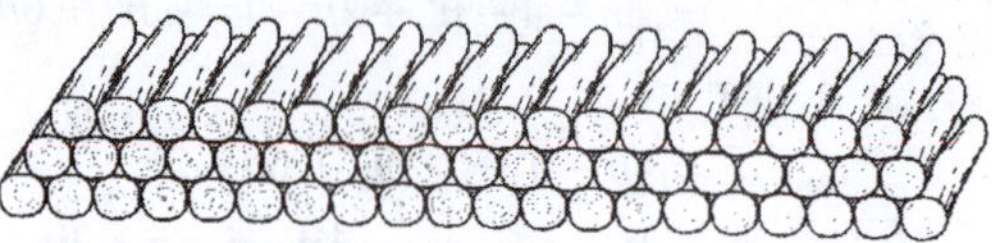

Sol. Number of logs stacked in each row form a sequence 20, 19, 18, 17,...., which is an AP with first term, $a = 20$ and common difference, $d = 19 - 20 = -1$.

Suppose number of rows is n, then $S_n = 200$

$\Rightarrow \frac{n}{2}[2 \times 20 + (n - 1)(-1)] = 200$

$\left[\because S_n = \frac{n}{2}\{2a + (n - 1)d\}\right]$

$\Rightarrow \quad 400 = 40n - n^2 + n$

$\Rightarrow \quad n^2 - 41n + 400 = 0$

$\Rightarrow \quad n^2 - 25n - 16n + 400 = 0$ [by factorisation]

$\Rightarrow \quad n(n - 25) - 16(n - 25) = 0$

$\Rightarrow \quad (n - 25)(n - 16) = 0$

$\Rightarrow \quad n = 16$ or $n = 25$

Hence, the number of rows is either 25 or 16.

When $n = 16$,

$a_n = a + (n - 1)d = 20 + (16 - 1)(-1) = 20 - 15 = 5$

When $n = 25$,

$a_n = a + (n - 1)d = 20 + (25 - 1)(-1)$

$= 20 - 24 = -4$

[$\because$ number of logs cannot be negative]

Hence, the number of rows is 16 and number of logs in the top row is 5.

Q 20. **In a potato race, a bucket is placed at the starting point, which is 5 m from the first potato and the other potatoes are placed 3 m apart in a straight line. There are ten potatoes in the line (see below figure).**

A competitor starts from the bucket, picks up the nearest potato, runs back with it, drops it in the bucket, runs back to pick up the next potato, runs to the bucket to drop it in and she continues in the same way until all the potatoes are in the bucket. What is the total distance the competitor has to run?

[**Hint** To pick up the first potato and the second potato, the total distance (in metres) run by a competitor is $2 \times 5 + 2 \times (5 + 3)$]

Sol. The distance run by the competitor to picks up the first potato, second potato, third potato, fourth potato, ... are respectively $2 \times 5, 2 \times (5+3), 2 \times (5+3+3)$, $2 \times (5+3+3+3)$ ... i.e. 10, 16, 22, 28, ...

Clearly, it is an AP with first term, $a = 10$ and common difference, $d = 16 - 10 = 6$.

$\because$ Sum of first n terms, $S_n = \frac{n}{2}[2a + (n-1)d]$

$\therefore$ Sum of first 10 terms, $S_{10} = \frac{10}{2}[2 \times 10 + (10-1) \times 6]$

[$\because n = 10$, given]

$= 5(20 + 54) = 5 \times 74 = 370$

Hence, the total distance the competitor has to run is 370 m.

EXERCISE 5.4

Q1. Which term of the AP : 121, 117, 113, ... is its first negative term?

[**Hint** Find n for which $a_n < 0$.]

Sol. Given, AP is 121, 117, 113, ...

Here, first term, $a = 121$

and common difference, $d = 117 - 121 = -4$

Let the nth term of this AP be the first negative term.

Then, $a_n < 0$

$\Rightarrow a + (n-1)d < 0 \Rightarrow 121 + (n-1)(-4) < 0$

$\Rightarrow 125 - 4n < 0 \Rightarrow 125 < 4n \Rightarrow 4n > 125$

$\Rightarrow n > \frac{125}{4} \Rightarrow n > 31\frac{1}{4}$

So, least integral value of n is 32.

Hence, 32nd term of the given AP is the first negative term.

Q2. The sum of the third and the seventh terms of an AP is 6 and their product is 8. Find the sum of first sixteen terms of the AP.

Sol. Let the first term and the common difference of the given AP be a and d, respectively.

According to the question,

Third term + Seventh term = 6

$\Rightarrow [a + (3-1)d] + [a + (7-1)d] = 6$ [$\because a_n = a + (n-1)d$]

$\Rightarrow (a + 2d) + (a + 6d) = 6$

$\Rightarrow a + 4d = 3$ ...(i)

and Third term $\times$ Seventh term = 8

$\Rightarrow (a + 2d)(a + 6d) = 8$

$\Rightarrow \{(a + 4d) - 2d\}\{(a + 4d) + 2d\} = 8$

$\Rightarrow (3 - 2d)(3 + 2d) = 8$ [using Eq. (i)]

$\Rightarrow 9 - 4d^2 = 8$

[$\because (a-b)(a+b) = a^2 - b^2$]

$\Rightarrow 4d^2 = 9 - 8$

$\Rightarrow d^2 = \frac{1}{4} \Rightarrow d = \pm\frac{1}{2}$

When $d = \frac{1}{2}$, then from Eq. (i), we get

$a + 4\left(\frac{1}{2}\right) = 3$

$\Rightarrow a + 2 = 3$

$\Rightarrow a = 3 - 2 \Rightarrow a = 1$

Now, sum of first sixteen terms of the AP,

$S_{16} = \frac{16}{2}[2a + (16-1)d]$ $\left[\because S_n = \frac{n}{2}\{2a + (n-1)d\}\right]$

$= 8[2a + 15d] = 8\left[2(1) + 15\left(\frac{1}{2}\right)\right]$

$= 8\left(2 + \frac{15}{2}\right) = 8\left(\frac{19}{2}\right) = 76$

When $d = -\frac{1}{2}$, then from Eq. (i), we get

$a + 4\left(-\frac{1}{2}\right) = 3 \Rightarrow a - 2 = 3 \Rightarrow a = 5$

Now, sum of first sixteen terms of this AP,

$S_{16} = \frac{16}{2}[2a + (16-1)d]$ $\left[\because S_n = \frac{n}{2}\{2a + (n-1)d\}\right]$

$= 8(2a + 15d) = 8\left[2(5) + 15\left(-\frac{1}{2}\right)\right]$

$= 8\left(10 - \frac{15}{2}\right) = 8\left(\frac{5}{2}\right) = 20$

Hence, the sum of first sixteen terms, $S_{16} = 20$ or 76.

Q3. A ladder has rungs 25 cm apart (see figure). The rungs decrease uniformly in length from 45 cm at the bottom to 25 cm at the top. If the top and the bottom rungs are $2\frac{1}{2}$ m apart, then what is the length of the wood required for the rungs?

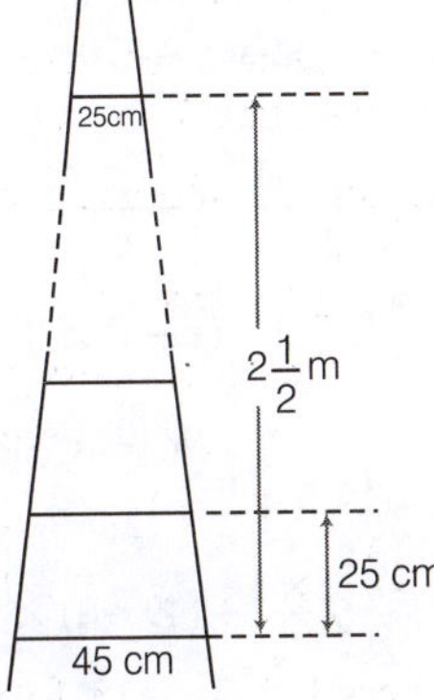

Hint Number of rungs

$= \frac{\text{Distance between top and bottom rungs}}{\text{Distance between two rungs}} + 1$

Sol. According to the question,

Number of rungs

$$= \frac{\text{Distance between top and bottom rungs}}{\text{Distance between two rungs}} + 1$$

$$= \frac{2\frac{1}{2}\text{m}}{25\text{ cm}} + 1 = \frac{\frac{5}{2} \times 100\text{ cm}}{25\text{ cm}} + 1 [\because 1\text{ m} = 100\text{ cm}]$$

$$= \frac{250\text{ cm}}{25\text{ cm}} + 1 = 10 + 1 = 11$$

Hence, there are 11 rungs.

The length of the wood required for the rungs

$$= \text{Sum of length of 11 rungs} = \frac{11}{2}(25 + 45)$$

$\left[\because \text{length of rungs forms an AP with first term } (a) = 25 \text{ and last term } (l) = 45 \text{ and } S_n = \frac{n}{2}(a + l)\right]$

$$= \frac{11}{2} \times 70 = 11 \times 35 = 385\text{ cm}$$

Hence, the length of the wood required for the rungs is 385 cm.

Q4. The houses of a row are numbered consecutively from 1 to 49. Show that there is a value of x such that the sum of the numbers of the houses preceding the house numbered x is equal to the sum of the numbers of the houses following it. Find the value of x. [Hint $S_{x-1} = S_{49} - S_x$]

Sol. The numbers on the houses of a row are 1, 2, 3, ..., 49.

Clearly, this list of numbers forms an AP with

$$a = 1 \text{ and } d = 2 - 1 = 1$$

According to the question, we have

$$S_{x-1} = S_{49} - S_x \quad \text{...(i)}$$

$$\because \quad S_n = \frac{n}{2}[2a + (n-1)d]$$

$$\therefore \quad S_{x-1} = \frac{x-1}{2}[2 \times 1 + (x - 1 - 1) \times 1]$$

$$= \frac{x-1}{2}(2 + x - 2)$$

$$= \frac{(x-1)x}{2} = \frac{x^2 - x}{2},$$

$$S_x = \frac{x}{2}[2 \times 1 + (x-1) \times 1]$$

$$= \frac{x}{2}(x+1) = \frac{x^2 + x}{2}$$

and $$S_{49} = \frac{49}{2}[2 \times 1 + (49 - 1) \times 1]$$

$$= \frac{49}{2}[2 + 48]$$

$$= \frac{49}{2} \times 50 = 49 \times 25 = 1225$$

Now, on substituting above values in Eq(i), we get

$$\frac{x^2 - x}{2} = 1225 - \frac{x^2 + x}{2}$$

$$\Rightarrow \quad \frac{x^2 - x}{2} + \frac{x^2 + x}{2} = 1225$$

$$\Rightarrow \quad \frac{x^2 - x + x^2 + x}{2} = 1225$$

$$\Rightarrow \quad x^2 = 1225 \Rightarrow x = \pm 35$$

Since, x is a counting number.

$\therefore$ Taking positive sign, we get $x = 35$.

Q5. A small terrace at a football ground comprises of 15 steps each of which is 50 m long and built of solid concrete. Each step has a rise of $\frac{1}{4}$ m and a tread of $\frac{1}{2}$ m (see figure). Calculate the total volume of concrete required to build the terrace.

[Hint Volume of concrete required to build the first step $= \frac{1}{4} \times \frac{1}{2} \times 50\text{ m}^3$]

Sol. Clearly, volume of concrete required to build the I step, II step, III step,.. are respectively,

$$\frac{1}{4} \times \frac{1}{2} \times 50, \left(2 \times \frac{1}{4}\right) \times \frac{1}{2} \times 50, \left(3 \times \frac{1}{4}\right) \times \frac{1}{2} \times 50, \ldots,$$

i.e. $$\frac{50}{8}, 2 \times \frac{50}{8}, 3 \times \frac{50}{8}, \ldots$$

Now, total volume of concrete,

$$V = \frac{50}{8} + 2 \times \frac{50}{8} + 3 \times \frac{50}{8} + \ldots = \frac{50}{8}[1 + 2 + 3 + \ldots]$$

Note that the numbers in the bracket forms an AP with first term $(a) = 1$, common difference $(d) = 2 - 1 = 1$ and number of terms $(n) = 15$

$$\therefore \quad V = \frac{50}{8} \times \frac{15}{2}[2 \times 1 + (15 - 1) \times 1]$$

$$\left[\because S_n = \frac{n}{2}\{2a + (n-1)d\}\right]$$

$$= \frac{50}{8} \times \frac{15}{2} \times (2 + 14)$$

$$= \frac{25 \times 15}{8} \times 16 = 750\text{ m}^3$$

Hence, the total volume of concrete required to build the terrace is 750 m^3.

REVIEW EXERCISE

Including Competency Based Questions

Part I

Multiple Choice Questions

1. If $k+7, 2k-2$ and $2k+6$ are three consecutive terms of an AP, then the value of k is **CBSE 2024 (Standard) Compartment**

(a) 15 (b) 17 (c) 5 (d) 1

2. What cannot be the difference between four consecutive terms of an arithmetic progression? **Competency Based Question**

(a) 0, 0, 0 (b) −2, −2, −2 (c) 2, 3, 4 (d) $\frac{2}{7}, \frac{2}{7}, \frac{2}{7}$

3. The common difference of the AP $\frac{1}{2x}, \frac{1-4x}{2x}, \frac{1-8x}{2x}, \ldots$ is **CBSE 2024 (Standard)**

(a) $-2x$ (b) −2 (c) 2 (d) $2x$

4. In an AP, if $a = 8$ and $a_{10} = -19$, then value of d is **CBSE 2024 (Basic)**

(a) 3 (b) $\frac{-11}{9}$ (c) $\frac{-27}{10}$ (d) −3

5. Is an sequence defined by $a_n = 2n^2 + 1$ forms an AP? **NCERT Exemplar**

(a) Yes (b) No
(c) Cannot be determined (d) None of these

6. The 21st term of an AP whose first two terms are −3 and 4, is

(a) 17 (b) 137 (c) 143 (d) − 143

7. The common difference of the AP whose nth term is given by $a_n = 3n + 7$, is **CBSE 2023 (Standard)**

(a) 7 (b) 3 (c) $3n$ (d) 1

8. Which term of the AP 5, 15, 25, ... will be 130 more than its 31st term? **NCERT Exemplar**

(a) 42 (b) 44 (c) 46 (d) 48

9. Two APs have the same common difference. The first term of one of these is − 1 and that of the other is − 8. Then, the difference between their 4th terms is **CBSE Sample Paper 2023 (Standard)**

(a) 1 (b) 8 (c) 7 (d) 9

10. The 7th term from the end of the AP − 8, − 5, − 2, ..., 49 is

(a) 67 (b) 13 (c) 31 (d) 10

11. Let a be a sequence defined by $a_1 = 1, a_2 = 1$ and $a_n = a_{n-1} + a_{n-2}$ for all $n > 2$, then the value of $\frac{a_4}{a_3}$ is **Competency Based Question**

(a) $\frac{2}{3}$ (b) $\frac{5}{4}$ (c) $\frac{4}{5}$ (d) $\frac{3}{2}$

12. If the sum of first n terms of an AP is given by $S_n = \frac{n}{2}(3n+1)$, then the first term of the AP is **CBSE 2025 (Basic)**

(a) 2 (b) $\frac{3}{2}$ (c) 4 (d) $\frac{5}{2}$

13. The sum of the first 50 odd natural numbers is **CBSE 2023 (Basic)**

(a) 5000 (b) 2500 (c) 2550 (d) 5050

Assertion-Reason Type Questions

14. **Assertion (A)** $-5, \frac{-5}{2}, 0, \frac{5}{2}, \ldots$ is an arithmetic progression.

Reason (R) The terms of an arithmetic progression cannot have both positive and negative rational numbers. **CBSE Sample Paper 2023 (Standard)**

(a) Both Assertion and Reason are correct and Reason is the correct explanation of Assertion.
(b) Both Assertion and Reason are correct but Reason is not the correct explanation of Assertion.
(c) Assertion is correct but Reason is incorrect.
(d) Assertion is incorrect but Reason is correct.

15. **Assertion (A)** The sequence −1, −1, −1, ..., −1 is an AP.

Reason (R) In an AP, $a_n - a_{n-1}$ is constant, where $n \geq 2$ and $n \in N$.

(a) Both Assertion and Reason are correct and Reason is the correct explanation of Assertion.
(b) Both Assertion and Reason are correct but Reason is not the correct explanation of Assertion.
(c) Assertion is correct but Reason is incorrect.
(d) Assertion is incorrect but Reason is correct.

16. **Assertion (A)** Sum of first 10 even natural numbers is 120.

Reason (R) If a is the first term, l is the last term and d is the common difference of an AP, then nth term from the end is given by $l-(n-1)d$.

(a) Both Assertion and Reason are correct and Reason is the correct explanation of Assertion.
(b) Both Assertion and Reason are correct but Reason is not the correct explanation of Assertion.
(c) Assertion is correct but Reason is incorrect.
(d) Assertion is incorrect but Reason is correct.

17. Assertion (A) If the nth term of an AP be $(2n^2 - 1)$, then the sum of its first n terms is n^3.

Reason (R) If a, l and n are first term, last term and number of terms of an AP, respectively, then $S_n = \frac{n}{2}(a + l)$.

(a) Both Assertion and Reason are correct and Reason is the correct explanation of Assertion.
(b) Both Assertion and Reason are correct but Reason is not the correct explanation of Assertion.
(c) Assertion is correct but Reason is incorrect.
(d) Assertion is incorrect but Reason is correct.

18. Assertion (A) In an AP, $S_n = n^2 + n$, then $T_{20} = 40$.

Reason (R) In an AP, $a_n - a_{n-1} = d$.

(a) Both Assertion and Reason are correct and Reason is the correct explanation of Assertion.
(b) Both Assertion and Reason are correct but Reason is not the correct explanation of Assertion.
(c) Assertion is correct but Reason is incorrect.
(d) Assertion is incorrect but Reason is correct.

Case Based Type Questions

19. A chair is available in two models with arms and without arms. A person bought 20 chairs of each model. After use, he stacked the chairs in a storeroom. The height of the storeroom is 1.55 m. The dimensions of the chair and how they are stacked is shown in the figure below.

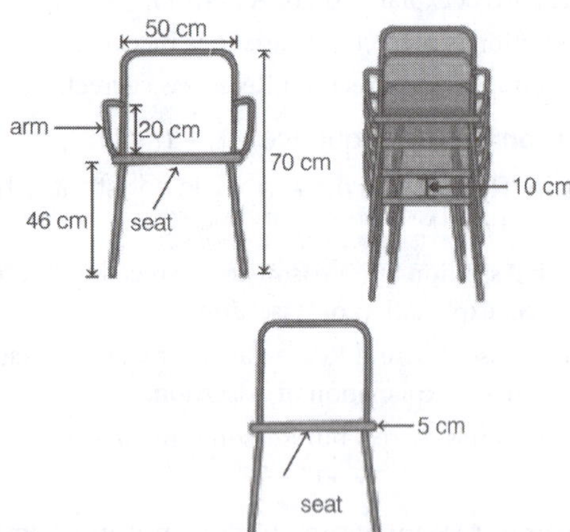

The dimensions of the seat (in cm) is $50 \times 40 \times 5$.
Based on the above information, answer the following questions. **CBSE QB**

(i) What is the height of the stack shown in the figure?
(a) 30 cm (b) 76 cm (c) 100 cm (d) 110 cm

(ii) What is the maximum number of chairs with arms that can be stacked in the storeroom?
(a) 4 (b) 8 (c) 9 (d) 10

(iii) What is the maximum number of chairs without arms that can be stacked in the storeroom?

(iv) What is the minimum number of columns (stacks) in which all chairs can be stacked in the storeroom?

(v) What can be the dimensions of the storeroom (in m)?
(a) $0.3 \times 1.5 \times 1.55$ (b) $0.4 \times 1.75 \times 1.55$
(c) $0.5 \times 0.4 \times 1.55$ (d) $1 \times 2.75 \times 1.55$

20. A school has decided to plant some endangered trees on 51st World Environment Day in the nearest park. They have decided to plant those trees in few concentric circular rows such that each succeeding row has 20 more trees than the previous one. The first circular row has 50 trees.

Based on the above given information, answer the following questions.

(i) How many trees will be planted in the 10th row ?

(ii) How many more trees will be planted in the 8th row than in the 5th row ?

(iii) (a) If 3200 trees are to be planted in the park, then how many rows are required?

Or

(b) If 3200 trees are to be planted in the park, then how many trees are still left to be planted after the 11th row ? **CBSE 2024 (Standard)] Compartment**

21. India is competitive manufacturing location due to the low cost of manpower and strong technical and engineering capabilities contributing to higher quality production runs. The production of TV sets in a factory increases uniformly by a fixed number every year. It produced 16000 sets in 6th year and 22600 in 9th year.

Based on the above information, answer the following questions.

(i) Find the production during 8th year.

(ii) (a) Find the production during first 3 yr.

Or

(b) In which year, the production is ₹ 29200.

(iii) Find the difference of the production during 7th year and 4th year.

22. Your elder brother wants to buy a car and plans to take loan from a bank for his car. He repays his total loan of ₹ 118000 by paying every month starting with the first installment of ₹ 1000. If he increases the installment by ₹ 100 every month, answer the following

(i) (a) Find the amount paid by him in 30th installment?

Or

(b) If total installments are 40, then amount paid in the last installment?

(ii) Find the total amount paid by him in the 30 installments?

(iii) Find the ratio of the 1st installment to the last installment.

23. The marathon is a long-distance foot race with a distance of 42.195 km, usually run as a road race but the distance can be covered on trail routes. The marathon can be completed by running or with a run/walk strategy. The marathon was one of the original modern Olympic events in 1896.

Neha, a student of class X, wishes to participate in a marathon. She decided to begin her practice by gradually increasing her running distance. In the first week, she decided to run 3 km each day and increase the distance by 2 km each week i.e. in the second week, she would run 5 km each day, in the third week, she would run 7 km each day and so on.

Based on the above information, answer the following questions

(i) What distance will Neha cover each day of the 8th week of her practice?

(ii) In which week would she be able to run for 45 km each day?

(iii) (a) What is the total distance covered by Neha after 11 weeks, if she practiced for 5 days in each week ?

Or

(b) Had she increased the distance by 3 km each week instead of 2 km each week, in how many weeks would she have trained herself to run for 42 km per day? **CBSE 2024 Basic Compartment**

24. Ms. Sheela visited a store near her house and found that the glass jars are arranged one above the other in a specific pattern.

On the top layer, there are 3 jars. In the next layer, there are 6 jars. In the 3rd layer from the top, there are 9 jars and so on till the 8th layer.

On the basis of the above situation, answer the following questions. **CBSE Sample Paper 2025 (Standard)**

(i) Write an AP whose terms represent the number of jars in different layers starting from top . Also, find the common difference.

(ii) Is it possible to arrange 34 jars in a layer if this pattern is continued? Justify your answer.

(iii) (a) If there are n number of rows in a layer, then find the expression for finding the total number of jars in terms of n. Hence, find S_8.

Or

(b) The shopkeeper added 3 jars in each layer. How many jars are there in the 5th layer from the top?

25. Manpreet Kaur is the national record holder for women in the shot-put discipline. Her throw of 18.86 m at the Asian Grand Prix in 2017 is the biggest distance for an Indian female athlete. **CBSE 2023 (Standard)**

Keeping her as a role model, Sanjitha is determined to earn gold in Olympics one day.

Initially her throw reached 7.56 m only. Being an athlete in school, she regularly practiced both in the mornings and in the evenings and was able to improve the distance by 9 cm every week.

During the special camp for 15 days, she started with 40 throws and every day kept increasing the number of throws by 12 to achieve this remarkable progress.

Based on the above information, answer the following questions.

(i) How many throws Sanjitha practiced on 11th day of the camp?

(ii) What would be Sanjitha's throw distance at the end of 6 months?

Or

When will she be able to achieve a throw of 11.16 m?

(iii) How many throws did she do during the entire camp of 15 days ?

Part II

Very Short Answer Type Questions

1. Find the 19th term of the following sequence.

$$t_n = \begin{cases} n^2, \text{ where } n \text{ is even} \\ n^2 - 1, \text{ where } n \text{ is odd} \end{cases}$$

2. Find the 7th term of the sequence whose nth term is given by $a_n = (-1)^{n-1} \cdot n^3$.

3. What is the difference between consecutive terms of an arithmetic progression $-13, -8, -3, 2$?

4. For what value of k will $k+9, 2k-1$ and $2k+7$ are the consecutive terms of an AP.

5. Find the common difference of the AP $\frac{1}{p}, \frac{1-p}{p}, \frac{1-2p}{p}, \dots$. **CBSE 2020 (Standard), 2013**

6. $\sqrt{2}, \sqrt{18}, \sqrt{50}, \sqrt{98} \dots$.
Is the above pattern in AP? Justify your answer. **Competency Based Question**

7. Consider the list of numbers given below.
$\frac{1}{2}+k, \frac{2}{3}+k, \frac{3}{4}+k, \frac{4}{5}+k, \dots$ where k is an integer.
Is the above list of numbers an arithmetic progression? Justify your answer. **Competency Based Question**

8. In an AP, if the common difference (d) is -4 and the seventh term (a_7) is 4, then find the first term. **CBSE 2018**

9. Find the common difference of the AP 4, 9, 14, ...
If the first term changes to 6 and the common difference remains the same, then write the new AP. **Competency Based Question**

10. Find the 25th term of the AP $-5, -\frac{5}{2}, 0, \frac{5}{2}, \dots$

11. If $a_n = 5 - 11n$, then find the common difference.

12. If the common difference of an AP is 5, then what is $a_{18} - a_{13}$? **NCERT Exemplar**

13. Find the value of $a_{25} - a_{15}$ for the AP 6, 9, 12, 15, ...

14. If 7 times the seventh term of the AP is equal to 5 times the fifth term, then find the value of its 12th term.

15. Which term of the AP 21, 42, 63, 84, ... is 210? **NCERT Exemplar**

16. Is 68 a term of the AP 7,10, 13,...?

17. Find the 7th term from the end of the AP 7, 10, 13, ... ,184.

18. The sum of the first 12 terms of an AP is 900. If its first term is 20, then find the common difference and 12th term. **CBSE Sample Paper 2025 (Basic)**

19. If the nth term of an AP is $(2n+1)$, then find the sum of its first three terms.

Short Answer Type Questions

20. In which of the following situations, do the list of numbers involved form an AP? Give reason for your answer.

(i) The number of bacteria in certain food item after each second, when they double in every second.

(ii) Number of students left in the school auditorium from the total strength of 800 students, when they leave the auditorium in batches of 20 students. **Competency Based Question**

21. The 3rd and the 14th terms of an arithmetic progression are -9 and 35, respectively.
Which term of this arithmetic progression is five times the 6th term? Show your work. **CBSE QB**

22. The 16th term of an AP is 1 more than twice its 8th term. If the 12th term of an AP is 47, then find its nth term.

23. The eighth term of an AP is half its second term and the eleventh term exceeds one-third of its fourth term by 1. Find the 15th term. **Competency Based Question**

24. The fourth term of an AP is 11. The sum of the fifth and seventh terms of the AP is 24. Find its common difference.

25. If the nth terms of the two AP's 9, 7, 5,... . and 24, 21, 18,... are the same, then find the value of n. Also, find that term. **NCERT Exemplar**

26. The angles of a triangle are in AP. The greatest angle is twice the least. Find all the angles of the triangle. **NCERT Exemplar**

27. Find the number of natural numbers between 101 and 999 which are divisible by both 2 and 5.

28. How many multiples of 9 lie between 10 and 300?

29. If four numbers are in AP such that their sum is 50 and the greatest number is 4 times the least, then find the numbers. **Competency Based Question**

30. Find how many two-digit numbers are divisible by 6.

31. The 4th term of an AP is zero. Prove that the 25th term of the AP is three times its 11th term.

32. Which term of the AP 120, 116, 112, ... is first negative term?

33. Split 207 into three parts such that these are in AP and the product of the two smaller parts is 4623.

34. Find the sum of first 8 multiples of 3. **CBSE 2018**

35. Find the sum of the first 25 terms of an AP, whose nth term is given by $a_n = 7 - 3n$.

36. An AP 5, 8, 11, ... has 40 terms. Find the last term. Also, find the sum of the last 10 terms.

37. If $\dfrac{1+3+5+\dots \text{ upto } n \text{ terms}}{2+5+8+\dots \text{ upto 8 terms}} = 9$, then find the value of n.

38. Sum of the first n terms of an AP is $5n^2 - 3n$. Find the AP and also find its 16th term.

39. Find the sum of first 24 terms of the AP $a_1, a_2, a_3 \dots$, if it is known that $a_1 + a_5 + a_{10} + a_{15} + a_{20} + a_{24} = 225$

40. The sum of first, third and seventeenth terms of an AP is 216. Find the sum of the first 13 terms of the AP.

41. The sum of 5th and 9th terms of an AP is 72 and sum of 7th and 12th terms is 97. Find the AP. **NCERT Exemplar**

42. If an AP has $a = 1, a_n = 20$ and $S_n = 399$, then find the value of n.

43. If 12th term of an AP is 213 and the sum of its four terms is 24, then what is the sum of its first 10 terms?

44. Find the common difference of an AP whose first term is 5 and the sum of its first 4 terms is half the sum of the next 4 terms.

45. The sum of the first three terms of an AP is 33. If the sum of the twice of first and the third term exceeds the third term by 28, then find the AP.

46. The sum of first and eighth terms of an AP is 32 and their product is 60. Find the first term and common difference of the AP. Hence, also find the sum of its first 20 terms. **CBSE 2024 (Standard)**

47. The sum of the first n terms of an AP whose first term is 8 and the common difference is 20, is equal to the sum of first $2n$ terms of another AP whose first term is -30 and the common difference is 8. Find the value of n. **NCERT Exemplar**

48. If S_n denotes the sum of first n terms of an AP, then show that the common difference d of the AP is given by $d = S_n - 2S_{n-1} + S_{n-2}$.

49. The sum of the first two terms of an arithmetic progression is the same as the sum of the first seven terms of the same arithmetic progression. Can such an arithmetic progression exist? Justify your answer. **Competency Based Question**

50. Find the sum of all three-digit natural numbers, which are multiples of 11.

51. Find the sum of all two-digit numbers greater than 50 which when divided by 7 leaves remainder 4.

52. Find the sum of those integers between 1 and 500, which are multiples of 2 as well as of 5. **NCERT Exemplar**

[**Hint** Take the LCM of 2 and 5.]

53. In an AP, if $S_n = n^2p$ and $S_m = m^2p$, $m \neq n$, then prove that $S_p = p^3$.

54. The sum of first n, $2n$ and $3n$ terms of an AP are S_1, S_2 and S_3, respectively.

Prove that $S_3 = 3(S_2 - S_1)$.

55. The sum of first n terms of three AP's are S_1, S_2 and S_3. The first term of each AP is unity and their common differences are 1, 2 and 3, respectively.

Prove that $S_1 + S_3 = 2S_2$. **Competency Based Question**

56. Show that the sum of first n even natural numbers is equal to $\left(1 + \dfrac{1}{n}\right)$ times the sum of first n odd natural numbers.

57. If there are $(2n + 1)$ terms in an AP, then prove that the ratio of the sum of odd terms and the sum of even terms is $(n + 1) : n$.

58. If a clock strikes one at one O'clock, two at two O'clock and so on, but does not strike at half hours, then total number of times the bell will be stuck in 24 h, are 156. Pradeep at once said, "It is true". Do you agree with Pradeep? **Competency Based Question**

Long Answer Type Questions

59. If the mth term of an AP is $\dfrac{1}{n}$ and nth term is $\dfrac{1}{m}$, then show that its mnth term is 1. **CBSE 2023 (Standard)**

60. 14, 21, 28, 35, ... and 26, 39, 52, 65, ... are two arithmetic progressions such that the pth term of the first arithmetic progression is the same as the qth term of the second arithmetic progression.

Derive a relationship between p and q.

Show your work. **Competency Based Question**

61. Two arithmetic progressions have the same first term. The common difference of one progression is 4 more than the other progression. 124th term of the first arithmetic progression is the same as 42nd term of the second.

Find one set of possible values of the common differences. Show your work. **Competency Based Question**

62. The pth, qth and rth terms of an AP are a, b and c, respectively. Show that $a(q - r) + b(r - p) + c(p - q) = 0$

CBSE Sample Paper 2021 Term I (Basic)

63. If $a_1, a_2, \dots, a_{n-2}, a_{n-1}, a_n$ are in AP, then prove that

$$\frac{1}{a_1 \cdot a_n} + \frac{1}{a_2 \cdot a_{n-1}} + \frac{1}{a_3 \cdot a_{n-2}} + \dots + \frac{1}{a_n \cdot a_1} = \frac{2}{a_1 + a_n}\left(\frac{1}{a_1} + \frac{1}{a_2} + \dots + \frac{1}{a_n}\right)$$

64. The sum of first four terms of an AP is 32 and the ratio of third and fourth term is 7:8. Find the terms of an AP. **CBSE 2020 (Standard)**

65. An AP consists of 37 terms. The sum of the three middle most terms is 225 and the sum of the last three terms is 429. Find the AP. **NCERT Exemplar**

66. Find the sum of the two middle most terms of the AP

$$-\frac{4}{3}, -1, \frac{-2}{3}, \ldots 4\frac{1}{3}.$$

[**Hint** Sum of the two middle most terms $= a_9 + a_{10}$]

NCERT Exemplar ; CBSE 2010

67. The ratio of the 11th term to the 18th term of an AP is 2 : 3. Find the ratio of 5th term to 21st term and also the ratio of the sum of the first 5 terms to sum of the first 21 terms. **CBSE 2023 (Standard)**

68. How many terms of the AP 27, 24, 21 ...... must be taken so that their sum is 105? Which term of the AP is zero? **CBSE 2024 (Basic)**

69. Solve the equation

$$-4 + (-1) + 2 + \ldots + x = 437.$$

CBSE 2023 (Standard), NCERT Exemplar

70. The first term of an AP is 22, the last term is –6 and the sum of all the terms is 64. Find the number of terms of the AP. Also, find the common difference. **CBSE 2023 (Basic)**

71. The sum of the first 7 terms of an AP is 63 and that of its next 7 terms is 161. Find the AP.

72. If the sum of first p terms of an AP is same as the sum of its first q terms ($p \neq q$), then show that the sum of its first ($p + q$) terms is zero.

73. Show that the sum of an AP whose first term is a, second term is b and the last term is c, is equal to

$$\frac{(b + c - 2a)(a + c)}{2(b - a)}$$

CBSE 2020 (Standard), NCERT Exemplar

74. A person buys cash certificates of ₹ 125. Thereafter, every year, he buys these certificates of the value exceeding previous year purchase by ₹ 25. Find the total value of certificates purchased by him in 20th year.

75. If pth term of an AP is a and qth term is b. Prove that the sum of its ($p + q$)th term is

$$\frac{p+q}{2}\left[a + b + \frac{(a-b)}{p-q}\right].$$

76. A student of class X gets pocket money from his mother everyday. Out of the pocket money, she saves money for poor people in her locality. On Ist day she saves ₹ 36. On each succeeding day she increases her saving by ₹ 4.5.

(i) Which mathematical concept and formula is being to used here for solving this question?

(ii) Find the amount saved by student 22th day.

77. Jaspal Singh repays his total loan of ₹ 118000 by paying every month starting with the first instalment of ₹ 1000. If he increases the instalment by ₹ 100 every month.

(i) What amount will be paid by him in the 30th instalment?

(ii) What amount of loan does he still have to pay after 30th instalment? **NCERT Exemplar; CBSE 2012, 11**

78. 360 bricks are stacked in the following manner, 30 bricks in the bottom row, 29 bricks in the next row, 28 bricks in the row next to it, and so on. In how many rows, 360 bricks are placed and how many bricks are there in the top row?

79. The students of a school decided to beautify the school on the annual day by fixing colourful flags on the straight passage of the school. They have 27 flags to be fixed at intervals of every 2 m. The flags are stored at the position of the middle most flag. Ruchi was given the responsibility of placing the flags. Ruchi kept her books where the flags were stored. She could carry only one flag at a time.

(i) How much distance did she cover in completing this job and returning back to collect her books?

(ii) What is the maximum distance she travelled carrying a flag? **Competency Based Question**

HINTS & SOLUTIONS

Part I

1. (b) Since, $k + 7, 2k - 2$ and $2k + 6$ are in AP.

$\therefore (2k - 2) - (k + 7) = (2k + 6) - (2k - 2)$

$\Rightarrow \quad 2k - 2 - k - 7 = 2k + 6 - 2k + 2$

$\Rightarrow \quad k = 8 + 9$

$\Rightarrow \quad k = 17$

2. (c) We know that in an AP the difference between two consecutive terms is fixed and is called the common difference of AP.

So, 2, 3, 4 is not the possible difference between four consecutive terms of an AP.

3. (b) Given AP is $\frac{1}{2x}, \frac{1-4x}{2x}, \frac{1-8x}{2x}, \ldots$

So, $a_1 = \frac{1}{2x}, a_2 = \frac{1-4x}{2x}, a_3 = \frac{1-8x}{2x}, \ldots$

$\therefore\ a_2 - a_1 = \frac{1-4x}{2x} - \frac{1}{2x} = \frac{1-4x-1}{2x} = \frac{-4x}{2x} = -2$

$a_3 - a_2 = \frac{1-8x}{2x} - \frac{1-4x}{2x}$

$= \frac{1-8x-1+4x}{2x} = \frac{-4x}{2x} = -2$

Since, $a_2 - a_1 = a_3 - a_2 = -2$

and common difference, $d = a_2 - a_1 = a_3 - a_2 =$ so on

$\therefore\ d = -2$

4. (b) Given, $a = 8$

and $a_{10} = -19$

$\Rightarrow\ a + 9d = -19$ $\quad [\because a_n = a + (n-1)d]$

$\Rightarrow\ 8 + 9d = -19$

$\Rightarrow\ 9d = -27 \Rightarrow d = -3$

5. (b) We have, $a_n = 2n^2 + 1$

Replacing n by $(n+1)$ in a_n, we get

$a_{n+1} = 2(n+1)^2 + 1 = 2n^2 + 4n + 3$

and $a_{n+1} - a_n = (2n^2 + 4n + 3) - (2n^2 + 1) = 4n + 2$

Clearly, $a_{n+1} - a_n$ is not independent of n.

So, the given sequence is not an AP.

6. (b) Given, first two terms of an AP are $a = -3$

and $a + d = 4 \Rightarrow -3 + d = 4$

Common difference, $d = 7$

$\therefore a_{21} = a + (21-1)d$ $\quad [\because a_n = a + (n-1)d]$

$= -3 + (20)7 = -3 + 140 = 137$

7. (b) Given, $a_n = 3n + 7$

If $n = 1, a_1 = 3(1) + 7 = 3 + 7 = 10$

So, first term $(a) = 10$

If $n = 2, a_2 = 3(2) + 7 = 6 + 7 = 13$

We know that $d = a_2 - a_1$

$\therefore\ d = 13 - 10 = 3$

8. (b) Solve as Example 5 of Topic 2.

9. (c) Let the common difference of two APs be d.

Given, first term of one AP $(a_1) = -1$

and first term of second AP $(b_1) = -8$

$\therefore$ Fourth term of 1st AP $(a_4) = a_1 + (4-1)d = -1 + 3d$

and Fourth term of 2nd AP $(b_4) = b_1 + (4-1)d$

$= -8 + 3d$

$\therefore\ a_4 - b_4 = (-1 + 3d) - (-8 + 3d)$

$= -1 + 3d + 8 - 3d = 7$

10. (c) Solve as Example 10 of Topic 2.

11. (d) We have, $a_1 = 1, a_2 = 1$

and $a_n = a_{n-1} + a_{n-2}$ for all $n > 2$

On putting $n = 3$ and 4, we get

$a_3 = a_2 + a_1 = 1 + 1 = 2$

$a_4 = a_3 + a_2 = 2 + 1 = 3$

Now, $\frac{a_4}{a_3} = \frac{3}{2}$

12. (a) Given, the sum of first n terms,

$$S_n = \frac{n}{2}(3n+1) \quad \ldots \text{(i)}$$

On putting $n = 1$ in Eq. (i), we get

$S_1 = \frac{1}{2}(3 \times 1 + 1) = \frac{1}{2}(3+1) = \frac{1}{2} \times 4 = 2$

We know that the first term of an AP is equal to the sum of the first term.

$\therefore$ First term $= S_1 = 2$

13. (b) First 50 odd natural numbers 1, 3, 5, 7, 4, 11, ... 50 terms. It forms an AP with first term $(a) = 1$, common difference $(d) = 3 - 1 = 2$

and number of terms $(n) = 50$

$S_n = \frac{n}{2}[2a + (n-1)d] \Rightarrow S_{50} = \frac{50}{2}[2(1) + (50-1)(2)]$

$= 25[2 + (49)(2)] = 25 \times 2 \times 50 = 2500$

14. (c) Solve as Question 4 of NCERT Folder Exercise 5.1.

15. (a) Given sequence is $-1, -1, -1, \ldots, -1$

For above sequence, $a_n - a_{n-1} = 0 =$ constant

Here, $a_n - a_{n-1}$ is constant, where $n \geq 2$ and $n \in N$.

So, both A and R are true and R is the correct explanation of A.

16. (d) **Hint** Solve as Example 10 of Topic 3.

17. (a) We have, $a_n = 2n^2 - 1$

$\therefore\ a_1 = 1$

Now, $S_n = \frac{n}{2}(a + l) = \frac{n}{2}(1 + 2n^2 - 1) = n^3$

18. (b) **Hint** Solve as Example 9 of Topic 3.

19. (i) (c) AP formed by the heights of the chairs,

70, 70 + 10, 70 + 10 + 10, 70 + 10 + 10 + 10

i.e. 70, 80, 90, 100

Here, first term, $a = 70$

and common difference, $d = 10$

Height of the stack = last term of AP = 100 cm

(ii) (c) Given, height of the storeroom = 1.55 m = 155 cm

$\therefore$ Maximum height of the stack ≤ 155

$\therefore\ a_n \leq 155$

$\Rightarrow\ a + (n-1)d \leq 155$

$\Rightarrow\ 70 + (n-1)10 \leq 155$

$\Rightarrow\ (n-1)10 \leq 85$

$\Rightarrow\ n - 1 \leq 8.5$

$\Rightarrow\ n \leq 9.5$

Since, number of chairs cannot be in decimal.

$\therefore\ n = 9$

(iii) AP formed by height of chairs without arms is

$70, 70+5, 70+5+5, 70+5+5+5, \ldots$

i.e. $70, 75, 80, 85, \ldots$

Here, first term, $a = 70$

and common difference, $d = 5$

Maximum height of the stack ≤ 155

$$\therefore \quad a_n \le 155$$
$$\Rightarrow \quad a+(n-1)d \le 155$$
$$\Rightarrow \quad 70+(n-1)5 \le 155$$
$$\Rightarrow \quad (n-1)5 \le 85$$
$$\Rightarrow \quad n-1 \le 17$$
$$\Rightarrow \quad n \le 18$$

$\therefore$ Maximum number of chairs that can be stacked in the storeroom = 18

(iv) Minimum number of columns (stacks) in which all chairs can be stacked in the storeroom = 4

(v) (d) Given, height of the storeroom = 1.55 m

Length of one chair = 0.5 m

and breadth of one chair = 0.4 m

Also, minimum number of columns (stacks) in which all chairs can be stacked in the storeroom = 4

$\therefore$ Only possible dimensions of the storeroom

$= 1 \times 2.75 \times 1.55$

20. Number of trees in first circular row = 50

$\because$ Each succeeding row has 20 more trees than previous one.

$\therefore$ Number of trees in second row = 50 + 20

Number of trees in third row = 50 + 20 + 20 and so on.

Thus, we get the following list of numbers,

50, 70, 90, ……

Clearly, it forms an AP.

Here, first term, $a = 50$

and common difference, $d = 70 - 50 = 20$

(i) Number of trees will be planted in 10th row,

$$a_{10} = a+(10-1)d = 50+9\times 20 = 230$$

(ii) Number of trees in 8th row,

$$a_8 = 50+7\times 20 = 190$$

Number of trees in 5th row, $a_5 = 50 + 4 \times 20 = 130$

Now, $a_8 - a_5 = 190 - 130 = 60$

Hence, 60 more trees will be planted in 8th row than the 5th row.

(iii) (a) Let 3200 trees are to be planted in n rows.

$$\therefore \quad S_n = 3200$$
$$\Rightarrow \quad \frac{n}{2}[2a+(n-1)d] = 3200$$
$$\Rightarrow \frac{n}{2}[2\times 50+(n-1)20] = 3200$$
$$\Rightarrow \quad n[50+10n-10] = 3200$$
$$\Rightarrow \quad n^2+4n-320 = 0 \quad \text{[dividing by 10]}$$
$$\Rightarrow n^2+20n-16n-320 = 0$$
$$\Rightarrow \quad (n+20)(n-16) = 0$$
$$\Rightarrow \quad n = 16 \text{ or } n = -20$$
$$\Rightarrow \quad n = 16$$

[$\because$ number of rows cannot be negative]

(b) **Hint** $S_{11} = \frac{11}{2}[2\times 50+10\times 20]$

$$\Rightarrow \quad S_{11} = \frac{11}{2}[100+200] \Rightarrow S_{11} = 1650$$

Hence, number of trees are left from 3200 trees after the 11th row = 3200 − 1650 = 1550

21. Let the production of TV sets in first year be a units. Then, production in the next consecutive years are $a+d, a+2d, \ldots$.

Thus, we get the sequence, $a, a+d, a+2d, \ldots$

This is an AP sequence, whose first term = a and common difference = d.

Given, $T_6 = 16000$ and $T_9 = 22600$

$$\therefore \quad a+(6-1)d = 16000$$

and $\quad a+(9-1)d = 22600 \quad [\because T_n = a+(n-1)d]$

$$\Rightarrow \quad a+5d = 16000 \quad \ldots(i)$$

and $\quad a+8d = 22600 \quad \ldots(ii)$

On subtracting Eq. (i) from Eq. (ii), we get

$$3d = 22600 - 16000$$
$$\Rightarrow \quad 3d = 6600$$
$$\Rightarrow \quad d = 2200$$

On putting $d = 2200$ in Eq. (i), we get

$$a+5\times 2200 = 16000$$
$$\Rightarrow \quad a = 16000 - 11000 = 5000$$

(i) The production during 8th yr is

$$T_8 = a+(8-1)d$$
$$= 5000+7\times 2200$$
$$= 5000+15400 = 20400$$

Hence, the production during 8th yr is 20400 sets.

(ii) (a) The production during first 3 yr,

$$S_3 = \frac{3}{2}[2a+(3-1)d]$$
$$= \frac{3}{2}[2\times 5000+2\times 2200]$$
$$= 3[5000+2200]$$
$$= 3\times 7200 = 21600$$

Or

(b) Let in nth year, the production is 29200.

$$\because \quad T_n = a+(n-1)d$$
$$\therefore \quad 29200 = 5000+(n-1)2200$$
$$\Rightarrow (n-1)2200 = 24200$$

$\Rightarrow \quad (n-1) = \dfrac{24200}{2200}$

$\Rightarrow \quad n - 1 = 11 \Rightarrow n = 12$

(iii) The difference of the production during 7th yr and 4th yr

$= T_7 - T_4$

$= a + (7-1)d - [a + (4-1)d]$

$= 6d - 3d = 3d$

$= 3 \times 2200 = 6600$

22. (i) (a) Since, he pays first installment of ₹ 1000 and next consecutive months he pay the installment are 1100, 1200, … .

Thus, we get the AP sequence, 1000, 1100, 1200, …

Here, $a = 1000$, $d = 1100 - 1000 = 100$

Now, $T_{30} = a + (30-1)d$

$= 1000 + 29 \times 100 = 1000 + 2900 = 3900$

Hence, the amount paid by him in 30th installment is ₹ 3900.

Or

(b) The amount in last 40th installment is

$T_{40} = a + (40-1)d$

$= 1000 + 39 \times 100$

$= 1000 + 3900 =$ ₹ 4900

(ii) Now, $S_{30} = \dfrac{30}{2}[2a + (30-1)d]$

$= 15(2 \times 1000 + 29 \times 100)$

$= 15(2000 + 2900) = 15 \times 4900 =$ ₹ 73500

(iii) The ratio of 1st installment to the last installment is $\dfrac{1000}{4900}$ i.e. $\dfrac{10}{49}$.

23. Given, distance ran by Neha in each day of first week

$= 3$ km

Distance ran by Neha in each day of second week

$= 3 + 2 = 5$ km

Distance ran by Neha in each day of third week

$= 3 + 2 + 2 = 7$ km and so on.

Thus, we get the following list of distances,

3, 5, 7, ...

Clearly, it forms an AP.

Here, first term, $a = 3$

and common difference, $d = 5 - 3 = 2$

(i) Distance covered by Neha in each day of 8th week,

$a_8 = a + (n-1)d$

$= 3 + 7 \times 2 = 17$ km

(ii) Let she would be able to run 45 km each day of nth week.

$\therefore \quad a_n = 45 = 3 + (n-1)2$

$\Rightarrow \quad 45 - 3 = (n-1)2$

$\Rightarrow \quad 21 = (n-1) \Rightarrow n = 22$

(iii) (a) The total distance for each week,

$A_n = 5 \times a_n$

$\therefore$ Total distance ran by Neha in first week

$= 5 \times 3 = 15$ km

and total distance ran by Neha in 11th week

$= 5 \times [3 + 10 \times 2] = 115$ km

Now, total distance covered by Neha after 11 weeks, if she practiced for 5 days in each week

$= \dfrac{11}{2}[15 + 115] \quad \left[\because S_n = \dfrac{n}{2}(a + l)\right]$

$= 11 \times 65 = 715$ km

(b) Now, she increased the distance by 3 km each week instead of 2 km each week, so we get the new series,

3, 6, 9, 12 ......

Here, $a = 3$ and $d = 6 - 3 = 3$

Let she would have trained herself to run for 42 km per day in n week.

$\therefore \quad a_n = 42 = a + (n-1)d$

$\Rightarrow \quad 42 = 3 + (n-1)3$

$\Rightarrow (n-1) = 13 \Rightarrow n = 14$

24. (i) According to the given condition,

first term = 3,

AP is 3, 6, 9, 12, ..., 24

$\therefore$ Common difference, $d = 6 - 3 = 3$

(ii) Since, nth term = 34

$\therefore \quad a + (n-1)d = 34 \quad [\because T_n = a + (n-1)d]$

$\Rightarrow \quad 3 + (n-1)3 = 34$

$\Rightarrow \quad n = \dfrac{34}{3}$

$= 11\dfrac{1}{3}$, which is not a positive integer.

Therefore, it is not possible to have 34 jars in a layer if the given pattern is continued.

(iii) (a) Let there are n numbers of rows in a layer.

$\because \quad S_n = \dfrac{n}{2}[2a + (n-1)d]$

$\Rightarrow \quad S_n = \dfrac{n}{2}[2 \times 3 + (n-1)3]$

$= \dfrac{n}{2}[6 + 3n - 3]$

$= \dfrac{n}{2}[3 + 3n] = \dfrac{3n}{2}[1 + n]$

$\therefore \quad S_8 = \dfrac{3 \times 8}{2}[1 + 8]$

$= 12 \times 9 = 108$

Or

(b) Given, the shopkeeper added 3 jars in each layer.

∴ AP will be 6, 9, 12, ...

Here, $a = 6$

and $d = 9 - 6 = 3$

Now, the number of jars in the 5th layer are,

$$t_5 = a + (5-1)d \quad [\because t_n = a + (n-1)d]$$
$$= 6 + 4 \times 3 = 18$$

Hence, there are 18 jars in the 5th layer from the top.

25. (i) Number of throws on first day $a = 40$

Number of throws on second day $= 40 + 12 = 52$

AP formed by number of throws is

40, 52, (52 + 12) ...
(I day) (II day) (III day)

Here, common difference, $d = 12$

Number of throws she practiced on 11th day

$$a_{11} = a + (11-1)d$$
$$= 40 + 10 \times 12 = 160$$

(ii) Distance of Sanjitha's throw on first day, $a = 7.56$ m

Distance of Sanjitha throw after a week

$= (7.56 + 0.09)$ m $= 7.65$ m

∴ AP formed by the distances is

7.56, 7.65, 7.65 + (0.09), ...
(I week) (II week) (III week)

Here, common difference, $d = 0.09$ m

Sanjitha's throw distance at the end of 6 months (i.e. 26 weeks)

$$a_{26} = a + (26-1)d$$
$$= 7.56 + 25 \times 0.09$$
$$= 7.56 + 2.25 = 9.81\text{m}$$

Or

Here, $a_n = 11.16 = a + (n-1)d$

$\Rightarrow 7.56 + (n-1)\,0.09 = 11.16$

$\Rightarrow \quad n - 1 = \dfrac{3.6}{0.09}$

$\Rightarrow \quad n = 41$

∴ On 41st week, she will be able to achieve a throw of 11.16 m.

(iii) Total throws done by her during the entire camp of 15 days $= S_n = \dfrac{n}{2}[2a + (n-1)d]$

where, n is total number of terms

$$\Rightarrow \quad S_{15} = \frac{15}{2}[2 \times 40 + 14 \times 12]$$
$$= 15[40 + 84]$$
$$= 15 \times 124$$
$$= 1860$$

Part II

1. Hint For 19th term i.e. for $n = 19$ which is odd, we take $t_n = n^2 - 1 = (19)^2 - 1 = 360$

2. Hint 7th term $(a_7) = (-1)^{7-1} \cdot (7)^3$. **Ans.** 343

3. $a_1 = -13, a_2 = -8, a_3 = -3, a_4 = 2$

$$a_2 - a_1 = -8 - (-13) = 5$$
$$a_3 - a_2 = -3 - (-8) = 5$$
$$a_4 - a_3 = 2 - (-3) = 5$$
$$\therefore a_2 - a_1 = a_3 - a_2 = a_4 - a_3 = 5$$

4. Hint $a_2 - a_1 = a_3 - a_2$

$\Rightarrow (2k-1) - (k+9) = (2k+7) - (2k-1)$ **Ans.** $k = 18$

5. Hint Common difference = Second term − First term

$$d = \frac{1-p}{p} - \frac{1}{p} \text{ **Ans.** } -1$$

6. $a_1 = \sqrt{2}, a_2 = \sqrt{18} = 3\sqrt{2}$,

$a_3 = \sqrt{50} = 5\sqrt{2}, a_4 = \sqrt{98} = 7\sqrt{2}$

So, $a_2 - a_1 = 3\sqrt{2} - \sqrt{2} = 2\sqrt{2}$

$a_3 - a_2 = 5\sqrt{2} - 3\sqrt{2} = 2\sqrt{2}$

$a_4 - a_3 = 7\sqrt{2} - 5\sqrt{2} = 2\sqrt{2}$

Since, $a_2 - a_1 = a_3 - a_2 = a_4 - a_3$

∴ The given series is in AP because the common difference is the same which is $2\sqrt{2}$.

7. Hint Solve as Question 4 of NCERT Folder Exercise 5.1. **Ans.** No

8. Given, $d = -4$ and $a_7 = 4$

Let first term of an AP be a.

$\because \quad a_n = a + (n-1)d$

$\therefore \quad a_7 = a + (7-1)(-4)$

$\Rightarrow \quad 4 = a + (6)(-4) \Rightarrow 4 = a - 24$

$\Rightarrow \quad a = 4 + 24 \Rightarrow a = 28$

9. Given AP, 4, 9, 14 ...

Common difference = 9 − 4 = 5

Now, we need to make new AP with first term 6 and common difference 5

∴ First term = 6, second term = 6 + 5 = 11

∴ New AP is 6, 11, 16, 21, ...

10. Hint $a = -5,\ d = -\dfrac{5}{2} + 5 = \dfrac{5}{2}$

∴ 25th term of given AP, $a_n = a + (n-1)d$

$$= -5 + (25-1) \times \frac{5}{2}$$

Ans. 55

11. Hint Common difference, $d = a_{n+1} - a_n$

$$= 5 - 11(n+1) - (5 - 11n)$$
$$= 5 - 11n - 11 - 5 + 11n$$

Ans. −11

12. Hint $a_{18} - a_{13} = (a + 17d) - (a + 12d) = 5d$ **Ans.** 25

13. Given AP, 6, 9, 12, 15 ......

So, $a = 6$ and $d = 9 - 6 = 3$

$$a_{25} - a_{15} = a + 24d - (a + 14d)$$
$$= a + 24d - a - 14d$$
$$= 10d = 10 \times 3 = 30$$

14. According to question,

7 times the 7th term = 5 times the 5th term

$$7a_7 = 5a_5$$
$$\Rightarrow \quad 7(a + 6d) = 5(a + 4d)$$
$$\Rightarrow \quad 7a + 42d = 5a + 20d$$
$$\Rightarrow \quad 2a = -22d$$
$$\Rightarrow \quad a = -11d$$

Then, $a_{12} = a + 11d = -11d + 11d$

$$a_{12} = 0$$

15. Hint Do same as Example 3 of Topic 2.

Ans. 10th term

16. Hint Do same as Question 6 of NCERT Folder Exercise 5.2.

Ans. No

17. Hint Do same as Example 10 of Topic 2. **Ans.** 166

18. Given, first term of AP, $a = 20$

and $S_{12} = 900$

Let common difference of given AP be d.

$$\because \quad S = \frac{n}{2}[2a + (n - 1)d]$$
$$\therefore \quad S_{12} = \frac{12}{2}[2 \times 20 + 11 \times d]$$
$$\Rightarrow \quad 900 = 6[40 + 11 \times d]$$
$$\Rightarrow \quad 66d = 900 - 240$$
$$\Rightarrow \quad d = \frac{900 - 240}{66} = \frac{660}{66} = 10$$

Hence, common difference d is 10.

Now, 12th term of AP,

$$a_{12} = 20 + (12 - 1) \times 10 \qquad [\because a_n = a + (n-1)d]$$
$$\Rightarrow a_{12} = 130$$

Hence, 12th term of AP is 130.

19. Hint Given, $a_n = 2n + 1$

On putting, $n = 1, 2, 3$, we get

$$a_1 = 2(1) + 1 = 3 = \text{First term} = (a)$$
$$a_2 = 2(2) + 1 = 5$$
$$a_3 = 2(3) + 1 = 7$$

Now, $S_n = \frac{n}{2}(a + l)$

$$\Rightarrow \quad S_3 = \frac{3}{2}[3 + 7]$$ **Ans.** 15

20. Hint Solve as Example 3 of Topic 1.

Ans. (i) It is not forming an AP.

(ii) It is forming an AP.

21. Let the first term and the common difference of the AP be a and d, respectively. Then,

$$a + 2d = -9 \qquad \text{...(i)}$$

and $$a + 13d = 35 \qquad \text{...(ii)}$$

On subtracting Eq. (i) from Eq. (ii), we get

$$11d = 44$$
$$\therefore \quad d = 4$$

On putting this value in Eq. (i), we get

$$a + 2 \times 4 = -9$$
$$\Rightarrow \quad a = -9 - 8$$
$$\therefore \quad a = -17$$

Now, let the nth term of this AP is 5 times the 6th term.

$$\therefore \quad a_n = 5a_6$$
$$a + (n - 1)d = 5[a + (6 - 1)d]$$
$$\Rightarrow \quad a + (n - 1)d = 5a + 25d$$
$$\Rightarrow \quad (n - 1)d = 4a + 25d$$
$$\Rightarrow \quad (n - 1) \times 4 = 4 \times (-17) + 25 \times 4$$
$$\Rightarrow \quad (n - 1) \times 4 = -68 + 100$$
$$\Rightarrow \quad n - 1 = \frac{32}{4}$$
$$\therefore \quad n = 8 + 1 = 9$$

Hence, the required term is 9th term.

22. Hint Given, $a_{12} = 47$

$$\Rightarrow \quad a + 11d = 47 \qquad \text{...(i)}$$

and $$a_{16} = 1 + 2a_8 \qquad \text{[by given condition]}$$
$$\Rightarrow [a + (16 - 1)d] = 1 + 2[a + (8 - 1)d]$$
$$\Rightarrow \quad a - d = -1 \qquad \text{...(ii)}$$

On solving Eqs. (i) and (ii), we get

$$d = 4 \text{ and } a = 3$$
$$\therefore \quad a_n = 3 + (n - 1)4 = 4n - 1$$

23. Hint We have, $a_8 = \frac{1}{2}a_2$ and $a_{11} = \frac{1}{3}a_4 + 1$

$$\Rightarrow \quad a + 13d = 0 \text{ and } 2a + 27d = 3.$$

Ans. 3

24. Hint Given, $a_4 = 11 \Rightarrow a + 3d = 11$ ...(i)

and $a_5 + a_7 = 24 \Rightarrow a + 5d = 12$ ...(ii)

On solving Eqs. (i) and (ii), we get

Ans. $d = \frac{1}{2}$

25. Hint Do same as Question 15 of NCERT Folder Exercise 5.2.

And then to find 13th term, put $n = 13$ in nth term of any of the two AP

Ans. $n = 13$ and nth term is -15.

26. Hint Let the angles be $a°$, $(a+d)°$, $(a+2d)°$

Then, we get $a+a+d+a+2d = 180$ and $a+2d = 2a$

Ans. 40°, 60°, 80

27. Hint Natural numbers between 101 and 999 divisible by both 2 and 5 i.e. divisible by 10, are

110, 120, 130, ..., 990

Here, $120 - 110 = 130 - 120 = \dots = 10$.

So, it is an AP with first term $(a) = 110$,

common difference $(d) = 120 - 110 = 10$ and

last term $(l) = 990$.

Let $l = a_n = a + (n-1)d$

Then, $990 = 110 + (n-1) \times 10$ **Ans.** $n = 89$

28. Hint Do same as Question 14 of NCERT Folder Exercise 5.2. **Ans.** 32

29. Hint Let $a + (a+d) + (a+2d) + (a+3d) = 50$

$\Rightarrow \quad 2a + 3d = 25 \quad \dots(i)$

and $\quad a + 3d = 4a$

$\Rightarrow \quad a = d \quad \dots(ii)$

On solving Eqs. (i) and Eqs. (ii), we get

$\therefore \quad a = d = 5$

Ans. 5, 10, 15 and 20

30. Hint Do same as Example 8 of Topic 2. **Ans.** 15

31. Hint Let a and d be the first term and common difference of the given AP, respectively.

Given $\quad a_4 = 0$

$\Rightarrow \quad a + 3d = 0$

$\Rightarrow \quad a = -3d \quad \dots(i)$

To prove $\quad a_{25} = 3a_{11}$

Proof Clearly, $\quad a_{25} = a + 24d$

$= -3d + 24d \quad$ [from Eq. (i)]

$\Rightarrow \quad a_{25} = 21d \quad \dots(ii)$

Also, $\quad a_{11} = a + 10d$

$= -3d + 10d \quad$ [from Eq. (i)]

$\Rightarrow \quad a_{11} = 7d$

$\Rightarrow \quad 3a_{11} = 21d \quad \dots(iii)$

From Eqs. (ii) and (iii), we get

$a_{25} = 3a_{11}$ **Hence proved.**

32. Hint Do same as Question 1 of NCERT Folder Exercise 5.4 **Ans.** 32nd term

33. Let the three parts be $a, a+d$ and $a+2d$ and let $d > 0$.

Then, $\quad a+a+d+a+2d = 207$

$\Rightarrow \quad a+d = 69 \quad \dots(i)$

and product of smaller parts = 4623

$\Rightarrow \quad a(a+d) = 4623$

$\Rightarrow \quad a = 67$

On putting $a = 67$ in Eq. (i), we get

$\Rightarrow \quad d = 2$

First part, $a = 67$

Second part, $a + d = 69$

Third part, $a + 2d = 71$

Hence, three parts of 207 are 67, 69 and 71.

34. Hint Do same as Q. 13 of NCERT Folder Exercise. 5.3. **Ans.** 108

35. Hint Do same as Example 4 of Topic 3. **Ans.** –800

36. Given AP, 5, 8, 11... upto 40 terms

Here, $a = 5, d = 3$ and $n = 40$

$a_{40} = a + (40-1)d$

$= 5 + 39 \times 3 = 5 + 117 = 122$

Hence, the last term is 122.

Now, we need to find sum of last 10 terms

Last 10 terms will be from the 31st to the 40th term.

Now, 31st term $= a_{31}$

$= a + (n-1)d$

$= 5 + (31-1)3$

$= 5 + 30 \times 3 = 95$

So, our last 10th term will be 95, 98, ..., 122

$$S_n = \frac{n}{2}[a + l] = \frac{10}{2}[95 + 122] = 5 \times 217 = 1085$$

$\therefore$ Required sum is 1085.

37. Hint Given, $\dfrac{1+3+5+\dots \text{ upto } n \text{ terms}}{2+5+8+\dots \text{ upto } 8 \text{ term}} = 9$

$$\Rightarrow \quad \frac{\frac{n}{2}[2(1) + (n-1)2]}{\frac{8}{2}[2(2) + (8-1)3]} = 9 \quad \textbf{Ans. } n = 30$$

38. Hint Do same as Q. 11 of NCERT Folder Exercise. 5.3. **Ans.** 2, 12, 22, ...

$a_{16} = 152$

39. Hint $a + (a+4d) + (a+9d) + (a+14d) + (a+19d) + (a+23d) = 225$

$\Rightarrow \quad 2a + 23d = 75 \dots(i)$

Now, $S_{24} = \frac{24}{2}[2a + (24-1)d]$

$= 12(2a + 23d)$ **Ans.** 900

40. Hint Third term $a_3 = a + 2d$

and seventeenth term $a_{17} = (a + 16d)$

Also, $\quad a_1 + a_3 + a_{17} = 216$

$\Rightarrow \quad a + a + 2d + a + 16d = 216$

$\Rightarrow \quad a + 6d = 72 \quad \dots(i)$

Now, $\quad S_{13} = \frac{13}{2}[2a + (13-1)d]$

$= \frac{13}{2}[2(a + 6d)]$ **Ans.** 936

41. Hint Do same as Question 18 of NCERT Folder Exercise 5.2. **Ans.** 6, 11, 16, 21, 26, ...

42. Hint Do same as Question 3 (vii) of NCERT Folder Exercise 5.3. **Ans.** $n = 38$

43. Hint $a_{12} = 213 \Rightarrow a + 11d = 213$ ...(i)

and $S_4 = 24$

$$\Rightarrow \frac{4}{2}[2a + (4 - 1)d] = 24$$

$$\Rightarrow 2a + 3d = 12 \quad \text{...(ii)}$$

On solving Eqs. (i) and (ii), we get

$$a = \frac{-507}{19} \text{ and } d = \frac{414}{19}$$

$$\text{Now, } S_{10} = \frac{10}{2}\left[2 \times \left(\frac{-507}{19}\right) + (10 - 1) \times \frac{414}{19}\right]$$

Ans. 713.68

44. Hint $S_4 = \frac{1}{2}(\text{Sum of } a_5, a_6, a_7, a_8) = \frac{1}{2}(S_8 - S_4)$

$$\Rightarrow 2S_4 = S_8 - S_4 \Rightarrow 3S_4 = S_8 \quad \text{...(i)}$$

$$\text{Clearly, } S_4 = \frac{4}{2}[2a + (4 - 1)d] \quad \left[\because S_n = \frac{n}{2}\{2a + (n - 1)d\}\right]$$

$$= 2[2(5) + 3 \times d] \quad [\because a = 5]$$

$$\Rightarrow S_4 = 20 + 6d$$

$$\text{and } S_8 = \frac{8}{2}[2 \times 5 + (8 - 1)d]$$

$$= \frac{8}{2}(10 + 7d) = 40 + 28d$$

On putting the values of S_4 and S_8 in Eq. (i), we get

$$3(20 + 6d) = 40 + 28d$$

$$\Rightarrow 60 + 18d = 40 + 28d$$

Ans. 2

45. Hint Let the three terms in AP be $a, a + d, a + 2d$.

$$a + a + d + a + 2d = 33$$

$$\Rightarrow a + d = 11$$

By second condtion,

$$2a + a + 2d = 28 + a + 2d \Rightarrow a = 14$$

Thus, $d = 11 - 14 = -3$

Ans. 14, 11, 8, ...

46. Given, $a + a_8 = 32$

$$\Rightarrow a + a + 7d = 32$$

$$\Rightarrow 2a + 7d = 32 \quad \text{...(i)}$$

Also, we have

$$a \times a_8 = 60$$

$$\Rightarrow a(a + 7d) = 60 \quad \text{...(ii)}$$

On solving Eqs. (i) and (ii), we get

$a = 30$, then $d = -4$

or $a = 2$, then $d = 4$

Now, sum of first 20 terms, when $a = 30$ and $d = -4$

$$S_{20} = \frac{20}{2}[60 + 19(-4)] \quad \left[\because S_n = \frac{n}{2}[2a + (n - 1)d]\right]$$

$$\Rightarrow S_{20} = 10[-16]$$

$$= -160$$

or sum of first 20 terms, when $a = 2$ and $d = 4$

$$S_{20} = \frac{20}{2}[4 + 19 \times 4]$$

$$= 10[80] = 800$$

47. Hint Given, $S_n = S_{2n}$

$$\frac{n}{2}[2 \times 8 + (n - 1) \times 20] = \frac{2n}{2}[2 \times (-30) + (2n - 1) \times 8]$$

After solving, we get value of n. **Ans.** $n = 11$

48. Hint RHS $= S_n - 2S_{n-1} + S_{n-2}$

$$= (S_n - S_{n-1}) - (S_{n-1} - S_{n-2})$$

$$= a_n - a_{n-1} \quad [\because a_n = S_n - S_{n-1}]$$

$$= [a + (n - 1)d] - [a + (n - 1 - 1)d]$$

$$[\because a_n = a + (n - 1)d]$$

$$= a + (n - 1)d - a - (n - 2)d$$

$$= (n - 1 - n + 2)d = d = \text{LHS}$$

$$\therefore d = S_n - 2S_{n-1} + S_{n-2}$$

49. Given, $S_2 = S_7$

$$\Rightarrow \frac{2}{2}[2a + (2 - 1)d] = \frac{7}{2}[2a + (7 - 1)d]$$

[where, a is the first term and d is the common difference]

$$\Rightarrow 2a + d = 7(a + 3d) \Rightarrow 5a = -20d$$

$$\Rightarrow a + 4d = 0 \Rightarrow a_5 = 0$$

Thus, 5th term is 0.

For example, if the series of AP is as follows :

$-4, -3, -2, -1, 0, 1, 2, \ldots$ where $a_5 = 0$ and sum of first two terms is -7 which is equal to sum of first seven terms.

$\therefore$ Such arithmetic progression can exist.

50. Hint All three-digit natural numbers, multiples of 11 are 110, 121, 132, ..., 990.

Here, common difference,

$$121 - 110 = 132 - 121 = \ldots = 11.$$

So, it is an AP with first term, $a = 110$, common difference, $d = 11$ and last term, $l = 990$.

$$\text{Let } l = a_n = a + (n - 1)d$$

$$\therefore 990 = 110 + (n - 1) \times 11$$

$$\Rightarrow n = 81$$

$$\because S_n = \frac{n}{2}[a + l]$$

$$\therefore S_{81} = \frac{81}{2}[110 + 990]$$

Ans. $S_{81} = 44550$

51. **Hint** All two-digit numbers greater than 50 which when divided by 7 leaves remainder 4, are

$$53, 60, 67, \ldots, 95.$$

which forms an AP with first term, $a = 53$,

common difference, $d = 60 - 53 = 7$ and last term, $l = 95$.

$$a_n = l = a + (n-1)d$$

$\therefore$ $95 = 53 + (n-1)7 \Rightarrow n = 7$

Now, required sum $= 53 + 60 + 67 + \ldots + 95$ **Ans.** 518

52. **Hint** Consider 10, 20, 30, 40, … 490.

According to question,

$$490 = 10 + (n-1) \times 10 \qquad [\because a = 10, a_n = 490]$$

On solving, we get $n = 49$

and $S_n = \frac{n}{2}[2 \times 10 + (n-1) \times 10]$ **Ans.** 12, 250

53. **Hint** $S_n = n^2 p$

$\Rightarrow$ $2a + (n-1)d = 2np$ …(i)

Also, $S_m = m^2 p$

$\Rightarrow$ $2a + (m-1)d = 2mp$ …(ii)

On subtracting Eqs. (ii) from Eq. (i), we get

$$2a + (n-1)d - 2a - (m-1)d = 2np - 2mp$$

$\Rightarrow$ $(n - 1 - m + 1)d = 2p(n-m)$

$\Rightarrow$ $(n-m)d = 2p(n-m)$

$\Rightarrow$ $d = 2p$ …(iii)

Put this in Eq. (i), we get

$$2a + (n-1)(2p) = 2np \Rightarrow a = p$$

Now, $S_p = \frac{p}{2}[2a + (p-1)d]$

$$= \frac{p}{2}[2p + (p-1)2p] = p^3$$

$\therefore$ $S_p = p^3$

54. According to the question,

$S_1 = S_n = \frac{n}{2}[2a + (n-1)d]$ …(i)

$S_2 = S_{2n} = \frac{2n}{2}[2a + (2n-1)d]$ …(ii)

and $S_3 = S_{3n} = \frac{3n}{2}[2a + (3n-1)d]$ …(iii)

Now, $S_2 - S_1 = \frac{2n}{2}[2a + (2n-1)d] - \frac{n}{2}[2a + (n-1)d]$

$$= \frac{n}{2}[2\{2a + (2n-1)d\} - \{2a + (n-1)d\}]$$

$$= \frac{n}{2}[2a + (3n-1)d]$$

$\therefore$ $3(S_2 - S_1) = \frac{3n}{2}[2a + (3n-1)d]$

$\Rightarrow$ $3(S_2 - S_1) = S_3$ [using Eq. (iii)]

or $S_3 = 3(S_2 - S_1)$ **Hence proved.**

55. **Hint** Do same as Question 54.

56. **Hint** $S_1 = 2 + 4 + 6 + \ldots + 2n$

$$= \frac{n}{2}[2 \times 2 + (n-1)2] = n(n+1)$$

$$S_2 = 1 + 3 + 5 + \ldots + 2n - 1$$

$$= \frac{n}{2}[2 \times 1 + (n-1) \times 2] = n^2$$

$\therefore$ $\frac{S_1}{S_2} = \frac{n(n+1)}{n^2}$

$$= \frac{n+1}{n} = 1 + \frac{1}{n}$$

$\therefore$ $S_1 = \left(1 + \frac{1}{n}\right)S_2$

57. Let a_k denotes the kth term of the given AP. Then,

$$a_k = a + (k-1)d$$

Now, let S_1 = Sum of odd terms

$\Rightarrow$ $S_1 = a_1 + a_3 + a_5 + \ldots + a_{2n+1}$

$\Rightarrow$ $S_1 = \frac{n+1}{2}(a_1 + a_{2n+1})$

$\Rightarrow$ $S_1 = \frac{n+1}{2}[a + a + (2n + 1 - 1)d]$

$\Rightarrow$ $S_1 = (n+1)(a + nd)$

and S_2 = Sum of even terms

$\Rightarrow$ $S_2 = a_2 + a_4 + a_6 + \ldots + a_{2n}$

$\Rightarrow$ $S_2 = \frac{n}{2}(a_2 + a_{2n})$

$\Rightarrow$ $S_2 = \frac{n}{2}[(a + d) + \{a + (2n-1)\}d]$

$\Rightarrow$ $S_2 = n(a + nd)$

Clearly, required ratio $= S_1 : S_2$

$$= (n+1)(a + nd) : n(a + nd)$$

$= (n+1) : n$ **Hence proved.**

58. **Hint** Yes, total number of times the bell will be struck

in first 12 h $= \frac{12(12+1)}{2} = 78$

$\therefore$ Total number of times the bell will be struck in

$$24 \text{ h} = 2 \times 78 = 156$$

59. Let a be the first term and d be the common difference of an AP.

mth term $= \frac{1}{n}$

So, $a_m = a + (m-1)d = \frac{1}{n}$ …(i)

nth term $= \frac{1}{n}$

So, $a_n = a + (n-1)d = \frac{1}{m}$ …(ii)

On subtracting Eq. (ii) from Eq. (i), we get

$$a + (m-1)d - a - (n-1)d = \frac{1}{n} - \frac{1}{m}$$

$$(m-1-n+1)d = \frac{m-n}{mn}$$

$$\Rightarrow \quad (m-n)d = \frac{(m-n)}{mn} \Rightarrow d = \frac{1}{mn}$$

From Eq. (i), we get

$$a + (m-1)\cdot\frac{1}{mn} = \frac{1}{n} \Rightarrow a = \frac{1}{mn}$$

Now, $a_{mn} = a + (mn-1)d$

$$= \frac{1}{mn} + (mn-1)\cdot\frac{1}{mn} = 1$$

60. Equate the p th term of the first arithmetic progression, a_p, to the q th term of the second arithmetic progression, b_q, as $a_p = b_q$.

Since, $a_p = b_q$

$$\Rightarrow \quad a + (p-1)\times d_1 = b + (q-1)\times d_2$$

where a, b are the first terms and d_1, d_2 are the common differences of the given arithmetic progressions, respectively.

$$\Rightarrow \quad 14 + (p-1)\times 7 = 26 + (q-1)\times 13$$

$$\Rightarrow \quad (p-1)7 - 13(q-1) = 12$$

$$\Rightarrow 7p - 13q = 12 + 7 - 13 = 6$$

$$\Rightarrow \quad 7p - 13q = 6$$

61. Considers $d_1 = d_2 + 4$ or $d_2 = d_1 + 4$, where d_1 and d_2 are the common differences of the two arithmetic progressions.

Also, $a_{124} = b_{42} \Rightarrow a_1 + 123d_1 = b_1 + 41d_2$

where a_1, a_{124}, b_1 and b_{42} are the 1st, 124th, 1st and 42nd terms of the two arithmetic progressions, respectively.

$$\Rightarrow \quad a_1 + 123d_1 = a_1 + 41d_2 \qquad [\because a_1 = b_1]$$

Solve the above two equations and the value of $d_1 = -2$ and $d_2 = -6$ or $d_1 = 2$ and $d_2 = 6$.

One set of possible value of common difference is as follows

When $d_1 = d_2 + 4$, then $d_1 = -2$ and $d_2 = -6$

62. Let A be the first term and D be the common difference of AP.

$$T_p = a = A + (p-1)D = (A-D) + pD \quad \ldots\text{(i)}$$

$$T_q = b = A + (q-1)D = (A-D) + qD \quad \ldots\text{(ii)}$$

$$T_r = c = A + (r-1)D = (A-D) + rD \quad \ldots\text{(iii)}$$

Here, we have got two unknowns A and D which are to eliminated.

We multiplying Eqs. (i), (ii) and (iii) by $q-r$, $r-p$ and $p-q$ respectively,

$$a(q-r) = (A-D)(q-r) + Dp(q-r)$$

$$b(r-p) = (A-D)(r-p) + Dq(r-p)$$

$$c(p-q) = (A-D)(p-q) + Dr(p-q)$$

On adding above three equations., we get

$$a(q-r) + b(r-p) + c(p-q) = (A-D)[q-r+r-p+p-q] + D[pq-pr+qr-pq+rp-rq] = 0$$

63. Consider, $\frac{1}{a_1} + \frac{1}{a_n} = \frac{a_1 + a_n}{a_1\cdot a_n}$

$$\frac{1}{a_2} + \frac{1}{a_{n-1}} = \frac{a_2 + a_{n-1}}{a_2\cdot a_{n-1}}$$

$$= \frac{a_1 + d + a_n - d}{a_2\cdot a_{n-1}}$$

$$[\because a_n - a_{n-1} = d \Rightarrow a_{n-1} = a_n - d]$$

$$= \frac{a_1 + a_n}{a_2\cdot a_{n-1}}$$

Similarly, $\frac{1}{a_3} + \frac{1}{a_{n-2}} = \frac{a_1 + a_n}{a_3\cdot a_{n-2}}$

$\vdots \quad \vdots \quad \vdots$

$$\frac{1}{a_n} + \frac{1}{a_1} = \frac{a_1 + a_n}{a_1\cdot a_n}$$

On adding all the above, we get

$$2\left[\frac{1}{a_1} + \frac{1}{a_2} + \frac{1}{a_3} + \ldots + \frac{1}{a_n}\right] = (a_1 + a_n)\left[\frac{1}{a_1\cdot a_n} + \frac{1}{a_2\cdot a_{n-1}} + \frac{1}{a_3\cdot a_{n-2}} + \ldots + \frac{1}{a_n\cdot a_1}\right]$$

$$\Rightarrow \frac{1}{a_1\cdot a_n} + \frac{1}{a_2\cdot a_{n-1}} + \frac{1}{a_3\cdot a_{n-2}} + \ldots + \frac{1}{a_n\cdot a_1} = \frac{2}{a_1 + a_n}\left(\frac{1}{a_1} + \frac{1}{a_2} + \ldots + \frac{1}{a_n}\right)$$ **Hence proved.**

64. Hint Let a_1, a_2, a_3, a_4 be the first four terms of AP.

$$\therefore \quad a_1 + a_2 + a_3 + a_4 = 32$$

$$a + a + d + a + 2d + a + 3d = 32$$

$$[\because a_1 = a, a_n = a + (n-1)d]$$

$$\Rightarrow \quad 4a + 6d = 32$$

$$\Rightarrow \quad 2a + 3d = 16 \quad \ldots\text{(i)}$$

Now, $\frac{a_3}{a_4} = \frac{7}{8}$

$$\Rightarrow \quad \frac{a+2d}{a+3d} = \frac{7}{8}$$

$$\Rightarrow \quad 8a + 16d = 7a + 21d$$

$$\Rightarrow \quad a = 5d \quad \ldots\text{(ii)}$$

From Eq. (i),

$$2a + 3d = 16$$
$$\Rightarrow \quad 2(5d) + 3d = 16$$
$$\Rightarrow \quad 10d + 3d = 16$$
$$\Rightarrow \quad 13d = 16$$
$$\therefore \quad d = \frac{16}{13}$$

Then, $a = 5 \times \frac{16}{13} = \frac{80}{13}$

$$\therefore \quad a = \frac{80}{13}, a + d = \frac{80}{13} + \frac{16}{13} = \frac{96}{13},$$
$$a + 2d = \frac{80}{13} + \frac{32}{13} = \frac{112}{13}$$
$$a + 3d = \frac{80}{13} + \frac{48}{13} = \frac{128}{13}$$

65. Hint $a_{18} + a_{19} + a_{20} = 225$

$a_{35} + a_{36} + a_{37} = 429$ **Ans.** 3, 7, 11, 15...

66. Hint $a = \frac{-4}{3}, d = -1 - \left(-\frac{4}{3}\right) = \frac{1}{3}$

Find $a_9 + a_{10}$ **Ans.** 3

67. Hint Given, $\frac{a + 10d}{a + 17d} = \frac{2}{3}$

Then, find $\frac{a + 4d}{a + 20d}$ and $\frac{\frac{5}{2}(2a + 4d)}{\frac{21}{2}(2a + 20d)}$ **Ans.** 1 : 3; 5 : 49.

68. Given, AP 27, 24, 21, ...

Let a and d be the first term and common difference of the AP, respectively.

$$a = 27 \text{ and } d = 24 - 27 = -3$$

Given, sum of n terms is 105.

$$S_n = 105$$
$$\Rightarrow \quad \frac{n}{2}[2a + (n - 1)d] = 105$$
$$\Rightarrow \quad n[2 \times 27 - 3(n - 1)] = 210$$
$$\Rightarrow \quad n[54 - 3n + 3] = 210$$
$$\Rightarrow \quad 3n^2 - 57n + 210 = 0$$
$$\Rightarrow \quad n^2 - 19n + 70 = 0 \qquad \text{[diving by 3]}$$
$$\Rightarrow \quad n^2 - 14n - 5n + 70 = 0$$
$$\Rightarrow \quad (n - 14)(n - 5) = 0$$
$$\Rightarrow \quad n = 14 \text{ or } n = 5$$

So, the sum of 5 terms of given AP

= sum of 14 terms of given AP = 105

Again, let pth term of the AP is zero.

$$a_p = a + (p - 1)d$$
$$\Rightarrow \quad 0 = 27 + (p - 1)(-3)$$
$$\Rightarrow \quad p - 1 = 9 \Rightarrow p = 10$$

Hence, 10th term of this AP is zero.

69. Hint – 4, – 1, 2, ..., x forms an AP with first term, $a = -4$ and common difference $d = -1 - (-4) = 3$

Also, last term, say $a_n = x$

$\because$ nth term of an AP, $a_n = a + (n - 1)d$

$$\Rightarrow \quad x = -4 + (n - 1)3$$
$$\Rightarrow \quad n = \frac{x + 7}{3} \qquad ...(ii)$$

$\because$ Sum of first n terms, $S_n = \frac{n}{2}[2a + (n - 1)d]$

$$S_{\frac{x+7}{3}} = \frac{x + 7}{2 \times 3}\left[2(-4) + \left(\frac{x + 4}{3}\right) \cdot 3\right]$$
$$\Rightarrow \quad x^2 + 3x - 2650 = 0$$

Ans. 50

70. Given, first term, $a = 22$

last term, $l = -6$

and sum of n terms, $S_n = 64$

$$\Rightarrow \quad \frac{n}{2}[a + l] = 64$$
$$\Rightarrow \quad \frac{n}{2}[22 - 6] = 64$$
$$\Rightarrow \quad n = 8$$

Now, $l = a + (n - 1)d$,

where d is the common difference.

$$\Rightarrow \quad -6 = 22 + 7d$$
$$\Rightarrow \quad 7d = -28$$
$$\Rightarrow \quad d = -4$$

71. Given, $S_7 = 63$

$$\therefore \quad \frac{7}{2}[2a + 6d] = 63 \qquad \left[\because S_n = \frac{n}{2}[2a + (n - 1)d]\right]$$
$$\Rightarrow \quad 2a + 6d = 18 \qquad ...(i)$$

Also, sum of next 7 terms is given 161.

$$\therefore S_{14} = S_{\text{first } 7} + S_{\text{next } 7} = 63 + 161 = 224$$
$$\Rightarrow \quad \frac{14}{2}[2a + 13d] = 224$$
$$\Rightarrow \quad 2a + 13d = 32 \qquad ...(ii)$$

On subtracting Eq (i) from Eq. (ii), we get

$$(2a + 13d) - (2a + 6d) = 32 - 18$$
$$\Rightarrow \quad 7d = 14$$
$$\Rightarrow \quad d = 2$$

Putting $d = 2$ in Eq (i), we get

$$2a + 6 \times 2 = 18$$
$$\Rightarrow \quad 2a = 18 - 12$$
$$\Rightarrow \quad 2a = 6$$
$$\Rightarrow \quad a = 3$$

$\therefore$ Required AP is $a, a + d, a + 2d, a + 3d, ...$

i.e. $\quad 3, 3 + 2, 3 + 2 \times 2, 3 + 3 \times 2, ...$

or $\quad 3, 5, 7, 9, ...$

72. Hint

$$S_p = S_q$$

$$\frac{p}{2}[2a + (p-1)d] = \frac{q}{2}[2a + (q-1)d]$$

$\Rightarrow \quad p[2a + (p-1)d] = q[2a + (q-1)d]$

$\Rightarrow \quad (p-q)[2a + (p+q)d - d] = 0$

$\Rightarrow \quad 2a + (p+q-1)d = 0$

$\left[\text{on multiplying both sides by } \frac{(p+q)}{2(p-q)}\right]$

$\Rightarrow \quad S_{p+q} = 0$

73. Hint From AP, we have

common difference, $d = b - a$

and last term, $l = c = a + (n-1)(b-a)$

$\Rightarrow \quad n = \dfrac{c + b - 2a}{b - a} \quad \ldots\text{(i)}$

and now we have to prove that $\left[S_n = \dfrac{(b + c - 2a)(a + c)}{2(b - a)}\right]$

Then, LHS $= S_n = \dfrac{n}{2}[2a + (n-1)d]$

$= \dfrac{n}{2}[2a + (n-1)(b-a)]$

$= \dfrac{c + b - 2a}{2(b-a)}[2a + c - a] \quad$ [using (i)]

$= \dfrac{(c + b - 2a)}{2(b-a)}(a + c) =$ RHS **Hence proved.**

74. Hint Do same as Question15 of NCERT Folder Exercise 5.3. **Ans.** ₹ 7250

75. Let the first term be A and common difference D.

Now, $T_p = a \Rightarrow A + (p-1)D = a$

$\Rightarrow \quad (A - D) + pD = a \quad \ldots\text{(i)}$

and $T_q = b \Rightarrow A + (q-1)D = b$

$\Rightarrow \quad (A - D) + qD = b \quad \ldots\text{(ii)}$

On subtracting Eq. (ii) from Eq. (i), we get

$(p-q)D = a - b$

$\Rightarrow \quad D = \dfrac{a-b}{p-q} \quad \ldots\text{(iii)}$

On adding Eqs. (i) and (ii), we get

$2A + (p+q-2)D = a + b$

$\Rightarrow 2A + (p+q-1)D = a + b + D = a + b + \dfrac{a-b}{p-q}$

[from Eq. (iii)] ...(iv)

Now, $S_{p+q} = \dfrac{p+q}{2}[2A + (p+q-1)D]$

$= \dfrac{p+q}{2}\left[a + b + \dfrac{a-b}{p-q}\right] \quad$ [from Eq. (iv)]

Hence proved.

76. (i) Arithmetic Progression

(ii) **Hint** Sum of AP $= \dfrac{n}{2}[2a + (n-1)d]$, where a is first term, d is common difference and n is number of terms of an AP.

Ans. ₹ 1831.5

77. (i) **Hint** Clearly, the amount (in ₹) of installment in the first month, second month, third month...are, respectively, 1000, 1100, 1200, 1300, ... which forms an AP, with first term, $a = 1000$

and common difference, $d = 100$.

Now, amount paid in 30th installment,

$a_{30} = 1000 + (30-1)100$

$=$ ₹ 3900

(ii) Amount paid in 30 installments,

$S_{30} = \dfrac{30}{2}[2 \times 1000 + (30-1)100]$

$=$ ₹ 73500

Remaining amount of loan that he has to pay

$=$ ₹ 118000 − ₹ 73500

$=$ ₹ 44500

78. Hint Do same as Question 19 of NCERT Folder Exercise 5.3.

Ans. 16 Rows 15 Bricks.

79. (i) **Hint** Since, distance between the store and first flag towards right side is 2 m.

2 m 2 m 2 m 2 m

Store

∴ Distance covered by Ruchi to place the flag first towards right side of the store = 4 m

Distance covered by Ruchi to place the second flag towards right side of the store = 8 m

Distance covered by Ruchi to place the third flag towards right side of the store = 12 m

Similarly, distance covered by Ruchi to place the thirteenth flag towards right side of the store

$= a + 12d$

$= 4 + 12 \times 4$

$= 52$ m

Now, total distance covered in completing the job

$= 2S_{13} = 2\left\{\dfrac{13}{2}(2 \times 4 + 12 \times 4)\right\}$

$= 13(8 + 48)$

$= 13 \times 56$

$= 728$ m

(ii) Maximum distance covered by Ruchi for carrying a flag is 52 m.

ARITHMETIC PROGRESSION (AP)

Sequence A list of numbers arranged in a definite order according to some rule is called sequence.

.e.g. 2, 4, 6, 8, ... each number is obtained by adding 2 to the preceding number, except first number.

Arithmetic Progression A list of numbers in which each term is obtained by adding a fixed number to the preceding term except the first term is called an arithmetic progression.

e.g. 3, 8, 13, 18, 23,...... is an AP, as each term is obtained by adding 5 to the preceding term.

Generally, $a_1, a_2, a_3, \ldots\ldots$ is an AP, where a_1 is the first term, a_2 is the second term and so on. Its nth term is denoted by a_n.

The fixed number is called the common difference *(d)*

i.e. $d = a_2 - a_1 = a_3 - a_2 = a_4 - a_3 = \ldots$

The terms of an AP are as follows

$a_1 = a$

$a_2 = a + d$

$a_3 = a + 2d$

$\vdots \quad \vdots \quad \vdots$

and so on.

nth Term of an AP If a is the first term and d is the common difference, then its nth term is

$a_n = a + (n-1)d$

The nth term of an AP is called its general term or last term l.

$\therefore l = a_n = a + (n-1)d$

nth Term from the End of an AP

Let a be the first term and d be the common difference and l be the last term of an AP, then nth term from the end can be found by the formula

nth term from the end $= l - (n-1)d$

Sum of First n Terms of an AP

If first term of an AP is a and its common difference is d, then the sum of its first n terms is given by

$S_n = \frac{n}{2}[2a + (n-1)d]$

$= \frac{n}{2}[a + a_n]$

where, a_n is nth term of an AP.

$= \frac{n}{2}[a + l] \qquad [\because l = a_n]$

Triangles

CHAPTER 6

In previous class, we have studied about triangles and their various properties. We have also studied about congruent figures. We know that two figures are called congruent, if they have the same shape and same size. In this chapter, we will study about those figures which have same shape but not necessarily in the same size.

TOPIC 01 Similar Figures and Similar Triangles

Similar Figures

Two geometrical figures are said to be similar figures, if they have same shape but not necessarily the same size. Some examples of similar figures are given below:

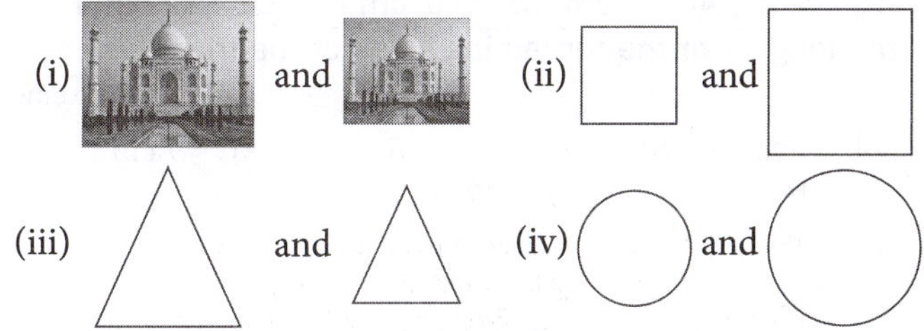

If two figures are similar, then one can be obtained from the other either by shrinking or by stretching without changing its shape. There is one-to-one correspondence between the parts of two similar figures. Concept of similarity is used in measuring the heights or distances of objects like mountain, moon etc.

From above discussion, we can say that all congruent figures are similar but the similar figures need not to be congruent.

Similar Polygons

Two polygons of same number of sides are similar, if

(i) all the corresponding angles are equal.

(ii) all the corresponding sides are in the same ratio (or proportion).

If only one condition from (i) and (ii) is true for two polygons, then they may not be similar.

It can be verified, if one polygon is similar to another polygon and the second polygon is similar to third polygon, then the first polygon is similar to the third polygon.

Scale Factor

The ratio that compares the measurements of two similar shapes, is called the scale factor or representative fraction. It is equal to the ratio of corresponding sides of two figures.

Example 1. Give two examples of pair of similar and non-similar figures.

Sol. (i) Examples of similar figures:

(a) Two squares of different sizes.

(b) Two regular hexagons of different sizes.

(ii) Examples of non-similar figures:

(a) Two isosceles triangles with different angle measures.

(b) Two rhombus with different angle measures.

Example 2. State whether the given quadrilaterals are similar or not.

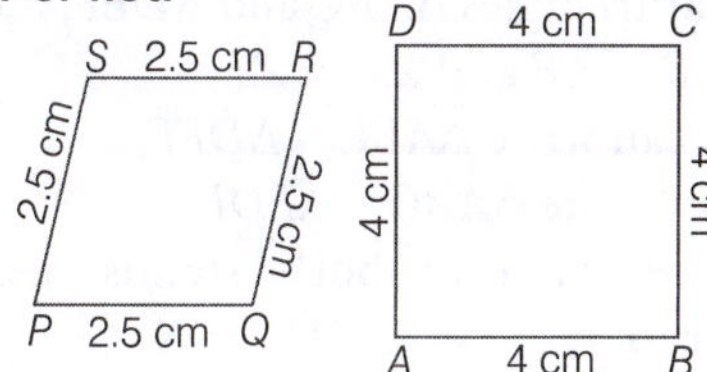

Sol. Here, $\frac{PQ}{AB}=\frac{2.5}{4}=\frac{25}{10\times4}=\frac{5}{8}$ and $\frac{RQ}{BC}=\frac{2.5}{4}=\frac{25}{10\times4}=\frac{5}{8}$

Clearly, the corresponding sides of quadrilaterals $ABCD$ and $PQRS$ are proportional but their corresponding angles are not equal. Hence, quadrilaterals $ABCD$ and $PQRS$ are not similar.

Example 3. **The given shapes are mathematically similar. Calculate the unknown side.**

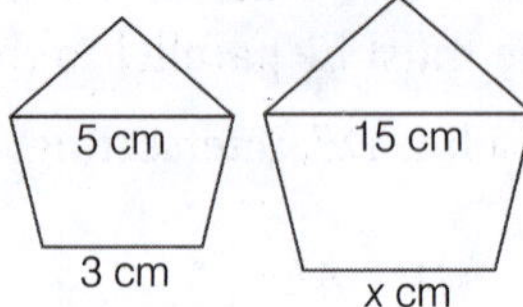

Sol. Given, both figures are similar.

So, the ratio of corresponding sides will be equal.

$$\therefore \quad \frac{3}{x}=\frac{5}{15} \Rightarrow x=\frac{3\times15}{5}=9 \text{ cm}$$

Similar Triangles

Two triangles are said to be similar, if

(i) their corresponding angles are equal.

(ii) their corresponding sides are proportional (i.e. the ratios of the lengths of corresponding sides are same).

e.g. In ΔABC and ΔPQR, if

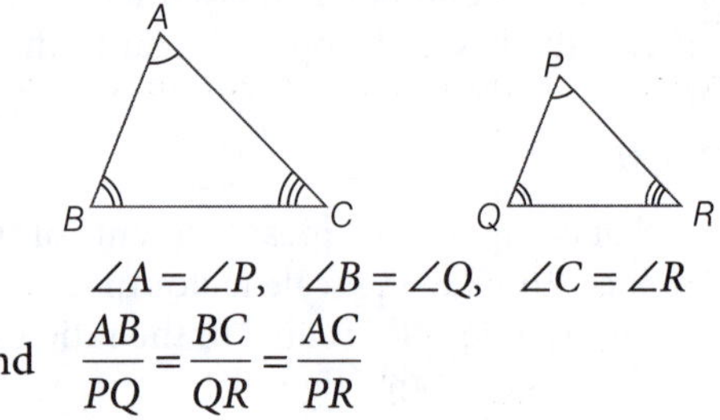

$$\angle A=\angle P,\quad \angle B=\angle Q,\quad \angle C=\angle R$$

and $\frac{AB}{PQ}=\frac{BC}{QR}=\frac{AC}{PR}$

Then, ΔABC is similar to ΔPQR.

Conversely

If ΔABC is similar to ΔPQR, then

$\angle A=\angle P, \angle B=\angle Q, \angle C=\angle R$ and $\frac{AB}{PQ}=\frac{BC}{QR}=\frac{AC}{PR}$.

Symbolic Representation of Two Similar Triangles

Similarity of two triangles can be expressed symbolically using correct correspondence of their vertices.

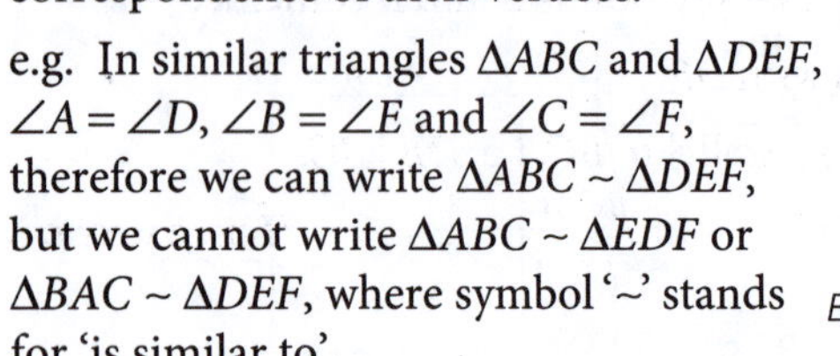

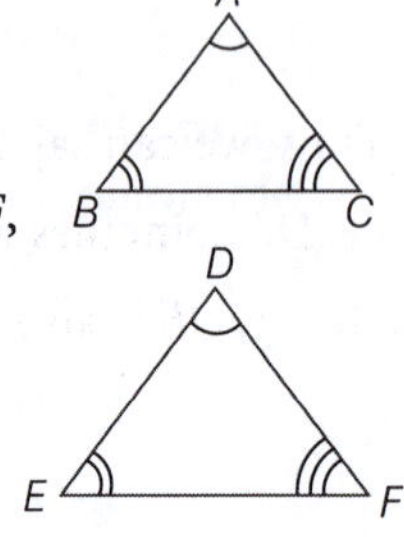

e.g. In similar triangles ΔABC and ΔDEF, $\angle A=\angle D, \angle B=\angle E$ and $\angle C=\angle F$, therefore we can write $\Delta ABC \sim \Delta DEF$, but we cannot write $\Delta ABC \sim \Delta EDF$ or $\Delta BAC \sim \Delta DEF$, where symbol '~' stands for 'is similar to'.

Note it
- If corresponding angles of two triangles are equal, then they are known as **equiangular triangles.**
- The ratio of any two corresponding sides in two equiangular triangle is always the same.

Example 4. **If $\Delta ABC \sim \Delta PQR$, $AB=6.5$ cm, $PQ=10.4$ cm and perimeter of $\Delta ABC=60$ cm, find the perimeter of ΔPQR.**

Sol. Given, $\Delta ABC \sim \Delta PQR$ with $AB=6.5$ cm and $PQ=10.4$ cm

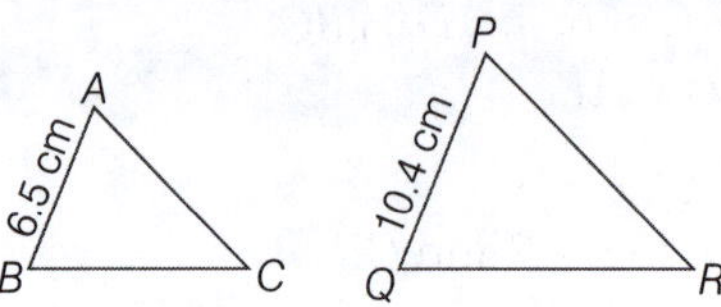

Since, $\Delta ABC \sim \Delta PQR$,

$$\therefore \quad \frac{AB}{PQ}=\frac{BC}{QR}=\frac{AC}{PR}=\frac{6.5}{10.4}=\frac{65}{104}$$

[$\because$ corresponding sides of similar triangles are proportional]

$$\Rightarrow \quad AB=\frac{65}{104}PQ,\ BC=\frac{65}{104}QR, AC=\frac{65}{104}PR$$

Also given, perimeter of $\Delta ABC=60$ cm

$$\therefore \quad AB+BC+AC=60$$

$$\Rightarrow \quad \frac{65}{104}(PQ+QR+PR)=60$$

$$\Rightarrow \quad PQ+QR+PR=\frac{60\times104}{65}=96 \text{ cm}$$

Hence, perimeter of ΔPQR is 96 cm.

Example 5. **It is given that $\Delta ABC \sim \Delta EDF$ such that $AB=5$ cm, $AC=7$ cm, $DF=15$ cm and $DE=12$ cm. Find the lengths of the remaining sides of the triangles.**

NCERT Exemplar

Sol. Given, $\Delta ABC \sim \Delta EDF$ with $AB=5$ cm, $AC=7$ cm, $DF=15$ cm and $DE=12$ cm. ...(i)

Since, $\Delta ABC \sim \Delta EDF$,

$$\therefore \quad \frac{AB}{ED}=\frac{AC}{EF}=\frac{BC}{DF}$$

[$\because$ corresponding sides of similar triangles are proportional]

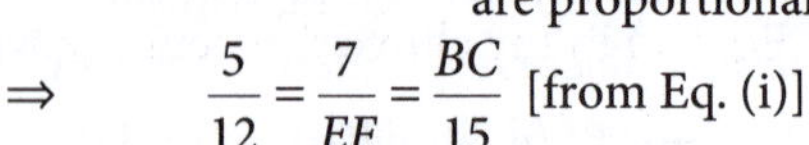

$$\Rightarrow \quad \frac{5}{12}=\frac{7}{EF}=\frac{BC}{15} \quad \text{[from Eq. (i)]}$$

On taking first and second ratios, we get

$$\frac{5}{12}=\frac{7}{EF}$$

$$\Rightarrow \quad EF=\frac{7\times12}{5}=16.8 \text{ cm}$$

On taking first and third ratios, we get

$$\frac{5}{12}=\frac{BC}{15} \Rightarrow BC=\frac{5\times15}{12}=6.25 \text{ cm}$$

Hence, lengths of the remaining sides of the triangles are $EF=16.8$ cm and $BC=6.25$ cm.

Basic Proportionality Theorem (BPT)

Theorem 1 If a line is drawn parallel to one side of a triangle to intersect the other two sides in distinct points, then the other two sides are divided in the same ratio. (This theorem is also known as Thales theorem)

CBSE 2025, 24 (Standard), 2023 (Basic)

Given ΔABC in which a line DE parallel to BC intersects AB at D and AC at E, i.e. $DE \parallel BC$.

To prove $\frac{AD}{DB} = \frac{AE}{EC}$

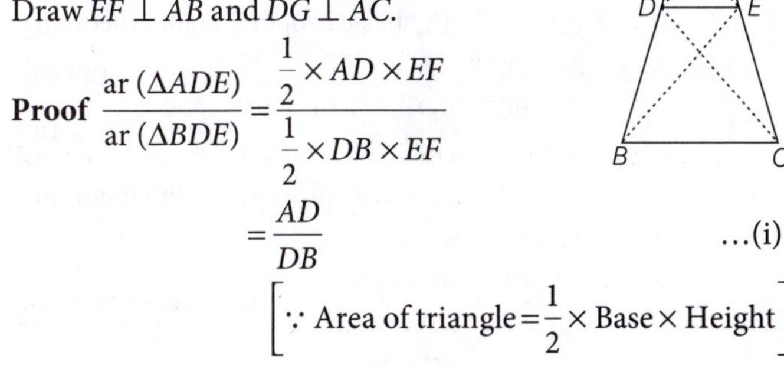

Construction Join BE and CD.

Draw $EF \perp AB$ and $DG \perp AC$.

Proof $\frac{\text{ar}(\Delta ADE)}{\text{ar}(\Delta BDE)} = \frac{\frac{1}{2} \times AD \times EF}{\frac{1}{2} \times DB \times EF}$

$= \frac{AD}{DB}$ ...(i)

$\left[\because \text{Area of triangle} = \frac{1}{2} \times \text{Base} \times \text{Height}\right]$

Similarly, $\frac{\text{ar}(\Delta ADE)}{\text{ar}(\Delta DEC)} = \frac{\frac{1}{2} \times AE \times DG}{\frac{1}{2} \times EC \times DG} = \frac{AE}{EC}$ ...(ii)

Since, ΔBDE and ΔDEC stand on the same base DE and between same parallel lines DE and BC.

$\therefore$ $\text{ar}(\Delta BDE) = \text{ar}(\Delta DEC)$ ...(iii)

From Eqs. (i), (ii) and (iii), we get

$\frac{AD}{DB} = \frac{AE}{EC}$ ...(iv) **Hence proved.**

Corollary (i) Prove that $\frac{AB}{DB} = \frac{AC}{EC}$ or $\frac{DB}{AB} = \frac{EC}{AC}$.

(ii) Prove that $\frac{AD}{AB} = \frac{AE}{AC}$ or $\frac{AB}{AD} = \frac{AC}{AE}$

Proof (i) From Eq. (iv) in the above theorem, we have

$$\frac{AD}{DB} = \frac{AE}{EC}$$

On adding 1 to both sides, we get

$$\frac{AD}{DB} + 1 = \frac{AE}{EC} + 1$$

$\Rightarrow$ $\frac{AD + DB}{DB} = \frac{AE + EC}{EC}$

$\Rightarrow$ $\frac{AB}{DB} = \frac{AC}{EC}$ or $\frac{DB}{AB} = \frac{EC}{AC}$

(ii) Similarly, by taking reciprocal of terms of Eq. (iv), we can prove that

$$\frac{AD}{AB} = \frac{AE}{AC}$$

or $\frac{AB}{AD} = \frac{AC}{AE}$

Theorem 2 Converse of Basic Proportionality Theorem If a line divides any two sides of a triangle in the same ratio, then the line must be parallel to the third side.

Given ΔABC and a line DE, intersecting AB at D and AC at E such that

$\frac{AD}{DB} = \frac{AE}{EC}$ ...(i)

To prove $DE \parallel BC$

Proof Let us assume that in ΔABC, DE is not parallel to BC. Now, draw a line DF parallel to BC, which intersects AC at point F.

On applying basic proportionality theorem, we get

$\frac{AD}{DB} = \frac{AF}{FC}$ ...(ii)

From Eqs. (i) and (ii), we get

$\frac{AE}{EC} = \frac{AF}{FC}$ ...(iii)

On adding 1 to both sides of Eq. (iii), we get

$$\frac{AE}{EC} + 1 = \frac{AF}{FC} + 1$$

$\Rightarrow$ $\frac{AE + EC}{EC} = \frac{AF + FC}{FC}$

$\Rightarrow$ $\frac{AC}{EC} = \frac{AC}{FC}$

$\Rightarrow$ $EC = FC$

Thus, we can say that the points E and F coincide, i.e. DF coincides with DE.

Hence, DE is also parallel to BC, i.e. $DE \parallel BC$.

Hence proved.

Problems Based on BPT and its Converse

Type I Sometimes we use BPT or its converse to prove some other results.

Example 6. In $\triangle ABC$, points P and Q are on CA and CB, respectively such that $CA = 16$ cm, $CP = 10$ cm, $CB = 30$ cm and $CQ = 25$ cm. Is $PQ \parallel AB$?

Sol. Given, $CQ = 25$ cm, $CB = 30$ cm, $CP = 10$ cm and $CA = 16$ cm

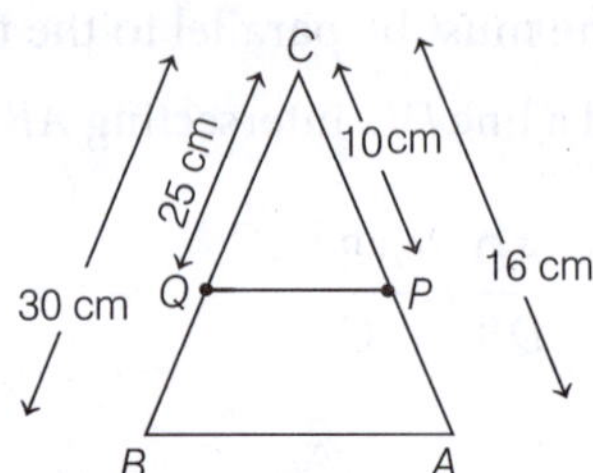

Here, $\frac{CQ}{CB} = \frac{25}{30} = \frac{5}{6}$

and $\frac{CP}{CA} = \frac{10}{16} = \frac{5}{8} \Rightarrow \frac{CQ}{CB} \neq \frac{CP}{CA}$

$\Rightarrow \frac{CB}{CQ} \neq \frac{CA}{CP} \Rightarrow \frac{CB}{CQ} - 1 \neq \frac{CA}{CP} - 1$

$\Rightarrow \frac{CB - CQ}{CQ} \neq \frac{CA - CP}{CP}$

$\Rightarrow \frac{QB}{CQ} \neq \frac{PA}{CP}$ or $\frac{CQ}{QB} \neq \frac{CP}{PA}$

Hence, by converse of basic proportionality theorem, PQ is not parallel to AB.

Example 7. If D and E are points on the respective sides AB and AC of $\triangle ABC$ such that $AD = 6$ cm, $BD = 9$ cm, $AE = 8$ cm and $EC = 12$ cm. Prove that $DE \parallel BC$.

Sol. In $\triangle ABC$, $\frac{AD}{DB} = \frac{6}{9} = \frac{2}{3}$

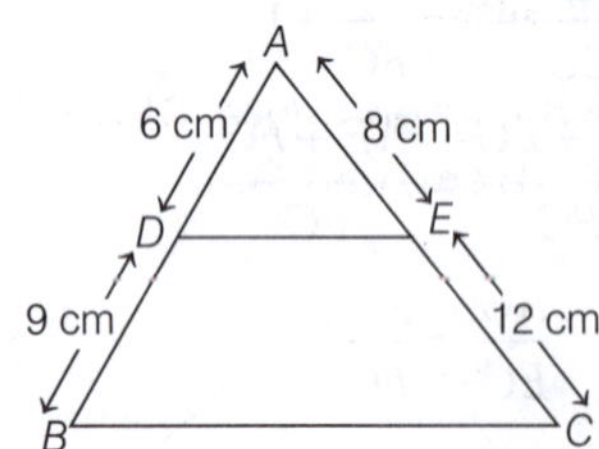

and $\frac{AE}{EC} = \frac{8}{12} = \frac{2}{3}$

Thus, $\frac{AD}{DB} = \frac{AE}{EC}$

Hence, $DE \parallel BC$

[by converse of basic proportionality theorem]

Hence proved.

Example 8. In the given figure of $\triangle ABC$, $DE \parallel AC$. If $DC \parallel AP$, where point P lies on BC produced, then prove that $\frac{BE}{EC} = \frac{BC}{CP}$. Also, find CP, if $BE = 20$ cm and $EC = 10$ cm.

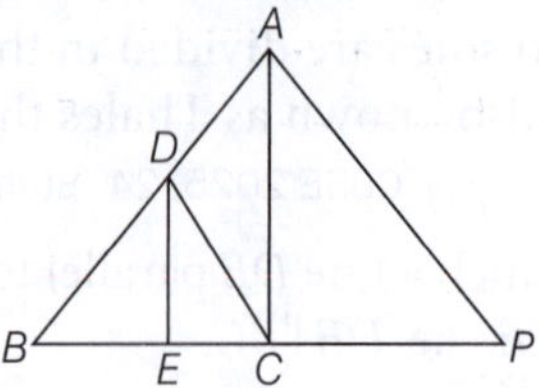

Sol. Given, in $\triangle ABC$, $DE \parallel AC$ [given]

So, $\frac{BE}{EC} = \frac{BD}{DA}$ ...(i)

[by basic proportionality theorem]

Also, in $\triangle ABP$, $DC \parallel AP$ [given]

So, $\frac{BC}{CP} = \frac{BD}{DA}$ ...(ii)

[by basic proportionality theorem]

From Eqs. (i) and (ii), we get

$\frac{BE}{EC} = \frac{BC}{CP}$ ...(iii) **Hence proved.**

Since, $BE = 20$ cm and $EC = 10$ cm

$\therefore BC = BE + EC = (20 + 10)$ cm $= 30$ cm

From Eq. (iii), we get

$\frac{20}{10} = \frac{30}{CP} \Rightarrow CP = 15$ cm

Example 9. In the adjoining figure, $\frac{AD}{BD} = \frac{AC}{EC}$ and $\angle BDE = \angle CED$. Prove that $\triangle ABC$ is an isosceles triangle.

CBSE 2025 (Standard)

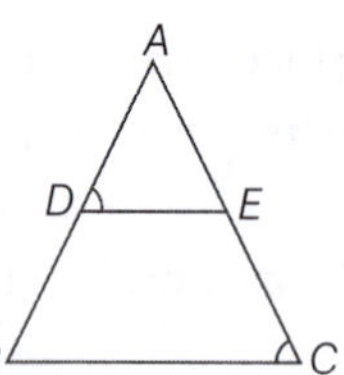

> Use converse of basic proportionality theorem to show $DE \parallel BC$ and then show $\triangle ABC$ an isosceles triangle, use the property that sides opposite to equal angles are also equal.

Sol. Given $\frac{AD}{BD} = \frac{AE}{EC}$ and $\angle BDE = \angle CED$

To prove $\triangle ABC$ is an isosceles triangle i.e. $AB = AC$.

Proof Since, $\frac{AD}{BD} = \frac{AE}{EC}$

$\therefore$ $DE \parallel BC$

[by converse of basic proportionality theorem]

Then, $\angle ADE = \angle AED$ [corresponding angles] ...(i)

Also, $\angle BDE = \angle CED$ [given] ...(ii)

From Eqs. (i) and (ii), we get

$\angle ADE = \angle AED$

$\Rightarrow$ $AB = AC$ [since sides opposite to equal angles of a triangle are also equal]

Hence, $\triangle ABC$ is an isosceles triangle.

Example 10. ***ABCD*** **is a trapezium with** $AB \parallel DC$. ***E*** **and** ***F*** **are two points on non-parallel sides** ***AD*** **and** ***BC*** **respectively, such that** ***EF*** **is parallel to** ***AB*****.**

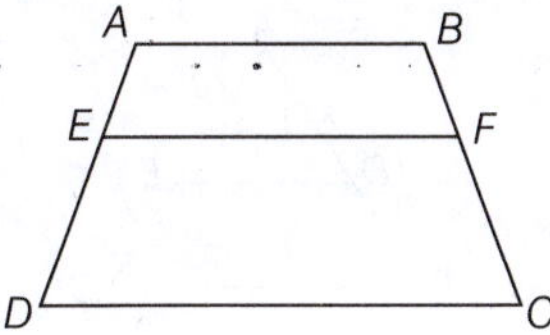

Show that $\frac{AE}{ED} = \frac{BF}{FC}$. [SQP 2023 (Basic)]

Or

In a trapezium, show that any line drawn parallel to the parallel sides of the trapezium, divides the non-parallel sides proportionally.

> Divide the given trapezium into two triangles by drawing a diagonal and then apply basic proportionality theorem in both triangles separately and then equate them to get the required result.

Sol. Given In trapezium *ABCD*,

$AB \parallel DC$ and $EF \parallel AB$

To prove $\frac{AE}{ED} = \frac{BF}{FC}$

Construction Join *AC* to intersect *EF* at *G*.

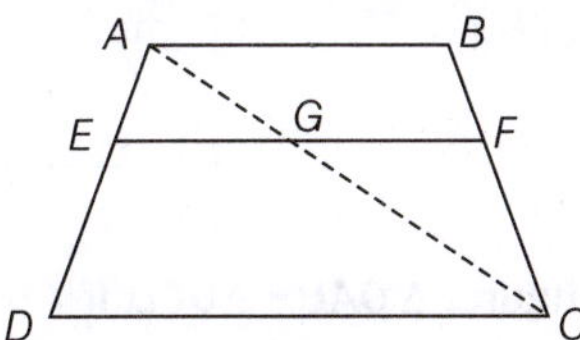

Proof Since, $AB \parallel DC$ and $EF \parallel AB$

$\therefore \quad EF \parallel DC$

[since lines parallel to the same line are also parallel to each other]

In ΔADC, $\quad EG \parallel DC \quad$ [$\because EF \parallel DC$]

By using basic proportionality theorem,

$$\frac{AE}{ED} = \frac{AG}{GC} \quad \text{...(i)}$$

In ΔABC, $\quad GF \parallel AB \quad$ [$\because EF \parallel AB$]

By using basic proportionality theorem,

$$\frac{CG}{AG} = \frac{CF}{BF}$$

or $$\frac{AG}{GC} = \frac{BF}{CF} \quad \text{...(ii)}$$

[on taking reciprocal of the terms]

From Eqs. (i) and (ii), we get

$$\frac{AE}{ED} = \frac{BF}{FC}$$

Hence proved.

Example 11. **In the given figure,** ΔABC **and** ΔDBC **have same base** ***BC*** **and lie on the same side of** ***BC*****. If** $PQ \parallel BA$ **and** $PR \parallel BD$**, then prove that** $QR \parallel AD$**.**

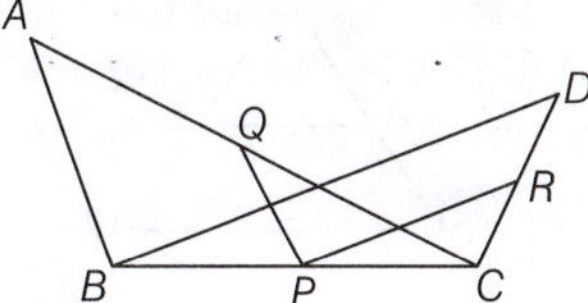

Sol. Given ΔABC and ΔDBC have same base *BC* and lie on the same side of *BC*.

To prove $QR \parallel AD$

Construction Join *QR* and *AD*.

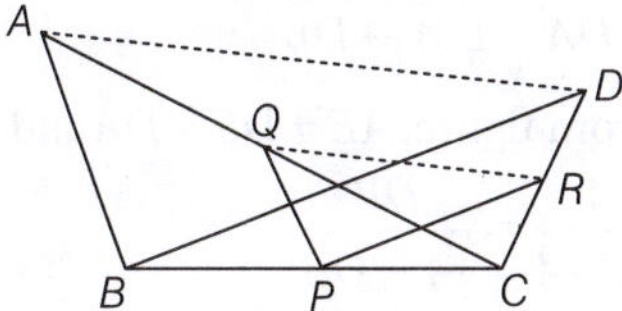

Proof Since,

$PQ \parallel BA$

So, $\quad \frac{CP}{PB} = \frac{CQ}{QA}$ [by basic proportionality theorem]...(i)

Also, $\quad PR \parallel BD$

$\therefore \quad \frac{CP}{PB} = \frac{CR}{RD}$ [by basic proportionality theorem]...(ii)

From Eqs. (i) and (ii), we get

$$\frac{CQ}{QA} = \frac{CR}{RD}$$

Hence, $QR \parallel AD$

[by converse of basic proportionality theorem]

Hence proved.

Type II Sometimes we use the basic proportionality theorem or its converse to find the length of unknown sides.

Example 12. **In the given figure,** $DE \parallel BC$**. If** $AD = 3$ **cm,** $DB = 4$ **cm and** $AE = 6$ **cm, find** ***EC*****.**

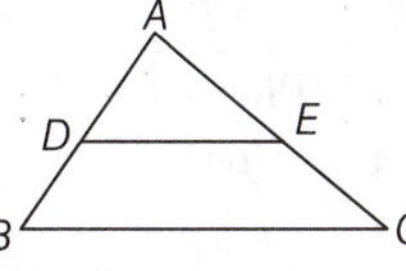

Sol. In ΔABC, $DE \parallel BC$

Let $EC = x$ cm, then $\frac{AD}{DB} = \frac{AE}{EC}$

[by basic proportionality theorem]

$\Rightarrow \quad \frac{3}{4} = \frac{6}{x} \Rightarrow x = \frac{4 \times 6}{3} = 8$ cm

$\therefore \quad EC = 8$ cm

Example 13. In ΔDEW, $AB \parallel EW$. If $AD = 4$ cm, $DE = 12$ cm and $DW = 24$ cm, find the length of DB.

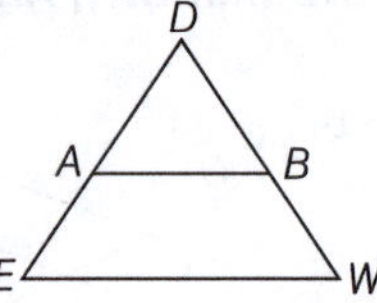

Sol. Given, $AB \parallel EW$

$$\therefore \quad \frac{DA}{AE} = \frac{DB}{BW}$$

[by basic proportionality theorem]

$$\Rightarrow \quad \frac{DA}{DE - DA} = \frac{DB}{DW - DB}$$

[$\because$ from figure, $AE = DE - DA$ and $BW = DW - DB$]

$$\Rightarrow \quad \frac{4}{12 - 4} = \frac{DB}{24 - DB}$$

$$\Rightarrow \quad \frac{4}{8} = \frac{DB}{24 - DB}$$

$$\Rightarrow \quad 24 - DB = 2DB$$

$$\Rightarrow \quad 24 = 3DB$$

$$\Rightarrow \quad DB = \frac{24}{3} = 8 \text{ cm}$$

Example 14. In ΔPQR, $ST \parallel QR$, $\frac{PS}{SQ} = \frac{3}{5}$ and $PR = 28$ cm, find the length of PT.

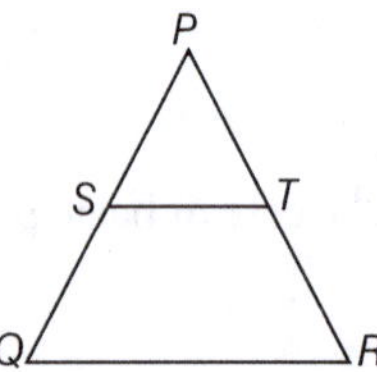

Sol. Given, $ST \parallel QR$, $PS/SQ = 3/5$ and $PR = 28$ cm

By using basic proportionality theorem, we get

$$\frac{PS}{SQ} = \frac{PT}{TR}$$

$$\Rightarrow \quad \frac{PS}{SQ} = \frac{PT}{PR - PT}$$

$$\Rightarrow \quad \frac{3}{5} = \frac{PT}{28 - PT}$$

$$\Rightarrow \quad 3(28 - PT) = 5PT$$

$$\Rightarrow \quad 84 = 5PT + 3PT$$

$$\Rightarrow \quad PT = \frac{84}{8}$$

$$\Rightarrow \quad PT = 10.5 \text{ cm}$$

Hence, the length of PT is 10.5 cm.

Example 15. In the given figure, ABC is a triangle in which $DE \parallel BC$. If $AD = x$, $DB = x - 2$, $AE = x + 2$ and $EC = x - 1$, then find the value of x. CBSE 2023 (Standard)

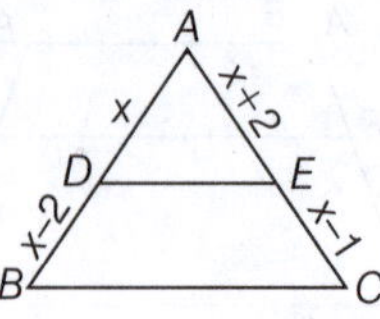

Sol. By basic proportionality theorem,

$$\frac{AD}{DB} = \frac{AE}{EC} \Rightarrow \frac{x}{x-2} = \frac{x+2}{x-1}$$

$$\Rightarrow \quad x(x-1) = (x+2)(x-2)$$

$$\Rightarrow \quad x^2 - x = x^2 - 4$$

$$\Rightarrow \quad x = 4$$

Try These 6.1

1. In ΔPQR and ΔMST, $\angle P = 55°$, $\angle Q = 25°$, $\angle M = 100°$ and $\angle S = 25°$. Is $\Delta QPR \sim \Delta TSM$? Why? NCERT Exemplar
2. If $\Delta ABC \sim \Delta DFE$, $\angle A = 30°$, $\angle C = 50°$, $AB = 5$ cm, $AC = 8$ cm and $DF = 7.5$ cm, then find DE and $\angle F$. NCERT Exemplar
3. Find the value of unknown variables, if ΔABC and ΔPQR are similar.

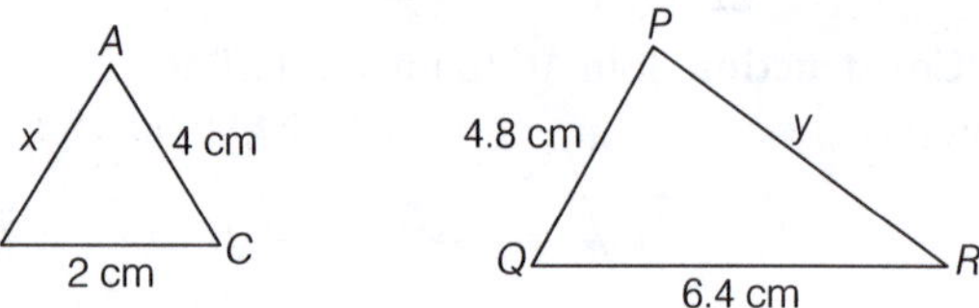

4. In the given figure, $\Delta OAB \sim \Delta OCD$. If $AB = 8$ cm, $BO = 6.4$ cm, $OC = 3.5$ cm and $CD = 5$cm, then find the values of OA and DO.

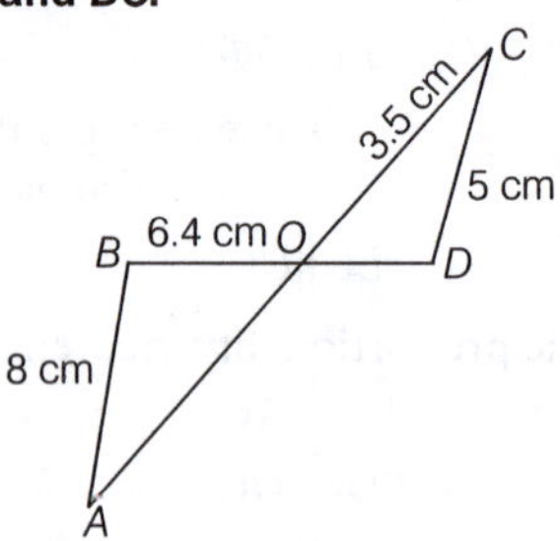

5. In the given figure, D and E are two points lying on side AB, such that $AD = BE$. If $DP \parallel BC$ and $EQ \parallel AC$, then prove that $PQ \parallel AB$.

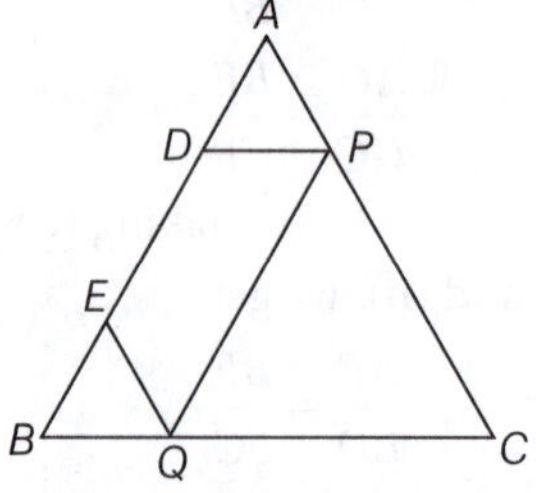

6. In the given figure, find the value of x, if $DE \parallel BC$.

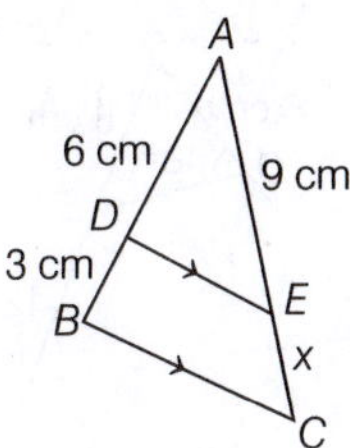

7. In the given figure, if $\Delta ADB \sim \Delta ADC$, then find the value of p.

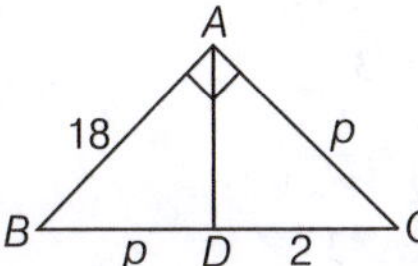

8. In ΔABC, P and Q are points on AB and AC such that $PQ \parallel BC$. If $AP = 4$ cm, $AQ = 3$ cm and $PB = 2$ cm, then find the value of AC.

9. In the given figure, $DE \parallel BC$, if $AD/DB = 3/5$ and $AC = 4.8$ cm, then find the value of AE.

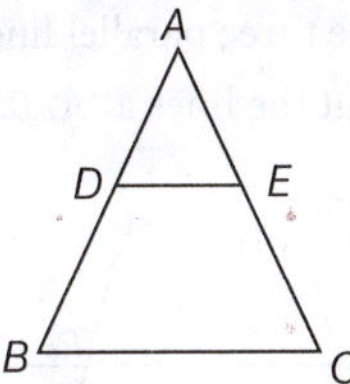

10. In the given figure, $DE \parallel BC$. Find the value of x.

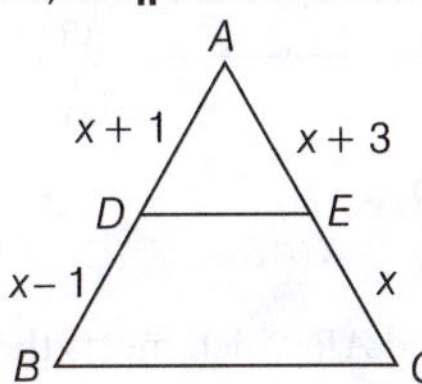

11. What value of a will make $DE \parallel AB$ in the figure given below?

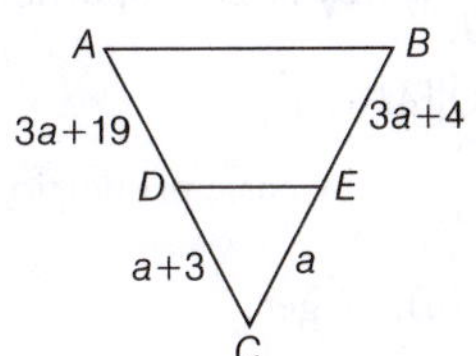

12. In the given figure, if $\dfrac{AD}{DC} = \dfrac{BE}{EC}$ and $\angle CDE = \angle CED$, then prove that ΔCAB is an isosceles triangle.

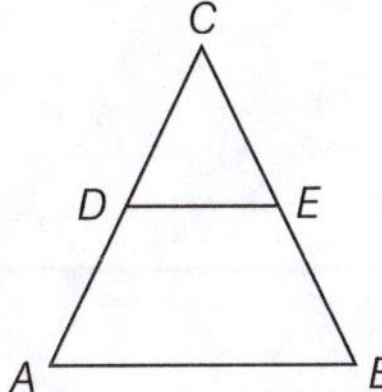

13. In the given figure, if $AD = 6$ cm, $DB = 9$ cm, $AE = 8$ cm and $EC = 12$ cm and $\angle ADE = 48^\circ$ find $\angle ABC$.

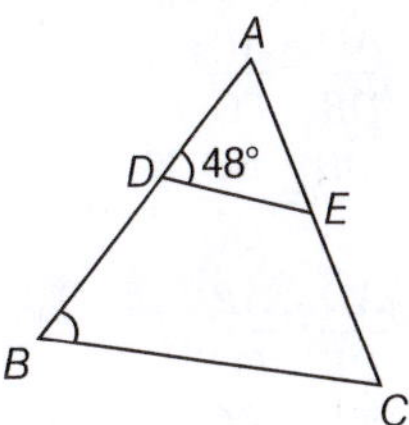

14. Prove that, if three or more parallel lines are intersected by two transversals, then intercepts made by them on the transversal are proportional.

Answers

1. Hint

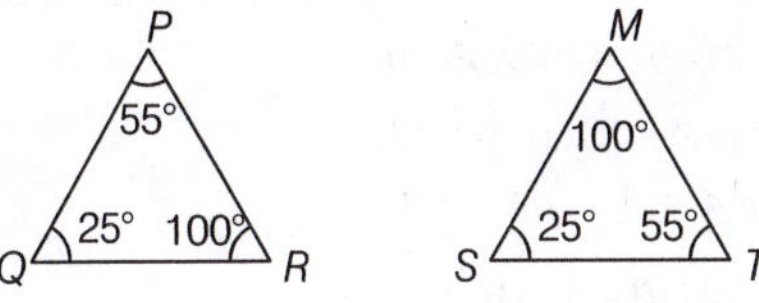

The correct correspondence will be $\Delta QRP \sim \Delta SMT$.

Ans. No

2. Hint As, $\Delta ABC \sim \Delta DFE$

$$\therefore \quad \angle F = \angle B = 180^\circ - (\angle A + \angle C)$$
$$= 180^\circ - (50^\circ + 30^\circ) = 100^\circ$$

Also, $\dfrac{AB}{DF} = \dfrac{AC}{DE}$

$$\Rightarrow \quad \frac{5}{7.5} = \frac{8}{DE}$$
$$\Rightarrow \quad DE = 12 \text{ cm}$$

Ans. $DE = 12$ cm, $\angle F = 100^\circ$

3. Hint As, ΔABC and ΔPQR are similar

$$\therefore \quad \frac{AB}{PQ} = \frac{BC}{QR}$$
$$\Rightarrow \quad \frac{x}{4.8} = \frac{2}{6.4}$$
$$\Rightarrow \quad x = 1.5$$

and $\dfrac{AC}{PR} = \dfrac{BC}{QR}$

$$\Rightarrow \quad \frac{4}{y} = \frac{2}{6.4}$$
$$\Rightarrow \quad y = 12.8$$

Ans. $x = 1.5$ cm and $y = 12.8$ cm.

4. Hint As, $\Delta OAB \sim \Delta OCD$

$$\therefore \quad \frac{OA}{OC} = \frac{AB}{CD} = \frac{BO}{OD}$$
$$\Rightarrow \quad \frac{OA}{3.5} = \frac{8}{5} = \frac{6.4}{DO}$$

Ans. $OA = 5.6$ cm and $DO = 4$ cm

5. Hint In ΔABC, we have

$$DP \parallel BC \text{ and } EQ \parallel AC$$

$\therefore$ $\frac{AD}{DB} = \frac{AP}{PC}$

and $\frac{BE}{EA} = \frac{BQ}{QC}$

$\Rightarrow$ $\frac{AD}{DB} = \frac{AP}{PC}$

and $\frac{AD}{DB} = \frac{BQ}{QC}$

[$\because EA = ED + DA = ED + BE = BD$ and $AD = BE$]

$\Rightarrow$ $\frac{AP}{PC} = \frac{BQ}{QC}$

[$\because$ in $\Delta ABC, P$ and Q divides sides CA and CB, respectively in the same ratio]

$\Rightarrow$ $PQ \parallel AB$

6. Hint Do same as Example 12.

Ans. $x = 4.5$ cm.

7. Hint As, $\Delta ADB \sim \Delta ADC$

$\Rightarrow$ $\frac{AB}{AC} = \frac{DB}{DC}$

$\Rightarrow$ $\frac{18}{p} = \frac{p}{2}$

Ans. $p = 6$ cm

8. Hint Do same as Example 13.

Ans. $AC = 4.5$ cm

9. Hint Do same as Example 14.

Ans. $AE = 1.8$ cm

10. Hint Do same as Example 15. **Ans.** $x = 3$

11. Hint Do same as Example 15. **Ans.** $a = 2$

12. Hint In ΔABC, $\frac{AD}{DC} = \frac{BE}{EC}$

$\Rightarrow$ $DE \parallel AB$ [by converse of BPT]

$\Rightarrow$ $\angle CDE = \angle A$ and $\angle CED = \angle B$ [corresponding angles]

Since, $\angle CDE = \angle CED$ [given]

$\therefore$ $\angle A = \angle B$

$\Rightarrow$ $CB = CA$ [$\because$ sides opposite to equal angles of a triangle are also equal]

Hence, ΔCAB is an isosceles triangle.

13.

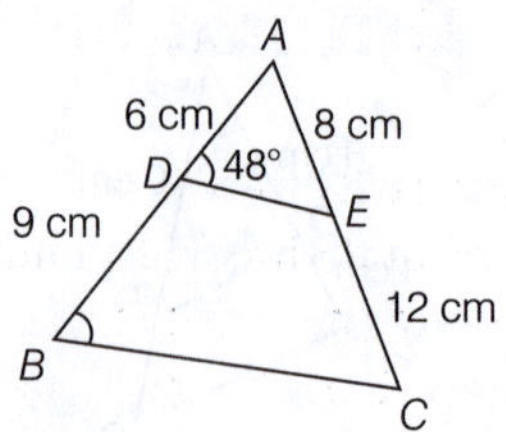

In ΔADE and ΔABC,

$$\frac{AD}{DB} = \frac{6}{9} = \frac{2}{3}$$

and $\frac{AE}{EC} = \frac{8}{12} = \frac{2}{3}$

$\Rightarrow$ $\frac{AD}{DB} = \frac{AE}{EC} = \frac{2}{3}$

$\therefore$ $DE \parallel BC$ [by converse of BPT]

Since, $DE \parallel BC$ and AB is the transversal

$\therefore$ $\angle ADE = \angle ABC$ [corresponding angles]

$\Rightarrow$ $\angle ABC = 48°$

14. Hint Let l, m and n be three parallel lines, t_1 and t_2 be any two transversals which cut the lines at A, B, C and P, Q, R, respectively.

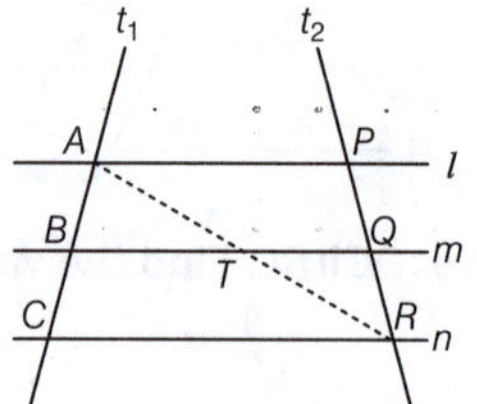

To prove $\frac{AB}{BC} = \frac{PQ}{QR}$

Construction Joined AR which meets the line m at T.

Proof Now, in ΔACR, $BT \parallel CR$

$\therefore$ $\frac{AB}{BC} = \frac{AT}{TR}$ [by basic proportionality theorem]...(i)

Also, in ΔAPR, $TQ \parallel AP$

$\therefore$ $\frac{AT}{TR} = \frac{PQ}{QR}$ [by basic proportionality theorem]...(ii)

From Eqs.(i) and (ii), we get

$$\frac{AB}{BC} = \frac{PQ}{QR}$$

Hence proved.

TOPIC 02 Criteria for Similarity of Triangles

For checking the similarity of two triangles, we look for all the equality relations of their corresponding angles and all the equality relations of the ratios of their corresponding sides. We have some criteria for congruency of two triangles involving only three pairs of corresponding parts (elements) of two triangles. Similarly, we have some criteria for similarity of two triangles involving relationship between less number of pairs of corresponding parts of two triangles instead of all the six pairs of **corresponding parts.**

These criteria are discussed below:

1. AAA (Angle-Angle-Angle) Similarity Criterion

Theorem *If in two triangles, corresponding angles are equal, then their corresponding sides are in the same ratio i.e. they are proportional and hence the two triangles are similar.*

Given In ΔABC and ΔDEF, we have

$$\angle A = \angle D, \angle B = \angle E \text{ and } \angle C = \angle F$$

To prove Corresponding sides are in the same ratio.

i.e. $$\frac{AB}{DE} = \frac{AC}{DF} = \frac{BC}{EF}$$

and then $\Delta ABC \sim \Delta DEF$

Construction Cut $DP = AB$ from DE and $DQ = AC$ from DF and join PQ.

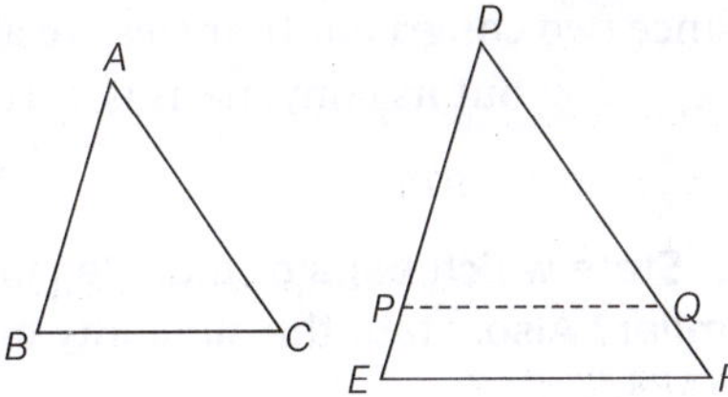

Proof In ΔABC and ΔDPQ,

$AB = DP$ [by construction] ...(i)

$AC = DQ$ [by construction] ...(ii)

and $\angle A = \angle D$ [given]

$\therefore$ $\Delta ABC \cong \Delta DPQ$ [by SAS congruency rule]

$\Rightarrow$ $\angle B = \angle P$ [by CPCT]

But $\angle B = \angle E$ [given]

$\therefore$ $\angle P = \angle E$

$\Rightarrow$ $PQ \parallel EF$ [since, corresponding angles are equal]

By basic proportionality theorem in ΔDEF, we get

$$\frac{DP}{PE} = \frac{DQ}{QF} \Rightarrow \frac{PE}{DP} = \frac{QF}{DQ}$$ [on taking reciprocal]

On adding 1 to both sides, we get

$$\frac{PE}{DP} + 1 = \frac{QF}{DQ} + 1$$

$$\Rightarrow \frac{PE + DP}{DP} = \frac{QF + DQ}{DQ}$$

$$\Rightarrow \frac{DE}{DP} = \frac{DF}{DQ}$$

$$\Rightarrow \frac{DE}{AB} = \frac{DF}{AC}$$ [from Eqs. (i) and (ii)]

or $$\frac{AB}{DE} = \frac{AC}{DF}$$ [on taking reciprocal] ...(iii)

Similarly, we can prove that

$$\frac{AB}{DE} = \frac{BC}{EF}$$ ...(iv)

From Eqs. (iii) and (iv), we get

$$\frac{AB}{DE} = \frac{AC}{DF} = \frac{BC}{EF}$$

$\therefore$ $\Delta ABC \sim \Delta DEF$ **Hence proved.**

Note it If two angles of one triangle are respectively equal to two angles of another triangle, then the two triangles are similar because by the angle sum property of a triangle their third angle will also be equal. AAA similarily criterion can be consider as **AA similarity criterion.**

2. SSS (Side-Side-Side) Similarity Criterion

Theorem *If in two triangles, sides of one triangle are proportional (i.e. in the same ratio) to the sides of the other triangle, then their corresponding angles are equal and hence the two triangles are similar.*

Given ΔABC and ΔDEF are such that

$$\frac{AB}{DE} = \frac{BC}{EF} = \frac{CA}{FD} (<1)$$ ...(i)

To prove Corresponding angles are equal.

i.e. $\angle A = \angle D, \angle B = \angle E, \angle C = \angle F$

and then $\Delta ABC \sim \Delta DEF$

Construction Cut $DP = AB$ from DE and $DQ = AC$ from DF and join PQ.

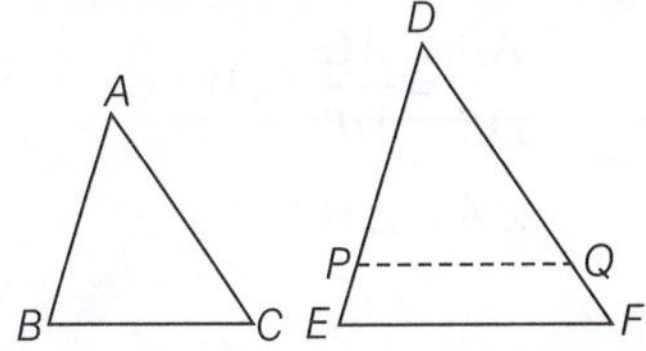

Proof It is given that

$$\frac{AB}{DE}=\frac{AC}{DF}$$

$\Rightarrow \quad \dfrac{DP}{DE}=\dfrac{DQ}{DF} \quad [\because DP=AB \text{ and } DQ=AC]$

$\Rightarrow \quad PQ \| EF$

[by converse of basic proportionality theorem]

Then, $\angle DPQ=\angle E$ and $\angle DQP=\angle F$ ...(ii)

In ΔDPQ and ΔDEF, we have

$\angle DPQ=\angle E$ and $\angle DQP=\angle F$

Therefore, by AA criterion of similarity, we have

$\Delta DPQ \sim \Delta DEF$

$\Rightarrow \quad \dfrac{DP}{DE}=\dfrac{DQ}{DF}=\dfrac{PQ}{EF}$

[since corresponding sides of similar triangles are proportional] ...(iii)

On putting $AB=DP$ and $AC=DQ$ in Eq. (i), we get

$\dfrac{DP}{DE}=\dfrac{DQ}{DF}=\dfrac{BC}{EF}$ ...(iv)

In ΔABC and ΔDPQ,

$BC=PQ$ [from Eqs. (iii) and (iv)]

$AB=DP$ [by construction]

and $AC=DQ$ [by construction]

$\therefore \quad \Delta ABC \cong \Delta DPQ$ [by SSS congruency rule]

So, $\angle A=\angle D, \angle B=\angle DPQ$

and $\angle C=\angle DQP$ [by CPCT]

$\Rightarrow \quad \angle A=\angle D, \angle B=\angle E$

and $\angle C=\angle F$ [from Eq. (ii)]

$\therefore \quad \Delta ABC \sim \Delta DEF$ **Hence proved.**

Note it In case of similarity of two triangles, it is not necessary to check both the conditions (AAA and SSS), because one condition implies the other.

3. SAS (Side-Angle-Side) Similarity Criterion

Theorem *If one angle of a triangle is equal to one angle of the other triangle and the sides including these angles are proportional, then the two triangles are similar.*

Given ΔABC and ΔDEF are such that

$\dfrac{AB}{DE}=\dfrac{AC}{DF} \;(<1)$ ...(i)

and $\angle A=\angle D$ ...(ii)

To prove $\Delta ABC \sim \Delta DEF$

Construction Cut $DP=AB$ from DE and $DQ=AC$ from DF and join PQ.

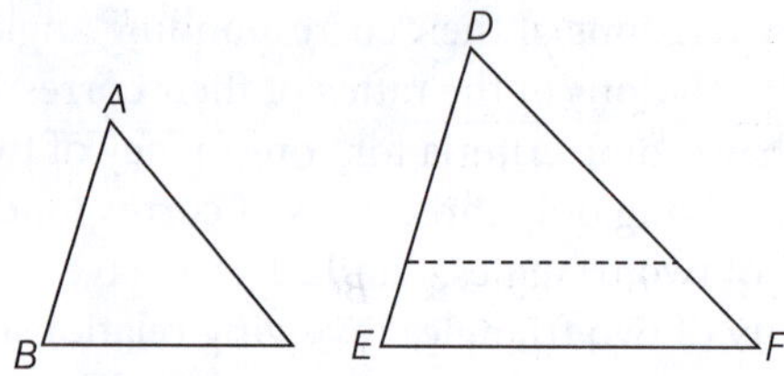

Proof In ΔABC and ΔDPQ,

$AB=DP$ [by construction]

$AC=DQ$ [by construction]

and $\angle A=\angle D$ [given]

$\therefore \quad \Delta ABC \cong \Delta DPQ$ [by SAS congruency rule] ...(iii)

From Eq. (i), $\dfrac{AB}{DE}=\dfrac{AC}{DF}$

$\Rightarrow \quad \dfrac{DP}{DE}=\dfrac{DQ}{DF} \quad [\because AB=DP \text{ and } AC=DQ]$

$\Rightarrow \quad PQ \| EF$

[by converse of basic proportionality theorem]

Now, $\angle DPQ=\angle E$

and $\angle DQP=\angle F$ [corresponding angles]

$\therefore \quad \Delta DPQ \sim \Delta DEF$ [by AA similarity criterion] ...(iv)

From Eqs. (iii) and (iv), we get

$\Delta ABC \sim \Delta DEF$

[since two congruent triangles are always similar but its converse is not true in general]

Hence proved.

Example 1. **State which pairs of triangles in the given figure are similar? Also, state the similarity criterion used.**

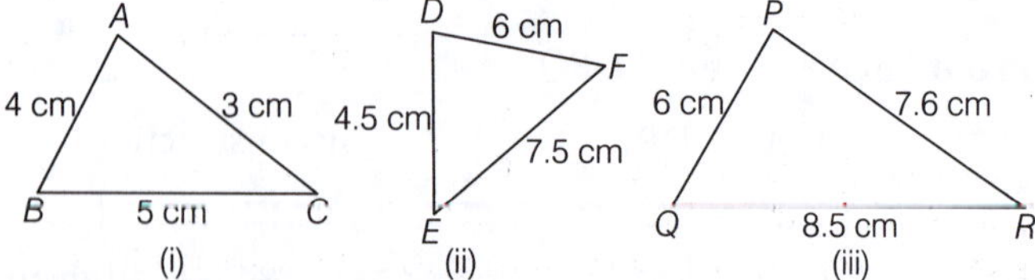

Sol. Here, $\dfrac{AB}{DF}=\dfrac{4}{6}=\dfrac{2}{3}, \dfrac{BC}{EF}=\dfrac{5}{7.5}=\dfrac{2}{3}, \dfrac{AC}{DE}=\dfrac{3}{4.5}=\dfrac{2}{3}$

As, $\dfrac{AB}{DF}=\dfrac{BC}{EF}=\dfrac{AC}{DE}$

So, $\Delta ABC \sim \Delta DFE$ [by SSS similarity criterion]

Hence, figures (i) and (ii) are similar triangles, but no other pairs of triangles in the given figure are similar.

Example 2. **State which of the two triangles given in the figure are similar. Also, state the similarity criterion used.**

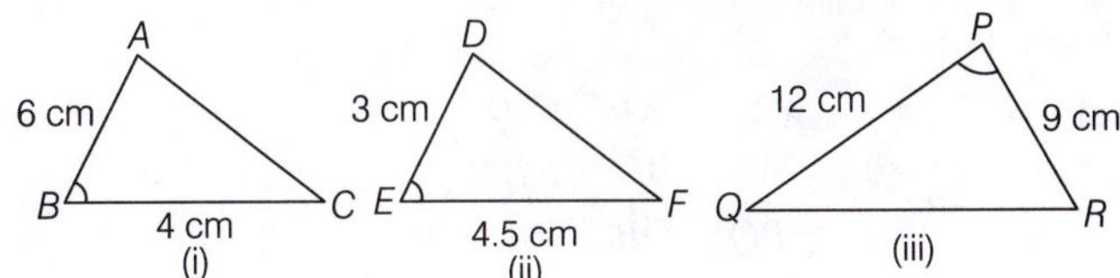

Sol. Here, $\frac{AB}{EF}=\frac{6}{4.5}=\frac{60}{45}=\frac{4}{3}, \frac{BC}{DE}=\frac{4}{3}$

$\Rightarrow \quad \frac{AB}{EF}=\frac{BC}{DE}$ and $\angle ABC=\angle FED$ [given]

So, $\Delta ABC \sim \Delta FED$ [by SAS similarity criterion]

Hence, figure (i) and (ii) are similar triangles, but no other pairs of triangles in the given figure are similar.

Example 3. **Find the value of each of the pronumerals in the given pair of triangles. Give reason for your answer.**

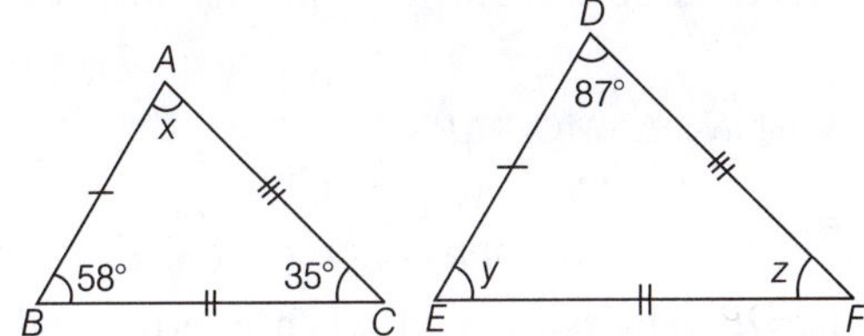

Sol. Given, $AB=DE, BC=EF$ and $AC=DF$

$\therefore \quad \Delta ABC \sim \Delta DEF$ [by SSS similarity criterion]

So, $\quad x=87°, y=58°$ and $z=35°$

[since corresponding angles of similar triangles are equal]

Example 4. **From the given figures, find $\angle P$.**

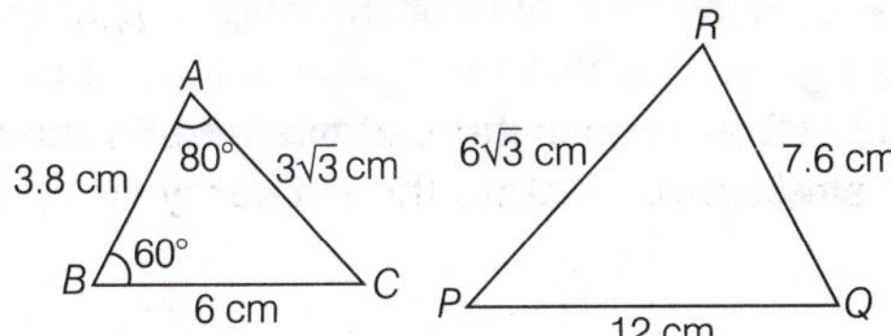

> First find the ratios of the sides. If ratios are equal, then triangles are similar and then corresponding angles are also equal. Also, use the property that sum of the angles of a triangle is 180° to find the third angle.

Sol. In ΔABC and ΔRQP,

$$\frac{AB}{RQ}=\frac{3.8}{7.6}=\frac{1}{2},$$

$$\frac{BC}{QP}=\frac{6}{12}=\frac{1}{2}$$

and $$\frac{CA}{PR}=\frac{3\sqrt{3}}{6\sqrt{3}}=\frac{1}{2}$$

Since, $\quad \frac{AB}{RQ}=\frac{BC}{QP}=\frac{CA}{PR}=\frac{1}{2}$

$\therefore \quad \Delta ABC \sim \Delta RQP$ [by SSS similarity criterion]

So, $\quad \angle P=\angle C$ ...(i)

[since corresponding angles of similar triangles are equal]

In ΔABC,

$\angle A+\angle B+\angle C=180°$

[by angle sum property of a triangle]

$\Rightarrow \quad 80°+60°+\angle C=180°$

[$\because \angle A=80°$ and $\angle B=60°$, given]

$\Rightarrow \quad \angle C=180°-140°=40°$

From Eq. (i), $\quad \angle P=40°$

Example 5. **In the given figure, *PQR* and *QST* are two right angled triangles, right angled at *R* and *T*, respectively. Prove that $QR \times QS = QP \times QT$.**

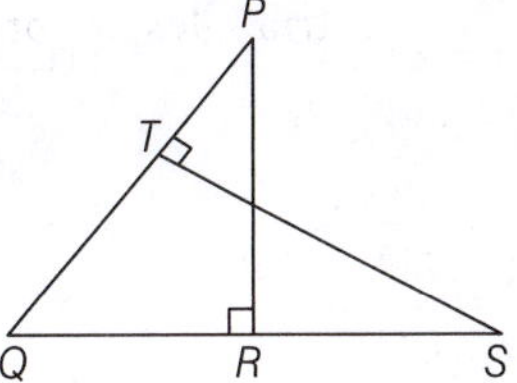

Sol. In ΔPRQ and ΔSTQ,

$\angle PRQ=\angle STQ$ [each 90°]

$\angle PQR=\angle SQT$ [common angle]

So, $\quad \Delta PRQ \sim \Delta STQ$ [by AA similarity criterion]

$\Rightarrow \quad \frac{QR}{QT}=\frac{QP}{QS}$

[since corresponding sides of similar triangles are proportional]

$\Rightarrow \quad QR \times QS = QP \times QT$ **Hence proved.**

Example 6. **In the given figure, *E* is a point on the side *CB* produced of an isosceles ΔABC with $AB = AC$. If $AD \perp BC$ and $EF \perp AC$, then prove that $\Delta ABD \sim \Delta ECF$.** CBSE 2023 (Standard)

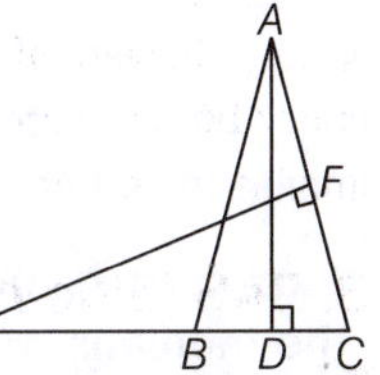

Sol. In ΔABC,

$AB=AC$

$\Rightarrow \quad \angle ABC=\angle ACB$

[angles opposite to equal sides of a triangle are equal]

$\Rightarrow \quad \angle ABD=\angle FCB$ ...(i)

Now, in ΔABD and ΔECF,

$\angle ABD=\angle ECF$ [using Eq. (i)]

and $\quad \angle ADB=\angle EFC=90°$

[$\because$ both 90°, as $AD \perp BC$ and $EF \perp AC$]

$\Rightarrow \quad \Delta ABD \sim \Delta ECF$ [AA similarity criterion]

Example 7. **ABCD is a parallelogram. Point P divides AB in the ratio 2 : 3 and point Q divides DC in the ratio 4 : 1.**

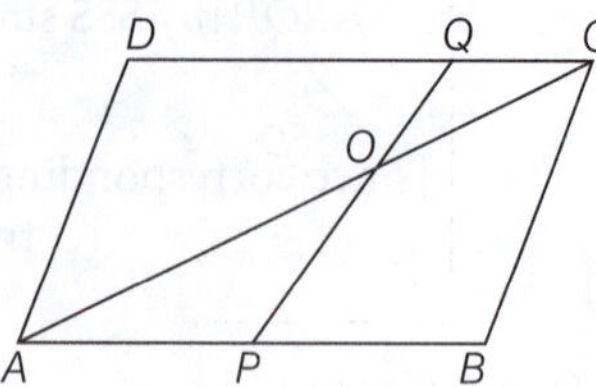

Prove that OC is half of OA. SQP 2023 (Standard)

Sol.

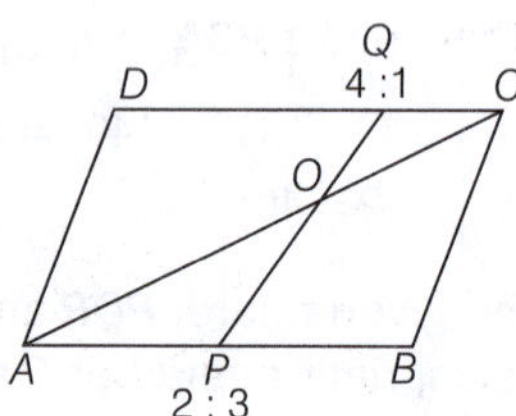

In ΔOAP and ΔOCQ,

$\therefore \quad \angle AOP = \angle COQ$ [vertically opposite angles]

$\therefore \quad \angle OAP = \angle OCQ$ [alternate angles]

$\Rightarrow \quad \Delta OAP \sim \Delta OCQ$ [by AA similarity criterion]

$$\therefore \quad \frac{OA}{OC} = \frac{AP}{CQ} \quad \text{... (i)}$$

Given, $\dfrac{AP}{PB} = \dfrac{2}{3}$ and $\dfrac{DQ}{QC} = \dfrac{4}{1}$

$\Rightarrow \quad \dfrac{AP}{AB} = \dfrac{2}{5}$ and $\dfrac{QC}{DC} = \dfrac{1}{5}$

$\Rightarrow \quad AP = \dfrac{2}{5}AB$ and $QC = \dfrac{1}{5}DC$

From Eq. (i),

$$\frac{OA}{OC} = \frac{\frac{2}{5}AB}{\frac{1}{5}DC} = 2$$

[$\because ABCD$ is a parallelogram; $\therefore AB = CD$]

$\Rightarrow \quad OC = \dfrac{1}{2}OA$ **Hence proved.**

Example 8. **In the given figure, CM and RN are respectively the medians ΔABC and ΔPQR. If $\Delta ABC \sim \Delta PQR$, then prove that**

(i) $\Delta AMC \sim \Delta PNR$ **(ii) $\dfrac{CM}{RN} = \dfrac{AB}{PQ}$**

[CBSE 2023 (Basic)]

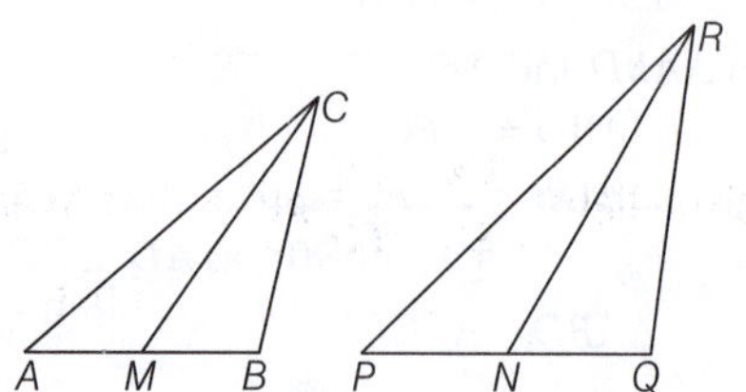

Write all the possible relations of similarity of triangles and use the result that the median bisects the opposite side. Further, prove the results.

Sol. (i) $\Delta ABC \sim \Delta PQR$ [given]

$$\Rightarrow \quad \frac{AB}{PQ} = \frac{BC}{QR} = \frac{AC}{PR} \quad \text{...(i)}$$

and $\angle A = \angle P, \angle B = \angle Q$ and $\angle C = \angle R$ ...(ii)

In ΔAMC and ΔPNR,

$2AM = AB$ and $2PN = PQ$

[$\because CM$ and RN are medians]

$\Rightarrow \quad \dfrac{2AM}{2PN} = \dfrac{CA}{RP}$ [from Eq. (i)]

$\Rightarrow \quad \dfrac{AM}{PN} = \dfrac{CA}{RP}$

Also, $\angle MAC = \angle NPR$ [from Eq. (ii)]

$\therefore \quad \Delta MAC \sim \Delta NPR$ [SAS similarity criterion]

Hence, $\Delta AMC \sim \Delta PNR$ [SAS similarity criterion]

Hence proved.

(ii) We have, $\Delta AMC \sim \Delta PNR$

$$\Rightarrow \quad \frac{AM}{PN} = \frac{AC}{PR} = \frac{CM}{RN}$$

[since triangles are similar, hence corresponding sides will be proportional]

$$\therefore \quad \frac{CM}{RN} = \frac{AC}{PR}$$

$\Rightarrow \quad \dfrac{CM}{RN} = \dfrac{AB}{PQ}$ [from Eq. (i)]

Hence proved.

Example 9. **Find the value of the height 'h' in the adjoining figure, at which the tennis ball must be hit, so that it will just pass over the net and land 6 m away from the base of the net.**

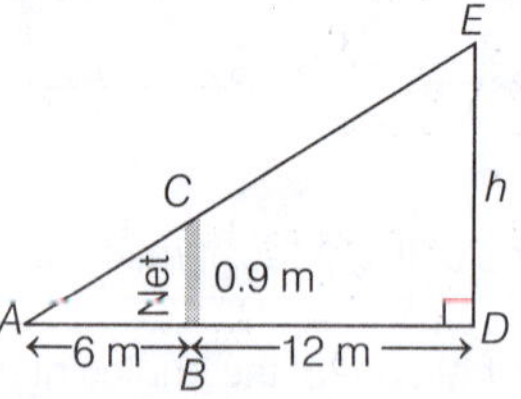

Sol. Since, the height h is measured vertically, so $\angle EDA$ is a right angle. We assume that the net (i.e. CB) is vertical. Here, ΔADE and ΔABC are similar

[by AA similarity criterion]

$\therefore \quad \dfrac{DE}{BC} = \dfrac{AD}{AB}$ [since corresponding sides of similar triangles are proportional]

$$\Rightarrow \quad \frac{h}{0.9} = \frac{18}{6} \Rightarrow \frac{h}{0.9} = 3$$

$$\Rightarrow \quad h = 0.9 \times 3 = 2.7 \text{ m}$$

Hence, the height at which the ball should be hit, is 2.7 m.

Example 10. **A girl of height 90 cm is walking away from the base of a lamp-post at a speed of 1.2 m/s. If the lamp is 3.6 m above the ground, then find the length of her shadow after 4s.**

Visualise the question carefully and draw a figure. Further, determine the distance of girl from lamp-post and show that two triangles are similar. At last, use the property of similar triangles (i.e. ratios of corresponding sides are same) and substitute the given values and simplify it.

Sol. Let AB be the lamp-post, CD be the girl and D be the position of girl after 4 s.

Again, let $DE = x$ m be the length of shadow of the girl.

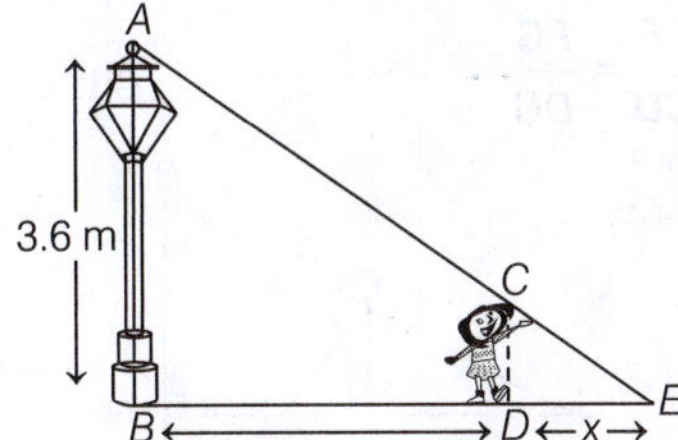

Given, $CD = 90\text{ cm} = 0.9\text{ m}$ and $AB = 3.6\text{ m}$ and speed of the girl = 1.2 m/s

$\therefore$ Distance of the girl from lamp-post after 4 s,

$BD = 1.2 \times 4 = 4.8\text{ m}$ [$\because$ distance = speed × time]

In ΔABE and ΔCDE,

$\angle B = \angle D$ [each 90°]

$\angle E = \angle E$ [common angle]

$\therefore$ $\Delta ABE \sim \Delta CDE$ [by AA similarity criterion]

$\Rightarrow \dfrac{BE}{DE} = \dfrac{AB}{CD}$ ...(i)

[since corresponding sides of similar triangles are proportional]

On substituting all the values in Eq. (i), we get

$\dfrac{4.8 + x}{x} = \dfrac{3.6}{0.9}$ [$\because BE = BD + DE = 4.8 + x$]

$\Rightarrow \dfrac{4.8 + x}{x} = 4$

$\Rightarrow 4.8 + x = 4x \Rightarrow 3x = 4.8$

$\Rightarrow x = \dfrac{4.8}{3} = 1.6\text{ m}$

Hence, the length of her shadow after 4 s is 1.6 m.

Try These 6.2

1. **In the given figures, find $\angle MLN$.**

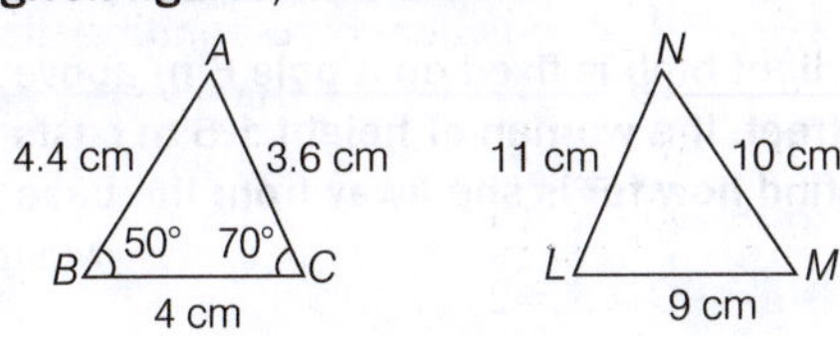

2. **In the given figure, $\angle ABC = 90°$ and $BD \perp AC$. If $BD = 6$ cm and $CD = 4$ cm, find the length of AD.**

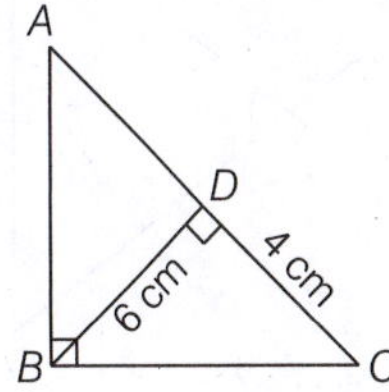

3. **In the given figure, two line segments AC and BD intersect each other at the point P such that $PA = 6$ cm, $PB = 3$ cm, $PC = 2.5$ cm, $PD = 5$ cm, $\angle APB = 50°$ and $\angle CDP = 30°$. Then, find $\angle PBA$.** NCERT Exemplar

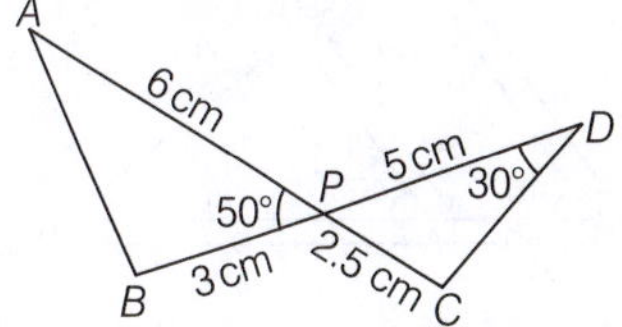

4. **In the given figure,**

$\angle ABC = \angle ACB$ and $\dfrac{BC}{BE} = \dfrac{BD}{AC}$.

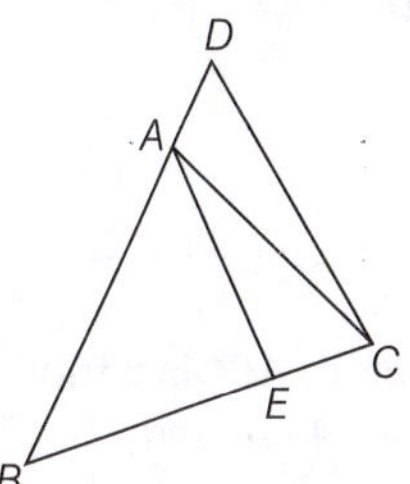

Show that $\Delta ABE \sim \Delta DBC$ and $AE \parallel DC$. CBSE 2024 (Basic)

5. **State whether the given pairs of triangles are similar or not. In case of similarity, mention the criterion.**

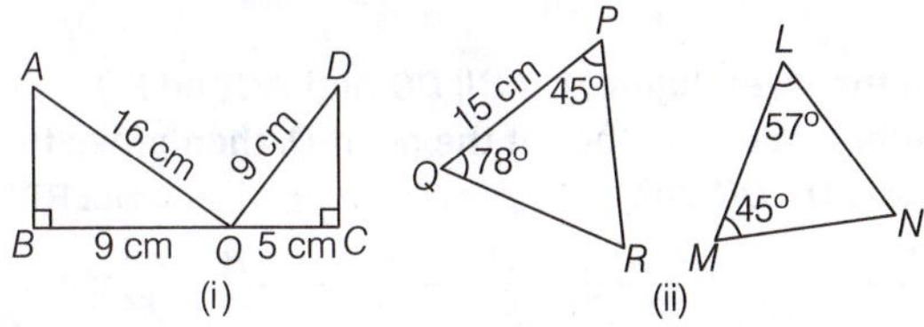

6. **ΔABC and ΔAMP are two right angled triangles, right angled at B and M, respectively. Prove that $CA \times MP = PA \times BC$.** NCERT Exemplar

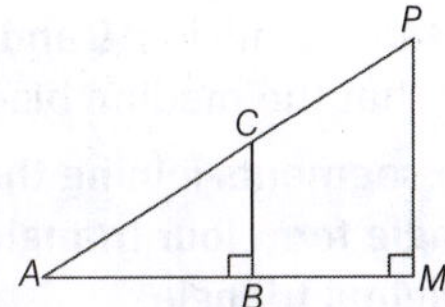

7. **In the given figure, $\dfrac{EA}{EC} = \dfrac{EB}{ED}$, prove that $\Delta EAB \sim \Delta ECD$.**

CBSE 2024 (Standard)

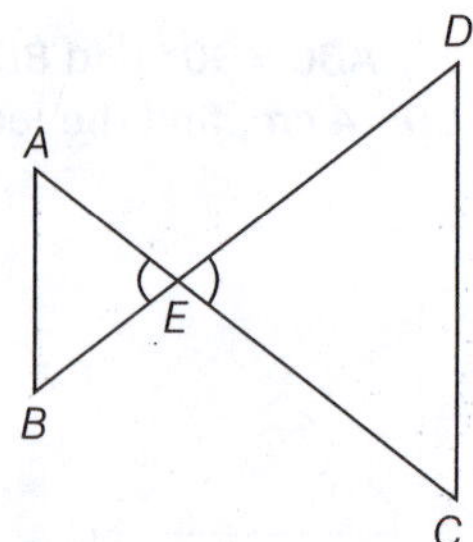

8. In the given figure, $\angle M = \angle N = 46°$. Express x in terms of a, b and c, where a, b and c are the lengths of LM, MN and NK, respectively.

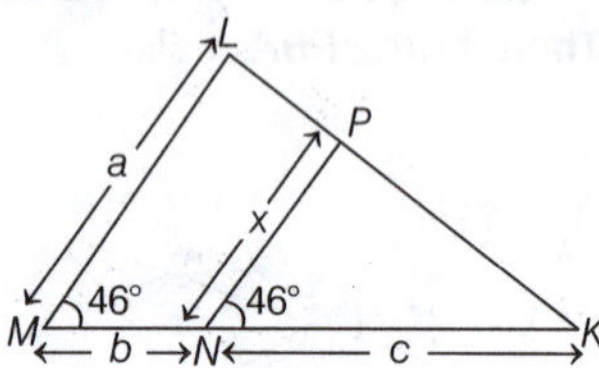

9. P and Q are the points on sides AB and AC, respectively of ΔABC. If $AP = 3$ cm, $PB = 6$ cm, $AQ = 5$ cm and $QC = 10$ cm, show that $BC = 3PQ$.

10. In the given figure, if $\angle BAC = 90°$ and $AD \perp BC$, prove that $AD^2 = BD \cdot CD$. NCERT Exemplar

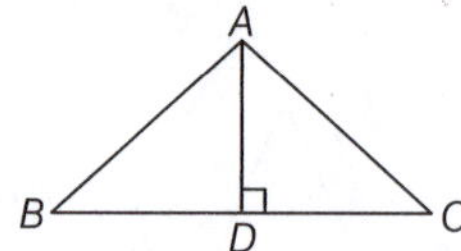

11. In the adjoining figure, ABC is a triangle right angled at B and $BD \perp AC$. If $AD = 4$ cm and $CD = 5$ cm, find BD and AB.

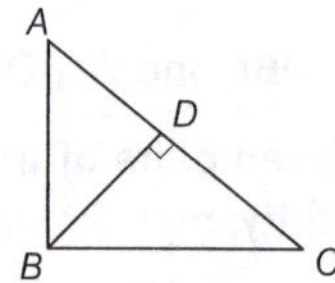

12. In the given figure, if $AB \| DC$ and AC and PQ intersect each other at the point O, then prove that $OA \cdot CQ = OC \cdot AP$. NCERT Exemplar

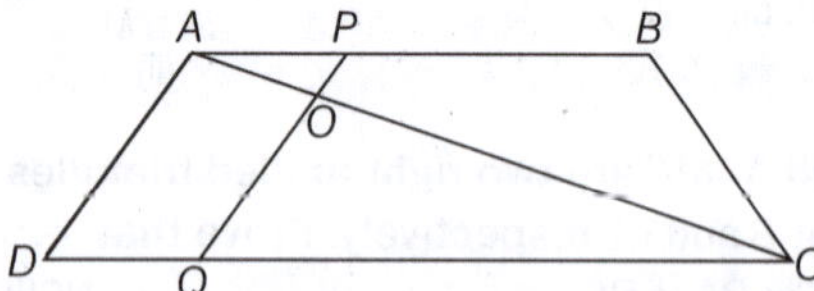

13. In a ΔABC, P and Q are points in AB and AC, respectively and $PQ \| BC$. Prove that the median bisects PQ.

14. Prove that the line segments joining the mid-points of the sides of a triangle form four triangles, each of which is similar to the original triangle.

15. In a trapezium $ABCD$, $AB \| DC$ and its diagonals intersect at O. Prove that $\frac{OA}{OC} = \frac{OB}{OD}$. CBSE 2025 (Basic)

16. In the given figure, $l \| m$ and line segments AB, CD and EF are concurrent at point P. Prove that $\frac{AE}{BF} = \frac{AC}{BD} = \frac{CE}{FD}$.

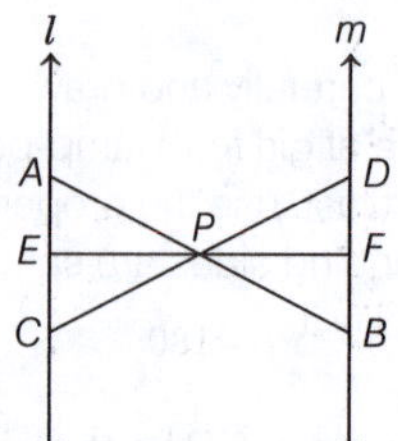

17. In the given figure, CD is the perpendicular bisector of AB. EF is perpendicular to CD. AE intersects CD at G. Prove that $\frac{CF}{CD} = \frac{FG}{DG}$. CBSE 2023 (Standard)

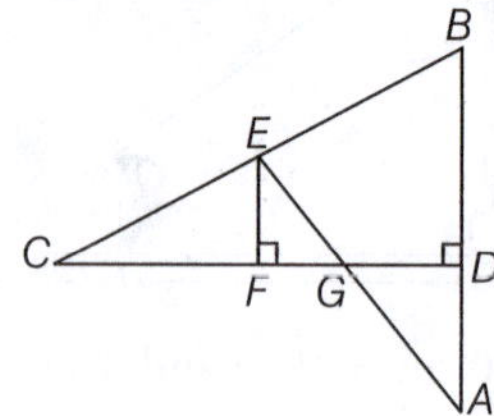

18. In the given figure, $ABCD$ is a parallelogram. BE bisects CD at M and intersects AC at L. Prove that $EL = 2BL$.

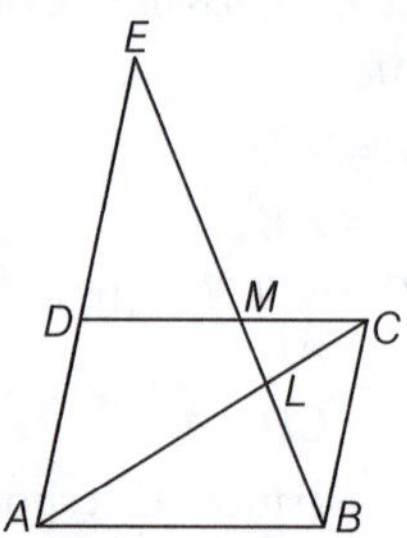

19. In the given figure, $AB \| PQ \| CD$, $AB = x$ units, $CD = y$ units and $PQ = z$ units. Prove that $\frac{1}{x} + \frac{1}{y} = \frac{1}{z}$.

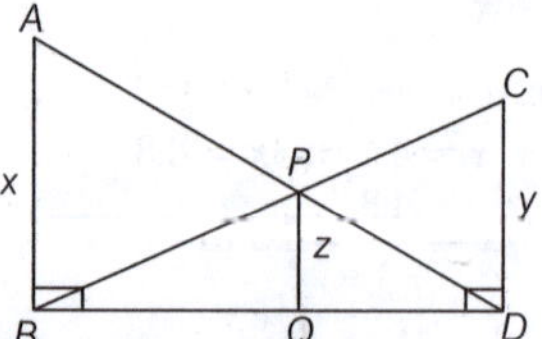

20. If two poles 5 m and 15 m high are 100 m apart, then find the height of the point of intersection of the line joining the top of each pole to the foot of the opposite pole.

21. A street light bulb is fixed on a pole 6 m above the level of the street. If a woman of height 1.5 m casts a shadow of 3 m, find how far is she away from the base of the pole? NCERT Exemplar

Answers

1. **Hint** Do same as Example 4. **Ans.** 60°
2. **Hint** Prove $\Delta DBA \sim \Delta DCB$

   Then, $\dfrac{DB}{DC} = \dfrac{DA}{DB}$

   Ans. $AD = 9$ cm
3. **Hint** Prove $\Delta APB \sim \Delta DPC$ [by SAS similarity]

   $\therefore$ $\angle A = \angle D = 30°$ [corresponding angles]

   In ΔAPB, $\angle A + \angle B + \angle APB = 180°$.

   Ans. 100°
4. **Hint** Given, $\angle ABC = \angle ACB$

   $\therefore$ $AB = AC$

   [$\because$ sides opposite to equal angles of a triangle are equal]

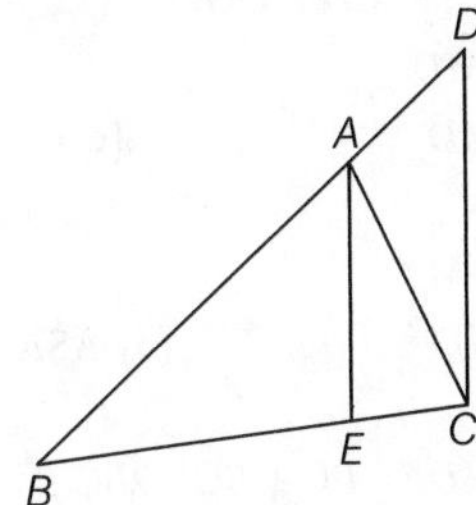

   In ΔABE and ΔDBC,

   $\angle ABE = \angle DBC$ [common]

   $\dfrac{BC}{BE} = \dfrac{BD}{AC}$ [given]

   $\Rightarrow$ $\dfrac{BC}{BE} = \dfrac{BD}{AB}$ [$\because AB = AC$]

   So, $\Delta ABC \sim \Delta DBE$ [by SAS similarity]

   Now, $\dfrac{BC}{BE} = \dfrac{BD}{AB}$

   Then, by converse of Basic Proportionality Theorem, if a line divides any two sides of a triangle in the same ratio, then the line must be parallel to the third side.

   $\therefore$ $AE \parallel DC$ **Hence proved.**
5. **Hint** In Fig. (i), corresponding sides are not in proportion.

   In Fig. (ii), in ΔLMN

   $\angle LMN + \angle MNL + \angle MLN = 180°$

   [by angle sum property of a triangle]

   $\Rightarrow$ $45° + \angle MNL + 57° = 180° \Rightarrow \angle MNL = 78°$

   $\therefore$ $\angle QPR = \angle LMN = 45°$

   $\therefore$ $\angle PQR = \angle MNL = 78°$

   So, $\Delta PQR \sim \Delta MNL$ [by AA similarity criterion]
6. **Hint** Prove that $\Delta ABC \sim \Delta AMP$ [by AA similarity criterion]
7. **Hint** In ΔEAB and ΔECD,

   $\dfrac{EA}{EC} = \dfrac{EB}{ED}$ [given]

   $\angle AEB = \angle CED$ [vertically opposite angles]

   $\therefore$ By SAS rule of similarity

   $\Delta EAB \sim \Delta ECD$ **Hence proved.**
8. **Hint** Prove ΔPNK and ΔLMK are similar by AA similarity criterion, then $\dfrac{NK}{MK} = \dfrac{PN}{LM}$

   $\Rightarrow$ $\dfrac{c}{b+c} = \dfrac{x}{a} \Rightarrow x = \dfrac{ac}{b+c}$
9. **Hint** Here, we have $\dfrac{AP}{AB} = \dfrac{AQ}{AC} = \dfrac{1}{3}$,

   Then, prove ΔAPQ and ΔABC are similar.

   Then, $\dfrac{AP}{AB} = \dfrac{AQ}{AC} = \dfrac{PQ}{BC} = \dfrac{1}{3} \Rightarrow BC = 3PQ$
10. **Hint** Prove $\Delta ADB \sim \Delta CDA$, then $\dfrac{BD}{AD} = \dfrac{AD}{CD}$

    $\Rightarrow AD^2 = BD \cdot CD$
11. **Hint** Prove ΔDBA and ΔDCB are similar.

    [by AA similarity criterion]

    $\dfrac{DB}{DC} = \dfrac{DA}{DB} \Rightarrow DB^2 = DA \times DC = 4 \times 5 \Rightarrow DB = 2\sqrt{5}$ cm

    In right angled ΔADB, $AB^2 = BD^2 + AD^2 = (2\sqrt{5})^2 + (4)^2$

    $\Rightarrow$ $AB = 6$ **Ans.** $AB = 6$ cm, $BD = 2\sqrt{5}$ cm
12. **Hint** Prove ΔAOP and ΔCOQ are similar.

    [by AA similarity criterion]

    Then, $\dfrac{OA}{OC} = \dfrac{AP}{CQ}$ [$\because$ corresponding sides of similar triangles are proportional]
13. **Hint** In ΔAPR and ΔABD,

    $\angle APR = \angle ABD$ [corresponding angles]

    $\angle ARP = \angle ADB$ [corresponding angles]

    $\therefore$ $\Delta APR \sim \Delta ABD$ [by AA similarity criterion]

    $\dfrac{PR}{BD} = \dfrac{AR}{AD}$ ...(i)

    Similarly, we can prove

    $\dfrac{AR}{AD} = \dfrac{RQ}{DC}$ ...(ii)

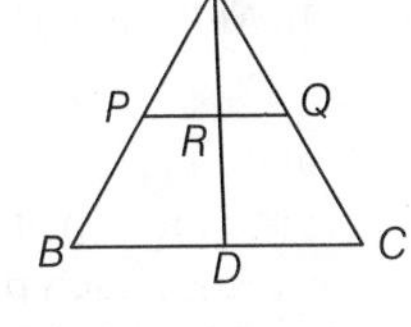

    From Eqs. (i) and (ii), we get

    $\dfrac{PR}{BD} = \dfrac{RQ}{DC}$

    $\Rightarrow$ $PR = RQ$

    [$\because AD$ is median]

    So, median AD bisects PQ.
14. **Hint** As, F and E are mid-points of AB and AC, respectively.

    $\therefore$ $FE \parallel BC$ [by mid-point theorem]

    $\Rightarrow$ $\angle AFE = \angle B$ [corresponding angles]

    Then, ΔAFE and ΔABC similar. [by AA similarity]

    Similarly, $\Delta FBD \sim \Delta ABC$, $\Delta EDC \sim \Delta ABC$.

    Now, we shall show that

    $\Delta DEF \sim \Delta ABC$

    Clearly, $ED \parallel AF$ and $DF \parallel EA$.

    $\therefore AFDE$ is a parallelogram.

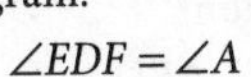

    $\angle EDF = \angle A$

    [$\because$ opposite angles of a parallelogram are equal]

    Similarly, $BDEF$ is a parallelogram

    $\angle DEF = \angle B$

    [$\because$ opposite angles of a parallelogram are equal]

Thus, in ΔABC and ΔDEF

$$\angle A = \angle EDF \text{ and } \angle B = \angle DEF$$

$\therefore$ $\Delta ABC \sim \Delta DEF$ [by AA similarity criterion]

15. Given in a trapezium $ABCD$, $AB || DC$ and its diagonals intersect at O.

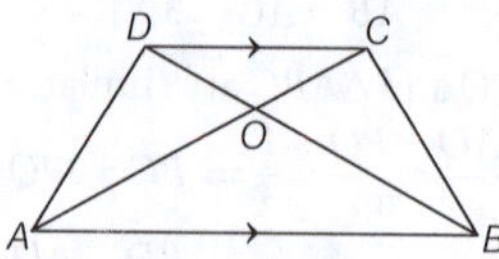

In ΔAOB and ΔCOD,

$\angle AOB = \angle COD$ [vertically opposite angles]

and $\angle OAB = \angle OCD$ [alternate angles]

$\therefore$ $\Delta AOB \sim \Delta COD$ [by AA similarity criterion]

$\Rightarrow$ $\dfrac{OA}{OC} = \dfrac{OB}{OD}$

[$\because$ corresponding sides of similar triangles are proportional]

16. Hint In ΔAPC and ΔBPD,

$\angle APC = \angle BPD$ [vertically opposite angles]

and $\angle PAC = \angle PBD$ [alternate angles]

$\therefore$ $\Delta APC \sim \Delta BPD$ [by AA similarity criterion]

$\Rightarrow$ $\dfrac{AP}{PB} = \dfrac{AC}{BD} = \dfrac{PC}{PD}$ ...(i)

[since, corresponding sides of similar triangles are proportional]

In ΔAPE and ΔBPF,

$\angle APE = \angle BPF$ [vertically opposite angles]

and $\angle PAE = \angle PBF$ [alternate angles]

$\therefore$ $\Delta APE \sim \Delta BPF$ [by AA similarity criterion]

$\Rightarrow$ $\dfrac{AP}{PB} = \dfrac{AE}{BF} = \dfrac{PE}{PF}$ ...(ii)

[since, corresponding sides of similar triangles are proportional]

In ΔPEC and ΔPFD,

$\angle EPC = \angle FPD$ [vertically opposite angles]

and $\angle PCE = \angle PDF$ [alternate angles]

$\therefore$ $\Delta PEC \sim \Delta PFD$ [by AA similarity criterion]

$\Rightarrow$ $\dfrac{PE}{PF} = \dfrac{PC}{PD} = \dfrac{EC}{FD}$ ...(iii)

[since corresponding sides of similar triangles are proportional]

From Eqs. (i), (ii) and (iii), we get

$$\frac{AP}{PB} = \frac{AC}{BD} = \frac{AE}{BF} = \frac{PE}{PF} = \frac{EC}{FD} = \frac{PC}{PD}$$

$\therefore$ $\dfrac{AE}{BF} = \dfrac{AC}{BD} = \dfrac{CE}{FD}$

17. In ΔEFC and ΔBDC, $\angle EFC = \angle BDC$ [90° each]

$\angle ECF = \angle BCD$ [common]

By AA similarity criterion,

$$\Delta EFC \sim \Delta BDC$$

$\Rightarrow$ $\dfrac{EF}{BD} = \dfrac{FC}{DC}$ ...(i)

[$\because$ corresponding sides of similar triangles are proportional]

Now, in ΔEFG and ΔDGA,

$\angle EGF = \angle DGA$ [vertically opposite angles]

$\angle EFG = \angle GDA$ [90° each]

By AA similarity criterion,

$$\Delta EFG \sim \Delta ADG$$

$\Rightarrow$ $\dfrac{EF}{AD} = \dfrac{FG}{DG}$

[$\because$ corresponding sides of similar triangles are proportional]

As, $AD = BD \Rightarrow \dfrac{EF}{BD} = \dfrac{FG}{DG}$ ...(ii)

From Eqs. (i) and (ii), $\dfrac{CF}{CD} = \dfrac{FG}{DG}$ **Hence proved.**

18. In ΔBMC and ΔEMD,

$\angle BMC = \angle EMD$ [vertically opposite angles]

$\Rightarrow$ $MC = DM$ [given]

$\angle BCM = \angle EDM$ [alternate angles]

$\therefore$ $\Delta BMC \cong \Delta EMD$ [by ASA congruency criteria]

$\Rightarrow$ $BC = DE$ [by CPCT] ...(i)

Now, $AE = AD + DE = BC + BC = 2BC$

[$\because AD = BC$ and and using Eq. (i)] ...(ii)

In ΔALE and ΔCLB,

$\angle LAE = \angle LCB$ [alternate angles]

and $\angle LEA = \angle LBC$ [alternate angles]

$\therefore$ $\Delta ALE \sim \Delta CLB$ [by AA similarity criterion]

$\Rightarrow$ $\dfrac{EL}{BL} = \dfrac{AE}{CB}$

[$\because$ corresponding sides of similar triangles are proportional]

$\Rightarrow$ $\dfrac{EL}{BL} = \dfrac{2BC}{BC}$ [from Eq. (ii)]

$\Rightarrow$ $\dfrac{EL}{BL} = 2 \Rightarrow EL = 2BL$ **Hence proved**

19. Hint Prove ΔDQP and ΔDBA are similar.

Then, $\dfrac{QP}{BA} = \dfrac{DQ}{DB} \Rightarrow \dfrac{z}{x} = \dfrac{DQ}{BD}$ ...(i)

Similar, $\dfrac{z}{y} = \dfrac{BQ}{BD}$ ...(ii)

On adding Eqs. (i) and (ii), we get

$$\frac{z}{x} + \frac{z}{y} = \frac{DQ}{BD} + \frac{BQ}{BD} = 1$$

$\Rightarrow$ $\dfrac{z}{x} + \dfrac{z}{y} = 1 \Rightarrow \dfrac{1}{x} + \dfrac{1}{y} = \dfrac{1}{z}$

20. Hint Do same as Question 19. **Ans.** $\dfrac{15}{4}$ m

21. Hint Do same as Example 9.

Ans. She is at 9 m from the base of the pole.

NCERT FOLDER

Complete Solutions of All Exercises of NCERT Textbook

EXERCISE 6.1

Q1. Fill in the blanks using the correct word given in brackets.

(i) All circles are .... (congruent, similar)

(ii) All squares are .... (similar, congruent)

(iii) All .... triangles are similar. (isosceles, equilateral)

(iv) Two polygons of the same number of sides are similar, if

(a) their corresponding angles are .... and

(b) their corresponding sides are .... (equal, proportional)

Sol. (i) All circles are similar because all circles have same shape but size can vary.

(ii) All squares are similar because all squares have same shape but size can vary.

(iii) All equilateral triangles are similar because all equilateral triangles have same shape but size can vary.

(iv) Two polygons of the same number of sides are similar, if

(a) their corresponding angles are equal and

(b) their corresponding sides are proportional.

Q2. Give two different examples of pair of

(i) similar figures. (ii) non-similar figures.

Sol. (i) (a) Pair of the equilateral triangles are similar figures.

(b) Pair of the squares are similar figures.

(ii) (a) A triangle and a quadrilateral form a pair of non-similar figures.

(b) A square and a circle form a pair of non-similar figures.

Q3. State whether the following quadrilaterals are similar or not.

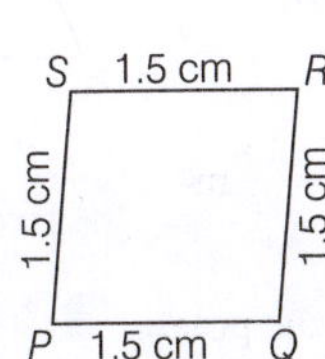

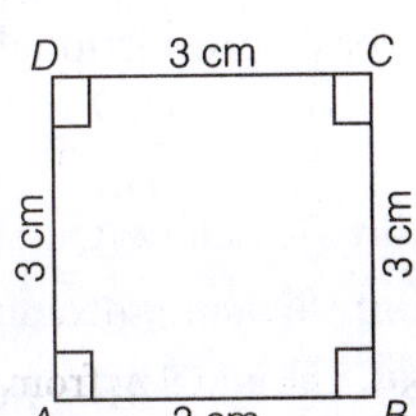

Sol. From the given two figures, we can see corresponding sides are in proportion but corresponding angles are different or unequal.

Therefore, they are not similar.

EXERCISE 6.2

Q1. In Fig. (i) and Fig. (ii), $DE \parallel BC$. Find EC in Fig. (i) and AD in Fig. (ii).

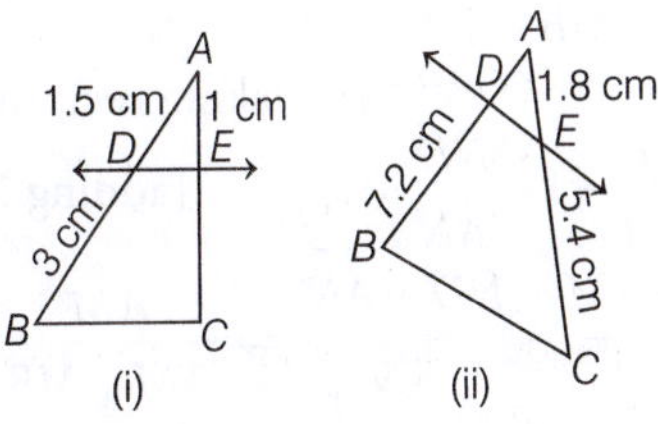

Sol. Do same as Example 12 of Topic 1.

Ans. (i) 2 cm (ii) 2.4 cm

Q2. E and F are points on the sides PQ and PR respectively of a ΔPQR. For each of the following cases, state whether $EF \parallel QR$.

(i) $PE = 3.9$ cm, $EQ = 3$ cm, $PF = 3.6$ cm and $FR = 2.4$ cm.

(ii) $PE = 4$ cm, $QE = 4.5$ cm, $PF = 8$ cm and $RF = 9$ cm.

(iii) $PQ = 1.28$ cm, $PR = 2.56$ cm, $PE = 0.18$ cm and $PF = 0.36$ cm.

First, find the values of $\frac{PF}{FR}$ and $\frac{PE}{EQ}$. If $\frac{PF}{FR} = \frac{PE}{EQ}$, then by converse of basic proportionality theorem, $EF \parallel QR$.

Sol. (i) Do same as Example 7 of Topic 1.

Ans. EF is not parallel to QR.

(ii) Do same as Example 7 of Topic 1.

Ans. $EF \parallel QR$

(iii) Do same as Example 6 of Topic 1.

Ans. $EF \parallel QR$

Q3. In the given figure, if $LM \parallel CB$ and $LN \parallel CD$, prove that $\frac{AM}{AB} = \frac{AN}{AD}$.

CBSE 2020, 2010 Sample Paper [Basic]

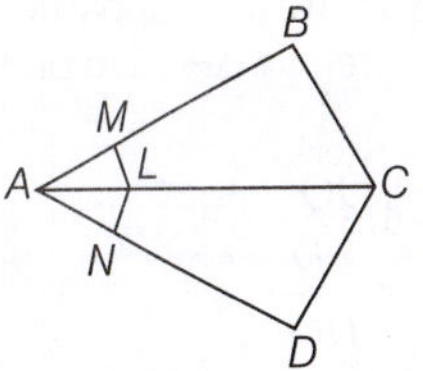

Use the basic proportionality theorem in both ΔACB and ΔACD.

Sol. In ΔACB, $LM \parallel CB$ [given]

$\Rightarrow \dfrac{AM}{MB} = \dfrac{AL}{LC}$ ...(i)

[by basic proportionality theorem]

In ΔACD, $LN \parallel CD$ [given]

$\Rightarrow \dfrac{AN}{ND} = \dfrac{AL}{LC}$ ...(ii)

[by basic proportionality theorem]

From Eqs. (i) and (ii), we get

$$\frac{AM}{MB} = \frac{AN}{ND} \Rightarrow \frac{MB}{AM} = \frac{ND}{AN}$$

[on taking reciprocal of the terms]

$\Rightarrow \dfrac{MB}{AM} + 1 = \dfrac{ND}{AN} + 1$ [adding 1 on both sides]

$\Rightarrow \dfrac{MB + AM}{AM} = \dfrac{ND + AN}{AN} \Rightarrow \dfrac{AM}{AM + MB} = \dfrac{AN}{AN + ND}$

[on taking reciprocal of the terms]

$\therefore \dfrac{AM}{AB} = \dfrac{AN}{AD}$ $\left[\begin{array}{l}\because AD = AN + ND \\ \text{and } AB = AM + MB\end{array}\right]$

Hence proved.

Q4. **In the given figure, if $DE \parallel AC$ and $DF \parallel AE$, prove that $\dfrac{BF}{FE} = \dfrac{BE}{EC}$.** CBSE 2020 Standard, CBSE 2015, 12, 11

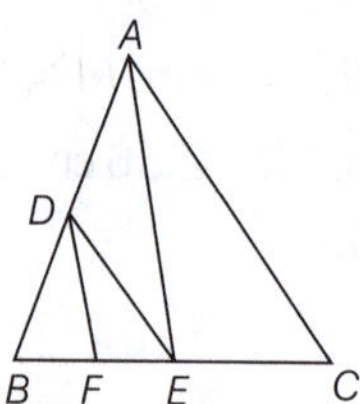

Sol. Do same as Example 8 of Topic 1.

Q5. **In the given figure, $DE \parallel OQ$ and $DF \parallel OR$. Show that $EF \parallel QR$.** CBSE 2012, 10

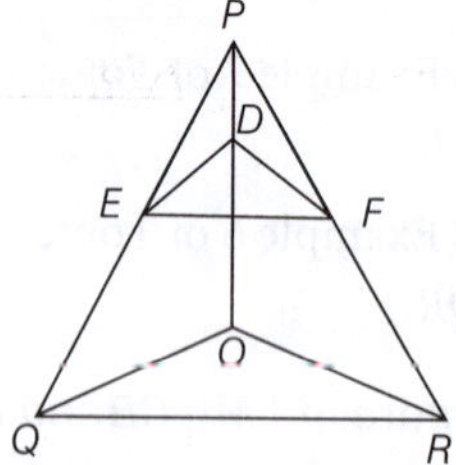

First, use the basic proportionality theorem in ΔPOQ and ΔPOR and equate them, then apply converse of basic proportionality theorem in ΔPQR to prove required result.

Sol. In ΔPOQ, $DE \parallel OQ$ [given]

$\therefore \dfrac{PE}{EQ} = \dfrac{PD}{DO}$ ...(i)

[by basic proportionality theorem]

In ΔPOR, $DF \parallel OR$ [given]

$\therefore \dfrac{PF}{FR} = \dfrac{PD}{DO}$ ...(ii)

[by basic proportionality theorem]

From Eqs. (i) and (ii), we get

$$\frac{PE}{EQ} = \frac{PF}{FR}$$

In ΔPQR, we have

$$\frac{PE}{EQ} = \frac{PF}{FR}$$

$\therefore EF \parallel QR$

[by converse of basic proportionality theorem]

Hence proved.

Q6. **In the given figure, A, B and C are points on OP, OQ and OR respectively such that $AB \parallel PQ$ and $AC \parallel PR$. Show that $BC \parallel QR$.**

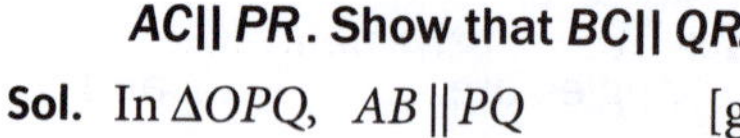

Sol. In ΔOPQ, $AB \parallel PQ$ [given]

$\therefore \dfrac{OA}{AP} = \dfrac{OB}{BQ}$ ...(i)

[by basic proportionality theorem]

Also, in ΔOPR,

$AC \parallel PR$ [given]

$\therefore \dfrac{OA}{AP} = \dfrac{OC}{CR}$ ...(ii)

From Eqs. (i) and (ii), $\dfrac{OB}{BQ} = \dfrac{OC}{CR}$

$\Rightarrow BC \parallel QR$

[by converse of basic proportionality theorem]

Hence proved.

Q7. **Using theorem (Thales theorem), prove that a line drawn through the mid-point of one side of a triangle parallel to another side, bisects the third side. (Recall that you have proved it in Class IX.)**

Sol. Consider ΔABC, in which D is the mid-point of AB.

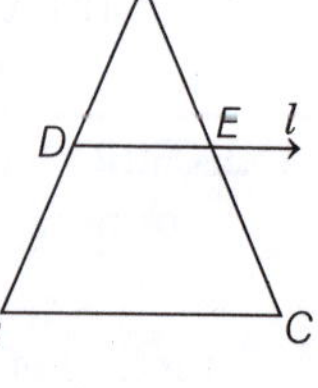

Then, $\dfrac{AD}{DB} = 1$ ...(i)

Line l is drawn through D such that $l \parallel BC$ and it meets AC at E.

By basic proportionality theorem,

$$\frac{AD}{DB} = \frac{AE}{EC}$$

$\Rightarrow \dfrac{AE}{EC} = 1$ [from Eq. (i)]

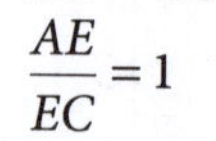

$\Rightarrow AE = EC$

So, E is the mid-point of AC.

Hence, a line drawn through the mid-point of one side of a triangle parallel to another side, bisects the third side.

Hence proved.

Q 8. Using theorem (converse of basic proportionality theorem), prove that the line joining the mid-points of any two sides of a triangle, is parallel to the third side. (Recall that you have done it in Class IX.)

Sol. Consider ΔABC, in which D and E are the mid-points of sides AB and AC, respectively.

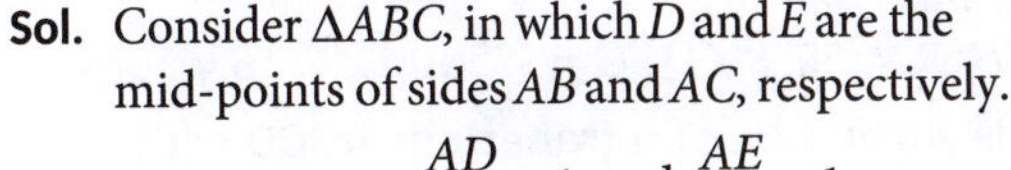

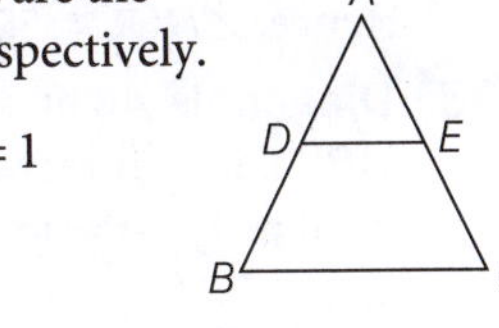

$\because \quad \frac{AD}{DB} = 1$ and $\frac{AE}{EC} = 1$

$\Rightarrow \quad \frac{AD}{DB} = \frac{AE}{EC}$

$\therefore \quad DE \parallel BC$

[by converse of basic proportionality theorem]

Hence, the line joining the mid-points of any two sides of a triangle, is parallel to the third side. **Hence proved.**

Q 9. *ABCD* is a trapezium, in which *AB* || *DC* and its diagonals intersect each other at the point *O*. Show that $\frac{AO}{BO} = \frac{CO}{DO}$. CBSE 2023, 15

Sol. Do same as Question 15 of Try these 6.2 of Topic 2.

Q 10. The diagonals of a quadrilateral *ABCD* intersect each other at the point *O*, such that $\frac{AO}{BO} = \frac{CO}{DO}$. Show that *ABCD* is a trapezium.

Sol. Given $ABCD$ is a quadrilateral. Its diagonals AC and BD intersect each other at O such that

$$\frac{AO}{BO} = \frac{CO}{DO} \Rightarrow \frac{AO}{CO} = \frac{BO}{DO} \quad \ldots(i)$$

To prove $ABCD$ is a trapezium.

Construction Through O, we draw $OE \parallel BA$.

Let OE meets AD at E.

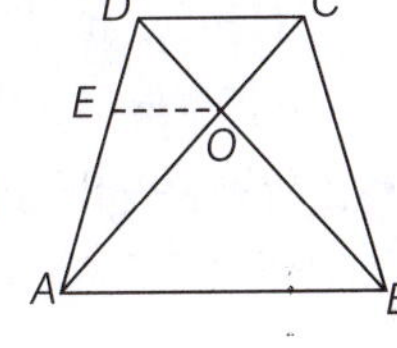

In ΔDAB, $\quad EO \parallel AB$

[by construction]

$\Rightarrow \quad \frac{DE}{EA} = \frac{DO}{BO}$

[by basic proportionality theorem]

or $\quad \frac{AE}{ED} = \frac{BO}{DO}$

[on taking reciprocal of the terms] ...(ii)

From Eqs. (i) and (ii), we get

$$\frac{AO}{CO} = \frac{AE}{ED} \Rightarrow OE \parallel DC$$

[by converse of basic proportionality theorem]

Now, $\quad BA \parallel OE$ and $OE \parallel CD$

$\therefore \quad AB \parallel DC$

[since lines parallel to the same line are also parallel to each other]

Hence, quadrilateral $ABCD$ is a trapezium. **Hence proved.**

EXERCISE 6.3

Q 1. State which pair of triangles in given figures, are similar? Write the similarity criterion used by you for answering the question and also write the pair of similar triangles in the symbolic form.

(i)

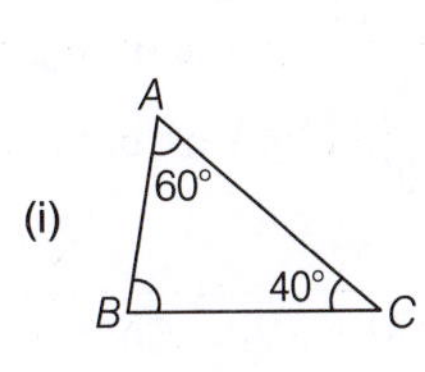

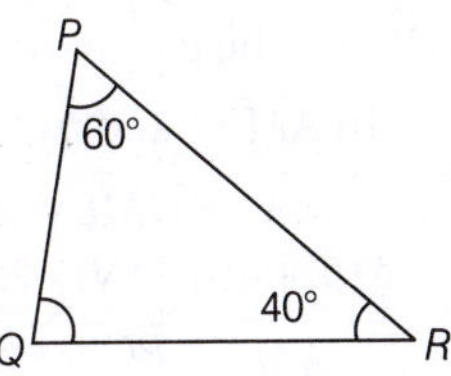

(ii)

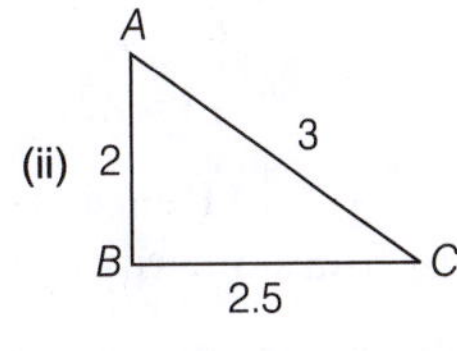

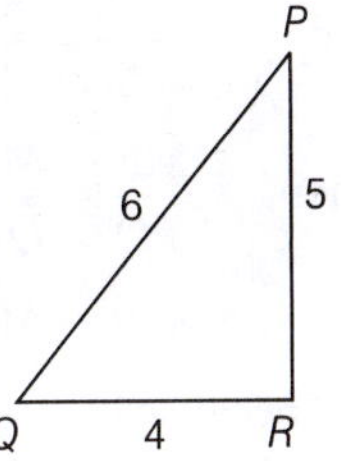

(iii)

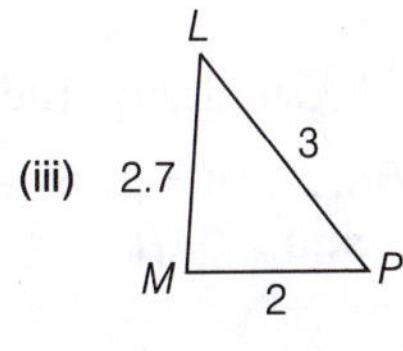

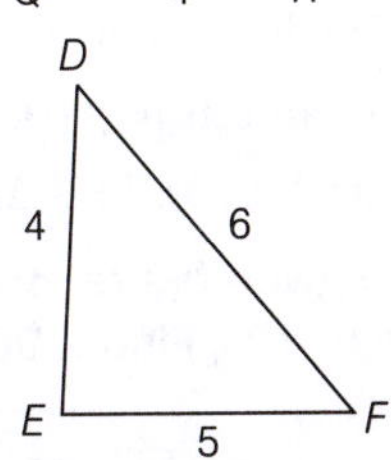

(iv)

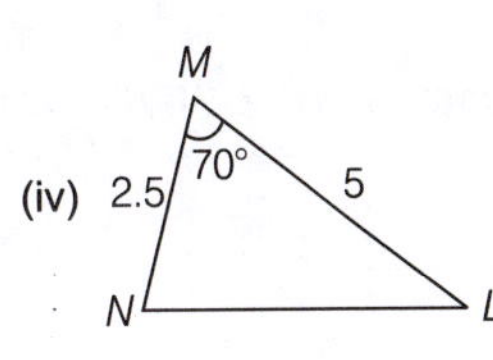

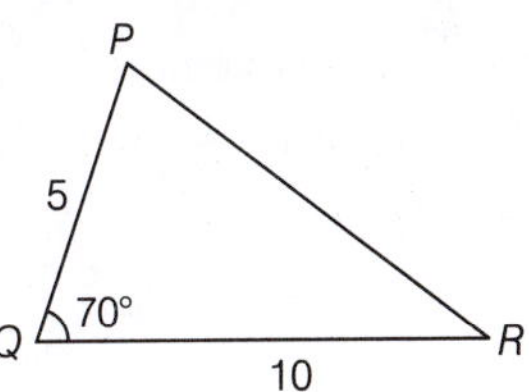

(v)

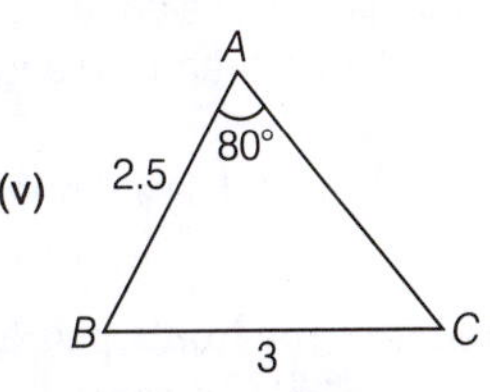

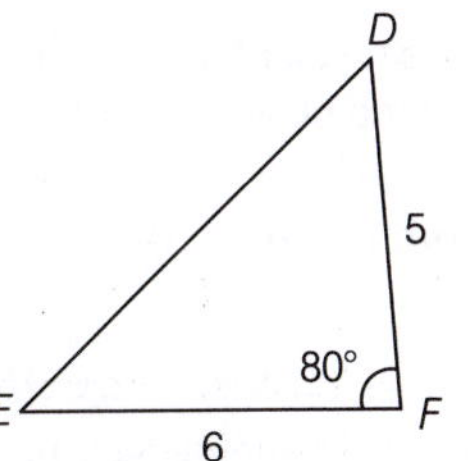

(vi)

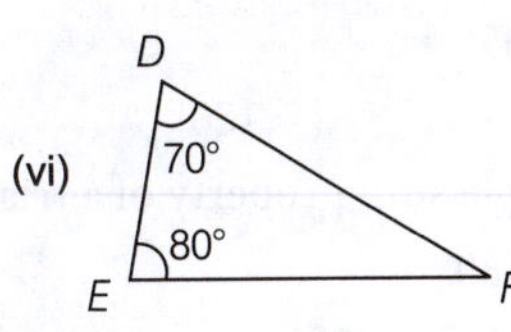

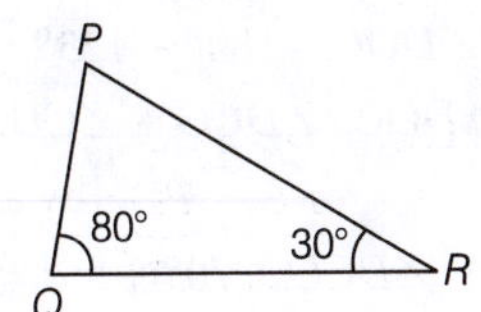

Sol. (i) Yes; The pair of triangles is similar.

In ΔABC and ΔPQR,

$$\angle A = \angle P = 60^\circ \text{ and } \angle C = \angle R = 40^\circ \quad \text{[given]}$$

Then, $\angle B = \angle Q = 180^\circ - 60^\circ - 40^\circ = 80^\circ$

$\therefore$ $\Delta ABC \sim \Delta PQR$ [by AAA similarity criterion]

(ii) Do same as Example 1 of Topic 2.

Ans. Yes, $\Delta ABC \sim \Delta QRP$ [by SSS similarity criterion]

(iii) Do same as Example 1 of Topic 2.

Ans. No, the two triangles are not similar.

(iv) Yes, the pair of triangles is similar.

In ΔMNL and ΔQPR,

$$\angle NML = \angle PQR = 70^\circ,$$

$$\frac{MN}{PQ} = \frac{2.5}{5} = \frac{1}{2}$$

and $$\frac{ML}{QR} = \frac{5}{10} = \frac{1}{2}$$

Then, $$\frac{MN}{PQ} = \frac{ML}{QR}$$

$\therefore$ $\Delta MNL \sim \Delta QPR$ [by SAS similarity criterion]

(v) No, because in ΔABC, $\angle BAC$ is given but the measure of included side AC is not given.

(vi) Do same as part (i).

Ans. Yes, $\Delta DEF \sim \Delta PQR$ [by AAA similarity criterion]

Q2. In the given figure, $\Delta ODC \sim \Delta OBA$, $\angle BOC = 125^\circ$ and $\angle CDO = 70^\circ$. Find $\angle DOC$, $\angle DCO$ and $\angle OAB$.

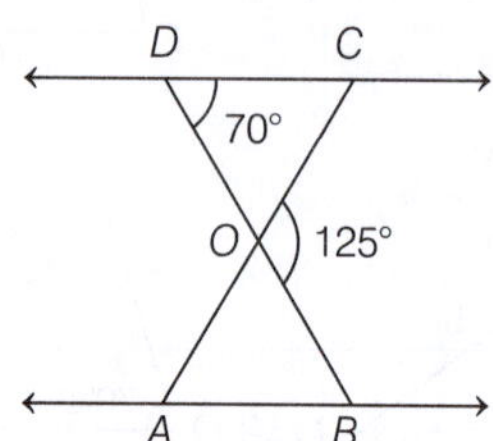

Use the result of angle sum property of a triangle and also use the criteria of similarity of triangles, to find the required angles.

Sol. From the given figure, it is clear that DOB is a straight line.

$\therefore$ $\angle DOC + \angle COB = 180^\circ$ [by linear pair axiom]

$\Rightarrow$ $\angle DOC + 125^\circ = 180^\circ$ [given, $\angle COB = 125^\circ$]

$\Rightarrow \angle DOC = 180^\circ - 125^\circ = 55^\circ$

In ΔDOC, $\angle DCO + \angle CDO + \angle DOC = 180^\circ$

[by angle sum property of a triangle]

$\Rightarrow$ $\angle DCO + 70^\circ + 55^\circ = 180^\circ$

[$\because \angle CDO = 70^\circ$ and $\angle DOC = 55^\circ$]

$\Rightarrow$ $\angle DCO + 125^\circ = 180^\circ$

$\Rightarrow \angle DCO = 180^\circ - 125^\circ = 55^\circ$ ...(i)

Also, $\Delta ODC \sim \Delta OBA$ [given]

$\Rightarrow$ $\angle OAB = \angle OCD = \angle DCO$

$\Rightarrow$ $\angle OAB = 55^\circ$ [from Eq. (i)]

Hence, $\angle DOC = 55^\circ$, $\angle DCO = 55^\circ$ and $\angle OAB = 55^\circ$

Q3. Diagonals AC and BD of a trapezium $ABCD$ with $AB \parallel DC$ intersect each other at the point O. Using a similarity criterion for two triangles, show that $\frac{OA}{OC} = \frac{OB}{OD}$.

Or **Prove that diagonals of a trapezium divide each other in the same ratio.**

Sol. Construct a trapezium $ABCD$ such that $AB \parallel DC$ and draw its diagonals AC and BD which intersect at point O.

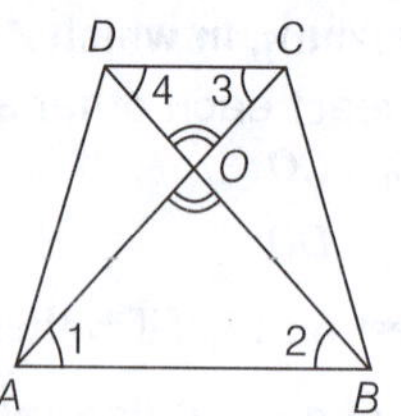

In ΔOCD and ΔOAB, $AB \parallel DC$ [given]

$\therefore$ $\angle 1 = \angle 3$, $\angle 2 = \angle 4$ [alternate interior angles]

Also, $\angle DOC = \angle BOA$ [vertically opposite angles]

$\therefore$ $\Delta OCD \sim \Delta OAB$ [by AAA similarity criterion]

$\Rightarrow$ $\frac{OC}{OA} = \frac{OD}{OB}$ [since ratios of the corresponding sides of the similar triangles are equal]

$\therefore$ $\frac{OA}{OC} = \frac{OB}{OD}$ [on taking reciprocal of the terms]

Hence, the diagonals of a trapezium divide each other in the same ratio. **Hence proved.**

Q4. In the given figure,

$$\frac{QR}{QS} = \frac{QT}{PR} \text{ and } \angle 1 = \angle 2.$$

Show that $\Delta PQS \sim \Delta TQR$. CBSE 2023 (Basic), 2010

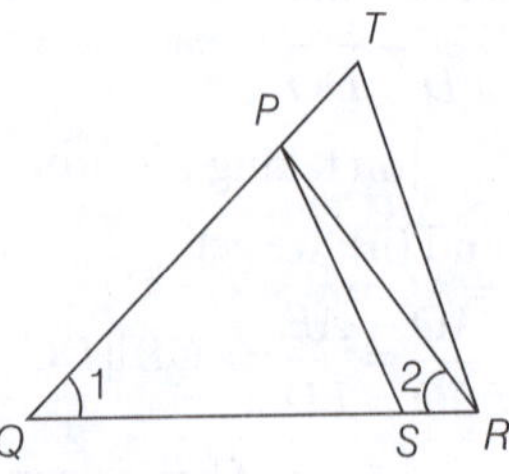

Sol. In ΔPQR, $\angle 1 = \angle 2$ [given]

$\Rightarrow$ $PR = PQ$

[since sides opposite to equal angles of a triangle are also equal]

Given that $\frac{QR}{QS} = \frac{QT}{PR} \Rightarrow \frac{QR}{QS} = \frac{QT}{PQ}$

[$\because PQ = PR$, proved above]

$\Rightarrow \quad \frac{QS}{QR} = \frac{PQ}{QT}$

[on taking reciprocal of the terms] ...(i)

In ΔPQS and ΔTQR, we have

$\angle PQS = \angle TQR$ [common]

and $\frac{QS}{QR} = \frac{QP}{QT}$ [from Eq. (i)]

$\therefore \quad \Delta PQS \sim \Delta TQR$ [by SAS similarity criterion]

Hence proved.

Q5. S and T are points on sides PR and QR of ΔPQR, such that $\angle P = \angle RTS$. Show that $\Delta RPQ \sim \Delta RTS$.

Sol. Draw ΔPQR, such that S and T are points on sides PR and QR, respectively. We join the points S and T.

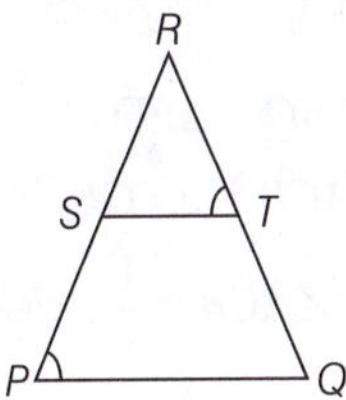

From the above figure, we have ΔRPQ and ΔRTS in which

$\angle RPQ = \angle RTS$ [given]

$\Rightarrow \quad \angle PRQ = \angle TRS$ [common angle]

$\therefore \quad \Delta RPQ \sim \Delta RTS$ [by AA similarity criterion]

Hence proved.

Q6. In the given figure, if $\Delta ABE \cong \Delta ACD$, show that $\Delta ADE \sim \Delta ABC$.

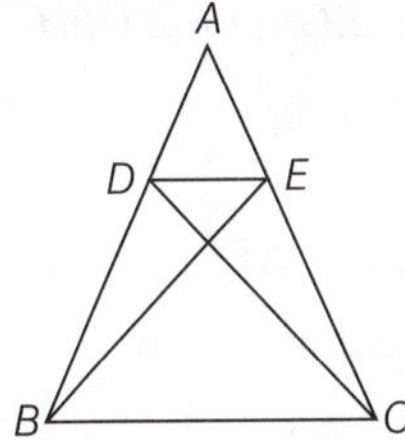

(i) Two triangles are congruent, if their corresponding angles and sides are equal.
(ii) Two triangles are similar, if their corresponding angles are equal and their corresponding sides are in the the same ratio.

Sol. Given, $\Delta ABE \cong \Delta ACD$

$\Rightarrow \quad AB = AC$ and $AE = AD$ [by CPCT]

$\Rightarrow \quad \frac{AB}{AC} = 1$

and $\frac{AD}{AE} = 1$

$\Rightarrow \quad \frac{AB}{AC} = \frac{AD}{AE}$ ...(i)

In ΔADE and ΔABC, we have

$\frac{AD}{AE} = \frac{AB}{AC}$ [from Eq. (i)]

$\Rightarrow \quad \frac{AD}{AB} = \frac{AE}{AC}$

and $\angle DAE = \angle BAC$ [common angle]

$\therefore \quad \Delta ADE \sim \Delta ABC$ [by SAS similarity criterion]

Hence proved.

Q7. In the given figure, altitudes AD and CE of ΔABC intersect each other at the point P.

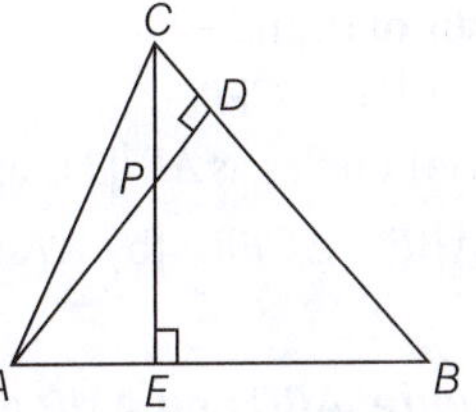

Show that

(i) $\Delta AEP \sim \Delta CDP$ (ii) $\Delta ABD \sim \Delta CBE$
(iii) $\Delta AEP \sim \Delta ADB$ (iv) $\Delta PDC \sim \Delta BEC$

Use AAA similarity criterion to prove the result.

Sol. Given, AD and CE are altitudes which intersect each other at the point P.

(i) In ΔAEP and ΔCDP,

$\angle AEP = \angle CDP$ [each 90°]

and $\angle APE = \angle CPD$ [vertically opposite angles]

$\therefore \quad \Delta AEP \sim \Delta CDP$ [by AA similarity criterion]

(ii) In ΔABD and ΔCBE,

$\angle ADB = \angle CEB$ [each 90°]

and $\angle ABD = \angle CBE$ [common angle]

$\therefore \quad \Delta ABD \sim \Delta CBE$ [by AA similarity criterion]

(iii) In ΔAEP and ΔADB,

$\angle AEP = \angle ADB$ [each 90°]

and $\angle PAE = \angle BAD$ [common angle]

$\therefore \quad \Delta AEP \sim \Delta ADB$ [by AA similarity criterion]

(iv) In ΔPDC and ΔBEC,

$\angle PDC = \angle BEC$ [each 90°]

and $\angle PCD = \angle BCE$ [common angle]

$\therefore \quad \Delta PDC \sim \Delta BEC$ [by AA similarity criterion]

Q8. E is a point on the side AD produced of a parallelogram ABCD and BE intersects CD at F. Show that $\Delta ABE \sim \Delta CFB$. CBSE 2023 (Basic)

In a parallelogram, opposite angles are equal to each other. Find the relation between angles of both triangles to show them similar.

Sol. Draw a parallelogram $ABCD$ and produce the line AD to E and join BE.

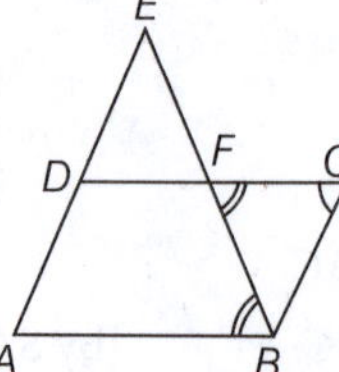

In parallelogram $ABCD$, $\angle A = \angle C$ ...(i)

[since opposite angles of a parallelogram are equal]

In ΔABE and ΔCFB,

$\angle EAB = \angle BCF$ [from Eq. (i)]

and $\angle ABE = \angle CFB$

[alternate interior angles as $AB \parallel FC$ and BE is transversal]

$\therefore$ $\Delta ABE \sim \Delta CFB$ [by AA similarity criterion]

Hence proved.

Q 9. In the given figure, ABC and AMP are two right angled triangles, right angled at B and M, respectively. Prove that

(i) $\Delta ABC \sim \Delta AMP$ (ii) $\dfrac{CA}{PA} = \dfrac{BC}{MP}$.

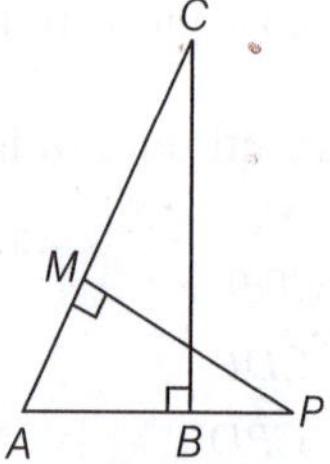

Sol. Do same as Example 5 of Topic 2

Q 10. CD and GH are respectively the bisectors of $\angle ACB$ and $\angle EGF$ such that D and H lie on sides AB and FE of ΔABC and ΔEFG, respectively. If $\Delta ABC \sim \Delta FEG$, show that

(i) $\dfrac{CD}{GH} = \dfrac{AC}{FG}$

(ii) $\Delta DCB \sim \Delta HGE$

(iii) $\Delta DCA \sim \Delta HGF$

Sol. Draw ΔABC and ΔFEG and then draw bisectors CD and GH of $\angle ACB$ and $\angle EGF$ such that D lies on AB and H lies on FE.

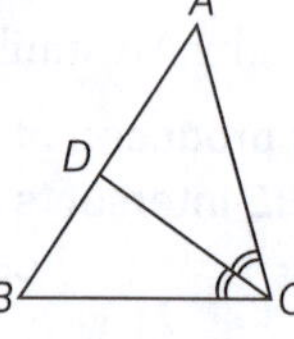

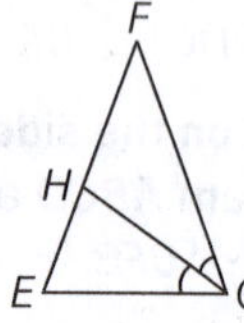

(i) Given, $\Delta ABC \sim \Delta FEG$

So, all corresponding angles are equal.

$\therefore$ $\angle CAB = \angle GFE$

or $\angle CAD = \angle GFH$ ...(i)

and $\angle ACB = \angle FGE$

$\Rightarrow$ $\dfrac{1}{2}\angle ACB = \dfrac{1}{2}\angle FGE$ [dividing both sides by 2]

$\Rightarrow$ $\angle ACD = \angle FGH$ ...(ii)

From Eqs. (i) and (ii),

$\Delta ACD \sim \Delta FGH$ [by AA similarity criterion]

$\therefore$ $\dfrac{CD}{GH} = \dfrac{AC}{FG}$

[since corresponding sides of two similar triangles are proportional]

(ii) In ΔDCB and ΔHGE,

$\angle DBC = \angle HEG$ ...(iii)

$\left[\begin{array}{l} \because \ \Delta ABC \sim \Delta FEG \\ \therefore \ \angle ABC = \angle FEG \Rightarrow \angle DBC = \angle HEG \end{array}\right]$

and $\angle DCB = \angle HGE$ ...(iv)

$\left[\begin{array}{l} \because \ \Delta ABC \sim \Delta FEG \\ \therefore \ \angle ACB = \angle FGE \\ \Rightarrow \dfrac{1}{2}\angle ACB = \dfrac{1}{2}\angle FGE \Rightarrow \angle DCB = \angle HGE \end{array}\right]$

From Eqs. (iii) and (iv),

$\Delta DCB \sim \Delta HGE$ [by AA similarity criterion]

(iii) In ΔDCA and ΔHGF,

$\angle DAC = \angle HFG$ ...(v)

$\left[\begin{array}{l} \because \ \Delta ABC \sim \Delta FEG \\ \therefore \ \angle CAB = \angle GFE \\ \Rightarrow \angle CAD = \angle GFH \text{ or } \angle DAC = \angle HFG \end{array}\right]$

and $\angle DCA = \angle HGF$ ...(vi)

$\left[\begin{array}{l} \because \Delta ABC \sim \Delta FEG \\ \therefore \ \angle ACB = \angle FGE \\ \Rightarrow \dfrac{1}{2}\angle ACB = \dfrac{1}{2}\angle FGE \Rightarrow \angle DCA = \angle HGF \end{array}\right]$

From Eqs. (v) and (vi),

$\Delta DCA \sim \Delta HGF$ [by AA similarity criterion]

Hence proved.

Q 11. In the given figure, E is a point on side CB produced of an isosceles ΔABC with $AB = AC$. If $AD \perp BC$ and $EF \perp AC$, prove that $\Delta ABD \sim \Delta ECF$.

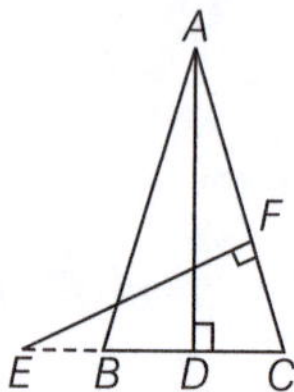

Sol. Given, ΔABC is an isosceles triangle with $AB = AC$. Also, we have $AD \perp BC$ and $EF \perp AC$.

To prove $\Delta ABD \sim \Delta ECF$

Proof In ΔABC, $AB = AC$

$\therefore \quad \angle B = \angle C$

[$\because$ angle opposite to equal sides are equal]

Now, consider ΔABD and ΔECF. In this we have

$\angle ABD = \angle ECF$ [$\because \angle B = \angle C$ proved above]

and $\angle ADB = \angle EFC$ [each 90°]

$\therefore \quad \Delta ABD \sim \Delta ECF$ [by AA similary criterion]

Hence proved.

Q 12. Sides *AB* and *BC* and median *AD* of ΔABC are respectively proportional to sides *PQ* and *QR* and median *PM* of ΔPQR. Show that $\Delta ABC \sim \Delta PQR$.

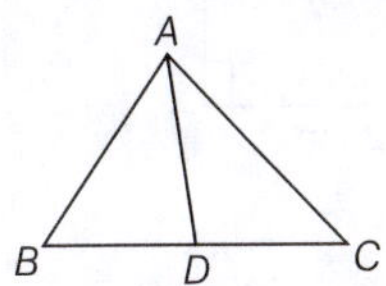

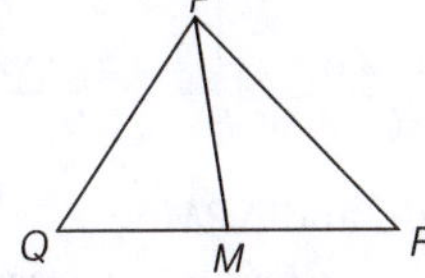

Use the result that median bisects the opposite sides, to show that the sides of ΔADB and ΔPMQ are proportional and then use the criterion of similar triangles to show $\Delta ABC \sim \Delta PQR$.

Sol. Given, ΔABC and ΔPQR in which AD and PM are their medians, respectively.

So, $\dfrac{AB}{PQ} = \dfrac{BC}{QR} = \dfrac{AD}{PM}$.

To prove $\Delta ABC \sim \Delta PQR$

Proof We have, $\dfrac{AB}{PQ} = \dfrac{BC}{QR} = \dfrac{AD}{PM}$ [given]

$\Rightarrow \quad \dfrac{AB}{PQ} = \dfrac{1/2BC}{1/2QR} = \dfrac{AD}{PM}$

[multiplying numerator and denominator of middle term by 1/2]

$\Rightarrow \quad \dfrac{AB}{PQ} = \dfrac{BD}{QM} = \dfrac{AD}{PM}$

[$\because$ medians AD and PM bisect the lines BC and QR, respectively, i.e. $BD = 1/2BC$ and $QM = 1/2QR$]

$\Rightarrow \quad \Delta ADB \sim \Delta PMQ$ [by SSS similarity criterion]

$\therefore \quad \angle B = \angle Q$ ...(i)

[$\because$ corresponding angles of similar triangles are equal]

In ΔABC and ΔPQR,

$\dfrac{AB}{PQ} = \dfrac{BC}{QR}$ [given]

and $\angle B = \angle Q$ [from Eq. (i)]

$\therefore \quad \Delta ABC \sim \Delta PQR$ [by SAS similarity criterion]

Hence proved.

Q 13. *D* is a point on the side *BC* of ΔABC such that $\angle ADC = \angle BAC$. Show that

$$CA^2 = CB \times CD.$$

Sol. Draw ΔABC such that D is a point on BC and join AD.

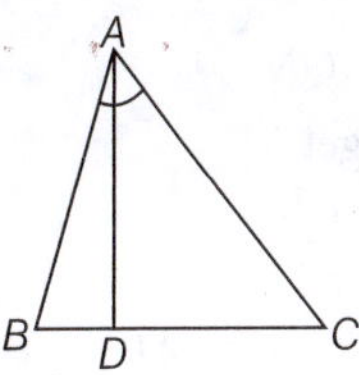

In ΔABC and ΔDAC, we have

$\angle BAC = \angle ADC$ [given]

and $\angle ACB = \angle DCA$ [common angle]

$\therefore \quad \Delta ABC \sim \Delta DAC$ [by AA similarity criterion]

$\Rightarrow \quad \dfrac{AC}{DC} = \dfrac{CB}{CA}$

[$\because$ corresponding sides of two similar triangles are proportional]

or $\quad \dfrac{CA}{CD} = \dfrac{CB}{CA}$

$\Rightarrow \quad CA \times CA = CB \times CD$

$\Rightarrow \quad CA^2 = CB \times CD$ **Hence proved.**

Q 14. Sides *AB* and *AC* and median *AD* of ΔABC are respectively proportional to sides *PQ* and *PR* and median *PM* of another ΔPQR. Show that $\Delta ABC \sim \Delta PQR$.

Sol. Given, in ΔABC and ΔPQR, AD and PM are their medians, respectively.

$\therefore \quad \dfrac{AB}{PQ} = \dfrac{AC}{PR} = \dfrac{AD}{PM}$ ...(i)

To prove $\Delta ABC \sim \Delta PQR$

Construction Produce AD to E such that $AD = DE$ and produce PM to N such that $PM = MN$.

Join BE, CE, QN and RN.

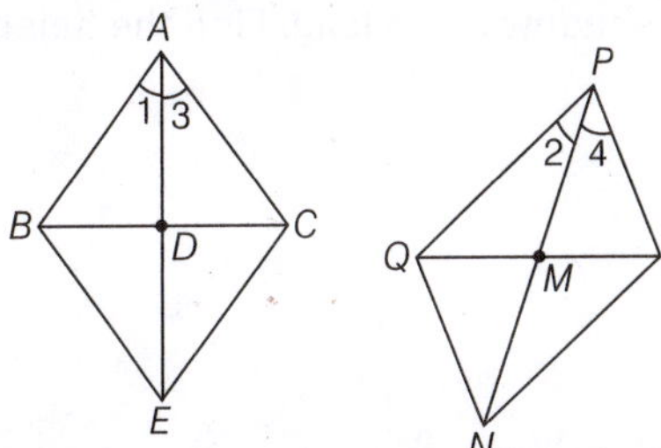

In above figures, quadrilaterals $ABEC$ and $PQNR$ are parallelograms because their diagonals bisect each other at D and M, respectively.

$\therefore \quad BE = AC$ and $QN = PR$

$\Rightarrow \quad \dfrac{BE}{AC} = 1$ and $\dfrac{QN}{PR} = 1$

$$\Rightarrow \quad \frac{BE}{AC} = \frac{QN}{PR} \text{ or } \frac{BE}{QN} = \frac{AC}{PR}$$

$$\Rightarrow \quad \frac{BE}{QN} = \frac{AB}{PQ} \quad \text{[from Eq. (i)]}$$

$$\text{or} \quad \frac{AB}{PQ} = \frac{BE}{QN} \quad \ldots\text{(ii)}$$

From Eq. (i), we get

$$\frac{AB}{PQ} = \frac{AD}{PM}$$

$$= \frac{2AD}{2PM} = \frac{AE}{PN}$$

[$\because$ diagonals bisect each other]

$$\Rightarrow \quad \frac{AB}{PQ} = \frac{AE}{PN} \quad \ldots\text{(iii)}$$

From Eqs. (ii) and (iii), we get

$$\frac{AB}{PQ} = \frac{BE}{QN} = \frac{AE}{PN}$$

$\Rightarrow \quad \Delta ABE \sim \Delta PQN$ [by *SSS* similarity criterion]

$\Rightarrow \quad \angle 1 = \angle 2$ ...(iv)

[$\because$ corresponding angles of two similar triangles are equal]

Similarly, we can prove that

$\Delta ACE \sim \Delta PRN$

$\Rightarrow \quad \angle 3 = \angle 4$ ...(v)

On adding Eqs. (iv) and (v), we get

$\angle 1 + \angle 3 = \angle 2 + \angle 4$

$\Rightarrow \quad \angle BAC = \angle QPR$

and $\quad \frac{AB}{PQ} = \frac{AC}{PR}$ [from Eq. (i)]

$\therefore \quad \Delta ABC \sim \Delta PQR$ [by *SAS* similarity criterion]

Hence proved.

Q 15. A vertical pole of length 6 m casts a shadow 4 m long on the ground and at the same time a tower casts a shadow 28 m long. Find the height of the tower.

Here, pole and tower both are perpendicular to the ground and they cast shadow at the same time, so sun makes equal angle with ground for both the triangles. Now, use the property of similar triangles and find the height of tower.

Sol. Let AB be a pole of length 6 m, BC = 4 m be the length of its shadow and θ be the angle which sun makes with ground. Also, at the same time, another tower casts shadow NM of length 28 m. Let $PM = h$ m be the height of the tower and θ be the angle which sun ray makes with ground.

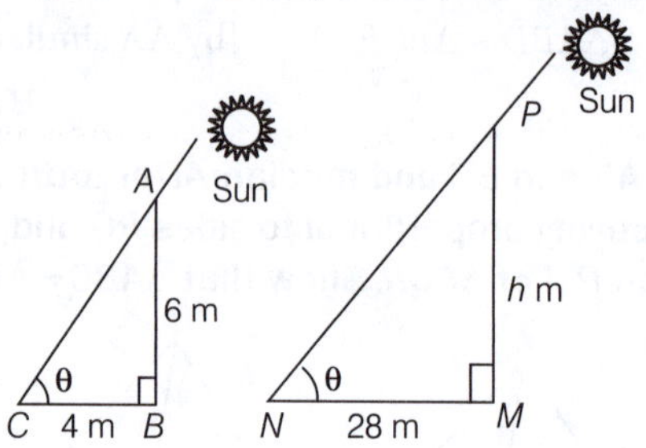

In ΔABC and ΔPMN,

$\angle ABC = \angle PMN$ [each 90°]

and $\quad \angle ACB = \angle PNM$ [each θ]

$\therefore \quad \Delta ABC \sim \Delta PMN$ [by AA similarity criterion]

Now, $\quad \frac{AB}{PM} = \frac{BC}{MN}$

$$\Rightarrow \quad \frac{AB}{BC} = \frac{PM}{MN}$$

$$\Rightarrow \quad \frac{6}{4} = \frac{h}{28}$$

[$\because AB = 6\text{m}, BC = 4\text{m and } MN = 28\text{m}$]

$$\Rightarrow \quad h = \frac{6 \times 28}{4} = 42 \text{ m}$$

Hence, the height of the tower is 42 m.

Q 16. If AD and PM are medians of ΔABC and ΔPQR respectively, where $\Delta ABC \sim \Delta PQR$, then prove that $\frac{AB}{PQ} = \frac{AD}{PM}$.

Sol. Do same as Example 8 of Topic 2.

REVIEW EXERCISE

Including Competency Based Questions

Part I

Multiple Choice Questions

1. If in the given figure, $DE \parallel BC$. If $AD = 2.8$ cm, $DB = 2.1$ cm and $EC = 4.8$ cm, then the value of x is **CBSE 2024 (Basic)**

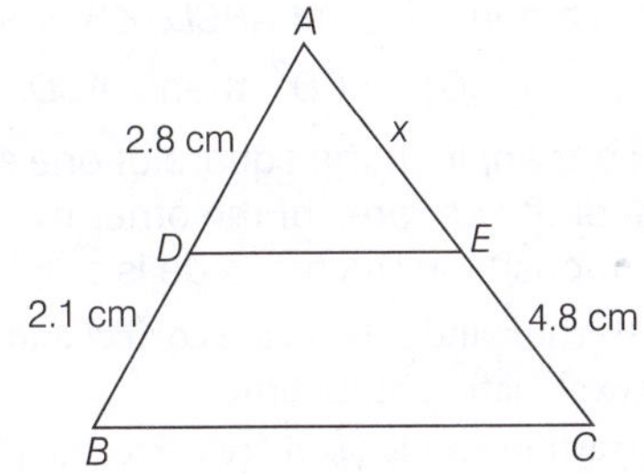

(a) 3.6 cm (b) 2.4 cm
(c) 6.4 cm (d) 4.8 cm

2. $\Delta ABC \sim \Delta DEF$ and their perimeters are 32 cm and 24 cm, respectively. If $AB = 10$ cm, then DE equals **CBSE 2023 (Basic)**

(a) 8 cm (b) 7.5 cm
(c) 15 cm (d) $5\sqrt{3}$ cm

3. If $\Delta PQR \sim \Delta ABC$, $PQ = 6$ cm, $AB = 8$ cm and the perimeter of ΔABC is 36 cm, then the perimeter of ΔPQR is

(a) 20.25 cm (b) 27 cm
(c) 48 cm (d) 64 cm

4. In ΔABC, $DE \parallel BC$. If $AE = (2x + 1)$ cm, $EC = 4$ cm, $AD = (x + 1)$ cm and $DB = 3$ cm, then value of x is **CBSE 2025 (Basic)**

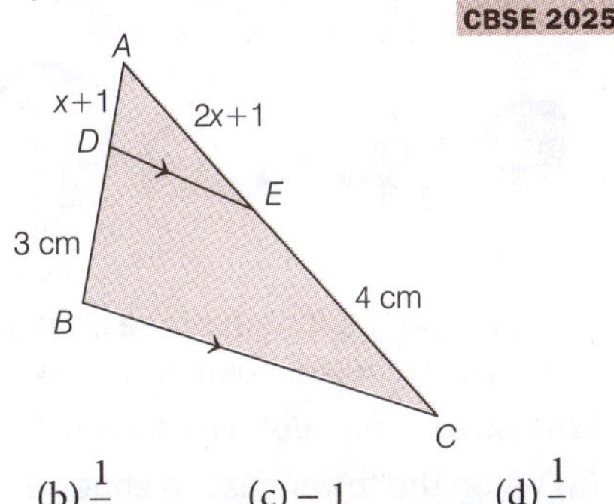

(a) 1 (b) $\frac{1}{2}$ (c) -1 (d) $\frac{1}{3}$

5. Which of the following is not the criterion for similarity of two triangles? **CBSE 2024 (Basic)**

(a) SAS (b) SSS
(c) AAA (d) RHS

6. In ΔABC, $DE \parallel BC$ (as shown in the figure). If $AD = 2$ cm, $BD = 3$ cm and $BC = 7.5$ cm, then the length of DE (in cm) is **CBSE 2024 (Standard)**

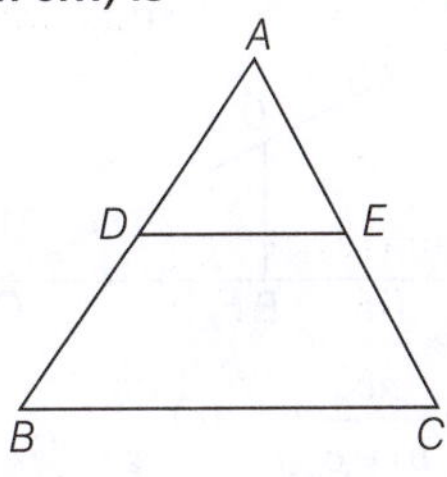

(a) 2.5 (b) 3 (c) 5 (d) 6

7. In the given figure, $PQ \parallel XY \parallel BC$, $AP = 2$ cm, $PX = 1.5$ cm and $BX = 4$ cm. If $QY = 0.75$ cm, then $AQ + CY$ is equal to **CBSE 2025 (Standard)**

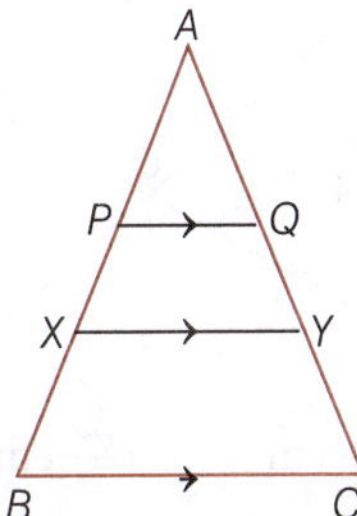

(a) 6 cm (b) 4.5 cm (c) 3 cm (d) 5.25 cm

8. In the given figure, if $\Delta OCA \sim \Delta OBD$, then $\angle OAC$ is equal to **CBSE Sample Paper 2025 (Basic)**

B D
58°
110° O
C
A

(a) 58° (b) 55° (c) 128° (d) 52°

9. In two ΔPQR and ΔABC, it is given that $\frac{AB}{BC} = \frac{PQ}{PR}$. For these two triangles to be similar, which of the following should be true? **CBSE 2023 (Basic)**

(a) $\angle A = \angle P$ (b) $\angle B = \angle Q$
(c) $\angle B = \angle P$ (d) $CA = QR$

10. In the given figure, ΔBAC is similar to **CBSE Sample Paper 2025 (Basic)**

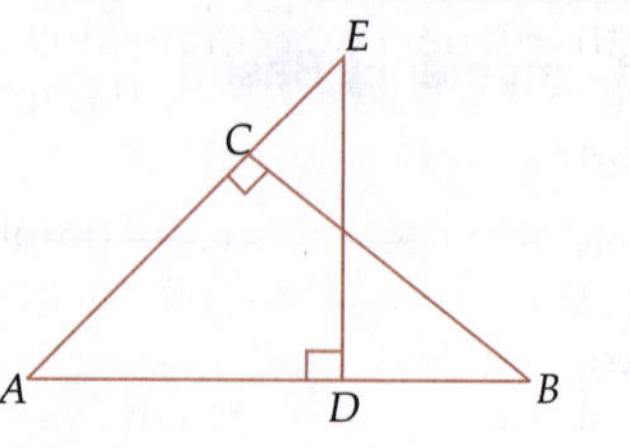

(a) ΔAED (b) ΔEAD (c) ΔACB (d) ΔBCA

11. In ΔABC, $DE \parallel AB$. If $AB = a$, $DE = x$, $BE = b$ and $EC = c$. Express x in terms of a, b and c.

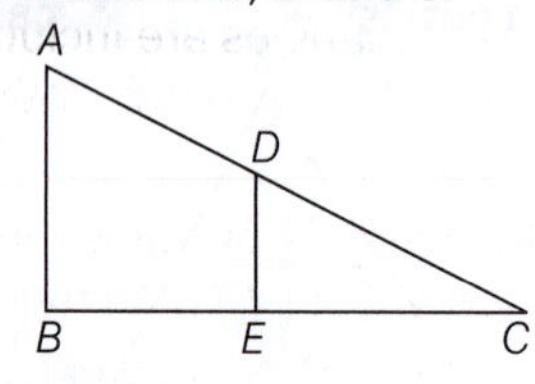

(a) $\frac{ac}{b}$ (b) $\frac{ac}{b+c}$ (c) $\frac{ab}{c}$ (d) $\frac{ab}{b+c}$

12. In the given figure, PA, QB and RC are each perpendicular to AC. If $x = 8$ cm and $z = 6$ cm, then y is equal to **CBSE 2022 (Standard)**

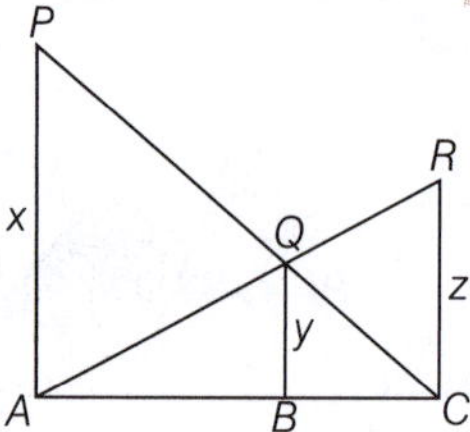

(a) $\frac{56}{7}$ cm (b) $\frac{7}{56}$ cm (c) $\frac{25}{7}$ cm (d) $\frac{24}{7}$ cm

13. In the given figure, $DE \parallel BC$. If $AD = 3$ cm, $AB = 7$ cm and $EC = 3$ cm, then the length of AE is **CBSE 2023 (Standard)**

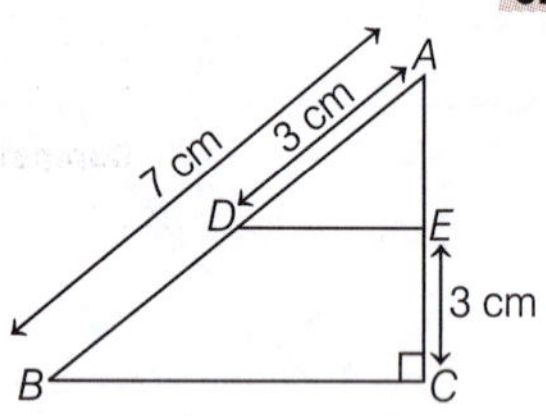

(a) 2 cm (b) 2.25 cm (c) 3.5 cm (d) 4 cm

14. In the given figure, $\angle ACB = \angle CDA$, $AC = 8$ cm and $AD = 3$ cm, then BD is **CBSE Sample Paper 2021 Term I (Basic)**

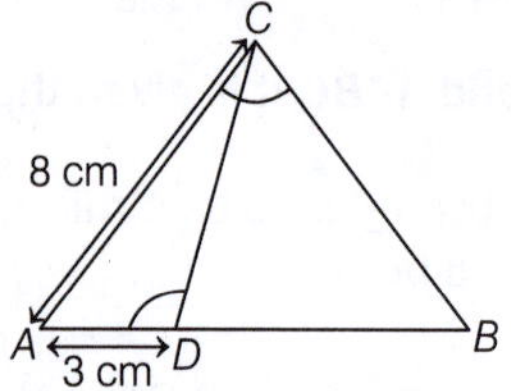

(a) 22/3 cm (b) 26/3 cm (c) 55/3 cm (d) 64/3 cm

Assertion-Reason Type Questions

15. **Assertion** In a rhombus of side 15 cm, one of the diagonals is 20 cm long. The length of the second diagonal is $10\sqrt{6}$ cm.

Reason The sum of the squares of the sides of a rhombus is equal to the sum of the squares of its diagonals.

(a) Both Assertion and Reason are correct and Reason is the correct explanation of Assertion.
(b) Both Assertion and Reason are correct but Reason is not the correct explanation of Assertion.
(c) Assertion is correct but Reason is incorrect.
(d) Assertion is incorrect but Reason is correct.

16. **Assertion** In a quadrilateral $ABCD$, $\angle B = 90°$. If $AD^2 = AB^2 + BC^2 + CD^2$, then $\angle ACD = 90°$.

Reason In a triangle, if the square of one side is equal to the sum of the squares of the other two sides, then the angle opposite to the first side is a right angle.

(a) Both Assertion and Reason are correct and Reason is the correct explanation of Assertion.
(b) Both Assertion and Reason are correct but Reason is not the correct explanation of Assertion.
(c) Assertion is correct but Reason is incorrect.
(d) Assertion is incorrect but Reason is correct.

Case Study Based Questions

17. Vijay is trying to find the average height of a tower near his house. He is using the properties of similar triangles.The height of Vijay's house, is 20 m when Vijay's house casts a shadow 10m long on the ground.

At the same time, the tower casts a shadow 50 m long on the ground and the house of Ajay casts 20 m shadow on the ground. **CBSE Question Bank**

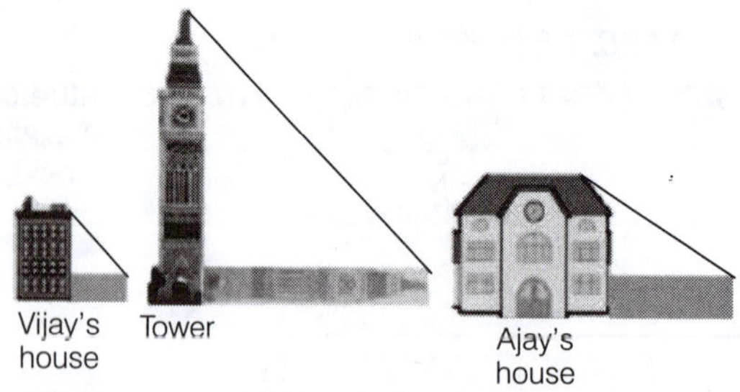

(i) What will be the length of the shadow of the tower when Vijay's house casts a shadow of 12 m?

(ii) What is the height of Ajay's house?

(iii) (a) When the tower casts a shadow of 40 m, same time what will be the length of the shadow of Ajay's house?

Or

(b) When the tower casts a shadow of 40 m, same time what will be the length of the shadow of Vijay's house?

18. Two hotels are at the ground level on either side of a mountain. On moving a certain distance towards the top of the mountain, two huts are situated as shown in the figure. The ratio between the distance from hotel B to top hut 2 and that of hut 2 to mountain top is 4 : 9.

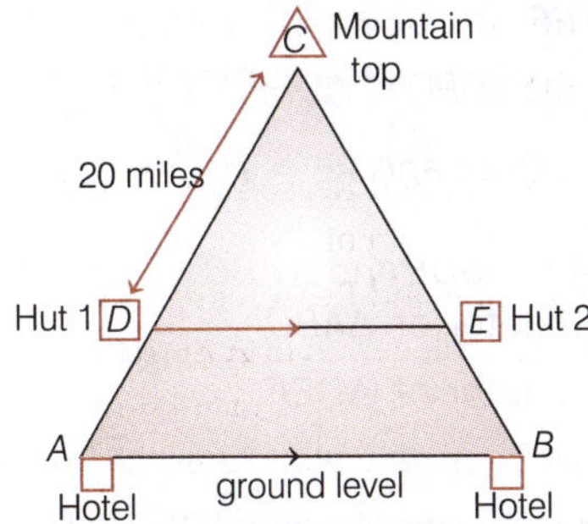

Based on the above information, answer the following questions.

(i) Find the distance between the hotel A and hut 1.

(ii) If the horizontal distance between the hut 1 and hut 2 is 15 miles, then find the distance between the two hotels.

(iii) (a) If the distance from mountain top to hut 1 is 7 miles more than that of distance from hotel B to mountain top, then what is the distance between hut 2 and mountain top?

Or (b) Find area of triangular region enclosed by hut 1, hut 2 and mountain top, if horizontal distance between hut 1 and hut 2 is 15 miles.

19. A boy is standing on the top of light house. He observed that Boat P and Boat Q are approaching the light house from opposite directions. He finds that angle of depression of Boat P is $45°$ and angle of depression of Boat Q is $30°$. He also knows that height of the light house is 100 m.

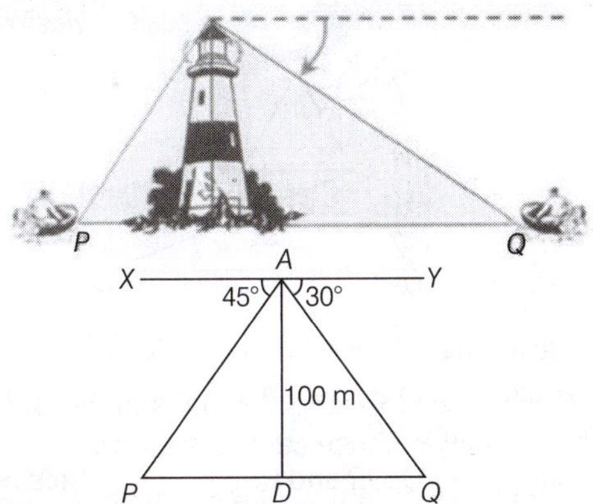

Based on the above information, answer the following questions. **CBSE Sample Paper 2023 (Basic)**

(i) What is the measure of $\angle APD$?

(ii) If $\angle YAQ = 30°$, then $\angle AQD$ is also $30°$. Why?

(iii) (a) How far is Boat P from the light house?

Or (b) How far is Boat Q from the light house?

20. Three villages X, Y and Z are situated at the three ends of a triangular region bounded by three roads. The lengths of the roads connecting X to Y, Y to Z and Z to X are in the ratio 5 : 3 : 4. The total lengths of the three roads are 180 km.

A new road is to be constructed parallel to the longest road. A team of three researchers Mayank, Biju and Shanti work on the technical specifications of the new road construction. Each of them makes a scale drawing of the region using different scale factors.

Based on the above information, answer the following questions. **Competency Based Question**

(i) Which types of triangles are included in their scale drawings, similar or congruent? Why?

(ii) The proposed road will meet the road between Y and Z in the middle. How far is the Village Y (in km) from the meeting point of the roads?

(iii) (a) In all the three scale drawings, the actual length of the new road is provided. Would the road length be the same in their maps? Justify your answer.

Or (b) Find the area of triangular region bounded by three roads.

21. A dollhouse with a triangular roof is shown below.

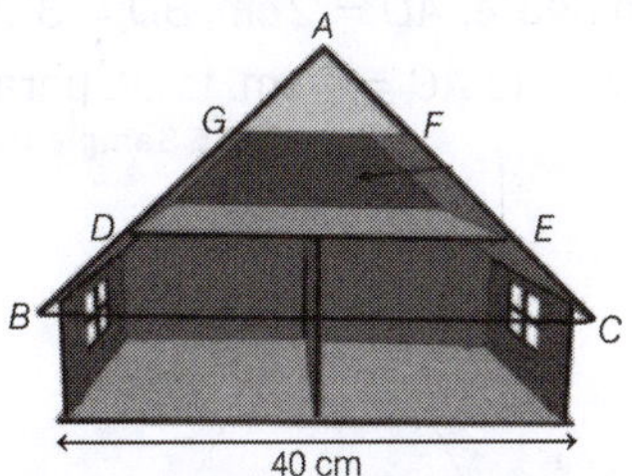

The front and back triangles are equilateral triangles. Panels parallel to the floor of the dollhouse are used to make the attic. The sides DE and GF of the panels divide the sides AB and AC into three equal parts.

Based on the above information, answer the following questions. **Competency Based Question**

(i) The area of ΔABC is 692 cm^2. What is the area of the plank AGF?

(ii) What is the height (in cm) of the attic?

(iii) (a) Find semiperimeter of ΔABC.

Or (b) Two overlapping right triangles are shown below. What is the value of x?

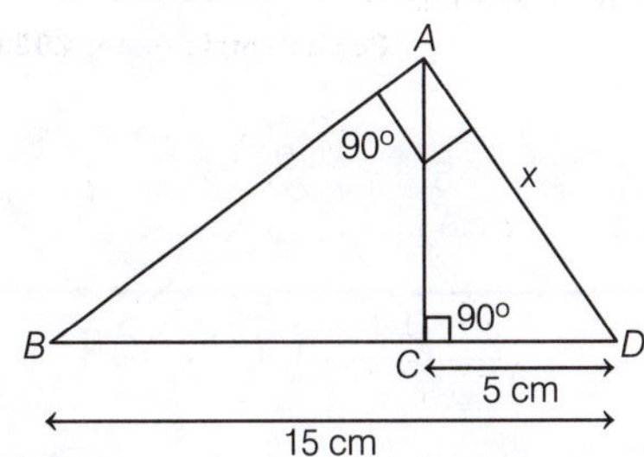

22. 

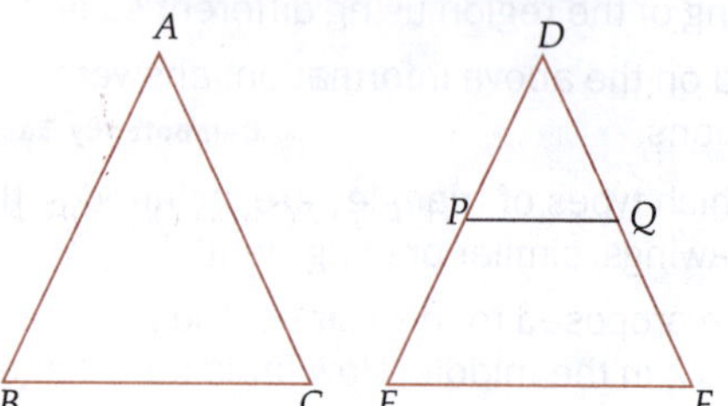

Triangle is a very popular shape used in interior designing. The picture given above shows a cabinet designed by a famous interior designer.

Here, the largest triangle is represented by ΔABC and smallest one with shelf is represented by ΔDEF. PQ is parallel to EF.

(i) Show that $\Delta DPQ \sim \Delta DEF$.

(ii) If $DP = 50$ cm and $PE = 70$ cm, then find $\frac{PQ}{EF}$.

(iii) (a) If $2AB = 5DE$ and $\Delta ABC \sim \Delta DEF$, then show that $\frac{\text{perimeter of } \Delta ABC}{\text{perimeter of } \Delta DEF}$ is constant.

Or

(b) If AM and DN are medians of ΔABC and ΔDEF respectively, then prove that $\Delta ABM \sim \Delta DEN$.

CBSE Sample Paper 2025 (Standard)

Part II

Very Short Answer Type Questions

1. In the given figure, $AD = 2$ cm, $BD = 3$ cm, $AE = 3.5$ cm and $AC = 7$ cm. Is DE parallel to BC?

CBSE Sample Paper 2020 (Basic)

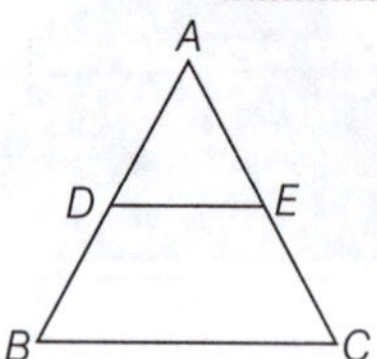

2. In ΔABC, $DE \parallel BC$, so that $AD = (7x - 4)$ cm, $AE = (5x - 2)$ cm, $DB = (3x + 4)$ cm and $EC = 3x$ cm. Then, find the value of x.

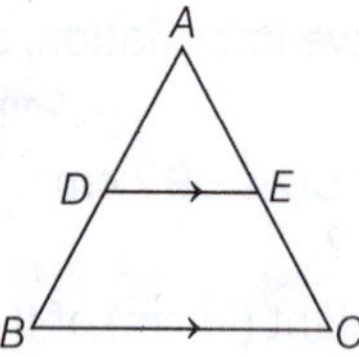

3. In the given figure, $\angle CAB = 90°$, $AD \perp BC$ and $\Delta BDA \sim \Delta BAC$. If $AC = 75$ cm, $AB = 1$ m and $BC = 1.25$ m, then find the value of AD.

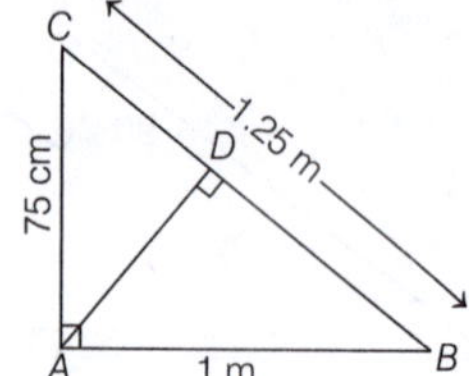

4. A vertical stick 1 m long casts a shadow 80 cm long. At the same time a tower casts a shadow 30 m long. Determine the height of the tower.

Short Answer Type Questions

5. $ABCD$ is a trapezium in which $AB \parallel DC$. P and Q are points on sides AD and BC, respectively such that $PQ \parallel AB$. If $PD = 18$ cm, $BQ = 35$ cm and $QC = 15$ cm, find the value of AD. **NCERT Exemplar**

6. In the given figure, if $\angle 1 = \angle 2$ and $\Delta NSQ \cong \Delta MTR$, prove that $\Delta PTS \sim \Delta PRQ$.

NCERT Exemplar

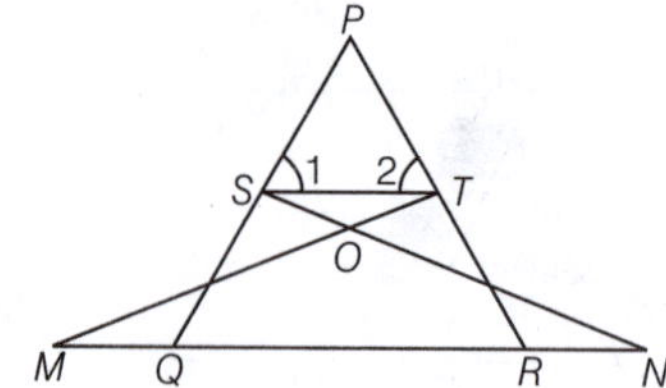

7. In the given figure PA, QB, RC and SD are all perpendiculars to a line l, $AB = 6$ cm, $BC = 9$ cm, $CD = 12$ cm and $SP = 36$ cm.

Then, find the PQ, QR and RS. **NCERT Exemplar**

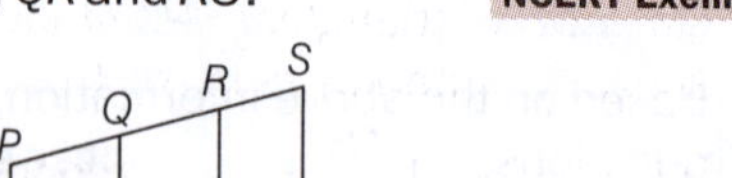

8. In the given figure, $PQ \parallel BA$ and $PR \parallel CA$. If $PD = 12$ cm, then find $BD \times CD$.

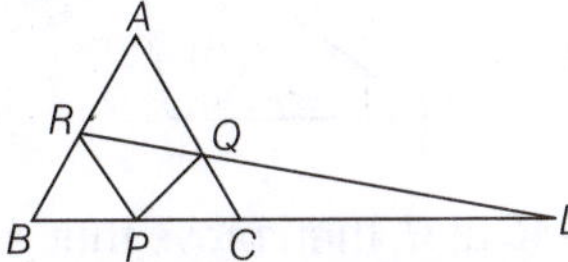

9. In the given figure, T is the exterior point on the diagonal PR of a parallelogram $PQRS$. SR produced meets QT at N and QR produced meets ST at M. Prove that $MN \parallel SQ$.

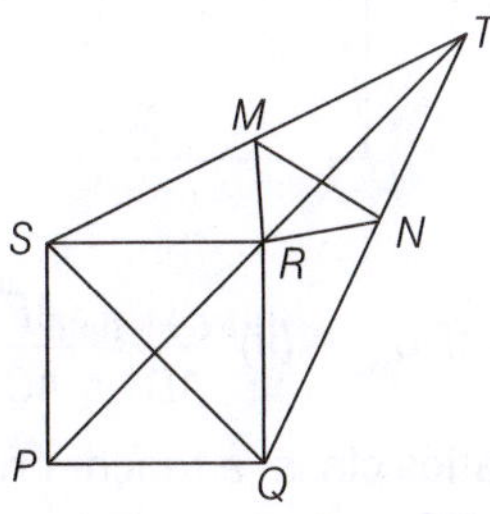

10. A girl of height 100 cm is walking away from the base of a lamp-post at a speed of 1.9 m/s. If the lamp is 5 m above the ground, find the length of her shadow after 4s.

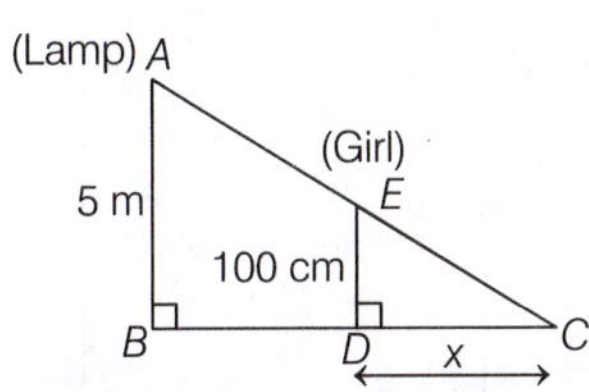

11. Are the two quadrilaterals shown below similar? Give a reason for your answer. **Competency Based Question**

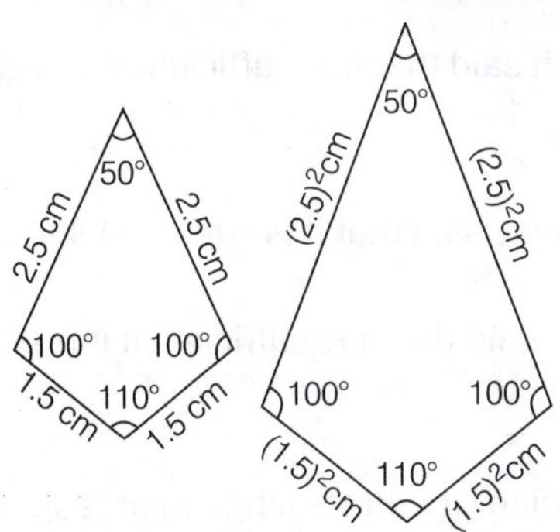

12. Two students of Class X, discuss on criteria for similarity of triangles. First student explain SSS similarity criterion as in ΔABC and ΔDEF such that $\angle A = \angle D$ and $\dfrac{AB}{DE} = \dfrac{AC}{DF}$, at once second student said, "It is wrong". If do you agree with second student, give correct explanation.

13. In the given figure, ABC is a right angled triangle, right angled at C and $DE \perp AB$.

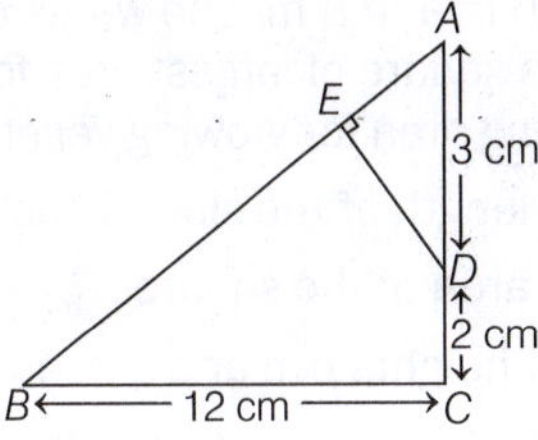

(i) Prove that $\Delta ABC \sim \Delta ADE$.

(ii) Find the lengths of AE and DE.

14. In ΔABC, $\angle A$ is obtuse, $PB \perp PC$ and $QC \perp QB$. Prove that $AB \times AQ = AC \times AP$.

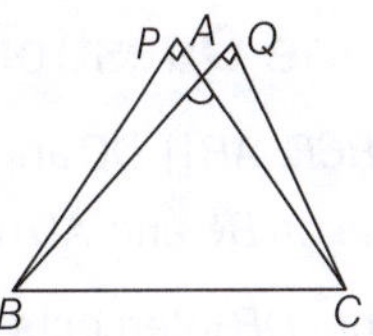

15. In the given figure, $DB \perp BC$ and $DE \perp AB$. Prove that $\dfrac{BE}{DE} = \dfrac{AC}{BC}$.

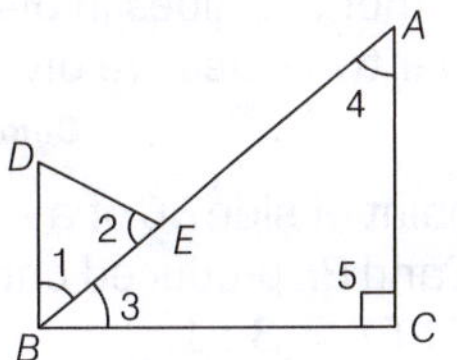

16. In the figure below, OPQ is a triangle with $OP = OQ$. RS is an arc of a circle with centre O.

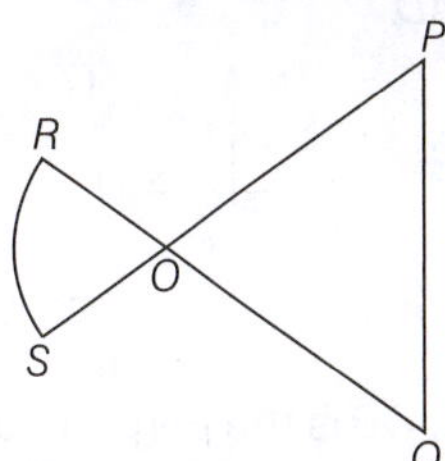

ΔOSR is similar to ΔOPQ. Is the above statement true or false? Justify your reason.

17. In given figure, ABC is an isosceles triangle with $AC = BC$. AB is produced on either side till P and Q respectively such that $AP \times BQ = AC^2$.

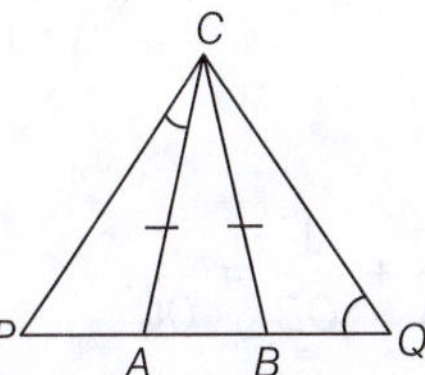

Prove that $\angle PCA = \angle CQB$.

18. A farmer has a field in the shape of a right angled triangle with legs (sides other than the hypotenuse) are of lengths 16 m and 8 m. She wants to leave a space in the form of a square of largest area for growing wheat and remaining area for growing vegetables.
(i) Find the length of the side of such a square.
(ii) Find the area of the square.

19. Two poles of heights p m and q m are standing vertically on a level ground, a metre apart. Prove that the height of the point of intersection of the line segments joining the top of each pole to the foot of the opposite pole is given by $\frac{pq}{p+q}$ m.

Long Answer Type Questions

20. In trapezium $ABCD$, $AB \parallel DC$ and $DC = 2AB$. $EF \parallel AB$, where E and F lie on BC and AD respectively, such that $\frac{BE}{EC} = \frac{4}{3}$. Diagonal DB intersects EF at G. Prove that $7EF = 11AB$.

21. If a line is drawn parallel to one side of a triangle to intersect the other two sides in distinct points, then prove that other two sides are divided in the same ratio. **Competency Based Question**

22. D is the mid-point of side BC of a $\Delta ABC \cdot AD$ is bisected at the point E and BE produced cuts AC at the point X. Prove that $BE : EX = 3 : 1$.

23. In the given figure, $AP = 3$ cm, $AR = 4.5$ cm, $AQ = 6$ cm, $AB = 5$ cm and $AC = 10$ cm. Determine the length of AD.

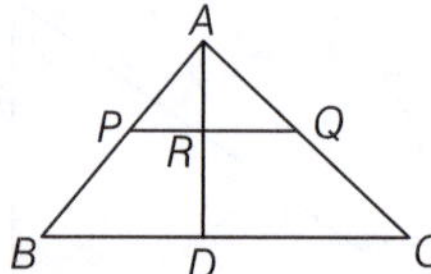

24. In given figure, OB is the perpendicular bisector of the line segment $DE \cdot FA \perp OB$ and FE intersects OB at the point C.

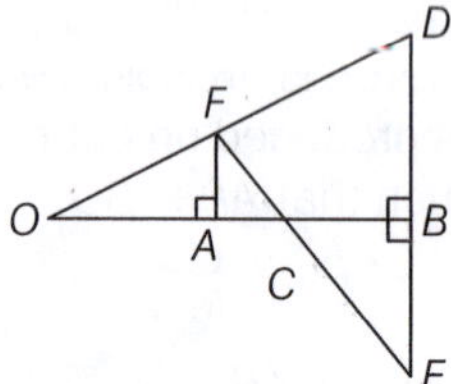

Prove that $\frac{1}{OA} + \frac{1}{OB} = \frac{2}{OC}$. **NCERT Exemplar**

25. $ABCD$ is a parallelogram in the given figure, AB is divided at P and CD at Q, so that $AP : PB = 3 : 2$ and $CQ : QD = 4 : 1$.

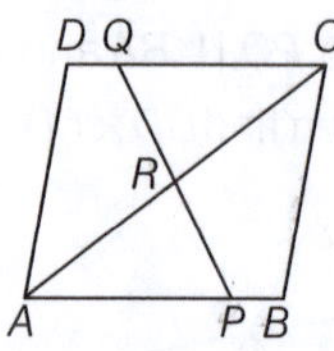

If PQ meets AC at R, then prove that $AR = \frac{3}{7} AC$.

26. In the given figure, $ABCD$ and $AEFG$ are two squares.

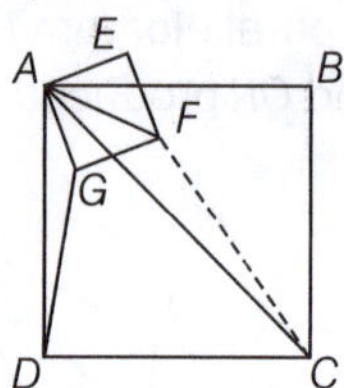

Prove that
(i) $\Delta AGF \sim \Delta ADC$ (ii) $\frac{AG}{AD} = \frac{AF}{AC}$

27. In a mathematics class, a teacher drew the following figure, where $\frac{TQ}{QR} = \frac{1}{3}$. She then asked, 'What is the sufficient condition required to prove that $\Delta TQP \sim \Delta RQS$?'

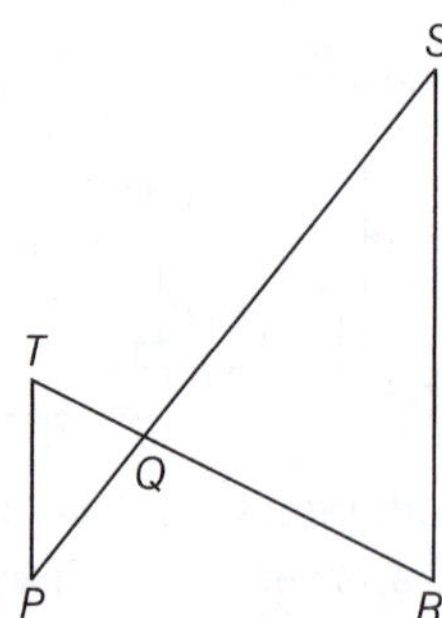

(i) Darsh said that it is sufficient if it is given that $\frac{TP}{SR} = \frac{1}{3}$.
(ii) Bhargav said that it is sufficient if it is given that $\angle P = \angle S$.
(iii) Tanvi said that it is sufficient if it is given that $\frac{PQ}{QS} = \frac{1}{3}$.
Examine whether each of their responses is correct or incorrect. Give reasons. **Competency Based Question**

28. In the given figure, if $PQRS$ is a parallelogram and $AB \parallel PS$, prove that $OC \parallel SR$. **NCERT Exemplar**

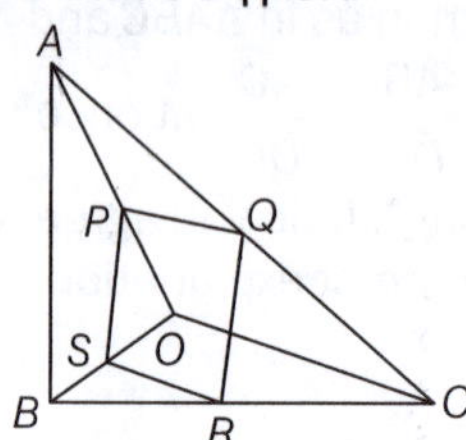

HINTS & SOLUTIONS

Part I

1. (c) Given, $DE \parallel BC$,

$\therefore \quad \dfrac{AD}{DB} = \dfrac{AE}{EC}$ [by Thales theorem]

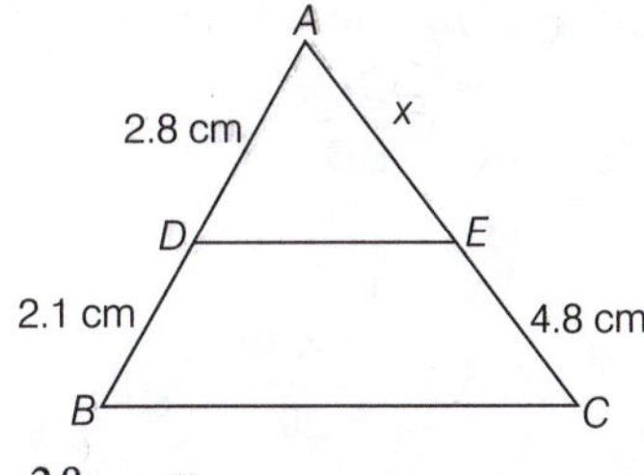

$\Rightarrow \quad \dfrac{2.8}{2.1} = \dfrac{x}{4.8}$

$\Rightarrow \quad x = \dfrac{2.8 \times 4.8}{2.1}$

$\Rightarrow \quad x = 6.4$

Hence, the value of x is 6.4 cm.

2. (b) **Hint** $\because \ \Delta ABC \sim \Delta DEF$

$\Rightarrow \quad \dfrac{AB}{DE} = \dfrac{BC}{EF} = \dfrac{CA}{FD} = \dfrac{AB + BC + CA}{DE + EF + FD}$

3. (b) **Hint** Do same as Question 2.

4. (b) **Hint** By BPT theorem,

$\therefore \quad \dfrac{AD}{DB} = \dfrac{AE}{EC}$

$\Rightarrow \quad \dfrac{x+1}{3} = \dfrac{2x+1}{4}$

5. (d) RHS is not the criterion for similarity of two triangles.

6. (b) In ΔABC, D and E are points on sides AB and AC respectively, such that $DE \parallel BC$.

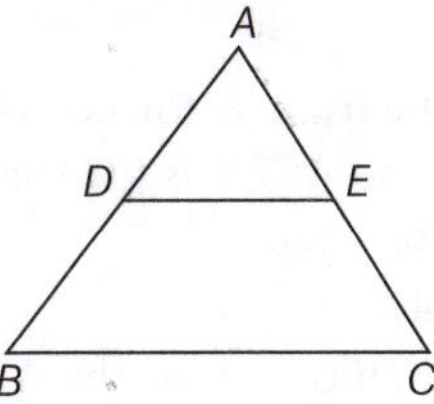

In ΔADE and ΔABC,

$\angle DAE = \angle BAC$ [common]

$\angle AED = \angle ACB$ [corresponding angles]

$\therefore \quad \Delta ADE \sim \Delta ABC$ [AA similarity]

$\Rightarrow \quad \dfrac{DE}{BC} = \dfrac{AD}{AB}$

[$\because$ if two triangles are similar, then their corresponding sides are proportional]

$\Rightarrow \quad \dfrac{DE}{7.5} = \dfrac{2}{2+3}$

$\Rightarrow \quad DE = \dfrac{2}{5} \times 7.5 = 3.0$

$\Rightarrow \quad DE = 3$

$\therefore$ The length of DE is 3 cm.

7. (c) **Hint** By BPT theorem,

$\because \quad \dfrac{AP}{PX} = \dfrac{AQ}{QY}$ [$\because PQ \parallel XY$]

$\dfrac{2}{1.5} = \dfrac{AQ}{0.75}$

$AQ = 1$

Again, $\dfrac{AX}{XB} = \dfrac{AY}{CY}$ [$\because XY \parallel BC$]

$\dfrac{3.5}{4} = \dfrac{1.75}{CY}$

$CY = 2$

Hence, $AQ + CY = 1 + 2 = 3$ cm

8. (d) Given, $\Delta OCA \sim \Delta OBD$

Also, given $\angle AOB = 110°$ and $\angle BDO = 58°$

$\because \quad \angle AOB = \angle COD$ [vertically opposite angles]

$\Rightarrow \quad 110° = \angle COD$

Now, $\angle AOC = 180° - \angle COD$ [linear pair]

$= 180° - 110° = 70°$

$\angle AOC = \angle BOD = 70°$

In ΔBOD,

$\angle BOD + \angle BDO + \angle DBO = 180°$

$\Rightarrow \quad 70° + 58° + \angle DBO = 180°$

$\Rightarrow \quad \angle DBO = 180° - 128° = 52°$

$\because \quad \Delta OCA \sim \Delta OBD$

$\therefore \quad \angle DBO = \angle OAC = 52°$

9. (c) **Hint** If $\angle B = \angle P$, then

$\Delta ABC \sim \Delta QPR$ [by SAS similarity criterion]

10. (b) In the given figure, we have

$\angle BCA = 90°$

and $\angle ADE = 90°$

Since, $\angle A$ is common.

So, it is clear that ΔBAC is similar to ΔEAD by AA similarity criterion.

11. (b) **Hint** $\Delta CED \sim \Delta CBA$ [by AA similarity criterion]

$\Rightarrow \quad \dfrac{CE}{CB} = \dfrac{ED}{BA}$

12. (d) **Hint** Do same as Question 19 of Try these 6.2.

13. (b) Given, $AD = 3\,cm$ and $AB = 7\,cm$

$\Rightarrow \quad DB = AB - AD = 7 - 3 = 4\,cm$

By basic proportionality theorem,

$$\frac{AD}{DB} = \frac{AE}{EC}$$

$\Rightarrow \quad \frac{3}{4} = \frac{AE}{3}$ [given, $EC = 3\,cm$]

$\Rightarrow \quad AE = \frac{9}{4} = 2.25\,cm$

14. (c) **Hint** $\Delta ACD \sim \Delta ABC$ [by AA similarity criterion]

$\therefore \quad \frac{AC}{AB} = \frac{AD}{AC}$

[$\because$ corresponding sides of similar triangles are proportional]

15. (d) Let $ABCD$ be a rhombus.

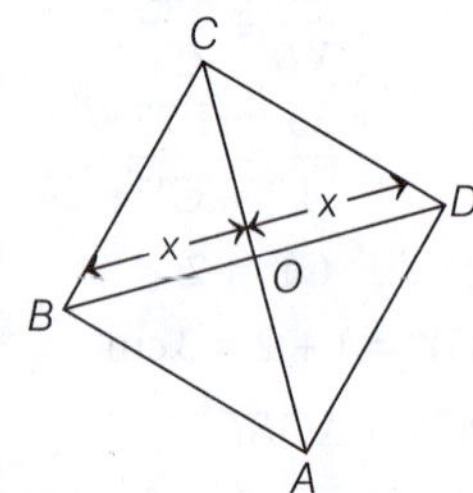

Given, $AB = BC = CD = DA = 15$ cm, $AC = 20$ cm

$\because$ In figure, $BO = OD = x$ cm (say)

Then, in ΔBOC, $x^2 + 10^2 = 15^2$

$\Rightarrow \quad x = 5\sqrt{5}$

$\therefore \quad 2x = 10\sqrt{5}$

So, Assertion is incorrect and Reason is correct.

16. (a) **Hint** Given, $AD^2 = AB^2 + BC^2 + CD^2$ ...(i)

In right ΔABC, $AC^2 = AB^2 + BC^2$ ...(ii)

[by Pythogoras theorem]

From Eqs. (i) and (ii), we get

$$AD^2 = AC^2 + CD^2$$

$\therefore$ ΔACD follows Pythagoras theorem.

$\therefore \quad \angle ACD = 90°$

Reason is also correct and correct explanation of Assertion.

17. Let $CD = h$ m be the height of the tower, $BE = 20$ m be the height of Vijay's house and GF be the height of Ajay's house.

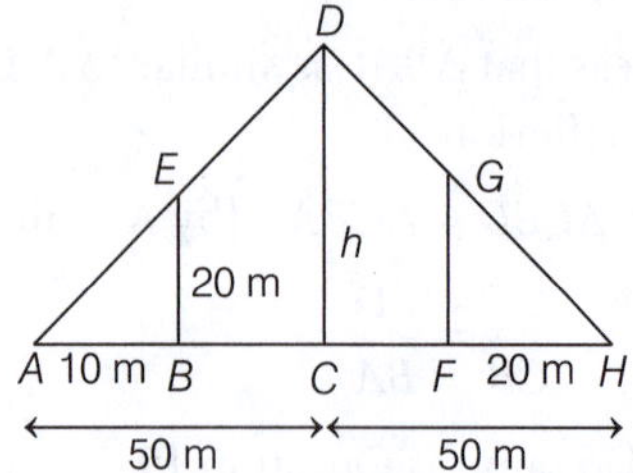

$\Delta ACD \sim \Delta ABE$

$\therefore \quad \frac{AC}{AB} = \frac{CD}{EB}$

$\Rightarrow \quad \frac{50}{10} = \frac{h}{20}$

$\Rightarrow \quad h = 100$ m

(i) Given, $AB = 12$ m, let $AC = x$

In similar ΔABE and ΔACD,

$$\frac{AB}{AC} = \frac{BE}{CD}$$

$\Rightarrow \quad \frac{12}{x} = \frac{20}{100}$

$\Rightarrow \quad x = \frac{12 \times 100}{20} = 12 \times 5 = 60$ m

(ii) Let the height of Ajay's house be $GF = h_1$

Since, $\Delta HFG \sim \Delta HCD$

$\therefore \quad \frac{HF}{HC} = \frac{FG}{CD}$

$\Rightarrow \quad \frac{20}{50} = \frac{h_1}{100} \Rightarrow h_1 = \frac{20 \times 100}{50} = 40$ m

(iii) (a) Given, $HC = 40$ m

Let length of the shadow of Ajay's house be $HF = l$ m

Since, $\Delta HFG \sim \Delta HCD$

$\therefore \quad \frac{HF}{HC} = \frac{FG}{CD}$

$\Rightarrow \quad \frac{l}{40} = \frac{40}{100} \Rightarrow l = \frac{40 \times 40}{100} = 16$ m

Or

(b) Given, $AC = 40$ m

Let length of the shadow of Vijay's house be $AB = l$ m

Since, $\Delta ABE \sim \Delta ACD$

$\therefore \quad \frac{AB}{AC} = \frac{EB}{CD}$

$\Rightarrow \quad \frac{l}{40} = \frac{20}{100} \Rightarrow l = \frac{20 \times 40}{100} = 8$ m

18. Let ΔABC be the triangle formed by both hotels and mountain top and ΔCDE is the triangle formed by both hut and mountain top.

Clearly, $DE \parallel AB$

So, $\Delta ABC \sim \Delta DEC$ [by AA similarity criterion]

Also given, $\frac{BE}{EC} = \frac{4}{9}$

(i) $\frac{CD}{AD} = \frac{CE}{EB} \Rightarrow \frac{20}{AD} = \frac{9}{4}$

$\Rightarrow AD = \frac{20 \times 4}{9} = 8.89$ miles

(ii) Here, $\frac{BC}{EC} = \frac{AB}{DE} \Rightarrow \frac{13}{9} = \frac{AB}{15}$

$\Rightarrow AB = \frac{13 \times 15}{9} = 21.67$ miles

(iii) (a) Given, $DC = 7 + BC$

$\Rightarrow \quad 20 - 7 = BC$

$\Rightarrow \quad BC = 13$ miles

Now, $\quad CE = \frac{9}{13} \times BC = \frac{9}{13} \times 13 = 9$ miles

Or

(b) $CD = 20$ miles, $DE = 15$ miles (DE = distance between hut 1and hut 2)

and $\quad CE = 9$ miles

Then, semi-perimeter, $s = \frac{20 + 9 + 15}{2}$

$= \frac{44}{2} = 22$ miles

$\therefore$ Area of triangular region

$= \sqrt{s(s - CD)(s - DE)(s - CE)}$

$= \sqrt{22\,(22 - 20)\,(22 - 15)\,(22 - 9)}$

$= \sqrt{22 \times 2 \times 7 \times 13}$

$= 63.28$ sq miles

19. (i) $XY \,||\, PQ$

$\therefore \angle XAP = \angle APQ = 45° = \angle APD$

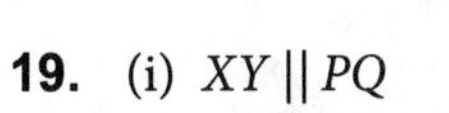

(ii) $\angle YAQ = \angle AQD = 30°$ [alternate angles]

(iii) (a) In right angled ΔADP,

$\tan 45° = \frac{AD}{PD}$

$\Rightarrow \quad 1 = \frac{100}{PD} \Rightarrow PD = 100$ m

Hence, the Boat P is at a distance of 100 m from the light house.

Or

(b) In right angled ΔADQ,

$\tan 30° = \frac{AD}{DQ}$

$\Rightarrow \quad \frac{1}{\sqrt{3}} = \frac{AD}{DQ}$

$\Rightarrow \quad DQ = 100\sqrt{3}$ m

Hence, the Boat Q is at a distance of $100\sqrt{3}$ m from the light house.

20. (i) Let the length of roads connecting X to Y, Y to Z and Z to X be $5x$, $3x$ and $4x$, respectively.

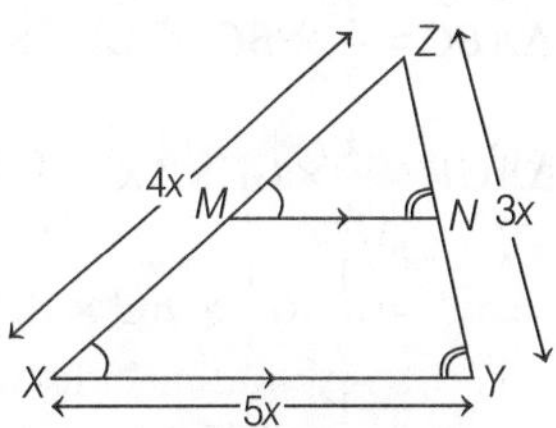

Given, total length of three roads = 180 km

$\Rightarrow \quad 5x + 3x + 4x = 180 \Rightarrow x = 15$

$\therefore$ Length of longest road is $5x = 5 \times 15 = 75$ km

Let MN be the road parallel to the longest road.

$\therefore \quad \Delta ZMN \sim \Delta ZXY$ [by AAA similarity criterion]

$\Rightarrow \quad \frac{ZM}{ZX} = \frac{MN}{XY} = \frac{ZN}{ZY}$

Mayank, Biju and Shanti had drawn similar triangles as angles in them are of same measure and sides in them are of same proportion.

(ii) **Hint** Distance of Village Y from the meeting point of the roads $= \frac{3}{2} \times x$

Ans. 22.5 km

(iii) (a) The length of the road would be the same in all three scale drawings as the line parallel to a side in a triangle and cutting the other two sides in a specific ratio is unique.

Or

(b) Sides of ΔXYZ are

$XY = 75$ km, $YZ = 45$ km and $ZX = 60$ km

Semi-perimeter of ΔXYZ, $s = \frac{75 + 45 + 60}{2}$

$= 90$

Then, ar$(\Delta XYZ) = \sqrt{s\,(s - XY)\,(s - YZ)\,(s - ZX)}$

$= \sqrt{90\,(90 - 75)\,(90 - 45)\,(90 - 60)}$

$= 1350$ km^2

21. First draw a perpendicular AZ from point A to BC.

$\therefore \quad AX = \frac{1}{3} AZ$ [by BPT]

and $\quad GF = \frac{1}{3} BC$ [by BPT]

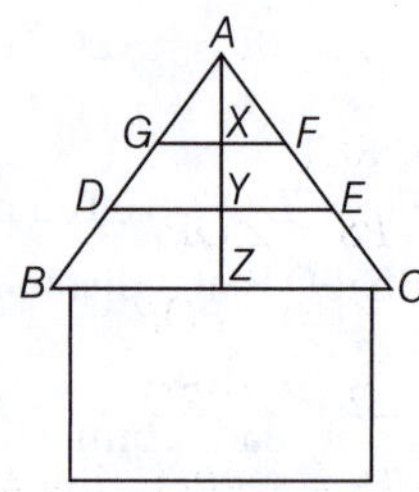

(i) Area of $\Delta ABC = \frac{1}{2} \times BC \times AZ = 876.8\ cm^2$ ...(i)

Area of $\Delta AGF = \frac{1}{2} \times GF \times AX = \frac{1}{2} \times \frac{1}{3} \times BC \times \frac{1}{3} \times AZ$

$= \frac{1}{9} \times \frac{1}{2} \times BC \times AZ$

$= \frac{1}{9} \times 876.8$ [from Eq. (i)]

$= 97.42\ cm^2$

(ii) Given, ABC is equilateral triangle of side 45 cm.

Height of attic $= XY = \frac{1}{3} \times AZ$ [by BPT]

$= \frac{1}{3} AB \sin 60°$

$= \frac{1}{3} \times 45 \times \frac{\sqrt{3}}{2} = \frac{15\sqrt{3}}{2}$ cm

(iii) (a) Semi-perimeter of $\Delta ABC = \frac{45 + 45 + 45}{2}$

$= \frac{135}{2} = 67.5$ cm

Or

(b) In ΔBAD and ΔACD,

$\angle BAD = \angle ACD$ [each 90°]

$\angle BDA = \angle ADA$ [common]

$\therefore$ $\Delta BAD \sim \Delta ACD$

[by *AA* similarity criterion]

$\therefore$ $\frac{AD}{CD} = \frac{BD}{AD} \Rightarrow (AD)^2 = BD \times CD$

$\Rightarrow$ $AD^2 = 15 \times 5 \Rightarrow AD = x = 5\sqrt{3}$ cm

22. (i) Given, ΔDEF, where PQ is parallel to EF.

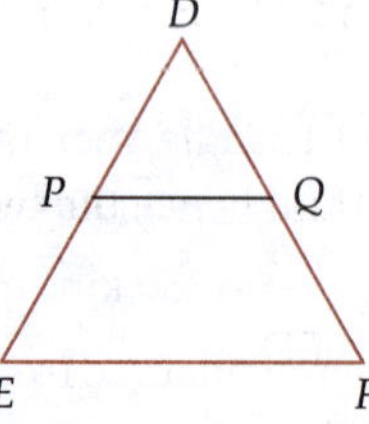

Since, $PQ \parallel EF$

$\angle DPQ = \angle DEF$ [corresponding angles]

$\angle PDQ = \angle EDF$ [common]

$\therefore$ By AA similarity criterion,

$\Delta DPQ \sim \Delta DEF$ **Hence proved**

(ii) Given, $DP = 50$ cm and $PE = 70$ cm

$\therefore$ $DE = DP + EP$

$= 50 + 70 = 120$ cm

$\because$ $\Delta DPQ \sim \Delta DEF$

$\frac{DP}{DE} = \frac{PQ}{EF}$ [$\because$ corresponding sides of similar triangles are proportional]

Therefore, $\frac{PQ}{EF} = \frac{50}{120}$ [$\because DP = 50$ and $DE = 120$]

$= \frac{5}{12}$

(iii) (a) Given, $2AB = 5DE$ and $\Delta ABC \sim \Delta DEF$

$\Rightarrow$ $\frac{AB}{DE} = \frac{5}{2}$ and $\frac{AB}{DE} = \frac{BC}{EF} = \frac{AC}{DF}$

$\Rightarrow$ $AB = \frac{5}{2} DE$

Now, $\frac{\text{perimeter of } \Delta ABC}{\text{perimeter of } \Delta DEF} = \frac{AB + BC + AC}{DE + EF + FD}$

$= \frac{\frac{5}{2}(DE + EF + FD)}{DE + EF + FD}$

$= \frac{5}{2}$ i.e. constant

Hence proved

Or

(b) Given AM and DN are medians of triangles ABC and DEF, respectively.

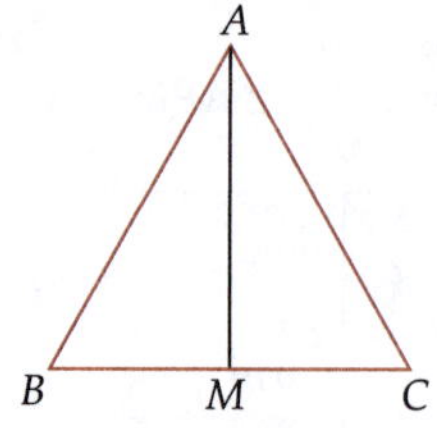

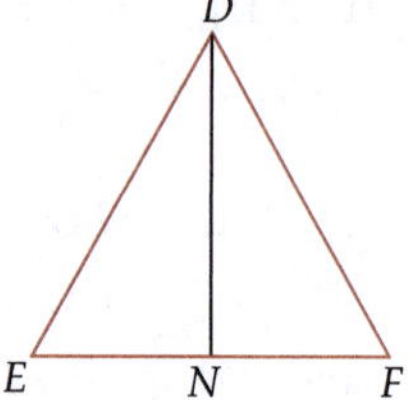

$\because$ $\Delta ABC \sim \Delta DEF$

$\Rightarrow$ $\frac{AB}{DE} = \frac{BC}{EF}$

[$\because$ corresponding sides of similar triangles are in proportion]

$\Rightarrow$ $\frac{AB}{DE} = \frac{\frac{BC}{2}}{\frac{EF}{2}}$

$\Rightarrow$ $\frac{AB}{DE} = \frac{BM}{EN}$

[$\because$ AM and DN are medians of triangles ABC and DEF]

Also, $\angle B = \angle E$

$\therefore$ $\Delta ABM \sim \Delta DEN$ [by SAS similarity criterion]

Hence proved

Part II

1. $\dfrac{AD}{BD} = \dfrac{2}{3}$

$\therefore \quad CE = AC - AE = 7 - 3.5 = 3.5$ cm

So, $\dfrac{AE}{EC} = \dfrac{3.5}{3.5} = 1$

Here, $\dfrac{AD}{BD} \neq \dfrac{AE}{EC}$

We know that if a line does not divides any two sides of a triangle in the same ratio, then the line is not parallel to the third side.

Hence, DE is not parallel to BC.

2. **Hint** Do same as Example 15 of Topic 1.

Ans. $x = 4$

3. **Hint** Since, $\Delta BDA \sim \Delta BAC$

$\therefore \quad \dfrac{AD}{AC} = \dfrac{BA}{BC}$

Ans. 60 cm

4. **Hint** Let h be the height of the tower.

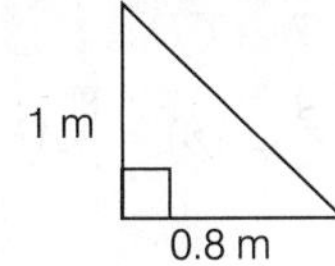

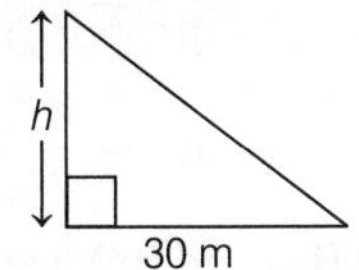

[$\because$ 80 cm = 0.8 m]

Since, it is clear that both the triangles will be similar.

$\therefore \quad \dfrac{1}{h} = \dfrac{0.8}{30} \Rightarrow h = \dfrac{30}{0.8}$

Ans. 37.5 m

5. **Hint** $\dfrac{AP}{PD} = \dfrac{BQ}{QC}$

and $AD = AP + PD$

Ans. 60 cm

6. **Given** $\Delta NSQ \cong \Delta MTR$ and $\angle 1 = \angle 2$

To prove $\Delta PTS \sim \Delta PRQ$

Proof Since, $\Delta NSQ \cong \Delta MTR$

$\therefore \quad SQ = TR \quad$ ...(i)

Also, $\quad \angle 1 = \angle 2$

$\Rightarrow \quad PT = PS \quad$ ...(ii)

[$\because$ sides opposite to equal angles are also equal]

From Eqs. (i) and (ii),

$$\frac{PS}{SQ} = \frac{PT}{TR}$$

$\Rightarrow \quad ST \parallel QR$

[by converse of basic proportionality theorem]

$\therefore \quad \angle 1 = \angle PQR$

and $\quad \angle 2 = \angle PRQ \quad$ [corresponding angles]

In ΔPTS and ΔPRQ,

$\angle TPS = \angle QPR \quad$ [common angle]

$\angle 1 = \angle PQR \quad$ [proved above]

and $\quad \angle 2 = \angle PRQ$

$\therefore \quad \Delta PTS \sim \Delta PRQ \quad$ [by AA similarity criterion]

Hence proved.

7. **Hint** If three or more parallel lines are intercepted by two transversals, the intercepts made by them on the transversal are proportional.

$\therefore PQ : QR : RS = AB : BC : CD = 6 : 9 : 12$

Let $PQ = 6x$, $QR = 9x$ and $RS = 12x$

Then, $6x + 9x + 12x = 36$

Ans. $PQ = 8$ cm, $QR = 12$ cm and $RS = 16$ cm.

8. **Hint** In ΔRDP, we have

$PR \parallel CQ \quad$ [$\because PR \parallel CA$]

$\therefore \quad \dfrac{DC}{DP} = \dfrac{DQ}{DR} \quad$ ...(i)

In ΔRDB, we have

$PQ \parallel BR \quad$ [$\because PQ \parallel BA$]

$\therefore \quad \dfrac{DP}{DB} = \dfrac{DQ}{DR} \quad$ ...(ii)

From Eqs. (i) and (ii), we get

$$\frac{DC}{DP} = \frac{DP}{DB}$$

$\Rightarrow \quad DC \times DB = DP^2$

or $\quad CD \times BD = PD^2$

Ans. 144 cm^2

9. **Hint** Use BPT in ΔSTP and ΔQTP and then apply converse of BPT.

10. **Hint** Do same as Example 10 of Topic 2. **Ans.** 190 cm.

11. **Hint** Given the two quadrilaterals are not similar because the corresponding sides of the quadrilaterals are not in the same ratio. **Ans.** No

12. Yes, in ΔABC and ΔDEF, SSS similarity criterion are as follows if sides of one triangle are proportional to the sides of the other triangle, then their corresponding angles are equal and hence the two triangles are similar.

i.e. $\dfrac{AB}{DE} = \dfrac{BC}{EF} = \dfrac{CA}{FD}$

13. (i) **Hint** Use AA similarity criterion to prove

$\Delta ABC \sim \Delta ADE$

(ii) **Hint** $\dfrac{AB}{AD} = \dfrac{BC}{DE} = \dfrac{AC}{AE}$

Ans. $AE = \dfrac{15}{13}$ cm and $DE = \dfrac{36}{13}$ cm

14. Hint Prove that $\Delta APB \sim \Delta AQC$

[by AA similarily criterion]

15. Hint Since, $DB \perp BC$ and $AC \perp BC$, therefore $DB \parallel AC$ and hence $\angle 1 = \angle 4$ [alternate angles]

Now, use AA similarity criteria in ΔBDE and ΔABC.

16. Hint In $\Delta OSR \sim \Delta OPQ$,

$\angle ROS = \angle POQ = x$ (say) [vertically opposite angles]

and $OR = OS$ [radii of circle formed]

$\Rightarrow \angle ORS = \angle OSR = \angle OPQ$

$= \angle OQP = \dfrac{180° - x}{2}$

[angle sum property of isosceles triangles]

$\therefore \quad \Delta OSR \sim \Delta OPQ$ [by AA similarity]

Ans. True

17. Hint In $\Delta ABC, AC = BC \Rightarrow \angle A = \angle B$

$\Rightarrow \quad 180° - \angle A = 180° - \angle B$

$\Rightarrow \quad \angle PAC = \angle QBC$

Also, we have $AP \times BQ = AC^2$

$\Rightarrow \quad \dfrac{AP}{AC} = \dfrac{AC}{BQ} \Rightarrow \dfrac{AP}{BC} = \dfrac{AC}{BQ}$ $[\because AC = BC]$

$\Rightarrow \Delta PAC \sim \Delta CBQ$ [by SAS similarity criterion]

18. (i) Let ABC be a right triangle right angled at B with $AB = 16$ m and $BC = 8$ m. Then, the largest square $BRSP$ which can be inscribed in this triangle will be as shown in the figure.

Let $PB = x$ m. So, $AP = (16 - x)$ m.

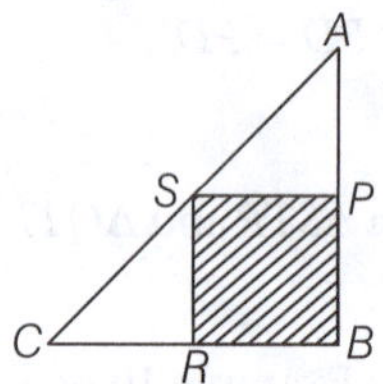

In ΔAPS and ΔABC, we have

$\angle A = \angle A$ and $\angle APS = \angle ABC = 90°$

$\therefore \quad \Delta APS \sim \Delta ABC$ [by AA similarity criterion]

$\Rightarrow \quad \dfrac{AP}{AB} = \dfrac{PS}{BC} \Rightarrow \dfrac{16 - x}{16} = \dfrac{x}{8}$

$\Rightarrow 128 - 8x = 16x \Rightarrow \quad x = \dfrac{16}{3}$ m

Thus, the side of the required square is $\dfrac{16}{3}$ m.

(ii) Area of square $BRSP = (\text{side})^2 = \left(\dfrac{16}{3}\right)^2 \text{m}^2$

$= \dfrac{256}{9} \text{m}^2$

19. Hint Do same as Question 20 of Try These 6.2.

20. Hint $\Delta DFG \sim \Delta DAB$ [by similarity criterion]

$\Rightarrow \quad \dfrac{DF}{DA} = \dfrac{FG}{AB}$ ...(i)

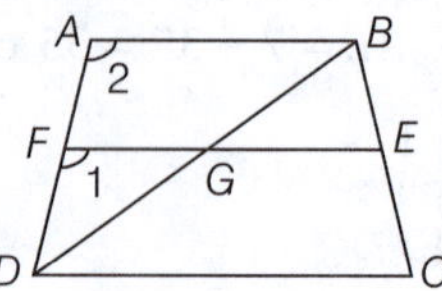

Again, $ABCD$ is trapezium.

$\therefore EF \| AB \| DC$

$\Rightarrow \quad \dfrac{AF}{DF} = \dfrac{BE}{EC} = \dfrac{4}{3}$

$\Rightarrow \quad \dfrac{AF}{DF} + 1 = \dfrac{4}{3} + 1 \Rightarrow \dfrac{AD}{DF} = \dfrac{7}{3}$

$\Rightarrow \quad \dfrac{DF}{AD} = \dfrac{3}{7}$ ...(ii)

From (i) and (ii), we get

$\dfrac{FG}{AB} = \dfrac{3}{7} \Rightarrow FG = \dfrac{3}{7}AB$ ...(iii)

Now, $\Delta BEG \sim \Delta BCD$ [by AA similarity criterion]

$\Rightarrow \quad \dfrac{BE}{BC} = \dfrac{EG}{CD} \Rightarrow \dfrac{4}{7} = \dfrac{EG}{CD}$

$\Rightarrow \quad EG = \dfrac{4}{7}CD = \dfrac{4}{7}(2AB) = \dfrac{8}{7}AB$ ...(iv)

Adding (iii) and (iv), we get

$FG + EG = \dfrac{3}{7}AB + \dfrac{8}{7}AB = \dfrac{11}{7}AB$

$\Rightarrow \quad EF = \dfrac{11}{7}AB$

21. Hint Do same as Theorem 1 of Topic 1.

22. Hint Draw $DY \| BX$.

Then, $\Delta BCX \sim \Delta DCY$ [by AA similarity criterion]

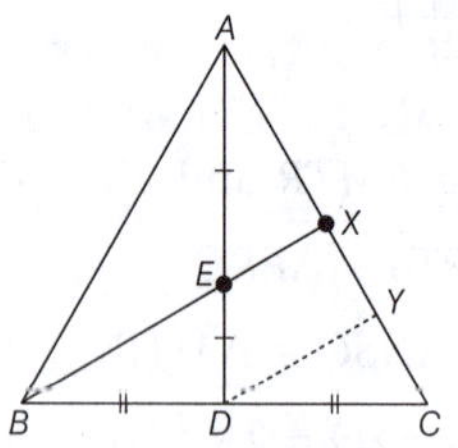

$\Rightarrow \quad \dfrac{BX}{DY} = \dfrac{BC}{DC} \Rightarrow \dfrac{BX}{DY} = 2$ ...(i)

Similarly, $\Delta AEX \sim \Delta ADY \Rightarrow \dfrac{EX}{DY} = \dfrac{1}{2}$ ...(ii)

From Eqs. (i) and (ii), we get

$\dfrac{BX}{EX} = 4 \Rightarrow \dfrac{BX}{EX} - 1 = 4 - 1$

$\Rightarrow \quad \dfrac{BX - EX}{EX} = \dfrac{3}{1} \Rightarrow \dfrac{BE}{EX} = \dfrac{3}{1}$

23. Hint Given, $AP = 3$ cm, $AR = 4.5$ cm,

$AQ = 6$ cm, $AB = 5$ cm and $AC = 10$ cm

Here, $\frac{AP}{AB} = \frac{3}{5}$ and $\frac{AQ}{AC} = \frac{6}{10} = \frac{3}{5} \Rightarrow \frac{AP}{AB} = \frac{AQ}{AC}$

Thus, $PQ \parallel BC$

[by converse of basic proportionality theorem]

In ΔARQ and ΔADC,

$\angle RAQ = \angle DAC$ [common angle]

$\angle ARQ = \angle ADC$ [corresponding angles]

So, $\Delta ARQ \sim \Delta ADC$ [by AA similarity criterion]

$\Rightarrow \frac{AR}{AD} = \frac{AQ}{AC}$

[$\because$ corresponding sides of similar triangles are proportional]

$\Rightarrow \frac{4.5}{AD} = \frac{6}{10}$

[$\because AR = 4.5$ cm, $AQ = 6$ cm and $AC = 10$ cm]

$\Rightarrow AD = \frac{45}{6} = \frac{15}{2} = 7.5\text{cm}$

24. Hint $\Delta AOF \sim \Delta BOD \Rightarrow \frac{OA}{OB} = \frac{FA}{DB}$ ...(i)

$\Delta FAC \sim \Delta EBC \Rightarrow \frac{FA}{EB} = \frac{AC}{BC}$

$\Rightarrow \frac{FA}{DB} = \frac{AC}{BC}$ ...(ii) [$\because EB = DB$]

From Eqs. (i) and (ii), we get

$\frac{OA}{OB} = \frac{AC}{BC} \Rightarrow \frac{OA}{OB} = \frac{OC - OA}{OB - OC}$

$\Rightarrow (OB + OA) \cdot OC = 2OA \cdot OB$

Divide both sides by $OA \cdot OB \cdot OC$.

25. Hint Do same as Example 7 of Topic 2.

26. Hint

(i) $\angle AGF = \angle ADC$ [each 90°]

and $\angle GAF = \angle DAC$ [each 45°]

$\therefore \Delta AGF \sim \Delta ADC$ [by AA similarity criterion]

(ii) $\angle DAC = \angle GAF$

[$\because \Delta AGF \sim \Delta ADC$, by CPCT]

$\Rightarrow \angle DAC - \angle GAC = \angle GAF - \angle GAC$

$\Rightarrow \angle DAG = \angle CAF$

and $\frac{AG}{AD} = \frac{AF}{AC}$ [from part (i)]

27. (i) In order to apply any of the similarity criterion, atleast one more piece of information is necessary.

So, Darsh's answer is incorrect.

(ii) $\angle TQP = \angle RQS$ [vertically opposite angles]

$\angle P = \angle S$ [given]

Hence, concludes that by AA criterion of similarity of triangles, $\Delta TQP \sim \Delta RQS$.

So, Bhargav's answer is correct.

(iii) $\frac{TQ}{QR} = \frac{1}{3}$ [given]

$\angle TQP = \angle RQS$ [vertically opposite angles]

$\frac{PQ}{QS} = \frac{1}{3}$ [given]

Hence, concludes that by SAS criterion of similarity of triangles, $\Delta TQP \sim \Delta RQS$.

Hence, Tanvi's answer is correct.

28. Given $PQRS$ is a parallelogram, so $PQ \parallel SR$ and $PS \parallel QR$.

Also, $AB \parallel PS$

To prove $OC \parallel SR$

Proof In ΔOPS and ΔOAB,

$PS \parallel AB$ [given]

$\angle POS = \angle AOB$ [common angle]

$\angle OSP = \angle OBA$ [corresponding angles]

$\therefore \Delta OPS \sim \Delta OAB$ [by AA similarity criterion]

Then, $\frac{PS}{AB} = \frac{OS}{OB}$ ...(i)

In ΔCQR and ΔCAB,

$QR \parallel PS \parallel AB$

$\angle QCR = \angle ACB$ [common angle]

$\angle CRQ = \angle CBA$ [corresponding angle]

$\therefore \Delta CQR \sim \Delta CAB$ [by AA similarity criterion]

Then, $\frac{QR}{AB} = \frac{CR}{CB}$

$\Rightarrow \frac{PS}{AB} = \frac{CR}{CB}$ ...(ii)

[since, $PQRS$ is a parallelogram, so $PS = QR$]

From Eqs. (i) and (ii), we get

$\frac{OS}{OB} = \frac{CR}{CB}$ or $\frac{OB}{OS} = \frac{CB}{CR}$

On subtracting 1 from both sides, we get

$\frac{OB}{OS} - 1 = \frac{CB}{CR} - 1$

$\Rightarrow \frac{OB - OS}{OS} = \frac{CB - CR}{CR} \Rightarrow \frac{BS}{OS} = \frac{BR}{CR}$

By converse of basic proportionality theorem,

$OC \parallel SR$ **Hence proved.**

TRIANGLES

Similar Figures

Two geometrical figures are said to be similar figures, if they have same shape but not necessarily the same size.

e.g.

(i)  and 

(ii) 

(iii) and

Similar Polygons

Two polygons of same number of sides are similar, if all the corresponding angles are equal and all the corresponding sides are in the same ratio (or proportion).

Similar Triangles

Two triangles are said to be similar, if their corresponding angles are equal or the ratio of the lengths of corresponding sides are same.

Basic Proportionality Theorem (BPT)

A ΔABC in which a line DE parallel to BC intersects AB at D and AC at E i.e. $DE \parallel BC$.

Then, $\frac{AD}{DB} = \frac{AE}{EC}$

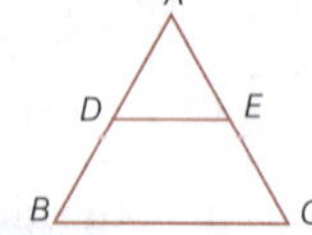

Note This theorem is also known as Thales theorem.

Converse of Basic Proportionality theorem (CBPT)

A ΔABC and a line DE, intersecting AB at D and AC at E such that

$$\frac{AD}{DB} = \frac{AE}{EC}$$

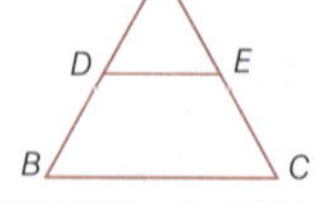

Then, $DE \parallel BC$

Criteria for Similarity of Triangles

We have some criteria for similarity of two triangles involving relationship between pairs of corresponding parts of two triangles.

(i) **AAA (Angle-Angle-Angle) Similarity Criterion**

In ΔABC and ΔDEF, we have

$\angle A = \angle D$, $\angle B = \angle E$ and $\angle C = \angle F$

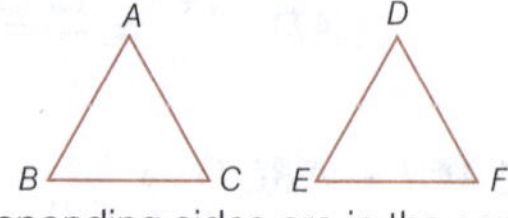

Corresponding sides are in the same ratio

i.e. $\frac{AB}{DE} = \frac{AC}{DF} = \frac{BC}{EF}$

then $\Delta ABC \sim \Delta DEF$

(ii) **SSS (Side-Side-Side) Similarity Criterion**

ΔABC and ΔDEF are such that

$$\frac{AB}{DE} = \frac{BC}{EF} = \frac{CA}{FD} (< 1)$$

Corresponding angles are equal.

i.e. $\angle A = \angle D$, $\angle B = \angle E$, $\angle C = \angle F$

then $\Delta ABC \sim \Delta DEF$

(iii) **SAS (Side-Angle-Side) Similarity Criterion**

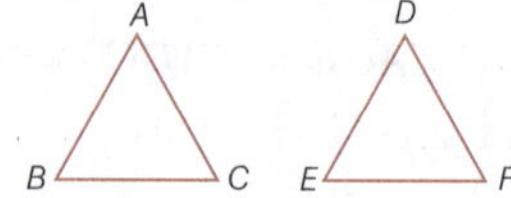

ΔABC and ΔDEF are such that

$$\frac{AB}{DE} = \frac{AC}{DF} (< 1)$$

and $\angle A = \angle D$

Then, $\Delta ABC \sim \Delta DEF$

CHAPTER 7

Coordinate Geometry

In class IXth, we have studied that to locate the position of a point on a plane, we require a pair of coordinate axes. The distance of a point from the Y-axis is called its **x-coordinate** or **abscissa.** The distance of a point from the X-axis is called its **y-coordinate** or ordinate. The coordinates of a point on the **X-axis** are of the form $(x, 0)$ and the coordinates of a point on the **Y-axis** are of the form $(0, y)$.

In this chapter, we will learn how to find the distance between two points whose coordinates are given and the coordinates of the point which divides a line segment joining two given points in a given ratio.

TOPIC 01 Distance Formula

Distance between any Two Points

The distance between any two points $P(x_1, y_1)$ and $Q(x_2, y_2)$ is given by

$$PQ = \sqrt{(x_2 - x_1)^2 + (y_2 - y_1)^2}$$

or $$PQ = \sqrt{(x_1 - x_2)^2 + (y_1 - y_2)^2}$$

i.e. $$PQ = \sqrt{(\text{Difference of abscissas})^2 + (\text{Difference of ordinates})^2}$$

where x-coordinates are called **abscissas** and y-coordinates are called **ordinates.**

Proof Let $X'OX$ and $Y'OY$ be the coordinate axes.

Let $P(x_1, y_1)$ and $Q(x_2, y_2)$ be the given points in XY-plane. Draw perpendicular lines PR and QS to the X-axis. Again, draw a perpendicular line from the point P on QS to meet it at the point T.

Now, $OR = x_1$ and $OS = x_2$

$\therefore$ $RS = OS - OR = x_2 - x_1 = PT$

Also, $SQ = y_2$ and $ST = PR = y_1$

$\therefore$ $QT = QS - ST = y_2 - y_1$

In right angled ΔPTQ,

$$PQ^2 = PT^2 + QT^2 \quad \text{[by Pythagoras theorem]}$$
$$= (x_2 - x_1)^2 + (y_2 - y_1)^2$$

$\Rightarrow$ $$PQ = \sqrt{(x_2 - x_1)^2 + (y_2 - y_1)^2}$$

Here, we will take only positive square root, because distance is always non-negative i.e. positive.

Note it Let $P(x, y)$ be a point and $O(0, 0)$ be the origin. Then, by distance formula, distance of P from O is

$$OP = \sqrt{(x-0)^2 + (y-0)^2} = \sqrt{x^2 + y^2}$$

Example 1. Find the distance between the points $P(-6, 7)$ and $Q(-1, -5)$.

Sol. Here, $x_1 = -6, y_1 = 7, x_2 = -1$ and $y_2 = -5$

$\therefore$ Distance between two points,

$$PQ = \sqrt{(x_2 - x_1)^2 + (y_2 - y_1)^2} \quad \text{[by distance formula]}$$
$$= \sqrt{(-1 + 6)^2 + (-5 - 7)^2}$$
$$= \sqrt{(5)^2 + (-12)^2}$$
$$= \sqrt{25 + 144} = \sqrt{169} = 13 \text{ units}$$

Example 2. **Find the distance of the point (20,15) from origin.**

Sol. Given, points are $P(20, 15)$ and origin $O(0, 0)$.

Here, $(x_1, y_1) = (20, 15)$ and $(x_2, y_2) = (0, 0)$

$\therefore$ Distance between two points,

$$PO = \sqrt{(x_2 - x_1)^2 + (y_2 - y_1)^2} \quad \text{[by distance formula]}$$

$$= \sqrt{(0-20)^2 + (0-15)^2} = \sqrt{(-20)^2 + (-15)^2}$$

$$= \sqrt{400 + 225} = \sqrt{625} = 25 \text{ units}$$

Example 3. **Find the values of x for which the distance between the points $A(x, 2)$ and $B(9, 8)$ is 10 units.** CBSE 2019

Sol. Given, points are $A(x, 2)$ and $B(9, 8)$.

According to the given condition, $AB = 10$

$$\Rightarrow \quad \sqrt{(9-x)^2 + (8-2)^2} = 10$$

$$\left[\because \text{distance} = \sqrt{(x_2 - x_1)^2 + (y_2 - y_1)^2}\right]$$

On squaring both sides, we get

$$81 + x^2 - 18x + (6)^2 = 100$$

$$\Rightarrow \quad x^2 - 18x = 100 - 36 - 81$$

$$\Rightarrow \quad x^2 - 18x + 17 = 0$$

$$\Rightarrow \quad x^2 - 17x - x + 17 = 0$$

$$\Rightarrow \quad x(x-17) - 1(x-17) = 0$$

$$\Rightarrow \quad (x-17)(x-1) = 0 \Rightarrow x = 1, 17$$

Hence, the values of x are 1 and 17.

Different Problems Related to Distance Formula

There are so many problems which can be solved using the distance formula. Some problems are given below.

Type I Problems Based on Collinearity of Points

Collinear points When three or more than three points lie on a same line, then they are called collinear points.

To show collinearity of three points say A, B and C, find AB, BC and CA and then show that sum of two shorter lengths is equal to the largest length

i.e. $AB + BC = AC$ or $AC + CB = AB$ or $BA + AC = BC$

If sum of shorter lengths is not equal to the largest length, then points are not collinear (or non-collinear.)

Example 4. **Check the points $(1, -1)$, $(5, 2)$ and $(9, 5)$ are collinear or not.**

Sol. Let $A = (1, -1)$, $B = (5, 2)$ and $C = (9, 5)$.

Then, $AB = \sqrt{(5-1)^2 + (2+1)^2}$

$$\left[\because \text{distance} = \sqrt{(x_2 - x_1)^2 + (y_2 - y_1)^2}\right]$$

$$= \sqrt{(4)^2 + (3)^2} = \sqrt{16+9} = \sqrt{25} = 5 \text{ units},$$

$$BC = \sqrt{(9-5)^2 + (5-2)^2}$$

$$= \sqrt{(4)^2 + (3)^2} = \sqrt{25} = 5 \text{ units}$$

and $AC = \sqrt{(9-1)^2 + (5+1)^2} = \sqrt{(8)^2 + (6)^2}$

$$= \sqrt{100} = 10 \text{ units}$$

$\because$ Here, $AC = AB + BC$

$\therefore$ A, B and C are collinear points.

Type II Problems Based on Equidistant Points

To find a point say X which is equidistant from two points say A and B, we take $AX = BX$ and then simplify.

Example 5. **If the point $P(x, y)$ is equidistant from the points $A(5, 1)$ and $B(1, 5)$, then prove that $x = y$.** CBSE 2024 (Standard)

Sol. Given, point $P(x, y)$ is equidistant from the points $A(5, 1)$ and $B(1, 5)$.

So, $$AP = BP$$

$$\Rightarrow \quad AP^2 = BP^2 \quad \text{[squaring both sides]}$$

$$\Rightarrow \quad (x-5)^2 + (y-1)^2 = (x-1)^2 + (y-5)^2$$

$$\left[\because \text{distance} = \sqrt{(x_2 - x_1)^2 + (y_2 - y_1)^2}\right]$$

$$\Rightarrow x^2 + 25 - 10x + y^2 + 1 - 2y = x^2 + 1 - 2x + y^2 + 25 - 10y$$

$$[\because (a-b)^2 = a^2 + b^2 - 2ab]$$

$$\Rightarrow \quad -10x + 2x = -10y + 2y$$

$$\Rightarrow \quad -8x = -8y \Rightarrow x = y \quad \textbf{Hence proved.}$$

Example 6. **Find the points on the X-axis each of which is at a distance of 10 units from the point $A(11, -8)$.** CBSE 2023 (Standard)

Sol. Let the points on X-axis be $(x_1, 0)$ and $(x_2, 0)$.

Using distance formula,

$$\sqrt{(11 - x_1)^2 + (-8-0)^2} = 10$$

and $\sqrt{(11 - x_2)^2 + (-8-0)^2} = 10$

On squaring both sides, we get

$$(11 - x_2)^2 + 64 = 100$$

$$\Rightarrow \quad (11 - x_2)^2 = 36 \Rightarrow 11 - x_2 = \pm 6$$

$$\Rightarrow \quad 11 - x_2 = 6 \text{ or } 11 - x_2 = -6 \Rightarrow x_2 = 5 \text{ or } x_2 = 17$$

Similarly, $x_1 = 5$ or 17

$\therefore$ The points on X-axis are $(5, 0)$ and $(17, 0)$.

Type III Problems Based on Geometrical Figures

Sometimes, three or four points are given and we have to show that the given points form a particular geometrical figure. To show that the given points form a

(i) **triangle**, prove that sum of lengths of any two sides is greater than the length of third side.

(ii) **isosceles triangle**, prove that two sides are equal.

(iii) **right angled triangle**, prove that sides of triangle satisfy Pythagoras theorem.

(iv) **equilateral triangle**, prove that all three sides are equal.

(v) **parallelogram**, prove that the opposite sides are equal.

(vi) **rectangle**, prove that opposite sides are equal and the diagonals are also equal.

(vii) **parallelogram but not a rectangle**, prove that its opposite sides are equal but the diagonals are not equal.

(viii) **square**, prove that the four sides are equal and the diagonals are also equal.

(ix) **rhombus**, prove that the four sides are equal.

(x) **rhombus but not a square**, prove that its all four sides are equal but the diagonals are not equal.

Calculate the length of different sides of a figure using distance formula and then show with the help of above results.

Note it To show that given quadrilateral $ABCD$ (say) is a square, we also use the following method.

First show that all four sides say AB, BC, CD and AD are equal and then find diagonal AC. Now, show that $AB^2 + BC^2 = AC^2$. Then, by converse of Pythagoras theorem, $\angle B = 90°$. Thus, given quadrilateral have four sides equal and one of the angle is 90°, so it forms a square.

Example 7. **Show that the points $A(3, 0)$, $B(6, 4)$ and $C(-1, 3)$ are vertices of a right-angled triangle.** CBSE 2023 (Basic)

Sol. Given, $A(3, 0)$, $B(6, 4)$ and $C(-1, 3)$.

Using distance formula,

$$AB^2 = (6-3)^2 + (4-0)^2 = 9 + 16 = 25$$

$$BC^2 = (-1-6)^2 + (3-4)^2 = 49 + 1 = 50$$

and $CA^2 = (3+1)^2 + (0-3)^2 = 16 + 9 = 25$

$\Rightarrow$ $BC^2 = AB^2 + CA^2$

$\Rightarrow$ ΔABC is a right angled triangle.

Example 8. **Show that $A(1, 2)$, $B(5, 4)$, $C(3, 8)$ and $D(-1, 6)$ are vertices of a parallelogram $ABCD$.** CBSE 2023 (Basic)

Sol. We know that the distance between the two points (x_1, y_1) and (x_2, y_2) is

$$d = \sqrt{(x_2 - x_1)^2 + (y_2 - y_1)^2}$$

$$\therefore AB = \sqrt{(5-1)^2 + (4-2)^2} = \sqrt{16+4} = \sqrt{20} = 2\sqrt{5} \text{ units}$$

$$BC = \sqrt{(3-5)^2 + (8-4)^2} = \sqrt{4+16}$$

$$= \sqrt{20} = 2\sqrt{5} \text{ units}$$

$$CD = \sqrt{(-1-3)^2 + (6-8)^2} = \sqrt{16+4}$$

$$= \sqrt{20} = 2\sqrt{5} \text{ units}$$

$$DA = \sqrt{(1+1)^2 + (2-6)^2} = \sqrt{4+16}$$

$$= \sqrt{20} = 2\sqrt{5} \text{ units}$$

We know that if the opposite sides have equal length, then $ABCD$ is a parallelogram.

Here, length of the opposite sides are equal

i.e. $AB = CD = 2\sqrt{5}$ units and $BC = DA = 2\sqrt{5}$ units

Hence, the given vertices are the vertices of a parallelogram.

Try These 7.1

1. Find the distance between the points
   (i) $(-6, 7)$ and $(-1, -5)$ (ii) $(-7, -3)$ and $(-5, -11)$
   (iii) $\left(\frac{-6}{5}, -3\right)$ and $\left(-4, \frac{-7}{5}\right)$ (iv) $(a, 0)$ and $(0, b)$
   (v) $(a+b, b+c)$ and $(a-b, c-b)$
2. Find the distance of the point $P(3, -4)$ from the origin.
3. Find the distance between the points $P(\cos\alpha, -\sin\alpha)$ and $Q(-\cos\alpha, \sin\alpha)$.
4. Find the points on the X-axis which are at a distance of $2\sqrt{5}$ units from the point $(7, -4)$. How many such points are there?
5. If the distance between the points $A(1, 1)$ and $B(x, 1)$ is 5 units, then find the value(s) of x.
6. If the distance between the points $(3, y)$ and $(3, -6)$ is 10 units, then what is the positive value of y?
7. The radius of a circle with centre at the origin is $\frac{1}{2}$ units. Find all the points on the circle which are of the form $(-y, y)$. Show your steps. CBSE CFPQ
8. Show that $(a, 1)$, $(b, 1)$ and $(c, 1)$ are collinear points.
9. Show that the points $(3, 2)$, $\left(4, \frac{5}{2}\right)$ and $(5, 3)$ are collinear.
10. Find the relation between x and y such that the point $P(x, y)$ is equidistant from $(7, 1)$ and $(3, 5)$. CBSE 2024 (Standard)
11. Point $P(x, y)$ is equidistant from points $A(6, 2)$ and $B(2, 6)$. Prove that $x = y$.
12. Find the point on Y-axis, equidistant from two points $A(-3, 4)$ and $B(3, 6)$ on the same plane.
13. If $Q(0, 1)$ is equidistant from $P(5, -3)$ and $R(x, 6)$, then find the values of x. Find distance QR.
14. If $A(x, y)$ is a point on the line joining the points $B(2, -3)$ and $C(-4, 5)$ and A is equidistant from B and C, then prove that $3x - 4y + 7 = 0$
15. Points $A(-1, y)$ and $B(5, 7)$ lie on a circle with centre $O(2, -3y)$. Find the value of y and radius of the circle.
16. Prove that the points $A(0, 1)$, $B(1, 4)$, $C(4, 3)$ and $D(3, 0)$ are the vertices of a square.
17. Show that the points $A(2, -2)$, $B(14, 10)$, $C(11, 13)$ and $D(-1, 1)$ are the vertices of a rectangle.
18. If two vertices of an equilateral triangle are $(0, 0)$ and $(3, \sqrt{3})$. Find the third vertex.
19. If two opposite vertices of a rectangle are $(-1, 3)$ and $(4, 0)$. Find the coordinates of other two vertices.
20. Show that the quadrilateral whose vertices are $(1, 3)$, $(2, 6)$, $(5, 7)$ and $(4, 4)$ is a rhombus.
21. Two vertices of an isosceles triangle are $(2, 8)$ and $(10, 2)$. Find the third vertex, if the length of the equal sides is 10 units.

22. **Show that the points (4,2), (7,5) and (9,7) do not form a triangle.**

23. **Find the area of a rhombus if its vertices are (– 3, 2), (– 5, – 5), (2, – 3) and (4, 4) taken in order.**

24. **Name the type of geometrical figure formed, if any by the following points, and given reasons for your answer.**

(i) (1, 1), (4, 1), (1, 4), (4, 4) (ii) (4, 2), (6, 2), (4, 5)

Answers

1. **Hint** Do same as Example 1.

Ans. (i) 13 units (ii) $\sqrt{68}$ units (iii) $\frac{\sqrt{260}}{5}$ units

(iv) $\sqrt{a^2+b^2}$ units (v) $2\sqrt{2}b$ units

2. **Hint** Do same as Example 2. **Ans.** 5 units

3. **Hint** Do same as Example 1. **Ans.** 2 units

4. **Hint** Do same as Example 6.

Ans. (9,0) and (5,0); Required number of points $=2$

5. **Hint** Do same as Example 3. **Ans.** $x=-4, 6$

6. **Hint** Do same as Example 3. **Ans.** 4

7. The distance between the origin and the point $(-y, y)$ is $\frac{1}{2}$ units.

$\because$ Using the distance formula, we have

$$(-y)^2+y^2=\left(\frac{1}{2}\right)^2$$

$$\Rightarrow \quad 2y^2=\frac{1}{4} \Rightarrow y^2=\frac{1}{8}$$

$$\Rightarrow \quad y=\frac{1}{\sqrt{8}} \text{ and } \frac{-1}{\sqrt{8}}$$

$\therefore$ The points are $\left(\frac{1}{\sqrt{8}}, \frac{-1}{\sqrt{8}}\right)$ and $\left(\frac{-1}{\sqrt{8}}, \frac{1}{\sqrt{8}}\right)$.

8. **Hint** Do same as Example 4.

9. **Hint** Do same as Example 4.

10. **Hint** Solve the equation

$\sqrt{(x-7)^2+(y-1)^2}=\sqrt{(3-x)^2+(5-y)^2}$ **Ans.** $x-y=2$

11. **Hint** Do same as Example 5.

12. **Hint** Let the point on Y-axis be $P(0, y)$.

Given, $P(0, y)$ is equidistant from the points $A(-3, 4)$ and $B(3, 6)$.

So, $\quad AP=BP$

$$\Rightarrow \sqrt{[0-(-3)]^2+(y-4)^2}=\sqrt{(0-3)^2+(y-6)^2}$$

[by distance formula]

$$\Rightarrow \quad 9+y^2+16-8y=9+y^2+36-12y$$

[squaring both sides]

$$\Rightarrow \quad 12y-8y=20 \Rightarrow 4y=20$$

$$\Rightarrow \quad y=5$$

Hence, the point on Y-axis is (0, 5).

Ans. (0, 5).

13. **Hint** $QP=QR$,

Ans. Coordinates of R are $(\pm 4, 6)$.

When $R=(4, 6)$, $QR=\sqrt{41}$ units, $PR=\sqrt{82}$ units

When $R=(-4, 6)$, $QR=\sqrt{41}$ units, $PR=9\sqrt{2}$ units

14. **Hint** Distance of AB = Distance of AC

15. **Hint** Since, O is the centre of circle and A, B are points on its circumference.

$\therefore \quad OA=OB$

Ans. $y=-1, 7$

When $y=-1$, radius $=5$ units

and when $y=7$, radius $=\sqrt{793}$ units

16. **Hint** See properties of Square.

17. **Hint** See properties of Rectangle.

18. **Hint** Let $O(0, 0)$ and $A(3, \sqrt{3})$.

Also, let the third vertex be $B(x, y)$.

Then, we get

$OB=OA$ [$\because$ ΔOAB is an equilateral triangle]

and $OA=AB$ **Ans.** $(0, 2\sqrt{3})$ or $(3, -\sqrt{3})$

19. **Hint** See properties of rectangle. **Ans** $(-1, 0)$ and $(4, 3)$

20. **Hint** See properties of rhombus.

21. **Hint** See properties of an isosceles triangle. **Ans.** (4,10)

22. **Hint** Show that sum of any two sides of a triangle is not greater than the third side.

23. **Hint** Find distance of $A(-3, 2)$ and $C(2, -3)$ and distance of $B(-5, -5)$ and $D(4, 4)$.

$\therefore$ Area of rhombus $=\frac{1}{2}\times AC\times BD$

Ans. 45 sq. units

24. (i) Let $A(1, 1)$, $B(4, 1)$, $C(4, 4)$ and $D(1, 4)$ be the given points.

Then, $AB=\sqrt{(4-1)^2+(1-1)^2}=\sqrt{9+0}=3$ units

$BC=\sqrt{(4-4)^2+(4-1)^2}=\sqrt{0+9}=3$ units

$CD=\sqrt{(4-4)^2+(1-4)^2}=\sqrt{9+0}=3$ units

$DA=\sqrt{(1-4)^2+(1-1)^2}=\sqrt{9+0}=3$ units

$AC=\sqrt{(4-1)^2+(4-1)^2}=\sqrt{9+9}=3\sqrt{2}$ units

$BD=\sqrt{(4-1)^2+(1-4)^2}=\sqrt{9+9}=3\sqrt{2}$ units

Since, $AB=BC=CD=DA$ and also, $AC=BD$

Thus, given coordinates formed a square.

(ii) Let $A(4, 2)$, $B(6, 2)$, $C(4, 5)$

Then, $AB=\sqrt{(6-4)^2+(2-2)^2}=\sqrt{4}=2$ units

$BC=\sqrt{(4-6)^2+(5-2)^2}=\sqrt{4+9}=\sqrt{13}$ units

$AC=\sqrt{(4-4)^2+(5-2)^2}=\sqrt{9}=3$ units

Now, $AB^2+AC^2=2^2+3^2=4+9=13$

and $BC^2=(\sqrt{13})^2=13$

Thus, given coordinates formed a right angled triangle.

TOPIC 02 Section Formula

In this topic, we will derive a formula to find the coordinates of a point which divides the given line segment internally in a given ratio.

Internal Division of a Line Segment

Let $A(x_1, y_1)$ and $B(x_2, y_2)$ be two points and $P(x, y)$ is a point on the line segment joining A and B such that $AP : BP = m_1 : m_2$, then point P divides line segment AB internally in the ratio $m_1 : m_2$.

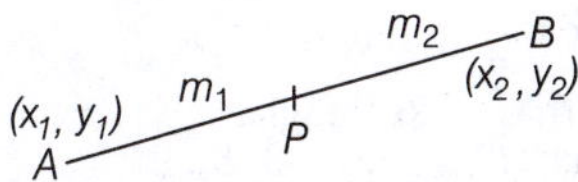

Coordinates of point P are given by

$$\left(\frac{m_1x_2 + m_2x_1}{m_1 + m_2}, \frac{m_1y_2 + m_2y_1}{m_1 + m_2}\right)$$

This formula is known as **section formula for internal division.**

Proof Consider any two points $A(x_1, y_1)$ and $B(x_2, y_2)$ and assume that point $P(x, y)$ divides AB internally in the ratio $m_1 : m_2$.

Then, $\frac{PA}{BP} = \frac{m_1}{m_2}$ ...(i)

Draw the perpendiculars AR, PS and BT on the X-axis from the points A, P and B, which intersect X-axis at R, S and T, respectively. Now, draw $AQ \perp PS$ and $PC \perp BT$, which are parallel to X-axis.

By AA similarity criterion, $\Delta AQP \sim \Delta PCB$

$$\therefore \quad \frac{PA}{BP} = \frac{AQ}{PC} = \frac{PQ}{BC} \quad \text{...(ii)}$$

Now, $AQ = RS = OS - OR = x - x_1$

$PC = ST = OT - OS = x_2 - x$

$PQ = PS - QS = PS - AR = y - y_1$ $\quad [\because QS = AR]$

and $BC = BT - CT = BT - PS = y_2 - y$ $\quad [\because CT = PS]$

On putting these values in Eq. (ii), we get

$$\frac{PA}{BP} = \frac{x - x_1}{x_2 - x} = \frac{y - y_1}{y_2 - y}$$

$$\Rightarrow \quad \underset{\text{I}}{\frac{m_1}{m_2}} = \underset{\text{II}}{\frac{x - x_1}{x_2 - x}} = \underset{\text{III}}{\frac{y - y_1}{y_2 - y}} \quad \text{[from Eq. (i)] ...(iii)}$$

On taking I and II terms of Eq. (iii), we get

$$\frac{m_1}{m_2} = \frac{x - x_1}{x_2 - x}$$

$$\Rightarrow \quad m_1(x_2 - x) = m_2(x - x_1)$$

$$\Rightarrow \quad -m_1x - m_2x = -m_1x_2 - m_2x_1$$

$$\Rightarrow \quad x(m_1 + m_2) = m_1x_2 + m_2x_1$$

$$\Rightarrow \quad x = \frac{m_1x_2 + m_2x_1}{m_1 + m_2}$$

On taking I and III terms of Eq. (iii), we get

$$\frac{m_1}{m_2} = \frac{y - y_1}{y_2 - y}$$

$$\Rightarrow \quad m_1(y_2 - y) = m_2(y - y_1)$$

$$\Rightarrow \quad m_1y_2 - m_1y = m_2y - m_2y_1$$

$$\Rightarrow \quad (m_1 + m_2)y = m_1y_2 + m_2y_1$$

$$\Rightarrow \quad y = \frac{m_1y_2 + m_2y_1}{m_1 + m_2}$$

Hence, the coordinates of the point P are

$$\left(\frac{m_1x_2 + m_2x_1}{m_1 + m_2}, \frac{m_1y_2 + m_2y_1}{m_1 + m_2}\right).$$

If the ratio in which P divides AB is $K : 1$, then the coordinates of the point P will be

$$\left(\frac{kx_2 + x_1}{k + 1}, \frac{ky_2 + y_1}{k + 1}\right)$$

Special Case

If a point divides the line segment joining the points (x_1, y_1) and (x_2, y_2) internally in the ratio 1:1, then we get mid-point of this line segment. Thus, coordinates of the mid-point P of the line segment joining the points $A(x_1, y_1)$ and $B(x_2, y_2)$ are $\left(\frac{x_1 + x_2}{2}, \frac{y_1 + y_2}{2}\right)$.

Example 1. **Find the coordinates of the point which divides the line segment joining the points (9, 4) and (3,5) in the ratio 2 : 1 internally.**

Sol. Let $P(x, y)$ be the required point.

Using the section formula, we get

$$x = \frac{2(3) + 1(9)}{2 + 1}$$

$$= \frac{6 + 9}{3} = \frac{15}{3} = 5$$

and $$y = \frac{2(5) + 1(4)}{2 + 1} = \frac{10 + 4}{3} = \frac{14}{3}$$

Hence, $\left(5, \frac{14}{3}\right)$ is the required point.

Example 2. **The line segment joining the points $A(4,-5)$ and $B(4, 5)$ is divided by the point P such that $AP : AB = 2:3$. Find the coordinates of P.** CBSE 2023 (Standard)

Sol.

2 : 3
A (4, –5) P (x, y) B (4, 5)

By section formula,

$$x = \frac{(2\times 4)+(4\times 3)}{2+3} \Rightarrow x = \frac{8+12}{5} = \frac{20}{5} = 4$$

and $$y = \frac{(2\times 5)+(3\times(-5))}{2+3} \Rightarrow y = \frac{10-15}{5} = \frac{-5}{5} = -1$$

$\therefore \quad x = 4$ and $y = -1$

So, coordinates of P are $(4, -1)$.

Example 3. **A line intersects X and Y-axes at points P and Q, respectively. If $R(2, 5)$ is the mid-point of line segment PQ, then find the coordinates of P and Q.** CBSE 2023 (Standard)

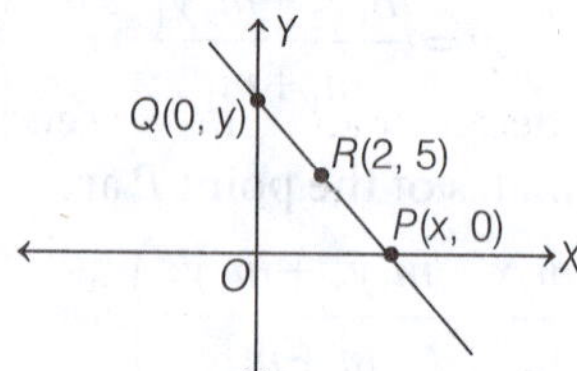

Sol. Let the coordinates of point P and Q be $(x, 0)$ and $(0, y)$, respectively.

$$\therefore \; (2, 5) = \left(\frac{0+x}{2}, \frac{y+0}{2}\right)$$

$\left[\because \text{ using mid-point formula, coordinates of mid-point are } \left(\frac{x_1+x_2}{2}, \frac{y_1+y_2}{2}\right)\right]$

$$\Rightarrow \quad (2, 5) = \left(\frac{x}{2}, \frac{y}{2}\right)$$

On comparing, we get

$$\frac{x}{2} = 2 \Rightarrow x = 4 \text{ and } \frac{y}{2} = 5 \Rightarrow y = 10$$

So, the coordinates of P and Q are $(4, 0)$ and $(0, 10)$, respectively.

Example 4. **Find the ratio in which the line segment joining the points $A(6, 3)$ and $B(-2, -5)$ is divided by X-axis.** CBSE 2023 (Standard)

Sol. Let $P(x, 0)$ be the point on the X-axis which divides the line joining the points $A(6, 3)$ and $B(-2, -5)$.

Let the ratio be $k : 1$.

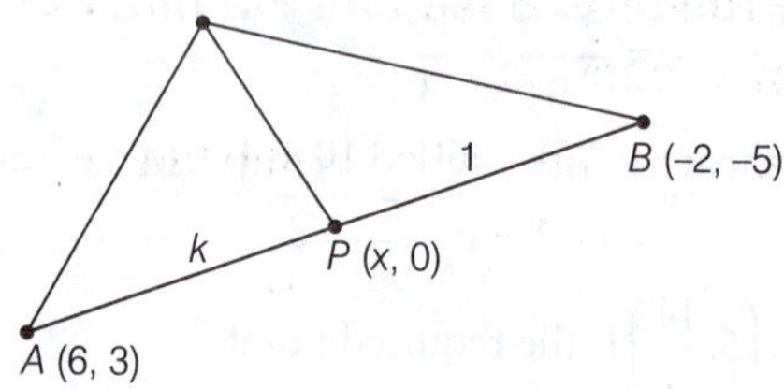

By section formula,

$$P(x, 0) = \left(\frac{k(-2)+1(6)}{k+1}, \frac{k(-5)+1(3)}{k+1}\right)$$

$$\left[\because x = \frac{m_1x_2+m_2x_1}{m_1+m_2} \text{ and } y = \frac{m_1y_2+m_2y_1}{m_1+m_2}\right]$$

On equating y-coordinates, we get

$$0 = \frac{-5k+3}{k+1}$$

$\Rightarrow \quad 5k = 3$

$\Rightarrow \quad k = \frac{3}{5}$

$\therefore$ The ratio is $k:1 = \frac{3}{5}:1 = 3:5$

Different Types of Problems Based on Section Formula

Type I To Show Collinearity Using Section Formula

To show collinearity of points say A, B and C by section formula, first assume that C divides AB in the ratio of $k:1$. Then, write coordinates of C by section formula and then equate it to original x and y-coordinates of C separately. If value of k from both equations is same, then A, B and C are collinear, otherwise not.

Example 5. **Using section formula, show that the points $A(-3,-1)$, $B(1, 3)$ and $C(-1, 1)$ are collinear.**

Sol. Let $C(-1, 1)$ divides AB in the ratio $k:1$.

k 1
A (–3,–1) C(–1,1) B (1, 3)

Then, using section formula,

Coordinates of C are $\left(\frac{k-3}{k+1}, \frac{3k-1}{k+1}\right)$.

Thus, $C(-1, 1) = C\left(\frac{k-3}{k+1}, \frac{3k-1}{k+1}\right)$

On equating x-coordinate from both sides, we get

$$-1 = \frac{k-3}{k+1} \quad \Rightarrow -k-1 = k-3$$

$\Rightarrow \quad -2k = -3+1 \Rightarrow -2k = -2 \Rightarrow k = 1$

On equating y-coordinate from both sides, we get

$$1 = \frac{3k-1}{k+1} \quad \Rightarrow k+1 = 3k-1$$

$\Rightarrow \quad 2k = 2 \Rightarrow k = 1$

Since, in both cases value of k is same. So, C divides AB in the ratio 1 : 1 i.e. C is the mid-point of AB.

Hence, A, B and C are collinear.

Type II Problems Based on Finding the Section Ratio and Section Point

Example 6. In what ratio does the X-axis divides the line segment joining the points (2, – 3) and (5, 6)? Also, find the coordinates of the point of intersection.

CBSE 2024 (Standard)

Sol. Let the given points be $A(2, -3)$ and $B(5, 6)$ and let AB be divided by the X-axis in the ratio $k:1$ at the point P.

Then, by section formula the coordinates of P are

$$(x, 0)=\left(\frac{5k+2}{k+1}, \frac{6k-3}{k+1}\right)$$

On comparing ordinate, we get

$$\frac{6k-3}{k+1}=0$$

$$\Rightarrow \quad 6k-3=0$$

$$\Rightarrow \quad 6k=3$$

$$\Rightarrow \quad k=\frac{3}{6}=\frac{1}{2}$$

$\therefore$ The required ratio is $\frac{1}{2}:1$ which is same as $1:2$.

Thus, the X-axis divides the line AB in the ratio $1:2$ at the point P.

Now, on applying $K=\frac{1}{2}$, we get the coordinates of point.

$$P\left(\frac{5k+2}{k+1}, 0\right)=P\left(\frac{5\times\frac{1}{2}+2}{\frac{1}{2}+1}, 0\right)$$

$$=P\left(\frac{\frac{5+4}{2}}{\frac{1+2}{2}}, 0\right)$$

$$=P\left(\frac{9}{3}, 0\right)$$

$$=P(3, 0)$$

Hence, the point of intersection of AB and the X-axis is $P(3, 0)$.

Type III Problems Based on Finding the Unknown Vertex of the Geometrical Figure

For finding the unknown vertex of a given geometrical figure (e.g. Parallelogram, triangle etc.) we use their properties.

Example 7. If the points $A(6,1)$, $B(8,2)$, $C(9,4)$ and $D(p,3)$ are the vertices of a parallelogram, taken in order, then find the value of p.

Sol. Given, vertices of a parallelogram are $A(6, 1)$, $B(8, 2)$, $C(9, 4)$ and $D(p, 3)$. Here, we have to find the value of p.

We know that diagonals of a parallelogram bisect each other.

$\therefore$ Coordinates of mid-point of diagonal AC

= Coordinates of mid-point of diagonal BD

$$\Rightarrow \quad \left(\frac{6+9}{2}, \frac{1+4}{2}\right)=\left(\frac{8+p}{2}, \frac{2+3}{2}\right)$$

$$\left[\because \text{mid - point}=\left(\frac{x_1+x_2}{2}, \frac{y_1+y_2}{2}\right)\right]$$

$$\Rightarrow \quad \left(\frac{15}{2}, \frac{5}{2}\right)=\left(\frac{8+p}{2}, \frac{5}{2}\right)$$

On equating x-coordinate from both sides, we get

$$\frac{15}{2}=\frac{8+p}{2} \Rightarrow 15=8+p$$

$$\Rightarrow \quad p=15-8 \Rightarrow p=7$$

Hence, the required value of p is 7.

Example 8. Find the coordinates of a point A, where AB is a diameter of the circle with centre $C(3,-1)$ and the point B is (2, 6).

CBSE 2019

Sol. Let AB be the diameter and C be the centre of the circle.

Let coordinates of A be (a, b).

Clearly, C will be the mid-point of AB.

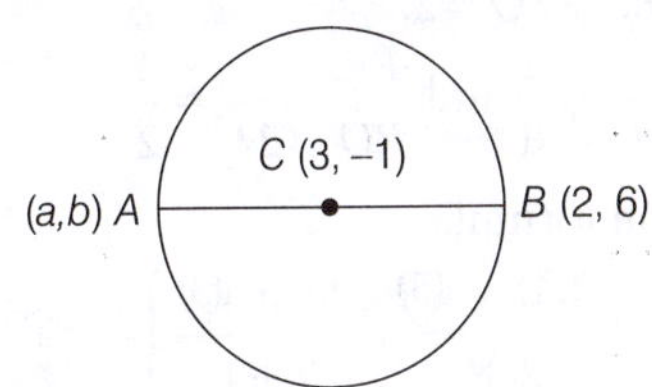

$$\therefore \text{ Coordinates of } C=\left(\frac{a+2}{2}, \frac{b+6}{2}\right)$$

$$\left[\because \text{coordinates of mid-point}=\left(\frac{x_1+x_2}{2}, \frac{y_1+y_2}{2}\right)\right]$$

$$\Rightarrow \quad (3, -1)=\left(\frac{a+2}{2}, \frac{b+6}{2}\right)$$

[$\because$ coordinates of $C=(3, -1)$ are given]

On comparing the coordinates x and y, we get

$$3=\frac{a+2}{2} \text{ and } -1=\frac{b+6}{2}$$

$$\Rightarrow \quad 6=a+2 \text{ and } -2=b+6$$

$$\Rightarrow \quad a=6-2 \text{ and } b=-2-6$$

$$\Rightarrow \quad a=4 \text{ and } b=-8$$

Hence, the coordinates of point A are $(4, -8)$.

Type IV Problems Based on Finding Points of Trisection

Trisection means a line is divided into three equal parts.

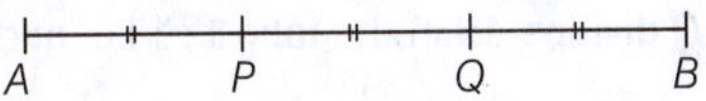

This can be done by finding two points P and Q on the line segment AB, such that $AP = PQ = QB$.

Let $\quad AP = PQ = QB = x$

Then, $\quad AP = x$ and $PB = PQ + QB = x + x = 2x$

$\therefore \quad AP : PB = x : 2x = 1 : 2$

Also, $AQ = AP + PQ = x + x = 2x$ and $QB = x$

$\therefore \; AQ : QB = 2x : x = 2 : 1$

Hence, to find points of trisection, we find two points P and Q (say) such that P divides AB in the ratio 1 : 2 and Q divides AB in the ratio 2 :1.

Example 9. Find the coordinates of the points of trisection of the line segment joining the points (5, 3) and (4, 5). CBSE 2023 (Standard)

Sol. Let $P \equiv (5, 3)$ and $Q \equiv (4, 5)$

Let the points of trisection be $R(a, b)$ and $S(c, d)$.

P (5, 3) — R (a, b) — S (c, d) — Q (4, 5)

Then, $PR = RS = SQ = \lambda$ (say)

$\therefore \quad PS = PR + RS = 2\lambda$

$RQ = RS + SQ = 2\lambda$

$\Rightarrow \dfrac{PS}{SQ} = \dfrac{2\lambda}{\lambda} = \dfrac{2}{1}$ and $\dfrac{PR}{RQ} = \dfrac{\lambda}{2\lambda} = \dfrac{1}{2}$

Using section formula,

$$S(c, d) = \left(\frac{2(4) + 1(5)}{2+1}, \frac{2(5) + 1(3)}{2+1}\right)$$

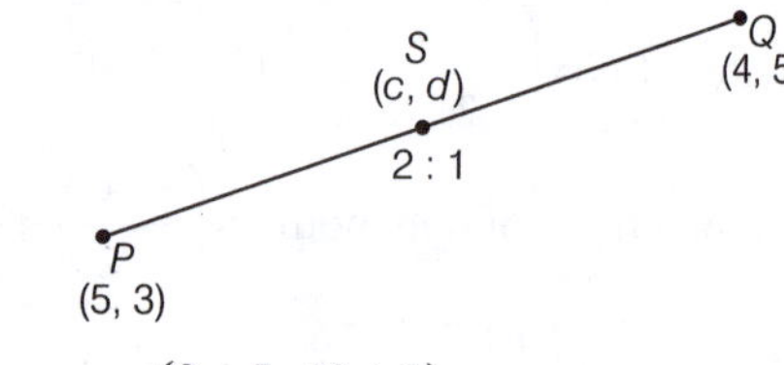

$$= \left(\frac{8+5}{3}, \frac{10+3}{3}\right)$$

$$\therefore \; S(c, d) = \left(\frac{13}{3}, \frac{13}{3}\right)$$

Similarly, $R(a, b) = \left(\dfrac{1(4) + 2(5)}{1+2}, \dfrac{1(5) + 2(3)}{1+2}\right) = \left(\dfrac{14}{3}, \dfrac{11}{3}\right)$

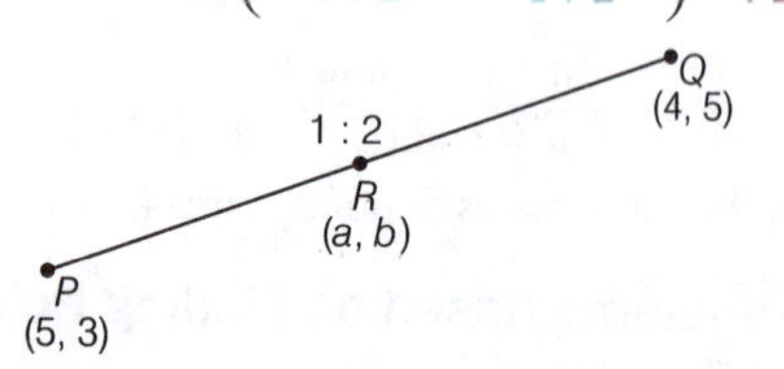

Note it If points P, Q and R divide the line segment AB into four equal parts, then P divides AB in the ratio 1 : 3, R divides AB in the ratio 3 : 1 and Q divides AB in the ratio 1 : 1 i.e. mid-point of AB.

A — P — Q — R — B

Try These 7.2

1. **Find the coordinates of the point which divides the line segment joining the points (3, 4) and (–5, – 7) internally in the following ratios:**
   (i) 3 : 2 (ii) 2 : 3 (iii) 1 : 3
   (iv) 3 : 1 (v) 4 : 5
2. **Find the coordinates of the mid-point of the line segment joining the following points:**
   (i) $A(4, 0)$ and $B\left(-\dfrac{7}{2}, 0\right)$
   (ii) $P(p+q, q+r)$ and $Q(p-q, r-q)$
   (iii) $M(-7, -4)$ and $N(1, 6)$
   (iv) $R(3, -4)$ and $S(-7, 8)$
   (v) $C(0, c)$ and $D(0, d)$
3. **If point P divides the line segment joining the points $A(2, 1)$ and $B(6, 5)$ in the ratio 1 : 3, then find the coordinates of P.**
4. **Find the coordinates of the point C, if the point $B\left(\dfrac{1}{2}, 6\right)$ divides the line segment joining the points $A(3, 5)$ and C in the ratio 1 : 3.**
5. **The mid-point of the line segment joining $P(3a, 4)$ and $B(-3, 4b)$ is (3, 4). Find the values of a and b.**
6. **If $P(9a - 2, -b)$ divides line segment joining $A(3a + 1, -3)$ and $B(8a, 5)$ in the ratio 3 : 1, then find the values of a and b. Also, determine the value of $a^2 + b^2$.** NCERT Exemplar
7. **Using section formula, show that the following points are collinear.**
   (i) $P(2, -1)$, $Q(0, 1)$ and $R(-3, 4)$
   (ii) $A(2, 3)$, $B(1, 4)$ and $C(-2, 7)$
8. **The points A, B and C are collinear and $AB = BC$. If the coordinates of A, B and C are $(3, a)$, $(1, 3)$ and $(b, 4)$ respectively, then find the values of a and b.**
9. **Find the ratio in which the line segment joining the points (5, 3) and (– 1, 6) is divided by Y-axis.** CBSE 2024 (Standard)
10. **Find the ratio in which the line segment joining the points (8, – 3) and (16, 5) is divided by (14, 3).**
11. **If the centre of a circle is $\left(\dfrac{4}{3}, -2\right)$ and one end of the diameter is (3, 2), then find the coordinates of the other end.**
12. **In the given figure, AD is a median of ΔABC. Find the coordinates of D.**

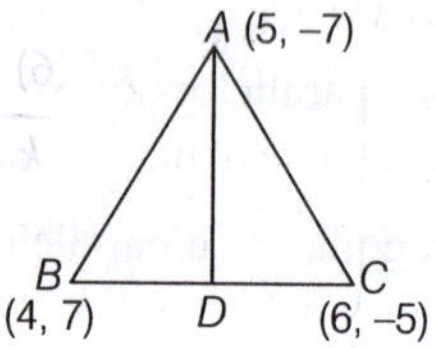

13. **Find the length of the median AD of ΔABC having vertices A (0, – 1), B(2, 1) and C (0, 3).** CBSE 2024 (Standard)

14. **If (1, 2), (4, y), (x, 6) and (4, 2) are the vertices of a parallelogram taken in order. Find x and y.**

15. **Find the coordinates of the point Q on the X-axis, which lies on the perpendicular bisector of the line segment joining the points A (–5, –2) and B (4, –2). Name the type of triangle formed by the points Q, A and B.** NCERT Exemplar

16. **Find the coordinates of the points which divide the line segment joining the points (– 4,0) and (0, 6) in four equal parts.**

Answers

1. Hint Do same as Example 1.

Ans.

(i) $\left(\frac{-9}{5}, \frac{-13}{5}\right)$ (ii) $\left(\frac{-1}{5}, \frac{-2}{5}\right)$ (iii) $\left(1, \frac{5}{4}\right)$

(iv) $\left(-3, -\frac{17}{4}\right)$ (v) $\left(\frac{-5}{9}, \frac{-8}{9}\right)$

2. Hint Do same as Example 3.

Ans.

(i) $\left(\frac{1}{4}, 0\right)$ (ii) (p, r) (iii) $(-3, 1)$

(iv) $(-2, 2)$ (v) $\left(0, \frac{c+d}{2}\right)$

3. Hint Do same as Example 2. **Ans.** (3,2)

4. Hint A (3, 5) —1 : 3— $B\left(\frac{1}{2}, 6\right)$ — C (x, y)

By section formula, we get

$$\left(\frac{1\times x+3\times 3}{4}, \frac{1\times y+3\times 5}{4}\right)=\left(\frac{1}{2}, 6\right)$$ **Ans.** (–7, 9)

5. Hint Do same as Example 3. **Ans.** $a=3$, $b=1$

6. Hint Use section formula with

$$m_1=3, m_2=1, x_1=3a+1, y_1=-3, x_2=8a, y_2=5$$

Ans. $a=1$ and $b=-3$; $a^2+b^2=10$

7. Hint Do same as Example 5.

8. Hint As, $AB=BC$. Thus, B is the mid-point of AC. Use mid-point formula to find a and b.

Ans. $a=2$ and $b=-1$

9. Hint Let a point $P(0, y)$ divides the line segment joining the points A (5, 3) and B(–1, 6) in the ratio $k:1$.

A(5, 3) —k— P(0, y) —1— B(–1, 6)

By section formula, we get

$$(0, y)=\left[\frac{k(-1)+1(5)}{k+1}, \frac{k(6)+1(3)}{k+1}\right]$$

$$(0, y)=\left(\frac{-k+5}{k+1}, \frac{6k+3}{k+1}\right) \quad \ldots(i)$$

On equating x-coordinate from both sides of Eq. (i), we get

$$0=\frac{-k+5}{k+1}$$

$\Rightarrow$ $-k+5=0 \Rightarrow k=5$

Hence, Y-axis divides the line segment joining the points (5, 3) and (–1, 6) in the ratio 5 : 1.

10. Hint Use the section formula. **Ans.** (3:1)

11. Hint Do same as Example 8. **Ans.** $\left(\frac{-1}{3}, -6\right)$

12. Hint D is the mid-point of BC. **Ans.** (5,1)

13. Hint Given, vertices of ΔABC are A (0, –1), B (2,1) and C (0, 3).

Let AD be the median of side BC.

Using mid-point formula,

$$\text{Coordinates of } D=\left(\frac{x_1+x_2}{2}, \frac{y_1+y_2}{2}\right)$$

$$=\left(\frac{2+0}{2}, \frac{1+3}{2}\right)=\left(\frac{2}{2}, \frac{4}{2}\right)=(1, 2)$$

Now, we find the length of median AD, by using distance formula $=\sqrt{(x_2-x_1)^2+(y_2-y_1)^2}$

$$\therefore \text{Length of } AD=\sqrt{(1-0)^2+(2+1)^2}$$

$$=\sqrt{(1)^2+(3)^2}$$

[$\because$ coordinates of $A=(0, -1)$ and coordinates of $D=(1, 2)$]

$$=\sqrt{1+9}=\sqrt{10} \text{ units}$$

14. Hint Do same as Example 7. **Ans.** $x=7, y=6$

15. Hint First plot the points A, B on cartesian plane and join them. Now, find mid-point P of AB. Then, draw a vertical line passing through the mid-point P, which cuts the X-axis at the point $Q\left(-\frac{1}{2}, 0\right)$, which are the required coordinates.

Ans. $Q\left(\frac{-1}{2}, 0\right)$, isosceles triangle.

16. Hint Let P, Q and R be the points which divide the line segment into four equal parts.

A (–4, 0) — P — Q — R — B (0, 6)

Then, $AP:PB=1:3, AQ:QB=2:2, AR:RB=3:1$

$$\text{So, coordinates of } P=\left(\frac{3(-4)+1(0)}{1+3}, \frac{3(0)+1(6)}{1+3}\right)$$

$$=\left(-3, \frac{3}{2}\right)$$

$$\text{Coordinates of } Q=\left(\frac{-4+0}{2}, \frac{0+6}{2}\right)=(-2, 3)$$

[$\because Q$ is the mid-point of AB]

$$\text{Coordinates of } R=\left(\frac{1(-4)+3(0)}{4}, \frac{1(0)+3(6)}{4}\right)=\left(-1, \frac{9}{2}\right)$$

$\therefore$ Three points are $\left(-3, \frac{3}{2}\right)$, $(-2, 3)$ and $\left(-1, \frac{9}{2}\right)$.

NCERT FOLDER

Complete Solutions of All Exercises of NCERT Textbook

EXERCISE 7.1

Q1. Find the distance between the following pairs of points.

(i) (2, 3), (4, 1)

(ii) (– 5, 7), (– 1, 3)

(iii) (*a*, *b*), (– *a*, – *b*)

Sol. (i) Let $A(2, 3)$ and $B(4, 1)$ be the given points.

Here, $x_1 = 2, y_1 = 3$ and $x_2 = 4, y_2 = 1$

Now, $AB = \sqrt{(x_2 - x_1)^2 + (y_2 - y_1)^2}$ [by distance formula]

$= \sqrt{(4-2)^2 + (1-3)^2}$

$= \sqrt{(2)^2 + (-2)^2} = \sqrt{4+4} = \sqrt{8} = 2\sqrt{2}$ units

(ii) Do same as Part (i). **Ans.** $4\sqrt{2}$ units

(iii) Do same as Part (i). **Ans.** $2\sqrt{a^2 + b^2}$ units

Q2. Find the distance between the points (0, 0) and (36, 15). Can you now find the distance between the two towns *A* and *B* discussed in NCERT section 7.2.

Sol. Do same as Example 2 of Topic 1. **Ans.** 39 and the distance between the towns *A* and *B* is 39 km.

Q3. Determine, if the points (1, 5), (2, 3) and (–2, –11) are collinear.

Sol. Do same as Example 4 of Topic 1.

Ans Non-collinear points

Q4. Check whether (5, – 2), (6, 4) and (7, – 2) are the vertices of an isosceles triangle.

Sol. Let $P(5, -2)$, $Q(6, 4)$ and $R(7, -2)$ be the given points.

Then, $PQ = \sqrt{(6-5)^2 + (4+2)^2}$

$[\because \text{distance} = \sqrt{(x_2 - x_1)^2 + (y_2 - y_1)^2}]$

$= \sqrt{(1)^2 + (6)^2} = \sqrt{1+36} = \sqrt{37}$ units

$QR = \sqrt{(7-6)^2 + (-2-4)^2} = \sqrt{(1)^2 + (-6)^2}$

$= \sqrt{1+36} = \sqrt{37}$ units

and $RP = \sqrt{(5-7)^2 + (-2+2)^2}$

$= \sqrt{(-2)^2 + 0} = \sqrt{4} = 2$ units

Here, $PQ = QR$

$\therefore$ *P*, *Q* and *R* will form the vertices of an isosceles triangle.

Q5. In a classroom, 4 friends are seated at the points *A*, *B*, *C* and *D* as shown in figure. Champa and Chameli walk into the class and after observing for a few minutes, Champa asks Chameli, "Don't you think *ABCD* is a square?", Chameli disagrees. Using distance formula, find which of them is correct?

CBSE 2020 (Basic)

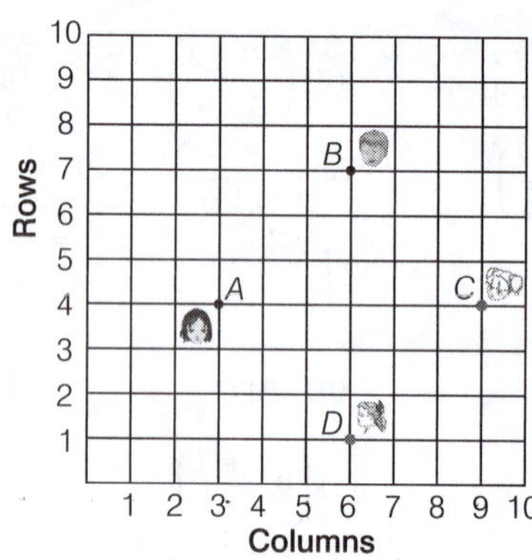

Sol. From the given figure, the coordinates of points *A*, *B*, *C* and *D* are (3, 4), (6, 7), (9, 4) and (6, 1), respectively.

Now, $AB = \sqrt{(6-3)^2 + (7-4)^2}$

$[\because \text{distance} = \sqrt{(x_2 - x_1)^2 + (y_2 - y_1)^2}]$

$= \sqrt{3^2 + 3^2} = \sqrt{9+9} = \sqrt{18} = 3\sqrt{2}$ units

$BC = \sqrt{(9-6)^2 + (4-7)^2}$

$= \sqrt{3^2 + (-3)^2} = \sqrt{9+9} = \sqrt{18} = 3\sqrt{2}$ units

$CD = \sqrt{(6-9)^2 + (1-4)^2}$

$= \sqrt{(-3)^2 + (-3)^2} = \sqrt{9+9}$

$= \sqrt{18} = 3\sqrt{2}$ units

$DA = \sqrt{(3-6)^2 + (4-1)^2}$

$= \sqrt{(-3)^2 + 3^2} = \sqrt{9+9}$

$= \sqrt{18} = 3\sqrt{2}$ units

$AC = \sqrt{(9-3)^2 + (4-4)^2}$

$= \sqrt{36+0} = \sqrt{36} = 6$ units

and $BD = \sqrt{(6-6)^2 + (1-7)^2}$

$= \sqrt{0+36} = \sqrt{36} = 6$ units

Here, all the four sides (*AB*, *BC*, *CD*, *DA*) are equal and diagonals (*AC*, *BD*) are equal.

Hence, *ABCD* is a square.

So, Champa is correct.

Alternate Method

Find four sides AB, BC, CD and DA and one diagonal say AC same as above.

Now, $AB^2 + BC^2 = (3\sqrt{2})^2 + (3\sqrt{2})^2 = 18 + 18 = 36 = (6)^2$

$\Rightarrow \quad AB^2 + BC^2 = AC^2$

Therefore, by converse of Pythagoras theorem, $\angle B = 90°$

Since, a quadrilateral with all four sides equal and one angle $90°$, is a square. So, $ABCD$ is a square.

Q6. Name the types of quadrilateral formed, if any, by the following points and give reasons for your answer.

(i) $(-1, -2), (1, 0), (-1, 2), (-3, 0)$

(ii) $(-3, 5), (3, 1), (0, 3), (-1, -4)$

(iii) $(4, 5), (7, 6), (4, 3), (1, 2)$

Sol. (i) Let $A(-1, -2)$, $B(1, 0)$, $C(-1, 2)$ and $D(-3, 0)$ be the given points.

Then, $AB = \sqrt{(1+1)^2 + (0+2)^2} = \sqrt{(2)^2 + (2)^2}$

$[\because \text{distance} = \sqrt{(x_2 - x_1)^2 + (y_2 - y_1)^2}]$

$= \sqrt{4+4} = \sqrt{8} = 2\sqrt{2}$ units

$BC = \sqrt{(-1-1)^2 + (2-0)^2} = \sqrt{(-2)^2 + (2)^2}$

$= \sqrt{4+4} = \sqrt{8} = 2\sqrt{2}$ units

$CD = \sqrt{(-3+1)^2 + (0-2)^2} = \sqrt{(-2)^2 + (-2)^2}$

$= \sqrt{4+4} = \sqrt{8} = 2\sqrt{2}$ units

$DA = \sqrt{(-1+3)^2 + (-2-0)^2}$

$= \sqrt{(2)^2 + (-2)^2} = \sqrt{4+4}$

$= \sqrt{8} = 2\sqrt{2}$ units

$AC = \sqrt{(-1+1)^2 + (2+2)^2} = \sqrt{0 + 4^2} = 4$ units

and $BD = \sqrt{(-3-1)^2 + (0-0)^2}$

$= \sqrt{(-4)^2 + 0} = 4$ units

Here, the four sides AB, BC, CD and DA are equal and also diagonals AC and BD are equal.

So, the quadrilateral $ABCD$ is a square.

(ii) **Hint** Do same as Part (i). **Ans.** Points A, B, C and D does not form a quadrilateral, because $AC + BC = AB$ i.e. A, B, C and D are collinear.

(iii) **Hint** Do same as part (i). **Ans.** The quadrilateral $ABCD$ is a parallelogram because $AB = CD = \sqrt{10}$, $BC = DA = 3\sqrt{2}$ and $AC \neq BD$.

Q7. Find the point on the X-axis which is equidistant from (2, - 5) and (- 2, 9).

Sol. Do same as Example 5 of Topic 1. **Ans.** $(-7, 0)$

Q8. Find the values of y for which the distance between the points P (2, – 3) and Q(10, y) is 10 units.

Sol. Do same as Example 3 of Topic 1. **Ans.** $y = -9$ or 3

Q9. If Q(0, 1) is equidistant from P(5, –3) and R(x, 6), then find the values of x. Also, find the distance QR and PR.

Sol. Given, point $Q(0, 1)$ is equidistant from $P(5, -3)$ and $R(x, 6)$.

$\therefore \quad QP = QR$

$\Rightarrow \quad QP^2 = QR^2$ [on squaring both sides]

$\Rightarrow (5-0)^2 + (-3-1)^2 = (x-0)^2 + (6-1)^2$

$[\because \text{distance} = \sqrt{(x_2 - x_1)^2 + (y_2 - y_1)^2}]$

$\Rightarrow \quad 5^2 + 4^2 = x^2 + 5^2$

$\Rightarrow \quad 25 + 16 = x^2 + 25$

$\Rightarrow \quad x^2 = 16$

$\Rightarrow \quad x = \pm 4$

Thus, coordinates of R are $(4, 6)$ or $(-4, 6)$.

Case I When coordinates of $R = (4, 6)$

QR = Distance between $Q(0, 1)$ and $R(4, 6)$

$= \sqrt{(4-0)^2 + (6-1)^2} = \sqrt{4^2 + 5^2}$

$= \sqrt{16+25} = \sqrt{41}$ units

and PR = Distance between $P(5, -3)$ and $R(4, 6)$

$= \sqrt{(4-5)^2 + (6+3)^2}$

$= \sqrt{(-1)^2 + (9)^2} = \sqrt{1+81} = \sqrt{82}$ units

Case II When coordinates of $R = (-4, 6)$

In this case, QR = Distance between $Q(0, 1)$ and $R(-4, 6)$

$= \sqrt{(-4-0)^2 + (6-1)^2}$

$= \sqrt{(-4)^2 + 5^2}$

$= \sqrt{16+25} = \sqrt{41}$ units

and PR = Distance between $P(5, -3)$ and $R(-4, 6)$

$= \sqrt{(-4-5)^2 + (6+3)^2}$

$= \sqrt{(-9)^2 + 9^2} = \sqrt{81+81}$

$= \sqrt{162} = 9\sqrt{2}$ units

Q10. Find a relation between x and y such that the point (x, y) is equidistant from the points (3, 6) and (–3, 4).

Sol. Do same as Example 5 of Topic 1.

Ans. $3x + y - 5 = 0$

EXERCISE 7.2

Q1. Find the coordinates of the point which divides the line segment joining of (– 1, 7) and (4, – 3) in the ratio 2 : 3.

Sol. Do same as Example 1 of Topic 2. **Ans** $(1, 3)$

Q2. Find the coordinates of the points of trisection of the line segment joining (4, – 1) and (– 2, – 3).

Sol. Do same as Example 9 of Topic 2.

Ans. $\left(2, -\frac{5}{3}\right)$ and $\left(0, -\frac{7}{3}\right)$

Q3. **To conduct Sports Day activities in your rectangular shaped school ground *ABCD*, lines have been drawn with chalk powder at a distance of 1m each. 100 flower pots have been placed at a distance of 1m from each other along *AD*, as shown in figure.**

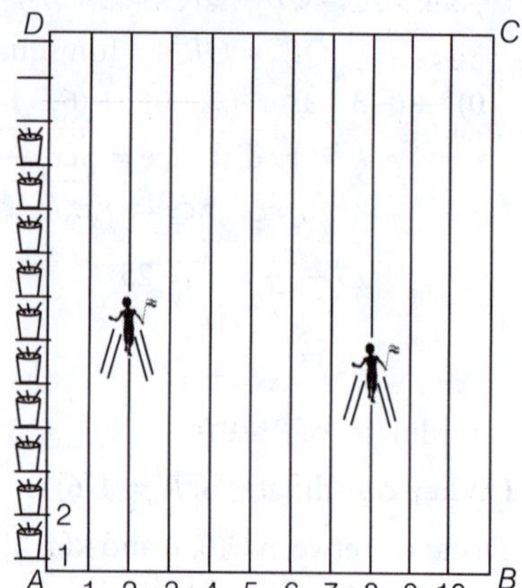

Niharika runs $\frac{1}{4}$ th the distance *AD* on the 2nd line and posts a green flag. Preet runs $\frac{1}{5}$ th the distance *AD* on the 8th line and posts a red flag. What is the distance between both the flags? If Rashmi has to post a blue flag exactly halfway between the line segment joining the two flags, where should she post her flag?

CBSE 2020 (Basic)

Sol. From the given figure, the position of green flag posted by Niharika is $M\left(2\times 1, \frac{1}{4}\times 100\right)$ i.e. $M(2, 25)$ and red flag posted by Preet is $N\left(8\times 1, \frac{1}{5}\times 100\right)$ i.e. $N(8, 20)$.

Now, $MN = \sqrt{(8-2)^2 + (20-25)^2}$

$[\because \text{distance} = \sqrt{(x_2 - x_1)^2 + (y_2 - y_1)^2}]$

$= \sqrt{(6)^2 + (-5)^2} = \sqrt{36+25} = \sqrt{61}$

Hence, the distance between flags is $\sqrt{61}$ m.

Let P be the position of the blue flag posted by Rashmi in the half way of line segment MN.

Then, coordinates of $P = \left(\frac{x_1 + x_2}{2}, \frac{y_1 + y_2}{2}\right)$

$= \left(\frac{2+8}{2}, \frac{25+20}{2}\right)$

$= \left(\frac{10}{2}, \frac{45}{2}\right) = (5, 22.5)$

Hence, the blue flag is on the 5th line at a distance of 22.5 m above it.

Q4. **Find the ratio, in which the line segment joining the points (– 3, 10) and (6, –8) is divided by (– 1, 6).**

Sol. Do same as Example 4 of Topic 2. **Ans.** 2 : 7

Q5. **Find the ratio, in which the line segment joining $A(1, -5)$ and $B(-4, 5)$ is divided by the *X*-axis. Also, find the coordinates of the point of division.**

Sol. Let *X*-axis divides the line joining the points $A(1, -5)$ and $B(-4, 5)$ in the ratio $k : 1$ at point M.

A (1, –5) —k— M —1— B (–4, 5)

By section formula, we get

$$\text{Coordinates of } M = \left(\frac{-4k+1}{k+1}, \frac{5k-5}{k+1}\right) \quad \text{...(i)}$$

Since, point M lies on *X*-axis.

$\therefore$ y-coordinate of $M = 0$

On equating y-coordinate of $M = 0$, we get

$$\frac{5k-5}{k+1} = 0$$

$\Rightarrow$ $5k - 5 = 0$

$\Rightarrow$ $k = 1$

On putting $k = 1$ in Eq. (i), we get

$$M = \left(\frac{-4\times 1+1}{1+1}, \frac{5\times 1 - 5}{1+1}\right) = \left(\frac{-4+1}{2}, \frac{5-5}{2}\right)$$

$\Rightarrow$ $M = \left(\frac{-3}{2}, 0\right)$

So, the required ratio is 1 : 1 and the coordinates of point of division M is $\left(\frac{-3}{2}, 0\right)$.

Q6. **If (1 , 2), (4 , *y*), (*x* , 6) and (3 , 5) are the vertices of a parallelogram taken in order, then find *x* and *y*.**

Sol. **Hint** Do same as Example 7 of Topic 2.

Ans. $x = 6$ and $y = 3$.

Q7. **Find the coordinates of a point *A*, where *AB* is the diameter of a circle whose centre is (2 , – 3) and *B* is (1, 4).**

Sol. Do same as Example 8 of Topic 2.

Ans. (3, – 10)

Q8. **If *A* and *B* are (– 2 , – 2) and (2 , – 4), respectively, then find the coordinates of *P* such that $AP = \frac{3}{7}AB$ and *P* lies on the line segment *AB*.**

Sol. **Hint** Do same as Example 2 of Topic 2.

Ans. Coordinates of the point P are $\left(-\frac{2}{7}, -\frac{20}{7}\right)$.

Q9. **Find the coordinates of the points which divide the line segment joining $A(-2, 2)$ and $B(2, 8)$ into four equal parts.**

Sol. Let P, Q and R be the points on line segment AB such that

$$AP = PQ = QR = RB$$

Let $AP = PQ = QR = RB = k$

(–2, 2) A —k— P —k— Q —k— R —k— B (2, 8)

Then, $\frac{AP}{PB} = \frac{k}{3k} = \frac{1}{3}$

$\Rightarrow$ P divides AB internally in the ratio 1 : 3.

$\therefore$ Coordinates of $P = \left[\frac{1\times 2 + 3(-2)}{1+3}, \frac{1\times 8 + 3\times 2}{1+3}\right]$

$\left[\text{using section formula i.e. } \left(\frac{m_1x_2 + m_2x_1}{m_1+m_2}, \frac{m_1y_2 + m_2y_1}{m_1+m_2}\right)\right]$

$$= \left(\frac{2-6}{4}, \frac{8+6}{4}\right) = \left(\frac{-4}{4}, \frac{14}{4}\right) = \left(-1, \frac{7}{2}\right)$$

Again, $\frac{AR}{RB} = \frac{3k}{k} = \frac{3}{1}$

$\Rightarrow$ R divides AB internally in the ratio 3 : 1.

$\therefore$ Coordinates of $R = \left[\frac{3\times 2 + 1\times(-2)}{3+1}, \frac{3\times 8 + 1\times 2}{3+1}\right]$

$$= \left(\frac{6-2}{4}, \frac{24+2}{4}\right) = \left(\frac{4}{4}, \frac{26}{4}\right) = \left(1, \frac{13}{2}\right)$$

Also, $\frac{AQ}{QB} = \frac{2k}{2k} = \frac{1}{1} \Rightarrow Q$ is the mid-point of AB.

$\therefore$ Coordinates of $Q = \left(\frac{-2+2}{2}, \frac{2+8}{2}\right)$

$\left[\because \text{coordinates of mid-point} = \left(\frac{x_1+x_2}{2}, \frac{y_1+y_2}{2}\right)\right]$

$\Rightarrow$ $Q = \left(\frac{0}{2}, \frac{10}{2}\right) = (0, 5)$

So, the required points are $\left(-1, \frac{7}{2}\right), \left(1, \frac{13}{2}\right)$ and $(0, 5)$.

Q 10. Find the area of a rhombus, if its vertices are (3, 0), (4, 5), (–1, 4) and (–2, –1) taken in order.

[Hint Area of a rhombus = $\frac{1}{2}$ (Product of its diagonals)]

Sol. Let $A(3, 0)$, $B(4, 5)$, $C(-1, 4)$ and $D(-2, -1)$ be the vertices of the rhombus $ABCD$.

$\therefore$ Diagonal, $AC = \sqrt{(-1-3)^2 + (4-0)^2}$

$\left[\because \text{distance} = \sqrt{(x_2-x_1)^2 + (y_2-y_1)^2}\right]$

$$= \sqrt{(-4)^2 + 4^2}$$

$$= \sqrt{32}$$

$$= 4\sqrt{2} \text{ units}$$

Diagonal, $BD = \sqrt{(-2-4)^2 + (-1-5)^2}$

$$= \sqrt{(-6)^2 + (-6)^2}$$

$$= \sqrt{36+36}$$

$$= \sqrt{72}$$

$$= 6\sqrt{2} \text{ units}$$

$\therefore$ Area of the rhombus $ABCD$

$$= \frac{1}{2} \times \text{Product of its diagonals}$$

$$= \frac{1}{2} \times AC \times BD$$

$$= \frac{1}{2} \times 4\sqrt{2} \times 6\sqrt{2}$$

$$= 2\times 6\times\sqrt{2}\times\sqrt{2}$$

$$= 12\times 2$$

$$= 24 \text{ sq units}$$

REVIEW EXERCISE

Including Competency Based Questions

Part I

Multiple Choice Questions

1. The distance of point $(a, -b)$ form X-axis is **CBSE 2025 (Standard)**

(a) a (b) $-a$ (c) b (d) $-b$

2. $ABCD$ is a rectangle with its vertices at $(2, -2)$, $(8, 4)$, $(4, 8)$ and $(-2, 2)$ taken in order. Length of its diagonal is **CBSE 2025 (Basic)**

(a) $4\sqrt{2}$ (b) $6\sqrt{2}$ (c) $4\sqrt{26}$ (d) $2\sqrt{26}$

3. The distance between the points $(a\cos\theta + b\sin\theta, 0)$ and $(0, a\sin\theta - b\cos\theta)$, is **Competency Based Question**

(a) $a^2 + b^2$ (b) $a^2 - b^2$ (c) $\sqrt{a^2 + b^2}$ (d) $\sqrt{a^2 - b^2}$

4. If the distances of the point $P(x, y)$ from $(1,0)$ and $(0,1)$ are equal, then which of the following is true? **CBSE 2024 (Basic)**

(a) $x + y = 0$ (b) $x = y + 1$
(c) $y = x + 1$ (d) $x = y$

5. The distance between the points $P\left(-\frac{11}{3}, 5\right)$ and $Q\left(-\frac{2}{3}, 5\right)$ is **CBSE 2023 (Standard)**

(a) 6 units (b) 4 units (c) 2 units (d) 3 units

6. The point on X-axis which is equidistant from the points $(5, -3)$ and $(4, 2)$ is **CBSE Compartment 2024 (Standard)**

(a) (4.5, 0) (b) (7, 0) (c) (0.5, 0) (d) (− 7, 0)

7. The point of intersection of the line represented by $3x - y = 3$ and Y-axis is given by **CBSE 2023 (Standard)**

(a) (0, −3) (b) (0, 3) (c) (2, 0) (d) (−2, 0)

8. The value of k, if $(6, k)$ lies on the line represented by $x - 3y + 6 = 0$, is **CBSE 2023 (Basic)**

(a) −4 (b) 12 (c) −12 (d) 4

9. The point that divides the line segment joining the points $(7, -6)$ and $(3, 4)$ in ratio $1 : 2$ internally lies in which quadrant? **NCERT Exemplar**

(a) I quadrant (b) II quadrant
(c) III quadrant (d) IV quadrant

10. Point P divides the line segment joining $R(-1, 3)$ and $S(9, 8)$ in ratio $k : 1$. If P lies on the line $x - y + 2 = 0$, then value of k is **Competency Based Question**

(a) 2/3 (b) 1/2 (c) 1/3 (d) 1/4

11. Find the ratio in which the line segment joining $(2, -3)$ and $(5, 6)$ is divided by X-axis. **CBSE Sample Paper 2023 (Standard)**

(a) 1 : 2 (b) 2 : 1 (c) 2 : 5 (d) 5 : 2

12. If $(2, 4)$ is the mid-point of the line segment joining $(6, 3)$ and $(a, 5)$, then the value of a is **CBSE 2023 (Basic)**

(a) 2 (b) 4 (c) −4 (d) −2

13. The origin divides the line segment AB joining the points $A(1, -3)$ and $B(-3, 9)$ in the ratio **CBSE 2022 (Basic)**

(a) 3 : 1 (b) 1 : 3 (c) 2 : 3 (d) 1 : 1

14. The line segment joining the points $P(-3, 2)$ and $Q(5, 7)$ is divided by the Y-axis in the ratio

(a) 3 : 1 (b) 3 : 4 (c) 3 : 2 (d) 3 : 5

15. ABC is a triangle such that $AB : BC = 1 : 2$. Point A lies on the Y-axis and the coordinates of B and C are known.

Which of the following formula can definitely be used to find the coordinates of A? **Competency Based Question**

(i) Section formula (ii) Distance formula

(a) only (i) (b) only (ii)
(c) both (i) and (ii) (d) neither (i) nor (ii)

16. Three vertices of a parallelogram $ABCD$ are $A(1, 4)$, $B(-2, 3)$ and $C(5, 8)$. The ordinate of the fourth vertex D is **CBSE 2022 (Basic)**

(a) 8 (b) 9 (c) 7 (d) 6

17. The vertices of a ΔOAB are $O(0, 0)$, $A(4, 0)$ and $B(0, 6)$. The median AD is drawn on OB. The length of AD is **CBSE 2021 Term I**

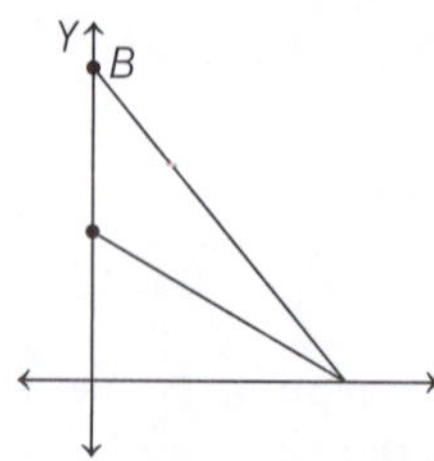

(a) $\sqrt{52}$ units (b) 5 units (c) 25 units (d) 10 units

Assertion-Reason Type Questions

18. Assertion If the points $A(4, 3)$ and $B(x, 5)$ lie on a circle with centre $O(2, 3)$, then the value of x is 2.

Reason Centre of a circle is the mid-point of each chord of the circle. **CBSE 2023 (Standard)**

(a) Both Assertion and Reason are correct and Reason is the correct explanation of Assertion.
(b) Both Assertion and Reason are correct but Reason is not the correct explanation of Assertion.
(c) Assertion is correct but Reason is incorrect.
(d) Assertion is incorrect but Reason is correct.

19. **Assertion** The distance of the point $(-3, 5)$ from the X-axis is 3 units.

Reason Abscissa of a point gives the distance from the Y-axis. **CBSE Compartment 2024 (Basic)**

(a) Both Assertion and Reason are correct and Reason is the correct explanation of Assertion.
(b) Both Assertion and Reason are correct but Reason is not the correct explanation of Assertion.
(c) Assertion is correct but Reason is incorrect.
(d) Assertion is incorrect but Reason is correct.

20. **Assertion** The distance of $P(a, b)$ from origin is $\sqrt{a^2 + b^2}$.

Reason The distance between two points $A(x_1, y_1)$ and $B(x_2, y_2)$ is $\sqrt{(x_2 - x_1)^2 + (y_2 - y_1)^2}$. **CBSE 2024 (Basic)**

(a) Both Assertion and Reason are correct and Reason is the correct explanation of Assertion.
(b) Both Assertion and Reason are correct but Reason is not the correct explanation of Assertion.
(c) Assertion is correct but Reason is incorrect.
(d) Assertion is incorrect but Reason is correct.

21. **Assertion** The point which divides the line segment joining the points $A(1, 2)$ and $B(-1, 1)$ internally in the ratio $1 : 2$ is $\left(\frac{-1}{3}, \frac{5}{3}\right)$.

Reason The coordinates of the point which divides the line segment joining the points $A(x_1, y_1)$ and $B(x_2, y_2)$ in the ratio $m_1 : m_2$ are $\left(\frac{m_1x_2 + m_2x_1}{m_1 + m_2}, \frac{m_1y_2 + m_2y_1}{m_1 + m_2}\right)$. **CBSE 2024 (Standard)**

(a) Both Assertion and Reason are correct and Reason is the correct explanation of Assertion.
(b) Both Assertion and Reason are correct but Reason is not the correct explanation of Assertion.
(c) Assertion is correct but Reason is incorrect.
(d) Assertion is incorrect but Reason is correct.

Case Study Based Questions

22. Ayush starts walking from his house to office. Instead of going to the office directly, he goes to a bank first, from there to his daughter's school and then reaches the office.

Based on the above information, answer the following questions. **NCERT Exemplar**

(i) What is the extra distance travelled by Ayush in reaching his office? [assume that all distances covered are in straight lines, if the house is situated at (2, 4), bank at (5, 8), school at (13, 14) and office at (13, 26) and coordinates are in kilometres].

(ii) How much far from bank to the office?

(iii) What is the mid-point between the line segment joining the school and bank?

Or

What is the difference in distance between house to bank and house to school?

23. Ronit is the captain of his school football team. He has decided to use a 4-4-2-1 formation in the next match. The figure below shows the positions of the players in a 4-4-2-1 formation on a coordinate grid.

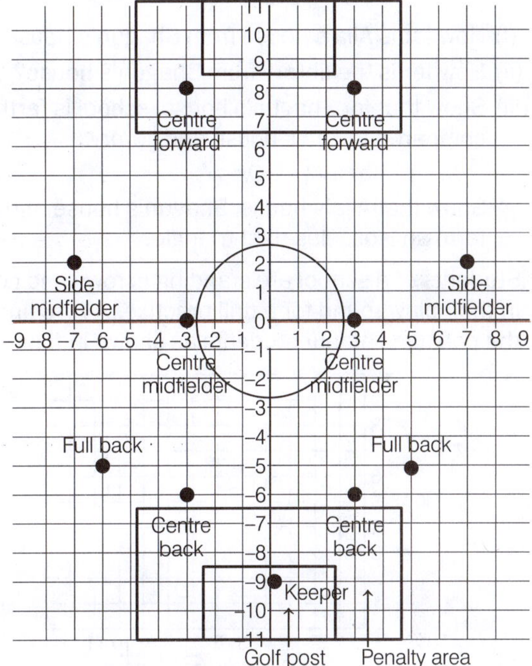

One square box represents 1 sq unit.

Based on the above information, answer the following questions.

(i) What is the distance between the two centre forward positions in Ronit's plan?

(ii) Mention two positions which are not equidistant from any axis.

(iii) What is the area (in sq units) of the football field enclosed by the lines joining the two centre back positions and the goalkeeper's position?

Or A ball hit from the left full back position travels uninterrupted to the right centre forward position. What can be the minimum distance travelled by the ball?

24. Alia and Shagun are friends living on the same street in Patel Nagar. Shagun's house is at the intersection of one street with another street on which there is a library. They both study in the same school and that is not far from Shagun's house. Suppose the school is situated at the point O i.e. the origin. Alia's house is at A, Shagun's house is at B and library is at C.

Based on the above information, answer the following questions. **CBSE Sample Paper 2023 (Basic)**

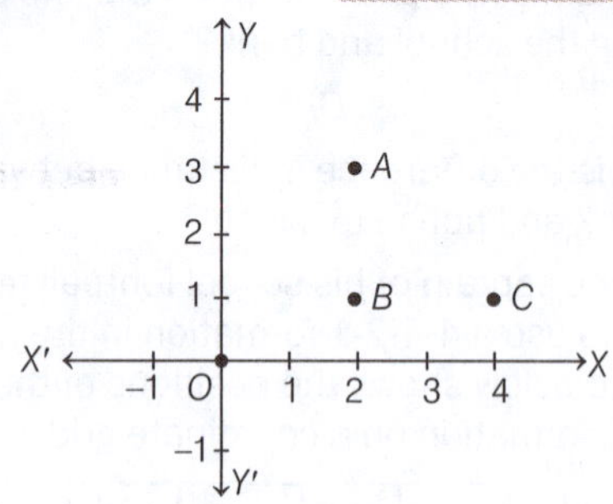

(i) How far is Alia's house from Shagun's house?

(ii) How far is the library from Shagun's house?

(iii) Show that for Shagun's house, school is farther as compared to Alia's house and library.

Or

Show that Alia's house, Shagun's house and library form an isosceles right triangle.

25. Students of a school are standing in rows and columns in their playground for a drill practice. A, B, C and D are the positions of four students as shown in figure.

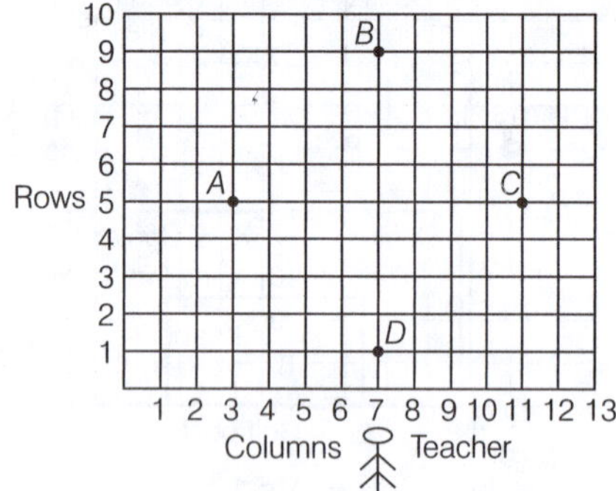

Based on the above information, answer the following questions. **NCERT Exemplar**

(i) Determine the distance between the points C and D, A and B.

(ii) Determine the distance between A and D, B and C.

(iii) Is it possible to place Jaspal in the drill in such a way that he is equidistant from each of the four students A, B, C and D? If so, what should be his position?

Or

Based on the positions of A, B, C and D, determine the type of quadrilateral formed by these points.

26. A part of a 'save trees' campaign, students designed triangular banners in the shape of a triangle which is as shown in the figure

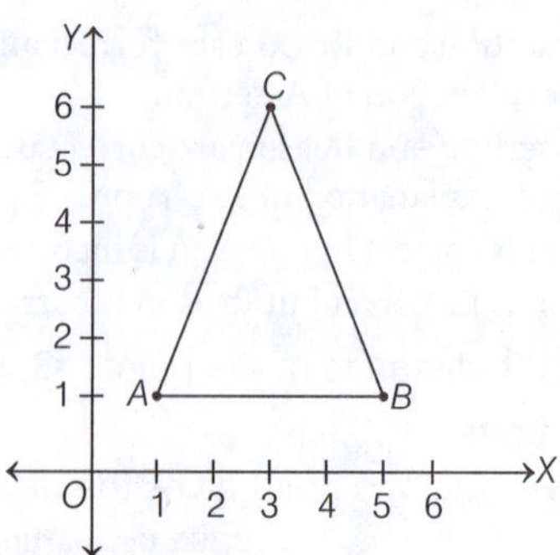

Based on the above information, answer the following questions.

(i) Find the coordinates of the mid-point of A and B.

(ii) Find the area of the ΔABC.

(iii) Find the point on X-axis, which is equidistant from points A and B.

Or

Find the centroid of the ΔABC.

27. Tharunya was thrilled to know that the football tournament is fixed with a monthly time frame from 20th July to 20th August 2023 and for the first time in the FIFA Women's World Cup's history, two nations host in 10 venues. Her father felt that the game can be better understood, if the position of players is represented as points on a coordinate plane. **CBSE Sample Paper 2023 (Standard)**

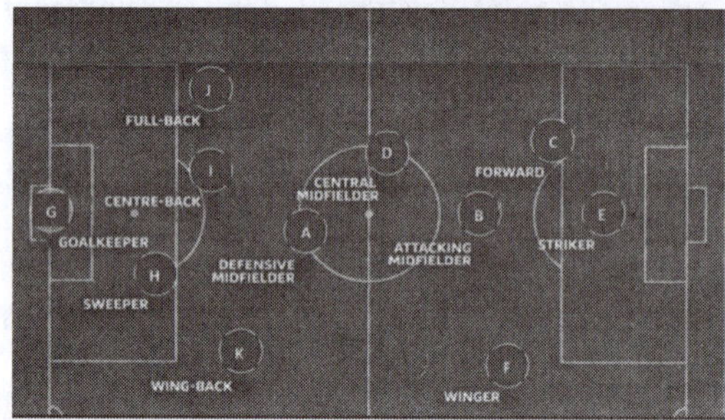

(i) At an instance, the midfielders and forward formed a parallelogram. Find the position of the central midfielder (D), if the position of other players who formed the parallelogram are $A(1, 2)$, $B(4, 3)$ and $C(6, 6)$.

(ii) Check if the Goal keeper $G(-3, 5)$, Sweeper $H(3, 1)$ and Wing-back $K(0, 3)$ fall on a same straight line.

Or Check if the Full-back $J(5, -3)$ and centre-back $I(-4, 6)$ are equidistant from forward $C(0,1)$ and if C is the mid-point of IJ.

(iii) If defensive midfielder $A(1, 4)$, Attacking midfielder $B(2, -3)$ and Striker $E(a, b)$ lie on the same straight line and B is equidistant from A and E, find the position of E.

Part II

Very Short Answer Type Questions

1. Find the distance of point $P(x, y)$ from the origin. **CBSE 2018**

2. Find the distance between the points $(a \cos 35°, 0)$ and $(0, a \cos 55°)$.

3. $P(x, y)$ is a point equidistant from the points $A(4, 3)$ and $B(3, 4)$. Prove that $x - y = 0$. **CBSE Sample Paper 2024-25 (Basic)**

4. Find the value(s) of x, for which the distance AB between the points $A(x, -5)$ and $B(3, 2)$ is $\sqrt{58}$ units.

5. If $Q(0,2)$ is equidistant from $P(5,-3)$ and $R(x, 7)$, then find the value(s) of x. **CBSE 2024 (Basic)**

6. Find the point on the X-axis which is equidistant from the points $(-1, 0)$ and $(5, 0)$.

7. Find the coordinates of the point, where the line $x - y = 5$ cuts Y-axis.

8. Find the radius of the circle whose end points of diameter are (24, 1) and (2, 23).

9. If the centre of a circle is $(2a, a - 7)$, then find the values of a, if the circle passes through the point $(11, -9)$ and has diameter $10\sqrt{2}$ units. **Competency Based Question**

10. If $\left(3, \frac{3}{4}\right)$ is the mid-point of the line segment joining the points $(k, 0)$ and $\left(7, \frac{3}{2}\right)$, then find the value of k.

11. PQ is a line segment such that the y-coordinate of P is -1 and Q lies on the Y-axis. The mid-point of PQ is $O(-3, -6)$. Find the coordinates of Q. Show your work. **Competency Based Question**

12. Find the coordinates of a point A, where AB is the diameter of a circle, whose centre is $(4, -3)$ and B is $(2, 6)$.

Short Answer Type Questions

13. Find the distance between the points $P\left(\frac{\sin\theta}{2}, 0\right)$ and $Q\left(0, \frac{\cos\theta}{2}\right)$.

14. If the distance between the points $(4, p)$ and $(1, 0)$ is 5 units, then find the value(s) of p. **NCERT Exemplar**

15. Find the values of k, for which the distance between the points $A(k, -5)$ and $B(2, 7)$ is 13 units.

16. Check whether the points $(1, 5)$, $(2, 3)$ and $(-2, -11)$ are collinear or not, using distance formula.

17. Check whether the points $(20, 3)$, $(19, 8)$ and $(2, -9)$ are all equidistant from the point $(7, 3)$.

18. If the point $P(2, 1)$ lies on the line segment joining the points $A(4, 2)$ and $B(8, 4)$, then find the relation between AP and AB. **NCERT Exemplar**

19. Prove that abscissa of a point P which is equidistant from points with coordinates $A(7, 1)$ and $B(3, 5)$ is 2 more than its ordinate. **CBSE 2025 (Standard)**

20. The line segment joining the points $A(2, 1)$ and $B(5, -8)$ is trisected at the points P and Q such that P is nearer to A. If P also lies on the line given by $2x - y + k = 0$, then find the value of k.

21. Find the angle subtended at the origin by the line segment whose end points are (0, 100) and (10, 0).

22. Find the angle subtended by these points $P(\sqrt{2}, \sqrt{2})$, $Q(-\sqrt{2}, -\sqrt{2})$ and $R(-\sqrt{6}, \sqrt{6})$. **NCERT Exemplar**

23. Find the perimeter of the triangle formed by points $(0, 0)$, $(1, 0)$ and $(0, 1)$.

24. ΔABC is a right angled triangle, in which $A(0, 2)$ and $B(2, 0)$ are given. Then, find the coordinates of C.

25. Check, whether the points $(-4, 0)$, $(4, 0)$ and $(0, 3)$ are the vertices of an isosceles triangle or equilateral triangle. **NCERT Exemplar**

26. The points $A(0, 3)$, $B(-2, a)$ and $C(-1, 4)$ are the vertices of ΔABC, right angled at A. Find the value of a.

27. If the points $A(4, 3)$ and $B(x, 5)$ are on the circle with centre $O(2, 3)$, then find the value of $x^2 + 5$.

28. Show that if a circle has its centre at the origin and a point $P(5, 0)$ lies on it, then the point $Q(6, 8)$ lies outside the circle. **NCERT Exemplar**

29. Show that quadrilateral $PQRS$ formed by vertices $P(22, 5)$, $Q(7, 10)$, $R(12, 11)$ and $S(3, 24)$ is not a parallelogram.

30. The point $P(x, y)$ divides the line segment joining the points $A(-1,3)$ and $B(9,8)$ such that $AP : PB = k : 1$. If the coordinates of P are such that $x = y$, then find the value of k. **CBSE 2024 (Basic)**

31. Prove that (5, 6), (2, 8), (0, 6) and (3, 4) are the vertices of a parallelogram. Is it a square?

32. The coordinates of one end point of a diameter of a circle are $(4, -1)$ and coordinates of the centre of the circle are $(1, -3)$. **Competency Based Question**

(i) Find the coordinates of the other end of the diameter.

(ii) Find the diameter of the circle.

(iii) Calculate the area of circle.

33. In the given figure, in ΔABC, D and E are the mid-points of the sides BC and AC respectively. Find the length of DE. Prove that

$$DE = \frac{1}{2} AB.$$

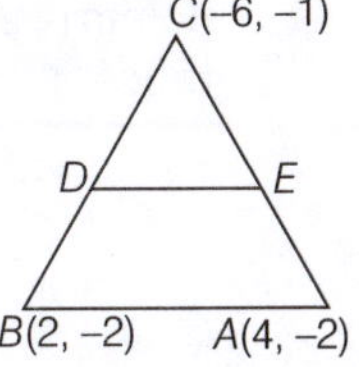

34. Show that ΔABC with vertices $A(-2, 0)$, $B(0, 2)$ and $C(2, 0)$ is similar to ΔDFE with vertices $D(-4, 0)$, $E(4, 0)$ and $F(0, 4)$. **NCERT Exemplar**

35. If the point $C(-1, 2)$ divides internally the line segment joining $A(2, 5)$ and $B(x, y)$ in the ratio $3:4$, find the coordinates of B. **CBSE 2020 (Standard)**

36. Find the coordinates of the point, which divides the line segment joining the points $(1, -3)$ and $(-3, 9)$ in the ratio $1:3$ internally.

37. $P(-2, 5)$ and $Q(3, 2)$ are two points. Find the coordinates of the point R on PQ such that $PR = 2QR$. **CBSE Sample Paper 2024 (Standard), 2020 (Standard)**

38. Find the ratio in which the point $\left(\frac{8}{5}, y\right)$ divides the line segment joining the points $(1, 2)$ and $(2, 3)$. Also, find the value of y. **CBSE 2024 (Standard)**

39. In what ratio, does the X-axis divide the line segment joining the points $(2, -3)$ and $(5, 6)$? Also, find the coordinates of the point of intersection.

40. In what ratio, does the Y-axis divide the line segment joining the points $P(-4, 5)$ and $Q(3, -7)$? Also, find the coordinates of the point of intersection.

41. Find the coordinates of the point R on the line segment joining the points $P(-1, 3)$ and $Q(2, 5)$ such that $PR = \frac{3}{5}PQ$. **NCERT Exemplar**

42. If P and Q are the points of trisection of the line segment joining the points $A(2, -2)$ and $B(-7, 4)$ such that P is nearer to A. Find the coordinates of P and Q.

43. Determine the ratio in which the point $P(a, -2)$ divides the line segment joining the points $A(-4, 3)$ and $B(2, -4)$. Also, find the value of a. **CBSE 2023 (Basic)**

44. In the given figure, in ΔABC points D and E are mid-points of sides BC and AC respectively. If given vertices are $A(4, -2)$, $B(2, -2)$ and $C(-6, -7)$, then verify the result

$$DE = \frac{1}{2}AB$$

CBSE 2023 (Basic)

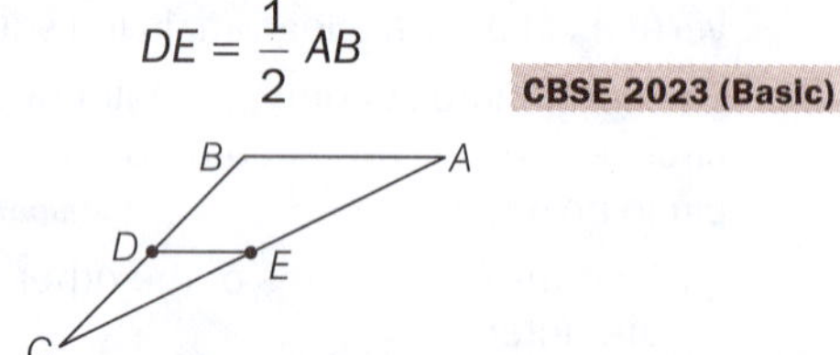

45. Line $4x + y = 4$ divides the line segment joining the points $(-2, -1)$ and $(3, 5)$ in a certain ratio. Find the ratio. **CBSE Sample Paper 2024-25 (Basic)**

46. On a playground, Parth, Qasim and Ragini are standing at the points $P(2, 4)$, $Q(8, 6)$ and $R(8, 9)$ respectively. Sameer is standing exactly halfway between Parth and Qasim on the line joining Parth and Qasim.
What is the shortest distance, in units, between Sameer and Ragini? Show your steps. **Competency Based Question**

47. If the mid-point of the line joining $(3, 4)$ and $(k, 7)$ is (x, y) and $2x + 2y + 1 = 0$, then find the value of k.

48. Find the point which lies on the perpendicular bisector of the line segment joining the points $A(-2, -5)$ and $B(2, 5)$. **NCERT Exemplar**

49. If (a, b) is the mid-point of the line segment joining the points $A(10, -6)$ and $B(k, 4)$ lies on $a - 2b = 18$. Find the value of k and the distance AB.

50. Find the ratio, in which the point $P\left(\frac{3}{4}, \frac{5}{12}\right)$ divides the line segment joining the points $A\left(\frac{1}{2}, \frac{3}{2}\right)$ and $B(2, -5)$. **NCERT Exemplar**

51. If the coordinates of one end of a diameter of a circle are $(2, 3)$ and the coordinates of its centre are $(-2, 5)$. Find the coordinates of the other end of the diameter? **Competency Based Question**

52. $AOBC$ is a rectangle whose three vertices are $A(0, 3)$, $O(0, 0)$ and $B(5, 0)$. What are the length of its diagonals? **NCERT Exemplar**

Long Answer Type Questions

53. Find the coordinates of the points which divide the line segment joining $A(-2, -2)$ and $B(2, 8)$ into four equal parts.

54. The points $(3, -4)$ and $(-6, 5)$ are the end points of a diagonal of a parallelogram. If one of the end points of the second diagonal is $(-2, 1)$, then find its other end point.

55. Points P, Q, R, S and T divide the line segment joining the points $A(1, 2)$ and $B(6, 7)$ in 6 equal parts. Find coordinates of the points P, Q, R, S and T.

56. The three vertices of a rhombus $PQRS$ are $P(2, -3)$, $Q(6, 5)$ and $R(-2, 1)$.

(i) Find the coordinates of the point where both the diagonals PR and QS intersect.

(ii) Find the coordinates of the fourth vertex S.

Show your steps and give valid reasons. **Competency Based Question**

HINTS & SOLUTIONS

Part I

1. (c) Let the given point is $A(a, -b)$ and the perpendicular from A on the X-axis intersects at B.

Point B lies on X-axis, so the coordinate of point B is $(a, 0)$.

Distance of given point from X-axis $= AB$

Using distance formula, we have

$$AB = \sqrt{(a-a)^2 + (0-(-b))^2}$$
$$= \sqrt{0 + b^2} = b \text{ units}$$

2. (d) $ABCD$ is a rectangle with its vertices at $(2, -2)$, $(8, 4)$, $(4, 8)$ and $(-2, 2)$.

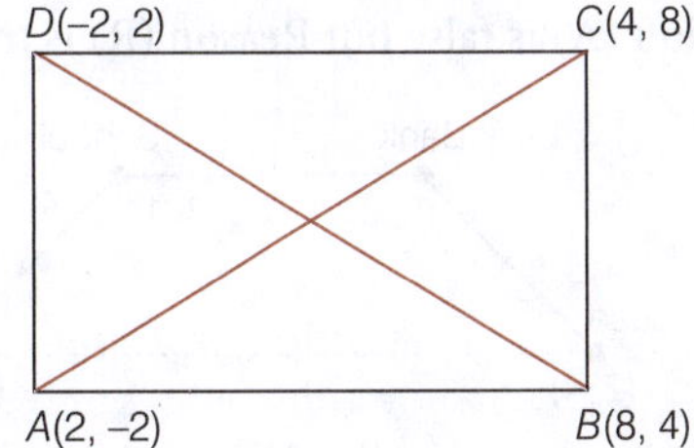

Now, length of diagonal AC by using distance formula, is

$$\sqrt{(x_2 - x_2)^2 + (y_2 - y_1)^2}$$
$$= \sqrt{(4-2)^2 + (8+2)^2}$$
$$[\because x_1 = 2, x_2 = 4, y_1 = -2, y_2 = 8]$$
$$= \sqrt{(2)^2 + (10)^2} = \sqrt{4 + 100}$$
$$= \sqrt{104} = 2\sqrt{26}$$

3. (c) **Hint** Do same as Example 1 of Topic 1.

4. (d) Let the points be $A(1, 0)$ and $B(0, 1)$.

Given that the distance of the point $P(x, y)$ from $(1, 0)$ and $(0, 1)$ are equal.

$$\therefore \quad PA = PB$$
$$\Rightarrow \quad PA^2 = PB^2$$
$$\Rightarrow (x-1)^2 + (y-0)^2 = (x-0)^2 + (y-1)^2$$
$$\Rightarrow \quad x^2 + 1 - 2x + y^2 = x^2 + y^2 + 1 - 2y$$
$$\Rightarrow \quad 1 - 2x = 1 - 2y$$
$$\Rightarrow \quad -2x = -2y$$
$$\Rightarrow \quad x = y$$

5. (d) **Hint** Do same Example 1 of Topic 1.

6. (b) Let the point on X-axis be $A(x, 0)$, which is equidistant from $B(5, -3)$ and $C(4, 2)$.

$$\therefore \quad AB^2 = AC^2$$
$$\Rightarrow (x-5)^2 + (0+3)^2 = (x-4)^2 + (0-2)^2$$
$$\Rightarrow \quad x = 7$$
$$\therefore \quad A \equiv (7, 0)$$

7. (a) Equation of Y-axis is $x = 0$.

Given, line is $3x - y = 3$

On substituting $x = 0$ in this equation, we get

$$3(0) - y = 3 \Rightarrow y = -3$$

$\therefore$ Point of intersection is $(0, -3)$.

8. (d) Since, the point $(6, k)$ lies on the line

$$x - 3y + 6 = 0$$
$$\therefore \quad 6 - 3(k) + 6 = 0$$
$$\Rightarrow \quad 3k = 12 \Rightarrow k = 4$$

9. (d) **Hint** Here, $x_1 = 7, y_1 = -6, x_2 = 3, y_2 = 4$, $m = 1$ and $n = 2$

$$\therefore \quad x = \frac{1(3) + 2(7)}{1+2}, y = \frac{1(4) + 2(-6)}{1+2}$$

[by section formula]

$$\Rightarrow \quad x = \frac{17}{3}, y = -\frac{8}{3}$$

So, $(x, y) = \left(\frac{17}{3}, -\frac{8}{3}\right)$ lies in IV quadrant.

[since, in IV quadrant, x-coordinate is positive and y-coordinate is negative]

10. (a) Point P divides the line segment joining $R(-1, 3)$ and $S(9, 8)$ in ratio $k : 1$.

$\therefore$ Coordinates of P are $\left(\frac{9k-1}{k+1}, \frac{8k+3}{k+1}\right)$.

Since, P lies on the line $x - y + 2 = 0$, then

$$\frac{9k-1}{k+1} - \frac{8k+3}{k+1} + 2 = 0$$
$$\Rightarrow \quad 9k - 1 - 8k - 3 + 2k + 2 = 0$$
$$\Rightarrow \quad 3k - 2 = 0$$
$$\Rightarrow \quad k = \frac{2}{3}$$

11. (a) **Hint** Do same as Example 4 of Topic 2.

12. (d) **Hint** Do same as Example 3 of Topic 2.

13. (b) **Hint** Let the ratio be $k : 1$.

Now, use section formula.

Ans. $k = \frac{1}{3}$

14. (d) **Hint** Let the ratio be $k : 1$.

Using section formula,

$$\left(\frac{-3+5k}{k+1}, \frac{2+7k}{k+1}\right) = (0, y)$$

[$\because$ coordinates of Y-axis are $(0, y)$]

$$\Rightarrow \quad \frac{-3+5k}{k+1} = 0 \Rightarrow k = \frac{3}{5}$$

15. (b) Let A lies on the Y-axis i.e. $(0, y)$ and let the coordinates of B and C be $(1, 2)$ and $(3, 4)$ respectively.

Now, $\quad \dfrac{AB}{BC} = \dfrac{1}{2}$

$\Rightarrow \quad 2AB = BC$

$\Rightarrow 2\sqrt{(1-0)^2 + (2-y)^2} = \sqrt{(3-1)^2 + (4-2)^2}$

$\Rightarrow \quad 2\sqrt{1 + 4 + y^2 - 4y} = \sqrt{4+4}$

$\Rightarrow \quad \sqrt{y^2 - 4y + 5} = \dfrac{2\sqrt{2}}{2} = \sqrt{2}$

$\Rightarrow \quad y^2 - 4y + 5 = 2 \Rightarrow y^2 - 4y + 3 = 0$

By solving this we get the coordinates of A.

But we cannot use the section formula in triangles.

$\therefore$ Coordinates of A can be found using only distance formula.

16. (b) **Hint** Do same as Example 7 of Topic 2.

17. (b) AD is median on OB in ΔAOB,

So, D is the mid-point of OB.

Coordinates of $D \equiv \left[\dfrac{0+0}{2}, \dfrac{0+6}{2}\right] = (0, 3)$

Length of $AD = \sqrt{(4-0)^2 + (0-3)^2}$

$= \sqrt{16+9} = 5$ units

18. (c) Given, $A(4, 3)$ and $B(x, 5)$ are two points on the circle with centre of circle $O(2, 3)$.

$\therefore \quad OA = OB \quad$ [radius of circle]

$\Rightarrow \quad OA^2 = OB^2$

$\Rightarrow (4-2)^2 + (3-3)^2 = (x-2)^2 + (5-3)^2$

[by distance formula]

$\Rightarrow \quad (x-2)^2 + 4 = 4 \Rightarrow (x-2)^2 = 0$

$\Rightarrow \quad x - 2 = 0 \Rightarrow x = 2$

19. (d)

(–3, 5) Y 5 X – 3 O

Clearly, we see that the distance of the given point $(-3, 5)$ is 5 units from the X-axis.

20. (a) **Assertion** (A) The distance of $P(a, b)$ from origin i.e. $(0, 0)$ is given by the distance formula,

$\sqrt{(x_2 - x_1)^2 + (y_2 - y_1)^2}$, where (x_1, y_1) and (x_2, y_2) are two points on a plane.

Here, $(x_1, y_1) = (a, b)$ and $(x_2, y_2) = (0, 0)$

On substituting the values in the formula, we get

$$\sqrt{(0-a)^2 + (0-b)^2} = \sqrt{a^2 + b^2}$$

Therefore, Assertion (A) is true.

Reason (R) The distance between the points $A(x_1, y_1)$ and $B(x_2, y_2)$ is given by the distance formula

$\sqrt{(x_2 - x_1)^2 + (y_2 - y_1)^2}$.

Therefore, Reason (R) is true.

Hence, both Assertion (A) and Reason (R) are true.

Also, Reason (R) is the correct explanation of Assertion (A).

21. (d) Let the point C divides $A(1, 2)$ and $B(-1, 1)$ internally in the ratio $1 : 2$.

Then, by section formula, we have

$$x = \frac{m_1 x_2 + m_2 x_1}{m_1 + m_2} \text{ and } y = \frac{m_1 y_2 + m_2 y_1}{m_1 + m_2}$$

So, $\quad x = \dfrac{2 \times 1 + 1 \times (-1)}{2+1}$ and $y = \dfrac{2 \times 2 + 1 \times 1}{2+1}$

$\Rightarrow \quad x = \dfrac{2-1}{3}$ and $y = \dfrac{4+1}{3} \Rightarrow x = \dfrac{1}{3}$ and $y = \dfrac{5}{3}$

$\therefore \quad x = \dfrac{1}{3}$ and $y = \dfrac{5}{3}$

$\therefore$ Assertion (A) is false but Reason (R) is true.

22. (i) **Hint**

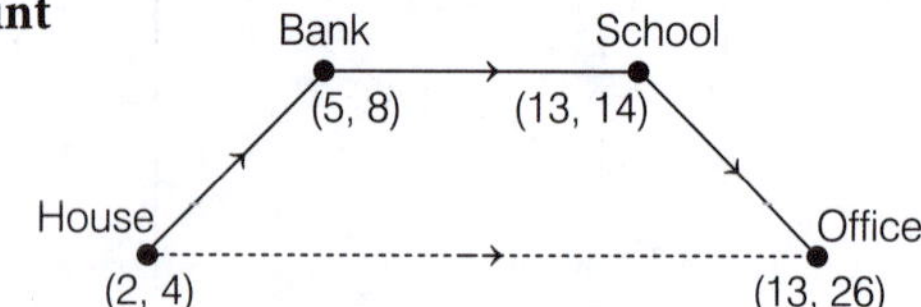

Extra distance travelled by Ayush

= Distance between house and office via Bank and School

– Direct distance between house and office

Now, using distance formula,

Extra distance

$= \sqrt{(5-2)^2 + (8-4)^2} + \sqrt{(13-5)^2 + (14-8)^2}$

$+ \sqrt{(13-13)^2 + (26-14)^2} - \sqrt{(13-2)^2 + (26-4)^2}$

Ans. 2.4 km

(ii) **Hint** $\sqrt{(13-5)^2 + (26-8)^2}$ **Ans.** $2\sqrt{97}$ km

(iii) **Hint** Mid-point $= \left(\dfrac{13+5}{2}, \dfrac{14+8}{2}\right) = (9, 11)$

Or **Hint** Difference

$= \sqrt{(13-2)^2 + (14-4)^2} - \sqrt{(5-2)^2 + (8-4)^2}$

≈ 14.87 km

23. (i) Coordinates of two centre forward positions in Ronit's plan are $(3, 8)$ and $(-3, 8)$.

Distance between the two positions

$= \sqrt{(-3-3)^2 + (8-8)^2} = \sqrt{36} = 6$ units

(ii) Two positions which are not equidistant from any axis are side mid-fielder and centre mid-fielder.

(iii) Let the coordinates of the position of right centre back be $A(3, -6)$, the coordinates of the position of left centre back be $B(-3, -6)$ and the coordinates of the position of goalkeeper be $C(0, -9)$.

Using distance formula, we get

$AB = 6$, $BC = 3\sqrt{2}$ and $AC = 3\sqrt{2}$

Here, $BC^2 + AC^2 = AB^2$

Hence, ΔABC is right angled triangle.

$\therefore$ Area of triangle formed by the positions A, B and C,

$$= \frac{1}{2} \times BC \times AC$$

$$= \frac{1}{2} \times 3\sqrt{2} \times 3\sqrt{2} = 9 \text{ sq units}$$

Or Coordinates of the position of left full back are (– 6, – 5) and coordinates of the position of right centre forward position are (3, 8).

$\therefore$ Minimum distance travelled by the ball

$$= \sqrt{\{3 - (-6)\}^2 + \{8 - (-5)\}^2}$$

$$= \sqrt{81 + 169} = \sqrt{250} = 5\sqrt{10} \text{ units}$$

24.

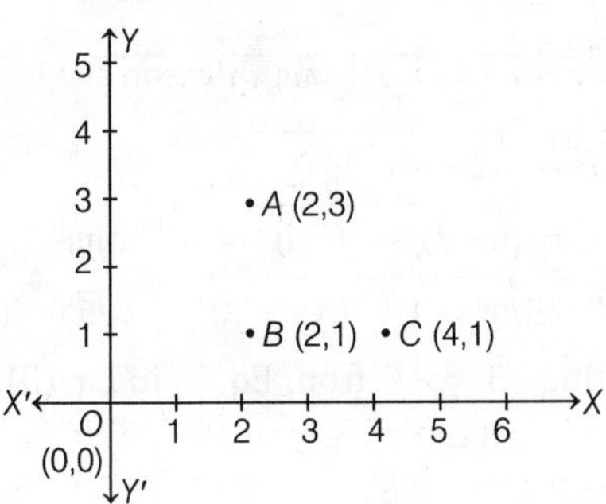

(i) Distance between Alia's house and Shagun's house

$$AB = \sqrt{(2-2)^2 + (1-3)^2} = \sqrt{(-2)^2} = 2 \text{ units}$$

(ii) Distance between library and Shagun's house,

$$BC = \sqrt{(4-2)^2 + (1-1)^2}$$

$$= \sqrt{4+0} = 2 \text{ units}$$

(iii) Distance between Shagun's house and school,

$$OB = \sqrt{(2-0)^2 + (1-0)^2}$$

$$= \sqrt{4+1}$$

$$= 5 \text{ units}$$

Distance between Alia's house and Shagun's house,

$AB = 2$ units

And distance between library and Shagun's house,

$CB = 2$ units

$\because$ $OB > AB$ and $OB > CB$

Hence, for Shagun's house, school is farther as compared to Alia's house and library.

Or

Distance between Shagun's house and library

$$BC = \sqrt{(4-2)^2 + (1-1)^2} = 2 \text{ units}$$

Now, $AC^2 = (2\sqrt{2})^2 = 8$ units

and $AB^2 + BC^2 = 2^2 + 2^2 = 8$ units

$\because$ $AC^2 = AB^2 + BC^2$

$\Rightarrow ABC$ is a right angled triangle, right angled at B.

Also, $AB = BC = 2$ units

$\therefore$ ABC is an isosceles right angled triangle.

25. (i) $CD = 4\sqrt{2}$ units, $AB = 4\sqrt{2}$ units

(ii) $AD = BC = 4\sqrt{2}$ units

(iii) Yes, Jaspal should be placed at the point (7, 5).

Or

Since, $AB = BC = CD = DA = 4\sqrt{2}$

and $AC = BD = 8$

$\therefore$ $ABCD$ is a square.

26. (i) The vertices of triangle ABC are $A(1, 1)$, $B(5, 1)$ and $C(3, 6)$.

$\therefore$ Mid-point of A and $B = \left(\frac{1+5}{2}, \frac{1+1}{2}\right) = (3, 1)$

(ii) Base of $\Delta ABC = AB = \sqrt{(5-1)^2 + (1-1)^2} = 4$ units

and height of ΔABC = Perpendicular distance from the vertex C to the base $AB = (6 - 1) = 5$ units

$\therefore$ Area of $\Delta ABC = \frac{1}{2} \times \text{base} \times \text{height}$

$$= \frac{1}{2} \times 4 \times 5 = 10 \text{ sq. units}$$

(iii) Let point on X-axis be $P(x, 0)$.

Then, $(PA)^2 = (PB)^2$

$$(x-1)^2 + (0-1)^2 = (x-5)^2 + (0-1)^2$$

$$\Rightarrow \quad (x-1)^2 + 1 = (x-5)^2 + 1$$

$$\Rightarrow \quad x^2 - 2x + 1 = x^2 - 10x + 25$$

$$\Rightarrow \quad x = 3$$

$\therefore$ Point on X-axis is (3, 0).

Or

$$\text{Centroid of the } \Delta ABC = \left(\frac{1+5+3}{3}, \frac{1+1+6}{3}\right)$$

$$= \left(3, \frac{8}{3}\right)$$

27. (i) **Hint**

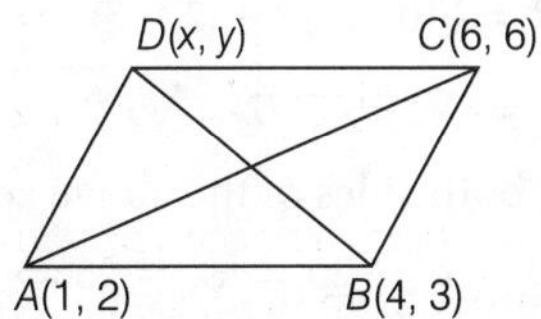

Let the coordinates of point D be (x, y).

$\therefore$ Mid-point of AC = Mid-point of BD

Now, use mid-point formula and find x, y.

Ans. $D = (3, 5)$

(ii) **Hint** Use distance formula and find GH, HK and GK.

Here, $GH + HK \neq GK$

$\therefore$ Points G, H and K are not on a same straight line.

Ans. No.

Or

Coordinates of mid-point of IJ

$$= \left(\frac{-4+5}{2}, \frac{6-3}{2}\right) = \left(\frac{1}{2}, \frac{3}{2}\right) \neq (0, 1)$$

$\therefore$ C is not the mid-point of IJ.

Distance between C and J,

$$CJ = \sqrt{(5-0)^2 + (-3-1)^2} = \sqrt{25+16} = \sqrt{41}$$

Distance between C and I,

$$CI = \sqrt{(-4-0)^2 + (6-1)^2} = \sqrt{16+25} = \sqrt{41}$$

$\because$ $CJ = CI$

$\therefore$ J and I are equidistant from C.

(iii) $\because B(2, -3)$ is equidistant from $A(1, 4)$ and $E(a, b)$.

A(1, 4) B(2, –3) E(a, b)

$\therefore B$ is the mid-point of AE

$$\Rightarrow \quad (2, -3) = \left(\frac{1+a}{2}, \frac{4+b}{2}\right)$$

$$\Rightarrow \quad a + 1 = 4 \text{ and } b + 4 = -6$$

$$\Rightarrow \quad a = 3 \text{ and } b = -10$$

Part II

1. **Hint** Do same as Example 2 of Topic 1.
   Ans. $\sqrt{x^2 + y^2}$ units
2. **Hint** Do same as Example 1 of Topic 1. **Ans.** a units
3. **Hint** Do same as Example 5 of Topic 1.
4. **Hint** Do same as Example 3 of Topic 1. **Ans.** $x = 0, 6$
5. **Hint** Given, $Q(0, 2)$ is equidistant from $P(5, -3)$ and $R(x, 7)$, which means $PQ = QR$.
   Find the distance of PQ and QR using distance formula,
   $\sqrt{(x_2 - x_1)^2 + (y_2 - y_1)^2}$
   $$PQ = \sqrt{(5-0)^2 + (-3-2)^2} = 5\sqrt{2}$$
   $$QR = \sqrt{(0-x)^2 + (2-7)^2} = \sqrt{x^2 + 25}$$
   Now, $\quad PQ = QR \Rightarrow 5\sqrt{2} = \sqrt{x^2 + 25}$
   On squaring both sides of the above equation, we get
   $$50 = x^2 + 25 \Rightarrow x^2 = 25 \Rightarrow x = \pm 5$$
   Therefore, the values of x are 5 and –5.
6. **Hint** Do same as Example 6 of Topic 1. **Ans.** (2, 0)
7. **Hint** Put $x = 0$ **Ans.** (0, –5)
8. **Hint** Diameter of circle,
   $d = \sqrt{(2-24)^2 + (23-1)^2}$ **Ans.** $11\sqrt{2}$ units
9. **Hint** Distance between $(2a, a-7)$ and $(11, -9)$
   = Radius of circle = $5\sqrt{2}$. **Ans.** $a = 5$ and 3
10. **Hint** By mid-point formula,
    $\left(3, \frac{3}{4}\right) = \left(\frac{k+7}{2}, \frac{3}{4}\right)$ **Ans.** $k = -1$
11. **Hint** The coordinates of Q are of the form $(0, y)$.
    Using the mid-point formula,
    $\left(\frac{-1+y}{2}\right) = -6 \Rightarrow y = -11$ **Ans.** (0, – 11).
12. **Hint** Do same as Example 8 of Topic 2. **Ans.** (6, –12)
13. **Hint** Do same as Example 1 of Topic 1. **Ans.** $\frac{1}{2}$
14. **Hint** Do same as Example 3 of Topic 1. **Ans.** ± 4
15. **Hint** Do same as Example 3 of Topic 1. **Ans.** $k = 7, -3$
16. **Hint** Do same as Example 4 of Topic 1.
    Ans. Non-collinear
17. **Hint** Do same as Example 5 of Topic 1. **Ans.** Yes.
18. **Hint** P(2, 1) A(4, 2) B(8, 4)
    Here, $AP = \sqrt{(2-4)^2 + (1-2)^2}$
    $= \sqrt{(-2)^2 + (-1)^2} = \sqrt{5}$ units ...(i)
    $AB = \sqrt{(8-4)^2 + (4-2)^2} = 2\sqrt{5}$ units ...(ii)
    On putting $\sqrt{5} = AP$ from Eq. (i) in Eq. (ii), we get
    $$AB = 2\sqrt{5} = 2AP$$
    $$\Rightarrow \quad AP = \frac{AB}{2}$$
19. **Hint** Let the coordinates of point P be (x, y).
    $\because$ Point P is equidistant from points with coordinates $A(7, 1)$ and $B(3, 5)$.
    So, by distance formula,
    $$\sqrt{(7-x)^2 + (1-y)^2} = \sqrt{(3-x)^2 + (5-y)^2}$$
    On squaring both sides and arrange as $x = y + 2$.
20. **Hint** Do same as Example 9 of Topic 2.
    We have, $P = (3, -2)$
    $\Rightarrow$ $P(3, -2)$ passes through $2x - y + k = 0 \Rightarrow k = -8$
21. **Hint** Use distance formula and then apply converse of Pythagoras theorem. **Ans.** 90°
22. **Hint** First find the type of triangle using distance formula and hence obtain the angles.
    Ans. 60°, equilateral triangle.
23. **Hint** The perimeter of a triangle is the sum of lengths of its three sides, so first find the length of three sides and then add them. **Ans.** $2 + \sqrt{2}$
24. **Hint** Use distance formula and then apply Pythagoras theorem. **Ans.** (0, 0).
25. **Hint** ΔABC is an isosceles triangle.
26. **Hint** Find AB, BC and AC using distance formula and then apply Pythagoras theorem.
    Ans. 1

27. **Hint** Since, $A(4,3)$ and $B(x,5)$ lie on the circle having centre $O(2,3)$.

$\therefore \quad OA = OB$ [radii of circle]

Ans. 9 units

28. **Hint** Here, $OP = \sqrt{(5-0)^2 + (0-0)^2}$

$= \sqrt{5^2} = 5$ units $=$ Radius of circle

Now, $OQ = \sqrt{(6-0)^2 + (8-0)^2} = 10$ units

$\because \quad OQ > OP$

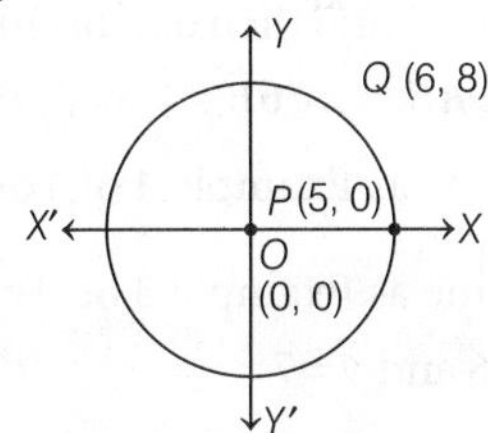

$\therefore$ $Q(6, 8)$ lies outside the circle.

29. **Hint** Given, vertices of a quadrilateral are $P(22, 5), Q(7, 10), R(12, 11)$ and $S(3, 24)$.

Now, $PQ = \sqrt{(7-22)^2 + (10-5)^2} = 5\sqrt{10}$ units

$QR = \sqrt{(12-7)^2 + (11-10)^2} = \sqrt{26}$ units

$RS = \sqrt{(3-12)^2 + (24-11)^2} = 5\sqrt{10}$ units

and $SP = \sqrt{(22-3)^2 + (5-24)^2} = 19\sqrt{2}$ units

Here, we see that opposite sides of a quadrilateral are not equal i.e. $QR \neq SP$.

Hence, given vertices of a quadrilateral are not forming a parallelogram.

30. **Hint**

$A(-1, 3) \quad \overset{k}{—} \quad P(x, y) \quad \overset{1}{—} \quad B(9, 8)$

Using section formula to find the coordinates of point P.

$$x = \frac{9k + (-1)}{k+1} = \frac{9k-1}{k+1} \text{ and } y = \frac{8k+3}{k+1}$$

Since, point P lies on the line $x - y = 0$, so it will satisfy the equation.

$$x - y = 0$$

$$\frac{9k-1}{k+1} - \frac{8k+3}{k+1} = 0$$

$$\Rightarrow \quad \frac{9k - 1 - 8k - 3}{k+1} = 0$$

$$\Rightarrow \quad k - 4 = 0 \Rightarrow k = 4$$

Hence, the value of k is 4.

31. **Hint** Do same as Example 8 of Topic 1. **Ans.** No

32. **Hint** Do same as Example 8 of Topic 2.

Now, diameter of circle

$=$ Distance between $(4, -1)$ and $(-2, -5)$.

Ans. (i) $(-2, -5)$ (ii) $2\sqrt{13}$ units (iii) 13π sq units

33. **Hint** First find coordinates of D and E, $DE = 1$ unit and then prove $DE = \frac{1}{2}AB$.

34. **Hint** Use distance formula and find in ΔABC, length of AB, BC and AC, in ΔDFE, the length of DF, FE and ED.

Here, we see that

$$\frac{AB}{DF} = \frac{BC}{FE} = \frac{CA}{ED}$$

$\therefore \quad \Delta ABC \sim \Delta DFE$ [by SSS criterion]

35. **Hint** Do same as Example 2 of Topic 2. **Ans.** $(-5, -2)$.

36. **Hint** Do same as Example 1 of Topic 2. **Ans.** $(0, 0)$

37. Since, $PR = 2QR$

Point R divides PQ in the ratio $2 : 1$.

$P(-2,5) \quad \overset{2}{—} \quad R(x, y) \quad \overset{1}{—} \quad Q(3, 2)$

Therefore,

$$\text{Coordinates of } R = \left[\frac{2(3) + (-2)1}{2+1}, \frac{2(2) + 1(5)}{2+1}\right]$$

$$= \left(\frac{6-2}{3}, \frac{4+5}{3}\right) = \left(\frac{4}{3}, 3\right)$$

38. **Hint**

$A(1, 2) \quad \overset{K}{—} \quad P\left(\frac{8}{5}, y\right) \quad \overset{1}{—} \quad B(2, 3)$

$$\therefore \quad \frac{8}{5} = \frac{2k+1}{k+1} \Rightarrow k = \frac{3}{2}$$

$\therefore$ Ratio is $3 : 2$.

Now, $y = \frac{13}{5}$

39. **Hint** Do same as Question 5 of NCERT Folder Exercise 7.2. **Ans.** $1 : 2$, $(3, 0)$

40. **Hint** Do same as Example 6 of Topic 2.

Ans. $4 : 3$; $\left(0, -\frac{13}{7}\right)$

41. **Hint** Do same as Example 2 of Topic 2. **Ans.** $\left(\frac{4}{5}, \frac{21}{5}\right)$

42. **Hint** Do same as Example 9 of Topic 2.

Ans. $(-1,0)$ and $(-4, 2)$.

43.

$A(-4, 3) \quad \overset{k:1}{—} \quad P(a, -2) \quad — \quad B(2, -4)$

By section formula,

$$a = \frac{2k-4}{k+1} \text{ and } -2 = \frac{-4k+3}{k+1} \Rightarrow k = \frac{5}{2}$$

$$\Rightarrow \quad a = \frac{2 \times \frac{5}{2} - 4}{\frac{5}{2} + 1} = \frac{5-4}{\frac{7}{2}} \Rightarrow a = \frac{2}{7}$$

Hence, ratio $= 5 : 2$ and $a = \frac{2}{7}$

44.

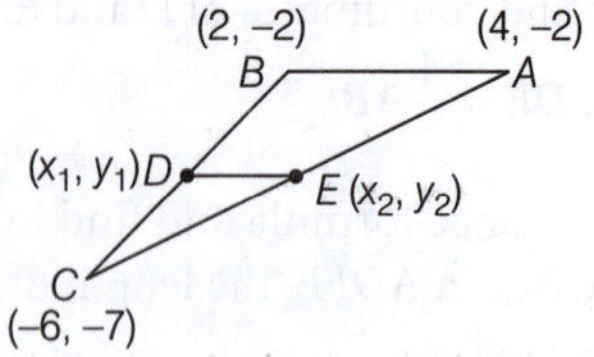

(2, −2) B, (4, −2) A, (x_1, y_1) D, E (x_2, y_2), C (−6, −7)

To prove $DE = \frac{1}{2}AB$

Since, D and E are mid-points of BC and AC respectively.
So, by mid-point formula,

$$x_1 = \frac{2-6}{2} = \frac{-4}{2} = -2,\ y_1 = \frac{-2-7}{2} = -\frac{9}{2}$$

and $$x_2 = \frac{4-6}{2} = -\frac{2}{2} = -1,\ y_2 = \frac{-2-7}{2} = -\frac{9}{2}$$

$\therefore D\left(-2, -\frac{9}{2}\right)$ and $E\left(-1, -\frac{9}{2}\right)$

Using distance formula,

$$DE = \sqrt{(-1+2)^2 + \left(-\frac{9}{2}+\frac{9}{2}\right)^2} = 1$$

$$AB = \sqrt{(2-4)^2 + (-2+2)^2} = 2$$

45. Hint

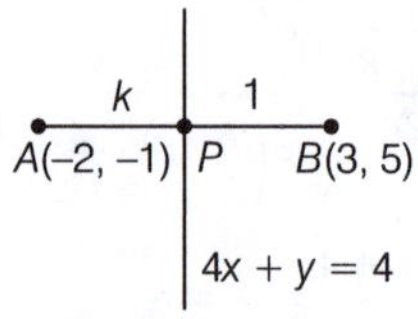

k, 1, A(−2, −1), P, B(3, 5), 4x + y = 4

Then, $P \equiv \left(\frac{3k-2}{k+1}, \frac{5k-1}{k+1}\right)$

Since, P lies on $4x + y = 4$.

$$\therefore\ 4\left(\frac{3k-2}{k+1}\right) + \left(\frac{5k-1}{k+1}\right) = 4$$

$$\Rightarrow\ k = 1$$

$\therefore$ Required ratio is 1 : 1.

46. By the mid-point formula, the coordinates of Sameer's location are $\left(\frac{2+8}{2}, \frac{4+6}{2}\right) = (5, 5)$

Now, the shortest distance between Sameer and Ragini is $\sqrt{\{(8-5)^2 + (9-5)^2\}} = 5$ units

47. Hint Coordinates of the mid-point satisfy the equaiton $2x + 2y + 1 = 0$. **Ans.** −15

48. Hint We know that the perpendicular bisector of any line segment divides the line segment into two equal parts i.e. the perpendicular bisector of the line segment always passes through the mid-point of the line segment.

$\therefore$ Mid-point of the line segment joining the points

$A(-2, -5)$ and $B(2, 5) = \left(\frac{-2+2}{2}, \frac{-5+5}{2}\right) = (0, 0)$

49. Hint According to the question,

$$\frac{10+k}{2} = a$$

and $$\frac{-6+4}{2} = b \qquad [\because (a, b) \text{ is mid-point, given}]$$

$$\Rightarrow\ 5 + \frac{k}{2} = a \text{ and } b = -1$$

Now, $a - 2b = 18 \Rightarrow 5 + \frac{k}{2} - 2(-1) = 18$

Now, solve for k and then use distance formula to find AB.

Ans. $k = 22, AB = 2\sqrt{61}$

50. Hint Do same as Example 4 of Topic 2. **Ans.** 1 : 5

51. Hint Do same as Example 8 of Topic 2.

Ans. $x = -6$ and $y = 7$

52. Hint In a rectangle, both diagonals are of same length.

Ans. Length of each diagonal is $\sqrt{34}$ units.

53. Hint Do same as Question 9 of NCERT Folder Exercise 7.2. **Ans.** $\left(-1, \frac{1}{2}\right), (0, 3), \left(1, \frac{11}{2}\right)$.

54. Hint Use properties of parallelogram.

Ans. (−1, 0)

55. Hint Do same as Question 9 of NCERT Folder Exercise 7.2.

Ans. $P\left(\frac{11}{6}, \frac{17}{6}\right), Q\left(\frac{8}{3}, \frac{11}{3}\right), R\left(\frac{7}{2}, \frac{9}{2}\right)$

$S\left(\frac{13}{3}, \frac{16}{3}\right)$ and $T\left(\frac{31}{6}, \frac{37}{6}\right)$

56. (i) We know that the diagonals of a rhombus bisect each other.

Thus, the point of intersection of both the diagonals is the mid-point of $P(2, -3)$ and $R(-2, 1)$.

So, $\left(\frac{2-2}{2}, \frac{-3+1}{2}\right) = (0, -1)$

(ii) The mid-point of $Q(6, 5)$ and $S(x, y)$ as $\left(\frac{6+x}{2}, \frac{5+y}{2}\right)$, where x and y are the coordinates of the fourth vertex S.

Uses the above steps and equates the respective coordinates of the mid-points to get the following relationships:

(a) $0 = \frac{6+x}{2} \Rightarrow x = -6$

(b) $-1 = \frac{5+y}{2} \Rightarrow y = -7$

Concludes that the coordinates of the fourth vertex S are $(-6, -7)$.

COORDINATE GEOMETRY

Distance Formula Distance between any two points $P(x_1, y_1)$ and $Q(x_2, y_2)$ is given by

$$PQ = \sqrt{(x_2 - x_1)^2 + (y_2 - y_1)^2}$$

i.e. $PQ = \sqrt{(\text{Difference of abscissas})^2 + (\text{Difference of ordinates})^2}$

Different Problems Related to Distance formula

***Type I* Problems Based on Collinearity of Points**

When three or more than three points lie on same line,they are called collinear points.

To show collinearity of three points say A, B and C, we find AB, BC and CA and show that sum of two shorter lengths is equal to largest length, otherwise non-collinear.

i.e. $AB + BC = AC$ or $AC + BC = AB$ or $BA + AC = BC$

***Type II* Problems Based on Equidistant Points**

A point say X which is equidistant from two points say A and B, then we take $AX = BX$ and simplify.

***Type III* Problems Based on Geometrical Figures**

Sometimes three or four points are given and using distance formula we show that the given points form a particular geometrical figure.

e.g. To prove given three coordinates form an isosceles triangle, first we find the sides of an isosceles triangle using distance formula and then that two sides are equal or not. If two sides are equal they formed an isosceles triangle.

Section Formula

Internal Division of a Line Segment Let $A(x_1, y_1)$ and $B(x_2, y_2)$ be two points and $P(x, y)$ is a point on the line segment joining A and B such that $AP : BP = m_1 : m_2$, then point P is said to divide the line segment AB internally in the ratio $m_1 : m_2$.

$A(x_1, y_1)$ ← m_1 → P ← m_2 → $B(x_2, y_2)$

$\therefore$ Coordinates of P are $\left(\dfrac{m_1x_2 + m_2x_1}{m_1 + m_2}, \dfrac{m_1y_2 + m_2y_1}{m_1 + m_2}\right)$

Mid-point of a Line Segment If a point P divides the line segment AB in the ratio 1 : 1, then we get mid-point of this line segment.

$\therefore$ Coordinates of P are $\left(\dfrac{x_1 + x_2}{2}, \dfrac{y_1 + y_2}{2}\right)$.

If the ratio in which P divides AB is $k : 1$, then the coordinates of the point P are

$$\left(\frac{kx_2 + x_1}{k + 1}, \frac{ky_2 + y_1}{k + 1}\right)$$

Different Problems Based on Section Formula

***Type I* Show Collinearity using Section Formula**

To show collinearity of three points A, B and C using section formula, first assume, C divides AB in the ratio of $k : 1$.

Then, write coordinates of C by section formula and equate it to original coordinates of C separately.

If value of k from both equations is same, then A, B and C are collinear, otherwise not.

***Type II* Problems Based on Finding Section Ratio and Section Point**

If end points of line segment and an axis which divides this line segment is given,then using section formula, we can find section ratio and section point.

***Type III* Problems Based on Finding the Unknown Vertex of a Geometrical figure**

For finding the unknown vertex of a given geometrical figure (e.g. parallelogram, triangle, circle etc.) we use their respective properties and section formula.

e.g. If A, B and C are three vertices of a parallelogram and we have to find vertex D. So,

we use the section formula to find the coordinates of mid-point of diagonal AC and coordinates of mid-point of diagonal BD.

And then using parallelogram property i.e. diagonals of a parallelogram bisect each other, we can find the fourth vertex D.

Introduction to Trigonometry

CHAPTER 8

The word **trigonometry** is derived from the Greek words 'tri ' (meaning three), 'gon' (meaning sides) and 'metron' (meaning measure).

Trigonometry is the study of the relationships between the sides and angles of a triangle. In this chapter, we will study ratios of the sides of a right angled triangle with respect to its acute angles. First, we will define the values of trigonometric ratios for angles of measure between 0° and 90°. Then, we will also calculate trigonometric ratios for some specific angles and establish some identities involving these ratios, which are called trigonometric identities.

TOPIC 01 Trigonometric Ratios

The ratios of the sides of a right angled triangle with respect to its acute angles, are called **trigonometric ratios**. Trigonometric ratios are also called ***T*-ratios.**

To understand the trigonometric ratios, first of all we will understand the concept of perpendicular, base and hypotenuse in a right angled triangle. For any acute angle (which is also known as the **angle of reference**) in a right angled triangle, the side opposite to the acute angle is called the **perpendicular** (P), the side adjacent to this acute angle is called the **base** (B) and side opposite to the right angle is called the **hypotenuse** (H).

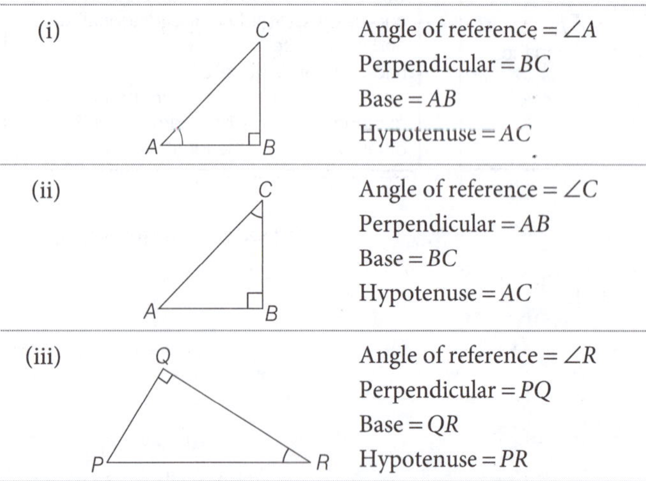

(i)	A, B, C	Angle of reference $= \angle A$ Perpendicular $= BC$ Base $= AB$ Hypotenuse $= AC$
(ii)	A, B, C	Angle of reference $= \angle C$ Perpendicular $= AB$ Base $= BC$ Hypotenuse $= AC$
(iii)	P, Q, R	Angle of reference $= \angle R$ Perpendicular $= PQ$ Base $= QR$ Hypotenuse $= PR$

Trigonometric ratios of $\angle A$ in right angled ΔABC are defined as follows:

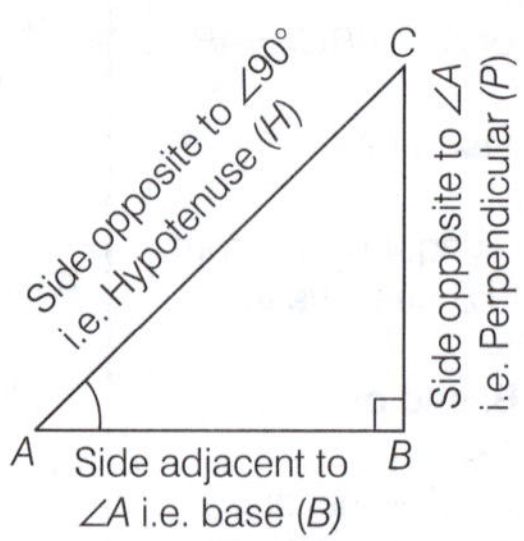

(i) sine of $\angle A$ or $\sin A = \dfrac{\text{Perpendicular}}{\text{Hypotenuse}} = \dfrac{P}{H} = \dfrac{BC}{AC}$

(ii) cosine of $\angle A$ or $\cos A = \dfrac{\text{Base}}{\text{Hypotenuse}} = \dfrac{B}{H} = \dfrac{AB}{AC}$

(iii) tangent of $\angle A$ or $\tan A = \dfrac{\text{Perpendicular}}{\text{Base}} = \dfrac{P}{B} = \dfrac{BC}{AB}$

(iv) cosecant of $\angle A$ or $\operatorname{cosec} A = \dfrac{\text{Hypotenuse}}{\text{Perpendicular}} = \dfrac{H}{P} = \dfrac{AC}{BC}$

(v) secant of $\angle A$ or $\sec A = \dfrac{\text{Hypotenuse}}{\text{Base}} = \dfrac{H}{B} = \dfrac{AC}{AB}$

(vi) cotangent of $\angle A$ or $\cot A = \dfrac{\text{Base}}{\text{Perpendicular}} = \dfrac{B}{P} = \dfrac{AB}{BC}$

Similarly, trigonometric ratios of $\angle C$ in right angled ΔABC are as follows :

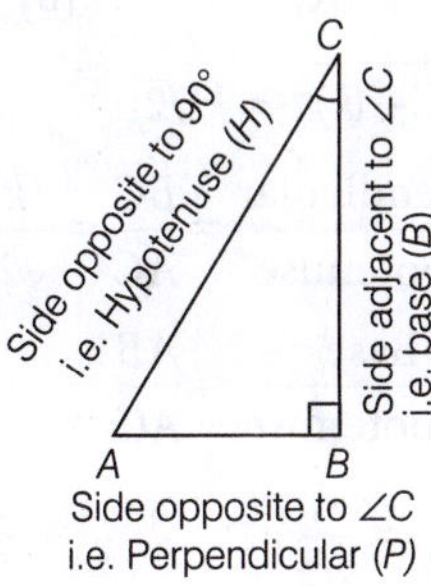

(i) $\sin C = \dfrac{AB}{AC}$ (ii) $\cos C = \dfrac{BC}{AC}$

(iii) $\tan C = \dfrac{AB}{BC}$ (iv) $\text{cosec } C = \dfrac{AC}{AB}$

(v) $\sec C = \dfrac{AC}{BC}$ (vi) $\cot C = \dfrac{BC}{AB}$

A Popular Technique to Remember *T*-ratios

$\sin\theta$	$\cos\theta$	$\tan\theta$
Pandit (*P*)	Badari (*B*)	Prasad (*P*)
Har (*H*)	Har (*H*)	Bholay (*B*)

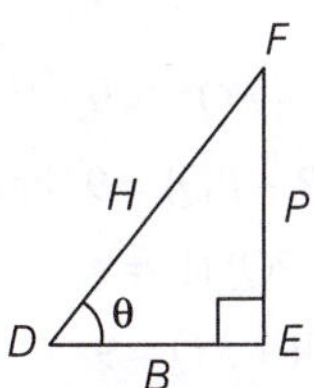

Then, $\sin\theta = \dfrac{P}{H}$, $\cos\theta = \dfrac{B}{H}$, $\tan\theta = \dfrac{P}{B}$,

$\text{cosec }\theta = \dfrac{H}{P}$, $\sec\theta = \dfrac{H}{B}$, $\cot\theta = \dfrac{B}{P}$

where, *P* is perpendicular, *B* is base and *H* is hypotenuse.

Some Important Points

(i) The symbol sin *A* is used as an abbreviation for 'the sine of $\angle A$.' sin *A* is not the product of 'sin' and '*A*'. 'sin' separated from '*A*' has no meaning. This interpretation follows for other trigonometric ratios also.

(ii) Each trigonometric ratio is a real number and has no unit.

(iii) The value of each of the trigonometric ratio of an angle does not depend on the size of the triangle. It depends only on the angle.

(iv) The values of the trigonometric ratios of an angle do not vary with the lengths of the sides of the triangle, if the angle remains the same.

(v) If one of the trigonometric ratios of an acute angle is known, then the remaining trigonometric ratios of that angle can be easily determined.

(vi) In an isosceles right angled ΔABC, right angled at *B*, the trigonometric ratios obtained by taking either $\angle A$ or $\angle C$, gives the same value.

(vii) As we know that the hypotenuse is the longest side in a right angled triangle, so the value of sin *A* or cos *A* is always less than 1 (or in particular case equal to 1), whereas the value of sec *A* or cosec *A* is always greater than or equal to 1.

Pythagoras Theorem

In right angled triangle, the square of the hypotenuse is equal to the sum of the squares of the other two sides.

In ΔABC, $AC^2 = BC^2 + AB^2$

$\Rightarrow \quad c^2 = a^2 + b^2$

or $\quad a^2 = c^2 - b^2$

or $\quad b^2 = c^2 - a^2$

Note it (i) $(\sin A)^2 = \sin^2 A \neq \sin A^2$ (ii) $(\sin A)^{-1} = \dfrac{1}{\sin A} \neq \sin^{-1} A$

Example 1. **Indicate the perpendicular, the hypotenuse and the base (in that order) with respect to the angle marked *x*.**

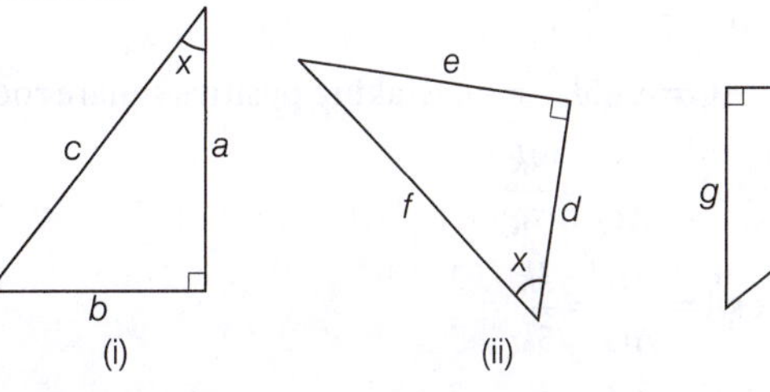

Sol. With reference to angle *x*,

(i) perpendicular $= b$, hypotenuse $= c$ and base $= a$

(ii) perpendicular $= e$, hypotenuse $= f$ and base $= d$

(iii) perpendicular $= g$, hypotenuse $= i$ and base $= h$

Example 2. **From the following figure, find**

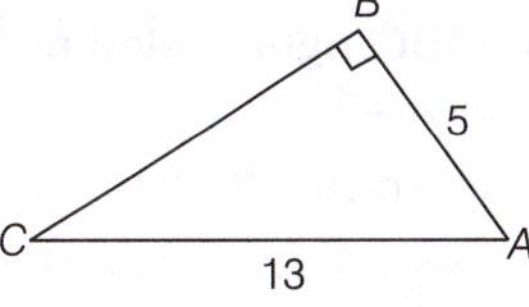

(i) sin *A* **(ii) cos *C*** **(iii) tan *A*** **(iv) cosec *C***

Sol. Given, $\angle ABC = 90°$, $AC = 13$ and $AB = 5$

Now, in right angled ΔABC, $AC^2 = AB^2 + BC^2$ [by Pythagoras theorem]

$\Rightarrow \quad 13^2 = 5^2 + BC^2$

$\Rightarrow \quad BC^2 = 169 - 25 = 144$

$\therefore \quad BC = \sqrt{144} = 12$ [taking positive square root]

(i) $\sin A = \frac{\text{Perpendicular}}{\text{Hypotenuse}} = \frac{BC}{AC} = \frac{12}{13}$

(ii) $\cos C = \frac{\text{Base}}{\text{Hypotenuse}} = \frac{BC}{AC} = \frac{12}{13}$

(iii) $\tan A = \frac{\text{Perpendicular}}{\text{Base}} = \frac{BC}{AB} = \frac{12}{5}$

(iv) $\text{cosec}\, C = \frac{\text{Hypotenuse}}{\text{Perpendicular}} = \frac{AC}{AB} = \frac{13}{5}$

Example 3. **If $\tan A = \frac{4}{3}$, find the other trigonometric ratios of $\angle A$.**

Sol. First, draw a ΔABC, right angled at B.

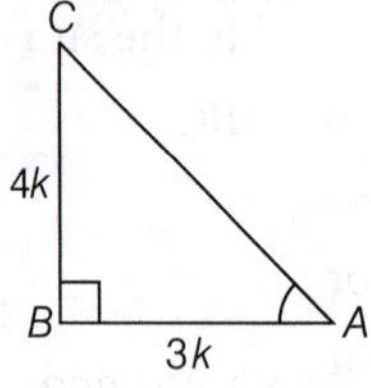

Given, $\tan A = \frac{4}{3}$

$\Rightarrow \frac{\text{Perpendicular}}{\text{Base}} = \frac{4}{3}$

$\Rightarrow \frac{BC}{AB} = \frac{4}{3}$

Let, $BC = 4k$ and $AB = 3k$ where, k is any positive integer.

Using Pythagoras theorem in ΔABC,

$AC^2 = BC^2 + AB^2$

$\Rightarrow AC^2 = (4k)^2 + (3k)^2 = 16k^2 + 9k^2$

$\Rightarrow AC^2 = 25k^2$

$\Rightarrow AC = \sqrt{25k^2} = 5k$ [taking positive square root]

Now, $\sin A = \frac{BC}{AC} = \frac{4k}{5k} = \frac{4}{5}$,

$\cos A = \frac{AB}{AC} = \frac{3k}{5k} = \frac{3}{5}$,

$\cot A = \frac{AB}{BC} = \frac{3k}{4k} = \frac{3}{4}$,

$\text{cosec} A = \frac{AC}{BC} = \frac{5k}{4k} = \frac{5}{4}$,

and $\sec A = \frac{AC}{AB} = \frac{5k}{3k} = \frac{5}{3}$.

Example 4. **In a ΔABC, right angled at B, if $\tan A = 1$, verify that $2 \sin A \cos A = 1$.**

Sol. Given, a ΔABC in which $\angle B = 90°$.

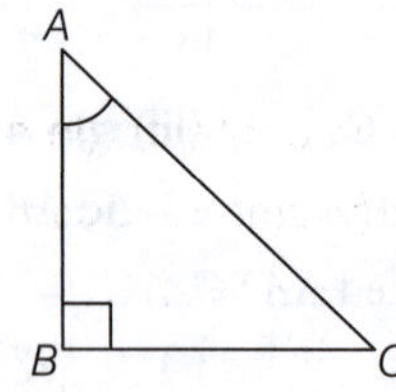

In ΔABC, $\tan A = \frac{\text{Perpendicular}}{\text{Base}} = \frac{BC}{AB} = 1$ [given]

$\Rightarrow BC = AB$

Let $AB = BC = k$, where k is a positive number.

Now, $AC = \sqrt{AB^2 + BC^2}$ [by Pythagoras theorem]

$= \sqrt{(k)^2 + (k)^2} = k\sqrt{2}$

$\therefore \sin A = \frac{\text{Perpendicular}}{\text{Hypotenuse}} = \frac{BC}{AC} = \frac{k}{\sqrt{2}k} = \frac{1}{\sqrt{2}}$

and $\cos A = \frac{\text{Base}}{\text{Hypotenuse}} = \frac{AB}{AC}$

$= \frac{k}{\sqrt{2}k} = \frac{1}{\sqrt{2}}$

Now, $2 \sin A \cos A = 2\left(\frac{1}{\sqrt{2}}\right)\left(\frac{1}{\sqrt{2}}\right) = 1$ **Hence proved.**

Example 5. **In ΔPQR right angled at Q, $QR = 3$ cm and $PR - PQ = 1$ cm. Determine the values of $\sin R$, $\cos R$ and $\tan R$.**

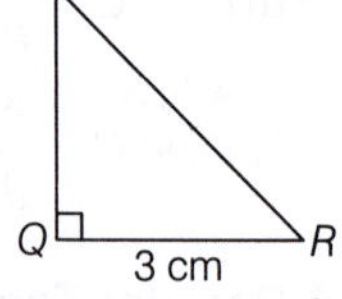

Sol. Given, a ΔPQR in which $\angle Q = 90°$ and $QR = 3$ cm.

Also, $PR - PQ = 1$ ...(i)

On applying Pythagoras theorem in ΔPQR, we get

$PR^2 = PQ^2 + QR^2$

$\Rightarrow QR^2 = PR^2 - PQ^2$

$\Rightarrow (3)^2 = PR^2 - PQ^2$ [given $QR = 3$ cm]

$\Rightarrow PR^2 - PQ^2 = 9$

$\Rightarrow (PR + PQ)(PR - PQ) = 9$ [$\because a^2 - b^2 = (a+b)(a-b)$]

$\Rightarrow (PR + PQ)(1) = 9$ [from Eq. (i)]

$\Rightarrow PR + PQ = 9$ ...(ii)

On adding Eqs. (i) and (ii), we get

$PR - PQ + PR + PQ = 1 + 9$

$\Rightarrow 2PR = 10 \Rightarrow PR = 5$ cm

On substituting $PR = 5$ cm in Eq. (i), we get

$5 - PQ = 1 \Rightarrow PQ = 4$ cm

$\therefore PR = 5$ cm and $PQ = 4$ cm

Now, $\sin R = \frac{PQ}{PR} = \frac{4}{5}$, $\cos R = \frac{QR}{PR} = \frac{3}{5}$ and $\tan R = \frac{PQ}{QR} = \frac{4}{3}$

Example 6. **If $\angle B$ and $\angle Q$ are acute angles such that $\sin B = \sin Q$, then prove that $\angle B = \angle Q$.**

Sol. Let us consider two right angled triangles, ΔABC and ΔPQR, where $\sin B = \sin Q$.

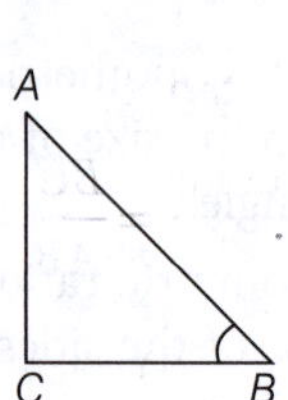

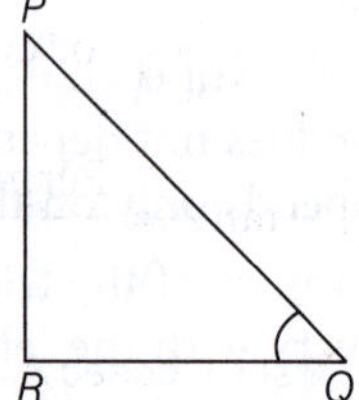

We have, $\sin B=\frac{AC}{AB}$ and $\sin Q=\frac{PR}{PQ}$

Then, $\frac{AC}{AB}=\frac{PR}{PQ}$

Therefore, $\frac{AC}{PR}=\frac{AB}{PQ}=k$, say ...(i)

Now, using Pythagoras theorem,

$$BC=\sqrt{AB^2-AC^2} \text{ and } QR=\sqrt{PQ^2-PR^2}$$

So, $$\frac{BC}{QR}=\frac{\sqrt{AB^2-AC^2}}{\sqrt{PQ^2-PR^2}}=\frac{\sqrt{k^2PQ^2-k^2PR^2}}{\sqrt{PQ^2-PR^2}}$$

$$=\frac{k\sqrt{PQ^2-PR^2}}{\sqrt{PQ^2-PR^2}}=k \quad ...(ii)$$

From Eqs. (i) and (ii), we have

$$\frac{AC}{PR}=\frac{AB}{PQ}=\frac{BC}{QR}$$

Then, using SSS criterion $\Delta ACB \sim \Delta PRQ$ and therefore $\angle B=\angle Q$.

Relations between Trigonometric Ratios

The relations between trigonometric ratios can be studied under the two heads (categories) given below:

Reciprocal Relation

Relations between trigonometric ratios and their reciprocals are given below :

(i) $\sin A=\frac{1}{\text{cosec } A}$ or $\text{cosec} A=\frac{1}{\sin A}$

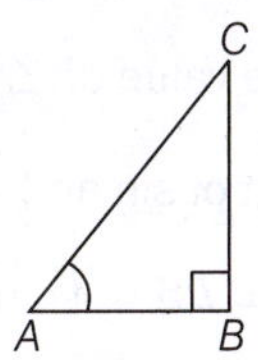

$$\left[\because \sin A=\frac{\text{Perpendicular}}{\text{Hypotenuse}}=\frac{BC}{AC}=\frac{1}{AC/BC}=\frac{1}{\text{cosec} A}\right]$$

(ii) $\cos A=\frac{1}{\sec A}$ or $\sec A=\frac{1}{\cos A}$

$$\left[\because \cos A=\frac{\text{Base}}{\text{Hypotenuse}}=\frac{AB}{AC}=\frac{1}{AC/AB}=\frac{1}{\sec A}\right]$$

(iii) $\tan A=\frac{1}{\cot A}$ or $\cot A=\frac{1}{\tan A}$

$$\left[\because \tan A=\frac{\text{Perpendicular}}{\text{Base}}=\frac{BC}{AB}=\frac{1}{AB/BC}=\frac{1}{\cot A}\right]$$

Note it (i) $\sin A\cdot\text{cosec } A=1$ (ii) $\cos A\cdot\sec A=1$
(iii) $\tan A\cdot\cot A=1$

Quotient Relation

Draw a ΔABC right angled at B. Then,

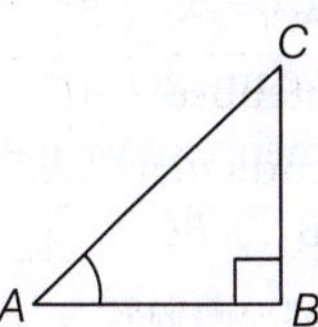

(i) $\tan A=\frac{\sin A}{\cos A}$

$$\left[\because \tan A=\frac{\text{Perpendicular}}{\text{Base}}=\frac{BC}{AB}=\frac{BC/AC}{AB/AC}=\frac{\sin A}{\cos A}\right]$$

(ii) $\cot A=\frac{\cos A}{\sin A}$

$$\left[\because \cot A=\frac{\text{Base}}{\text{Perpendicular}}=\frac{AB}{BC}=\frac{AB/AC}{BC/AC}=\frac{\cos A}{\sin A}\right]$$

Example 7. If $m\cot A=n$, then find the value of $\frac{m\sin A-n\cos A}{n\cos A+m\sin A}$.

Sol. Given, $m\cot A=n$

$$\Rightarrow \quad m\cdot\frac{1}{\tan A}=n \qquad \left[\because \cot\theta=\frac{1}{\tan\theta}\right]$$

$$\Rightarrow \quad \tan A=\frac{m}{n} \quad ...(i)$$

Now, $$\frac{m\sin A-n\cos A}{n\cos A+m\sin A}=\frac{m\cdot\frac{\sin A}{\cos A}-n}{n+m\cdot\frac{\sin A}{\cos A}}$$

[dividing numerator and denominator by $\cos A$]

$$=\frac{m\tan A-n}{n+m\tan A}=\frac{m\cdot\frac{m}{n}-n}{n+m\cdot\frac{m}{n}} \quad \text{[from Eq. (i)]}$$

$$=\frac{\frac{m^2-n^2}{n}}{\frac{n^2+m^2}{n}}$$

$$=\frac{m^2-n^2}{m^2+n^2}$$

Example 8. If θ is an acute angle and $3\sin\theta=4\cos\theta$, then find the value of $4\sin^2\theta-3\cos^2\theta+2$.

Sol. Given, equation is $3\sin\theta=4\cos\theta$

$$\Rightarrow \quad \frac{\sin\theta}{\cos\theta}=\frac{4}{3} \Rightarrow \tan\theta=\frac{4}{3} \quad ...(i)$$

Now, draw a right angled ΔABC such that $\angle B=90°$ and let $\angle A=\theta$.

From Eq. (i), $\tan\theta = \dfrac{4}{3} = \dfrac{\text{Perpendicular}}{\text{Base}} = \dfrac{BC}{AB}$

Let $BC = 4k$ and $AB = 3k$

where, k is a positive integer.

Using Pythagoras theorem, we have

$$AC^2 = AB^2 + BC^2$$

$\Rightarrow \quad AC^2 = (3k)^2 + (4k)^2 = 9k^2 + 16k^2$

$\Rightarrow \quad AC^2 = 25k^2$

$\Rightarrow \quad AC = 5k$ [taking positive square root both sides]

Now, $\quad \sin\theta = \dfrac{\text{Perpendicular}}{\text{Hypotenuse}} = \dfrac{BC}{AC} = \dfrac{4k}{5k} = \dfrac{4}{5}$

and $\quad \cos\theta = \dfrac{\text{Base}}{\text{Hypotenuse}} = \dfrac{AB}{AC} = \dfrac{3k}{5k} = \dfrac{3}{5}$

Now, $4\sin^2\theta - 3\cos^2\theta + 2 = 4\left(\dfrac{4}{5}\right)^2 - 3\left(\dfrac{3}{5}\right)^2 + 2$

$$= 4\left(\frac{16}{25}\right) - 3\left(\frac{9}{25}\right) + 2 = \frac{64}{25} - \frac{27}{25} + 2$$

$$= \frac{64 - 27 + 50}{25} = \frac{87}{25} = 3\frac{12}{25}$$

Try These 8.1

1. In each of the following, one of the six trigonometric ratios is given. Find the values of the other trigonometric ratios.

   (i) $\sin A = \dfrac{12}{13}$ (ii) $\tan\theta = \dfrac{a}{b}$ (iii) $\sin A = \dfrac{3}{5}$ (iv) $\cot A = \dfrac{8}{15}$

2. If $\tan A = \dfrac{3}{4}$, then show that $\sin A \cos A = \dfrac{12}{25}$.

   NCERT Exemplar

3. In the following figure, find $\tan P - \cot R$.

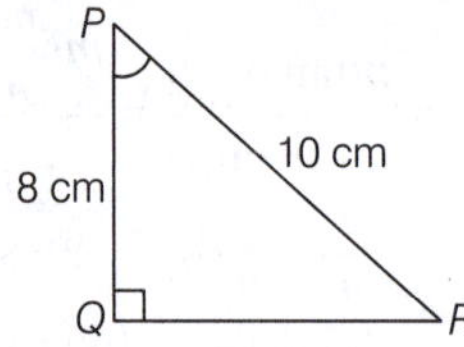

4. If $\sin\theta = \dfrac{24}{25}$, then find the value of $\sin^2\theta + \cos^2\theta$.

5. If $\sin A = \dfrac{3}{5}$, then find the value of $\sin A \cos B + \cos A \sin B$, where $\angle C$ is 90°.

6. In a ΔABC, $\angle B = 90°$. If $AB = 2$ cm and $AC = 3$ cm, then find the value of $\sin A$.

7. If $\sin\alpha = \dfrac{1}{2}$ and α is an acute angle, then find the value of $(3\cos\alpha - 4\cos^3\alpha)$.

8. If $\cos\theta = \dfrac{2}{3}$, then find the value of $2\sec^2\theta + 2\tan^2\theta - 9$.

9. In ΔABC, right angled at B, $AC + BC = 49$ cm, $AB = 7$ cm. Determine the values of $\sin A$, $\cos A$, $\tan C$ and $\sec C$.

10. In a ΔPQR, $\angle Q = 90°$. If $PQ = 10$ cm and $PR = 15$ cm, then find the value of $\tan^2 P + \sec^2 P + 1$.

11. If $17\cos A = 8$, then find $15\,\text{cosec}\,A - 8\sec A$.

12. If $\sec\theta = \dfrac{4}{\sqrt{7}}$, then prove that $\sqrt{\dfrac{2\tan^2\theta - \text{cosec}^2\theta}{2\cos^2\theta - \cot^2\theta}} = \dfrac{20}{7}$.

13. In a ΔABC, right angle at B, having $AB = 5$ cm, and $BC = 12$ cm, then find $\sin A$, $\cos C$ and $\tan A$.

14. If $3\tan A = 4$, then prove that

    (i) $\sqrt{\dfrac{\sec A - \text{cosec}\,A}{\sec A + \text{cosec}\,A}} = \dfrac{1}{\sqrt{7}}$ (ii) $\sqrt{\dfrac{1 - \sin A}{1 + \cos A}} = \dfrac{1}{2\sqrt{2}}$

15. If $\angle A$ and $\angle Q$ are acute angles such that $\tan A = \tan Q$, then show that $\angle A = \angle Q$.

16. If $\tan\theta = \dfrac{4}{3}$, then find $\dfrac{\sin\theta + \cos\theta}{\sin\theta - \cos\theta}$.

17. If $5\tan\alpha = 4$, then prove that $\dfrac{5\sin\alpha - 3\cos\alpha}{5\sin\alpha + 2\cos\alpha} = \dfrac{1}{6}$.

18. If $3\tan A = 4\sin A$, then find the relation between cosec A and cot A.

19. If $\sqrt{3}\sin\theta = \cos\theta$, then find the value of $\dfrac{\sin\theta\tan\theta(1 + \cot\theta)}{\sin\theta + \cos\theta}$.

20. If $22\cos A - 3\sin A = 20\sin A$, then find the value of $\tan^2 A + \sin^2 A \cdot \sec^2 A$.

21. Prove that $(1 + \tan A + \cot A)(\sin A - \cos A) = \sin A \tan A - \cot A \cos A$.

22. State whether the following are true or false. Justify your answer.

    (i) The value of $\tan A$ is always greater than 1.

    (ii) $\sec A = \dfrac{4}{3}$ for some value of $\angle A$.

    (iii) $\sin A$ is the product of sin and A.

    (iv) $\sin\theta = \dfrac{12}{5}$ for some $\angle\theta$.

Answers

1. **Hint** Do same as Example 3.

Ans. (i) $\cos A = \dfrac{5}{13}$, $\tan A = \dfrac{12}{5}$, $\cot A = \dfrac{5}{12}$, $\sec A = \dfrac{13}{5}$, $\text{cosec}A = \dfrac{13}{12}$

(ii) $\sin\theta = \dfrac{a}{\sqrt{a^2 + b^2}}$, $\cos\theta = \dfrac{b}{\sqrt{a^2 + b^2}}$, $\cot\theta = \dfrac{b}{a}$,

$\sec\theta = \dfrac{\sqrt{a^2 + b^2}}{b}$, $\text{cosec}\theta = \dfrac{\sqrt{a^2 + b^2}}{a}$

(iii) $\cos A = \dfrac{4}{5}$, $\tan A = \dfrac{3}{4}$, $\cot A = \dfrac{4}{3}$, $\sec A = \dfrac{5}{4}$, $\text{cosec}\,A = \dfrac{5}{3}$

(iv) $\sin A = \dfrac{15}{17}$, $\cos A = \dfrac{8}{17}$, $\tan A = \dfrac{15}{8}$, $\sec A = \dfrac{17}{8}$, $\text{cosec}\,A = \dfrac{17}{15}$

2. **Hint** Do same as Example 4.

3. Hint Use Pythagoras theorem, to find QR, then find $\tan P$ and $\cot R$. **Ans.** 0

4. Hint Use Pythagoras theorem to find the base, after using it, find the value of $\cos\theta$, then put in given expression. **Ans.** 1

5. Hint Use Pythagoras theorem, to find base, then on the basis of angle find $\sin B$ and $\cos B$ and then put the values in given expression. **Ans.** 1

6. Hint Do same as Example 2 (i). **Ans.** $\frac{\sqrt{5}}{3}$

7. Hint As, $\sin\alpha = \frac{1}{2} = \frac{P}{H}$

Using Pythagoras theorem,

$$(1)^2 + B^2 = (2)^2 \Rightarrow B = \sqrt{3}$$

Now, $\cos\alpha = \frac{B}{H} = \frac{\sqrt{3}}{2}$

Put the value in the given expression. **Ans.** 0

8. Hint Do same as Question 7. **Ans.** -2

9. Hint Do same as Example 5.

Ans. $\sin A = \frac{24}{25}, \tan C = \frac{7}{24}, \cos A = \frac{7}{25}$ and $\sec C = \frac{25}{24}$.

10. Hint Use Pythagoras theorem to find QR and then find $\sec P$, $\tan P$ and put in given expression. **Ans.** $\frac{9}{2}$

11. Hint As, $\cos A = \frac{8}{17} = \frac{B}{H}$

Using Pythagoras theorem,

$$P^2 + 8^2 = 17^2 \Rightarrow P = 15$$

Then, $15 \operatorname{cosec} A - 8 \sec A$

$$= 15\left(\frac{H}{P}\right) - 8\left(\frac{H}{B}\right) = 15\left(\frac{17}{15}\right) - 8\left(\frac{17}{8}\right) = 17 - 17 = 0$$

12. Hint As, $\sec\theta = \frac{4}{\sqrt{7}} = \frac{H}{B}$

Using Pythagoras theorem,

$$P^2 = H^2 - B^2 = 16 - 7 = 9 \Rightarrow P = 3$$

Now, $\tan\theta = \frac{P}{B} = \frac{3}{\sqrt{7}}, \operatorname{cosec}\theta = \frac{H}{P} = \frac{4}{3}, \cos\theta = \frac{B}{H} = \frac{\sqrt{7}}{4}, \cot\theta = \frac{\sqrt{7}}{3}$

Now, put these values in LHS of given expression.

13. Hint Do same as Example 2.

Ans. $\sin A = \frac{12}{13}, \cos C = \frac{12}{13}, \tan A = \frac{12}{5}$

14. Hint As, $3\tan A = 4 \Rightarrow \tan A = \frac{4}{3} = \frac{P}{B}$

Using Pythagoras theorem, $H^2 = 4^2 + 3^2 \Rightarrow H = 5$

$$\sec A = \frac{H}{B} = \frac{5}{3}, \operatorname{cosec} A = \frac{H}{P} = \frac{5}{4}$$

$$\cos A = \frac{B}{H} = \frac{3}{5}, \sin A = \frac{P}{H} = \frac{4}{5}$$

Now, put these values in LHS of given equations in part (i) and (ii).

15. Hint Do same as Example 6.

16. Hint Do same as Example 7. **Ans.** 7

17. Hint Do same as Example 7.

18. Hint We have, $3\tan A = 4\sin A$

$$\Rightarrow \frac{1}{3\tan A} = \frac{1}{4\sin A} \Rightarrow 4\cot A = 3\operatorname{cosec} A$$

19. Hint As, $\sqrt{3}\sin\theta = \cos\theta \Rightarrow \tan\theta = \frac{1}{\sqrt{3}}$

$$\therefore \frac{\sin\theta\tan\theta(1+\cot\theta)}{\sin\theta + \cos\theta} = \frac{\tan\theta\tan\theta(1+\cot\theta)}{\tan\theta + 1}$$ **Ans.** $\frac{1}{\sqrt{3}}$

20. Hint Given, $22\cos A - 3\sin A = 20\sin A$

$$\Rightarrow \frac{22}{20}\cot A - \frac{3}{20} = 1 \Rightarrow \cot A = \frac{23}{22} \Rightarrow \tan A = \frac{22}{23}$$

Now, put in given expression and simplify. **Ans.** $2 \times \left(\frac{22}{23}\right)^2$

21. Hint LHS $= (1 + \tan A + \cot A)(\sin A - \cos A)$

$$= \left(1 + \frac{\sin A}{\cos A} + \frac{\cos A}{\sin A}\right)(\sin A - \cos A)$$

$$= \left(\frac{\sin A\cos A + \sin^2 A + \cos^2 A}{\sin A\cos A}\right)(\sin A - \cos A)$$

$$= \frac{\sin^3 A - \cos^3 A}{\sin A\cos A} = \frac{\sin^2 A}{\cos A} - \frac{\cos^2 A}{\sin A}$$

$$= \sin A\tan A - \cos A\cot A = \text{RHS}$$ **Hence proved.**

22. (i) False (ii) True (iii) False (iv) False

TOPIC 02 Trigonometric Ratios of Some Specific Angles

Determination of trigonometric ratios of some specific angles by geometrical method is discussed below:

Trigonometric Ratios for an Angle of 45°

Let ΔABC be an isosceles right angled triangle in which $\angle B = 90°$ and $\angle A = 45°$, then third angle will also be 45° i.e. $\angle C = 45°$.

Here, $\angle A = \angle C \Rightarrow BC = AB = a$

[since, sides opposite to equal angles of a triangle are also equal]

Then, $AC = \sqrt{2}a$ units [by Pythagoras theorem]

Now, by the definitions of the trigonometric ratios, we have,

$$\sin 45° = \frac{P}{H} = \frac{BC}{AC} = \frac{a}{\sqrt{2}a} = \frac{1}{\sqrt{2}}$$

Similarly, we can find other trigonometric ratios.

Trigonometric Ratios for Angles of 60° and 30°

Let ΔABC be an equilateral triangle with each side equal to $2a$. Then, each angle of the triangle is 60°

i.e. $\angle A = \angle B = \angle C = 60°$

Now, draw perpendicular AD from A to the side BC.

Here, $\Delta ADB \cong \Delta ADC$ [by RHS congruency rule]

Thus, $BD = DC = a$ units

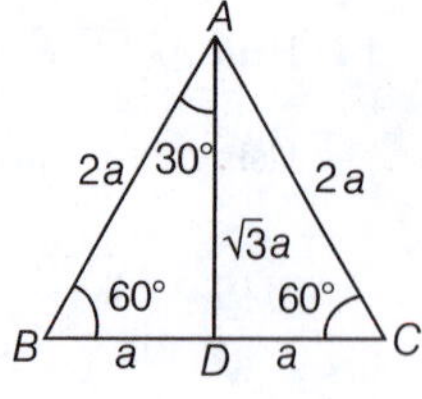

On applying Pythagoras theorem in right angled ΔADB, we get

$$AD = \sqrt{AB^2 - BD^2}$$

$$= \sqrt{4a^2 - a^2} = \sqrt{3}a$$

For angle 60°

In right angled ΔADB, we have

$$\sin 60° = \frac{P}{H} = \frac{AD}{AB} = \frac{\sqrt{3}a}{2a} = \frac{\sqrt{3}}{2};$$

Similarly, we can find other trigonometric ratios.

For angle 30°

In right angled ΔADB, we have

$$\sin 30° = \frac{P}{H} = \frac{BD}{AB} = \frac{a}{2a} = \frac{1}{2}$$

Similarly, we can find other trigonometric ratios.

Trigonometric Ratios for Angles of 0° and 90°

For angle 0°

In ΔABC, as $\angle A$ gets smaller and smaller, the length of the side BC decreases and the point C gets closer to point B.

Finally, when $\angle A$ becomes very close to 0°, AC becomes almost the same as AB

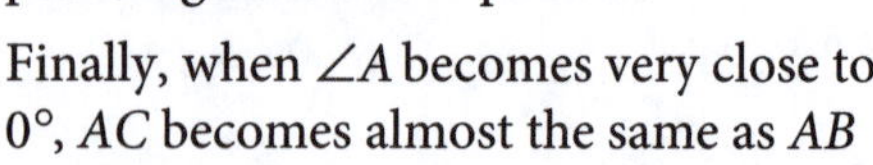

and BC gets very close to 0, so the value of $\sin A = \frac{BC}{AC}$ is very close to 0 and the value of $\cos A = \frac{AB}{AC}$ is very close to 1.

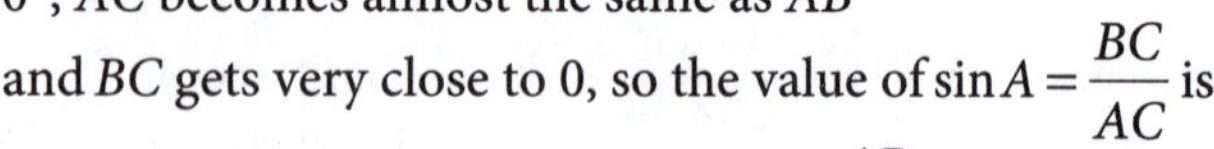

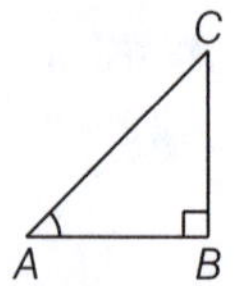

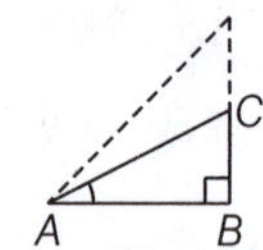

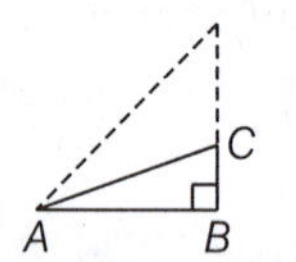

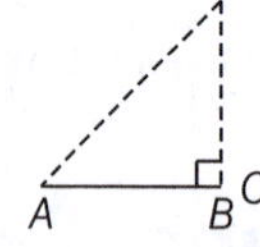

Thus, when $\angle A = 0°$, $\sin 0° = \frac{BC}{AC} = \frac{0}{AC} = 0$

and $\cos 0° = \frac{AB}{AC} = \frac{AB}{AB} = 1.$

For angle 90°

In ΔABC, as $\angle A$ gets larger and larger, $\angle C$ gets smaller and smaller and the length of the side AB goes on decreasing i.e. point A gets closer to point B. Finally, when $\angle A$ is very close to 90°, $\angle C$ becomes very close to 0° and the side AC almost coincides with side BC and the side AB is nearly zero. So, $\sin A = \frac{P}{H} = \frac{BC}{AC}$ is very close to 1 and

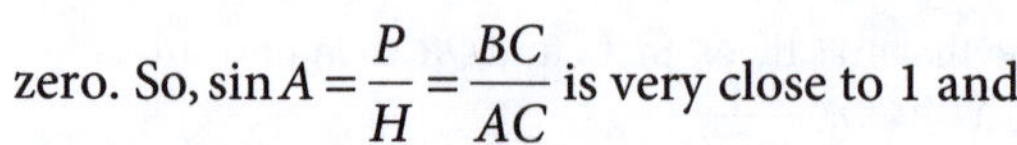

$\cos A = \frac{B}{H} = \frac{AB}{AC}$ is very close to 0.

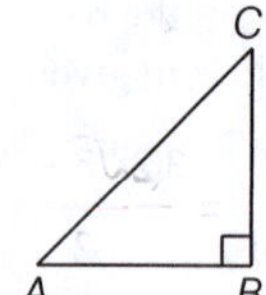

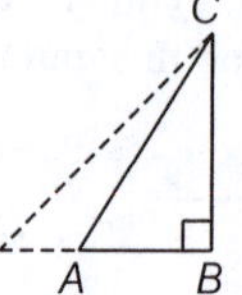

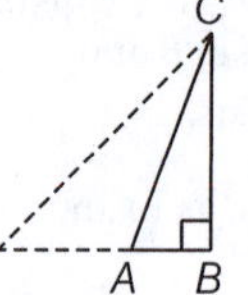

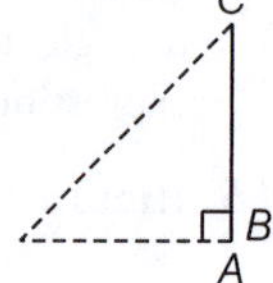

Thus, when

$$\angle A = 90°,$$

$$\sin 90° = \frac{BC}{AC} = \frac{BC}{BC} = 1,$$

$$\cos 90° = \frac{AB}{AC} = \frac{0}{AC} = 0$$

Using these, we can find other trigonometric ratios.

Values of Trigonometric Ratios for Some Specific Angles

Angles	0° or 0	30° or $\frac{\pi}{6}$	45° or $\frac{\pi}{4}$	60° or $\frac{\pi}{3}$	90° or $\frac{\pi}{2}$
$\sin\theta$	0	$\frac{1}{2}$	$\frac{1}{\sqrt{2}}$	$\frac{\sqrt{3}}{2}$	1
$\cos\theta$	1	$\frac{\sqrt{3}}{2}$	$\frac{1}{\sqrt{2}}$	$\frac{1}{2}$	0
$\tan\theta$	0	$\frac{1}{\sqrt{3}}$	1	$\sqrt{3}$	∞
$\text{cosec}\,\theta$	∞	2	$\sqrt{2}$	$\frac{2}{\sqrt{3}}$	1
$\sec\theta$	1	$\frac{2}{\sqrt{3}}$	$\sqrt{2}$	2	∞
$\cot\theta$	∞	$\sqrt{3}$	1	$\frac{1}{\sqrt{3}}$	0

Here, '∞' stands for undefined (not defined) value.

Note it

(i) The value of $\sin\theta$ increases from 0 to 1 and $\cos\theta$ decreases from 1 to 0, where $0 \le \theta \le 90°$.

(ii) Division by 0 is not allowed, hence 1/0 is an indeterminate (not defined) value.

(iii) In the case of $\tan\theta$, the values increase from 0 to ∞, where $0 \le \theta \le 90°$.

(iv) In the case of $\cot\theta$, the values decrease from ∞ to 0, where $0 \le \theta \le 90°$.

(v) In the case of $\text{cosec}\,\theta$, the values decrease from ∞ to 1, where $0 \le \theta \le 90°$.

(vi) In the case of $\sec\theta$, the values increase from 1 to ∞, where $0 \le \theta \le 90°$.

Example 1. Evaluate $\dfrac{\sin 30^\circ + \tan 45^\circ}{\sec 30^\circ + \cot 45^\circ}$. CBSE 2023 (Basic)

Sol. We have, $\dfrac{\sin 30^\circ + \tan 45^\circ}{\sec 30^\circ + \cot 45^\circ} = \dfrac{\frac{1}{2}+1}{\frac{2}{\sqrt{3}}+1} = \dfrac{3}{2} \times \dfrac{\sqrt{3}}{2+\sqrt{3}}$

$$= \frac{3\sqrt{3}}{2(2+\sqrt{3})} \times \frac{2-\sqrt{3}}{2-\sqrt{3}} = \frac{6\sqrt{3}-9}{2(4-3)} = \frac{3(2\sqrt{3}-3)}{2}$$

Example 2. Evaluate $\dfrac{\cos 45^\circ + \sin 60^\circ}{\sec 30^\circ + \operatorname{cosec} 30^\circ}$.

CBSE 2024 (Standard)

Sol. We know that

$\cos 45^\circ = \dfrac{1}{\sqrt{2}}, \sin 60^\circ = \dfrac{\sqrt{3}}{2}, \sec 30^\circ = \dfrac{2}{\sqrt{3}}$ and $\operatorname{cosec} 30^\circ = 2$

Now, $\dfrac{\cos 45^\circ + \sin 60^\circ}{\sec 30^\circ + \operatorname{cosec} 30^\circ} = \dfrac{\frac{1}{\sqrt{2}}+\frac{\sqrt{3}}{2}}{\frac{2}{\sqrt{3}}+2} = \dfrac{\frac{2+\sqrt{6}}{2\sqrt{2}}}{\frac{2+2\sqrt{3}}{\sqrt{3}}}$

$$= \frac{(2+\sqrt{6})\sqrt{3}}{2\sqrt{2}(2+2\sqrt{3})} = \frac{2\sqrt{3}+\sqrt{18}}{4\sqrt{2}+4\sqrt{6}}$$

$$= \frac{2\sqrt{3}+3\sqrt{2}}{4\sqrt{2}+4\sqrt{6}} = \frac{2\sqrt{3}+3\sqrt{2}}{4\sqrt{2}+4\sqrt{6}} \times \frac{4\sqrt{2}-4\sqrt{6}}{4\sqrt{2}-4\sqrt{6}}$$

$$= \frac{8\sqrt{6}-8\sqrt{18}+12\times 2-12\sqrt{12}}{32-96}$$

$$= \frac{8\sqrt{6}-24\sqrt{2}+24-24\sqrt{3}}{-64} = \frac{-\sqrt{6}+3\sqrt{2}-3+3\sqrt{3}}{8}$$

$$= \frac{\sqrt{2}(-\sqrt{3}+3)+\sqrt{3}(-\sqrt{3}+3)}{8} = \frac{(-\sqrt{3}+3)(\sqrt{2}+\sqrt{3})}{8}$$

$$\therefore \frac{\cos 45^\circ + \sin 60^\circ}{\sec 30^\circ + \operatorname{cosec} 30^\circ} = \frac{(-\sqrt{3}+3)(\sqrt{2}+\sqrt{3})}{8}$$

Example 3. Evaluate $8\sqrt{3} \operatorname{cosec}^2 30^\circ \sin 60^\circ \cos 60^\circ \cos^2 45^\circ \sin 45^\circ \tan 30^\circ \operatorname{cosec}^3 45^\circ$.

Sol. We have,

$8\sqrt{3} \operatorname{cosec}^2 30^\circ \sin 60^\circ \cos 60^\circ \cos^2 45^\circ \sin 45^\circ \tan 30^\circ \operatorname{cosec}^3 45^\circ$

$$= 8\sqrt{3}(\operatorname{cosec} 30^\circ)^2 \sin 60^\circ \cdot \cos 60^\circ (\cos 45^\circ)^2 \sin 45^\circ \tan 30^\circ (\operatorname{cosec} 45^\circ)^3$$

$$= 8\sqrt{3}(2)^2 \times \frac{\sqrt{3}}{2} \cdot \frac{1}{2} \times \left(\frac{1}{\sqrt{2}}\right)^2 \times \left(\frac{1}{\sqrt{2}}\right) \times \frac{1}{\sqrt{3}} \times (\sqrt{2})^3$$

$$\left[\because \operatorname{cosec} 30^\circ = 2, \sin 60^\circ = \frac{\sqrt{3}}{2}, \cos 60^\circ = \frac{1}{2}, \sin 45^\circ = \cos 45^\circ = \frac{1}{\sqrt{2}}, \tan 30^\circ = \frac{1}{\sqrt{3}} \text{ and } \operatorname{cosec} 45^\circ = \sqrt{2}\right]$$

$$= 8\sqrt{3} \times \sqrt{3} \times \frac{1}{2} \times \frac{1}{\sqrt{2}} \times \frac{1}{\sqrt{3}} \times 2\sqrt{2} = 8\sqrt{3}$$

Example 4. Verify that $\sin 2A = \dfrac{2\tan A}{1+\tan^2 A}$, for $A = 30^\circ$.

CBSE 2025 (Basic)

Sol. LHS $= \sin 2A = \sin(2\times 30^\circ) = \sin 60^\circ = \dfrac{\sqrt{3}}{2}$

$$\text{RHS} = \frac{2\tan A}{1+\tan^2 A} = \frac{2\times \tan 30^\circ}{1+\tan^2 30^\circ} = \frac{2\times \frac{1}{\sqrt{3}}}{1+\left(\frac{1}{\sqrt{3}}\right)^2}$$

$$= \frac{\frac{2}{\sqrt{3}}}{1+\frac{1}{3}} = \frac{2}{\sqrt{3}} \times \frac{3}{4} = \frac{3}{2\sqrt{3}} = \frac{3\sqrt{3}}{2\times 3} = \frac{\sqrt{3}}{2}$$

LHS = RHS **Hence verified.**

Example 5. If $A = 60^\circ$ and $B = 30^\circ$, verify that $\sin(A+B) = \sin A \cos B + \cos A \sin B$ CBSE 2024 (Standard)

Sol. Given, $A = 60^\circ$ and $B = 30^\circ$

and given expression is

$\sin(A+B) = \sin A \cos B + \cos A \sin B$

$\text{LHS} = \sin(A+B) = \sin(60^\circ + 30^\circ) = \sin 90^\circ = 1$

$\text{RHS} = \sin A \cos B + \cos A \sin B$

$= \sin 60^\circ \cos 30^\circ + \cos 60^\circ \sin 30^\circ$

$= \dfrac{\sqrt{3}}{2} \times \dfrac{\sqrt{3}}{2} + \dfrac{1}{2} \times \dfrac{1}{2} = \dfrac{3}{4} + \dfrac{1}{4} = \dfrac{4}{4} = 1$

LHS = RHS **Hence verified.**

Example 6. If $\sin(A-B) = \dfrac{1}{2}$, $\cos(A+B) = \dfrac{1}{2}$, $0^\circ < A+B \leq 90^\circ$, $A > B$, then find the values of A and B.

CBSE Sample Paper 2025

Sol. Given, $\sin(A-B) = \dfrac{1}{2}$

$\Rightarrow \sin(A-B) = \sin 30^\circ$ $[\because \sin 30^\circ = 1/2]$

On equating both sides, we get

$A - B = 30^\circ$ ...(i)

Also, $\cos(A+B) = \dfrac{1}{2}$

$\Rightarrow \cos(A+B) = \cos 60^\circ$ $[\because \cos 60^\circ = 1/2]$

On equating both sides, we get

$A + B = 60^\circ$ ...(ii)

On adding Eqs. (i) and (ii), we get

$2A = 90^\circ$

$\Rightarrow A = 45^\circ$

On putting $A = 45^\circ$ in Eq. (i), we get

$45^\circ - B = 30^\circ$ $[\because A = 45^\circ]$

$\Rightarrow B = 45^\circ - 30^\circ$

$\therefore B = 15^\circ$

Hence, $A = 45^\circ$ and $B = 15^\circ$.

Example 7. **If $\sin x+\cos y=1$, $x=30^\circ$ and y is an acute angle, then find the value of y.** CBSE 2019

Sol. Given, equation is $\sin x+\cos y=1$

Put $x=30^\circ$, we get $\sin 30^\circ+\cos y=1$

$$\Rightarrow \quad \cos y=1-\sin 30^\circ \Rightarrow \cos y=1-\frac{1}{2}$$

$$\Rightarrow \quad \cos y=\frac{1}{2} \Rightarrow \cos y=\cos 60^\circ$$

$\Rightarrow y=60^\circ$, which is an acute angle.

Example 8. **In a ΔABC, right angled at B, $\angle A=\angle C$, find the value of**

(i) $\sin A\cos C+\cos A\sin C$. (ii) $\sin A\sin B+\cos A\cos B$.

Sol. Given, $\angle A=\angle C$

Now, $\angle A+\angle B+\angle C=180^\circ$

[by angle sum property of triangle]

$$\Rightarrow \quad 90^\circ+\angle A+\angle C=180^\circ \quad [\because \angle B=90^\circ]$$

$$\Rightarrow \quad \angle A+\angle C=90^\circ$$

$$\Rightarrow \quad 2\angle A=90^\circ \text{ and } 2\angle C=90^\circ \quad [\because \angle A=\angle C]$$

$$\Rightarrow \quad \angle A=45^\circ \text{ and } \angle C=45^\circ$$

(i) $\sin A\cos C+\cos A\sin C=\sin 45^\circ\cos 45^\circ+\cos 45^\circ\sin 45^\circ$

$$=\frac{1}{\sqrt{2}}\times\frac{1}{\sqrt{2}}+\frac{1}{\sqrt{2}}\times\frac{1}{\sqrt{2}}=\frac{1}{2}+\frac{1}{2}=1$$

$$\left[\because \sin 45^\circ=\cos 45^\circ=\frac{1}{\sqrt{2}}\right]$$

(ii) $\sin A\sin B+\cos A\cos B$

$$=\sin 45^\circ\sin 90^\circ+\cos 45^\circ\cos 90^\circ$$

$$=\frac{1}{\sqrt{2}}\times 1+\frac{1}{\sqrt{2}}\times 0=\frac{1}{\sqrt{2}}+0=\frac{1}{\sqrt{2}}$$

$$[\because \sin 90^\circ=1 \text{ and } \cos 90^\circ=0]$$

Example 9. **Find acute angles A and B, if $\sin(A+2B)=\frac{\sqrt{3}}{2}$ and $\cos(A+4B)=0^\circ$, $A>B$.** CBSE 2019

Sol. We have, $\sin(A+2B)=\frac{\sqrt{3}}{2}=\sin 60^\circ \quad \left[\because \sin 60^\circ=\frac{\sqrt{3}}{2}\right]$

$$\Rightarrow \quad A+2B=60^\circ \quad \text{...(i)}$$

Again, $\cos(A+4B)=0^\circ=\cos 90^\circ \quad [\because \cos 90^\circ=0]$

$$\Rightarrow \quad A+4B=90^\circ \quad \text{...(ii)}$$

On subtracting Eq. (i) from Eq. (ii), we get

$$A+4B-A-2B=90^\circ-60^\circ \Rightarrow 2B=30^\circ \Rightarrow B=15^\circ$$

On substituting $B=15^\circ$ in Eq. (i), we get

$$A+2\times 15^\circ=60^\circ \Rightarrow A+30^\circ=60^\circ \Rightarrow A=60^\circ-30^\circ=30^\circ$$

Hence, $A=30^\circ$ and $B=15^\circ$

Problems Based on Trigonometric Ratios of Some Specific Angles

There are many different problems in which one or more angles is given to us and we have to find the side or sides of a triangle using these trigonometric ratios of specific angles. For these problems, we have no particular method to solve but we can understand method of solving these type of problems with the help of examples.

Example 10. **In right angled ΔABC, right angled at B, $AB=5$ cm and $\angle ACB=30^\circ$. Determine the length of the sides BC and AC.**

Sol. Given, $\angle C=\angle ACB=30^\circ$ and $AB=5$ cm

Now, $\tan 30^\circ=\frac{AB}{BC}=\frac{5}{BC} \quad \left[\because \tan\theta=\frac{\text{Perpendicular}}{\text{Base}}\right]$

$$\Rightarrow \quad \frac{1}{\sqrt{3}}=\frac{5}{BC} \quad \left[\because \tan 30^\circ=\frac{1}{\sqrt{3}}\right]$$

$$\Rightarrow \quad BC=5\sqrt{3}\text{ cm}$$

By Pythagoras theorem, we have

$$AC=\sqrt{AB^2+BC^2}=\sqrt{5^2+(5\sqrt{3})^2}$$

$$=\sqrt{25+75}=\sqrt{100}=10$$

$$\Rightarrow \quad AC=10\text{ cm} \quad \text{[taking positive square root]}$$

$\therefore$ Length of side $BC=5\sqrt{3}$ cm and $AC=10$ cm.

Example 11. **In the following figure, ΔPQR is right angled at Q, $PQ=3$ cm and $PR=6$ cm. Determine $\angle QPR$ and $\angle PRQ$.**

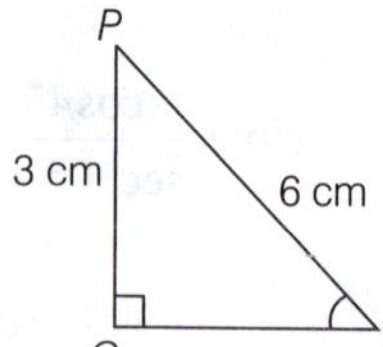

Sol. Given, $PQ=3$ cm and $PR=6$ cm

$$\therefore \quad \sin R=\frac{\text{Perpendicular}}{\text{Hypotenuse}}=\frac{PQ}{PR}$$

$$\Rightarrow \quad \sin R=\frac{3}{6} \Rightarrow \sin R=\frac{1}{2} \Rightarrow \sin R=\sin 30^\circ \left[\because \sin 30^\circ=\frac{1}{2}\right]$$

$$\therefore \quad R=30^\circ \text{ or } \angle PRQ=30^\circ$$

In ΔPQR, $\angle P+\angle Q+\angle R=180^\circ$

[by angle sum property of triangle]

$$\Rightarrow \quad \angle P+90^\circ+30^\circ=180^\circ \Rightarrow \angle P=180^\circ-120^\circ$$

$$\therefore \quad \angle P=60^\circ \text{ or } \angle QPR=60^\circ$$

Try These 8.2

1. Evaluate $5\sin^2 45^\circ-\sec 60^\circ\cot^2 30^\circ$. CBSE 2024 (Basic)
2. Evaluate $2\sqrt{2}\cos 45^\circ\sin 30^\circ+2\sqrt{3}\cos 30^\circ$. CBSE 2024 (Standard)
3. Find the value of $(\sin 30^\circ+\cos 30^\circ)-(\sin 60^\circ+\cos 60^\circ)$.
4. Evaluate $\frac{\cos 45^\circ}{\tan 30^\circ+\sin 60^\circ}$. CBSE 2025 Basic
5. If $\tan A+\sin^2 45^\circ-\cos^2 30^\circ-\operatorname{cosec}^2 45^\circ\sec^2 60^\circ=4$, then find $\tan A$.
6. Find the value of x in each of the following
   (i) $x\tan 45^\circ\cos 60^\circ=\sin 60^\circ\cot 60^\circ$
   (ii) $-x\sin 90^\circ\cos 30^\circ+\sin 30^\circ\cos 90^\circ=\frac{4}{5}$
   (iii) $\cos 2x=\cos 60^\circ\cos 30^\circ+\sin 60^\circ\sin 30^\circ$
7. Evaluate $\frac{2\sin^2 60^\circ-\tan^2 30^\circ}{\sec^2 45^\circ}$. CBSE Sample paper 2025 (Standard)
8. Show that $(\sqrt{3}+1)(3-\cot 30^\circ)=\tan^3 60^\circ-2\sin 60^\circ$. NCERT Exemplar

9. If ΔABC is right angled at C, then find the value of $\cos(A+B)$. NCERT Exemplar

10. State whether the following statements are true or false. Justify your answer.
(i) $\cos(A+B)=\cos A+\cos B$
(ii) $\tan\theta=\cot\theta$ for all values of θ.

11. Find the value of $3\tan^2\theta+2\sin\theta\cos\theta$, for $\theta=45°$.

12. Find the value of $\text{cosec}^2 A-2\sin A+\tan A\cos A+5$, for $A=60°$.

13. If $\sin\theta-\cos\theta=0$, $(0\le\theta\le 90°)$, then find the value of θ.

14. Determine the value of x, such that
$$2\,\text{cosec}^2 30°+x\sin^2 60°-\frac{3}{4}\tan^2 30°=10.$$

15. Prove the following
(i) $2(\cos^2 45°+\tan^2 60°)-6(\sin^2 45°-\tan^2 30°)=6$
(ii) $2(\cos^4 60°+\sin^4 30°)-(\tan^2 60°-\cot^2 45°)+3\sec^2 30°=9/4$

16. If $\cos(A+B)=\frac{1}{2}$ and $\tan(A-B)=\frac{1}{\sqrt{3}}$, where $0\le A+B\le 90°$, then find the value of $\sec(2A-3B)$.
CBSE 2024 (Standard) Compartment

17. In an acute ΔABC, if $\tan(A+B-C)=1$ and $\sec(B+C-A)=2$, then find the values of $\angle A$, $\angle B$ and $\angle C$.

18. In the following figure, ΔPQR is right angled at Q, $PQ=5$ cm, $PR=10$ cm. Determine $\angle QPR$ and $\angle PRQ$.

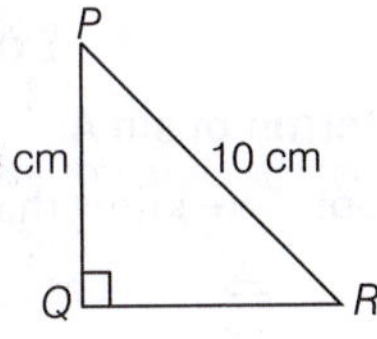

Answers

1. **Hint** We have, $5\sin^2 45°-\sec 60°\cot^2 30°$
$$=\left[5\times\left(\frac{1}{\sqrt{2}}\right)^2\right]-(2\times(\sqrt{3})^2)=-\frac{7}{2}$$

2. 4 3. 0 4. $\frac{\sqrt{6}}{5}$ 5. $\frac{49}{4}$

6. (i) 1 (ii) $\frac{-8}{5\sqrt{3}}$ (iii) 15 7. $\frac{7}{12}$

9. **Hint** $A+B+C=180°\Rightarrow A+B=180°-C\Rightarrow A+B=90°$ **Ans.** 0

10. (i) **Hint** Let $A=60°$ and $B=30°$. Then, $\cos(60°+30°)=\cos 90°=0$ and $\cos 60°+\cos 30°=\frac{1}{2}+\frac{\sqrt{3}}{2}$ **Ans.** (i) False (ii) False

11. 4 12. $\frac{38-3\sqrt{3}}{6}$

13. $\sin\theta-\cos\theta=0\Rightarrow\sin\theta=\cos\theta\Rightarrow\tan\theta=1\Rightarrow\theta=45°$

14. $x=3$ 16. **Hint** Do same as Example 9. **Ans.** $\sqrt{2}$

17. **Hint** Solve the following equations to find A, B, C.
$A+B-C=45°, B+C-A=60°, A+B+C=180°$
Ans. $A=60°, B=\frac{105°}{2}, C=\frac{135°}{2}$

18. **Hint** Do same as Example 11.
Ans. $\angle QPR=60°$ and $\angle PRQ=30°$.

TOPIC 03 Trigonometric Identities

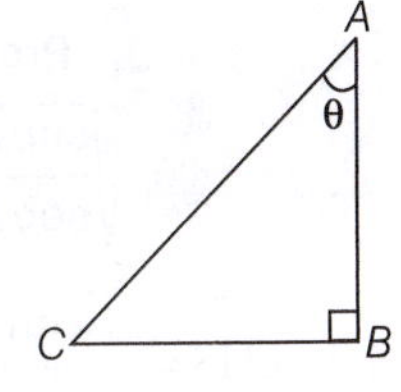

We know that, an equation is called **an identity** when it is true for all values of the variables involved. Similarly, an equation involving trigonometric ratios of an angle is called **a trigonometric identity**, if it is true for all values of the angle (s) involved. For any acute angle θ, we have three identities

i.e. (i) $\sin^2\theta+\cos^2\theta=1$ (ii) $1+\tan^2\theta=\sec^2\theta$ (iii) $\cot^2\theta+1=\text{cosec}^2\theta$

Conversion of Trigonometric Ratios in Terms of Other Trigonometric Ratios

	$\sin\theta$	$\cos\theta$	$\tan\theta$	$\cot\theta$	$\sec\theta$	$\text{cosec}\,\theta$
$\sin\theta$	$\sin\theta$	$\sqrt{1-\cos^2\theta}$	$\frac{\tan\theta}{\sqrt{1+\tan^2\theta}}$	$\frac{1}{\sqrt{1+\cot^2\theta}}$	$\frac{\sqrt{\sec^2\theta-1}}{\sec\theta}$	$\frac{1}{\text{cosec}\,\theta}$
$\cos\theta$	$\sqrt{1-\sin^2\theta}$	$\cos\theta$	$\frac{1}{\sqrt{1+\tan^2\theta}}$	$\frac{\cot\theta}{\sqrt{1+\cot^2\theta}}$	$\frac{1}{\sec\theta}$	$\frac{\sqrt{\text{cosec}^2\theta-1}}{\text{cosec}\theta}$
$\tan\theta$	$\frac{\sin\theta}{\sqrt{1-\sin^2\theta}}$	$\frac{\sqrt{1-\cos^2\theta}}{\cos\theta}$	$\tan\theta$	$\frac{1}{\cot\theta}$	$\sqrt{\sec^2\theta-1}$	$\frac{1}{\sqrt{\text{cosec}^2\theta-1}}$
$\cot\theta$	$\frac{\sqrt{1-\sin^2\theta}}{\sin\theta}$	$\frac{\cos\theta}{\sqrt{1-\cos^2\theta}}$	$\frac{1}{\tan\theta}$	$\cot\theta$	$\frac{1}{\sqrt{\sec^2\theta-1}}$	$\sqrt{\text{cosec}^2\theta-1}$
$\sec\theta$	$\frac{1}{\sqrt{1-\sin^2\theta}}$	$\frac{1}{\cos\theta}$	$\sqrt{1+\tan^2\theta}$	$\frac{\sqrt{1+\cot^2\theta}}{\cot\theta}$	$\sec\theta$	$\frac{\text{cosec}\theta}{\sqrt{\text{cosec}^2\theta-1}}$
$\text{cosec}\,\theta$	$\frac{1}{\sin\theta}$	$\frac{1}{\sqrt{1-\cos^2\theta}}$	$\frac{\sqrt{1+\tan^2\theta}}{\tan\theta}$	$\sqrt{1+\cot^2\theta}$	$\frac{\sec\theta}{\sqrt{\sec^2\theta-1}}$	$\text{cosec}\,\theta$

Note it $\sin^2\theta=(\sin\theta)^2$ but $\sin\theta^2\neq(\sin\theta)^2$. The same is true for all other trigonometric ratios.

Example 1. **Express the ratios cos *A*, tan *A* and sec *A* in terms of sin *A*.**

Sol. We know that $\cos^2 A+\sin^2 A=1$,

$$\Rightarrow \quad \cos^2 A=1-\sin^2 A$$

$$\Rightarrow \quad \cos A=\sqrt{1-\sin^2 A}$$

Now, $\tan A=\dfrac{\sin A}{\cos A}=\dfrac{\sin A}{\sqrt{1-\sin^2 A}}$

and $\sec A=\dfrac{1}{\cos A}=\dfrac{1}{\sqrt{1-\sin^2 A}}$

Example 2. **Prove that** $\dfrac{1+\sec A}{\sec A}=\dfrac{\sin^2 A}{1-\cos A}$

CBSE 2023 (Basic)

Sol. LHS $=\dfrac{1+\sec A}{\sec A}=\dfrac{1+\dfrac{1}{\cos A}}{\dfrac{1}{\cos A}}$

$$=\frac{\cos A+1}{\cos A}\times \cos A=\cos A+1$$

RHS $=\dfrac{\sin^2 A}{1-\cos A}=\dfrac{1-\cos^2 A}{1-\cos A}$ $\quad [\because \sin^2\theta+\cos^2\theta=1]$

$$=\frac{(1+\cos A)(1-\cos A)}{1-\cos A}=1+\cos A$$

$\therefore$ LHS = RHS **Hence proved.**

Example 3. **Prove that**

$$\sqrt{\frac{\sec A-1}{\sec A+1}}+\sqrt{\frac{\sec A+1}{\sec A-1}}=2\operatorname{cosec} A$$

CBSE 2023 (Standard)

Sol. LHS $=\sqrt{\dfrac{\sec A-1}{\sec A+1}}+\sqrt{\dfrac{\sec A+1}{\sec A-1}}$

$$=\frac{\sec A-1+\sec A+1}{\sqrt{(\sec A+1)(\sec A-1)}}$$

$$=\frac{2\sec A}{\sqrt{\sec^2 A-1}}$$

$$=\frac{2\sec A}{\sqrt{\tan^2 A}} \quad [\because \sec^2\theta-\tan^2\theta=1]$$

$$=\frac{2\sec A}{\tan A}=2\times\frac{1}{\cos A}\times\frac{\cos A}{\sin A}$$

$$=2\operatorname{cosec} A$$

= RHS **Hence proved.**

Example 4. **Prove that**

$$\frac{\sin A+\cos A}{\sin A-\cos A}+\frac{\sin A-\cos A}{\sin A+\cos A}=\frac{2}{2\sin^2 A-1}.$$

CBSE 2024 (Standard)

Sol. LHS $=\dfrac{\sin A+\cos A}{\sin A-\cos A}+\dfrac{\sin A-\cos A}{\sin A+\cos A}$

$$=\frac{(\sin A+\cos A)^2+(\sin A-\cos A)^2}{(\sin A-\cos A)(\sin A+\cos A)}$$

$$=\frac{\left[\begin{array}{l}\sin^2 A+2\sin A\cos A+\cos^2 A+\sin^2 A\\ -2\sin A\cos A+\cos^2 A\end{array}\right]}{\sin^2 A-\cos^2 A}$$

$$[\because (a\pm b)^2=a^2+b^2\pm 2ab]$$

$$=\frac{2\sin^2 A+2\cos^2 A}{\sin^2 A-\cos^2 A}$$

$$=\frac{2(\sin^2 A+\cos^2 A)}{\sin^2 A-\cos^2 A}$$

$$=\frac{2}{\sin^2 A-\cos^2 A}$$

$$=\frac{2}{\sin^2 A-(1-\sin^2 A)}$$

$$=\frac{2}{\sin^2 A-1+\sin^2 A}$$

$$=\frac{2}{2\sin^2 A-1}$$

= RHS **Hence proved.**

Example 5. **If $\cos\theta+\sin\theta=1$, then prove that $\cos\theta-\sin\theta=\pm 1$.**

CBSE Sample Paper 2025 (Standard)

Sol. Given, $\cos\theta+\sin\theta=1$

$$(\cos\theta+\sin\theta)^2+(\cos\theta-\sin\theta)^2=2(\cos^2\theta+\sin^2\theta)=2$$

$$\Rightarrow (1)^2+(\cos\theta-\sin\theta)^2=2 \quad [\because \cos\theta+\sin\theta=1 \text{ (given)}]$$

$$\Rightarrow \quad (\cos\theta-\sin\theta)^2=2-1$$

$$\Rightarrow \quad (\cos\theta-\sin\theta)^2=1$$

$$\Rightarrow \quad \cos\theta-\sin\theta=\pm 1$$

Hence proved.

Example 6. **If $a\sec\theta+b\tan\theta=m$ and $b\sec\theta+a\tan\theta=n$, prove that $a^2+n^2=b^2+m^2$.**

CBSE 2025 (Standard)

Sol. Given, $a\sec\theta+b\tan\theta=m$ ...(i)

and $b\sec\theta+a\tan\theta=n$ ...(ii)

On squaring and subtracting Eqs. (i) and (ii), we get

$$(a\sec\theta+b\tan\theta)^2-(b\sec\theta+a\tan\theta)^2=m^2-n^2$$

$$\Rightarrow a^2\sec^2\theta+b^2\tan^2\theta+2ab\sec\theta\cdot\tan\theta-b^2\sec^2\theta-a^2\tan^2\theta-2ab\sec\theta\cdot\tan\theta=m^2-n^2$$

$$\Rightarrow a^2(\sec^2\theta-\tan^2\theta)-b^2(\sec^2\theta-\tan^2\theta)=m^2-n^2$$

$$\Rightarrow a^2-b^2=m^2-n^2 \quad [\because \sec^2-\tan^2\theta=1]$$

$$\Rightarrow a^2+n^2=m^2+b^2$$

Hence proved.

Example 7. If $\tan\theta + \sin\theta = m$ and $\tan\theta - \sin\theta = n$, then show that $(m^2 - n^2)^2 = 16\,mn$ or $(m^2 - n^2) = 4\sqrt{mn}$.

Sol. Given, $\tan\theta + \sin\theta = m$ ...(i)

and $\tan\theta - \sin\theta = n$ ...(ii)

On adding Eqs. (i) and (ii), we get

$$2\tan\theta = m + n \Rightarrow \tan\theta = \frac{m+n}{2}$$

$$\therefore \quad \cot\theta = \frac{1}{\tan\theta} = \frac{2}{m+n} \quad \text{...(iii)}$$

On subtracting Eq. (ii) from Eq. (i), we get

$$2\sin\theta = m - n$$

$$\Rightarrow \quad \sin\theta = \frac{m-n}{2}$$

$$\therefore \quad \operatorname{cosec}\theta = \frac{1}{\sin\theta} = \frac{2}{m-n} \quad \text{...(iv)}$$

We know that $\operatorname{cosec}^2\theta - \cot^2\theta = 1$

$$\Rightarrow \quad \left(\frac{2}{m-n}\right)^2 - \left(\frac{2}{m+n}\right)^2 = 1 \quad \text{[from Eqs. (iii) and (iv)]}$$

$$\Rightarrow \quad \frac{4}{(m-n)^2} - \frac{4}{(m+n)^2} = 1$$

$$\Rightarrow \quad 4\left[\frac{1}{(m-n)^2} - \frac{1}{(m+n)^2}\right] = 1$$

$$\Rightarrow \quad 4\left[\frac{(m+n)^2 - (m-n)^2}{(m-n)^2\,(m+n)^2}\right] = 1$$

$$\Rightarrow \quad 4\left[\frac{(m^2 + n^2 + 2mn) - (m^2 + n^2 - 2mn)}{(m-n)^2 (m+n)^2}\right] = 1$$

$$[\because (A \pm B)^2 = A^2 + B^2 \pm 2AB]$$

$$\Rightarrow \quad 4\left[\frac{2mn + 2mn}{(m-n)^2\,(m+n)^2}\right] = 1$$

$$\Rightarrow \quad \frac{16mn}{[(m-n)\,(m+n)]^2} = 1$$

$$\Rightarrow \quad \frac{16mn}{(m^2 - n^2)^2} = 1$$

$$\Rightarrow \quad (m^2 - n^2)^2 = 16mn$$

$$\therefore \quad (m^2 - n^2) = 4\sqrt{mn}$$

[taking positive square root]

Hence proved.

Try These 8.3

1. Express the trigonometric ratios $\cos A$, $\cot A$ and $\operatorname{cosec} A$ in terms of $\tan A$.
2. Write all the other trigonometric ratios of $\angle A$ in term of $\operatorname{cosec} A$.

Directions (Q. Nos. 3-7) Show that

3. $\sqrt{\frac{1+\cos A}{1-\cos A}} = \operatorname{cosec} A + \cot A$.
4. $(1 - \sin A + \cos A)^2 = 2\,(1 - \sin A)\,(1 + \cos A)$
5. $\frac{\sin\theta}{1+\cos\theta} + \frac{1+\cos\theta}{\sin\theta} = 2\operatorname{cosec}\theta$
6. $\sqrt{(1-\cos^2\theta)\sec^2\theta} = \tan\theta$
7. Prove that $(\cot\theta - \operatorname{cosec}\theta)^2 = \frac{1-\cos\theta}{1+\cos\theta}$. CBSE 2024 (Basic)
8. If $\frac{\cot A}{1+\operatorname{cosec} A} - \frac{\cot A}{1-\operatorname{cosec} A} = \frac{k}{\cos A}$, then find the value of k.
9. Find the values of the constant a and b for which $\sin x \cdot \cos x\,(5\tan x + 2\cot x) = a + b\sin^2 x$.

Directions (Q. Nos. 10-26) Prove that

10. $(1 + \tan^2\theta) + \left(1 + \frac{1}{\tan^2\theta}\right) = \frac{1}{\sin^2\theta - \sin^4\theta}$.
11. $(1 + \cot\theta - \operatorname{cosec}\theta)\,(1 + \tan\theta + \sec\theta) = 2$.
12. $\tan^2\theta + \cot^2\theta + 2 = \sec^2\theta + \operatorname{cosec}^2\theta$.
13. $\tan\theta - \cot\theta = \frac{2\sin^2\theta - 1}{\sin\theta \cdot \cos\theta}$.
14. $\frac{\tan\theta}{1-\cot\theta} + \frac{\cot\theta}{1-\tan\theta} = 1 + \sec\theta\operatorname{cosec}\theta$ CBSE 2024, 23 (Standard)
15. $\frac{1-\cos A+\sin A}{\sin A+\cos A-1} = \frac{1+\sin A}{\cos A}$.
16. Prove that $(\operatorname{cosec} A - \sin A)\,(\sec A - \cos A) = \frac{1}{\tan A + \cot A}$. CBSE Sample Paper 2025
17. $\sqrt{\frac{\sin A+1}{1-\sin A}} + \sqrt{\frac{1-\sin A}{\sin A+1}} = 2\sec A$.
18. $\sqrt{\frac{\sec A-\tan A}{\sec A+\tan A}}\sqrt{\frac{\operatorname{cosec} A-\cot A}{\operatorname{cosec} A+\cot A}} = (\sec A - \tan A)\,(\operatorname{cosec} A - \cot A)$.
19. $\sec^2\theta - \frac{\sin^2\theta - 2\sin^4\theta}{2\cos^4\theta - \cos^2\theta} = 1$.
20. $\frac{1+\tan^3\theta}{1+\tan\theta} + \tan\theta - \sec^2\theta = 0$.
21. $(\tan\theta + \sec\theta - 1)\,(\tan\theta + 1 + \sec\theta) = \frac{2\sin\theta}{1-\sin\theta}$.
22. $\frac{\cos A}{1-\tan A} + \frac{\sin^2 A}{\sin A - \cos A} = \sin A + \cos A$.
23. $\frac{\operatorname{cosec}\theta + \cot\theta}{\operatorname{cosec}\theta - \cot\theta} = (\operatorname{cosec}\theta + \cot\theta)^2 = 1 + 2\cot^2\theta + 2\operatorname{cosec}\theta \cdot \cot\theta$.

24. $\dfrac{\sin A+\sin B}{\cos A+\cos B}+\dfrac{\cos A-\cos B}{\sin A-\sin B}=0.$

25. $\dfrac{\sin A}{1+\cos A}+\dfrac{\sin A}{1-\cos A}=\sqrt{\dfrac{1+\cos A}{1-\cos A}}+\sqrt{\dfrac{1-\cos A}{1+\cos A}}=2\operatorname{cosec} A.$

26. $\left(\dfrac{\sin A}{1+\cos A}+\dfrac{1+\cos A}{\sin A}\right)\left(\dfrac{\sin A}{1-\cos A}-\dfrac{1-\cos A}{\sin A}\right)$
$=4\operatorname{cosec} A\cot A.$

27. If $\sin\theta+\cos\theta=p$ and $\sec\theta+\operatorname{cosec}\theta=q$, then prove that $q(p^2-1)=2p$. CBSE 2023 (Standard)

28. Given that
$$2\sin A\cos A+(\cos A+\sin A)^2-(2\cos A+\sin A)^2$$
$=p\sin^2 A+q$. Find the value of p and q.

29. If $\sec\theta+\tan\theta=p$, show that $\sec\theta-\tan\theta=\dfrac{1}{p}$.

Hence, find the value of $\cos\theta$ and $\sin\theta$.

30. If $\cos\theta-\sin\theta=\sqrt{2}\sin\theta$, then prove that
$\cos\theta+\sin\theta=\sqrt{2}\cos\theta$.

31. Show that $2(\sin^6\theta+\cos^6\theta)-3(\sin^4\theta+\cos^4\theta)+1=0$.

32. If $m=\cos\theta-\sin\theta$ and $n=\cos\theta+\sin\theta$,

show that $\sqrt{\dfrac{m}{n}}+\sqrt{\dfrac{n}{m}}=\dfrac{2}{\sqrt{1-\tan^2\theta}}$.

Answers

1. **Hint** $\cos A=\dfrac{1}{\sec A}=\dfrac{1}{\sqrt{1+\tan^2 A}}$

$[\because \sec^2 A=1+\tan^2 A\Rightarrow \sec A=\sqrt{1+\tan^2 A}]$

and $\cot A=\dfrac{1}{\tan A}$

Now, $\operatorname{cosec} A=\sqrt{1+\cot^2 A}$

$[\because \operatorname{cosec}^2 A=1+\cot^2 A\Rightarrow \operatorname{cosec} A=\sqrt{1+\cot^2 A}]$

$=\sqrt{1+\left(\dfrac{1}{\tan A}\right)^2}=\sqrt{1+\dfrac{1}{\tan^2 A}}$

$=\sqrt{\dfrac{\tan^2 A+1}{\tan^2 A}}=\dfrac{\sqrt{1+\tan^2 A}}{\tan A}$

2. (i) **Hint** We know that $\sin^2 A+\cos^2 A=1$

$\Rightarrow \cos^2 A=1-\sin^2 A$

$\Rightarrow \cos A=\sqrt{1-\sin^2 A}$ [taking positive square root]

$\Rightarrow \cos A=\sqrt{1-\dfrac{1}{\operatorname{cosec}^2 A}}$

$\Rightarrow \cos A=\sqrt{\dfrac{\operatorname{cosec}^2 A-1}{\operatorname{cosec}^2 A}}=\dfrac{\sqrt{\operatorname{cosec}^2 A-1}}{\operatorname{cosec} A}$ $[\because \sqrt{a^2}=a]$

(ii) **Hint** $\sin A=\dfrac{1}{\operatorname{cosec} A}$

(iii) **Hint** We know that $\operatorname{cosec}^2 A-\cot^2 A=1$

$\Rightarrow \cot^2 A=\operatorname{cosec}^2 A-1$ [taking positive square root]

$\Rightarrow \cot A=\sqrt{\operatorname{cosec}^2 A-1}$

(iv) **Hint** $\tan A=\dfrac{1}{\cot A}=\dfrac{1}{\sqrt{\operatorname{cosec}^2 A-1}}$ [using part (iii)]

(v) **Hint** $\sec A=\dfrac{1}{\cos A}=\dfrac{\operatorname{cosec} A}{\sqrt{\operatorname{cosec}^2 A-1}}$ [using part (i)]

3. **Hint** LHS $=\sqrt{\dfrac{1+\cos A}{1-\cos A}\times\dfrac{1+\cos A}{1+\cos A}}$

4. **Hint** LHS $=(1-\sin A+\cos A)^2$

$=(1)^2+\sin^2 A+\cos^2 A-2\sin A(1)-2\sin A\cdot\cos A+2\cos A$

5. **Hint** LHS $=\dfrac{\sin^2\theta+\cos^2\theta+2\cos\theta+1}{(1+\cos\theta)\sin\theta}=\dfrac{1+2\cos\theta+1}{(1+\cos\theta)\sin\theta}$

6. **Hint** Use $1-\cos^2\theta=\sin^2\theta$ in LHS, then simplify it.

7. LHS $=(\cot\theta-\operatorname{cosec}\theta)^2$

$=\left[\dfrac{\cos\theta}{\sin\theta}-\dfrac{1}{\sin\theta}\right]^2$ $\left[\because \operatorname{cosec} A=\dfrac{1}{\sin A}\right.$ and $\left.\cot A=\dfrac{\cos A}{\sin A}\right]$

$=\left[\dfrac{\cos\theta-1}{\sin\theta}\right]^2=\dfrac{(\cos\theta-1)^2}{1-\cos^2\theta}$

$=\dfrac{1-\cos\theta}{1+\cos\theta}=$ RHS **Hence proved.**

8. **Hint** $\dfrac{\cot A}{1+\operatorname{cosec} A}-\dfrac{\cot A}{1-\operatorname{cosec} A}=\dfrac{k}{\cos A}$

Taking LHS $=\dfrac{\cot A}{1+\operatorname{cosec} A}-\dfrac{\cot A}{1-\operatorname{cosec} A}$

$=\dfrac{\frac{\cos A}{\sin A}}{1+\frac{1}{\sin A}}-\dfrac{\frac{\cos A}{\sin A}}{1-\frac{1}{\sin A}}$ $\left[\because \operatorname{cosec} A=\dfrac{1}{\sin A}\right.$ and $\left.\cot A=\dfrac{\cos A}{\sin A}\right]$

$=\dfrac{\cos A}{1+\sin A}+\dfrac{\cos A}{\sin A-1}$

$=\dfrac{\cos A[(\sin A-1)-(1+\sin A)]}{(1-\sin^2 A)}$

$=\dfrac{-2\cos A}{\cos^2 A}$ $[\because 1-\sin^2 A=\cos^2 A]$

$=\dfrac{-2}{\cos A}$

Ans. $k=-2$

9. **Hint** $\sin x\cdot\cos x\left(\dfrac{5\sin x}{\cos x}+\dfrac{2\cos x}{\sin x}\right)=a+b\sin^2 x$

Ans. $a=2, b=3$

10. **Hint** LHS $=\sec^2\theta+\dfrac{1+\tan^2\theta}{\tan^2\theta}$ $[\because \sec^2 A-\tan^2 A=1]$

$=\sec^2\theta+\dfrac{\sec^2\theta}{\sec^2\theta-1}$

$=\dfrac{\sec^4\theta-\sec^2\theta+\sec^2\theta}{\sec^2\theta-1}$

$=\dfrac{\frac{1}{\cos^4\theta}}{\frac{1}{\cos^2\theta}-1}=\dfrac{1}{\cos^4\theta\,\frac{(1-\cos^2\theta)}{\cos^2\theta}}$ $\left[\because \sec A=\dfrac{1}{\cos A}\right]$

$$=\frac{1}{\cos^2\theta\cdot\sin^2\theta}=\frac{1}{(1-\sin^2\theta)\sin^2\theta}$$

$$=\frac{1}{\sin^2\theta-\sin^4\theta}=\text{RHS}$$ **Hence proved.**

11. Hint $\text{LHS}=1+\tan\theta+\sec\theta+\cot\theta+\cot\theta\cdot\tan\theta+\cot\theta\cdot\sec\theta-\operatorname{cosec}\theta-\operatorname{cosec}\theta\cdot\tan\theta-\operatorname{cosec}\theta\cdot\sec\theta$

$$=1+\tan\theta+\sec\theta+\cot\theta+1+\operatorname{cosec}\theta-\operatorname{cosec}\theta-\sec\theta-\operatorname{cosec}\theta\cdot\sec\theta$$

$$=2+\frac{\sin\theta}{\cos\theta}+\frac{\cos\theta}{\sin\theta}-\frac{1}{\cos\theta\cdot\sin\theta}$$

$$=\frac{2\cos\theta\cdot\sin\theta+\sin^2\theta+\cos^2\theta-1}{\cos\theta\cdot\sin\theta}=2=\text{RHS}$$

$[\because \cos^2 A+\sin^2 A=1]$ **Hence proved.**

12. Hint $\text{LHS}=(1+\tan^2\theta)+(1+\cot^2\theta)=\sec^2\theta+\operatorname{cosec}^2\theta$

$=\text{RHS}$ **Hence proved.**

13. Hint $\text{RHS}=\frac{2\sin^2\theta-1}{\sin\theta\cdot\cos\theta}=\frac{\sin^2\theta+\sin^2\theta-1}{\sin\theta\cdot\cos\theta}$

14. Hint $\text{LHS}=\frac{\tan\theta}{1-\cot\theta}+\frac{\cot\theta}{1-\tan\theta}$

$$=\frac{\tan\theta}{1-\frac{1}{\tan\theta}}+\frac{\frac{1}{\tan\theta}}{1-\tan\theta}$$

$$=\frac{\tan^2\theta}{\tan\theta-1}+\frac{1}{\tan\theta(1-\tan\theta)}=\frac{1-\tan^3\theta}{\tan\theta(1-\tan\theta)}$$

$$=\frac{(1-\tan\theta)(1+\tan\theta+\tan^2\theta)}{\tan\theta(1-\tan\theta)}$$

$$=\frac{\sec^2\theta+\tan\theta}{\tan\theta}\qquad[\because 1+\tan^2 A=\sec^2 A]$$

$$=\frac{\sec^2\theta}{\tan\theta}+1=\frac{1}{\cos^2\theta}\times\frac{\cos\theta}{\sin\theta}+1$$

$=\sec\theta\operatorname{cosec}\theta+1=\text{RHS}$ **Hence proved.**

15. Hint $\text{LHS}=\frac{1-\cos A+\sin A}{\sin A+\cos A-1}=\frac{\sec A+\tan A-1}{1-(\sec A-\tan A)}$

[dividing numerator and denominator by $\cos A$]

$$=\frac{(\sec A+\tan A)-1}{1-(\sec A-\tan A)}\times\frac{1+(\sec A-\tan A)}{1+(\sec A-\tan A)}$$

$$=\frac{(\sec A+\tan A)+(\sec^2 A-\tan^2 A)-1-(\sec A-\tan A)}{1-(\sec^2 A+\tan^2 A-2\tan A\sec A)}$$

$$=\frac{2\tan A}{2\tan A(\sec A-\tan A)}\qquad[\because \sec^2 A-\tan^2 A=1]$$

$$=\frac{1}{\sec A-\tan A}$$

$$=\frac{\sec A+\tan A}{(\sec A-\tan A)(\sec A+\tan A)}$$

$$=\frac{\sec A+\tan A}{1}$$

$$=\frac{1+\sin A}{\cos A}=\text{RHS}$$ **Hence proved.**

16. $\text{LHS}=(\operatorname{cosec}A-\sin A)(\sec A-\cos A)$

$$=\left(\frac{1}{\sin A}-\sin A\right)\left(\frac{1}{\cos A}-\cos A\right)\qquad\left[\because \operatorname{cosec}A=\frac{1}{\sin A}\text{ and }\sec A=\frac{1}{\cos A}\right]$$

$$=\left(\frac{1-\sin^2 A}{\sin A}\right)\left(\frac{1-\cos^2 A}{\cos A}\right)$$

$$=\frac{\cos^2 A}{\sin A}\times\frac{\sin^2 A}{\cos A}\qquad\left[\because 1-\sin^2 A=\cos^2 A\text{ and }1-\cos^2 A=\sin^2 A\right]$$

$$=\sin A\cdot\cos A\qquad\ldots(\text{i})$$

$$\text{RHS}=\frac{1}{\tan A+\cot A}$$

$$=\frac{1}{\frac{\sin A}{\cos A}+\frac{\cos A}{\sin A}}$$

$$=\frac{1}{\frac{\sin^2 A+\cos^2 A}{\sin A\cdot\cos A}}$$

$$=\sin A\cdot\cos A\qquad[\because \sin^2 A+\cos^2 A=1]\quad\ldots(\text{ii})$$

From Eq. (i) and (ii), we get

$\text{LHS}=\text{RHS}$ **Hence proved.**

17. Hint $\text{LHS}=\sqrt{\frac{1+\sin A}{1-\sin A}\times\frac{1+\sin A}{1+\sin A}}+\sqrt{\frac{1-\sin A}{1+\sin A}\times\frac{1-\sin A}{1-\sin A}}$

$$=\frac{1+\sin A}{\cos A}+\frac{1-\sin A}{\cos A}=2\sec A=\text{RHS}$$ **Hence proved.**

18. Hint Do same as Question 17.

19. Hint $\text{LHS}=\sec^2\theta-\dfrac{\frac{\sin^2\theta}{\cos^4\theta}-\frac{2\sin^4\theta}{\cos^4\theta}}{\frac{2\cos^4\theta}{\cos^4\theta}-\frac{\cos^2\theta}{\cos^4\theta}}$

$$=\sec^2\theta-\frac{\tan^2\theta\cdot\sec^2\theta-2\tan^4\theta}{2-\sec^2\theta}$$

$$=\sec^2\theta-\frac{\tan^2\theta(\sec^2\theta-2\tan^2\theta)}{2-\sec^2\theta}$$

$$=\sec^2\theta-\frac{\tan^2\theta(2-\sec^2\theta)}{2-\sec^2\theta}$$

$$=\sec^2\theta-\tan^2\theta$$

$=1=\text{RHS}$ **Hence proved.**

20. Hint $\text{LHS}=\frac{1^3+\tan^3\theta}{1+\tan\theta}+\tan\theta-\sec^2\theta$

$$=\frac{(1+\tan\theta)(1^2+\tan^2\theta-\tan\theta)}{(1+\tan\theta)}+\tan\theta-\sec^2\theta$$

$$=1+\tan^2\theta-\tan\theta+\tan\theta-\sec^2\theta$$

$$=1+\tan^2\theta-\tan\theta+\tan\theta-1-\tan^2\theta=0$$

21. Hint $\text{LHS}=(\sec\theta+\tan\theta-1)(\sec\theta+\tan\theta+1)$

$$=(\sec\theta+\tan\theta)^2-1$$

$$=1+\tan^2\theta+\tan^2\theta+2\sec\theta\tan\theta-1$$

$[\because \sec^2\theta=1+\tan^2\theta]$

$$=2\tan^2\theta+2\sec\theta\tan\theta$$
$$=2\tan\theta(\tan\theta+\sec\theta)$$
$$=\frac{2\sin\theta}{\cos\theta}\left(\frac{\sin\theta}{\cos\theta}+\frac{1}{\cos\theta}\right)$$

22. Hint LHS, write $\tan A=\dfrac{\sin A}{\cos A}$

23. Hint LHS $=\dfrac{\operatorname{cosec}\theta+\cot\theta}{\operatorname{cosec}\theta-\cot\theta}\times\dfrac{\operatorname{cosec}\theta+\cot\theta}{\operatorname{cosec}\theta+\cot\theta}$
$$=\frac{(\operatorname{cosec}\theta+\cot\theta)^2}{\operatorname{cosec}^2\theta-\cot^2\theta}=(\operatorname{cosec}\theta+\cot\theta)^2$$
$$=\operatorname{cosec}^2\theta+\cot^2\theta+2\operatorname{cosec}\theta\cdot\cot\theta$$

24. Hint LHS $=\dfrac{\sin^2A-\sin^2B+\cos^2A-\cos^2B}{(\cos A+\cos B)(\sin A-\sin B)}$
$$=\frac{1-1}{(\cos A+\cos B)(\sin A-\sin B)}=0$$

25. Hint First term $=\sin A\left(\dfrac{1-\cos A+1+\cos A}{1-\cos^2A}\right)=\sin A\cdot\dfrac{2}{\sin^2A}$
$$=\frac{2}{\sin A}=2\operatorname{cosec}A\qquad\left[\because\frac{1}{\sin\theta}=\operatorname{cosec}\theta\right]$$
$=$ Third term

Second term $=\sqrt{\dfrac{1+\cos A}{1-\cos A}}+\sqrt{\dfrac{1-\cos A}{1+\cos A}}$
$$=\sqrt{\frac{1+\cos A}{1-\cos A}\times\frac{1+\cos A}{1+\cos A}}+\sqrt{\frac{1-\cos A}{1+\cos A}\times\frac{1-\cos A}{1-\cos A}}$$
$$=\frac{1+\cos A}{\sqrt{\sin^2A}}+\frac{1-\cos A}{\sqrt{\sin^2A}}\qquad[\because\sin^2\theta+\cos^2\theta=1]$$
$$=\frac{1+\cos A+1-\cos A}{\sin A}=\frac{2}{\sin A}=2\operatorname{cosec}A$$
$=$ Third term $\qquad\left[\because\dfrac{1}{\sin\theta}=\operatorname{cosec}\theta\right]$

Hence proved.

26. Hint Given, $\left(\dfrac{\sin A}{(1+\cos A)}+\dfrac{1+\cos A}{\sin A}\right)\left(\dfrac{\sin A}{1-\cos A}-\dfrac{1-\cos A}{\sin A}\right)$
$$=\left(\frac{\sin^2A+1+\cos^2A+2\cos A}{\sin A(1+\cos A)}\right)\left(\frac{\sin^2A-(1+\cos^2A-2\cos A)}{\sin A(1-\cos A)}\right)$$
$$=\left(\frac{2+2\cos A}{\sin A(1+\cos A)}\right)\left(\frac{1-\cos^2A-1-\cos^2A+2\cos A}{\sin A(1-\cos A)}\right)$$
$$[\because\sin^2A=1-\cos^2A]$$
$$=\frac{2(1+\cos A)}{\sin A(1+\cos A)}\cdot\frac{2\cos A(1-\cos A)}{\sin A(1-\cos A)}$$
$$=4\operatorname{cosec}A\cdot\cot A=\text{RHS}$$

27. Hint Given, $\sin\theta+\cos\theta=p$ ...(i)

and $\sec\theta+\operatorname{cosec}\theta=q$

$\Rightarrow\ \dfrac{1}{\cos\theta}+\dfrac{1}{\sin\theta}=q\Rightarrow\dfrac{\sin\theta+\cos\theta}{\sin\theta\cos\theta}=q$ ...(ii)

On squaring Eq. (i), we get
$$(\sin\theta+\cos\theta)^2=p^2$$
$$\Rightarrow\ \sin^2\theta+\cos^2\theta+2\sin\theta\cos\theta=p^2$$
$$\Rightarrow\ 1+2\sin\theta\cos\theta=p^2\qquad[\because\sin^2A+\cos^2A=1]$$

On subtracting 1 from both the sides, we get

$\Rightarrow\ 2\sin\theta\cos\theta=p^2-1$ ...(iii)

From Eq. (ii), we get
$$\frac{2(\sin\theta+\cos\theta)}{2\sin\theta\cos\theta}=q$$
$$\Rightarrow\ 2(\sin\theta+\cos\theta)=2q\sin\theta\cos\theta$$
$$\Rightarrow\ 2p=q(p^2-1)\qquad[\text{using Eqs. (i) and (iii)}]$$

Hence proved.

28. Hint First, expand the terms in left hand side of the given equation and simplify them.

Then, compare the value of LHS with RHS of identity to get required values.

Ans. $p=3$ and $q=-3$

29. Hint Given, $\sec\theta+\tan\theta=p$ ...(i)
$$\text{LHS}=\sec\theta-\tan\theta\times\frac{\sec\theta+\tan\theta}{\sec\theta+\tan\theta}$$
$$=\frac{1}{\sec\theta+\tan\theta}=\frac{1}{p}\qquad\text{...(ii)}$$

On adding Eqs. (i) and (ii), we get
$$2\sec\theta=p+\frac{1}{p}$$
$$\Rightarrow\ \cos\theta=\frac{2p}{p^2+1}$$
$$\therefore\ \sin\theta=\sqrt{1-\left(\frac{2p}{p^2+1}\right)^2}=\frac{p^2-1}{p^2+1}$$

30. Hint Given, $\cos\theta-\sin\theta=\sqrt{2}\sin\theta$
$$\Rightarrow\ \cos\theta=\sqrt{2}\sin\theta+\sin\theta=\sin\theta(\sqrt{2}+1)$$
$$\Rightarrow\ \sin\theta=\frac{\cos\theta}{(\sqrt{2}+1)}\Rightarrow\sin\theta=\frac{\cos\theta}{\sqrt{2}+1}\times\frac{\sqrt{2}-1}{\sqrt{2}-1}$$
$$\Rightarrow\ \sin\theta=\frac{(\sqrt{2}-1)\cos\theta}{2-1}=\sqrt{2}\cos\theta-\cos\theta$$
$$\therefore\ \cos\theta+\sin\theta=\sqrt{2}\cos\theta$$

Hence proved.

31. Hint LHS $=2(\sin^6\theta+\cos^6\theta)-3(\sin^4\theta+\cos^4\theta)+1$
$$=2[(\sin^2\theta)^3+(\cos^2\theta)^3]-3(\sin^4\theta+\cos^4\theta)+1$$
$$=2[(\sin^2\theta+\cos^2\theta)(\sin^4\theta+\cos^4\theta-\sin^2\theta\cos^2\theta)]-3\sin^4\theta-3\cos^4\theta+1$$
$$=-\sin^4\theta-\cos^4\theta-2\sin^2\theta\cos^2\theta+1$$
$$=1-(\sin^4\theta+\cos^4\theta+2\sin^2\theta\cos^2\theta)$$
$$=1-[(\sin^2\theta+\cos^2\theta)^2]$$
$$=1-1=0=\text{RHS}$$

Hence proved.

32. Hint LHS $=\sqrt{\dfrac{m}{n}}+\sqrt{\dfrac{n}{m}}=\sqrt{\dfrac{\cos\theta-\sin\theta}{\cos\theta+\sin\theta}}+\sqrt{\dfrac{\cos\theta+\sin\theta}{\cos\theta-\sin\theta}}$
$$=\frac{\cos\theta-\sin\theta}{\sqrt{\cos^2\theta-\sin^2\theta}}+\frac{\cos\theta+\sin\theta}{\sqrt{\cos^2\theta-\sin^2\theta}}$$
$$=\frac{2\cos\theta}{\sqrt{\cos^2\theta-\sin^2\theta}}$$

NCERT FOLDER

Complete Solutions of All Exercises of NCERT Textbook

EXERCISE 8.1

Q1. In ΔABC, right angled at B, $AB = 24$ cm and $BC = 7$ cm. Determine

(i) $\sin A, \cos A$. (ii) $\sin C, \cos C$.

Sol. In right angled ΔABC,

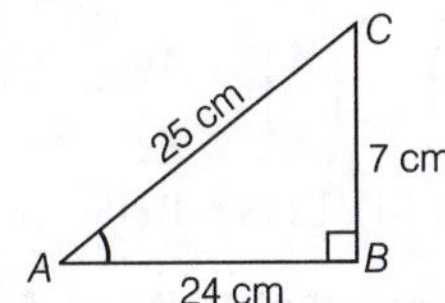

$$AB = 24 \text{ cm}, BC = 7 \text{ cm}$$

Now, $AC^2 = AB^2 + BC^2$ [by Pythagoras theorem]

$\Rightarrow AC^2 = (24)^2 + (7)^2 = 576 + 49 = 625$

$\Rightarrow AC = \sqrt{625} = 25$ [taking positive square root]

$\therefore AC = 25$ cm [since, side cannot be negative]

(i) With reference to $\angle A$, we have

Base $= AB = 24$ cm, perpendicular $= BC = 7$ cm

and hypotenuse $= AC = 25$ cm

$\therefore \sin A = \dfrac{P}{H} = \dfrac{BC}{AC} = \dfrac{7}{25}$ and $\cos A = \dfrac{B}{H} = \dfrac{AB}{AC} = \dfrac{24}{25}$

(ii) Do same as part (i). **Ans.** $\sin C = \dfrac{24}{25}$, $\cos C = \dfrac{7}{25}$

Q2. In the following figure, find $\tan P - \cot R$.

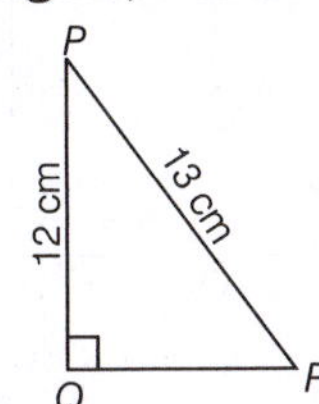

Sol. In right angled ΔPQR,

$PQ = 12$ cm, $PR = 13$ cm [given]

Then, $PQ^2 + QR^2 = PR^2$ [by Pythagoras theorem]

$\Rightarrow (12)^2 + QR^2 = (13)^2$

$\Rightarrow 144 + QR^2 = 169 \Rightarrow QR^2 = 169 - 144 = 25$

$\Rightarrow QR = 5$ cm [taking positive square root since, side cannot be negative]

Now, $\tan P = \dfrac{P}{B} = \dfrac{QR}{PQ} = \dfrac{5}{12}$ and $\cot R = \dfrac{B}{P} = \dfrac{QR}{PQ} = \dfrac{5}{12}$

$\therefore \tan P - \cot R = \dfrac{5}{12} - \dfrac{5}{12} = 0$

Q3. If $\sin A = \dfrac{3}{4}$, calculate $\cos A$ and $\tan A$.

Sol. Given, $\sin A = \dfrac{3}{4} \Rightarrow \dfrac{P}{H} = \dfrac{3}{4} \Rightarrow \dfrac{BC}{AC} = \dfrac{3}{4}$

Let $BC = 3k, AC = 4k$

where, k is any positive integer.

In right angled ΔABC, we have

$BC^2 + AB^2 = AC^2$ [by Pythagoras theorem]

$\Rightarrow (3k)^2 + AB^2 = (4k)^2$

$\Rightarrow 9k^2 + AB^2 = 16k^2$

$\Rightarrow AB^2 = 16k^2 - 9k^2 = 7k^2 \Rightarrow AB = k\sqrt{7}$

[taking positive square root since, side cannot be negative]

$\therefore \cos A = \dfrac{B}{H} = \dfrac{k\sqrt{7}}{4k} = \dfrac{\sqrt{7}}{4}$

and $\tan A = \dfrac{P}{B} = \dfrac{3k}{k\sqrt{7}} = \dfrac{3}{\sqrt{7}}$

Q4. Given, $15 \cot A = 8$, find $\sin A$ and $\sec A$.

Sol. Do same as Question 3. **Ans.** $\sin A = \dfrac{15}{17}$, $\sec A = \dfrac{17}{8}$

Q5. Given, $\sec\theta = \dfrac{13}{12}$, calculate all other trigonometric ratios.

Sol. Do same as Example 3 of Topic 1.

Ans.

$\sin\theta = \dfrac{5}{13}$, $\cos\theta = \dfrac{12}{13}$, $\tan\theta = \dfrac{5}{12}$, $\operatorname{cosec}\theta = \dfrac{13}{5}$, $\cot\theta = \dfrac{12}{5}$

Q6. If $\angle A$ and $\angle B$ are acute angles such that $\cos A = \cos B$, show that $\angle A = \angle B$.

Sol. Draw a right angled ΔABC, right angled at C. With reference to $\angle A$, base $= AC$, hypotenuse $= AB$ and with reference to $\angle B$, base $= BC$ and hypotenuse $= AB$

Given, $\cos A = \cos B$

$\Rightarrow \dfrac{AC}{AB} = \dfrac{BC}{AB}$

$\Rightarrow AC = BC$

$\therefore \angle B = \angle A$

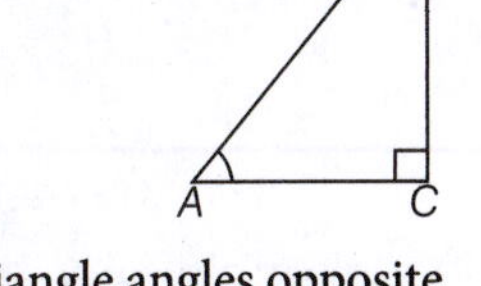

[since, in a triangle angles opposite to equal sides are also equal] **Hence proved.**

Q7. If $\cot\theta = \frac{7}{8}$, evaluate

(i) $\frac{(1+\sin\theta)(1-\sin\theta)}{(1+\cos\theta)(1-\cos\theta)}$ (ii) $\cot^2\theta$

Sol. Given, $\cot\theta = \frac{7}{8} \Rightarrow \frac{B}{P} = \frac{7}{8}$

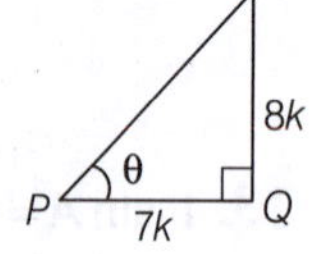

Let $B = 7k$ and $P = 8k$

where, k is any positive integer.

Draw a right angled ΔPQR, right angled at Q.

In right angled ΔPQR,

$$H^2 = B^2 + P^2 \quad \text{[by Pythagoras theorem]}$$

$$\Rightarrow H^2 = (7k)^2 + (8k)^2$$

$$\Rightarrow H^2 = 49k^2 + 64k^2 = 113k^2$$

$$\Rightarrow H = k\sqrt{113} \quad \text{[taking positive square root since, side cannot be negative]}$$

$$\therefore \sin\theta = \frac{P}{H} = \frac{8k}{k\sqrt{113}} = \frac{8}{\sqrt{113}}$$

and $\cos\theta = \frac{B}{H} = \frac{7k}{k\sqrt{113}} = \frac{7}{\sqrt{113}}$

(i) $$\frac{(1+\sin\theta)(1-\sin\theta)}{(1+\cos\theta)(1-\cos\theta)} = \frac{1^2 - \sin^2\theta}{1^2 - \cos^2\theta}$$

$$[\because (a+b)(a-b) = a^2 - b^2]$$

$$= \frac{1-\left(\frac{8}{\sqrt{113}}\right)^2}{1-\left(\frac{7}{\sqrt{113}}\right)^2} = \frac{1-\frac{64}{113}}{1-\frac{49}{113}} = \frac{\frac{113-64}{113}}{\frac{113-49}{113}} = \frac{49}{64}$$

(ii) $$\cot^2\theta = \left(\frac{\cos\theta}{\sin\theta}\right)^2 = \left(\frac{7}{8}\right)^2 = \frac{49}{64}$$

Q8. If $3\cot A = 4$, check whether

$$\frac{1-\tan^2 A}{1+\tan^2 A} = \cos^2 A - \sin^2 A \text{ or not.}$$

Sol. Given, $3\cot A = 4$

$$\Rightarrow \cot A = \frac{4}{3} \Rightarrow \frac{B}{P} = \frac{4}{3}$$

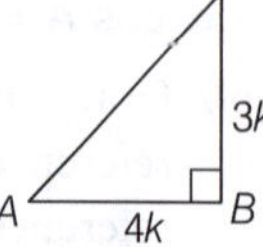

Let $B = 4k$ and $P = 3k$

where, k is any positive integer.

Draw a right angled ΔABC, right angled at B.

In right angled ΔABC,

$$H^2 = P^2 + B^2 \quad \text{[by Pythagoras theorem]}$$

$$\Rightarrow H^2 = (3k)^2 + (4k)^2$$

$$= 9k^2 + 16k^2 = 25k^2$$

$$\Rightarrow H = 5k \quad \text{[taking positive square root, since side cannot be negative]}$$

$$\therefore \tan A = \frac{1}{\cot A} = \frac{3}{4} \quad \left[\because \tan\theta = \frac{1}{\cot\theta}\right]$$

$$\cos A = \frac{B}{H} = \frac{4k}{5k} = \frac{4}{5} \text{ and } \sin A = \frac{P}{H} = \frac{3k}{5k} = \frac{3}{5}$$

Now, $$\text{LHS} = \frac{1-\tan^2 A}{1+\tan^2 A} = \frac{1-\left(\frac{3}{4}\right)^2}{1+\left(\frac{3}{4}\right)^2} \quad \left[\because \tan\theta = \frac{3}{4}\right]$$

$$= \frac{1-\frac{9}{16}}{1+\frac{9}{16}} = \frac{\frac{16-9}{16}}{\frac{16+9}{16}} = \frac{7}{25} \quad \text{...(i)}$$

and $$\text{RHS} = \cos^2 A - \sin^2 A$$

$$= \left(\frac{4}{5}\right)^2 - \left(\frac{3}{5}\right)^2 = \frac{16}{25} - \frac{9}{25} = \frac{16-9}{25} = \frac{7}{25} \quad \text{...(ii)}$$

From Eqs. (i) and (ii), LHS = RHS **Hence proved.**

Q9. In ΔABC, right angled at B, if $\tan A = \frac{1}{\sqrt{3}}$, then find the value of

(i) $\sin A \cos C + \cos A \sin C$.

(ii) $\cos A \cos C - \sin A \sin C$.

Sol. Given, $\tan A = \frac{1}{\sqrt{3}}$

$$\Rightarrow \frac{P}{B} = \frac{1}{\sqrt{3}}$$

Let $P = k$ and $B = \sqrt{3}k$, where k is any positive integer.

Draw a right angled ΔABC, right angled at B.

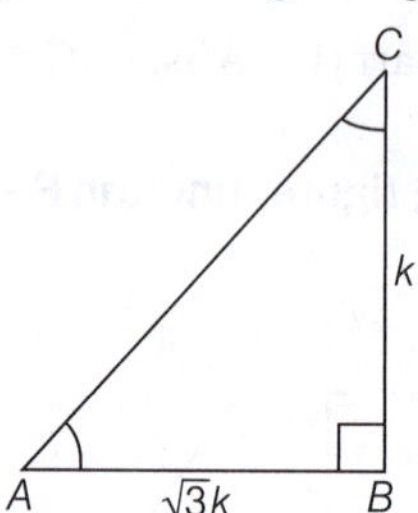

In right angled ΔABC,

$$H^2 = B^2 + P^2 \quad \text{[by Pythagoras theorem]}$$

$$\Rightarrow H^2 = (\sqrt{3}k)^2 + (k)^2 = 3k^2 + k^2 = 4k^2$$

$$\therefore H = 2k \quad \text{[taking positive square root since, side cannot be negative]}$$

With reference to $\angle A$, we have

Base $= AB = \sqrt{3}k$, perpendicular $= BC = k$

and hypotenuse $= AC = 2k$

With reference to $\angle C$, we have

Base $= BC = k$, perpendicular $= AB = \sqrt{3}k$

and hypotenuse $= AC = 2k$

(i) $\sin A \cos C + \cos A \sin C = \left(\frac{BC}{AC}\right)\left(\frac{BC}{AC}\right) + \left(\frac{AB}{AC}\right)\left(\frac{AB}{AC}\right)$

$$\left[\because \sin\theta = \frac{P}{H} \text{ and } \cos\theta = \frac{B}{H}\right]$$

$$= \left(\frac{k}{2k}\right)\left(\frac{k}{2k}\right) + \left(\frac{\sqrt{3}k}{2k}\right)\left(\frac{\sqrt{3}k}{2k}\right)$$

$$= \frac{k^2}{4k^2} + \frac{3k^2}{4k^2} = \frac{4k^2}{4k^2} = 1$$

(ii) Do same as Part (i). **Ans.** 0

Q 10. **In ΔPQR, right angled at Q, $PR + QR = 25$ cm and $PQ = 5$ cm. Determine the values of $\sin P$, $\cos P$ and $\tan P$.**

Sol. Let $QR = x$ and $PR = y$

Then, $PR + QR = 25$ [given]

$\Rightarrow y + x = 25$

$\Rightarrow y = 25 - x$ ...(i)

In right angled ΔPQR,

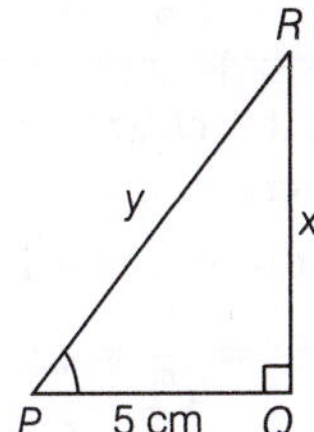

$RQ^2 + PQ^2 = PR^2$ [by Pythagoras theorem]

$\Rightarrow x^2 + (5)^2 = y^2$

$\Rightarrow x^2 + 25 = (25 - x)^2$ [from Eq. (i)]

$\Rightarrow x^2 + 25 = 625 + x^2 - 50x$

$[\because (a-b)^2 = a^2 + b^2 - 2ab]$

$\Rightarrow x^2 - x^2 + 50x = 625 - 25$

$\Rightarrow 50x = 600$

$\Rightarrow x = \frac{600}{50} = 12 = QR$

From Eq. (i),

$y = 25 - x = 25 - 12 = 13 = PR$

Now, $\sin P = \frac{P}{H} = \frac{RQ}{PR} = \frac{12}{13}$

$\cos P = \frac{B}{H} = \frac{PQ}{PR} = \frac{5}{13}$ and $\tan P = \frac{P}{B} = \frac{QR}{PQ} = \frac{12}{5}$

Q 11. **State whether the following statements are true or false. Justify your answer.**

(i) The value of $\tan A$ is always less than 1.

(ii) $\sec A = \frac{12}{5}$ for some value of $\angle A$.

(iii) $\cos A$ is the abbreviation used for the cosecant of $\angle A$.

(iv) $\cot A$ is the product of cot and A.

(v) $\sin\theta = \frac{4}{3}$ for some $\angle\theta$.

Sol. (i) False, because the value of $\tan A$ lies between $-\infty$ and $+\infty$.

(ii) True, because $\sec A$ is always greater than 1.

(iii) False, because $\cos A$ is the abbreviation of cosine of $\angle A$ and for cosecant of $\angle A$, the abbreviation is $\operatorname{cosec} A$.

(iv) False, because $\cot A$ is just a symbol and cannot be separated.

(v) False, because the value of $\sin\theta$ is always less than or equal to 1. Here, $\sin\theta = 4/3$ which is greater than 1, so it is not possible for any θ.

EXERCISE 8.2

Q 1. **Evaluate the following.**

(i) $\sin 60° \cos 30° + \sin 30° \cos 60°$

(ii) $2\tan^2 45° + \cos^2 30° - \sin^2 60°$

(iii) $\dfrac{\cos 45°}{\sec 30° + \operatorname{cosec} 30°}$

(iv) $\dfrac{\sin 30° + \tan 45° - \operatorname{cosec} 60°}{\sec 30° + \cos 60° + \cot 45°}$

(v) $\dfrac{5\cos^2 60° + 4\sec^2 30° - \tan^2 45°}{\sin^2 30° + \cos^2 30°}$

Sol. (i) $\sin 60° \cos 30° + \sin 30° \cos 60° = \frac{\sqrt{3}}{2} \times \frac{\sqrt{3}}{2} + \frac{1}{2} \times \frac{1}{2}$

$$\left[\because \sin 60° = \cos 30° = \frac{\sqrt{3}}{2} \text{ and } \sin 30° = \cos 60° = \frac{1}{2}\right]$$

$$= \frac{3}{4} + \frac{1}{4} = \frac{3+1}{4} = \frac{4}{4} = 1$$

(ii) Do same as part (i). **Ans.** 2

(iii) Do same as part (i) **Ans.** $\frac{3\sqrt{2} - \sqrt{6}}{8}$

(iv) $\dfrac{\sin 30° + \tan 45° - \operatorname{cosec} 60°}{\sec 30° + \cos 60° + \cot 45°}$

$$= \frac{\frac{1}{2} + \frac{1}{1} - \frac{2}{\sqrt{3}}}{\frac{2}{\sqrt{3}} + \frac{1}{2} + \frac{1}{1}} = \frac{\frac{\sqrt{3} + 2\sqrt{3} - 4}{2\sqrt{3}}}{\frac{4 + \sqrt{3} + 2\sqrt{3}}{2\sqrt{3}}}$$

$$\left[\because \sin 30° = \cos 60° = \frac{1}{2}, \operatorname{cosec} 60° = \sec 30° = \frac{2}{\sqrt{3}}, \cot 45° = \tan 45° = 1\right]$$

$$= \frac{3\sqrt{3} - 4}{4 + 3\sqrt{3}} = \frac{3\sqrt{3} - 4}{4 + 3\sqrt{3}} \times \frac{4 - 3\sqrt{3}}{4 - 3\sqrt{3}}$$

[multiplying numerator and denominator by the conjugate of $4 + 3\sqrt{3}$ i.e. $4 - 3\sqrt{3}$]

$$= \frac{12\sqrt{3} - 27 - 16 + 12\sqrt{3}}{(4)^2 - (3\sqrt{3})^2}$$

$[\because (a+b)(a-b) = a^2 - b^2]$

$$= \frac{24\sqrt{3} - 43}{16 - 27} = \frac{-(43 - 24\sqrt{3})}{-11} = \frac{43 - 24\sqrt{3}}{11}$$

(v) Do same as part (iv). **Ans.** $\frac{67}{12}$

Q 2. Choose the correct option and justify your choice.

CBSE 2023 Standard

(i) $\frac{2\tan 30^\circ}{1 + \tan^2 30^\circ}$ is equal to

(a) $\sin 60^\circ$ (b) $\cos 60^\circ$ (c) $\tan 60^\circ$ (d) $\sin 30^\circ$

(ii) $\frac{1 - \tan^2 45^\circ}{1 + \tan^2 45^\circ}$ is equal to

(a) $\tan 90^\circ$ (b) 1 (c) $\sin 45^\circ$ (d) 0

(iii) $\sin 2A = 2\sin A$ is true, when A is equal to

(a) 0° (b) 30° (c) 45° (d) 60°

(iv) $\frac{2\tan 30^\circ}{1 - \tan^2 30^\circ}$ is equal to

(a) $\cos 60^\circ$ (b) $\sin 60^\circ$ (c) $\tan 60^\circ$ (d) $\sin 30^\circ$

Sol. (i) (a) $\frac{2\tan 30^\circ}{1 + \tan^2 30^\circ} = \frac{2\left(\frac{1}{\sqrt{3}}\right)}{1 + \left(\frac{1}{\sqrt{3}}\right)^2} = \frac{\frac{2}{\sqrt{3}}}{\left(1 + \frac{1}{3}\right)}$ $\left[\because \tan 30^\circ = \frac{1}{\sqrt{3}}\right]$

$$= \frac{\frac{2}{\sqrt{3}}}{\left(\frac{3+1}{3}\right)} = \frac{2}{\sqrt{3}} \times \frac{3}{4} = \frac{\sqrt{3}}{2} = \sin 60^\circ \quad \left[\because \sin 60^\circ = \frac{\sqrt{3}}{2}\right]$$

(ii) (d) $\frac{1 - \tan^2 45^\circ}{1 + \tan^2 45^\circ} = \frac{1 - (1)^2}{1 + (1)^2}$ $[\because \tan 45^\circ = 1]$

$$= \frac{1-1}{1+1} = \frac{0}{2} = 0$$

(iii) (a) Given, $\sin 2A = 2\sin A$

When $A = 0^\circ$, then $\sin(2 \times 0^\circ) = 2\sin(0^\circ)$

Now, $2\sin(0^\circ) = 2(0) = 0$ $[\because \sin 0^\circ = 0]$

$\therefore \quad 0 = 0$

So, for $A = 0^\circ$, the given statement is true.

(iv) (c) Do same as part (i). **Ans.** $\tan 60^\circ$

Q 3. If $\tan(A+B) = \sqrt{3}$ and $\tan(A-B) = 1/\sqrt{3}$, $0^\circ < A + B \le 90^\circ$, $A > B$, find the values of A and B.

CBSE 2020 (Basic), 12, 11, 10

Sol. Do same as Example 6 of Topic 2. **Ans.** $A = 45^\circ$ and $B = 15^\circ$

Q 4. State whether the following statements are true or false. Justify your answer.

(i) $\sin(A+B) = \sin A + \sin B$.

(ii) The value of $\sin\theta$ increases as θ increases.

(iii) The value of $\cos\theta$ increases as θ increases.

(iv) $\sin\theta = \cos\theta$ for all values of θ.

(v) $\cot A$ is not defined for $A = 0^\circ$.

Sol. (i) False, let $A = 60^\circ$ and $B = 30^\circ$

Then, $\sin(A+B) = \sin(60^\circ + 30^\circ) = \sin 90^\circ = 1$

and $\sin A + \sin B = \sin 60^\circ + \sin 30^\circ = \frac{\sqrt{3}}{2} + \frac{1}{2} = \frac{\sqrt{3}+1}{2}$

Hence $\sin(A+B) \ne \sin A + \sin B$.

(ii) True, consider the table given below

θ	0°	30°	45°	60°	90°
$\sin\theta$	0	$\frac{1}{2}$	$\frac{1}{\sqrt{2}}$	$\frac{\sqrt{3}}{2}$	1

From this table, it is clear that the value of $\sin\theta$ increases as θ increases.

(iii) False, consider the table given below

θ	0°	30°	45°	60°	90°
$\cos\theta$	1	$\frac{\sqrt{3}}{2}$	$\frac{1}{\sqrt{2}}$	$\frac{1}{2}$	0

From this table, it is clear that the value of $\cos\theta$ decreases as θ increases.

(iv) False, because it is only true for $\theta = 45^\circ$

$\because \quad \sin 45^\circ = \frac{1}{\sqrt{2}} = \cos 45^\circ$

(v) True, because if $A = 0^\circ$, then $\cot A = \frac{1}{\tan A}$

$$= \frac{1}{\tan 0^\circ} = \frac{1}{0} = \infty \quad \text{[not defined]}$$

EXERCISE 8.3

Q 1. Express the trigonometric ratios $\sin A$, $\tan A$ and $\sec A$ in terms of $\cot A$.

Sol. (i) $\sin A = \frac{1}{\operatorname{cosec} A} = \frac{1}{\sqrt{1 + \cot^2 A}}$

$[\because \operatorname{cosec}^2\theta = 1 + \cot^2\theta \Rightarrow \operatorname{cosec}\theta = \sqrt{1 + \cot^2\theta}]$

(ii) $\tan A = \frac{1}{\cot A}$ $[\because \tan\theta \cot\theta = 1]$

(iii) $\sec A = \sqrt{1 + \tan^2 A}$

$[\because \sec^2\theta = 1 + \tan^2\theta \Rightarrow \sec\theta = \sqrt{1 + \tan^2\theta}]$

$$= \sqrt{1 + \left(\frac{1}{\cot A}\right)^2} \quad \left[\because \tan\theta = \frac{1}{\cot\theta}\right]$$

$$= \sqrt{1 + \frac{1}{\cot^2 A}} = \sqrt{\frac{\cot^2 A + 1}{\cot^2 A}} = \frac{\sqrt{1 + \cot^2 A}}{\cot A}$$

$[\because \sqrt{a^2} = a]$

Q2. Write all the other trigonometric ratios of $\angle A$ in terms of sec A.

Sol. (i) We know that

$$\sin^2 A + \cos^2 A = 1$$

$$\Rightarrow \quad \sin^2 A = 1 - \cos^2 A$$

$$\Rightarrow \quad \sin A = \sqrt{1 - \cos^2 A}$$

[taking positive square root]

$$= \sqrt{1 - \frac{1}{\sec^2 A}} \qquad \left[\because \cos\theta = \frac{1}{\sec\theta}\right]$$

$$= \sqrt{\frac{\sec^2 A - 1}{\sec^2 A}} = \frac{\sqrt{\sec^2 A - 1}}{\sec A}$$

$[\because \sqrt{a^2} = a]$

(ii) $\cos A = \dfrac{1}{\sec A}$

(iii) We know that $\sec^2 A - \tan^2 A = 1$

$\Rightarrow \tan^2 A = \sec^2 A - 1$

$\therefore \quad \tan A = \sqrt{\sec^2 A - 1}$ [taking positive square root]

(iv) $\cot A = \dfrac{1}{\tan A} = \dfrac{1}{\sqrt{\sec^2 A - 1}}$ [using part (iii)]

(v) $\operatorname{cosec} A = \dfrac{1}{\sin A} = \dfrac{\sec A}{\sqrt{\sec^2 A - 1}}$ [using part (i)]

Q3. Choose the correct option. Justify your choice.

(i) $9\sec^2 A - 9\tan^2 A$ is equal to

(a) 1 (b) 9 (c) 8 (d) 0

(ii) $(1+\tan\theta+\sec\theta)(1+\cot\theta-\operatorname{cosec}\theta)$ is equal to

(a) 0 (b) 1 (c) 2 (d) -1

(iii) $(\sec A + \tan A)(1 - \sin A)$ is equal to

[CBSE 2023 (Basic)]

(a) sec A (b) sin A (c) cosec A (d) cos A

(iv) $\dfrac{1+\tan^2 A}{1+\cot^2 A}$ is equal to

(a) $\sec^2 A$ (b) -1 (c) $\cot^2 A$ (d) $\tan^2 A$

Sol. (i) (b) $9\sec^2 A - 9\tan^2 A = 9(\sec^2 A - \tan^2 A)$

$= 9 \times 1 = 9 \quad [\because \sec^2 A - \tan^2 A = 1]$

(ii) (c) $(1+\tan\theta+\sec\theta)(1+\cot\theta-\operatorname{cosec}\theta)$

$$= \left(1 + \frac{\sin\theta}{\cos\theta} + \frac{1}{\cos\theta}\right)\left(1 + \frac{\cos\theta}{\sin\theta} - \frac{1}{\sin\theta}\right)$$

$$\left[\because \tan A = \frac{\sin A}{\cos A}, \sec A = \frac{1}{\cos A}, \cot A = \frac{\cos A}{\sin A} \text{ and } \operatorname{cosec} A = \frac{1}{\sin A}\right]$$

$$= \left[\frac{(\cos\theta+\sin\theta)+1}{\cos\theta}\right] \times \left[\frac{(\sin\theta+\cos\theta)-1}{\sin\theta}\right]$$

$$= \frac{(\cos\theta+\sin\theta)^2 - 1^2}{\cos\theta\sin\theta}$$

$[\because (a+b)(a-b) = a^2 - b^2]$

$$= \frac{\cos^2\theta + \sin^2\theta + 2\cos\theta\sin\theta - 1}{\cos\theta\sin\theta}$$

$[\because (a+b)^2 = a^2 + b^2 + 2ab]$

$$= \frac{1 + 2\cos\theta\sin\theta - 1}{\cos\theta\sin\theta} \qquad [\because \cos^2 A + \sin^2 A = 1]$$

$$= \frac{2\cos\theta\sin\theta}{\cos\theta\sin\theta} = 2$$

(iii) (d) $(\sec A + \tan A)(1 - \sin A)$

$$= \left(\frac{1}{\cos A} + \frac{\sin A}{\cos A}\right)(1 - \sin A) \qquad \left[\because \sec\theta = \frac{1}{\cos\theta} \text{ and } \tan\theta = \frac{\sin\theta}{\cos\theta}\right]$$

$$= \frac{(1+\sin A)(1-\sin A)}{\cos A} = \frac{1-\sin^2 A}{\cos A}$$

$[\because (a+b)(a-b) = a^2 - b^2]$

$$= \frac{\cos^2 A}{\cos A} = \cos A$$

$[\because \sin^2\theta + \cos^2\theta = 1 \Rightarrow \cos^2\theta = 1 - \sin^2\theta]$

(iv) (d) $$\frac{1+\tan^2 A}{1+\cot^2 A} = \frac{\sec^2 A}{\operatorname{cosec}^2 A} \qquad \left[\because 1+\tan^2\theta = \sec^2\theta \text{ and } 1+\cot^2\theta = \operatorname{cosec}^2\theta\right]$$

$$= \frac{\frac{1}{\cos^2 A}}{\frac{1}{\sin^2 A}} \qquad \left[\because \sec\theta = \frac{1}{\cos\theta} \text{ and } \operatorname{cosec}\theta = \frac{1}{\sin\theta}\right]$$

$$= \frac{1}{\cos^2 A} \times \frac{\sin^2 A}{1} = \tan^2 A$$

$$\left[\because \tan\theta = \frac{\sin\theta}{\cos\theta}\right]$$

Q4. Prove the following identities, where the angles involved are acute angles for which the expressions are defined.

(i) $(\operatorname{cosec}\theta - \cot\theta)^2 = \dfrac{1-\cos\theta}{1+\cos\theta}$

(ii) $\dfrac{\cos A}{1+\sin A} + \dfrac{1+\sin A}{\cos A} = 2\sec A$

(iii) $\dfrac{\tan\theta}{1-\cot\theta} + \dfrac{\cot\theta}{1-\tan\theta} = 1 + \sec\theta \operatorname{cosec}\theta$

CBSE 2025 (Basic)

(iv) $\dfrac{1+\sec A}{\sec A}=\dfrac{\sin^2 A}{1-\cos A}$

(v) $\dfrac{\cos A-\sin A+1}{\cos A+\sin A-1}=\operatorname{cosec} A+\cot A$, using the identity $\operatorname{cosec}^2 A=1+\cot^2 A$.

(vi) $\sqrt{\dfrac{1+\sin A}{1-\sin A}}=\sec A+\tan A$

(vii) $\dfrac{\sin\theta-2\sin^3\theta}{2\cos^3\theta-\cos\theta}=\tan\theta$ CBSE 2024 (Standard)

(viii) $(\sin A+\operatorname{cosec} A)^2+(\cos A+\sec A)^2$
$=7+\tan^2 A+\cot^2 A$ CBSE 2024 (Basic)

(ix) $(\operatorname{cosec} A-\sin A)(\sec A-\cos A)=\dfrac{1}{\tan A+\cot A}$

(x) $\left(\dfrac{1+\tan^2 A}{1+\cot^2 A}\right)=\left(\dfrac{1-\tan A}{1-\cot A}\right)^2=\tan^2 A$

CBSE 2024 (Standard) Compartment

Sol. (i) LHS $=(\operatorname{cosec}\theta-\cot\theta)^2=\left(\dfrac{1}{\sin\theta}-\dfrac{\cos\theta}{\sin\theta}\right)^2$

$\left[\because \operatorname{cosec} A=\dfrac{1}{\sin A},\ \cot A=\dfrac{\cos A}{\sin A}\right]$

$=\left(\dfrac{1-\cos\theta}{\sin\theta}\right)^2=\dfrac{(1-\cos\theta)^2}{\sin^2\theta}=\dfrac{(1-\cos\theta)^2}{1-\cos^2\theta}$

$[\because \sin^2 A=1-\cos^2 A]$

$=\dfrac{(1-\cos\theta)(1-\cos\theta)}{(1+\cos\theta)(1-\cos\theta)}$ $[\because a^2-b^2=(a+b)(a-b)]$

$=\dfrac{1-\cos\theta}{1+\cos\theta}=$ RHS **Hence proved.**

(ii) LHS $=\dfrac{\cos A}{1+\sin A}+\dfrac{1+\sin A}{\cos A}=\dfrac{\cos^2 A+(1+\sin A)^2}{(1+\sin A)\cos A}$

$=\dfrac{\cos^2 A+\sin^2 A+1+2\sin A}{(1+\sin A)\cos A}$

$[\because (a+b)^2=a^2+b^2+2ab]$

$=\dfrac{1+1+2\sin A}{(1+\sin A)\cos A}$ $[\because \sin^2\theta+\cos^2\theta=1]$

$=\dfrac{2+2\sin A}{(1+\sin A)\cos A}$

$=\dfrac{2(1+\sin A)}{(1+\sin A)\cos A}$

$=\dfrac{2}{\cos A}=2\sec A$ $\left[\because \dfrac{1}{\cos\theta}=\sec\theta\right]$

= RHS **Hence proved.**

(iii) LHS $=\dfrac{\tan\theta}{1-\cot\theta}+\dfrac{\cot\theta}{1-\tan\theta}=\dfrac{\frac{\sin\theta}{\cos\theta}}{1-\frac{\cos\theta}{\sin\theta}}+\dfrac{\frac{\cos\theta}{\sin\theta}}{1-\frac{\sin\theta}{\cos\theta}}$

$\left[\because \tan A=\dfrac{\sin A}{\cos A},\ \cot A=\dfrac{\cos A}{\sin A}\right]$

$=\dfrac{\frac{\sin\theta}{\cos\theta}}{\frac{\sin\theta-\cos\theta}{\sin\theta}}+\dfrac{\frac{\cos\theta}{\sin\theta}}{\frac{\cos\theta-\sin\theta}{\cos\theta}}$

$=\dfrac{\sin\theta}{\cos\theta}\times\dfrac{\sin\theta}{\sin\theta-\cos\theta}+\dfrac{\cos\theta}{\sin\theta}\times\dfrac{\cos\theta}{\cos\theta-\sin\theta}$

$=\dfrac{\sin^2\theta}{\cos\theta(\sin\theta-\cos\theta)}-\dfrac{\cos^2\theta}{\sin\theta(\sin\theta-\cos\theta)}$

$=\dfrac{\sin^3\theta-\cos^3\theta}{\cos\theta\sin\theta(\sin\theta-\cos\theta)}$

$=\dfrac{(\sin\theta-\cos\theta)(\sin^2\theta+\cos^2\theta+\sin\theta\cos\theta)}{\cos\theta\sin\theta(\sin\theta-\cos\theta)}$

$[\because x^3-y^3=(x-y)(x^2+y^2+xy)]$

$=\dfrac{1+\sin\theta\cos\theta}{\cos\theta\sin\theta}$ $[\because \sin^2 A+\cos^2 A=1]$

$=\dfrac{1}{\cos\theta\sin\theta}+\dfrac{\sin\theta\cos\theta}{\sin\theta\cos\theta}=\dfrac{1}{\cos\theta\sin\theta}+1$

$=1+\sec\theta\operatorname{cosec}\theta$

$\left[\because \dfrac{1}{\cos A}=\sec A \text{ and } \dfrac{1}{\sin A}=\operatorname{cosec} A\right]$

= RHS **Hence proved.**

(iv) LHS $=\dfrac{1+\sec A}{\sec A}=\dfrac{1+\frac{1}{\cos A}}{\frac{1}{\cos A}}$ $\left[\because \sec\theta=\dfrac{1}{\cos\theta}\right]$

$=\dfrac{\frac{\cos A+1}{\cos A}}{1/\cos A}=\dfrac{\cos A+1}{\cos A}\times\dfrac{\cos A}{1}$

$=\cos A+1=1+\cos A$ ...(i)

RHS $=\dfrac{\sin^2 A}{1-\cos A}=\dfrac{1-\cos^2 A}{1-\cos A}$

$[\because \sin^2\theta+\cos^2\theta=1\Rightarrow \sin^2\theta=1-\cos^2\theta]$

$=\dfrac{(1+\cos A)(1-\cos A)}{(1-\cos A)}$ $[\because a^2-b^2=(a+b)(a-b)]$

$=1+\cos A$ ...(ii)

From Eqs. (i) and (ii), LHS = RHS **Hence proved.**

(v) LHS $= \dfrac{\cos A - \sin A + 1}{\cos A + \sin A - 1}$

On dividing numerator and denominator by $\sin A$, we get

$$= \frac{\dfrac{\cos A}{\sin A} - \dfrac{\sin A}{\sin A} + \dfrac{1}{\sin A}}{\dfrac{\cos A}{\sin A} + \dfrac{\sin A}{\sin A} - \dfrac{1}{\sin A}} = \frac{\cot A - 1 + \operatorname{cosec} A}{\cot A + 1 - \operatorname{cosec} A}$$

$$\left[\because \frac{\cos\theta}{\sin\theta} = \cot\theta \text{ and } \frac{1}{\sin\theta} = \operatorname{cosec}\theta\right]$$

$$= \frac{\cot A + \operatorname{cosec} A - 1}{\cot A + 1 - \operatorname{cosec} A}$$

$$= \frac{(\cot A + \operatorname{cosec} A) - (\operatorname{cosec}^2 A - \cot^2 A)}{\cot A + 1 - \operatorname{cosec} A}$$

$$[\because 1 = \operatorname{cosec}^2 A - \cot^2 A]$$

$$= \frac{(\cot A + \operatorname{cosec} A) - [(\operatorname{cosec} A + \cot A)(\operatorname{cosec} A - \cot A)]}{\cot A + 1 - \operatorname{cosec} A}$$

$$[\because a^2 - b^2 = (a+b)(a-b)]$$

$$= \frac{(\cot A + \operatorname{cosec} A)[1 - (\operatorname{cosec} A - \cot A)]}{\cot A + 1 - \operatorname{cosec} A}$$

$$= \frac{(\cot A + \operatorname{cosec} A)[1 - \operatorname{cosec} A + \cot A]}{(\cot A + 1 - \operatorname{cosec} A)}$$

$= \cot A + \operatorname{cosec} A$

$=$ RHS **Hence proved.**

(vi) LHS $= \sqrt{\dfrac{1+\sin A}{1-\sin A}} = \sqrt{\dfrac{1+\sin A}{1-\sin A} \times \dfrac{1+\sin A}{1+\sin A}}$

[multiplying numerator and denominator by $\sqrt{(1+\sin A)}$]

$$= \sqrt{\frac{(1+\sin A)^2}{1-\sin^2 A}} = \sqrt{\frac{(1+\sin A)^2}{\cos^2 A}}$$

$$[\because \sin^2\theta + \cos^2\theta = 1 \Rightarrow 1 - \sin^2\theta = \cos^2\theta]$$

$$= \frac{1+\sin A}{\cos A} = \frac{1}{\cos A} + \frac{\sin A}{\cos A}$$

$$= \sec A + \tan A \left[\because \frac{1}{\cos\theta} = \sec\theta \text{ and } \tan\theta = \frac{\sin\theta}{\cos\theta}\right]$$

$=$ RHS **Hence proved.**

(vii) LHS $= \dfrac{\sin\theta - 2\sin^3\theta}{2\cos^3\theta - \cos\theta} = \dfrac{\sin\theta(1 - 2\sin^2\theta)}{\cos\theta(2\cos^2\theta - 1)}$

$$= \frac{\sin\theta[1 - 2(1-\cos^2\theta)]}{\cos\theta\,(2\cos^2\theta - 1)}$$

$$[\because \sin^2 A + \cos^2 A = 1 \Rightarrow \sin^2 A = 1 - \cos^2 A]$$

$$= \frac{\sin\theta(1 - 2 + 2\cos^2\theta)}{\cos\theta\,(2\cos^2\theta - 1)}$$

$$= \frac{\sin\theta(2\cos^2\theta - 1)}{\cos\theta(2\cos^2\theta - 1)}$$

$$= \frac{\sin\theta}{\cos\theta} = \tan\theta = \text{RHS} \qquad \left[\because \tan A = \frac{\sin A}{\cos A}\right]$$

Hence proved.

(viii) LHS $= (\sin A + \operatorname{cosec} A)^2 + (\cos A + \sec A)^2$

$$= \sin^2 A + \operatorname{cosec}^2 A + 2\sin A \operatorname{cosec} A + \cos^2 A + \sec^2 A + 2\cos A \sec A$$

$$[\because (a+b)^2 = a^2 + b^2 + 2ab]$$

$$= (\sin^2 A + \cos^2 A) + (1 + \cot^2 A) + 2\sin A\frac{1}{\sin A} + (1 + \tan^2 A) + 2\cos A\frac{1}{\cos A}$$

$$\left[\because \operatorname{cosec}^2\theta = 1 + \cot^2\theta, \sec^2\theta = 1 + \tan^2\theta, \operatorname{cosec}\theta = \frac{1}{\sin\theta} \text{ and } \sec\theta = \frac{1}{\cos\theta}\right]$$

$$= 1 + 1 + \cot^2 A + 2 + 1 + \tan^2 A + 2$$

$$[\because \sin^2\theta + \cos^2\theta = 1]$$

$= 7 + \tan^2 A + \cot^2 A =$ RHS **Hence proved.**

(ix) LHS $= (\operatorname{cosec} A - \sin A)(\sec A - \cos A)$

$$= \left(\frac{1}{\sin A} - \frac{\sin A}{1}\right)\left(\frac{1}{\cos A} - \frac{\cos A}{1}\right)$$

$$\left[\because \operatorname{cosec}\theta = \frac{1}{\sin\theta} \text{ and } \sec\theta = \frac{1}{\cos\theta}\right]$$

$$= \left(\frac{1 - \sin^2 A}{\sin A}\right)\left(\frac{1 - \cos^2 A}{\cos A}\right) = \frac{\cos^2 A}{\sin A} \times \frac{\sin^2 A}{\cos A}$$

$$[\because \sin^2\theta + \cos^2\theta = 1]$$

$= \cos A \sin A$ ...(i)

$$\text{RHS} = \frac{1}{\tan A + \cot A} = \frac{1}{\left(\dfrac{\sin A}{\cos A} + \dfrac{\cos A}{\sin A}\right)}$$

$$\left[\because \tan\theta = \frac{\sin\theta}{\cos\theta}, \cot\theta = \frac{\cos\theta}{\sin\theta}\right]$$

$$= \frac{1}{\left(\dfrac{\sin^2 A + \cos^2 A}{\cos A \sin A}\right)} = \frac{1}{\dfrac{1}{\cos A \sin A}}$$

$$[\because \sin^2\theta + \cos^2\theta = 1]$$

$= 1 \times \dfrac{\cos A \sin A}{1} = \cos A \sin A$ ...(ii)

From Eqs. (i) and (ii), LHS = RHS **Hence proved.**

(x) First, put $\tan A$ and $\cot A$ in terms of $\sin A$ and $\cos A$. Then, simplify it.

REVIEW EXERCISE

Including Competency Based Questions

Part I

Multiple Choice Questions

1. If $\tan A = \frac{3}{4}$, then $\frac{\sin^2 A + \cos^2 A}{\sec A}$ is equal to **CBSE 2024 (Basic) Compartment**

(a) $\frac{4}{3}$ (b) $\frac{4}{5}$ (c) $\frac{3}{5}$ (d) $\frac{5}{4}$

2. If $3 \cot A = 4$, where $0° < A < 90°$, then $\sec A$ is equal to **CBSE Sample Paper 2025**

(a) $\frac{5}{4}$ (b) $\frac{4}{3}$ (c) $\frac{5}{3}$ (d) $\frac{3}{4}$

3. In a right ΔABC, right angled at A. If $\sin B = \frac{1}{4}$ then the value of $\sec B$ is **CBSE 2025 (Standard)**

(a) 4 (b) $\frac{\sqrt{15}}{4}$ (c) $\sqrt{15}$ (d) $\frac{4}{\sqrt{15}}$

4. ΔABC is an isosceles triangle, with $AB = BC$. A semi-circle of the area equal to that of the triangle is combined with it.

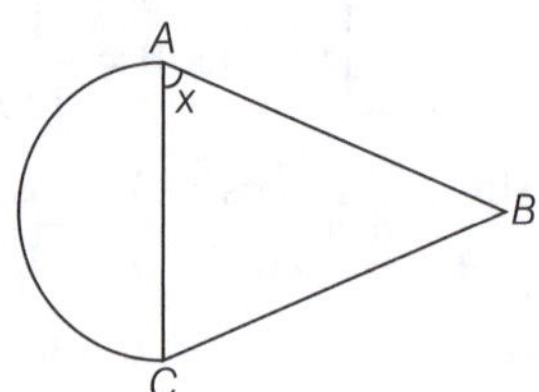

What is the value of $\tan x$? **Competency Based Question**

(a) 1 (b) $\frac{1}{4}\pi$ (c) $\frac{1}{2}\pi$ (d) π

5. $\frac{1 - \tan^2 30°}{1 + \tan^2 30°}$ is equal to **CBSE Sample Paper 2025**

(a) $\cos 60°$ (b) $\sin 60°$ (c) 1 (d) $\tan^2 60°$

6. If $\cos(\alpha + \beta) = 0$, then value of $\cos\left(\frac{\alpha + \beta}{2}\right)$ is equal to **CBSE 2024 (Standard)**

(a) $\frac{1}{\sqrt{2}}$ (b) $\frac{1}{2}$ (c) 0 (d) $\sqrt{2}$

7. If θ is an acute angle and $\tan\theta + \cot\theta = 2$, then the value of $\sin^3\theta + \cos^3\theta$ is **CBSE 2021 Term I (Standard)**

(a) 1 (b) $\frac{1}{2}$ (c) $\frac{\sqrt{2}}{2}$ (d) $\sqrt{2}$

8. If $\cos\theta = \frac{\sqrt{3}}{2}$ and $\sin\phi = \frac{1}{2}$, then $\tan(\theta + \phi)$ is **CBSE 2024 (Standard)**

(a) $\sqrt{3}$ (b) $\frac{1}{\sqrt{3}}$

(c) 1 (d) not defined

9. If $\tan^2\theta + \cot^2\alpha = 2$, where $\theta = 45°$ and $0° \le \alpha \le 90°$, then the value of α is **CBSE 2024 (Standard) Compartment**

(a) 30° (b) 45° (c) 60° (d) 90°

10. The value of $\left(\sin^2\theta + \frac{1}{1 + \tan^2\theta}\right)$ is **CBSE 2024 (Standard) Compartment**

(a) 0 (b) 2 (c) 1 (d −1

11. In a right-angled ΔPQR, $\angle Q = 90°$. If $\angle P = 45°$, then value of $\tan P - \cos^2 R$ is

(a) 0 (b) 1 (c) 1/2 (d) 3/2

Directions (Q. Nos. 12 to 13) In the figure given below, $PQRS$ is a quadrilateral. PR is perpendicular to QR and PS.

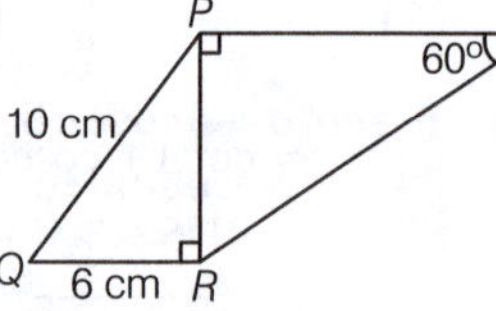

Based on the above information, answer the following questions. **Competency Based Question**

12. What is the value of $\tan Q$?

(a) $\frac{3}{5}$ (b) $\frac{1}{2}$ (c) 1 (d) $\frac{4}{3}$

13. What is the length of RS?

(a) 8 units (b) 10 units (c) $8\sqrt{2}$ units (d) $\frac{16}{3}\sqrt{3}$ units

14. $(\cos^4 A - \sin^4 A)$ on simplified form, gives **CBSE 2023 (Standard)**

(a) $2\sin^2 A - 1$ (b) $2\sin^2 A + 1$

(c) $2\cos^2 A + 1$ (d) $2\cos^2 A - 1$

15. If θ is an acute angle of a right angled triangle, then which of the following equation is not true?

(a) $\sin\theta\cot\theta = \cos\theta$ (b) $\cos\theta\tan\theta = \sin\theta$

(c) $\mathrm{cosec}^2\theta - \cot^2\theta = 1$ (d) $\tan^2\theta - \sec^2\theta = 1$

16. If $x\sin^3\theta + y\cos^3\theta = \sin\theta\cos\theta$ and $x\sin\theta = y\cos\theta$, then $x^2 + y^2$ is equal to **CBSE 2023 (Standard)**

(a) 0 (b) 1/2 (c) 1 (d) 3/2

17. If $\sec\theta - \tan\theta = m$, then the value of $\sec\theta + \tan\theta$ is **CBSE 2024 (Standard)**

(a) $1-\frac{1}{m}$ (b) m^2-1 (c) $\frac{1}{m}$ (d) $-m$

18. $\frac{\cos^2\theta}{\sin^2\theta} - \frac{1}{\sin^2\theta}$, in simplified form, is

(a) $\tan^2\theta$ (b) $\sec^2\theta$ (c) 1 (d) -1

19. If $\sec\theta - \tan\theta = \frac{1}{3}$, then the value of $(\sec\theta + \tan\theta)$ is **CBSE 2023 (Standard)**

(a) $\frac{4}{3}$ (b) $\frac{2}{3}$ (c) $\frac{1}{3}$ (d) 3

20. $(1+\tan^2 A)(1+\sin A)(1-\sin A)$ is equal to

(a) $\frac{\cos^2 A}{\sec^2 A}$ (b) 1 (c) 0 (d) 2

21. If $\sin\theta = \frac{3}{4}$, then $\frac{(\sec^2\theta - 1)\cos^2\theta}{\sin\theta}$ equals **CBSE 2023 (Basic)**

(a) $\frac{3}{5}$ (b) $\frac{3}{4}$ (c) $\frac{4}{3}$ (d) $\frac{9}{16}$

22. If $\sec\theta + \tan\theta = p$, then $\tan\theta$ is **CBSE 2021 Term I (Standard)**

(a) $\frac{p^2+1}{2p}$ (b) $\frac{p^2-1}{2p}$ (c) $\frac{p^2-1}{p^2+1}$ (d) $\frac{p^2+1}{p^2-1}$

23. Given that $\sin\theta = \frac{a}{b}$, find $\cos\theta$

(a) $\frac{b}{\sqrt{b^2-a^2}}$ (b) $\frac{b}{a}$ (c) $\frac{\sqrt{b^2-a^2}}{b}$ (d) $\frac{a}{\sqrt{b^2-a^2}}$

24. If $a\cot\theta + b\,\text{cosec}\,\theta = p$ and $b\cot\theta + a\,\text{cosec}\,\theta = q$, then $p^2 - q^2$ is equal to **CBSE 2022 (Standard)**

(a) a^2-b^2 (b) b^2-a^2 (c) a^2+b^2 (d) $b-a$

Assertion-Reason Type Questions

25. Assertion The value of $\frac{1}{\sqrt{\cot^2\theta+1}}$ is equal to $\sin\theta$.

Reason Trigonometric ratio of $\sin\theta$ in term of $\tan\theta$ is $\frac{\tan\theta}{\sqrt{1+\tan^2\theta}}$.

(a) Both Assertion and Reason are correct and Reason is the correct explanation of Assertion.
(b) Both Assertion and Reason are correct but Reason is not the correct explanation of Assertion.
(c) Assertion is correct but Reason is incorrect.
(d) Assertion is incorrect but Reason is correct.

26. Assertion The equation $\sec^2\theta = \frac{4xy}{(x+y)^2}$ is only possible, when $x = y$.

Reason $\sec^2\theta \geq 1$ and therefore $(x-y)^2 \leq 0$.

(a) Both Assertion and Reason are correct and Reason is the correct explanation of Assertion.
(b) Both Assertion and Reason are correct but Reason is not the correct explanation of Assertion.
(c) Assertion is correct but Reason is incorrect.
(d) Assertion is incorrect but Reason is correct.

27. Assertion For $0 < \theta \leq 90°$, $\text{cosec}\,\theta - \cot\theta$ and $\text{cosec}\,\theta + \cot\theta$ are reciprocal of each other.

Reason $\text{cosec}^2\theta - \cot^2\theta = 1$ **CBSE 2023 (Basic)**

(a) Both Assertion and Reason are correct and Reason is the correct explanation of Assertion.
(b) Both Assertion and Reason are correct but Reason is not the correct explanation of Assertion.
(c) Assertion is correct but Reason is incorrect.
(d) Assertion is incorrect but Reason is correct.

28. Assertion $\cos^2 A - \sin^2 A = 1$ is a trigonometric identity.

Reason An equation involving trigonometric ratios of an angle is called trigonometric identity, if it is true for all values of the angles involved.

(a) Both Assertion and Reason are correct and Reason is the correct explanation of Assertion.
(b) Both Assertion and Reason are correct but Reason is not the correct explanation of Assertion.
(c) Assertion is correct but Reason is incorrect.
(d) Assertion is incorrect but Reason is correct.

Case Study Based Questions

29. Shown below is the rough figure of the view of a proposed water slide which has to be constructed in a water park.

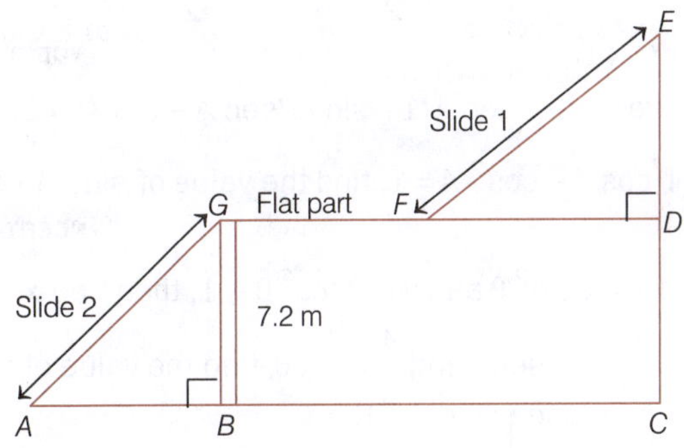

[take $\sqrt{2} = 1.4$, $\sqrt{3} = 1.7$, wherever required]

Based on the above information, answer the following questions.

(i) What should be the measure of the angle between slide 2 and ground if the length of AB is $2.4\sqrt{3}$ m?

(ii) What should be the value of $\tan x$, if length of slide 2 is 12 m?

(iii) (a) If slide 1 makes an angle of $150°$ with the flat part and $FD = 17$ m, then what is the height of the top point of slide 1 from the ground (EC)?

Or

(b) What should be the length of slide 2 if the angle between slide 2 and ground is $30°$?

30. A moving camera at the top of a 4 m high building captures the images of a walking man at five different positions. The five positions are shown in the figure below.

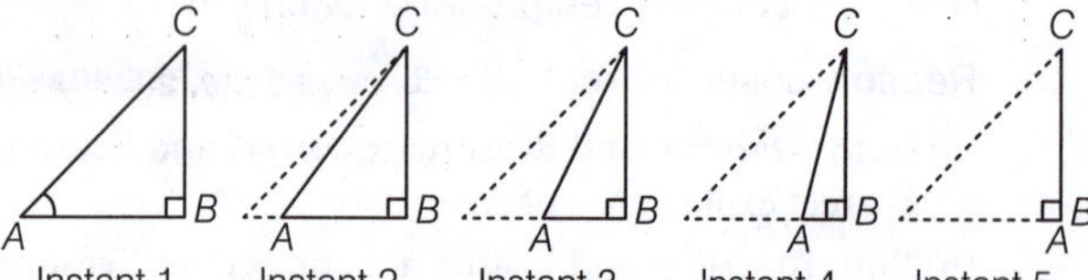

Based on the above information, answer the following questions.

(i) Describe the change in the value of $\sin A$.

(ii) If for position 1, $AB = BC$ and ΔABC is right angled at B, then find the value of $\sin A$.

(iii) (a) If ΔABC is right angled at B, then find the value of $\sin(A+C)$.

Or

(b) For a isosceles ΔABC right angled at B, prove that $\dfrac{\tan A+\tan C}{1+2\sin A\cos C}=1$.

Part II

Very Short Answer Type Questions

1. If $\tan A = 3/4$, then find the value of $\dfrac{1}{\sin A}+\dfrac{1}{\cos A}$. **CBSE Sample Paper 2020 (Standard)**

2. If $7\tan\theta = 4$, then find the value of $\dfrac{7\sin\theta-3\cos\theta}{7\sin\theta+3\cos\theta}$.

3. If $\sqrt{3}\tan\theta = 3\sin\theta$, then find the value of $\sin^2\theta-\cos^2\theta$. **Competency Based Question**

4. Evaluate $\sin^2 60° + 2\tan 45° - \cos^2 30°$. **CBSE Sample Paper 2023 (Basic)**

5. Given that, $\sin\alpha = \dfrac{1}{2}$ and $\cos\beta = \dfrac{1}{2}$, what is the value of $(\alpha+\beta)$? **NCERT Exemplar**

6. Prove that $\sec A(1-\sin A)(\sec A+\tan A)=1$.

7. If $\cos A+\cos^2 A = 1$, find the value of $\sin^2 A+\sin^4 A$. **NCERT Exemplar**

8. If $x = 2\sin^2\theta$ and $y = 2\cos^2\theta + 1$, then find $x+y$.

9. If $4x = \operatorname{cosec}\theta$ and $\dfrac{4}{x} = \cot\theta$, find the value of $4\left[x^2-\dfrac{1}{x^2}\right]$. **Competency Based Question**

Short Answer Type Questions

10. If $\tan A = \sqrt{2}-1$, prove that $\dfrac{\tan A}{1+\tan^2 A}=\dfrac{\sqrt{2}}{4}$.

11. In right angled ΔACB, $\angle C = 90°$, $AB = 29$ units and $BC = 21$ units. If $\angle ABC = \theta$, find $\cos^2\theta-\sin^2\theta$ and $\sin^2\theta+\cos^2\theta$.

12. Consider the statement given below.

In a right triangle, the value of $\cos A = \sqrt{2}$ for some acute angle A. Is the statement true or false? Give a valid reason. **CBSE QB**

13. If $\cos A = \dfrac{5}{13}$, then verify that $\dfrac{\cos A}{1-\tan A}+\dfrac{\sin A}{1-\cot A}=\cos A+\sin A$ **CBSE 2024 (Basic)**

14. In the given figure, ΔABC is right angled triangle, right angle at B. ΔBSC is right angled triangle, right angle at S and ΔBRS is right angled triangle, right angle at R, $AB = 18$ cm, $BC = 7.5$ cm, $RS = 5$ cm, $RB = 6$ cm, $\angle BSR = x$ and $\angle SAB = y$. **Competency Based Question**

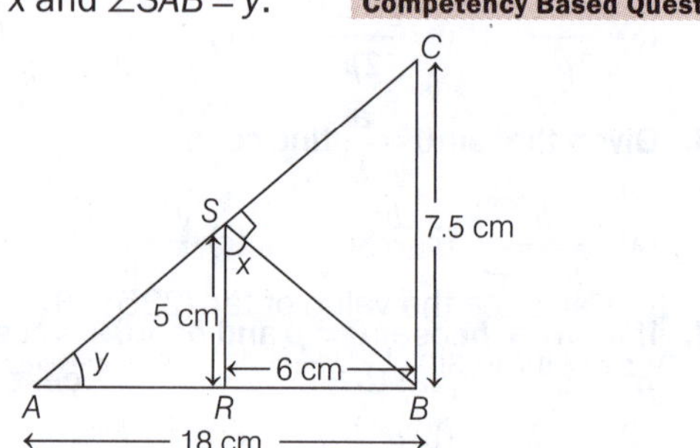

Find the following

(i) $\tan x$ (ii) $\sin y$ (iii) $\cos y$

15. In the given figure, ΔABC is a right angled triangle, right angle at B. If $BC = 7$ cm and $AC - AB = 1$ cm, find the value of $\sin A+\cos A$. **Competency Based Question**

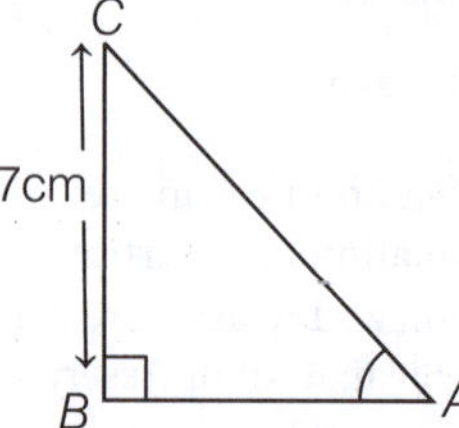

16. In the given figure, if D is the mid-point of BC, find the value of $\dfrac{\tan x}{\tan y}$.

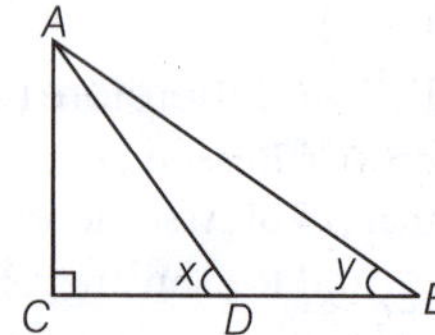

17. If $\tan\theta + \frac{1}{\tan\theta} = 2$, find the value of $\cot^2\theta + \frac{1}{\cot^2\theta}$.

18. Prove that $\sqrt{\frac{\sec A + \tan A}{\sec A - \tan A}} \cdot \sqrt{\frac{\operatorname{cosec} A - 1}{\operatorname{cosec} A + 1}} = 1$.

19. If $\sqrt{3}\cot^2\theta - 4\cot\theta + \sqrt{3} = 0$, then find the value of $\tan^2\theta + \cot^2\theta$.

20. If $\tan\theta = 1$ and $\sin\phi = \frac{1}{\sqrt{2}}$, then find the value of $\cos(\theta + \phi)$, where θ and ϕ are both acute angles.

Competency Based Question

21. Find the value of x such that

$3\tan^2 60° - x\sin^2 45° + \frac{3}{4}\sec^2 30° = 2\operatorname{cosec}^2 30°$.

CBSE 2024 (Standard) Compartment

22. Two famous bowlers of Indian Cricket team Navdeep Saini and Jaspreet Bumrah throw a ball at an angle of A and B respectively in such a way that $\sin(A-B) = \frac{1}{2}$ and $\cos(A+B) = 0$, $0° < A+B \leq 90°$, $A > B$.

(i) Find the angles of both bowlers at which they throw a ball.

(ii) Find the values of the following trigonometric ratios $\tan A$, $\operatorname{cosec}(A-B)$, $\sec B$.

Competency Based Question

23. Suppose $\sin\theta_1 + \sin\theta_2 + \sin\theta_3 = 3$, $0° < \theta_1, \theta_2, \theta_3 \leq 90°$,

(i) Find the value of $\cos\theta_1 + \cos\theta_2 + \cos\theta_3$.

(ii) Calculate the value of $\tan(225° - \theta_1 - \theta_2)$.

(iii) Evaluate $\sin(120° - \theta_3)$.

Competency Based Question

24. Calculate $A+B$ when $\tan A = \frac{2}{3}$ and $\tan B = \frac{3}{2}$, if it is given that $\tan(A+B) = \frac{\tan A + \tan B}{1 - \tan A \tan B}$

where, A and B are acute angles.

Competency Based Question

25. If $\operatorname{cosec}(A-B) = 2$, $\cot(A+B) = \frac{1}{\sqrt{3}}$, $0° < (A+B) \leq 90°$, $A > B$, then find A and B.

26. If $\tan\theta = \frac{20}{21}$, then prove that $\frac{1 - \sin\theta + \cos\theta}{1 + \sin\theta + \cos\theta} = \frac{3}{7}$.

27. Prove that $\frac{1}{1+\sin\theta} + \frac{1}{1-\sin\theta} = 2\sec^2\theta$.

CBSE 2020 (Basic)

28. Use the identity $\sin^2 A + \cos^2 A = 1$ to prove that $\tan^2 A + 1 = \sec^2 A$. Hence, find the value of $\tan A$, when $\sec A = \frac{5}{3}$, where A is an acute angle.

CBSE 2025 (Standard)

29. Prove that $\frac{\sin^4\theta + \cos^4\theta}{1 - 2\sin^2\theta \cdot \cos^2\theta} = 1$.

30. Simplify $\frac{\sin^3\theta + \cos^3\theta}{\sin\theta + \cos\theta} + \sin\theta\cos\theta$.

31. Prove that $\frac{\cot A - \cos A}{\cot A + \cos A} = \frac{\cos^2 A}{(1 + \sin A)^2}$.

CBSE 2023 (Basic)

32. Prove that $\frac{\cot\theta + \operatorname{cosec}\theta - 1}{\cot\theta - \operatorname{cosec}\theta + 1} = \frac{1 + \cos\theta}{\sin\theta}$.

CBSE 2020, 2016 (Standard)

33. If $\sin^6 A + \cos^6 A + 3\sin^2 A \cdot \cos^2 A + 4 = k$, then find the value of k.

34. If $\sec\theta = x + \frac{1}{4x}$, then find the value of $\sec\theta + \tan\theta$.

35. If $\cot\theta = 3x - \frac{1}{12x}$, then show that

$\cot\theta + \operatorname{cosec}\theta = 6x$ or $-\frac{1}{6x}$.

36. Prove that $\sqrt{\sec^2\theta + \operatorname{cosec}^2\theta} = \tan\theta + \cot\theta$.

NCERT Exemplar

37. Eliminate θ from the following equations.

(i) $x = a\sec\theta$, $y = b\tan\theta$

(ii) $x = k + a\cos\theta$, $y = h + b\sin\theta$

38. If $m\sin\theta + n\cos\theta = p$ and $m\cos\theta - n\sin\theta = q$, then prove that $m^2 + n^2 = p^2 + q^2$.

39. Prove that $\frac{\sin\theta}{\cot\theta + \operatorname{cosec}\theta} = 2 + \frac{\sin\theta}{\cot\theta - \operatorname{cosec}\theta}$.

40. If $7\sin^2 A + 3\cos^2 A = 4$, prove that $\tan A = \frac{1}{\sqrt{3}}$.

41. If $\cos\theta + \sin\theta = \sqrt{2}\cos\theta$, prove that $\cos\theta - \sin\theta = \sqrt{2}\sin\theta$.

CBSE 2019, 16, 12

42. Ram was trying hard to prove $a\cos\theta - b\sin\theta = \pm\sqrt{a^2 + b^2 - c^2}$, when $a\sin\theta + b\cos\theta = c$. Her classmate Swati gave her a hint of squaring both sides of $a\sin\theta + b\cos\theta = c$ and proceed further. With her hint, Ram was able to solve the problem and he thanks Swati for this hint. So, write the solution of the above problem.

Competency Based Question

43. Prove that $\frac{\sin A - \cos A + 1}{\sin A + \cos A - 1} = \frac{1}{\sec A - \tan A}$.

CBSE Sample Paper 2020 (Basic)

44. If $\cos\theta - \sin\theta = x$ and $\sin\theta + \cos\theta = y$, then show that $x^2 + y^2 = 2$.

45. If $\frac{\cos\alpha}{\cos\beta} = m$ and $\frac{\cos\alpha}{\sin\beta} = n$, show that $(m^2 + n^2)\cos^2\beta = n^2$.

Competency Based Question

46. Prove that $\frac{1}{(\sec x - \tan x)} - \frac{1}{\cos x} = \frac{1}{\cos x} - \frac{1}{\sec x + \tan x}$.

47. Prove that $(1 + \tan A\tan B)^2 + (\tan A - \tan B)^2 = \sec^2 A\sec^2 B$.

48. If $a\cos\theta - b\sin\theta = c$, prove that

$$a\sin\theta + b\cos\theta = \pm\sqrt{a^2+b^2-c^2}.$$

49. If $\sin\theta + 2\cos\theta = 1$, prove that $2\sin\theta - \cos\theta = 2$.

NCERT Exemplar

50. If $\sin A = \frac{1}{\sqrt{5}}$ and $\sin B = \frac{1}{\sqrt{10}}$, find the values of $\cos A$ and $\cos B$. Hence, using the formula $\cos(A+B) = \cos A\cos B - \sin A\sin B$, show that $A+B = 45°$. **Competency Based Question**

51. Prove that $\sec^2 A - \left(\frac{\sin^2 A - 2\sin^4 A}{2\cos^4 A - \cos^2 A}\right) = 1.$

52. If $1+\sin^2\theta = 3\sin\theta\cos\theta$, prove that $\tan\theta = 1$ or $\frac{1}{2}$.

NCERT Exemplar

Long Answer Type Questions

53. In the figure below, $5\sin P = 4$.

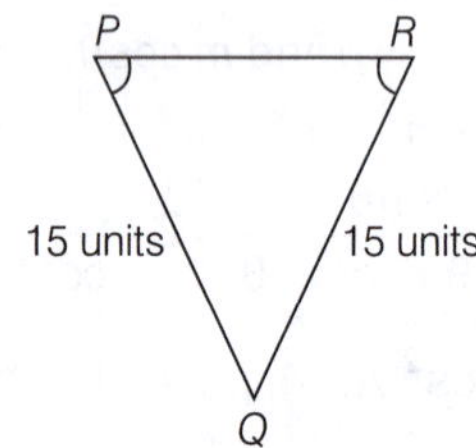

(**Note** The figure is not to scale)

What is the length of PR? Draw a diagram and show your steps. **Competency Based Question**

54. Shown below is a cuboid. Its length is l units, breadth b units and height h units.

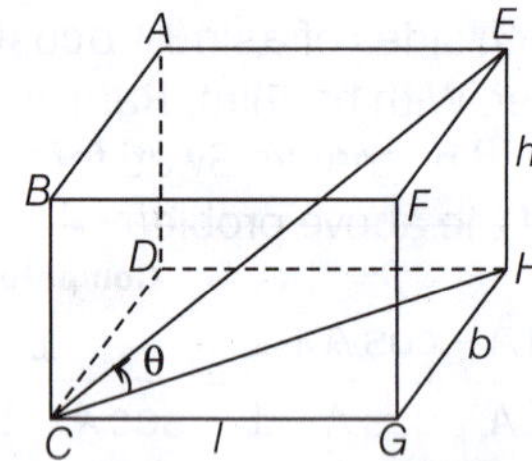

(i) Express $\cos\theta$ in terms of l, b and h.

(ii) If the figure was a cube, what would be the value of $\cos\theta$?

Show your work. **Competency Based Question**

55. Prove that $\cot^2 A\left[\frac{\sec A - 1}{1+\sin A}\right] + \sec^2 A\left[\frac{\sin A - 1}{1+\sec A}\right] = 0.$

56. Prove that $\frac{\sin A - 2\sin^3 A}{2\cos^3 A - \cos A} = \tan A.$

57. $\frac{1}{\operatorname{cosec}\theta - \cot\theta} - \frac{\cot\theta}{\cos\theta} = \cot\theta$ **Competency Based Question**

58. If $\frac{1}{\sin\theta - \cos\theta} = \frac{\operatorname{cosec}\theta}{\sqrt{2}}$, prove that

$$\left(\frac{1}{\sin\theta+\cos\theta}\right)^2 = \frac{\sec^2\theta}{2}.$$

Competency Based Question

59. Prove that $\frac{\operatorname{cosec}^2 x - \sin^2 x\cot^2 x - \cot^2 x}{\sin^2 x} = 1.$

60. Prove that $\left[\frac{1}{\sec^2\theta - \cos^2\theta} + \frac{1}{\operatorname{cosec}^2\theta - \sin^2\theta}\right]$

$$\sin^2\theta\cos^2\theta = \frac{1-\sin^2\theta\cos^2\theta}{2+\sin^2\theta\cos^2\theta}.$$

61. Prove that

$$\frac{(1+\cot\theta+\tan\theta)(\sin\theta-\cos\theta)}{\sec^3\theta - \operatorname{cosec}^3\theta} = \sin^2\theta\cos^2\theta.$$

62. If $\tan A = a\tan B$ and $\sin A = b\sin B$, prove that

$$\cos^2 A = \frac{b^2-1}{a^2-1}.$$

63. If $\operatorname{cosec}\theta - \sin\theta = m$ and $\sec\theta - \cos\theta = n$, then prove that $(m^2n)^{2/3} + (mn^2)^{2/3} = 1$.

64. If $\tan\theta + \sec\theta = l$, then prove that $\sec\theta = \frac{l^2+1}{2l}$.

NCERT Exemplar

65. If $\sec A = \frac{17}{8}$, show that $\frac{3-4\sin^2 A}{4\cos^2 A - 3} = \frac{3-\tan^2 A}{1-3\tan^2 A}$.

66. Show that $(\sin^8 A - \cos^8 A)$

$$= (2\sin^2 A - 1)(1 - 2\sin^2 A\cos^2 A).$$

67. If $\operatorname{cosec}\theta + \cot\theta = p$, then prove that $\cos\theta = \frac{p^2-1}{p^2+1}$.

NCERT Exemplar

68. Prove that $\frac{\cot A - \cos A}{\cot A + \cos A} = (\sec A - \tan A)^2$

CBSE 2024 (Basic) Compartment

69. If $\operatorname{cosec} A - \cot A = q$, show that $\frac{q^2-1}{q^2+1} + \cos A = 0.$

70. Prove that $2\sec^2\theta - \sec^4\theta - 2\operatorname{cosec}^2\theta$

$$+ \operatorname{cosec}^4\theta = \cot^4\theta - \tan^4\theta.$$

71. If $x = r\sin A\cos B$, $y = r\sin A\sin B$ and $z = r\cos A$, show that $x^2+y^2+z^2 = r^2$.

72. Prove that

$$\left(\tan\theta + \frac{1}{\cos\theta}\right)^2 + \left(\tan\theta - \frac{1}{\cos\theta}\right)^2 = 2\left(\frac{1+\sin^2\theta}{1-\sin^2\theta}\right).$$

73. Prove that $l^2m^2(l^2+m^2+3) = 1$, if $\operatorname{cosec}\theta - \sin\theta = l$ and $\sec\theta - \cos\theta = m$.

HINTS & SOLUTIONS

Part I

1. (b) Given, $\tan A = \frac{3}{4}$

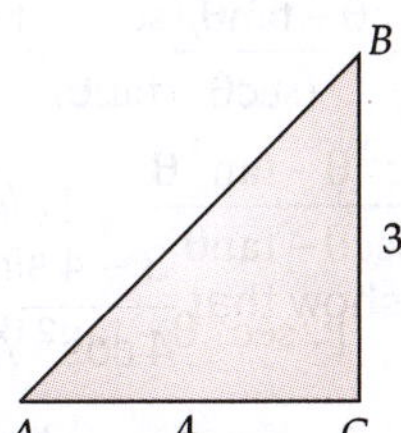

In right angled ΔABC,

$AB = 4$ and $BC = 3$

By Pythagoras theorem,

$$AC^2 = AB^2 + BC^2$$

$$\Rightarrow \quad AC^2 = (4)^2 + (3)^2$$

$$\Rightarrow \quad AC^2 = 16 + 9$$

$$\Rightarrow \quad AC = 5 \quad \text{[neglecting } -ve \text{ sign]}$$

$$\therefore \quad \sec A = \frac{AC}{AB} = \frac{5}{4}$$

Now, $\frac{(\sin^2 A + \cos^2 A)}{\sec A} = \frac{1}{\frac{5}{4}} = \frac{4}{5}$ $\quad [\because \sin^2 A + \cos^2 A = 1]$

2. (a) Given, $3 \cot A = 4$, where $0° < A < 90°$

$$\Rightarrow \quad \cot A = \frac{4}{3} = \frac{\text{Base}}{\text{Perpendicular}}$$

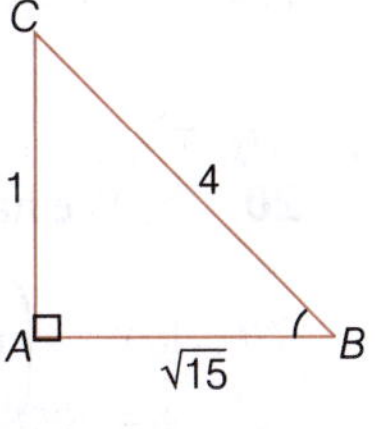

In right angled ΔABC, using Pythagoras theorem,

$$AB = \sqrt{16 + 9} \Rightarrow AB = 5$$

So, $\sec A = \frac{\text{Hypotenuse}}{\text{Base}}$

$$= \frac{AB}{AC} = \frac{5}{4}$$

3. (d) **Hint** $\sin B = \frac{1}{4} = \frac{\text{Perpendicular}}{\text{Hypotenuse}}$

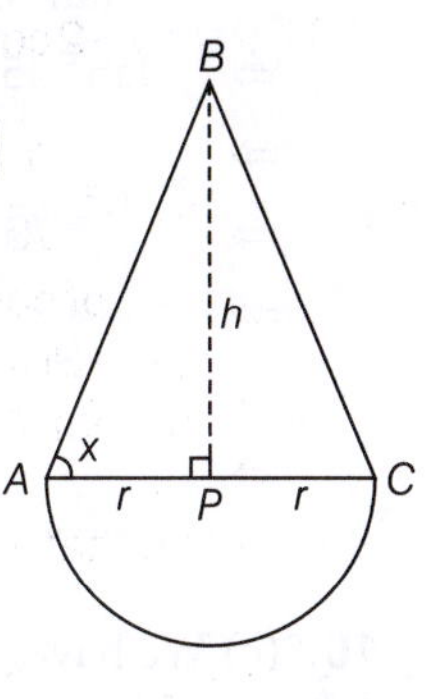

Use Pythagoras theorem and find base.

Base $= \sqrt{15}$

Now, $\sec B = \frac{\text{Hypotenuse}}{\text{Base}} = \frac{4}{\sqrt{15}}$

4. (c) In the isosceles ΔABC, BP is perpendicular to AC.

Let $BP = h$

Since, area of semi-circle = Area of triangle

$$\therefore \quad \frac{1}{2}\pi r^2 = \frac{1}{2} \cdot 2r \cdot h$$

$$\Rightarrow \quad \frac{1}{2}\pi r = h$$

[r = Radius of semi-circle]

$$\Rightarrow \quad h = \frac{\pi r}{2}$$

Now, $\tan x = \frac{\text{Perpendicular}}{\text{Base}} = \frac{h}{r}$

$$= \frac{\pi r}{2} \cdot \frac{1}{r}$$

$$\Rightarrow \quad \tan x = \frac{\pi}{2}$$

5. (a) We have, $\frac{1 - \tan^2 30°}{1 + \tan^2 30°} = \frac{1 - \left(\frac{1}{\sqrt{3}}\right)^2}{1 + \left(\frac{1}{\sqrt{3}}\right)^2}$ $\left[\because \tan 30° = \frac{1}{\sqrt{3}}\right]$

$$= \frac{1 - \frac{1}{3}}{1 + \frac{1}{3}} = \frac{2}{3} \times \frac{3}{4} = \frac{1}{2}$$

$$= \cos 60° \quad \left[\because \cos 60° = \frac{1}{2}\right]$$

6. (a) Given, $\cos(\alpha + \beta) = 0$

$$\Rightarrow \quad \cos(\alpha + \beta) = \cos 90° \quad [\because \cos 90° = 0]$$

$$\Rightarrow \quad \alpha + \beta = 90°$$

$$\therefore \quad \cos\left(\frac{\alpha + \beta}{2}\right) = \cos\left(\frac{90°}{2}\right)$$

$$= \cos 45°$$

$$= \frac{1}{\sqrt{2}}$$

7. (c) If $\theta = 45°$, then $\tan\theta + \cot\theta = 2$

Now, $\sin^3 45° + \cos^3 45°$ $\quad [\because \theta = 45°]$

$$= \left(\frac{1}{\sqrt{2}}\right)^3 + \left(\frac{1}{\sqrt{2}}\right)^3$$

$$= \frac{1}{2\sqrt{2}} + \frac{1}{2\sqrt{2}} = \frac{2}{2\sqrt{2}} = \frac{1}{\sqrt{2}} \times \frac{\sqrt{2}}{\sqrt{2}} = \frac{\sqrt{2}}{2}$$

8. (a) Given, $\cos\theta = \frac{\sqrt{3}}{2}$ and $\sin\phi = \frac{1}{2}$

Since, $\cos\theta = \frac{\sqrt{3}}{2} = \cos 30° \Rightarrow \theta = 30°$

and $\quad \sin\phi = \frac{1}{2} = \sin 30° \Rightarrow \phi = 30°$

$\because \tan(\theta + \phi) = \tan(30° + 30°) = \tan(60°) = \sqrt{3}$

$\therefore \tan(\theta + \phi) = \sqrt{3}$

9. (b) Given, $\theta = 45°$ and $0° \le \alpha \le 90°$

Now, we have

$$\tan^2\theta + \cot^2\alpha = 2$$
$$\Rightarrow \tan^2 45° + \cot^2\alpha = 2 \quad [\text{putting } \theta = 45°]$$
$$\Rightarrow 1 + \cot^2\alpha = 2$$
$$\Rightarrow \cot^2\alpha = 2 - 1$$
$$\Rightarrow \cot^2\alpha = 1$$
$$\Rightarrow \cot\alpha = 1$$
$$\Rightarrow \cot\alpha = \cot 45°$$
$$\Rightarrow \alpha = 45° \quad [\because 0° \le \alpha \le 90°]$$

10. (c) We have, $\sin^2\theta + \dfrac{1}{1+\tan^2\theta}$

$$= \sin^2\theta + \frac{1}{1+\dfrac{\sin^2\theta}{\cos^2\theta}}$$
$$= \sin^2\theta + \frac{\cos^2\theta}{\cos^2\theta + \sin^2\theta}$$
$$[\because \sin^2\theta + \cos^2\theta = 1]$$
$$= \sin^2\theta + \cos^2\theta$$
$$= 1$$

11. (c) Given, in ΔPQR,

$\angle Q = 90°$

and $\angle P = 45°$

So, $\angle R = 180° - (P + Q)$,

$\angle R = 180° - (90° + 45°)$

and $\angle R = 45°$

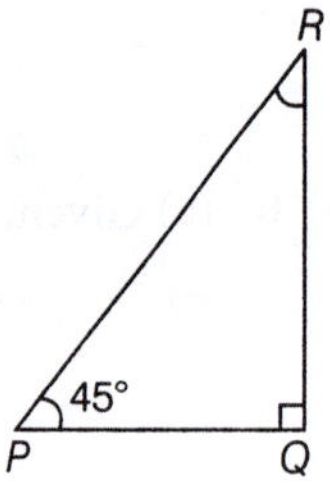

So, $\tan P - \cos^2 R = \tan 45° - \cos^2 45° \quad \left[\begin{array}{l}\because \tan 45° = 1 \text{ and} \\ \cos 45° = 1/\sqrt{2}\end{array}\right]$

$$= 1 - \left(\frac{1}{\sqrt{2}}\right)^2$$

$\therefore \tan P - \cos^2 R = 1/2$

12. (d) Using Pythagoras theorem in ΔPQR, we get

$PR = 8$ cm

Now, in ΔPRQ, $\tan Q = \dfrac{PR}{QR} = \dfrac{8}{6} = \dfrac{4}{3}$

13. (d) **Hint** Similar as Question 12. **Ans.** $\dfrac{16\sqrt{3}}{3}$

14. (d) We have, $\cos^4 A - \sin^4 A$

$$= (\cos^2 A + \sin^2 A)(\cos^2 A - \sin^2 A)$$
$$= 1(\cos^2 A - \sin^2 A) \quad [\because \sin^2\theta + \cos^2\theta = 1]$$
$$= \cos^2 A - (1 - \cos^2 A) = 2\cos^2 A - 1$$

15. (d) From option (a),

$$\sin\theta\cot\theta = \sin\theta \times \frac{\cos\theta}{\sin\theta} = \cos\theta$$

$\therefore$ Option (a) is true

From option (b), $\cos\theta\tan\theta = \cos\theta \times \dfrac{\sin\theta}{\cos\theta} = \sin\theta$

$\therefore$ Option (b) is true

From option (c), $\operatorname{cosec}^2\theta - \cot^2\theta = \dfrac{1}{\sin^2\theta} - \dfrac{\cos^2\theta}{\sin^2\theta}$

$$= \frac{1-\cos^2\theta}{\sin^2\theta} = \frac{\sin^2\theta}{\sin^2\theta} = 1$$
$$[\because \sin^2 A + \cos^2 A = 1]$$

$\therefore$ Option (c) is true.

16. (c) We have, $x\sin^3\theta + y\cos^3\theta = \sin\theta\cos\theta$

$$\Rightarrow (x\sin\theta)\sin^2\theta + (y\cos\theta)\cos^2\theta = \sin\theta\cos\theta$$
$$\Rightarrow x\sin\theta(\sin^2\theta) + (x\sin\theta)\cos^2\theta = \sin\theta\cos\theta$$
$$[\because y\cos\theta = x\sin\theta(\text{given})]$$
$$\Rightarrow x\sin\theta(\sin^2\theta + \cos^2\theta) = \sin\theta\cos\theta$$
$$\Rightarrow x\sin\theta = \sin\theta\cos\theta \quad [\because \sin^2\theta + \cos^2\theta = 1]$$
$$\Rightarrow x = \cos\theta$$

Now, $x\sin\theta = y\cos\theta$

$$\Rightarrow \cos\theta\sin\theta = y\cos\theta \Rightarrow y = \sin\theta$$

Hence, $x^2 + y^2 = \cos^2\theta + \sin^2\theta = 1$

17. (c) Given, $\sec\theta - \tan\theta = m$ ...(i)

We have,

$$\sec\theta + \tan\theta = \frac{(\sec\theta + \tan\theta)(\sec\theta - \tan\theta)}{(\sec\theta - \tan\theta)}$$
$$= \frac{\sec^2\theta - \tan^2\theta}{\sec\theta - \tan\theta} \quad [\because (a+b)(a-b) = a^2 - b^2]$$
$$= \frac{1}{m} \quad [\because \sec^2\theta - \tan^2\theta = 1 \text{ and using Eq. (i)}]$$

18. (d) Given, $\dfrac{\cos^2\theta}{\sin^2\theta} - \dfrac{1}{\sin^2\theta} = \dfrac{\cos^2\theta - 1}{\sin^2\theta} = \dfrac{-\sin^2\theta}{\sin^2\theta} = -1$

$$[\because \sin^2 A + \cos^2 A = 1 \Rightarrow \cos^2 A - 1 = -\sin^2 A]$$

19. (d) We know that, $\sec^2\theta - \tan^2\theta = 1$

$$\Rightarrow (\sec\theta - \tan\theta)(\sec\theta + \tan\theta) = 1$$
$$\Rightarrow \frac{1}{3}(\sec\theta + \tan\theta) = 1$$
$$\left[\because \text{given}, \sec\theta - \tan\theta = \frac{1}{3}\right]$$
$$\Rightarrow \sec\theta + \tan\theta = 3$$

20. (b) We have, $(1 + \tan^2 A)(1 + \sin A)(1 - \sin A)$

$$= \left(1 + \frac{\sin^2 A}{\cos^2 A}\right)(1 - \sin^2 A) \quad \left[\begin{array}{l}\because \tan A = \dfrac{\sin A}{\cos A}, \\ (a-b)(a+b) = a^2 - b^2\end{array}\right]$$
$$= \frac{\cos^2 A + \sin^2 A}{\cos^2 A}(1 - \sin^2 A)$$
$$= \frac{1}{\cos^2 A} \cdot \cos^2 A \quad \left[\begin{array}{l}\because \cos^2 A + \sin^2 A = 1 \text{ and} \\ \cos^2 A = 1 - \sin^2 A\end{array}\right]$$
$$= 1$$

21. (b) Given, $\sin\theta = \frac{3}{4}$

We know that $\sin^2\theta + \cos^2\theta = 1$

$\Rightarrow \quad \cos^2\theta = 1 - \sin^2\theta$

$\Rightarrow \quad \cos^2\theta = 1 - \left(\frac{3}{4}\right)^2 = 1 - \frac{9}{16} = \frac{7}{16}$

We know, $\sec^2\theta = \frac{1}{\cos^2\theta} = \frac{16}{7}$

Thus, $\frac{(\sec^2\theta - 1)\cos^2\theta}{\sin\theta} = \frac{\left(\frac{16}{7} - 1\right)\frac{7}{16}}{\frac{3}{4}} = \frac{9}{7} \times \frac{7}{16} \times \frac{4}{3} = \frac{3}{4}$

22. (b) $\sec\theta + \tan\theta = p$ ... (i)

$\therefore \quad \sec\theta - \tan\theta = \frac{1}{p}$ $[\because \sec^2 A - \tan^2 A = 1]$ ... (ii)

On subtracting Eq. (ii) from Eq. (i), we get

$2\tan\theta = p - \frac{1}{p}$

$\Rightarrow \quad \tan\theta = \frac{1}{2}\left[\frac{p^2 - 1}{p}\right]$

23. (c) Given, $\sin\theta = \frac{a}{b}$

We know that $\sin^2\theta + \cos^2\theta = 1 \Rightarrow \cos^2\theta = 1 - \frac{a^2}{b^2}$

$\Rightarrow \quad \cos\theta = \frac{\sqrt{b^2 - a^2}}{b}$

24. (a) We have, $a\cot\theta + b\,\text{cosec}\,\theta = p$,

$b\cot\theta + a\,\text{cosec}\,\theta = q$

After squaring both sides, we get

$a^2\cot^2\theta + b^2\text{cosec}^2\theta + 2ab\cot\theta\,\text{cosec}\,\theta = p^2$ ...(i)

$b^2\cot^2\theta + a^2\text{cosec}^2\theta + 2ab\cot\theta\,\text{cosec}\,\theta = q^2$ ...(ii)

Now, $p^2 - q^2 = (a^2 - b^2)\cot^2\theta - (a^2 - b^2)\,\text{cosec}^2\theta$

[using Eqs. (i) and (ii)]

$= (a^2 - b^2)(\cot^2\theta - \text{cosec}^2\theta)$

$[\because \cot^2\theta - \text{cosec}^2\theta = 1]$

$= a^2 - b^2$

25. (b) We know that

the trigonometric ratio of $\sin\theta$ in term of $\tan\theta$ is given by $\frac{\tan\theta}{\sqrt{1 + \tan^2\theta}}$ and the trigonometric ratio of $\sin\theta$ in term of $\cot\theta$ is $\frac{1}{\sqrt{\cot^2\theta + 1}}$.

Hence, Assertion and Reason both are correct but Reason is not correct explanation of Assertion.

26. (a) Since, $\sec^2\theta = \frac{4xy}{(x+y)^2} \geq 1$

$\Rightarrow \quad 4xy \geq (x+y)^2$

$\Rightarrow \quad x^2 + y^2 + 2xy - 4xy \leq 0$

$\Rightarrow \quad (x-y)^2 \leq 0 \Rightarrow x = y$

27. (a) Given, $\text{cosec}\,\theta - \cot\theta$

Reciprocal of this expression $= \frac{1}{\text{cosec}\,\theta - \cot\theta}$

On multiplying and dividing by $\text{cosec}\,\theta + \cot\theta$,

$\frac{1}{\text{cosec}\,\theta - \cot\theta} \times \frac{\text{cosec}\,\theta + \cot\theta}{\text{cosec}\,\theta + \cot\theta} = \frac{\text{cosec}\,\theta + \cot\theta}{\text{cosec}^2\theta - \cot^2\theta}$

$= \text{cosec}\,\theta + \cot\theta \quad [\because \text{cosec}^2\theta - \cot^2\theta = 1]$

28. (d) **Hint** We have,

$\cos^2 A - \sin^2 A = 1$

Put $A = 45°$, we get

$\cos^2 45° - \sin^2 45° = \left(\frac{1}{\sqrt{2}}\right)^2 - \left(\frac{1}{\sqrt{2}}\right)^2$

$= \frac{1}{2} - \frac{1}{2} = 0$

$\therefore$ This is not a trigonometry identity.

29.

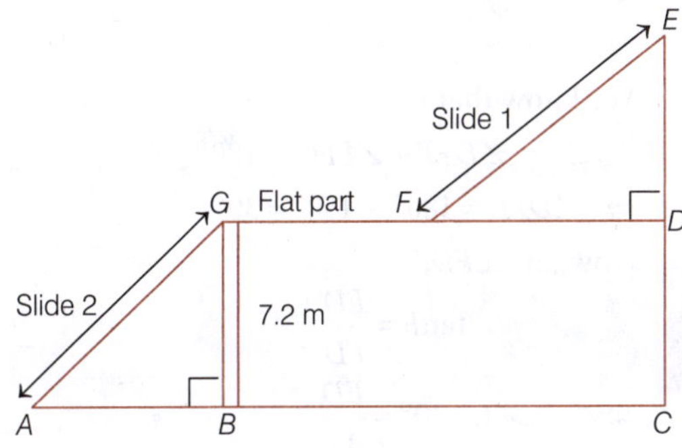

(i) In ΔAGB, $BG = 7.2$ m

and $AB = 2.4\sqrt{3}$ m

Now, $\tan A = \frac{BG}{AB}$

$= \frac{7.2}{2.4\sqrt{3}} = \frac{3}{\sqrt{3}}$

$= \sqrt{3} = \tan 60°$

$A = 60°$

Hence, the angle between slide 2 and ground is 60°.

(ii) In ΔAGB, $BG = 7.2$ m

and length of slide 2 $(AG) = 12$ m

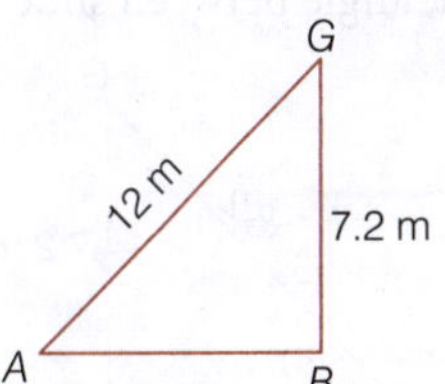

By Pythagoras theorem,

$$AG^2 = AB^2 + BG^2$$

$$\Rightarrow \quad AB^2 = AG^2 - BG^2$$

$$= (12)^2 - (7.2)^2$$

$$= 144 - 51.84$$

$$= 92.16$$

$$\Rightarrow \quad AB = 9.6 \text{ m}$$

Now, $\tan x = \frac{AB}{BG}$ $\quad [\because \angle AGB = x]$

$$= \frac{9.6}{7.2} = \frac{4}{3}$$

(iii) (a) Given, $FD = 17$ m

and $\angle EFG = 150°$

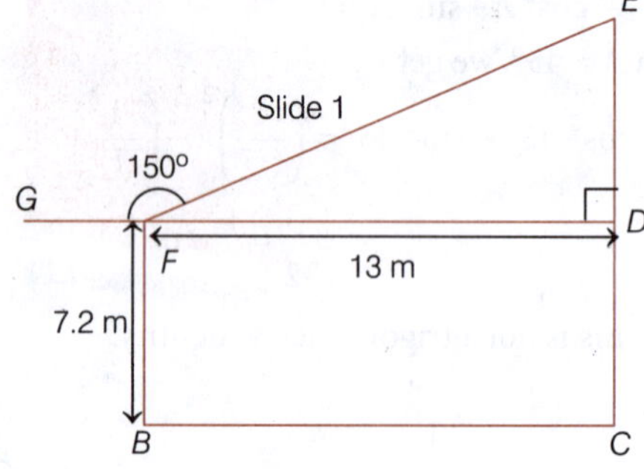

We know that

$$\angle DFE + \angle EFG = 180°$$

$$\Rightarrow \angle DFE = 180° - 150° = 30°$$

Now, in ΔEFD,

$$\tan F = \frac{ED}{FD}$$

$$\Rightarrow \quad \tan 30° = \frac{ED}{17}$$

$$\Rightarrow \quad \frac{1}{\sqrt{3}} = \frac{ED}{17}$$

$$\Rightarrow \quad \frac{1}{1.7} = \frac{ED}{17}$$

$$\Rightarrow \quad ED = 10 \text{ m}$$

Thus, the height of the top point of slide 1 from ground

$$= CD + DE$$

$$= 7.2 + 10 = 17.2 \text{ m}$$

Or

(b) Given, angle between slide 2 and ground = 30°

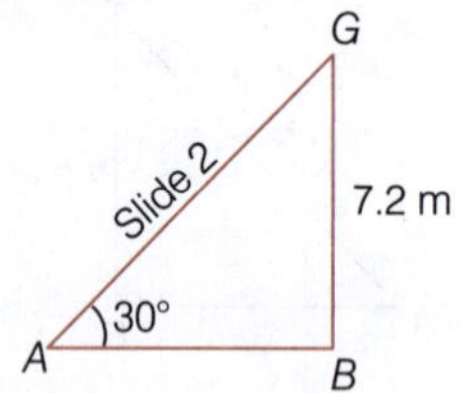

In ΔGAB,

$$BG = 7.2 \text{ m and } \angle GAB = 30°$$

$$\because \sin 30° = \frac{7.2}{AG} \Rightarrow \frac{1}{2} = \frac{7.2}{AG}$$

$$\therefore \quad AG = 14.4 \text{ m}$$

Hence, the length of slide 2 is 14.4 m.

30. (i) The value of $\sin A$ increases as the measure of $\angle A$ increases. It reaches to 1, when the person comes directly under the camera.

(ii) Given, $AB = BC$

and $\angle B = 90°$

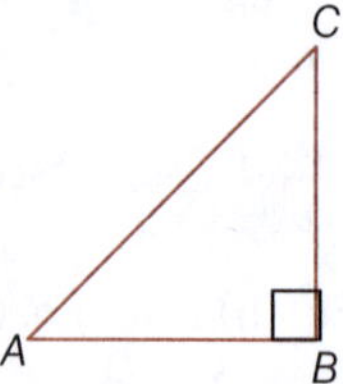

Therefore, ΔABC is an isosceles triangle.

i.e. $\quad \angle A = \angle C$

$$\therefore \angle A + \angle B + \angle C = 180°$$

$$\Rightarrow \angle A + 90° + \angle A = 180° \quad [\because \angle A = \angle C]$$

$$\Rightarrow \quad \angle A = 45°$$

and $\quad \angle C = 45°$

$$\therefore \sin A = \sin 45° = \frac{1}{\sqrt{2}}$$

(iii) (a) Given, ΔABC is right angled at B.

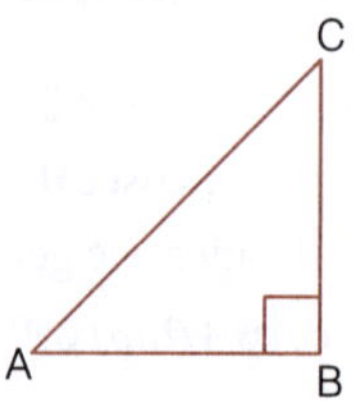

$$\because \angle A + \angle B + \angle C = 180°$$

$$\Rightarrow \quad \angle A + \angle C = 90°$$

$$\therefore \quad \sin(A + C) = \sin 90° = 1$$

Or

(b) Given, ΔABC is isosceles right angled triangle at B.

$$\therefore \angle A = \angle C = 45°$$

Now, LHS $= \frac{\tan A + \tan C}{1 + 2\sin A \cos C}$

$$= \frac{\tan 45° + \tan 45°}{1 + 2\sin 45° \cos 45°}$$

$$= \frac{1+1}{1 + 2\left(\frac{1}{\sqrt{2}}\right)\left(\frac{1}{\sqrt{2}}\right)}$$

$= \frac{2}{2} = 1 =$ RHS **Hence proved.**

Part II

1. Given, $\tan A = \frac{3}{4}$

$\Rightarrow \quad \tan A = \frac{P}{B} = \frac{3}{4}$

Let $\quad P = 3k$ and $B = 4k$

As $\quad H = \sqrt{(3k)^2 + (4k)^2} = 5k$

Now, $\quad \sin A = \frac{P}{H} = \frac{3k}{5k} = \frac{3}{5}$

and $\quad \cos A = \frac{B}{H} = \frac{4k}{5k} = \frac{4}{5}$

$\therefore \frac{1}{\sin A} + \frac{1}{\cos A} = \frac{5}{3} + \frac{5}{4} = \frac{20+15}{12} = \frac{35}{12}$

2. Hint $\tan\theta = \frac{4}{7}$,

Now, on dividing numerator and denominator by $\cos\theta$ in given expression, we get

$$\frac{7\tan\theta - 3}{7\tan\theta + 3}$$

Then, put value of $\tan\theta$ and simplify.

Ans. $\frac{1}{7}$

3. Hint $\sqrt{3}\tan\theta = 3\sin\theta \Rightarrow \frac{\sqrt{3}\sin\theta}{\cos\theta} - 3\sin\theta = 0$

$\Rightarrow \sqrt{3}\sin\theta\left(\frac{1}{\cos\theta} - \sqrt{3}\right) = 0$

$\Rightarrow \quad \sin\theta = 0$ or $\cos\theta = \frac{1}{\sqrt{3}}$

$\Rightarrow \sin\theta = 0$ or $\sin\theta = \sqrt{1-\cos^2\theta} = \sqrt{\frac{2}{3}}$

Now, put value of $\sin\theta$ after rewriting the given expression as $2\sin^2\theta - 1$ **Ans.** -1 or $\frac{1}{3}$.

4. $\sin^2 60° + 2\tan 45° - \cos^2 30°$

$= \left(\frac{\sqrt{3}}{2}\right)^2 + 2(1)^2 - \left(\frac{\sqrt{3}}{2}\right)^2$

$= \frac{3}{4} + 2 - \frac{3}{4} = 2$

5. Hint Given, $\sin\alpha = \frac{1}{2}$ and $\cos\beta = \frac{1}{2}$

$\Rightarrow \quad \sin\alpha = \sin 30° \quad \left[\because \sin 30° = \frac{1}{2}\right]$

and $\quad \cos\beta = \cos 60° \quad \left[\because \cos 60° = \frac{1}{2}\right]$

$\Rightarrow \quad \alpha = 30°$ and $\beta = 60°$

$\therefore \quad \alpha + \beta = 30° + 60° = 90°$

Ans. 90°

6. Hint Express $\sec A$ and $\tan A$ in terms of $\sin A$ and $\cos A$, then use $\cos^2\theta = 1 - \sin^2\theta$

7. Hint $\cos A = 1 - \cos^2 A \Rightarrow \cos A = \sin^2 A$ **Ans.** 1

8. $x + y = 2\sin^2\theta + 2\cos^2\theta + 1 = 2[\sin^2\theta + \cos^2\theta] + 1$

$= 2 + 1 \quad [\because \sin^2 A + \cos^2 A = 1]$

$= 3$

9. Hint $4x = \operatorname{cosec}\theta \Rightarrow x = \frac{\operatorname{cosec}\theta}{4}$

and $\frac{4}{x} = \cot\theta \Rightarrow \frac{1}{x} = \frac{\cot\theta}{4}$

Now, $4\left[x^2 - \frac{1}{x^2}\right] = 4\left[\left(\frac{\operatorname{cosec}\theta}{4}\right)^2 - \left(\frac{\cot\theta}{4}\right)^2\right]$

Ans. 1/4

10. Hint Put the value of $\tan A$ in LHS and simplify.

11. Hint First do same as Question 1 of NCERT Folder Exercise 8.1, then put value of $\cos\theta$ and $\sin\theta$ in given expression.

Ans. $\frac{41}{841}$, 1

12. Given statement, $\cos A = \sqrt{2}$

Where, A is an acute angle.

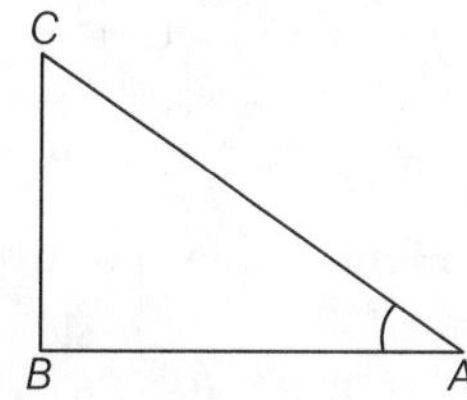

In right angled triangle,

$$\cos A = \frac{AB}{AC}$$

$\because \quad AC > AB$

[as length of hypotenuse is greater than other two sides in a right angled triangle]

$\therefore \quad \frac{AB}{AC} < 1$

$\Rightarrow \quad \cos A < 1$

But $\sqrt{2} \not< 1$

Hence, the statement is false.

13. Given, $\cos A = \frac{5}{13} = \frac{\text{Base}(B)}{\text{Hypotenuse}(H)}$

By Pythagoras theorem, we get

$H^2 = P^2 + B^2$

$\Rightarrow \quad (13)^2 = P^2 + (5)^2$

$\Rightarrow \quad 169 = P^2 + 25 \Rightarrow 169 - 25 = P^2$

$\Rightarrow \quad 144 = P^2 \Rightarrow P = 12$

Now, we have to verify that

$$\frac{\cos A}{1-\tan A}+\frac{\sin A}{1-\cot A}=\cos A+\sin A$$

$$\text{LHS}=\frac{\cos A}{1-\tan A}+\frac{\sin A}{1-\cot A}$$

$$=\frac{\frac{5}{13}}{1-\frac{12}{5}}+\frac{\frac{12}{13}}{1-\frac{5}{12}}$$

$$=\frac{\frac{5}{13}}{\frac{5-12}{5}}+\frac{\frac{12}{13}}{\frac{12-5}{12}}=\frac{5}{13}\times\left(-\frac{5}{7}\right)+\frac{12}{13}\times\frac{12}{7}$$

$$=-\frac{25}{91}+\frac{144}{91}=\frac{119}{91}=\frac{17}{13}$$

$$\text{RHS}=\cos A+\sin A$$

$$=\frac{5}{13}+\frac{12}{13}=\frac{17}{13}$$

LHS = RHS **Hence proved.**

14. Hint Given, $\angle CBA=90°$, $\angle BRS=90°$, $\angle BSC=90°$, $BC=7.5$ cm, $RS=5$ cm, $BR=6$ cm and $AB=18$ cm

Then, $AR=AB-RB=18-6=12$ cm

In ΔARS, using Pythagoras theorem, we get

$$AS^2=AR^2+RS^2=(12)^2+(5)^2$$

$$\Rightarrow \quad AS^2=144+25=169$$

$$\Rightarrow \quad AS=\sqrt{169}$$

$\therefore$ $AS=13$ cm [taking positive square root since, side cannot be negative]

(i) In ΔBRS, $\tan x=\frac{P}{B}=\frac{BR}{RS}=\frac{6}{5}$

(ii) In ΔARS, $\sin y=\frac{P}{H}=\frac{SR}{AS}=\frac{5}{13}$

(iii) In ΔARS, $\cos y=\frac{B}{H}=\frac{AR}{AS}=\frac{12}{13}$

15. Hint Do same as Example 5 of Topic 1. **Ans.** $\frac{31}{25}$

16. Hint Use $\tan\theta=\frac{P}{B}$ and $BC=2CD$. **Ans.** 2

17. Hint Given, $\tan\theta+\frac{1}{\tan\theta}=2$

On squaring both sides, we get

$$\left(\tan\theta+\frac{1}{\tan\theta}\right)^2=(2)^2 \quad \textbf{Ans. } 2$$

18. Hint Use $\sec A=\frac{1}{\cos A}$, $\tan A=\frac{\sin A}{\cos A}$ and $\operatorname{cosec} A=\frac{1}{\sin A}$ in LHS of given equation and simplify.

19. Hint Let $\cot\theta=x$

So, the given equation can be rewritten as

$$\sqrt{3}x^2-4x+\sqrt{3}=0$$

Using quadratic formula, we get

$$x=\sqrt{3},\frac{1}{\sqrt{3}} \text{ i.e. } \cot\theta=\sqrt{3},\frac{1}{\sqrt{3}}$$

So, $\tan\theta=\frac{1}{\sqrt{3}},\sqrt{3}$. **Ans.** $\frac{10}{3}$

20. Hint Since, $\tan\theta=1$ and $\sin\phi=\frac{1}{\sqrt{2}}$,

$\therefore$ $\theta=45°$ and $\phi=45°$

Now, $\cos(\theta+\phi)=\cos(45°+45°)=\cos(90°)=0$

21. We have,

$$3\tan^2 60°-x\sin^2 45°+\frac{3}{4}\sec^2 30°=2\operatorname{cosec}^2 30°$$

$$\Rightarrow 3\times(\sqrt{3})^2-x\times\left(\frac{1}{\sqrt{2}}\right)^2+\frac{3}{4}\times\left(\frac{2}{\sqrt{3}}\right)^2=2\times(2)^2$$

$$\Rightarrow \quad 3\times3-x\times\frac{1}{2}+\frac{3}{4}\times\frac{4}{3}=2\times4$$

$$\Rightarrow \quad 9-\frac{x}{2}+1=8$$

$$\Rightarrow \quad 10-\frac{x}{2}=8$$

$$\Rightarrow \quad 10-8=\frac{x}{2}\Rightarrow x=4$$

22. (i) Given, $\sin(A-B)=\frac{1}{2}$

$$\Rightarrow \quad \sin(A-B)=\sin 30°$$

$$\Rightarrow \quad A-B=30° \quad \ldots\text{(i)}$$

and $\quad \cos(A+B)=0$

$$\Rightarrow \quad \cos(A+B)=\cos 90°$$

$$\Rightarrow \quad A+B=90° \quad \ldots\text{(ii)}$$

On solving Eqs. (i) and (ii), we get

$$A=60° \text{ and } B=30°$$

Navdeep Saini and Jaspreet Bumrah throwing ball at an angle of 60° and 30°, respectively.

(ii) $\tan A=\sqrt{3}$, cosec $(A-B)=2$ and $\sec B=\frac{2}{\sqrt{3}}$

23. (i) We know that the maximum value of $\sin\theta$ is 1.

$$\because \quad \sin\theta_1+\sin\theta_2+\sin\theta_3=3$$

$$\Rightarrow \quad \sin\theta_1=\sin\theta_2=\sin\theta_3=1$$

$$\Rightarrow \quad \theta_1=\theta_2=\theta_3=90°$$

Now, $\cos\theta_1+\cos\theta_2+\cos\theta_3$

$$=\cos 90°+\cos 90°+\cos 90°$$

$$=0+0+0=0$$

(ii) **Hint** $225°-\theta_1-\theta_2=225°-90°-90°=45°$

Ans. 1

(iii) **Hint** $120°-\theta_3=120°-90°=30°$ **Ans.** $\frac{1}{2}$

24. Hint Given, $\tan A = 2/3, \tan B = 3/2$

Since, $\tan(A+B) = \dfrac{\tan A + \tan B}{1 - \tan A \tan B}$

$$\tan(A+B) = \frac{2/3 + 3/2}{1 - 2/3 \cdot 3/2} = \frac{(4+9)/6}{0}$$

$$\tan(A+B) = \frac{13}{0} = \infty$$

$$A + B = 90°$$

25. Hint Do same as Example 6 of Topic 2

Ans. $A = 45°, B = 15°$

26. Hint $\sec\theta = \sqrt{1+\tan^2\theta} = \sqrt{1+\left(\frac{20}{21}\right)^2} = \sqrt{1+\frac{(20)^2}{(21)^2}} = \frac{29}{21}$

On dividing numerator and denominator of LHS by $\cos\theta$, we get $\dfrac{\sec\theta - \tan\theta + 1}{\sec\theta + \tan\theta + 1}$.

Now, put the value of $\sec\theta$ and $\tan\theta$ then simplify.

27. Hint LHS $= \dfrac{1}{1+\sin\theta} + \dfrac{1}{1-\sin\theta} = \dfrac{1-\sin\theta + 1 + \sin\theta}{(1+\sin\theta)(1-\sin\theta)}$

$$= \frac{2}{(1-\sin^2\theta)} = \frac{2}{\cos^2\theta} \quad [\because 1-\sin^2 A = \cos^2 A]$$

$= 2\sec^2\theta = \text{RHS}$ **Hence proved.**

28. Given, $\sin^2 A + \cos^2 A = 1$ ...(i)

On dividing Eq. (i) by $\cos^2 A$, we get

$$\frac{\sin^2 A}{\cos^2 A} + \frac{\cos^2 A}{\cos^2 A} = \frac{1}{\cos^2 A}$$

$\Rightarrow \tan^2 A + 1 = \sec^2 A$ **Hence proved.**

$$\left[\because \tan\theta = \frac{\sin\theta}{\cos\theta} \text{ and } \sec\theta = \frac{1}{\cos\theta}\right]$$

Also, given $\sec A = \dfrac{5}{3}$

On squaring both sides, we get

$$\sec^2 A = \left(\frac{5}{3}\right)^2$$

$$\Rightarrow \sec^2 A = \frac{25}{9}$$

We know that

$$\tan^2 A + 1 = \sec^2 A$$

$$\therefore \tan A = \sqrt{\sec^2 A - 1}$$

$$= \sqrt{\frac{25}{9} - 1} = \sqrt{\frac{16}{9}}$$

$$\therefore \tan A = \frac{4}{3} \quad [\because A \text{ is an acute angle}]$$

29. Hint In LHS add and subtract the term $(2\sin^2\theta\cos^2\theta)$ in the numerator and then simplify the expression and use $\sin^2\theta + \cos^2\theta = 1$.

30. Hint Given, $\dfrac{\sin^3\theta + \cos^3\theta}{\sin\theta + \cos\theta} + \sin\theta\cos\theta$

$$= \frac{(\sin\theta + \cos\theta)(\sin^2\theta + \cos^2\theta - \sin\theta\cos\theta)}{(\sin\theta + \cos\theta)} + (\sin\theta\cos\theta)$$

$$[\because a^3 + b^3 = (a^2 - ab + b^2)(a+b)]$$

Ans. 1

31. LHS $= \dfrac{\cot A - \cos A}{\cot A + \cos A} = \dfrac{\frac{\cos A}{\sin A} - \cos A}{\frac{\cos A}{\sin A} + \cos A}$ $\left[\because \cot A = \dfrac{\cos A}{\sin A}\right]$

$$= \frac{\cos A - \cos A \sin A}{\cos A + \cos A \sin A} = \frac{\cos A(1-\sin A)}{\cos A(1+\sin A)}$$

$$= \frac{(1-\sin A)}{(1+\sin A)}\frac{(1+\sin A)}{(1+\sin A)} = \frac{1-\sin^2 A}{(1+\sin A)^2}$$

$= \dfrac{\cos^2 A}{(1+\sin A)^2} = \text{RHS}$ **Hence proved.**

32. LHS $= \dfrac{\cot\theta + \operatorname{cosec}\theta - 1}{\cot\theta - \operatorname{cosec}\theta + 1}$

$$= \frac{(\cot\theta + \operatorname{cosec}\theta) - (\operatorname{cosec}^2\theta - \cot^2\theta)}{\cot\theta - \operatorname{cosec}\theta + 1}$$

$$[\because \operatorname{cosec}^2 A - \cot^2 A = 1]$$

$$= \frac{(\operatorname{cosec}\theta + \cot\theta)\{1 - (\operatorname{cosec}\theta - \cot\theta)\}}{\cot\theta - \operatorname{cosec}\theta + 1}$$

$$= \frac{(\operatorname{cosec}\theta + \cot\theta)(1 - \operatorname{cosec}\theta + \cot\theta)}{\cot\theta - \operatorname{cosec}\theta + 1}$$

$$= \operatorname{cosec}\theta + \cot\theta = \frac{1}{\sin\theta} + \frac{\cos\theta}{\sin\theta} = \frac{1+\cos\theta}{\sin\theta} = \text{RHS}$$

33. Hint Given, $\sin^6 A + \cos^6 A + 3\sin^2 A\cos^2 A + 4 = k$

$$[\because a^3 + b^3 = (a+b)^3 - 3ab(a+b)]$$

$$(\sin^2 A)^3 + (\cos^2 A)^3 + 3\sin^2 A\cos^2 A + 4$$

$$= (\sin^2 A + \cos^2 A)^3 - 3\sin^2 A\cos^2 A(\sin^2 A + \cos^2 A) + 3\sin^2 A\cos^2 A + 4$$

$$= 1 - 3\sin^2 A\cos^2 A + 3\sin^2 A\cos^2 A + 4 = 5$$

$$[\because \sin^2 A + \cos^2 A = 1]$$

Ans. $k = 5$

34. Hint $\sec\theta = x + \dfrac{1}{4x}$

$$\Rightarrow \sec^2\theta = x^2 + \left(\frac{1}{4x}\right)^2 + 2\cdot x\cdot\frac{1}{4x}$$

$$\Rightarrow \sec^2\theta - 1 = x^2 + \frac{1}{16x^2} - \frac{1}{2}$$

$$\Rightarrow \tan^2\theta = \left(x - \frac{1}{4x}\right)^2$$

$$\Rightarrow \tan\theta = \pm\left(x - \frac{1}{4x}\right)$$

Ans. $2x, 1/2x$

35. Hint Do same as Question 34.

36. Hint Use $\sec\theta = \frac{1}{\cos\theta}$ and $\operatorname{cosec}\theta = \frac{1}{\sin\theta}$ in LHS

and $\tan\theta = \frac{\sin\theta}{\cos\theta}, \cot\theta = \frac{\cos\theta}{\sin\theta}$ in RHS

37. (i) **Hint** First we have, $\sec\theta = \frac{x}{a}$ and $\tan\theta = \frac{y}{b}$,

then use $\sec^2\theta - \tan^2\theta = 1$ **Ans.** $\frac{x^2}{a^2} - \frac{y^2}{b^2} = 1$

(ii) **Hint** First we have, $\cos\theta = \frac{x-k}{a}, \sin\theta = \frac{y-h}{b}$,

then use $\sin^2\theta + \cos^2\theta = 1$

Ans. $\frac{(x-k)^2}{a^2} + \frac{(y-h)^2}{b^2} = 1$

38. Hint Given, $m\sin\theta + n\cos\theta = p$ ...(i)

$m\cos\theta - n\sin\theta = q$ ...(ii)

On squaring Eqs.(i) and (ii) and adding them, we get

$$(m\sin\theta + n\cos\theta)^2 + (m\cos\theta - n\sin)^2 = p^2 + q^2$$

Now, simplify the above equation to get the required expression.

39. Hint Simplify LHS and RHS separately and use $\sin^2\theta + \cos^2\theta = 1$

40. Hint Given, $7\sin^2 A + 3\cos^2 A = 4$

$\Rightarrow \cos^2 A(7\tan^2 A + 3) = 4$

$\Rightarrow 7\tan^2 A + 3 = 4\sec^2 A$

Now use, $\sec^2 A - \tan^2 A = 1$

41. Hint Given, $\cos\theta + \sin\theta = \sqrt{2}\cos\theta$

On squaring both sides, we get

$\cos^2\theta + \sin^2\theta + 2\sin\theta\cos\theta = 2\cos^2\theta$

$\Rightarrow \sin^2\theta = \cos^2\theta - 2\sin\theta\cos\theta$

$\Rightarrow \sin^2\theta + \sin^2\theta = \cos^2\theta - 2\sin\theta\cos\theta + \sin^2\theta$

$\Rightarrow 2\sin^2\theta = (\cos\theta - \sin\theta)^2$

42. Given that $a\sin\theta + b\cos\theta = c$

On squaring both sides of above equation, we get

$$(a\sin\theta + b\cos\theta)^2 = c^2$$

$\Rightarrow a^2\sin^2\theta + b^2\cos^2\theta + 2ab\sin\theta\cos\theta = c^2$

$\Rightarrow a^2(1-\cos^2\theta) + b^2(1-\sin^2\theta) + 2ab\sin\theta\cos\theta = c^2$

$\Rightarrow a^2 - a^2\cos^2\theta + b^2 - b^2\sin^2\theta + 2ab\sin\theta\cos\theta = c^2$

$\Rightarrow a^2 + b^2 - c^2 = a^2\cos^2\theta + b^2\sin^2\theta - 2ab\sin\theta\cos\theta$

$\Rightarrow (a\cos\theta - b\sin\theta)^2 = a^2 + b^2 - c^2$

$\Rightarrow a\cos\theta - b\sin\theta = \pm\sqrt{a^2 + b^2 - c^2}$ **Hence proved.**

43. Hint Divide numerator and denominator by $\cos A$ and use the identity $\sec^2 A - \tan^2 A = 1$ to get the desired result.

44. Hint Given $\cos\theta - \sin\theta = x$ ...(i)

$\sin\theta + \cos\theta = y$ ...(ii)

On squaring Eq. (i) and (ii) both side, we get

$\cos^2\theta + \sin^2\theta - 2\sin\theta\cos\theta = x^2$

$\sin^2\theta + \cos^2\theta + 2\sin\theta\cos\theta = y^2$

Now, $x^2 + y^2 = 2\cos^2\theta + 2\sin^2\theta - 2\sin\theta\cos\theta + 2\sin\theta\cos\theta$

$= 2(\cos^2\theta + \sin^2\theta)$

$= 2$ $[\because \sin^2\theta + \cos^2\theta = 1]$

45. Hint Put the values of m and n in LHS and RHS of given equation separately and show the equality.

46. Hint Convert $\sec x$ and $\tan x$ into $\sin x$ and $\cos x$ using, $\sec x = \frac{1}{\cos x}$ and $\tan x = \frac{\sin x}{\cos x}$ in both LHS and RHS separately and simplify.

47. Hint First, simplify the LHS of given equation using $(a+b)^2 = a^2 + 2ab + b^2$ and $(a-b)^2 = a^2 - 2ab + b^2$, then use $1 + \tan^2\theta = \sec^2\theta$.

48. Hint $(a\cos\theta - b\sin\theta)^2 + (a\sin\theta + b\cos\theta)^2$

$= (a^2\cos^2\theta + b^2\sin^2\theta - 2ab\sin\theta\cos\theta)$

$+ (a^2\sin^2\theta + b^2\cos^2\theta + 2ab\sin\theta\cos\theta)$

$\Rightarrow c^2 + (a\sin\theta + b\cos\theta)^2 = a^2 + b^2$

49. Hint Given, $\sin\theta + 2\cos\theta = 1$

On squaring both sides, we get

$\sin^2\theta + 4\cos^2\theta + 4\sin\theta\cos\theta = \sin^2\theta + \cos^2\theta$

$\Rightarrow \sin^2\theta + 4\cos^2\theta = \sin^2\theta + \cos^2\theta - 4\sin\theta\cos\theta$

$\Rightarrow 4\sin^2\theta + 4\cos^2\theta = 4\sin^2\theta + \cos^2\theta - 4\sin\theta\cos\theta$

[$\because$ adding $3\sin^2\theta$ both sides]

$\Rightarrow 4(\sin^2\theta + \cos^2\theta) = (2\sin\theta - \cos\theta)^2$

50. Hint Use, $\cos^2\theta = 1 - \sin^2\theta$ to find $\cos A$ and $\cos B$.

51. Hint Let LHS $= \frac{1}{\cos^2 A} - \frac{\sin^2 A(1 - 2\sin^2 A)}{\cos^2 A(2\cos^2 A - 1)}$

$\left[\because \sec^2\theta = \frac{1}{\cos^2\theta}\right]$

$= \frac{1}{\cos^2 A} - \frac{\sin^2 A[1 - 2(1 - \cos^2 A)]}{\cos^2 A(2\cos^2 A - 1)}$

$[\because \sin^2\theta = 1 - \cos^2\theta]$

52. Hint Given, $1+\sin^2\theta = 3\sin\theta\cos\theta$

[dividing both sides by $\cos^2\theta$]

$\Rightarrow \quad \sec^2\theta + \tan^2\theta = 3\tan\theta$

$\Rightarrow \quad 2\tan^2\theta - 3\tan\theta + 1 = 0 \quad [\because \sec^2\theta = 1+\tan^2\theta]$

Let, $\tan\theta = x$, so above equation becomes $2x^2 - 3x + 1$.

Solve for $x = \tan\theta$ using quadratic formula.

53. Given, $5\sin P = 4$

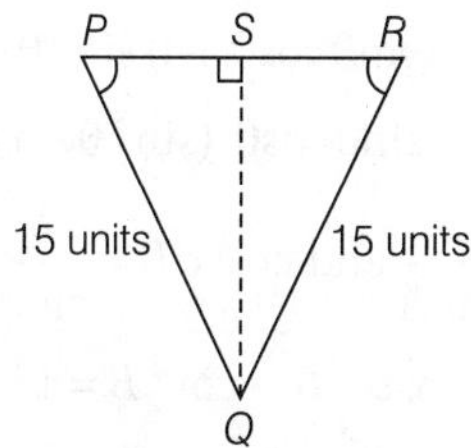

From figure, in ΔPSQ

$$\sin P = \frac{SQ}{PQ}$$

$$\Rightarrow \quad SQ = PQ \times \sin P = 15 \times 4/5 = 12 \text{ units}$$

By Pythagoras theorem, we get

$$PS^2 = PQ^2 - SQ^2 = 15^2 - 12^2 = 225 - 144 = 81$$

So, $PS = 9$

So, length of $PR = 2 \times 9 = 18$ units.

54. In ΔHGC,

By Pythagoras theorem,

$$CH^2 = CG^2 + GH^2$$

$$\Rightarrow \quad CH^2 = l^2 + b^2$$

$$\Rightarrow \quad CH = \sqrt{l^2+b^2}$$

Now, in ΔCHE

$$CE^2 = CH^2 + HE^2 = (\sqrt{l^2+b^2})^2 + h^2$$

$$\Rightarrow \quad CE^2 = l^2 + b^2 + h^2$$

$$\Rightarrow \quad CE = \sqrt{l^2+b^2+h^2}$$

(i) $\cos\theta = \dfrac{\text{Base}}{\text{Hypotenuse}} = \dfrac{CH}{CE} = \dfrac{\sqrt{l^2+b^2}}{\sqrt{l^2+b^2+h^2}}$

(ii) In cube, all sides are equal. So, $l = b = h$

$$\therefore \quad \cos\theta = \frac{\sqrt{l^2+l^2}}{\sqrt{l^2+l^2+l^2}} = \sqrt{\frac{2}{3}}$$

55. Hint Use $\cot A = \dfrac{\cos A}{\sin A}$ and $\sec A = \dfrac{1}{\cos A}$ in LHS of given equation and simplify it.

56. To prove $\dfrac{\sin A - 2\sin^3 A}{2\cos^3 A - \cos A} = \tan A$

$$\text{Let LHS} = \frac{\sin A - 2\sin^3 A}{2\cos^3 A - \cos A} = \frac{\sin A(1-2\sin^2 A)}{\cos A(2\cos^2 A - 1)}$$

$$= \frac{\sin A(\sin^2 A + \cos^2 A - 2\sin^2 A)}{\cos A(2\cos^2 A - (\sin^2 A + \cos^2 A))}$$

$[\because \sin^2 A + \cos^2 A = 1]$

$$= \frac{\sin A(\cos^2 A - \sin^2 A)}{\cos A(\cos^2 A - \sin^2 A)}$$

$= \tan A =$ RHS **Hence proved.**

57. Given, $\dfrac{1}{\operatorname{cosec}\theta - \cot\theta} - \dfrac{\cot\theta}{\cos\theta} = \cot\theta$

$$\text{Taking LHS} = \frac{1}{\operatorname{cosec}\theta - \cot\theta} - \frac{\cot\theta}{\cos\theta}$$

$$= \frac{1}{\frac{1}{\sin\theta} - \frac{\cos\theta}{\sin\theta}} - \frac{\cos\theta}{\sin\theta\cos\theta}$$

$\left[\because \operatorname{cosec}\theta = \dfrac{1}{\sin\theta} \text{ and } \cot\theta = \dfrac{\cos\theta}{\sin\theta}\right]$

$$= \frac{\sin\theta}{1-\cos\theta} - \frac{1}{\sin\theta}$$

$$= \frac{\sin^2\theta - 1 + \cos\theta}{\sin\theta(1-\cos\theta)}$$

$$= \frac{1-\cos^2\theta - 1 + \cos\theta}{\sin\theta(1-\cos\theta)} \quad [\because \sin^2\theta = 1-\cos^2\theta]$$

$$= \frac{\cos\theta(1-\cos\theta)}{\sin\theta(1-\cos\theta)} = \frac{\cos\theta}{\sin\theta}$$

$= \cot\theta$

$=$ RHS

58. Given, $\dfrac{1}{\sin\theta - \cos\theta} = \dfrac{\operatorname{cosec}\theta}{\sqrt{2}}$

On squaring both sides, we get

$$\frac{1}{\sin^2\theta + \cos^2\theta - 2\sin\theta\cos\theta} = \frac{\operatorname{cosec}^2\theta}{2}$$

$[\because (a-b)^2 = a^2 + b^2 - 2ab]$

$$\Rightarrow \quad \frac{1}{1-2\sin\theta\cos\theta} = \frac{\operatorname{cosec}^2\theta}{2}$$

$[\because \sin^2\theta + \cos^2\theta = 1]$

$$\Rightarrow \frac{2}{\operatorname{cosec}^2\theta} = 1 - 2\sin\theta\cos\theta$$

$$\Rightarrow 2\cos\theta\sin\theta = 1 - 2\sin^2\theta$$

$$\Rightarrow 2\cos\theta\sin\theta = \sin^2\theta + \cos^2\theta - 2\sin^2\theta$$

$$\Rightarrow 2\cos\theta\sin\theta = \cos^2\theta - \sin^2\theta \quad [\because \sin^2\theta = 1 - \cos^2\theta]$$

$$= 2\cos^2\theta - 1$$

$$\Rightarrow 2\cos^2\theta = 1 + 2\sin\theta\cos\theta$$

$$\Rightarrow \frac{2}{\sec^2\theta} = 1 + 2\sin\theta\cos\theta$$

$$\Rightarrow \frac{\sec^2\theta}{2} = \frac{1}{\sin^2\theta + \cos^2\theta + 2\sin\theta\cos\theta}$$

$$\Rightarrow \frac{\sec^2\theta}{2} = \frac{1}{(\sin\theta + \cos\theta)^2}$$

Hence proved.

59. Given, $\frac{\operatorname{cosec}^2 x - \sin^2 x \cot^2 x - \cot^2 x}{\sin^2 x} = 1$

$$= \frac{\frac{1}{\sin^2 x} - \sin^2 x \cdot \frac{\cos^2 x}{\sin^2 x} - \frac{\cos^2 x}{\sin^2 x}}{\sin^2 x}$$

$$\left[\because \operatorname{cosec} x = \frac{1}{\sin x} \text{ and } \cot x = \frac{\cos x}{\sin x}\right]$$

$$= \frac{\frac{1 - \cos^2 x}{\sin^2 x} - \cos^2 x}{\sin^2 x}$$

$$= \frac{\frac{\sin^2 x}{\sin^2 x} - \cos^2 x}{\sin^2 x} \quad [\because \sin^2 x = 1 - \cos^2 x]$$

$$= \frac{1 - \cos^2 x}{\sin^2 x}$$

$$= \frac{\sin^2 x}{\sin^2 x}$$

$$= 1$$

60. Hint LHS $= \left[\frac{1}{\frac{1}{\cos^2\theta} - \cos^2\theta} + \frac{1}{\frac{1}{\sin^2\theta} - \sin^2\theta}\right]$ $\sin^2\theta\cos^2\theta$

$$= \left[\frac{\cos^2\theta}{1 - \cos^4\theta} + \frac{\sin^2\theta}{1 - \sin^4\theta}\right]\sin^2\theta\cos^2\theta$$

$$= \left[\frac{\cos^2\theta}{(1 + \cos^2\theta)(1 - \cos^2\theta)} + \frac{\sin^2\theta}{(1 - \sin^2\theta)(1 + \sin^2\theta)}\right]$$

$\sin^2\theta\cos^2\theta$

$$= \left[\frac{\cos^2\theta}{(1 + \cos^2\theta)\sin^2\theta} + \frac{\sin^2\theta}{\cos^2\theta(1 + \sin^2\theta)}\right]$$

$\sin^2\theta\cos^2\theta$

61. Hint Let LHS $= \frac{\left[1 + \frac{\cos\theta}{\sin\theta} + \frac{\sin\theta}{\cos\theta}\right](\sin\theta - \cos\theta)}{\frac{1}{\cos^3\theta} - \frac{1}{\sin^3\theta}}$

$$= \frac{(\sin\theta\cos\theta + 1)\sin^3\theta \cdot \cos^3\theta}{\sin\theta\cos\theta \cdot (\sin^3\theta - \cos^3\theta)}(\sin\theta - \cos\theta)$$

62. Hint $\cot B = \frac{a}{\tan A}$ and $\operatorname{cosec} B = \frac{b}{\sin A}$

We know that $\operatorname{cosec}^2 B - \cot^2 B = 1$

$$\Rightarrow \frac{b^2}{\sin^2 A} - \frac{a^2}{\tan^2 A} = 1$$

63. Hint Given, $\operatorname{cosec}\theta - \sin\theta = m$

and $\sec\theta - \cos\theta = n$

$$\Rightarrow \frac{1}{\sin\theta} - \sin\theta = m \text{ and } \frac{1}{\cos\theta} - \cos\theta = n$$

$$\Rightarrow \frac{1 - \sin^2\theta}{\sin\theta} = m \text{ and } \frac{1 - \cos^2\theta}{\cos\theta} = n$$

$$\Rightarrow \frac{\cos^2\theta}{\sin\theta} = m \text{ and } \frac{\sin^2\theta}{\cos\theta} = n$$

Now, put the values of m and n in LHS of given equation.

64. Hint Given,

$$\sec\theta + \tan\theta = l \quad \ldots(i)$$

$$\Rightarrow \frac{(\sec\theta + \tan\theta)(\sec\theta - \tan\theta)}{(\sec\theta - \tan\theta)} = l$$

$$\Rightarrow \frac{\sec^2\theta - \tan^2\theta}{\sec\theta - \tan\theta} = l$$

$$\Rightarrow \sec\theta - \tan\theta = \frac{1}{l} \quad \ldots(ii)$$

Hence, find $\sec\theta$ using Eqs. (i) and (ii).

65. Hint First $\tan A = \sqrt{\sec^2 A - 1}$

$$= \sqrt{\left(\frac{17}{8}\right)^2 - 1} = \frac{15}{8}$$

Now, LHS $= \frac{3 - 4\sin^2 A}{4\cos^2 A - 3}$

$$= \frac{3\sec^2 A - 4\tan^2 A}{4 - 3\sec^2 A}$$

[dividing numerator and denominator by $\cos^2 A$]

Now, put values of $\sec^2 A$ and $\tan^2 A$ in LHS and RHS and hence verify the equality.

66. Hint Let LHS $= (\sin^4 A)^2 - (\cos^4 A)^2$

$$= (\sin^4 A - \cos^4 A)(\sin^4 A + \cos^4 A)$$

$$[\because (a^2 - b^2) = (a+b)(a-b)]$$

$$= [(\sin^2 A)^2 - (\cos^2 A)^2][(\sin^2 A)^2 + (\cos^2 A)^2]$$

$$= (\sin^2 A + \cos^2 A)(\sin^2 A - \cos^2 A)$$

$$[(\sin^2 A + \cos^2 A)^2 - 2\sin^2 A\cos^2 A]$$

$$[\because a^2 + b^2 = (a+b)^2 - 2ab]$$

$$= 1\cdot[\sin^2 A - (1 - \sin^2 A)][1^2 - 2\sin^2 A\cos^2 A]$$

$$[\because \sin^2\theta + \cos^2\theta = 1]$$

$$= (2\sin^2 A - 1)(1 - 2\sin^2 A\cos^2 A)$$

= RHS **Hence proved.**

67. Hint Put the value of p in RHS of given equality and simplify to obtain it equal to LHS.

68. LHS $= \dfrac{\cot A - \cos A}{\cot A + \cos A}$

$$= \frac{\dfrac{\cos A}{\sin A} - \cos A}{\dfrac{\cos A}{\sin A} + \cos A}$$

$$= \frac{(1 - \sin A)\times(1 - \sin A)}{(1 + \sin A)\times(1 - \sin A)}$$

$$= \frac{(1 - \sin A)^2}{1 - \sin^2 A}$$

$$= \left(\frac{1 - \sin A}{\cos A}\right)^2 \quad [\because 1 - \sin^2\theta = \cos^2\theta]$$

$$= (\sec A - \tan A)^2$$

= RHS **Hence proved.**

69. Hint Put value of q in LHS of given equation and simplify it.

70. Hint Consider, simplify it

$$\text{LHS} = \sec^2\theta(2 - \sec^2\theta) - \text{cosec}^2\theta\,(2 - \text{cosec}^2\theta)$$

$$= \sec^2\theta(2 - 1 - \tan^2\theta) - \text{cosec}^2\theta(2 - 1 - \cot^2\theta)$$

$$= (1 + \tan^2\theta)(1 - \tan^2\theta) - (1 + \cot^2\theta)(1 - \cot^2\theta)$$

$$[\because \sec^2 A = 1 + \tan^2 A \text{ and } \text{cosec}^2 A = 1 + \cot^2 A]$$

71. Hint $x^2 + y^2 + z^2 = r^2\sin^2 A\cos^2 B$

$$+ r^2\sin^2 A\sin^2 B + r^2\cos^2 A$$

$$= r^2\sin^2 A(\cos^2 B + \sin^2 B) + r^2\cos^2 A$$

72. Hint Let LHS $= \left(\dfrac{\sin\theta}{\cos\theta} + \dfrac{1}{\cos\theta}\right)^2 + \left(\dfrac{\sin\theta}{\cos\theta} - \dfrac{1}{\cos\theta}\right)^2$

$$= \frac{(\sin\theta + 1)^2}{\cos^2\theta} + \frac{(\sin\theta - 1)^2}{\cos^2\theta}$$

73. Hint Simplify l and m in terms of $\sin\theta$ and $\cos\theta$ and then put the value of l and m in LHS of the equation.

INTRODUCTION TO TRIGONOMETRY

Study of relationships between the sides and angles of a right triangle

Trigonometric Identities

(i) $\sin^2 A + \cos^2 A = 1$

(ii) $1 + \tan^2 A = \sec^2 A$

(iii) $\cot^2 A + 1 = \text{cosec}^2 A$

e.g. Express the ratios $\cos A$, $\tan A$ and $\sec A$ in terms of $\sin A$.

$\sin^2 A + \cos^2 A = 1$

$\cos^2 A = 1 - \sin^2 A$

$\cos A = \sqrt{1 - \sin^2 A}$

$\tan A = \dfrac{\sin A}{\sqrt{1 - \sin^2 A}}$

$\sec A = \dfrac{1}{\sqrt{1 - \sin^2 A}}$

Trigonometric Ratios

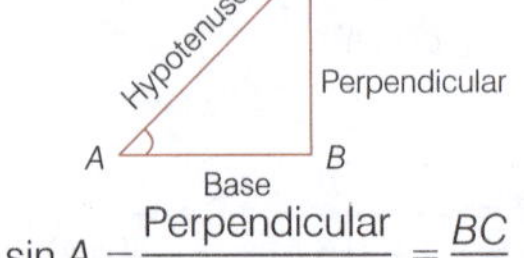

$\sin A = \dfrac{\text{Perpendicular}}{\text{Hypotenuse}} = \dfrac{BC}{AC}$

$\cos A = \dfrac{\text{Base}}{\text{Hypotenuse}} = \dfrac{AB}{AC}$

$\tan A = \dfrac{\text{Perpendicular}}{\text{Base}} = \dfrac{BC}{AB}$

$\text{cosec } A = \dfrac{\text{Hypotenuse}}{\text{Perpendicular}} = \dfrac{AC}{BC}$

$\sec A = \dfrac{\text{Hypotenuse}}{\text{Base}} = \dfrac{AC}{AB}$

$\cot A = \dfrac{\text{Base}}{\text{Perpendicular}} = \dfrac{AB}{BC}$

Trigonometric Ratios of Some Specific Angles

$\angle A$	0°	30°	45°	60°	90°
sin A	0	$1/2$	$1/\sqrt{2}$	$\sqrt{3}/2$	1
cos A	1	$\sqrt{3}/2$	$1/\sqrt{2}$	$1/2$	0
tan A	0	$1/\sqrt{3}$	1	$\sqrt{3}$	∞
cot A	∞	$\sqrt{3}$	1	$1/\sqrt{3}$	0
sec A	1	$2/\sqrt{3}$	$\sqrt{2}$	2	∞
cosec A	∞	2	$\sqrt{2}$	$2/\sqrt{3}$	1

Some Applications of Trigonometry

CHAPTER 9

Measuring height and distances is an important application of trigonometry. In this chapter, we shall study the use of trigonometry in measuring the height and distances of towers, buildings and other objects. In solving problems of height and distances of different objects, we need to define few terms as discuss below.

Line of Sight

The line of sight is the line drawn from the eye of an observer to the point in the object viewed by the observer.

Angle of Elevation

The angle of elevation of an object viewed, is the angle formed by the line of sight with the horizontal, when it is above the horizontal level, i.e. the case when we raise our head to look at object.

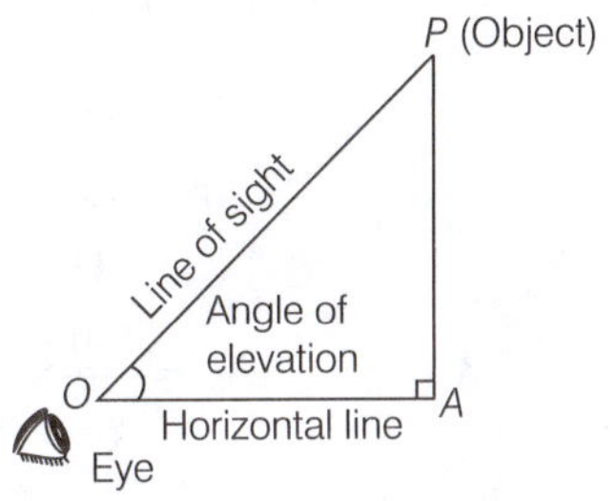

Let P be the position of the object above the horizontal line OA and O be the eye of the observer. Then, OP is the line of sight and $\angle AOP$ is called **angle of elevation**, because the observer has to elevate (raise) his/her line of sight from the horizontal OA to see the object P.

Some Important Points

(i) A plane level parallel to Earth's surface is called the horizontal plane level and a line drawn parallel to horizontal plane is called a horizontal line.

(ii) If the observer moves towards the perpendicular line (tower/building), then angle of elevation increases and if the observer moves away from the perpendicular line (tower/building), then angle of elevation decreases.

(iii) If the height of tower is doubled and the distance between the observer and foot of the tower is also doubled, then the angle of elevation remains same.

(iv) If the angle of elevation of Sun, above a tower decreases, then the length of shadow of a tower increases and *vice-versa*.

Angle of Depression

The angle of depression of an object viewed, is the angle formed by the line of sight with the horizontal, when it is below the horizontal level i.e. the case when we lower our head to look at the object.

Let P be the position of the object below the horizontal level OA and O be the eye of the observer. Then, OP is the line of sight and $\angle AOP$ is called an **angle of depression**, because the observer has to depress (lower) his/her line of sight from the horizontal OA to see the object P.

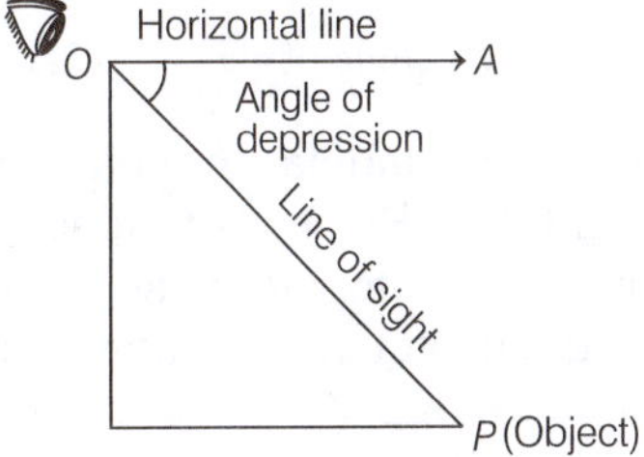

Some Important Points

(i) The angle of elevation of a point P as seen from a point O is always equal to the angle of depression of O as seen from P.

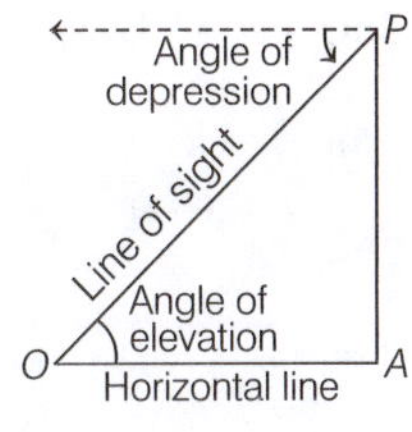

(ii) The angles of elevation and depression are always acute angles.

(iii) In solving problems, observer is represented by a point and object is represented by a line segment or a point.

Example 1. **A tower stands vertically on the ground. From a point on the ground which is $15\sqrt{3}$ m away from the foot of the tower, the angle of elevation of the top of the tower is found to be 30°. Find the height of the tower.**

Sol. Let the height of the tower be H m.

So, $AB = H$ m

Distance of the point from the foot of the tower $= 15\sqrt{3}$ m

$\Rightarrow \quad CB = 15\sqrt{3}$ m

$\therefore \quad \tan 30° = \dfrac{AB}{BC}$

$\Rightarrow \quad \dfrac{1}{\sqrt{3}} = \dfrac{AB}{15\sqrt{3}}$

$\Rightarrow \quad AB = 15$ m

Hence, the height of the tower is 15 m.

Example 2. **If $300\sqrt{3}$ m high tower makes angle of elevation at a point on ground which is 300 m away from its foot, then find the angle of elevation.**

Sol. Let AB be the tower whose height is $300\sqrt{3}$ m, i.e. $AB = 300\sqrt{3}$ m.

Again, let C be the point at a distance of 300 m from the foot of the tower, i.e. $AC = 300$ m.

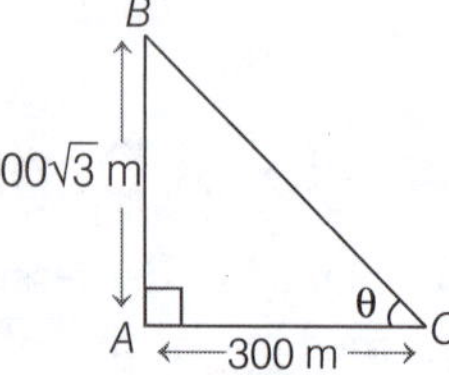

Here, the angle of elevation is unknown, so let it be θ.

Since, here base and perpendicular are given.

So, in right angled ΔBAC,

$$\tan\theta = \frac{\text{Perpendicular}}{\text{Base}} = \frac{AB}{AC} = \frac{300\sqrt{3}}{300}$$

$\Rightarrow \quad \tan\theta = \sqrt{3} = \tan 60°$

$\therefore \quad \theta = 60°$

Hence, the required angle of elevation is 60°.

Example 3. **An electrician has to repair an electric fault on a pole of height 4 m. He needs to reach a point 1 m below the top of the pole to undertake the repair work. What should be the length of the ladder that he should use, when inclined at an angle of 60° to the horizontal, which would enable him to reach the required position? [take $\sqrt{3} = 1.73$]**

Sol. Let AC be the pole and BD be the ladder.

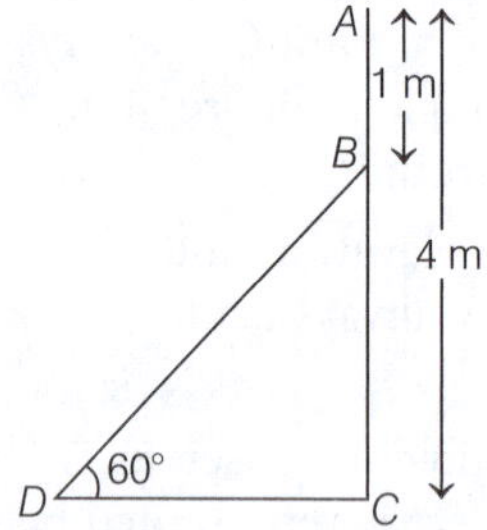

We have, $AC = 4$ m, $AB = 1$ m and $\angle BDC = 60°$

and $BC = AC - AB = 4 - 1 = 3$ m

In ΔBDC, $\sin 60° = \dfrac{BC}{BD}$

$\Rightarrow \quad \dfrac{\sqrt{3}}{2} = \dfrac{3}{BD} \qquad \left[\because \sin 60° = \dfrac{\sqrt{3}}{2}\right]$

$\Rightarrow \quad BD = \dfrac{3 \times 2}{\sqrt{3}}$

$\Rightarrow \quad BD = 2 \times 1.73$

$\therefore \quad BD = 3.46$ m

Hence, the length of the ladder should be 3.46 m.

Example 4. **A bridge on a river makes an angle of 45° with its edge. If the length along the bridge from one edge to the other is 150 m, then find the width of the river.**

Sol. Let BC be the width of the river and A, B be the ends of bridge such that $AB = 150$ m = Length of the bridge [given]

and $\angle BAC = 45°$.

In right angled ΔACB,

$\sin 45° = \dfrac{P}{H}$

$\Rightarrow \quad \dfrac{1}{\sqrt{2}} = \dfrac{BC}{AB} = \dfrac{BC}{150} \qquad \left[\because \sin 45° = \dfrac{1}{\sqrt{2}}\right]$

$\therefore \quad BC = \dfrac{150}{\sqrt{2}} \times \dfrac{\sqrt{2}}{\sqrt{2}}$

[by rationalising denominator]

$= \dfrac{150}{2}\sqrt{2} = 75\sqrt{2}$

$= 75 \times 1.414 \qquad [\because \sqrt{2} = 1.414]$

$= 106.05$ m (approx.)

Hence, the width of the river is 106.05 m.

Example 5. **A straight tree is broken due to thunderstorm. The broken part is bent in such a way that the peak of the tree touches the ground at an angle of 60° at a distance of $2\sqrt{3}$ m. Find the whole height of the tree.**

Here, angle of elevation and base of triangle is given and we have to find the whole height of the tree i.e. AB, for this we have to find AC (or CD) and BC.

Sol. Let AB be the tree whose part AC breaks and touches the ground at D.

Then, $BD = 2\sqrt{3}$ m [given]

and $AC = CD$

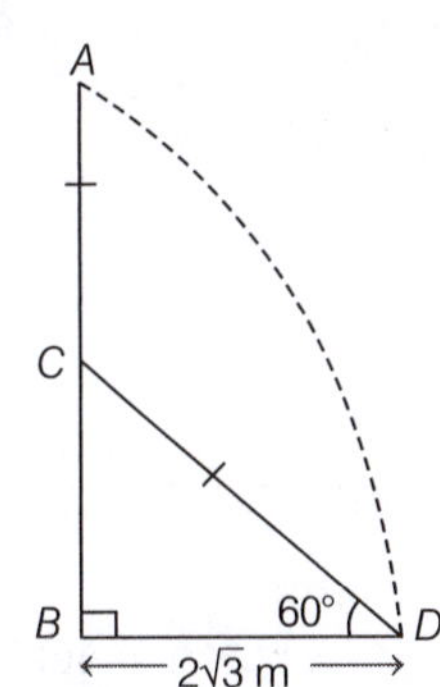

In right angled ΔCBD, $\cos 60° = \frac{B}{H} = \frac{BD}{CD}$

$\Rightarrow \quad \frac{1}{2} = \frac{2\sqrt{3}}{CD} \quad \left[\because \cos 60° = \frac{1}{2} \text{ and } BD = 2\sqrt{3} \text{ m}\right]$

$\Rightarrow \quad CD = 2 \times 2\sqrt{3} = 4\sqrt{3}$ m

$= 4 \times 1.732 = 6.928$ m $\quad [\because \sqrt{3} = 1.732]$

$\therefore \quad AC = CD = 6.928$ m

Again, in right angled ΔCBD,

$\tan 60° = \frac{P}{B} = \frac{BC}{BD}$

$\Rightarrow \quad \sqrt{3} = \frac{BC}{2\sqrt{3}} \quad [\because \tan 60° = \sqrt{3} \text{ and } BD = 2\sqrt{3} \text{ m}]$

$\Rightarrow \quad BC = \sqrt{3} \times 2\sqrt{3} = 6$ m

Now, $AB = AC + BC$

$= 6.928 + 6$

$= 12.928$ m (approx.)

Hence, the height of the tree is 12.928 m.

Example 6. **One observer estimates the angle of elevation to the basket of a hot air balloon to be 60°, while another observer 100 m away estimates the angle of elevation to be 30°. Find**

(i) the height of the basket from the ground.

(ii) the distance of the basket from the first observer's eye.

(iii) the horizontal distance of the second observer from the basket. [take $\sqrt{3} = 1.732$] CBSE 2023 (Standard)

Sol. (i)

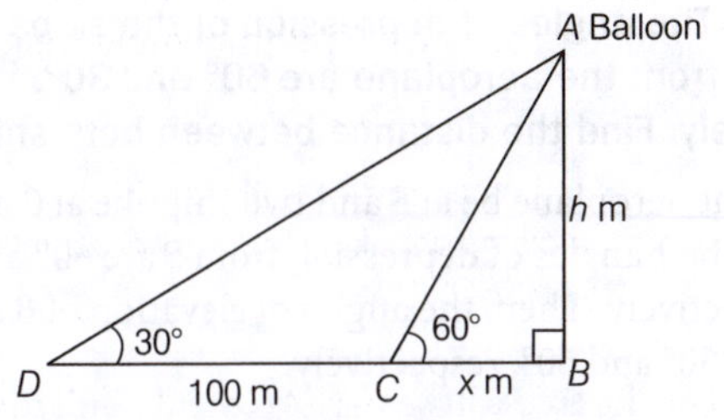

In ΔABC,

$\tan 60° = \frac{AB}{BC} \Rightarrow \sqrt{3} = \frac{h}{x}$

$\Rightarrow \quad h = \sqrt{3}x \quad$ ...(i)

In ΔABD,

$\tan 30° = \frac{AB}{BD} \Rightarrow \frac{1}{\sqrt{3}} = \frac{h}{100 + x}$

$\Rightarrow \quad 100 + x = \sqrt{3}h$

$\Rightarrow \quad 100 + x = \sqrt{3}(\sqrt{3}x) \quad$ [from Eq. (i)]

$\Rightarrow \quad 100 = 2x \Rightarrow x = 50$ m

Height of basket $= h = \sqrt{3}x$

$= \sqrt{3} \times 50 = 50 \times 1.732 = 86.60$ m

(ii) In ΔABC,

$\cos 60° = \frac{BC}{AC}$

$\Rightarrow \quad \frac{1}{2} = \frac{50}{AC}$

$\Rightarrow \quad AC = 100$ m

$\therefore$ Distance of the basket from first observer's eye

$= 100$ m

(iii) Horizontal distance of the second observer from the basket $= BD = BC + CD$

$= 50 + 100 = 150$ m

Example 7. **Two pillars are standing on either side of a 80 m wide road. Height of one pillar is 20 m more than the height of the other pillar. From a point on the road between the pillars, the angle of elevation of the higher pillar is 60°, whereas that of the other pillar is 30°. Find the position of the point between the pillars and the height of each pillar. [take $\sqrt{3} = 1.73$]** CBSE 2023 (Standard)

Sol.

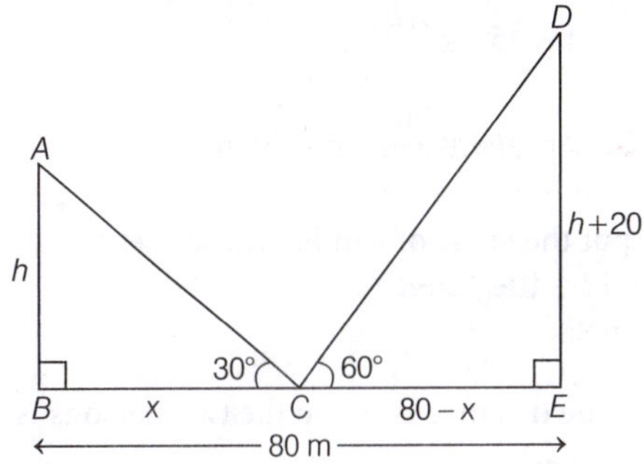

In ΔABC, $\tan 30° = \frac{h}{x}$

$\Rightarrow \quad \frac{1}{\sqrt{3}} = \frac{h}{x}$

$\Rightarrow \quad x = \sqrt{3}h \quad$ ...(i)

In ΔCDE, $\tan 60° = \frac{h + 20}{80 - x} \Rightarrow \sqrt{3} = \frac{h + 20}{80 - x}$

$\Rightarrow \quad \sqrt{3}(80-\sqrt{3}h) = h+20$ [from Eq. (i)]

$\Rightarrow \quad 80\sqrt{3} - 3h = h + 20 \Rightarrow 80\sqrt{3} - 20 = 4h$

$\Rightarrow \quad h = 20\sqrt{3} - 5 \Rightarrow h = 20(1.73) - 5 = 29.6$ m

From Eq. (i), $x = 1.73 \times 29.6 = 51.208$ m

Hence, the height of both pillars are 29.6 m and (29.6 + 20) m = 49.6 m

Position of point between the pillars are 51.208 m and (80 − 51.208) m = 28.792 m.

Example 8. **Two persons standing on the same side of a tower in a straight line with it, measure the angles of elevation of the top of the tower as 30° and 45°, respectively. If the height of the tower is 70 m, then find the distance between the two persons.**

Sol. Let P and Q be the positions of two persons and AB be the height of tower.

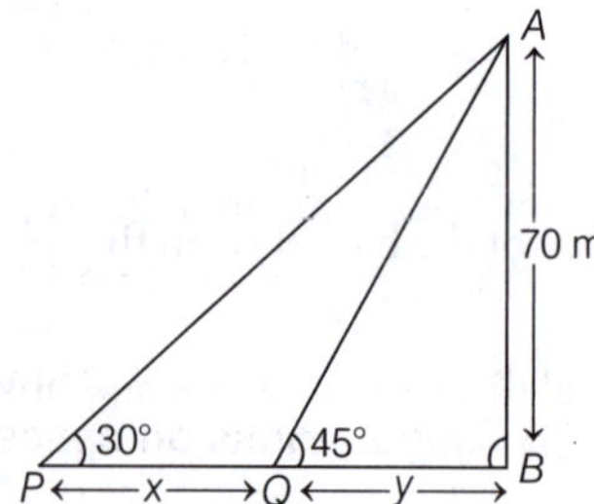

Let $PQ = x$ m and $QB = y$ m

In ΔAPB,

$$\tan 30^\circ = \frac{AB}{PB}$$

$$\Rightarrow \quad \frac{1}{\sqrt{3}} = \frac{70}{x+y}$$

$$\Rightarrow \quad x + y = 70\sqrt{3} \quad \ldots(i)$$

and in ΔAQB,

$$\tan 45^\circ = \frac{AB}{QB}$$

$$\Rightarrow \quad 1 = \frac{70}{y} \Rightarrow y = 70 \text{ m}$$

Now, put the value of y in Eq. (i), we get

$$x + 70 = 70\sqrt{3}$$

$$\Rightarrow \quad x = 70(\sqrt{3}-1) \text{ m}$$

Hence, the distance between the two persons is $70(\sqrt{3}-1)$ m.

Example 9. **A pole 6m high is fixed on the top of a tower. The angle of elevation of the top of the pole observed from a point P on the ground is 60° and the angle of depression of the point P from the top of the tower is 45°. Find the height of the tower and the distance of point P from the foot of the tower.**

[use $\sqrt{3} = 1.73$] CBSE 2024 (Standard)

Sol. Let QR be the tower of height h m and RS be the pole of height 6 m.

And the distance of point P from the foot of the tower be x m.

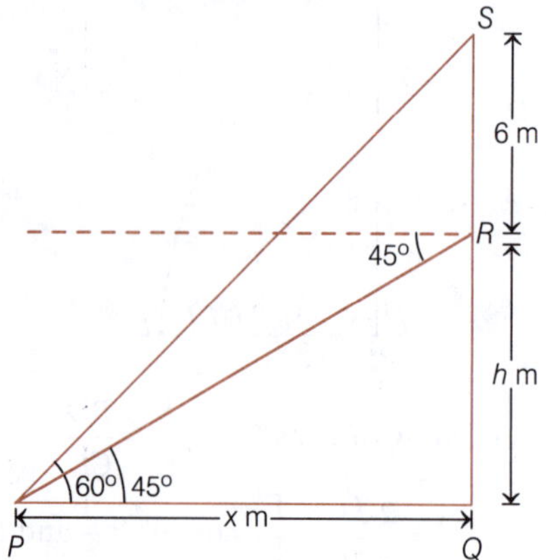

In right angled ΔPQR,

$$\tan 45^\circ = \frac{QR}{PQ}$$

$$\Rightarrow \quad 1 = \frac{h}{x} \Rightarrow x = h \quad \ldots(i)$$

Now, in ΔPQS,

$$\tan 60^\circ = \frac{QS}{PQ}$$

$$\Rightarrow \quad \sqrt{3} = \frac{h+6}{x}$$

$$\Rightarrow \quad \sqrt{3}x = h + 6$$

$$\Rightarrow \quad \sqrt{3}x = x + 6 \quad \text{[from Eq. (i)]}$$

$$\Rightarrow \quad x = \frac{6(\sqrt{3}+1)}{(\sqrt{3}-1)(\sqrt{3}+1)}$$

$$\Rightarrow \quad x = \frac{6(\sqrt{3}+1)}{2}$$

$$\Rightarrow \quad x = 3 \times (1.73 + 1) = 8.19 \text{ m}$$

Now, put the value of x in Eq. (i), we get

$$h = 8.19 \text{ m}$$

Hence, the height of the tower and distance of point P from the foot of the tower is 8.19 m.

Example 10. **An aeroplane is at an altitude of 1200 m find that two ships are sailing towards it in the same direction. The angles of depression of the ships as observed from the aeroplane are 60° and 30°, respectively. Find the distance between both ships.**

Sol. Let the aeroplane be at B and two ships be at C and D such that their angles of depression from B are 60° and 30°, respectively. Then, the angles of elevation of B from D and C are 30° and 60°, respectively.

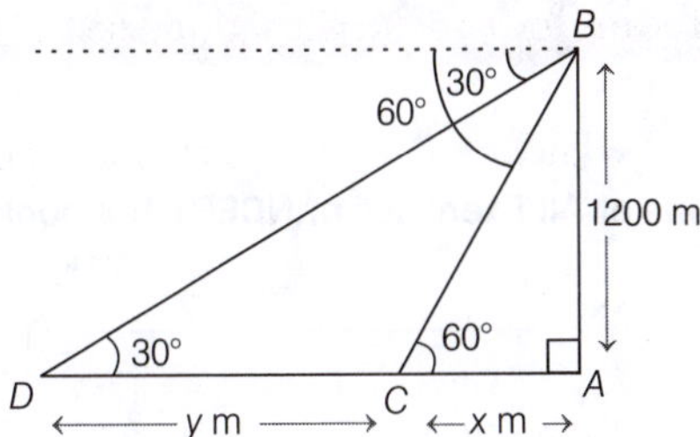

We have, $AB = 1200$ m

Let $AC = x$ m and $CD = y$ m

In right angled ΔBAC, we have

$$\tan 60° = \frac{P}{B} = \frac{AB}{AC}$$

$$\Rightarrow \quad \sqrt{3} = \frac{1200}{x} \quad [\because \tan 60° = \sqrt{3}]$$

$$\Rightarrow \quad x = \frac{1200}{\sqrt{3}} \times \frac{\sqrt{3}}{\sqrt{3}} \text{ [by rationalising denominator]}$$

$$\Rightarrow \quad x = \frac{1200\sqrt{3}}{3} = 400\sqrt{3} \text{ m} \quad \text{...(i)}$$

In right angled ΔBAD, we have

$$\tan 30° = \frac{AB}{AD} = \frac{AB}{DC + CA} \quad [\because AD = DC + CA]$$

$$\Rightarrow \quad \frac{1}{\sqrt{3}} = \frac{1200}{x + y}$$

$$\Rightarrow \quad x + y = 1200\sqrt{3} \quad \left[\because \tan 30° = \frac{1}{\sqrt{3}}\right]$$

$$\Rightarrow \quad y = 1200\sqrt{3} - x \quad \text{...(ii)}$$

On putting the value of x from Eq. (i) in Eq. (ii), we get

$$y = 1200\sqrt{3} - 400\sqrt{3} = 800\sqrt{3}$$

$$= 800 \times 1.732 \quad [\because \sqrt{3} = 1.732]$$

$$= 1385.6 \text{ m}$$

Hence, the distance between both ships is 1385.6 m.

Example 11. **The angle of depression of the top and bottom of 9 m tall building from the top of a multistoried building are 30° and 60°, respectively. Find the height of the multistoried building and the distance between the two buildings. [use $\sqrt{3} = 1.73$]** CBSE 2025 (Basic)

Sol. Let the multistoried building AB be h m and the distance between the two buildings be d m and CD be the tall building of 9 m. Then, according to the question,

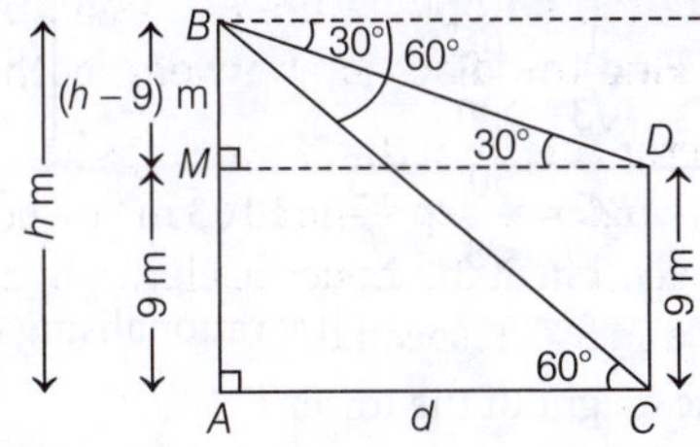

In ΔBMD,

$$\tan 30° = \frac{BM}{MD} \Rightarrow \frac{h-9}{d} = \frac{1}{\sqrt{3}} \quad \left[\because \tan 30° = \frac{1}{\sqrt{3}}\right]$$

$$\Rightarrow \quad \sqrt{3}(h - 9) = d \quad \text{...(i)}$$

Now, in ΔBAC,

$$\tan 60° = \frac{AB}{AC} \Rightarrow \frac{h}{d} = \sqrt{3} \quad [\because \tan 60° = \sqrt{3}]$$

$$\Rightarrow \quad h = \sqrt{3}d \quad \text{...(ii)}$$

On putting the value of h from Eq. (ii) in Eq. (i), we get

$$\sqrt{3}(\sqrt{3}d - 9) = d$$

$$\Rightarrow \quad 3d - 9\sqrt{3} = d$$

$$\Rightarrow \quad (3 - 1)d = 9\sqrt{3}$$

$$\Rightarrow \quad d = \frac{9\sqrt{3}}{2}$$

$$\Rightarrow \quad d = 7.785 \text{ m}$$

Now, $h = \sqrt{3}d = 13.468$ m

So, the height of the multistoried building and the distance between the two buildings is 13.468 m.

Example 12. **From a point of a bridge across a river, the angle of depression of the banks on opposite sides of the river are 30° and 45°, respectively. If the bridge is at a height of 10 m from the banks, then find the width of the river. [use $\sqrt{3} = 1.73$]**

Sol. Let AC represent the width of the river. P is a point on the bridge at a height of 10 m i.e. $PD = 10$ m, then

According to the question,

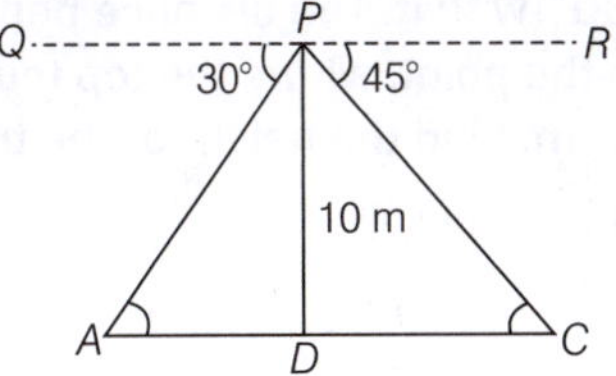

$$\text{In } \Delta APD, \ \tan 30° = \frac{PD}{AD}$$

$$\Rightarrow \quad \frac{1}{\sqrt{3}} = \frac{10}{AD}$$

$$\Rightarrow \quad AD = 10\sqrt{3} \text{ m} \quad \text{...(i)}$$

$$\text{In } \Delta CPD, \ \tan 45° = \frac{PD}{DC}$$

$$\Rightarrow \quad 1 = \frac{10}{DC}$$

$$\Rightarrow \quad DC = 10 \text{ m} \quad \text{...(ii)}$$

Width of the river, $AC = AD + DC$

$$= 10\sqrt{3} + 10 = 10(\sqrt{3} + 1) \text{ m}$$

$$= 27.3 \text{ m}$$

Hence, the width of the river is 27.3 m.

NCERT FOLDER

Complete Solutions of All Exercises of NCERT Textbook

EXERCISE 9.1

Q1. A circus artist is climbing a 20 m long rope, which is tightly stretched and tied from the top of a vertical pole to the ground. Find the height of the pole, if the angle made by the rope with ground level is 30° (see the figure).

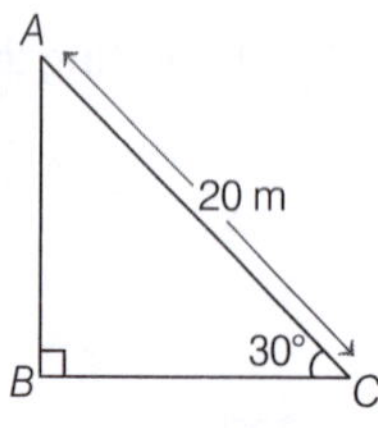

Sol. In the given figure, AB is the height of the pole and $AC = 20$ m is the length of rope, which is tied from the top of the pole to the ground at point C.

In right angled ΔABC,

$$\sin 30° = \frac{P}{H} = \frac{AB}{AC} = \frac{AB}{20}$$

$$\Rightarrow \frac{1}{2} = \frac{AB}{20} \quad \left[\because \sin 30° = \frac{1}{2}\right]$$

$$\therefore \quad AB = \frac{20}{2} = 10 \text{ m}$$

Hence, the height of the pole is 10 m.

Q2. A tree breaks due to storm and the broken part bends, so that the top of the tree touches the ground making an angle 30° with it. The distance between the foot of the tree to the point, where the top touches the ground is 8 m. Find the height of the tree.

Sol. Do same as Example 5.

Ans. $8\sqrt{3}$ m

Q3. A contractor plans to install two slides for the children to play in a park. For the children below the age of 5 years, she prefers to have a slide whose top is at a height of 1.5 m and is inclined at an angle of 30° to the ground, whereas for elder children, she wants to have a steep slide at a height of 3 m and inclined at an angle of 60° to the ground. What should be the length of the slide in each case?

Sol. ***Case* I Slide for the children below age of 5 yr.**

Let $BC = 1.5$ m be the height of the slide and let slide AC be inclined at an angle of 30° to the ground.

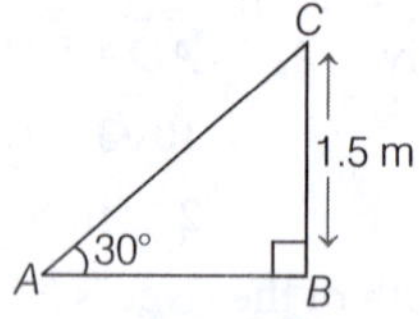

In right angled ΔABC,

$$\sin 30° = \frac{BC}{AC} \quad \left[\because \sin\theta = \frac{P}{H}\right]$$

$$\Rightarrow \frac{1}{2} = \frac{1.5}{AC} \quad \left[\because \sin 30° = \frac{1}{2}\right]$$

$$\Rightarrow AC = 3 \text{ m}$$

***Case* II Slide for the elder children.**

Let $RQ = 3$ m be the height of the slide and let slide PR be inclined at an angle of 60° to the ground.

In right angled ΔPQR,

$$\sin 60° = \frac{RQ}{PR}$$

$$\Rightarrow \frac{\sqrt{3}}{2} = \frac{3}{PR} \quad \left[\because \sin 60° = \frac{\sqrt{3}}{2}\right]$$

$$\Rightarrow PR = \frac{3 \times 2}{\sqrt{3}} = \frac{6}{\sqrt{3}} \times \frac{\sqrt{3}}{\sqrt{3}} = 2\sqrt{3} \text{ m}$$

[by rationalising denominator]

Hence, the length of slides in each case are 3m and $2\sqrt{3}$ m.

Q4. The angle of elevation of the top of a tower from a point on the ground, which is 30 m away from the foot of the tower, is 30°. Find the height of the tower.

Sol. Let BC be the height of the tower which is standing on the ground. Let A be a point on the ground which is 30 m away from the foot of tower.

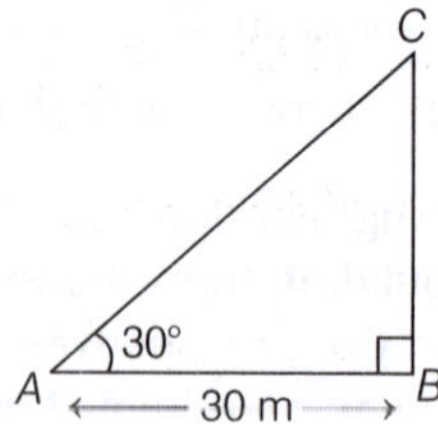

Then, $AB = 30$ m and $\angle BAC = 30°$

In right angled ΔABC,

$$\tan 30° = \frac{BC}{AB} \quad \left[\because \tan\theta = \frac{P}{B}\right]$$

$$\Rightarrow \frac{1}{\sqrt{3}} = \frac{BC}{30} \quad \left[\because \tan 30° = \frac{1}{\sqrt{3}}\right]$$

$$\Rightarrow BC = \frac{30}{\sqrt{3}} \times \frac{\sqrt{3}}{\sqrt{3}} = 10\sqrt{3} \text{ m}$$

[by rationalising denominator]

Hence, the height of the tower is $10\sqrt{3}$ m.

Q5. **A kite is flying at a height of 60 m above the ground. The string attached to the kite is temporarily tied to a point on the ground. The inclination of the string with the ground is 60°. Find the length of the string, assuming that there is no slack in the string.**

Sol. Let C be the position of the kite and AC be the length of the string which makes an angle of 60° on the ground. The height of the kite from the ground is $BC = 60$ m.

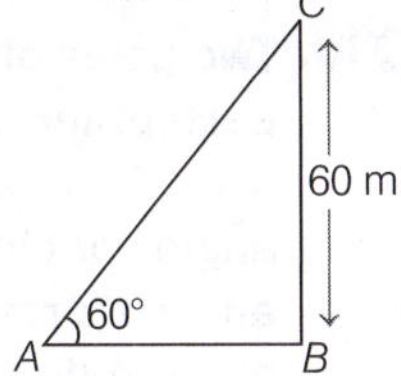

In right angled ΔABC,

$$\sin 60° = \frac{P}{H} = \frac{BC}{AC}$$

$$\Rightarrow \quad \frac{\sqrt{3}}{2} = \frac{60}{AC} \qquad \left[\because \sin 60° = \frac{\sqrt{3}}{2}\right]$$

$$\therefore \quad AC = \frac{60 \times 2}{\sqrt{3}} \times \frac{\sqrt{3}}{\sqrt{3}}$$

[by rationalising denominator]

$$= \frac{120\sqrt{3}}{3} = 40\sqrt{3} \text{ m}$$

Hence, the length of the string is $40\sqrt{3}$ m.

Q6. **A 1.5 m tall boy is standing at some distance from a 30 m tall building. The angle of elevation from his eyes to the top of the building increases from 30° to 60° as he walks towards the building. Find the distance he walked towards the building.**

Sol. Let $AB = 30$ m be the height of the building and $DC = 1.5$ m be the height of the boy. The point D be the boy's eyes.

Draw the line $DF \parallel CA$.

Then, $CD = AF = 1.5$ m

The angle of elevation is $\angle BDF = 30°$.

Let he walked $DE = x$ m towards the building. Then, the angle of elevation is $\angle BEF = 60°$.

Let $EF = y$ m

Now, $BF = AB - AF = 30 - 1.5 = 28.5$ m.

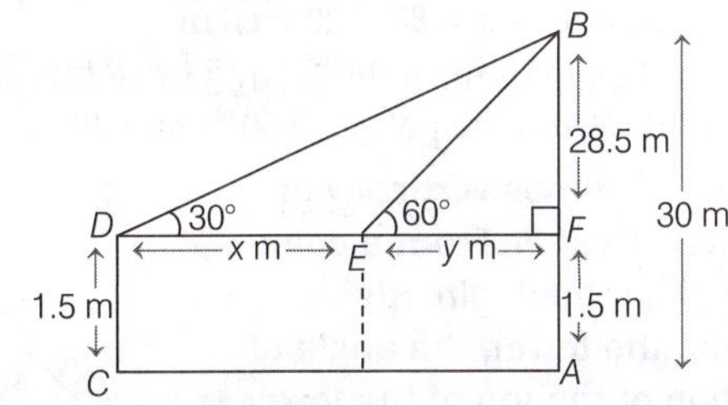

In right angled ΔBFD,

$$\tan 30° = \frac{P}{B} = \frac{BF}{DF} = \frac{BF}{DE + EF} \qquad [\because DF = DE + EF]$$

$$\Rightarrow \quad \frac{1}{\sqrt{3}} = \frac{28.5}{x + y} \qquad \left[\because \tan 30° = \frac{1}{\sqrt{3}}\right]$$

$$\Rightarrow \quad x + y = 28.5\sqrt{3} \text{ m} \qquad \ldots\text{(i)}$$

and in right angled ΔBFE,

$$\tan 60° = \frac{BF}{EF}$$

$$\Rightarrow \quad \sqrt{3} = \frac{28.5}{y} \qquad [\because \tan 60° = \sqrt{3}]$$

$$\Rightarrow \quad y = \frac{28.5}{\sqrt{3}} \text{ m}$$

On putting $y = \frac{28.5}{\sqrt{3}}$ in Eq. (i), we get

$$x + \frac{28.5}{\sqrt{3}} = 28.5\sqrt{3}$$

$$\Rightarrow \quad x = 28.5\left(\sqrt{3} - \frac{1}{\sqrt{3}}\right) = 28.5\left(\frac{3-1}{\sqrt{3}}\right)$$

$$= \frac{28.5 \times 2}{\sqrt{3}} \times \frac{\sqrt{3}}{\sqrt{3}}$$

[by rationalising denominator]

$$= \frac{57\sqrt{3}}{3} = 19\sqrt{3} \text{ m}$$

Hence, the distance he walked towards the building is $19\sqrt{3}$ m.

Q7. **From a point on the ground, the angles of elevation of the bottom and the top of a transmission tower fixed at the top of a 20 m high building are 45° and 60°, respectively. Find the height of the tower.**

CBSE 2024, 20 (Standard)

Sol. Do same as Example 9. **Ans.** 14.64 m

Q8. **A statue, 1.6 m tall, stands on the top of a pedestal. From a point on the ground, the angle of elevation of the top of the statue is 60° and from the same point, the angle of elevation of the top of the pedestal is 45°. Find the height of the pedestal.**

Sol. Let $BC = h$ m be the height of the pedestal and $CD = 1.6$m be the length of the statue, which is standing on the pedestal.

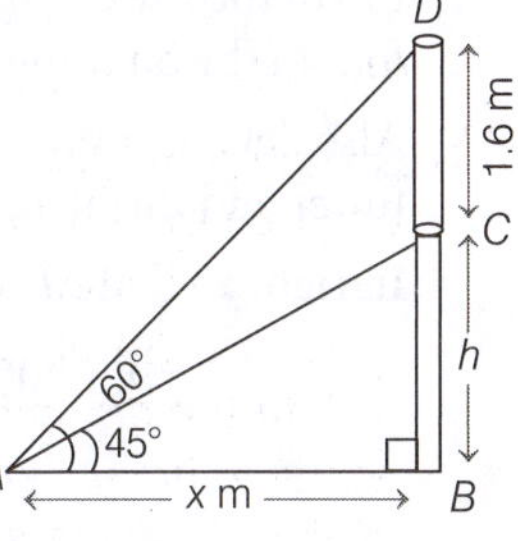

Again, let point A be a fixed point on the ground such that the angles of elevation of the top of the statue and bottom of the statue (i.e. top of the pedestal) are $\angle DAB = 60°$ and $\angle CAB = 45°$.

Also, let $AB = x$ m.

In right angled ΔABD,

$$\tan 60° = \frac{P}{B} = \frac{BD}{AB}$$

$$\Rightarrow \quad \sqrt{3} = \frac{BC + CD}{x} \qquad [\because \tan 60° = \sqrt{3}]$$

$$\Rightarrow \quad \sqrt{3} = \frac{h + 1.6}{x} \Rightarrow h = \sqrt{3}x - 1.6 \qquad \ldots\text{(i)}$$

In right angled ΔCBA,

$$\tan 45° = \frac{BC}{AB}$$

$$\Rightarrow \quad 1 = \frac{h}{x} \quad [\because \tan 45° = 1]$$

$$\Rightarrow \quad x = h$$

On putting $x = h$ in Eq. (i), we get

$$h = \sqrt{3}h - 1.6$$

$$\Rightarrow \quad h(\sqrt{3} - 1) = 1.6$$

$$\Rightarrow \quad h = \frac{1.6}{(\sqrt{3}-1)} \times \frac{\sqrt{3}+1}{\sqrt{3}+1} \quad \text{[rationalising]}$$

$$= \frac{1.6(\sqrt{3}+1)}{(\sqrt{3})^2 - (1)^2}$$

$$[\because (a+b)(a-b) = a^2 - b^2]$$

$$= \frac{1.6}{2}(\sqrt{3}+1)$$

$$= 0.8(\sqrt{3}+1) \text{ m}$$

Hence, the height of the pedestal is $0.8(\sqrt{3}+1)$ m.

Q 9. The angle of elevation of the top of a building from the foot of the tower is 30° and the angle of elevation of the top of the tower from the foot of the building is 60°. If the tower is 50 m high, find the height of the building.

Sol. Let $BC = 50$ m be the height of the tower and $AD = h$ m be the height of the building. Angle of elevation of the top of the building from the foot of the tower is $\angle DBA = 30°$ and angle of elevation of the top of the tower from the foot of the building $\angle CAB = 60°$.

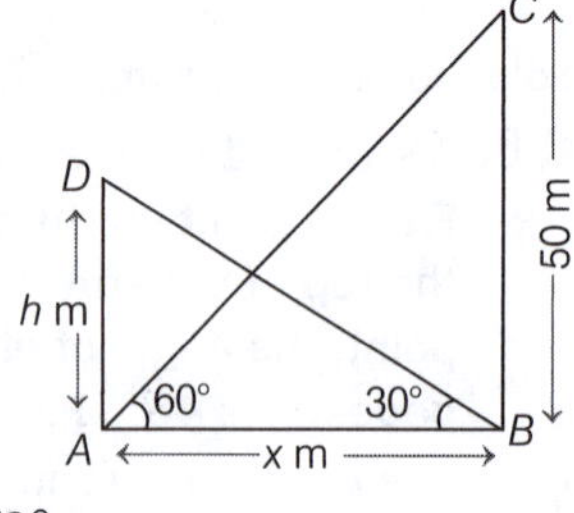

Also, let $AB = x$ m be the distance between foots of the tower and the building.

In right angled ΔBAD,

$$\tan 30° = \frac{P}{B} = \frac{AD}{AB}$$

$$\Rightarrow \quad \frac{1}{\sqrt{3}} = \frac{h}{x} \quad \left[\because \tan 30° = \frac{1}{\sqrt{3}}\right]$$

$$\Rightarrow \quad h = \frac{x}{\sqrt{3}} \quad \ldots(i)$$

and in right angled ΔCBA,

$$\tan 60° = \frac{BC}{AB}$$

$$\Rightarrow \quad \sqrt{3} = \frac{50}{x} \quad [\because \tan 60° = \sqrt{3}]$$

$$\Rightarrow \quad x = \frac{50}{\sqrt{3}} \text{ m}$$

On putting $x = \frac{50}{\sqrt{3}}$ in Eq. (i), we get

$$h = \frac{50}{\sqrt{3}} \times \frac{1}{\sqrt{3}} = \frac{50}{3} = 16\frac{2}{3} \text{ m}$$

Hence, the height of the building is $16\frac{2}{3}$ m.

Q 10. Two poles of equal heights are standing opposite to each other on either side of the road, which is 80m wide. From a point between them on the road, the angles of elevation of the top of the poles are 60° and 30°, respectively. Find the height of the poles and the distances of the point from the poles.

CBSE 2015, 2019 CBSE Sample paper 2020 (Standard)

Sol. Let $AB = 80$ m be the width of the road. On both sides of the road, poles $AE = BD = h$ m are standing. Let C be any point on AB such that from point C, angles of elevation are $\angle BCD = 60°$ and $\angle ACE = 30°$.

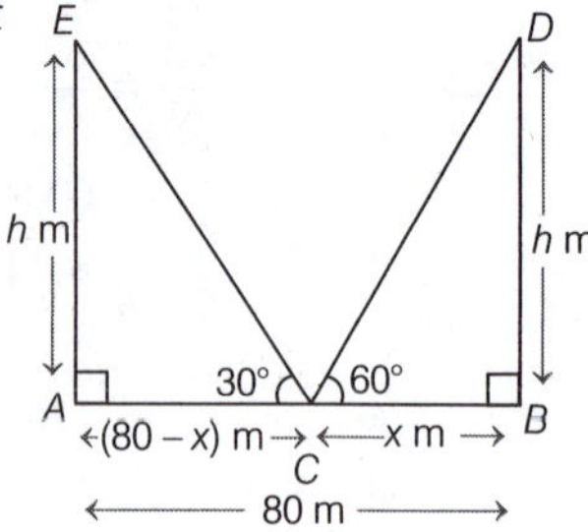

Let $BC = x$ m.

Then, $AC = AB - BC = (80 - x)$ m

In right angled ΔCAE, $\tan 30° = \frac{P}{B} = \frac{AE}{AC}$

$$\Rightarrow \quad \frac{1}{\sqrt{3}} = \frac{h}{80 - x} \quad \left[\because \tan 30° = \frac{1}{\sqrt{3}}\right]$$

$$\Rightarrow \quad 80 - x = h\sqrt{3} \Rightarrow h\sqrt{3} + x = 80 \quad \ldots(i)$$

and in right angled ΔCBD,

$$\tan 60° = \frac{BD}{BC} \Rightarrow \sqrt{3} = \frac{h}{x} \quad [\because \tan 60° = \sqrt{3}]$$

$$\Rightarrow \quad h = \sqrt{3}x \quad \ldots(ii)$$

On putting $h = \sqrt{3}x$ in Eq. (i), we get

$$\sqrt{3}x(\sqrt{3}) + x = 80 \Rightarrow 3x + x = 80$$

$$\Rightarrow \quad 4x = 80 \Rightarrow x = 20 \text{ m}$$

On putting $x = 20$ m in Eq. (ii), we get

$$h = 20\sqrt{3} \text{ m}$$

Now, $\quad AC = 80 - x = 80 - 20 = 60$ m

Hence, the height of the poles is $20\sqrt{3}$ m and the distances of the point C from the poles are 60 m and 20 m.

Q 11. A TV tower stands vertically on a bank of a canal. From a point on the other bank directly opposite the tower, the angle of elevation of the top of the tower is 60°. From another point 20 m away from this point on the line joining this point to the foot of the tower, the angle of elevation of the top of the tower is 30° (see the figure). Find the height of the tower and the width of the canal.

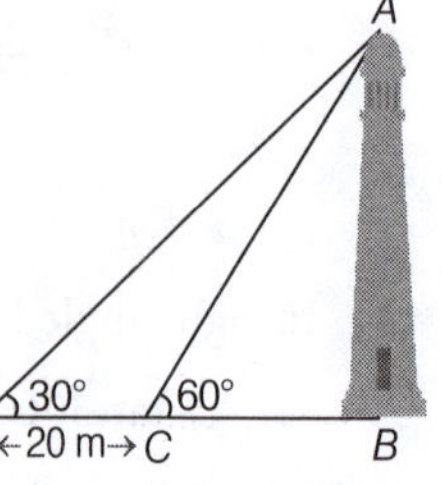

Sol. Let $BC = x$ m be the width of the canal and $AB = h$ m be the height of the tower.

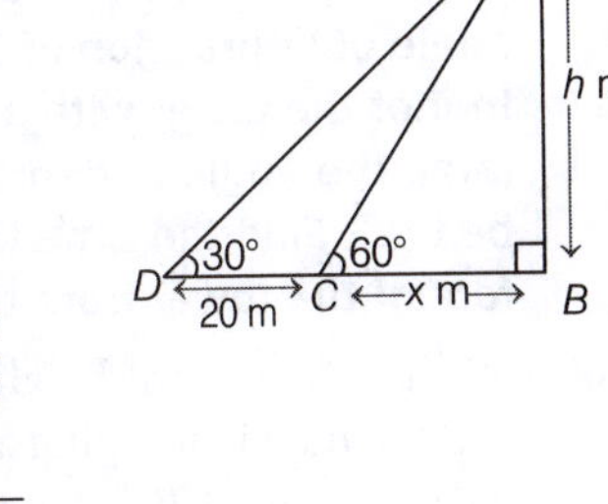

Given, $\angle ACB = 60°$ and $\angle ADB = 30°$

In right angled ΔABD,

$$\tan 30° = \frac{P}{B} = \frac{AB}{DB}$$

$$\Rightarrow \quad \frac{1}{\sqrt{3}} = \frac{h}{DC + CB}$$

$$\left[\because \tan 30° = \frac{1}{\sqrt{3}} \text{ and } DB = DC + CB\right]$$

$$\Rightarrow \quad \frac{1}{\sqrt{3}} = \frac{h}{20 + x} \Rightarrow 20 + x = \sqrt{3}h \quad \ldots\text{(i)}$$

and in right angled ΔABC,

$$\tan 60° = \frac{AB}{BC} \Rightarrow \sqrt{3} = \frac{h}{x} \quad [\because \tan 60° = \sqrt{3}]$$

$$\Rightarrow \quad h = \sqrt{3}x \quad \ldots\text{(ii)}$$

On putting $h = \sqrt{3}x$ in Eq. (i), we get

$$20 + x = \sqrt{3}(\sqrt{3}x)$$

$$\Rightarrow \quad 20 + x = 3x \Rightarrow 2x = 20 \Rightarrow x = 10 \text{ m}$$

On putting $x = 10$ m in Eq. (ii), we get

$$h = \sqrt{3}(10) \Rightarrow h = 10\sqrt{3} \text{ m}$$

Hence, the height of the tower is $10\sqrt{3}$ m and width of the canal is 10 m.

Q 12. From the top of a 7 m high building, the angle of elevation of the top of a cable tower is 60° and the angle of depression of its foot is 45°. Determine the height of the tower. CBSE 2020 (Standard)

Sol. Let $AD = 7$ m be the height of the building and $BC = h$ m be the height of the cable tower. From the top of the building D, the angles of elevation and depression are $\angle CDE = 60°$ and $\angle EDB = 45°$.

$\because DE \parallel AB$.

$\therefore \angle EDB = \angle ABD = 45°$ [alternate angles]

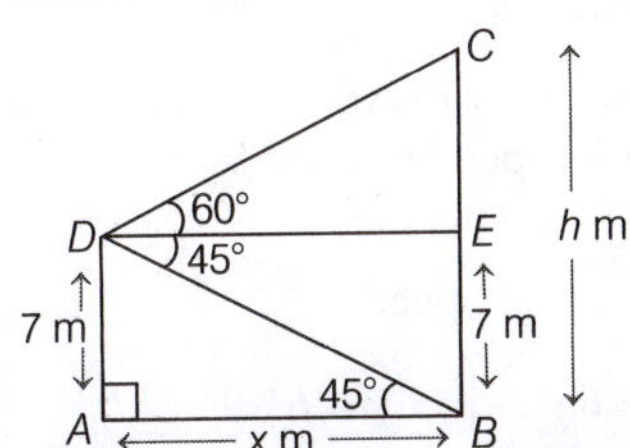

Also, $AB = DE = x$ m be the distance between building and tower.

In right angled ΔBAD,

$$\tan 45° = \frac{P}{B} = \frac{AD}{AB}$$

$$\Rightarrow \quad 1 = \frac{7}{x} \quad [\because \tan 45° = 1]$$

$$\Rightarrow \quad x = 7 \text{ m} \quad \ldots\text{(i)}$$

and in right angled ΔCED,

$$\tan 60° = \frac{CE}{DE} = \frac{CB - BE}{AB} \quad [\because CE = CB - BE]$$

$$\Rightarrow \quad \sqrt{3} = \frac{h - 7}{x} \quad [\because \tan 60° = \sqrt{3}]$$

$$\Rightarrow \quad h - 7 = x\sqrt{3}$$

$$\Rightarrow \quad h = x\sqrt{3} + 7$$

$$\Rightarrow \quad h = 7\sqrt{3} + 7 \quad \text{[from Eq. (i)]}$$

$$\Rightarrow \quad h = 7(\sqrt{3} + 1) \text{ m}$$

Hence, the height of the tower is $7(\sqrt{3} + 1)$ m.

Q 13. As observed from the top of a 75 m high lighthouse from the sea level, the angles of depression of two ships are 30° and 45°. If one ship is exactly behind the other on the same side of the lighthouse, then find the distance between the two ships.

Sol. Let $CD = 75$ m be the height of the lighthouse from the sea level. Let A and B be the positions of two ships on the sea level. From point D of the lighthouse, the angles of depression of two ships A and B are

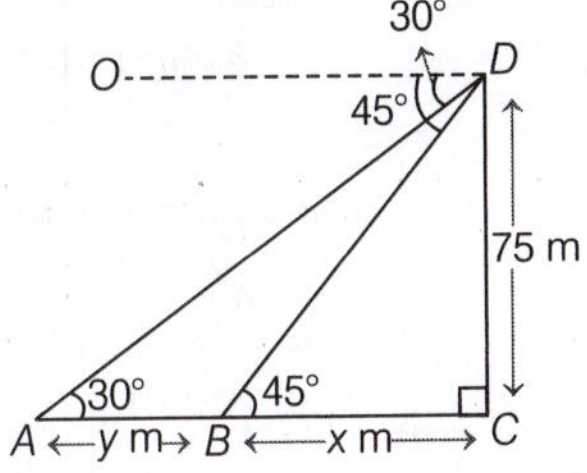

$$\angle ODA = 30° \text{ and } \angle ODB = 45°$$

$\therefore \quad \angle CAD = \angle ODA = 30°$ [alternate angles]

and $\quad \angle CBD = \angle ODB = 45°$ [alternate angles]

Let distance between two ships be $AB = y$ m and $BC = x$ m.

In right angled ΔACD,

$$\tan 30° = \frac{P}{B} = \frac{CD}{AC}$$

$$\Rightarrow \quad \frac{1}{\sqrt{3}} = \frac{75}{AB + BC}$$

$$\left[\because \tan 30° = \frac{1}{\sqrt{3}} \text{ and } AC = AB + BC\right]$$

$$\Rightarrow \quad \frac{1}{\sqrt{3}} = \frac{75}{y + x} \Rightarrow x + y = 75\sqrt{3} \quad \ldots\text{(i)}$$

and in right angled ΔDCB,

$$\tan 45° = \frac{CD}{BC}$$

$$\Rightarrow \quad 1 = \frac{75}{x} \quad [\because \tan 45° = 1]$$

$$\Rightarrow \quad x = 75 \text{ m}$$

On putting $x = 75$ m in Eq. (i), we get

$$75 + y = 75\sqrt{3} \Rightarrow y = 75(\sqrt{3} - 1) \text{ m}$$

Hence, the distance between two ships is $75(\sqrt{3} - 1)$ m.

Q 14. **A 1.2 m tall girl spots a balloon moving with the wind in a horizontal line at a height of 88.2 m from the ground. The angle of elevation of the balloon from the eyes of the girl at any instant is 60°. After sometime, the angle of elevation reduces to 30° (see the figure). Find the distance travelled by the balloon during the interval.** CBSE 2009, CBSE Sample Paper 2020 (Basic)

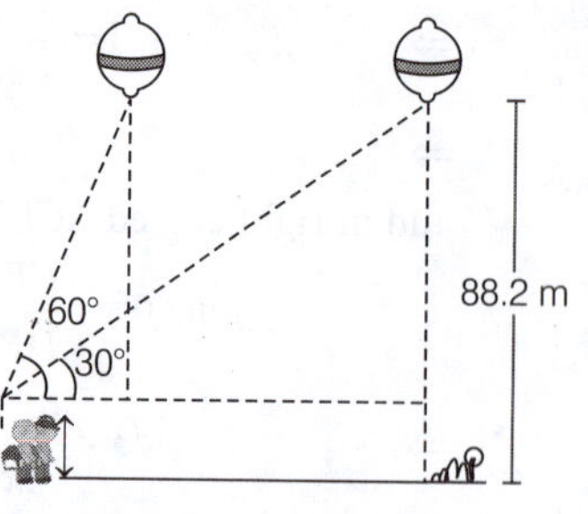

Sol. Let $AD = 1.2$ m be the height of girl standing on the horizontal line AB and let $FH = EB = 88.2$ m be the height of balloon from the line AB. At the eyes of the girl, the angles of elevation are $\angle FDC = 60°$ and $\angle EDC = 30°$.

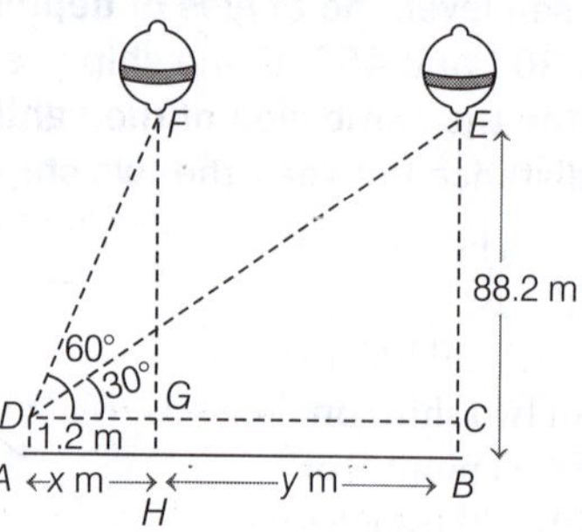

Now, $FG = EC = 88.2 - 1.2 = 87$ m

Let the distance travelled by the balloon, $HB = y$ m and $AH = x$ m.

$\therefore$ $DG = AH = x$ m and $GC = HB = y$ m

In right angled ΔFGD,

$$\tan 60° = \frac{P}{B} = \frac{FG}{DG} \Rightarrow \sqrt{3} = \frac{87}{x} \quad [\because \tan 60° = \sqrt{3}]$$

$$\Rightarrow \quad x = \frac{87}{\sqrt{3}} \quad \ldots(i)$$

In right angled ΔECD, $\tan 30° = \dfrac{EC}{DC} \Rightarrow \dfrac{1}{\sqrt{3}} = \dfrac{87}{DG + GC}$

$$\left[\because \tan 30° = \frac{1}{\sqrt{3}} \text{ and } DC = DG + GC\right]$$

$$\Rightarrow \quad \frac{1}{\sqrt{3}} = \frac{87}{x+y} \Rightarrow x + y = 87\sqrt{3} \quad \ldots(ii)$$

$$\frac{87}{\sqrt{3}} + y = 87\sqrt{3} \Rightarrow y = 87\left(\sqrt{3} - \frac{1}{\sqrt{3}}\right) \text{[from Eq. (i)]}$$

$$\Rightarrow \quad y = \frac{87\,(3-1)}{\sqrt{3}} = \frac{87 \times 2}{\sqrt{3}} \times \frac{\sqrt{3}}{\sqrt{3}} = \frac{87 \times 2\sqrt{3}}{3}$$

[rationalising]

$$= 29 \times 2\sqrt{3} = 58\sqrt{3} \text{ m}$$

Hence, the distance travelled by the balloon during the interval is $58\sqrt{3}$ m.

Q 15. **A straight highway leads to the foot of a tower. A man standing at the top of the tower observes a car at an angle of depression of 30°, which is approaching the foot of the tower with a uniform speed. Six seconds later, the angle of depression of the car is found to be 60°. Find the time taken by the car to reach the foot of the tower from this point.**

Sol. Let $CD = h$ m be the height of the tower. At point D of the tower, a man is standing and observes the car at an angle of depression of 30°. After six seconds, the angle of depression of the car is 60°.

i.e. $\angle ODA = 30°$ and $\angle ODB = 60°$

$\Rightarrow$ $\angle DAC = \angle ODA = 30°$ [alternate angles]

and $\angle DBC = \angle ODB = 60°$ [alternate angles]

Let $AB = y$ m and $BC = x$ m

In right angled ΔBCD,

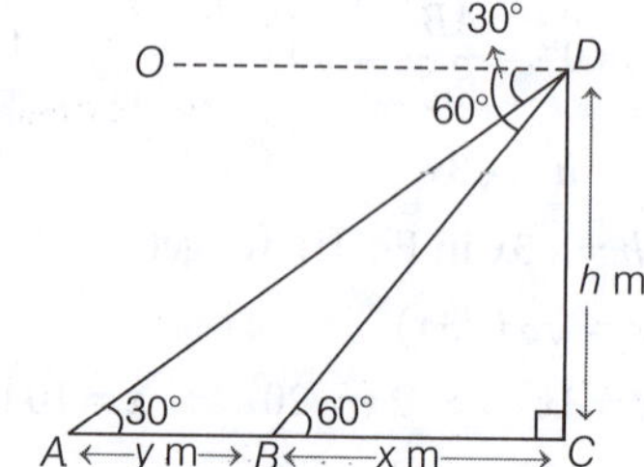

$$\tan 60° = \frac{P}{B} = \frac{CD}{BC}$$

$$\Rightarrow \quad \sqrt{3} = \frac{h}{x} \quad [\because \tan 60° = \sqrt{3}]$$

$$\Rightarrow \quad h = \sqrt{3}x \quad \ldots(i)$$

In right angled ΔACD,

$$\tan 30° = \frac{CD}{AC} = \frac{CD}{AB + BC} \quad [\because AC = AB + BC]$$

$$\Rightarrow \quad \frac{1}{\sqrt{3}} = \frac{h}{x+y} \quad \left[\because \tan 30° = \frac{1}{\sqrt{3}}\right]$$

$$\Rightarrow \quad x + y = h\sqrt{3}$$

$$\Rightarrow \quad x + y = \sqrt{3}x\,(\sqrt{3}) \quad \text{[from Eq. (i)]}$$

$$\Rightarrow \quad x + y = 3x \quad \ldots(ii)$$

It is given that a car moves from point A to B in six seconds. Let its speed be k km/s.

$$\therefore \quad \text{Time} = \frac{\text{Distance}}{\text{Speed}}$$

$$\Rightarrow \quad 6 = \frac{y}{k} \Rightarrow y = 6k$$

On putting $y = 6k$ in Eq. (ii), we get

$$x + 6k = 3x \Rightarrow 6k = 2x \Rightarrow x = 3k$$

$$\therefore \quad \text{Time} = \frac{\text{Distance}}{\text{Speed}} = \frac{x}{k} = \frac{3k}{k} = 3\text{s}$$

Hence, the car moves from point B to point C in 3 sec .

REVIEW EXERCISE

Including Competency Based Questions

Part I

Multiple Choice Questions

1. If the height of the tower is equal to the length of its shadow, then the angle of elevation of the Sun is **CBSE 2023 (Basic)**

(a) 30° (b) 45° (c) 60° (d) 90°

2. A car is moving away from the base of a 30 m high tower. The angle of elevation of the top of the tower from the car at an instant, when the car is $10\sqrt{3}$ m away from the base of the tower, is **CBSE 2024 (Basic) Compartment**

(a) 30° (b) 45° (c) 90° (d) 60°

3. An observer, 1.5 m tall is 20.5 away from a tower 22 m high, then the angle of elevation of the top of the tower from the eye of the observer is **NCERT Exemplar**

(a) 30° (b) 45° (c) 60° (d) 90°

4. From a point on the ground which is 30 m away from the foot of a vertical tower, the angle of elevation of the top of the tower is found to be 60°. The height (in metres) of the tower is **CBSE 2024 (Standard)**

(a) $10\sqrt{3}$ (b) $30\sqrt{3}$ (c) 60 (d) 30

5. A circus artist is climbing a 30 m long rope, which is tightly stretched and tied from the top of a vertical pole to the ground, then the height of pole, if the angle made by the rope with the ground level is 30°, is **Competency Based Question**

(a) 5 m (b) 10 m (c) 15 m (d) 20 m

6. If the length of the shadow on the ground of a pole is $\sqrt{3}$ times the height of the pole, then the angle of elevation of the Sun is **CBSE 2025 (Basic)**

(a) 30° (b) 45° (c) 60° (d) 90°

7. A kite is flying at a height of 80 m above the ground. The string attached to the kite is temporarily tied to a point on the ground. The inclination of the string with ground is 60°, then the length of the string is **Competency Based Question**

(a) 62.37 m (b) 92.37 m (c) 52.57 m (d) 72.57 m

8. The length of a string between a kite and a point on the ground is 85 m. If the string makes an angle θ with level ground such that $\tan\theta = \frac{15}{8}$, then the height of kite is **Competency Based Question**

(a) 75 m (b) 78.05 m
(c) 226 m (d) None of these

9. A pole, whose height is *h* units, is standing straight in the ground. The top of the pole subtends an angle β with a specific point on the ground.

Which of these gives the distance from the bottom of the pole to the point on the ground?

(a) $h \times \cos\beta$ (b) $h \times \tan\beta$
(c) $\frac{h}{\tan\beta}$ (d) $\frac{h}{\cot\beta}$

10. The top of two poles of height 20 m and 14 m are connected by a wire. If the wire makes an angle of 30° with the horizontal, then the length of the wire is

(a) 12 m (b) 10 m (c) 8 m (d) 6 m

11. From the top of a 8 m high building the angle of elevation of the top of a cable tower is 60° and the angle of depression of its foot is 45°, then the height of the tower is

(a) 14.124 m (b) 17.124 m
(c) 21.856 m (d) 15.124 m

12. Seaweed is found under 80 m deep seafloor. To reach it, a diver makes a 45° dive from a boat. What is the distance travelled by the diver to reach the seafloor? **Competency Based Question**

(a) 80 m (b) 80.2 m
(c) $80\sqrt{2}$ m (d) $80\sqrt{3}$ m

13. Two persons are watching a game in a stadium. The distance between them is 1.5 m as shown in the figure.

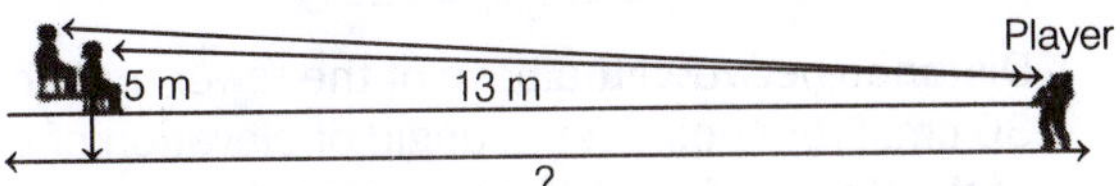

Based on the above information, what is the distance of the second person from the player?

(a) 10 m (b) 12 m (c) 13.5 m (d) 14.5 m

Case Study Based Questions

14. A short circuit can happen on electric poles due to several reasons, like

(a) If the insulation is damaged or old, it may allow the hot wires to touch with neutral. This will cause a short circuit.

(b) If there are any loose wire connections or attachments, it will allow the live and neutral wires to touch. **CBSE 2024 (Basic) Compartment**

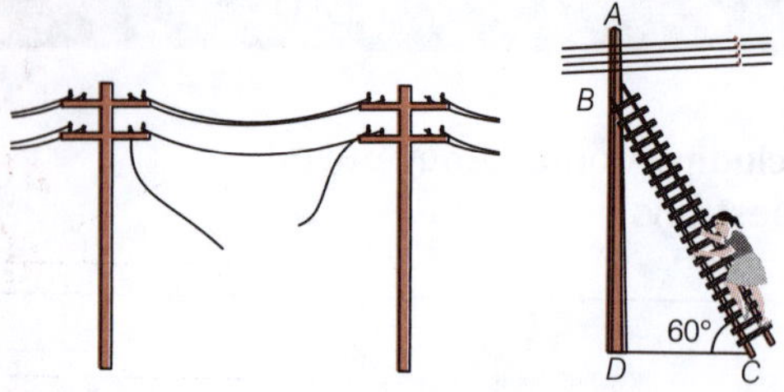

An electrician has to repair an electric fault on a pole of height 5 m. He needs to reach a point 1 m below the top of the pole to undertake the repair work.

Based on the above information, answer the following questions.

(i) What should be the length of the ladder that he should use which inclined at an angle of 60° to the horizontal, enables him to reach the required position?

(ii) (a) How far from the foot of the pole should he place the foot of the ladder?

Or

(b) What is the length of the ladder, if its foot is kept at a distance of 4 m from the foot of the pole?

15. Radio towers are used for transmitting a range of communication services including radio and television. The tower will either act as an antenna itself or support one or more antennas on its structure. On a similar concept, a radio station tower was built in two Sections *A* and *B*. Tower is supported by wires from a point *O*.

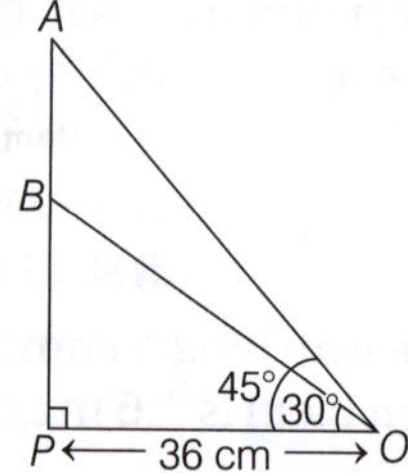

Distance between the base of the tower and point *O* is 36 cm. From point *O*, the angle of elevation of the top of the Section *B* is 30° and the angle of elevation of the top of Section *A* is 45°.

Based on the above information, answer the following questions :

(i) Find the length of the wire from the point *O* to the top of Section *B*.

(ii) Find the distance *AB*.

(iii) (a) Find the height of the Section *A* from the base of the tower.

Or (b) Find the area of ΔOPB. **CBSE 2023 (Standard)**

16. One evening, Kaushik was in a park. Children were playing cricket. Birds were singing on a nearby tree of height 80m. He observed a bird on the tree at an angle of elevation of 45°.

When a sixer was hit, a ball flew through the tree frightening the bird to fly away. In 2 s, he observed the bird flying at the same height at an angle of elevation of 30° and the ball flying towards him at the same height at an angle of elevation of 60°. **CBSE Sample paper 2023 (Standard)**

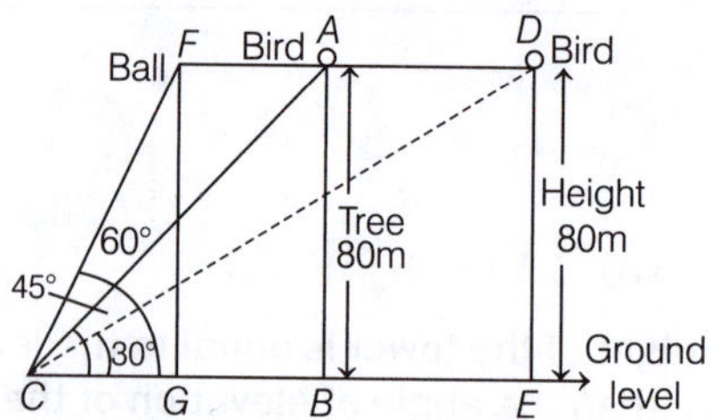

(i) At what distance from the foot of the tree was he observing the bird sitting on the tree?

(ii) How far did the bird fly in the mentioned time?

Or After hitting the tree, how far did the ball travel in the sky when Kaushik saw the ball?

(iii) What is the speed of the bird in m/min, if it had flown $20(\sqrt{3}+1)$ m?

17. Due to short circuit, a fire has broken out in New Home Complex. Two buildings, namely *X* and *Y* have mainly been affected. The fire engine has arrived and it has been stationed at a point which is between two buildings. A ladder at point *O* is fixed in front of the fire engine.

The ladder inclined at an angle 60° to the horizontal is leaning against the wall of the terrace (top) of the building *Y*. The foot of the ladder is kept fixed and after sometime it is made to lean against the terrace (top) of the opposite building *X* at an angle of 45° with the ground. Both the buildings along with the foot of the ladder, fixed at *O* are in a straight line. **CBSE 2024 (Standard Compartment)**

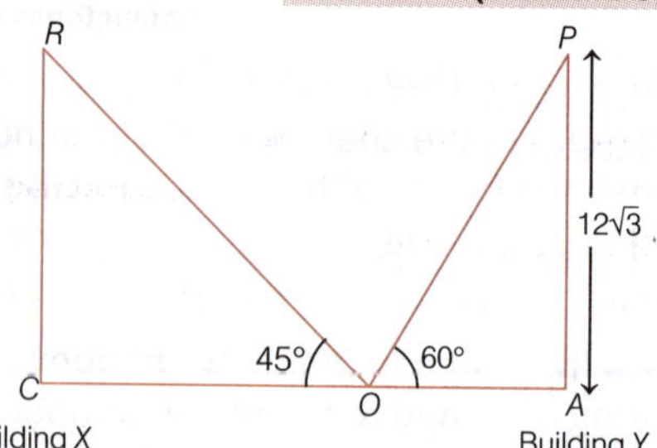

Based on the above information, answer the following questions.

(i) Find the length of the ladder.

(ii) Find the distance of the building *Y* from point *O*, i.e. *OA*.

(iii) (a) Find the horizontal distance between both buildings.

Or

(b) Find the height of the building *X*.

Part II

Very Short Answer Type Questions

1. In the given figure, the height of the girl is 1.5 m and the height of the tree is 13.5 m. **Competency Based Question**

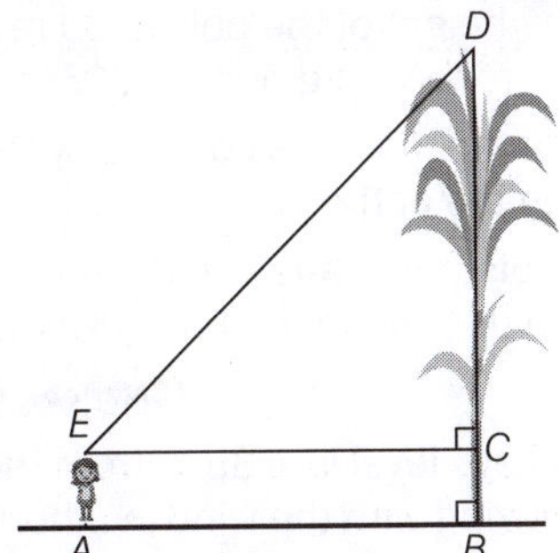

(**Note** The figure is not to scale.)

If $AB = 12\sqrt{3}$ m, what is the angle of elevation of the top of the tree from her eyes? Show your steps.

2. At the toll plaza, a traffic monitoring camera is installed at a height of 6.2 m. It takes pictures of moving vehicles at regular intervals.

The diagram below shows the position of the camera and a car moving away from it after paying the toll in four instances. The speed of the car is 5 m/s.

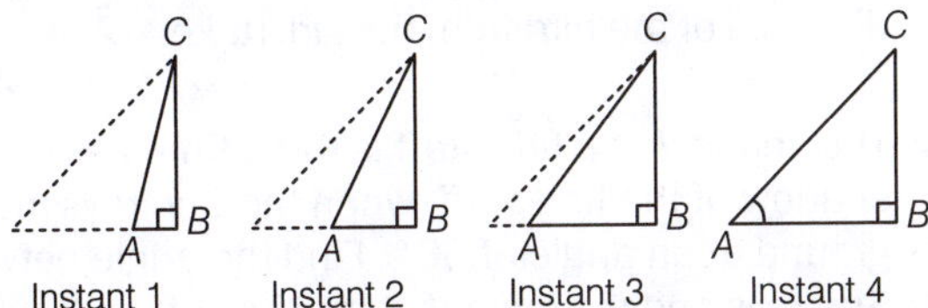

Based on the above information, answer the following questions.

The angle made by the camera to the car in instance 1 is 30° and changes to 60° in instance 4. What is the distance moved by the car? (take, $\sqrt{3} = 1.73$) **Competency Based Question**

3. Find the length of the shadow on the ground on a pole of height 18 m when angle of elevation θ of the Sun is such that $\tan\theta = \frac{6}{7}$. **CBSE 2023 (Standard)**

4. If the length of the shadow of a tower is increasing, then the angle of elevation of the Sun is also increasing. Is it true? Justify your answer. **NCERT Exemplar**

5. If the angles of elevation of the top of the candle from two coins distant a cm and b cm $(a > b)$ from its base and in the same straight line from it are 30° and 60°, then find the height of the candle. **CBSE Sample Paper 2020 (Standard)**

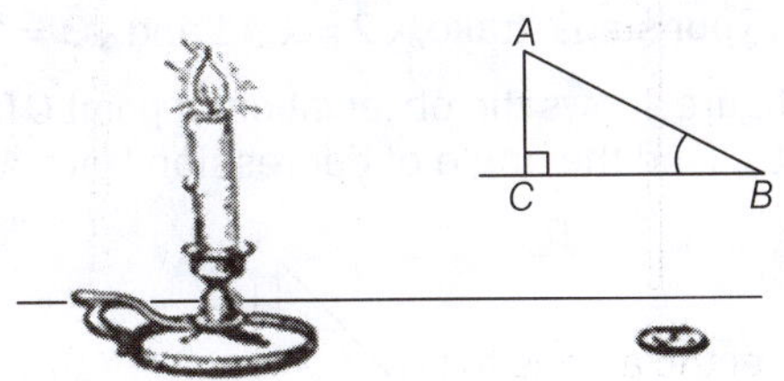

6. Find the angle of elevation of the Sun when the shadow of a pole h m high is $\sqrt{3}h$ m long. **NCERT Exemplar**

7. A tower stands vertically on the ground. From a point on the ground which is 20 m away from of the foot of the tower, the angle of elevation of the top of the tower is found to be 60°. Find the height of the tower.

8. A peacock sitting on the top of a tree of height 10 m observe a snake moving on the ground. If the snake is $10\sqrt{3}$ m away from the base of the tree, then angle of depression of the snake from the eye of the peacock is **CBSE 2025 (Standard)**

(a) 30° (b) 45° (c) 60° (d) 90°

9. The angle of elevation of the top of a building 150 m high, from a point on the ground is 45°. Find the distance of the point from foot of the building.

10. Shown below is a submarine scouting an enemy ship in the ocean using a sonar device. Sonar devices send out a sound pulse from a transducer, and then precisely measure the time it takes for the sound pulses to be reflected back to the transducer.

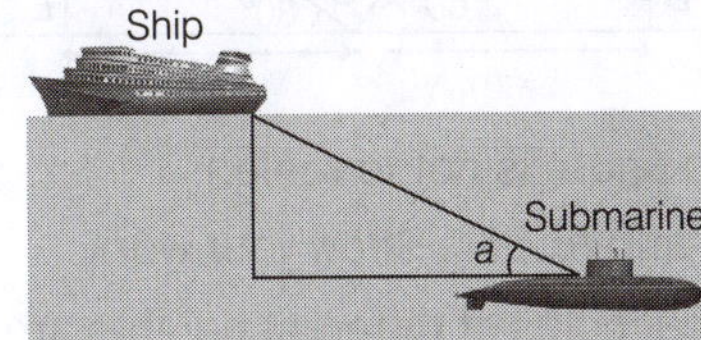

A sonar wave sent by the submarine hits the ship and returns back in 2 sec. The speed of a sonar wave underwater is 1500 m/s and the submarine is diving at a depth of 750 m below sea level.

Find the angle of elevation a of the ship from the submarine. Show your steps. **Competency Based Question**

11. The position of an Eagle and two identical geese are shown in the figure below. All the birds are at the same height from the ground. Assume that the Eagle can fly at the same speed in all directions and that the geese are unaware of the Eagle's intention and will not move from their positions.

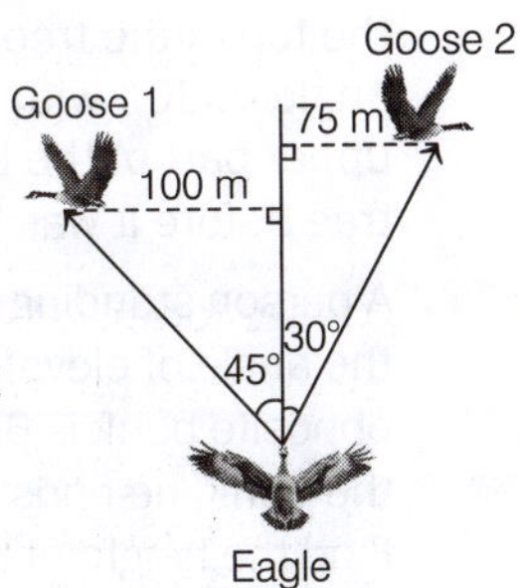

(**Note** The figure is not to scale.)

If the Eagle wants to attack the goose that is nearer to it, which one should it attack?
Show your steps. (take, $\sqrt{2}=1.41$ and $\sqrt{3}=1.73$)

12. The figure shows the observation of point C from point A. Find the angle of depression from A.

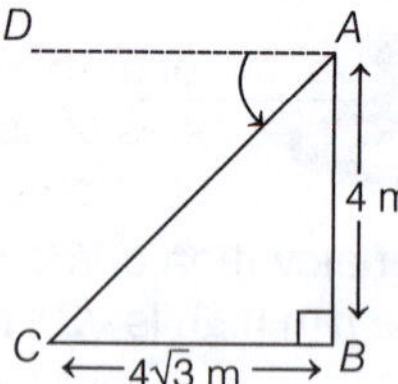

13. The angle of depression of car parked on the road from the top of a 150 m high tower is 30°. Find the distance of the car from the tower.

Short Answer Type Questions

14. Two poles of height h_1 m and h_2 m subtend angles 60° and 30°, respectively. At the mid-point of the line joining their feet. The distance from the point on the ground to both poles is given by x m as shown in the figure below. **CBSE QB**

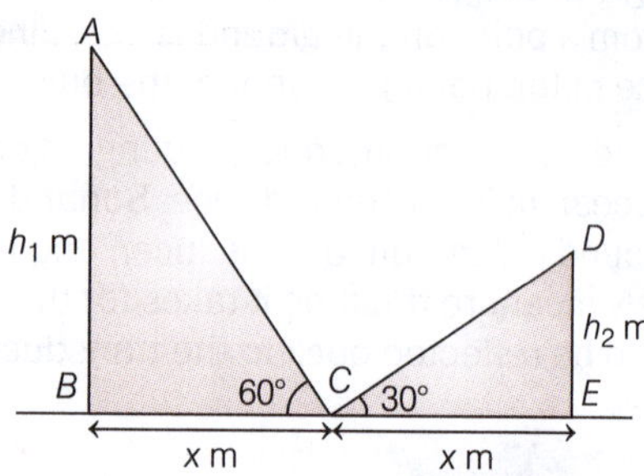

(**Note** The figure is not to scale.)

Find the ratio $h_1 : h_2$. Show your work.

15. Two vertical poles of different heights are standing 20m away from each other on the level ground. The angle of elevation of the top of the first pole from the foot of the second pole is 60° and angle of elevation of the top of the second pole from the foot of the first pole is 30°. Find the difference between the heights of two poles. [take, $\sqrt{3}=1.732$]

16. A tree is broken due to the storm in such a way that the top of the tree touches the ground and makes an angle of 30° with the ground. Length of the broken upper part of the tree is 8 m. Find the height of the tree before it was broken.

17. A person standing on the bank of a river observes that the angle of elevation of the top of tree standing on the opposite bank is 60°. When he moves 40 m away from the bank, he finds the angle of elevation to be 30°. Find the height of the tree and the width of the river. [take, $\sqrt{3}=1.732$]

18. Sachin is a fireman worker. When he throws water on the fire of burning house, he notice that one child is crying for getting help. At once Sachin tied a rope at the top of a pole near the burning house and its other end tied at the ground. He climbed the rope and from the top of the pole picked the child and save his life. Suppose the height of the pole is 20 m and the angle made by the rope with ground is 60°.

(i) Calculate the distance covered by the fireman to reach the top of the pole.

(ii) Find the distance between the foot of the pole and where he tied the rope at the ground.

Competency Based Question

19. A boy whose eye level is 1.35 m from the ground, spots a balloon moving with the wind in a horizontal line at some height from the ground. The angle of elevation of the balloon from the eyes of the boy at an instant is 60°. After 12 sec, the angle of elevation reduces to 30°. If the speed of the wind is 3 m/sec, then find the height of the balloon from the ground.
[take, $\sqrt{3}=1.73$] **CBSE Sample Paper 2025 (Standard)**

20. A boy standing on a horizontal plane finds a bird flying at a distance of 100 m from him at an elevation of 30°. A girl standing on the roof of a 20 m high building, finds the elevation of the same bird to be 45°. The boy and the girl are on the opposite sides of the bird. Find the distance of the bird from the girl. [take, $\sqrt{2}=1.414$] **CBSE 2019**

21. The shadow of a flag staff is three times as long as the shadow of the flag staff, when the Sun rays meet the ground at an angle of 60°. Find the angle between the Sun rays and the ground at the time of longer shadow.

22. The angle of elevation of a jet plane from a point A, on the ground is 60°. After a flight of 30 s, the angle of elevation changes to 30°. If the jet plane is flying at a constant height of $3600\sqrt{3}$ m, find the speed of the jet plane. **CBSE 2024 (Standard)**

23. There is a small island in the middle of a 100 m wide river and a tall tree stands on the island. P and Q are points directly opposite to each other on two banks and in line with the tree. Suppose the angles of elevation of the top of the tree from P and Q are respectively 30° and 45°.

(i) Find the height of the tree. [take, $\sqrt{3}=1.732$]

(ii) Determine the distance of point P from foot of tree.

(iii) Which point is farthest from the island?

Competency Based Question

24. The angle of elevation of the top Q of a vertical tower PQ from a point X on the ground is 60°. At a point R, 40 m vertically above X, the angle of elevation of the top Q of tower is 45°. Find the height of the tower PQ and the distance PX. [take, $\sqrt{3}=1.732$]

25. Sunita is an electrician and she has to repair an electric fault on a pole of height 8 m. She needs to reach to a point on the pole 3 m below the top of the pole to undertake the repair work.

(i) What should be the length of the ladder that she should use which when inclined at an angle of 30° from the horizontal, would enable her to reach the required position?

(ii) How far from the foot of the pole should she place the foot of the ladder.

(iii) The space between the pole and ladder is in the triangular shape, find its area.

26. A vertical tower stands on a horizontal plane and is surmounted by a vertical flag staff of height h. At a point on the plane, the angles of elevation of the bottom and the top of the flag staff are α and β, respectively. Prove that the height of the tower is $\left(\frac{h\tan\alpha}{\tan\beta - \tan\alpha}\right)$.

27. Two trees are $2d$ m apart. Ajay stood at a point midway between them and started walking in a direction perpendicular to the line connecting the two trees. After walking d metres, he observed the angle of elevations to the tops of the two trees and found them to be complementary.

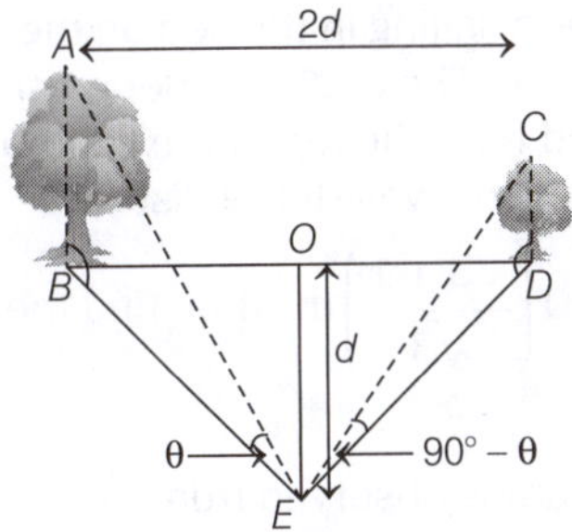

(**Note** The figure is not to scale.)

If one of the trees is thrice as tall as the other, find the height of the shorter tree, in terms of d.

Show your work. **Competency Based Question**

28. A player sitting on the top of a tower of height 20 m observes the angle of depression of a ball lying on the ground as 60°. Find the distance between the foot of the tower and the ball.

29. A peacock is sitting on the top of a tree. It observes a serpent on the ground making an angle of depression of 30°. The peacock catches the serpent in 12 s with the speed of 300 m/min. What is the height of the tree?

30. From the top of a hill, the angles of depression of two consecutive kilometre stones due East are found to be 30° and 45°. Find the height of the hill.

31. As observed from the top of a lighthouse, 100 m high above sea level, the angle of depression of a ship sailing directly towards it, changes from 30° to 60°. Determine the distance travelled by the ship during the period of observation. [take, $\sqrt{3} = 1.732$] **CBSE 2022 (Basic)**

32. As observed from the top of a 75 m high lighthouse from the sea level, the angles of depression of two ships are 30° and 45°. If one ship is exactly behind the other on the same side of the lighthouse, find the distance between the two ships. [take, $\sqrt{3} = 1.732$] **CBSE Sample Paper 2025 (Basic)**

33. From the top of a building 50 m high, the angles of depression of the top and bottom of a tower are observed to be 30° and 60°. Find the height of the tower and distance between the building and the tower. [take, $\sqrt{3} = 1.73$] **CBSE 2023 (Basic)**

34. A ship was moving towards the shore at a uniform speed of 36 km/h. Initially, the ship was 1.3 km away from the foot of a lighthouse which is 173.2 m in height.

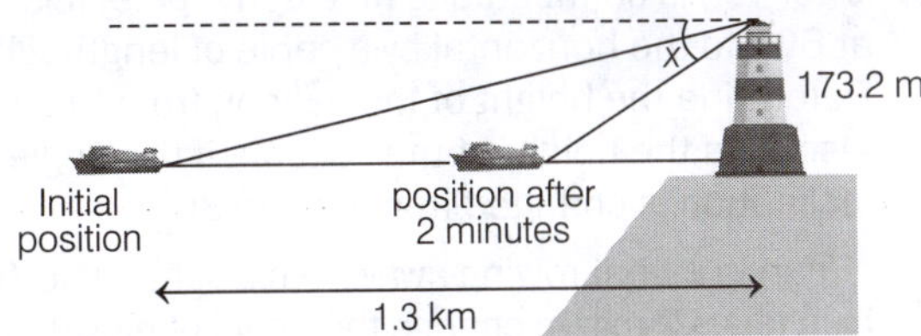

(**Note** The figure is not to scale.)

Find the angle of depression x of the top of the lighthouse from the ship after the ship had been moving for 2 min. Show your steps and give reasons.

(take, $\sqrt{3} = 1.732$ and $\sqrt{2} = 1.414$)

Competency Based Question

35. A window in a building is at a height of 10 m from the ground. The angle of depression of a point P on the ground from the window is 30°. The angle of elevation of the top of the building from the point P is 60°. Find the height of the building.

36. A man standing on the deck of a ship, which is 10 m above the water level. He observes the angle of elevation of the top of a hill is 60° and the angle of depression of the base of the hill is 30°. Calculate the distance of the hill from the ship and height of the hill. **Competency Based Question**

37. A window of a house is h m above the ground. From the window, the angles of elevation and depression of the top and the bottom of another house situated on the opposite side of the lane are found to be α and β, respectively. Prove that the height of the other house is $h(1 + \tan\alpha \cot\beta)$ m.

Long Answer Type Questions

38. The angle of elevation θ of the top of a lighthouse as seen by a person on the ground is such that $\tan\theta = \frac{5}{12}$. When the person moves a distance of 240 m towards the lighthouse, the angle of elevation becomes ϕ, such that $\tan\phi = \frac{3}{4}$. Find the height of the lighthouse.

39. The shadow of a tower standing on a level ground is found to be 40 m longer when the Sun's altitude is $30°$ than when it was $60°$. Find the height of the tower and the length of original shadow. [take, $\sqrt{3} = 1.73$] **CBSE 2024 (Basic)**

40. The angle of elevation of the top of a tower at a distance of 120 m from a point A on the ground is $45°$. If the angle of elevation of the top of a flag staff fixed at the top of the tower at A is $60°$, then find the height of the flag staff. [take, $\sqrt{3} = 1.732$]

41. A balloon is connected to an electric pole. It is inclined at $60°$ to the horizontal by a cable of length 215 m. Determine the height of the balloon from the ground. Also, find the height of the balloon, if the angle of inclination is changed from $60°$ to $30°$.

42. A man in a boat rowing away from a lighthouse 100 m high takes 2 min to change the angle of elevation of the lighthouse from $60°$ to $45°$. Find the speed of boat.

43. The angle of elevation of the top of a building from the foot of the tower is $30°$ and the angle of elevation of the top of the tower from the foot of the building is $60°$. If the tower is 60 m high, then find the height of the building. **CBSE 2020 (Basic), 2013**

44. At the foot of mountain, the elevation of its summit is $45°$. After ascending 1000 m towards to mountain up a slope of $30°$ inclination, the elevation is found to be $60°$. Find the height of the mountain.

45. A ladder leaning against a vertical wall at an inclination α to the horizontal. Its foot is pulled away from the wall through a distance p, so that its upper end slides a distance q down the wall and then the ladder makes an angle β to the horizontal.

(i) Show that $\frac{p}{q} = \frac{\cos\beta - \cos\alpha}{\sin\alpha - \sin\beta}$.

(ii) Check whether the above result is true for $\alpha = \beta$.

46. A triangle is drawn inside a square of side length 6 cm as shown in figure given below. **Competency Based Question**

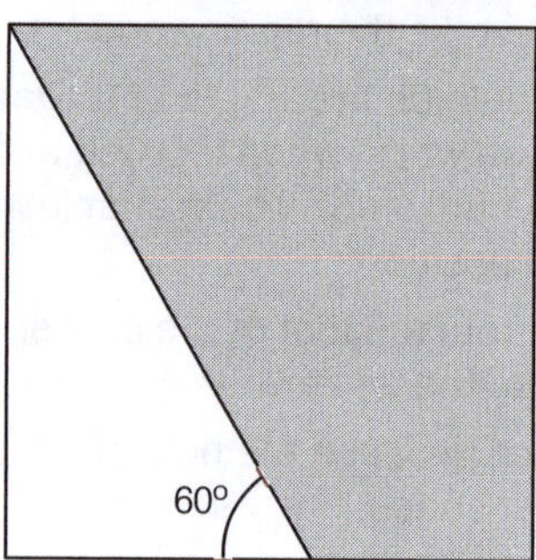

What is the area of the shaded region?

47. In the figure below, PQU is a right angled triangle with $\angle PQU = 90°$. ST is parallel to RQ, $PS = RQ$ and $ST = RU$. Calculate the length of SR. **Competency Based Question**

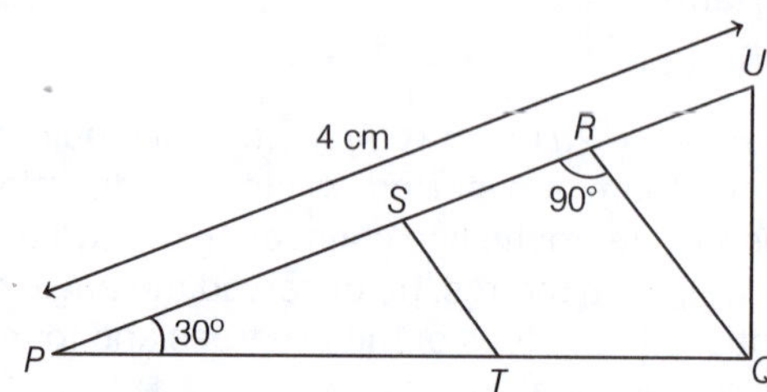

48. Two ships are sailing in the sea on the either side of the lighthouse. The angles of depression of two ships as observed from the top of the lighthouse are $60°$ and $45°$, respectively. If the distance between the ships is $100\left(\frac{\sqrt{3}+1}{\sqrt{3}}\right)$ m, then find the height of the lighthouse.

49. A moving boat is observed from the top of a 150 m high cliff moving away from the cliff. The angle of depression of the boat changes from $60°$ to $45°$ in 2 min. Find the speed of the boat in (m/h).

50. A man on a cliff observes a boat at an angle of depression of $30°$ which is approaching the shore to the point immediately beneath the observer with a uniform speed. Six minutes later, the angle of depressions of the boat is found to be $60°$. Find the time taken by the boat from here to reach the shore. **CBSE 2024 (Standard)**

HINTS & SOLUTIONS

Part I

1. (b) Let AB be the tower and BC be its shadow.

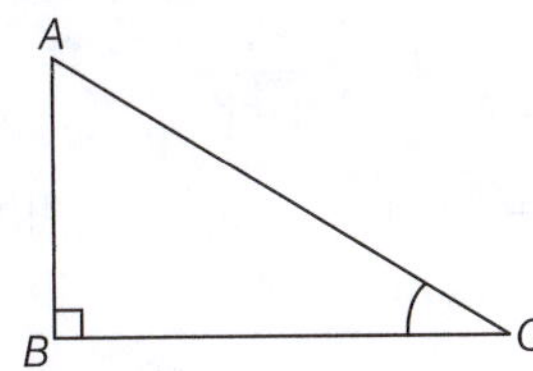

Given, $AB = BC$

In right angled ΔABC,

$$\tan C = \frac{\text{Perpendicular}}{\text{Base}} = \frac{AB}{BC} = 1$$

$\Rightarrow \tan C = \tan 45°$ $[\because \tan 45° = 1]$

$\therefore C = 45°$

2. (d)

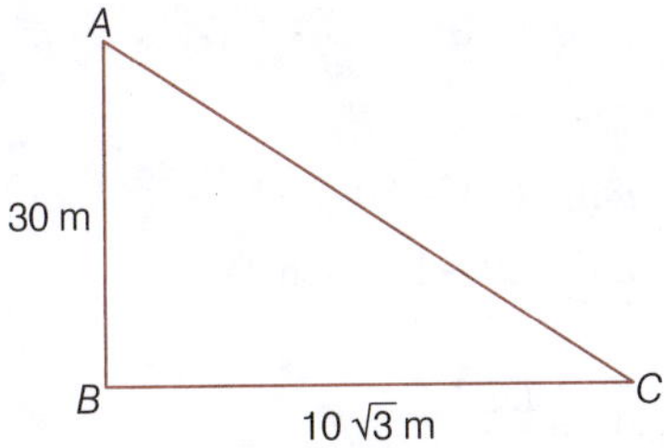

Let $AB = 30$ m be the height of the tower and distance of the car from the base of the tower $BC = 10\sqrt{3}$ m.

In right angled ΔABC,

$$\tan C = \frac{AB}{BC}$$

$$\Rightarrow \tan C = \frac{30}{10\sqrt{3}}$$

$$\Rightarrow \tan C = \sqrt{3}$$

$$\Rightarrow \tan C = \tan 60°$$

$$\therefore \angle C = 60°$$

3. (b) Let $BE = 22$ m be the height of the tower and $AD = 1.5$ m be the height of the observer. The point D be the observer's eye. Draw $DC \parallel AB$.

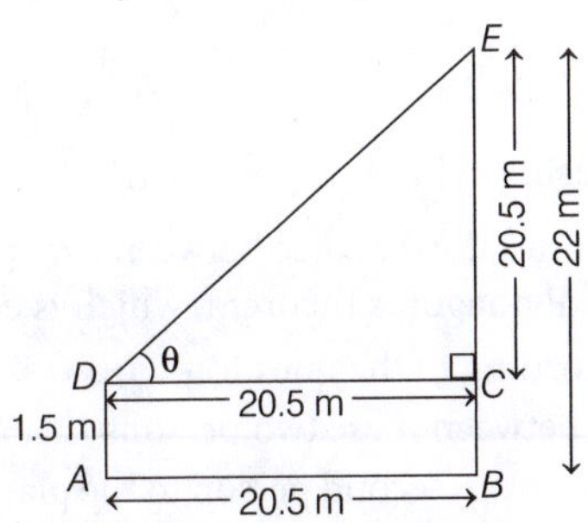

Then, $AB = 20.5$ m $= DC$ and $EC = BE - BC$

$= BE - AD = 22 - 1.5 = 20.5$ m $[\because BC = AD]$

Let θ be the angle of elevation make by observer's eye to the top of the tower i.e. $\angle EDC = \theta$.

In right angled ΔDCE,

$$\tan\theta = \frac{P}{B} = \frac{CE}{DC} = \frac{20.5}{20.5}$$

$$\Rightarrow \tan\theta = 1 \Rightarrow \tan\theta = \tan 45° \Rightarrow \theta = 45°$$

4. (b) Let the height of the tower AB be h m.

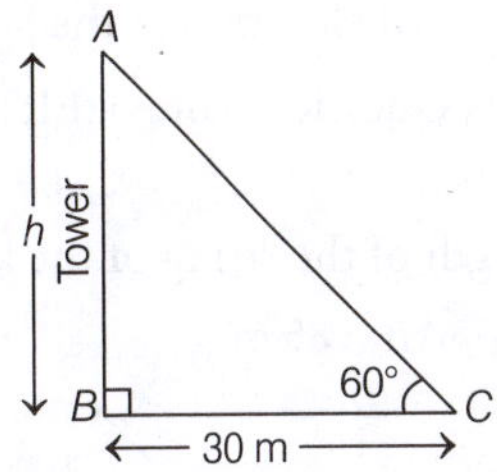

In right angled ΔABC,

$$\tan 60° = \frac{P}{B} = \frac{AB}{BC}$$

$$\Rightarrow \sqrt{3} = \frac{h}{30} \Rightarrow h = 30\sqrt{3}$$

$\therefore$ The height of the tower is $30\sqrt{3}$ m.

5. (c) Let AB be the vertical pole and CA be the 30 m long rope such that its one end A is tied from the top of the vertical pole AB and the other end C is tied to a point C on the ground.

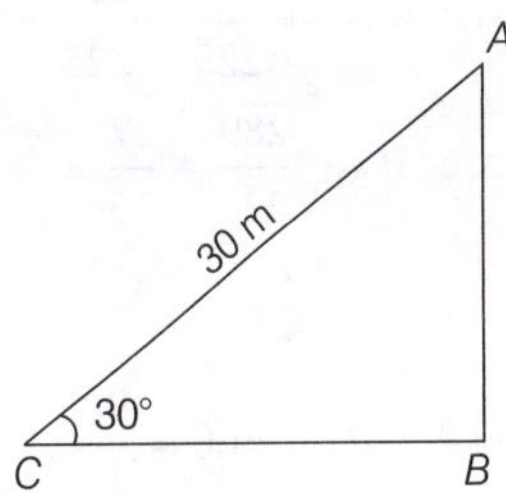

In right angled ΔABC, we have

$$\sin 30° = \frac{AB}{AC} \Rightarrow \frac{1}{2} = \frac{AB}{30}$$

$$\Rightarrow AB = 15 \text{ m}$$

Hence, the height of the pole is 15 m.

6. (a)

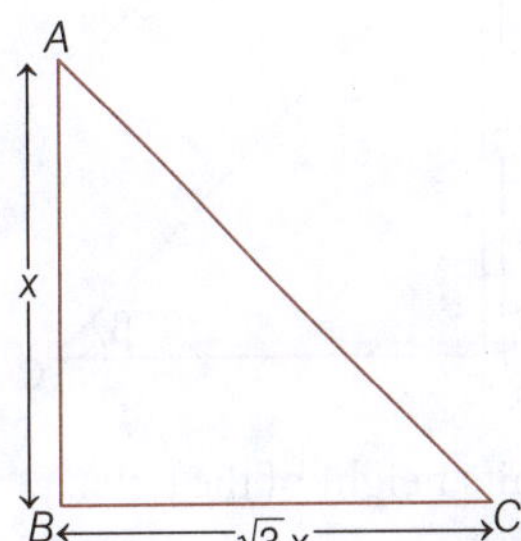

Let $AB = x$ be the height of the pole and $BC = \sqrt{3}x$ be the length of the shadow.

In right angled ΔABC,

$$\tan C = \frac{AB}{BC}$$

$$\Rightarrow \quad \tan C = \frac{x}{\sqrt{3}x}$$

$$\Rightarrow \quad \tan C = \frac{1}{\sqrt{3}}$$

$$\Rightarrow \quad C = 30°$$

Hence, the angle of elevation of the Sun is 30°.

7. (b) Do same as Question 5 of NCERT Folder Exercise 9.1.

8. (a) Given, length of the string of the kite,

$$AB = 85 \text{ m}$$

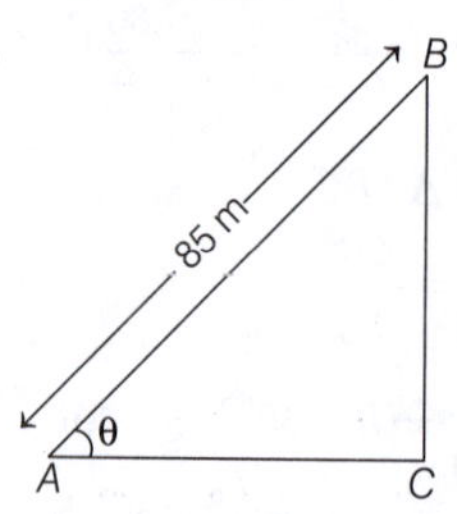

and $\quad \tan\theta = \frac{15}{8} \Rightarrow \cot\theta = \frac{8}{15}$

$$\Rightarrow \quad \text{cosec}^2\theta - 1 = \frac{64}{225}$$

$$\Rightarrow \quad \text{cosec}^2\theta = 1 + \frac{64}{225} = \frac{289}{225}$$

$$\Rightarrow \quad \text{cosec}\,\theta = \sqrt{\frac{289}{225}} = \frac{17}{15}$$

$$\Rightarrow \quad \sin\theta = \frac{15}{17}$$

In right angled ΔABC, $\sin\theta = \frac{BC}{AB}$

$$\Rightarrow \quad \frac{15}{17} = \frac{BC}{85} \Rightarrow BC = 75 \text{ m}$$

$\therefore$ Height of kite = 75 m

9. (c)

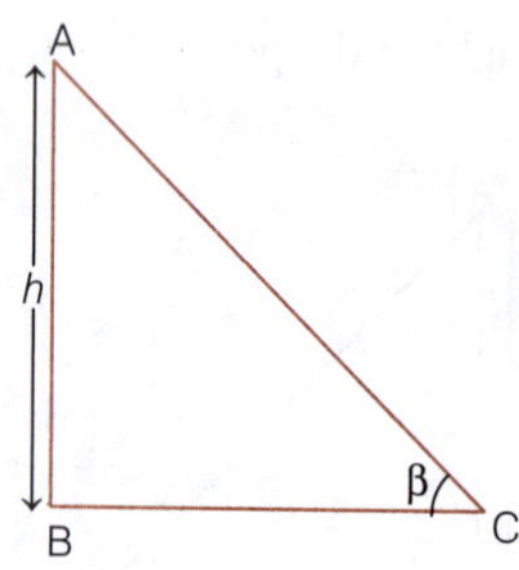

Let $AB = h$ units height of the pole.

In right angled ΔABC,

$$\Rightarrow \quad \tan C = \frac{AB}{BC}$$

$$\Rightarrow \quad \tan\beta = \frac{h}{BC}$$

$$\Rightarrow \quad BC = \frac{h}{\tan\beta}$$

10. (a) Here, $CD = 20$ m [height of big pole]

$AB = 14$ m [height of small pole]

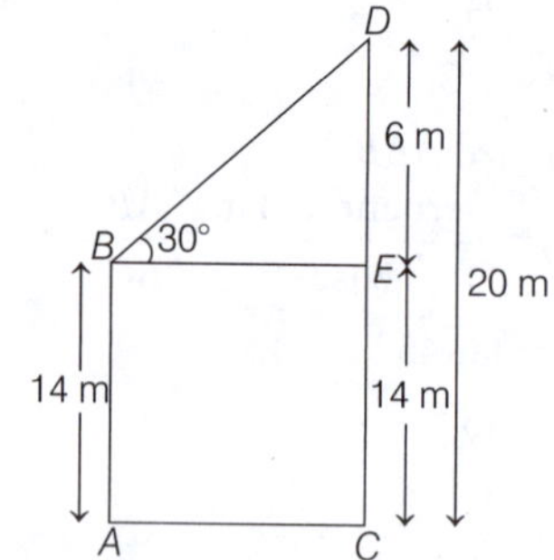

$$\therefore \quad DE = CD - CE$$

$$\Rightarrow \quad DE = CD - AB \qquad [\because AB = CE]$$

$$\Rightarrow \quad DE = 20 - 14 = 6 \text{ m}$$

In ΔBDE,

$$\sin 30° = \frac{DE}{BD}$$

$$\Rightarrow \quad \frac{1}{2} = \frac{6}{BD} \Rightarrow BD = 12 \text{ m}$$

$\therefore$ Length of wire = 12 m

11. (c) **Hint** Do same as Question 12 of NCERT Folder Exercise 9.1.

12. (c) **Hint** Since, diver makes an angle of 45° from the boat, it is an angle of depression.

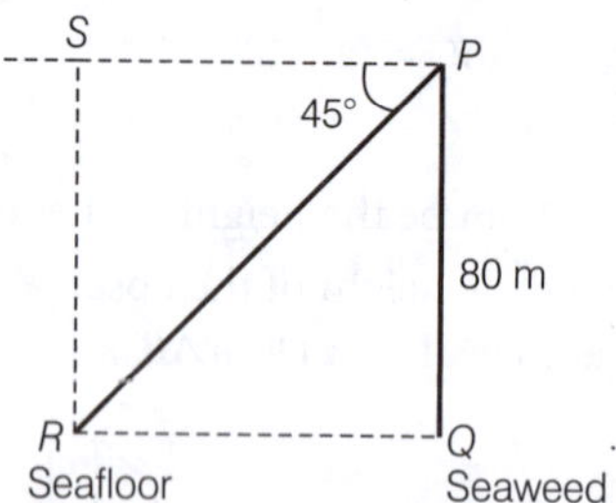

Find PR using suitable trigonometric ratio.

13. (c) **Hint** Find the distance between first person and the player by Pythagoras theorem, which is equal to 12 m.

Now, according to the question,

Distance between these two persons is 1.5 m.

$\therefore$ Distance from second person to the player = 12 + 1.5 m

= 13.5 m

14. Hint Do same as Example 3.

Ans. (i) $\frac{8\sqrt{3}}{3}$ m, (ii) (a) $\frac{4}{\sqrt{3}}$ m *Or* (b) $4\sqrt{2}$ m

15. (i) In right angled ΔOPB,

$$\cos 30° = \frac{OP}{OB} = \frac{36}{OB}$$

$$\Rightarrow \quad OB = \frac{36}{\cos 30°} = \frac{36}{\frac{\sqrt{3}}{2}} = \frac{72}{\sqrt{3}} \times \frac{\sqrt{3}}{\sqrt{3}}$$

$$\therefore \quad OB = 24\sqrt{3} \text{ cm}$$

(ii) In right angled ΔOPB,

$$\tan 30° = \frac{BP}{OP}$$

$$\Rightarrow \quad \frac{1}{\sqrt{3}} = \frac{BP}{36}$$

$$\Rightarrow \quad BP = \frac{36}{\sqrt{3}} \times \frac{\sqrt{3}}{\sqrt{3}}$$

$$\Rightarrow \quad BP = 12\sqrt{3} \text{ cm} \quad \ldots\text{(i)}$$

In right angled ΔAPO,

$$\tan 45° = \frac{AP}{OP}$$

$$\Rightarrow \quad OP = AP \quad [\because \tan 45° = 1]$$

$$\Rightarrow \quad AP = 36 \text{ cm} \quad \ldots\text{(ii)}$$

$\therefore$ Distance, $AB = AP - BP$

$$= 36 - 12\sqrt{3} = 12(3 - \sqrt{3}) \text{ cm}$$

(iii) (a) Height of the Section *A* from the base of the tower

$$AP = 36 \text{ cm} \quad \text{[using Eq (ii)]}$$

Or

(b) $BP = 12\sqrt{3}$ cm [using Eq. (i)]

$$\therefore \text{ Area of } \Delta OPB = \frac{1}{2} \times OP \times BP$$

$$= \frac{1}{2} \times 36 \times 12\sqrt{3} = 216\sqrt{3} \text{ cm}^2$$

16. (i) In right angled ΔABC,

$$\tan 45° = \frac{AB}{BC}$$

$$\Rightarrow \quad BC = AB = 80 \text{ m} \quad \ldots\text{(i)}$$

$$[\because AB = 80 \text{ m and } \tan 45° = 1]$$

$\therefore$ Required distance = 80 m

(ii) In right angled ΔDEC,

$$\tan 30° = \frac{DE}{EC}$$

$$\Rightarrow \quad \frac{1}{\sqrt{3}} = \frac{80}{EC}$$

$$\left[\because DE = 80 \text{ m and } \tan 30° = \frac{1}{\sqrt{3}}\right]$$

$$\Rightarrow \quad EC = 80\sqrt{3} \text{ m}$$

$$\therefore \quad BE = EC - BC$$

$$= 80\sqrt{3} - 80 \quad \text{[using Eq. (i)]}$$

$$= 80(\sqrt{3} - 1) \text{ m}$$

Hence, distance the bird flew

$$= AD = BE$$

$$= 80(\sqrt{3} - 1) \text{ m}$$

Or

In right angled ΔCGF,

$$\tan 60° = \frac{GF}{GC}$$

$$\Rightarrow \quad \sqrt{3} = \frac{80}{GC}$$

$$[\because GF = ED = 80 \text{ m and } \tan 60° = \sqrt{3}]$$

$$\Rightarrow \quad GC = \frac{80\sqrt{3}}{3} \text{ m} \quad \ldots\text{(ii)}$$

Distance travelled by the ball after hitting the tree

$$= AF = BG$$

and $BG = BC - GC$

$$= \left(80 - \frac{80\sqrt{3}}{3}\right)$$

$$= 80\left(\frac{3 - \sqrt{3}}{3}\right) \text{ m}$$

[using Eqs. (i) and (ii)]

(iii) Speed of the bird $= \frac{\text{Distance}}{\text{Time}}$

$$= \frac{20(\sqrt{3} + 1)}{2} \text{ m/sec}$$

$$= 10(\sqrt{3} + 1) \text{ m/sec}$$

$$= 600(\sqrt{3} + 1) \text{ m/min}$$

$$\left[\because 1 \text{ sec} = \frac{1}{60} \text{ min}\right]$$

17. Let the length of the ladder be l m

i.e. $OP = OR = l$ m and $OA = x$ m, $OC = y$ m

(i) In right angled ΔOAP,

$$\sin 60° = \frac{AP}{OP}$$

$$\Rightarrow \quad \frac{\sqrt{3}}{2} = \frac{12\sqrt{3}}{OP} \Rightarrow l = OP = 24 \text{ m}$$

Hence, the length of the ladder = 24 m

(ii) Again, in right angled ΔOAP,

$$\tan 60° = \frac{AP}{OA}$$

$$\Rightarrow \quad \sqrt{3} = \frac{12\sqrt{3}}{x} \Rightarrow x = 12 \text{ m}$$

Hence, the distance of the building *Y* from point *O* is 12 m.

(iii) (a) In right angled ΔOCR,

$$\cos 45° = \frac{OC}{OR}$$

$$\Rightarrow \quad \frac{1}{\sqrt{2}} = \frac{OC}{24}$$

$$\Rightarrow \quad y = OC = 12\sqrt{2} \text{ m}$$

Horizontal distance between the buildings

$$= (x + y) = 12(\sqrt{2} + 1) \text{ m}$$

Or

(b) Again, in right angled ΔOCR,

$$\tan 45° = \frac{RC}{OC}$$

$$\Rightarrow \quad 1 = \frac{RC}{12\sqrt{2}}$$

$$\Rightarrow \quad x = RC = 12\sqrt{2} \text{ m}$$

Height of building x is $12\sqrt{2}$ m.

Part II

1. According to the figure,

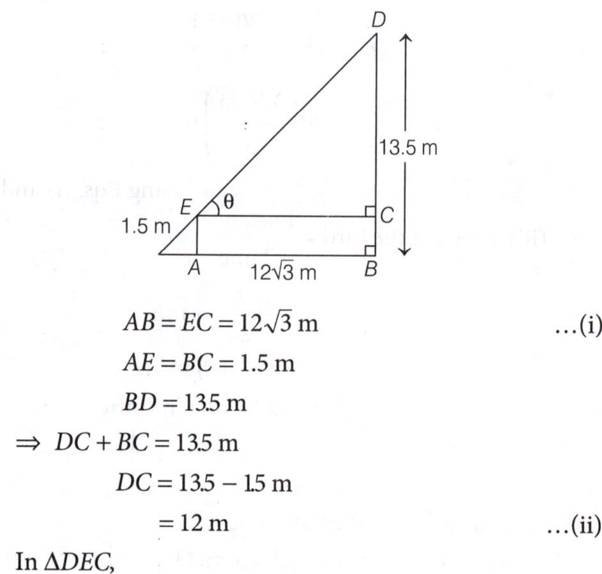

$$AB = EC = 12\sqrt{3} \text{ m} \quad \ldots\text{(i)}$$

$$AE = BC = 1.5 \text{ m}$$

$$BD = 13.5 \text{ m}$$

$$\Rightarrow DC + BC = 13.5 \text{ m}$$

$$DC = 13.5 - 1.5 \text{ m}$$

$$= 12 \text{ m} \quad \ldots\text{(ii)}$$

In ΔDEC,

$$\tan\theta = \frac{DC}{EC}$$

$$= \frac{12}{12\sqrt{3}} \quad \text{[from Eqs. (i) and (ii)]}$$

$$\tan\theta = \frac{1}{\sqrt{3}}$$

$$\therefore \quad \theta = 30° \quad \left[\because \tan 30° = \frac{1}{\sqrt{3}}\right]$$

Hence, angle of elevation of top of the tree from her eyes is 30°.

2. Hint In instance 1, $\angle ACB = 30°$ and in instance 4, $\angle ACB = 60°$

Then, with the help of suitable trigonometric ratio, find the distance.

Ans. 7.16 m

3. Hint Let AB be the pole of height 18 m and BC be the length of the shadow.

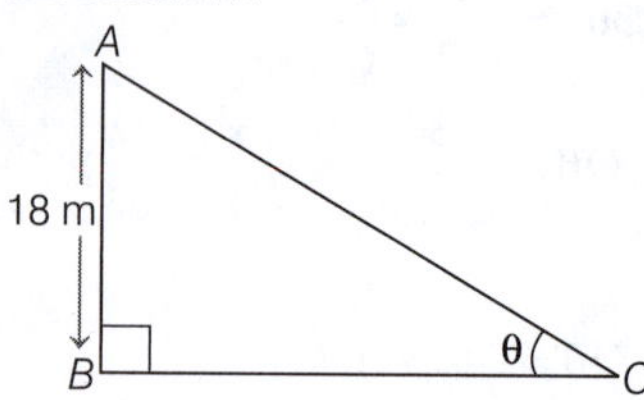

In right angled ΔABC,

$$\tan\theta = \frac{AB}{BC} = \frac{18}{BC} = \frac{6}{7} \quad \left[\text{given}, \tan\theta = \frac{6}{7}\right]$$

Ans. 21 m

4. False, because when length of shadow increases, the angle of elevation of the Sun decreases and *vice-versa*.

5. Given, the angle of elevation of the top of candle from two coins distant a cm and b cm from its base.

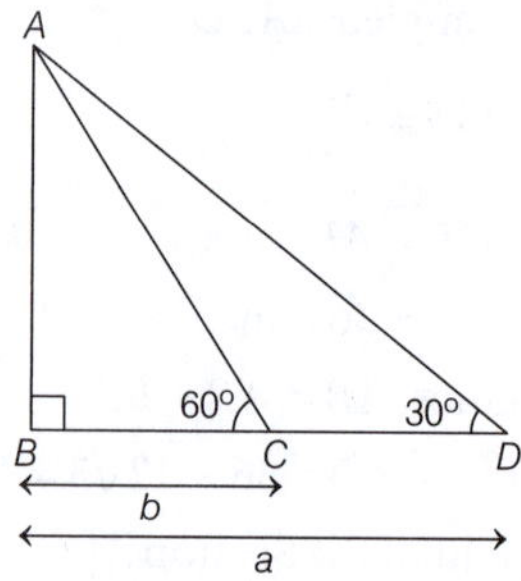

$$\text{In } \Delta ABC, \quad \tan 60° = \frac{AB}{BC} \Rightarrow \sqrt{3} = \frac{AB}{b} \quad \ldots\text{(i)}$$

$$\text{In } \Delta ABD, \quad \tan 30° = \frac{AB}{BD} \Rightarrow \frac{1}{\sqrt{3}} = \frac{AB}{a} \quad \ldots\text{(ii)}$$

On multiplying Eqs. (i) and (ii), we get

$$\Rightarrow \quad \sqrt{3} \times \frac{1}{\sqrt{3}} = \frac{AB \times AB}{a \times b}$$

$$\Rightarrow \quad AB^2 = ab$$

$$\Rightarrow \quad AB = \sqrt{ab}$$

6. Hint Let SQ be the pole of height h and PQ be the shadow of a pole.

According to the question,

$$SQ = h \text{ and } PQ = \sqrt{3}h$$

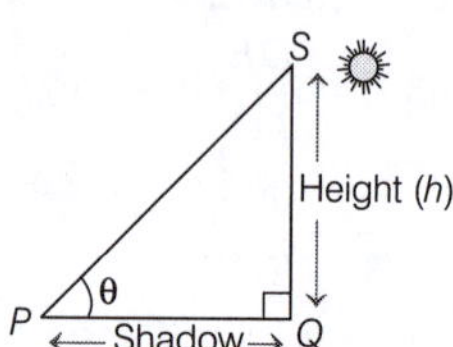

Again, let the angle of elevation of the Sun be θ.

In right angled ΔPQS,

$$\tan\theta = \frac{P}{B} = \frac{QS}{PQ}$$

$$\Rightarrow \quad \tan\theta = \frac{h}{\sqrt{3}h} = \frac{1}{\sqrt{3}}$$

Ans. 30°

7. **Hint** Do same as Question 4. of NCERT Folder Exercise 9.1. **Ans.** $20\sqrt{3}$ m

8. Let height of tree, $AB = 10$ m and $BC = 10\sqrt{3}$ m

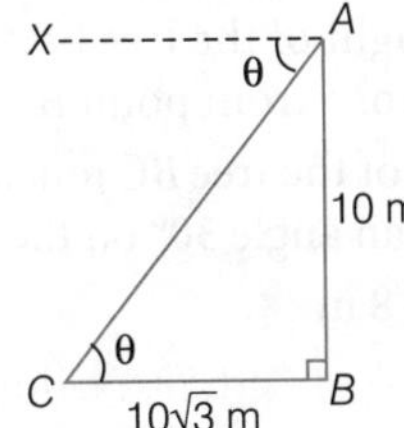

Again, let θ be the angle of depression.

Therefore, $\angle XAC = \angle ACB = \theta$

Now, in ΔACB, $\tan\theta = \frac{AB}{BC}$

$$\Rightarrow \quad \tan\theta = \frac{10}{10\sqrt{3}} = \frac{1}{\sqrt{3}}$$

$$\Rightarrow \quad \tan\theta = \tan 30° \qquad \left[\because \tan 30° = \frac{1}{\sqrt{3}}\right]$$

$$\Rightarrow \quad \theta = 30°$$

Hence, angle of depression is 30°.

9. **Hint** Let $AB = 150$ m be the height of building and C be a point on the ground such that

$$\angle ACB = 45°$$

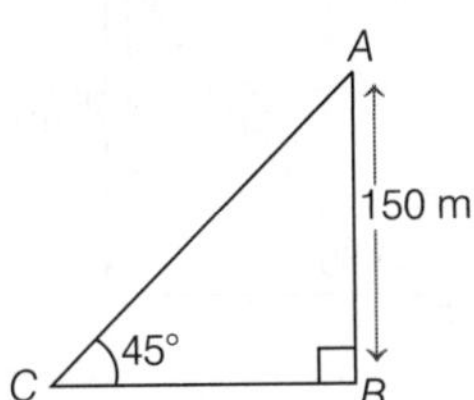

In right angled ΔABC,

$$\tan 45° = \frac{P}{B} = \frac{AB}{BC}$$ **Ans.** 150 m

10. Time taken from both side = 2sec

Speed underwater = 1500 m/s

Distance travelled = $1500 \times 2 = 3000$ m

Since, distance travelled by sonar wave to ship and back = 3000 m

So, distance between ship and sonar $\frac{3000}{2} = 1500$ m

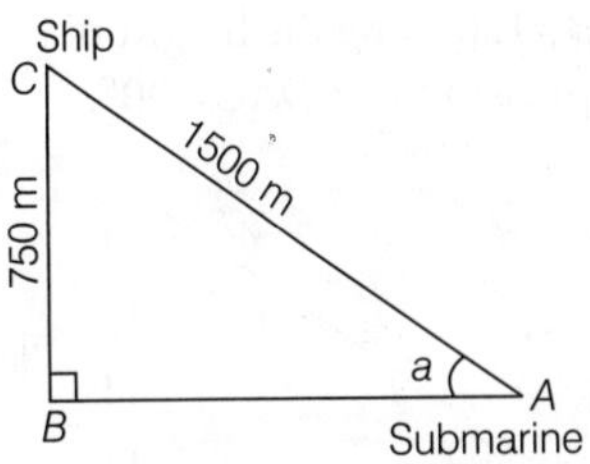

In ΔABC, $\sin a = \frac{BC}{AC} = \frac{750}{1500} = \frac{1}{2}$

$$\therefore \quad \sin a = \sin 30° \qquad \left[\because \sin 30° = \frac{1}{2}\right]$$

Thus, $a = 30°$

11. Let Eagle is at position A.

Goose 1 at B

Goose 2 at E

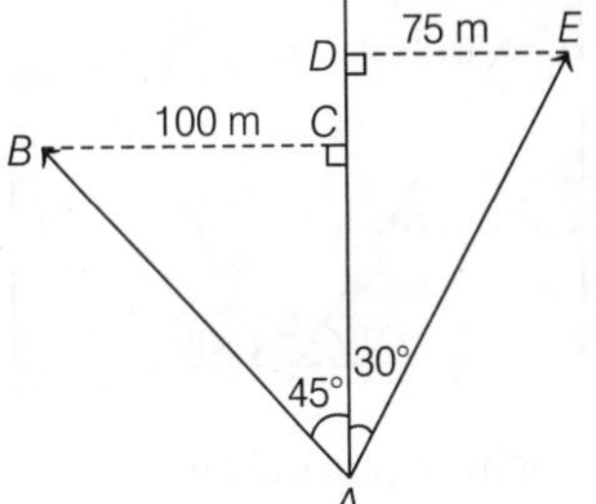

Now, in right angled ΔABC,

$$\sin 45° = \frac{BC}{AB}$$

$$\Rightarrow \quad \frac{1}{\sqrt{2}} = \frac{100}{AB} \qquad \left[\because \sin 45° = \frac{1}{\sqrt{2}}\right]$$

$$= 100 \times 1.41$$

$$AB = 141\text{m} \qquad \ldots\text{(i)}$$

In right angled ΔADE,

$$\sin 30° = \frac{DE}{AE}$$

$$\frac{1}{2} = \frac{75}{AE} \qquad \left[\because \sin 30° = \frac{1}{2}\right]$$

$$AE = 150 \text{ m} \qquad \ldots\text{(ii)}$$

Thus, as Goose 1 is closer, so the Eagle would attack it.

12. **Hint** In right angled ΔABC,

$$\angle B = 90°$$

Let $\quad \angle DAC = \theta$

Then, $\angle ACB = \angle DAC = \theta$ [alternate angles]

Now, $\quad \tan\theta = \frac{P}{B} = \frac{AB}{BC}$

$$= \frac{4}{4\sqrt{3}} = \frac{1}{\sqrt{3}} = \tan 30°$$

Ans. 30°

13. Hint Let $AB=150$ be the height of the tower and angle of depression is $\angle DAC=30°$.

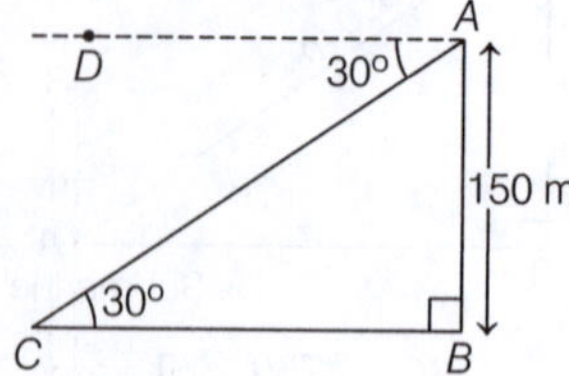

Then, $\angle ACB = \angle DAC = 30°$ [alternate angles]

Now, in right angled ΔABC,

$$\tan 30° = \frac{P}{B} = \frac{AB}{BC}$$

Ans. $150\sqrt{3}$ m

14.

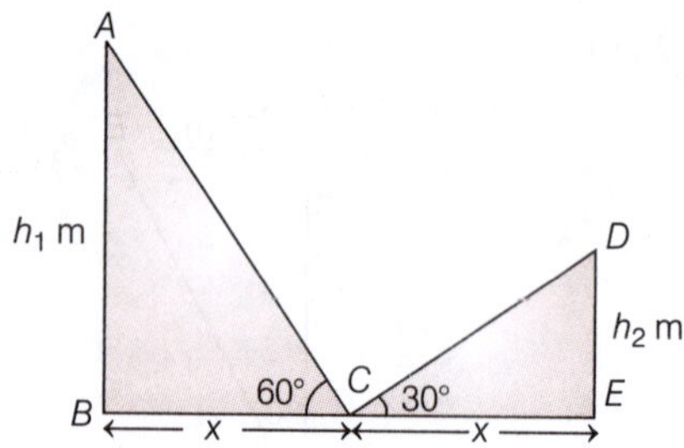

Given, the height of poles are h_1 m and h_2 m.

So, $\tan 60° = \frac{AB}{BC}$

$\Rightarrow \sqrt{3} = \frac{h_1}{x}$

$\Rightarrow h_1 = \sqrt{3}x$

and $\tan 30° = \frac{DE}{CE}$

$\Rightarrow \frac{1}{\sqrt{3}} = \frac{h_2}{x}$

$\Rightarrow h_2 = \frac{x}{\sqrt{3}}$

$\therefore h_1 : h_2$

$\sqrt{3}x : \frac{x}{\sqrt{3}} = \frac{3}{1} = 3:1$

15. Let two poles be AB and CD.

Given, distance between both the poles = 20 m

So, $BC = 20$ m

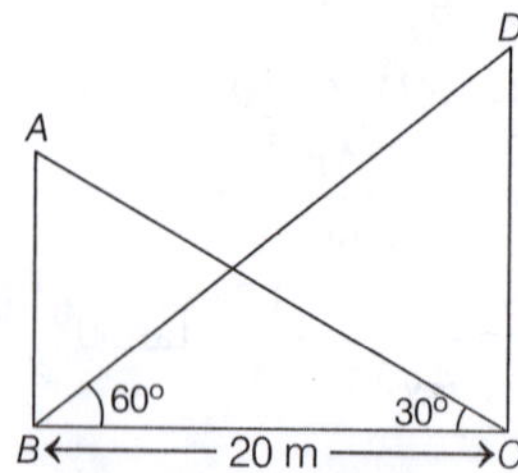

Also, $\angle ACB = 30°$ and $\angle DBC = 60°$

In right angled $\Delta ABC, \angle ABC = 90°$

$$\tan 30° = \frac{AB}{BC} \Rightarrow AB = \frac{20}{\sqrt{3}} \text{ m} \quad \dots\text{(i)}$$

Now, in right angled ΔDBC,

$$\tan 60° = \frac{DC}{BC} \Rightarrow DC = 20\sqrt{3} \text{ m}$$

Distance between heights $= CD - AB$

$$= 20\sqrt{3} - \frac{20}{\sqrt{3}} = \left(\frac{40}{3}\sqrt{3}\right) \text{m}$$

$$= 23.09 \text{ m}$$

16. Let the initial height of the tree be AC, when the storm come, the tree broke from point B.

The broken part of the tree BC touches the ground at point D, making an angle 30° on the ground.

Also, given $BD = 8$ m

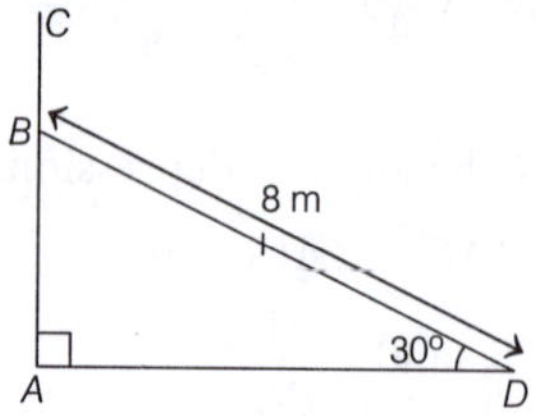

In right ΔABD, $\sin 30° = \frac{AB}{BD} \Rightarrow AB = \frac{8}{2} = 4$ m

$\therefore$ $AC = AB + BC = AB + BD$ [$\because BC = BD$]

$= 4 + 8 = 12$ m

17. Hint Do same as Question 11 of NCERT Folder Exercise 9.1

Ans. Height of tree = 34.64 m and width of river = 20 m

18. Hint (i) Find AB using suitable trigonometric ratio,

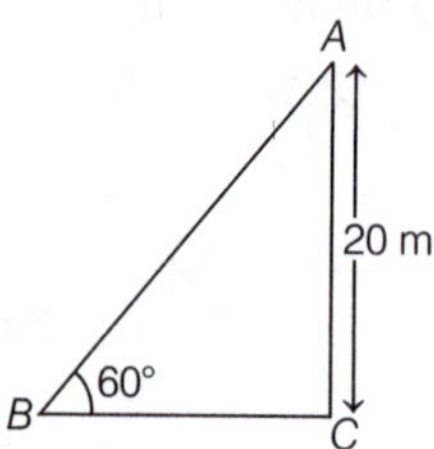

(ii) Find BC

Ans. (i) $\frac{40}{\sqrt{3}}$ m (ii) $\frac{20}{\sqrt{3}}$ m

19. Let A be the eye level and B, C are positions of balloon.

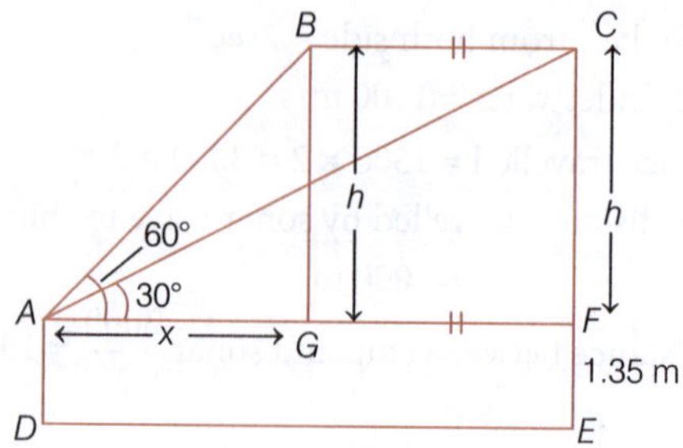

Distance covered by balloon in 12 sec

$$= 3 \times 12 = 36 \text{ m}$$

$\Rightarrow \quad BC = GF = 36 \text{ m}$

In ΔABG,

$$\tan 60° = \frac{BG}{AG} \Rightarrow \sqrt{3} = \frac{h}{x} \quad [\because \tan 60° = \sqrt{3}]$$

$\Rightarrow \quad h = \sqrt{3}x \quad$ ...(i)

In ΔACF,

$$\tan 30° = \frac{CF}{AF} \Rightarrow \frac{1}{\sqrt{3}} = \frac{h}{x+36}$$

$$\left[\because \tan 30° = \frac{1}{\sqrt{3}} \text{ and } AF = AG + GF\right]$$

$\Rightarrow \quad h = \dfrac{x+36}{\sqrt{3}} \quad$ ...(ii)

On solving Eqs. (i) and (ii), we get

$$\sqrt{3}x = \frac{x+36}{\sqrt{3}}$$

$\Rightarrow \quad 3x = x + 36 \Rightarrow x = 18$

So, $h = 18\sqrt{3} = 18 \times 1.73 = 31.14$ m

$\therefore$ Height of balloon from ground

$$= 1.35 + 31.14 = 32.49 \text{ m}$$

20. Let C be the position of bird, and B and E be the position of boy and girl, respectively.
Let the height of building be $DE = 20$ m
Let the distance of girl from bird be $EC = x$ m

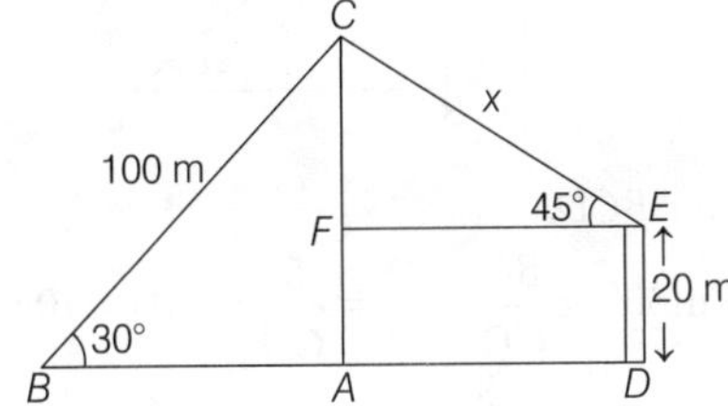

In right ΔBAC,

$$\sin 30° = \frac{AC}{BC}$$

$\Rightarrow \quad \dfrac{1}{2} = \dfrac{AC}{100}$

$\Rightarrow \quad AC = \dfrac{100}{2} = 50$ m

Now, $\quad CF = AC - AF = 50 - 20 = 30$ m $\quad [\because AF = DE]$

In right ΔEFC,

$$\sin 45° = \frac{CF}{CE} \Rightarrow \frac{1}{\sqrt{2}} = \frac{30}{x}$$

$\Rightarrow \quad x = 30 \times \sqrt{2} = 30 \times 1.414 = 42.42$ m

Hence, the distance of girl from bird is 42.42 m.

21. Hint Let AB be the flag staff of height h units and $AC = x$ units be length of its shadow, when the Sun rays meet the ground at an angle of 60°.

Also, let θ be the angle between the Sun rays and the ground, when the length of the shadow of the flag staff is $AD = 3x$ units.

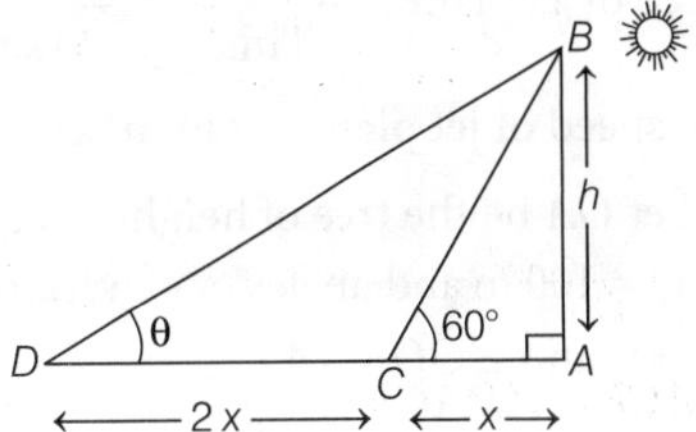

In right angled ΔCAB,

$$\tan 60° = \frac{AB}{AC} \quad \left[\because \tan\theta = \frac{\text{Perpendicular}}{\text{Base}}\right]$$

$\Rightarrow \quad \sqrt{3} = \dfrac{h}{x} \quad [\because \tan 60° = \sqrt{3}]$

$\Rightarrow \quad h = \sqrt{3}x \quad$ ...(i)

Now, in right angled ΔDAB,

$$\tan\theta = \frac{AB}{AD} = \frac{AB}{DC + CA} \quad [\because AD = DC + CA]$$

$\Rightarrow \quad \tan\theta = \dfrac{h}{2x + x} = \dfrac{h}{3x}$ **Ans.** 30°

22. Let the point on ground be A.
Since, jet plane is flying at a height of $3600\sqrt{3}$ m.

$$BP = CQ = 3600\sqrt{3} \text{ m}$$

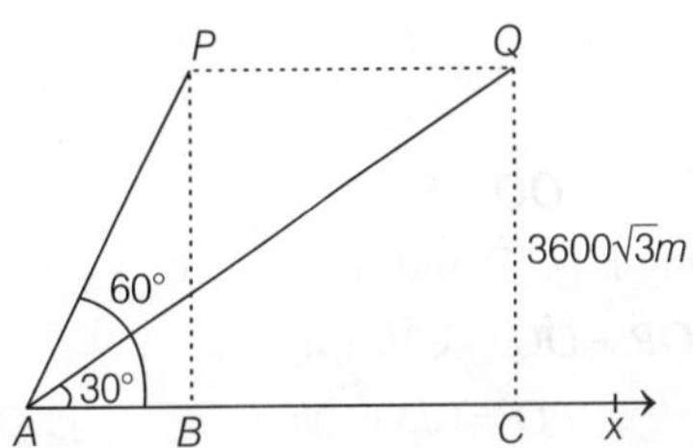

To find speed, we need to find distance travelled by jet plane in 30 sec i.e. BC

Let $\quad BC = x$

In ΔABP, $\tan A = \dfrac{BP}{AB} \quad \left[\because \tan\theta = \dfrac{\text{perpendicular}}{\text{base}}\right]$

$\Rightarrow \quad \tan 60° = \dfrac{3600\sqrt{3}}{AB} \Rightarrow \sqrt{3} = \dfrac{3600\sqrt{3}}{AB} \quad [\because \tan 60° = \sqrt{3}]$

$\Rightarrow \quad AB = 3600$ m

In ΔACQ, $\tan A = \dfrac{CQ}{AC}$

$$\tan 30° = \frac{3600\sqrt{3}}{AB + BC} \quad [\because AC = AB + BC]$$

$\Rightarrow \quad \dfrac{1}{\sqrt{3}} = \dfrac{3600\sqrt{3}}{3600 + x} \quad \left[\because \tan 30° = \dfrac{1}{\sqrt{3}}\right]$

$\Rightarrow \quad 3600 + x = 3600 \times 3 \Rightarrow 3600 + x = 10800$

$\Rightarrow \quad x = 10800 - 3600 = 7200$

$\Rightarrow \quad BC = 7200$ m

Hence, the distance travelled by jet plane in 30 sec = 7200 m

Now, speed of jet plane $= \frac{\text{Distance}}{\text{Time}} = \frac{7200 \text{ m}}{30 \text{ sec}} = 240 \text{ m/sec}$

Thus, the speed of jet plane is 240 m/sec.

23. (i) **Hint** Let OA be the tree of height h m.
Given, $PQ = 100$ m and angles of elevation are $\angle APO = 30°$ and $\angle OQA = 45°$.

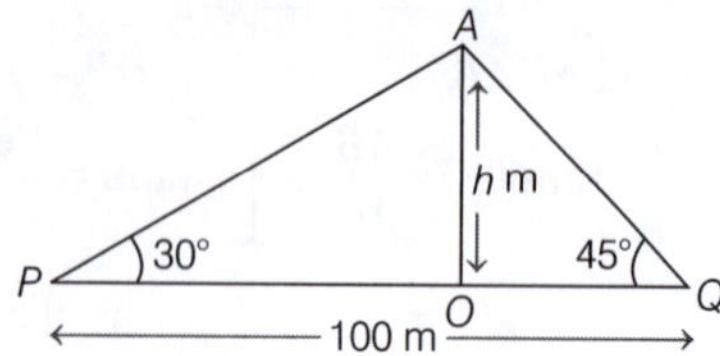

In right angled ΔPOA,

$$\tan 30° = \frac{P}{B} = \frac{OA}{OP}$$

$$\Rightarrow \quad \frac{1}{\sqrt{3}} = \frac{h}{OP} \qquad \left[\because \tan 30° = \frac{1}{\sqrt{3}}\right]$$

$$\Rightarrow \quad OP = \sqrt{3}h \qquad \text{...(i)}$$

Now, in right angled ΔQOA,

$$\tan 45° = \frac{OA}{OQ}$$

$$\Rightarrow \quad 1 = \frac{h}{OQ} \qquad [\because \tan 45° = 1]$$

$$\Rightarrow \quad OQ = h \qquad \text{...(ii)}$$

On adding Eqs. (i) and (ii), we get

$$OP + OQ = \sqrt{3}h + h$$

$$\Rightarrow \quad PQ = (\sqrt{3} + 1)h \qquad [\because OP + OQ = PQ]$$

$$\Rightarrow \quad 100 = (\sqrt{3} + 1)h \qquad [\because PQ = 100 \text{ m, given}]$$

Ans. (i) 36.6 m, (ii) 63.39 m, (iii) Point P

24. **Hint** Let h be the height of tower,
i.e. $PQ = h$ m and $PX = y$ m

Now, draw $RS \| XP$.

Then, we have $RX = 40 \text{ m} = SP$, $\angle QXP = 60°$ and $\angle QRS = 45°$

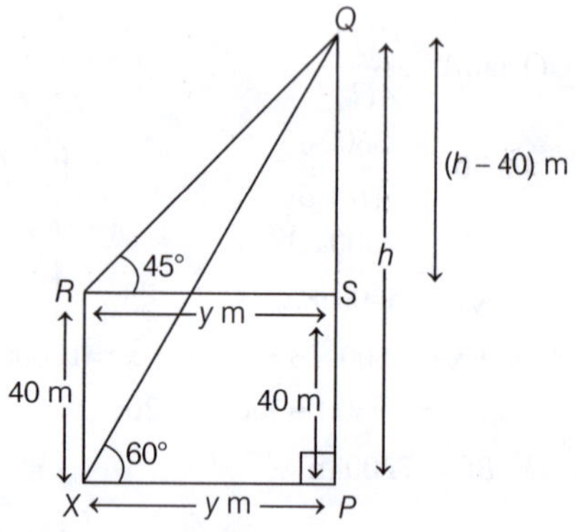

In right angled ΔXPQ,

$$\tan 60° = \frac{P}{B} = \frac{PQ}{XP}$$

$$\Rightarrow \quad \frac{\sqrt{3}}{1} = \frac{h}{y} \qquad [\because \tan 60° = \sqrt{3}]$$

$$\Rightarrow \quad y = \frac{h}{\sqrt{3}} \qquad \text{...(i)}$$

In right angled ΔRSQ,

$$\tan 45° = \frac{QS}{RS} \Rightarrow \tan 45° = \frac{PQ - SP}{XP}$$

$$[\because QS = PQ - SP \text{ and } RS = XP]$$

$$\Rightarrow \quad 1 = \frac{h - 40}{y} \qquad [\because \tan 45° = 1]$$

$$\Rightarrow \quad y = h - 40 \qquad \text{...(ii)}$$

Now, solve Eqs. (i) and (ii), to find h and y.

Ans. $PQ = 94.64$ m and $PX = 54.64$ m

25. (i) Let AB be the pole and C be the point 3 m below the top A of the pole. Also, let D be the point on the ground, where ladder CD be placed.

So, $\angle CDB = 30°$ and $BC = (8 - 3) = 5$ m.

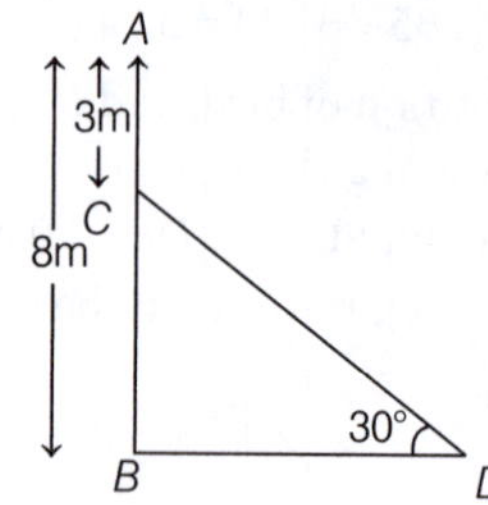

In ΔBCD,

$$\sin 30° = \frac{BC}{CD} \Rightarrow \frac{1}{2} = \frac{5}{CD} \Rightarrow CD = 10 \text{ m}$$

(ii) $\tan 30° = \frac{BC}{BD} \Rightarrow \frac{1}{\sqrt{3}} = \frac{5}{BD} \Rightarrow BD = 5\sqrt{3}$ m

(iii) $\therefore$ Area of $\Delta BCD = \frac{1}{2} \times BD \times BC$

$$= \frac{1}{2} \times 5\sqrt{3} \times 5 = \frac{25\sqrt{3}}{2} \text{ m}$$

26. **Hint** Let the height of the tower OP be H and R be a point on the plane such that the angle of elevation of the bottom and top of the flag staff are α and β respectively.

Given, height of flag staff, say $PF = h$

Now, $\angle PRO = \alpha$, $\angle FRO = \beta$

Clearly, in right angled ΔPOR,

$$\tan\alpha = \frac{PO}{RO} = \frac{H}{x}$$

$$\Rightarrow \quad x = \frac{H}{\tan\alpha} \qquad \text{...(i)}$$

and in right angled ΔFOR,

$$\tan\beta = \frac{FO}{RO} = \frac{FP+PO}{RO} = \frac{h+H}{x}$$

$$\Rightarrow \quad x = \frac{h+H}{\tan\beta} \quad \ldots\text{(ii)}$$

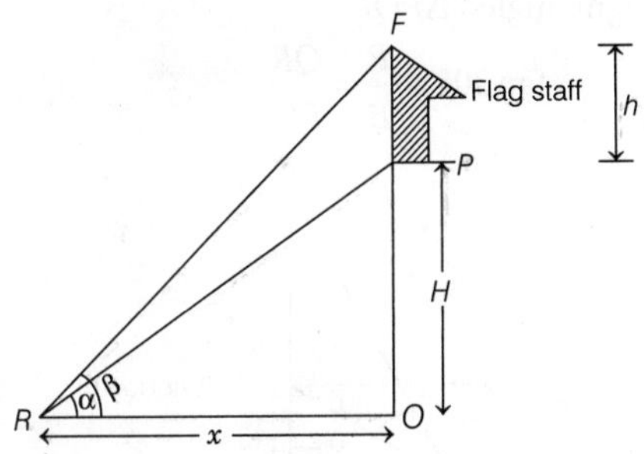

From Eqs. (i) and (ii), we get

$$\frac{H}{\tan\alpha} = \frac{h+H}{\tan\beta}$$

27.

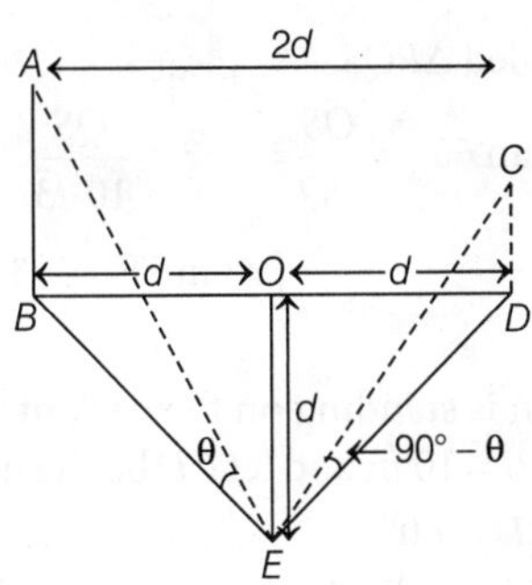

Since, Ajay stands midway between two trees.

$\therefore BO = OD = d$ m.

Now, in right angled ΔBOE,

$$BE^2 = BO^2 + OE^2 \quad \text{[by Pythagoras theorem]}$$

$$BE^2 = d^2 + d^2 = 2d^2$$

$$BE = \sqrt{2}d \quad \ldots\text{(i)}$$

Similarly, $DE = \sqrt{2}d$ ...(ii)

Let $DC = h$ m ...(iii)

Then, $AB = 3h$ m ...(iv)

In right angled ΔEBA,

$$\tan\theta = \frac{AB}{BE}$$

$$\tan\theta = \frac{3h}{\sqrt{2}d} \quad \ldots\text{(v)}$$

[from Eq. (i) and (iv)]

Similarly, in right angled ΔEDC,

$$\tan(90^\circ - \theta) = \frac{CD}{ED}$$

$$\Rightarrow \quad \cot\theta = \frac{h}{\sqrt{2}d} \quad \ldots\text{(vi)}$$

[$\because \tan(90^\circ - \theta) = \cot\theta$ and from Eqs. (ii) and (iii)]

On multiplying Eqs. (v) and (vi), we get

$$\tan\theta \times \cot\theta = \frac{3h}{\sqrt{2}d} \times \frac{h}{\sqrt{2}d}$$

$$1 = \frac{3h^2}{2d^2} \quad [\because \tan\theta \times \cot\theta = 1]$$

$$\Rightarrow \quad \frac{2}{3}d^2 = h^2$$

Thus, $h = d \times \sqrt{\frac{2}{3}}$

28. Hint Let $AB = 20$ m be the height of tower and let the ball lying on the ground at point C.

Given, angle of depression,

$$\angle TAC = 60^\circ = \angle ACB$$

[alternate angles]

In right angled ΔABC,

$$\tan 60^\circ = \frac{P}{B} = \frac{AB}{BC}$$

Ans. 11.55 m

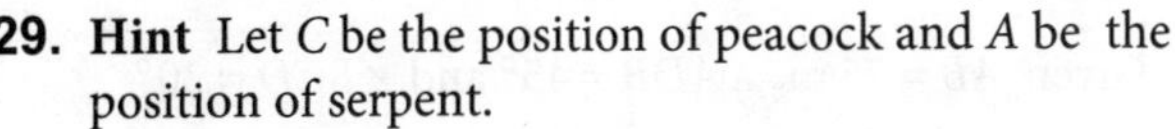

29. Hint Let C be the position of peacock and A be the position of serpent.

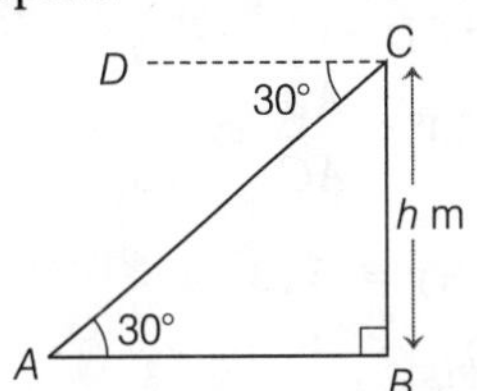

Given, $\angle DCA = 30^\circ$

$\Rightarrow \quad \angle BAC = \angle DCA = 30^\circ$ [alternate angles]

$\because$ Distance = Speed × Time

$\therefore \quad AC = 300 \times \frac{12}{60} \quad \left[\because 12\,\text{sec} = \frac{12}{60}\,\text{min}\right]$

$\Rightarrow \quad AC = 60$ m

In right angled ΔABC, $\sin 30^\circ = \frac{P}{H} = \frac{BC}{AC} = \frac{h}{60}$ **Ans.** 30 m

30. Hint Let $AB = h$ km be the height of the hill and C, D be two consecutive stones such that $CD = 1$ km

Let BC be x km, then

$$BD = BC + CD = (x+1) \text{ km}$$

Now, $\angle ADB = \angle XAD = 30^\circ$ [alternate angles]

and $\angle ACB = \angle XAC = 45^\circ$ [alternate angles]

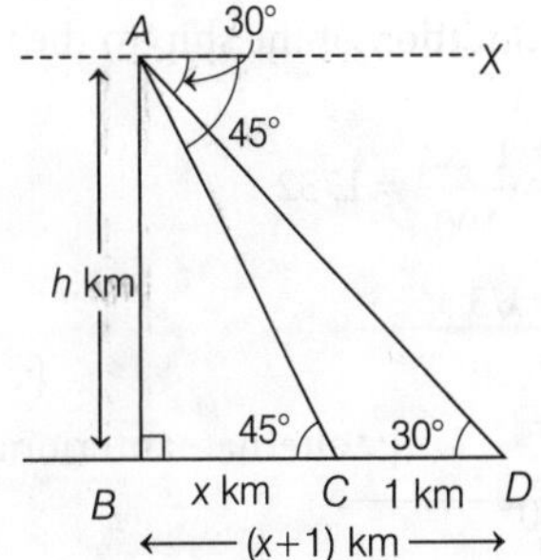

In right angled ΔABC,

$$\tan 45° = \frac{P}{B} = \frac{AB}{BC} \Rightarrow 1 = \frac{h}{x} \Rightarrow x = h$$

Now, in right angled ΔABD,

$$\tan 30° = \frac{AB}{BD} \Rightarrow \frac{1}{\sqrt{3}} = \frac{h}{x+1} \qquad \left[\because \tan 30° = \frac{1}{\sqrt{3}}\right]$$

Ans. $\left(\frac{\sqrt{3}+1}{2}\right)$ km

31. **Hint** Do same as Question 13 of NCERT Folder Exercise 9.1. **Ans.** 115.47m

32. Let AB be the lighthouse, C and D be positions of ships.

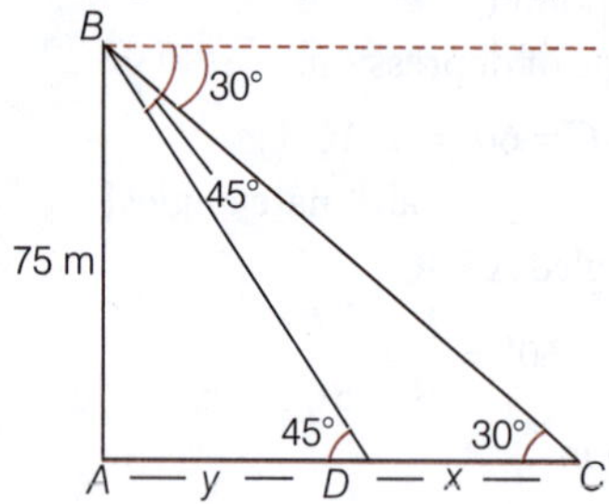

Given, $AB = 75$ m, $\angle ADB = 45°$ and $\angle BCD = 30°$

Let $AD = y$ and $CD = x$

In ΔBAC, $\tan 30° = \frac{AB}{AC} \Rightarrow \frac{1}{\sqrt{3}} = \frac{75}{x+y}$

$$\Rightarrow \qquad x + y = 75\sqrt{3} \qquad \text{...(i)}$$

Now, in ΔBAD,

$$\tan 45° = \frac{AB}{AD} \Rightarrow 1 = \frac{75}{y} \Rightarrow y = 75 \qquad \text{...(ii)}$$

On putting the value $y = 75$ in Eq. (i), we get

$$x + 75 = 75\sqrt{3}$$

$$\Rightarrow \qquad x = 75(\sqrt{3}-1) \Rightarrow x = 75 \times 0.732 = 54.9 \text{ m}$$

Hence, distance between the ships is 54.9 m.

33. **Hint** Do same as Example 11. **Ans.** 33.33 m, 28.9 m

34. Speed of ship = 36 km/h

Time taken = 2 min

$\therefore$ Distance covered by ship in 2 min $= 36 \times \frac{2}{60} = 1.2$ km

Distance of ship from foot of lighthouse $= 1.3 - 1.2$

$= 0.1 \text{km} = 100$ m

Let angle of elevation of the ship to the top of the lighthouse $= y°$

Then, $\tan y = \frac{173.2}{100} = 1.732$

$\Rightarrow \quad \tan y = \sqrt{3} \qquad [\because 1.732 = \sqrt{3}]$

$\Rightarrow \quad y = 60° \qquad [\because \tan\sqrt{3} = \tan 60°]$

Now, $y = x°$ $\qquad$ [$\because$ alternate interior angles are equal]

Thus, $x° = 60°$

35. **Hint** Let QS be the building and R be the position of window.

Given, height of the window, $QR = 10$ m

$\angle QPR = \angle XRP = 30°$ $\qquad$ [alternate angles]

and $\qquad \angle SPQ = 60°$

In right angled ΔPQR,

$$\tan 30° = \frac{P}{B} = \frac{QR}{PQ}$$

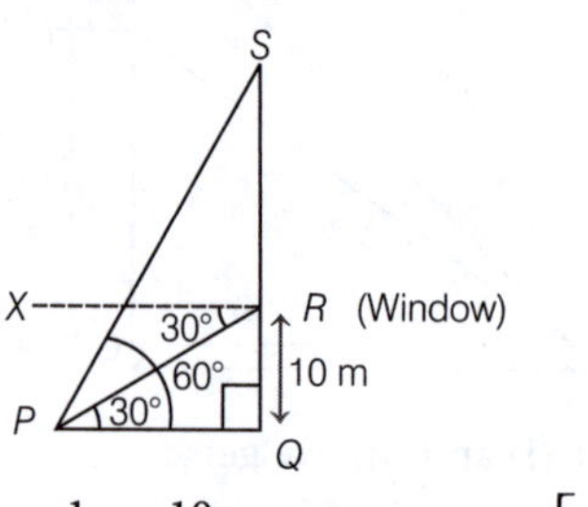

$\Rightarrow \qquad \frac{1}{\sqrt{3}} = \frac{10}{PQ} \qquad \left[\because \tan 30° = \frac{1}{\sqrt{3}}\right]$

$\Rightarrow \qquad PQ = 10\sqrt{3} \qquad \text{...(i)}$

In right angled ΔPQS,

$$\tan 60° = \frac{QS}{PQ} \Rightarrow \sqrt{3} = \frac{QS}{10\sqrt{3}}$$

[$\because \tan 60° = \sqrt{3}$ and from Eq. (i)]

Ans. 30 m

36. **Hint** A man is standing on the deck of a ship at point A such that $AB = 10$ m and let CD be the hill.

Then, $\angle EAD = 60°$

and $\quad \angle CAE = \angle BCA = 30°$ $\qquad$ [alternate angles]

Let $\quad BC = x \text{ m} = AE$ and $DE = h$ m

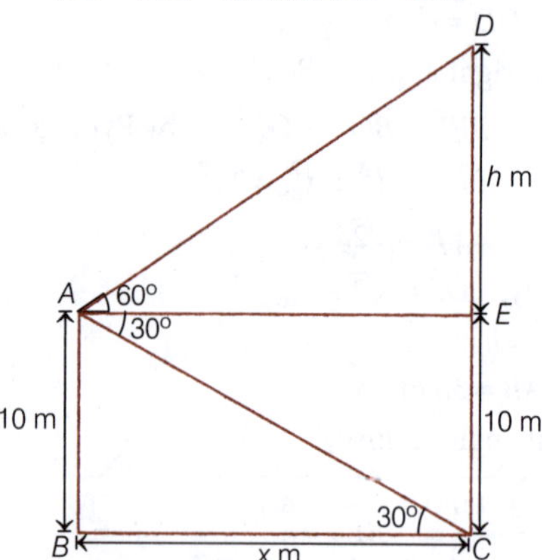

In right angled ΔAED,

$$\tan 60° = \frac{P}{B} = \frac{DE}{EA} = \frac{h}{x}$$

In right angled ΔABC,

$$\tan 30° = \frac{AB}{BC} \Rightarrow \frac{1}{\sqrt{3}} = \frac{10}{x} \qquad \left[\because \tan 30° = \frac{1}{\sqrt{3}}\right]$$

Ans. Distance of the hill from the ship is $10\sqrt{3}$ m and height of the hill is 40 m.

37. Hint Let W denote the window and OQ denote the height of the other house.

Now, draw $WM \parallel OB$.

Given, height of the window $= WB = h$ m

Then, $OM = BW = h$ m,

$\angle QWM = \alpha$ and $\angle OWM = \beta = \angle WOB$ [alternate angles]

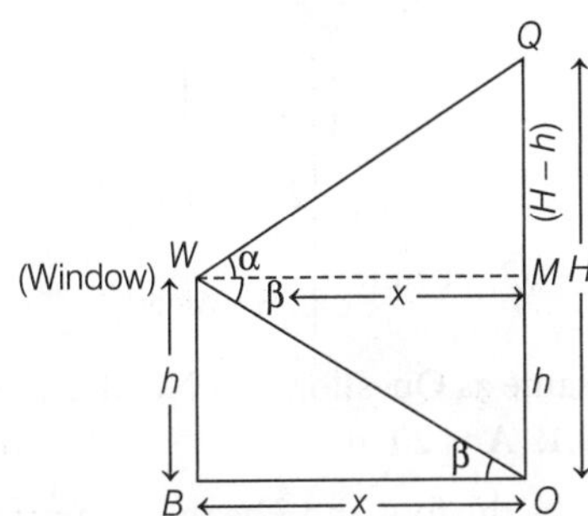

Now, in right angled ΔWBO,

$$\tan\beta = \frac{WB}{OB} = \frac{h}{x}$$

$$\Rightarrow \quad x = \frac{h}{\tan\beta} \quad \text{...(i)}$$

and in right angled ΔQMW,

$$\tan\alpha = \frac{QM}{WM} = \frac{OQ - MO}{WM}$$

$$\Rightarrow \quad \tan\alpha = \frac{H-h}{x}$$

$$\Rightarrow \quad x = \frac{H-h}{\tan\alpha} \quad \text{...(ii)}$$

From Eqs. (i) and (ii), we get

$$\frac{h}{\tan\beta} = \frac{H-h}{\tan\alpha}$$

$$\therefore \quad H = h\left(1 + \tan\alpha \cdot \frac{1}{\tan\beta}\right)$$

$$= h\,(1 + \tan\alpha \cdot \cot\beta) \quad \left[\because \frac{1}{\tan\theta} = \cot\theta\right]$$

38. Hint Let the height of lighthouse AB be h m and C, D be the positions of the person, such that

$\angle ADB = \theta, \angle ACB = \phi$ and $DC = 240$ m.

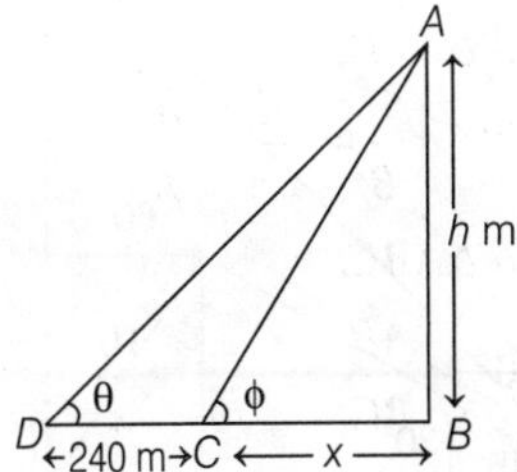

Let $BC = x$ m.

In right angled ΔABC,

$$\tan\phi = \frac{AB}{BC} \Rightarrow \frac{3}{4} = \frac{AB}{BC} \quad \left[\because \tan\phi = \frac{3}{4}, \text{ given}\right]$$

$$\Rightarrow \quad h = \frac{3}{4} \times x \quad \text{...(i)}$$

and in right angled ΔABD,

$$\tan\theta = \frac{AB}{BD} \Rightarrow \frac{5}{12} = \frac{AB}{DC + CB}$$

$$\left[\because \tan\theta = \frac{5}{12}, \text{ given and } BD = DC + CB\right]$$

$$\Rightarrow \quad \frac{5}{12} = \frac{h}{240 + x} \quad \text{...(ii)}$$

Now, solve Eqs. (i) and (ii) to find h.

Ans. 225 m

39. Hint Do same as Question 21.

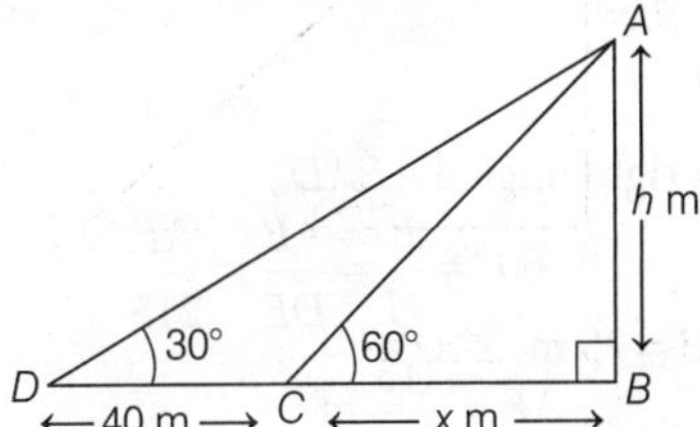

Ans. 34.6 m and 20 m.

40. Hint Let height of the tower, $BC = h$ m and height of the flag staff $CD = H$ m.

$$\therefore \quad BD = BC + CD = (h + H) \text{ m} \quad \text{...(i)}$$

Given, $AB = 120$ m, $\angle CAB = 45°$

and $\angle DAB = 60°$

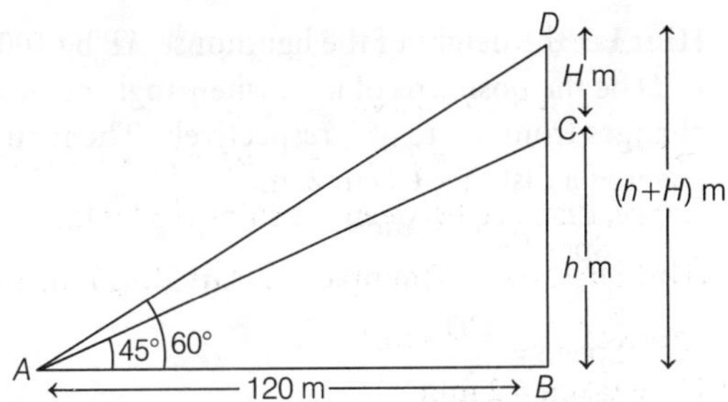

In right angled ΔABC, we get

$$\tan 45° = \frac{BC}{AB} \quad \left[\because \tan\theta = \frac{P}{B}\right]$$

$$\Rightarrow \quad h = 120 \text{ m} \quad \text{...(ii)}$$

Now, in right angled ΔABD, we get

$$\tan 60° = \frac{BD}{AB}$$

$$\Rightarrow \quad \sqrt{3} = \frac{h+H}{120} \quad \text{...(iii)}$$

$[\because \tan 60° = \sqrt{3}$ and from Eq. (i)$]$

Now, solve Eq. (iii) using Eq. (ii). **Ans.** 87.84 m

41. Hint Let D be the position of the balloon, when it is inclined at angle of 60° and AB be the height of the pole.

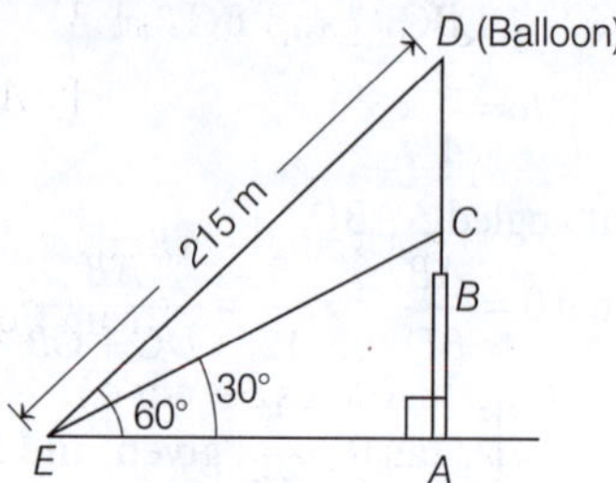

Given, length of cable,

$$DE = 215 \text{ m}$$

In right angled ΔEAD,

$$\sin 60° = \frac{P}{H} = \frac{AD}{ED} \Rightarrow AD = \frac{215\sqrt{3}}{2} \text{ m}$$

Hence, height of the balloon from the ground is $\frac{215\sqrt{3}}{2}$ m.

Again, in right angled ΔEAD,

$$\cos 60° = \frac{B}{H} = \frac{AE}{DE} = \frac{AE}{215}$$

$$\Rightarrow \quad AE = \frac{215}{2} \text{ m} \quad \text{...(i)}$$

Now, the angle of inclination is changed, say $\angle CEA = 30°$.

In right angled ΔEAC, $\tan 30° = \frac{P}{B} = \frac{AC}{EA}$

Ans. $\frac{215}{2\sqrt{3}}$ m

42. Hint Let the height of the lighthouse AB be 100 m and C, D be the positions of man when angle of elevation changes from 60° to 45°, respectively. The man has covered a distance CD in 2 min.

$$\because \quad \text{Speed} = \frac{\text{Distance}}{\text{Time}}$$

$$\Rightarrow \quad \text{Speed} = \frac{CD}{2} \quad \text{...(i)}$$

In right angled ΔABC,

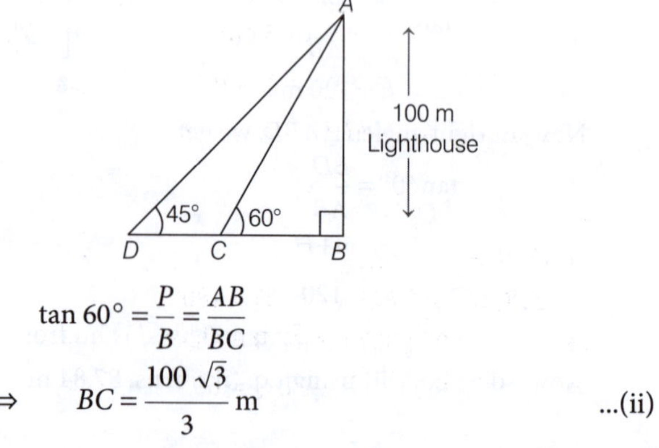

$$\tan 60° = \frac{P}{B} = \frac{AB}{BC}$$

$$\Rightarrow \quad BC = \frac{100\sqrt{3}}{3} \text{ m} \quad \text{...(ii)}$$

In right angled ΔABD,

$$\tan 45° = \frac{AB}{BD}$$

$$\Rightarrow \quad BD = 100 \text{ m}$$

Now, $\quad CD = BD - BC$

and $\quad \text{speed} = \frac{CD}{2}$

$$= \frac{100\left(\frac{3-\sqrt{3}}{3}\right)}{2}$$

Ans. $\frac{50}{3}(3-\sqrt{3})$ m/min

43. Hint Do same as Question 9 of NCERT folder Exercise 9.1. **Ans** 20 m

44. Hint Let F be the foot and S be the summit of the mountain FOS. Also, let the height of mountain be h km.

Then, $\angle OFS = 45°$

and so $\angle OSF = 45°$

$$\Rightarrow \quad OF = OS = h \text{ km}$$

[$\because$ sides opposite to equal angles are equal]

Let $FP = 1000 \text{ m} = 1 \text{ km}$ be the slope, so that

$$\angle OFP = 30°$$

Draw $PM \perp OS$ and $PL \perp OF$

Join PS.

Clearly, $\angle MPS = 60°$ [given]

Now, in right angled ΔFLP,

$$\sin 30° = \frac{PL}{PF}$$

$$\Rightarrow \quad PL = PF \sin 30°$$

$$= 1 \times \frac{1}{2} = \frac{1}{2} \text{ km} \quad \left[\because \sin 30° = \frac{1}{2}\right]$$

$$\Rightarrow \quad OM = PL = \frac{1}{2} \text{ km}$$

Now, $SM = OS - OM = \left(h - \frac{1}{2}\right)$ km ...(i)

Also, in right angled ΔFLP,

$$\cos 30° = \frac{FL}{PF}$$

$$\Rightarrow \quad FL = PF \cos 30°$$

$$= \left(1 \times \frac{\sqrt{3}}{2}\right)$$

$$= \frac{\sqrt{3}}{2} \text{ km}$$

Now, $OL = OF - FL$

$$\Rightarrow \quad OL = \left(h - \frac{\sqrt{3}}{2}\right) \quad \left[\because LF = \frac{\sqrt{3}}{2}\right]$$

$$\Rightarrow \quad PM = h - \frac{\sqrt{3}}{2} \quad [\because OL = PM] \ldots\text{(ii)}$$

In right angled ΔSMP,

$$\tan 60° = \frac{SM}{PM}$$

Now, put value of SM and PM from Eqs. (i) and (ii) and hence find h.

Ans. 1.366 km

45. (i) Let AB and SQ be two positions of the ladder making inclination α and β with the horizontal, respectively.

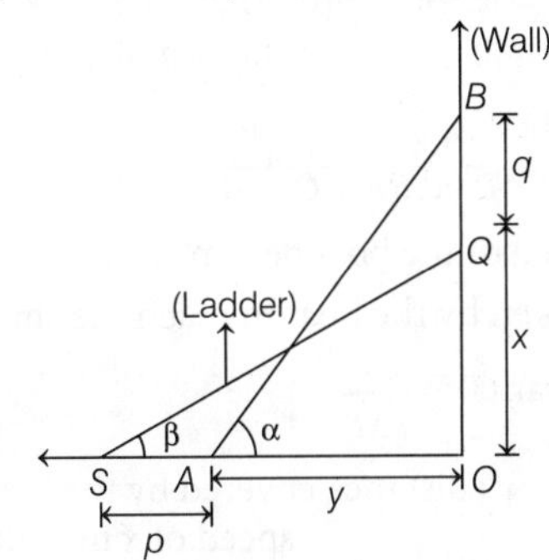

Let $OQ = x$ and $OA = y$

Given that $BQ = q$ and $SA = p$

Clearly, now in ΔBAO,

$$\cos\alpha = \frac{OA}{AB}$$

$$\Rightarrow \quad \cos\alpha = \frac{y}{AB}$$

$$\Rightarrow \quad y = AB\cos\alpha = OA \quad \ldots\text{(i)}$$

and $\sin\alpha = \dfrac{OB}{AB}$

$$\Rightarrow \quad OB = BA\sin\alpha \quad \ldots\text{(ii)}$$

Now, in ΔQSO,

$$\cos\beta = \frac{OS}{SQ}$$

$$\Rightarrow \quad OS = SQ\cos\beta = AB\cos\beta$$

$$[\because AB = SQ] \ldots\text{(iii)}$$

and $\sin\beta = \dfrac{OQ}{SQ}$

$$\Rightarrow \quad OQ = SQ\sin\beta = AB\sin\beta$$

$$[\because AB = SQ] \ldots\text{(iv)}$$

Now, $SA = OS - AO$

$$p = AB\cos\beta - AB\cos\alpha$$

[from Eqs. (i) and (iii)]

$$\Rightarrow \quad p = AB(\cos\beta - \cos\alpha) \quad \ldots\text{(v)}$$

and $BQ = BO - QO$

$$\Rightarrow \quad q = BA\sin\alpha - AB\sin\beta$$

[from Eqs. (ii) and (iv)]

$$\Rightarrow \quad q = AB(\sin\alpha - \sin\beta) \quad \ldots\text{(vi)}$$

On dividing Eq. (v) by Eq. (vi), we get

$$\frac{p}{q} = \frac{AB(\cos\beta - \cos\alpha)}{AB(\sin\alpha - \sin\beta)}$$

$$\Rightarrow \quad \frac{p}{q} = \frac{\cos\beta - \cos\alpha}{\sin\alpha - \sin\beta}$$ **Hence proved.**

(ii) No

46. In ΔABC, $\tan 60° = \dfrac{AB}{BC}$

$$\Rightarrow \quad \sqrt{3} = \frac{6}{x}$$

$$\therefore \quad x = \frac{6}{\sqrt{3}} = 2\sqrt{3} \text{ cm}$$

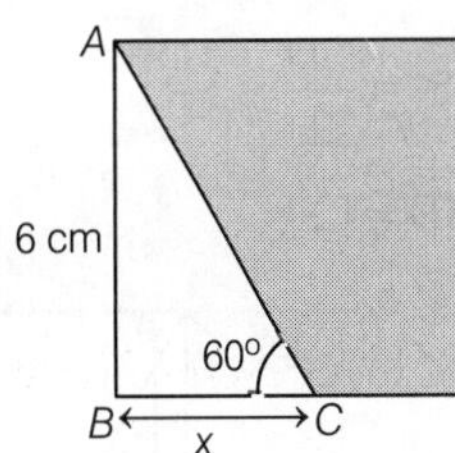

So, area of $\Delta ABC = \dfrac{1}{2} \times 6 \times 2\sqrt{3}$

$$= 6\sqrt{3} \text{ cm}^2$$

Hence, area of shaded region

$$= \text{Area of square} - \text{Area of } \Delta ABC$$

$$= 36 - 6\sqrt{3} \text{ cm}^2$$

$$= 6(6 - \sqrt{3}) \text{ cm}^2$$

47. In ΔPQU, $\sin 30° = \dfrac{QU}{4}$

$$\Rightarrow \quad QU = 2 \text{ cm}$$

In ΔPQU,

$$\angle PQU + \angle UPQ + \angle PUQ = 180°$$

$$\Rightarrow \quad 90° + 30° + \angle PUQ = 180°$$

$$\Rightarrow \quad \angle PUQ = 60°$$

In ΔQRU,

$$\cos 60° = \frac{RU}{QU} = \frac{RU}{2}$$

$\Rightarrow \quad RU = 1\text{cm}$

and $\quad \tan 60° = \frac{RQ}{RU}$

$\Rightarrow \quad \sqrt{3} = \frac{RQ}{1}$

$\Rightarrow \quad RQ = \sqrt{3}\text{ cm} = PS$

$\therefore \quad PS + SR + RU = 4\text{ cm}$

$\Rightarrow \quad SR = 4 - PS - RU$

$= 4 - \sqrt{3} - 1$

$\Rightarrow \quad SR = (3 - \sqrt{3})\text{ cm}$

Ans. $(3 - \sqrt{3})$ cm

48. **Hint** Let $CD = h$ m be the height of the lighthouse and A, B be two ships on either side of lighthouse, such that their angles of depression are 60° and 45°, respectively.

i.e. $\quad \angle XCB = \angle CBD = 45°$ [alternate angles]

and $\quad \angle YCA = \angle CAD = 60°$ [alternate angles]

Given, the distance between the ships A and B is

$$AB = \frac{100(\sqrt{3}+1)}{\sqrt{3}}\text{ m}$$

In right angled ΔBDC,

$$\tan 45° = \frac{CD}{BD} \quad \left[\because \tan\theta = \frac{P}{B}\right]$$

$\Rightarrow \quad BD = CD \quad$ ...(i)

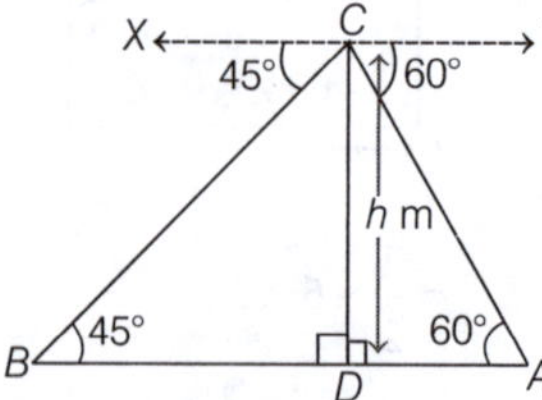

and in right angled ΔADC,

$$\tan 60° = \frac{CD}{AD}$$

$\Rightarrow \quad CD = \sqrt{3}\,AD$

$\Rightarrow \quad AD = \frac{CD}{\sqrt{3}} \quad$ ...(ii)

Ans. 100 m

49. **Hint** Let the speed of boat be x m/min.

$\therefore CD = 2x$

In ΔABC,

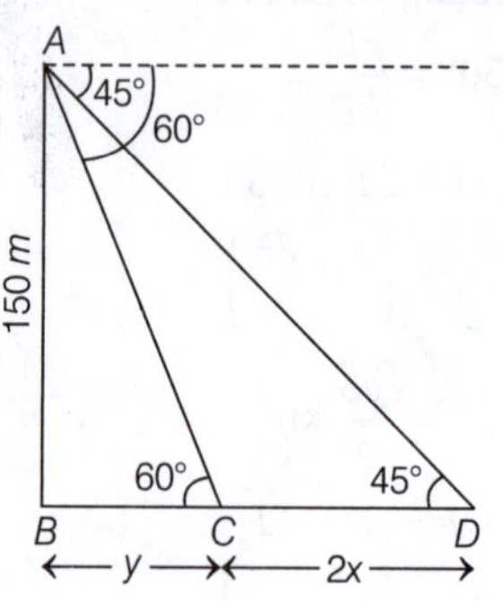

$$\frac{150}{y} = \tan 60° \Rightarrow y = \frac{150}{\sqrt{3}} = 50\sqrt{3}\text{ m}$$

In ΔABD, $\frac{150}{y+2x} = \tan 45°$

$\Rightarrow \quad 150 = 50\sqrt{3} + 2x \Rightarrow x = 25(3-\sqrt{3})$ m/min

$= 25 \times 60(3-\sqrt{3})$ m/h $= 1500(3-\sqrt{3})$ m/h

50. Let AD be a cliff of height h.

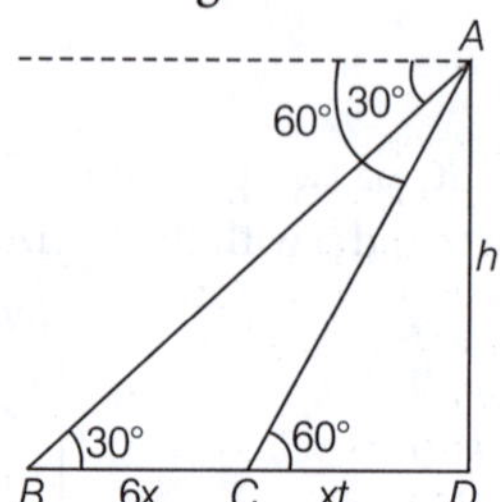

Let the speed of the boat be x m/min.

Let time taken by the boat to reach the shore be t.

In ΔADC, $\tan 60° = \frac{h}{xt}$

[$\because$ distance covered by the boat at a uniform speed of x m/min in t time is xt]

$$\sqrt{3} = \frac{h}{xt} \Rightarrow h = \sqrt{3}xt \quad \text{...(i)}$$

In ΔABD, $\tan 30° = \frac{h}{x(t+6)} \quad \left[\because \tan\theta = \frac{P}{B}\right]$

[$\therefore$ distance covered by the boat at a uniform speed of x m/min in 6 min is $6x$]

$$\frac{1}{\sqrt{3}} = \frac{h}{x(t+6)} \Rightarrow h = \frac{x(t+6)}{\sqrt{3}} \quad \text{...(ii)}$$

From Eqs. (i) and (ii), we get

$$\sqrt{3}xt = \frac{xt+6x}{\sqrt{3}}$$

$$3xt = xt + 6x \Rightarrow 3t = t + 6$$

$$2t = 6 \Rightarrow t = 3\text{ min}$$

Mind Map

SOME APPLICATIONS OF TRIGONOMETRY

Measuring height or length of an object or the distance between two distant objects is an important application of trigonometry. It can be determined with the help of trigonometric ratios.

Line of Sight

The line of sight is the line drawn from eye of an observer to the point in the object viewed by observer.

Angle of Elevation

The angle of elevation of an object viewed, is the angle formed by the line of sight with the horizontal when it is above the horizontal level, i.e. the case when we raise our head to look at the object.

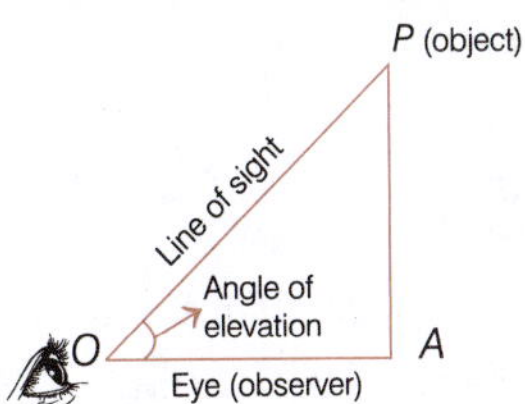

Angle of Depression

The angle of depression of an object viewed, is the angle formed by the line of sight with the horizontal when it is below the horizontal level, when we lower our head to look at the object.

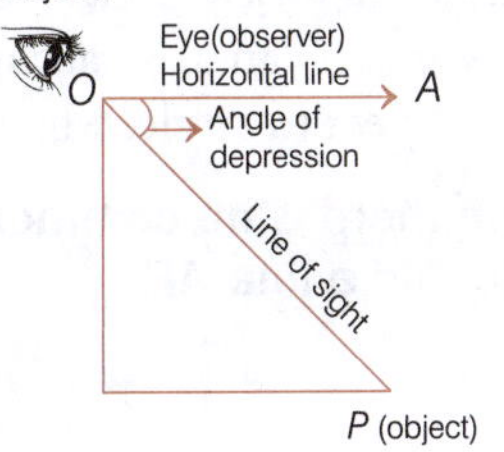

Circles

CHAPTER 10

In previous classes, we have studied about circle which is a collection of all point in a plane and which are at a constant distance (radius) from a fixed point (centre) and various terms related to it like chord, segment, sector, arc, etc. In this chapter, we will discuss different situations that can arise when a circle and a line are given in a plane.

TOPIC 01 Tangent to a Circle

Consider, a line AB and a circle. Now, there can be three possible cases which can arise according to the position of line AB with respect to circle, which are given below.

Case I When there is no common point between a circle and a line AB.

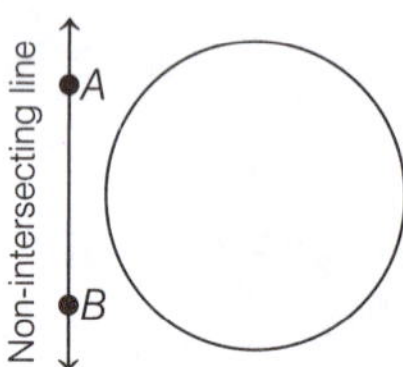

In this case, the line AB is said to be **non-intersecting line** with respect to a circle.

Case II When there are two common points P and Q between a circle and a line AB.

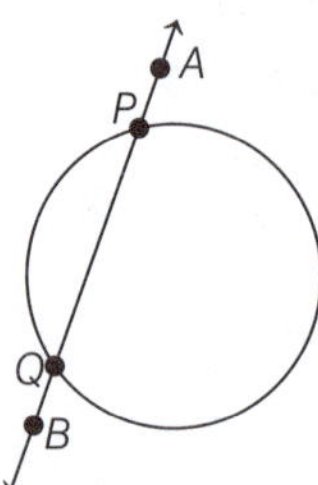

In this case, line AB intersects the circle at two points, so this line is called **secant** of the circle.

Case III When there is only one common point between a circle and a line AB.

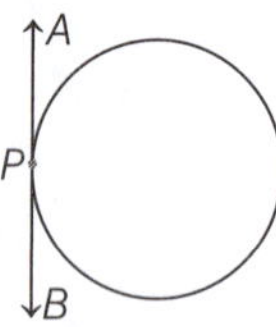

In this case, the line AB is said to be the **tangent** to the circle at point P.

Tangent to a Circle

A tangent to a circle is a line that intersects or touches the circle at only one point. The common point of the tangent and the circle is called the **point of contact**.

Also, we can say that the tangent to a circle is a special case of the secant, when the two end points of its corresponding chord coincide. There is only one tangent at a point of the circle.

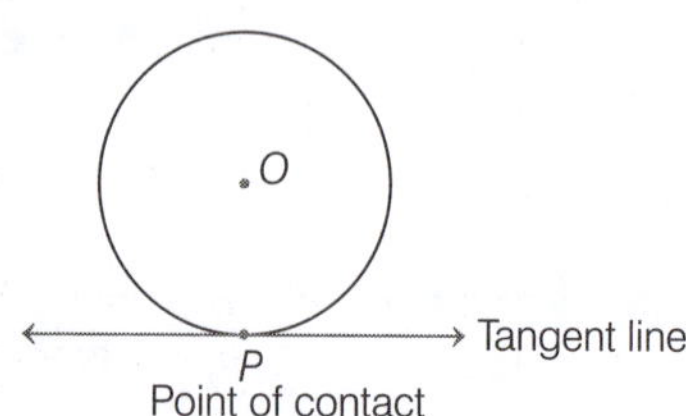

Length of Tangent

The length of the segment of the tangent, between the given point (on the tangent) and the point of contact with the circle is called the length of tangent from the given point.

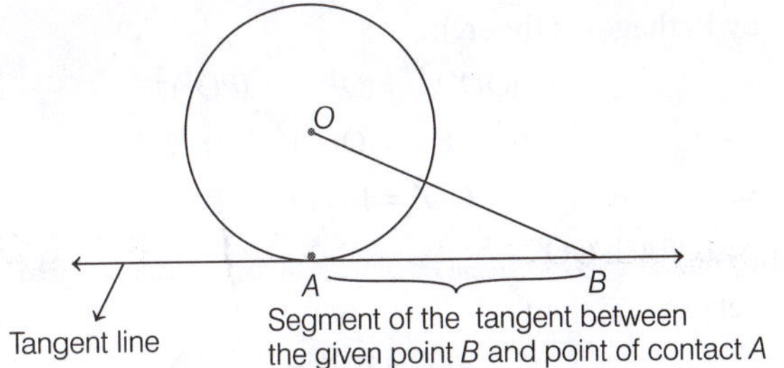

In the figure, AB is called the length of tangent.

Properties of a Tangent

Theorem The tangent at any point of a circle is perpendicular to the radius through the point of contact. CBSE 2020 (Basic) 13, 12, 11

Given A circle with centre O and a tangent AB at a point P on the circle.

To prove $OP \perp AB$

Construction Take any point Q, other than P on the tangent AB and join OQ.

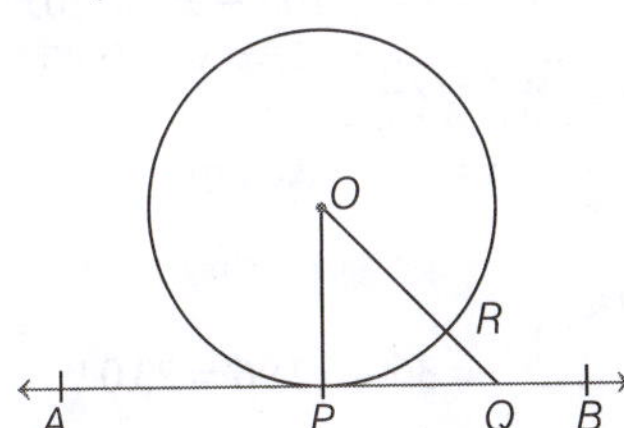

Proof Here, Q is a point on the tangent AB, other than the point of contact P. So, Q lies outside the circle [if Q lies inside the circle, then AB becomes a secant and not a tangent to the circle].

Let OQ intersects the circle at R.

$\therefore \quad OP = OR$ [radii of the same circle]

Now, $\quad OQ = OR + RQ$

$\Rightarrow \quad OQ > OR$

$\Rightarrow \quad OQ > OP$ or $OP < OQ$ $\quad [\because OP = OR]$

Thus, OP is shorter than any other segment joining O to any point of AB. Also, we know that the shortest distance between a point and a line is perpendicular distance from the point to the line. So, OP is perpendicular to AB.

i.e. $\quad OP \perp AB$ **Hence proved.**

Note it Its converse is also true, i.e. a line drawn through the end point of a radius and perpendicular to it, is a tangent to the circle.

Example 1. From a point P, the length of the tangent to a circle is 24 cm and the distance of P from the centre of the circle is 25 cm. Find the radius of the circle. CBSE 2023 (Standard)

Sol. Let PQ be the tangent drawn to the circle with centre O.

$PQ \perp OQ$

[$\because$ tangent to a circle is perpendicular to the radius through the point of contact]

$\Rightarrow \quad \angle OQP = 90^\circ$

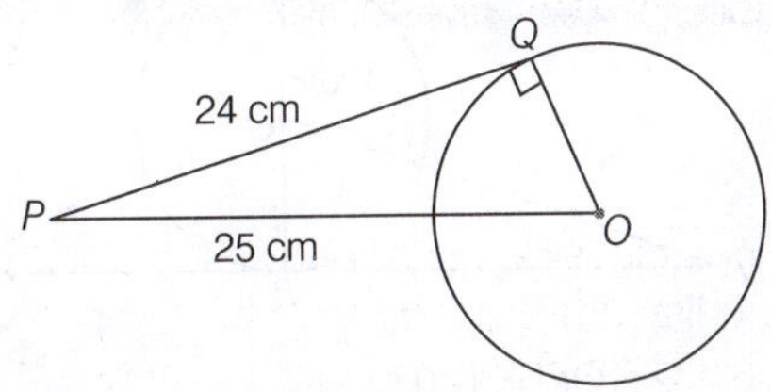

In right angled ΔOQP,

By Pythagoras theorem,

$$OP^2 = OQ^2 + PQ^2$$

$$\Rightarrow \quad 25^2 = OQ^2 + 24^2$$

$$\Rightarrow \quad OQ^2 = 25^2 - 24^2$$

$$= 625 - 576$$

$$\Rightarrow \quad OQ = \sqrt{49}$$

$$\Rightarrow \quad OQ = 7 \text{ cm}$$

Example 2. In the given figure, AP is tangent to a circle with centre O. If $\angle APO = 30^\circ$ and $OA = 2.5$ cm then find the length of OP. CBSE 2025 (Basic)

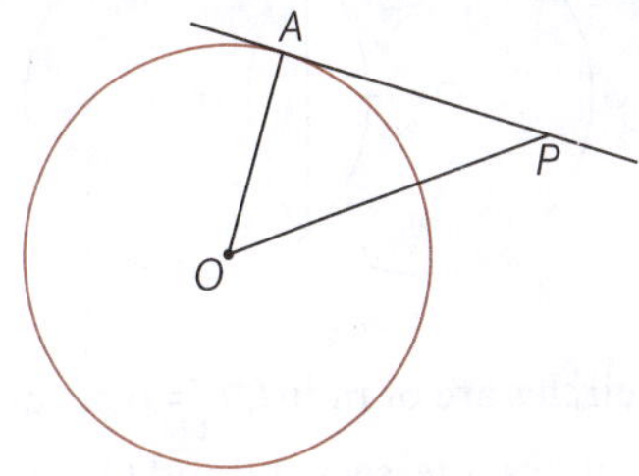

Sol. Given, AP is a tangent, $OA = 2.5$ cm and $\angle APO = 30^\circ$

We know that tangent at any point of a circle is perpendicular to the radius through the point of contact.

$\therefore \quad OA \perp AP$

Now, in right angled ΔOAP,

$$\sin 30^\circ = \frac{OA}{OP} \quad \left[\because \sin\theta = \frac{P}{H}\right]$$

$$\Rightarrow \quad \frac{1}{2} = \frac{2.5}{OP} \quad \left[\because \sin 30^\circ = \frac{1}{2}\right]$$

$$\Rightarrow \quad OP = 2 \times 2.5$$

$$\Rightarrow \quad OP = 5 \text{ cm}$$

Example 3. **If AB is a tangent drawn from a point A to a circle with centre O and BOC is a diameter of the circle such that $\angle AOC = 120°$, then find $\angle OAB$.**

Sol. Given, AB and BOC are the tangent and diameter of the circle with centre O, respectively.

We know that tangent at any point on a circle is perpendicular to the radius through the point of contact.

$\therefore \quad OB \perp AB \Rightarrow \angle OBA = 90°$

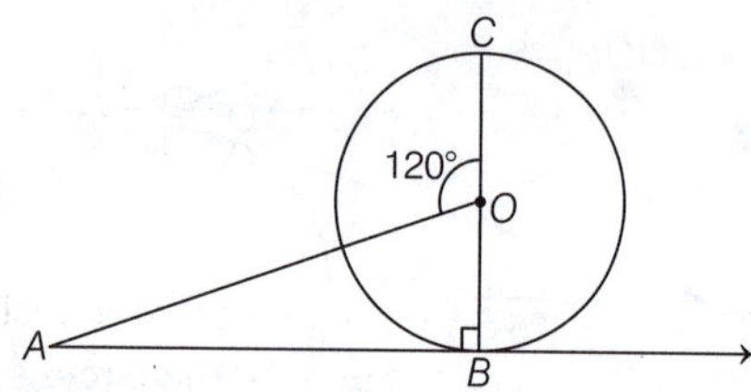

Given, $\angle AOC = 120°$

In ΔABO, $\angle AOC = \angle OAB + \angle OBA$

[$\because$ external angle = sum of opposite internal angles]

$\Rightarrow \quad 120° = \angle OAB + 90°$

$\Rightarrow \quad \angle OAB = 120° - 90°$

$\Rightarrow \quad \angle OAB = 30°$

Example 4. **Two circles with centres O and O' of radii 6 cm and 8 cm, respectively intersect at two points P and Q such that OP and $O'P$ are tangents to the two circles. Find the length of the common chord PQ.**

CBSE 2023 (Standard)

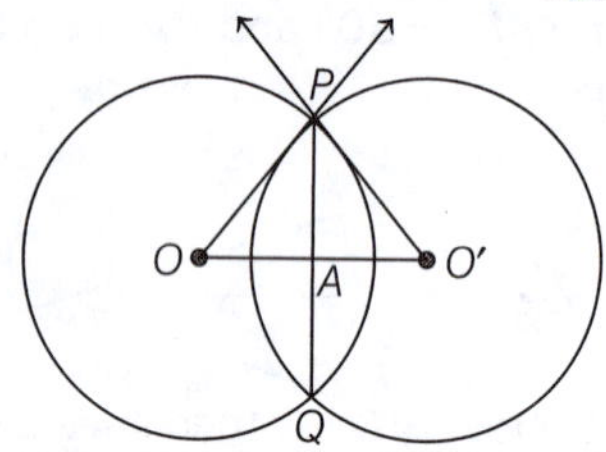

Sol. Here, two circles are of radii $OP = 6$ cm and $O'P = 8$ cm

These two circles intersect at P and Q.

Here, OP and $O'P$ are two tangents drawn at point P.

$\therefore \quad \angle OPO' = 90°$

[tangent at any point of circle is perpendicular to radius through the point of contact]

In $\Delta OPO'$,

by Pythagoras theorem,

$$(OO')^2 = (OP)^2 + (PO')^2$$

$\Rightarrow \quad 6^2 + 8^2 = (OO')^2$

$\Rightarrow \quad OO' = 10$ cm

Also, $PA \perp OO'$.

Let $OA = x$, then

$$AO' = 10 - x$$

In ΔOAP,

$$(OP)^2 = (OA)^2 + (AP)^2$$

[by Pythagoras theorem]

$\Rightarrow \quad (AP)^2 = 6^2 - x^2 = 36 - x^2 \quad \ldots$(i)

Now, in $\Delta APO'$,

$$(PO')^2 = (PA)^2 + (AO')^2$$

[by Pythagoras theorem]

$\Rightarrow \quad (PA)^2 = 8^2 - (10 - x)^2 \quad \ldots$(ii)

From Eqs. (i) and (ii), we get

$$36 - x^2 = 64 - (10 - x)^2$$

$\Rightarrow \quad 36 - x^2 = 64 - 100 - x^2 + 20x$

$\Rightarrow \quad 20x = 72$

$\Rightarrow \quad x = \frac{18}{5} = 3.6$ cm

From Eq. (i),

$$AP^2 = 36 - 12.96 = 23.04$$

$\Rightarrow \quad AP = 4.8$ cm

Since, the perpendicular drawn from the centre of a circle to a chord bisect it.

$\therefore$ Length of common chord $= PQ$

$= 2AP$

$= 2 \times 4.8$

$= 9.6$ cm

Try These 10.1

1 **Find the length of the tangents to the circle from a point at any distance of x cm from centre of the circle of radius r cm.**

(i) $x = 5, r = 3$

(ii) $x = 13, r = 12$

(iii) $x = 25, r = 24$

(iv) $x = 3\sqrt{3}, r = 3\sqrt{2}$

2 **The length of a tangent from a point A at distance 5cm from the centre of the circle is 4cm. Find the radius of the circle.** SQP 2023 (Basic)

3 **In the given figure, PA is a tangent to the circle drawn from the external point P and PBC is the secant to the circle with BC as diameter.** CBSE 2023 (Standard)

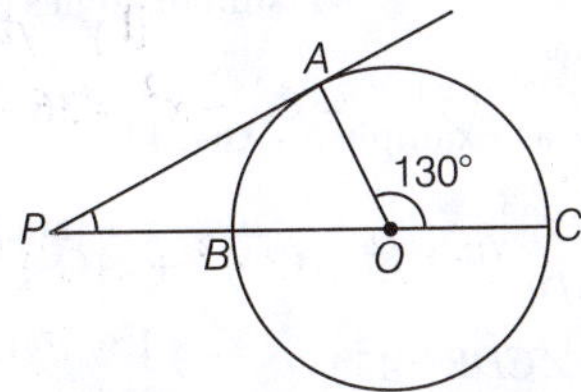

If $\angle AOC = 130°$, then find the measure of $\angle APB$, where O is the centre of the circle.

4 **In the given figure, AT is a tangent to the circle with centre O such that $OT = 4$ cm and $\angle OTA = 30°$. Find the length of AT.**

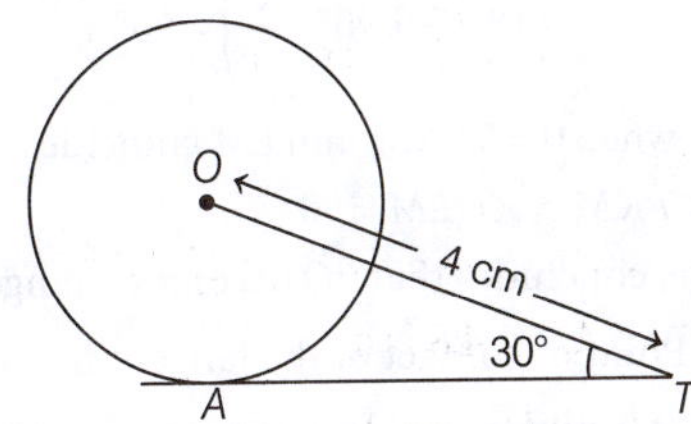

5 **If AB is a tangent drawn from a point B to a circle with centre C and radius 1.5 cm such that $\angle CBA = 30°$, then find the length of a tangent AB and a line CB.**

6 **If PQ is a tangent drawn from an external point P to a circle with centre O and QOR is a diameter where length of QOR is 8 cm such that $\angle POR = 120°$, then find OP and PQ.**

7 **In the given figure, PA is a tangent from an external point P to a circle with centre O. If $\angle POB = 115°$, then find $\angle APO$.**

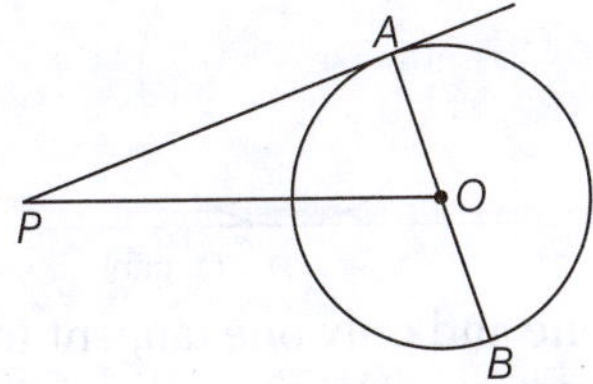

8 (i) In the given figure, find the value of x.

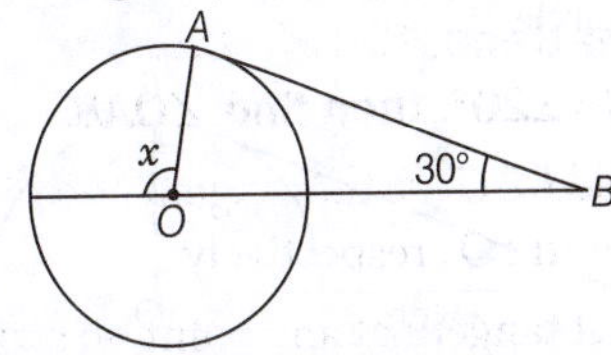

(ii) From the given figure, find the value of $x + y$.

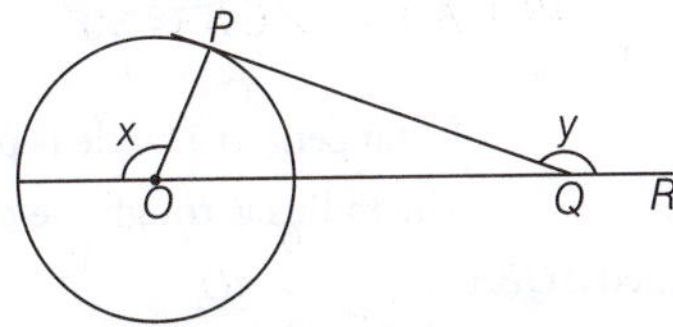

9 **PQ is a tangent drawn from a point P to a circle with centre O and QOR is a diameter of the circle such that $\angle POR = 135°$, then find $\angle OPQ$.**

10 **In the given figure, FG is a tangent to the circle with centre A. If $\angle DCB = 15°$ and $CE = DE$, then find $\angle GCE$ and $\angle BCE$.**

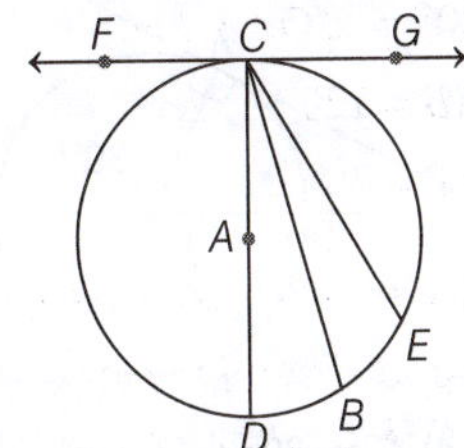

11 **Shown below is a circle with centre M. PQ is a secant and $\angle KML = \theta$.**

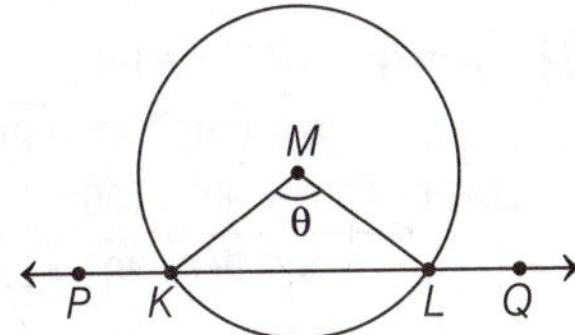

(i) Show that when $\theta = 0°$, PQ becomes a tangent to the circle.

(ii) What is the point of contact of the tangent in part (i) with the circle? CBSE CFPQ

Answers

1. (i) Given, $OB = x$ cm and radius $OA = r$ cm

Use Pythagoras theorem in right ΔOAB, to find AB

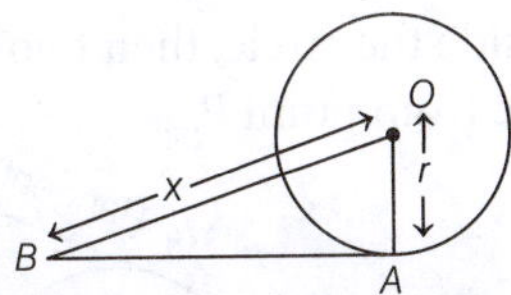

Ans. 4 cm

(ii) **Hint** Do same as part (i). **Ans.** 5 cm

(iii) **Hint** Do same as part (i). **Ans.** 7 cm

(iv) **Hint** Do same as part (i). **Ans.** 3 cm

2. Let O be the centre of circle and let B be the point of contact of tangent and circle.

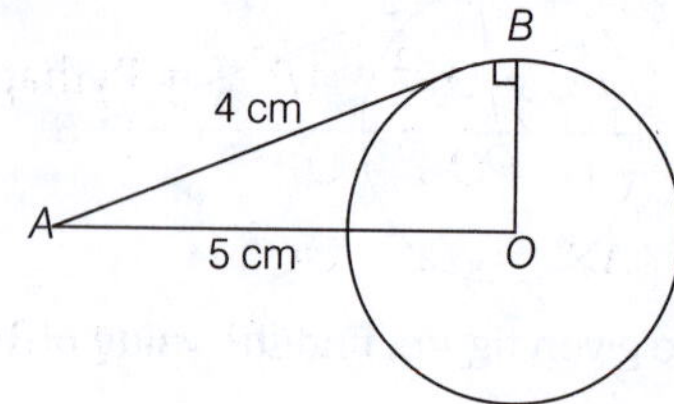

Then, $OB \perp AB$

[$\because$ tangent to a circle is perpendicular to the radius through the point of contact]

In right angled ΔOBA,

$$OA^2 = OB^2 + AB^2 \quad \text{[by Pythagoras theorem]}$$

$\Rightarrow$ $5^2 = OB^2 + 4^2$

$\Rightarrow$ $OB^2 = 9 \Rightarrow OB = 3$ cm

3. $OA \perp PA$ (tangent to a circle is perpendicular to the radius through the point of contact)

$\Rightarrow$ $\angle OAP = 90°$

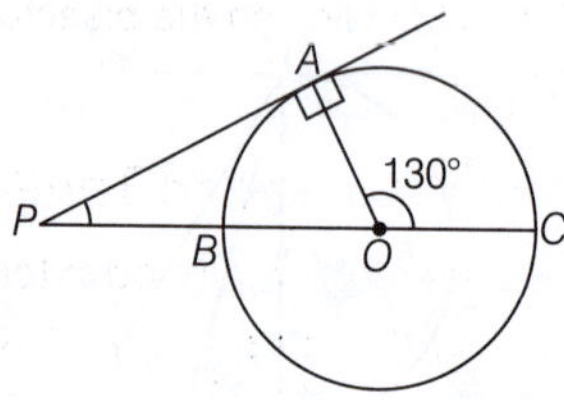

Also, $\angle AOP + \angle AOC = 180°$ [linear pair]

$\Rightarrow$ $\angle AOP + 130° = 180° \Rightarrow \angle AOP = 50°$

Now, in ΔAPO,

$\angle APO + \angle AOP + \angle OAP = 180°$

[angle sum property of triangle]

$\Rightarrow$ $\angle APO + 50° + 90° = 180°$

$\Rightarrow$ $\angle APO = 40° = \angle APB$

4. **Hint** Do same as Example 2. **Ans.** $2\sqrt{3}$ cm

5. **Hint** Do same as Example 2.

Ans. Line $CB = 3$ cm and tangent $AB = \frac{3\sqrt{3}}{2}$ cm

6. **Hint** Do same as Example 2.

Ans. 8 cm and $4\sqrt{3}$ cm

7. **Hint** Do same as Example 3. **Ans.** 25°

8. (i) **Hint** Do same as Example 3.

Ans. 120°

(ii) **Hint** In given figure, we have

$\angle OPQ = 90°$, [$\because$ tangent to a circle is perpendicular to the radius through the point of contact]

$\angle POQ = 180° - x$ and $\angle PQO = 180° - y$

$\because \angle OPQ + \angle POQ + \angle PQO = 180°$

[sum of angles of a triangle is 180°]

Ans. 270°

9. **Hint** Do same as Example 3. **Ans.** 45°

10. **Hint** $\angle CED = 90°$ [angle in a semi-circle]

$\because$ $CE = DE$

$\therefore$ $\angle ECD = \angle CDE = 45°$

Ans. 45° and 30°

11. (i) **Hint** ΔKLM is an isosceles triangle.

$\therefore \angle KLM = \angle LKM = \frac{180° - \theta}{2}$

and $\angle PKM = \angle QLM$

$$= 180° - \left(90° - \frac{\theta}{2}\right) = 90° + \frac{\theta}{2}$$

Now, when $\theta = 0°$, KM and LM coincide and $\angle PKM = \angle QLM = 90°$

Hence, concludes that PQ becomes a tangent to the circle.

(ii) **Hint** Point of contact of the tangent in part (i) with the circle is K and L.

TOPIC 02 Number of Tangents from a Point on a Circle

The number of tangents drawn from a point on a circle depends upon the position of the point with respect to the circle. So, three cases are possible.

Case I When point P lies outside the circle.

If point P lies outside the circle, then two tangents can be drawn to the circle from point P.

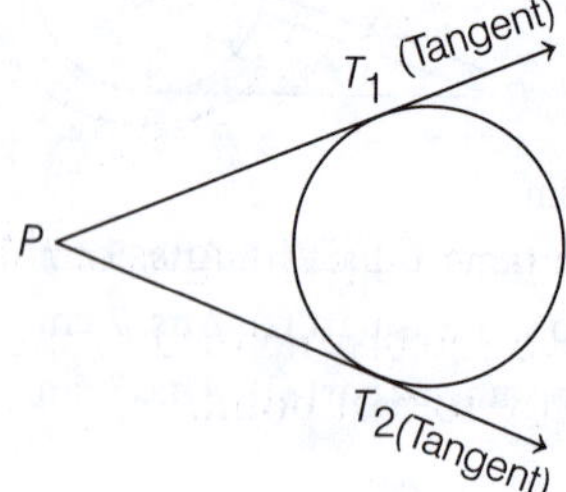

Hence, there are exactly two tangents (PT_1 and PT_2) from a point lying outside the circle.

Case II When point P lies on the circle.

If point P lies on the circle, then there is one and only one line passing through point P which touch the circle at one point.

Hence, there is one and only one tangent to the circle passing through a point P lying on the circle and this point P will be its point of contact.

Case III When point P lies inside the circle.

If a point P lies inside the circle, then any line passing through the point P will intersect the circle at two points.

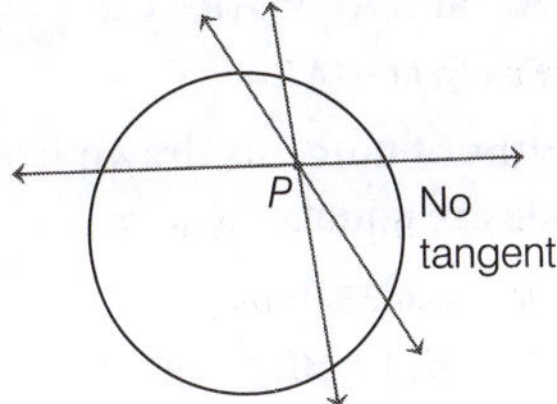

Hence, there is no tangent to a circle passing through a point lying inside the circle.

Length of Tangents Drawn from an External Point

The length of the segment of the tangent between the external point 'P' (say) and the point of contact of tangent with the circle is called **length of the tangent.**

If two tangents are drawn from an external point, then they are equal in length.

This result is proved in the form of following theorem.

Theorem The lengths of tangents drawn from an external point to a circle are equal

CBSE Sample Paper 2025 (Basic), CBSE 2020 (Basic)

Let AP and AQ be two tangents from a point A to a circle with centre O.

To prove $AP = AQ$

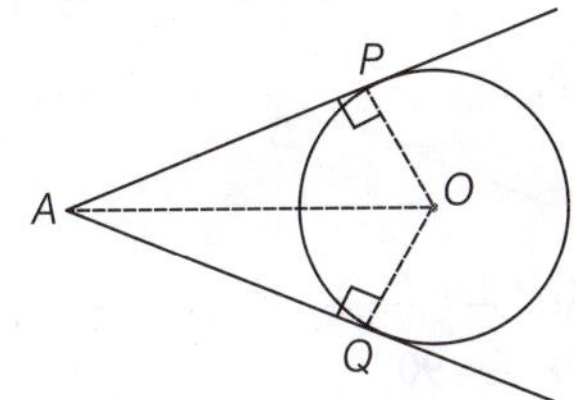

Construction Join OP, OQ and OA.

Proof We know that a tangent at any point of a circle is perpendicular to the radius through the point of contact.

Here, AP is a tangent and OP is the radius of the circle through P.

$\therefore \quad OP \perp AP$

Similarly, $\quad OQ \perp AQ$

$\Rightarrow \quad \angle OPA = \angle OQA = 90° \quad$ ...(i)

First Method

In ΔOPA and ΔOQA, we have

$OP = OQ$ [radii of a circle]

$\angle OPA = \angle OQA = 90°$ [from Eq. (i)]

$OA = OA$ [common sides]

So, $\Delta OPA \cong \Delta OQA$ [by RHS congruence rule]

$\therefore \quad AP = AQ$ [by CPCT]

Second Method

In right angled ΔOPA,

$OA^2 = OP^2 + AP^2$ [by Pythagoras theorem]

$\Rightarrow \quad AP^2 = OA^2 - OP^2$

$\Rightarrow \quad AP^2 = OA^2 - OQ^2 \quad$ ...(ii)

[$\because OP = OQ =$ Radii of a circle]

Now, in right angled ΔOQA,

$OA^2 = OQ^2 + AQ^2$

$\Rightarrow \quad AQ^2 = OA^2 - OQ^2 \quad$ ...(iii)

From Eqs. (ii) and (iii), we get

$AP^2 = AQ^2$

$\Rightarrow \quad AP = AQ \quad$ **Hence proved.**

Note it From the above theorem,

$\angle OAP = \angle OAQ \quad [\because \Delta OPA \cong \Delta OQA]$

$\Rightarrow$ OA is the angle bisector of $\angle PAQ$.

Thus, the centre of the circle lies on the bisector of the angle between the two tangents.

Important Results Related to Tangent to a Circle

(i) If two circles touch internally or externally, then point of contact lies on the straight line through the two centres.

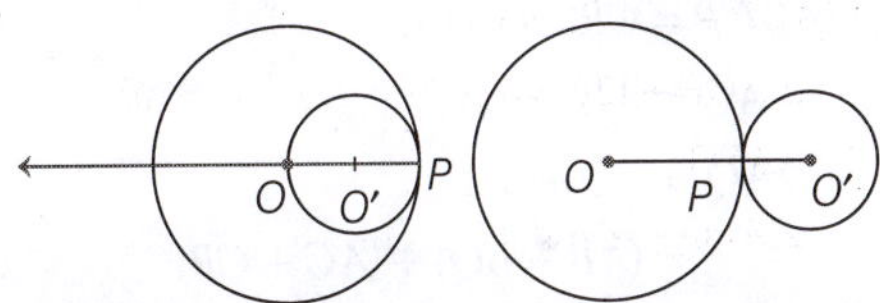

(ii) A pair of tangents drawn at two points of a circle are either parallel or they intersect each other at a point outside the circle.

(iii) If two tangents drawn to a circle are parallel to each other, then the line segment joining their point of contact is a diameter of the circle.

(iv) If two tangents are drawn to a circle from an external point, then

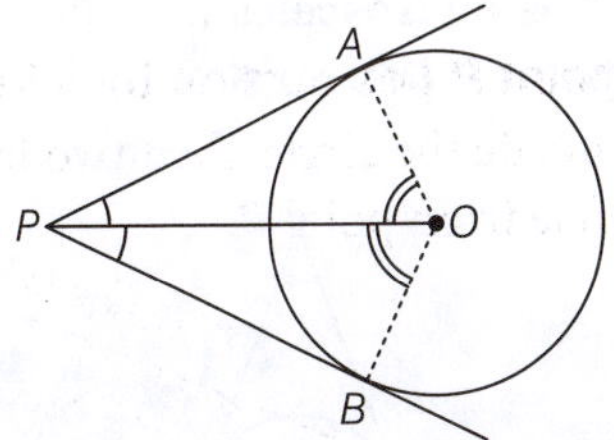

(a) They subtend equal angles at the centre.

(b) They are equally inclined to the segment, joining the centre to that point.

(v) The opposite sides of a quadrilateral circumscribing a circle subtend supplementary angles at the centre of the circle.

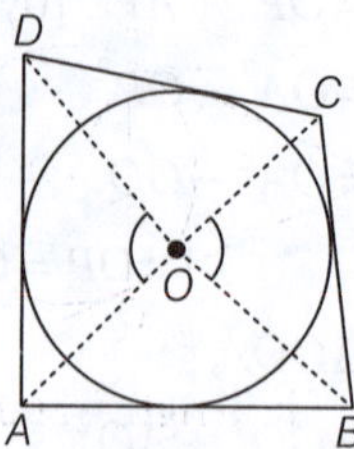

Example 1. A circle touches the side BC of a ΔABC at a point P and touches AB and AC when produced at Q and R respectively. Show that $AQ = \frac{1}{2}$ (Perimeter of ΔABC).

CBSE 2023, 20, 09, (Standard) 12,11

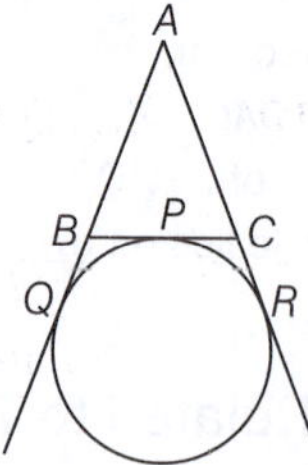

Sol. $BQ = BP$ (length of tangents drawn from an external point to a circle are equal) ...(i)

$$CP = CR \quad \text{...(ii)}$$

and $AQ = AR$

$$\therefore \quad 2AQ = AQ + AR$$
$$= (AB + BQ) + (AC + CR)$$
$$= (AB + BP) + (AC + CP)$$

[using Eqs. (i) and (ii)]

$$\Rightarrow \quad 2AQ = AB + AC + (BP + CP)$$
$$\Rightarrow \quad 2AQ = AB + AC + BC$$
$$\Rightarrow \quad AQ = \frac{1}{2}(AB + BC + AC)$$
$$\Rightarrow \quad AQ = \frac{1}{2} \text{ Perimeter of } \Delta ABC$$

Example 2. ABC is an isosceles triangle with $AB = AC$, circumscribed about a circle. Prove that BC is bisected at E.

CBSE 2023 (Basic)

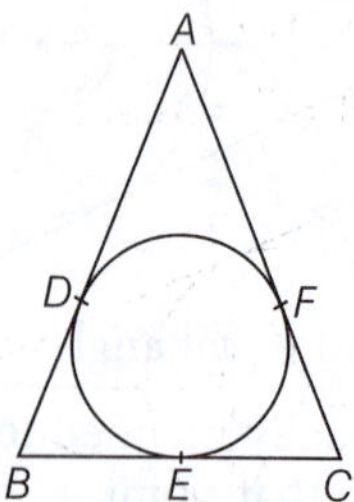

Sol. **Given** $AB = AC$

To prove $BE = CE$

Proof Since, ΔABC is an isosceles triangle. So, $AB = AC$

$\because AB = BD + AD$ and $AC = AF + CF$

$$\Rightarrow \quad BD + AD = AF + CF \quad \text{...(i)}$$

Since, the lengths of tangents drawn from an external point to a circle are equal.

$$\therefore \quad AD = AF \quad \text{...(ii)}$$
$$BD = BE \quad \text{...(iii)}$$
$$CF = CE \quad \text{...(iv)}$$

From Eqs. (i) and (ii),

$$BD + AF = AF + CF$$
$$\Rightarrow \quad BD = CF$$
$$\Rightarrow \quad BE = CE \quad \text{[from Eqs. (iii) and (iv)]}$$

Hence proved.

Example 3. O is the centre of a circle of radius 5 cm. T is a point such that $OT = 13$ cm and OT intersects the circle at E. If AB is the tangent to the circle at E, then find the length of AB.

NCERT Exemplar

Sol. Given, radius of circle = 5 cm and $OT = 13$ cm.

We know that tangent at any point of a circle is perpendicular to the radius through the point of contact.

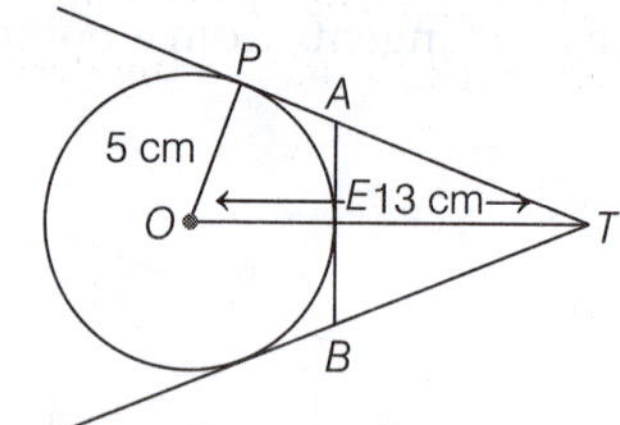

So, $OP \perp PT$

$$\Rightarrow \quad \angle OPT = 90^\circ$$

In right angled ΔOPT,

$$OT^2 = OP^2 + PT^2 \quad \text{[by Pythagoras theorem]}$$
$$\Rightarrow \quad 13^2 = 5^2 + PT^2$$
$$\Rightarrow \quad PT^2 = 169 - 25 = 144$$
$$\therefore \quad PT = 12 \text{ cm}$$

[taking positive square root as length cannot be negative]

Also, we know that length of tangents drawn from a point to a circle are equal.

Therefore, $AP = AE = x$ (say)

Now, $AT = PT - AP = (12 - x)$ cm

Since, AB is the tangent to the circle at point E and OE is radius.

Therefore, $OE \perp AB$

$$\Rightarrow \quad \angle OEA = 90^\circ$$
$$\Rightarrow \quad \angle AET = 90^\circ$$

[$\because OT$ is a straight line, so $\angle OEA + \angle AET = 180^\circ$]

Now, in right angled ΔAET,

$$AT^2 = AE^2 + ET^2$$

[by Pythagoras theorem]

$$\Rightarrow \quad (12 - x)^2 = x^2 + (13 - 5)^2$$

$[\because ET = OT - OE = 13 - 5]$

$$\Rightarrow 144 - 24x + x^2 = x^2 + 64 \quad [\because (a-b)^2 = a^2 + b^2 - 2ab]$$

$$\Rightarrow \quad -24x = -80$$

$$\Rightarrow \quad x = \frac{10}{3} \text{ cm}$$

$$\therefore \quad AE = \frac{10}{3} \text{ cm}$$

Similarly, $BE = \frac{10}{3}$ cm

Hence, $AB = AE + BE$

$$= \frac{10}{3} + \frac{10}{3} = \frac{20}{3} \text{ cm}$$

Example 4. **ABC is a right angled triangle with $\angle B = 90°$, $BC = 3$ cm and $AB = 4$ cm. A circle with centre O and radius r cm has been inscribed in ΔABC. Find the radius of the incircle.**

Sol. Let D, E and F be the points where the incircle touches the sides AB, BC and CA, respectively. Join OA, OB and OC.

In ΔABC, $AC^2 = AB^2 + BC^2$ [by Pythagoras theorem]

$$= 4^2 + 3^2 = 25$$

$$\therefore \quad AC = 5 \text{ cm}$$

[taking positive square root as length cannot be negative]

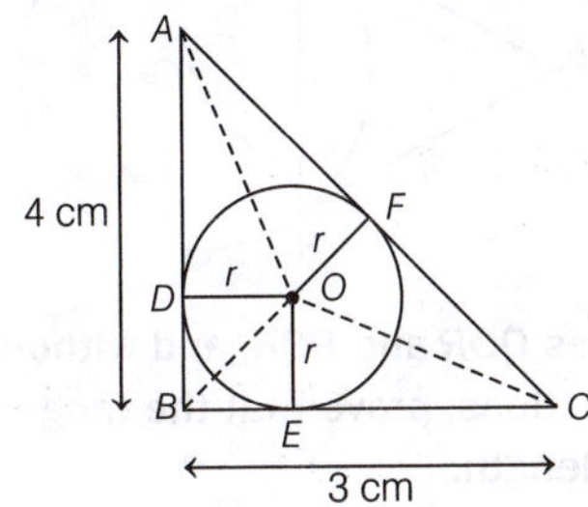

Let the radius of incircle $= r$ cm

Now, $\text{ar}(\Delta OAB) = \frac{1}{2} \times OD \times AB = \frac{1}{2} \times r \times 4 = \frac{4r}{2} \text{ cm}^2$

$$\text{ar}(\Delta OBC) = \frac{1}{2} \times OE \times BC = \frac{1}{2} \times r \times 3 = \frac{3r}{2} \text{ cm}^2$$

and $\text{ar}(\Delta OAC) = \frac{1}{2} \times OF \times AC = \frac{1}{2} \times r \times 5 = \frac{5r}{2} \text{ cm}^2$

$\therefore$ ar (ΔABC) = ar (ΔOAB) + ar (ΔOBC) + ar (ΔOAC)

$$\Rightarrow \frac{1}{2} \times AB \times BC = \frac{4r}{2} + \frac{3r}{2} + \frac{5r}{2}$$

$$\Rightarrow \frac{1}{2} \times 3 \times 4 = \frac{12r}{2}$$

$$\Rightarrow \quad r = 1 \text{ cm}$$

Example 5. **Two tangents TP and TQ are drawn to a circle with centre O from an external point T. Prove that $\angle PTQ = 2\angle OPQ$.** CBSE 2023, 20, 13, 12, 11, 09 (Standard)

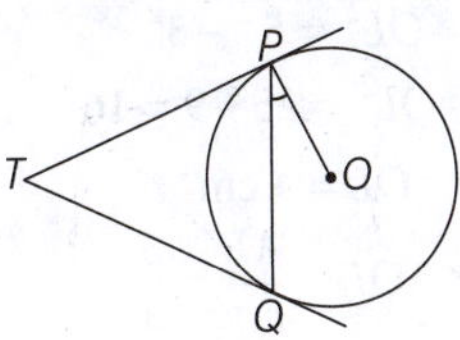

Sol. $TP = TQ$ [$\because$ length of tangents drawn from an external point are equal]

$\therefore$ In ΔTPQ,

$\angle TPQ = \angle TQP$ [angles opposite to equal sides are equal]

Also, $OP \perp TP$ [tangent to a circle is perpendicular to the radius through the point of contact] ...(i)

$$\Rightarrow \quad \angle TPO = 90°$$

$$\therefore \quad \angle TPQ = \angle TPO - \angle OPQ = 90° - \angle OPQ \quad \text{...(ii)}$$

Now in ΔTPQ,

$$\angle TPQ + \angle TQP + \angle PTQ = 180°$$

[sum of interior angles of a triangle is 180°]

$$\Rightarrow \quad 2\angle TPQ + \angle PTQ = 180° \quad \text{[using Eq. (i)]}$$

$$\Rightarrow \quad \angle PTQ = 180° - 2\angle TPQ$$

$$= 180° - 2(90° - \angle OPQ)$$

[using Eq. (ii)]

$$\Rightarrow \quad \angle PTQ = 2\angle OPQ$$ **Hence proved.**

Example 6. **In the given figure, AB is chord of length 6 cm of a circle of radius 5 cm. The tangents at A and B intersect at a point P. Find the length of PB.** CBSE 2024 (Basic)

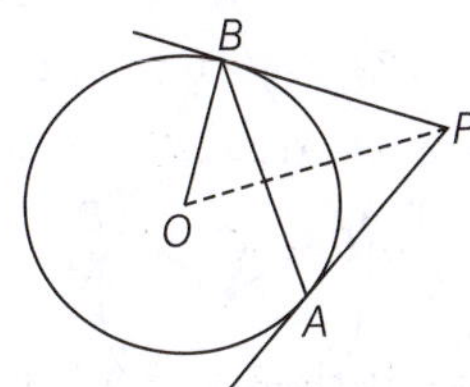

Sol. **Given** $AB = 6$ cm and radius, $OA = OB = 5$ cm

To find Length of PB

Construction Join OA, so $OA = 5$ cm

OL is perpendicuar to AB.

$$AL = LB = \frac{6}{2} = 3 \text{ cm} \quad [\because OL \text{ bisect } AB]$$

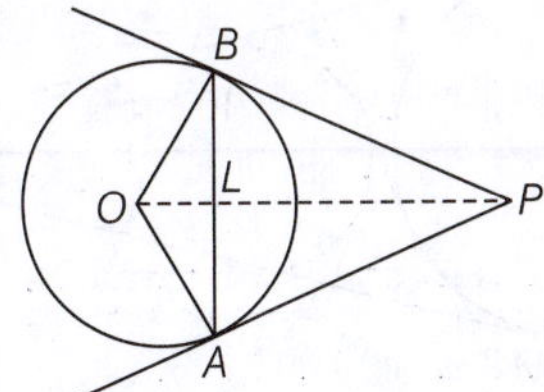

Proof By Pythagoras theorem in ΔOLA,

$$OL^2 + LA^2 = OA^2$$
$$\Rightarrow \quad OL^2 = OA^2 - LA^2$$
$$\Rightarrow \quad OL^2 = 5^2 - 3^2$$
$$\Rightarrow \quad OL^2 = 25 - 9 = 16$$
$$\therefore \quad OL = 4 \text{ cm}$$

We have, $\tan \angle AOL = \frac{AL}{OL} = \frac{3}{4}$

From ΔOAP,

$$\tan\angle AOP = \frac{PA}{OA}$$
$$\Rightarrow \quad \tan\angle AOL = \frac{PA}{OA} \quad [\because \angle AOL = \angle AOP]$$
$$\Rightarrow \quad \frac{3}{4} = \frac{PA}{5} \Rightarrow PA = \frac{3\times5}{4} = \frac{15}{4} \text{ cm}$$

Length of $PA = \frac{15}{4} = 3.75$ cm

Since, $PA = PB$ [length of tangents drawn from an external points to a circle are equal]

$\therefore PB = 3.75$ cm

Try These 10.2

1. If the radius of a circle is 5 cm, then find the distance between two parallel tangents.
2. Anu says, 'A circle of radius 10 cm can have 100 tangents.' Is Anu correct? Give a reason to justify your answer. Competency Based Question
3. If AB and BC are two tangents to a circle with centre O such that $\angle AOC = 120°$, then find $\angle ABC$.
4. In the figure below, a circle with centre O is inscribed inside ΔLMN. A and B are the points of tendency.

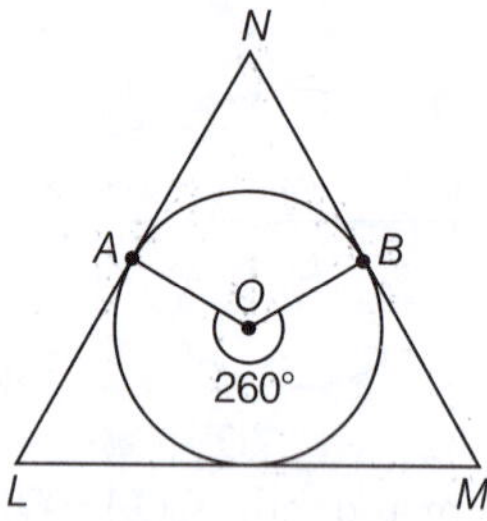

Find $\angle ANB$. Show your steps. CBSE CFPQ

5. In the given figure, PT and PM are two tangents to the circle with centre O. If $OT = 6$ cm and $OP = 10$ cm, then find the length of PT and PM.

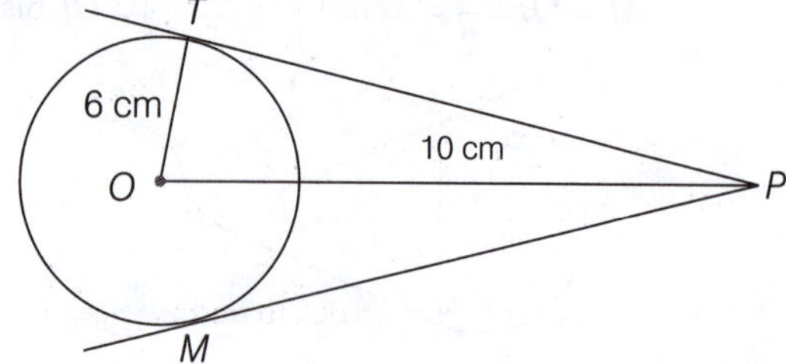

6. In the given figure, PA and PB are tangents to the given circle such that $PA = 5$ cm and $\angle APB = 60°$.

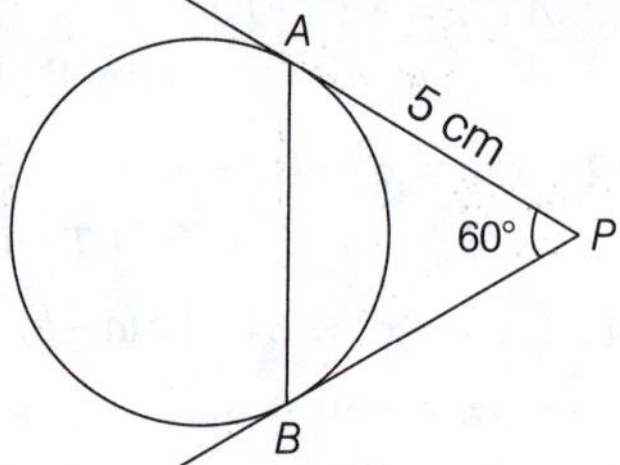

Find the length of chord AB.

7. Shown below is a circle with centre O and radius 5 units. PM and PN are tangents and the length of chord MN is 6 units.

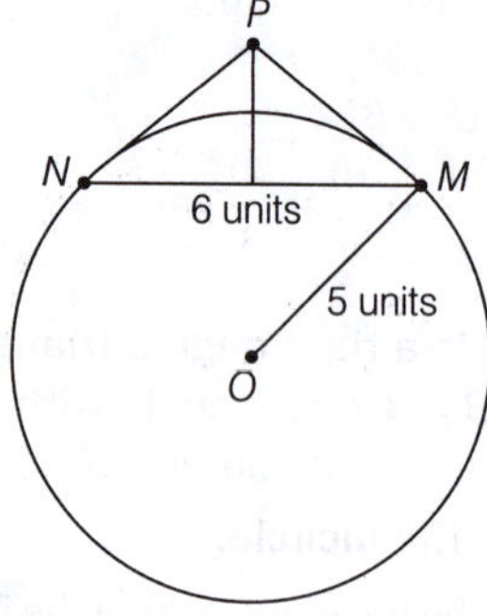

Find the length of $(PM + PN)$. Show your work. CBSE CFPQ

8. Shown below is a circle with centre O and tangents PQ and PR.

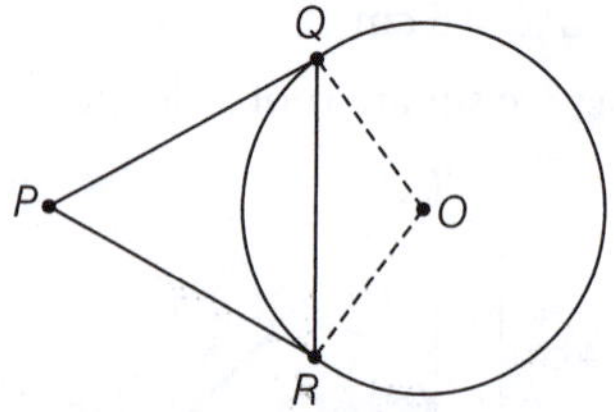

Using triangles QOR and PQR, and without doing any extra constructions, prove that the tangents PQ and PR are equal in length.

9. From an external point P, tangents PA and PB are drawn to a circle with centre O. If CD is the tangent to the circle at a point E and $PA = 14$ cm, then find the perimeter of ΔPCD.

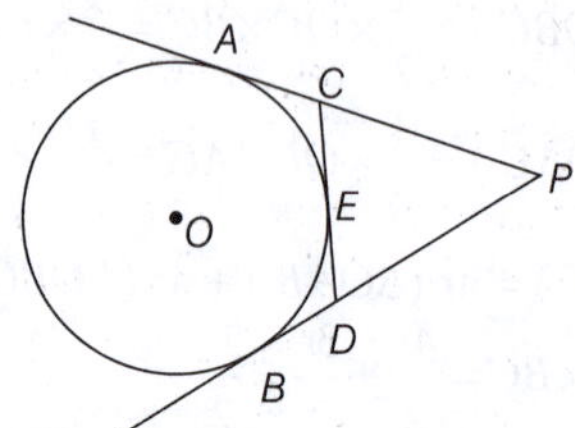

10. In a right angled ΔABC, right angled at B, $BC = 15$ cm and $AB = 8$ cm. A circle is inscribed in ΔABC. Find the radius of a circle.

11. In the given figure, an isosceles ΔABC with $AB = AC$, circumscribes a circle. Prove that point of contact P bisects the base BC.

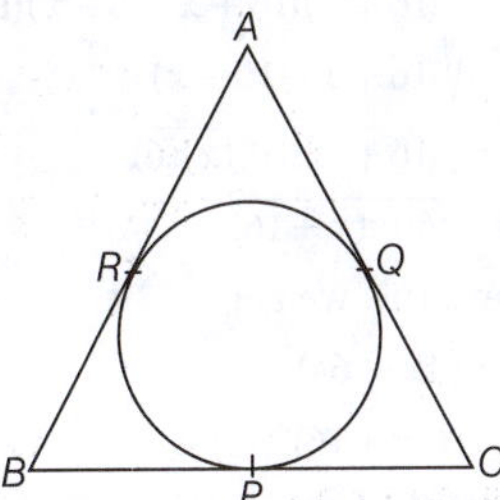

12. The given figure shows a circle with centre O and radius 4 cm circumscribed by ΔABC. BC touches the circle at D such that $BD = 6$ cm, $DC = 10$ cm. Find the length of AE.

CBSE 2025 (Basic)

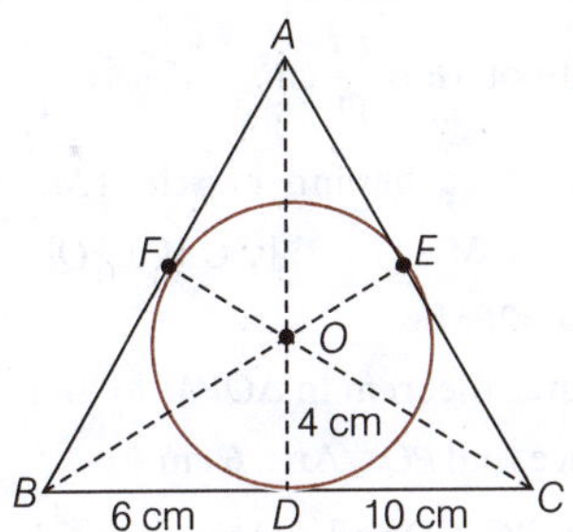

13. In the given figure, O is the centre of two concentric circles of radii 4 cm and 5 cm, respectively. PQ is the chord of outer circle which touches the inner circle. Find the length of chord PQ.

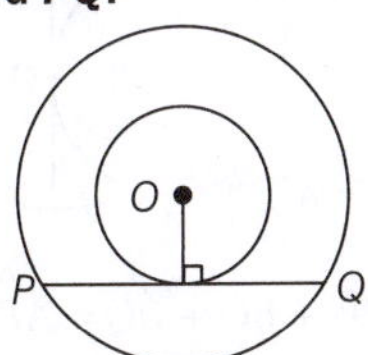

14. In the given figure, a circle touches all the four sides of a quadrilateral $ABCD$ whose three sides are $AB = 6$ cm, $BC = 7$ cm and $CD = 4$ cm. Find the length of AD.

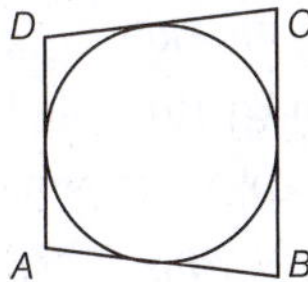

15. In two concentric circles, a chord of length 24 cm of larger circle becomes a tangent to the smaller circle whose radius is 5 cm. Find the radius of the larger circle.

16. In the given figure, PP' and QQ' are the two common tangents of the two circles. Show that $PP' = QQ'$.

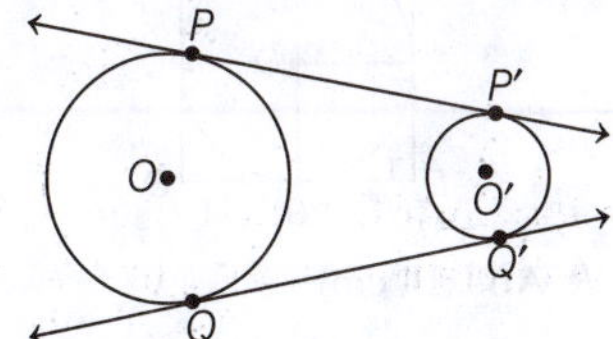

17. Given below is the diagram of a pair of pulleys.

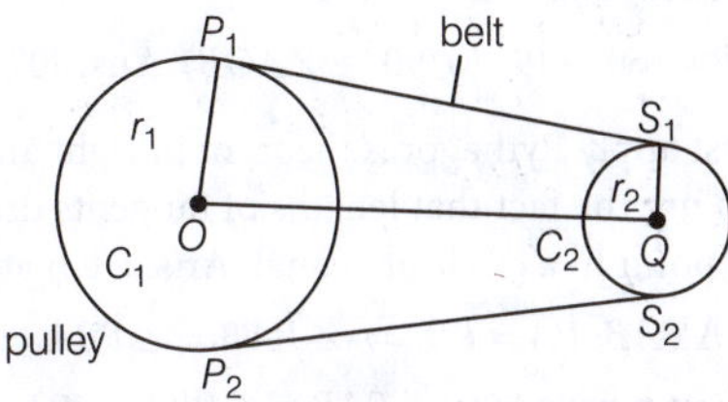

C_1 and C_2 are two pulleys attached with a belt. P_1 and P_2 are points of contact, where the belt meets C_1. S_1 and S_2 are points of contact, where belt meets C_2. O and Q are the centres of C_1 and C_2, respectively.

Identify the common tangents to the two circles (pulleys)?

Competency Based Question

18. In the given figure, O is the centre of two concentric circles of radii 4 cm and 6 cm, respectively. PA and PB are tangents to the outer and inner circles, respectively. If $PA = 10$ cm, then find the length of PB upto one place of decimal.

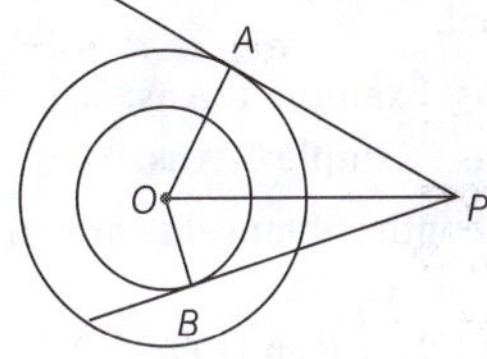

19. $ABCD$ is a quadrilateral such that $\angle D = 90°$. A circle $C(O, r)$ touches the sides AB, BC, CD and DA at P, Q, R and S, respectively. If $BC = 38$ cm, $CD = 25$ cm and $BP = 27$ cm, then find the value of r.

20. In the given figure, AB is a chord of length 9.6 cm of a circle with centre O and radius 6 cm. The tangents at A and B intersects at P. Find the length of PA.

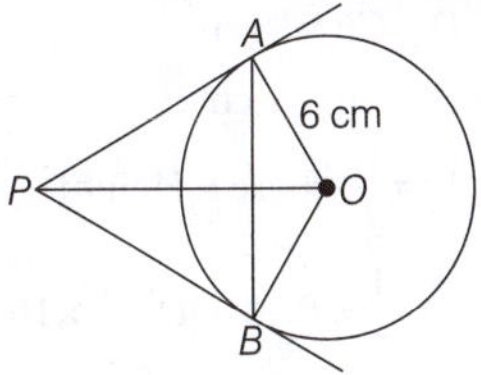

Answers

1. **Hint** The distance between two parallel tangents is equal to diameter of the circle. **Ans.** 10 cm
2. Yes, Anu is correct as a tangent to a circle can be made at any point on the circle and a circle has infinitely many points.
3. **Hint** Join OB,
   Thus, $\angle AOC = 2\ \angle AOB$ and $\angle ABC = 2\ \angle ABO$

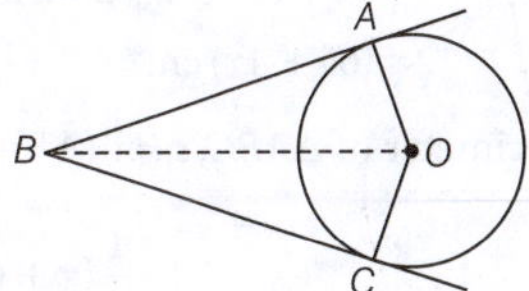

Use angle sum property in ΔABO, to find $\angle ABO$ and hence find $\angle ABC$ **Ans.** 60°

4. Hint $\angle AOB = 360° - 260° = 100°$

$\therefore \angle ANB = 360° - (90° + 90° + \angle AOB)$ **Ans.** 80°

5. Hint First apply Pythagoras theorem in right angled ΔOTP and then use the fact that lengths of tangents drawn from an external point to a circle are equal. **Ans.** 8 cm and 8 cm

6. Hint In ΔPAB, $PA = PB \Rightarrow \angle PAB = \angle PBA$

By angle sum property, $\angle PAB = \angle PBA = 60°$

$\Rightarrow \Delta PAB$ is equilateral. **Ans.** 5 cm

7. Hint Join P and O, intersecting MN at T (let).

$PO \perp MN$

$\therefore MT = NT = 3$ units

Now, apply Pythagoras theorem in ΔOTM and find OT.

Similarly, apply Pythagoras theorem in ΔPTM and ΔPMO and solve to find the value of $PM + PN$. **Ans.** 7.5 units

8. Hint Assume the base angles of ΔQOR as θ each as angles opposite equal sides are equal.

$\therefore \angle PRQ = \angle PQR = (90 - \theta)°$

PQ and PR are equal as sides opposite to equal angle in a triangle are equal.

9. Hint Do same as Example 1. **Ans.** 28 cm

10. Hint Do same as Example 4. **Ans.** 3 cm

11. We know that lengths of tangents drawn from an external point to a circle are equal.

$\therefore \quad AR = AQ, BR = BP$ and $CQ = CP$

Given, $AB = AC \Rightarrow AB - AR = AC - AQ$

[on subtracting AR from both sides]

$\Rightarrow BR = CQ \Rightarrow BP = CP$

12. Given, $BD = 6$ cm and $DC = 10$ cm

We know that tangents drawn from an external point to the circle are equal in length.

$\therefore \quad BD = BF = 6$ cm

$CD = CE = 10$ cm

and $\quad AF = AE = x$ cm (say)

Area of ΔOBC, $A_1 = \frac{1}{2} \times \text{Base} \times \text{Height}$

$= \frac{1}{2} \times BC \times OD = \frac{1}{2} \times 16 \times 4 = 32 \text{ cm}^2$,

area of ΔOBA, $A_2 = \frac{1}{2} \times AB \times OF = \frac{1}{2} \times (6 + x) \times 4$

$= (12 + 2x) \text{ cm}^2$

and area of ΔOAC, $A_3 = \frac{1}{2} \times AC \times OE = \frac{1}{2} \times (10 + x) \times 4$

$= (20 + 2x) \text{ cm}^2$

Thus, area of $\Delta ABC = A_1 + A_2 + A_3$

$= 32 + 12 + 2x + 20 + 2x$

$= (64 + 4x) \text{ cm}^2$ ...(i)

Now, semi-perimeter of ΔABC, $s = \frac{1}{2}(AB + BC + CA)$

$\Rightarrow \quad s = \frac{1}{2}(x + 6 + 16 + 10 + x)$

$\Rightarrow \quad s = \frac{1}{2}(32 + 2x) = (16 + x)$ cm

Using Heron's formula,

area of $\Delta ABC = \sqrt{s(s-a)(s-b)(s-c)}$

$= \sqrt{\begin{matrix}(16+x)(16+x-6-x)(16+x-16) \\ (16+x-10-x)\end{matrix}}$

$= \sqrt{(16+x)(10)(x)(6)}$

$= \sqrt{60x(x+16)}$ ...(ii)

From Eqs. (i) and (ii), we get

$\sqrt{60x(x+16)} = (4x + 64)$

$\Rightarrow 60x(x+16) = 16(x+16)^2$

$\Rightarrow \quad 60x = 16(x+16)$

$\Rightarrow \quad 15x = 4(x+16)$

$\Rightarrow \quad 15x = 4x + 64$

$\Rightarrow \quad 11x = 64 \Rightarrow x = \frac{64}{11}$

Hence, length of AE is $\frac{64}{11}$ cm.

13. Hint Chord PQ touches inner circle at M.

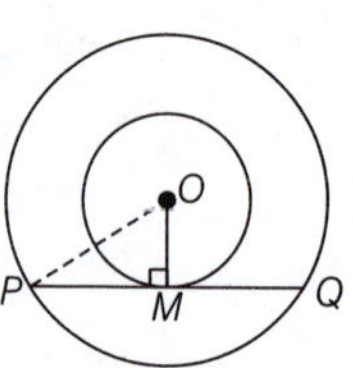

$\therefore \quad PM = QM \quad [\because OM \perp PQ]$

$\Rightarrow \quad PQ = 2PM$

Use Pythagoras theorem in ΔOPM to find PM and hence find PQ. **Ans.** 6 cm

14. Hint Let AB, BC, CD and AD touch the circle at points P, Q, R and S respectively, then

$AS = AP, BQ = BP, CQ = CR$ and $DS = DR$

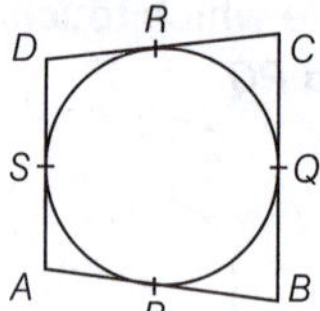

On adding, $AS + DS + BQ + CQ = AP + DR + BP + CR$

$\Rightarrow AD + BC = AB + CD \Rightarrow AD = (6 + 4 - 7)$ cm $= 3$ cm

15. Hint Do same as Question 13 **Ans.** 13 cm

16. Hint Produce PP' and QQ' to meet at point R (say).

Now, $\quad RP' = RQ'$ ...(i)

$RP = RQ$ ...(ii)

Subtract Eq. (i) from Eq. (ii) to find $PP' = QQ'$.

17. Hint P_1S_1 and P_2S_2 are two common tangents to the two circles.

18. Hint $OA \perp AP$ and $OB \perp BP$.

Use Pythagoras theorem in ΔOAP and ΔOBP. **Ans.** 10.9 cm

19. Hint Join OS and OR.

$\therefore \quad \angle OSD = \angle ORD = 90° \Rightarrow ORDS$ is a square.

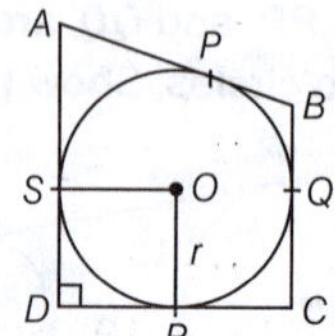

Hence, $r = DR$ **Ans.** 14 cm

20. Hint Do same as Example 6. **Ans.** 8 cm

NCERT FOLDER

Complete Solutions of All Exercises of NCERT Textbook

EXERCISE 10.1

Q1. How many tangents can a circle have?

Sol. From every point of a circle, we can draw a tangent. Therefore, infinite tangents can be drawn.

Q2. Fill in the blanks.

(i) A tangent to a circle intersects it in ...... point(s).

(ii) A line intersecting a circle in two points is called a ......

(iii) A circle can have ...... parallel tangents at the most.

(iv) The common point of a tangent to a circle and the circle is called ......

Sol. (i) one (ii) secant

(iii) two (iv) point of contact

Q3. A tangent *PQ* at a point *P* of a circle of radius 5 cm meets a line through the centre *O* at a point *Q*, so that $OQ = 12$ cm. Length of *PQ* is

(a) 12 cm (b) 13 cm

(c) 8.5 cm (d) $\sqrt{119}$ cm

Sol. (d) Here, PQ is a tangent, which touches the circle at point P and $OP = 5$ cm is the radius of circle. Join $OQ = 12$ cm. We know that tangent at any point of a circle is perpendicular to the radius through the point of contact.

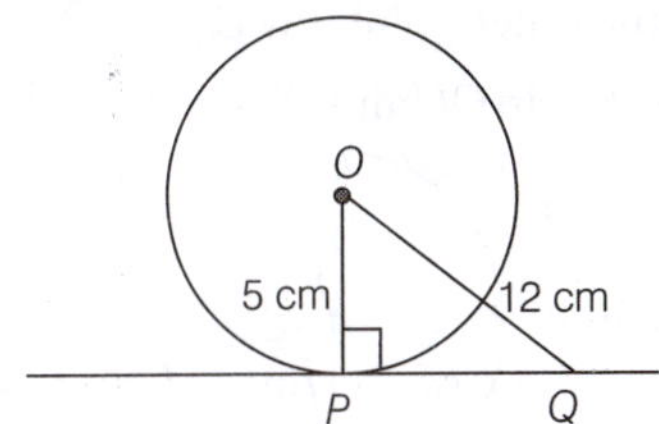

So, $OP \perp PQ$

Now, in right angled ΔOPQ,

$$OQ^2 = OP^2 + PQ^2$$

[by Pythagoras theorem]

$$\Rightarrow (12)^2 = (5)^2 + PQ^2$$

$$\Rightarrow PQ^2 = 144 - 25 = 119$$

$$\Rightarrow PQ = \sqrt{119} \text{ cm}$$

[taking positive square root as length cannot be negative]

Q4. Draw a circle and two lines parallel to a given line such that one is a tangent and the other a secant to the circle.

Sol. First, draw a circle with centre O and draw a line l. Now, we draw two lines parallel to l, such that one line say m, is a tangent to the circle and another say n, is a secant to the circle.

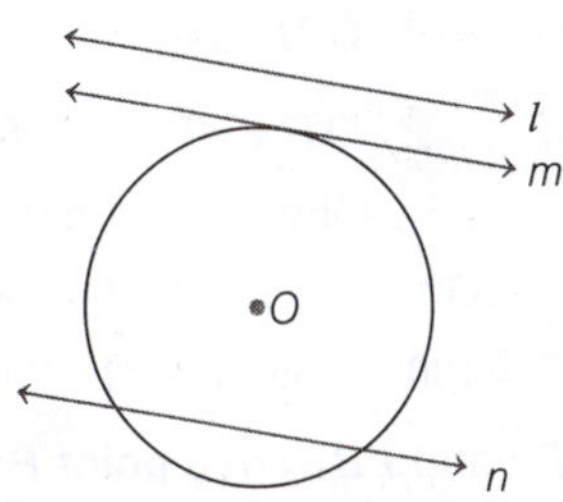

EXERCISE 10.2

Directions (Q. Nos. 1 to 3) *Choose the correct option and give justification.*

Q1. From a point Q, the length of the tangent to a circle is 24 cm and the distance of Q from the centre is 25 cm. The radius of the circle is

(a) 7 cm (b) 12 cm (c) 15 cm (d) 24.5 cm

Sol. (a) Do same as Q.3 of NCERT Folder Exercise 10.1.

Q2. In the given figure, if *TP* and *TQ* are the two tangents to a circle with centre *O*, so that $\angle POQ = 110°$, then $\angle PTQ$ is equal to

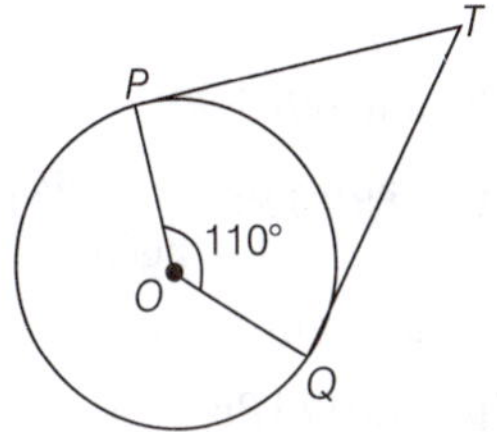

(a) 60° (b) 70° (c) 80° (d) 90°

Sol. (b) Given, TP and TQ are two tangents to a circle and $\angle POQ = 110°$. Join PQ.

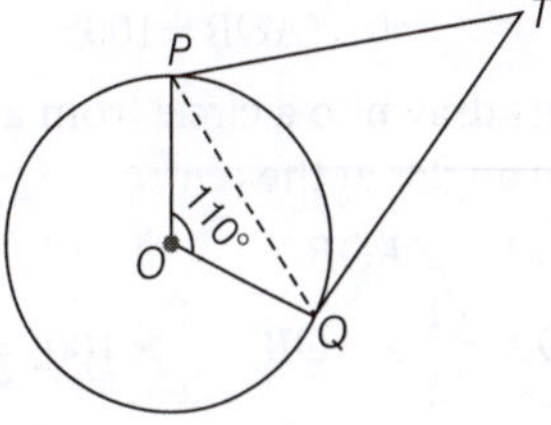

In ΔOPQ, $OP = OQ$ [radii of circle]

$\Rightarrow \angle OPQ = \angle OQP$

[angles corresponding to equal sides are equal]

Then, $\angle OPQ = \angle OQP = \dfrac{180^\circ - 110^\circ}{2} = 35^\circ$

[by angle sum property of isosceles triangle]

Since, $OP \perp PT$

[$\because$ radius of a circle is perpendicular to the tangent at the point of contact]

$\therefore \angle OPT = 90^\circ \Rightarrow \angle OPQ + \angle QPT = 90^\circ$

$\Rightarrow 35^\circ + \angle QPT = 90^\circ \Rightarrow \angle QPT = 55^\circ$

Similarly, $\angle PQT = 55^\circ$

Now, in ΔPTQ,

$$\angle QPT + \angle PQT + \angle PTQ = 180^\circ$$

[by angle sum property of triangle]

$\Rightarrow 55^\circ + 55^\circ + \angle PTQ = 180^\circ$

$\Rightarrow \angle PTQ = 180^\circ - (55^\circ + 55^\circ) = 70^\circ$

Q3. If tangents *PA* and *PB* from a point *P* to a circle with centre *O* are inclined to each other at angle of 80°, then $\angle POA$ is equal to CBSE 2020 (Basic)

(a) 50° (b) 60° (c) 70° (d) 80°

Sol. (a) Given, PA and PB are two tangents drawn from a point P, such that $\angle APB = 80^\circ$.

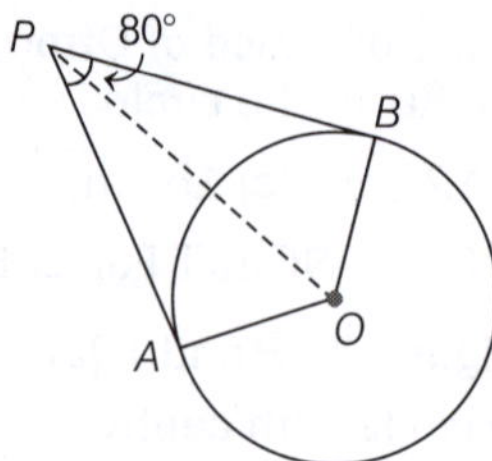

Join OA and OB.

Clearly, $OA \perp PA$ and $OB \perp PB$

[$\because$ radius of a circle is perpendicular to the tangent at the point of contact]

$\therefore \angle OAP = 90^\circ$ and $\angle OBP = 90^\circ$

Now, in quadrilateral $OAPB$,

$$\angle OAP + \angle APB + \angle OBP + \angle AOB = 360^\circ$$

[$\because$ sum of all interior angles $= 360^\circ$]

$\Rightarrow 90^\circ + 80^\circ + 90^\circ + \angle AOB = 360^\circ$

$\Rightarrow \angle AOB = 100^\circ$

Since, tangents drawn to a circle from an external point subtend equal angles at the centre.

$\therefore \angle POA = \angle POB$

$\Rightarrow \angle POA = \dfrac{1}{2}\angle AOB = \dfrac{1}{2} \times 100^\circ = 50^\circ$

Q4. Prove that the tangents drawn at the ends of a diameter of a circle are parallel.

CBSE 2023 (Standard), CBSE 2020 (Basic), 19

Sol. Let AB be a diameter of a given circle and LM and PQ be the tangent lines drawn to the circle at points A and B, respectively.

To prove $LM \parallel PQ$

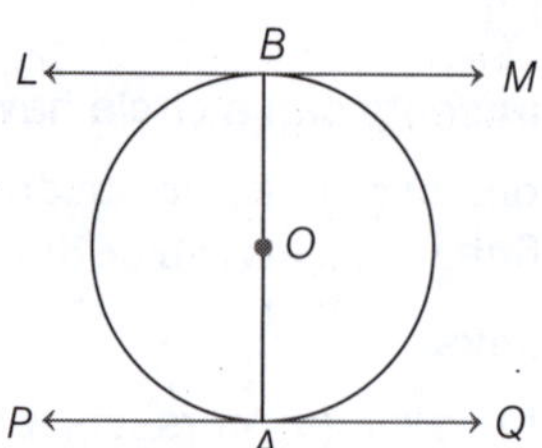

Proof We know that the tangent at any point of a circle is perpendicular to the radius through the point of contact.

$\therefore OA \perp PQ$ and $OB \perp LM$

$\Rightarrow AB \perp PQ$ and $AB \perp LM$

$\Rightarrow \angle PAB = 90^\circ$ and $\angle ABM = 90^\circ$

$\Rightarrow \angle PAB = \angle ABM$ [each 90°]

But these are alternate angles.

$\therefore PQ \parallel LM$

Hence, the tangents drawn at the ends of a diameter of a circle are parallel. **Hence proved.**

Q5. Prove that the perpendicular at the point of contact to the tangent to a circle passes through the centre.

Sol. Let AB be the tangent drawn at a point C on the circle with centre O.

To prove Perpendicular at point C passes through the centre O. If possible, let the perpendicular passing through some other point, say O'.

Construction Join OC and $O'C$.

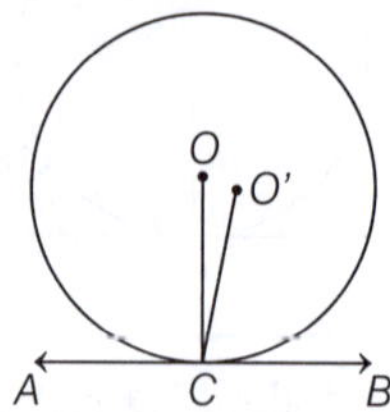

Proof Since, tangent at any point of a circle is perpendicular to the radius through the point of contact.

$\therefore OC \perp AB \Rightarrow \angle OCB = 90^\circ$

Also, $\angle O'CB = 90^\circ$ [as it is supposed that $CO' \perp AB$]

$\therefore \angle OCB = \angle O'CB$

which is possible only when points O and O' coincide.

So, our assumption is wrong.

Hence, the perpendicular at the point of contact to the tangent to a circle always passes through the centre.

Hence proved.

Q6. **The length of a tangent from a point *A* at a distance 5 cm from the centre of the circle is 4 cm. Find the radius of the circle.**

Sol. Do same as Example 1 of Topic 1. **Ans.** 3 cm

Q7. **Two concentric circles are of radii 5 cm and 3 cm. Find the length of the chord of the larger circle which touches the smaller circle.** CBSE 2020 (Standard)

Sol. Let C_1 and C_2 be two circles of radii, $r_1 = 3$ cm and $r_2 = 5$ cm and having common centre O.

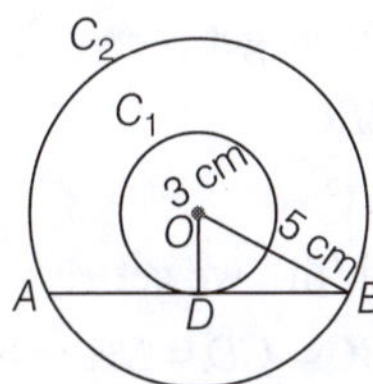

Now, let AB be the chord of circle C_2 such that it touches the circle C_1 at point D. Clearly, AB be the tangent to the circle C_1 at point D.

$\therefore \quad OD \perp AB$ [$\because$ radius is perpendicular to the tangent at the point of contact]

$\Rightarrow \quad AD = BD$ [$\because$ perpendicular from centre to the chord bisect the chord]

Now, in right angled ΔODB,

$OB^2 = OD^2 + DB^2$ [by Pythagoras theorem]

$\Rightarrow \quad 5^2 = 3^2 + DB^2$

$\Rightarrow \quad DB^2 = 25 - 9 = 16$

$\Rightarrow \quad DB = 4$ cm [taking positive square root]

$\therefore$ Length of chord $= AB = 2DB = 2 \times 4 = 8$ cm

Q8. **A quadrilateral *ABCD* is drawn to circumscribe a circle (see figure). Prove that *AB*+ *CD*= *AD*+ *BC*.**

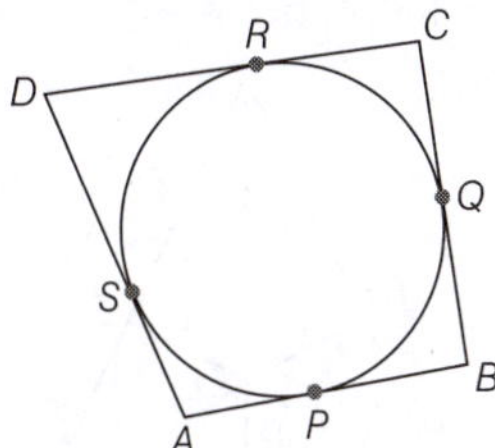

Sol. **Given** A quadrilateral $ABCD$, circumscribing a circle.

To prove $AB + CD = AD + BC$

Proof We know that the lengths of tangents drawn from an external point to a circle are equal.

$\therefore \quad AP = AS \quad$ ...(i)

[$\because$ both are tangents to a circle from point A]

Similarly, $\quad BP = BQ \quad$ ...(ii)

$CR = CQ \quad$ ...(iii)

and $\quad DR = DS \quad$ ...(iv)

On adding Eqs. (i), (ii), (iii) and (iv), we get

$(AP + BP) + (CR + DR) = (AS + BQ) + (CQ + DS)$

$\Rightarrow \quad AB + CD = (AS + DS) + (BQ + CQ)$

$\Rightarrow \quad AB + CD = AD + BC$ **Hence proved.**

Q9. **In the given figure, *XY* and *X′ Y′* are two parallel tangents to a circle with centre *O* and another tangent *AB* with point of contact *C* intersecting *XY* at *A* and *X′ Y′* at *B*. Prove that $\angle AOB = 90°$.**

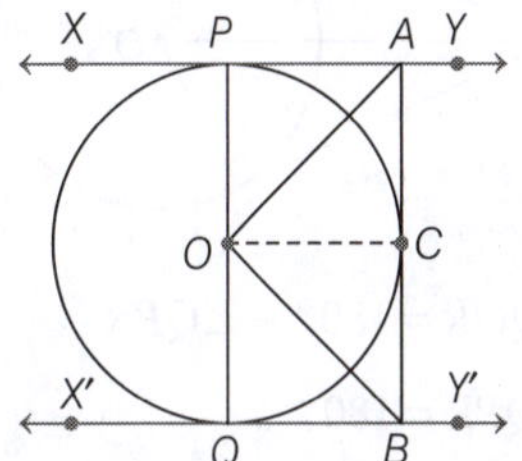

Sol. **Given** XY and $X'Y'$ are two parallel tangents. Another tangent AB touches the circle at C and intersect XY at A and $X'Y'$ at B.

To prove $\angle AOB = 90°$

Proof We know that tangents drawn from an external point to a circle are equal in length.

$\therefore \quad AP = AC$ [$\because A$ is an external point]...(i)

Thus, in ΔAPO and ΔACO, $AP = AC$ [from Eq. (i)]

$AO = AO$ [common sides]

$OP = OC$ [radii of circle]

$\Delta APO \cong \Delta ACO$ [by SSS congruence rule]

Then, $\quad \angle OAP = \angle OAC$ [by CPCT] ...(ii)

$\Rightarrow \quad \angle PAC = 2\angle CAO \quad$ ...(iii)

Similarly, we can prove that

$\angle CBO = \angle OBQ$

$\Rightarrow \quad \angle CBQ = 2\angle CBO \quad$ ...(iv)

Since, $\quad XY \| X'Y'$ [given]

$\therefore \quad \angle PAC + \angle QBC = 180°$

[$\because$ sum of interior angles on the same side of transversal is 180°]

$\Rightarrow \quad 2\angle CAO + 2\angle CBO = 180°$ [from Eqs. (iii) and (iv)]

$\Rightarrow \quad \angle CAO + \angle CBO = 90° \quad$ ...(v)

Now, in ΔAOB,

$\angle CAO + \angle CBO + \angle AOB = 180°$

[by angle sum property of triangle]

$\Rightarrow \quad \angle CAO + \angle CBO = 180° - \angle AOB \quad$ ...(vi)

From Eqs. (v) and (vi), we get

$180° - \angle AOB = 90°$

$\Rightarrow \quad \angle AOB = 90°$ **Hence proved.**

Q10. Prove that the angle between the two tangents drawn from an external point to a circle is supplementary to the angle subtended by the line segment joining the points of contact at the centre.

Sol. Let PQ and PR be two tangents drawn from an external point P to a circle with centre O.

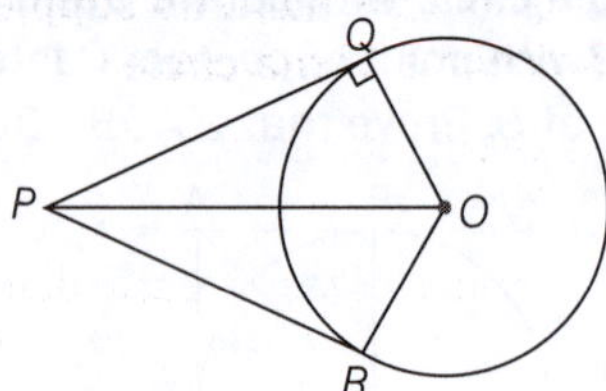

To prove $\angle QOR = 180° - \angle QPR$

or $\angle QOR + \angle QPR = 180°$

Proof In ΔOQP and ΔORP,

$PQ = PR$ [$\because$ tangents drawn from an external point are equal in length]

$OQ = OR$ [radii of circle]

$OP = OP$ [common sides]

$\therefore$ $\Delta OQP \cong \Delta ORP$ [by SSS congruence rule]

Then, $\angle QPO = \angle RPO$ [by CPCT]

and $\angle POQ = \angle POR$ [by CPCT]

$\Rightarrow$ $\left.\begin{aligned}\angle QPR &= 2\angle OPQ\\ \angle QOR &= 2\angle POQ\end{aligned}\right\}$ ...(i)

and

Now, in right angled ΔOQP,

$\angle QPO + \angle QOP = 90°$

$\Rightarrow$ $\angle QOP = 90° - \angle QPO$

$\Rightarrow$ $2\angle QOP = 180° - 2\angle QPO$

[multiplying both sides by 2]

$\Rightarrow$ $\angle QOR = 180° - \angle QPR$ [from Eq. (i)]

$\Rightarrow$ $\angle QOR + \angle QPR = 180°$ **Hence proved.**

Q11. Prove that the parallelogram circumscribing a circle is a rhombus.

Sol. Let $ABCD$ be a parallelogram circumscribing a circle.

To prove $ABCD$ is a rhombus.

i.e. To prove $AB = BC = CD = DA$

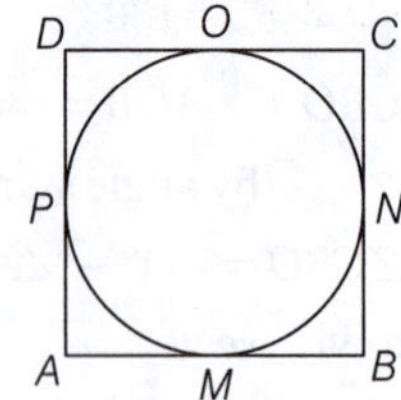

Proof We know that the tangents to a circle from an external point are equal in length.

$\therefore$ $AM = AP, BM = BN,$

$CO = CN$ and $DO = DP$

On adding all above equations, we get

$(AM + BM) + (CO + DO) = AP + BN + CN + DP$

$\Rightarrow$ $AB + CD = (AP + PD) + (BN + NC)$

$= AD + BC$ ...(i)

Given, $ABCD$ is a parallelogram.

$\therefore$ $AB = CD$ and $BC = AD$ ...(ii)

[$\because$ opposite sides of a parallelogram are equal]

Then, from Eq. (i), we get

$2AB = 2BC$

$\Rightarrow$ $AB = BC$ ...(iii)

From Eqs. (ii) and (iii), we get

$AB = BC = CD = DA$

$\Rightarrow ABCD$ is a rhombus.

Hence, the parallelogram circumscribing a circle is a rhombus. **Hence proved.**

Q12. A ΔABC is drawn to circumscribe a circle of radius 4 cm such that the segments BD and DC into which BC is divided by the point of contact D are of lengths 8 cm and 6 cm, respectively (see figure). Find the sides AB and AC.

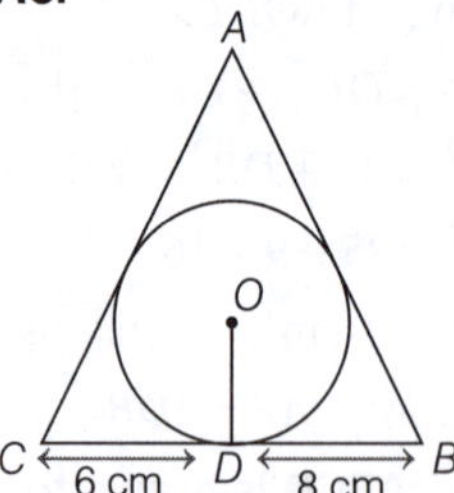

Sol. Given, $CD = 6$ cm, $BD = 8$ cm and radius $= 4$ cm

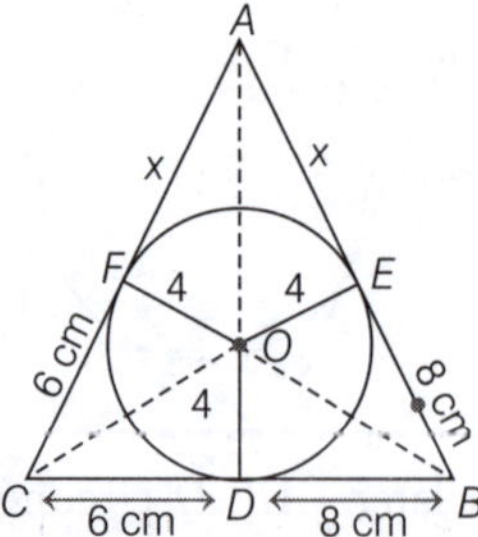

Join OC, OA and OB.

Let the circle touches the other sides AB and AC at points E and F, respectively.

We know that tangents drawn from an external point to the circle are equal in length.

$\therefore$ $CD = CF = 6$ cm [$\because C$ is an external point]

$BD = BE = 8$ cm [$\because B$ is an external point]

and $AF = AE = x$ cm (say) [$\because A$ is an external point]

Area of ΔOCB, $A_1 = \frac{1}{2} \times \text{Base} \times \text{Height}$

$$= \frac{1}{2} \times CB \times OD$$

$$= \frac{1}{2} \times 14 \times 4 = 28 \text{ cm}^2$$

$[\because CB = CD + BD = 6 + 8 = 14]$

Area of ΔOCA, $A_2 = \frac{1}{2} \times AC \times OF$

$$= \frac{1}{2}(6 + x) \times 4$$

$$= (12 + 2x) \text{ cm}^2$$

and area of ΔOBA,

$$A_3 = \frac{1}{2} \times AB \times OE$$

$$= \frac{1}{2}(8 + x) \times 4$$

$$= (16 + 2x) \text{ cm}^2$$

Thus, area of $\Delta ABC = A_1 + A_2 + A_3$

$$= [28 + (12 + 2x) + (16 + 2x)]$$

$$= (56 + 4x) \text{ cm}^2 \quad \ldots\text{(i)}$$

Now, semi-perimeter of $\Delta ABC = \frac{1}{2}(AB + BC + CA)$

$$\Rightarrow \quad s = \frac{1}{2}(x + 8 + 14 + 6 + x)$$

$$\Rightarrow \quad s = (14 + x) \text{ cm}$$

Using Heron's formula,

area of $\Delta ABC = \sqrt{s(s-a)(s-b)(s-c)}$

$$= \sqrt{(14 + x)(14 + x - 14)(14 + x - x - 6)(14 + x - x - 8)}$$

$$= \sqrt{(14 + x) \times x \times 8 \times 6}$$

$$= \sqrt{(14 + x)\, 48x} \quad \ldots\text{(ii)}$$

From Eqs. (i) and (ii), we get

$$\sqrt{(14 + x)\, 48x} = 56 + 4x$$

$$= 4(14 + x)$$

On squaring both sides, we get

$$(14 + x)\, 48\, x = 4^2 (14 + x)^2$$

$$\Rightarrow \quad 3x = 14 + x$$

$$\Rightarrow \quad 2x = 14$$

$$\Rightarrow \quad x = 7$$

$\therefore$ Length of $AC = 6 + x = 6 + 7 = 13$ cm

and length of $AB = 8 + x = 8 + 7 = 15$ cm

Q13. Prove that opposite sides of a quadrilateral circumscribing a circle subtend supplementary angles at the centre of the circle.

Sol. Let $ABCD$ be a quadrilateral circumscribing a circle with centre O.

Let circle touches the sides of a quadrilateral at points E, F, G and H.

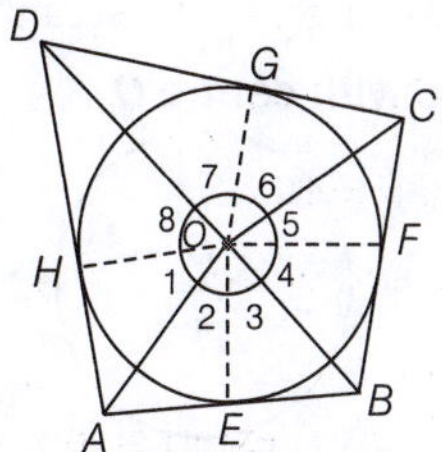

To prove $\angle AOB + \angle COD = 180°$

and $\angle AOD + \angle BOC = 180°$

Construction Join OE, OF, OG and OH.

Proof We know that two tangents drawn from an external point to a circle subtend equal angles at the centre.

$$\left.\begin{aligned} \angle 1 &= \angle 2 \\ \angle 3 &= \angle 4 \\ \angle 5 &= \angle 6 \\ \angle 7 &= \angle 8 \end{aligned}\right\}$$

and

Also, we know that the sum of all angles subtended at a point is 360°.

$\therefore \angle 1 + \angle 2 + \angle 3 + \angle 4 + \angle 5 + \angle 6 + \angle 7 + \angle 8 = 360° \quad \ldots\text{(ii)}$

$$\Rightarrow \quad 2(\angle 2 + \angle 3 + \angle 6 + \angle 7) = 360°$$

$$\Rightarrow \quad (\angle 2 + \angle 3) + (\angle 6 + \angle 7) = 180°$$

$$\Rightarrow \quad \angle AOB + \angle COD = 180°$$

Similarly, we have

$2(\angle 1 + \angle 8 + \angle 4 + \angle 5) = 360°$ [from Eqs. (i) and (ii)]

$\Rightarrow (\angle 1 + \angle 8) + (\angle 4 + \angle 5) = 180°$

$\Rightarrow \quad \angle AOD + \angle BOC = 180°$ **Hence proved.**

REVIEW EXERCISE

Including Competency Based Questions

Part I

Multiple Choice Questions

1. A line which intersects a circle in two distinct points, is called a **CBSE 2024 (Basic)**

(a) chord (b) tangent (c) secant (d) diameter

2. Here is a circle with centre O.

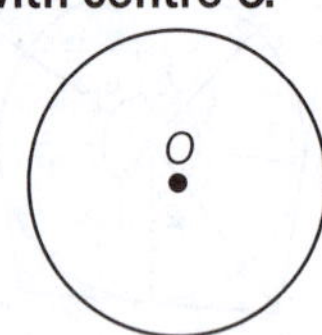

Manu wants to draw a tangent RS to the circle. What is the number of points at which the line RS will meet the circle? **Competency Based Question**

(a) 0 (b) 1 (c) 2 (d) 3

3. PQ is tangent to a circle centered at O. If the radius of the circle is 5 cm, then the length of the tangent PQ is

CBSE 2023 (Standard)

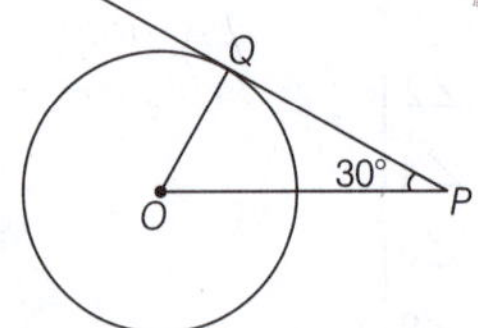

(a) $5\sqrt{3}$ cm (b) $\frac{10}{\sqrt{3}}$ cm (c) 10 cm (d) $\frac{5}{\sqrt{3}}$ cm

4. In the adjoining figure, TS is a tangent to a circle with centre O. The value of $2x°$ is

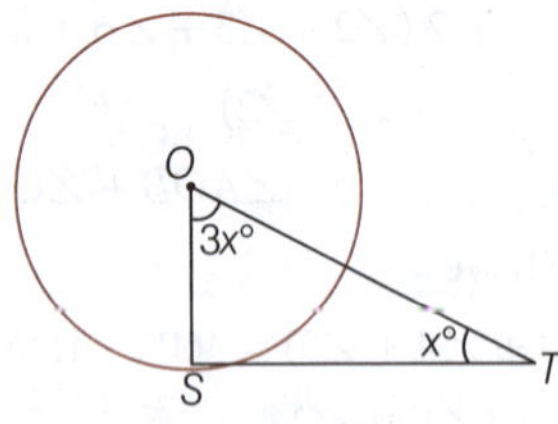

(a) 22.5 (b) 45 (c) 67.5 (d) 90

5. In the given figure, O is the centre of the circle and PA is a tangent to the circle. If $\angle OAB = 60°$, then $\angle OPA$ is equal to **CBSE 2023 (Basic)**

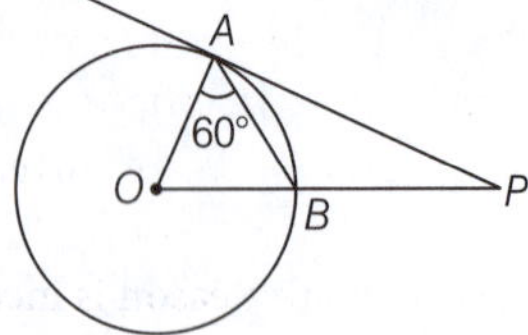

(a) 60° (b) 30° (c) 15° (d) 20°

6. In figure, if O is the centre of a circle, PQ is a chord and the tangent PR at P makes an angle of 50° with PQ, then $\angle POQ$ is equal to

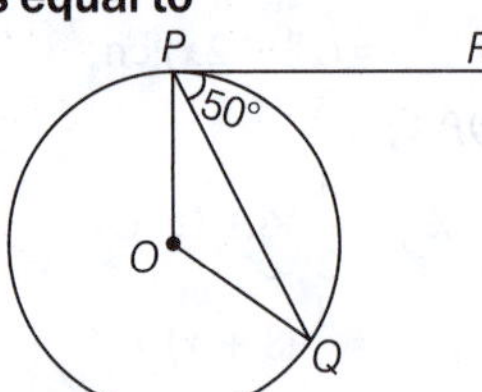

NCERT Exemplar, CBSE 2020 (Basic), SQP 2023 (Standard)

(a) 100° (b) 80° (c) 90° (d) 75°

7. In the given figure, PA and PB are two tangents drawn to the circle with centre O and radius 5 cm. If $\angle APB = 60°$, then the length of PA is **CBSE 2024 (Standard)**

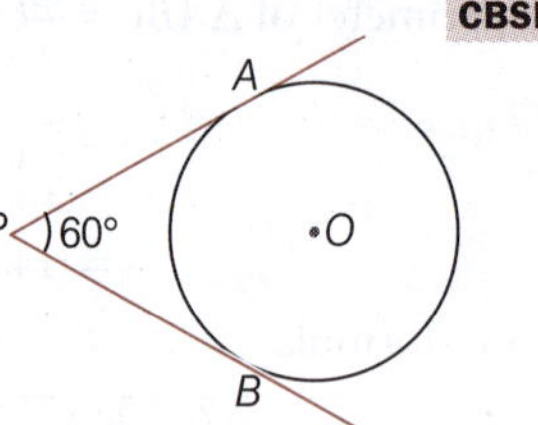

(a) $\frac{5}{\sqrt{3}}$ cm (b) $5\sqrt{3}$ cm (c) $\frac{10}{\sqrt{3}}$ cm (d) 10 cm

8. In the given figure, tangents PA and PB drawn from P to circle are inclined to each other at an angle of 80°. The measure of $\angle PAB$ is **Competency Based Question**

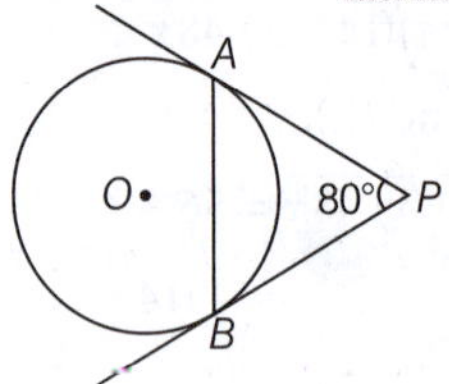

(a) 80° (b) 60° (c) 50° (d) 40°

9. In the adjoining figure, PA and PB are tangents to a circle with centre O such that $\angle P = 90°$. If $AB = 3\sqrt{2}$ cm, then the diameter of the circle is **CBSE 2025 (Standard)**

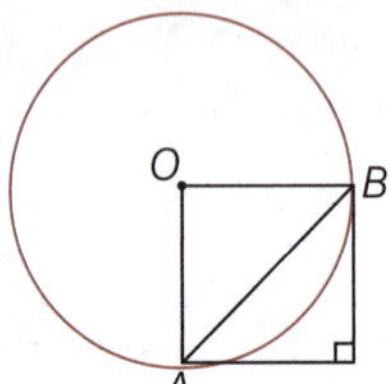

(a) $3\sqrt{2}$ cm (b) $6\sqrt{2}$ cm (c) 3cm (d) 6 cm

10. In the given figure, AC and AB are tangents to a circle centered at O. If $\angle COD = 120°$, then $\angle BAO$ is equal to

CBSE 2023 (Standard)

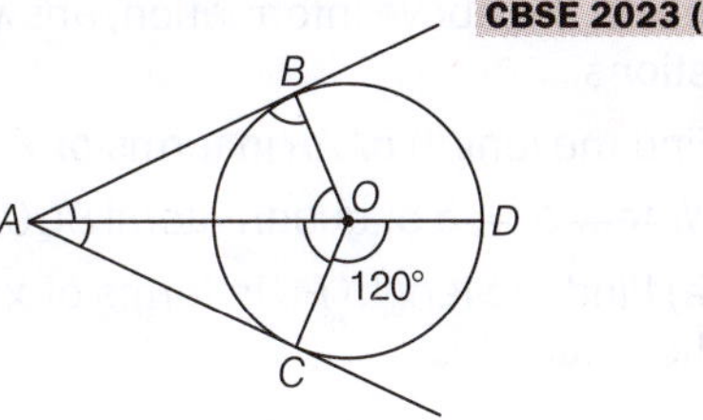

(a) 30° (b) 60° (c) 45° (d) 90°

11. In the given figure, PA and PB are tangents from external point P to a circle with centre C and Q is any point on the circle. Then, the measure of $\angle AQB$ is

CBSE 2023 (Standard)

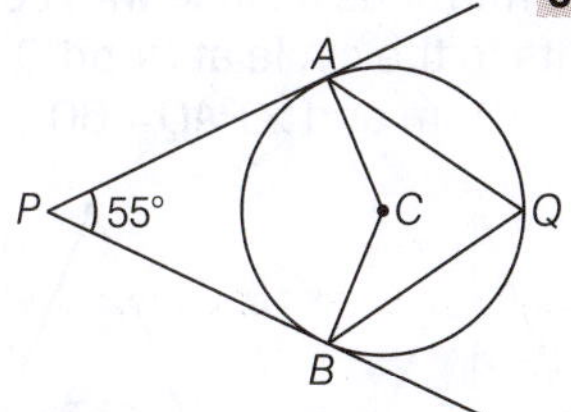

(a) 62.5° (b) 125° (c) 55° (d) 90°

12. From a point P which is at a distance of 13 cm from the centre O of a circle of radius 5 cm, the pair of tangents PQ and PR to the circle is drawn. Then, the area of the quadrilateral $PQOR$ is **NCERT Exemplar**

(a) 60 cm^2 (b) 65 cm^2 (c) 30 cm^2 (d) 32.5 cm^2

13. In two concentric circles centred at O, a chord AB of the larger circle touches the smaller circle at C. If $OA = 3.5$ cm, $OC = 2.1$ cm, then AB is equal to

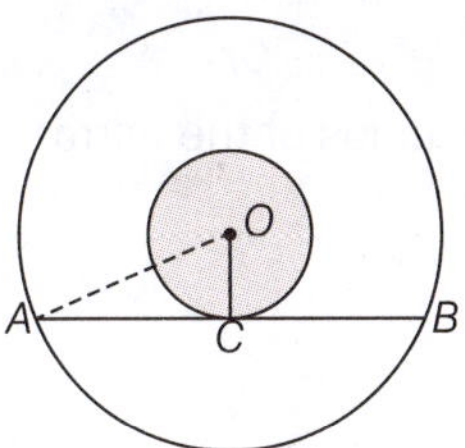

(a) 5.6 cm (b) 2.8 cm (c) 3.5 cm (d) 4.2 cm

14. A quadrilateral $PQRS$ is drawn to circumscribe a circle. If $PQ = 12$ cm, $QR = 15$ cm and $RS = 14$ cm, then find the length of SP.

(a) 15 cm (b) 14 cm (c) 12 cm (d) 11 cm

15. In figure, if $\angle AOB = 125°$, then $\angle COD$ is equal to

Competency Based Question

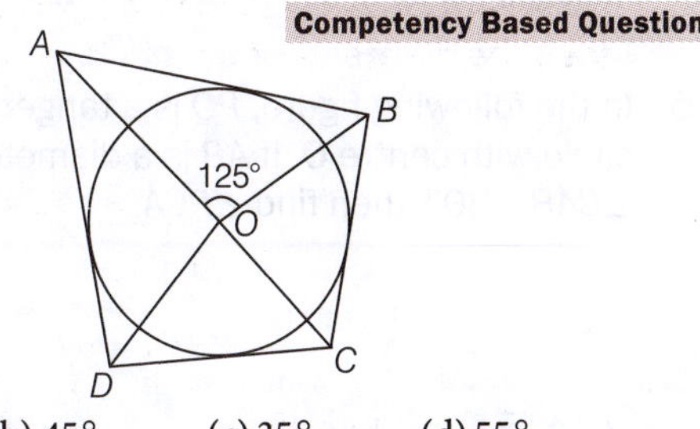

(a) 62.5° (b) 45° (c) 35° (d) 55°

Assertion-Reason Type Questions

16. Assertion TA and TB are two tangents drawn from an external point T to a circle with centre O. If $\angle TBA = 75°$, then $\angle ABO = 25°$.

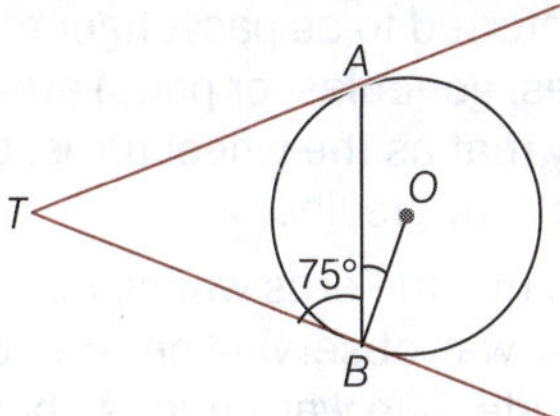

Reason The tangent drawn at any point of a circle is perpendicular to the radius through the point of contact. **CBSE 2024 (Standard)**

(a) Both Assertion and Reason are correct and Reason is the correct explanation of Assertion.
(b) Both Assertion and Reason are correct but Reason is not the correct explanation of Assertion.
(c) Assertion is correct but Reason is incorrect.
(d) Assertion is incorrect but Reason is correct.

17. Assertion If tangents PA and PB from a point P to a circle with centre O are inclined to each other at angle of 76°, then $\angle POA$ is 52°.

Reason Two tangents AP and AQ are drawn to a circle with centre O from a point A. Then, $\angle APO = \angle AQO$.

(a) Both Assertion and Reason are correct and Reason is the correct explanation of Assertion.
(b) Both Assertion and Reason are correct but Reason is not the correct explanation of Assertion.
(c) Assertion is correct but Reason is incorrect.
(d) Assertion is incorrect but Reason is correct.

18. Assertion If TA and TB are tangents to the circle with centre O such that $\angle ATB = 70°$, then $\angle OAB = 35°$.

Reason Two tangents TP and TQ are drawn to a circle with centre O from an external point T, then $\angle PTQ = 2\angle OPQ$.

(a) Both Assertion and Reason are correct and Reason is the correct explanation of Assertion.
(b) Both Assertion and Reason are correct but Reason is not the correct explanation of Assertion.
(c) Assertion is correct but Reason is incorrect.
(d) Assertion is incorrect but Reason is correct.

19. Assertion The tangents drawn at the end points of a diameter of a circle, are parallel.

Reason Diameter of a circle is the longest chord. **CBSE 2024 (Standard)**

(a) Both Assertion and Reason are correct and Reason is the correct explanation of Assertion.
(b) Both Assertion and Reason are correct but Reason is not the correct explanation of Assertion.
(c) Assertion is correct but Reason is incorrect.
(d) Assertion is incorrect but Reason is correct.

Case Study Based Questions

20. A Ferris wheel (or a big wheel in the United Kingdom) is an amusement ride consisting of a rotating upright wheel with multiple passenger-carrying components (commonly referred to as passenger cars, cabins, tubs, capsules, gondolas, or pods) attached to the rim in such a way that as the wheel turns, they are kept upright, usually by gravity.

After taking a ride in Ferris wheel, Aarti came out from the crowd and was observing her friends who were enjoying the ride. She was curious about the different angles and measures that the wheel will form. She forms the figure as given below.

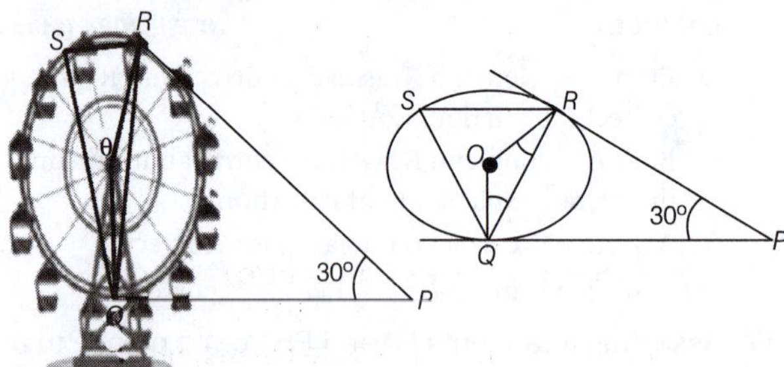

(i) In the given figure, find $\angle ROQ$.

(ii) Find $\angle RQP$.

(iii) (a) Find $\angle RSQ$.

Or

(b) Find $\angle ORP$.

21. A backyard is in the shape of a triangle ABC with right angle at B. $AB = 7$ m and $BC = 15$ m. A circular pit was dug inside it such that it

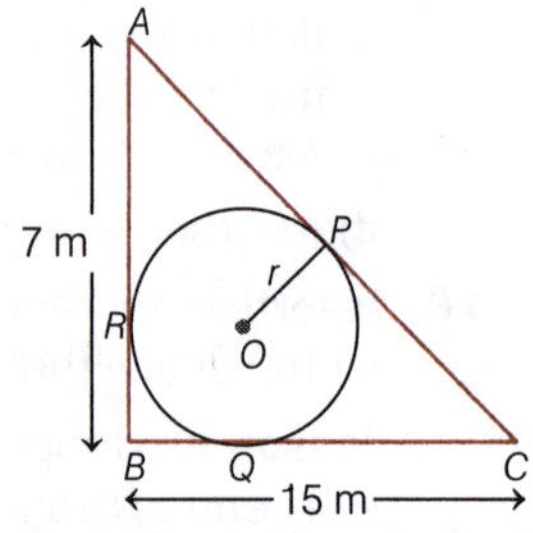

Part II

Very Short Answer Type Questions

1. What term will you use for a line which intersect a circle at two distinct points?

2. What do you say about the line which is perpendicular to the radius of the circle through the point of contact?

3. A point is 26 cm away from the centre of a circle and the length of tangent drawn from P to the circle is 24cm. Find the radius of the circle.

4. In the given figure, AB is a chord of a circle and AOC is its diameter such that $\angle ACB = 50°$. If AT is the tangent to the circle at point A, then find $\angle BAT$. **NCERT Exemplar**

touches the walls AC, BC and AB at P, Q and R respectively such that $AP = x$ metre.

Based on the above information, answer the following questions.

(i) Find the length of AR in terms of x.

(ii) Write the type of quadrilateral $BQOR$.

(iii) (a) Find the length PC in terms of x and hence find the value of x.

Or

(b) Find x and hence find the radius r of circle. **CBSE 2024 (Standard)**

22. The picture given below shows a circular mirror hanging on the wall with a cord. The diagram represents the mirror as a circle with centre O. AP and AQ are tangents to the circle at P and Q, respectively such that $AP = 30$ cm and $\angle PAQ = 60°$.

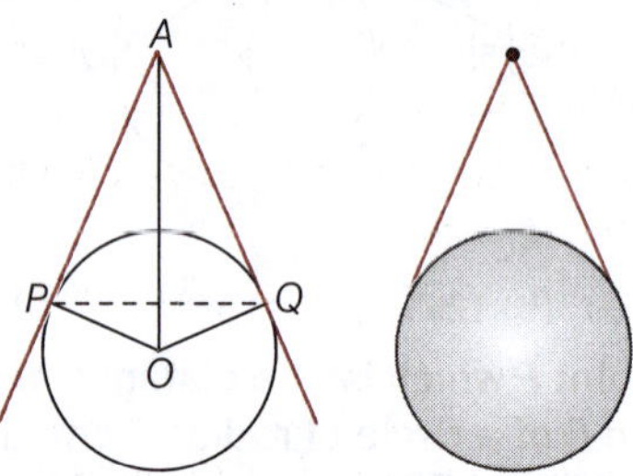

Based on the above information, answer the following questions.

(i) Find the length PQ.

(ii) Find $\angle POQ$.

(iii) (a) Find the length OA.

Or

(b) Find the radius of the mirror. **CBSE 2024 (Basic)**

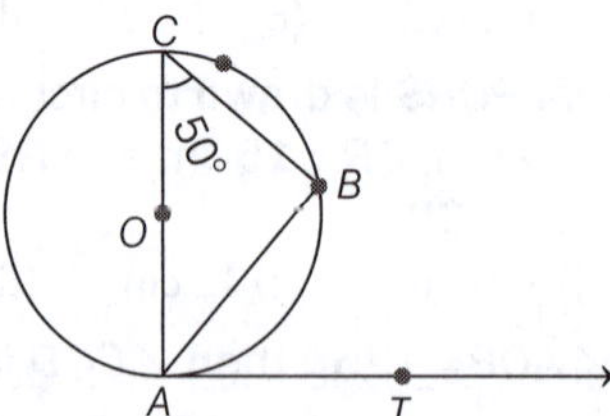

5. In the following figure, PQ is a tangent at a point C to circle with centre O. If AB is a diameter and $\angle CAB = 30°$, then find $\angle PCA$. **CBSE 2019**

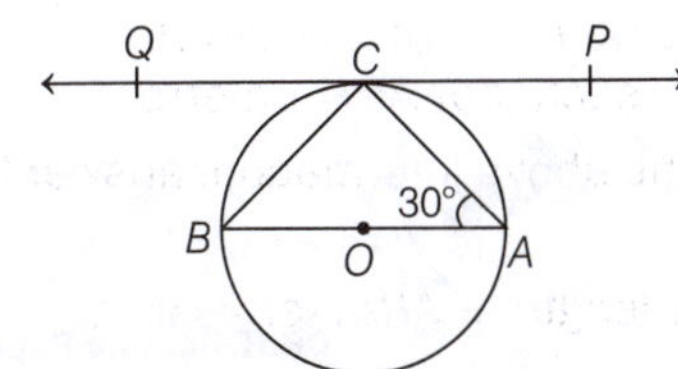

6. In the given figure, if PQR is the tangent to a circle at Q whose centre is O, AB is a chord parallel to PR and $\angle BQR = 70°$, then find $\angle AQB$. **NCERT Exemplar**

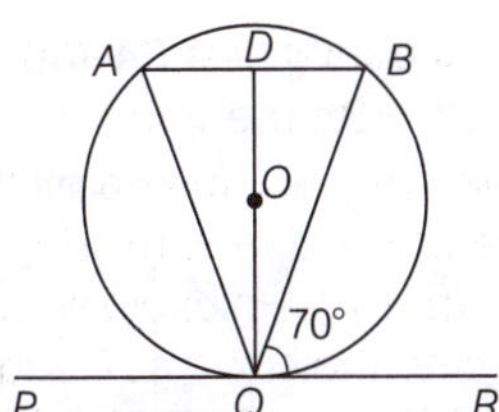

7. Write the number of tangents to a circle which are parallel to a secant.

8. Find the distance between two parallel tangents of a circle of radius 3 cm.

9. In the given figure, O is the centre of the circle and PA and PB are tangents drawn to the circle from an external point P. If $OP = 10$ cm and $PA = 8$ cm, then find the length of a diameter of the circle. **CBSE 2024 (Basic)**

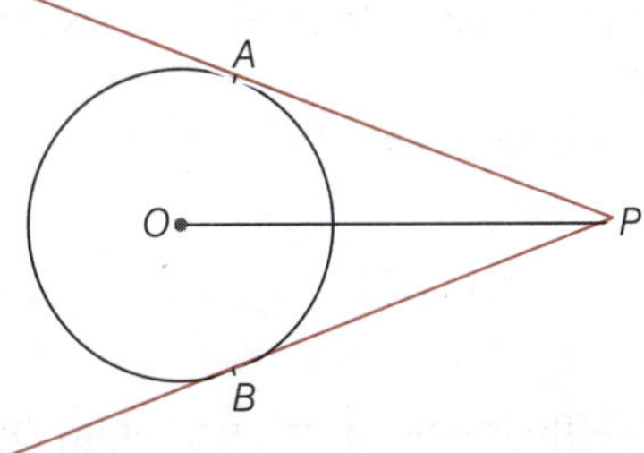

10. In the given figure, PA and PB are tangents from P to a circle with centre O. If $\angle AOB = 130°$, then find $\angle APB$.

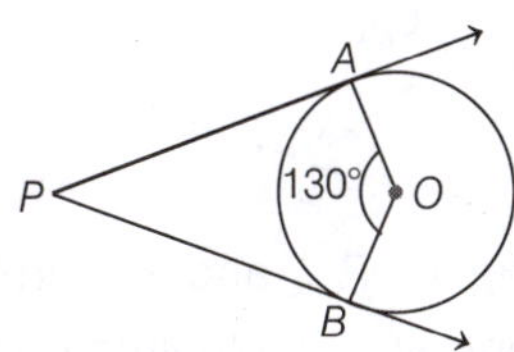

11. In the given figure, tangents AB and AC are drawn to a circle centred at O. $\angle OAB = 60°$ and $OB = 5$ cm, then find the length OA and AC. **Competency Based Question**

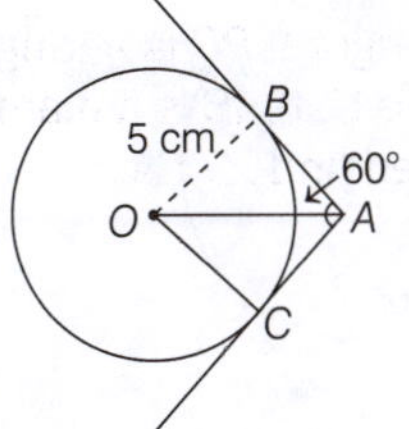

12. In the given figure, if $\angle AOB = 120°$, then find $\angle COD$. **Competency Based Question**

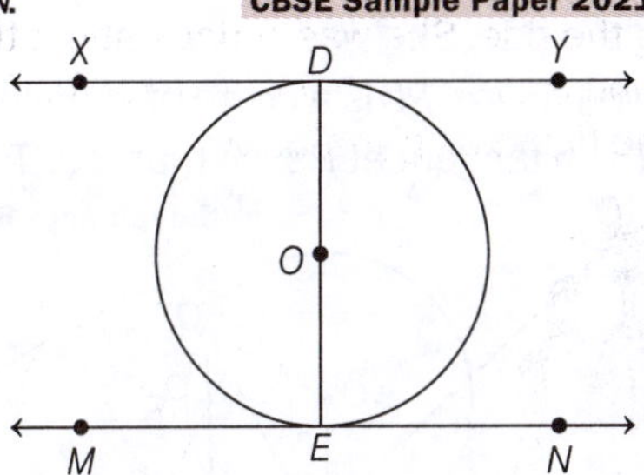

13. XY and MN are the tangents drawn at the end points of the diameter DE of the circle with centre O. Prove that $XY \parallel MN$. **CBSE Sample Paper 2021 Term I (Basic)**

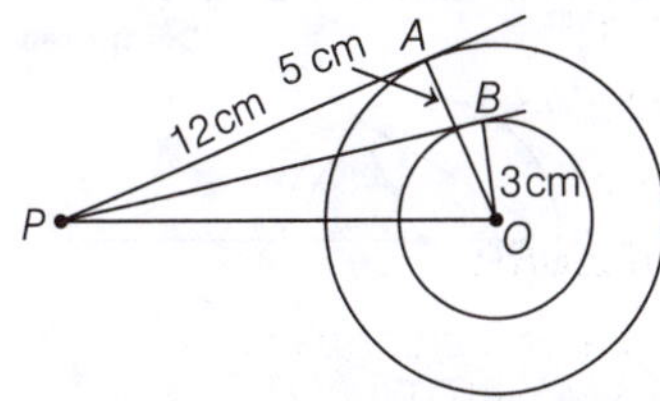

14. Two concentric circles with centre O are of radii 5 cm and 3 cm. From an external point P, two tangents PA and PB are drawn to these circles, respectively. If $PA = 12$ cm, then find length of PB. **Competency Based Question**

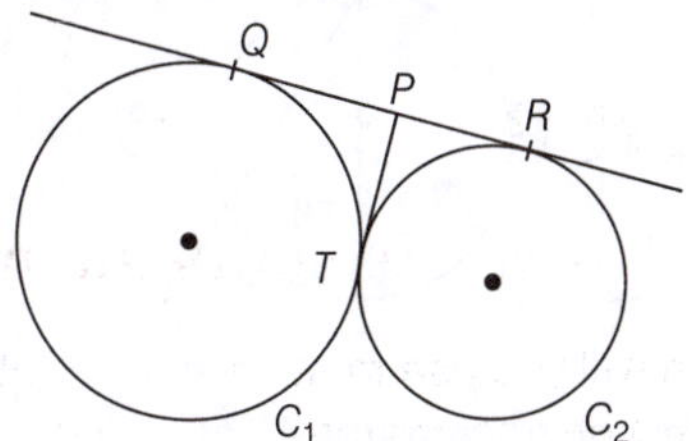

15. In the given figure, QR is common tangent to the circles C_1 and C_2 touching externally at T. Find the length of QR, if $QP = 3.2$ cm.

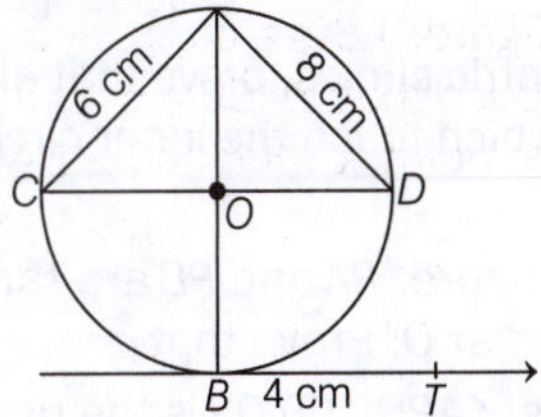

Short Answer Type Questions

16. In the given figure, $AD = 8$ cm, $AC = 6$ cm and TB is the tangent at B to the circle with centre O. Find OT, if BT is 4 cm.

17. PA is a tangent to the circle with centre O. If $BC = 3$ cm, $AC = 4$ cm and $\Delta ACB \sim \Delta PAO$, then find OA and $\frac{OP}{AP}$.
Competency Based Question

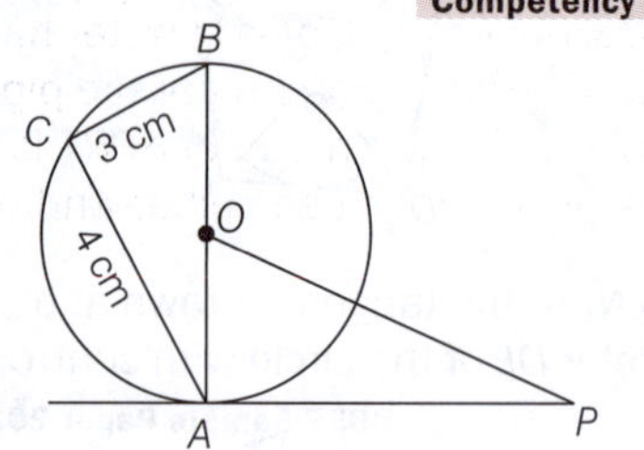

18. In the given figure, PQ is a chord of a circle with centre O and PT is a tangent at P such that $\angle QPT = 60°$, then find $\angle PRQ$.
Competency Based Question

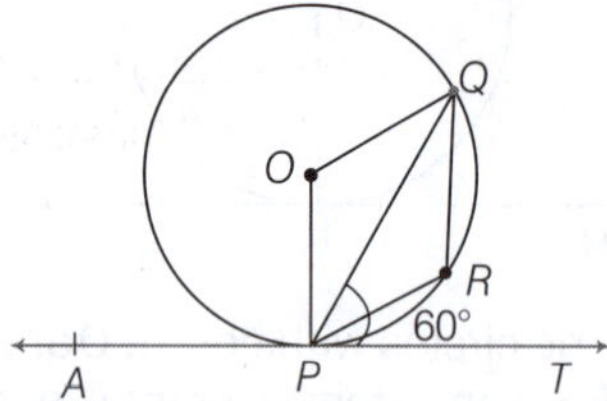

19. In the given figure, O is the centre of a circle, BOA is its diameter and the tangent at the point P meets BA extended at T. If $\angle PBO = 30°$, then find $\angle PTA$.
Competency Based Question

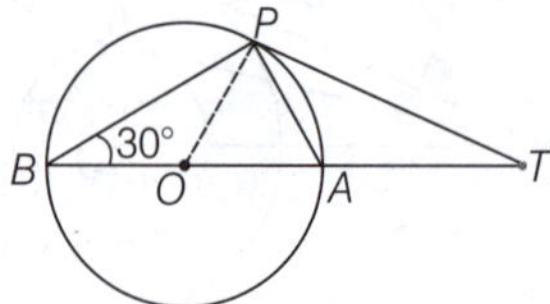

20. In the given figure, AB is diameter of a circle with centre O and AT is tangent. If $\angle AOQ = 58°$, find $\angle ATQ$.

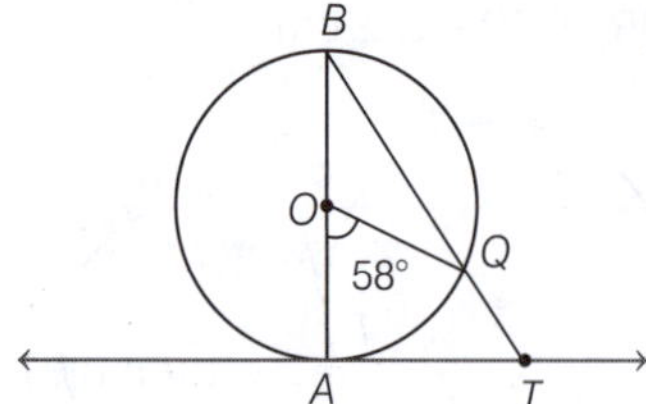

21. At one end A of a diameter AB of a circle of radius 5 cm, tangent XAY is drawn to the circle. Find the length of the chord CD parallel to XY and at a distance 8 cm from A.
NCERT Exemplar

22. Prove that the lengths of tangents drawn from an external point to a circle are equal.
CBSE Sample Paper 2025 (Basic)

23. In two concentric circles, prove that all chords of the outer circle which touch the inner circle are of equal length.

24. In the given figure, PA and PB are tangents to a circle centred at O. Prove that
(i) OP bisects $\angle APB$ (ii) OP is the right bisector of AB.

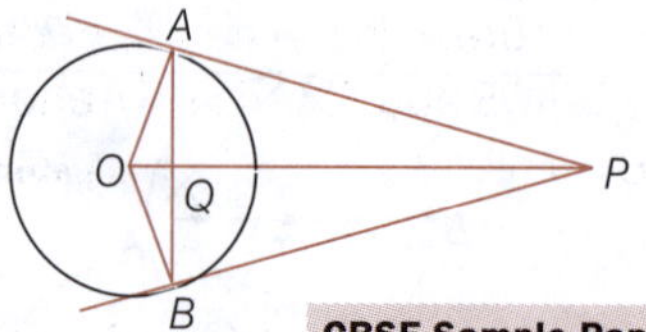

CBSE Sample Paper 2025 (Basic)

25. The radii of two concentric circles are 13 cm and 8 cm. AB is a diameter of the bigger circle. BD is a tangent to the smaller circle touching it at D. Find the length of AD.

26. From a point P, two tangents PA and PB are drawn to a circle $C(O, r)$. If $OP = 2r$, then find $\angle APB$. What type of triangle is APB?
Competency Based Question

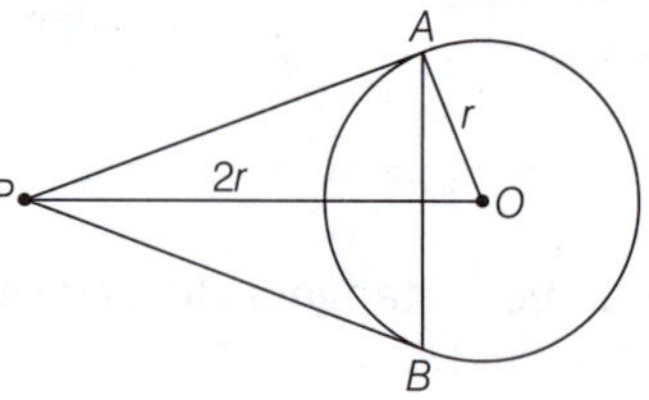

27. In the given figure, from an external point P, two tangents PT and PS are drawn to a circle with centre O and radius r. If $OP = 2r$, then show that $\angle OTS = \angle OST = 30°$

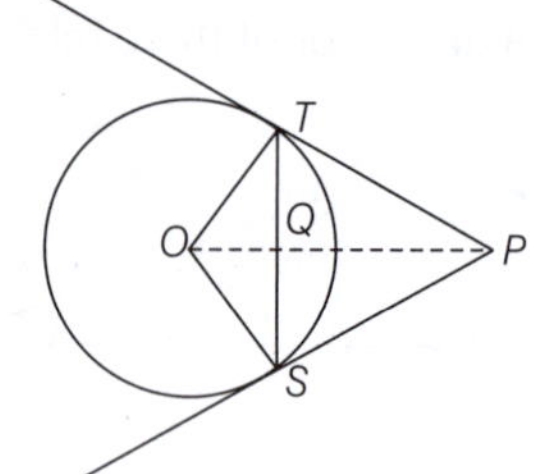

28. In the given figure, if $\angle ACB = 50°$, then find $\angle ATO$.

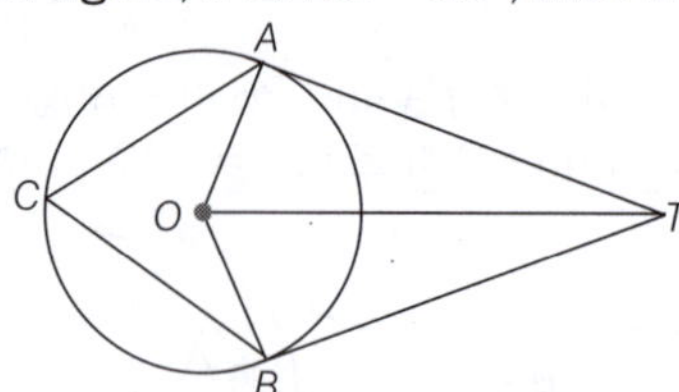

29. In the given figure, PAQ and PBR are tangents to the circle with centre O at the points A and B, respectively. If T is a point on the circle such that $\angle QAT = 45°$ and $\angle TBR = 65°$, then find $\angle ATB$.
CBSE 2024 (Standard)

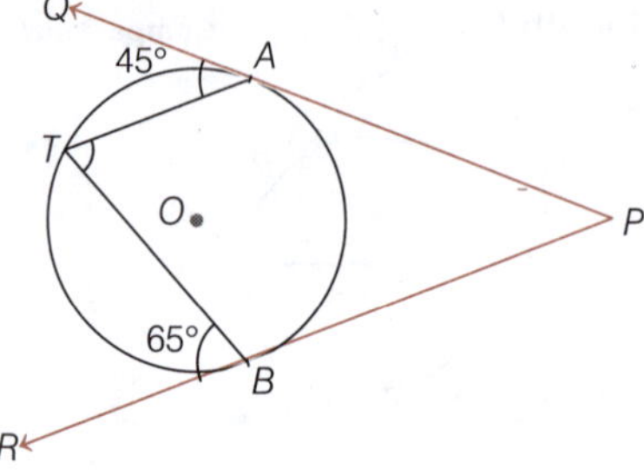

30. In the given figure, O is the centre of the circle. Determine $\angle AQB$ and $\angle AMB$, if PA and PB are tangents and $\angle APB = 75°$. **Competency Based Question**

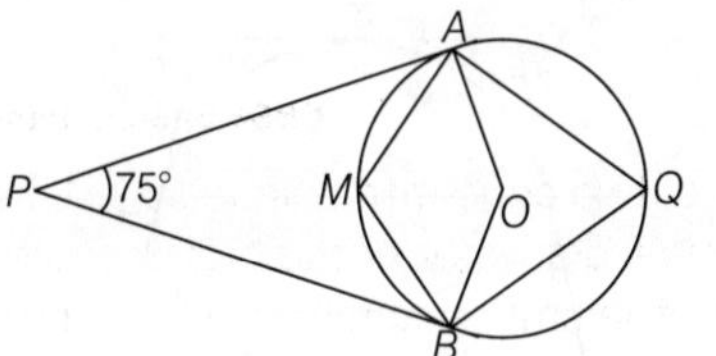

31. In the figure, two circles touch each other at a point C. Prove that the common tangent to the circles at C, bisects the common tangent at P and Q. **Competency Based Question**

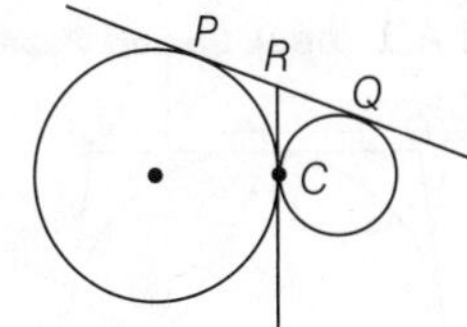

32. In the given figure, common tangents AB and CD to two circles intersect at E. Prove that $AB = CD$. **NCERT Exemplar**

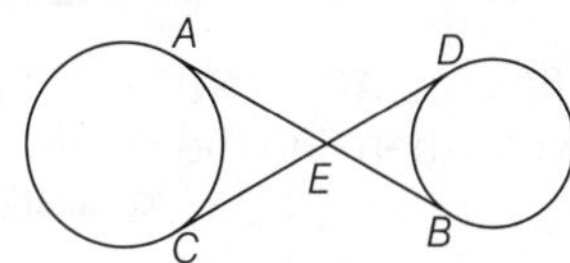

33. In the given figure, ΔPQR circumscribes the circle. If $PX = 10$ cm, $QY = 8$ cm and $RZ = 6$ cm, then find the perimeter of ΔPQR. **CBSE 2024 (Basic)**

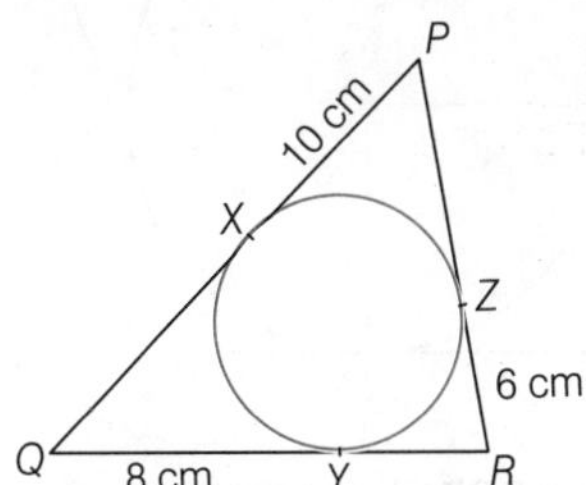

34. Prove that a diameter AB of a circle bisects all those chords which are parallel to the tangent at the point A.

35. PA and PB are tangents drawn to a circle of centre O from an external point P. Chord AB makes an angle of 30° with the radius at the point of contact.

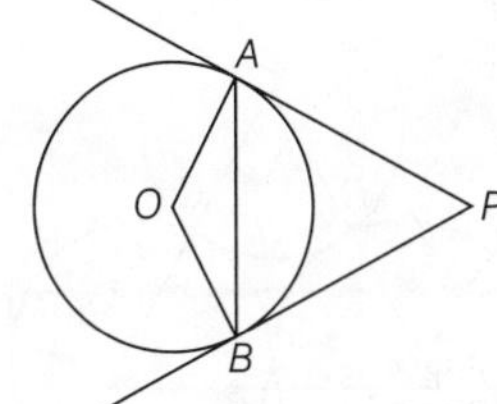

If length of the chord is 6 cm, find the length of the tangent PA and the length of the radius OA. **CBSE Sample Paper 2023 (Standard)**

36. Vistrit prepared a model for rain water harvesting. In the following figure PA and PB are the pipes touching the circular pond. If perimeter of ΔPRT is 72 cm, then determine the length of each pipes and verify our answer.

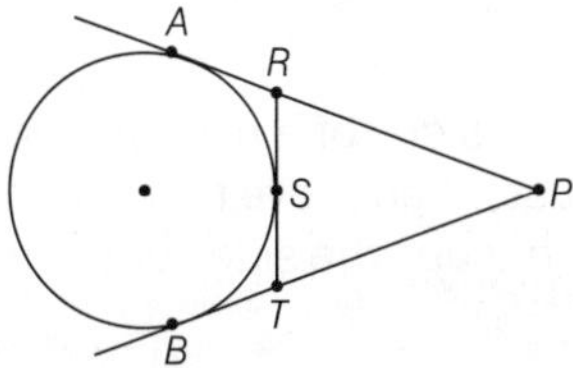

37. If $PQ = 28$ cm, then find the perimeter of ΔPLM. **CBSE Sample Paper 2020**

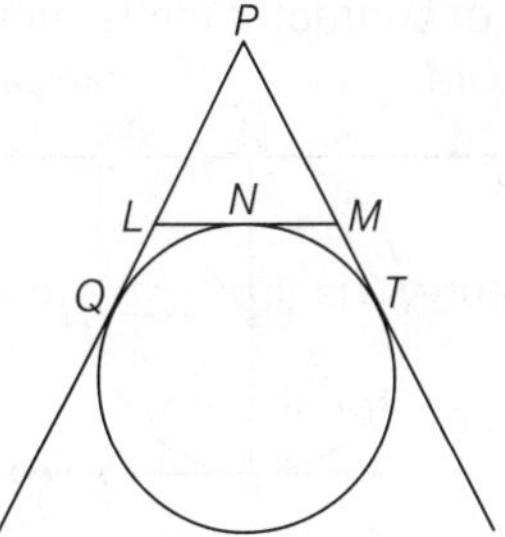

38. In the given figure, PQ is the common tangent to both the circles. SR and PT are tangents. If $SR = 4$ cm and $PT = 7$ cm, then find RP. **Competency Based Question**

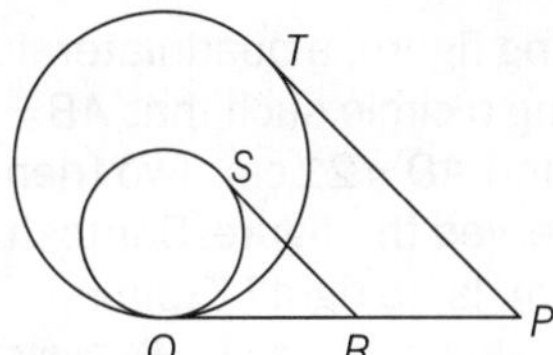

39. Out of the two concentric circles, the diameter of the outer circle is 10 cm and the chord AC of length 8 cm is a tangent to the inner circle, then find the diameter of the inner circle.

40. In the given figure, a right angled ΔABC, circumscribes a circle of radius r. If AB and BC are of lengths 8 cm and 6 cm respectively, then find the value of r.

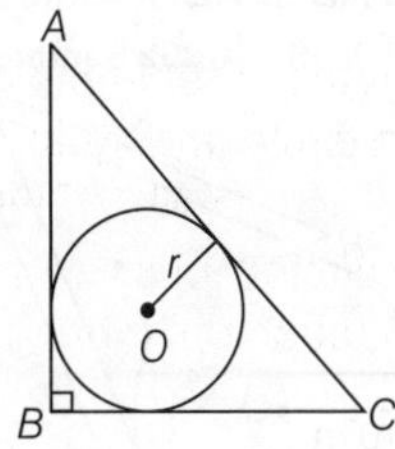

41. A circle is inscribed in a ΔABC having sides $AB = 8$ cm, $BC = 10$ cm and $CA = 12$ cm as shown in figure. Find AD, BE and CF.

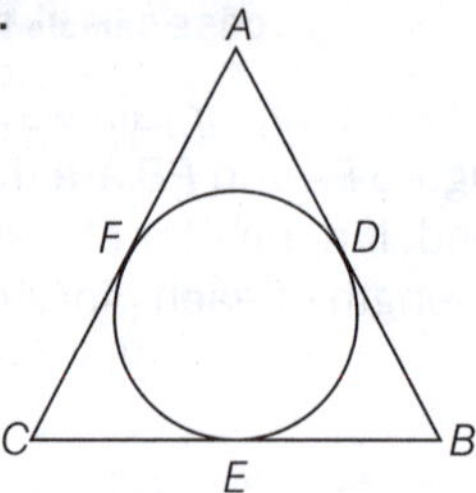

42. If a, b, c are the sides of a right angled triangle, where c is hypotenuse, then prove that the radius r of the circle which touches the sides of the triangle is given by $r = \dfrac{a+b-c}{2}$. **NCERT Exemplar**

43. In the given figure, PQ and $P'Q'$ are two parallel tangents to a circle with centre O and another tangent LM with point of contact N intersecting PQ at L and $P'Q'$ at M. Find $\angle LOM$. **Competency Based Question**

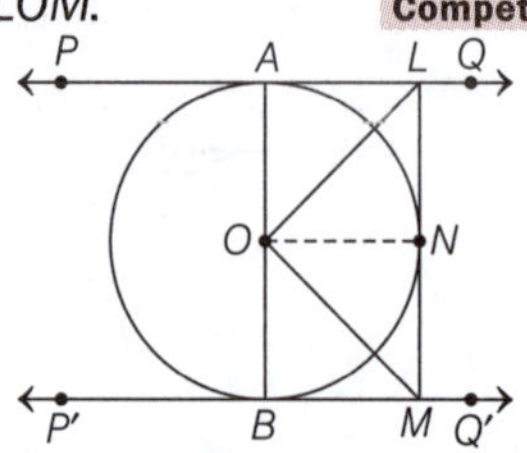

44. The tangents drawn at the end points of two perpendicular diameters of a circle are parallel to each other, which form of a square and whose length of side is 2 cm. Find the radius of circle.

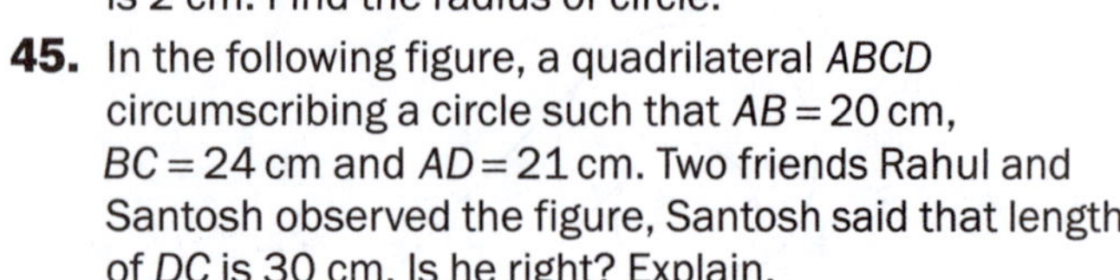

45. In the following figure, a quadrilateral $ABCD$ circumscribing a circle such that $AB = 20$ cm, $BC = 24$ cm and $AD = 21$ cm. Two friends Rahul and Santosh observed the figure, Santosh said that length of DC is 30 cm. Is he right? Explain. **Competency Based Question**

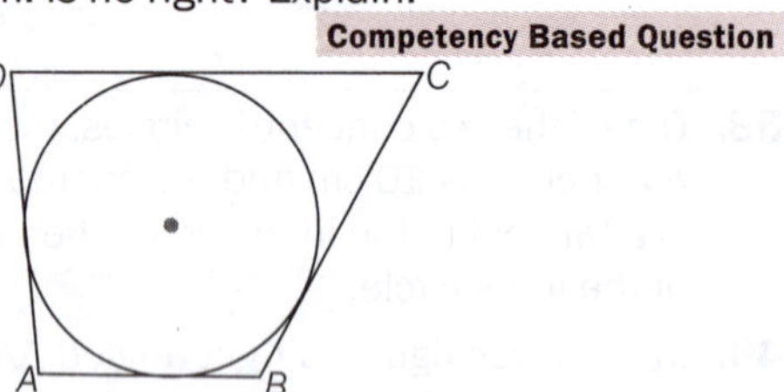

46. In the figure, quadrilateral $ABCD$ is circumscribing a circle with centre O and $AD \perp AB$. If radius of incircle is 10 cm, then the value of x is **CBSE Sample Paper 2020 (Standard)**

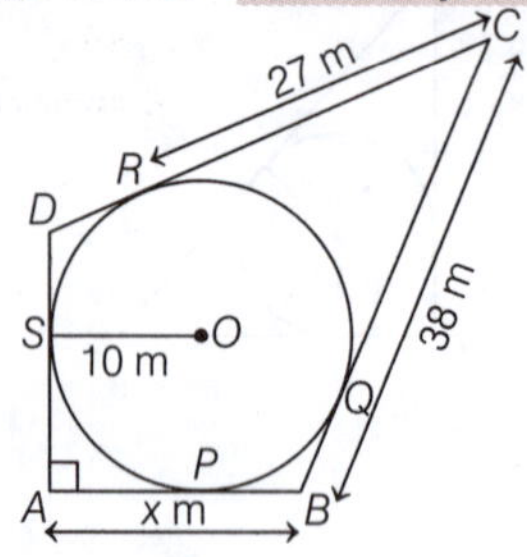

47. In the given figure, quadrilateral $ABCD$ is circumscribed, touching the circle at P, Q, R and S. If $AP = 5$ cm, $BC = 7$ cm and $CS = 3$ cm, then find the length of AB.

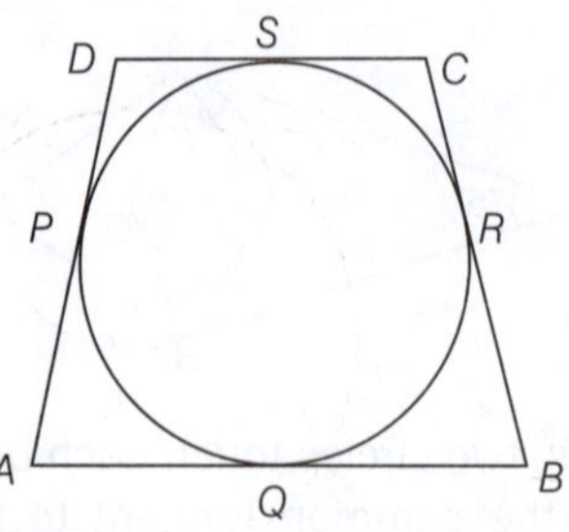

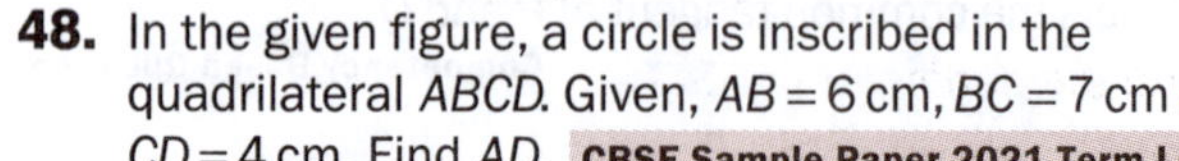

48. In the given figure, a circle is inscribed in the quadrilateral $ABCD$. Given, $AB = 6$ cm, $BC = 7$ cm and $CD = 4$ cm. Find AD. **CBSE Sample Paper 2021 Term I (Basic)**

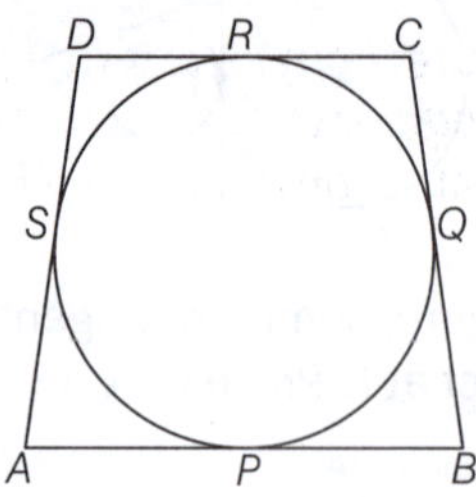

49. In the given figure, $\angle ADC = 90°$, $BC = 38$ cm, $CD = 28$ cm and $BP = 25$ cm, then find the radius of the circle.

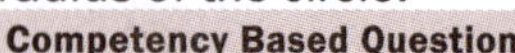

Competency Based Question

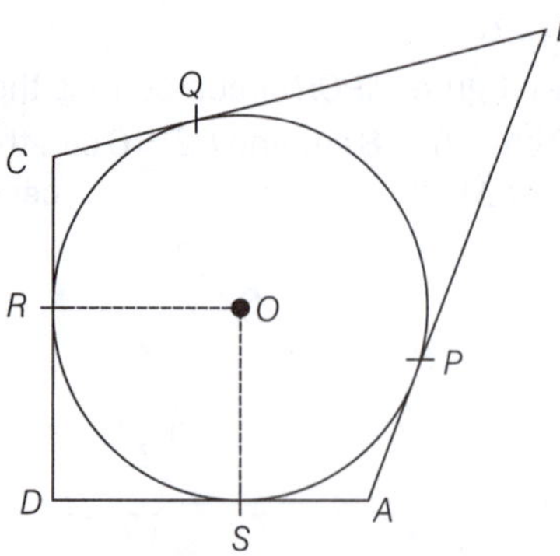

50. If a hexagon $ABCDEF$ circumscribes a circle, prove that

$$AB + CD + EF = BC + DE + FA$$ **NCERT Exemplar**

51. In the given figure, three circles with centres, A, B and C, respectively touch each other externally. If $AB = 5$ cm, $BC = 7$ cm and $CA = 6$ cm, then find the radius of the circle with centre A. **Competency Based Question**

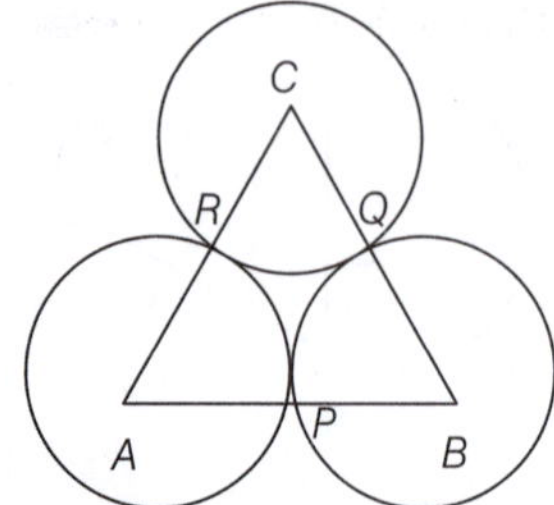

Long Answer Type Questions

52. In the figure below, PQ and PR are tangents to the circle. **CBSE QB**

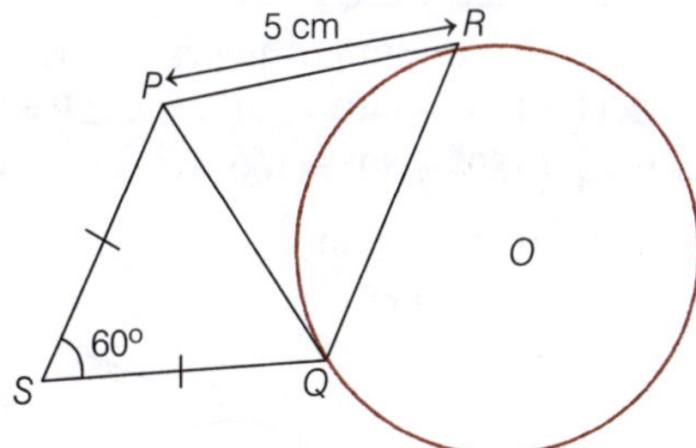

Find the perimeter of ΔSQP.

Show your work.

53. In the given figure, from an external point P, a tangent PT and a line segment drawn to a circle with centre O. ON is perpendicular on the chord AB.

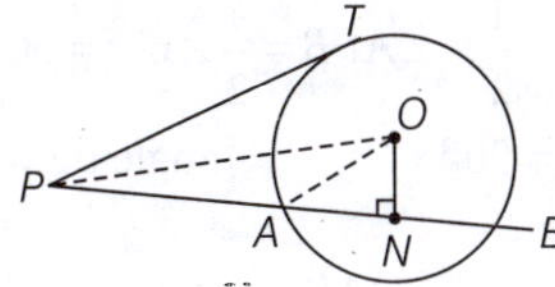

Prove that

(i) $PA \cdot PB = PN^2 - AN^2$

(ii) $PN^2 - AN^2 = OP^2 - OT^2$

(iii) $PA \cdot PB = PT^2$ **NCERT Exemplar**

54. The figure shown below represents a circle with centre O and diameter 12 cm.

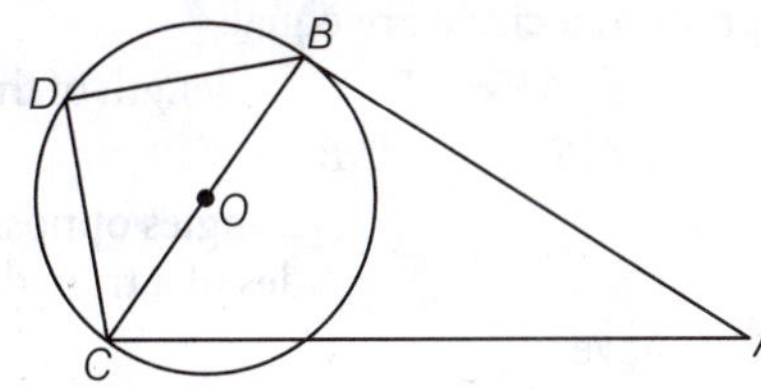

In ΔDBA, $\angle DBC = \angle BCD$ and $\angle A = 50°$.

(i) What is the measure of $\angle DCA$?

(ii) Dhruv said that, 'The quadrilateral $DBAC$ is a cyclic quadrilateral.' Is Dhruv correct? Give a reason to support your answer.

(iii) In ΔBAC, the length of side $CA = 2.5$ times OB. What is the length of side BA? **Competency Based Question**

55. As a part of a campaign, a huge balloon with message of "AWARENESS OF CANCER" was displayed from the terrace of a tall building.It was held by strings of length 8 m each, which inclined at an angle of 60° at the point, where it was tied as shown in the figure.

(i) What is the length of AB?

(ii) If the perpendicular distance from the centre of the circle to the chord AB is 3 m, then find the radius of the circle.

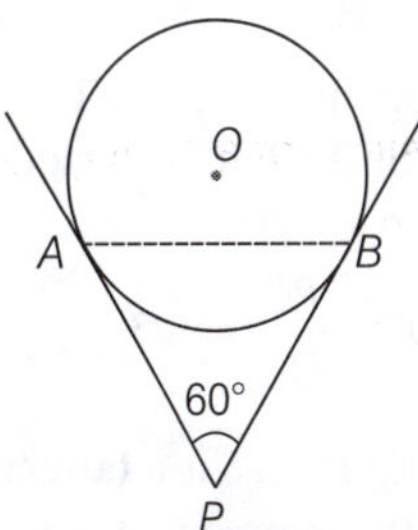

(iii) Which method should be apply to find the radius of circle? **Competency Based Question**

56. A ΔABC is drawn to circumscribe a circle of radius 2 cm such that the segment BD and DC into which BC is divided by the point of contact D are of lengths of 4 cm and 3 cm respectively. If area of ΔABC is 21 cm^2, find the length of AB and AC.

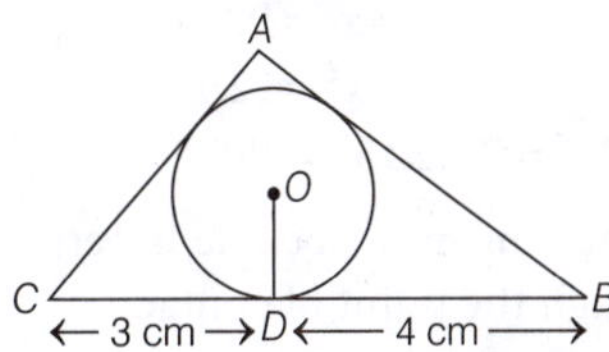

57. Prove that the parallelogram circumscribing a circle is a rhombus. Also, find area of the rhombus, if radius of circle is 3cm and length of one side of the rhombus is 10 cm. **CBSE 2024 (Basic)**

58. In the figure below, PQ and RQ are tangents to the circle with centre O and radius $6\sqrt{3}$ cm.

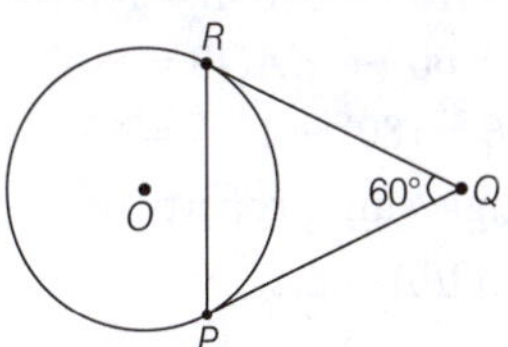

(i) Prove that ΔPQR is an equilateral triangle.

(ii) Find the length of RP. Show your steps along with a diagram and give valid reasons. **Competency Based Question**

HINTS & SOLUTIONS

Part I

1. (c) A line which intersects circle at two distinct points is known as secant.

2. (b) **Hint** A tangent is a line touching a circle only at one point.

3. (a) Since, the tangent to a circle is perpendicular to the radius through the point of contact.

$\therefore \quad \angle OQP = 90°$

In ΔOQP, $\cot 30° = \frac{PQ}{OQ} \Rightarrow \sqrt{3} = \frac{PQ}{5} \Rightarrow PQ = 5\sqrt{3}$ cm

4. (b) In the given figure, *TS* is a tangent.

We know that the tangent at any point of a circle is perpendicular to the radius through the point of contact.

$\therefore \quad OS \perp TS$

So, $\angle OST = 90°$

Now, in ΔOST, we have

$\angle OST + \angle STO + \angle TOS = 180°$ [angle sum property of triangle]

$\Rightarrow \quad 90° + x° + 3x° = 180°$

$\Rightarrow \quad 4x° = 90°$

$\Rightarrow \quad x° = 22.5°$

Therefore, $2x° = 2 \times 22.5° = 45°$

5. (b) Since, the tangent to a circle is perpendicular to the radius through the point of contact.

$\therefore \quad \angle OAP = 90°$

Now, $\quad OA = OB$ [radii of a circle]

$\Rightarrow \quad \angle OAB = \angle OBA$ [angles opposite to equal sides are equal]

$\Rightarrow \quad \angle OBA = 60°$

By angle sum property of triangle in ΔAOB,

$\angle OAB + \angle OBA + \angle AOB = 180°$

$\Rightarrow \quad 60° + 60° + \angle AOB = 180°$

$\Rightarrow \quad \angle AOB = 180° - 120° = 60°$

Now, using angle sum property of triangle in ΔOAP,

$\angle OAP + \angle OPA + \angle AOP = 180°$

$\Rightarrow \quad 90° + \angle OPA + 60° = 180°$

$\Rightarrow \quad \angle OPA = 180° - 150° = 30°$

6. (a) Given, $\angle QPR = 50°$

We know that the tangent at any point of a circle is perpendicular to the radius through the point of contact.

$\therefore \quad \angle OPR = 90°$

$\Rightarrow \quad \angle OPQ + \angle QPR = 90°$ [from figure]

$\Rightarrow \quad \angle OPQ = 90° - 50° = 40°$ [$\because \angle QPR = 50°$]

Now, $\quad OP = OQ$ [radii of a circle]

$\therefore \quad \angle OQP = \angle OPQ = 40°$ [since, angles opposite to equal sides are equal]

In ΔOPQ, $\angle O + \angle P + \angle Q = 180°$ [since, sum of angles of a triangle = 180°]

$\Rightarrow \quad \angle O = 180° - (40° + 40°)$ [$\because \angle P = 40° = \angle Q$]

$\Rightarrow \quad \angle POQ = 180° - 80° = 100°$

7. (b) Given, radius $OA = 5$ cm

and $\quad \angle APB = 60°$

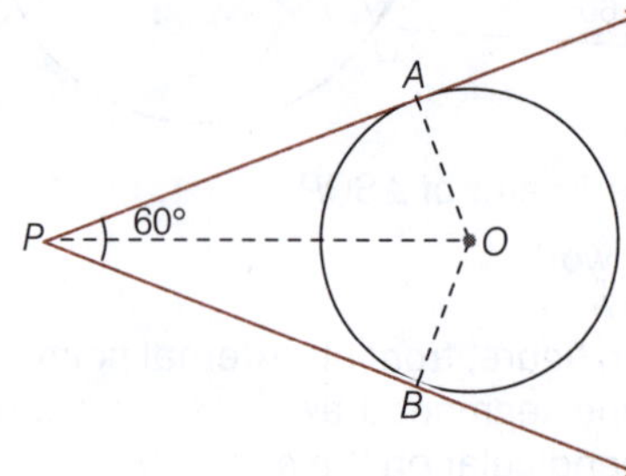

Now, $\angle OPA = \frac{1}{2} \times \angle APB = \frac{1}{2} \times 60° = 30°$

and $\quad \angle OAP = 90°$ [angle between tangent and radius of a circle]

So, in right angled ΔOAP, we get

$\tan \angle OPA = \frac{OA}{PA}$

$\Rightarrow \quad \tan 30° = \frac{5}{PA}$

$\Rightarrow \quad \frac{1}{\sqrt{3}} = \frac{5}{PA} \Rightarrow PA = 5\sqrt{3}$ cm

8. (c) We know that the lengths of tangents drawn from an external point to a circle are equal.

$\therefore \quad AP = BP$ [length of the tangents]

$\Rightarrow \quad \angle PBA = \angle PAB$ ...(i)

[$\because$ angles opposite to equal sides of a triangle are equal]

In ΔPAB, we have

$\angle PAB + \angle PBA + \angle APB = 180°$ [by angle sum property]

$\Rightarrow \quad \angle PAB + \angle PAB + 80° = 180°$ [using Eq. (i) and $\angle APB = 80°$]

$\Rightarrow \quad 2\angle PAB = 100°$

$\Rightarrow \quad \angle PAB = 50°$

Hence, the measure of $\angle PAB$ is 50°.

9. (d) Given, *PA* and *PB* are tangents to a circle with centre *O* such that $\angle P = 90°$ and $AB = 3\sqrt{2}$ cm.

Since, *PA* and *PB* are tangents from the same point *P*, they are equal in length i.e. $PA = PB$ ...(i)

In ΔPAB, $AB^2 = PA^2 + PB^2$ [using Pythagoras theorem]

$\Rightarrow \quad (3\sqrt{2})^2 = PA^2 + PA^2$ [using Eq. (i)]

$\Rightarrow \quad 2PA^2 = 18 \Rightarrow PA^2 = 9$

$\Rightarrow \quad PA = 3$ cm

10. (a) $\because$ $\angle AOC$ and $\angle COD$ form a linear pair.

$\Rightarrow \quad \angle AOC + \angle COD = 180°$

$\Rightarrow \quad \angle AOC = 180° - \angle COD$

$= 180° - 120° = 60°$

We know that the tangent to a circle is perpendicular to the radius through the point of contact.

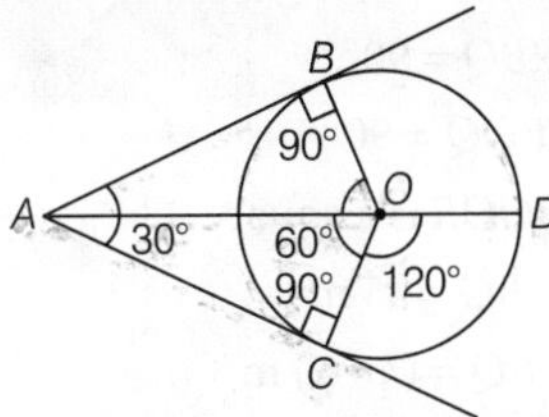

$\therefore \quad \angle ABO = \angle ACO = 90°$

In ΔAOC, using angle sum property of triangle,

$\angle AOC + \angle OCA + OAC = 180°$

$\Rightarrow \quad 60° + 90° + \angle OAC = 180°$

$\Rightarrow \quad \angle OAC = 30°$

$\Rightarrow \quad \angle BAO = 30° \quad [\because \angle OAC = \angle OAB]$

11. (a) $CA \perp PA$ and $CB \perp PB$

[$\because$ tangents to a circle perpendicular to the radius through the point of contact]

$\Rightarrow \quad \angle CAP = 90°$ and $\angle CBP = 90°$

Now, in quadrilateral $APBC$,

$\angle APB + \angle PBC + \angle BCA + \angle CAP = 360°$

[angle sum property of a quadrilateral]

$\Rightarrow 55° + 90° + \angle BCA + 90° = 360°$

$\Rightarrow \quad \angle BCA = 125°$

But $\quad \angle BCA = 2\angle BQA$

[$\because$ angle subtended by an arc at the centre is twice the angle subtended by it at any point on the remaining part of the circle]

$\therefore \quad \angle BQA = \frac{1}{2}\angle BCA$

$= \frac{1}{2} \times 125° = 62.5°$

12. (a) Firstly, draw a circle of radius 5 cm having centre O. P is a point at a distance of 13 cm from O. A pair of tangents PQ and PR are drawn.

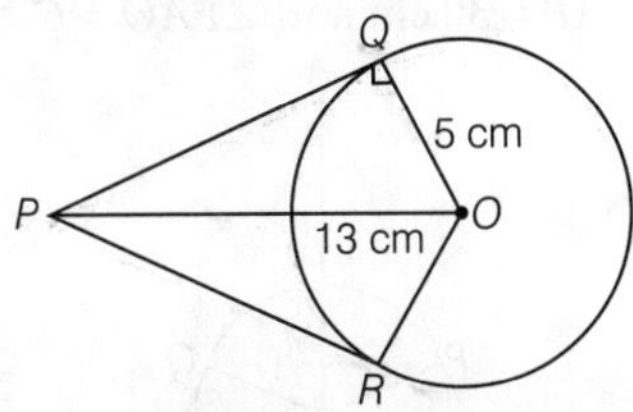

Thus, quadrilateral $PQOR$ is formed.

$\because \quad OQ \perp QP$

[since, QP is a tangent line]

In right angled ΔPQO, $OP^2 = OQ^2 + QP^2$

$\Rightarrow \quad 13^2 = 5^2 + QP^2$

$\Rightarrow \quad QP = 12$ cm

Now, area of $\Delta OQP = \frac{1}{2} \times QP \times QO = \frac{1}{2} \times 12 \times 5$

$= 30 \text{ cm}^2$

$\therefore$ Area of quadrilateral $QORP = 2 \times$ (area of ΔOQP)

$= 2 \times 30 \text{ cm}^2 = 60 \text{ cm}^2$

13. (a) A radius drawn to the point of tangency is perpendicular to the tangent line.

Since, OC is perpendicular to AB, so ΔOCA is a right angled triangle.

$\therefore \quad AC^2 + OC^2 = OA^2$ [by Pythagoras theorem]

$\Rightarrow \quad AC^2 + (2.1)^2 = (3.5)^2$

$\Rightarrow \quad AC^2 + 4.41 = 12.25$

$\Rightarrow \quad AC^2 = 12.25 - 4.41$

$\Rightarrow \quad AC^2 = 7.84$

$\Rightarrow \quad AC = \sqrt{7.84}$

$\Rightarrow \quad AC = 2.8$ cm

Since, OC is perpendicular to chord AB, C is the mid-point of AB.

$\therefore \quad AB = 2 \times AC$

$\Rightarrow \quad AB = 2 \times 2.8 = 5.6$ cm

$\therefore$ The length of AB is 5.6 cm.

14. (d) **Hint** $SP + RQ = PQ + RS$. **Ans.** 11

15. (d) We know that the opposite sides of a quadrilateral circumscribing a circle subtend supplementary angles at the centre of the circle.

i.e. $\quad \angle AOB + \angle COD = 180°$

$\Rightarrow \quad \angle COD = 180° - \angle AOB$

$= 180° - 125° = 55°$

16. (d) **Assertion** TA and TB are tangents.

OB is radius of circle.

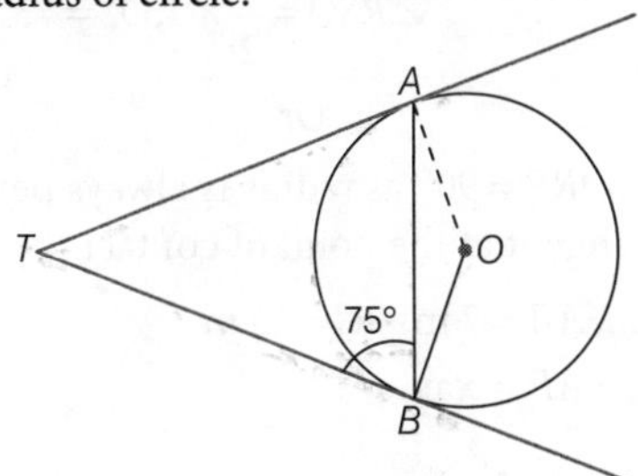

Thus, $\angle OBT = 90°$ [angle between tangent and radius]

$\therefore \quad \angle OBA = \angle OBT - \angle ABT$

$= 90° - 75° = 15° \neq 25°$

Reason Tangent drawn from an external point to a circle is perpendicular to the radius through the point of contact.

Hence, Assertion is incorrect but Reason is correct.

17. (a) **Hint** Do same as Question 3 of NCERT folder Exercise 10.2.

18. (a) **Hint** Do same as Example 5 of Topic 2.

19. (b) **Assertion** Two parallel tangents always lie at the end points of diameter.

Reason Diameter is the longest chord of a circle passes through the centre joining the two points on the circumference of a circle.

20. (i) In quadrilateral $PQOR$, we have

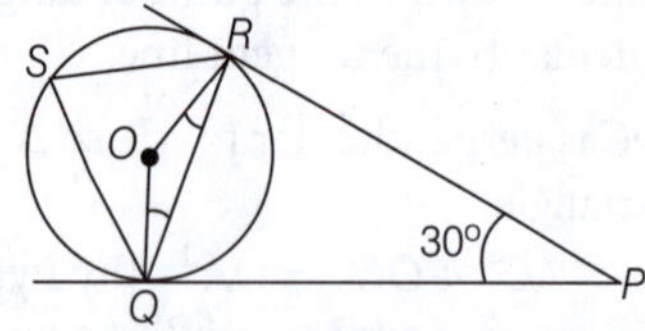

$$\angle QPR + \angle PRO + \angle PQO + \angle ROQ = 360°$$

$\Rightarrow$ $30° + 90° + 90° + \angle ROQ = 360°$

[$\because$ radius is always perpendicular to the tangent at point of contact]

$\Rightarrow$ $\angle ROQ = 360° - 210° = 150°$

(ii) In ΔQOR, $OQ = OR$ [radii of a circle]

$\therefore$ $\angle ORQ = \angle OQR$

Now, $\angle ROQ + \angle ORQ + \angle OQR = 180°$

$\Rightarrow$ $2\angle OQR = 180° - 150°$

$\Rightarrow$ $2\angle OQR = 30°$

$\Rightarrow$ $\angle OQR = 15°$

Again, $\angle OQP = 90°$ [$\because OQ \perp QP$]

$\Rightarrow$ $\angle OQR + \angle RQP = 90°$

$\Rightarrow$ $\angle RQP = 90° - 15° = 75°$

(iii) (a) We know that angle subtended by an arc at centre is double the angle subtended by it at the remaining part of the circle.

$\therefore$ $2\angle RSQ = \angle ROQ$

$\Rightarrow$ $\angle RSQ = \frac{1}{2} \times 150° = 75°$

Or

(b) $\angle ORP = 90°$ as radius is always perpendicular to the tangent at the point of contact.

21. (i) Given, $AB = 7$ m, $BC = 15$ m

and $AP = x$ m

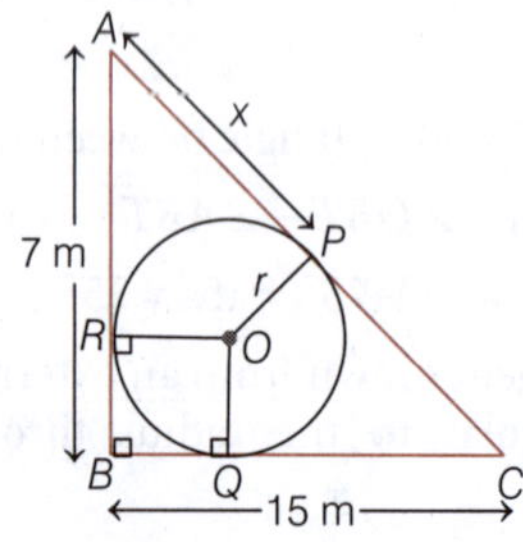

Here, $AP = AR$

[tangents drawn from an external points are equal in length]

$\therefore$ $AR = x$ m

(ii) Since, $AR = x$ and $AB = 7$ m

$\therefore$ $RB = (7 - x)$ m

Also, $RB = BQ$ [tangents drawn from an external points are equal in length]

$OR = OQ$ [radii of same circle]

$\angle ORB = 90°$ [angle between radius and tangent]

Also, $\angle RBQ = 90°$

Thus, $\angle ROQ = 90°$

Hence, $BQOR$ is a square.

(iii) (a) Here, $BC = 15$ m

and $BQ = (7 - x)$ m

$\therefore$ $QC = 15 - (7 - x) = (8 + x)$ m

Also, $QC = PC$

[tangents drawn from an external points are equal in length]

$\therefore$ $PC = (8 + x)$ m

In ΔABC,

$$AC^2 = AB^2 + BC^2$$
$$= 7^2 + 15^2 = 274$$

$\Rightarrow$ $AC^2 = 274$

$\Rightarrow$ $AC = \sqrt{274} = 16.55$

Since, $AC = AP + PC$

$\Rightarrow$ $AP + PC = 16.55$

$\Rightarrow$ $x + 8 + x = 16.55$

$\Rightarrow$ $2x = 8.55$

$\Rightarrow$ $x = 4.275$

$\Rightarrow$ $x = 4.28$ m

Or

(b) As we get $x = 4.28$ m [from part (iii) (a)]

We know that $BROQ$ is a square.

$\therefore$ $BQ = OQ$

$\Rightarrow$ $r = 7 - x$

$\Rightarrow$ $r = 7 - 4.28 \Rightarrow r = 2.72$ m

22. (i) Given, AP and AQ are tangents to the circle at P and Q, respectively.

$AP = 30$ cm and $\angle PAQ = 60°$

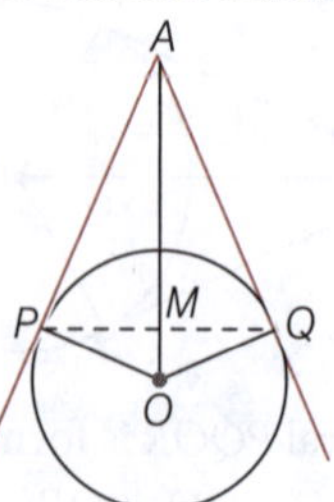

Since, $AP = AQ$

[tangents drawn from an external points are equal in length]

$\therefore$ $AQ = 30$ cm

Now, in ΔPAQ, we get

$$\angle PAQ = 60° \quad \text{[given]}$$
$$AP = AQ$$
$$\therefore \quad \angle APQ = \angle AQP$$

[angles corresponding to equal sides are equal in a triangle]

$$\therefore \; \angle PAQ + \angle APQ + \angle AQP = 180°$$

[angle sum property of a triangle]

$$\Rightarrow \quad 60° + 2\angle APQ = 180°$$
$$\Rightarrow \quad \angle APQ = 60°$$
$$\therefore \quad \angle AQP = 60°$$

Thus, ΔPAQ is an equilateral triangle

$$\Rightarrow \quad PQ = 30 \text{ cm}$$

$[AP = AQ = 30 \text{ cm}]$

(ii) $\angle POQ = 2\angle PAQ$

[angle subtended by an arc at the centre is twice the angle subtended by any point on the remaining part of the circle]

$$\Rightarrow \angle POQ = 2 \times 60°$$
$$= 120°$$

(iii) (a) Since, $\angle PAO = 30°$ $\quad \left[\because \angle PAO = \frac{1}{2} \times \angle PAQ\right]$

$$\angle APO = 90°$$

[angle between tangent and radius]

$\therefore$ In right angled ΔAPO,

$$\cos \angle PAO = \frac{AP}{AO}$$
$$\Rightarrow \quad \cos 30° = \frac{AP}{AO}$$
$$\Rightarrow \quad \frac{\sqrt{3}}{2} = \frac{30}{AO}$$
$$\Rightarrow \quad AO = \frac{60}{\sqrt{3}} = \frac{20\sqrt{3} \times \sqrt{3}}{\sqrt{3}}$$
$$= 20\sqrt{3} \text{ cm}$$

Or

(b) In right angled ΔAPO,

$$\tan 30° = \frac{OP}{AP} \quad [\because \angle PAO = 30°]$$
$$\Rightarrow \quad \frac{1}{\sqrt{3}} = \frac{OP}{30}$$
$$\Rightarrow \quad OP = \frac{30}{\sqrt{3}} = \frac{10\sqrt{3} \times \sqrt{3}}{\sqrt{3}}$$
$$\Rightarrow \quad OP = 10\sqrt{3} \text{ cm}$$

Part II

1. The term used for a line which intersects a circle at two distinct points is secant.

2. The line which is perpendicular to the radius of the circle through the point of contact will be tangent to the circle.

3. Hint Do same as Example 1 of Topic 1.

Ans. 10 cm

4. Hint $\angle ABC = 90°$

[$\because$ diameter subtends an angle 90° at the circle]

$$\Rightarrow \quad \angle OAB = 180° - (90° + 50°)$$

[by angle sum property of a triangle]

$$= 40°$$
$$\Rightarrow \quad \angle BAT = 90° - \angle OAB \quad \textbf{Ans. } 50°$$

5. Hint Given, $\angle CAB = 30°$

Join OC.

$$\therefore \quad OA = OC \quad [\because \text{radii of a circle}]$$
$$\Rightarrow \quad \angle OCA = \angle OAC$$

[$\because$ angles opposite to equal sides of a triangle are equal]

$$\Rightarrow \quad \angle OCA = 30° \quad [\because \angle OAC = 30°] \;...(i)$$

Since, a tangent is perpendicular to the radius at the point of contact.

$$\therefore \quad OC \perp PQ \Rightarrow \angle OCP = 90°$$
$$\Rightarrow \quad \angle OCA + \angle PCA = 90°$$
$$\Rightarrow \quad 30° + \angle PCA = 90° \quad \text{[using Eq.(i)]}$$
$$\Rightarrow \quad \angle PCA = 90° - 30°$$

Ans. $\angle PCA = 60°$

6. Hint As $OQ \perp PR \Rightarrow AB \perp OD$

$$\Rightarrow \quad AD = BD$$

[$\because$ perpendicular from centre bisects the chord]

and $\Delta ADQ \cong \Delta BDQ$ [by SAS congruency]

$\therefore \; \angle AQD = \angle BQD$ [by CPCT]

$\therefore \; \angle AQD = \angle BQD = 90° - 70° = 20°$

$\therefore \; \angle AQB = 40°$ **Ans.** 40°

7. Number of tangents to a circle which are parallel to a secant is 2.

8. Distance between two parallel tangents,

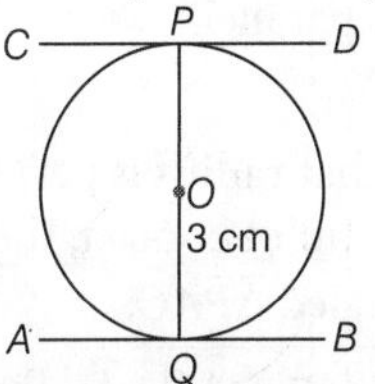

$$PQ = OP + OQ = 3 + 3 = 6 \text{ cm}$$

9. Given, PA and PB are two tangents drawn from an external point P.

$OP = 10$ cm and $PA = 8$ cm

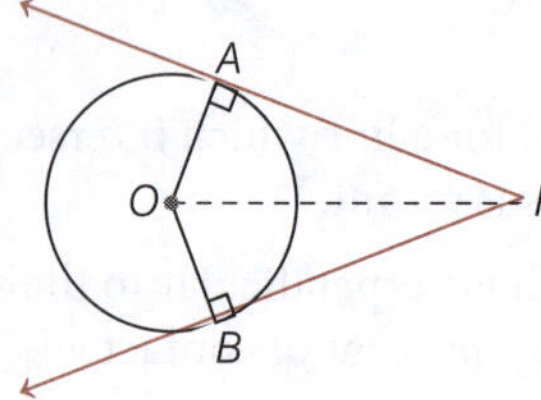

Since, $\angle OAP = 90°$

[angle between tangent and radius of a circle]

$\therefore$ In right angled ΔOAP, we get

$$OP^2 = AP^2 + OA^2 \quad \text{[by Pythagoras theorem]}$$

$$\Rightarrow \quad 10^2 = 8^2 + OA^2 \Rightarrow 100 = 64 + OA^2$$

$$\Rightarrow \quad 100 - 64 = OA^2 \Rightarrow OA^2 = 36$$

$$\Rightarrow \quad OA = 6 \text{ cm}$$

$$\therefore \quad \text{Diameter} = 2 \times OA = 2 \times 6 = 12 \text{ cm}$$

10. **Hint** Do same as Question 2 of NCERT Folder Exercise 10.2. **Ans.** 50°

11. We know that the tangents to a circle is perpendicular to the radius through the point of contact.

$$\therefore \quad \angle OBA = \angle OCA = 90°$$

In right angled ΔOBA, $\operatorname{cosec} 60° = \frac{OA}{OB} \Rightarrow \frac{2}{\sqrt{3}} = \frac{OA}{5}$

$$\Rightarrow \quad \sqrt{3}\, OA = 10 \Rightarrow OA = \frac{10}{\sqrt{3}} \text{ cm}$$

Since, $\angle OAB = \angle OAC = 60°$

In right angled ΔOCA, $\cot 60° = \frac{AC}{OC} \Rightarrow \frac{1}{\sqrt{3}} = \frac{AC}{5}$

$$\therefore \quad AC = \frac{5}{\sqrt{3}} \text{ cm}$$

12. **Hint** Use the result that opposite sides of a quadrilateral circumscribing a circle subtend supplementary angles at the centre of the circle. **Ans.** 60°

13. Given, XY and MN are tangents and DE is the diameter.

Since, tangent is perpendicular to radius

$$XY \perp DE \text{ and } MN \perp DE$$

$$\therefore \quad \angle YDE = 90° \text{ and } \angle NED = 90°$$

For lines XY and MN with transversal DE,

$$\angle YDE = \angle NED$$

Thus, co-interior angles are equal.

$\therefore$ Lines must be parallel.

Hence, $XY \| MN$

14. **Hint** We know that radius is perpendicular to the tangent at the point of contact, therefore $AO \perp AP$.

Now, in right angled ΔPAO,

$$OP = \sqrt{PA^2 + AO^2} \quad \text{[by Pythagoras theorem]}$$

$$= \sqrt{169} = 13 \text{ cm}$$

Similarly, in right angled ΔPBO,

$$PB = \sqrt{OP^2 - OB^2} = \sqrt{160}$$

[$\because$ radius, $OB = 3$ cm, given]

Ans. $4\sqrt{10}$ cm

15. **Hint** $QP = PT$ and $PT = PR$ **Ans.** 6.4 cm

16. **Hint** Clearly, $\angle CAD = 90°$ [angle in a semi-circle]

So, in right angled ΔCAD,

$$CD^2 = AC^2 + AD^2 \quad \text{[by Pythagoras theorem]}$$

$$= 36 + 64 = 100$$

$$\Rightarrow \quad CD = 10 \text{ cm}$$

Therefore, $OC = OD = OB = 5$ cm [$\because$ radius of a circle]

Join OT.

Since, $\angle OBT = 90°$ [angle between radius and tangent]

So, in right angled ΔOBT,

$$OT^2 = OB^2 + BT^2 \quad \text{[by Pythagoras theorem]}$$

$$= 25 + 16 = 41 \quad \textbf{Ans. } OT = \sqrt{41} \text{ cm}$$

17. In ΔACB,

$$\angle BCA = 90° \quad \text{[angle in a semi-circle]}$$

$$\therefore \quad AB^2 = AC^2 + BC^2 \quad \text{[by Pythagoras theorem]}$$

$$\Rightarrow \quad AB^2 = 4^2 + 3^2$$

$$\Rightarrow \quad AB = 5 \text{ cm}$$

$$\Rightarrow \quad OA = \frac{5}{2} \text{ cm} \quad \left[\because OA = \frac{AB}{2}\right]$$

Also given, $\Delta ACB \sim \Delta PAO$

$$\therefore \quad \frac{AB}{AC} = \frac{OP}{AP}$$

$$\Rightarrow \quad \frac{OP}{AP} = \frac{5}{4}$$

18. **Hint** Take a point Q' on circle and join PQ' and QQ'.

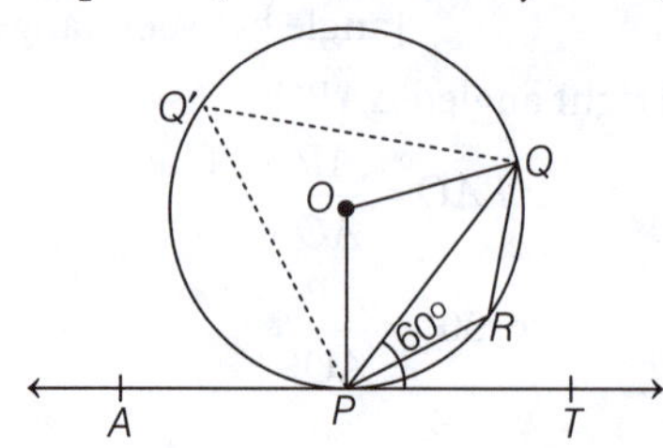

Now, $\angle OPQ = 90° - 60° = 30°$ [$\because \angle OPT = 90°$]

$\Rightarrow \quad \angle OQP = 30°$

[angles opposite to equal sides are equal]

$\Rightarrow \quad \angle POQ = 120°$ [angle sum property of a triangle]

$\Rightarrow \quad \angle PQ'Q = 60°$

[angle subtended by an arc at centre is twice the angle subtended by it at remaining part of circle]

$\Rightarrow \quad \angle PRQ = 120°$

[$\because$ opposite angles are supplementary in a cyclic quadrilateral $PQ'QR$]

19. **Hint** $\angle OPB = 30°$

[$\because$ angles opposite to equal sides are equal]

and $\angle OPT = 90°$ [$\because$ angle between radius and tangent]

$\therefore \quad \angle BPT = 90° + 30° = 120°$

Now, in ΔBPT, $\angle PTB = 180° - (\angle TBP + \angle BPT)$

[angle sum property of a triangle]

Ans. 30°

20. Hint $\angle ABQ = \frac{1}{2}\angle AOQ$

[angle subtended by an arc twice the angle subtended at remaining part of circle]

$\therefore \angle ABQ = 29°$

and $\angle BAT = 90°$ [angle between radius and tangent]

In ΔABT, we get

$\angle ATB = 180° - (29° + 90°)$

[angle sum property of a triangle]

$\therefore \angle ATQ = \angle ATB = 61°$. **Ans.** 61°

21. Hint Since, $OA \perp AY$

$\therefore \angle OAY = 90°$

[$\because$ radius is perpendicular to the tangent of the circle at the point of contact]

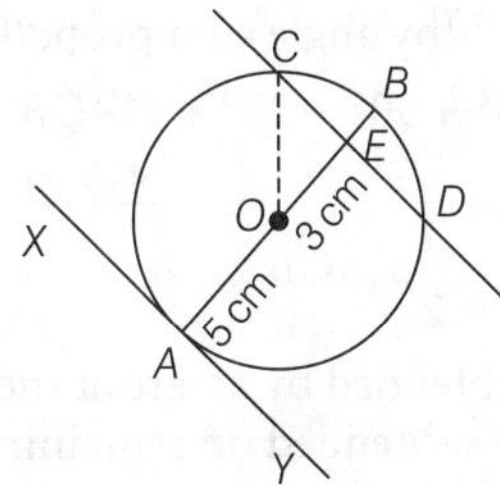

Now, $\angle OAY + \angle OED = 180°$

[$\because XY \parallel CD$, therefore sum of cointerior angles of a transversal is 180°]

$\therefore \angle OED = 90°$

Now, in right angled ΔOEC,

$OC^2 = OE^2 + EC^2$ [by Pythagoras theorem]

$\Rightarrow EC^2 = 25 - 9 = 16 \Rightarrow EC = 4$ cm

Hence, length of chord

$CD = 2\ CE = 2 \times 4 = 8$ cm

[$\because$ perpendicular from centre to the chord bisects the chord]

Ans. 8 cm

22. Do same as Theorem of Topic-2.

23. Let the chord AB and CD of outer circle, touch the inner circle at M and N.

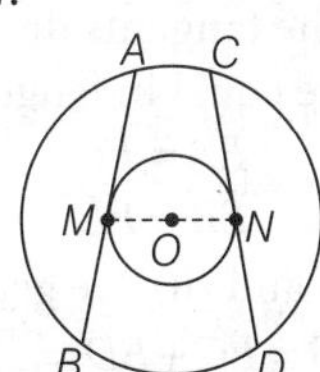

To prove $AB = CD$

Construction Join OM and ON.

Proof Since, OM and ON are radii of the inner circle through the points of contact M and N of the tangents AB and CD, respectively.

$\therefore OM \perp AB$ and $ON \perp CD$.

Also, $OM = ON$ [radii of the inner circle]

Thus, AB and CD are two chords of the outer circle which are equidistant from its centre O.

Hence, $AB = CD$ **Hence proved.**

24. Given, PA and PB are tangents to the circle centred at O.

(i) $OA = OB$ [radii of the circle]

$PA = PB$

[tangents from an external point to a circle are equal length]

$OP = OP$ [common side]

$\therefore \Delta OAP \cong \Delta OBP$

So, $\angle APO = \angle BPO$

Thus, OP bisects $\angle P$. **Hence proved.**

(ii) It is clear that

$\Delta AQP \cong \Delta BQP$

$\Rightarrow AQ = QB$

and $\angle AQP = \angle BQP$

AB is a straight line.

Therefore, $\angle AQP = \angle BQP = 90°$

Hence, OP is right bisector of AB. **Hence proved.**

25. Hint Produce BD to meet the bigger circle at E. Join AE.

Then, $\angle AEB = 90°$ [$\because$ angle in semi-circle]

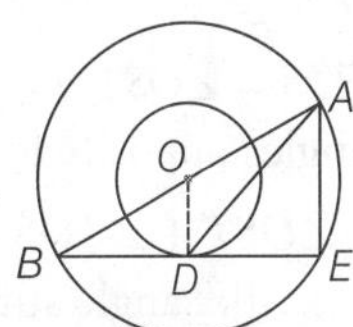

Clearly, $OD \perp BE$

[$\because BE$ is tangent to the smaller circle at D and OD is its radius]

$\therefore BD = DE$

[$\because BE$ is a chord of the bigger circle and $OD \perp BE$]

Now, in ΔAEB, O and D are the mid-points of AB and BE, respectively.

Therefore, by mid-point theorem, we have

$OD = \frac{1}{2}AE \Rightarrow AE = 2 \times 8 = 16$ cm

[$\because OD$ = radius of smaller circle = 8 cm]

In right angled ΔODB,

$OB^2 = OD^2 + BD^2$ [by Pythagoras theorem]

$\Rightarrow BD^2 = 169 - 64 = 105$

$\Rightarrow BD = \sqrt{105}$ cm $= DE$ [$\because BD = DE$]

Now, in right angled ΔAED,

$AD^2 = AE^2 + ED^2$ [by Pythagoras theorem]

$\Rightarrow AD = \sqrt{(16)^2 + (\sqrt{105})^2}$

Ans. 19 cm

26. Let $\angle APB = 2\theta$

By symmetry, $\angle APO = \angle BPO = \frac{1}{2}\angle APB$

$\Rightarrow \quad \angle APO = \angle BPO = \theta$

Also, we know that radius is perpendicular to tangent.

$\therefore \quad \angle OAP = 90°$

In right angled ΔOAP, $\sin\theta = \frac{OA}{OP} = \frac{r}{2r} = \frac{1}{2} \Rightarrow \theta = 30°$

$\therefore \angle APB = 2\theta = 2 \times 30° = 60°$

By angle sum property in ΔAPB,

$\Rightarrow \quad \angle APB + \angle PAB + \angle PBA = 180°$

$\Rightarrow \quad 60° + \angle PAB + \angle PAB = 180°$

[$PA = PB$, $\angle PAB = \angle PBA$]

$\Rightarrow \quad 2\angle PAB = 180° - 60°$

$\Rightarrow \quad \angle PAB = \frac{120°}{2} = 60°$

$\therefore \Delta APB$ is an equilateral triangle.

27. Hint $\because$ A tangent is perpendicular to the radius at the point of contact.

$\therefore \quad OT \perp PT \Rightarrow \angle OTP = 90°$

Now, right angled ΔOTP,

$$\cos\angle TOP = \frac{OT}{OP} \Rightarrow \cos\angle TOP = \frac{r}{2r} = \frac{1}{2}$$

$\Rightarrow \quad \angle TOP = 60° \Rightarrow \angle TOS = 2\angle TOP = 120°$

[$\because OP$ is the bisector of $\angle TOS$]

In ΔOTS, $\quad OT = OS \quad$ [$\because$ radii of a circle]

$\therefore \quad \angle OTS = \angle OST$

[$\because$ angles opposite to equal sides are equal]

Now, $\quad \angle OTS + \angle OST + \angle TOS = 180°$

[by angle sum property of triangle]

$\Rightarrow \quad 2\angle OTS + 120° = 180°$

$\Rightarrow \quad \angle OTS = \angle OST = 30°$

28. Hint $\angle OAT = 90°$ [$\because$ angle between radius and tangent]

Now, $\angle BOA = 100°$ [angle subtended by an arc at centre is twice the angle subtended by it at remaining part of circle]

$\Rightarrow \quad \angle ATO = 180° - (\angle TOA + \angle OAT)$

[angle sum property of a triangle]

$\Rightarrow \quad \angle ATO = 180° - (50° + 90°) = 40° \quad$ [$\because \angle TOA = 50°$]

Ans. 40°

29. Join OA, OB and OT.

Now, $\angle OAT = \angle OAQ - \angle QAT = 90° - 45° = 45°$

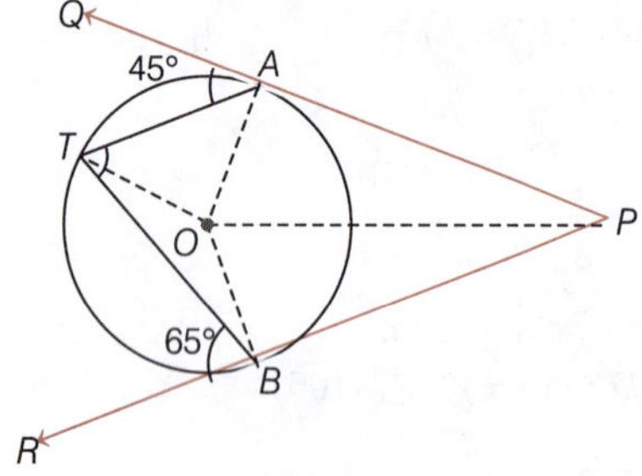

Similarly, $\angle OBT = 25°$

In ΔOTB, $\angle OBT = \angle OTB$

[angles corresponding to equal sides are equal]

Similarly, in ΔOAT, $\angle OAT = \angle OTA$

[angles corresponding to equal sides are equal]

Now, $\angle ATB = \angle OTA + \angle OTB$

$= 45° + 25° = 70° \quad \left[\begin{array}{l}\because \angle OAT = \angle OTA \\ \text{and } \angle OBT = \angle OTB\end{array}\right]$

30. Hint In quadrilateral $APBO$, $AO \perp PA$ and $BO \perp PB$

[$\because$ radius is perpendicular to tangent at the point of contact]

$\therefore \quad \angle PAO = \angle PBO = 90°$

$\because \quad \angle APB + \angle PAO + \angle PBO + \angle AOB = 360°$

[by angle sum property of a quadrilateral]

$\therefore \quad 75° + 90° + 90° + \angle AOB = 360°$

$\Rightarrow \quad \angle AOB = 105°$

Here, $\angle AQB = \frac{1}{2}\angle AOB$

[angle subtended by an arc at the centre is double of the angle subtended on remaining part of the circle]

$= \frac{1}{2} \times 105° = 52\frac{1°}{2}$

In cyclic quadrilateral $AQBM$,

$\angle AQB + \angle AMB = 180°$

[sum of opposite angles of a cyclic quadrilateral = 180°]

$\Rightarrow \quad 52\frac{1°}{2} + \angle AMB = 180°$

Ans. $\angle AQB = 52\frac{1°}{2}$ and $\angle AMB = 127\frac{1°}{2}$

31. As we know that the tangents drawn from an external point to a circle are equal in length.

Then, in given figure, $PR = RC$ ...(i)

and $\quad RQ = RC$ ...(ii)

From Eqs. (i) and (ii), we get $PR = RQ$

Hence, R is the mid-point of PQ and it bisects the common tangent at P and Q.

32. As we know that the tangents drawn from an exterior point to a circle are equal in length.

$\therefore \quad EA = EC$ ...(i)

and $\quad EB = ED$ ...(ii)

On adding Eqs. (i) and (ii), we get

$EA + EB = EC + ED \Rightarrow AB = CD$

33.

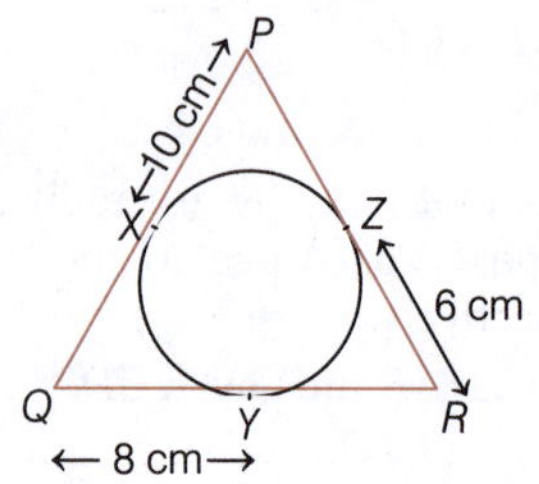

Given, $PX = 10$ cm, $QY = 8$ cm and $RZ = 6$ cm

Now, $PX = PZ$ [tangents drawn from external points are equal in length]

$\therefore\ PZ = 10$ cm

$RZ = RY$ [tangents drawn from external points are equal in length]

$\therefore\ RY = 6$ cm

$QY = QX$ [tangents drawn from external points are equal in length]

$\therefore QX = 8$ cm

Now, $QP = QX + XP = 8 + 10 = 18$ cm,

$PR = PZ + RZ = 10 + 6 = 16$ cm

and $QR = QY + YR = 8 + 6 = 14$ cm

$\therefore$ Perimeter of $\Delta PQR = QP + PR + QR$

$= 18 + 16 + 14 = 48$ cm

34. Let CD be a chord parallel to tangent MN to a circle with centre O. AB is a diameter of circle.

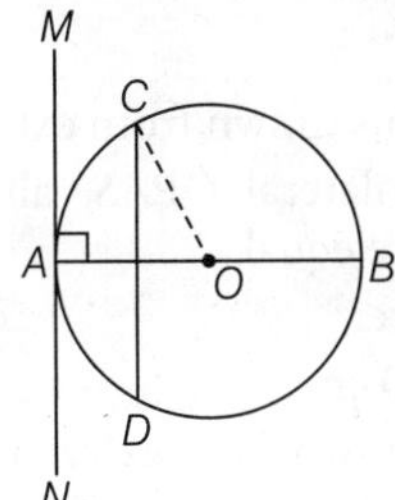

Given, $CD \parallel MN$

$\angle OAM = 90^\circ$

$\angle CEO = 90^\circ$ [corresponding angle]

$CE = ED$

[$\because OE \perp CD$ and perpendicular drawn from the centre of the circle always bisect the chord]

Hence, the diameter AB bisects the chord CD.

35.

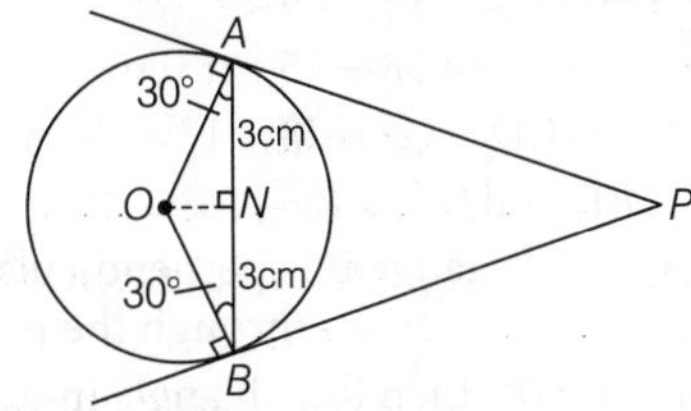

In ΔOAB,

$\angle OAB + \angle OBA + \angle AOB = 180^\circ$

$\Rightarrow\ \angle AOB + 2 \times 30^\circ = 180^\circ$ [$\because \angle OBA = \angle OAB$]

$\angle AOB = 120^\circ$

Draw $ON \perp AB$

$\Rightarrow\ AN = \frac{6}{2} = 3$ cm

[$\because$ perpendicular from centre to a chord bisects the chord]

In right angled ΔONA,

$\cos 30^\circ = \frac{AN}{AO} \Rightarrow \frac{\sqrt{3}}{2} = \frac{3}{AO}$

$\Rightarrow\ AO = 2\sqrt{3}$ cm

Now, $OB \perp BP$ [tangent to a circle is perpendicular to the radius through the point of contact]

$\Rightarrow\ \angle OBP = 90^\circ$

$\Rightarrow\ \angle ABP = 90^\circ - \angle OBA$

$= 90^\circ - 30^\circ = 60^\circ$

Similarly, $\angle BAP = 60^\circ$

$\therefore$ In ΔABP, $\angle APB = 60^\circ$

$\Rightarrow \Delta ABP$ is an equilateral triangle

$\therefore\ AB = BP = PA = 6$ cm

36. Hint Length of each pipe $= \frac{1}{2}$ (perimeter of ΔPRT)

Ans. 36 cm

37. $PQ = PT$ [because tangents drawn from an external points to the circle are equal in length]

$\Rightarrow\ PL + LQ = PM + MT$

$\Rightarrow\ PL + LN = PM + MN$ ... (i)

[$\because LQ = LN, MT = MN$]

[because tangents drawn from an external point to the circle are equal in length]

$\therefore$ Perimeter $(\Delta PLM) = PL + LM + PM$

$= PL + LN + MN + PM$

$= PL + LN + PL + LN$ [using Eq. (i)]

$= 2(PL + LN)$

$= 2(PL + LQ) = 2(PQ)$ [$\because LQ = LN$]

$= 2 \times 28 = 56$ cm

[because tangent drawn from an external point to the circle are equal in length]

38. Hint $SR = QR$ and $TP = QP$

[lengths of two tangents drawn from an external point are equal]

Ans. 3 cm

39. Hint Do same as Question 7 of NCERT Folder Exercise 10.2. **Ans.** 6 cm

40. Hint Do same as Example 4 of Topic 2.

Ans. 2 cm

41. We know that tangents drawn from an exterior point to a circle are equal in length.

$\therefore\ AD = AF = x$ cm [say]

$BD = BE = y$ cm [say]

$CE = CF = z$ cm [say]

Given, $AB = 8$ cm

$\Rightarrow\ AD + BD = 8$

$\Rightarrow\ x + y = 8$ ...(i)

$\because\ BC = 10$ cm

$\Rightarrow\ BE + CE = 10$

$\Rightarrow\ y + z = 10$ ...(ii)

and $CA = 12$ cm

$\Rightarrow\ CF + AF = 12$

$\Rightarrow\ z + x = 12$ ...(iii)

On adding Eqs. (i), (ii) and (iii), we get

$$2(x+y+z)=30$$

$\Rightarrow$ $x+y+z=15$ ...(iv)

On subtracting Eq. (ii) from Eq. (iv), we get

$$x=15-10=5$$

On subtracting Eq. (iii) from Eq. (iv), we get

$$y=15-12=3$$

On subtracting Eq. (i) from Eq. (iv), we get

$$z=15-8=7$$

$\therefore$ $AD=x\text{ cm}=5\text{ cm}$, $BE=y\text{ cm}=3\text{ cm}$ and $CF=z\text{ cm}=7\text{ cm}$

42. Let a, b and c be the sides of right angled ΔABC, such that $BC=a$, $CA=b$ and $AB=c$.

Let the circle touches the sides BC, CA, AB at D, E and F, respectively.

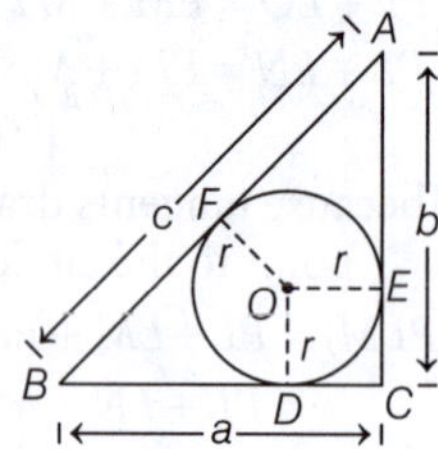

Then, $AE=AF$,

$BD=BF$ and $CD=CE$

[$\because$ tangents drawn from an external point are equal in length]

In quadrilateral $OECD$ each angle is 90°. So, $OECD$ is a square therefore, we have

$$OE=EC=CD=OD=r$$

$\therefore$ $AF=AE=b-r$ and $BF=BD=a-r$

$\Rightarrow AF+BF=(b-r)+(a-r)$

$\Rightarrow$ $AB=b-r+a-r$

$\Rightarrow$ $c=a+b-2r$ [$\because AB=c$]

$\therefore$ $r=\dfrac{a+b-c}{2}$ **Hence proved.**

43. Hint Do same as Question 9 of NCERT Folder Exercise 10.2.

Ans. $\angle LOM=90°$

44. Hint Let AB and CD be two perpendicular diameters of a circle with centre O and T_1, T_2 are tangents to circle at A, B and T_3 and T_4 are tangents to circle at C and D, respectively.

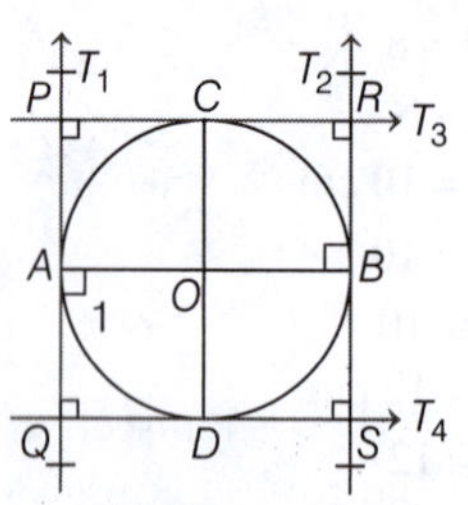

From figure, $PQSR$ is a square. [given]

$\because$ $PQ\parallel RS$

$\therefore$ $AP\parallel BR$ ...(i)

Also, $\angle CPQ=\angle OAQ=90°$

$\therefore$ $PR\parallel AB$ ...(ii)

[$\because$ corresponding angles are equal]

From Eqs. (i) and (ii), we get

$APRB$ is a parallelogram.

$\therefore$ $AB=2\text{ cm}$

[$\because$ opposite sides of parallelogram are equal]

So, radius of circle $=\dfrac{AB}{2}=\dfrac{2}{2}=1\text{ cm}$

45. Hint $AB+DC=BC+AD$ **Ans.** No

46. Since, tangent is perpendicular to radius .

$\therefore$ $OS\perp AD$ and $OP\perp AB$.

Thus, $\angle OSA=90°$, $\angle OPA=90°$ and $\angle SOP=90°$

[$\because \angle SAP=90°$]

Also, $AS=AP$

[tangents drawn from external points are equal]

Thus, in quadrilateral $OPAS$, all angles are 90° and adjacent sides are equal.

$\therefore$ $OPAS$ is square.

So, $AP=OS=10\text{ cm}$

Also, tangents drawn from external points are equal.

$\therefore$ $CQ=CR=27\text{ cm}$ and $BP=BQ$

Now, $CQ+BQ=38$

$\Rightarrow$ $27+BP=38\Rightarrow BP=11\text{ cm}$

Thus, $x=AB=AP+BP=10+11=21\text{ cm}$

47. Do same as Question 14 of Try These 10.2.

Ans. 9 cm

48. Do same as Question 45. **Ans.** $AD=3\text{ cm}$

49. Hint $CR=CQ=BC-BQ$

$$=38-25=13\text{ cm}$$

$\therefore$ $RD=CD-CR=28-13=15\text{ cm}$

Here, $OR\perp RD$ and $OS\perp DA$

[$\because$ tangent is perpendicular to the radius through the point of contact]

Also, $\angle ADC=90°$, then fourth angle in quadrilateral $ORDS$ will be 90°.

Thus, $ORDS$ will be a rectangle.

$\because$ D is an external point of a circle.

$\therefore$ $DR=DS$

Also, opposites sides of rectangle are equal.

$\therefore$ $RD=OR=OS=SD$

Hence, quadrilateral $DROS$ is a square.

$\therefore$ Radius $=OR=RD=15\text{ cm}$

50. Hint Since, tangents drawn from an external point to a circle are equal in length.

$\therefore$ $AQ=AP$, $BQ=BR$, $CR=CS$, $DS=DT$, $ET=EU$ and $FP=FU$

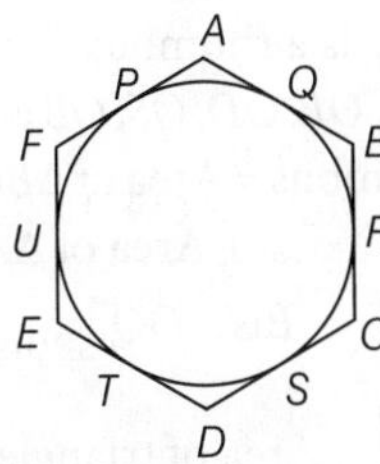

So, $AB + CD + EF = (AQ + QB) + (CS + SD) + (EU + UF)$

$= AP + BR + CR + DT + ET + FP$

$= (AP + FP) + (BR + CR) + (DT + ET)$

$\Rightarrow \quad AB + CD + EF = AF + BC + DE$

51. **Hint** Let radius of circle with center A be x cm.

$\Rightarrow \quad AP = AR = x,$

$CR = CQ = 6 - x$ and $BP = BQ = 5 - x$

$\Rightarrow \quad (6 - x) + (5 - x) = 7$ **Ans.** 2 cm

52. In the given figure, we have

PQ and PR are tangents to the circle with centre O.

$PR = 5$ cm and $\angle PSQ = 60°$,

also given, $PS = QS$

We know, $PQ = PR = 5$ cm

[$\because$ tangents from a point to the circle are equal]

$\Rightarrow \quad PQ = 5\text{ cm} \quad \ldots\text{(i)}$

$\because$ In ΔPQS,

$PS = QS$ [given]

$\therefore \quad \angle SQP = \angle QPS$

$\because \angle QSP + \angle SQP + \angle QPS = 180°$

[$\because$ sum of angles of a triangle is 180°]

$\Rightarrow \quad \angle SQP = \angle QPS = \dfrac{180° - 60°}{2}$

[$\because \angle QSP = 60°$, given]

$= 60°$

So, ΔSQP is an equilateral triangle.

So, perimeter of $\Delta SQP = 3 \times PQ$

$= 3 \times 5$ [using Eq. (i)]

$= 15$ cm

53. (i) **Hint** $PA \cdot PB = (PN - AN)(PN + BN)$

$= (PN - AN)(PN + AN)$

[$\because AN = BN$ as ON perpendicular to chord AB, so bisect it]

$= PN^2 - AN^2$

(ii) **Hint** $PN^2 - AN^2 = (OP^2 - ON^2) - AN^2$

[$\because$ in $\Delta ONP, OP^2 = ON^2 + PN^2 \Rightarrow PN^2 = OP^2 - ON^2$]

$= OP^2 - (ON^2 + AN^2) = OP^2 - OA^2$

[$\because$ in $\Delta ONA, OA^2 = ON^2 + AN^2$]

$= OP^2 - OT^2$

[$\because OA = OT =$ radii of circle]

(iii) **Hint** From parts (i) and (ii), we get

$PA \cdot PB = OP^2 - OT^2$

$\Rightarrow \quad PA \cdot PB = PT^2$

[$\because$ in $\Delta OTP, OP^2 = OT^2 + PT^2$]

54. (i) $\angle CDB = 90°$ [angle in a semi-circle]...(i)

In ΔBCD, $\angle BCD + \angle DBC + \angle CDB = 180°$

$\Rightarrow \quad 2\angle BCD = 90°$

[$\because \angle DBC = \angle BCD$]

$\Rightarrow \quad \angle BCD = 45°$

$\therefore \quad \angle BCD = \angle DBC = 45° \quad \ldots\text{(ii)}$

Now, $OB \perp AB$ [tangent is perpendicular to the radius through the point of contact]

$\Rightarrow \quad \angle OBA = 90° \quad \ldots\text{(iii)}$

In quadrilateral $ACDB$,

$\angle ACD + \angle CDB + \angle DBA + \angle BAC = 360°$

$\Rightarrow (\angle ACB + \angle BCD) + 90° + (\angle DBC + \angle CBA) + 50° = 360°$

[$\because \angle BAC = 50°$, using Eq. (i)]

$\Rightarrow \quad \angle ACB + 45° + 90° + 45° + 90° + 50° = 360°$

[using Eqs. (ii) and (iii)]

$\Rightarrow \quad \angle ACB = 40°$

$\therefore \quad \angle DCA = \angle DCB + \angle ACB$

$= 45° + 40° = 85°$

(ii) No, Dhruv is not correct as the sum of the opposite angles of the quadrilateral $DBAC$ is not 180°. Thus, the quadrilateral $DBAC$ is not a cyclic quadrilateral.

(iii) $OB = \dfrac{12}{2} = 6$ cm

$\therefore \ CA = 2.5 \times OB = 2.5 \times 6 = 15$ cm

In right angled ΔABC,

$AC^2 = BC^2 + AB^2$

$\Rightarrow \quad (15)^2 = (12)^2 + AB^2 \quad [\because BC = 12\text{ cm}]$

$\Rightarrow \quad 225 - 144 = AB^2$

$\Rightarrow \quad AB^2 = 81 \Rightarrow AB = 9$ cm

55. (i) Given, $PA = PB = 8$ m

Clearly, PA and PB are tangents to the circle.

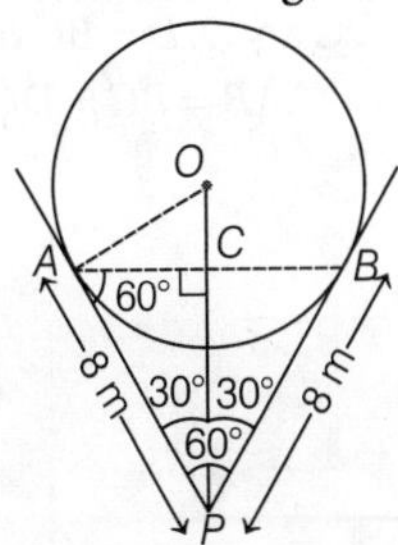

Now, draw OP which bisects $\angle APB$ and perpendicular to the chord AB.

Thus, we have

$$\angle APC = \angle BPC = 30^\circ \text{ and } \angle ACP = \angle BCP = 90^\circ$$

In ΔACP, $\angle APC + \angle ACP + \angle PAC = 180^\circ$

[$\because$ sum of all angles of triangle is 180°]

$\Rightarrow$ $30^\circ + 90^\circ + \angle PAC = 180^\circ$

$\Rightarrow$ $\angle PAC = 180^\circ - 120^\circ = 60^\circ$

Similarly, $\angle PBC = 60^\circ$

Thus, ΔAPB is an equilateral triangle.

$\therefore$ $AB = AP = BP = 8$ m

(ii) Given, $OC = 3$ m

We know that if a perpendicular drawn from the centre of the circle to the chord, then it bisects the chord.

$\therefore$ $AC = BC = \dfrac{AB}{2} = \dfrac{8}{2} = 4$ m

In right angled ΔACO,

$OA^2 = AC^2 + OC^2$ [by Pythagoras theorem]

$\Rightarrow$ $OA = \sqrt{(4)^2 + (3)^2} = 5$ m,

which is the radius of the circle.

(iii) Pythagoras theorem.

56. Hint Do same as Question 12 of Try These 10.2.

Ans. $AB = 7.5$ cm, $AC = 6.5$ cm.

57. Given $ABCD$ be a parallelogram circumscribing a circle with centre O.

To prove $ABCD$ is a rhombus.

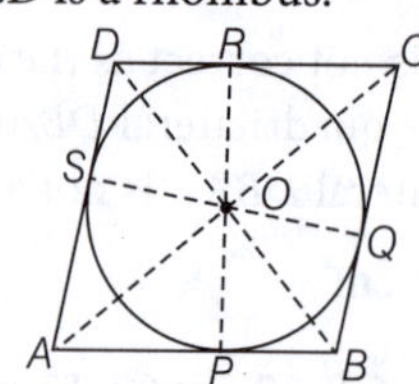

Proof We know that the tangents drawn to a circle from an exterior point are of equal length.

$\therefore AP = AS, BP = BQ, CR = CQ$ and $DR = DS$

On adding the above four equations, we get

$$AP + BP + CR + DR = AS + BQ + CQ + DS$$

$$\Rightarrow (AP + BP) + (CR + DR) = (AS + DS) + (BQ + CQ)$$

$\therefore$ $AB + CD = AD + BC$

or $2AB = 2AD$

[$\because AB = DC$ and $AD = BC$ of parallelogram $ABCD$]

$\therefore$ $AB = BC = DC = AD$

Therefore, $ABCD$ is a rhombus.

Join $OC, OP, OQ, OR, OD, OS, OB$ and OA

Now, area of rhombus = Area of ΔBOC + Area of ΔAOB + Area of ΔAOD + Area of ΔCOD

Area of $\Delta BOC = \dfrac{1}{2} \times BC \times OQ$

$\left[\because \text{Area of triangle} = \dfrac{1}{2} \times \text{Base} \times \text{Height}\right]$

$= \dfrac{1}{2} \times 10 \times 3 = 15 \text{ cm}^2$

$\therefore$ Area of ΔBOC = Area of ΔAOB

= Area of ΔAOD

= Area of ΔCOD

$= 15 \text{ cm}^2$

Area of rhombus $= 4 \times$ Area of ΔBOC

$= 4 \times 15 \text{ cm}^2 = 60 \text{ cm}^2$

Therefore, area of rhombus is 60 cm^2.

58. Hint

(i) $PQ = RQ$ [the length of tangents drawn from an external point to a circle are equal]

In ΔPQR, $\angle RPQ = \angle PRQ = 60^\circ$

[by angles sum property]

(ii) Join OP and OQ.

$\because$ $\angle OPQ = 90^\circ$

$\therefore$ $\angle OPS = \angle OPQ - \angle SPQ$

$= 90^\circ - 60^\circ = 30^\circ$

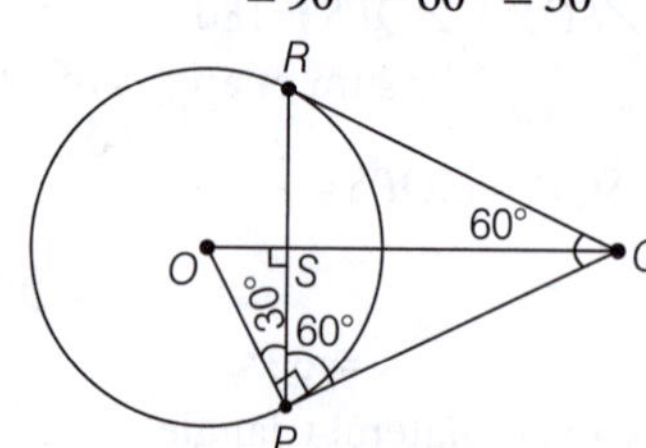

In ΔOPQ, $\angle POQ = 60^\circ$

In ΔOPS, $\angle OSP = 90^\circ$

Now, in ΔOPS, $\sin 60^\circ = \dfrac{PS}{PO} \Rightarrow PS = 9$ cm

$\therefore$ $RS = PS = 9$ cm

[the perpendicular from the centre of a circle to a chord bisects the chord]

$\therefore$ $RP = RS + PS = 9 + 9 = 18$ cm

CIRCLES

Tangent to a Circle
A tangent to a circle is a line that intersects or touches the circle at only one point. The common point of the tangent and the circle is called the point of contact.

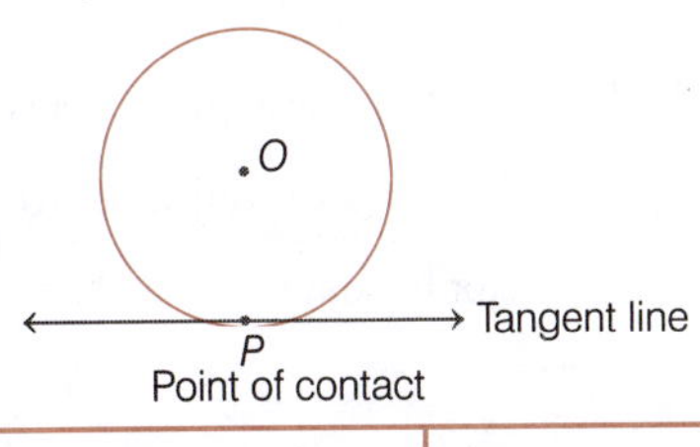

Length of Tangent
The length of the segment of the tangent, between the given point (on the tangent) and the point of contact with the circle is called the length of tangent from the given point.

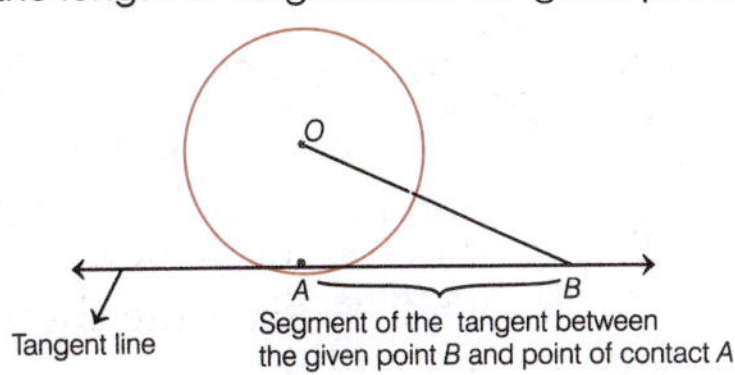

In the figure, AB is called the length of tangent.

Theorem The tangent at any point of a circle is perpendicular to the radius through the point of contact.
e.g. A circle with centre O and a tangent AB at a point P on the circle.
Then, OP is perpendicular to AB
i.e. $OP \perp AB$

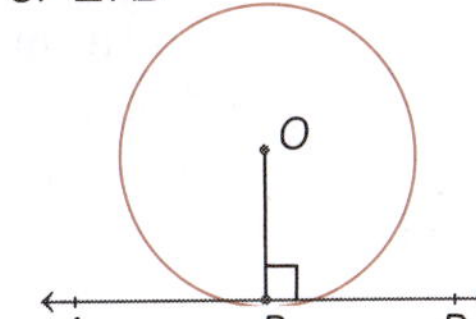

Number of Tangents from a Point on a Circle
(i) If point P lies outside the circle, then two tangents can be drawn to the circle from point P.

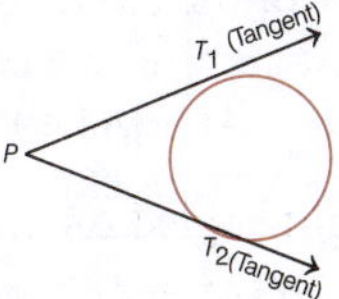

(ii) If point P lies on the circle, then there is one and only one line passing through point P which touch the circle in one point.

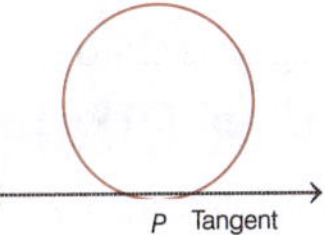

(iii) If the point P lies inside the circle, then there are no tangent draw to a circle from the point P.

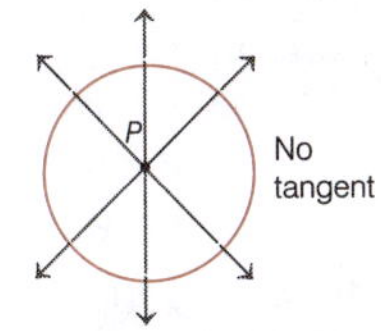

Theorem
The lengths of tangents drawn from an external point to a circle are equal.
e.g. Let AP and AQ be two tangents from a point A to a circle with centre O.

$$AP = AQ$$

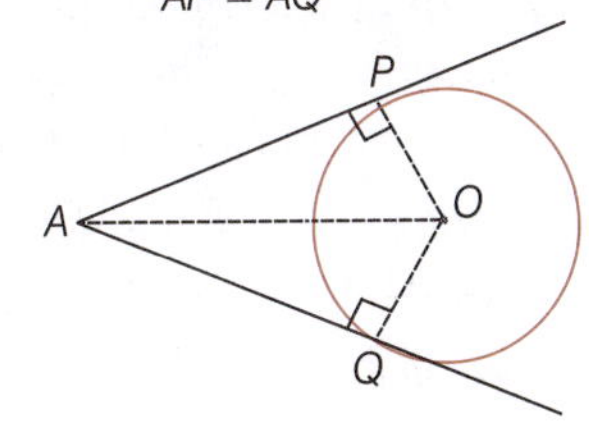

Areas Related to Circles

Many objects that we come across in our daily life, are related to circular shape in some form or other like cycle wheels, round cake, papad, bangles, flower beds, etc. In this chapter, we shall find the areas of two special parts of a circular region known as **sector** and **segment.**

Sector of a Circle

The portion of the circular region enclosed by two radii and the corresponding arc of a circle is called the sector of circle.

In the given figure, shaded region *OAPBO* is a sector of the circle with centre *O*. Here, $\angle AOB$ is called the **angle of sector**. The sector containing minor arc is called **minor sector** (shaded region *OAPBO*) and the sector containing major arc is called **major sector** (unshaded region *OACBO*).

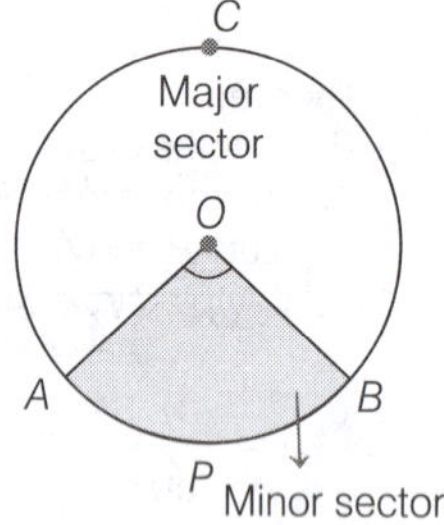

Angle of minor sector is less than 180° and angle of major sector is more than 180°. The sum of angles of major and minor sector is 360°.

Area of Sector of a Circle

Let there be a circle of radius *r* having a minor sector with angle θ. Then,

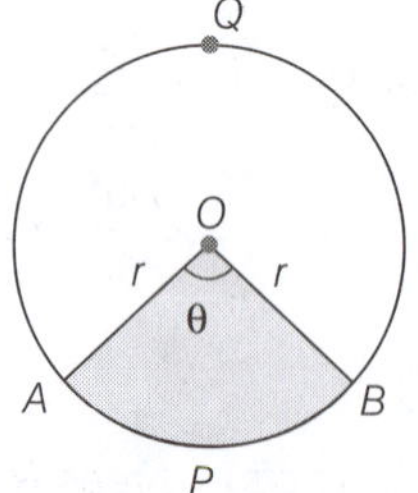

$$\text{Area of the sector} = \frac{\theta}{360°} \times \pi r^2$$

Also,

Area of major sector $= \pi r^2$ – Area of minor sector

Area of minor sector $= \pi r^2$ – Area of major sector

Note it
- If $\theta = 180°$, then sector becomes a semi-circular region and its area $= \frac{1}{2}\pi r^2$
- If $\theta = 90°$, then sector becomes a quadrant of a circle and its area $= \frac{1}{4}\pi r^2$

Example 1. **The length of minute hand of a clock is 14 cm. Find the area swept by the minute hand in 1 min.** $\left[\text{take, } \pi = \frac{22}{7}\right]$

Sol. The minute hand of a clock describes a circle of radius equal to its length i.e. 14 cm in 1 hour.

So, the angle described by minute hand in 60 min = 360°

$\therefore$ Angle described by minute hand in 1 min

$$= \frac{360°}{60} = 6°$$

So, the area swept by the minute hand in 1 min is the area of a sector of angle 6° in a circle of radius 14 cm.

$$\therefore \text{ Required area} = \frac{\theta}{360°} \times \pi r^2$$

$$= \frac{6°}{360°} \times \frac{22}{7} \times (14)^2$$

$$= \frac{1}{60} \times \frac{22}{7} \times 14 \times 14$$

$$= 10.27 \text{ cm}^2$$

Length of an Arc of a Sector

The arc corresponding to a sector is called the arc of the sector.

If the radius of a circle is r and the angle of sector is θ, then

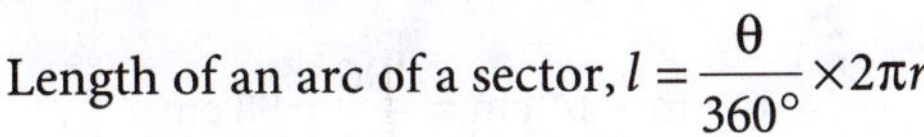

Length of an arc of a sector, $l = \dfrac{\theta}{360^\circ} \times 2\pi r$

Also, area of sector in terms of length of arc $= \dfrac{1}{2} lr$

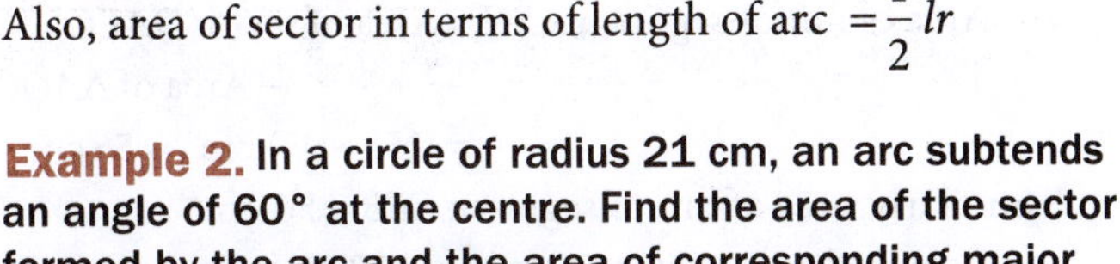

Example 2. **In a circle of radius 21 cm, an arc subtends an angle of 60° at the centre. Find the area of the sector formed by the arc and the area of corresponding major sector. Also, find the length of the arc.**

Sol. Given, radius $(r) = 21\text{cm}$

and angle of the sector, $\theta = 60^\circ$

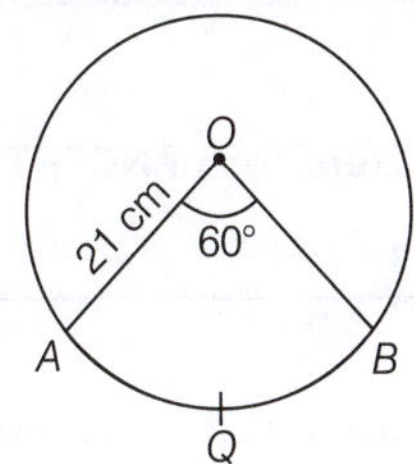

$\therefore$ Area of the sector of angle $\theta = \dfrac{\theta}{360^\circ} \times \pi r^2$

$= \dfrac{60^\circ}{360^\circ} \times \dfrac{22}{7} \times 21 \times 21 = 231 \text{cm}^2$

Length of the arc $= \dfrac{\theta}{360^\circ} \times 2\pi r$

$= \dfrac{60^\circ}{360^\circ} \times 2 \times \dfrac{22}{7} \times 21 = 22 \text{ cm}$

Area of corresponding major sector

$= \pi r^2$ – Area of sector $OAQB$

$= \dfrac{22}{7} \times 21 \times 21 - 231$

$= 1155 \text{ cm}^2$

Segment of a Circle

The portion of the circular region enclosed between by a chord and the corresponding arc of the circle is called the **segment of the circle.**

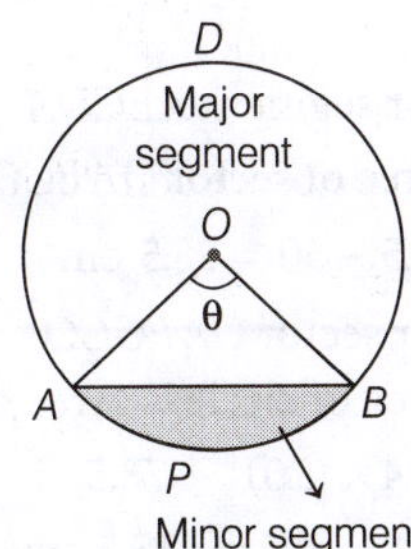

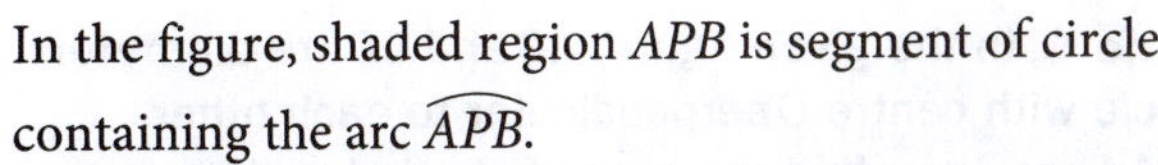

In the figure, shaded region APB is segment of circle containing the arc $\widehat{APB}$.

The segment containing the minor arc is called the **minor segment** and the segment containing the major arc is called the **major segment.**

In other words, we can say that, the segment which is less than semi-circular region is called a minor segment and the other segment is called major segment.

Area of a segment

= Area of corresponding sector – Area of triangle formed by chord and the radii of the circle

Also,

Area of major segment $= \pi r^2 -$ Area of minor segment

Area of minor segment $= \pi r^2 -$ Area of major segment

Note it When we write segment and sector, we will mean the 'minor segment' and the 'minor sector' respectively, unless stated otherwise.

Example 3. **In the given figure, AB is a chord of a circle of radius 7 cm and centred at O. Find the area of the shaded region if $\angle AOB = 90^\circ$. Also, find length of minor arc AB.** CBSE 2023 (Standard)

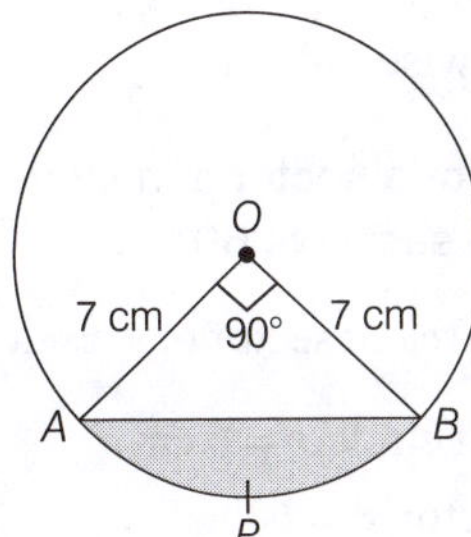

Sol. $\therefore$ Area of $\Delta OAB = \dfrac{1}{2} \times \text{Base} \times \text{Height}$

$= \dfrac{1}{2} \times OA \times OB = \dfrac{1}{2} \times 7 \times 7 = \dfrac{49}{2} \text{cm}^2$

$\therefore$ Area of sector $OAB = \dfrac{\theta}{360^\circ} \times \pi r^2$

$= \dfrac{90^\circ}{360^\circ} \times \dfrac{22}{7} \times 7 \times 7 = \dfrac{77}{2} \text{cm}^2$

$\therefore$ Area of shaded region = Area of sector $OAPB$ – Area of ΔAOB

$= \left(\dfrac{77}{2} - \dfrac{49}{2}\right) \text{cm}^2$

$= \dfrac{28}{2} \text{cm}^2 = 14 \text{ cm}^2$

Length of minor arc $AB = \dfrac{\theta}{360^\circ} \times 2\pi r$

$= \dfrac{90^\circ}{360^\circ} \times 2 \times \dfrac{22}{7} \times 7 = 11 \text{cm}$

Example 4. **In the given figure, AB and CD are diameters of a circle with centre O perpendicular to each other. If $OA = 14$ cm, then find the area of shaded region.**

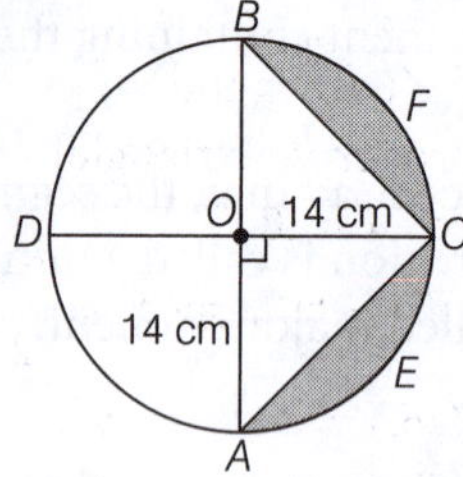

Sol. Given, $OA = 14$ cm

$\therefore \quad OC = 14$ cm

Also, $AB \perp CD$

$\Rightarrow \angle AOC = 90°$

$\therefore$ Area of sector $OAEC = \dfrac{90°}{360°} \times \pi r^2$, [$r$ is the radius]

$= \dfrac{1}{4} \times \dfrac{22}{7} \times 14 \text{ cm} \times 14 \text{ cm} = 154 \text{ cm}^2$

Area of $\Delta AOC = \dfrac{1}{2} \times OA \times OC$

$= \dfrac{1}{2} \times 14 \text{ cm} \times 14 \text{ cm} = \dfrac{196}{2} = 98 \text{ cm}^2$

$\therefore$ Area of minor segment AEC = Area of sector $OAEC$ − Area of ΔAOC

$= (154 - 98) \text{ cm}^2 = 56 \text{ cm}^2$

Similarly, area of minor segment $CFB = 56 \text{ cm}^2$

$\therefore$ Required area $= (56 + 56) \text{ cm}^2 = 112 \text{ cm}^2$

NCERT FOLDER

Complete Solutions of All Exercises of NCERT Textbook

Exercise 11.1

Unless stated otherwise, take $\pi = \dfrac{22}{7}$.

Q1. **Find the area of a sector of a circle with radius 6 cm, if angle of the sector is 60°.**

Sol. We know that area of sector of a circle $= \dfrac{\theta}{360°} \times \pi r^2$

Given, radius of circle, $r = 6$ cm

and angle of sector, $\theta = 60°$

$\therefore$ Area of sector of a circle $= \dfrac{60°}{360°} \times \dfrac{22}{7} \times (6)^2 = \dfrac{132}{7} \text{ cm}^2$

Q2. **Find the area of a quadrant of a circle whose circumference is 22 cm.**

Sol. Given, circumference of a circle = 22 cm

$\Rightarrow \; 2\pi r = 22 \Rightarrow 2 \times \dfrac{22}{7} \times r = 22 \Rightarrow r = \dfrac{22 \times 7}{2 \times 22} = \dfrac{7}{2}$ cm

Now, area of a quadrant of a circle $= \dfrac{90°}{360°} \times \pi r^2$

$= \dfrac{22}{7} \times \dfrac{\left(\dfrac{7}{2}\right)^2}{4}$ [$\because \theta = 90°$]

$= \dfrac{11}{14} \times \dfrac{49}{4} = \dfrac{77}{8} \text{ cm}^2$

Q3. **The length of the minute hand of a clock is 14 cm. Find the area swept by the minute hand in 5 min.**

Sol. Do same as Example 1. **Ans.** $\dfrac{154}{3} \text{ cm}^2$

Q4. **A chord of a circle of radius 10 cm subtends a right angled at the centre. Find the area of the corresponding**

(i) minor segment. (ii) major sector. [take, $\pi = 3.14$]

Sol. Given, radius of a circle, $AO = 10$ cm and $\angle AOC = 90°$

Area of $\Delta AOC = \dfrac{1}{2} \times OA \times OC = \dfrac{1}{2} \times 10 \times 10 = 50 \text{ cm}^2$

Area of sector $OAECO = \dfrac{\theta}{360°} \times \pi r^2$

$= \dfrac{90°}{360°} \times 3.14 \times (10)^2$ [$\because \pi = 3.14$]

$= \dfrac{314}{4} = 78.5 \text{ cm}^2$

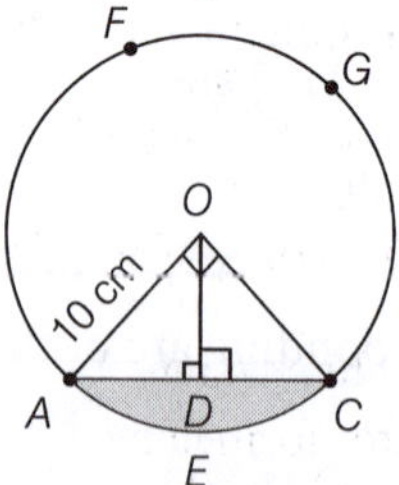

(i) Area of minor segment $AECDA$

= Area of sector $OAECO$ − Area of ΔAOC

$= 78.5 - 50 = 28.5 \text{ cm}^2$

(ii) Area of major sector $OAFGCO$

= Area of circle − Area of sector $OAECO$

$= 3.14 \times (10)^2 - 78.5$

$= 314 - 78.5 = 235.5 \text{ cm}^2$

Q5. In a circle of radius 21 cm, an arc subtends an angle of 60° at the centre. Find

(i) the length of the arc.

(ii) area of the sector formed by the arc.

(iii) area of the segment formed by the corresponding chord.

Sol. Given, arc ABC subtends an angle 60° at the centre.

$\therefore$ $\theta = 60°$ and radius, $r = 21$ cm

(i) Length of the arc $ABC = \dfrac{\theta}{360°} \times 2\pi r$

$$= \frac{60°}{360°} \times 2 \times \frac{22}{7} \times 21$$

$$= \frac{44}{6} \times 3 = 22 \text{ cm}$$

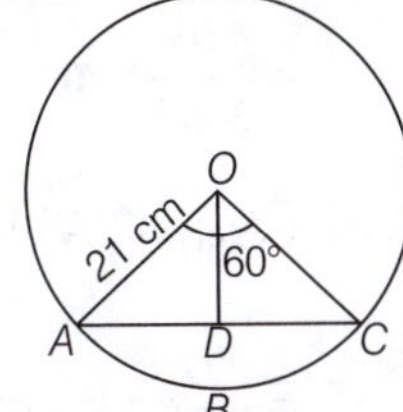

(ii) Area of the sector formed by the arc

$$= \frac{60°}{360°} \times \frac{22}{7} \times (21)^2$$

$$= \frac{22}{6 \times 7} \times 21 \times 21 = \frac{9702}{42} = 231 \text{ cm}^2$$

(iii) Given, $\angle AOC = 60°$ and $OA = OC$ [radii of circle]

Let $\angle OAC = \angle OCA = x$

[$\because$ angle opposite to equal sides are also equal]

In ΔOAC, $\angle OAC + \angle AOC + \angle OCA = 180°$

$\Rightarrow$ $60° + x + x = 180°$

$\Rightarrow$ $60° + 2x = 180°$

$\Rightarrow$ $2x = 120° \Rightarrow x = 60°$

$\therefore$ $\angle A = \angle O = \angle C = 60°$

$\Rightarrow$ ΔOAC is an equilateral triangle.

So, area of $\Delta OAC = \dfrac{\sqrt{3}}{4} \times (21)^2 = \dfrac{441\sqrt{3}}{4}$ cm^2

$\left[\because \text{area of equilateral triangle} = \dfrac{\sqrt{3}}{4}(\text{side})^2\right]$

Hence, area of the segment

= Area of sector formed by the arc − Area of ΔOAC

$$= \left(231 - \frac{441\sqrt{3}}{4}\right) \text{cm}^2 = 40.04 \text{ cm}^2$$

Q6. A chord of a circle of radius 15 cm subtends an angle of 60° at the centre. Find the areas of the corresponding minor and major segments of the circle. [take, $\pi = 3.14$ and $\sqrt{3} = 1.73$]

Sol. Given, chord AB subtends an angle 60° at the centre.

$\therefore$ $\angle AOB = 60°$ and $OA = OB$ [radii of circle]

$\therefore$ $\angle OBA = \angle OAB = x$ [let]

[$\because$ angles opposite to equal sides are also equal]

In ΔAOB,

$\angle AOB + \angle OBA + \angle OAB = 180°$

[by angle sum property of triangle]

$\Rightarrow$ $60° + x + x = 180°$

$\Rightarrow$ $2x = 180° - 60° \Rightarrow x = \dfrac{120°}{2} = 60°$

$\Rightarrow$ $\angle OBA = \angle OAB = 60° = \angle AOB$

$\therefore$ ΔAOB is an equilateral triangle.

Now, area of $\Delta AOB = \dfrac{\sqrt{3}}{4} \times (15)^2$

$\left[\because \text{area of equilateral triangle} = \dfrac{\sqrt{3}}{4}(\text{side})^2\right]$

$$= 56.25 \times 1.73 = 97.3125 \text{ cm}^2$$

Area of sector $OACBO = \dfrac{\theta}{360°} \times \pi r^2$

$$= \frac{60°}{360°} \times 3.14 \times (15)^2$$

$$= \frac{3.14 \times 225}{6} = \frac{706.5}{6}$$

$$= 117.75 \text{ cm}^2$$

$\therefore$ Area of minor segment $ACBDA$

= Area of sector $OACBO$ − Area of ΔAOB

$= (117.75 - 97.3125)$ cm^2 $= 20.4375$ cm^2

Now, area of major segment

= Area of circle − Area of minor segment

$= \pi\,(15 \text{ cm})^2 - 20.4375 \text{ cm}^2$

$= 3.14 \times 225 \text{ cm}^2 - 20.4375 \text{ cm}^2$

$= 706.5 \text{ cm}^2 - 20.4375 \text{ cm}^2 = 686.0625 \text{ cm}^2$

Q7. A chord of a circle of radius 12 cm subtends an angle of 120° at the centre. Find the area of the corresponding segment of the circle. [take, $\pi = 3.14$ and $\sqrt{3} = 1.73$] CBSE 2023

Sol. Do same as Example 3. **Ans.** 88.44 cm^2

Q8. A horse is tied to a peg at one corner of a square shaped grass field of side 15 m by means of a 5 m long rope (see the figure). Find CBSE 2023

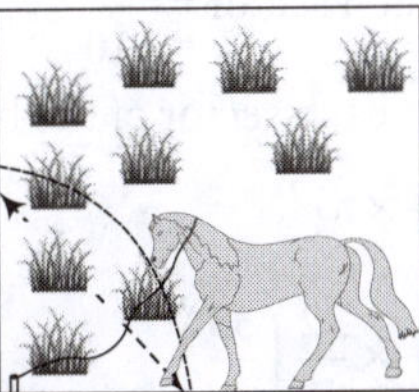

(i) the area of the part of the field in which the horse can graze.

(ii) the increase in the grazing area if the rope were 10 m long instead of 5 m. [take, $\pi = 3.14$]

Sol. Given, side of a square = 15 m

$\therefore$ Area of square $= (15)^2 = 225\ m^2$

[$\because$ area of square $= (\text{side})^2$]

Also given, length of rope = 5 m

$\therefore$ Radius of arc = 5 m

(i) Area of the field graze by the horse,

$$A_1 = \frac{\theta}{360°} \times \pi r^2 = \frac{90°}{360°} \times 3.14 \times (5\ m)^2$$

[$\because$ each angle of a square is 90°]

$$= \frac{3.14 \times 25 m^2}{4} = \frac{78.5}{4} m^2 = 19.625\ m^2$$

(ii) If length of rope $= 10\ m = r_1$ (say)

Then, area of the field graze by the horse,

$$A_2 = \frac{\theta}{360°} \times \pi r_1^2 = \frac{90°}{360°} \times 3.14 \times (10\ m)^2$$

$$= \frac{3.14 \times 100\ m^2}{4} = \frac{314}{4} = 78.5\ m^2$$

$\therefore$ Required increase in the grazing area

$= A_2 - A_1$

$= 78.5 - 19.625 = 58.875\ m^2$

Q 9. A brooch is made with silver wire in the form of a circle with diameter 35 mm. The wire is also used in making 5 diameters which divide the circle into 10 equal sectors as shown in the figure.

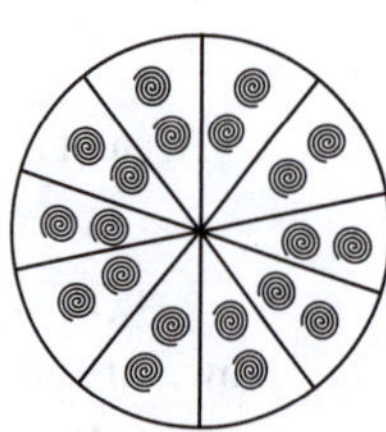

Find

(i) the total length of the silver wire required.

(ii) the area of each sector of the brooch.

Sol. Given, diameter of circle, $d = 35$ mm

$\therefore$ Circumference of circle $= \pi d$ [$\because d = 2r$]

$$= \frac{22}{7} \times 35\ mm = 110\ mm$$

Now, length of 5 diameters $= 5 \times 35 = 175$ mm

(i) Total length of the silver wire $= \pi d + 5d$

$= 110 + 175 = 285$ mm

(ii) Here, we see that total circle is divided into 10 sectors.

$\therefore$ Angle of each sector $= \frac{360°}{10} = 36°$

Then, area of each sector of the brooch

$$= \frac{\theta}{360°} \times \pi r^2$$

$$= \frac{36°}{360°} \times \frac{22}{7}\left(\frac{35}{2}\right)^2 \quad \left[\because r = \frac{d}{2} = \frac{35}{2} mm\right]$$

$$= \frac{1}{10} \times \frac{22}{1} \times \frac{5}{2} \times \frac{35}{2}$$

$$= \frac{11 \times 35}{2 \times 2} = \frac{385}{4} mm^2$$

Q 10. An umbrella has 8 ribs which are equally spaced (see the figure). Assuming umbrella to be a flat circle of radius 45 cm, find the area between the two consecutive ribs of the umbrella.

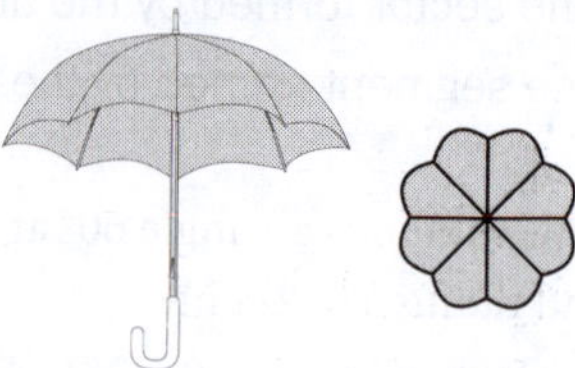

Sol. Given, umbrella to be a flat circle. So, the central angle of an umbrella is 360°.

Since, umbrella has 8 ribs.

$\therefore$ Angle between two ribs $= \frac{360°}{8} = 45°$

Area between two ribs = Area of one sector of the umbrella

$$= \frac{\theta}{360°} \times \pi r^2$$

$$= \frac{45°}{360°} \times \frac{22}{7} \times (45\ cm)^2$$

[$\because r = 45$, given]

$$= \frac{22}{7 \times 8}(45\ cm)^2$$

$$= \frac{22275}{28} cm^2$$

Q 11. A car has two wipers which do not overlap. Each wiper has a blade of length 25 cm sweeping through an angle of 115°. Find the total area cleaned at each sweep of the blades.

Sol. Given, length of wiper blade $= 25\ cm = r$ [let]

and angle made by this blade, $\theta = 115°$

$\therefore$ Area cleaned by one blade

= Area of sector formed by blade

$$= \frac{\theta}{360°} \times \pi r^2 = \frac{115°}{360°} \times \frac{22}{7} \times (25\ cm)^2$$

$$= \frac{23 \times 22}{72 \times 7} \times 625\ cm^2 = \frac{23 \times 11 \times 625}{36 \times 7} cm^2$$

$$= \frac{158125}{252} cm^2$$

$\therefore$ Total area cleaned by both blades

$= 2 \times$ Area cleaned by one blade

$$= \frac{2 \times 158125}{252} = \frac{158125}{126} cm^2$$

Q 12. To warn ships for underwater rocks, a light house spreads a red coloured light over a sector of angle 80° to a distance of 16.5 km. Find the area of the sea over which the ships are warned. [take, $\pi = 3.14$]

Sol. Given, sector angle, $\theta = 80°$

and distance or radius, $r = 16.5$ km

$$\therefore \text{ Area of sector} = \frac{\theta}{360^\circ} \times \pi r^2$$

$$= \frac{80^\circ}{360^\circ} \times 3.14 \times (16.5)^2$$

$$= \frac{2 \times 3.14 \times 272.25}{9}$$

$$= \frac{1709.73}{9}$$

$$= 189.97 \text{ km}^2$$

which is the required area of the sea over which the ships are warned.

Q 13. A round table cover has six equal designs as shown in the figure. If the radius of the cover is 28 cm, then find the cost of making the designs at the rate of ₹ 0.35 per cm². [take, $\sqrt{3} = 1.732$]

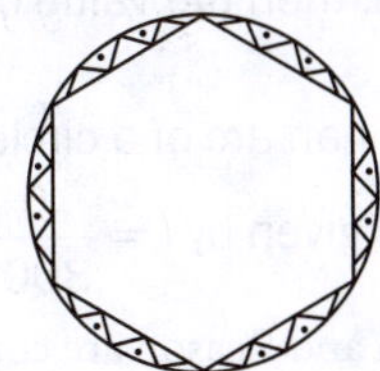

Sol. We know that the central angle of a circle is 360°.

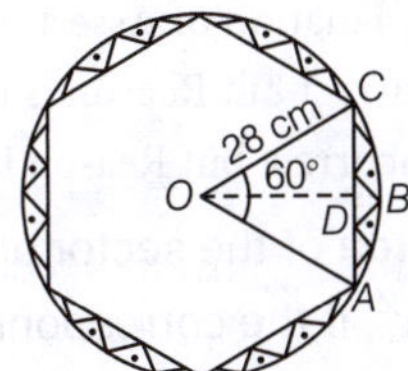

$$\therefore \text{ Angle of each sector} = \frac{360^\circ}{6} = 60^\circ$$

$\therefore \quad \angle AOC = 60^\circ$ and $OA = OC$ [radii of circle]

$\therefore \quad \angle OAC = \angle OCA = x$ [let]

[$\because$ angles opposite to equal sides of a triangle are also equal]

In ΔAOC, $\angle AOC + \angle OAC + \angle OCA = 180^\circ$

[by angle sum property of triangle]

$\Rightarrow \quad 60^\circ + x + x = 180^\circ$

$\Rightarrow \quad 2x = 180^\circ - 60^\circ$

$\Rightarrow \quad x = \frac{120^\circ}{2}$

$\Rightarrow \quad x = 60^\circ$

$\Rightarrow \quad \angle OAC = \angle OCA = 60^\circ = \angle AOC$

$\therefore$ ΔAOC is an equilateral triangle.

$$\text{Area of } \Delta AOC = \frac{\sqrt{3}}{4} \times (28)^2$$

$= 339.472 \text{ cm}^2$ [$\because \sqrt{3} = 1.732$]

$\left[\because \text{area of an equilateral triangle} = \frac{\sqrt{3}}{4}(\text{side})^2\right]$

$$\text{Now, area of sector } OABCO = \frac{\theta}{360^\circ} \times \pi r^2$$

$$= \frac{60^\circ}{360^\circ} \times \frac{22 \times (28)^2}{7}$$

$$= \frac{22 \times 4 \times 28}{6} = 410.67 \text{ cm}^2$$

$\therefore$ Area of segment $ABCA$

$= \text{Area of sector } OABCO - \text{Area of } \Delta AOC$

$= 410.67 - 339.472$

$= 71.198 \simeq 71.20 \text{ cm}^2$

Now, area of six segments $= 6 \times 71.20$

$= 427.2 \text{ cm}^2$

Since, the cost of making the design is ₹ 0.35 per cm².

$\therefore$ Total cost $= 427.72 \times 0.35 =$ ₹ 149.52

Q 14. Tick the correct answer in the following question. Area of a sector of angle p (in degrees) of a circle with radius R is

(i) $\frac{p}{180^\circ} \times 2\pi R$ (ii) $\frac{p}{180^\circ} \times \pi R^2$

(iii) $\frac{p}{360^\circ} \times 2\pi R$ (iv) $\frac{p}{720^\circ} \times 2\pi R^2$

Sol. (iv) Given, sector angle $= p$ and radius of circle $= R$

$$\therefore \text{ Area of sector} = \frac{\theta}{360^\circ} \times \pi r^2$$

$$= \frac{p}{360^\circ} \times \pi R^2$$

$$= \frac{p}{720^\circ} \times 2\pi R^2$$

REVIEW EXERCISE

Including Competency Based Questions

Part I

Multiple Choice Questions

1. Area of a quadrant of a circle of radius 7 cm is **CBSE 2023 (Standard)**

(a) 154 cm^2 (b) 77 cm^2

(c) $\frac{77}{2} \text{ cm}^2$ (d) $\frac{77}{4} \text{ cm}^2$

2. If the area of a sector of a circle is $\frac{7}{20}$ of the area of the circle, then the angle at the centre is equal to **CBSE 2024 (Standard)**

(a) 110° (b) 130° (c) 100° (d) 126°

3. In the given figure, two concentric circles of radii 5 cm and 3 cm have their centre *O*. *OAB* is a sector of outer circle making an angle of 60° at the centre while *OCD* is the sector of smaller circle. The area of the shaded region is **CBSE 2024 (Basic)**

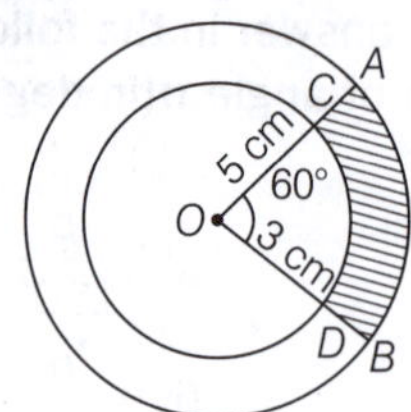

(a) $\frac{7\pi}{2} \text{ cm}^2$ (b) $\frac{8\pi}{3} \text{ cm}^2$

(c) $\frac{25\pi}{6} \text{ cm}^2$ (d) $\frac{3\pi}{2} \text{ cm}^2$

4. Perimeter of a sector of a circle whose central angle is 90° and radius 7 cm is **CBSE 2024 (Standard)**

(a) 35 cm (b) 11 cm (c) 22 cm (d) 25 cm

5. *OAB* is sector of a circle with centre *O* and radius 7 cm. If length of arc $\widehat{AB} = \frac{22}{3}$ cm, then $\angle AOB$ is equal to **CBSE 2025 (Basic)**

(a) $\left(\frac{120}{7}\right)^\circ$ (b) 45° (c) 60° (d) 30°

6. If length of an arc of a circle subtending an angle θ at the centre is numerically equal to the area of the sector formed by it, then the radius of the circle is **CBSE 2024 (Basic) Compartment**

(a) 1 unit (b) 2 units

(c) 3 units (d) $\frac{1}{2}$ unit

Assertion-Reason Type Questions

7. Assertion In the figure, *O* is the centre of a circle.

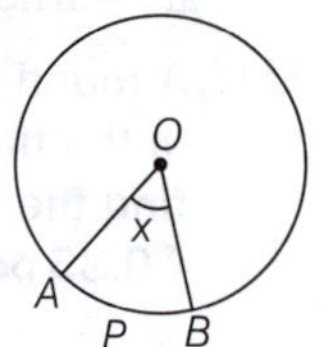

The area of sector *OAPB* is $\frac{5}{18}$ of the area of the circle, then the value of x is 100°.

Reason Length of an arc of a circle with radius r and central angle θ is given by $l = \frac{\theta}{360^\circ} \times \pi r^2$

(a) Both Assertion and Reason are correct and Reason is the correct explanation of Assertion.
(b) Both Assertion and Reason are correct, but Reason is not the correct explanation of Assertion.
(c) Assertion is correct but Reason is incorrect.
(d) Assertion is incorrect but Reason is correct.

8. Assertion The area of the sector of a circle of radius 5 cm is 9.75 cm^2, if the corresponding arc length is 3.5 cm.

Reason Area of a sector of a circle of radius r and central angle θ is $\frac{\theta}{360^\circ} \times \pi r^2$.

(a) Both Assertion and Reason are correct and Reason is the correct explanation of Assertion.
(b) Both Assertion and Reason are correct, but Reason is not the correct explanation of Assertion.
(c) Assertion is correct but Reason is incorrect.
(d) Assertion is incorrect but Reason is correct.

9. Assertion If the radius of sector of a circle is reduced to its half and angle is doubled, then the perimeter of the sector remains the same.

Reason The length of the arc subtending angle θ at the centre of a circle of radius, $r = \frac{\pi r \theta}{180^\circ}$.

CBSE Sample Paper 2025 (Standard)

(a) Both Assertion and Reason are correct and Reason is the correct explanation of Assertion.
(b) Both Assertion and Reason are correct, but Reason is not the correct explanation of Assertion.
(c) Assertion is correct but Reason is incorrect.
(d) Assertion is incorrect but Reason is correct.

Case Study Based Questions

10. A stable owner has four horses. He usually tie these horses with 7 m long rope to pegs at each corner of a square shaped grass field of 20 m length, to graze in his farm. But tying with rope sometimes results in injuries to his horses, so he decided to build fence around the area, so that each horse can graze. **CBSE 2024**

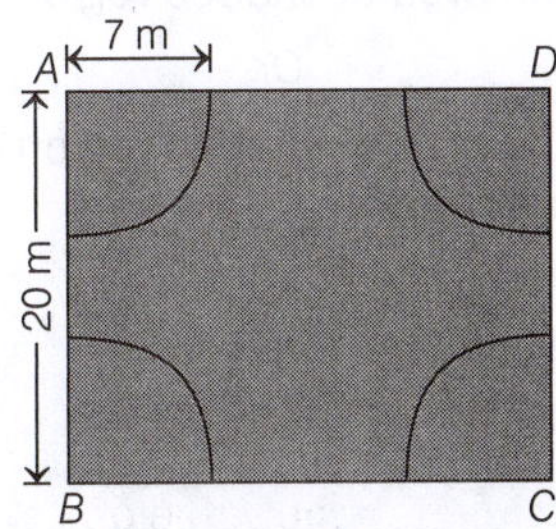

Based on the above information, answer the following questions.

(i) Find the area of the square shaped grass field.

(ii) (a) Find the area of the total field in which these horses can graze.

Or

(b) If the length of the rope of each horse is increased from 7m to 10m, then find the area grazed by one horse. [take, $\pi = 3.14$]

(iii) What is area of the field that is left ungrazed, if the length of the rope of each horse is 7 cm?

11. Heena hold a Japanese fan in her hand as shown in the figure. It is shaped like a sector of a circle and made of a thin material such as paper or feather. The inner and outer radii are 6 cm and 10 cm, respectively. The fan has three colours i.e. pink, blue and black.

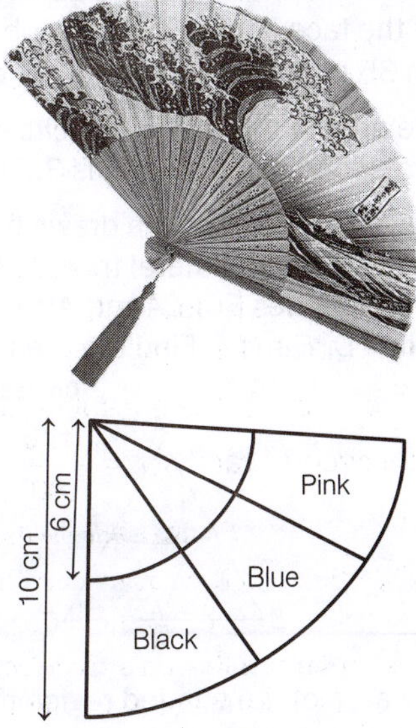

Based on the above information, answer the following questions.

(i) (a) If the region containing blue colour makes an angle of 80° at the centre, then find the area of the region having blue colour.

Or

(b) If the region containing black colour makes an angle of 40° at the centre, then find the area of the region having black colour.

(ii) If the region containing pink colour makes an angle of 30° at the centre, then find the perimeter of the region containing pink colour.

(iii) Find the area of the region having radius 6 cm.

12. A ferris wheel is rotating upright wheel with multiple passenger cars attached to the rim. The passenger cars are installed at equal distance from each other. Neeraj takes a picture of a ferris wheel.

He then makes a drawing of the picture and labels some points to make some calculations as under.

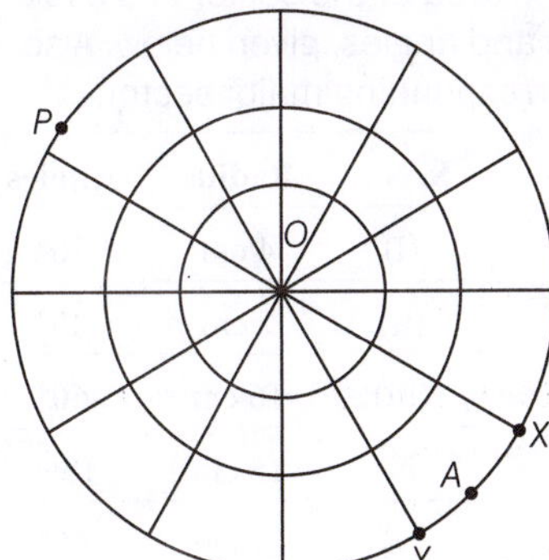

Point X and Y show the position of two consecutive passenger cars. The centre of the wheel is labelled O. The radius of the wheel is 16 m.

Based on the above information, answer the following questions.

(i) What is the measure of $\angle XOY$?

(ii) Each sector of the ferris wheel is to be decorated with lights of different colours. What is the area decorated by each light?

(iii) (a) What number should the area of sector $OYAX$ be multiplied with to get the area of sector $OYPX$?

Or

(b) What is the area of major sector $OYPXO$.

13. NSS (National Service Scheme) aims to connect the students to the community and to involve them in problem solving process.

NSS symbol is based on the 'Rath' wheel of the Konark Sun Temple situated in Odisha. The wheel signifies the progress cycle of life. The diagrammatic representation of the symbol is given below.

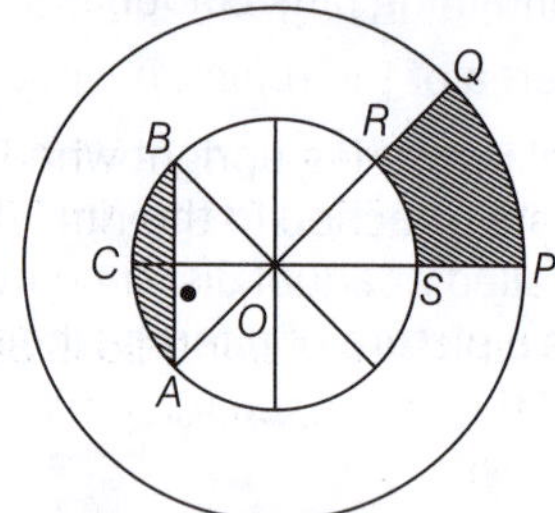

Observe the figure given above. The diameters of inner circle are equally placed. Given that $OP = 21$ cm and $OS = 10$ cm :

Based on the above information answer the following questions.

(i) Find $\angle ROS$

(ii) Find the perimeter of sector OPQ

(iii) (a) Find the area of shaded region $PQRS$.

Or

(b) Find the area of shaded region ACB i.e. the segment ACB. **CBSE 2024 (Basic)**

Part II

Very Short Answer Type Questions

1. The length of hour hand of a clock is 7 cm. Find the area swept by the hour hand in one hour.

2. If the area of a sector of a circle is $\frac{7}{18}$th of the area of that circle, then find the central angle of the sector.

3. Find the area of the sector of a circle with the following radius and angles, given below. Also, find the area of the corresponding major sector.

S. No.	Radius	Angles
(i)	4 cm	30°
(ii)	7 cm	45°
(iii)	16 cm	60°
(iv)	15 cm	135°
(v)	21 cm	90°

4. What will be the length of an arc of a sector of a circle with radius r and angle θ ?

5. In a circle of diameter 28 cm, if an arc subtends an angle of 60° at the centre where $\pi = \frac{22}{7}$, then what will be the length of arc? **Competency Based Question**

6. In a circle of radius 28 cm an arc subtends an angle of 60° at the centre. Find the length of the arc.

7. Area of a sector of a circle of radius 36 cm is 54π cm^2. Find the length of the corresponding arc of sector.

8. A circle has radius 5 cm. Three chords of lengths 6 cm, 8 cm and 10 cm are drawn. Which chord subtends the largest angle on its minor arc? **Competency Based Question**

Short Answer Type Questions

9. The minute hand of a wall clock is 18 cm long. Find the area of the face of the clock described by the minute hand in 35 min. **CBSE Sample Paper 2025 (Standard)**

10. The minute hand of a clock is 12 cm long. Find the area of the face of the clock described by the minute hand in 35 min. **CBSE 2020 (Standard)**

11. Find the area of the sector of a circle of radius 5 cm, if the corresponding arc length is 3.5 cm. **NCERT Exemplar**

12. In the given figure, arcs are drawn by taking vertices A, B and C of an equilateral triangle of side 10 cm, to intersect the sides BC, CA and AB at their respective mid-points D, E and F. Find the area of the shaded region. **Competency Based Question**

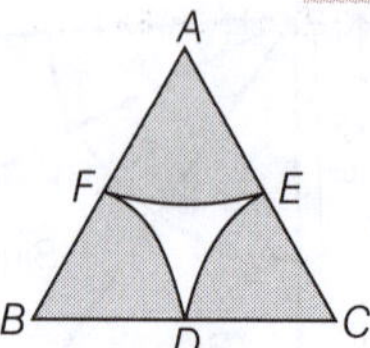

13. Find the area of the shaded region if length of radius of each circle is 7 cm. Each circle touches the other two externally. **CBSE 2024 (Standard) Compartment**

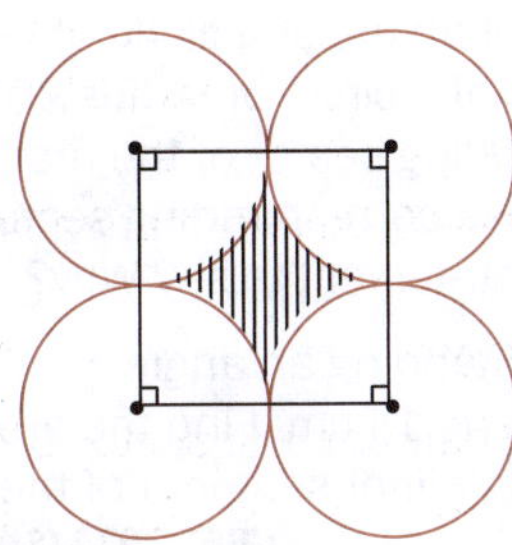

14. In the given figure, $ABCD$ is a square of side 10 cm. A sector of radius 5 cm is cut out from one of the corners. Find the area of the shaded region.

[take, $\pi = 3.14$] **CBSE 2024 Basic Compartment**

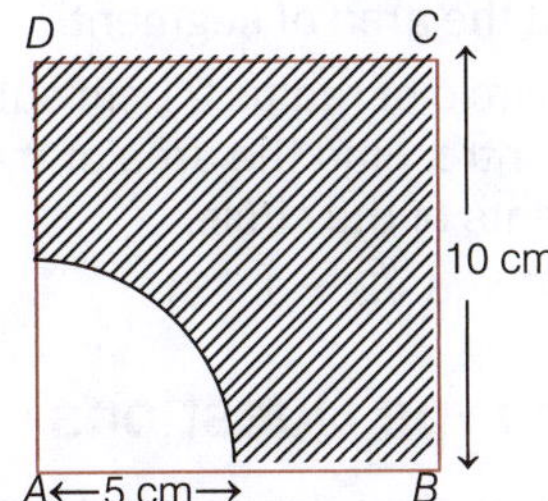

15. In the given figure, O is the centre of the concentric circles. Radius of the inner circle is half the radius of the outer circle. If $\angle DOC = 135°$ and $OD = 14$ cm, then calculate the area of the shaded region.

[leave your answer in terms of π]

Competency Based Question

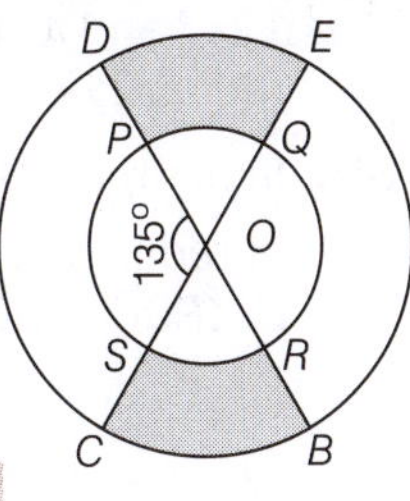

16. In the given figure, three sectors of a circle of radius 7 cm, making angles of 60°, 80° and 40° at the centre are shaded. Find the area of the shaded region. **CBSE 2019**

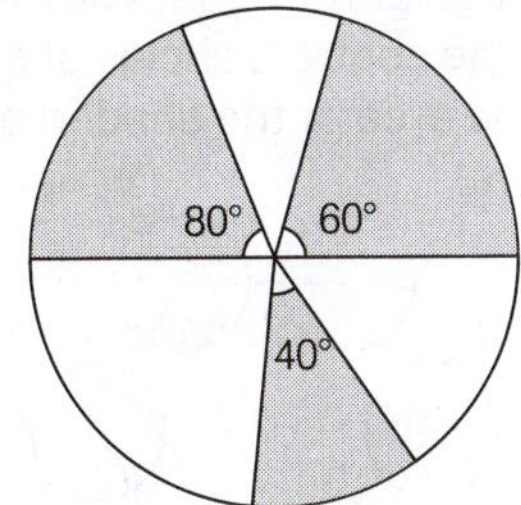

17. In the given figure, arcs have been drawn with radius 14 cm each and with centres P, Q and R. Find the area of the shaded region. **NCERT Exemplar; CBSE 2023 (Standard)**

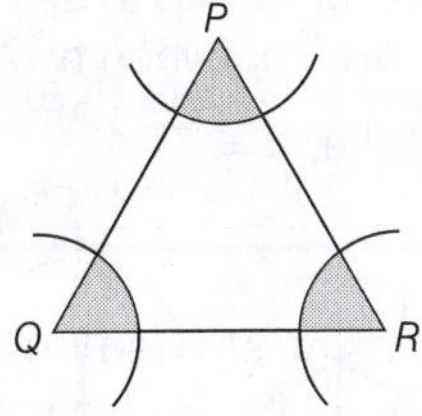

18. The figure below is a part of a circle with centre O. Its area is $\left(\frac{1250\pi}{9}\right)$ cm² and the 10 sectors are identical.

[**Note** The figure is not to scale]

Find the value of β, in degrees. Show your steps.

Competency Based Question

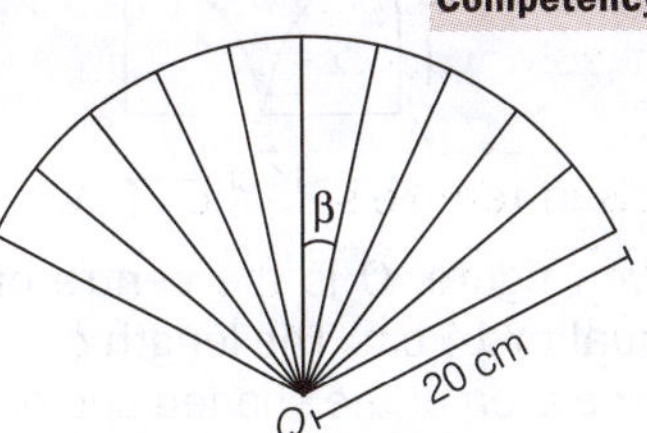

19. In a circular agricultural field, a sector subtending an angle of 120° at the centre is dedicated to growing sugarcane.

If the radius of the circular field is 30 m, then what is the area of the land used for growing sugarcane? Show your work. **CBSE QB**

(**Note** take, $\pi = 3.14$)

20. A Sonar system is deployed in a maritime environment to detect and alert submarines about potential underwater obstacles. The Sonar covers a sector with a central angle of 120° and has a maximum detection range of 3 km under water.

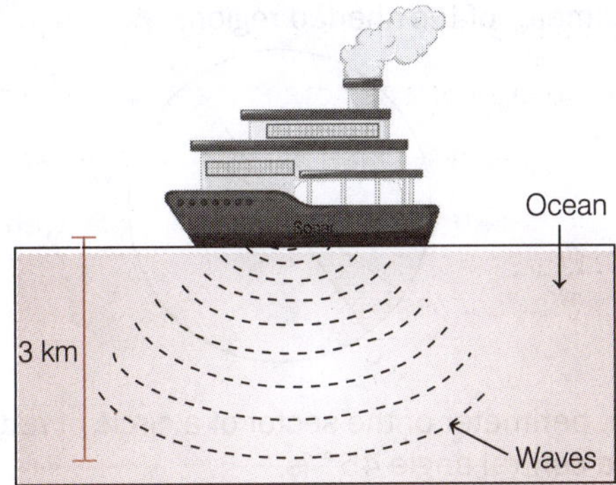

Approximately, how much area is covered by the Sonar during the monitoring period? Show your work. **CBSE QB**

(**Note** take, $\pi = 3.14$ if required)

21. In the given figure, $OABC$ is a square of side 7 cm. If $OAPC$ is a quadrant of a circle with centre O, then find the area of the shaded region.

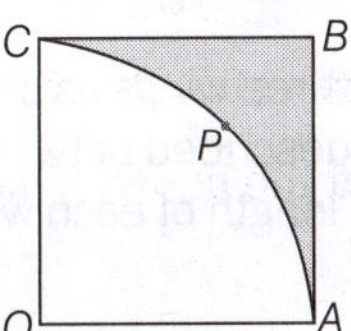

22. The length of the minute hand of a clock is 5 cm. Find the area swept by the minute hand during the time period 6 : 05 am and 6 : 40 am. **NCERT Exemplar**

23. Find the area of the shaded portion from the given figure.

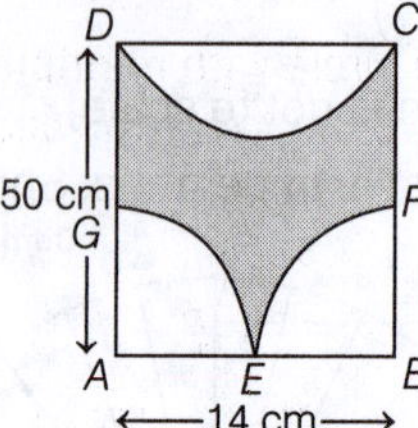

24. In the given figure, O is the centre of the circle with radius equal to 14 cm. The length of the arc $AB = 13.2$ cm. Find the area of the shaded sector of the circle.

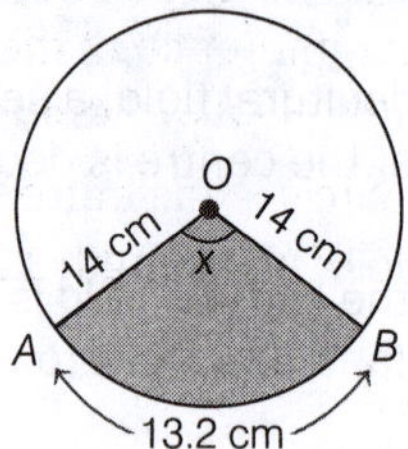

25. The radius of a circle is 17.5 cm. Find the area of the sector of the circle enclosed by two radii and an arc 44 cm in length. **CBSE 2020 (Basic)**

26. *AB* and *CD* are diameters of a circle with centre *O* and radius 7cm. If $\angle BOD = 30°$ then find the area and perimeter of the shaded region.

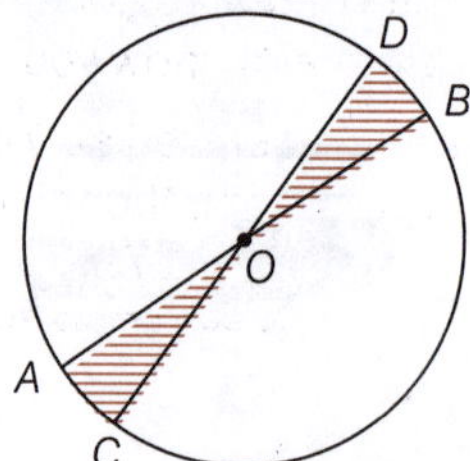

27. The perimeter of the sector of a circle of radius 14 cm and central angle 45° is **CBSE 2022**

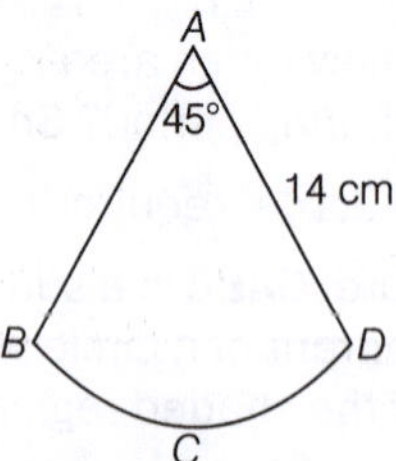

28. A ceiling fan has three wings as shown in the figure. Find the length of arc described between two consecutive wings, where the length of each wing is 0.98 m. **Competency Based Question**

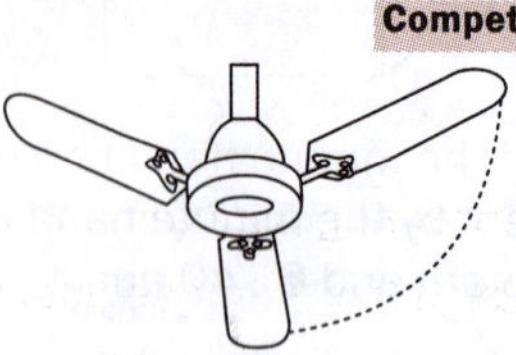

29. If the length of an arc of a circle of radius *r* is equal to that of an arc of a circle of radius 2*r*, then the angle of the corresponding sector of the first circle is double the angle of the corresponding sector of the other circle. Is this statement false? Why? **NCERT Exemplar**

30. A chord is subtending an angle of 90° at the centre of a circle of radius 14 cm. Find the area of the corresponding minor segment of the circle. **CBSE 2024 (Standard) Compartment**

31. A chord of a circle of radius 20 cm subtends an angle of 90° at the centre. Find the area of the corresponding major segment of the circle. [take, $\pi = 3.14$]

32. A chord 10 cm long is drawn in a circle whose radius is $\sqrt{50}$ cm. Find the area of segment.

33. A chord of a circle of radius 21 cm subtends an angle 60° at the centre. Find the area of the corresponding minor segments of the circle.
[use $\pi = 3.14$ and $\sqrt{3} = 1.73$]

Long Answer Type Questions

34. Find the difference of the areas of a sector of angle 120° and its corresponding major sector of a circle of radius 21 cm. **NCERT Exemplar**

35. In figure, $\overset{\frown}{PQ}$ and $\overset{\frown}{AB}$ are two arcs of concentric circles of radii 7 cm and 3.5 cm, respectively with centre *O*. If $\angle POQ = 30°$, then find the area of shaded region. **CBSE 2020 (Basic)**

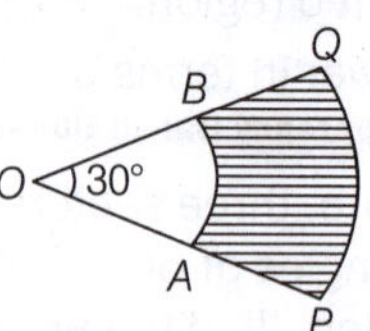

36. *ABCDEF* is a regular hexagon. With vertices *A, B, C, D, E* and *F* as the centres, circles of same radius *r* are drawn. Find the area of the shaded portion shown in the given figure. **Competency Based Question**

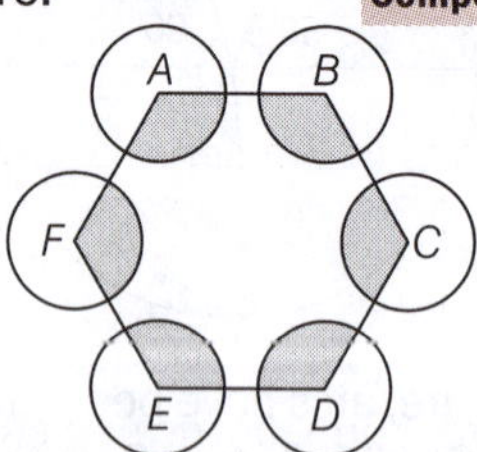

37. An umbrella has 6 ribs which are equally spaced (see figure). Assuming umbrella to be a flat circle of radius 35 cm, find the area between two consecutive ribs of the umbrella. $\left(\text{take, } \pi = \frac{22}{7}\right)$ **Competency Based Question**

38. Given below is a geometrical shape.

C is the centre of the circle with radius $BC = 21$ cm ABC is an isosceles right triangle. Calculate the area of the triangle outside the circular region? (take, $\pi = 3.14$) **Competency Based Question**

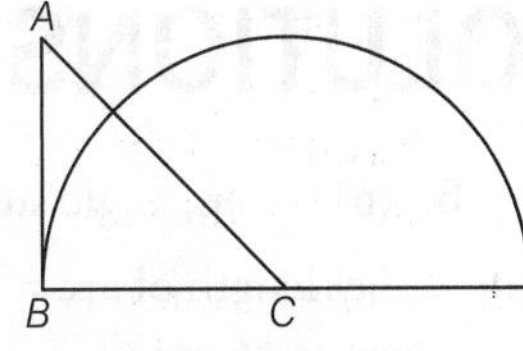

39. Avikant bought a pair of glasses with wiper blades. He was curious to know the area being cleaned by each of the wiper blades. With the help of a ruler and a protractor, he found the length of each blade as 3 cm and the angle swept as 60°.

(**Note** The figure is for visual representation only)

(i) Find the area that each wiper cleans in one swipe, in terms of π.

(ii) If the diameter of each circular glass is 5 cm, that what percent of the area of the glass will be cleaned by the blade in one swipe ?

Show your work. **Competency Based Question**

40. Shown below are two overlapping sectors of a circle. The radii of the sectors are 6 cm and 8 cm. The figure is divided into three regions I, II and III.

(**Note** the figure is not to scale)

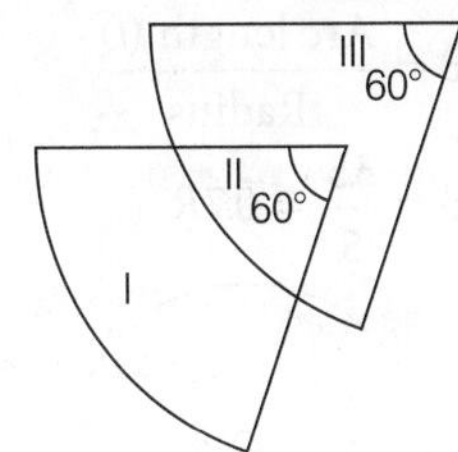

Find the difference in the areas of regions I and III.

Show your work. $\left[\text{take, } \pi = \frac{22}{7}\right]$

Competency Based Question

41. Shown below are 3 concentric circles with centre O. The tangent to the second circle AB, has a length of 5 cm. **Competency Based Question**

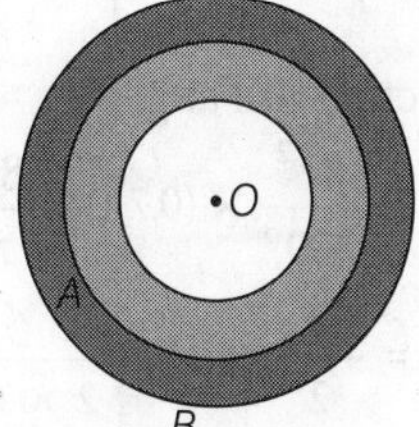

(**Note** The figure is not to scale.)

Find the area of the shaded region in terms of π. Draw a rough figure and show your work.

42. Shown below is a circle with multiple chords. One of the chords is the diameter of the circle.

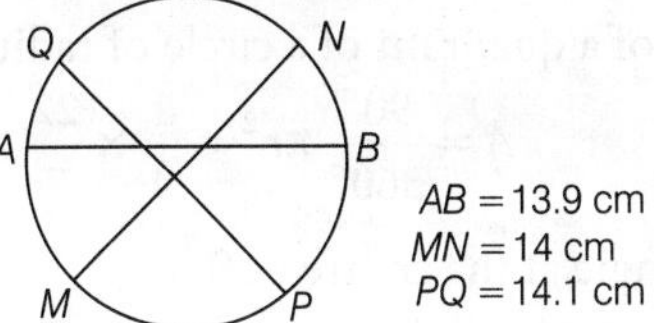

(**Note** The figure is not to scale.)

Find the measure of the angle subtended by an arc 4.7π cm at the circumference of the circle. Show your work and give valid reasons. **Competency Based Question**

43. Shown below is a circle with centre O. PQR is an equilateral triangle of side length 12 cm.

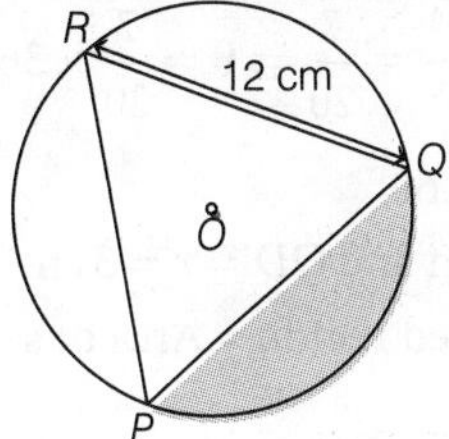

(**Note** The figure is not to scale.)

Find the area of the shaded region in terms of π. Draw a rough diagram and show your work.

44. AB is a chord of a circle centred at O such that $\angle AOB = 60°$. If $OA = 14$ cm, then find the area of the minor segment. (take, $\sqrt{3} = 1.73$)

CBSE Sample Paper 2025 (Standard)

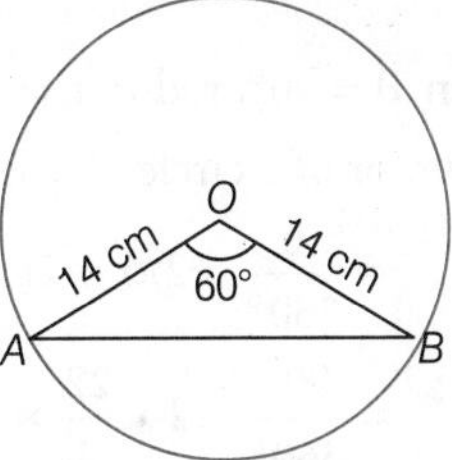

45. The perimeter of sector $OACB$ of the circle centred at O of radius 24, is 73.12 cm. **CBSE Sample Paper 2025 (Basic)**

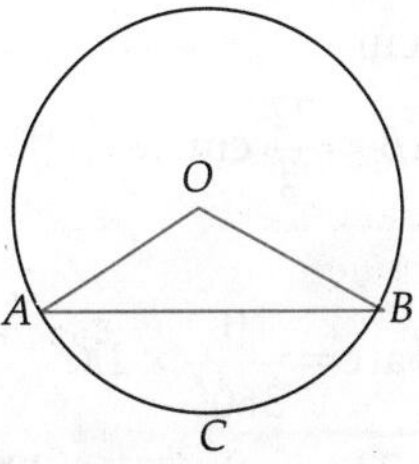

(i) Find the central angle $\angle AOB$.

(ii) Find the area of the minor segment ACB.

(take, $\pi = 3.14$ and $\sqrt{3} = 1.73$)

HINTS & SOLUTIONS

Part I

1. (c) Area of a quadrant of a circle of radius r is given by

$$A = \frac{90^\circ}{360^\circ}\pi r^2 = \frac{1}{4}\times\frac{22}{7}\times 7^2 = \frac{77}{2}\text{ cm}^2$$

2. (d) Let angle at the centre be θ.

We know that

Area of a sector of a circle $= \frac{\theta}{360^\circ}\times \pi r^2$

and area of circle $= \pi r^2$

According to the question,

$$\frac{\theta}{360^\circ}\times\pi r^2 = \frac{7}{20}\times \pi r^2$$

$$\Rightarrow \frac{\theta}{360^\circ} = \frac{7}{20} \Rightarrow \theta = \frac{7}{20}\times 360^\circ = 126^\circ$$

3. (b) Given, $\theta = 60^\circ$

$OA = R = 5$ cm and $OD = r = 3$ cm

$\therefore$ Area of shaded region = Area of sector OAB − Area of sector OCD

$$= \frac{\theta}{360^\circ}\times\pi R^2 - \frac{\theta}{360^\circ}\times \pi r^2$$

$$= \frac{\theta}{360^\circ}\pi(R^2 - r^2)$$

$$= \frac{60^\circ}{360^\circ}\pi(5^2 - 3^2) = \frac{8}{3}\pi$$

Hence, the area of shaded region is $\frac{8}{3}\pi$ cm^2.

4. (d) **Hint** Given, $\theta = 90^\circ$, radius $r = 7$ cm

Perimeter of sector of a circle

$$= \frac{\theta}{360^\circ}\times 2\pi r + 2r$$

$$= \frac{90^\circ}{360^\circ}\times 2\times\frac{22}{7}\times 7 + 2\times 7$$

$$= 11 + 14 = 25$$

$\therefore$ Perimeter of sector of circle is 25 cm.

5. (c) Radius = 7 cm

Length of arc $\widehat{AB} = \frac{22}{3}$ cm

Let $\angle AOB = \theta$

Now, length of arc $= \frac{\theta}{360^\circ}\times 2\pi r$

$$\Rightarrow \frac{22}{3} = \frac{\theta}{360^\circ}\times 2\times\frac{22}{7}\times 7$$

$$\Rightarrow \frac{22\times 360}{3\times 2\times 22} = \theta \Rightarrow \theta = 60^\circ$$

6. (b) Given, angle subtended by the arc $= \theta$

Let length of arc = Area of sector $= x$

We know that

$$\text{Area of sector} = \frac{1}{2}\times\text{Length of arc}\times\text{Radius}$$

$$\Rightarrow x = \frac{1}{2}\times x\times\text{Radius}$$

$\therefore$ Radius = 2 units

7. (c) Area of sector $OAPB = \frac{x}{360^\circ}\times\pi r^2$

$$\Rightarrow \frac{x}{360^\circ}\times\pi r^2 = \frac{5}{18}\pi r^2$$

$$\Rightarrow \frac{x}{360^\circ} = \frac{5}{18}$$

$$\Rightarrow x = 100^\circ$$

So, Assertion is correct.

Now, length of an arc of a circle using radius r and central angle θ, $l = \frac{\theta^\circ}{360^\circ}\times 2\pi r$

So, Reason is incorrect.

8. (d) Let the central angle of the sector be θ.

Given that radius of the sector of circle, $r = 5$ cm

and arc length, $l = 3.5$ cm

$\therefore$ Central angle of the sector,

$$\theta = \frac{\text{Arc length }(l)}{\text{Radius}}$$

$$\Rightarrow \theta = \frac{3.5}{5} = 0.7R \qquad \left[\because \theta = \frac{l}{r}\right]$$

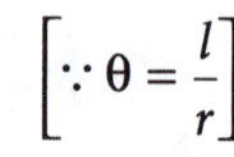

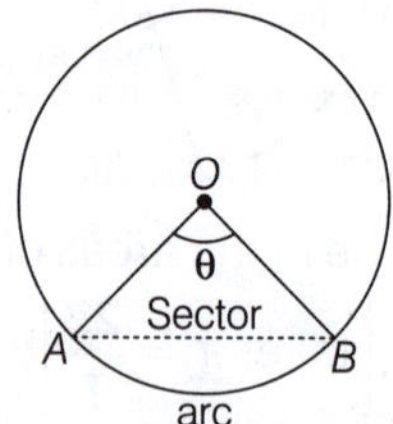

$$\Rightarrow \theta = \left(0.7\times\frac{180}{\pi}\right)^\circ$$

$$\left[\because 1\text{ radian} = \frac{180^\circ}{\pi}\text{ degree}\right]$$

Now, area of sector with angle θ

$$= \frac{\pi r^2}{360^\circ}\times(0.7)\times\frac{180^\circ}{\pi}$$

$$= \frac{(5)^2}{2}\times 0.7 = \frac{25\times 7}{2\times 10} = 8.75\text{ cm}^2$$

Hence, Assertion is incorrect but Reason is correct.

9. (d) Let r be the radius and θ be the angle of the sector.

$\therefore$ Perimeter, $P = 2r + r\theta$

When radius is reduced to half and angle is doubled.

$\therefore$ Perimeter, $P' = 2\left(\frac{r}{2}\right) + \frac{r}{2} \cdot 2\theta = r + r\theta$

$\Rightarrow \quad P' \neq P$

Hence, perimeter of sector are not the same.

Reason The length of the arc subtending angle θ at the centre of a circle of radius, $r = \frac{\pi r\theta}{180°}$

So, Assertion is incorrect but Reason is correct.

10. (i) Length of the square shaped grass field = 20 m

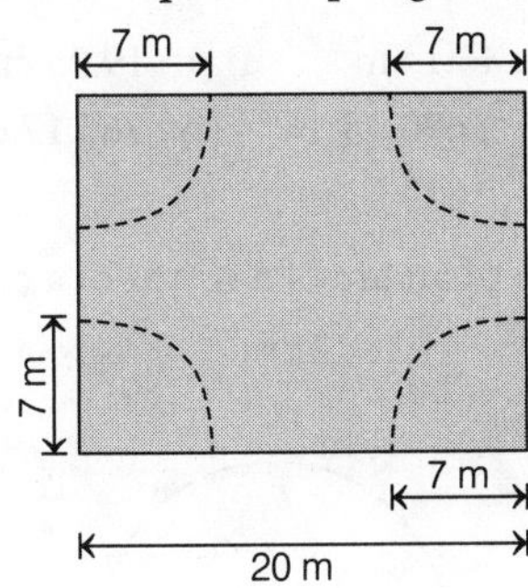

$\therefore$ Area of the square shaped grass field

$= 20 \times 20 = 400 \text{ m}^2$

(ii) (a) Length of the rope = 7 m

Thus, each horse can graze upto 7 m of distance along the side.

The grazed area is making a complete circle by taking all the four grazed parts.

So, area of grazed part $= \pi r^2$

$= \frac{22}{7} \times 7^2 = 22 \times 7 = 154 \text{ m}^2$

Therefore, area of the total field in which these horses can graze is 154 m^2.

Or

(b) New length of the rope of each horse = 10 m

Area grazed by one horse $= \frac{1}{4}\pi r^2$

$= \frac{1}{4} \times 3.14 \times 10^2 = \frac{314}{4} = 78.5 \text{ m}^2$

Therefore, the required area grazed by one horse is 78.5 m^2.

(iii) Length of rope of each horse = 7 m

Area of square shaped grass field = 400 m^2 [from part (i)]

Area of total field grazed by horses = 154 m^2 [from part (ii) (a)]

Area of field left ungrazed

= Area of square field

– Area of grazed field by horses

$= 400 - 154 = 246 \text{ m}^2$

Therefore, area of field left ungrazed is 246m^2.

11. Hint (i) (a) Area of region having blue colour

$= \frac{80°}{360°} \pi [(10)^2 - (6^2)]$ **Ans.** 44.69 cm^2

Or

(b) Area of region having black colour

$= \frac{40°}{360°} \pi [(10)^2 - (6)^2]$

Ans. 22.34 cm^2

(ii) Perimeter of the region having pink colour

= 2 (10 – 6) + Length of arc having radius 6 cm

+ Length of arc having radius 10 cm

Ans. 16.38 cm

(iii) Area of region $= \frac{150°}{360°} \times \pi r^2$

Ans. 47.14 cm^2

12. (i) Since, there are 12 equal sectors, therefore angle of each sector $= \frac{360°}{12} = 30°$

$\therefore \quad \angle XOY = 30°$

(ii) Angle of each sector = 30°

Given, radius of the wheel = 16 m

$\therefore$ Area of each sector $= \frac{30°}{360°} \times \pi r^2$

$= \frac{1}{12} \times 16 \times 16 \times \pi$

$= 21.33 \, \pi \text{ m}^2$

(iii) (a) Sector *OYPX* consists of 11 equal sector, therefore 11 should be multiplied by area of sector *OYAX* to get the area of sector *OYPX*.

Or

(b) Area of major sector *OYPXO*

= Area of circle

– Area of minor sector *OYAXO*.

$= \pi r^2 - \frac{30°}{360°} \pi r^2$

$= \pi \times 16^2 \left[1 - \frac{1}{12}\right]$

$= \pi \times 256 \times \frac{11}{12}$

$= 737.23 \text{ cm}^2$

13.

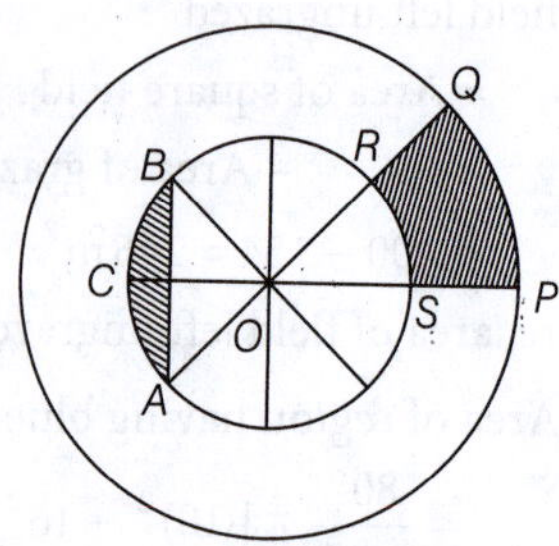

Given, $OP = 21\text{cm}$ and $OS = 10$ cm

(i) The inner circle is divided into 8 equal sectors.

Central angle of circle = 360°

$\angle ROS = \frac{360°}{8} = 45°$

Therefore, $m\angle ROS = 45°$

(ii) We know that perimeter of sector OPQ

$= \frac{\theta}{360°} \times 2\pi r + 2r = \frac{45}{360} \times 2 \times \frac{22}{7} \times 21 + 2 \times 21$

[$\because$ given $OP = 21$cm and $m\angle ROS = 45°$]

$= 16.5 \text{ cm} + 42 \text{ cm} = 58.5 \text{ cm}$

(iii) (a) Area of shaded region $PQRS$

= Area of sector OPQ – Area of sector ORS

$= \frac{\theta}{360°} \times \pi(OP)^2 - \frac{\theta}{360°} \times \pi(OS)^2$

$= \frac{\theta}{360°} \times \pi[(OP)^2 - (OS)^2]$

$= \frac{45}{360} \times \frac{22}{7}[(21)^2 - (10)^2]$

$= \frac{1}{8} \times \frac{22}{7} \times [441 - 100]$

$= \frac{1}{8} \times \frac{22}{7} \times 341 = 133.96 \text{ cm}^2$

(b) From figure, we have

$\angle AOB = 90°$

$\therefore$ Area of segment ACB

$= \pi(OA)^2 \frac{90°}{360°} - \text{ar } \Delta(AOB)$

$= \pi \times 100 \times \frac{1}{4} - \frac{1}{2} \times 10 \times 10$

$= 25\pi - 100 \times \frac{1}{2}$

$= 25\pi - 50$

$= 25(\pi - 2)$

$= 25\left(\frac{22}{7} - 2\right)$

$= 25 \times \frac{8}{7}$

$= \frac{200}{7} \text{ cm}^2$

Part II

1. **Hint** Angle described by hour hand in 1 h $= \frac{360°}{12} = 30°$

$\therefore$ Area swept $= \frac{30°}{360°} \times \pi \times (7)^2 \text{ cm}^2$ **Ans.** 12.83 cm^2

2. **Hint** Area of sector of circle

$= \frac{7}{18} \times$ Area of the same circle

$\Rightarrow \frac{\theta}{360°} \times \pi r^2 = \frac{7}{18} \times \pi r^2$ [$\because r$ = radius of circle]

Ans. 140°

3. **Hint** Do same as Example 2.

Ans.

(i) $4.19 \text{ cm}^2, 46.1 \text{ cm}^2$ (ii) $19.25 \text{ cm}^2, 134.74 \text{ cm}^2$

(iii) $134.09 \text{ cm}^2, 670.48 \text{cm}^2$ (iv) $265.17 \text{ cm}^2, 441.97 \text{ cm}^2$

(v) $346.5 \text{ cm}^2, 1039.5 \text{ cm}^2$

4. **Hint** Length of an arc of a sector of a circle with radius r and angle θ is $\frac{\theta}{360°} \times 2\pi r$ i.e. $\frac{\theta}{180°} \times \pi r$.

5.

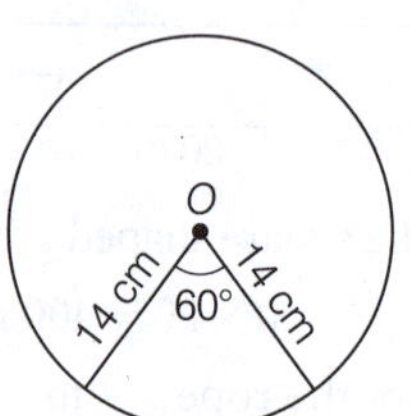

Length of arc $= \frac{\theta}{360°} \times 2\pi r$

$= \frac{60°}{360°} \times 2 \times \frac{22}{7} \times 14 = 14.6 \text{ cm}$

6. **Hint** Do same as Example 2. **Ans.** 29.33 cm

7. **Hint** Length of arc $= \frac{2 \times \text{Area of sector}}{\text{Radius}}$ **Ans.** 3π cm

8. Radius = 5 cm, chords of lengths 6 cm, 8 cm and 10 cm.

$\therefore \sin\theta = \frac{3}{5} = 0.6 = 36.87°$

[$\because$ perpendicular drawn from the centre of a circle bisects the chord]

$\sin\theta = \frac{4}{5} = 0.8 = 53.13°$

$\sin\theta = \frac{5}{5} = 1 = 90°$

$\therefore$ The chord of lengths 10 cm subtends the largest angle on its minor arc.

9. Angle described by minute hand in 5 min = 30°

Length of minute hand = 18 cm = r

Angle described by minute hand in 35 min

$= 7 \times 30° = 210°$

$\therefore$ Area swept by minute hand in 35 min

$$= \frac{\theta}{360^\circ} \times \pi r^2$$

$$= \frac{210^\circ}{360^\circ} \times \frac{22}{7} \times 18 \times 18 = 594 \text{ cm}^2$$

10. We have,

Angle described by the minute hand in 1 min = 6°

Angle described by the minute hand in 35 min

$= 6 \times 35^\circ = 210^\circ$

$\therefore$ Area swept by the minute hand in 35 min

= Area of a sector of angle 210° in a circle of radius 12 cm

$$= \frac{210^\circ}{360^\circ} \times \frac{22}{7} \times (12)^2 = \frac{1}{12} \times 22 \times 12 \times 12 = 264 \text{ cm}^2$$

11. Hint Area of sector of circle having radius (r) and length (l) $= \frac{1}{2} rl$ **Ans.** 8.75 cm^2

12. Hint Total area of shaded region

= 3 × Area of each sector

= 3 × Area of sector $AFEA$

$$= 3 \times \frac{60^\circ}{360^\circ} \times \pi \times (5)^2$$

Ans. 39.29 cm^2

13. Hint Given, radius of circle = 7 cm

According to figure, side of square = 7 + 7 = 14 cm

Area of square = $(14)^2$ = 196 cm^2

$$\text{Area of one sector} = \frac{90^\circ}{360^\circ} \times \pi \times (7)^2$$

$$= \frac{1}{4} \times \frac{22}{7} \times (7)^2 = \frac{77}{2} \text{ cm}^2$$

Now, area of shaded region

= Area of square − 4 × Area of sector

$$= 196 - 4 \times \frac{77}{2} = 196 - 154 = 42 \text{ cm}^2$$

14. Hint Area of shaded region

= Area of square − Area of sector

$$= 10^2 - \frac{90^\circ}{360^\circ} \times 3.14 \times 25$$

$= 100 - 19.625 = 80.375$ cm^2

15. Hint $\angle DOE = \angle COB = \theta$ [let]

[vertically opposite angles]

$\Rightarrow \angle DOE + 135^\circ = 180^\circ$ [by linear pair as EOC is a line]

$\therefore \quad \theta = 45^\circ$

Area of shaded region

= 2 (area of sector DOE − area of sector POQ)

Ans. $\frac{147}{4} \pi$ cm^2

16. Hint Area of shaded region

= Sum of area of three sectors

$$= \frac{60^\circ}{360^\circ} \pi r^2 + \frac{80^\circ}{360^\circ} \pi r^2 + \frac{40^\circ}{360^\circ} \pi r^2$$

$$= \frac{\pi r^2}{360^\circ} [60^\circ + 80^\circ + 40^\circ]$$

$$= \frac{22}{7} \times 49 \times \frac{180^\circ}{360^\circ}$$

$= 77$ cm^2

17. Hint Area of sector with central $\angle P$

$$= \frac{\angle P}{360^\circ} \times \pi \times (14)^2$$

Area of sector with central $\angle Q$

$$= \frac{\angle Q}{360^\circ} \times \pi \times (14)^2$$

and area of sector with central $\angle R$

$$= \frac{\angle R}{360^\circ} \times \pi \times (14)^2$$

Now, area of shaded region

$$= (14)^2 \times \pi \frac{(\angle P + \angle Q + \angle R)}{360^\circ}$$

$$= 196 \times \pi \times \frac{180^\circ}{360^\circ}$$

[by angle sum property of triangle]

Ans. 308 cm^2

18. Area of sector $= \frac{1250\pi}{9}$ cm^2 [given]

$\Rightarrow \quad \frac{\theta}{360^\circ} \times \pi \times (20)^2 = \frac{1250\pi}{9}$ [$\because$ radius = 20 cm]

$\Rightarrow \quad \theta = \frac{1250\pi}{9} \times \frac{360^\circ}{\pi \times 400}$

$\Rightarrow \quad \theta = 125^\circ$

θ = value of 10 sectors

$\therefore \quad \beta = \frac{\theta}{10} = \frac{125^\circ}{10^\circ} = 12.5^\circ$

Thus, value of $\beta = 12.5^\circ$

19. Given, angle subtended by a sector of a circular field = 120°

and radius of the circular field = 30 m

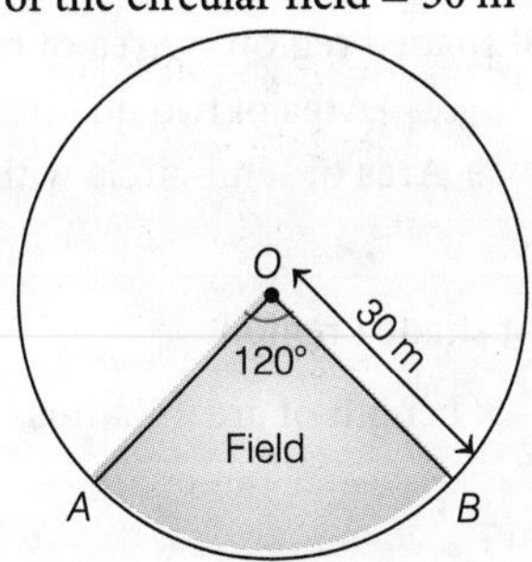

∴ Area of the land used for growing sugarcane

= Area of sector of the circle.

$$= \pi r^2 \times \frac{\theta}{360°} = 3.14 \times 30 \times 30 \times \frac{120°}{360°}$$

$$= 314 \times 9 \times \frac{1}{3} = 314 \times 3 = 942 \text{ m}^2$$

Hence, the area of land used for growing sugarcane is 942 m^2.

20. Given maximum detection range of Sonar = 3 km

i.e. Radius of sector of circle = 3 km

Angle made by sector to the centre = 120°

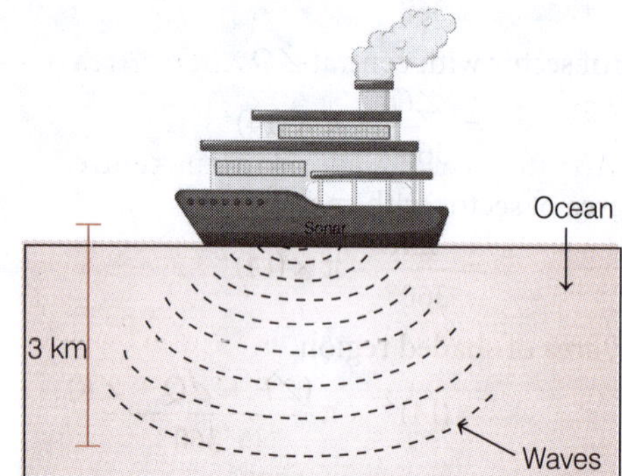

∵ The area covered by Sonar during the monitoring period

= Area of sector of the circle

$$= \pi r^2 \times \frac{\theta}{360°} = 3.14 \times 3 \times 3 \times \frac{120°}{360°}$$

$$= 3.14 \times 9 \times \frac{1}{3} = 3.14 \times 3 = 9.42 \text{ km}^2$$

Hence, the area covered by Sonar during the monitoring period is 9.42 km^2.

21. Hint Area of shaded region

= Area of square $OABC$ – Area of quadrant $OAPCO$

$$= (OA)^2 - \frac{1}{4} \times \pi (OA)^2$$

Ans. 10.5 cm^2

22. Hint Do same as Example 1.

Ans. $45\frac{5}{6}$ cm^2

23. Hint Area of shaded region = Area of rectangle $ABCD$

– (Area of two quadrants AEG and EBF

+ Area of semi-circle with CD as diameter)

Ans. 546 cm^2

24. Hint Area of shaded region

$$= \frac{1}{2} \times \text{Length of arc} \times \text{Radius}$$

Ans. 92.4 cm^2

25. Given, radius = 17.5 cm and length of the arc = 44 cm

Now, length of the arc $= \frac{2\pi r}{360°} \times \theta$

$$\Rightarrow \quad 44 = 2 \times \frac{22}{7} \times 17.5 \times \frac{\theta}{360°}$$

$$\Rightarrow \quad \theta = \frac{44 \times 7 \times 360°}{44 \times 17.5} = 144°$$

Also, area of the sector $= \frac{\pi r^2 \theta}{360°} = \frac{22}{7} \times 17.5 \times 17.5 \times \frac{144°}{360°}$

$$= 385 \text{ cm}^2$$

26. Hint Area of sector $= \frac{\theta}{360°} \times \pi r^2$

$$= \frac{30°}{360°} \times \pi \times 7 \times 7 = \frac{49\pi}{12}$$

Area of shaded region = 2 × Area of one sector

$$= 2 \times \frac{49\pi}{12} = \frac{49\pi}{6} \text{ cm}^2$$

Length of arc $= \frac{\theta}{360°} \times 2\pi r$

$$= \frac{30°}{360°} \times 2 \times \pi \times 7$$

$$= \frac{14\pi}{12} = \frac{7\pi}{6} \text{ cm}$$

∴ Perimeter of shaded region = 2 × Length of arc + $4r$

$$= 2 \times \frac{7\pi}{6} + 4 \times 7$$

$$= \frac{7\pi}{3} + 28 \text{ cm}$$

27. We have, radius = 14 cm

$\angle BAD = 45°$

According to the question,

Perimeter = 2 (Radius) + arc BCD

∴ Length of arc $= \frac{\theta}{360°} \times 2\pi r = \frac{45°}{360°} \times 2 \times \frac{22}{7} \times 14$

$= 11$ cm

∴ Perimeter = 2 × 14 + 11 = 28 + 11 = 39 cm

Hence, perimeter of the sector $ABCDA$ is 39 cm.

28. Hint Area of each sector

$$= \frac{120°}{360°} \times \text{Area of circle form by wings of fan}$$

$$= \frac{1}{3} \times \frac{22}{7} \times (0.98)^2 \quad \ldots\text{(i)}$$

Area of each sector $= \frac{1}{2} \times 0.98 \times l$ ...(ii)

From Eqs.(i) and (ii), we get

$$\frac{1}{2} \times 0.98 \times l = \frac{1}{3} \times \frac{22}{7} \times (0.98)^2$$

Ans. 2.05 m

29. Hint No; Let two circles be C_1 and C_2 of radii r and $2r$ with centres O and O', respectively.

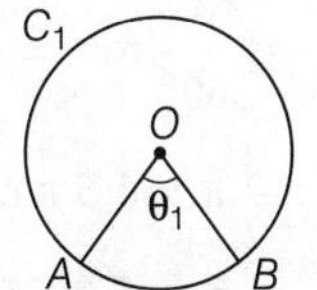

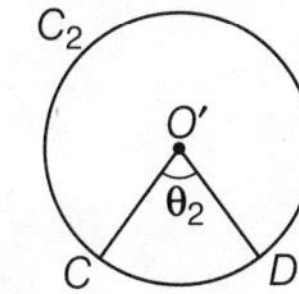

It is given that the arc length AB of C_1 is equal to arc length CD of C_2 i.e. $\widehat{AB} = \widehat{CD}$ ...(i)

Now, let θ_1 be the angle subtended by arc AB and θ_2 be the angle subtended by arc CD at the centre.

$\therefore \quad \widehat{AB} = \frac{\theta_1}{360^\circ} \times 2\pi r$

and $\quad \widehat{CD} = \frac{\theta_2}{360^\circ} \times 2\pi(2r) = \frac{\theta_2}{360^\circ} \times 4\pi r$

From Eq. (i), $\widehat{AB} = \widehat{CD}$

$\Rightarrow \quad \frac{\theta_1}{360^\circ} \times 2\pi r = \frac{\theta_2}{360^\circ} \times 4\pi r$

$\Rightarrow \quad \theta_1 = 2\theta_2$

i.e. angle of the corresponding sector of C_1 is double the angle of the corresponding sector of C_2.

Hence, the statement is true.

30. Hint Given, $\theta = 90^\circ$ and $r = 14$ cm

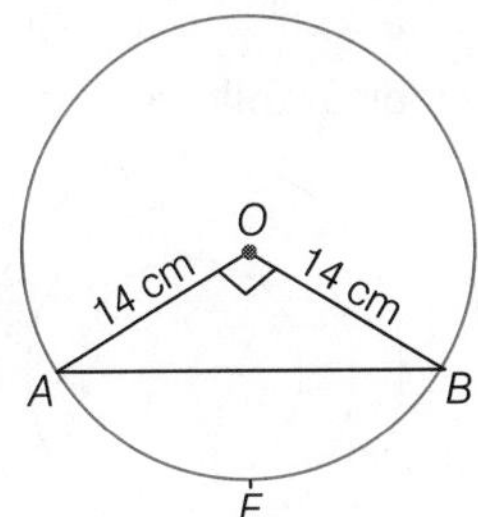

Area of $\Delta AOB = \frac{1}{2} \times OA \times OB$

$= \frac{1}{2} \times 14 \times 14 = 98 \text{ cm}^2$

Area of sector $OAEBO = \frac{\theta}{360^\circ} \times \pi r^2$

$= \frac{90^\circ}{360^\circ} \times \frac{22}{7} \times 14 \times 14$

$= 154 \text{ cm}^2$

Area of minor segment of the circle

$AEBA = 154 - 98$

$= 56 \text{ cm}^2$

31. Hint For finding area of minor segment, refer Example 3

Area of major segment = Area of circle − Area of minor segment

Ans. 1142 cm^2

32. Hint Since, OM bisects chord AB

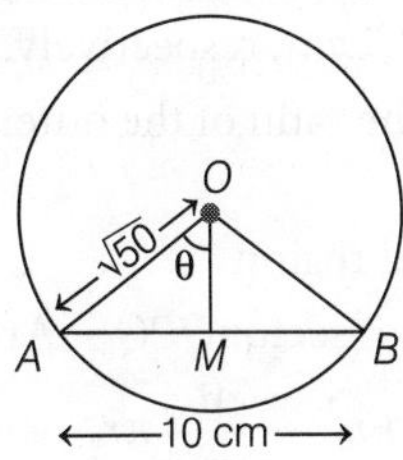

$\therefore \quad AM = \frac{AB}{2} = 5$ cm

In ΔOMA, $\sin\theta = \frac{AM}{OA} = \frac{1}{\sqrt{2}}$ $\left[\because \sin\theta = \frac{\text{perpendicular}}{\text{hypotenuse}}\right]$

$\Rightarrow \quad \theta = 45^\circ$

Area of segment = Area of sector ABO − Area of ΔOAB

Ans. 14.28 cm^2

33. Chord AB subtends an angle 60° at the centre.

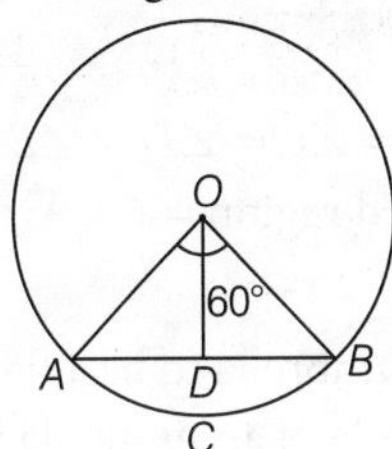

$\therefore \quad \angle AOB = 60^\circ$ and $\angle OAB = \angle OBA = x$ [let]

[$\because$ angles opposite to equal sides are equal]

In ΔAOB, $\angle AOB + \angle OBA + \angle OAB = 180^\circ$

$\Rightarrow \quad 60^\circ + x + x = 180^\circ \Rightarrow x = 60^\circ$

So, ΔAOB is an equilateral triangle.

Now, area of $\Delta AOB = \frac{\sqrt{3}}{4}a^2 = \frac{\sqrt{3}}{4} \times (21)^2 = 190.95 \text{ cm}^2$

Area of sector $OACBD = \frac{\theta}{360^\circ} \times \pi r^2$

$= \frac{60^\circ}{360^\circ} \times 3.14 \times (21)^2 = 230.79 \text{ cm}^2$

$\therefore$ Area of minor segment $ACBDA$

= Area of sector $OACBO$ − Area of ΔAOB

$= (230.79 - 190.95) \text{ cm}^2 = 39.84 \text{ cm}^2$

34. Hint Difference of the area of minor sector $AOBA$ and its corresponding major sector $ABOA$

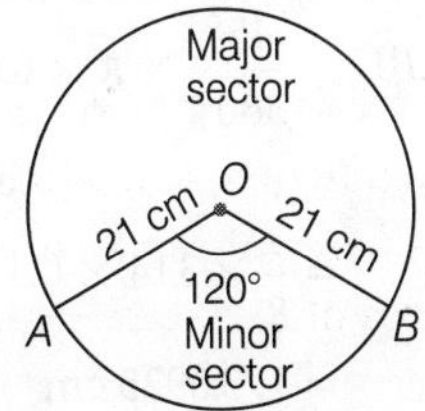

= Area of major sector $ABOA$ − Area of minor sector $AOBA$

= (Area of circle − Area of minor sector $AOBA$) − Area of minor sector $AOBA$

Ans. 462 cm^2

35. PQ and AB are the arcs of two concentric circles of radii 7 cm and 3.5 cm, respectively.

Let r_1 and r_2 be the radii of the outer and inner circle, respectively.

$\therefore$ Area of shaded region

$$= \text{Area of sector } OPQ - \text{Area of sector } OAB$$
$$= \frac{\theta}{360^\circ}\pi r_1^2 - \frac{\theta}{360^\circ}\pi r_2^2$$
$$= \frac{30^\circ}{360^\circ}\times\frac{22}{7}[7^2 - 3.5^2] = \frac{1}{12}\times\frac{22}{7}[49 - 12.25]$$
$$= \frac{1}{12}\times\frac{22}{7}\times 36.75 = 9.625$$

Therefore, the area of the shaded region is $9.625\ \text{cm}^2$.

36. Hint Each angle of regular hexagon $= \dfrac{\text{Sum of all angles}}{\text{Number of sides}}$

$$= \frac{(6-2)\times 180^\circ}{6} = 120^\circ$$

$\therefore \angle A = \angle B = \angle C = \angle D = \angle E = \angle F = 120^\circ$

Area of shaded region $= 6 \times$ Area of sector with $\angle A$.

Ans. $2\pi r^2$

37. Hint Given, umbrella to be a flat circle.

So, central angle of an umbrella is 360°.

$\therefore$ Angle between two ribs $= \dfrac{360^\circ}{6} = 60^\circ$

So, area between two ribs = Area of one sector of umbrella

Ans. $\dfrac{1925}{3}\ \text{cm}^2$

38. Given, radius $BC = 21\text{cm}$

$AB = BC$ [$\because \Delta ABC$ is an isosceles triangle]

$\Rightarrow \angle A = \angle C$ [angles opposite to equal sides]

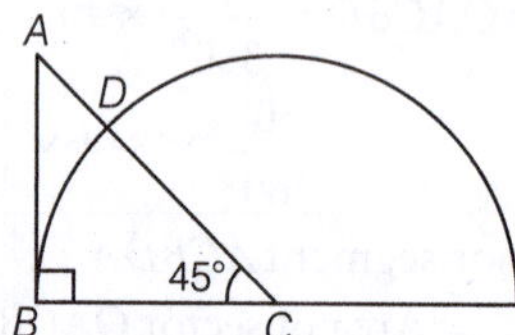

In ΔABC, $\angle A + \angle B + \angle C = 180^\circ$

$\Rightarrow \angle C + 90^\circ + \angle C = 180^\circ$ [$\because \angle A = \angle C$]

$\Rightarrow 2\angle C = 90^\circ \Rightarrow \angle C = 45^\circ$

Area of sector $CBD = \dfrac{45^\circ}{360^\circ}\times\pi\times(BC)^2$

[$\because$ angle of sector is 45°]

$$= \frac{1}{8}\times 3.14\times(21\times 21)\ [\because BC = 21\text{cm}]$$
$$= 173.0925\ \text{cm}^2$$

Area of $\Delta = \dfrac{1}{2}\times BC\times AB = \dfrac{1}{2}\times 21\times 21 = 220.5\ \text{cm}^2$

Area of the triangle outside the circular region

$$= \text{Area of } \Delta ABC - \text{Area of sector } CBD$$
$$= 220.5 - 173.0925 = 47.4075\ \text{cm}^2$$

39. (i) Radius = Length of wiper = 3 cm and Angle, $\theta = 60^\circ$

$\therefore$ Area that wiper cleans = Area of sector

$$= \frac{\theta}{360^\circ}\pi r^2 = \frac{60^\circ}{360^\circ}\times\pi\times(3)^2$$
$$= \frac{3}{2}\pi = 1.5\pi\ \text{cm}^2$$

(ii) Area of glass $= \pi r^2 = \pi\times\dfrac{5}{2}\times\dfrac{5}{2} = \dfrac{25}{4}\pi\ \text{cm}^2$

Percentage of area cleaned $= \dfrac{1.5\pi}{\frac{25}{4}\pi}\times 100$

$$= 1.5\pi\times\frac{4}{25\pi}\times 100 = 24\%$$

40. Let radius of sector (I + II) = 8 cm

and radius of sector (II + III) = 6 cm

Area of sector (I + II) $= \dfrac{60^\circ}{360^\circ}\times\pi\times 8\times 8 = \dfrac{64}{6}\pi\ \text{cm}^2$

Area of sector (II + III) $= \dfrac{60^\circ}{360^\circ}\times\pi\times 6\times 6 = \dfrac{36}{6}\pi\ \text{cm}^2$

Difference in areas of region I and III

$$= \frac{64}{6}\pi - \frac{36}{6}\pi = \frac{28}{6}\pi = \frac{28}{6}\times\frac{22}{7} = \frac{44}{3}\ \text{cm}^2$$

41. Join OA and OB to make ΔOAB and assume the radius of the second circle as x cm.

The figure may look as follows:

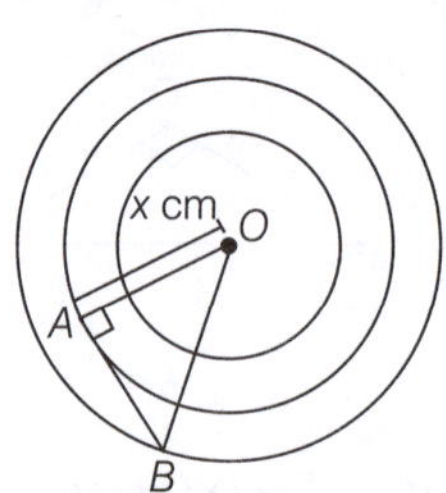

(**Note** The figure is not to scale.)

Use Pythagoras theorem to find the length of OB as $\sqrt{(x^2 + 25)}$ cm.

The area of the second circle $\pi x^2\ \text{cm}^2$ and the area of the largest circle as $\pi(x^2 + 25)\ \text{cm}^2$.

$\therefore$ The area of the shaded region as

$$\pi(x^2 + 25) - \pi x^2 = 25\pi\ \text{cm}^2$$

42. Given, $AB = 13.9$ cm, $MN = 14$ cm and $PQ = 14.1$ cm

Diameter of circle is the longest chord.

Therefore, diameter $= PQ = 14.1$ cm

Length of arc $= \dfrac{2\pi r\theta}{360^\circ}$

$$\Rightarrow 4.7\pi = 2\times\pi\times\frac{14.1}{2}\times\frac{\theta}{360^\circ} \Rightarrow \frac{4.7\times 2\times 360^\circ}{14.1\times 2} = \theta$$

$\Rightarrow \quad \theta = 120°$

Where, θ = central angle

Measure of angle subtended by an arc at the circumference

$= \frac{1}{2} \times \text{Central angle} = \frac{1}{2} \times 120° = 60°$

43. Join OQ and OP.

Given that ΔPQR is an equilateral triangle.

and $\quad PQ = RQ = PR = 12$ cm $\quad$ [given]

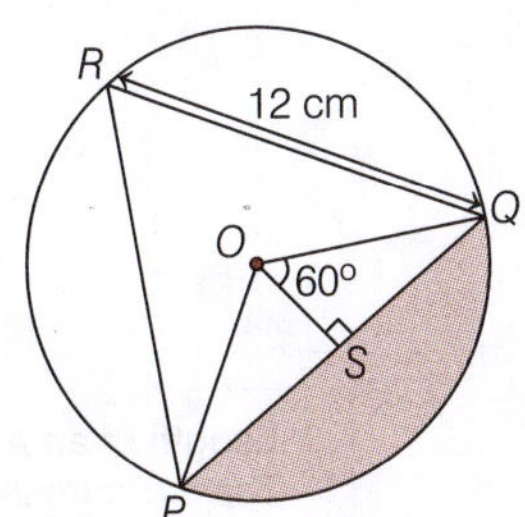

$\because \quad \angle PRQ = 60°$

$\therefore \quad \angle POQ = 120°$

[angle subtended by a chord at the centre is double that of the circumference]

$\because$ OS is perpendicular to PQ.

So, $\angle QOS = 60°$ and $SQ = 6$ cm

$\therefore$ Length of the radius, $OQ = \frac{SQ}{\sin 60°}$

$= \frac{6}{\sin 60°} = 4\sqrt{3}$ cm

and length of $OS = OQ \cdot \cos 60°$

$= 4\sqrt{3} \times \frac{1}{2} = 2\sqrt{3}$ cm

Now, the area of $\Delta OPQ = \frac{1}{2} \times PQ \times OS$

$= \frac{1}{2} \times 12 \times 2\sqrt{3} = 12\sqrt{3}$ cm^2

The area of sector $POQ = \frac{120°}{360°} \times \pi \times (4\sqrt{3})^2$

$= 16\,\pi$ cm^2

Hence, the area of shaded region

= Area of sector POQ – Area of ΔOPQ

$= (16\,\pi - 12\sqrt{3})$ cm^2

44. Given, AB is a chord of a circle centred at O such that $\angle AOB = 60°$ and $OA = 14$ cm.

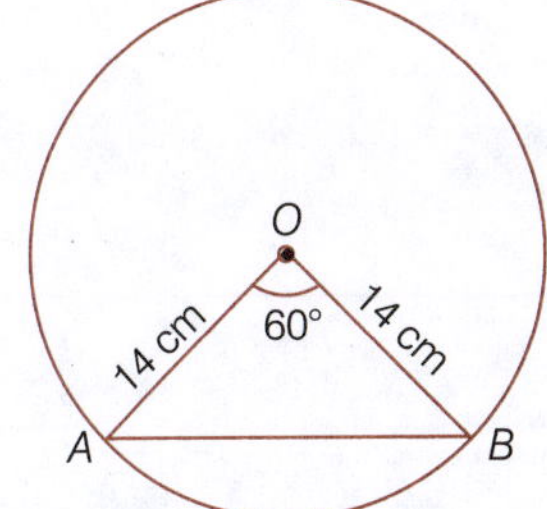

In ΔAOB, $\angle A = \angle B$ [angle opposite to the equal sides]

$\because \angle A = \angle B = \angle O = 60°$

$\therefore$ ΔABO is an equilateral triangle.

$\therefore$ Area of equilateral $\Delta ABO = \frac{\sqrt{3}}{4} \times (OA)^2$

$= \frac{\sqrt{3}}{4} \times (14)^2$

Now, area of sector $OABO = \frac{\theta}{360°}(\pi r^2)$

$= \frac{60°}{360°} \times \frac{22}{7} \times (14)^2$

So, area of minor segment = Area of sector $OABO$

– Area of ΔOAB

$= \frac{60°}{360°} \times \frac{22}{7} \times 14 \times 14 - \frac{\sqrt{3}}{4} \times 14 \times 14$

$= 102.66 - 84.77 = 17.89$ cm^2.

45. Given, perimeter of sector $OACB = 73.12$ cm

and radius = 24 cm

Let θ be the angle of sector $OACB$.

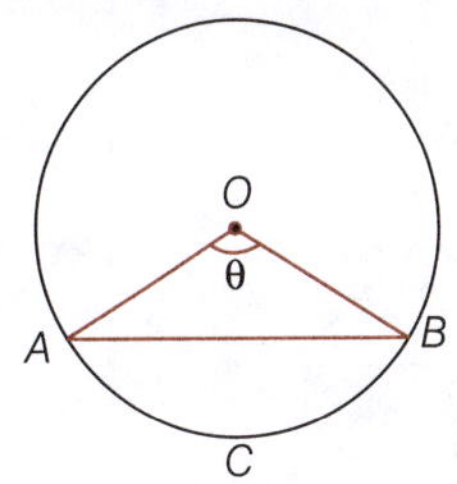

(i) $\because$ Perimeter of sector $OACB = 2r + \frac{2\pi r\theta}{360°} = 73.12$

$\Rightarrow 2 \times 24 + \frac{2 \times 3.14 \times 24 \times \theta}{360} = 73.12$

$\Rightarrow \quad 48 + \frac{48 \times 3.14 \times \theta}{360} = 73.12 \Rightarrow \theta = 60°$

(ii) In ΔOAB, $\angle OAB = \angle OBA$

[$\because$ $OA = OB$ = radii of circle]

$\therefore \angle OAB + \angle OBA + 60° = 180°$

$\Rightarrow \quad \angle OAB + \angle OAB = 180° - 60°$

$\Rightarrow \quad 2\angle OAB = 120° \Rightarrow \angle OAB = 60°$

$\Rightarrow \quad \angle OAB = \angle OBA = 60°$

$\Rightarrow$ ΔOAB is an equilateral triangle.

$\therefore$ Area of minor segment $ACB = \frac{\pi r^2\theta}{360°} - \frac{\sqrt{3}}{4}r^2$

$= \frac{3.14 \times 24 \times 24 \times 60}{360} - \frac{1.73}{4} \times 24 \times 24$

$= (301.44 - 249.12)$

$= 52.32$ cm^2

Mind Map

AREA RELATED TO CIRCLES

Segment of a Circle

The region bounded by a chord and the corresponding arc of the circle is called the segment of the circle. The segment containing the minor arc is called the minor segment and the segment containing the major arc is called major segment.

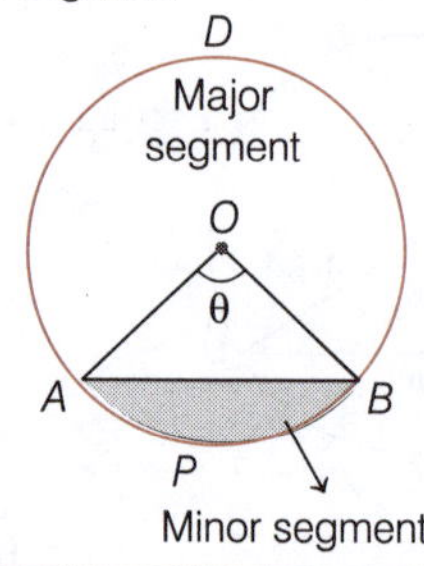

Area of Segment of a Circle

Area of a segment

= Area of corresponding sector

– Area of triangle formed by chord and the radii of the circle

Also,

Area of major segment $= \pi r^2 -$ Area of minor segment

Area of minor segment $= \pi r^2 -$ Area of major segment

Length of an Arc of a Sector

The arc corresponding to a sector is called the arc of the sector.

Length of an arc of a sector,

$$l = \frac{\theta}{360^\circ} \times 2\pi r$$

Area of sector in terms of length of arc $= \frac{1}{2} lr$

Sector

The region enclosed by two radii and the corresponding arc of a circle is called the sector of circle. The sector containing minor arc is called minor sector and the sector containing major arc is called major sector.

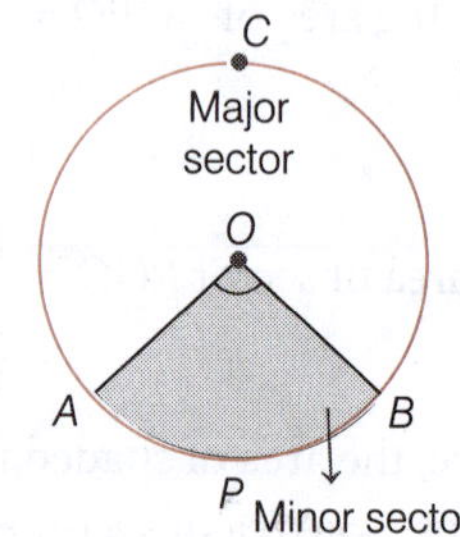

Area of Sector of a Circle

Area of the sector $= \frac{\theta}{360^\circ} \times \pi r^2$

Area of the major sector $= \pi r^2 -$ Area of minor sector

Area of minor sector $= \pi r^2 -$ Area of major sector

Surface Areas and Volumes

CHAPTER 12

In earlier classes, we have learnt how to find the surface area and volume of solid figures, like cuboid, cube, cylinder, cone, sphere and hemisphere etc. In this chapter, we will learn how to find the surface area and volume of combination of solid figures.

Before starting topics of this chapter, we will review some important definitions and formulae that will be used frequently in this chapter.

Solid Figures

The objects having definite shape, size and occupies a fixed amount of space in three dimensions are called **solids** such as cube, cuboid, cylinder, cone, sphere and hemisphere etc.

Surface Area (SA)

Surface area of a solid body is the area of all of its surfaces together and it is always measured in **square units.**

e.g. A cube has 6 surfaces and each surface is in a square shape. Therefore, its surface area will be $6a^2$ sq units, where a^2 is the area of each surface of the cube.

Volume

Space occupied by an object/solid body is called the **volume** of that particular object/solid. Volume is always measured in **cubic units**.

e.g. Suppose, a cube has edge of length a units. Volume of a cube is equal to the product of area of base and height of a cube i.e. $a^2 \times a = a^3$ cu units.

Important Formulae (Related to Some Solid Figures)

1. Cuboid

A cuboid is a solid figure having 6 rectangular faces. Let its length $= l$ units, breadth $= b$ units and height $= h$ units.

Then,

(i) Total surface area of cuboid (TSA)

$$= 2(lb + bh + hl) \text{ sq units}$$

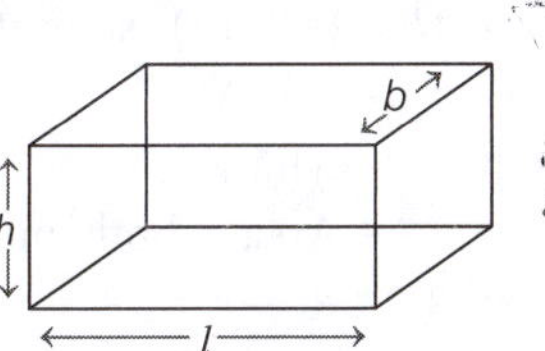

(ii) Lateral surface area of cuboid $= 2(l + b)h$ sq units

or Lateral surface area = Area of the 4 faces

(iii) Diagonal of the cuboid $= \sqrt{l^2 + b^2 + h^2}$ units

(iv) Volume of cuboid $= l \times b \times h$ cu units

2. Cube

Cube is a special case of cuboid which has 6 equal square faces.

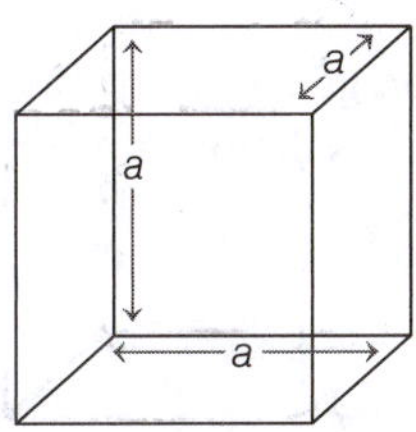

Let its length = Breadth = Height = a units

$\therefore$ Each edge of cube $= a$ units

Then,

(i) Total surface area (TSA) of a cube

$$= 6 \times (\text{Edge})^2 = 6a^2 \text{ sq units}$$

(ii) Lateral surface area of cube

$$= 4 \times (\text{Edge})^2 = 4a^2 \text{ sq units}$$

(iii) Diagonal of a cube $= \sqrt{3} \times$ Edge $= \sqrt{3}a$ units

(iv) Volume of a cube $= (\text{Edge})^3 = a^3$ cu units

3. Right Circular Cylinder

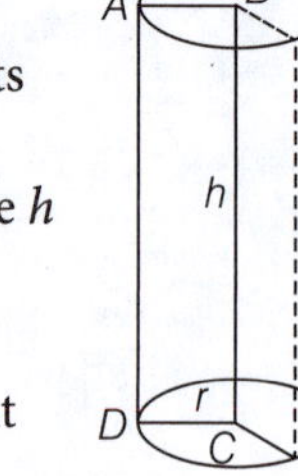

Cylinder is a solid figure obtained by revolving the rectangle, say $ABCD$, about its one side, say BC. Let base radius of right circular cylinder be r units and its height be h units. Then,

(i) Curved surface area (CSA)
$= \text{Circumference of the base} \times \text{Height}$
$= 2\pi rh$ sq units

(ii) Total surface area (TSA)
$= \text{Curved surface area (CSA)} + \text{Area of two ends}$
$= 2\pi rh + 2\pi r^2 = 2\pi r(h + r)$ sq units

(iii) Volume of the cylinder = Area of base × Height
$= \pi r^2 h$ cu units

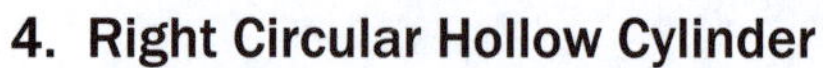

4. Right Circular Hollow Cylinder

Let R units and r units be the external and internal radii of the hollow cylinder, respectively and h units be its height. Then,

(i) Curved surface area (CSA)
= CSA of outer cylinder + CSA of inner cylinder

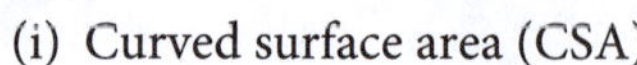

$= 2\pi Rh + 2\pi rh = 2\pi(R + r)h$ sq units

(ii) Total surface area (TSA)
= CSA of hollow cylinder
+ Area of both ends
$= 2\pi(R + r)h + 2\pi(R^2 - r^2)$
$= 2\pi(R + r)h + 2\pi(R + r)(R - r)$
$= 2\pi(R + r)[h + R - r]$ sq units

(iii) Total outer surface area
$= 2\pi Rh + 2\pi(R^2 - r^2)$ sq units

(iv) Volume of hollow cylinder
= Volume of outer cylinder
− Volume of inner cylinder
$= \pi R^2 h - \pi r^2 h = \pi(R^2 - r^2)h$ cu units

5. Sphere

A sphere is a solid generated by the revolution of a semi-circle about its diameter. Let radius of sphere be r units. Then,

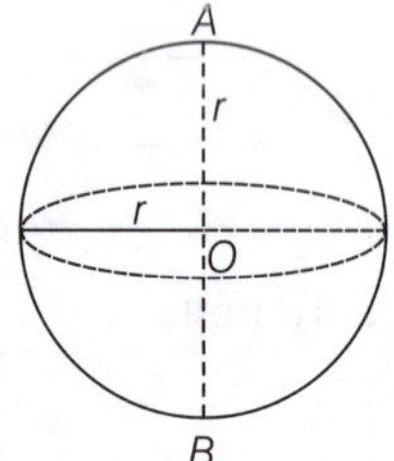

(i) Surface area (SA) of sphere $= 4\pi r^2$ sq units

(ii) Volume of sphere $= \frac{4}{3}\pi r^3$ cu units

6. Spherical Shell

If R and r are respectively the outer and inner radii of a spherical shell, then

(i) Volume of a hollow sphere
$= \frac{4}{3}\pi(R^3 - r^3)$ cu units

(ii) Outer surface area $= 4\pi R^2$ sq units

7. Hemisphere

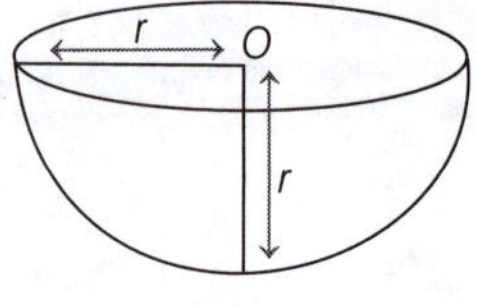

A plane passing through the centre, cuts the sphere in two equal parts, each part is called a hemisphere. Let radius of hemisphere be r units. Then,

(i) Curved surface area (CSA) of hemisphere
$= 2\pi r^2$ sq units

(ii) Total surface area (TSA) of hemisphere = CSA of hemisphere + Area of one end $= 2\pi r^2 + \pi r^2$
$= 3\pi r^2$ sq units

(iii) Volume of hemisphere $= \frac{2}{3}\pi r^3$ cu units

8. Right Circular Cone

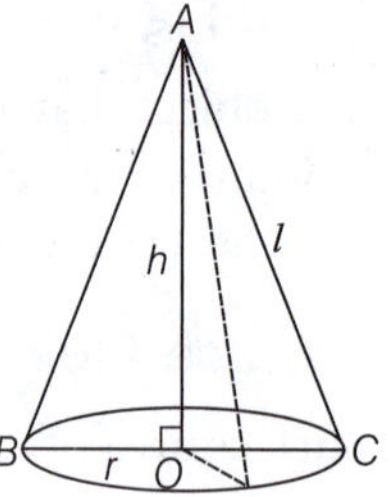

A right circular cone is a solid generated by the revolution of a right angled triangle about one of its sides containing the right angle as axis as shown in figure. Let height of a right circular cone be h units and its radius be r units. Then,

(i) Slant height of the cone,
$l = AC = \sqrt{r^2 + h^2}$ units

(ii) Curved surface area (CSA) of cone $= \pi rl$ sq units

(iii) Total surface area (TSA) of a cone
= Curved surface area (CSA) + Area of the base
$= \pi rl + \pi r^2 = \pi r(l + r)$ sq units

(iv) Volume of cone $= \frac{1}{3}\pi r^2 h$ cu units

Surface Area and Volume of Combination of Solids

In our day-to-day life we come across some complex solid figures, e.g. a circus tent consisting of a cylindrical base surmounted by a conical roof, a toy in the form of cone mounted on a hemisphere etc. All of these are combination of two or more basic solids.

In this topic, we will learn how to find the surface areas and volumes of combination of two or more similar or different solid figures.

Different Types of Problems Based on Various Combination of Solids

Type I When combination of two or more than two figures of same type is given

Method of solving this type of problems can be understood with the help of the following examples.

Example 1. **Three cubes each of side 5 cm are joined end to end. Find the surface area of the resulting solid.**

Sol. Here, on joining three cubes, we get a cuboid whose length, $l = 5 + 5 + 5 = 15$ cm, breadth, $b = 5$ cm and height, $h = 5$ cm

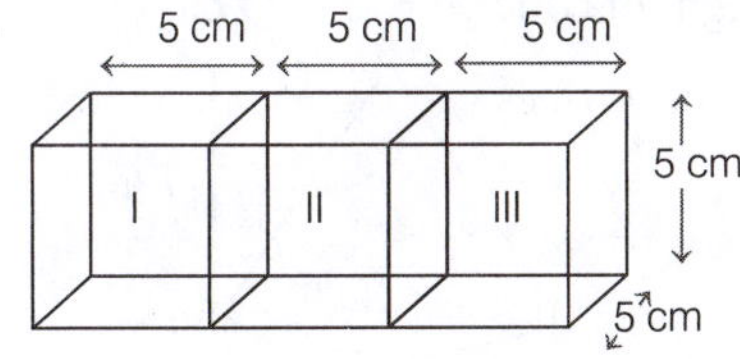

$\therefore$ Required surface area of the resulting solid

$= $ Surface area of new cuboid

$= 2(lb + bh + hl) = 2(15 \times 5 + 5 \times 5 + 5 \times 15)$

$= 2(75 + 25 + 75) = 2(175) = 350 \text{ cm}^2$

Example 2. **An iron pole consists of a cylinder of height 240 cm and base diameter 26 cm, which is surmounted by another cylinder of height 66 cm and radius 10 cm. Find the mass of the pole given that 1 cm^3 of iron has approximately 8 g mass. [take, $\pi = 3.14$]**

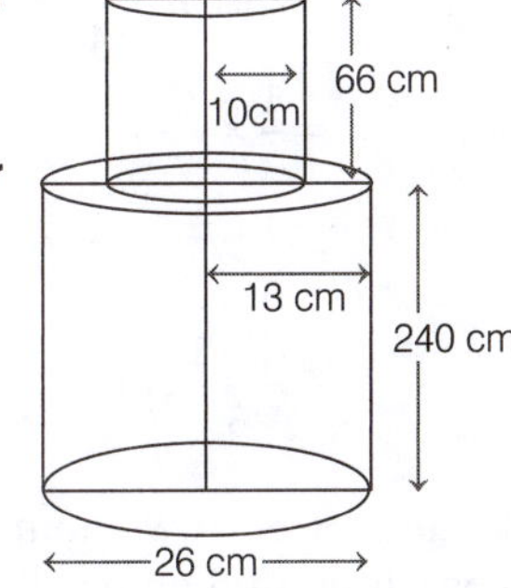

Sol. Here, solid iron pole is a combination of two cylinders.

For first cylinder, Height $= 240$ cm

Base diameter $= 26$ cm

$\therefore$ Base radius $= \frac{26}{2}$ cm $= 13$ cm

For second cylinder,

Height $= 66$ cm, Radius $= 10$ cm

We know that

Volume of cylinder $= \pi r^2 h$

$\therefore$ Total volume of iron pole $=$ Volume of first cylinder $+$ Volume of second cylinder

$= \pi (13)^2 \times 240 + \pi (10)^2 \times 66$

$= \pi [169 \times 240 + 100 \times 66]$

$= 3.14 [40560 + 6600]$

$= 3.14 \times 47160 = 148082.4 \text{ cm}^3$

Hence, total mass of the iron pole

$= 148082.4 \times 8 \text{ g} = 1184659.2$ g

[given, mass of 1 cm^3 iron pole ≈ 8 g]

$= \frac{1184659.2}{1000}$ kg $\quad \left[\because 1 \text{g} = \frac{1}{1000} \text{kg}\right]$

$= 1184.66$ kg

Type II When combination of sphere (or hemisphere) and cube/cuboid is given

Method of solving this type of problems can be understood with the help of following example.

Example 3. **The decorative block shown in the following figure is made of two solids, a cube and a hemisphere.**

The base of the block is a cube with edge 6 cm and the hemisphere fixed on the top has a diameter of 2.1 cm, then find the total surface area of the block and find the total area to be painted. $\left[\textbf{take, } \pi = \frac{22}{7}\right]$

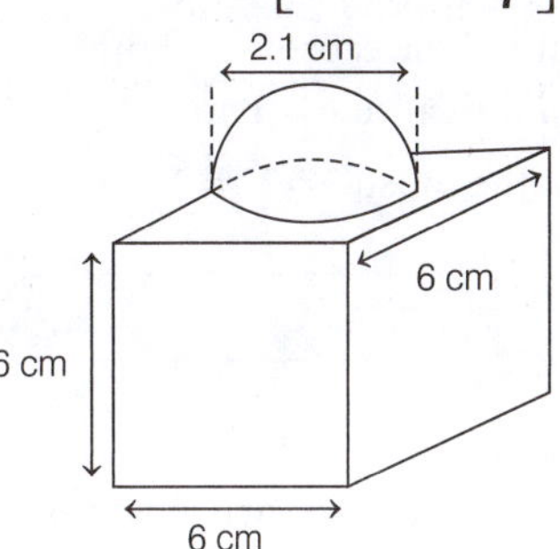

Sol. Here, the decorative block is a combination of a cube and a hemisphere.

For cubical portion,

Each edge $= 6$ cm

For hemispherical portion,

Diameter $= 2.1$ cm

$\therefore$ Radius, $r = \frac{2.1}{2}$ cm

Now, total surface area of the cube

$= 6 \times (\text{Edge})^2 = 6 \times 6 \times 6 = 216 \text{ cm}^2$

Here, the part of the cube where the hemisphere is attached, is not included in the surface area.

So, the total surface area of the decorative block

$=$ Total surface area of cube $-$ Area of base of hemisphere $+$ Curved surface area of hemisphere

$= 216 - \pi r^2 + 2\pi r^2 = 216 + \pi r^2$

$= 216 + \frac{22}{7} \times \frac{2.1}{2} \times \frac{2.1}{2}$

$= 216 + 3.465 = 219.465 \text{ cm}^2$

Clearly, the total area to be painted

$=$ Total surface area of the decorative block $-$ Area of base of cube

$= 219.465 - 6^2 = 219.465 - 36 = 183.465 \text{ cm}^2$

Note It In calculating the surface area, we do not add the surface areas of the two or more individual solids because some part of the surface area disappears in the process of joining them.

Type III When combination of cylinder and hemisphere is given

Method of solving this type of problems can be understood with the help of following examples.

Example 4. **A medicine capsule is in the shape of a cylinder with two hemispheres stuck to each of its ends. The length of the entire capsule is 14 mm and the diameter of the capsule is 4 mm. Find its surface area. Also, find its volume.** CBSE 2024 (Standard)

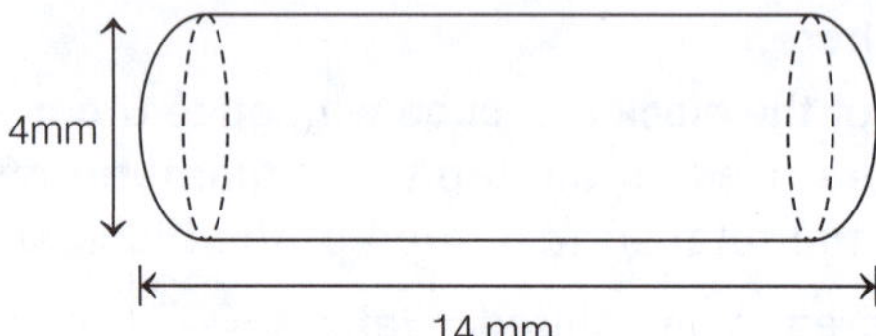

Sol. Given, length of the capsule = 14 mm

Diameter of the capsule = 4 mm

$\therefore$ Radius of the capsule $= \frac{4}{2} = 2$ mm

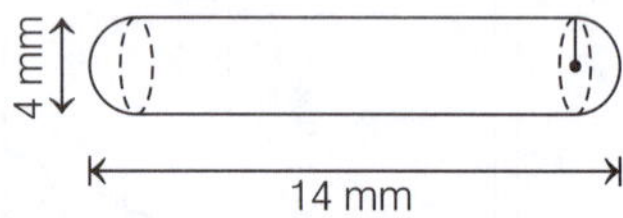

Length of the cylinder = Total length of capsule − Radius of left hemisphere − Radius of right hemisphere

$= 14 - 2 - 2 = 10$ mm

Surface area of capsule = Curved surface area of cylinder + Surface area of left hemisphere + Surface area of right hemisphere

$= 2\pi rh + 2\pi r^2 + 2\pi r^2$

$= 2\pi rh + 4\pi r^2$

$= 2 \times \frac{22}{7} \times 2 \times 10 + 4 \times \frac{22}{7} \times 2 \times 2$

$= 125.71 + 50.29$

$= 176 \text{ mm}^2$

Thus, the required surface area of the capsule is 176 mm^2.

Now, volume of capsule = Volume of cylinder + Volume of left hemisphere + Volume of right hemisphere

$= \pi r^2 h + \frac{2}{3}\pi r^3 + \frac{2}{3}\pi r^3$

$= \pi r^2 h + \frac{4}{3}\pi r^3$

$= \frac{22}{7} \times 2 \times 2 \times 10 + \frac{4}{3} \times \frac{22}{7} \times 2 \times 2 \times 2$

$= 125.71 + 33.52$

$= 159.23 \text{ mm}^3$

Type IV When combination of cone and hemisphere/cylinder is given

Method of solving this type of problems can be understood with the help of following examples.

Example 5. **A solid is in the shape of a right-circular cone surmounted on a hemisphere, the radius of each of them being 7 cm and the height of the cone is equal to its diameter. Find the volume of the solid.** $\left[\text{use } \pi = \frac{22}{7}\right]$

CBSE 2023 (Standard)

Sol. Given, radius of cone $(r) = 7$ cm

and height of cone $(h) = 2r = 14$ cm

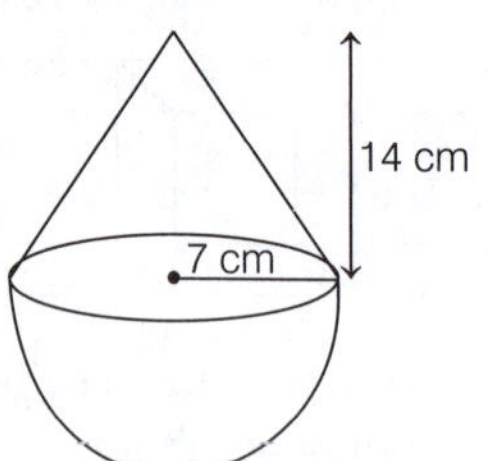

$\therefore$ Volume of the solid = Volume of cone + Volume of hemisphere

$= \frac{1}{3}\pi r^2 h + \frac{2}{3}\pi r^3$

$= \frac{1}{3} \times \frac{22}{7} \times 7^2 \times 14 + \frac{2}{3} \times \frac{22}{7} \times (7)^3$

$= \frac{1}{3} \times \frac{22}{7} \times 7^3 (2 + 2) = \frac{22}{3} \times 7^2 \times 4$

$= \frac{4312}{3} \text{ cm}^3$

Example 6. **A wooden toy rocket is in the shape of a cone mounted on a cylinder, as shown in figure. The height of the entire rocket is 24 cm, while the height of the conical part is 4 cm. The base of the conical portion has a diameter of 6 cm, while the base diameter of the cylindrical portion is 4 cm. If the conical portion is to be painted orange and the cylindrical portion yellow, then find the area of the rocket painted with each of these colours. [take, $\pi = 3.14$]**

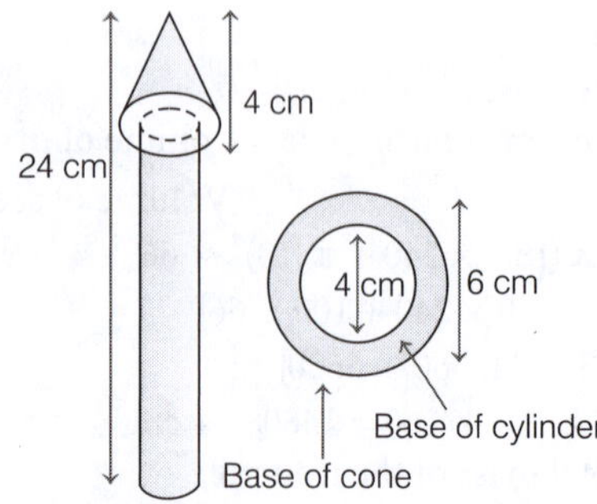

Sol. Here, the given wooden toy rocket is combination of a cone and a cylinder.

For conical portion,

Diameter = 6 cm

$\therefore$ Radius, $r_1 = \frac{6}{2}$ cm = 3 cm

Height, h_1 = 4 cm

Then, slant height, $l = \sqrt{3^2 + 4^2}$ $\quad [\because l = \sqrt{r^2 + h^2}]$

$= \sqrt{9 + 16} = \sqrt{25} = 5$ cm

For cylindrical portion,

Diameter = 4 cm

$\therefore$ Radius, $r_2 = \frac{4}{2}$ cm = 2 cm

Height, h_2 = Total height of rocket – Height of cone

= 24 – 4 $\quad$ [$\because$ total height of rocket = 24 cm]

= 20 cm

Here, we have to find the area of the rocket painted with orange and yellow colours separately.

Since, radius of base of cone is larger than radius of base of cylinder and cone is mounted on cylinder.

$\therefore$ Area to be painted orange

= Curved surface area of cone

+ Area of base of cone – Area of base of cylinder

[$\because$ area of base of cylinder is common in area of base of cone]

$= \pi r_1 l + \pi r_1^2 - \pi r_2^2$

$= 3.14 \times 3 \times 5 + 3.14 \times (3)^2 - 3.14 \times (2)^2$

$= 3.14\,[15 + 9 - 4]$

$= 3.14 \times 20$

$= 62.8\ \text{cm}^2$

Now, area to be painted yellow

= Curved surface area of cylinder

+ Area of base of cylinder

$= 2\pi r_2 h_2 + \pi r_2^2$

$= 2 \times 3.14 \times 2 \times 20 + 3.14 \times (2)^2$

$= 3.14\,[80 + 4] = 3.14 \times 84 = 263.76\ \text{cm}^2$

Example 7. A solid toy is in the form of a hemisphere surmounted by a right circular cone. The height of the cone is 2 cm and the diameter of the base is 4 cm. Determine the volume of the toy. CBSE 2024 (Basic)

Sol. Given, height of cone $(h) = OA = 2$ cm

and diameter of cone = 4 cm

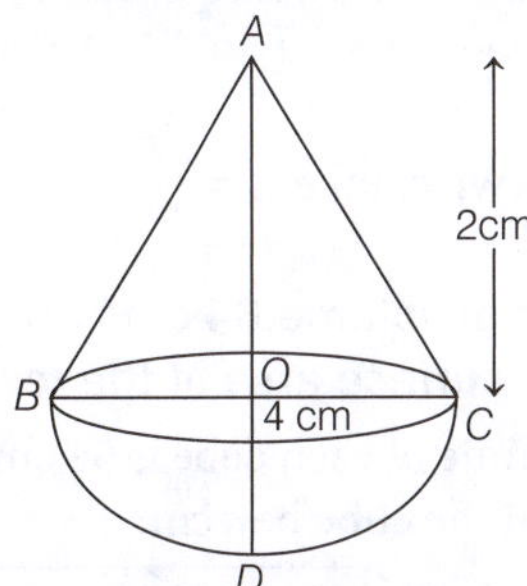

So, radius $= r = \frac{\text{Diameter}}{2} = \frac{4}{2} = 2$ cm

Now, volume of toy = Volume of cone

+ Volume of hemisphere

Volume of cone $= \frac{1}{3}\pi r^2 h$

$= \frac{1}{3} \times \frac{22}{7} \times (2)^2 \times 2$

$= \frac{176}{21}\ \text{cm}^3$

and volume of hemisphere $= \frac{2}{3}\pi r^3$

$= \frac{2}{3} \times \frac{22}{7} \times (2)^3$

$= \frac{352}{21}\ \text{cm}^3$

$\therefore$ Volume of toy $= \frac{176}{21} + \frac{352}{21} = \frac{528}{21}$

$= 25.14\ \text{cm}^3$

Hence, volume of toy is 25.14 cm^3.

NCERT FOLDER

Complete Solutions of All Exercises of NCERT Textbook

EXERCISE 12.1

Unless stated otherwise, take $\pi = \frac{22}{7}$.

Q1. 2 cubes each of volume 64 cm^3 are joined end to end. Find the surface area of the resulting cuboid.

Sol. Given, the volume of each cube is 64 cm^3.
Let each side of the cube be a cm.

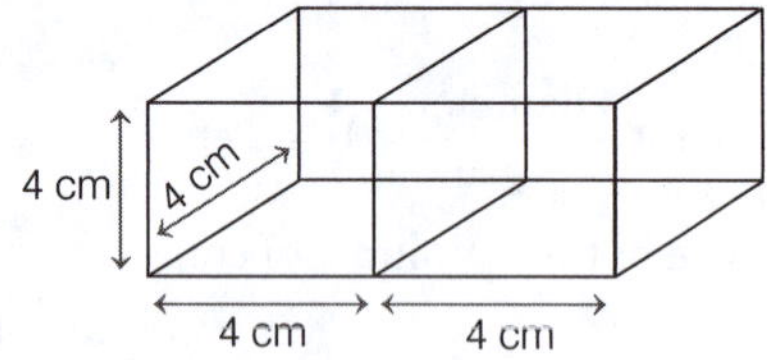

$\because$ Volume of cube = (Side)^3

$\therefore \quad 64 = a^3 \quad$ [given]

$\Rightarrow \quad a = 4$ cm

When two cubes are joined end to end, then we get a cuboid whose length, $l = (4 + 4) = 8$ cm, breadth, $b = 4$ cm and height, $h = 4$ cm.

Now, surface area of the resulting cuboid

$= 2(lb + bh + hl) = 2(8 \times 4 + 4 \times 4 + 4 \times 8)$

$= 2(32 + 16 + 32) = 2(80) = 160 \text{ cm}^2$

Q2. A vessel is in the form of a hollow hemisphere mounted by a hollow cylinder. The diameter of the hemisphere is 14 cm and the total height of the vessel is 13 cm. Find the inner surface area of the vessel.

CBSE 2024 (Standard)

Sol. Here, vessel is a combination of a hollow hemisphere and a hollow cylinder.

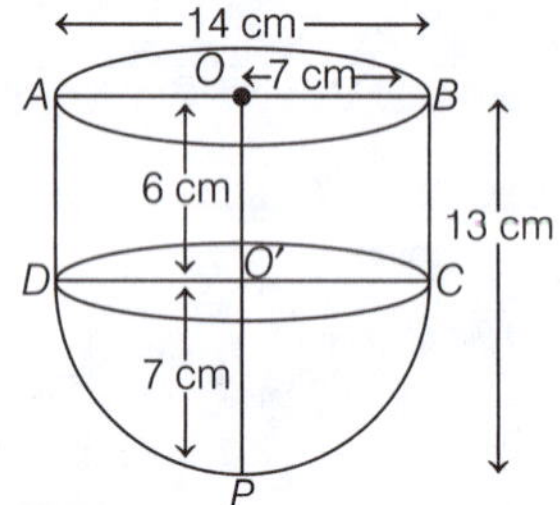

For cylindrical portion,

Diameter = $AB = DC = 14$ cm

$\therefore$ Radius = $OB = O'C = O'P$

$= \frac{AB}{2} = \frac{14}{2} = 7$ cm

Total length of vessel, $PO = 13$ cm

$\therefore$ Length of cylinder, $OO' = PO - O'P = 13 - 7 = 6$ cm

For hemispherical portion,

Radius of hemisphere = Height of hemisphere = 7 cm

Now, the inner surface area of the vessel

= Curved surface area of cylinder + Curved surface area of hemisphere

$= 2\pi rh + 2\pi r^2$

$= 2 \times \frac{22}{7} \times 7 \times 6 + 2 \times \frac{22}{7} \times (7)^2$

$= 2 \times 22 \times 6 + 2 \times 22 \times 7$

$= 44(6 + 7) = 44 \times 13 = 572 \text{ cm}^2$

Q3. A toy is in the form of a cone of radius 3.5 cm mounted on a hemisphere of same radius. The total height of the toy is 15.5 cm. Find the total surface area of the toy. CBSE 2020 (Basic), CBSE 2024 (Standard)

Sol. Here, toy is a combination of a hemisphere and a cone.

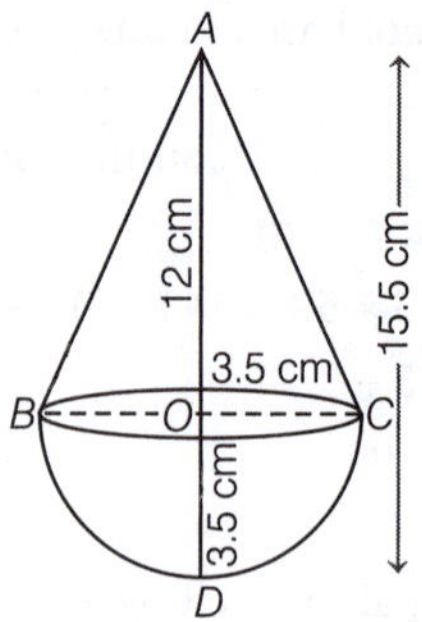

Given, total height of toy,

$AD = 15.5$ cm

For hemispherical portion,

Radius, $OC = OD = OB = 3.5$ cm

For conical portion,

Height, $OA = AD - OD$

$= 15.5 - 3.5 = 12$ cm

and radius = 3.5 cm

Now, total surface area of the toy

= Curved surface area of cone + Curved surface area of hemisphere

$= \pi rl + 2\pi r^2 = \pi r\sqrt{h^2 + r^2} + 2\pi r^2 \quad [\because l = \sqrt{h^2 + r^2}]$

$= \frac{22}{7} \times 3.5 \times \sqrt{(12)^2 + (3.5)^2} + 2 \times \frac{22}{7} \times (3.5)^2$

$= 11\sqrt{144 + 12.25} + 22 \times 3.5$

$= 11\sqrt{156.25} + 11 \times 7$

$= 11(12.5) + 77$

$= 137.5 + 77 = 214.5 \text{ cm}^2$

Q4. A cubical block of side 7 cm is surmounted by a hemisphere. What is the greatest diameter the hemisphere can have? Find the surface area of the solid.

Sol. Given, a cubical block is surmounted by a hemisphere. Therefore, diameter of hemisphere must be equal to the side of cubical block and it is the greatest diameter of hemisphere.

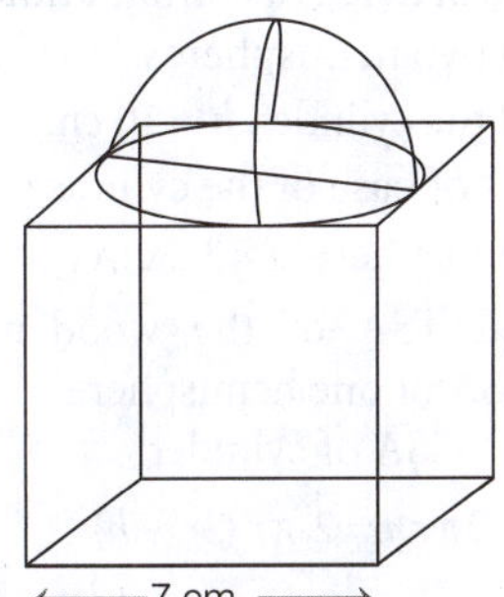

For cubical portion,

$$\text{Edge} = 7 \text{ cm}$$

For hemispherical portion,

$$\text{Diameter} = 7 \text{ cm}$$

$$\therefore \quad \text{Radius, } r = \frac{7}{2} \text{ cm}$$

Now, required surface area of solid

= TSA of the cube + CSA of hemisphere − Area of circular base of hemisphere.

$$= 6 \times (\text{Edge})^2 + 2\pi r^2 - \pi r^2$$

$$= 6 \times (7)^2 + 2 \times \frac{22}{7} \times \frac{7}{2} \times \frac{7}{2} - \frac{22}{7} \times \frac{7}{2} \times \frac{7}{2}$$

$$= 294 + 11 \times 7 - \frac{11 \times 7}{2}$$

$$= 294 + 77 - \frac{77}{2}$$

$$= 371 - 38.5 = 332.5 \text{ cm}^2$$

Q5. A hemispherical depression is cut-out from one face of a cubical wooden block such that the diameter *l* of the hemisphere is equal to the edge of the cube. Determine the surface area of the remaining solid.

Sol. Given, side of the cube = Diameter of the hemisphere = l units

$$\therefore \text{ Radius of the hemisphere, } r = \frac{l}{2} \text{ units}$$

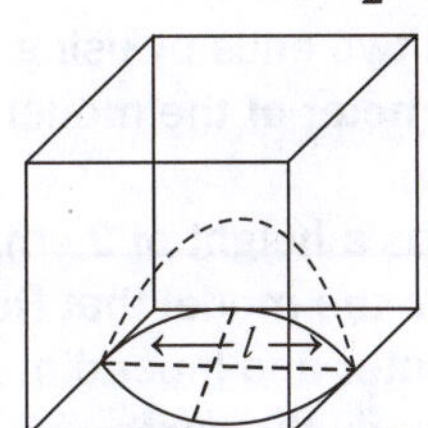

Now, required surface area of the remaining solid

= TSA of the cube + CSA of hemisphere − Area of circular base of hemisphere

$$= 6 \times (\text{Edge})^2 + 2\pi r^2 - \pi r^2$$

$$= 6 \times l^2 + 2\pi \times \left(\frac{l}{2}\right)^2 - \pi\left(\frac{l}{2}\right)^2$$

$$= 6l^2 + 2\pi \times \frac{l^2}{4} - \pi\frac{l^2}{4} = 6l^2 + \pi\frac{l^2}{4}$$

$$= \frac{l^2}{4}(\pi + 24) \text{ sq units}$$

Q6. A medicine capsule is in the shape of a cylinder with two hemispheres stuck to each of its ends (see below figure). The length of the entire capsule is 14 mm and the diameter of the capsule is 5 mm. Find its surface area.

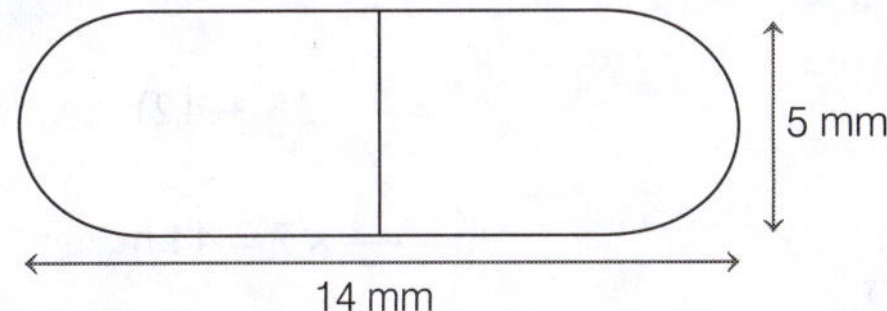

Sol. Given that medicine capsule is a combination of two hemispheres and one cylinder.

Also, given diameter of the capsule = 5 mm

$$\therefore \text{ Radius} = \frac{5}{2} = 2.5 \text{ mm}$$

and length of the capsule = 14 mm

∴ Length of the cylindrical portion = 14 − (2.5 + 2.5) = 9 mm

2.5 mm
2.5 mm
14 mm
9 mm
2.5 mm
5 mm

Now, CSA of one hemispherical portion

$$= 2\pi r^2 = 2 \times \frac{22}{7} \times 2.5 \times 2.5 = \frac{275}{7} \text{ mm}^2$$

and CSA of the cylindrical portion

$$= 2\pi rh = 2 \times \frac{22}{7} \times 2.5 \times 9 = \frac{22}{7} \times 45 = \frac{990}{7} \text{ mm}^2$$

Now, required surface area of medicine capsule

= 2 × CSA of one hemispherical portion + CSA of the cylindrical portion

$$= 2 \times \frac{275}{7} + \frac{990}{7} = \frac{550}{7} + \frac{990}{7} = \frac{1540}{7} = 220 \text{ mm}^2$$

Q7. A tent is in the shape of a cylinder surmounted by a conical top. If the height and diameter of the cylindrical part are 2.1 m and 4 m respectively, and the slant height of the top is 2.8 m, then find the area of the canvas used for making the tent. Also, find the cost of the canvas of the tent at the rate of ₹500 per m^2.

[Note The base of the tent will not be covered with canvas.] CBSE 2016

Sol. Given that tent is a combination of a cylinder and a cone.

For conical portion,

Slant height, $l = 2.8$ m

Radius, r = Radius of cylinder

$$= \frac{\text{Diameter}}{2} = \frac{4}{2} = 2 \text{ m}$$

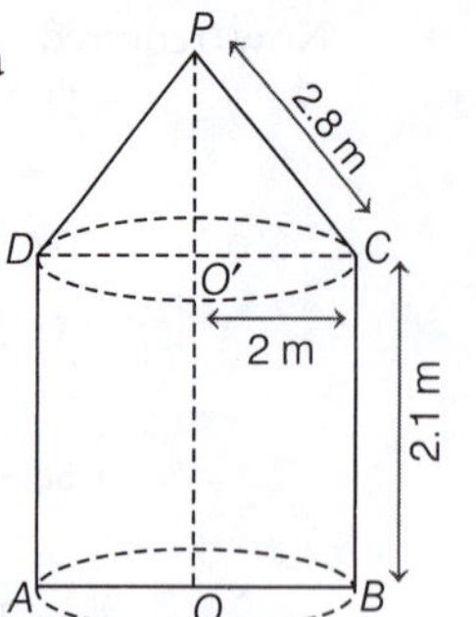

For cylindrical portion,

Radius, $r = \frac{4}{2} = 2$ m

Height, $h = 2.1$ m

$\therefore$ Required surface area of the tent

= CSA of cone + CSA of cylinder

$$= \pi r l + 2\pi r h = \pi r (l + 2h)$$

$$= \frac{22}{7} \times 2 \times (2.8 + 2 \times 2.1)$$

$$= \frac{44}{7}(2.8 + 4.2)$$

$$= \frac{44}{7} \times 7 = 44 \text{ m}^2$$

Now, cost of the canvas of the tent at the rate of ₹ 500 per m^2

= Surface area × Cost per m^2 = 44 × 500 = ₹ 22000

Q8. From a solid cylinder whose height is 2.4 cm and diameter 1.4 cm, a conical cavity of the same height and same diameter is hollowed out. Find the total surface area of the remaining solid to the nearest cm^2.

Sol. Given, diameter of cylinder

= Diameter of conical cavity

= 1.4 cm

$\therefore$ Radius of cylinder

= Radius of conical cavity

$$= \frac{\text{Diameter}}{2} = \frac{1.4}{2} = 0.7 \text{ cm}$$

Height of the cylinder

= Height of the conical cavity

= 2.4 cm

$\therefore$ Slant height of the conical cavity,

$$l = \sqrt{h^2 + r^2} = \sqrt{(2.4)^2 + (0.7)^2}$$

$$= \sqrt{5.76 + 0.49}$$

$$= \sqrt{6.25} = 2.5 \text{ cm}$$

Now, TSA of remaining solid

= CSA of conical cavity + CSA of cylinder + Area of the base of the cylinder

$$= \pi r l + 2\pi r h + \pi r^2$$

$$= \pi r (l + 2h + r)$$

$$= \frac{22}{7} \times 0.7 \times (2.5 + 2 \times 2.4 + 0.7)$$

$$= 22 \times 0.1 \times (2.5 + 4.8 + 0.7)$$

$$= 2.2 \times 8$$

$$= 17.6 \approx 18 \text{ cm}^2$$

Q9. A wooden article was made by scooping out a hemisphere from each end of a solid cylinder, as shown in adjacent figure. If the height of the cylinder is 10 cm and its base is of radius 3.5 cm, then find the total surface area of the article.

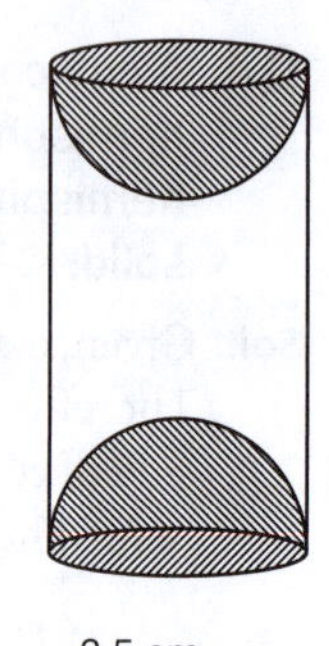

Sol. Given, wooden article is a combination of a cylinder and two hemispheres.

Here, height of the cylinder, $h = 10$ cm

Clearly, Radius of base of the cylinder

= Radius of hemisphere, $r = 3.5$ cm

Now, required TSA of the wooden article = 2 × CSA of one hemisphere + CSA of cylinder

$$= 2 \times (2\pi r^2) + 2\pi r h = 2\pi r(2r + h)$$

$$= 2 \times \frac{22}{7} \times 3.5 \times (2 \times 3.5 + 10)$$

$$= \frac{22}{7} \times 7 \times (7 + 10) = 22 \times 17 = 374 \text{ cm}^2$$

EXERCISE 12.2

Unless stated otherwise, take $\pi = \frac{22}{7}$

Q1. A solid is in the shape of a cone standing on a hemisphere with both their radii being equal to 1 cm and the height of the cone is equal to its radius. Find the volume of the solid in terms of π. CBSE 2024 (Basic)

Sol. Given, solid is a combination of a cone and a hemisphere.

Also, radius of the cone, r

= Radius of the hemisphere

= 1 cm

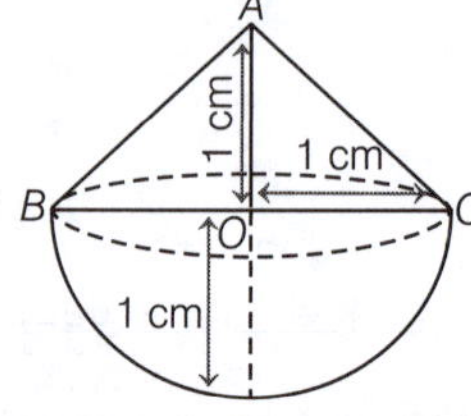

Height of the cone, $h = 1$ cm

$\therefore$ Required volume of the solid

= Volume of the cone + Volume of the hemisphere

$$= \frac{1}{3}\pi r^2 h + \frac{2}{3}\pi r^3 = \frac{1}{3}\pi (1)^2 (1) + \frac{2}{3}\pi (1)^3$$

$$= \frac{\pi}{3} + \frac{2}{3}\pi = \frac{(\pi + 2\pi)}{3} = \frac{3\pi}{3} = \pi \text{ cm}^3$$

Q2. Rachel, an engineering student, was asked to make a model shaped like a cylinder with two cones attached at its two ends by using a thin aluminium sheet. The diameter of the model is 3 cm and its length is 12 cm.

If each cone has a height of 2 cm, find the volume of air contained in the model that Rachel made. (Assume the outer and inner dimensions of the model to be nearly the same.)

Sol. Given, model is a combination of a cylinder and two cones. Clearly, volume of the air will be equal to the sum of the volumes of two cones and one cylinder.

We have, diameter of the model, $BC = ED = 3$ cm

$\therefore$ Radius of cone = Radius of cylinder, $r = \frac{3}{2} = 1.5$ cm

Length of cone, $h_1 = 2$ cm

Total length of the model, $AF = 12$ cm

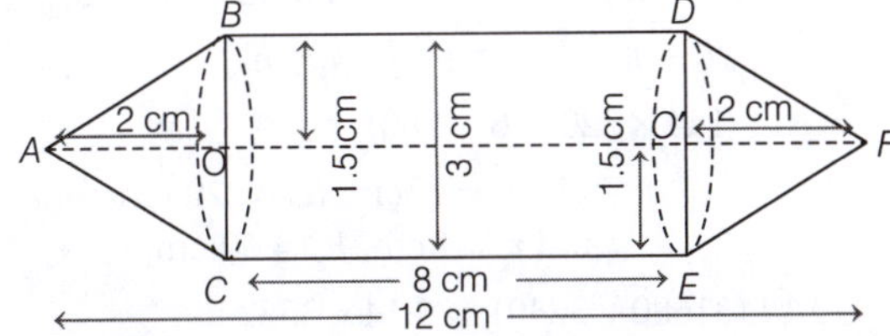

$\therefore$ Length of the cylinder, $OO' = AF - (AO + O'F)$

$$= 12 - (2 + 2) = 8 \text{ cm} = h_2$$

Now, volume of the air inside the model

$$= \text{Volume of air inside (cone + cylinder + cone)}$$

$$= \left(\frac{1}{3}\pi r^2 h_1 + \pi r^2 h_2 + \frac{1}{3}\pi r^2 h_1\right)$$

$$= \frac{1}{3}\pi r^2 (h_1 + 3h_2 + h_1)$$

$$= \frac{1}{3} \times \frac{22}{7} \times 1.5 \times 1.5\ (2 + 3 \times 8 + 2)$$

$$= \frac{22}{7} \times \frac{2.25}{3} \times (2 + 24 + 2)$$

$$= \frac{22}{7} \times 0.75 \times 28 = 22 \times 3 = 66 \text{ cm}^3$$

Q3. A gulab jamun, contains sugar syrup up to about 30% of its volume. Find approximately how much syrup would be found in 45 gulab jamuns, each shaped like a cylinder with two hemispherical ends with length 5 cm and diameter 2.8 cm (see figure).

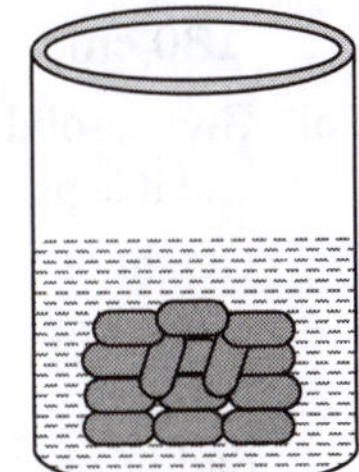

Sol. Given, one gulab jamun is a combination of a cylinder and two hemispheres. Here, total length of one gulab jamun = 5 cm and diameter = 2.8 cm

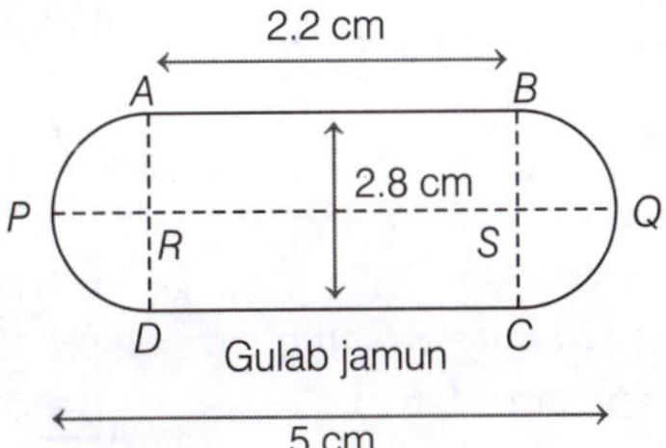

$\therefore$ Radius of cylindrical part = Radius of hemispherical part

$$= r = \frac{2.8}{2} = 1.4 \text{ cm}$$

Height of cylindrical part,

$$h = PQ - (PR + SQ) = 5 - (1.4 + 1.4)$$
$$= 5 - 2.8 = 2.2 \text{ cm}$$

$\therefore$ Volume of one gulab jamun

$$= 2 \times \text{Volume of hemispherical part} + \text{Volume of cylindrical part}$$

$$= 2 \times \left[\frac{2}{3}\pi r^3\right] + \pi r^2 h = \frac{4}{3}\pi r^3 + \pi r^2 h$$

$$= \pi r^2 \left[\frac{4r}{3} + h\right] = \frac{22}{7} \times 1.4 \times 1.4 \left[\frac{4}{3} \times 1.4 + 2.2\right]$$

$$= \frac{22}{7} \times \frac{14}{10} \times \frac{14}{10}\left[\frac{4}{3} \times \frac{14}{10} + \frac{22}{10}\right]$$

$$= 22 \times \frac{1}{5} \times \frac{7}{5}\left[\frac{28}{15} + \frac{11}{5}\right] = \frac{154}{25} \times \frac{61}{15} = \frac{9394}{375} \text{ cm}^3$$

Now, volume of 45 gulab jamuns

$$= 45 \times \frac{9394}{375} = \frac{3 \times 9394}{25} = \frac{28182}{25} = 1127.28 \text{ cm}^3$$

Since, one gulab jamun contains sugar syrup upto about 30% of its volume.

Hence, quantity of syrup found in 45 gulab jamuns

$$= 1127.28 \times \frac{30}{100} = 1127.28 \times \frac{3}{10} = 338.184 \approx 338 \text{ cm}^3$$

Q4. A pen stand made of wood is in the shape of a cuboid with four conical depressions to hold pens. The dimensions of the cuboid are 15 cm × 10 cm × 3.5 cm. The radius of each of the depressions is 0.5 cm and the depth is 1.4 cm. Find the volume of wood in the entire stand (see figure).

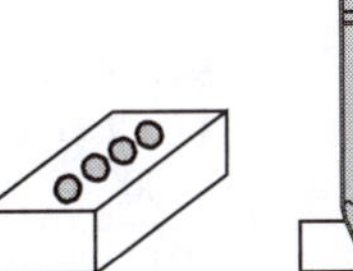

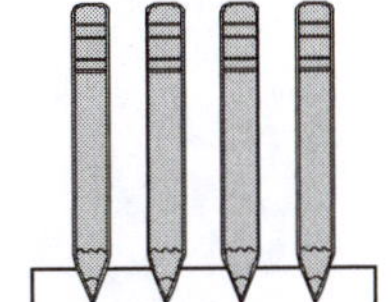

Sol. Given, length of cuboid $(l) = 15$ cm,

Breadth of cuboid $(b) = 10$ cm

and height of cuboid $(h) = 3.5$ cm

$\therefore$ Volume of cuboid $= l \times b \times h$

$$= 15 \times 10 \times 3.5 = 525 \text{ cm}^3$$

Also, radius of conical depression, $r = 0.5$ cm

and height of conical depression, $h = 1.4$ cm

$\therefore$ Volume of one conical depression $= \frac{1}{3}\pi \times r^2 \times h$

$$= \frac{1}{3} \times \frac{22}{7} \times 0.5 \times 0.5 \times 1.4$$

$$= \frac{22}{3} \times \frac{1}{2} \times \frac{1}{2} \times \frac{2}{10} = \frac{11}{30} \text{ cm}^3$$

Now, volume of 4 conical depressions = 4 × Volume of one conical depression

$$= 4 \times \frac{11}{30} = \frac{22}{15} \text{ cm}^3$$

Hence, the volume of wood in the entire stand

$= $ Volume of cuboid – Volume of 4 conical depressions

$= 525 - \frac{22}{15} = 525 - 1.47$

$= 523.53 \text{ cm}^3$

Q5. A vessel is in the form of an inverted cone. Its height is 8 cm and the radius of its top, which is open, is 5 cm. It is filled with water upto the brim. When lead shots, each of which is a sphere of radius 0.5 cm are dropped into the vessel, one-fourth of the water flows out. Find the number of lead shots dropped in the vessel.

Sol. Here, a cone and spherical lead shots are given. Since, lead shots are dropped into the vessel, so the water which flows out from the vessel is equal to the volume of lead shots.

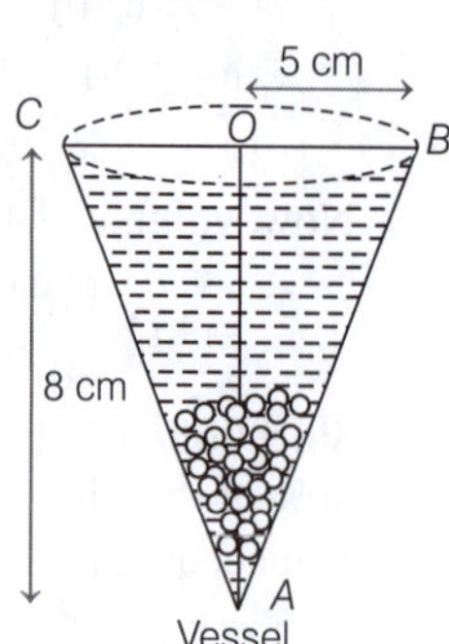

Vessel

Given, height of the vessel, $h = 8$ cm and radius of the vessel, $r = 5$ cm.

$\therefore$ Volume of water filled in a vessel

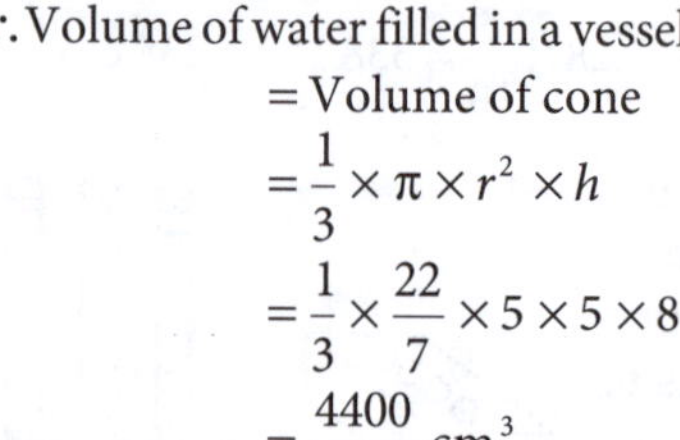

$= $ Volume of cone

$= \frac{1}{3} \times \pi \times r^2 \times h$

$= \frac{1}{3} \times \frac{22}{7} \times 5 \times 5 \times 8$

$= \frac{4400}{21} \text{ cm}^3$

Also, radius of a spherical lead shot $= 0.5$ cm

$\therefore$ Volume of one spherical lead shot $= \frac{4}{3} \times \pi \times r^3$

$= \frac{4}{3} \times \frac{22}{7} \times \frac{1}{2} \times \frac{1}{2} \times \frac{1}{2} = \frac{11}{21} \text{ cm}^3$

Let n be the number of lead shots dropped in the vessel, then according to the question,

$n \times$ Volume of one spherical lead shot

$= \frac{1}{4} \times$ Volume of water filled in a vessel

$\Rightarrow \quad n \times \frac{11}{21} = \frac{4400}{21} \times \frac{1}{4}$

$\Rightarrow \quad n \times 11 = 1100$

$\Rightarrow \quad n = 100$

Hence, required number of lead shots is 100.

Q6. A solid iron pole consists of a cylinder of height 220 cm and base diameter 24 cm, which is surmounted by another cylinder of height 60 cm and radius 8 cm. Find the mass of the pole, given that 1 cm^3 of iron has approximately 8 g mass. [take, $\pi = 3.14$]

Sol. Here, the given solid is a combination of two cylinders.

Given, height of the first cylinder, $h_1 = 220$ cm

and radius of the first cylinder, $r_1 = \frac{24}{2} = 12$ cm

Height of the second cylinder, $h_2 = 60$ cm

and radius of the second cylinder, $r_2 = 8$ cm

Now, volume of iron pole

$= $ Volume of first cylinder + Volume of second cylinder

$= \pi r_1^2 h_1 + \pi r_2^2 h_2 = \pi (r_1^2 h_1 + r_2^2 h_2)$

$= 3.14 (144 \times 220 + 64 \times 60)$

$[\because r_1 = 12 \text{cm}, h_1 = 220 \text{ cm}$ and $r_2 = 8 \text{cm}, h_2 = 60 \text{ cm}]$

$= 3.14 (31680 + 3840) = 3.14 \times 35520$

$= 111532.8 \text{ cm}^3$

16 cm

60 cm

220 cm

24 cm

Pole

$\because 1 \text{ cm}^3$ of iron pole has approximately mass $= 8$ g

$= \frac{8}{1000}$ kg $\left[\because 1\text{g} = \frac{1}{1000} \text{kg}\right]$

$\therefore$ 111532.8 cm^3 iron has approximately mass

$= 111532.8 \times \frac{8}{1000}$

$= \frac{892262.4}{1000} = 892.26$ kg

Q7. A solid consisting of a right circular cone of height 120 cm and radius 60 cm standing on a hemisphere of radius 60 cm is placed upright in a right circular cylinder full of water such that it touches the bottom. Find the volume of water left in the cylinder, if the radius of the cylinder is 60 cm and its height is 180 cm.

Sol. Given, solid is a combination of a cone and a hemisphere and it is placed into a right circular cylinder.

Height of the cylinder, $h = 180 \text{ cm} = 1.8$ m

$\left[\because 1 \text{cm} = \frac{1}{100} \text{m}\right]$

Radius of the cylinder,

$r = 60 \text{ cm} = 0.6$ m

$\therefore$ Volume of water filled in a right circular cylinder $= \pi r^2 h$

$= \frac{22}{7} \times 0.6 \times 0.6 \times 1.8$

$= \frac{14.256}{7} \text{m}^3$

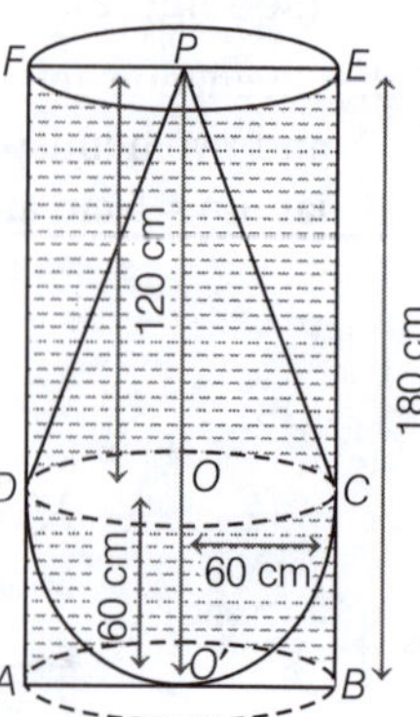

For conical portion,

Height, $h_1 = 120 \text{ cm} = 1.2$ m

Radius, $r_1 = 60 \text{ cm} = 0.6$ m

For hemispherical portion,

Radius, $r_2 = 60 \text{ cm} = 0.6$ m

$\therefore$ Volume of the solid

$= \text{Volume of the cone} + \text{Volume of the hemisphere}$

$= \frac{1}{3} \times \pi r_1^2 h_1 + \frac{2}{3} \pi r_2^3$

$= \frac{1}{3} \times \frac{22}{7} \times (0.6)^2 \times (1.2) + \frac{2}{3} \times \frac{22}{7} \times (0.6)^3$

$= \frac{22}{21} \times (0.6)^2 \,[1.2 + 2 \times 0.6]$

$= \frac{22}{21} \times 0.36\,(1.2 + 1.2)$

$= \frac{22}{21} \times 0.36 \times 2.4$

$= \frac{19.008}{21} = \frac{6.336}{7} \text{ m}^3$

Clearly, volume of water left in the cylinder

$= \text{Volume of water filled in a right circular cylinder} - \text{Volume of the solid}$

$= \frac{14.256}{7} - \frac{6.336}{7} = \frac{7.92}{7}$

$= 1.131429 \text{ m}^3 \approx 1.131 \text{ m}^3$

Note It When a solid is placed in the right circular cylinder full of water, then the volume of water which flows out from the cylinder will be equal to volume of solid. Thus, if we need to find the volume of water left in the cylinder, then we subtract the volume of the solid from volume of the cylinder filled with water.

Q 8. A spherical glass vessel has a cylindrical neck 8 cm long, 2 cm in diameter; the diameter of the spherical part is 8.5 cm. By measuring the amount of water it holds, a child finds its volume to be 345 cm^3. Check whether she is correct, taking the above as the inside measurements, and $\pi = 3.14$.

Sol. Given, spherical glass vessel is a combination of a sphere as its base and a cylinder as its neck.

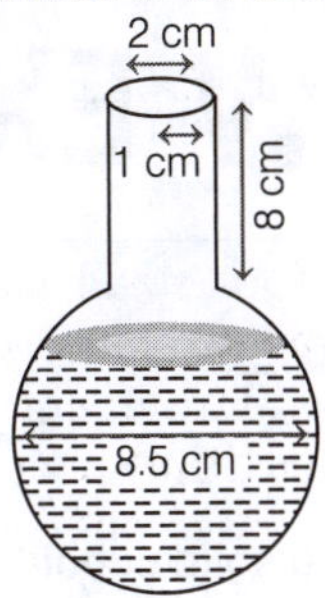

For cylindrical portion,

Height of the cylinder, $h_1 = 8$ cm

Radius of the cylinder,

$r_1 = \frac{2}{2} = 1 \text{ cm}$

For spherical portion,

Radius of the sphere,

$r_2 = \frac{8.5}{2} \text{ cm}$

$\therefore$ Volume of water filled in a spherical glass vessel

$= \text{Volume of the cylinder} + \text{Volume of the sphere}$

$= \pi r_1^2 h_1 + \frac{4}{3} \pi r_2^3$

$= 3.14 \times 1 \times 1 \times 8 + \frac{4}{3} \times 3.14 \times \frac{8.5}{2} \times \frac{8.5}{2} \times \frac{8.5}{2}$

$= 25.12 + \frac{1928.3525}{6}$

$= 25.12 + 321.39 = 346.51$

So, the correct answer is 346.51 cm^3.

REVIEW EXERCISE

Including Competency Based Questions

Part I

Multiple Choice Questions

1. **Figure 1 below is a solid cuboid made of unit cubes. Figure 2 is obtained after removing some unit cubes from figure 1.** Competency Based Question

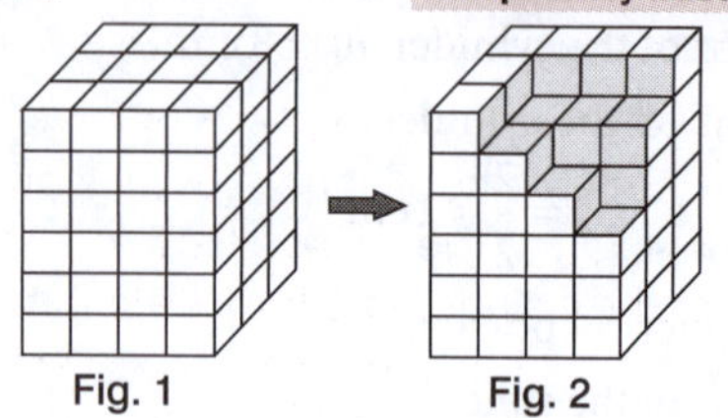

Fig. 1 Fig. 2

(Note The figures are not to scale.)

Based on the figures shown above, the surface area of the cuboid in Figure 1 is .... the surface area of the solid in Figure 2.

(a) less than (b) more than (c) equal to
(d) cannot be concluded with the given information

2. **The volume of a solid hemisphere is $\frac{396}{7}$ cm^3. The total surface area of the solid hemisphere (in sq cm) is** CBSE Sample Paper 2024-25 (Standard)

(a) $\frac{396}{7}$ (b) $\frac{594}{7}$ (c) $\frac{549}{7}$ (d) $\frac{604}{7}$

3. **The radius of the base of a right circular cone and the radius of a sphere are each 5 cm in length. If the volume of the cone is equal to the volume of the sphere, then the height of the cone is** CBSE Sample Paper 2024-25 (Standard)

(a) 5 cm (b) 20 cm (c) 10 cm (d) 4 cm

4. **If a cone of greatest possible volume is hollowed out from a solid wooden cylinder then the ratio of the volume of remaining wood to the volume of cone hollowed out is** CBSE 2025 (Standard)

(a) 1 : 1 (b) 1 : 3 (c) 2 : 1 (d) 3 : 1

5. **The volume of air in a hollow cylinder is 450 cm^3. A cone of same height and radius as that of cylinder is kept inside it. The volume of empty space in the cylinder is** CBSE 2025 (Basic)

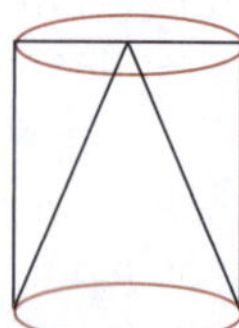

(a) 225 cm^3 (b) 150 cm^3 (c) 250 cm^3 (d) 300 cm^3

Assertion-Reason Type Questions

6. **Assertion** The surface area of largest sphere that can be inscribed in a hollow cube of side a cm is πa^2 cm^2.

Reason The surface area of a sphere of radius r is $\frac{4}{3}\pi r^3$. CBSE 2023 (Basic)

(a) Both Assertion and Reason are correct and Reason is the correct explanation of Assertion.
(b) Both Assertion and Reason are correct but Reason is not the correct explanation of Assertion.
(c) Assertion is correct but Reason is incorrect.
(d) Assertion is incorrect but Reason is correct.

7. **Assertion** Total surface area of the toy is the sum of the curved surface area of the hemisphere and the curved surface area of the cone.

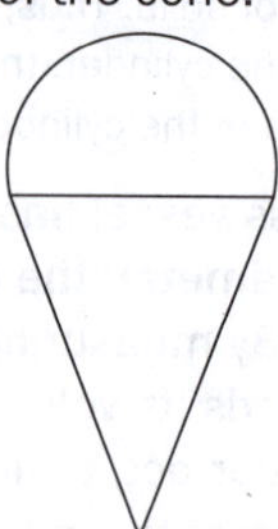

Reason Toy is obtained by fixing the plane surfaces of the hemisphere and cone together. CBSE Sample Paper 2023 (Standard)

(a) Both Assertion and Reason are correct and Reason is the correct explanation of Assertion.
(b) Both Assertion and Reason are correct but Reason is not the correct explanation of Assertion.
(c) Assertion is correct but Reason is incorrect.
(d) Assertion is incorrect but Reason is correct.

Case Study Based Questions

8. Metallic silos are used by farmers for storing grains. Farmer Girdhar has decided to build a new metallic silo to store his harvested grains. It is in the shape of a cylinder mounted by a cone.

Dimensions of the conical part of a silo is as follows.

Radius of base = 1.5 m

Height = 2 m

Dimensions of the cylindrical part of a silo is as follow.

Radius of base = 1.5 m

Height = 7 m

On the basis of the above information, answer the following questions.

(i) Calculate the slant height of the conical part of one silo.

(ii) Find the curved surface area of the conical part of one silo.

(iii) (a) Find the cost of metal sheet used to make the curved cylindrical part of 1 silo at the rate of ₹ 2000 per m^2.

(b) Find the total capacity of one silo to store grains.

CBSE Sample Paper 2024-25 (Standard)

Part II

Very Short Answer Type Questions

1. If two cubes of edge 5 cm, each are joined end-to-end, then find the surface area of the resulting cuboid.

2. If two solid hemispheres of same base of radius r are joined together along their bases, then find curved surface area of this new solid.

Competency Based Question

3. A solid ball is exactly fitted inside the cubical box of side a. What is the volume of remaining space inside the cubical box?

4. From a circular cylinder of diameter 10 cm and height 12 cm, a conical cavity of the same base radius and of the same height is hollowed out. Find the volume of the remaining solid. [take, $\pi = 3.14$]

5. Find the volume of the largest right circular cone that can be cut-out from a cube of edge 4.2 cm.

NCERT Exemplar

Short Answer Type Questions

6. Three cubes of volume 27 cm^3 each are joined end-to-end to form a solid. Find the surface area of the cuboid so formed.

7. Two cones with same base radius 8 cm and height 15 cm are joined together along their bases. Find the surface area of the shape so formed. **NCERT Exemplar**

8. An hour glass is made using identical double glass cones of diameter 10 cm each. If total height is 24 cm, then find the surface area of the glass used in making it.

Competency Based Question

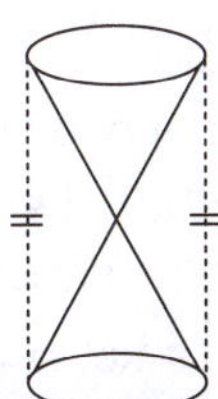

9. A solid toy is in the form of a hemisphere surmounted by a right circular cone. Ratio of the radius of the cone to its slant height is 3 : 5. If the volume of the toy is $240\pi \text{ cm}^3$, then find the total height of the toy.

CBSE 2024 (Standard) Compartment

10. A hemispherical depression is cut out from one face of a cubical wooden block such that the diameter 4 units of the hemisphere is equal to the edge of the cube. Determine the surface area of the remaining solid.

11. A metal container is in the form of a cylinder surmounted by a hemisphere of the same radius. The internal height of the cylinder is 7 m and the internal radius of the cylinder is 3.5 m. Calculate the total surface area of the container. **CBSE 2024 (Standard)**

12. A solid is composed of a cylinder with hemispherical ends. If the whole length of the solid is 108 cm and the diameter of the hemispherical ends is 36 cm, find the cost of polishing the surface of the solid at the rate of 7 paise per sq cm. $\left[\text{take, } \pi = \frac{22}{7}\right]$

Competency Based Question

13. From a solid cylinder whose height is 15 cm and the diameter is 16 cm, a conical cavity of the same height and same diameter is hollowed out. Find the total surface area of remaining solid.

[give your answer in terms of π] **CBSE 2020 (Basic)**

14. A circus tent is cylindrical upto a height of 4 m and conical above it. If the diameter of the base is 98 m and the slant height of the conical part is 33 m, then find the total canvas used in making the tent.

15. A tent is in the shape of a right circular cylinder upto a height of 3 m and conical above it. The total height of the tent is 13.5 m above the ground. Calculate the cost of painting the inner side of the tent at the rate of ₹ 2 per m^2, if the radius of the base is 14 m.

CBSE 2024 (Standard)

16. A circus tent is made up using two different coloured cloth material. Red coloured material is used to make cylindrical part upto a height of 3 m and green coloured material to make conical part above it. If the diameter of the base is 105 m and slant height of the conical part is 53 m, find the red coloured material and green coloured material required.[assuming no stitching margins.] **Competency Based Question**

17. A wooden article as shown in the figure was made from a cylinder by scooping out a hemisphere from one end and a cone from the other end. Find the total surface area of the article. **CBSE 2024 (Basic)**

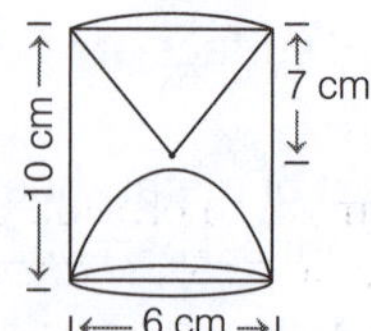

18. A conical hole is drilled in a circular cylinder of height 15 cm and radius 8 cm, which has same height and same base radius. Find the total surface area after drilling of cone. [take, $\pi = 3.14$]

19. A warehouse is used as a granary. It is in the shape of a cuboid surmounted by a half-cylinder. The base of the warehouse is 6 m × 14 m and its height is 8 m. Find the surface area of the non-cuboidal part of the warehouse. **Competency Based Question**

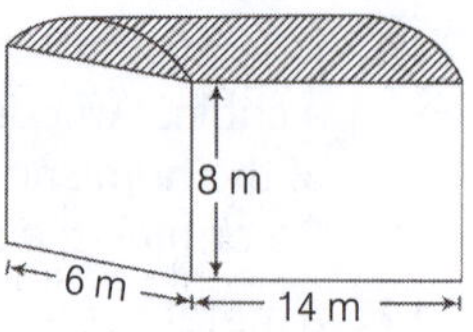

20. 50 circular plates, each of radius 7 cm and thickness 0.5 cm, are placed one above another to form a solid right circular cylinder. Find the total surface area and the volume of the cylinder so formed.

21. A building is in the form of a cylinder surmounted by a hemispherical vaulted dome and contains $41\frac{19}{21}\ m^3$ of air. If the internal diameter of dome is equal to its total height above the floor. Find the height of the building. **NCERT Exemplar**

22. A rocket is in the form of a right circular cylinder closed at the lower end and surmounted by a cone with the same radius as that of the cylinder. The diameter and height of the cylinder are 6 cm and 12 cm, respectively. If the slant height of the conical portion is 5 cm, find the total surface area and volume of the rocket. [take, $\pi = 3.14$] **NCERT Exemplar**

23. A small terrace at a hockey ground comprises of 10 steps each of which 20 m long and built of solid concrete. Each step has a rise of $\frac{1}{4}$ m and a tread of $\frac{1}{2}$ m. Calculate the total volume of concrete required to build the terrace.

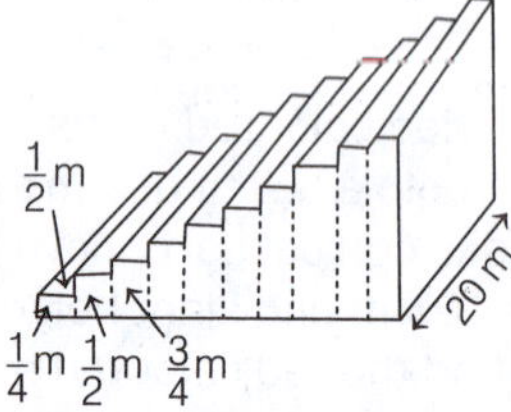

24. A wooden article was made by scooping out a hemisphere from one face of a cubical wooden block. If each edge of cube is 10 cm and diameter of base of hemisphere is 7 cm, then find the volume of wooden article. **CBSE 2024 (Standard)**

25. A juice seller was serving his customers using glasses as shown in figure. The inner diameter of the cylindrical glass was 5 cm but bottom of the glass had a hemispherical raised portion which reduced the capacity of the glass. If the height of a glass was 10 cm, find the apparent and actual capacity of the glass. [take, $\pi = 3.14$] **CBSE 2019**

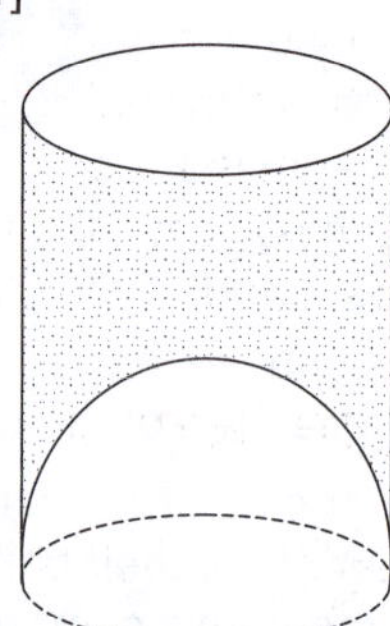

26. A spherical glass vessel has a cylindrical neck 7 cm long, 4 cm in diameter, the diameter of the spherical part is 21 cm. Find the quantity of water it can hold. $\left[\text{take, } \pi = \frac{22}{7}\right]$

27. A vessel is in the form of a hemisphere bowl mounted by a hollow cylinder. The diameter of the hemisphere is 16 cm and the total of height of the vessel is 15 cm. Find the capacity of the vessel. $\left[\text{take, } \pi = \frac{22}{7}\right]$

28. A trophy awarded to the best student in the class is in the form of a solid cylinder mounted on a solid hemisphere with the same radius and is made from some metal. This trophy is mounted on a wooden cuboid as shown in the figure. The diameter of the hemisphere is 21 cm and the total height of the trophy is 24.5 cm. Find the weight of the metal used in making the trophy, if the weight of 1 cm^3 of the metal is 1.2 g.

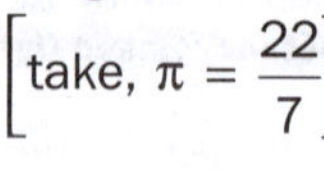

$\left[\text{take, } \pi = \frac{22}{7}\right]$ **Competency Based Question**

29. From a circular cylinder of diameter 14 cm and height 15 cm, a conical cavity of the same base radius and of the same height is hollowed out. Find the volume of the remaining solid. $\left[\text{take, } \pi = \frac{22}{7}\right]$

30. A solid is in the shape of a right-circular cone surmounted on a hemisphere the radius of each of them being 3.5 cm and the total height of the solid is 9.5 cm. Find the volume of the solid. **CBSE 2023 (Standard)**

31. From a solid cube of side 7 cm, a conical cavity of height 7 cm and radius 3 cm is hollowed out. Find the volume of the remaining solid. **NCERT Exemplar**

32. A pen stand made of wood is in the shape of a cuboid with four conical depressions and a cubical depression to hold the pens and pins, respectively. The dimensions of cuboid are 10 cm, 5 cm and 4 cm. The radius of each of the conical depressions is 0.5 cm and the depth is 2.1 cm. The edge of the cubical depression is 3 cm. Find the volume of the wood in the entire stand. **Competency Based Question**

Long Answer Type Questions

33. Dinesh is building a greenhouse in his farm as shown below. The base of the greenhouse is circular having a diameter of 12 m and it has a hemispherical dome on top.

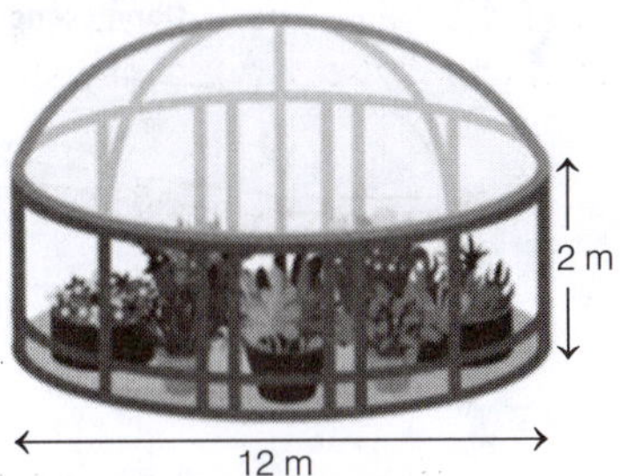

(**Note** The image is not to scale.)

How much will it cost him to cover the walls and top of the greenhouse with transparent plastic, if the plastic sheet costs ₹ 77 per sq m? Show your steps.

$\left[\text{take, } \pi = \frac{22}{7}\right]$ **Competency Based Question**

34. A tent is in the shape of a cylinder surmounted by a conical top. If the height and radius of the cylindrical part are 3 m and 14 m respectively and the total height of the tent is 13.5 m, find the area of the canvas required for making the tent, keeping a provision of 26 m^2 of canvas for stitching and wastage. Also, find the cost of the canvas to be purchased at the rate of ₹ 500 per m^2. **CBSE Sample Paper 2023 (Standard)**

35. A solid is in the form of cone mounted on a hemisphere in such a way that the centre of the base of the cone just coincide with the centre of the base of the hemisphere.

Slant height of the cone is l and radius of the base of the cone is $\frac{1}{2}r$, where r is the radius of the hemisphere. Prove that the total surface area of the solid is $\frac{\pi}{4}(11r + 2l)r$ sq unit.

36. Due to heavy floods in a state, thousands were rendered homeless. 50 schools collectively offered to the state government to provide place and the canvas for 1500 tents to be fixed by the government and decided to share their whole expenditure equally. The lower part of each tent is cylindrical of base radius 2.8 m and height 3.5 m, with conical upper part of same base radius but of height 2.1 m. If the canvas used to make the tents cost ₹ 120 per m^2, then find the amount shared by each school to set up the tents.

$\left[\text{take, } \pi = \frac{22}{7}\right]$ **Competency Based Question**

37. From one face of a solid cube of side 14 cm, the largest possible cone is carved out. Find the volume and surface area of the remaining solid.

$\left[\text{use } \pi = \frac{22}{7}, \sqrt{5} = 2.2\right]$ **CBSE 2025 (Standard)**

38. Shown below is a cake that Subodh is baking for his brother's birthday. The cake is 21 cm tall and has a radius of 15 cm. He wants to surprise his brother by filling gems inside the cake. In order to do that, he removes a cylindrical portion of cake out of the centre as shown. The piece that is removed is 21 cm tall.

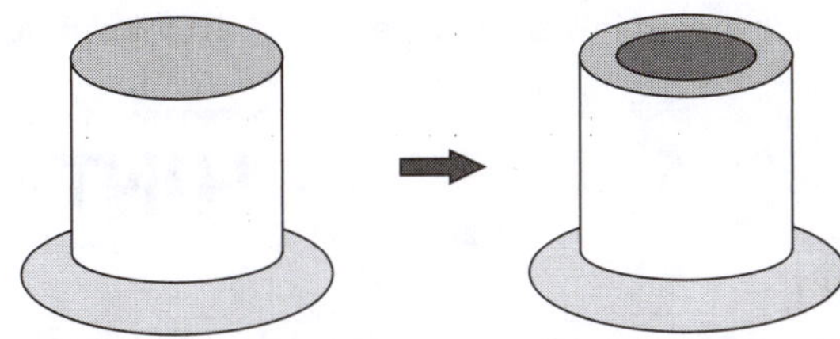

If the cake weights 0.5 g per cubic cm and the weight of the cake that is left after removing the central portion is 6600 g, find the radius of the central portion that is cut. Show your steps.

$\left[\text{take, } \pi = \frac{22}{7}\right]$ **Competency Based Question**

39. A building is in the form of a cylinder surmounted by a hemispherical dome (see the figure). The base diameter of the dome is equal to $\frac{2}{3}$ of the total height of the building. Find the height of the building, if it contains $67\frac{1}{21}$ m^3 of air. **CBSE 2023 (Standard)**

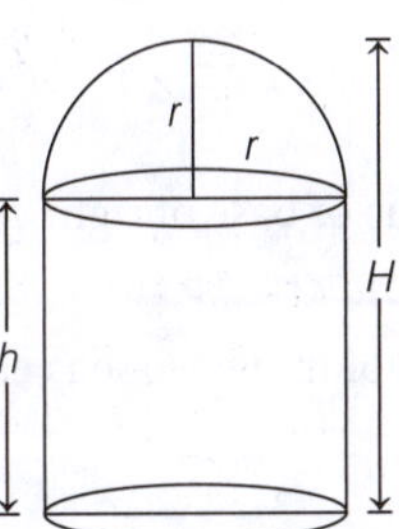

40. Shown below is a solid made of a cone, a cylinder and a hemisphere.

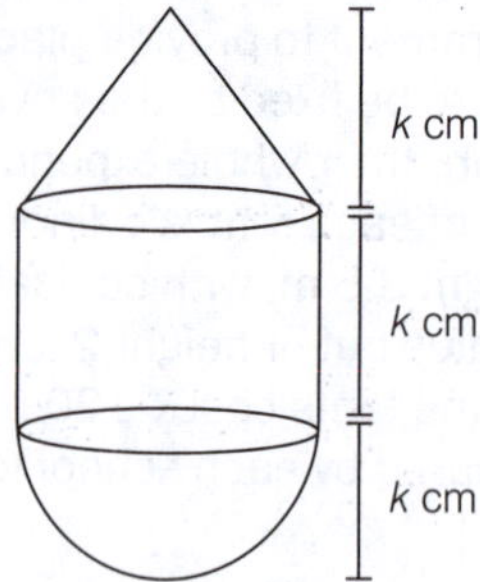

(**Note** The figure is not to scale.)

Prove that the total volume of the solid is twice the volume of the cylinder. **Competency Based Question**

41. Water is flowing at the rate of 15 km/h through a pipe of diameter 14 cm into a cuboidal pond which is 50 m long and 44 m wide. In what time will the level of water in pond rise by 21 cm?

What should be the speed of water, if the rise in water level is to be attained in 1 h? **CBSE Sample Paper 2023 (Standard)**

42. An ice-cream filled cone having radius 5 cm and height 10 cm is as shown in the figure. Find the volume of the ice-cream in 7 such cones. **CBSE 2023 (Basic)**

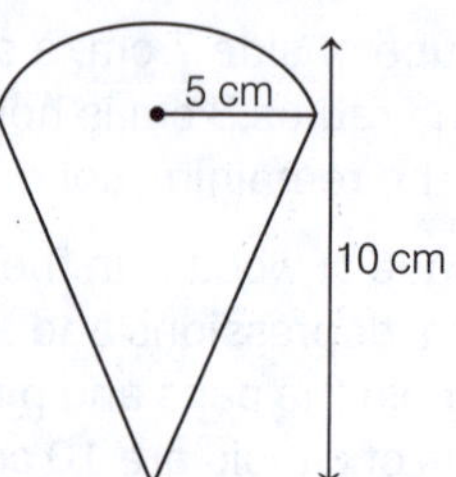

43. Neetu runs an industry in a shed which is in the shape of a cuboid surmounted by a half cylinder see in the figure. If the base of the shade is of dimension 7 m × 15 m and height of the cuboidal portion is 8 m. Find the volume of air that the shed can hold. Further suppose the machinery in the shed occupies a total space of 400 m^3 and there are 15 workers, each of whom occupy about 0.08 m^3 space on average. Then, how much air in the shed?

$\left[\text{take, } \pi = \frac{22}{7}\right]$

Competency Based Question

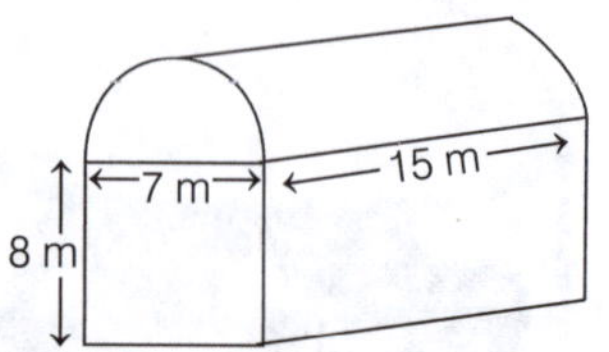

HINTS & SOLUTIONS

Part I

1. (c) **Hint** We know, the surface area of any given object is the area or region occupied by the surface of the object.

Thus, both figures have equal surface area.

2. (b) Let r be the radius of hemisphere.

Given, volume of a solid hemisphere is $\frac{396}{7}$ cm^3

$$\therefore \quad \frac{2}{3}\pi r^3 = \frac{396}{7}$$

$$\Rightarrow \quad r^3 = \frac{396 \times 3 \times 7}{2 \times 22 \times 7} = 27$$

$$\Rightarrow \quad r = 3\,\text{cm}$$

Total surface area of the solid hemisphere

$$= 3\pi r^2 = 3 \times \frac{22}{7} \times 3^2 = \frac{594}{7}\ \text{cm}^2$$

3. (b) Given, radius of base of right circular cone = 5 cm and radius of a sphere = 5 cm

It is given that volume of cone is equal to the volume of sphere i.e. $\frac{1}{3}\pi r^2 h = \frac{4}{3}\pi r^3$

$$\Rightarrow \quad \frac{1}{3}\pi(5)^2 h = \frac{4}{3}\pi(5)^3$$

$$\therefore \quad h = 20\ \text{cm}$$

4. (c) Let r and h be the radius and height of the cylinder, respectively.

$\therefore$ Volume of cylinder $= \pi r^2 h$

Since, the cone is hollowed out from the cylinder with the greatest possible volume, therefore it has same radius and height as the cylinder.

$\therefore$ Volume of cone $= \frac{1}{3}\pi r^2 h$

Volume of remaining wood = Volume of cylinder − Volume of cone

$$= \pi r^2 h - \frac{1}{3}\pi r^2 h = \frac{2}{3}\pi r^2 h$$

Now, $\frac{\text{Volume of remaining wood}}{\text{Volume of cone hollowed out}}$

$$= \frac{\frac{2}{3}\pi r^2 h}{\frac{1}{3}\pi r^2 h} = \frac{2}{1}$$

Hence, the ratio of volume of remaining wood to the volume of cone hollowed out is 2 : 1.

5. (a) Volume of cylinder, $V_{\text{cylinder}} = 450 \text{ cm}^3$

Since, the cone has the same radius and height as the cylinder, so its volume is

$$V_{\text{cone}} = \frac{1}{3}\pi r^2 h = \frac{1}{3} \times V_{\text{cylinder}} = \frac{1}{3} \times 450 = 150 \text{ cm}^3$$

$$V_{\text{empty}} = V_{\text{cylinder}} - V_{\text{cone}} = 450 - 150 = 300 \text{ cm}^3$$

6. (c) Given, side of cube = a cm

and diameter of sphere = a cm

$\therefore$ Radius of sphere = $\frac{a}{2}$ cm

We know that surface area of sphere = $4\pi r^2$

$$= 4\pi \times \frac{a}{2} \times \frac{a}{2} = a^2 \pi \text{ cm}^2$$

7. (a) Total surface area (TSA) of toy

= CSA of hemisphere + CSA of cone

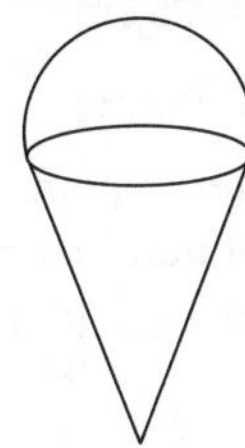

So, Assertion is true.

Reason Since, the top is obtained by joining hemisphere and cone together, we can calculate its area by adding curved surface area of both cone and hemisphere, which is true.

8. Given dimension of conical part of a silo is radius of base = 1.5 m

Height = 2 m

And dimension of the cylindrical part of a silo is radius of base = 1.5 m

Height = 7 m

(i) We know that slant height

$$l = \sqrt{r^2 + h^2} = \sqrt{(1.5)^2 + (2)^2} = 2.5 \text{ m}$$

(ii) Curved surface area of cone = $\pi r l$

$$= \frac{22}{7} \times 1.5 \times 2.5 = 11.78 \text{ m}^2$$

(iii) (a) Curved surface area of cylinder = $2\pi r h$

$$= 2 \times \frac{22}{7} \times 1.5 \times 7 = 66 \text{ m}^2$$

Cost of 1 m^2 of metal sheet = ₹ 2000

$\therefore$ Cost of metal sheet used = 66×2000 = ₹ 132000

Or

(b) Volume of cylinder = $\pi r^2 h$

$$= \frac{22}{7} \times (1.5)^2 \times 7 = 49.5 \text{ m}^3$$

Volume of cone = $\frac{1}{3}\pi r^2 h$

$$= \frac{1}{3} \times \frac{22}{7} \times (1.5)^2 \times 2 = 4.71 \text{ m}^3$$

Thus, total capacity of 1 silo = 49.5 + 4.71= 54.21 m^3.

Part II

1. **Hint** Do same as Example 1. **Ans.** 250 cm^2

2. **Hint** We know that

Curved surface area of a hemisphere = $2\pi r^2$

So, when two solids hemispheres of same base radius are joined together along their bases, then curved surface area of newly formed solid sphere = $2 \times 2\pi r^2 = 4\pi r^2$

Ans. $4\pi r^2$ sq units

3. **Hint** Diameter of solid ball

= Length of edge of cubical box = a

$\therefore$ Volume of remaining space inside the box

= Volume of cubical box – Volume of solid ball.

Ans. $\frac{a^3}{6}(6 - \pi)$ cu units

4. **Hint** Volume of remaining solid = Volume of cylinder – Volume of a conical cavity

Ans. 628 cm^3

5. **Hint** Height of the cone = Edge of the cube = 4.2 cm

and diameter of the cone = Edge of cube = 4.2 cm

Ans. 19.404 cm^3

6. **Hint** Do same as Question 1 of NCERT Folder Exercise 12.1. **Ans.** 126 cm^2

7. **Hint** If two cones with same base and height are joined together along their bases, then the shape so formed looks likes as figure shown.

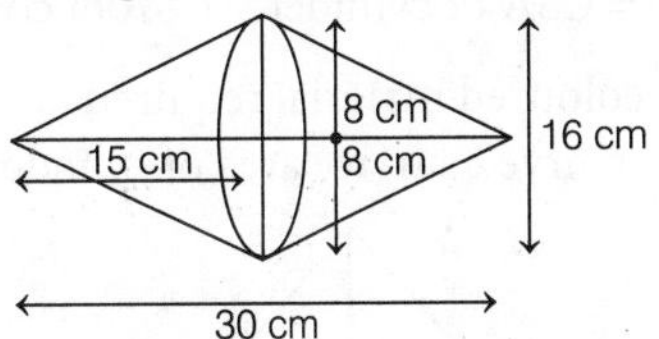

Given that radius of cone, r = 8 cm

and height of cone h = 15 cm

So, surface area of the shape so formed

= Curved area of first cone + Curved surface area of second cone

= 2 (Curved surface area of a cone)

[since, both cones are identical]

Ans. 855 cm^2 (approx.)

8. Hint Let l be the slant height of each cone given,

radius of each cone $= \frac{10}{2} = 5$ cm

and height of each cone $= \frac{24}{2} = 12$ cm

Now, we know that,

$$l = \sqrt{r^2 + h^2} \Rightarrow l = \sqrt{5^2 + 12^2} = 13 \text{ cm}$$

$\therefore$ Total surface area of two cones $= 2(\pi rl + \pi r^2)$

Ans. $180\ \pi\ \text{cm}^2$

9. Hint Let $r = 3k$ and $l = 5k$

$\Rightarrow \quad h = \sqrt{(5k)^2 - (3k)^2} = 4k$

Given, $\frac{1}{3}\pi r^2 h + \frac{2}{3}\pi r^3 = 240\pi$

$\Rightarrow \frac{1}{3}\pi(3k)^2 \cdot 4k + \frac{2}{3}\pi(3k)^3 = 240\pi$

$\Rightarrow \quad k = 2$

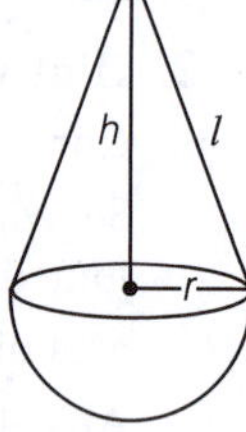

$\therefore$ Height of toy $= r + h$

Ans. 14 cm

10. Hint SA of remaining solid

= TSA of cubical wooden block

+ CSA of hemisphere

− Area of circular base of hemisphere

Ans. $4(24 + \pi)$ sq units.

11. Hint TSA of container = TSA of cylinder

+ CSA of hemisphere

− Area of circular base of cylinder

Ans. $269.5\ \text{m}^2$

12. Hint Do same as Example 4. **Ans.** ₹ 855.36

13. Hint Do same as Question 8 of NCERT Folder Exercise 12.1. **Ans.** $440\pi\ \text{cm}^2$

14. Hint Do same as Question 7 of NCERT Folder Exercise 12.1. **Ans.** $6314\ \text{m}^2$

15. Hint Required surface area

= CSA of cylinder + CSA of cone. **Ans.** ₹ 2068

16. Hint Red coloured material required

= Curved surface area of cylinder

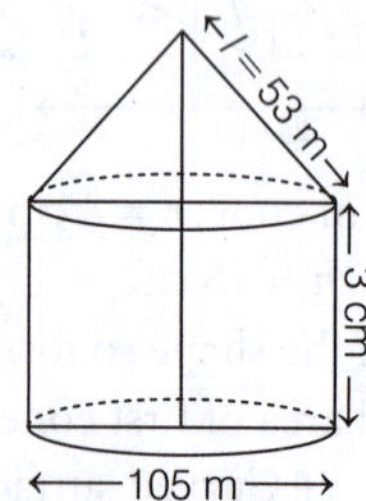

and green coloured material required

= Curved surface area of cone

Ans. 990m^2 and 8745m^2

17. Hint Total surface area of the article

= CSA of cylinder + CSA of cone + CSA of hemisphere

Ans. $316.94\ \text{cm}^2$

18. Hint TSA $= 2\pi r(r + h) + \pi rl - \pi r^2$

$= 2\pi r^2 + 2\pi rh + \pi rl - \pi r^2$

$= 2\pi rh + \pi rl + \pi r^2$

Ans. $1381.6\ \text{cm}^2$

19. Hint Radius of cylinder,

$$r = \frac{\text{Breadth of cuboid}}{2} = \frac{6}{2} = 3 \text{ m}$$

and height of cylinder = Length of cuboid = 14 m

$\therefore$ Surface area of the non-cuboidal part

= Curved surface area of half cylinder

+2 × Area of one semi-circle.

Ans. $\frac{1122}{7}\ \text{m}^2$

20. Hint Given, radius of cylinder formed, $r = 7$ cm

Also, we get, height of the cylinder formed, h

= Thickness of 50 plates

$= 50 \times 0.5 = 25$ cm

Ans. $1408\ \text{cm}^2$ and $3850\ \text{cm}^3$

21. Hint Given, diameter of hemisphere = Diameter of cylinder = Height of building = H (say)

$\therefore$ Radius of hemisphere = Radius of cylinder

$= \frac{H}{2}$

and height of cylinder $= H - \frac{H}{2} = \frac{H}{2}$

Now, Volume of building = Volume of hemisphere

+ Volume of cylinder

Ans. 4 m

22. Hint Rocket is the combination of a right circular cylinder and a cone.

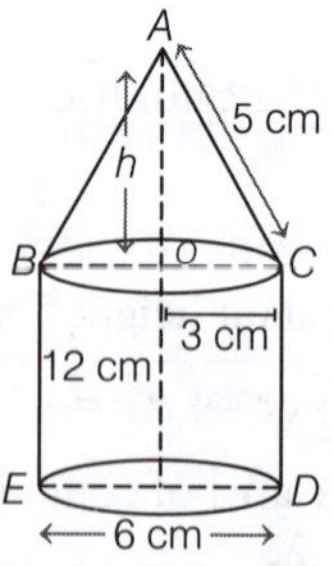

$\therefore$ Total surface area of the rocket

= CSA of cylinder + CSA of cone

+ Base area of cylinder

and total volume of the rocket

= Volume of the cylinder + Volume of the cone

Ans. $301.44\ \text{cm}^2$ and $376.8\ \text{cm}^3$

23. Hint It is clear from the figure, length = 20 m and width = $\frac{1}{2}$ m of each step.

And height of Ist step which is in the bottom = $\frac{1}{4}$ m

$\therefore$ Height of second step = $2 \times \frac{1}{4} = \frac{1}{2}$ m

Height of third step = $3 \times \frac{1}{4} = \frac{3}{4}$ m

$\vdots \qquad \vdots$

Height of tenth step = $10 \times \frac{1}{4} = \frac{10}{4}$ m

Total volume of the concrete used

$$= 20 \times \frac{1}{2} \times \frac{1}{4} + 20 \times \frac{1}{2} \times \frac{2}{4} + 20 \times \frac{1}{2} \times \frac{3}{4} + \dots + 20 \times \frac{1}{2} \times \frac{10}{4}$$

$[\because \text{volume of cuboid} = l \times b \times h]$

$$= 20 \times \frac{1}{2} \times \frac{1}{4} [1 + 2 + 3 + \dots + 10]$$

$$= 20 \times \frac{1}{2} \times \frac{1}{4} \times \frac{10 \times 11}{2} \quad \left[\because 1 + 2 + \dots + n = \frac{n(n+1)}{2}\right]$$

Ans. 137.5 m^3

24. Hint Volume of wooden article = Volume of cubical wooden block – Volume of hemisphere

Ans. 910.17 cm^3

25. Given height of glass, h = 10 cm

and inner diameter of the glass, d = 5 cm

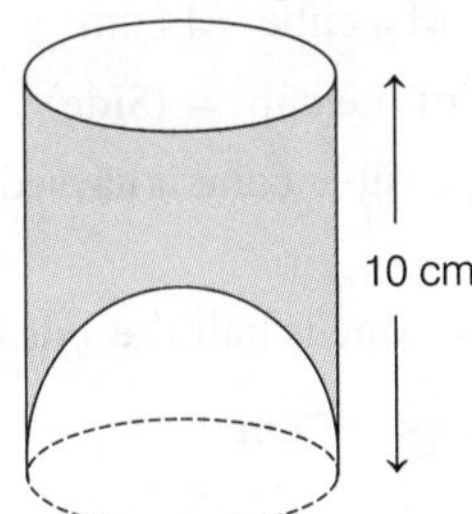

$\therefore$ Radius of glass, $r = \frac{5}{2}$ cm = 2.5 cm

Now, apparent capacity of glass

= Volume of cylindrical glass = $\pi r^2 h$

= $3.14 \times (2.5)^2 \times 10$

= 196.25 cm^3

Now, volume of hemisphere = $\frac{2}{3} \pi r^3$

$= \frac{2}{3} \times 3.14 \times (2.5)^3$

$= \frac{2}{3} \times 3.14 \times 15.625$

= 32.71 cm^3

$\therefore$ The actual capacity of the glass

= Volume of cylindrical glass – Volume of hemisphere

= 196.25 – 32.71 = 163.54 cm^3

26. Hint Quantity of water a spherical glass vessel can hold = Volume of cylindrical neck + Volume of spherical part

Ans. 4939 cm^3

27. Hint Capacity of the vessel = Volume of hemispherical bowl + Volume of the cylinder **Ans.** 2480.7619 cm^3

28. Hint Height of cylinder = Height of trophy – Radius of hemisphere

Volume of the metal used in the trophy

= Volume of cylinder + Volume of hemisphere

Weight of metal = Volume of the metal used in the trophy × 1.2 g

Ans. 8.7318 kg

29. Hint Volume of the remaining solid

= Volume of cylinder – Volume of cone

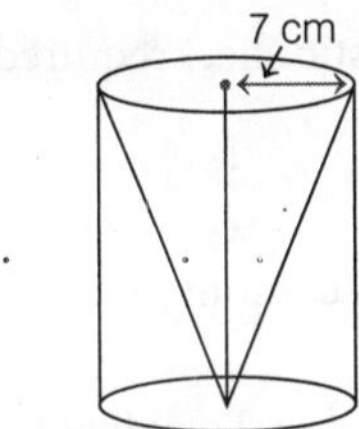

Ans. 1540 cm^3

30. Hint Radius of cone and hemisphere (r) = 3.5 cm

Height of cone (h) = Total height of the solid – Radius of hemisphere

= 9.5 – 3.5 = 6 cm

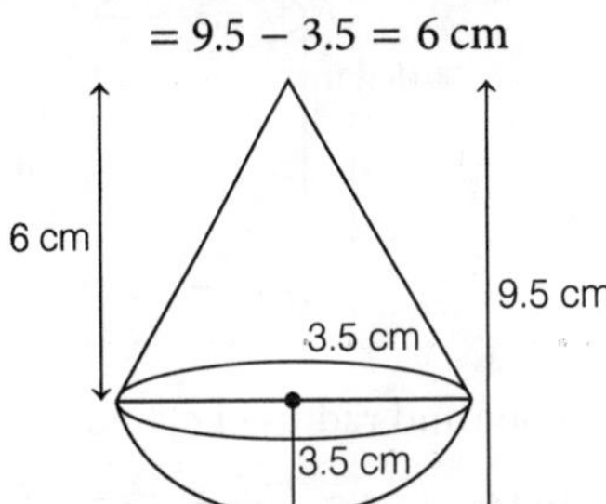

$\therefore$ Volume of the solid = Volume of cone + Volume of hemisphere

Ans. 166.83 cm^3

31. Hint

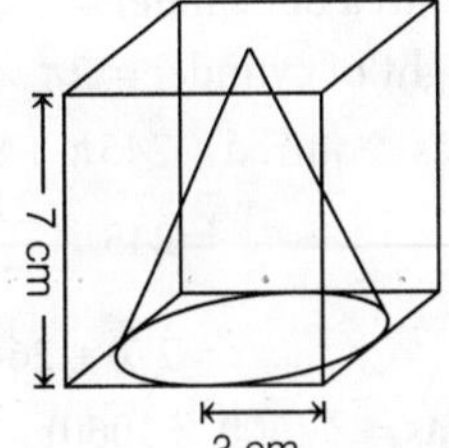

According to the question,
Volume of remaining solid

= Volume of cube – Volume of conical cavity

Ans. 277 cm^3

32. Hint Volume of the wood in the entire stand

= Volume of cuboid – 4 × Volume of each cone

– Volume of a cube

Ans. 170.8 cm^3

33. Hint Given, diameter of base of the greenhouse is circular = 12 m

Radius = 6 m

Height of greenhouse cylindrical wall = 2 m

$\therefore$ CSA of the hemispherical roof $= 2 \times \pi \times 6^2 \text{ m}^2$

$= 72\pi \text{ m}^2$

and CSA of the cylindrical wall $= 2 \times \pi \times 6 \times 2 \text{ m}^2$

$= 24\pi \text{ m}^2$

TSA of the greenhouse to be covered $= 72\pi + 24\pi$

$= 96\pi \text{ m}^2$

The cost of the plastic sheet required to cover the entire greenhouse $= 96\pi \times 77$

Ans. ₹ 23232

34. Given that tent is a combination of a cylinder and a cone.

Height of the cone, h_1 = Total height – Height of cylinder

$= 13.5 - 3 = 10.5$ m

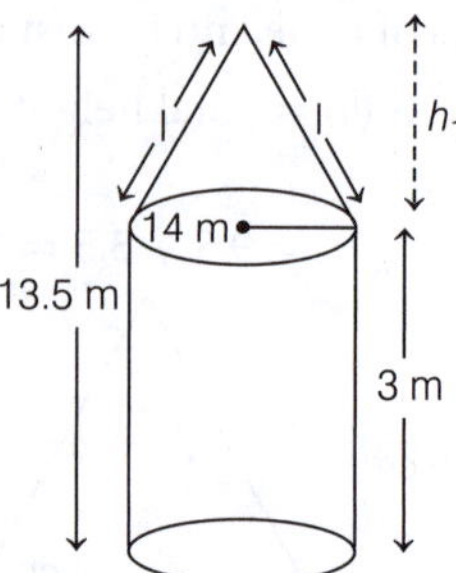

Radius of cone and radius of cylinder $r = 14$ m

Slant height l of cone $= \sqrt{h_1^2 + r^2} = \sqrt{(10.5)^2 + (14)^2}$

$= 17.5$ m

Curved surface area of cone $= \pi rl$

$= \pi \times 14 \times 17.5 = 245\ \pi \text{ m}^2$

Curved surface area of cylinder $= 2\pi r h_2$,

where h_2 is height of cylinder $= 2\pi \times 14 \times 3 = 84\ \pi \text{ m}^2$

$\therefore$ Area of canvas required $= 245\pi + 84\pi + 26$

$= 245 \times \dfrac{22}{7} + 84 \times \dfrac{22}{7} + 26$

$= 770 + 264 + 26 = 1060 \text{ m}^2$

$\therefore$ Cost of canvas = ₹ (500 × 1060) = ₹ 530000

35. Given, radius of base of cone $= \dfrac{r}{2}$,

slant height of cone $= l$

and radius of hemisphere $= r$

$\therefore$ Total surface area of solid = TSA of hemisphere

$-2 \times$ Area of base of cone + TSA of cone

$$= 3\pi r^2 + \frac{\pi r}{2}\left(\frac{r}{2} + l\right) - 2\frac{\pi r^2}{4}$$

$$= 3\pi r^2 + \frac{\pi r^2}{4} + \frac{\pi rl}{2} - \frac{\pi r^2}{2}$$

$$= 3\pi r^2 + \frac{\pi rl}{2} - \frac{\pi r^2}{4}$$

$$= \frac{11}{4}\pi r^2 + \frac{\pi rl}{2}$$

$$= \frac{\pi r}{4}(11r + 2l) \text{ sq units.}$$

Hence proved.

36. Hint Canvas required for one tent

= Curved surface area of cylinder

+ Curved surface area of cone

So, canvas required for 1500 tents

= 1500 × Canvas required for one tent.

Thus, cost of the canvas

= ₹ 120 × Canvas required for 1500 tents

Hence, amount shared by each school

$= \dfrac{\text{Cost of the canvas}}{50}$

Ans. ₹ 332640

37. Given, the side of a cube = 14 cm

$\therefore$ The volume of the cube $= (\text{Side})^3 = (14)^3 = 2744 \text{ cm}^3$

$\because$ The largest possible cone is carved out from one face of cube.

$\therefore$ The radius of cone is half the side of the cube

i.e. $r = \dfrac{14}{2} = 7$ cm

and height of the cone is equal to the side of the cube

i.e. $h = 14$ cm

$\therefore$ The volume of the cone $= \dfrac{1}{3} \times \pi r^2 h$

$= \dfrac{1}{3} \times \dfrac{22}{7} \times 7 \times 7 \times 14$

$= \dfrac{2156}{3} \text{ cm}^3$

So, the volume of remaining solid

= Volume of cube – Volume of cone

$= 2744 - \dfrac{2156}{3}$

$= \dfrac{8232 - 2156}{3} = \dfrac{6076}{3} \text{ cm}^3$

Now, surface area of cube $= 6 \times (\text{Side})^2$

$$= 6 \times (14)^2 = 1176 \text{ cm}^2$$

and the curved surface area of the cone

$$= \pi rl$$

$$= \pi r\sqrt{h^2 + r^2} \quad [\because l^2 = h^2 + r^2]$$

$$= \frac{22}{7} \times 7 \times \sqrt{14^2 + 7^2}$$

$$= \frac{22}{7} \times 7 \times 7 \times \sqrt{5}$$

$$= 22 \times 7 \times 2.23$$

$$= 343.42$$

The area of the base of the cone $= \pi r^2$

$$= \frac{22}{7} \times 7^2 = 154 \text{ cm}^2$$

So, the surface area of the remaining solid

= Surface area of cube

+ Curved surface area of cone

– Base area of cone

$$= 1176 - 154 + 343.42$$

$$= 1365.42 \text{ cm}^2$$

38. Given, height of the cylindrical cake = 21cm

Height of the piece that is removed = 21cm

Radius of cake = 15 cm

We know, volume of cylinder $= \pi r^2 h$

$$= \frac{22}{7} \times 15 \times 15 \times 21$$

$$= 14850 \text{ cm}^3$$

Weight of cake per 1 $\text{cm}^3 = 0.5$ g

Then, weight of cake per 14850 $\text{cm}^3 = 14850 \times 0.5$

$$= 7425 \text{ g}$$

Given, weight of the cake that is left after removing the central portion is 6600 g.

Thus, the weight of the portion removed $= 7425 - 6600$

$$= 825 \text{ g}$$

The volume of portion removed $= \dfrac{825}{0.5} = 1650 \text{ cm}^3$

$\therefore$ Volume of the portion removed.

$$1650 \text{ cm}^3 = \pi r^2 \times 21$$

$$r^2 = \frac{1650 \times 7}{21 \times 22}$$

$$\Rightarrow \quad r^2 = 25$$

$$\Rightarrow \quad r = 5 \text{ cm}$$

Hence, radius of the central portion that is cut is 5 cm.

39. Hint Let r be the radius of the hemispherical dome and total height of building be Hm.

It is given that diameter of dome

$$= \frac{2}{3} \times \text{Total height of the building}$$

$$\Rightarrow \quad r = \frac{1}{3} H \text{ m}$$

Let h m be the height of the cylinder.

$$\therefore \quad h = H - r = \frac{2}{3} H \text{ m}$$

Volume of the air inside the building = Volume of air inside the dome + Volume of air inside the cylinder

$$= \frac{2}{3}\pi r^3 + \pi r^2 h = \frac{8}{81}\pi H^3 \text{ m}^3$$

Given, volume of the air inside the building

$$= 67\frac{1}{21} \text{ m}^3$$

$$\therefore \quad \frac{8}{81}\pi H^3 = \frac{1408}{21}$$

Ans. 6 m

40. Given, radius of hemisphere $= k$ cm

and height of cylinder $= k$ cm

So, volume of cylinder $= \pi r^2 h = \pi k^3$ ...(i)

Volume of cone $= \dfrac{1}{3}\pi r^2 h = \dfrac{1}{3}\pi k^3$

and volume of hemisphere $= \dfrac{2}{3}\pi r^3 = \dfrac{2}{3}\pi k^3$

$\therefore$ Total volume of solid $= \pi k^3 + \dfrac{1}{3}\pi k^3 + \dfrac{2}{3}\pi k^3$

$= \pi k^3 + \pi k^3 = 2\pi k^3 \text{ cm}^3$ ...(ii)

From Eqs. (i) and (ii), we get

The volume of solid $= 2 \times$ Volume of cylinder

41. Given, diameter of cylindrical pipe = 14 cm

$\therefore$ Radius of cylindrical pipe $(r) = 7$ cm

Also, length of the pond $(l) = 50$ m,

Breadth of the pond $(b) = 44$ m

and height of the water level in the pond $(h) = 21$cm

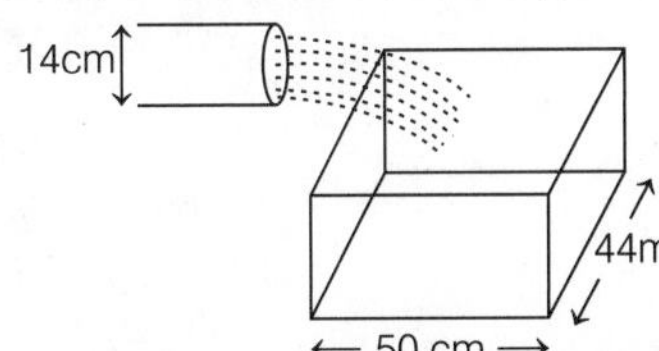

Let t h be the time taken to raise the level of water by 21 cm.

Length of the water column in t h $= (15 \times t)$ km

$$= 15000\, t \text{ m}^3$$

Volume of water column that come out from cylindrical pipe in t h $= \pi \times \left(\frac{7}{100}\right)^2 \times 15000\, t$

$\therefore$ Volume of water column

$= $ Volume of cuboid with height h

$\Rightarrow \pi \times \left(\frac{7}{100}\right)^2 \times 15000t = 50 \times 44 \times \frac{21}{100}$

$\Rightarrow \quad \frac{22}{7} \times \frac{7^2}{10} \times 15t = 22 \times 21$

$\Rightarrow \quad 7 \times 15t = 210 \Rightarrow t = 2h$

Hence, in 2 h, level of water in pond rise by 21 cm.

Let v km/h be the speed of water.

Length of the water column in 1 h $= v$ km

$= (v \times 1000)$ m

$\therefore$ Volume of water column $= \pi \times \left(\frac{7}{100}\right)^2 \times v \times 1000$

$= \frac{22 \times 7 \times v}{10}$ m^3

$\therefore \quad \frac{22 \times 7 \times v}{10} = 50 \times 44 \times \frac{21}{100} \Rightarrow v = 30$ km/h

Hence, speed of water is 30 km/h.

42. Given, radius (r) of hemispherical part = 5 cm

Height of the conical part (h)

= Total height – Radius of hemispherical part

$= 10 - 5 = 5$ cm

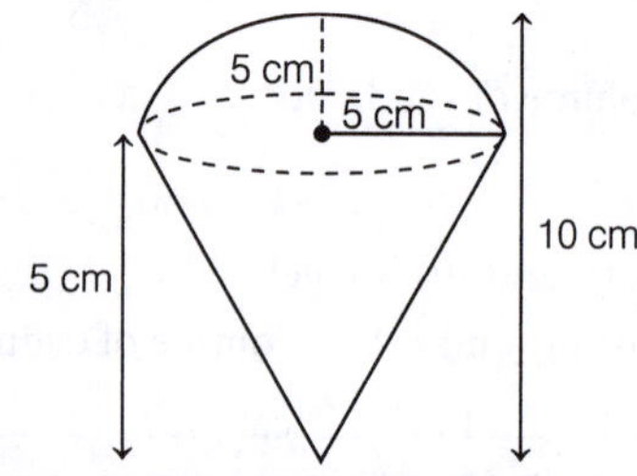

$\therefore$ Volume of ice-cream in one cone

= Volume of hemispherical part + Conical part

$= \frac{2}{3}\pi r^3 + \frac{1}{3}\pi r^2 h$

$= \frac{1}{3}\pi r^2 (2r + h)$

$= \frac{1}{3} \times \frac{22}{7} \times 5^2 (10 + 5)$

$= \frac{22}{21} \times 25 \times 15$

$= 392.86$ cm^3

$\therefore$ The volume of the ice-cream in 7 such cones

$= 7 \times 392.86$

$= 2750.02$ cm^3

43. Hint Required volume = Volume of the cuboid

$+ \frac{1}{2} \times$ Volume of the cylinder

$= 15 \times 7 \times 8 + \frac{1}{2} \times \frac{22}{7} \times \frac{7}{2} \times \frac{7}{2} \times 15$

$= 1128.75$ m^3

Total space occupied by the machinery = 400 m^3 and total space occupied by the workers

$= 15 \times 0.08$

$= 1.2$ m^3

$\therefore$ Total volume of the air, when there are machinery and workers $= 1128.75 - 400 - 1.2$

Ans. 727.55 m^3

Statistics

Statistics is the study of collection, organisation, presentation, analysis and interpretation of data. In the previous class, we have studied the classification of given data into ungrouped and grouped frequency distribution, representation of data (such as bar graphs, histograms, frequency polygon) and mean, median, mode for the ungrouped data.

In this chapter, we shall extend the study of measures of central tendency i.e., mean, median and mode, from ungrouped data to that of grouped data.

TOPIC 01 Mean of Grouped Data

Grouped and Ungrouped Data

Grouped data is the data that has been organised into several groups, called classes, whereas **ungrouped data** is the data that is obtained in original form, it is just a list of numbers.

Method to Convert Ungrouped Data into Grouped Data

Ungrouped data can be converted into grouped data by forming class intervals of equal width with allocation of frequencies to each class interval. Remember that observation falling in any upper class limit would be considered in the next class.

e.g. 6 students who obtained 60 marks, would be considered in the class interval 60-75 and not in 45-60 (here, width of the class interval is 15).

Sometimes, the grouped data is discontinuous (e.g. 1-4, 5-8, 9-12,...). Then, we convert it into continuous data by subtracting $\frac{5-4}{2} = 0.5$ from lower limit and adding 0.5 to upper limit in each interval.

(i.e. 0.5-4.5, 4.5-8.5, 8.5-12.5, ...).

Class Mark

For each class interval, we require a point which would serve as the representative of the whole class. It is assumed that the frequency of each class-interval is centred around its **mid-point**. So, the mid-point (or class mark) of each class can be chosen to represent the observations falling in the class.

$$\text{Thus, Class mark} = \frac{\text{Lower class limit} + \text{Upper class limit}}{2}$$

Arithmetic Mean or Mean or Average

The arithmetic mean of a set of observations is obtained by dividing the sum of the values of all observations by the total number of observations.

Thus, the mean of n observations $x_1, x_2, x_3, \ldots, x_n$, is defined as

$$\text{Mean } (\bar{x}) = \frac{x_1 + x_2 + x_3 + \ldots + x_n}{n} = \frac{\sum_{i=1}^{n} x_i}{n}$$

where, the Greek letter 'Σ' (sigma) means 'Summation.'

Let $x_1, x_2, \ldots, x_n$ be n observations with respective frequencies $f_1, f_2, \ldots, f_n$. This means observation x_1 occurs f_1 times, x_2 occurs f_2 times and so on.

Then, sum of the values of all the observations

$$= f_1x_1 + f_2x_2 + \ldots + f_nx_n = \sum_{i=1}^{n} f_ix_i$$

and total number of respective frequencies

$$= f_1 + f_2 + \ldots + f_n = \sum_{i=1}^{n} f_i$$

$$\therefore \quad \text{Mean } (\bar{x}) = \frac{\sum_{i=1}^{n} f_ix_i}{\sum_{i=1}^{n} f_i}$$

It can also be written as

$$\bar{x} = \frac{\Sigma f_ix_i}{\Sigma f_i}$$

Here, it is understood that i varies from 1 to n.

Note It $\bar{x}$ is read as 'x bar'.

Example 1. **Find the mean of the following data.**

x	10	30	50	70	89
f	7	8	10	15	10

Sol. Table for the given data is

x_i	f_i	f_ix_i
10	7	70
30	8	240
50	10	500
70	15	1050
89	10	890
Total	$\Sigma f_i = 50$	$\Sigma f_ix_i = 2750$

Here, $\Sigma f_i = 50$ and $\Sigma f_ix_i = 2750$

$$\therefore \quad \text{Mean } (\bar{x}) = \frac{\Sigma f_ix_i}{\Sigma f_i} = \frac{2750}{50} = 55$$

Hence, the mean of the given data is 55.

Example 2. **The mean of the following data is 14. Find the value of k.**

x	5	10	15	20	25
f	7	k	8	4	5

Sol. Table for the given data is

x_i	f_i	f_ix_i
5	7	35
10	k	$10k$
15	8	120
20	4	80
25	5	125
Total	$\Sigma f_i = k + 24$	$\Sigma f_ix_i = 10k + 360$

Here, $\Sigma f_i = k + 24$ and $\Sigma f_ix_i = 10k + 360$

Given, $\quad \text{mean} = 14$

$$\therefore \quad \frac{\Sigma f_i x_i}{\Sigma f_i} = 14$$

$$\Rightarrow \quad \frac{10k + 360}{k + 24} = 14$$

$$\Rightarrow \quad 10k + 360 = 14(k + 24)$$

$$\Rightarrow \quad 10k + 360 = 14k + 336$$

$$\Rightarrow \quad 14k - 10k = 360 - 336$$

$$\Rightarrow \quad 4k = 24$$

$$\therefore \quad k = \frac{24}{4} = 6$$

Hence, the value of k is 6.

Method of Calculating Mean of Grouped Data

To calculate the mean of grouped data, we have following three methods:

1. Direct method
2. Assumed mean method
3. Step deviation method

The process of finding mean by these methods are given below:

1. Direct Method

In this method, find the class marks of each class interval. These class marks would serve as the representative of whole class and are represented by x_i.

In general, for the ith class interval, we have the frequency f_i corresponding to the class mark x_i. The sum of the values in the last column gives us Σf_ix_i, so the mean $\bar{x}$ of the given data is given by

$$\bar{x} = \frac{\Sigma f_ix_i}{\Sigma f_i}$$

Example 3. **The marks obtained by 30 students of Class X of a certain school in a Mathematics paper consisting of 100 marks are presented in table below**

Class interval	10-25	25-40	40-55	55-70	70-85	85-100
Number of students	2	3	7	6	6	6

Find the mean of the marks obtained by the students.

CBSE 2020 (Basic)

Sol. Let us make the following table for the given data.

Class interval	Frequency (f_i)	Class marks (x_i)	$f_i x_i$
10-25	2	$\frac{10+25}{2}=17.5$	35.0
25-40	3	$\frac{25+40}{2}=32.5$	97.5
40-55	7	$\frac{40+55}{2}=47.5$	332.5
55-70	6	$\frac{55+70}{2}=62.5$	375.0
70-85	6	$\frac{70+85}{2}=77.5$	465.0
85-100	6	$\frac{85+100}{2}=92.5$	555.0
Total	$\Sigma f_i = 30$		$\Sigma f_i x_i = 1860.0$

Here, $\Sigma f_i = 30$ and $\Sigma f_i x_i = 1860.0$

On putting the values of $\Sigma f_i x_i$ and Σf_i in the formula,

$$\bar{x} = \frac{\Sigma f_i x_i}{\Sigma f_i}, \text{ we get}$$

$$\bar{x} = \frac{1860.0}{30} = 62$$

Hence, the mean marks obtained by the students are 62.

Example 4. **The arithmetic mean of the following frequency distribution is 53. Find the value of *k*.** CBSE 2019

Class	0-20	20-40	40-60	60-80	80-100
Frequency	12	15	32	k	13

Sol. Table for given data is

Class	Class marks (x_i)	Frequency (f_i)	$f_i x_i$
0-20	10	12	120
20-40	30	15	450
40-60	50	32	1600
60-80	70	k	$70k$
80-100	90	13	1170
Total		$\Sigma f = 72 + k$	$\Sigma f_i x_i = 3340 + 70k$

Here, $\Sigma f_i = 72 + k$ and $\Sigma f_i x_i = 3340 + 70k$

$$\therefore \quad \text{Mean } (\bar{x}) = \frac{\Sigma f_i x_i}{\Sigma f_i}$$

$$\Rightarrow \quad 53 = \frac{3340 + 70k}{72 + k}$$

$$\Rightarrow \quad 3816 + 53k = 3340 + 70k$$

$$\Rightarrow \quad 17k = 476 \Rightarrow k = 28$$

Hence, the value of k is 28.

2. Assumed Mean Method

The cases, in which numerical values of x_i and f_i are large and computation of product of x_i and f_i becomes tedious and time consuming, assumed mean method is used. In this method, first of all, one among x_i's is chosen as the **assumed mean** denoted by 'a'. After that, the difference d_i between a and each of the x_i's i.e. $d_i = x_i - a$ is calculated.

Then, arithmetic mean is given by

$$\bar{x} = a + \frac{\Sigma f_i d_i}{\Sigma f_i}$$

where, $\quad d_i = x_i - a$

Note it We may take a to be that x_i which lies in the middle of $x_1, x_2, \ldots, x_n$.

Example 5. **Find the mean of the following frequency distribution using assumed mean method.**

Class	2-8	8-14	14-20	20-26	26-32
Frequency	6	3	12	11	8

Sol. Let us make the following table.

Class	Frequency (f_i)	x_i	$d_i = x_i - a$	$f_i d_i$
2-8	6	$\frac{2+8}{2}=5$	$5-17=-12$	$6(-12)=-72$
8-14	3	$\frac{8+14}{2}=11$	$11-17=-6$	$3(-6)=-18$
14-20	12	$\frac{14+20}{2}=17=a$	$17-17=0$	$12\times0=0$
20-26	11	$\frac{20+26}{2}=23$	$23-17=6$	$11\times6=66$
26-32	8	$\frac{26+32}{2}=29$	$29-17=12$	$8\times12=96$
Total	$\Sigma f_i = 40$			$\Sigma f_i d_i = 72$

Here, $a = 17$, $\Sigma f_i = 40$ and $\Sigma f_i d_i = 72$

$$\therefore \text{ Mean } (\bar{x}) = a + \frac{\Sigma f_i d_i}{\Sigma f_i} = 17 + \frac{72}{40} = 17 + 1.8 = 18.8$$

3. Step Deviation Method

Step deviation method is used in the cases, where the deviations from the assumed mean are multiples of a common number. If the values of d_i for each class is a multiple of h (say), the calculation becomes simpler by taking

$$u_i = \frac{d_i}{h} = \frac{x_i - a}{h}$$

Here, h is the class size of each class interval. Generally, the value of h is equal to the difference between upper and lower class limits of a class or the difference between two consecutive class marks. The arithmetic mean is given by

$$\bar{x} = a + \left(\frac{\Sigma f_i u_i}{\Sigma f_i}\right) \times h, \text{ where } u_i = \frac{x_i - a}{h}$$

Note it
- If the class sizes are not equal for each class interval, then we take h to be a suitable divisor of all the d_i's.
- The mean obtained by all the three methods is always the same.
- The assumed mean method and step deviation method are just simplified forms of the direct method.
- If the given data is discontinuous, there is no need to convert it into continuous data, while finding the mean, because mid-value x_i of each class interval would be same either class interval is continuous or not continuous.

Example 6. **Find mean of the following data.**

Class	0-15	15-30	30-45	45-60	60-75	75-90
frequency	12	15	11	20	16	6

CBSE 2023 (Basic)

Sol. Here, class width $(h) = 15$

Table for the given data is

Classes	f_i	x_i	$d_i = x_i - a$	$u_i = \frac{x_i - a}{h}$	$f_i u_i$
0 - 15	12	7.5	−30	−2	−24
15 - 30	15	22.5	−15	−1	−15
30 - 45	11	$a = 37.5$	0	0	0
45 - 60	20	52.5	15	1	20
60 - 75	16	67.5	30	2	32
75 - 90	6	82.5	45	3	18
Total	$\Sigma f_i = 80$				$\Sigma f_i u_i = 31$

$$\therefore \text{ Mean } (\bar{x}) = a + h\left(\frac{\Sigma f_i u_i}{\Sigma f_i}\right) = 37.5 + 15 \times \frac{31}{80}$$

$$= 37.5 + 5.8125$$

$$= 43.3125$$

Selection of Method for Calculating Mean

The value of mean obtained by all the three methods is the same.

So, the choice of method to be used depends on the numerical values of x_i and f_i.

- If x_i and f_i are sufficiently small, then we use the direct method.
- If x_i and f_i are numerically large numbers, then we can use assumed mean method or step deviation method.
- The step deviation method will be convenient to apply if all d_i's have a common factor.
- If the class sizes are unequal and x_i's are numerically large, we can still apply the step deviation method by taking h to be a suitable divisor of all the d_i's.

Example 7. **In a health check up, the number of heart beats of 40 women were recorded in the following table:**

Number of heart beats/minute	65-69	70-74	75-79	80-84
Number of women	2	18	16	4

Find the mean of the data.

Sol. Here, class intervals are not continuous. But mid-value x_i of each class interval would be same either class interval is continuous or not continuous.

So, we solve it without making it continuous.

Also, x_i's are larger, so we apply step-deviation method.

Here, class width $(h) = 5$.

Table for the given data is

Number of heart beats/ minute	Class marks (x_i)	Number of women (f_i)	$u_i = \frac{x_i - 72}{5}$	$f_i u_i$
65-69	67	2	−1	−2
70-74	$72 = a$	18	0	0
75-79	77	16	1	16
80-84	82	4	2	8
Total		$\Sigma f_i = 40$		$\Sigma f_i u_i = 22$

Now, we have, $a = 72, h = 5, \Sigma f_i = 40$

and $\Sigma f_i u_i = 22$

$\therefore$ By step deviation method,

$$\text{Mean } (\bar{x}) = a + \frac{\Sigma f_i u_i}{\Sigma f_i} \times h$$

$$= 72 + \frac{22}{40} \times 5$$

$$= 72 + 2.75$$

$$= 74.75$$

Example 8. **In a class test, marks obtained by 120 students are given in the following frequency distribution. If it is given that mean is 59, then find the missing frequencies *x* and *y*.**

Marks	Number of students
0-10	1
10-20	3
20-30	7
30-40	10
40-50	15
50-60	x
60-70	9
70-80	27
80-90	18
90-100	y

Sol. Here, width of class interval, $h = 10$.

Let the assumed mean, $a = 55$.

Now, let us make the following table for given data

Marks	Class marks (x_i)	Number of students (f_i)	$u_i = \frac{x_i - a}{h}$	$f_i u_i$
0-10	5	1	−5	−5
10-20	15	3	−4	−12
20-30	25	7	−3	−21
30-40	35	10	−2	−20
40-50	45	15	−1	−15
50-60	$55 = a$	x	0	0
60-70	65	9	1	9
70-80	75	27	2	54
80-90	85	18	3	54
90-100	95	y	4	$4y$
Total		$N = \Sigma f_i = 90 + x + y$		$\Sigma f_i u_i = 44 + 4y$

Now, we have, $N = 90 + x + y$

$\Rightarrow \quad 120 = 90 + x + y$

$\Rightarrow \quad x + y = 30 \quad \ldots(i)$

$\because \quad \text{Mean} = 59 \quad$ [given]

$$\Rightarrow \quad a + \left(\frac{\Sigma f_i u_i}{N}\right) \times h = 59$$

$$\Rightarrow \quad 55 + \left(\frac{44 + 4y}{120}\right) \times 10 = 59$$

$$\Rightarrow \quad \frac{11 + y}{3} = 4$$

$\Rightarrow \quad 11 + y = 12$

$\Rightarrow \quad y = 1$

On putting the value of y in Eq. (i), we get

$x + 1 = 30$

$\Rightarrow \quad x = 29$

Hence, $x = 29$ and $y = 1$.

Try These 13.1

1 **Find the mean of the following distribution by direct method.**

Class interval	0-10	10-20	20-30	30-40	40-50
Number of workers	7	10	15	8	10

2 **Find the mean of the following data by direct method.**

Class	25-35	35-45	45-55	55-65	65-75
Frequency	6	10	8	12	4

3 **The table below shows the daily expenditure on food of 50 households in a locality.**

Daily Expenditure (in ₹)	0-100	100-200	200-300	300-400	400-500
Number of workers	6	9	15	12	8

Find the mean daily expenditure on food by direct method.

4 **Find the mean of following data by direct method.**

Class	7.5-12.5	12.5-17.5	17.5-22.5	22.5-27.5	27.5-32.5
Frequency	5	10	7	8	2

5 **Calculate the mean of the following data.**

Class	4-7	8-11	12-15	16-19
Frequency	5	4	9	10

NCERT Exemplar

6 **Find the mean of the following frequency distribution.**

Class	0-20	20-40	40-60	60-80	80-100
Frequency	17	28	32	24	19

CBSE 2019

7 **Calculate the mean of the scores of 20 students in a Mathematics test.**

Marks	10-20	20-30	30-40	40-50	50-60
Number of students	2	4	7	6	1

NCERT Exemplar

8 The length of 40 leaves of a plant are measured correct to nearest millimetre and the data obtained is represented in the following table.

Length [in mm]	Number of leaves
118-126	3
127-135	5
136-144	9
145-153	12
154-162	5
163-171	4
172-180	2

Find the average length of the leaves.

SQP 2023 (Standard)

9 If the mean of given data is 50, find the value of p.

Class interval	0-20	20-40	40-60	60-80	80-100
Frequency	17	28	32	p	19

10 Find the missing frequency for the given frequency distribution table, if the mean of the distribution is 18.

Class interval	11-13	13-15	15-17	17-19	19-21	21-23	23-25
Frequency	3	6	9	13	f	5	4

CBSE 2020 (Standard), 2011

11 If the mean of the following distribution is 27, then find the value of p.

Class	0-10	10-20	20-30	30-40	40-50
Frequency	8	p	12	13	10

12 Find p, if mean of the following data is 15.45.

Class	0-6	6-12	12-18	18-24	24-30
Frequency	6	8	p	9	7

13 Find the mean of the following frequency distribution by assumed mean method. CBSE 2023

Class	25-30	30-35	35-40	40-45	45-50	50-55	55-60
Frequency	14	22	16	6	5	3	4

14 The data on number of patients attending a hospital in a month are given below. Find the average number of patients attending the hospital. (use assumed mean method)

Number of patients	0-10	10-20	20-30	30-40	40-50	50-60	60-70
Number of days	4	4	7	20	12	8	5

15 An office admin has the following absentee record of 54 employees of a office for the whole term. Find the mean number of days the employee was absent.

Number of days	0-6	6-10	10-14	14-20	20-28	28-38	38-40
Number of employees	13	12	9	6	6	5	3

16 The following table gives the distribution of the life time of 400 neon lamps CBSE 2023 (Basic)

Life time (in hours)	Number of lamps
1500-2000	14
2000-2500	56
2500-3000	60
3000-3500	86
3500-4000	74
4000-4500	62
4500-5000	48

Find the average life time of a lamp.

17 Using assumed mean method find the mean of the following frequency distribution.

Class	63-65	66-68	69-71	72-74	75-77
Frequency	4	3	7	8	3

18 Find the mean of the following data by using step deviation method.

Class	0-20	20-40	40-60	60-80	80-100
Frequency	17	28	32	24	19

19 Monthly pocket money of students of a class is given in the following frequency distribution:

Pocket money (in ₹)	100-125	125-150	150-175	175-200	200-225
Number of students	14	8	12	5	11

Find the mean of pocket money using step deviation method.

20 Calculate the mean of the following distribution.

Class	10-30	30-50	50-70	70-90	90-110
Frequency	15	18	25	10	2

21 **Find the mean of the following distribution.**

Class interval	Frequency
50-75	5
75-100	6
100-125	3
125-150	4
150-175	3
175-200	7
200-225	5
225-250	4
250-275	8
275-300	5

22 **The following table represents the number of illiterate females in the age group (10-34) in a town**

Age group	10-14	15-19	20-24	25-29	30-34
Number of females	300	980	800	580	290

Find the mean of the above data by using step deviation method.

23 **To find out the concentration of SO_2 in the air (in parts per million i.e. ppm), the data was collected for 35 localities in Bareilly city and is presented below.**

Concentration of SO_2 (in ppm)	Frequency
0.00-0.06	5
0.06-0.12	10
0.12-0.18	10
0.18-0.24	2
0.24-0.30	5
0.30-0.36	3

Find the mean concentration of SO_2 in the air.

24 **If the mean of the distribution is 33.2 and the sum of all frequencies is 100. Find the missing frequencies f_1 and f_2.**

Class	Frequency
6-14	11
14-22	21
22-30	f_1
30-38	15
38-46	14
46-54	8
54-62	f_2
62-70	6

Answers

1. **Hint** Do same as Example 3. **Ans.** 25.8
2. **Hint** Do same as Example 3. **Ans.** 49.5
3. **Hint** Do same as Example 3. **Ans.** ₹ 264
4. **Hint** Do same as Example 3. **Ans.** 18.75
5. **Hint** Here, class intervals are not continuous. But it does not affect mid-values (x_i). So, we will solve it without making it continuous.

Class	Class marks (x_i)	Frequency (f_i)	$f_i x_i$
4-7	5.5	5	27.5
8-11	9.5	4	38
12-15	13.5	9	121.5
16-19	17.5	10	175
Total		$\Sigma f_i = 28$	$\Sigma f_i x_i = 362$

$\therefore$ Mean $(\bar{x}) = \dfrac{\Sigma f_i x_i}{\Sigma f_i}$

Ans. 12.93

6. **Hint** Do same as Example 3. **Ans.** 50
7. **Hint** Do same as Example 3. **Ans.** 35
8. Table for the given data is

Length (in mm)	Number of leaves (f_i)	Class mark (x_i)	$f_i x_i$
117.5-126.5	3	122	366
126.5-135.5	5	131	655
135.5-144.5	9	140	1260
144.5-153.5	12	149	1788
153.5-162.5	5	158	790
162.5-171.5	4	167	668
171.5-180.5	2	176	352
Total	$\Sigma f_i = 40$		$\Sigma f_i x_i = 5879$

$\therefore$ Average length of the leaves $= \dfrac{\Sigma f_i x_i}{\Sigma f_i}$

$= \dfrac{5879}{40} = 146.975$

9. **Hint** Do same as Example 4. **Ans.** $p = 24$
10. **Hint** Do same as Example 4. **Ans.** $f = 8$
11. **Hint** Do same as Example 4. **Ans.** $p = 7$
12. **Hint** Do same as Example 4. **Ans.** $p = 10$
13. **Hint** Do same as Example 5. **Ans.** 36.85
14. **Hint** Do same as Example 5. **Ans.** 37.66
15. **Hint** Do same as Example 5. **Ans** 14.28

16. Table for the given data is

Life time (in hours)	Number of lamps (f_i)	Class mark (x_i)	$d_i = x_i - a$	$f_i d_i$
1500-2000	14	1750	−1500	−21000
2000-2500	56	2250	−1000	−56000
2500-3000	60	2750	−500	−30000
3000-3500	86	$3250 = a$	0	0
3500-4000	74	3750	500	37000
4000-4500	62	4250	1000	62000
4500-5000	48	4750	1500	72000
Total	$\Sigma f_i = 400$			$\Sigma f_i d_i = 64000$

Assumed mean, $a = 3250$

$$\therefore \quad \bar{x} = a + \frac{\Sigma f_i d_i}{\Sigma f_i} = 3250 + \frac{64000}{400} = 3250 + 160 = 3410$$

17. **Hint** Do same as Example 5. **Ans.** 70.36

18. **Hint** Do same as Example 6. **Ans.** 50

19. **Hint** Do same as Example 6. **Ans.** ₹158

20. **Hint** Do same as Example 6. **Ans.** 50.28

21. **Hint** Do same as Example 6. **Ans.** 181.5

22. **Hint** Do same as Example 7. **Ans.** 21.28

23. Table for the given data is

Concentration of SO_2 (in ppm)	Frequency (f_i)	Class marks (x_i)	$u_i = \frac{x_i - 0.15}{0.06}$	$f_i u_i$
0.00-0.06	5	0.03	−2	−10
0.06-0.12	10	0.09	−1	−10
0.12-0.18	10	$0.15 = a$	0	0
0.18-0.24	2	0.21	1	2
0.24-0.30	5	0.27	2	10
0.30-0.36	3	0.33	3	9
Total	$n = 35$			$\Sigma f_i u_i = 1$

Here, $a = 0.15, h = 0.06, n = 35$ and $\Sigma f_i u_i = 1$

By step deviation method,

$$\text{Mean } (\bar{x}) = a + \left(\frac{\Sigma f_i u_i}{n}\right) \times h$$

$$= 0.15 + \left(\frac{1}{35}\right) \times 0.06 = 0.15 + \frac{0.06}{35} = 0.151$$

Hence, the mean concentration SO_2 in air is 0.15 ppm.

24. **Hint** Do same as Example 8. **Ans.** $f_1 = 16, \ f_2 = 9$

TOPIC 02 Mode of Grouped Data

Mode

The observation, which occurs most frequently among the given observations, i.e. the value of the observation having maximum frequency is called **mode**. e.g. Mode of the numbers 2, 3, 4, 4, 6, 6, 6, 6, 7 and 9 is 6 because it is repeated maximum number of times i.e. 4 times.

Sometimes, it is possible that more than one value may have the same maximum frequency. In this situation, the data is said to be **multimodal**. Here, we will discuss the problems having single mode only. In case of ungrouped data, the mode is the observation with maximum frequency.

Example 1. **In a class of 72 students, marks obtained by the students in a class test (out of 10) are given below:**

Marks obtained (out of 10)	1	2	3	4	6	7	9	10
Number of students	3	5	12	18	23	8	2	1

Find the mode of the data.

Sol. The mode of the given data is 6 as it has the maximum frequency i.e. 23 among all the observations.

Modal Class

In a grouped frequency distribution, it is not possible to determine the mode by looking at the frequencies.

So, here we first locate a class with the maximum frequency. This class is called modal class.

e.g.

Class interval	0-10	10-20	20-30	30-40	40-50	50-60
Number of students	2	9	14	20	22	8

Here, the highest frequency is of the class 40-50, which is 22.

Hence, the modal class is 40-50.

Mode of Grouped Data

In grouped data, mode is a value that lies in the modal class and it is given by the formula,

$$\text{Mode} = l + \left\{\frac{f_1 - f_0}{2f_1 - f_0 - f_2}\right\} \times h$$

where, l = Lower limit of the modal class

h = Size of the class intervals (assuming all class sizes to be equal)

f_1 = Frequency of the modal class

f_0 = Frequency of the class preceding the modal class

f_2 = Frequency of the class succeeding the modal class

Example 2. **Find the mode of the following frequency distribution.** CBSE 2019

Class	0-10	10-20	20-30	30-40	40-50	50-60	60-70
Frequency	8	10	10	16	12	6	7

Sol. Here, the maximum frequency is 16 and the corresponding class is 30-40. So, this is the modal class.

We have, $l = 30, h = 10, f_1 = 16, f_0 = 10$ and $f_2 = 12$

$$\therefore \text{ Mode} = l + \frac{f_1 - f_0}{2f_1 - f_0 - f_2} \times h$$

$$= 30 + \frac{16 - 10}{2(16) - 10 - 12} \times 10$$

$$= 30 + \frac{6}{32 - 22} \times 10 = 30 + \frac{6}{10} \times 10 = 30 + 6$$

$$\Rightarrow \text{Mode} = 36$$

Example 3. **An NGO working for welfare of cancer patients, maintained its records as follows:**

Age of patients (in years)	0-20	20-40	40-60	60-80
Number of patients	35	315	120	50

Find mode.

Sol. Here, maximum frequency is 315 and the class corresponding to this frequency is 20-40. So, the modal class is 20-40.

Age of patients (in years)	0-20	20-40	40-60	60-80
Number of patients	$35 = f_0$	$315 = f_1$	$120 = f_2$	50

$\therefore l = 20, f_1 = 315, f_0 = 35, f_2 = 120$ and $h = 20$

$$\text{Now, mode} = l + \left(\frac{f_1 - f_0}{2f_1 - f_0 - f_2}\right) \times h$$

$$= 20 + \left(\frac{315 - 35}{2 \times 315 - 35 - 120}\right) \times 20$$

$$= 20 + \frac{280}{475} \times 20 = 20 + 11.79 = 31.79$$

Hence, the mode of given grouped data is 31.79.

Example 4. **If mode of the following series is 54, then find the value of f.**

Class interval	0-15	15-30	30-45	45-60	60-75	75-90
Frequency	3	5	f	16	12	7

Find the modal class in which the given mode lies and find the value of f by using the formula,

$$\text{mode} = l + \left\{\frac{f_1 - f_0}{2f_1 - f_0 - f_2}\right\} \times h.$$

Sol. Here, given mode is 54, which lies between 45-60. Therefore, the modal class is 45-60.

$\therefore \quad l = 45, f_1 = 16, f_0 = f, f_2 = 12$ and $h = 15$

$$\because \quad \text{Mode} = l + \left(\frac{f_1 - f_0}{2f_1 - f_0 - f_2}\right) \times h$$

$$\therefore \quad 54 = 45 + \left(\frac{16 - f}{2 \times 16 - f - 12}\right) \times 15$$

$$\Rightarrow \quad 9 = \frac{16 - f}{20 - f} \times 15$$

$$\Rightarrow \quad 9(20 - f) = 15(16 - f)$$

$$\Rightarrow \quad 180 - 9f = 240 - 15f$$

$$\Rightarrow \quad 6f = 240 - 180 = 60 \Rightarrow f = 10$$

Hence, the required value of f is 10.

Example 5. **A box contains 250 apples and each apple was weighted, the distribution of masses of the apples is given in the following table.**

Mass (in grams)	80-100	100-120	120-140	140-160	160-180
Number of apples	20	60	70	x	60

(i) Find the value of x and the mean mass of the apples.

(ii) Find the modal mass of the apples.

Sol.

Mass (in grams)	Number of apples (f_i)	Class mark (x_i)	$f_i x_i$
80 - 100	20	90	1800
100 - 120	60	110	6600
120 - 140	70	130	9100
140 - 160	x	150	$150x$
160 - 180	60	170	10200
Total	$\Sigma f_i = 210 + x$		$\Sigma f_i x_i = 27700 + 150x$

$$\therefore \quad \Sigma f_i = 20 + 60 + 70 + x + 60$$

$$\Rightarrow \quad 250 = 210 + x \Rightarrow x = 40 \quad [\because \Sigma f_i = 250 \text{ given}]$$

$$\therefore \quad \Sigma f_i x_i = 27700 + 150 \times 40 = 33700$$

$$\text{Mean,} \quad \bar{x} = \frac{\Sigma f_i x_i}{\Sigma f_i} = \frac{33700}{250} = 134.8$$

Now, modal class = 120-140,

Lower limit (l) of modal class = 120,

Class size (h) = 20,

Frequency (f_1) of the modal class = 70,

Frequency (f_0) of class preceding the modal class = 60,

Frequency (f_2) of class succeeding the modal class x = 40.

$$\therefore \text{Mode} = l + \left(\frac{f_1 - f_0}{2f_1 - f_0 - f_2}\right) \times h$$

$$= 120 + \left(\frac{70 - 60}{2 \times 70 - 60 - 40}\right) \times 20$$

$$= 120 + \frac{10 \times 20}{140 - 100}$$

$$= 120 + \frac{200}{40}$$

$$= 125 \text{ g}$$

Hence, the modal mass of the apple is 125g.

Try These 13.2

1 Find the mode of the given data.

Marks	0-20	20-40	40-60	60-80
Frequency	15	6	18	10

2 For the following data, find the mode.

Class	1-3	3-5	5-7	7-9	9-11
Frequency	14	16	4	4	2

3 Find the mode of the given data.

Marks	0-10	10-20	20-30	30-40	40-50
Frequency	20	24	40	36	20

4 Find the mode of the following frequency distribution

CBSE 2019

Class	10-14	14-18	18-22	22-26	26-30	30-34	34-38
Frequency	8	6	11	20	25	22	10

5 The following table shows the age distribution of cases of a certain disease admitted during a year in a particular hospital

Age (in years)	Number of cases
0-10	5
10-20	8
20-30	7
30-40	12
40-50	28
50-60	20
60-70	10
70-80	10

Find the average age for which maximum cases occurred.

6 The weight of coffee in 70 packets are shown in the following table

Weight (in g)	Number of packet
200-201	12
201-202	26
202-203	20
203-204	9
204-205	2
205-206	1

Determine the modal weight. NCERT Exemplar

7 Find the missing frequency f for the following data, if the mode for the following data is 39.

Class	5-15	15-25	25-35	35-45	45-55	55-65	65-75
Frequency	2	3	f	7	4	2	2

8 Monthly consumption of electricity of some consumers is given below as a distribution. Find the missing frequency (x), if mode of distribution is given to be 200 units.

Monthly consumption (in units)	Number of consumers
90-120	20
120-150	15
150-180	x
180-210	75
210-240	50

9 Some surnames were picked up from a local telephone directory and the frequency distribution of the number of letters of the English alphabets was obtained as follows:

Number of letters	1-4	4-7	7-10	10-13	13-16	16-19
Number of surnames	10	25	35	x	12	8

If it is given that mode of the distribution is 8, then find the missing frequency (x).

10 Find mean and mode of the following data.

CBSE 2025 (Basic)

Class	15-20	20-25	25-30	30-35	35-40	40-45
Frequency	12	10	15	11	7	5

11 Find the mode of the following data.

Class interval	1-10	11-20	21-30	31-40	41-50	51-60
Frequency	12	15	21	17	19	6

12 **Given below is the frequency distribution of the heights of players in a school.**

Height (in cm)	Number of students
160-163	18
164-167	116
168-171	142
172-175	129
176-179	80
180-183	15

Determine the modal height.

13 **A box contains 125 orange and each orange was weighted, the distribution of mass of the oranges is given in following table.**

Mass (in grams)	80-100	100-120	120-140	140-160	160-180
Number of oranges	10	30	35	$x+10$	30

(i) Find the value of x and mean mass of the oranges.

(ii) Find the modal mass of the oranges.

14 **On sports day of a school, age-wise participation of students is shown in the following distribution.**

Age (in years)	5-7	7-9	9-11	11-13	13-15	15-17	17-19
Number of students	x	15	18	30	50	48	x

Find the mode of the data. Also, find missing frequencies when sum of frequencies is 181.

CBSE 2016, 15

Answers

1. **Hint** Do same as Example 2. **Ans.** 52
2. **Hint** Do same as Example 2. **Ans.** 3.28
3. **Hint** Do same as Example 2. **Ans.** 28
4. **Hint** Do same as Example 2. **Ans.** 28.50
5. **Hint** Do same as Example 3. **Ans.** 46.67 yr
6. **Hint** Do same as Example 3. **Ans.** 201.7 g
7. **Hint** Do same as Example 4. **Ans.** $f=5$
8. **Hint** Do same as Example 4. **Ans.** $x=25$
9. **Hint** Do same as Example 4. **Ans.** $x=15$
10. **Hint** From the given data, we have the maximum frequency $=15$

So, modal class is 25-30.

$\because$ $l=25$, $f_1=15$, $f_0=10$, $f_2=11$ and $h=5$

Use formula,

$$\text{Mode} = l + \left\{\frac{f_1 - f_0}{2f_1 - f_0 - f_2}\right\} \times h$$

To find mean, let the assumed mean, $a=30$ and find mean by formula,

$$\text{Mean} = a + \left(\frac{\Sigma f_i u_i}{n}\right) \times h, \text{ where } u_i = \frac{x_i - a}{h}$$

Ans. Mode $=27.78$, Mean $=28$

11. Here, the given frequency distribution is not continuous. So, first we make it continuous by subtracting 0.5 from lower limit and adding 0.5 to upper limit.

Class interval	Continuous class interval	Frequency
1-10	0.5 - 10.5	12
11-20	10.5 - 20.5	15
21-30	20.5 - 30.5	21 (modal class)
31-40	30.5 - 40.5	17
41-50	40.5 - 50.5	19
51-60	50.5 - 60.5	6

$\therefore$ $l=20.5$, $f_1=21$, $f_0=15$, $f_2=17$ and $h=10$

Now, $$\text{mode} = 20.5 + \frac{21-15}{42-15-17} \times 10$$

$$= 20.5 + 6 = 26.5$$

12. **Hint** Do same as Question 11.

Ans. 169.5 cm

13. **Hint** Do same as Example 5.

Ans. (i) $x=10$, mean mass of the oranges $=134.8$ g

(ii) Modal mass of the orange $=125$ g

14. **Hint** Since, sum of frequencies $=181$

$\therefore$ $x+15+18+30+50+48+x=181$

$\Rightarrow$ $2x=181-161=20$

$\Rightarrow$ $x=10$

Now, maximum frequency is 50. So, modal class is 13-15.

$\therefore$ $l=13$, $f_1=50$, $f_0=30$, $f_2=48$ and $h=2$

Now, $$\text{mode} = l + \left(\frac{f_1 - f_0}{2f_1 - f_0 - f_2}\right) \times h$$

Ans. 14.82

TOPIC 03 Median of Grouped Data

Median

Median is defined as the middle-most or the central observation, when the observations are arranged either in ascending or descending order of their magnitudes.

Median divides the arranged series into two equal parts, i.e. 50% of the observations lie below the median and the remaining are above the median.

Let n be the total number of observations and let they are arranged in ascending or descending order.

Median of the data depends on the number of observations (n).

Case I If n is odd, then

$$\text{Median} = \text{Value of } \left(\frac{n+1}{2}\right)\text{th observation}$$

e.g. If five girls of different heights are made to stand in a row, in descending order of their heights, then the height of the third girl from either end is median height.

Since, $n = 5$ is odd.

$$\therefore \text{ Median} = \left(\frac{n+1}{2}\right)\text{th observation} = \frac{5+1}{2}$$

$$= \frac{6}{2} = 3\text{rd observation}$$

Height of the 3rd girl is median height.

Case II If n is even, then

$$\text{Median} = \text{Mean of value of } \left(\frac{n}{2}\right)\text{th and } \left(\frac{n}{2}+1\right)\text{th observations}$$

$$= \frac{1}{2} \times \text{Value of} \left[\left(\frac{n}{2}\right)\text{th} + \left(\frac{n}{2}+1\right)\text{th}\right] \text{ observations}$$

e.g. If six girls of different heights are made to stand in a row, in descending order of their heights, then the mean height of third and fourth girl from either end is the median height.

Since, $n = 6$ is even.

So, $\frac{n}{2} = \frac{6}{2} = 3\text{rd observation}$

and $\left(\frac{n}{2}+1\right) = \frac{6}{2}+1 = \frac{6+2}{2} = 4\text{th observation}$

$\therefore$ Median = Mean of 3rd and 4th observations

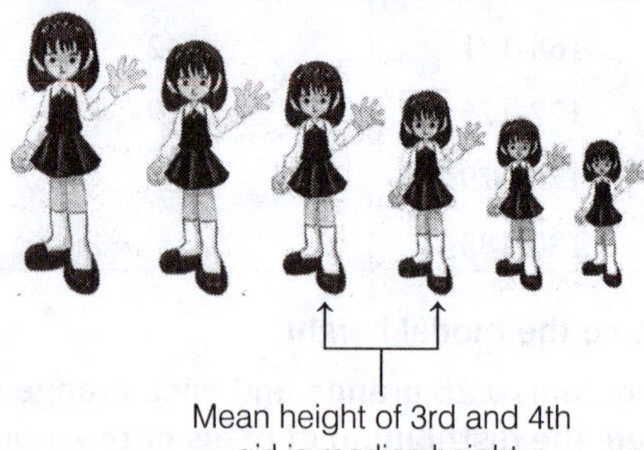

Mean height of 3rd and 4th girl is median height.

Example 1. Find the median of the first ten prime numbers.

Sol. First ten prime numbers in ascending order are 2, 3, 5, 7, 11, 13, 17, 19, 23 and 29.

Here, $n = 10$ (even)

$\therefore$ Median

$$= \frac{1}{2} \times \text{Value of} \left[\left(\frac{n}{2}\right)\text{th} + \left(\frac{n}{2}+1\right)\text{th}\right] \text{ observations}$$

$$= \frac{1}{2} \times \text{Value of} \left[\left(\frac{10}{2}\right)\text{th} + \left(\frac{10}{2}+1\right)\text{th}\right] \text{ observations}$$

$$= \frac{1}{2}[\text{Value of 5th observation} + \text{Value of 6th observation}]$$

$$= \frac{1}{2}(11+13) = \frac{24}{2} = 12$$

Cumulative Frequency

The frequency of an observation in a data refers to how many times that observation occur in the data. The cumulative frequency is the total of frequencies, in which the frequency of the first class interval is added to the frequency of the second class interval and then the sum is added to the frequency of third class interval and so on. Hence, cumulative frequency of a class is defined as the sum of all frequencies up to the given class.

The cumulative frequency is usually observed by constructing a **cumulative frequency table.**

Example 2. The set of data given below shows the ages of participants in a certain summer camp. Draw a cumulative frequency table for the data.

Age (in years)	10	11	12	13	14	15
Frequency	3	18	13	12	7	27

Sol. The cumulative frequency of first observation is the same as its frequency, since there is no frequency before it. Now, the cumulative frequency table is

Age (in years)	Frequency	Cumulative frequency (*cf*)
10	3	3
11	18	$3+18=21$
12	13	$21+13=34$
13	12	$34+12=46$
14	7	$46+7=53$
15	27	$53+27=80$

Cumulative Frequency Distribution

Cumulative frequency distribution is of two types **Less than type** and **more than type**. Formation of these two distributions can be understood with the help of following example.

Example 3. Consider a grouped frequency distribution of marks obtained, out of 100, by 58 students, in a certain examination, as follows:

Marks	Number of students
0-10	5
10-20	7
20-30	4
30-40	2
40-50	3
50-60	6
60-70	7
70-80	9
80-90	8
90-100	7

Form the cumulative frequency distribution of less than type and more than type.

Sol. Cumulative frequency distribution of the less than type : Here, the number of students who have scored marks less than 10 are 5. The number of students who have scored marks less than 20 includes the number of students who have scored marks from 0-10 as well as the number of students who have scored marks from 10-20.

Thus, the total number of students with marks less than 20 is $5+7$ i.e. 12. So, the cumulative frequency of the class 10-20 is 12.

Similarly, on computing the cumulative frequencies of the other classes i.e., the number of students with marks less than 30, less than 40, ... less than 100, we get the distribution which is called the cumulative frequency distribution of the less than type.

Marks obtained	Number of students (cumulative frequency)
Less than 10	5
Less than 20	$5+7=12$
Less than 30	$12+4=16$
Less than 40	$16+2=18$
Less than 50	$18+3=21$
Less than 60	$21+6=27$
Less than 70	$27+7=34$
Less than 80	$34+9=43$
Less than 90	$43+8=51$
Less than 100	$51+7=58$

Here, 10, 20, 30,..., 100 are the upper limits of the respective class intervals.

Cumulative frequency distribution of the more than type : For this type of distribution, we make the table for the number of students with scores, more than or equal to 0, more than or equal to 10, more than or equal to 20 and so on. From the question, we observed that all 58 students have scored marks more than or equal to 0.

There are 5 students scoring marks in the interval 0-10, it shows that there are $58-5=53$ students getting more than or equal to 10 marks. In the same manner, the number of students scoring 20 marks or above $=53-7=46$ students, scoring 30 or above $=46-4=42$ students and so on.

Similarly, computing the cumulative frequencies of the other classes i.e. the number of students with marks more than or equal to 40, more than or equal to 50,..., we get the distribution which is called the cumulative frequency distribution of the more than type.

Marks obtained	Number of students (cumulative frequency)
More than or equal to 0	58
More than or equal to 10	$58-5=53$
More than or equal to 20	$53-7=46$
More than or equal to 30	$46-4=42$
More than or equal to 40	$42-2=40$
More than or equal to 50	$40-3=37$
More than or equal to 60	$37-6=31$
More than or equal to 70	$31-7=24$
More than or equal to 80	$24-9=15$
More than or equal to 90	$15-8=7$

Here, 0, 10, 20, 30,..., 90 are the lower limits of the respective class intervals.

Example 4. The following distribution gives cumulative frequencies of 'more than type.'

Marks obtained (more than or equal to)	5	10	15	20
Number of students (cumulative frequency)	30	23	8	2

Change the above data into a continuous grouped frequency distribution.

Sol. Given distribution is the more than type distribution.

Here, we observe that all 30 students have obtained marks more than or equal to 5. Further, since 23 students have obtained score more than or equal to 10. So, $30-23=7$ students lie in the class 5-10. Similarly, we can find the other classes and their corresponding frequencies. Now, we construct the continuous grouped frequency distribution as

Class (marks obtained)	Number of students
5-10	$30-23=7$
10-15	$23-8=15$
15-20	$8-2=6$
More than or equal to 20	2

Example 5. The following distribution gives the daily income of 50 workers of a factory

Daily income (in ₹)	100-120	120-140	140-160	160-180	180-200
Number of workers	12	14	8	6	10

Write the above distribution as 'less than type' cumulative frequency distribution.

Sol. We construct a cumulative frequency distribution of the less than type as follows:

Daily income (in ₹)	Cumulative frequency (cf)
Less than 120	12
Less than 140	$12+14=26$
Less than 160	$26+8=34$
Less than 180	$34+6=40$
Less than 200	$40+10=50$

Median for Discrete Series

A series having observations $x_1, x_2, x_3, \ldots, x_n$ with respective frequencies $f_1, f_2, f_3 \ldots, f_n$ is known as **discrete series.**

Method to Find the Median of the Discrete Series

Firstly, we arrange the data in the ascending or descending order of x_i, then we find the cumulative frequencies of all the observations.

Let n be the total number of observations (sum of frequencies), then median of the data depends on the number of observations (n).

If n is odd, then Median = Value of $\left(\frac{n+1}{2}\right)$th observation.

If n is even, then

Median = Mean of $\left(\frac{n}{2}\right)$th and $\left(\frac{n}{2}+1\right)$th observations

$= \frac{1}{2} \times$ Value of $\left[\left(\frac{n}{2}\right)\text{th} + \left(\frac{n}{2}+1\right)\text{th}\right]$ observations

Here, for the value of observation, first look at the cumulative frequency just greater than (and nearest to) the position of required observations. Then, determine the corresponding value of the observation.

Example 6. Find the median of the following data.

Marks obtained	20	29	28	42	19	35	51
Number of students	3	4	5	7	9	2	3

Sol. Let us arrange the data in ascending order of x_i and make a cumulative frequency table.

Marks obtained (x_i)	Number of students (f_i)	cf
19	9	9
20	3	$9+3=12$
28	5	$12+5=17$
29	4	$17+4=21$
35	2	$21+2=23$
42	7	$23+7=30$
51	3	$30+3=33$

Here, $n=33$ (odd)

$\therefore$ Median = Value of $\left(\frac{n+1}{2}\right)$th observation

= Value of $\left(\frac{33+1}{2}\right)$th observation

= Value of 17th observation

Corresponding value of 17th observation of cumulative frequency in x_i is 28. Hence, median is 28.

Example 7. Obtain the median for the following frequency distribution.

x	1	2	3	4	5	6	7	8	9
f_i	8	10	11	16	20	25	15	9	6

Sol. Here, the given data is in ascending order of x_i.
Cumulative frequency table for the given data is

x_i	f_i	cf
1	8	8
2	10	18
3	11	29
4	16	45
5	20	65
6	25	90
7	15	105
8	9	114
9	6	120

Here, $n = 120$ (even)

$$\therefore \text{Median} = \frac{1}{2}\left[\text{value of } \left\{\left(\frac{n}{2}\right)\text{th} + \left(\frac{n}{2}+1\right)\text{th}\right\}\right] \text{observations}$$

$$= \frac{1}{2}\left[\text{value of } \left\{\left(\frac{120}{2}\right)\text{th} + \left(\frac{120}{2}+1\right)\text{th}\right\}\right] \text{observations}$$

$$= \frac{1}{2}[\text{value of 60th observation} + \text{value of 61th observation}]$$

Both 60th and 61th observations lie in the cumulative frequency 65 and its corresponding value of x_i is 5.

$$\therefore \quad \text{Median} = \frac{1}{2}(5+5) = 5$$

Median for Grouped Data

In a grouped data, we may not find the middle observation by looking at the cumulative frequencies, since the middle observation will be some value in a class interval, so it is necessary to find the value inside a class that divides the whole distribution into two halves.

For this, we find the cumulative frequencies of all the classes and $\frac{n}{2}$, where n = number of observations.

Now, locate the class whose cumulative frequency is greater than (and nearest to) $\frac{n}{2}$ and this class is called **median class.** After finding the median class, use the following formula for calculating the median.

$$\text{Median} = l + \left\{\frac{\frac{n}{2} - cf}{f}\right\} \times h$$

where, l = Lower limit of median class

n = Number of observations

cf = Cumulative frequency of the class preceding the median class

f = Frequency of the median class

h = Class width (assuming class sizes to be equal)

Note it The median of grouped data with unequal class sizes can also be calculated. However, we shall not discuss it here.

Example 8. A survey condcuted on 20 households in a locality by a group of students resulted in the following frequency table for the number of family members in a household

Family size	1-3	3-5	5-7	7-9	9-11
Number of Families	7	8	2	2	1

Find the median of this data.

CBSE 2023 (Basic), CBSE 2024 (Standard)

Sol. The cumulative frequency table of given data is

Family Size	Number of families (f)	Cumulative frequency (cf)
1 - 3	7	7
3 - 5	8	15
5 - 7	2	17
7 - 9	2	19
9 - 11	1	20

Here, $\frac{n}{2} = \frac{20}{2} = 10$

Since, the cumulative frequency just greater than 10 is 15 and the corresponding class interval is 3-5.

$\therefore$ Median class is 3-5.

$\therefore$ $l = 3$, $cf = 7$, $f = 8$ and $h = 2$

$$\therefore \quad \text{Median} = l + \left(\frac{\frac{n}{2} - cf}{f}\right) \times h = 3 + \left(\frac{\frac{20}{2} - 7}{8}\right) \times 2$$

$$= 3 + \frac{3}{8} \times 2 = \frac{30}{8} = 3.75$$

Example 9. A survey regarding the heights (in cm) of 51 boys of Class X of a school was conducted and the following data was obtained:

Heights (in cm)	Number of boys
Less than 140	4
Less than 145	11
Less than 150	29
Less than 155	40
Less than 160	46
Less than 165	51

Find the median height.

Sol. To calculate the median height, we need to convert the given data in the continuous grouped frequency distribution.

Given distribution is of less than type and 140, 145, 150, ..., 165 gives the upper limits of the corresponding class intervals. So, the classes should be below 140, 140-145, 145-150, ..., 160-165.

Clearly, the frequency of class interval below 140 is 4, since there are 4 boys with height less than 140. For the frequency of class interval 140-145 subtract the number of boys having height less than140 from the number of boys having height less than 145.

Thus, the frequency of class interval 140 - 145 is $11-4=7$. Similarly, we can calculate the frequencies of other class intervals and get the following table

Class interval	Frequency	Cumulative frequency (cf)
Below 140	4	4
140-145	$11-4=7$	11 (cf)
145-150	$29-11=18=f$	29
150-155	$40-29=11$	40
155-160	$46-40=6$	46
160-165	$51-46=5$	51

Here, $n=51$

$\therefore \quad \frac{n}{2}=\frac{51}{2}=25.5$

Since, the cumulative frequency just greater than 25.5 is 29 and the corresponding class interval is 145-150.

$\therefore$ Median class = 145-150

Now, $l=145,\ f=18, cf=11$ and $h=5$

$$\therefore \quad \text{Median}=l+\left\{\frac{\frac{n}{2}-cf}{f}\right\}\times h$$

$$=145+\left\{\frac{25.5-11}{18}\right\}\times 5$$

$$=145+\frac{72.5}{18}$$

$$=145+4.03=149.03$$

Hence, the required median height is 149.03 cm.

Example 10. Find the missing frequencies in the following frequency distribution table, if $n=100$ and median is 32. CBSE 2024 (Basic), CBSE 2019

Marks obtained	0-10	10-20	20-30	30-40	40-50	50-60	Total
Number of students	10	?	25	30	?	10	100

Sol. Given, median = 32 and $n=\Sigma f=100$

Let f_1 and f_2 be the missing frequencies of the class interval 10-20 and 40-50, respectively.

Since, sum of frequencies = 100

$\therefore \quad 10+f_1+25+30+f_2+10=100$

$\Rightarrow \quad f_1+f_2=100-75 \Rightarrow f_1+f_2=25$

$\Rightarrow \quad f_2=25-f_1 \quad$ ...(i)

Now, the cumulative frequency table for given distribution is

Class interval	Frequency (f)	Cumulative frequency (cf)
0-10	10	10
10-20	f_1	$10+f_1$
20-30	25	$35+f_1$ (cf)
30-40	$30=f$	$65+f_1$
40-50	f_2	$65+f_1+f_2$
50-60	10	$75+f_1+f_2$
Total	$n=f_1+f_2+75$	

Here, $n=100 \Rightarrow \frac{n}{2}=50$

Given, median = 32, which belongs to the class 30-40.

So, the median class is 30-40.

Then, $l=30, h=10,\ f=30$ and $cf=35+f_1$

$$\because \quad \text{Median}=l+\left\{\frac{\frac{n}{2}-cf}{f}\right\}\times h$$

$$\therefore \quad 32=30+\left\{\frac{50-35-f_1}{30}\right\}\times 10$$

$$\Rightarrow \quad 32-30=\frac{15-f_1}{3}$$

$$\Rightarrow \quad 2\times 3=15-f_1$$

$$\Rightarrow \quad f_1=15-6=9$$

On putting the value of f_1 in Eq. (i), we get

$$f_2=25-9=16$$

Hence, the missing frequencies are $f_1=9$ and $f_2=16$.

Relationship between Mean, Median and Mode

There is an empirical relationship between the three measures of central tendency, which is given by

$$\text{Mode} = 3(\text{Median})-2(\text{Mean})$$

or $$\text{Mean}=\frac{3\,(\text{Median})-\text{Mode}}{2}$$

or $$\text{Median}=\frac{\text{Mode}+2\,(\text{Mean})}{3}$$

Example 11. If median = 137 units and mean = 137.05 units, then find the mode.

Sol. Given, median = 137 units and mean = 137.05 units.

We know that

$$\text{Mode} = 3(\text{Median}) - 2(\text{Mean})$$
$$= 3(137) - 2(137.05)$$
$$= 411 - 274.10$$
$$= 136.90$$

Hence, the value of mode is 136.90 units.

Try These 13.3

1 Write the frequency distribution table for the following data :

Marks	Below 10	Below 20	Below 30	Below 40	Below 50	Below 60
Number of students	0	15	20	30	35	40

2 Given below is a cumulative frequency distribution of 'more than type':

Marks	Number of students
More than or equal to 60	11
More than or equal to 50	23
More than or equal to 40	43
More than or equal to 30	58
More than or equal to 20	72
More than or equal to 10	82

Change the above data into a continuous grouped frequency distribution.

3 The number of students absent in a school was recorded everyday for 147 days and the row data was presented in the form of the following frequency table:

Number of students	Number of days
5	1
6	5
7	11
8	14
9	16
10	13
11	10
12	70
13	4
15	1
18	1
20	1

Find the median of the above data.

4 In the following distribution, find the upper limit of median class.

Class interval	0-8	8-16	16-24	24-32	32-40	40-48
Frequency	7	9	10	8	12	8

5 Find the median of the following frequency distribution.

x	1	2	3	4	5	6	7	8	9	10
f_i	2	3	6	8	16	12	10	13	9	15

6 The following table gives the literacy rate (in %) of 25 cities.

Literacy rate (in per cent)	50-60	60-70	70-80	80-90
Number of cities	9	6	8	2

Find the median class and modal class.

7 Calculate the median from the following distribution.

Class	Frequency
5-10	5
10-15	6
15-20	15
20-25	16
25-30	5
30-35	4
35-40	2
40-45	2

8 During an examination, percentages of marks scored by the students are recorded and are shown in the following table:

Marks	Number of students
0-10	1
10-20	3
20-30	2
30-40	8
40-50	20
50-60	15
60-70	13
70-80	25
80-90	18
90-100	10

Find the mode and median for the above data.

9 The maximum bowling speed (in km/h) of 33 players at a cricket coaching centre are given below:

Speed (in km/h)	85-100	100-115	115-130	130-145
Number of players	11	9	8	5

Calculate the median bowling speed. NCERT Exemplar

10 Compute the median marks for the following data.

Marks	Number of students
0 and above	50
10 and above	46
20 and above	40
30 and above	20
40 and above	10
50 and above	3
60 and above	0

11 If median of the following frequency distribution is 24, then find the missing frequency x.

Age (in years)	0-10	10-20	20-30	30-40	40-50
Number of persons	5	25	x	18	7

12 Find median for the following data.

Height (in cm) [less than]	120	140	160	180	200
Number of students	12	26	34	40	50

13 If median of the following frequency distribution is 35, then find the value of x.

Class interval	0-10	10-20	20-30	30-40	40-50	50-60	60-70
Frequency	2	3	x	6	5	3	2

14 The number of bags sold by Sarah in the initial days of her business is given below. **CBSE QB**

Number of bags sold	Number of Days
0 – 5	x
5 – 10	4
10 – 15	15
15 – 20	5
20 – 25	8

She misplaces the data for the number of days on which less than 5 bags were sold. She knows that the median of her entire data is 12 bags.

Find the number of days on which less than 5 bags were sold. Show your steps.

15 If the median of the following distribution is 58 and the sum of all the frequencies is 140. Find the values of x and y.

Variable	15-25	25-35	35-45	45-55	55-65	65-75	75-85	85-95
Frequency	8	10	x	25	40	y	15	7

16 Following distribution shows the marks of 230 students in a particular subject. If the median marks are 46, then find the values of x and y. **CBSE 2025 (Standard)**

Marks	Number of students
10-20	12
20-30	30
30-40	x
40-50	65
50-60	y
60-70	25
70-80	18

17 The weights (in kg) of 45 students of a class are given in the following distribution table. Determine the value of weight x which is such that the number of students having weight less than x kg is same as the number of students having weight more than x kg.

Weight (in kg)	Cumulative frequency
Below 45	5
Below 50	11
Below 55	15
Below 60	22
Below 65	38
Below 70	45

18 In a certain distribution, mean and median are 9.5 and 10, respectively. Find the mode of the distribution, using an empirical relation?

19 Mode and mean of a data are $12k$ and $15k$, respectively. Find the median of the data.

20 During medical check up of 200 students of school, their weights were recorded as follows:

Weight (in kg)	30-39	40-49	50-59	60-69	70-79	80-89
Number of students	5	22	63	74	30	6

Find the median weight of students.

21 Find the mean, mode and median of the following data

Class interval	11-15	16-20	21-25	26-30	31-35	36-40	41-45	46-50
Frequency	2	3	6	7	14	12	4	2

Answers

1.

Marks	Number of students
10-20	15
20-30	20-15 = 5
30-40	30-20 = 10
40-50	35-30 = 5
50-60	40-35 = 5

2. **Hint** Do same as Example 4.
3. **Hint** Do same as Example 6. **Ans.** 12

4. Hint In given data, $\frac{n}{2}=\frac{54}{2}=27$

Since, cumulative frequency just greater than 27 is 34 and corresponding class is 24-32

$\therefore$ Median class = 24-32

Hence, the upper limit of median class is 32. **Ans** 32

5. Hint Do same as Example 7. **Ans.** 6

6.

Literary rate (in per cent)	50-60	60-70	70-80	80-90
Number of cities	9	6	8	2

Here, $\frac{n}{2}=\frac{25}{2}=12.5$

Since, cumulative frequency just greater than 12.5 is 15 and corresponding class is 60-70.

$\therefore$ Median class = 60-70

Since, highest frequency is 9 and corresponding class is 50-60.

$\therefore$ Modal class = 50-60

7. Hint Do same as Example 8. **Ans.** 20.47

8. Hint Do same as Example 8. **Ans.** Median = 66.54

Hint Do same as Example 3 of Topic 2. **Ans.** Mode = 76.31

9. Hint Do same as Example 8. **Ans.** 109.17 km/h

10. To find median marks, we convert the given data into continuous grouped frequency distribution

Marks	Number of students	Cumulative frequency
0-10	50-46 = 4	4
10-20	46-40 = 6	10
20-30	40-20 = 20	30
30-40	20-10 = 10	40
40-50	10-3 = 7	47
50-60	3-0 = 3	50

Here, $\frac{n}{2}=\frac{50}{2}=25$

$\therefore$ Median class = 20-30

$$\therefore \text{ Median} = l+\frac{\frac{n}{2}-cf}{f}\times h = 20+\frac{25-10}{20}\times 10 = 20+7.5 = 27.5$$

11.

Age (in years)	Number of persons	Cumulative frequency
0-10	5	5
10-20	25	30
20-30	x	$30+x$
30-40	18	$48+x$
40-50	7	$55+x$

Since, median is 24. Therefore, median class is 20-30.

$$\therefore \text{ Median} = l+\left(\frac{\frac{n}{2}-cf}{f}\right)\times h$$

$$\Rightarrow 24 = 20+\frac{\frac{55+x}{2}-30}{x}\times 10 \Rightarrow 4=\frac{x-5}{2x}\times 10$$

$$\Rightarrow 8x = 10x-50 \Rightarrow x=\frac{50}{2}=25$$

12. Hint Do same as Example 9. **Ans.** 138.57 cm

13. Hint Do same as Question 12. **Ans.** $x=5$

14. Given,

Median of entire data = 12 bags

Table for given data is

Number of bags	Number of days	cf
0-5	x	x
5-10	4	$x+4$
10-15	15	$x+19$
15-20	5	$x+24$
20-25	8	$x+32$

$\because$ Median of the data = 12.

$\therefore$ Median class of the data = (10 – 15)

$\therefore$ $l=10, f=15, cf=x+4, h=5$

and $\frac{n}{2}=\frac{x+32}{2}$

We know that

$$\text{Median} = l+\left[\frac{\frac{n}{2}-cf}{f}\right]\times h$$

$$\Rightarrow 12 = 10+\left[\frac{\frac{x+32}{2}-(x+4)}{15}\right]\times 5$$

$$\Rightarrow 2=\frac{\frac{x}{2}+16-x-4}{3}$$

$$\Rightarrow 6 = 12-\frac{x}{2} \Rightarrow \frac{x}{2}=6 \Rightarrow x=12$$

Hence, the number of days on which less than 5 bags were sold are 12.

15. Hint Do same as Example 10. **Ans.** $x=15, y=20$

16. Hint Do same as Example 10. **Ans.** $x=34, y=46$

17. Hint Here, we are required to find median weight of students. Do same as Example 9. **Ans.** 60.16 kg

18. Hint Do same as Example 11. **Ans.** 11

19. Hint Median $=\frac{\text{Mode}+2\ (\text{Mean})}{3}=\frac{12k+2\times 15k}{3}=\frac{42k}{3}=14k$

20. Hint Convert the given distribution into continuous grouped frequency distribution and find the median.

Ans. 60.85 kg

21. Hint Do same as Example 7 of Topic 1 **Ans.** Mean = 32

Hint Do same as Example 2 of Topic 2. **Ans.** Mode = 34.38

Hint Use relation,

Mode = 3 (Median) – 2 (Mean) **Ans.** Median = 32.79

NCERT FOLDER

For Practice and more Study of this Exercise

EXERCISE 13.1

Q1. A survey was conducted by a group of students as a part of their environment awareness programme, in which they collected the following data regarding the number of plants in 20 houses in a locality. Find the mean number of plants per house. How environment awareness programme for students makes environment healthy?

Number of plants	0-2	2-4	4-6	6-8	8-10	10-12	12-14
Number of houses	1	2	1	5	6	2	3

Which method will you use for finding the mean and why?

First, calculate the class mark of each class interval, then find $f_i x_i$ and use the formula, $\bar{x} = \frac{\Sigma f_i x_i}{\Sigma f_i}$ to calculate the mean.

Sol. Here, all the values of f_i and x_i are small, so we use direct method to calculate mean.

Table for given data is

Number of plants	Number of houses (f_i)	Class marks (x_i)	$f_i x_i$
0-2	1	1	1
2-4	2	3	6
4-6	1	5	5
6-8	5	7	35
8-10	6	9	54
10-12	2	11	22
12-14	3	13	39
Total	$N = 20$		$\Sigma f_i x_i = 162$

We have, $N = \Sigma f_i = 20$ and $\Sigma f_i x_i = 162$

$$\therefore \quad \text{Mean } (\bar{x}) = \frac{1}{N} \times \Sigma f_i x_i$$

$$= \frac{1}{20} \times 162 = 8.1$$

Hence, the required mean number of plants per house is 8.1.

The environment awareness programme for students makes environment healthier, because

(i) as they plant more and more trees, it is good for the environment.

(ii) they will not make any type of pollution.

Q2. Consider the following distribution of daily wages of 50 workers of a factory.

Daily wages (in ₹)	Number of workers
500-520	12
520-540	14
540-560	8
560-580	6
580-600	10

Find the mean daily wages of the workers of the factory by using an appropriate method.

Sol. Do same as Example 6 of Topic 1. **Ans.** ₹ 545.20

Q3. The following distribution shows the daily pocket allowance of children of a locality. The mean pocket allowance is ₹ 18. Find the missing frequency *f*.

Daily pocket allowance (in ₹)	Number of children
11-13	7
13-15	6
15-17	9
17-19	13
19-21	f
21-23	5
23-25	4

First, calculate the class mark of each class interval, then find $d_i = x_i - a$ and $f_i d_i$, where a = assumed mean. Use the formula, $\bar{x} = a + \frac{\Sigma f_i d_i}{N}$ to calculate mean in terms of f. Then, equate this value of mean to given mean and determine the value of f.

Sol. Table for the given data is

Daily pocket allowance (in ₹)	Number of children (f_i)	Class marks (x_i)	$d_i = x_i - 18$	$f_i d_i$
11-13	7	12	– 6	– 42
13-15	6	14	– 4	– 24
15-17	9	16	– 2	–18
17-19	13	$18 = a$	0	0
19-21	f	20	2	$2f$
21-23	5	22	4	20
23-25	4	24	6	24
Total	$N = 44 + f$			$\Sigma f_i d_i = 2f - 40$

Here, $a = 18, N = 44 + f$ and $\Sigma f_i d_i = 2f - 40$

$\therefore$ Mean $(\bar{x}) = a + \frac{1}{N} \times \Sigma f_i d_i$

$$= 18 + \frac{1}{(44+f)} \times (2f - 40) \quad \ldots\text{(i)}$$

But mean = 18 [given]...(ii)

On equating Eqs. (i) and (ii), we get

$$18 = 18 + \frac{1}{(44+f)} \times (2f - 40)$$

$$\Rightarrow \quad 0 = \frac{2f - 40}{44 + f}$$

$$\Rightarrow \quad 2f - 40 = 0 \Rightarrow 2f = 40$$

$$\therefore \quad f = \frac{40}{2} = 20$$

Hence, the missing frequency is 20.

Q4. Thirty women were examined in a hospital by a doctor and the number of heart beats per minute were recorded and summarised as follows:

Number of heart beats per minute	65-68	68-71	71-74	74-77	77-80	80-83	83-86
Number of women	2	4	3	8	7	4	2

Find the mean heart beats per minute for these women, choosing a suitable method.

Sol. Do same as Example 7 of Topic 1. **Ans.** 75.9

Q5. In a retail market, fruit vendors were selling mangoes kept in packing boxes. These boxes contained varying number of mangoes. The following was the distribution of mangoes according to the number of boxes.

Number of mangoes	50-52	53-55	56-58	59-61	62-64
Number of boxes	15	110	135	115	25

Find the mean of mangoes kept in a packing box. Which method of finding the mean did you choose?

Sol. Do same as Example 7 of Topic 1. **Ans.** 57.19

Q6. The table below shows the daily expenditure on food of 25 households in a locality. CBSE 2019

Daily expenditure (in ₹)	100-150	150-200	200-250	250-300	300-350
Number of households	4	5	12	2	2

Find the mean daily expenditure on food by a suitable method.

Sol. Do same as Example 7 of Topic 1. **Ans.** ₹ 211

Q7. To find out the concentration of SO_2 in the air (in parts per million i.e. ppm), the data was collected for 30 localities in a certain city and is presented below:

Concentration of SO_2 (in ppm)	Frequency
0.00-0.04	4
0.04-0.08	9
0.08-0.12	9
0.12-0.16	2
0.16-0.20	4
0.20-0.24	2

Find the mean concentration of SO_2 in the air.

Sol. Do same as Question 23 of Try these 13.1.
Ans. 0.099 ppm

Q8. A class teacher has the following absentee record of 40 students of a class for the whole term. Find the mean number of days a student was absent.

Number of days	0-6	6-10	10-14	14-20	20-28	28-38	38-40
Number of students	11	10	7	4	4	3	1

Sol. Here, the class size varies but value of x_i are large, so we will use assumed mean method.

Now, do same as Example 5 of Topic 1. **Ans.** 12.475 days

Q9. The following table gives the literacy rate (in percentage) of 35 cities. Find the mean literacy rate.

Literacy rate (in %)	45-55	55-65	65-75	75-85	85-95
Number of cities	3	10	11	8	3

Sol. Do same as Example 6 of Topic 1. **Ans.** 69.43%

EXERCISE 13.2

Q1. The following table shows the ages of the patients admitted in a hospital during a year:

Age (in years)	5-15	15-25	25-35	35-45	45-55	55-65
Number of patients	6	11	21	23	14	5

Find the mode and the mean of the data given above. Compare and interpret the two measures of central tendency.

Observe the maximum frequency and find the modal class, then calculate mode by using the formula, Mode $= l+\left\{\frac{f_1-f_0}{2f_1-f_0-f_2}\right\}\times h$. Also, use the step deviation method for calculating mean according to which mean $= a+\left(\frac{\Sigma f_i u_i}{N}\right)\times h$ and compare the mode and mean.

Sol. From the given data, we have the maximum frequency is 23. So, the modal class is 35-45.

So, $l=35, f_1=23, f_0=21, f_2=14$ and $h=10$

$$\therefore \text{ Mode} = l+\left\{\frac{f_1-f_0}{2f_1-f_0-f_2}\right\}\times h$$

$$= 35+\left\{\frac{23-21}{46-21-14}\right\}\times 10 \quad [\because 2f_1 = 2\times 23 = 46]$$

$$= 35+\frac{20}{11} = 36.82 \text{ yr}$$

Let the assumed mean, $a = 30$ and width of the class, $h = 10$

For finding mean, table for given data is

Age (in years)	Number of patients (f_i)	Class marks (x_i)	$u_i = \frac{x_i - 30}{10}$	$f_i u_i$
5-15	6	10	− 2	− 12
15-25	11	20	− 1	− 11
25-35	21	30 = a	0	0
35-45	23	40	1	23
45-55	14	50	2	28
55-65	5	60	3	15
Total	$N = 80$			$\Sigma f_i u_i = 43$

We have, $N = 80$ and $\Sigma f_i u_i = 43$

By step deviation method,

$$\text{Mean} = a+\left(\frac{\Sigma f_i u_i}{N}\right)\times h = 30+\left(\frac{43}{80}\right)\times 10$$

$$= 30+5.375 = 35.375$$

$\therefore$ Mode = 36.82 yr and mean = 35.375 yr

So, we conclude that maximum number of patients admitted in the hospital are of age 36.82 yr (approx.), whereas the average age of a patient admitted in the hospital is 35.375 yrs.

Q2. The following data gives the information on the observed lifetimes (in hours) of 225 electrical components:

Lifetimes (in hours)	0-20	20-40	40-60	60-80	80-100	100-120
Frequency	10	35	52	61	38	29

Determine the modal lifetime of the components.

Sol. Do same as Example 3 of Topic 2. **Ans.** 65.625 h

Q3. The following data gives the distribution of total monthly household expenditure of 200 families of a village. Find the modal monthly expenditure of the families. Also, find mean monthly expenditure.

Expenditure (in ₹)	Number of families
1000-1500	24
1500-2000	40
2000-2500	33
2500-3000	28
3000-3500	30
3500-4000	22
4000-4500	16
4500-5000	7

Sol. Do same as Q.1.

Ans. Mode = ₹ 1847.83 and mean = ₹ 2662.50

Q4. The following distribution gives the statewise teacher-student ratio in higher secondary schools of India. Find the mode and mean of this data. Interpret the two measures.

Number of students per teacher	Number of states/UT
15-20	3
20-25	8
25-30	9
30-35	10
35-40	3
40-45	0
45-50	0
50-55	2

Sol. Do same as Q. 1. **Ans.** Mode = 30.625 and Mean = 29.21

We conclude that most states/UT have a student-teacher ratio of 30.6 and on an average, the ratio is 29.2.

Q5. **The given distribution shows the number of runs scored by some top batsmen of the world in one-day international cricket matches.**

Runs scored	Number of batsmen
3000-4000	4
4000-5000	18
5000-6000	9
6000-7000	7
7000-8000	6
8000-9000	3
9000-10000	1
10000-11000	1

Find the mode of the data.

Sol. Do same as Example 2 of Topic 2. **Ans.** 4608.7 runs

Q6. **A student noted the number of cars passing through a spot on a road for 100 periods each of 3 min and summarised it in the table given below:**

Number of cars	0-10	10-20	20-30	30-40	40-50	50-60	60-70	70-80
Frequency	7	14	13	12	20	11	15	8

Find the mode of the data. CBSE 2014

Sol. Do same as Example 3 of Topic 2. **Ans.** 44.7 cars

EXERCISE 13.3

Q1. **The following frequency distribution gives the monthly consumption of electricity of 68 consumers of a locality. Find (i) median, (ii) mean and (iii) mode of the data and compare them.**

Monthly consumption (in units)	Number of consumers
65-85	4
85-105	5
105-125	13
125-145	20
145-165	14
165-185	8
185-205	4

Sol. (i) Do same as Example 8 of Topic 3.

Ans. Median = 137 units

(ii) Do same as Example 6 of Topic 1.

Ans. Mean = 137.05 units

(iii) Do same as Example 2 of Topic 2.

Ans. Mode = 135.77 units

Q2. **If median of the distribution given below is 28.5, then find the values of x and y.**

Class interval	Frequency
0-10	5
10-20	x
20-30	20
30-40	15
40-50	y
50-60	5
Total	60

Sol. Do same as Example 10 of Topic 3. **Ans.** $x = 8, y = 7$

Q3. **A life insurance agent found the following data for distribution of ages of 100 policy holders:**

Age (in years)	Number of policy holders
Below 20	2
Below 25	6
Below 30	24
Below 35	45
Below 40	78
Below 45	89
Below 50	92
Below 55	98
Below 60	100

Calculate the median age, if policies are given only to persons having age 18 yr onwards but less than 60 yr.

Sol. Do same as Example 9 of Topic 3. **Ans.** 35.76yr

Q4. **The length of 40 leaves of a plant are measured correct to the nearest millimetre and the data obtained is represented in the following table:**

Length (in mm)	Number of leaves
118-126	3
127-135	5
136-144	9
145-153	12
154-162	5
163-171	4
172-180	2

Find the median length of the leaves.

Sol. Here, the given data is not in continuous classes, so we convert it into continuous classes for finding, the median. For this, change the classes to 117.5-126.5, 126.5-135.5, ..., 171.5-180.5 i.e., subtract 0.5 from lower limit of each class interval and add 0.5 to upper limit of each class interval.

Then, cumulative frequency table for given distribution is

Lengths (in mm)	Number of leaves (f_i)	Cumulative frequency (cf)
117.5-126.5	3	$3=3$
126.5-135.5	5	$3+5=8$
135.5-144.5	9	$8+9=17$
144.5-153.5	12	$17+12=29$
153.5-162.5	5	$29+5=34$
162.5-171.5	4	$34+4=38$
171.5-180.5	2	$38+2=40$
Total	$n=40$	

Here, $n=40$

$$\Rightarrow \quad \frac{n}{2}=\frac{40}{2}=20$$

The cumulative frequency just greater than 20 is 29 and the corresponding class is 144.5-153.5. Thus, we have the median class 144.5 -153.5.

Now, $l=144.5$, $f=12$, $cf=17$, $h=9$.

$$\therefore \quad \text{Median}=l+\left\{\frac{\frac{n}{2}-cf}{f}\right\}\times h$$

$$=144.5+\left\{\frac{20-17}{12}\right\}\times 9$$

$$=144.5+\frac{9}{4}$$

$$=144.5+2.25$$

$$=146.75 \text{ mm}$$

Q5. The following table gives the distribution of the lifetime of 400 neon lamps

Lifetime (in hours)	Number of lamps
1500-2000	14
2000-2500	56
2500-3000	60
3000-3500	86
3500-4000	74
4000-4500	62
4500-5000	48

Find the median lifetime of a lamp.

Sol. Do same as Example 8 of Topic 3. **Ans.** 3406.98 h

Q6. 100 surnames were randomly picked up from a local telephone directory and the frequency distribution of the number of letters in the English alphabets in the surnames was obtained as follows:

Number of letters	1-4	4-7	7-10	10-13	13-16	16-19
Number of surnames	6	30	40	16	4	4

Determine

(i) median number of letters in the surnames.

(ii) mean number of letters in the surnames.

(iii) modal size of the surnames.

Sol. (i) Do same as Example 8 of Topic 3. **Ans.** Median $=8.05$

(ii) Do same as Example 6 of Topic 1. **Ans.** Mean $=8.32$

(iii) Do same as Example 2 of Topic 2. **Ans.** Mode $=7.88$

Q7. The distribution given below, gives the weights of 30 students of a class. Find the median weight of the students. 2020 (Basic)

Weight (in kg)	40-45	45-50	50-55	55-60	60-65	65-70	70-75
Number of students	2	3	8	6	6	3	2

Sol. Do same as Example 8 of Topic 3. **Ans.** 56.67 kg

REVIEW EXERCISE

Including Competency Based Questions

Part I

Multiple Choice Questions

1. If the mean of 6, 7, x, 8, y, 14 is 9, then **CBSE 2023 (Basic)**

(a) $x+y=21$ (b) $x+y=19$
(c) $x-y=19$ (d) $x-y=21$

2. If the mean of five observations x, $x+2$, $x+4$, $x+6$ and $x+8$ is 11, then the values of x is **CBSE 2024 (Standard)**

(a) 4 (b) 7 (c) 11 (d) 6

3. If the maximum number of students has obtained 52 marks out of 80 then **CBSE 2025 (Standard)**

(a) 52 is the mean of the data
(b) 52 is the median of the data
(c) 52 is the mode of the data
(d) 52 is the range of the data

4. If for a distribution $\sum_{1}^{n} f_i x_i = 132 + 5p$, $\sum_{1}^{n} f_i = 20$ and mean of the distribution is 8.1, then the value of p is **CBSE 2024 (Basic)**

(a) 3 (b) 6 (c) 4 (d) 5

5. The mean of five observations is 15. If the mean of first three observations is 14 and that of the last three observations is 17, then the third observation is **CBSE 2024 (Standard)**

(a) 20 (b) 19 (c) 18 (d) 17

6. Consider the frequency distribution of 45 observations.

Class	0-10	10-20	20-30	30-40	40-50
Frequency	5	9	15	10	6

The upper limit of median class is **CBSE Sample Paper 2025 (Standard)**

(a) 20 (b) 10 (c) 30 (d) 40

7. The median of first seven prime numbers is **CBSE 2023 (Basic)**

(a) 5 (b) 7 (c) 11 (d) 13

8. The following distribution shows the marks distribution of 80 students.

Marks	Below 10	Below 20	Below 30	Below 40	Below 50	Below 60
Number of students	2	12	28	56	76	80

The median class is **CBSE Sample Paper 2025 (Basic)**

(a) 20-30 (b) 40-50
(c) 30-40 (d) 10-20

9. If the mean and median of a data are 10 and 11 respectively, then mode of the data is **CBSE 2024 (Basic)**

(a) 12 (b) 8 (c) 20 (d) 13

10. If the mode of some observations is 10 and sum of mean and median is 25 then the mean and median respectively are **CBSE 2025 (Standard)**

(a) 12 and 13 (b) 13 and 12
(c) 10 and 15 (d) 15 and 10

Assertion-Reason Type Questions

11. **Assertion** The mean of the following distribution is 6.

Observations	2	4	6	10	12
Frequency	3	2	3	1	2

Reason Mean of grouped data can be found by using formula $\bar{x} = a + \frac{\Sigma f_i d_i}{\Sigma f_i}$, where a = assumed mean and $d_i = x_i - a$.

(a) Both Assertion and Reason are correct and Reason is the correct explanation of Assertion.
(b) Both Assertion and Reason are correct but Reason is not the correct explanation of Assertion.
(c) Assertion is correct but Reason is incorrect.
(d) Assertion is incorrect but Reason is correct.

12. **Assertion** For the following distribution

Class	5-10	10-15	15-20	20-25	25-30	30-35
Frequency	8	12	15	25	20	18

The sum of lower limit and upper limit of the modal class is 45.

Reason The algebraic sum of deviation of each variate from its arithmetic mean is always zero.

(a) Both Assertion and Reason are correct and Reason is the correct explanation of Assertion.
(b) Both Assertion and Reason are correct but Reason is not the correct explanation of Assertion.
(c) Assertion is correct but Reason is incorrect.
(d) Assertion is incorrect but Reason is correct.

13. Assertion The median class of the following distribution is 40-50.

Class interval	0-10	10-20	20-30	30-40	40-50	50-60
Frequency	8	10	12	22	30	18

Reason The median is a measure of central tendency which gives the value of the middle-most observation in the data.

(a) Both Assertion and Reason are correct and Reason is the correct explanation of Assertion.
(b) Both Assertion and Reason are correct but Reason is not the correct explanation of Assertion.
(c) Assertion is correct but Reason is incorrect.
(d) Assertion is incorrect but Reason is correct.

Case Study Based Questions

14. Arti owns a manufacturing company. She hires 5 supervisors and 20 operators for a six month project. The table given below shows their salary breakup.

Position	Salary for the first two months	Salary for the remaining four months
Supervisor	Between ₹ 18000 to ₹ 20000	Between ₹ 22000 to ₹ 25000
Operator	Between ₹ 8000 to ₹ 10000	Between ₹ 13000 to ₹ 15000

Based on the above information, answer the following questions.

(i) The mean salary of the supervisors for the first two months is ₹ 19000. The salary of three supervisors are ₹ 18000, ₹ 18500 and ₹ 20000, respectively. What could be the salary of other two supervisors?
(ii) Arti agrees to pay the maximum decided amount as salary to the operators. What would be the total amount (in ₹) that Arti will have to pay the operators for the first two months?

15. A table in a restaurant is in the shape of a hemisphere.

Claim amount (in hundred dollars)	Number of claims
No claims	368
$>5 \leq 15$	3
$>15 \leq 25$	610
$>25 \leq 35$	1255
$>35 \leq 45$	1067
$>45 \leq 55$	555
$>55 \leq 65$	1280

Based on the above information, answer the following questions.

(i) What is the mean claim amount in dollars?
(ii) How many claim requests of up to \$3500 did the company receive?
(iii) What is the modal range of the claim amount in dollars?

16. A table in a restaurant is in the shape of a hemisphere.

Salary (in ₹)	Number of operators
13000	5
13500	3
14000	2
14500	4
15000	6

Based on the above information, answer the following questions.

(i) What is the median salary of the operators after two months?
(ii) What is the salary received by most of the operators?

17. Gurpreet is very fond of doing research on plants. She collected some leaves from different plants and measured their lengths in mm. **CBSE 2024 (Basic)**

The data obtained is represented in the following table.

Length (in mm)	Number of leaves
70-80	3
80-90	5
90-100	9
100-110	12
110-120	5
120-130	4
130-140	2

Based on the above information, answer the following questions.

(i) Write the median class of the data.
(ii) How many leaves are of length equal to or more than 10 cm?
(iii) (a) Find median of the data.

Or

(b) Write the modal class and find the mode of the data.

18. Vocational training complements traditional education by providing practical skills and hands on experience. While education equips individuals with a broad knowledge base, vocational training focuses on job-specific skills, enhancing employability, thus making the student self-reliant. Keeping this in view, a teacher made the following table giving the frequency distribution of students/adults undergoing vocational training from the training institute.

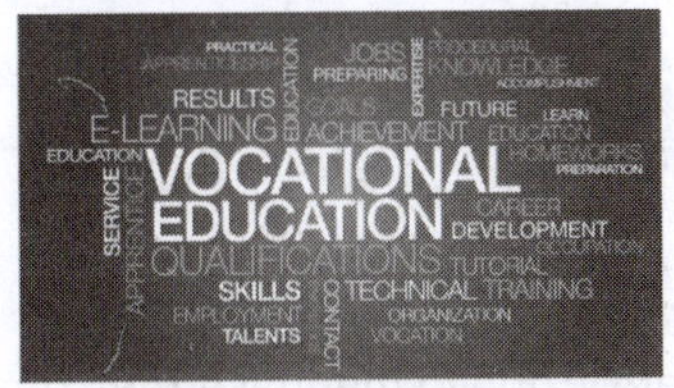

Age (in years)	15-19	20-24	25-29	30-34	35-39	40-44	45-49	50-54
Number of participants	62	132	96	37	13	11	10	4

From the above, answer the following questions.

(i) What is the lower limit of the modal class of the above data?

(ii) (a) Find the median class of the above data.

Or

(b) Find the number of participants of age less than 50 yr who undergo vocational training.

(iii) Give the empirical relationship between mean, median and mode. **CBSE 2024 (Standard)**

Part II

Very Short Answer Type Questions

1. If x_i's are the mid-points of the class intervals of grouped data, f_i's are corresponding frequencies and $\bar{x}$ is the mean, then find the value of $\Sigma(f_i x_i - \bar{x})$. **NCERT Exemplar**

2. If the mean of the following distribution is 6, then find the value of a.

x_i	2	4	6	10	$a+5$
f_i	3	2	3	1	2

3. If the mean of the following distribution is 2.6, then find the value of y.

Variable	1	2	3	4	5
Frequency	4	5	y	1	2

4. The distribution given below shows the runs scored by batsmen in one-day cricket matches. Find the mean number of runs. **Competency Based Question**

Runs scored	0-40	40-80	80-120	120-160	160-200
Number of batsmen	12	20	35	30	23

5. If $u_i = \frac{x_i - 20}{10}$, $\Sigma f_i u_i = 30$ and $\Sigma f_i = 40$, then find the value of $\bar{x}$.

6. For the following distribution, then find the modal class. **NCERT Exemplar**

Marks	Below 10	Below 20	Below 30	Below 40	Below 50	Below 60
Number of students	3	12	27	57	75	80

7. A ketchup manufacturing company sells ketchup in three different bottle sizes. Now, it wants to sell only one size in the market. It has data on how the three sizes perform in the market.

Based on which measure of central tendency, should the company fix the size of the ketchup bottle? Justify your answer. **Competency Based Question**

8. In an arranged series of $4n$ terms, which term is median?

9. In the following distribution, find the number of families having income range 16000-19000 (in ₹).

Monthly income range (in ₹)	Number of families
Income more than ₹ 10000	100
Income more than ₹ 13000	85
Income more than ₹ 16000	69
Income more than ₹ 19000	50
Income more than ₹ 22000	33
Income more than ₹ 25000	15

NCERT Exemplar

10. Given below is a cumulative frequency distribution of 'less than type'

Marks obtained	Less than 20	Less than 30	Less than 40	Less than 50
Number of students (cumulative frequency)	8	13	19	24

Change the above data into a continuous grouped frequency distribution.

11. The time (in seconds) taken by 150 athletes to run a 110m hurdle race are tabulated below.

Class interval	Frequency
13.8-14.0	2
14.0-14.2	4
14.2-14.4	5
14.4-14.6	71
14.6-14.8	48
14.8-15.0	20

Find the number of athletes, who completed the race in less than 14.6 s. **NCERT Exemplar**

12. Write the empirical relationship between the three measures of central tendency.

13. Find the mode of the data, using an empirical formula, when it is given that median = 41.25 and mean = 33.75.

14. If mode = 80 and mean = 110, then find the median.

Short Answer Type Questions

15. Find the value of k, if the mean of the following distribution is 20.

x_i	15	17	19	$20+k$	23
f_i	2	3	4	$5k$	6

16. In the following distribution, if mean of the distribution is 86, then find the value of p.

Wages (in ₹)	50-60	60-70	70-80	80-90	90-100	100-110
Number of workers	5	3	4	p	2	13

17. If the sum of deviations of a set of values $x_1, x_2, x_3, \dots x_n$ measured from 50 is −10 and the sum of deviations of the values from 46 is 70. Rohit solve this question and get the mean of the data is 49.5. Is he right? Explain. **Competency Based Question**

18. In a class test, the mean score of the class is 60. Half the students of the class scored 80 marks or above in the test.

Dipti said, 'Each of the remaining half of the students would have definitely got 40 marks or below in the test for the mean to be 60 marks'.

Prove or disprove Dipti's statement with a valid example. **Competency Based Question**

19. The mean temperature of a certain city for 31 consecutive days was found to be 35.7 °C. Further, the mean temperature of the first 8 days was 28.4 °C. The mean temperature of the next 12 days was 36.4 °C.

Find the mean temperature of the rest of the days. Show your work.

(**Note** Round the numbers to one decimal point.) **Competency Based Question**

20. The frequency distribution of daily rainfall in a town during a certain period is shown below.

Rainfall (in mm)	Number of days
0-20	7
20- 40	x
40 - 60	10
60 - 80	4

Unfortunately, due to manual errors, the information on the 20-40 mm range got deleted from the data.

If the mean daily rainfall for the period was 35 mm, find the number of days when the rainfall ranged between 20-40 mm. Show your work. **Competency Based Question**

21. Find the mean of the following distribution **CBSE 2020 (Standard)**

Class	3-5	5-7	7-9	9-11	11-13
Frequency	5	10	10	7	8

22. The weight (in kg) of 50 wrestlers are recorded in the following table:

Weight (in kg)	100-110	110-120	120-130	130-140	140-150
Number of wrestlers	4	14	21	8	3

Find the mean weight of the wrestlers. **NCERT Exemplar**

23. The government rescued 100 people after a train accident. Their ages were recorded in the following table. Find their mean age. **CBSE 2024 (Standard) Compartment**

Age (in years)	Number of people rescued
10-20	9
20-30	14
30-40	15
40-50	21
50-60	23
60-70	12
70-80	6

24. The daily income of a sample of 50 employees are tabulated as follows: **NCERT Exemplar**

Income (in ₹)	1-200	201-400	401-600	601-800
Number of employees	14	15	14	7

Find the mean daily income of employees.

25. Using step deviation method, then find the mean of the following data.

Class interval	Frequency
135-140	4
140-145	9
145-150	18
150-155	28
155-160	24
160-165	10
165-170	5
170-175	2

26. The mean of the following distribution is 132 and sum of frequencies is 50. Find the values of x and y.

Class interval	0-40	40-80	80-120	120-160	160-200	200-240
Frequency	4	7	x	12	y	9

27. Find the mode of the following data. **CBSE 2020 (Standard)**

Class	0-20	20-40	40-60	60-80	80-100	100-120	120-140
Frequency	6	8	10	12	6	5	3

28. The mode of the following frequency distribution is 38. Find the value of x. **CBSE Sample Paper 2022 Term II (Basic)**

Class interval	0-10	10-20	20-30	30-40	40-50	50-60	60-70
Frequency	7	9	12	16	x	6	11

29. The mode of a distribution is 55 and the modal class is 45-60 and the frequency preceding the modal class is 5 and the frequency after the modal class is 10. Find the frequency of the modal class.

30. Convert the following data into a 'more than type' distribution.

Class interval	50-55	55-60	60-65	65-70	70-75	75-80
Frequency	2	8	12	24	38	16

31. Shown below is a table representing the percentage distribution of mental health disorders of Asian countries in 2019.

Percentage of citizens with mental health disorders	Number of Asian countries
7.5-10	1
10-12.5	25
12.5-15	11
15-17.5	4
17.5-20	1

Can the median of the above data be greater than 12.5%? Give a valid reason. **Competency Based Question**

32. The following is the distribution of weights (in kg) of 40 persons

Weight (in kg)	40-45	45-50	50-55	55-60	60-65	65-70	70-75	75-80
Number of persons	4	4	13	5	6	5	2	1

Construct a cumulative frequency distribution (of the 'less than type') table for the data above. **NCERT Exemplar**

33. Construct the frequency distribution table for the given data.

Marks	Number of students
Less than 10	14
Less than 20	22
Less than 30	37
Less than 40	58
Less than 50	67
Less than 60	75

34. Convert the given cumulative frequency table into a frequency distribution table.

Marks	Number of students
0 and above	120
20 and above	108
40 and above	90
60 and above	75
80 and above	50
100 and above	24
120 and above	9
140 and above	0

35. Form the frequency distribution table from the following data.

Marks (out of 90)	Number of candidates
More than or equal to 80	4
More than or equal to 70	6
More than or equal to 60	11
More than or equal to 50	17
More than or equal to 40	23
More than or equal to 30	27
More than or equal to 20	30
More than or equal to 10	32
More than or equal to 0	34

NCERT Exemplar

36. Consider the following data

Class interval	65-85	85-105	105-125	125-145	145-165	165-185	185-205
Frequency	4	5	13	20	14	7	4

Find the difference of the upper limit of the median class and the lower limit of the modal class.

NCERT Exemplar

37. In the following frequency distribution table, find the missing values.

Class interval	0-8	8-16	16-24	24-32	32-40	40-48
Frequency	15	f_1	f_2	18	9	f_3
Cumulative frequency	15	28	43	61	f_4	80

38. Find the unknown entries *m*, *n*, *o*, *p*, *q* and *r* in the following distribution of heights of students in a class and the total number of students is 50.

Competency Based Question

Height (in cm)	150-155	155-160	160-165	165-170	170-175	175-180
Frequency	12	n	10	p	q	2
Cumulative frequency	m	25	o	43	48	r

39. In a class test, 50 students obtained marks as follows.

Marks obtained	0-20	20-40	40-60	60-80	80-100
Number of students	4	6	25	10	5

Find the modal class and the median class.

40. An inter house cricket match was organized by a school. Distribution of runs made by the students is given below. Find the median runs scored.

CBSE Sample Paper 2022 Term II (Basic)

Runs scored	0-20	20-40	40-60	60-80	80-100
Number of students	4	6	5	3	4

41. In the following data, find the values of *p* and *q*. Also, find the median class and modal class.

Class interval	100-200	200-300	300-400	400-500	500-600	600-700
Frequency	11	12	10	q	20	14
Cumulative frequency	11	p	33	46	66	80

42. While allocating frequencies to each class interval, students falling in any upper class-limit would be considered in the next class, this statement explain using a example.

43. Find the median for the given frequency distribution

CBSE 2020 (Basic)

Class	40-45	45-50	50-55	55-60	60-65	65-70	70-75
Frequency	2	3	8	6	6	3	2

44. Following is the distribution of the long jump competition in which 250 students participated. Find the median distance jumped by the students. Interpret the median

CBSE Sample Paper 2022 Term II (Standard)

Distance (in m)	0-1	1-2	2-3	3-4	4-5
Number of Students	40	80	62	38	30

45. Compute the median for the following data.

Class interval (less than)	20	30	40	50	60	70	80	90	100
Cumulative frequency	0	4	16	30	46	66	82	92	100

46. An incomplete distribution is given as follows:

Class interval	Frequency
0-10	10
10-20	20
20-30	?
30-40	40
40-50	?
50-60	25
60-70	15

The median value is 35 and the sum of all the frequencies is 170. Using the median formula, fill up the missing frequencies.

47. The median of the following data is 525. Find the values of *x* and *y*, if total frequency is 100.

CBSE 2020 (Standard)

Class	Frequency
0-100	2
100-200	5
200-300	x
300-400	12
400-500	17
500-600	20
600-700	y
700-800	9
800-900	7
900-1000	4

48. Find the mean of the following data and hence find the mode, given that median of the data is 42.5.

Class interval	10-20	20-30	30-40	40-50	50-60	60-70	70-80
Frequency	4	8	10	12	10	4	2

Long Answer Type Questions

49. The monthly expenditure on milk in 200 families of a Housing Society is given below.

Monthly Expenditure (in ₹)	Number of families
1000-1500	24
1500-2000	40
2000-2500	33
2500-3000	x
3000-3500	30
3500-4000	22
4000-4500	16
4500-5000	7

Find the value of x and also find the mean expenditure. **CBSE Sample Paper 2025 (Standard)**

50. The mean of the following frequency distribution is 50, but the frequencies f_1 and f_2 in classes 20-40 and 60-80, respectively are missing. Find the missing frequencies. **NCERT Exemplar**

Class interval	0-20	20-40	40-60	60-80	80-100	Total
Frequency	17	f_1	32	f_2	19	120

51. The following distribution shows the weekly pocket allowance of 64 children of a locality. If the mean pocket allowance is ₹ 180, then find the values of x and y. **CBSE 2024 (Basic) Compartment**

Pocket allowance (in ₹)	Number of children
110-130	7
130-150	6
150-170	9
170-190	13
190-210	x
210-230	5
230-250	y

52. Determine the mean of the following distribution.

Marks	Number of students
Below 10	5
Below 20	9
Below 30	17
Below 40	29
Below 50	45
Below 60	60
Below 70	70
Below 80	78
Below 90	83
Below 100	85

NCERT Exemplar

53. Following is the cumulative frequency distribution (of less than type) of 1000 persons each of age 20 yr and above. Determine the mean age. **NCERT Exemplar**

Age (in years)	Number of persons
Below 30	100
Below 40	220
Below 50	350
Below 60	750
Below 70	950
Below 80	1000

54. A survey was conducted to give the percentage distribution of doctors in hospitals of rural areas of various states and Union Territories (UT) of India are given in the following table:

Percentage of doctors	Number of states/UT
15-25	6
25-35	11
35-45	7
45-55	4
55-65	4
65-75	2
75-85	1

(i) Find the mean percentage of doctors of rural areas of various states and union territories.

(ii) Suppose there are two persons Ram and Shyam. If Ram find out the mean by direct method and Shyam find out the mean by step deviation method, then whether both of them get the same value. Explain the reason. **Competency Based Question**

55. Calculate the mode of the following frequency distribution table.

Marks	Number of students
25 or more than 25	52
35 or more than 35	47
45 or more than 45	37
55 or more than 55	17
65 or more than 65	8
75 or more than 75	2
85 or more than 85	0

56. Calculate the mode from the following data.

Monthly salary (in ₹)	Number of employees
Less than 5000	90
Less than 10000	240
Less than 15000	340
Less than 20000	420
Less than 25000	490
Less than 30000	500

57. Find the mean and median of the following data.
CBSE Sample Paper 2025 (Standard)

Class	Frequency
85-90	15
90-95	22
95-100	20
100-105	18
105-110	20
110-115	25

58. The median class of a frequency distribution is 125-145. The frequency and cumulative frequency of the class preceding to the median class are 20 and 22, respectively. Find the sum of the frequencies, if the median is 137. **CBSE 2011**

59. Find the mode of the following data

Class	1-3	3-5	5-7	7-9	9-11
Frequency	7	8	2	2	1

If mean $= 4.2$, then find the median using empirical relationship. **CBSE 2024 (Basic) Compartment**

60. The marks obtained by 45 students of a class in a test are given below

Marks	40-45	45-50	50-55	55-60	60-65	65-70
Number of students	8	9	10	9	5	4

Find the mean and median marks. **CBSE 2024 (Basic)**

61. A health officer took an initiative organising a medical camp in a remote village. The medical checkup of 35 students of the age group of 10 yr and their weights were recorded as follows:

Weight (in kg)	38-40	40-42	42-44	44-46	46-48	48-50	50-52
Number of students	3	2	4	5	14	4	3

(i) Find the mean weight of students using step deviation method.

(ii) Calculate the median of the given data.

Competency Based Question

HINTS & SOLUTIONS

Part I

1. (b) $\text{Mean} = \dfrac{\text{Sum of the terms}}{\text{Number of terms}}$

$\therefore \quad 9 = \dfrac{6+7+x+8+y+14}{6}$

$\Rightarrow \quad x+y+35 = 54 \Rightarrow x+y = 19$

2. (b) $\text{Mean} = \dfrac{\text{Sum of given observations}}{\text{Total number of observations}}$

$\therefore \quad 11 = \dfrac{x+x+2+x+4+x+6+x+8}{5}$

$\Rightarrow \quad 55 = 5x+20 \Rightarrow 55-20 = 5x \Rightarrow 5x = 35$

$\Rightarrow \quad x = \dfrac{35}{5} = 7$

3. (c) Given, maximum number of students has obtained 52 marks out of 80.

We know that the mode is the value that appears most often in a set of data.

Since, the score 52 is obtained by the maximum number of students, therefore 52 is the mode of the data.

4. (b) Given, $\sum_{i=1}^{n} f_i x_i = 132+5p, \sum_{i=1}^{n} f_i = 20$

and the mean of the distribution is 8.1

We know that

$$\text{Mean,} \quad \bar{x} = \frac{\sum_{i=1}^{n} f_i x_i}{\sum_{i=1}^{n} f_i} \Rightarrow 8.1 = \frac{132+5p}{20}$$

$\Rightarrow \quad 132+5p = 162.0 \Rightarrow 5p = 30 \Rightarrow p = 6$

Hence, the value of p is 6.

5. (c) Mean $\bar{x} = \dfrac{\text{Sum of all the observations}}{\text{Number of observations}}$

$= \dfrac{x_1 + x_2 + \ldots + x_n}{n}$

Here, mean of five observations is 15.

i.e. $n = 5$, and $\bar{x} = 15$

and mean of first three obsrevations is 14.

and that of last three observations is 17.

i.e. $x_1 + x_2 + x_3 = 14 \times 3 = 42$ ...(i)

and $x_3 + x_4 + x_5 = 17 \times 3 = 51$ ...(ii)

On adding Eqs. (i) and (ii), we get

$x_1 + x_2 + 2x_3 + x_4 + x_5 = 93$ ...(iii)

and $\bar{x} = \dfrac{x_1 + x_2 + x_3 + x_4 + x_5}{5}$

$\Rightarrow 15 = \dfrac{x_1 + x_2 + x_3 + x_4 + x_5}{5}$

$\Rightarrow x_1 + x_2 + x_3 + x_4 + x_5 = 75$ ...(iv)

On subtracting Eq. (iv) from Eq. (iii), we get

$x_3 = 18$

∴ Third observation is 18.

6. (c) The cumulative frequency table of given data is

Class	Frequency (f_i)	Cumulative Frequency (cf)
0-10	5	5
10-20	9	14
20-30	15	29
30-40	10	39
40-50	6	45
	$\Sigma f_i = 45$	

Here, $n = 45 \Rightarrow \dfrac{n}{2} = 22.5$

Since, the cumulative frequency just greater than 22.5 is 29 and the corresponding interval is 20-30.

∴ Median class = 20 – 30

Hence, the upper limit of median class is 30.

7. (b) First seven prime numbers are 2, 3, 5, 7, 11, 13, 17

∴ Median = Middle element = 7

8. (c) Here,

Class Intervals	Number of students (Frequency)	Cumulative frequency
Below 10	2	2
10-20	10	12
20-30	16	28
30-40	28	56
40-50	20	76
50-60	4	80
Total	$n = 80$	

Here, $n = 80$

∴ $\dfrac{n}{2} = \dfrac{80}{2} = 40$

Since, the cumulative frequency just greater than 40 is 56.

∴ The median class is 30-40.

9. (d) Given, mean = 10 and median = 11

We know that

Mode = 3 Median – 2 Mean

$= 3(11) - 2(10)$

$= 33 - 20 = 13$

Hence, mode of the data is 13.

10. (b) Given, mode = 10

and mean + median = 25

⇒ mean = 25 – median

We know that mode = 3 median – 2 mean

⇒ 10 = 3 median – 2(25 – median)

⇒ 10 = 3 median – 50 + 2 median

⇒ 5 median = 60

⇒ median = 12

∴ Mean = 25 – median

= 25 – 12 = 13

11. (a) 12. (b) 13. (d)

14. (i) Given, mean salary of the supervisors = ₹ 19000

∴ Total salary of 5 supervisors = 5 × ₹ 19000 = ₹ 95000

But, salary of 3 supervisors are ₹ 18000, ₹ 18500 and ₹ 20000.

Total salary of 3 supervisors

= ₹ (18000 + 18500 + 20000) = ₹ 56500

∴ Total salary of remaining 2 supervisors

= Total salary of 5 supervisors – Total salary of 3 supervisors

= ₹ (95000 – 56500)

= ₹ 38500

∵ Salary of supervisors for the first two months is between ₹ 18000 and ₹ 20000.

∴ Possible salaries of other two supervisors are ₹ 19250 and ₹ 19250 or ₹ 19500 and ₹ 19000 or ₹ 18500 and ₹ 20000, etc. (any combination between ₹ 18000 to ₹ 20000 which gives a sum of ₹ 38500).

(ii) (b) Maximum salary that an operator can get for the first two months = ₹ 10000

∵ There are 20 operators for the project.

∴ Total amount Arti will have to pay the operators for first two months = 20 × 10000

= ₹ 200000

15. (i) Frequency distribution table for the given data is

Class interval	Number of claims (f_i)
No claims	368
6-15	3
16-25	610
26-35	1255
36-45	1067
46-55	555
56-65	1280

Since, the given data is not continuous. So, we subtract 0.5 from the lower limit and add 0.5 to the upper limit of each class to make the data continuous.

Class interval	Frequency (f_i)	Class mark (x_i)	$f_i x_i$
No claims	368		
5.5-15.5	3	10.5	31.5
15.5-25.5	610	20.5	12505
25.5-35.5	1255	30.5	38277.5
35.5-45.5	1067	40.5	43213.5
45.5-55.5	555	50.5	28027.5
55.5-65.5	1280	60.5	77440
	$\Sigma f_i = 5138$		$\Sigma f_i x_i = 199495$

∴ Mean claim amount,

$$\bar{x} = \frac{\Sigma f_i x_i}{\Sigma f_i}$$

$$= \frac{199495}{5138}$$

$$= 38.827 \text{ hundred dollars}$$

(ii) Number of claims upto $ 3500, the company received $= 368 + 3 + 610 + 1255 = 2236$

(iii) Model class $= 55.5 - 65.5$ (i.e. the class with maximum frequency).

16. (i) Cumulative frequency table for the given data is

Salary (in ₹)	Number of operators (f_i)	Cumulative frequency
13000	5	5
13500	3	8
14000	2	10
14500	4	14
15000	6	20
	$\Sigma f_i = n = 20$	

Here, $n = 20$ (even)

$$\therefore \text{Median} = \frac{1}{2}\left[\text{Value of } \left(\frac{20}{2}\right)\text{th} + \left(\frac{20}{2}+1\right)\text{th}\right] \text{ observation}$$

$$= \frac{1}{2}(10\text{th} + 11\text{th}) \text{ observation}$$

$$= \frac{1}{2}(14000 + 14500) = \frac{28500}{2} = ₹\ 14250$$

(ii) Since, number of operators corresponding to the salary ₹ 15000 is more. Therefore, salary received by most of the operators is ₹ 15000.

17. Table for the given data

Length (in mm)	Frequency (f)	Cumulative frequency (cf)
70-80	3	3
80-90	5	8
90-100	9	17
100-110	12	29
110-120	5	34
120-130	4	38
130-140	2	40

(i) We have, $N = 40$

$$\frac{N}{2} = 20$$

So, median class is 90 – 100.

(ii) We know that 10 cm = 100 mm

Number of leaves greater than 100 mm

$$= 12 + 5 + 4 + 2 = 23$$

(iii) (a) Median of class is 100 – 110.

So, $l = 100$, $f = 12$, $cf = 17$ and $h = 10$

$$\because \text{Median} = l + \frac{\left(\frac{N}{2} - cf\right)}{f} \times h$$

$$\Rightarrow \text{Median} = 100 + \left(\frac{20-17}{12}\right) \times 10$$

$$= 100 + \frac{30}{12} = 100 + 2.5$$

$$\Rightarrow \text{Median} = 102.5$$

(b) We have, modal class as 100 – 110.

So, $l = 100$, $f_1 = 12$, $f_0 = 9$, $f_2 = 5$ and $h = 10$

We know that mode $= l + \dfrac{f_1 - f_0}{2f_1 - f_0 - f_2} \times h$

$$\text{Mode} = 100 + \frac{12-9}{24-9-5} \times 10$$

$$= 100 + 3 = 103$$

18. (i) Modal class is the class interval in a frequency distribution table which has the highest frequency. According to the given data, the highest frequency is 132 and the class interval corresponding to it is 20-24.

Thus, the modal class of the above data is 20-24.

Hence, lower limit of the modal class is 20.

(ii) (a) Convert the given data as continuous classes and calculate the cumulative frequency.

Class interval (Age)	Frequency (f)	Cumulative frequency (cf)
14.5-19.5	62	62
19.5-24.5	132	194
24.5-29.5	96	290
29.5-34.5	37	327
34.5-39.5	13	340
39.5-44.5	11	351
44.5-49.5	10	361
49.5-54.5	4	365

Here, $N = 365$ (odd)

$$\frac{N}{2} = \frac{365}{2} = 182.5$$

Cumulative frequency greater than and nearer to 182.5 is 194 which belongs to the class interval 19.5-24.5.

$\therefore$ The median class of the above data is 19.5 - 24.5.

(b) Number of participants of age less than 50 yr who undergo vocational training

$$= 62 + 132 + 96 + 37 + 13 + 11 + 10 = 361$$

Therefore, required number of participants is 361.

(iii) The empirical relationship between mean, median and mode is given by

$$\text{Mode} = 3\,\text{Median} - 2\,\text{Mean}$$

Part II

1. We know that $\bar{x} = \dfrac{\Sigma f_i x_i}{n}$

$\Rightarrow \quad \Sigma f_i x_i = n\bar{x}$

Now, $\Sigma(f_i x_i - \bar{x}) = \Sigma f_i x_i - \Sigma\bar{x} = n\bar{x} - n\bar{x} \quad [\because \Sigma\bar{x} = n\bar{x}]$

$= 0$

2. Hint $\because \Sigma f_i = 11$

and $\Sigma f_i x_i = 6 + 8 + 18 + 10 + 2(a + 5)$

$= 42 + 2\,(a + 5)$

$$\therefore \text{ Mean} = \frac{\Sigma f_i x_i}{\Sigma f_i} = \frac{42 + 2\,(a + 5)}{11} = 6$$

Ans. $a = 7$

3. Hint Do same as Example 2 of Topic 1. **Ans.** $y = 8$

4. Table for the given data is

Runs Scored (class interval)	Number of students (f_i)	Mid-value (x_i)	$f_i x_i$
0-40	12	20	240
40-80	20	60	1200
80-120	35	100	3500
120-160	30	140	4200
160-200	23	180	4140
Total	120		13280

Here, $\Sigma f_i = 120$ and $\Sigma f_i x_i = 13280$

$$\therefore \text{Mean} = \frac{\Sigma f_i x_i}{\Sigma f_i} = \frac{13280}{120} = 110.66$$

Hence, the mean of given data is 110.66.

5. Given, $\Sigma f_i u_i = 30, \Sigma f_i = 40$ and $u_i = \dfrac{x_i - 20}{10}$

We know that $u_i = \dfrac{x_i - a}{h}$

On comparing, we get $a = 20, h = 10$

$$\therefore \quad \bar{x} = a + \left\{\frac{\Sigma f_i u_i}{\Sigma f_i}\right\} \times h = 20 + \left\{\frac{30}{40}\right\} \times 10$$

$$= 20 + \frac{30}{4} = \frac{80 + 30}{4} = \frac{110}{4} = 27.5$$

6. Frequency distribution table with cumulative frequency is

Marks	Class interval	Number of students	Cumulative frequency
Below 10	0-10	3	3
Below 20	10-20	9	12
Below 30	20-30	15	27
Below 40	30-40	30	57
Below 50	40-50	18	75
Below 60	50-60	5	80

Here, the highest frequency is 30, which lies in the interval 30-40. So, it is the modal class i.e. 30-40.

7. Hint Writes that the company should fix the size of the ketchup bottle based on the mode.

Writes that the mode gives the information about the size that is sold most often.

8. Hint Here, number of terms, $N = 4n$, which is an even number.

$$\therefore \text{ Median} = \text{Mean of} \left(\frac{N}{2}\right)\text{th term and} \left(\frac{N}{2} + 1\right)\text{th term}$$

i.e. Median = Mean of [$(2n)$th term and $(2n + 1)$th term].

9. We prepare a continuous grouped frequency distribution table.

Monthly income range (in ₹)	Number of families (f_i)
10000-13000	$100 - 85 = 15$
13000-16000	$85 - 69 = 16$
16000-19000	$69 - 50 = 19$
19000-22000	$50 - 33 = 17$
22000-25000	$33 - 15 = 18$
More than 25000	15
	$\Sigma f_i = 100$

Observing the above table, we find that there are 19 families having income range 16000-19000 (in ₹).

10. Do same as Example 9 of Topic 3.

Ans.

Class interval	Frequency
Below 20	8
20-30	5
30-40	6
40-50	5

11. Hint The less than type frequency distribution of given table is

Class interval	Frequency	Time taken	Cumulative frequency
13.8-14.0	2	Less than 14	2
14.0-14.2	4	Less than 14.2	$2+4=6$
14.2-14.4	5	Less than 14.4	$6+5=11$
14.4-14.6	71	Less than 14.6	$11+71=82$
14.6-14.8	48	Less than 14.8	$82+48=130$
14.8-15.0	20	Less than 15.0	$130+20=150$

Hence, the required number of athletes, who completed the race in less than 14.6s is 82.

12. Mode = 3(Median) − 2(Mean)

13. Hint Use formula used in Q.12. **Ans.** 56.25

14. Hint Use formula used in Q.12. **Ans.** 100

15. Table for the given data is

x_i	f_i	$f_i x_i$
15	2	30
17	3	51
19	4	76
$20+k$	$5k$	$100k+5k^2$
23	6	138
Total	$\Sigma f_i = 5k+15$	$\Sigma f_i x_i = 295 + 100k + 5k^2$

Here, $\Sigma f_i = 5k+15$ and $\Sigma f_i x_i = 295+100k+5k^2$

Given, mean = 20

We know that mean $= \dfrac{\Sigma f_i x_i}{\Sigma f_i}$

$$\Rightarrow \frac{295+100k+5k^2}{5k+15} = 20$$

$$\Rightarrow (295+100k+5k^2) = 20(5k+15)$$

$$\Rightarrow 295+100k+5k^2 = 100k+300$$

$$\Rightarrow 295+100k+5k^2-100k-300 = 0$$

$$\Rightarrow 5k^2 - 5 = 0 \Rightarrow k^2 - 1 = 0$$

$$\Rightarrow (k+1)(k-1) = 0 \quad [\because a^2 - b^2 = (a+b)(a-b)]$$

If $k+1=0$, then $k=-1$ [here, negative value is not possible, as frequency cannot be negative]

If $k-1=0$, then $k=1$

Hence, the required value of k is 1.

16. Hint Do same as Example 4 of Topic 1. **Ans.** $p = 3$

17. Yes,

Hint $\displaystyle\sum_{i=1}^{n}(x_i - 50) = -10$

$$\Rightarrow \sum_{i=1}^{n} x_i - 50n = -10 \quad \ldots\text{(i)}$$

and $\displaystyle\sum_{i=1}^{n}(x_i - 46) = 70$

$$\Rightarrow \sum_{i=1}^{n} x_i - 46n = 70 \quad \ldots\text{(ii)}$$

Now, solve Eq. (i) and (ii) and find the value of $\displaystyle\sum_{i=1}^{n} x_i$ and n.

18. Hint Dipti's claim is not correct.
e.g. Consider there are 4 students in the class with scores, 80, 90, 20 and 50. The mean is 60 marks, half of them got 80 or above, but one score in the remaining half is above 40.

19. Hint The number of days remaining as $31 - 8 - 12 = 11$
Sum of the temperatures of all the 31 days as $35.7°C \times 31 = 1106.7°C$.
The sum of the temperatures of first 8 days as $28.4°C \times 8 = 227.2°C$.
The sum of the temperatures of next 12 days as $36.4°C \times 12 = 436.8°C$.
$\therefore$ The sum of the temperatures of last 11 days as $1106.7°C - 227.2°C - 436.8°C = 442.7°C$.
$\therefore$ The mean temperature of the last 11 days $= \dfrac{442.7}{11}$

Ans. 40.2°C

20. Hint Completes the frequency distribution table as

Rainfall (in mm)	Number of days /Frequency (f_i)	Class-mark (x_i)	($f_i x_i$)
0-20	7	10	70
20-40	x	30	$30x$
40-60	10	50	500
60-80	4	70	280
Total	$21+x$		$850+30x$

$\therefore$ Mean $= \dfrac{850+30x}{21+x} = 35$ **Ans.** $x = 23$

21. Hint Do same as Example 6 of Topic 1.
Ans. Mean $= 8.15$

22. Hint Do same as Example 7 of Topic 1. **Ans.** 123.4 kg

23. Hint Do same as Example 7 of Topic 1. **Ans.** 44.5 yr

24. Since, the given data is not continuous, so we subtract 0.5 from the lower limit and add 0.5 in the upper limit of each class. The table for given data becomes

Income (in ₹)	Class marks (x_i)	Number of employees (f_i)	$u_i = \dfrac{x_i - a}{h}$	$f_i u_i$
0.5-200.5	100.5	14	-1	-14
200.5-400.5	a=300.5	15	0	0
400.5-600.5	500.5	14	1	14
600.5-800.5	700.5	7	2	14
Total		$n = \Sigma f_i = 50$		$\Sigma f_i u_i = 14$

Here, assumed mean, $a = 300.5$
Class width, $h = 200$
and total number of observations, $n = 50$
By step deviation method,

$$\therefore \text{Mean} = a + \left\{\frac{\sum_{i=1}^{50} f_i u_i}{n}\right\} \times h = 300.5 + \left\{\frac{14}{50}\right\} \times 200$$

$$= 300.5 + 56 = 356.5$$

Note it Above question also can be solved without changing the intervals.

25. Do same as Example 6 of Topic 1. **Ans.** 153.45

26. Hint Do same as Example 8 of Topic 1. **Ans.** $x = 10, y = 8$

27. Do same as Example 2 of Topic 2. **Ans.** 65

28. Hint Do same as Example 4 of Topic 2. **Ans.** $x = 15$

29. Hint Mode $= l + \dfrac{f_1 - f_0}{2f_1 - f_0 - f_2} \times h$. **Ans.**15

30. Hint Do same as Example 3 of Topic 3.

31. Hint Writes that the median of the given data cannot be greater than 12.5% as 10-12.5 is the median class.

32. Table for the given data is

Weight (in Kg)	Number of Persons (cumulative frequency)
Less than 45	4
Less than 50	$4+4=8$
Less than 55	$8+13=21$
Less than 60	$21+5=26$
Less than 65	$26+6=32$
Less than 70	$32+5=37$
Less than 75	$37+2=39$
Less than 80	$39+1=40$

33. Hint Do same as Example 9 of Topic 3.
Ans.

Marks	Number of students
0-10	14
10-20	$22-14=8$
20-30	$37-22=15$
30-40	$58-37=21$
40-50	$67-58=9$
50-60	$75-67=8$

34. Hint

Marks	Number of students
0-20	$120-108=12$
20-40	$108-90=18$
40-60	$90-75=15$
60-80	$75-50=25$
80-100	$50-24=26$
100-120	$24-9=15$
120-140	$9-0=9$

35. Hint Do same as Example 4 of Topic 3.

36. The cumulative frequency table for given data is

Class interval	Frequency	Cumulative frequency
65-85	4	4
85-105	5	9
105-125	13	22
125-145	20	42
145-165	14	56
165-185	7	63
185-205	4	67

Here, $\frac{n}{2}=\frac{67}{2}=33.5$

The cumulative frequency just greater than 33.5 is 42 and the corresponding class is 125-145.

Thus, we have median class 125-145.

Also, the maximum frequency is of the class 125-145. Therefore, the modal class is 125-145.

$\therefore$ Difference of the upper limit of median class and the lower limit of modal class = 145 − 125 = 20

37. Hint $15+f_1=28, 28+f_2=43,$

$61+9=f_4,\ f_3+f_4=80$

Ans. $f_1=13, f_2=15, f_3=10, f_4=70$

38. Hint Given, distribution table is

Height (in cm)	Frequency	Cumulative frequency
150-155	12	m
155-160	n	25
160-165	10	o
165-170	p	43
170-175	q	48
175-180	2	r

We know that cumulative frequency of an interval is equal to the sum of frequency of that interval and of previous intervals.

Here, $m=12$

$\therefore\quad m+n=25 \Rightarrow 12+n=25 \Rightarrow n=13$

and $\quad 25+10=o \Rightarrow o=35$

Also, $\quad o+p=43 \Rightarrow 35+p=43$

$\Rightarrow\quad p=8$

$43+q=48 \Rightarrow q=48-43=5$

and $\quad 48+2=r \Rightarrow r=50$

Hence, the required values are

$m=12, n=13, o=35, p=8, q=5$ and $r=50$.

39. Hint Do same as Question 37.

Ans Modal class = 40-60, Median class = 40-60

40.

Class interval	Frequency	Commutative frequency
0-20	4	4
20-40	6	10
40-60	5	15
60-80	3	18
80-100	4	22
Total	22(=n)	

$n=22$

$\Rightarrow\quad \frac{n}{2}=\frac{22}{2}=11$ (near to 15)

$\therefore$ Median class is 40-60.

Now, median $=l+\frac{\left[\frac{n}{2}-cf\right]}{f}\times h$

where, l = Lower limit of median class

cf = Cumulative frequency just before median class

h = Size of median class.

f = Frequency of median class

$\therefore$ Median $=40+\frac{11-10}{5}\times 20=44$

Hence, the required median score is 44 runs.

41. Hint Do same as Question 36 and 37.

Ans. $p=23, q=13,$

Median class = 400-500, Modal class = 500-600.

42. 10 students who have obtained 60 marks would be considered in the class interval 60-70 and not in 50-60.

43. Do same as Example 8 of Topic 3. **Ans.** Median = 56.67

44.

Class interval (distance in m)	Frequency (number of students)	cf
0-1	40	40
1-2	80	120
2-3	62	182
3-4	38	220
4-5	30	250
Total	250 (=n)	

$\therefore\quad \frac{n}{2}=\frac{250}{2}=125$, which lies in the interval 2-3.

$\therefore$ Median $=l+\frac{\left(\frac{n}{2}-cf\right)}{f}\times h=2+\frac{125-120}{62}\times 1$

$=2+\frac{5}{62}=2+0.08=2.08$ m

Hence, we observe that 50% of students jump below 2.08 m and 50% above it.

45. Do same as Example 9 of Topic 3. **Ans.** 62

46. Hint Do same as Example 10 of Topic 3.

Ans. $f_1=35$ and $f_2=25$

47. Do same as Example 10 of Topic 3.

Ans. $x=9$ and $y=15$

48. Hint Do same as Example 6 of Topic 1. Also, use the empirical formula.

Ans. Mean = 42.2, Mode = 43.1.

49. The table for the given data is

Monthly expenditure	f_i	x_i	f_ix_i
1000-1500	24	1250	30000
1500-2000	40	1750	70000
2000-2500	33	2250	74250
2500-3000	x	2750	$2750x$
3000-3500	30	3250	97500
3500-4000	22	3750	82500
4000-4500	16	4250	68000
4500-5000	7	4750	33250
	$\Sigma f_i = 172 + x$		$\Sigma f_ix_i = 2750x + 455500$

We have, $172 + x = 200 \Rightarrow x = 28$

So, $2750x = 2750 \times 28 = 77000$

Now, Mean $= \dfrac{\Sigma f_ix_i}{\Sigma f_i}$

$$= \frac{455500 + 77000}{200} = \frac{532500}{200} = 2662.5$$

50. Hint Do same as Example 8 of Topic 1.

Ans. $f_1 = 28, f_2 = 24$

51. Hint Do same as Example 8 of Topic 1.

Ans. $x = 20$ and $y = 4$

52. Here, we observe that 5 students have scored marks below 10 i.e. it lies between class interval 0-10 and 9 students have scored marks below 20.

So, $(9-5) = 4$ students lie in the class interval 10-20. Continuing in the same manner, we get the following frequency distribution table for given data.

Marks	Number of students (f_i)	Class marks (x_i)	$u_i = \dfrac{x_i - 45}{h}$	f_iu_i
0-10	5	5	-4	-20
10-20	$9-5=4$	15	-3	-12
20-30	$17-9=8$	25	-2	-16
30-40	$29-17=12$	35	-1	-12
40-50	$45-29=16$	$45=a$	0	0
50-60	$60-45=15$	55	1	15
60-70	$70-60=10$	65	2	20
70-80	$78-70=8$	75	3	24
80-90	$83-78=5$	85	4	20
90-100	$85-83=2$	95	5	10
Total	$N = \Sigma f_i = 85$			$\Sigma f_iu_i = 29$

Here, assumed mean $(a) = 45$

and class width $(h) = 10$

By step deviation method,

$$\text{Mean } (\bar{x}) = a + \left\{\frac{\Sigma f_iu_i}{\Sigma f_i}\right\} \times h = 45 + \left\{\frac{29}{85}\right\} \times 10$$

$$= 45 + \frac{58}{17} = 45 + 3.41 = 48.41$$

53. Do same as Question 52. **Ans.** 51.3 yr

54. (i) **Ans.** 39.72%

(ii) Yes, the mean will be same i.e. 39.72. Because, step deviation method is just simplified form of direct method.

55. Hint Convert it into frequency distribution table and then do same as Example 2 of Topic 2. **Ans.** 49.76

56. Hint Convert it into frequency distribution table and then do same as Example 2 of Topic 2.

Ans. 7727.27

57. The table for the given data is

Class	x_i	f_i	$u = \dfrac{x - 102.5}{5}$	f_iu_i
85-90	87.5	15	-3	-45
90-95	92.5	22	-2	-44
95-100	97.5	20	-1	-20
100-105	102.5	18	0	0
105-110	107.5	20	1	20
110-115	112.5	25	2	50
		$\Sigma f_i = 120$		$\Sigma f_iu_i = -39$

We know, mean, $\bar{x} = A + \left(\dfrac{\Sigma f_iu_i}{\Sigma f_i}\right) \times h$

Here, $A = 102.5, \Sigma f_iu_i = -39, \Sigma f_i = 120$

and $h = 5$

$\therefore \quad \bar{x} = 102.5 - \left(\dfrac{39}{120}\right) \times 5$

$= 100.875$

The cumulative frequency table for the given data is

Class	f	cf
85-90	15	15
90-95	22	37
95-100	20	57 (cf)
100-105	18 (f)	75
105-110	20	95
110-115	25	120
	$\Sigma f = 120$	

$\because \quad n = 120$

$\Rightarrow \quad \frac{n}{2} = 60$

Since, the cumulative frequency just greater than 60 is 75 an d the corresponding class is 100-105.

$\therefore$ Median class = 100 − 105

Here, $l = 100$, $f = 18$, $cf = 57$ and $h = 5$

$$\therefore \text{Median} = l + \left(\frac{\frac{n}{2} - cf}{f}\right) \times h$$

$$= 100 + \left(\frac{60 - 57}{18}\right) \times 5$$

$$= 100 + \frac{3}{18} \times 5$$

$$= 100.83$$

58. Hint Use the formula, median $= l + \left\{\frac{\frac{n}{2} - cf}{f}\right\} \times h.$

Ans. 68

59. Do same as Example 2 of Topic 2 and after use empirical relationship and find the median.

Ans. Mode = 3.28

Median = 3.89

60. We have,

Marks	Number of students (f_i)	Mid-point (x_i)	$x_i f_i$	cf
40-45	8	42.5	340	8
45-50	9	47.5	427.5	17
50-55	10	52.5	525	27
55-60	9	57.5	517.5	36
60-65	5	62.5	312.5	41
65-70	4	67.5	270	45
	$\Sigma f_i = 45$		$\Sigma f_i x_i = 2392.5$	

$$\text{Mean} = \frac{\Sigma f_i x_i}{\Sigma f_i} = \frac{2392.5}{45} = 53.167$$

Size of $\left(\frac{N}{2}\right)$th item is $\frac{45}{2}$ i.e. 22.5

which lies in the class interval 50-55.

Here, $l = 50$, $h = 5$, $f = 10$, $cf = 17$

$$\text{Median} = l + \frac{\frac{N}{2} - cf}{f} \times h = 50 + \frac{22.5 - 17}{10} \times 5 = 52.75$$

Therefore, mean is 53.167 and median marks is 52.75.

61. Hint (i) Do same as Example 6 of Topic 1. **Ans.** 45.8 kg

(ii) Do same as Example 8 of Topic 3. **Ans.** 46.5

Grouped Data
The data that has been organised into several groups, called classes.

Ungrouped Data
The data that is obtained in original form, it is just a list of numbers.

Arithmetic Mean or Average
The arithmetic mean of a set of observations is obtained by dividing the sum of the values of all observations by the total number of observations
i.e. mean of n observations $x_1, x_2, \ldots, x_n$ is

$$\text{Mean } (\bar{x}) = \frac{x_1 + x_2 + \ldots + x_n}{n} = \frac{\sum_{i=1}^{n} x_i}{n}$$

If n observations $x_1, x_2 \ldots, x_n$ is given with their respective frequencies $f_1, f_2 \ldots f_n$.

$$\text{Then, mean } (\bar{x}) = \frac{f_1 x_1 + f_2 x_2 + \ldots + f_n x_n}{f_1 + f_2 + \ldots + f_n} = \frac{\sum_{i=1}^{n} f_i x_i}{\sum_{i=1}^{n} f_i}$$

where, $\bar{x}$ is read as 'x bar'.

Method of Calculating Mean of Grouped Data

1. Direct Method
For ith class interval, the frequency f_i corresponding to the class mark x_i, the sum of the values in last column gives $\Sigma f_i x_i$.

$$\therefore \bar{x} = \frac{\Sigma f_i x_i}{\Sigma f_i}$$

2. Assumed Mean Method
When numerical values x_i and f_i are large and computation of product of x_i and f_i becomes tedious and time consuming, we use assumed mean method.
First choose x_i's as assumed mean 'a',
then $d_i = x_i - a$

$$\therefore \text{ Arithmetic mean is } \bar{x} = a + \frac{\Sigma f_i d_i}{\Sigma f_i}$$

where x_i's are given observations and f_i are their respective frequencies.

3. Step Deviation Method
For $d_i = x_i - a$ for each class, where a is assumed mean of x_i's we take the deviation from the assumed mean that are multiples of common number. If the values of d_i for each class is a multiple of h, then we have

$$u_i = \frac{d_i}{h} = \frac{x_i - a}{h}$$

where, h is the class size of each class interval i.e. the difference between upper and lower class limits of a class. Thus, the arithmetic mean is

$$x = \left(a + \frac{\Sigma f_i u_i}{\Sigma f_i} \times h\right)$$

STATISTICS

Mode
The value of observation having maximum frequency is called mode.
e.g. Mode of the numbers, 2, 3,4, 4, 6, 6, 6, 6, 7 and 9 is 6 because it is repeated maximum numbers of times.

Mode of Grouped Data
In a grouped frequency distribution, it is not possible to determine the mode by looking at the frequencies, so first locate a class with the maximum frequency.

$$\therefore \text{ Mode} = l + \left[\frac{f_1 - f_0}{2f_1 - f_0 - f_2}\right] \times h$$

where, l = Lower limit of the modal class
h = Size of the class interval
f_1 = Frequency of the modal class
f_0 = Frequency of the class preceding the modal class
f_2 = Frequency of the class succeeding the modal class.

Median Median is the middle-most or the central observation when the observations are arranged either in ascending or descending order of their magnitudes.
Let n be total number of observations. Thus, median of arranged data is

Case I If n is odd,

$$\text{Median} = \text{Value of } \left(\frac{n+1}{2}\right)\text{th observation}$$

Case II If n is even,

$$\text{Median} = \text{Mean of value of } \left(\frac{n}{2}\right)\text{th and } \left(\frac{n}{2}+1\right)\text{th observations}$$

$$= \frac{1}{2}\left[\text{Value of } \left(\frac{n}{2}\right)\text{th} + \left(\frac{n}{2}+1\right)\text{th observations}\right]$$

Cumulative Frequency It is the sum of all frequencies up to the given class.

Median for Discrete Series A series having observations $x_1, x_2, \ldots x_n$ with their respective frequencies $f_1, f_2, \ldots, f_n$ is known as discrete series.
So, first arrange the data in ascending or descending order. Then,

$$\text{Median} = \left[\text{Value of } \left(\frac{n+1}{2}\right)\text{th}\right] \text{ observations, } n = \text{Odd}$$

$$= \frac{1}{2}\left[\text{value of } \left(\frac{n}{2}\right)\text{th} + \left(\frac{n}{2}+1\right)\text{th}\right] \text{observation, } n = \text{Even}$$

Median for Grouped Data For given grouped data,

$$\text{Median} = l + \left[\frac{\frac{n}{2} - cf}{f}\right] \times h$$

where, l = Lower limit of median class
n = Number of observations
cf = Cumulative frequency of the class preceding the median class.
f = Frequency of the median class
h = Class width (assuming class sizes to be equal)

Probability

CHAPTER 14

In this chapter, we shall first recall the study of probability done in earlier classes and then continue it to study theoretical (classical) definition of probability and problems based on it.

Meaning of Probability

Probability is the study of the chances (or likelihood) of events happening. By means of probability, the chance (or likelihood) of events is measured by a number lying between 0 and 1.

Experiment

An operation which produces some well-defined outcomes, is called an experiment.

e.g. Tossing a coin, throwing a die, etc.

There are two types of experiment

(i) Random experiment

(ii) Deterministic experiment

Random Experiment

If an experiment, when repeated under identical conditions, do not produce the same outcome every time but the outcome produced in each trial is one of the several possible outcomes, then it is known as a random or probabilistic experiment.

Tossing a fair coin is a random experiment because if we toss a coin, then either a head or a tail will come up. If we toss a coin again and again, then each time outcome will not be the same but it will be sure either head or tail.

Note it An experiment whose outcome is known, is not a random experiment.

e.g. Throwing a stone upward is not a random experiment because when a stone is thrown upward, it is sure that the stone will fall downward.

Deterministic Experiment

An experiment which when repeated under identical conditions produce the same result or outcome, is known as deterministic experiment.

e.g. Tossing of an unfair coin (having either tail or head on both sides) is a deterministic experiment, as it gives same result while tossing the coin any number of times.

Event

An event for an experiment is the collection of some outcomes of the experiment. We generally denote it by capital letter E.

e.g. Getting an even number in a single throw of a die is an event. This event would consist of three outcomes, namely 2, 4 and 6.

Elementary Event

An event having only one outcome of the random experiment is called an elementary event.

e.g. In tossing of a coin, the possible outcomes are head (H) and tail (T). Getting H or T are known as elementary events.

Occurrence of an Event

An event E associated to a random experiment is said to be occur (or happen) in a trial, if the outcome of trial is one of the outcomes that favours E.

e.g. If a die is rolled and the outcome of a trial is 4, then we say that event getting an even number has happened (or occurred).

Probability of an Event (or Probability of occurrence of an Event)

If E is an event associated with a random experiment, then probability of E, denoted by $P(E)$, represents the chance of occurrence of event E.

e.g. If E denotes the event of getting an even number in a single throw of a die, then $P(E)$ represents the chance of occurrence of event E i.e. the chance of getting 2, 4 or 6.

Probability-An Experimental Approach

The empirical (or experimental) probability of an event E is given by

$$P(E) = \frac{\text{Number of trials in which the event happened}}{\text{Total number of trials}}$$

e.g. If a coin is tossed 1000 times with the following frequencies as Head : 455 times, Tail : 545 times and if E_1 is the event of getting a head and E_2 is the event of getting a tail, then $P(E_1)$ = Probability of occurrence of head

$$= \frac{455}{1000} = 0.455$$

and $P(E_2)$ = Probability of occurrence of tail

$$= \frac{545}{1000} = 0.545$$

Probability-A Theoretical Approach

A theoretical approach of probability has some limitations, like repetition of experiment is not possible in every situation as it may be very expensive or unfeasible.

e.g. Repeating the experiment of launching a satellite in order to compute the empirical probability of its failure during launching, will be very expensive.

Note it The basic difference between these two approaches of probability is that in the experimental approach, the probability of an event is based on what has been actually happened while in theoretical approach, we try to predict what will happen without actually performing the experiment.

Compound Event

A collection of two or more elementary events associated with an experiment is called a compound event.

e.g. In the random experiment of tossing of two coins simultaneously, if we define the event of getting exactly one head, then it is a collection of elementary events (or outcomes) HT and TH. So, it is a compound event.

Equally Likely Outcomes

The outcomes of a random experiment are said to be equally likely, when each outcome is as likely to occur as the other i.e. when we have no reason to believe that one is more likely to occur than the other.

e.g. When a die is thrown, all the six outcomes i.e. 1, 2, 3, 4, 5 and 6 are equally likely to appear. So, the outcomes 1, 2, 3, 4, 5 and 6 are equally likely outcomes.

Favourable Outcomes

The outcomes which ensure the occurrence of an event are called favourable outcomes to the event.
e.g. The favourable outcomes to the event of getting an even number when a die is thrown are 2, 4 and 6.

Complement of an Event/Negation of an Event

Let E be an event associated with a random experiment. Then, we can define the complement of event E or negation of event E, denoted by $\overline{E}$, as an event which occurs if and only if E does not occur.

e.g. Let E be the event of getting an even number in a single throw of a die. Then, its complement can be define as event $\overline{E}$ of getting an odd number, as E is consisting 2, 4 and 6. Therefore, $\overline{E}$ would consist 1, 3 and 5.

Note it E and $\overline{E}$ are called complementary events.

Theoretical Definition (Classical definition) of Probability

Let us assume all the outcomes of an experiment are equally likely and E is an event associated with the experiment, then the theoretical probability (or classical probability) of the event E is given by

$$P(E) = \frac{\text{Number of outcomes favourable to } E}{\text{Total number of outcomes}}$$

Example 1. **If a die is thrown, then find the probability of getting 4.**

Sol. When a die is thrown, there are six possible outcomes i.e. 1, 2, 3, 4, 5, 6.
So, total number of outcomes is 6.
Let E be the event of getting 4.
$\therefore$ Number of outcome favourable to $E = 1$ (i.e. 4)

Hence, $P(E) = \frac{\text{Number of outcomes favourable to } E}{\text{Total number of outcomes}} = \frac{1}{6}$

Important Results Related to Probability

1. The experimental probability of an event approaches to its theoretical probability, if the number of trials of an experiment is very large.
2. The probability of happening of an event always lies between 0 to 1 (0 and 1 inclusive) i.e. $0 \le P(E) \le 1$. Also, probability can be expressed as a percentage by multiplying it by 100. Thus, probability (in percentage) lies between 0% to 100% (0 and 100 inclusive).

3. Probability of an event can never be negative.
4. The sum of the probabilities of complementary events of an experiment is 1

i.e. if E and $\bar{E}$ are complementry events.

Then, $P(E)+P(\bar{E})=1$ or $P(\bar{E})=1-P(E)$

or $P(E)=1-P(\bar{E})$

where, $P(E)$ represents the probability of occurrence of an event E and $P(\bar{E})$ represents the probability of non-occurrence of an event E.

Justification If m outcomes are favourable to an event E out of n possible outcomes, then the number of outcomes which ensure the non-occurrence of event E is $n-m$.

Thus, we have

$$P(\bar{E})=\frac{n-m}{n}=1-\frac{m}{n}=1-P(E) \Rightarrow P(\bar{E})+P(E)=1$$

Note it

- The ratio $P(E):P(\bar{E})$ i.e. $m:n-m$ known as odd in favour of occurrence of event E.
- The ratio $P(\bar{E}):P(E)$ i.e. $n-m:m$ known as odd in against of the occurrence of event E.

Some Special Events

Impossible Event

An event which is impossible to occur, is called an impossible event and probability of an impossible event is always zero.

e.g. In throwing a die, there are only six possible outcomes 1, 2, 3, 4, 5 and 6. Let we are interested in getting a number 7 on throwing a die. Since, no face of the die is marked with 7. So, 7 cannot come in any throw. Hence, getting 7 is an impossible event.

Then, $P(\text{getting a number } 7)=\frac{0}{6}=0$

Sure Event or Certain Event

An event which is sure to occur, is called a sure event or a certain event and probability of sure event is always 1.

e.g. Suppose we want to find the probability of getting a number less than 7 in a single throw of a die having numbers 1 to 6 on its six faces.

We are sure that, we shall always get a number less than 7, whenever we throw a die. So, getting a number less than 7 is a sure event.

Then, $P(\text{getting a number less than } 7)=\frac{6}{6}=1$

Different Types of Problems Related to Probability of an Event

Let us discuss the procedure of finding probability for the problems of following types

Type I Problems Based on Tossing a Coin

A coin has two sides, head (H) and tail (T). If we toss one or more coins, then their possible outcomes are as follows :

(i) In case of one coin, possible outcomes are H and T.

(ii) In case of two coins, possible outcomes are HH, HT, TH, TT.

(iii) In case of three coins, possible outcomes are $HHH, HHT, HTH, HTT, THH, THT, TTH, TTT$.

Note it

- When we talk about a coin, we assume that it to be 'fair', i.e. symmetrical so that there is no reason for it to come down more often on one side than the other. This property of the coin is said to be 'unbiased'.
- **Random toss of a coin** It is a phrase which means that the coin is allowed to fall freely without any bias or interference.

Example 2. **Two coins are tossed simultaneously. Find the probability of getting**

(i) exactly two head. **(ii) atleast one head.**

CBSE 2020 (Basic)

Sol. When two coins are tossed simultaneously, then possible outcomes are (H, H), (H, T), (T, H) and (T, T).

$\therefore$ Total number of outcomes = 4

We know that for an event E

$$P(E)=\frac{\text{Number of outcomes favourable to } E}{\text{Total number of outcomes}}$$

(i) Let E_1 be the event of getting exactly two head. Then, the outcomes favourable to E_1 is (H, H).

$\therefore$ Number of outcome favourable to $E_1=1$

$\therefore \quad P(E_1)=\frac{1}{4}$

(ii) Let E_2 be the event of getting atleast one head i.e. one head or two head. Then, outcomes favourable to E_2 are (H,T), (T,H) and (H, H)

$\therefore$ Number of outcomes favourable to $E_2=3$

$\therefore \quad P(E_2)=\frac{3}{4}$

Type II Problems Based on Throwing a Die

A die has six faces marked as 1, 2, 3, 4, 5 and 6. If we have more than one die, then all dice are considered as distinct, unless stated otherwise .

If we throw one die or two dice, then their possible outcomes are as follows

(i) In case of a die, possible outcomes are 1, 2, 3, 4, 5 and 6.

(ii) In case of two dice, possible outcomes are (1, 1), (1, 2), (1, 3), (1, 4), (1, 5), (1, 6), (2, 1), (2, 2), (2, 3), (2, 4), (2, 5), (2, 6), (3, 1), (3, 2), (3, 3), (3, 4), (3, 5), (3, 6), (4, 1), (4, 2), (4, 3), (4, 4), (4, 5), (4, 6), (5, 1), (5, 2), (5, 3), (5, 4), (5, 5), (5, 6),(6, 1), (6, 2), (6, 3), (6, 4), (6, 5) and (6, 6).

Example 3. **Suppose we throw a die once.**

(i) What is the probability of getting a number greater than 4?

(ii) What is the probability of getting a number less than or equal to 4? NCERT Exemplar

Sol. Possible outcomes of the experiment are 1, 2, 3, 4, 5 and 6.

$\therefore$ Total number of outcomes = 6

(i) Let E be the event of getting a number greater than 4. Then, outcomes favourable to E are 5 and 6, as 5 and 6 are greater than 4.

Therefore, the number of outcomes favourable to $E = 2$

$\therefore P(E) = P(\text{number greater than 4}) = \frac{2}{6} = \frac{1}{3}$

(ii) Let F be the event of getting a number less than or equal to 4.

Then, outcomes favourable to the event F are 1, 2, 3 and 4.

So, the number of outcomes favourable to $F = 4$

$\therefore P(F) = P(\text{number less than or equal to 4}) = \frac{4}{6} = \frac{2}{3}$

Example 4. **Two dice are thrown simultaneously.**

(i) Find the probability of getting a multiple of 2 on one die and a multiple of 3 on the other die.

(ii) Find the probability that the sum of the two numbers appearing on the top of the dice is 9.

Sol. Here, two dice are thrown, so possible outcomes are

(1, 1), (1, 2), (1, 3), (1, 4), (1, 5), (1, 6)
(2, 1), (2, 2), (2, 3), (2, 4), (2, 5), (2, 6)
(3, 1), (3, 2), (3, 3), (3, 4), (3, 5), (3, 6)
(4, 1), (4, 2), (4, 3), (4, 4), (4, 5), (4, 6)
(5, 1), (5, 2), (5, 3), (5, 4), (5, 5), (5, 6)
(6, 1), (6, 2), (6, 3), (6, 4), (6, 5) and (6, 6)

$\therefore$ Total number of outcomes = 36

(i) Let E be the event of getting a multiple of 2 on one die and a multiple of 3 on the other die.

Here, multiples of 2 are 2, 4 and 6, and multiples of 3 are 3 and 6. So, favourable outcomes for event E are (2, 3), (4, 3), (6, 3), (2, 6), (4, 6), (6, 6), (3, 2), (3, 4), (3, 6), (6, 2) and (6, 4).

$\therefore$ Number of outcomes favourable to $E = 11$

$\therefore$ Required probability $= P(E)$

$$= \frac{\text{Number of outcomes favourable to } E}{\text{Total number of outcomes}} = \frac{11}{36}$$

(ii) The outcomes favourable to the event, 'the sum of two numbers is 9' denoted by F, are (3, 6), (4, 5), (5, 4), (6, 3).

$\therefore$ Number of outcomes favourable to $F = 4$

Hence, required probability $= P(F) = \frac{4}{36} = \frac{1}{9}$

Note it According to the question, a multiple of 2 occurs on one die and a multiple of 3 occurs on other. So, here we take two cases. In first case, we will take (2, 4, 6) on first die and (3, 6) on second and in second case, we will take (3, 6) on first die and (2, 4, 6) on other. Thus, we get 11 favourable outcomes.

Type III Problems Based on Playing Cards

A deck of playing cards consists of 52 cards out of which 26 are black cards and other 26 are red cards, where red cards consist of 13 cards of heart (♥), 13 cards of diamond (♦) and black cards consist of 13 cards of spades (♠) and 13 cards of club (♣).

Thus, 52 playing cards are divided into four parts (called suits) of 13 cards each, namely heart, diamond, spades and club.

Also, 13 cards in each suit are ace, king, queen, jack, 10, 9, 8, 7, 6, 5, 4, 3 and 2.

Tree diagram of playing cards

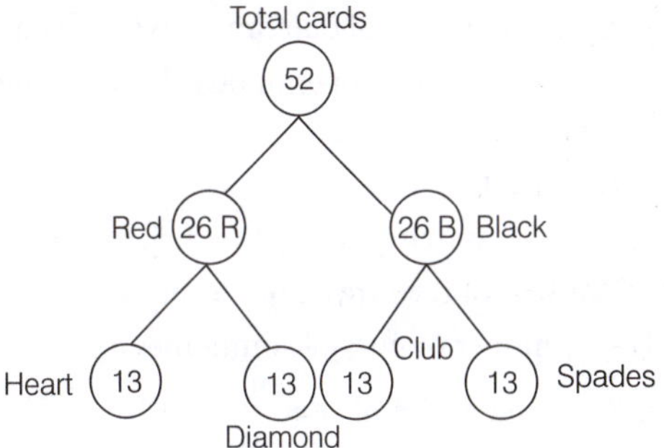

Face Cards King, Queen and Jack are called face cards. So, total number of face cards = 12

Example 5. **One card is drawn at random from a well shuffled deck of 52 cards. Find the probability that the card drawn**

(i) is queen of hearts.

(ii) is not a jack. CBSE 2024 (Standard)

Sol. Total number of cards in one deck of card is 52.

$\therefore$ Total number of outcomes = 52

(i) Let E_1 = Event of getting a queen of heart

$\therefore$ Number of outcome favourable to $E_1 = 1$

Hence, probability of getting a queen of heart,

$$P(E_1) = \frac{1}{52}$$

(ii) Let E_2 = Event of getting a card is not a jack

$\therefore$ Number of outcomes favourable to $E_2 = 48$

Hence, probability of getting a card is not a jack,

$$P(E_2) = \frac{48}{52} = \frac{12}{13}$$

Type IV Problems Based on Selection of an Object from a Bag/Box

In this type of problems, we have to find the probability of selecting an item/object of particular colour/type from a bag/box containing items/objects (like 5 balls, 4 marbles, 8 oranges, 7 bulbs etc.) in more than one colour/type.

Example 6. A box contains 20 discs which are numbered from 1 to 20. If one disc is drawn at random from the box, then find the probability that the number on the drawn disc is a CBSE 2023 (Basic)

(i) 2-digit number.

(ii) number less than 10.

Sol. (i) Let E be the event of getting a 2-digit number.

Outcomes favourable to E are

10, 11, 12, 13, 14, 15, 16, 17, 18, 19, 20.

$\therefore$ Number of outcomes favourable to $E = 11$

Total number of possible outcomes = 20

$$\therefore \quad P(E) = \frac{\text{Number of outcomes favourable to } E}{\text{Total number of possible outcomes}} = \frac{11}{20}$$

(ii) Favourable outcomes = 1, 2, 3, 4, 5, 6, 7, 8, 9

$\therefore$ Number of favourable outcomes = 9

Total number of possible outcomes = 20

$\therefore$ Required probability $= \frac{9}{20}$

Example 7. The number of red balls in a bag is three more than the number of black balls. If the probability of drawing a red ball at random from the given bag is $\frac{12}{23}$, find the total number of balls in the given bag.

Sol. Let the number of red and black balls in a bag be x and y, respectively.

$\therefore$ Total number of balls $= x + y$

According to the question,

$$x = y + 3$$

$$\Rightarrow \quad x - y = 3 \quad \text{...(i)}$$

Given, the probability of drawing a red ball is $\frac{12}{23}$.

$$\therefore \quad P(\text{a red ball}) = \frac{x}{x+y}$$

$$\Rightarrow \quad \frac{12}{23} = \frac{x}{x+y}$$

$$\Rightarrow \quad 12x + 12y = 23x$$

$$\Rightarrow \quad 12y = 11x$$

$$\Rightarrow \quad x = \frac{12}{11}y \quad \text{...(ii)}$$

On putting the value of x in Eq. (i), we get

$$\frac{12}{11}y - y = 3$$

$$\Rightarrow \quad 12y - 11y = 33$$

$$\Rightarrow \quad y = 33$$

On substituting $y = 33$ in Eq. (i), we get

$$x - 33 = 3 \Rightarrow x = 36$$

Hence, the total number of balls in bag is $33 + 36$ i.e. 69.

Example 8. Cards numbered 1, 2, 3, 4, 5, ..., 17 are put in a box and mixed thoroughly. One person draws a card from the box. Find the probability that the number on the card is

(i) an odd number.

(ii) a prime number.

(iii) divisible by both 2 and 3.

(iv) a multiple of 3 or 5.

Sol. There are 17 cards numbered 1, 2, 3, 4, 5,...,17 in a box.

Out of 17 cards, one card can be drawn in 17 ways.

$\therefore$ Total number of outcomes = 17

(i) There are 9 odd numbered cards, namely 1, 3, 5, 7, 9, 11, 13, 15 and 17.

$\therefore$ Number of outcomes favourable = 9

Hence, P (getting an odd number)

$$= \frac{\text{Number of outcomes favourable}}{\text{Total number of outcomes}} = \frac{9}{17}$$

(ii) There are 7 prime numbered cards, namely 2, 3, 5, 7, 11, 13 and 17.

$\therefore$ Number of outcomes favourable = 7

Hence, P (getting a prime number)

$$= \frac{\text{Number of outcomes favourable}}{\text{Total number of outcomes}} = \frac{7}{17}$$

(iii) If a number is divisible by both 2 and 3, then it must be a multiple of 6. In cards bearing number 1, 2, 3, 4, ..., 17, there are only 2 cards which bear a number divisible by both 2 and 3 i.e. by 6. These cards bearing numbers 6 and 12.

$\therefore$ Number of outcomes favourable = 2

Hence, P (getting a card bearing number divisible by both 2 and 3)

$$= \frac{\text{Number of outcomes favourable}}{\text{Total number of outcomes}} = \frac{2}{17}$$

(iv) There are 7 numbered cards, which are multiple of 3 or 5 namely, 3, 6, 9, 12, 15, 5 and 10.

$\therefore$ Number of favourable outcomes = 7

Hence,

P (getting a card bearing a number multiple of 3 or 5)

$$= \frac{\text{Number of outcomes favourable}}{\text{Total number of outcomes}} = \frac{7}{17}$$

Type V Problems Based on Geometry

In this type of problems, a geometrical figure is given to us and we have to find the probability that, a given element lies inside the small part of the geometrical figure. For this, we first find the area/volume of both geometrical figures (small and big) separately and then find the required probability by taking area/volume of small part as number of favourable outcomes and area/volume of whole part as total number of outcomes.

Example 9. A missing helicopter is reported to have crashed somewhere in the rectangular region shown in figure. What is the probability that it crashed inside the lake shown in the figure?

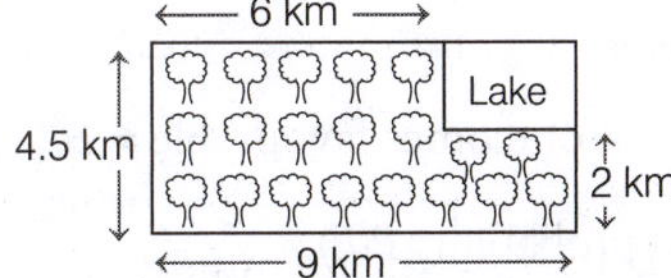

Sol. Here, the helicopter is equally likely to crash anywhere in the region. The given geometrical figure is a rectangle and its small part i.e. lake is also a rectangle.

For rectangular region, length = 9 km

and breadth = 4.5 km

$\therefore$ Area of entire rectangular region, where the helicopter can crash $= 4.5 \times 9 = 40.5 \text{ km}^2$

For rectangular lake,

Length $= 9 - 6 = 3$ km

Breadth $= 4.5 - 2 = 2.5$ km

$\therefore$ Area of the lake $= 2.5 \times 3 = 7.5 \text{ km}^2$

Hence, probability that helicopter crashed inside the lake

$$= \frac{\text{Area of favourable region}}{\text{Total area of region}} = \frac{7.5}{40.5} = \frac{75}{405} = \frac{5}{27}$$

Type VI Miscellaneous Problems

Sometimes the given problem is not of the type I to V which are discussed before.

Example 10. A lot consists of 48 mobile phones of which 42 are good, 3 have only minor defect and 3 have major defect. Varnika will buy a phone, if it is good but the trader will only buy a mobile, if it has no major defect. One phone is selected at random from the lot. What is the probability that it is

(i) acceptable to Varnika?

(ii) acceptable to the trader? NCERT Exemplar

Sol. Given, total number of mobile phones is 48. So, number of possible outcomes = 48

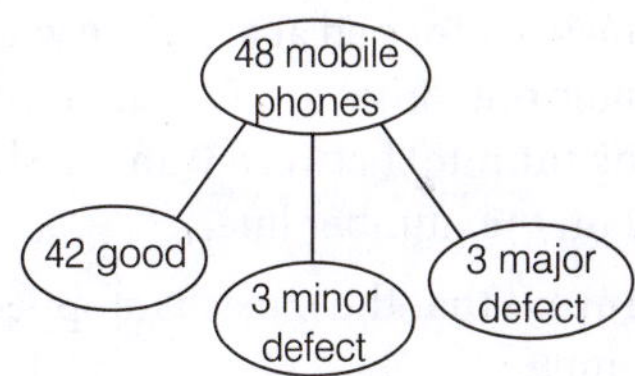

(i) Let E_1 be the event that phone is acceptable to Varnika i.e. E_1 be the event of getting a good phone.

$\therefore$ Number of outcomes favourable to $E_1 = 42$

Hence, probability that phone is acceptable to Varnika,

$$P(E_1) = \frac{42}{48} = \frac{7}{8}$$

(ii) Let E_2 be the event that phone is acceptable to the trader i.e. E_2 be the event of getting a good phone or a phone with minor defect.

$\therefore$ Number of outcomes favourable to E_2

= Number of good phones

+ Number of phones with minor defect

$= 42 + 3 = 45$

Hence, probability that phone is acceptable to the trader,

$$P(E_2) = \frac{45}{48} = \frac{15}{16}$$

Example 11. **Savita and Hamida are friends. What is the probability that both will have**

(i) the same birthday?

(ii) different birthdays? (ignoring a leap year)

Sol. There are 365 days in a year, so Savita's birthday can be at any day of 365 days in the year.

Similarly, Hamida's birthday can be at any day of 365 days in the year. So, total number of outcomes $= 365 \times 365$

(i) If both have same birthday, then the number of favourable outcomes for their birthday $= 365$

$\therefore$ P (Savita and Hamida have same birthday)

$$= \frac{365}{365 \times 365}$$

$$= \frac{1}{365}$$

(ii) P (Savita and Hamida have different birthdays)

$= 1 - P$ (Savita and Hamida have same birthday)

$[\because P(E) + P(\bar{E}) = 1]$

$$= 1 - \frac{1}{365} = \frac{364}{365}$$

Example 12. **In a musical chair game, the person playing the music has been advised to stop playing the music at any time within 2 mins after she starts playing. What is the probability that the music will stop within the first half-minute after starting?**

Sol. Here, the music is stopped at any time within 2 mins. So, the possible outcomes are all real numbers (representing minute) between 0 and 2 which are represented on the number line.

Let E be the event that the music is stopped within the first half-minute.

Then, outcomes favourable to E are points on the number line from 0 to $\frac{1}{2}$.

0 $\frac{1}{2}$ 1 $1\frac{1}{2}$ 2

Here, all the outcomes are equally likely.

So, total number of outcomes

$=$ Total distance from 0 to 2 $= 2$

and number of outcomes favourable to event E

$=$ Distance from 0 to $\frac{1}{2} = \frac{1}{2}$

Hence, required probability $= P(E)$

$$= \frac{1/2}{2} = \frac{1}{4}$$

Example 13. **Two players Neha and Shivani play a tennis match. It is known that the probability of Neha winning the match is 0.62. What is the probability of Shivani winning the match?**

Sol. Let E and F denote the events that Neha and Shivani win the match, respectively.

It is clear that, if Neha wins the match, then Shivani losses the match and if Shivani wins the match, then Neha losses the match.

Thus, E and F are complementary events.

$\therefore$ $P(E) + P(F) = 1$

Since, probability of Neha's winning the match

i.e. $P(E) = 0.62$

$\therefore$ Probability of Shivani's winning the match,

$P(F) = P$ (Neha losses the match)

$= 1 - P(E)$ $[\because P(E) + P(F) = 1]$

$= 1 - 0.62$

$= 0.38$

Example 14. **Find the probability that a number selected at random from the numbers 3, 4, 4, 4, 5, 5, 6, 6, 6, 7 will be their mean.** CBSE 2019

Sol. Given, numbers are 3, 4, 4, 4, 5, 5, 6, 6, 6, 7.

Here, $n = 10$

$\because$ Number of all possible outcomes $= 10$

Now, mean of given numbers,

$$\bar{x} = \frac{3+4+4+4+5+5+6+6+6+7}{10}$$

$$= \frac{50}{10} = 5$$

Let E be the event of getting a mean from given numbers.

Here, we see that mean 5 is repeated in the given numbers are two times.

So, number of outcomes favourable $= 2$

$\therefore$ Required probability $P(E) = \frac{2}{10} = \frac{1}{5}$

NCERT FOLDER

Complete Solutions of All Exercises of NCERT Textbook

Exercise 14.1

Q1. Complete the following statements

(i) Probability of an event E+ Probability of the event 'not E' = ...

(ii) The probability of an event that cannot happen is .... Such an event is called ....

(iii) The probability of an event that is certain to happen is .... Such an event is called ....

(iv) The sum of the probabilities of all the elementary events of an experiment is ....

(v) The probability of an event is greater than or equal to .... and less than or equal to ....

Sol. (i) 1, because the sum of probabilities of complementary events is equal to one.

(ii) 0, impossible event.

(e.g. Suppose a die is thrown and we have to determine the probability of getting 8. This type of event is called an impossible event and probability of this event is 0.)

(iii) 1, sure event.

(e.g. The event of getting a number less than 7 in a single throw of a die is a sure event and its probability is 1.)

(iv) 1, (e.g. Suppose a die is thrown, then

$P(\text{getting } 1) + P(\text{getting} 2) + P(\text{getting } 3) + P(\text{getting } 4) + P(\text{getting } 5) + P(\text{getting } 6) = 1)$

(v) 0, 1

Since, the probability of each event lies between 0 and 1.

Q2. Which of the following experiments have equally likely outcomes? Explain.

(i) A driver attempts to start a car. The car starts or does not start.

(ii) A player attempts to shoot a basketball. She/He shoots or misses the shot.

(iii) A trial is made to answer a true-false question. The answer is right or wrong.

(iv) A baby is born. It is a boy or a girl.

Sol. (i) The car starts normally but when there is some defect, then car does not start. So, the outcomes are not equally likely.

(ii) The outcomes in this situation are not equally likely because the outcomes depends on many factors such as training of the player, quality of basketball, etc.

(iii) The outcomes in trial of true-false question is either true or false. Hence, the two outcomes are equally likely.

(iv) A new baby can be either a boy or a girl, so both the outcomes are equally likely.

Q3. Why is tossing a coin considered to be a fair way of deciding which team should get the ball at the beginning of a football game?

Sol. When we toss a coin, we get either head or tail which are equally likely outcomes. Hence, the result of the toss of a coin is completely unpredictable or unbiased. So, tossing a coin is a fair way of deciding.

Q4. Which of the following cannot be the probability of an event?

(i) $\frac{2}{3}$ (ii) -1.5 (iii) 15% (iv) 0.7

Sol. (ii) The probability of an event is always lies from 0 to 1. So, the probability of an event cannot be negative in any case.

Q5. If $P\ E = 0.05$, what is the probability of 'not E'?

Sol. Given, $P(E) = 0.05$

We know that,

$P(E) + P(\overline{E}) = 1$

$\therefore \quad P(\overline{E}) = 1 - P(E) \Rightarrow P(\overline{E}) = 1 - 0.05 = 0.95.$

Q6. A bag contains lemon flavoured candies only. Malini takes out one candy without looking into the bag. What is the probability that she takes out

(i) an orange flavoured candy?

(ii) a lemon flavoured candy?

Sol. (i) Let E be an event of getting an orange flavoured candy. All possible outcomes are against to the event E because in a bag, all candies are lemon flavoured.

So, $P(E) = 0$

(ii) Let F be an event of getting a lemon flavoured candy. All possible outcomes are favourable to event F because all the candies in the bag are lemon flavoured.

So, $P(F) = 1$

Q7. It is given that in a group of 3 students, the probability of 2 students not having the same birthday is 0.992. What is the probability that the 2 students have the same birthday?

Sol. Do same as Example 13. **Ans.** 0.008

Q8. **A bag contains 3 red balls and 5 black balls. A ball is drawn at random from the bag. What is the probability that the ball drawn is**

(i) red? (ii) not red?

Sol. Do same as Example 7. **Ans.** (i) $\frac{3}{8}$ (ii) $\frac{5}{8}$

Q9. **A box contains 5 red marbles, 8 white marbles and 4 green marbles. One marble is taken out of the box at random. What is the probability that the marble taken out will be**

(i) red? (ii) white? (iii) not green?

Sol. (i) Do same as Example 7. **Ans.** $\frac{5}{17}$

(ii) Do same as Example 7. **Ans.** $\frac{8}{17}$

(iii) Let E_3 be the event of drawing a marble which is not green

i.e. E_3 be the event of drawing either red or white marble.

$\therefore$ Number of outcomes favourable to $E_3 = 5 + 8 = 13$

So, probability of taken out not a green marble,

$P(E_3) = \frac{13}{17}$

Q10. **A piggy bank contains hundred 50 paise coins, fifty ₹ 1 coins, twenty ₹ 2 coins and ten ₹ 5 coins. If it is equally likely that one of the coins will fall out when the bank is turned upside down, then what is the probability that the coin**

(i) will be a 50 paise coin?

(ii) will not be a ₹ 5 coin?

Sol. Given, number of 50 paise coins = 100,

number of ₹ 1 coins = 50,

number of ₹ 2 coins = 20

and number of ₹ 5 coins = 10

$\therefore$ Total number of coins = 100 + 50 + 20 + 10 = 180

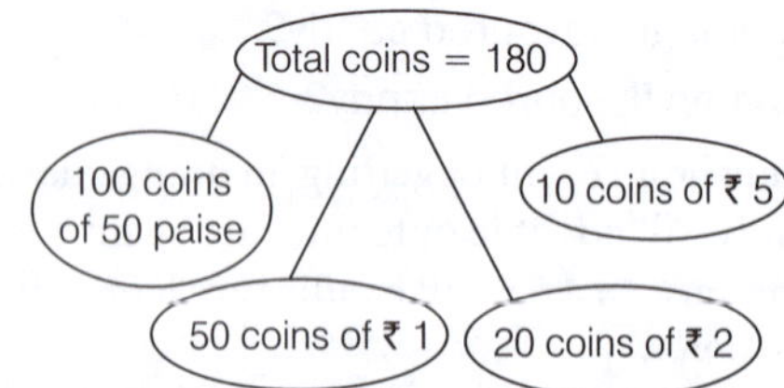

(i) $P(\text{50 paise coin}) = \frac{\text{Number of 50 paise coins}}{\text{Total number of coins}}$

$= \frac{100}{180} = \frac{5}{9}$

(ii) Number of coins which are not of ₹ 5

= Total number of coins − Number of ₹ 5 coins

= 180 − 10 = 170

$\therefore$ P(that the coin will not be a ₹ 5 coin) $= \frac{170}{180} = \frac{17}{18}$

Q11. **Gopi buys a fish from a shop for her aquarium. The shopkeeper takes out one fish at random from a tank containing 5 male fishes and 8 female fishes (see figure). What is the probability that the fish taken out is a male fish?**

Sol. Total number of fishes in the tank

= 5 male fishes + 8 female fishes = 13

$\therefore$ Probability of taken out a male fish

$= \frac{\text{Number of male fishes}}{\text{Total number of fishes}} = \frac{5}{13}$

Q12. **A game of chance consists of spinning an arrow which comes to rest pointing at one of the numbers 1, 2, 3, 4, 5, 6, 7 and 8 (see figure) and these are equally likely outcomes.**

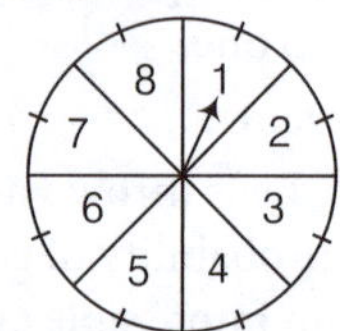

What is the probability that it will point at

(i) 8?

(ii) an odd number?

(iii) a number greater than 2?

(iv) a number less than 9?

Sol. Total number of points on the circle = 8

(i) Let E_1 be the event of getting arrow at number 8.

$\therefore$ Number of outcome favourable to $E_1 = 1$

$\therefore$ Probability that arrow comes at number 8,

$P(E_1) = \frac{1}{8}$

(ii) Let E_2 be the event of getting arrow at an odd number.

Here, odd numbers are 1, 3, 5 and 7.

$\therefore$ Number of outcomes favourable to $E_2 = 4$

$\therefore$ Probability that arrow comes at an odd number,

$P(E_2) = \frac{4}{8} = \frac{1}{2}$

(iii) Let E_3 be the event of getting arrow at a number greater than 2 i.e. at 3, 4, 5, 6, 7 or 8.

$\therefore$ Number of outcomes favourable to $E_3 = 6$

$\therefore$ Probability that arrow comes at a number greater than 2, $P(E_3) = \frac{6}{8} = \frac{3}{4}$

(iv) Do same as Part (iii). **Ans.** 1

Q13. A die is thrown once. Find the probability of getting

(i) a prime number. CBSE 2020 (Standard)

(ii) a number lying between 2 and 6. CBSE 2019

(iii) an odd number.

Sol. On a die, there are six numbers 1, 2, 3, 4, 5 and 6.

$\therefore$ Total number of possible outcomes = 6

(i) Let E_1 be the event of getting a prime number.

Then, E_1 would consist of three outcomes namely 2, 3 and 5.

$\therefore$ Number of outcomes favourable to $E_1 = 3$

$\therefore$ Probability of getting a prime number,

$$P(E_1) = \frac{3}{6} = \frac{1}{2}$$

(ii) Let E_2 be the event of getting a number lying between 2 and 6.

Then, E_2 would consist of three outcomes, namely 3, 4 and 5.

$\therefore$ Number of outcomes favourable to $E_2 = 3$

$\therefore$ Probability of getting a number lying between 2 and 6,

$$P(E_2) = \frac{3}{6} = \frac{1}{2}$$

(iii) Do same as Q. 12 (ii). **Ans.** $\frac{1}{2}$

Q14. One card is drawn from a well-shuffled deck of 52 cards. Find the probability of getting

(i) a king of red colour.

(ii) a face card.

(iii) a red face card.

(iv) the jack of hearts.

(v) a spade.

(vi) the queen of diamonds.

Sol. Total number of cards in one deck of cards is 52.

$\therefore$ Total number of outcomes = 52

(i) Let E_1 be the event of getting a king of red colour.

$\therefore$ Number of outcomes favourable to $E_1 = 2$

[$\because$ there are four kings in a deck of playing cards out of which two are red and two are black]

Hence, probability of getting a king of red colour,

$$P(E_1) = \frac{2}{52} = \frac{1}{26}$$

(ii) Let E_2 be the event of getting a face card.

$\therefore$ Number of outcomes favourable to $E_2 = 12$

[$\because$ in a deck of cards, there are 12 face cards, namely 4 kings, 4 jacks, 4 queens]

Hence, probability of getting a face card,

$$P(E_2) = \frac{12}{52} = \frac{3}{13}$$

(iii) Do same as Part (ii). **Ans.** $\frac{3}{26}$

(iv) Let E_4 be the event of getting a jack of heart.

$\therefore$ Number of outcomes favourable to $E_4 = 1$

[$\because$ there are four jack cards in a deck, namely 1 of heart, 1 of club, 1 of spade and 1 of diamond]

Hence, probability of getting a jack of heart,

$$P(E_4) = \frac{1}{52}$$

(v) Let E_5 be the event of getting a spade

$\therefore$ Number of outcomes favourable to $E_5 = 13$

[$\because$ in a deck of cards, there are 13 spades, 13 clubs, 13 hearts and 13 diamonds]

Hence, probability of getting a spade,

$$P(E_5) = \frac{13}{52} = \frac{1}{4}$$

(vi) Do same as Part (iv). **Ans.** $\frac{1}{52}$

Q15. Five cards — the ten, jack, queen, king and ace of diamonds are well-shuffled with their face downwards. One card is then picked up at random.

(i) What is the probability that the card is the queen?

(ii) If the queen is drawn and put aside, then what is the probability that the second card picked up is

(a) an ace? (b) a queen?

Sol. (i) Total number of cards = 5

$\therefore$ Number of all possible outcomes = 5

P (picking a queen card) $= \frac{1}{5}$

[$\because$ as there is only one queen]

(ii) Suppose a queen is drawn and put aside. Then, four cards are left namely, ten, jack, king and ace of diamonds.

Now, number of all possible outcomes = 4

(a) P (the second card picked up is an ace) $= \frac{1}{4}$

(b) P (the second card picked up is a queen) $= \frac{0}{4} = 0$

[$\because$ queen is drawn before]

Q16. 12 defective pens are accidentally mixed with 132 good ones. It is not possible to just look at a pen and tell whether or not it is defective. One pen is taken out at random from this lot. Determine the probability that the pen taken out is a good one.

Sol. Total number of pens = 12 defective + 132 good

= 144

Let E be the event of selecting a good pen.

Then, number of outcomes favourable to $E = 132$

$\therefore$ Probability of selecting a good pen, $P(E) = \frac{132}{144} = \frac{11}{12}$

Q17. (i) A lot of 20 bulbs contain 4 defective ones. One bulb is drawn at random from the lot. What is the probability that this bulb is defective?

(ii) Suppose the bulb drawn in (i) is not defective and is not replaced. Now, one bulb is drawn at random from the rest. What is the probability that this bulb is not defective?

Sol. (i) Total number of bulbs is 20.

$\therefore$ Number of all possible outcomes = 20

Let E be the event of getting a defective bulb.

Then, the number of outcomes favourable to $E = 4$

$\therefore$ Probability of selecting a defective bulb,

$$P(E) = \frac{4}{20} = \frac{1}{5}$$

(ii) Suppose one good bulb is drawn and put outside.

Then, 15 good bulbs and 4 defective bulbs are remain in a lot.

Now, total number of bulbs = 19

$\therefore$ Number of all possible outcomes = 19

Let E_1 be the event of selecting a good bulb.

Then, the number of outcomes favourable to $E_1 = 15$

$\therefore$ Required probability $= P(E_1) = \dfrac{15}{19}$

Q18. A box contains 90 discs, which are numbered from 1 to 90. If one disc is drawn at random from the box, find the probability that it bears

(i) a two-digit number.

(ii) a perfect square number.

(iii) a number divisible by 5.

Sol. (i) Total number of discs in a box = 90

$\therefore$ Number of all possible outcomes = 90

Let E_1 be the event of getting a disc bearing a two-digit number.

Here, two-digit numbers are 10, 11, ..., 90

$\therefore$ Number of outcomes favourable to $E_1 = 81$

Hence, probability of getting a disc bearing a two-digit number, $P(E_1) = \dfrac{81}{90} = \dfrac{9}{10}$

(ii) Let E_2 be the event of getting a disc bearing a perfect square number.

Here, perfect square numbers are 1, 4, 9, 16, 25, 36, 49, 64 and 81.

$\therefore$ Number of outcomes favourable to $E_2 = 9$

Hence, probability of getting a disc bearing a perfect square number, $P(E_2) = \dfrac{9}{90} = \dfrac{1}{10}$

(iii) Let E_3 be the event of getting a disc bearing a number divisible by 5 .

Here, the numbers divisible by 5 are 5, 10, 15, 20, 25, 30, 35, 40, 45, 50, 55, 60, 65, 70, 75, 80, 85 and 90.

$\therefore$ Number of outcomes favourable to $E_3 = 18$

Hence, required probability $= P(E_3) = \dfrac{18}{90} = \dfrac{1}{5}$

Q19. A child has a die whose six faces show the letters as given below

A | B | C | D | E | A

The die is thrown once. What is the probability of getting

(i) A? (ii) D? CBSE 2020 (Standard)

Sol. Total number of outcomes in a single throw of a six faces die = 6

(i) Let E_1 be the event of getting a letter A.

Then, number of outcomes favourable to $E_1 = 2$

Hence, probability of getting a letter A,

$$P(E_1) = \frac{2}{6} = \frac{1}{3}$$

(ii) Let E_2 be the event of getting a letter D.

Then, number of outcome favourable to $E_2 = 1$

Hence, probability of getting a letter D,

$$P(E_2) = \frac{1}{6}$$

Q20. Suppose, you drop a die at random on the rectangular region shown in figure. What is the probability that it will land inside the circle of diameter 1 m?

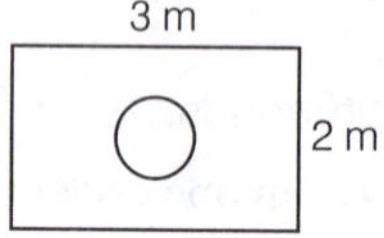

Sol. Area of rectangle $= 3 \times 2 = 6\ m^2$

and area of circle of radius $\frac{1}{2}$ m $= \pi\left(\frac{1}{2}\right)^2 = \frac{\pi}{4}\ m^2$

$$\left[\because \text{diameter} = 1\text{m} \Rightarrow \text{radius} = \frac{1}{2}\text{m}\right]$$

Now, probability that the die land inside the circle

$$= \frac{\text{Area of circle}}{\text{Area of rectangle}} = \frac{\pi/4}{6} = \frac{\pi}{24}$$

Q21. A lot consists of 144 ball pens of which 20 are defective and the others are good. Nuri will buy a pen if it is good, but will not buy if it is defective. The shopkeeper draws one pen at random and gives it to her. What is the probability that

(i) she will buy it?

(ii) she will not buy it?

Sol. Total number of ball pens = 144

$\therefore$ Number of all possible outcomes = 144

(i) Let E be the event of getting a good ball pen.

Then, number of outcomes favourable to E

$$= \text{Total number of ball pens} - \text{Number of defective ball pens}$$

$$= 144 - 20 = 124$$

She will buy a pen, if it is a good pen.

$\therefore$ Required probability $= P(E) = \frac{124}{144} = \frac{31}{36}$

(ii) She will not buy a pen, if it is not a good pen.

$\therefore$ Required probability

$= 1-$ Probability of getting a good pen $\quad [\because P(E) + P(\bar{E}) = 1]$

$$= 1 - P(E) = 1 - \frac{31}{36} = \frac{5}{36}$$

Q22. Two dice, one blue and one grey, are thrown at the same time. Then

(i) Complete the following table:

Event : Sum on 2 dice	2	3	4	5	6	7	8	9	10	11	12
Probability	$\frac{1}{36}$						$\frac{5}{36}$				$\frac{1}{36}$

(ii) A student argues that there are 11 possible outcomes 2, 3, 4, 5, 6, 7, 8, 9, 10, 11 and 12. Therefore, each of them has a probability $\frac{1}{11}$. Do you agree with this argument? Justify your answer.

Sol. (i) Total possible outcomes on throwing two dice are

(1,1),(1,2),(1,3),(1,4),(1,5), (1,6)

(2, 1),(2,2),(2,3),(2,4),(2,5),(2,6)

(3,1),(3,2),(3,3),(3,4),(3,5),(3,6)

(4,1),(4,2),(4,3),(4,4),(4,5),(4,6)

(5,1),(5,2),(5,3), (5,4),(5,5),(5,6)

(6,1),(6,2),(6,3),(6,4),(6,5) and (6,6)

$\therefore$ Number of all possible outcomes = 36

(a) Let E_1 be the event of getting sum on two dice is 3.

Then, E_1 would consist of two outcomes, namely (1, 2) and (2, 1).

$\therefore$ Number of outcomes favourable to $E_1 = 2$

Hence, $P(E_1) = \frac{2}{36} = \frac{1}{18}$

(b) Let E_2 be the event of getting sum on two dice is 4.

Then, E_2 would consist of three outcomes, namely (1, 3), (2, 2) and (3, 1).

$\therefore$ Number of outcomes favourable to $E_2 = 3$

Hence, $P(E_2) = \frac{3}{36} = \frac{1}{12}$

(c) Let E_3 be the event of getting sum on two dice is 5.

Then, E_3 would consist of four outcomes, namely (1, 4), (2, 3), (3, 2) and (4, 1).

$\therefore$ Number of outcomes favourable to $E_3 = 4$

Hence, $P(E_3) = \frac{4}{36} = \frac{1}{9}$

(d) Let E_4 be the event of getting sum on two dice is 6.

Then, E_4 would consist of five outcomes, namely (1, 5), (2, 4), (3, 3), (4, 2) and (5, 1).

$\therefore$ Number of outcomes favourable to $E_4 = 5$

Hence, $P(E_4) = \frac{5}{36}$

(e) Let E_5 be the event of getting sum on two dice is 7.

Then, E_5 would consist of six outcomes, namely (1, 6), (2, 5), (3, 4), (4, 3), (5, 2) and (6, 1).

$\therefore$ Number of outcomes favourable to $E_5 = 6$

Hence, $P(E_5) = \frac{6}{36} = \frac{1}{6}$

(f) Let E_6 be the event of getting sum on two dice is 9.

Then, E_6 would consist of four outcomes, namely (3, 6), (4, 5), (5, 4) and (6, 3).

$\therefore$ Number of outcomes favourable to $E_6 = 4$

Hence, $P(E_6) = \frac{4}{36} = \frac{1}{9}$

(g) Let E_7 be the event of getting sum on two dice is 10.

Then, E_7 would consist of three outcomes, namely (4, 6), (5, 5) and (6, 4).

$\therefore$ Number of outcomes favourable to $E_7 = 3$

Hence, $P(E_7) = \frac{3}{36} = \frac{1}{12}$

(h) Let E_8 be the event of getting sum on two dice is 11.

Then, E_8 would consist of two outcomes, namely (6, 5) and (5, 6).

$\therefore$ Number of outcomes favourable to $E_8 = 2$

Hence, $P(E_8) = \frac{2}{36}$

$$= \frac{1}{18}$$

(ii) No, we do not agree with the given argument because the events of eleven sums are not equally likely.

Q23. **A game consists of tossing a one rupee coin 3 times and noting its outcome each time. Hanif wins if all the tosses give the same result i.e. three heads or three tails, and loses otherwise. Calculate the probability that Hanif will lose the game.**

CBSE 2019

Sol. The total possible outcomes on tossing a coin three times are $(HHH), (HHT), (HTH), (THH), (HTT),$
$(THT), (TTH)$ and (TTT).

$\therefore$ Number of all possible outcomes = 8

Let E be the event that Hanif will lose the game.

Hanif will lose the game, if all tosses do not have same result i.e. if outcomes are

$(HHT), (HTH), (THH), (HTT), (THT)$ or (TTH).

$\therefore$ Number of outcomes favourable to $E = 6$

Hence, required probability $= P(E) = \dfrac{6}{8}$

$= \dfrac{3}{4}$

Q24. **A die is thrown twice. What is the probability that**

(i) 5 will not come up either time?

(ii) 5 will come up atleast once?

Hint Throwing a die twice and throwing two dice simultaneously are treated as the same experiment.

Sol. Total number of outcomes = 36

(i) Let E be the event that 5 will not come up either time. Then, E would consist of 25 outcomes, namely (1, 1), (1, 2), (1, 3), (1, 4), (1, 6), (2, 1), (2, 2), (2, 3), (2, 4), (2, 6), (3, 1), (3, 2), (3, 3), (3, 4), (3, 6), (4, 1), (4, 2), (4, 3), (4, 4), (4, 6), (6, 1), (6, 2), (6, 3), (6, 4), (6, 6)

$\therefore$ Number of outcomes favourable to $E = 25$

Hence, probability that 5 will not come up either time,

$$P(E) = \frac{25}{36}$$

(ii) Probability that 5 will come up at least once,

$$P(\overline{E}) = 1 - P(E)$$
$$= 1 - \frac{25}{36} = \frac{11}{36}$$

Q25. **Which of the following arguments are correct and which are not correct? Give reasons for your answer.**

(i) If two coins are tossed simultaneously, there are three possible outcomes—two heads, two tails or one of each. Therefore, for each of these outcomes, the probability is $\frac{1}{3}$.

(ii) If a die is thrown, there are two possible outcomes—an odd number or an even number. Therefore, the probability of getting an odd number is $\frac{1}{2}$.

Sol. (i) **Incorrect** We can classify the outcomes like this but they are not 'equally likely'. Reason is that 'one of each' can result in two ways– from a head on first coin and tail on the second coin or from a tail on the first coin and head on the second coin. This makes it twice as likely as two heads (or two tails).

(ii) **Correct** Since, the two outcomes considered in the question, are equally likely, therefore we can classify the outcomes as given in the question.

So, we have, P (getting an odd number)
$= P$ (getting an even number) ... (i)
[$\because$ outcomes are equally likely]

Also, we know that sum of probabilities of all elementary events of an experiment is 1.

Since, we have, P (getting an odd number) $+ P$ (getting an even number) $= 1$

$\Rightarrow 2P$ (getting an odd number) $= 1$ [using Eq. (i)]

$\Rightarrow P$ (getting an odd number) $= \dfrac{1}{2}$

REVIEW EXERCISE

Including Competency Based Questions

Part I

Multiple Choice Questions

1. Let k be the probability that a player wins a medium prize in his first attempt. If a player wins a small and a large prize in his first two attempts, then the probability that he wins a medium prize in his third attempt is **Competency Based Question**
   (a) equal to k
   (b) less than k
   (c) more than k
   (d) cannot be determined using the given information

2. Which of the following cannot be the probability of an event? **CBSE 2022 (Basic)**
   (a) 0.01 (b) 3% (c) $\frac{16}{17}$ (d) $\frac{17}{16}$

3. Which of the following numbers cannot be the probability of happening of an event? **CBSE 2023 (Standard)**
   (a) 0 (b) $\frac{7}{0.01}$
   (c) 0.07 (d) $\frac{0.07}{3}$

4. The probability of guessing the correct answer to a certain test question is $\frac{x}{6}$. If the probability of not guessing the correct answer to this question is $\frac{2}{3}$, then the value of x is **CBSE 2024 (Standard)**
   (a) 2 (b) 3 (c) 4 (d) 6

5. If probability of winning a game is p, then probability of losing the game is **CBSE 2024 (Basic)**
   (a) $1+p$ (b) $-p$ (c) $p-1$ (d) $1-p$

6. For an event E, $P(E)+P(\overline{E})=x$, then the value of x^3-3, is **CBSE 2021 Term I (Standard)**
   (a) -2 (b) 2 (c) 1 (d) -1

7. Two coins are tossed simultaneously. The probability of getting at most one tail is **CBSE 2024 (Standard)**
   (a) $\frac{1}{2}$ (b) $\frac{1}{4}$ (c) $\frac{3}{4}$ (d) 1

8. Two coins are tossed simultaneously. The probability of getting atleast one head is **CBSE 2025 (Standard)**
   (a) $\frac{1}{4}$ (b) $\frac{1}{2}$ (c) $\frac{3}{4}$ (d) 1

9. When a dice is thrown once, then the probability of getting an even number less than 4 is **Competency Based Question**
   (a) $\frac{1}{4}$ (b) 0 (c) $\frac{1}{2}$ (d) $\frac{1}{6}$

10. A dice is rolled twice. The probability that 6 will not come up either time is
    (a) $\frac{11}{36}$ (b) $\frac{1}{3}$ (c) $\frac{13}{36}$ (d) $\frac{25}{36}$

11. Two dice are rolled together. The probability of getting a sum more than 9 is **CBSE 2025 (Basic)**
    (a) $\frac{5}{6}$ (b) $\frac{5}{18}$ (c) $\frac{1}{6}$ (d) $\frac{1}{2}$

12. 2 cards of heart and 4 cards of spade are missing from a pack of 52 cards. What is the probability of getting a black card from the remaining pack? **CBSE Sample Paper 2023 (Basic)**
    (a) $\frac{22}{52}$ (b) $\frac{22}{46}$ (c) $\frac{24}{52}$ (d) $\frac{24}{46}$

13. One card is drawn at random from a well-shuffled deck of 52 playing cards. What is the probability of getting a black king? **CBSE 2023 (Basic)**
    (a) $\frac{1}{26}$ (b) $\frac{1}{13}$ (c) $\frac{1}{52}$ (d) $\frac{1}{2}$

14. From the data 1, 4, 7, 9, 16, 21, 25, if all the even numbers are removed, then the probability of getting at random a prime number from the remaining is **CBSE 2024 (Standard)**
    (a) $\frac{2}{5}$ (b) $\frac{1}{5}$ (c) $\frac{1}{7}$ (d) $\frac{2}{7}$

15. One card is drawn at random from a well-shuffled pack of 52 playing cards. The probability that the drawn card is a queen, is **CBSE 2023 (Standard)**
    (a) $\frac{4}{13}$ (b) $\frac{1}{13}$ (c) $\frac{2}{13}$ (d) $\frac{1}{26}$

16. Two dice are rolled together. The probability of getting sum of numbers on the two dice as 2, 3 or 5, is **CBSE 2024 (Standard)**
    (a) $\frac{7}{36}$ (b) $\frac{11}{36}$ (c) $\frac{5}{36}$ (d) $\frac{4}{9}$

17. A bag contains 8 red balls and some blue balls. If the probability of drawing a blue ball is three times the probability of drawing a red ball, then the number of blue balls in the bag is **Competency Based Question**
    (a) 12 (b) 18 (c) 24 (d) 36

18. **A box contains cards numbered 6 to 50. A card is drawn at random from the box. The probability that the drawn card has a number which is a perfect square like 4, 9 ...., is** **Competency Based Question**

(a) $\frac{1}{45}$ (b) $\frac{2}{15}$ (c) $\frac{4}{45}$ (d) $\frac{1}{9}$

19. **A box contains 90 discs, numbered from 1 to 90. If one disc is drawn at random from the box, the probability that it bears a prime number less than 23 is** **CBSE 2023 (Standard)**

(a) $\frac{7}{90}$ (b) $\frac{1}{9}$ (c) $\frac{4}{45}$ (d) $\frac{9}{89}$

20. **Two fair coins are tossed together. The probability of getting 2 heads is** **CBSE 2024 (Basic)**

(a) $\frac{1}{2}$ (b) $\frac{3}{4}$ (c) $\frac{1}{4}$ (d) $\frac{3}{8}$

21. **There is a green square board of side $2a$ unit circumscribing a red circle. Jayadev is asked to keep a dot on the above said board. Find the probability that he keeps the dot on the green region.** **CBSE Sample Paper 2023 (Basic)**

(a) $\frac{\pi}{4}$ (b) $\frac{4-\pi}{4}$ (c) $\frac{\pi-4}{4}$ (d) $\frac{4}{\pi}$

Assertion-Reason Type Questions

22. **Assertion** In a cricket match, a batsman hits a boundary 9 times out of 45 balls he plays. The probability that in a given ball, he does not hit the boundary is $\frac{4}{5}$. **CBSE 2024 (Standard)**

Reason $P(E)+P(\text{not } E)=1$

(a) Both Assertion and Reason are correct and Reason is the correct explanation of Assertion.
(b) Both Assertion and Reason are correct but Reason is not the correct explanation of Assertion.
(c) Assertion is correct but Reason is incorrect.
(d) Assertion is incorrect but Reason is correct.

23. **Assertion** When two coins are tossed together, the probability of getting no tail is $\frac{1}{4}$.

Reason The probability $P(E)$ of an event E satisfies $0 \le P(E) \le 1$. **CBSE 2023 (Basic)**

(a) Both Assertion and Reason are correct and Reason is the correct explanation of Assertion.
(b) Both Assertion and Reason are correct but Reason is not the correct explanation of Assertion.
(c) Assertion is correct but Reason is incorrect.
(d) Assertion is incorrect but Reason is correct.

24. In an experiment of throwing a die,

Assertion Event E_1 = getting a number less than 3 and Event E_2 = getting a number greater than 3 are complementary events.

Reason If two events E and F are complementary events then $P(E)+P(F)=1$. **CBSE 2025 (Standard)**

(a) Both Assertion and Reason are correct and Reason is the correct explanation of Assertion.
(b) Both Assertion and Reason are correct but Reason is not the correct explanation of Assertion.
(c) Assertion is correct but Reason is incorrect.
(d) Assertion is incorrect but Reason is correct.

25. **Assertion** In a lottery, there are 5 prizes and 20 blanks, the probability of not getting a prize is $\frac{4}{5}$.

Reason A die is tossed once, then the probability of getting a number less than 5 is $\frac{2}{3}$.

(a) Both Assertion and Reason are correct and Reason is the correct explanation of Assertion.
(b) Both Assertion and Reason are correct but Reason is not the correct explanation of Assertion.
(c) Assertion is correct but Reason is incorrect.
(d) Assertion is incorrect but Reason is correct.

Case Study Based Questions

26. A middle school decided to run the following spinner game as a fund-raiser on Christmas Carnival.

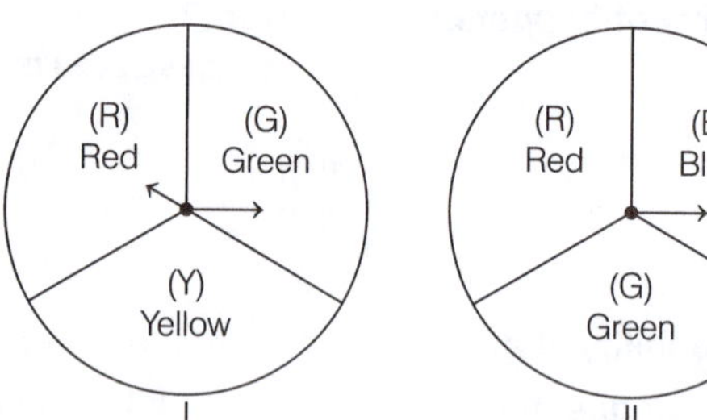

Making Purple : Spin each spinner once, blue and red make purple. So, if one spinner shows Red (R) and another Blue (B), then you 'win'. One such outcome is written as 'RB'. **CBSE 2023 (Standard)**

Based on the above, answer the following questions

(i) List all possible outcomes of the game.
(ii) Find the probability of 'Making Purple'.
(iii) For each win, a participant gets ₹ 10, but if he/she loses, he/she has to pay ₹5 to the school.
If 99 participants played, calculate how much fund could the school have collected.

Or

If the same amount of ₹ 5 has been decided for winnings or losing the game, then how much fund had been collected by school?
(Number of participants = 99)

27. 'Eight Ball' is a game played on a pool table with 15 balls numbered from 1 to 15 and a "cue ball" that is solid and white. Out of the 15 balls, eight are solid (non-white) coloured and numbered from 1 to 8 and seven are striped balls numbered from 9 to 15.

CBSE 2023 (Standard)

The 15 numbered pool balls (no cue ball) are placed in a large bowl and mixed, then one ball is drawn out at random.

Based on the above information, answer the following questions :

(i) What is the probability that the drawn ball bears number 8?

(ii) What is the probability that the drawn ball is a solid coloured and bears an even number?

(iii) What is the probability that the drawn ball bears an even number?

Or

What is the probability that the drawn ball bears a number, which is a multiple of 3?

28. Some students were asked to list their favourite colour. The measure of each colour is shown by the central angle of a pie-chart given below.

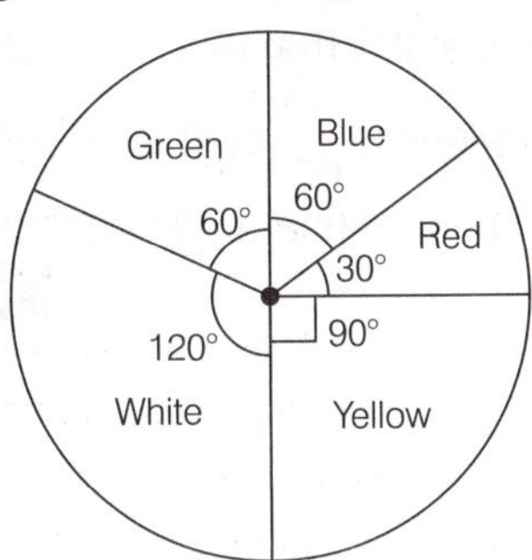

CBSE 2023 (Basic)

Study the pie-chart and answer the following questions.

(i) If a student is chosen at random, then find the probability of his/her favourite colour being white?

(ii) What is the probability of his/her favourite colour being blue or green?

(iii) If 15 students liked the colour yellow, how many students participated in the survey?

Or

What is the probability of the favourite colour being red or blue?

29. Nishant and Kapil are playing a game of dart. They use this dart board.

Here, are the rules of the game.

When your dart is placed in any circular region, you get the points mentioned in that region.

If your dart strikes outside the circles you get zero point.

During the game, all the darts of both Nishant and Kapil fall in the circular region.

The radius of the innermost circle is 7 cm and the width of all other circular regions is 7 cm.

Based on the above information, answer the following questions.

(i) Nishant throws the first dart. What is the probability of Nishant getting a score of 100 in the first throw?

(ii) Kapil threw a dart which hits the board. What is the probability of the dart hitting the outermost circular region on the board?

(iii) In the first three throw Nishant gets 75 points in two throw and 100 points in the third throw. What is the probability of Nishant getting a 75 in the next throw?

Or

Kapil gets 25 points each, in the first and second throw. How many possibilities are there for the total points Kapil can have after four throw?

30. A group of students conducted a survey to find out about the preferred mode of transportation to school among their classmates. They surveyed 200 students from their school. The results of the survey are as follows

120 students preferred to walk to school.

25% of the students preferred to use bicycles.

10% of the students preferred to take the bus.

Remaining students preferred to be dropped off by car.

Based on the above information, answer the following questions.

(i) What is the probability that a randomly selected student does not prefer to walk to school?

(ii) Find the probability of a randomly selected student who prefers to walk or use a bicycle.

(iii) (a) One day 50% of walking students decided to come by bicycle. What is the probability that a randomly selected student comes to school using a bicycle on that day?

Or

(b) What is the probability that a randomly selected student prefers to be dropped off by car?

CBSE Sample Paper 2025 (Basic)

31. Ross observed the food a few puppies preferred to eat. The table given below shows the number of puppies and their preferred food during day time.

Food	Number of puppies
Egg	10
Meat	20
Milk	7
Pet food	13

Based on the above information, answer the following questions.

(i) A puppy was chosen at random from the group that Ross observed. What is the probability that the chosen puppy prefers to have pet food during the day?

(ii) Sixty percent of the time, puppies prefers to have the same food at night, which they had eaten during the day. A puppy ate eggs during the day. What is the probability that the puppy will not eat eggs at night as well?

(iii) (a) What is the probability that chosen puppy neither prefers to have meat nor milk?

Or

(b) What is the probability that chosen puppy either prefers to have an egg or milk?

32. In a survey on holidays, 120 people were asked to state which type of transport they used on their last holiday. The following pie-chart shows the results of the survey.

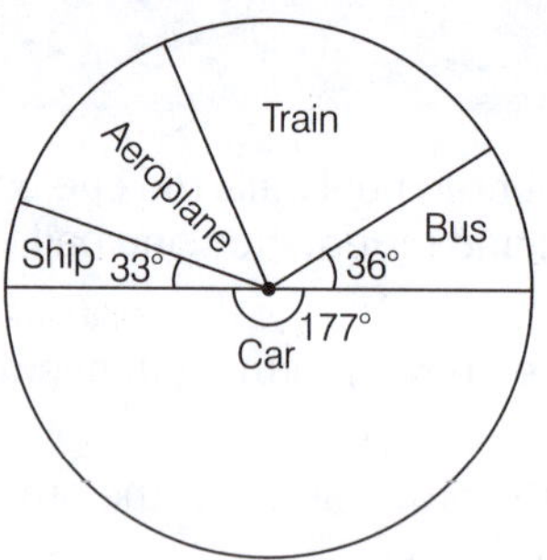

Observe the pie-chart and answer the following questions.

(i) If one person is selected at random, then find the probability that he/she travelled by bus or ship.

(ii) Which is most favourite mode of transport and how many people used it?

(iii) (a) A person is selected at random. If the probability that he did not use train is 4/5, find the number of people who used train.

Or

(b) The probability that randomly selected person used aeroplane is $\frac{7}{60}$. Find the revenue collected by air company at the rate of ₹ 5000 per person.

CBSE 2024 (Standard)

Part II

Very Short Answer Type Questions

1. What is the probability of non-occurrence of an event that is certain to happen?

2. The probability that it will rain today is 0.07. What is the probability that it will not rain today?

Or

If the probability of winning a game is 0.07, then what is the probability of losing it? **CBSE 2020 (Standard)**

3. Shivesh was tossing a fair coin. Shown below are the outcomes of his first 5 tosses.

Tail Tail Tail Tail Tail

Is the probability of Shivesh getting a head in his sixth toss higher than the probability of getting a tail? Give a valid reason. **Competency Based Question**

4. If I toss a coin 3 times and get head each time, then I should expect a tail to have a higher chance in the 4th toss. Is it true?

5. A child has a die whose 6 faces show the letters given below

A B C A A B

The die is thrown once. What is the probability of getting (i) A (ii) B?

6. A die is thrown once. What is the probability of getting a number less than 3? **CBSE 2020 (Standard)**

7. If a die is thrown, then what is the probability of getting a number less than 3 and greater than 2?

8. A die is thrown once. Find the probability of getting a number which is not a factor of 36.

9. In a throw of a pair of dice, what is the probability of getting a doublet or same numbers?

10. Cards marked with numbers 5 to 75 are placed in a box and mixed thoroughly. One card is drawn from the box. Find the probability that the number on the card is odd. **Competency Based Question**

11. A single letter is selected at random from the word 'PROBABILITY'. Find the probability that it is a vowel.

12. In a pack of 52 playing cards, one card is lost. From the remaining cards, a card is drawn at random. Find the probability that the drawn card is queen of heart, if the lost card is a black card. **CBSE 2024 (Standard)**

13. A letter is chosen at random from the English alphabet. What is the probability that it is a letter of the word 'RAMANUJAN'?

14. A school has five houses A, B, C, D and E. A class has 23 students, 4 from house A, 8 from house B, 5 from house C, 2 from house D and rest from house E. A single student is selected at random to be the class monitor. Find the probability that the selected students is not from houses A, B and C. **Competency Based Question**

15. Two dice are rolled together bearing numbers 4, 6, 7, 9, 11, 12. Find the probability that the product of numbers obtained is an odd number. **CBSE Sample Paper 2025 (Standard)**

16. A bag contains cards which are numbered from 5 to 100 such that each card bears a different number. A card is drawn at random. Find the probability that number on the card is
   (i) a perfect square
   (ii) a 2-digit number

17. Find the probability that a non-leap year selected at random will contain 53 Sundays. **CBSE 2016; NCERT Exemplar**

18. The probability of guessing the correct answer to certain question is $p/12$. If the probability of not guessing the correct answer to same question is $3/4$, then find the value of p.

19. A girl calculates that the probability of her winning the first prize in a lottery is 0.08. If 6000 tickets are sold, then how many tickets has she bought? **NCERT Exemplar**

20. A student says that, if you throw a die, it will show up 1 or not 1. Therefore, the probability of getting 1 or not 1 is equal to $\frac{1}{2}$. Is this correct? Give reasons.

21. How many positive three digit integers have the hundredths digit 8 and unit's digit 5? Find the probability of selecting one such number out of all three digit numbers. **CBSE Sample Paper 2025 (Standard)**

22. In a family having three children, there may be no girl, one girl, two girls or three girls. So, the probability of each is $\frac{1}{4}$. Is it true? **NCERT Exemplar**

23. A bag contains 4 red, 5 white and some yellow balls. If probability of drawing a red ball at random is $\frac{1}{5}$, then find the probability of drawing a yellow ball at random. **CBSE 2024 (Basic)**

24. In a cricket match a batsman hits the boundary 8 times out of 40 balls he plays. Find the probability that he did not hit the boundary.

25. A number x is chosen at random from the numbers $-4, -3, -2, -1, 0, 1, 2, 3, 4$. What is the probability that $|x| < 2$? **Competency Based Question**

Short Answer Type Questions

26. Which of the following experiments have equally likely outcomes? Explain.
   (i) A coin is tossed. It is head or tail.
   (ii) A player attempts to shoot a ballon. She/he shoots or misses the shot.
   (iii) A bag contains red, blue and green colour lemon flavoured candies. The man picked red or blue colour lemon candy.

27. Anu, Priya and Jyoti were fighting to get first chance in a game. Anu says, "Let us toss two coins. If both heads appear, Priya will take first chance, if both tails appear Jyoti will get it and if one head and one tail appears, I will get the chance".
   (i) What is the probability of Anu, Priya and Jyoti getting the first chance?
   (ii) Is her decision fair? **Competency Based Question**

28. Three different coins are tossed together. Find the probability of getting
   (i) exactly two tails.
   (ii) atleast two heads.
   (iii) atleast two tails.

29. In a game, the entry fee is ₹ 5. The game consists of tossing a coin 3 times. If one or two heads show, then Sweta gets her entry fee back. If she tosses 3 heads, then she receives double the entry fee. Otherwise, she will loss. For tossing a coin three times, find the probability that she

(i) losses the entry fee.

(ii) gets double entry fee.

(iii) just gets her entry fee. **NCERT Exemplar**

30. Two different dice are tossed together. Find the probability of getting a sum 10 of the numbers on the two dice.

31. Two dice, one red and one black are thrown simultaneously. A student of Class X makes the following table.

Event: Sum on 2 dice	1	6	12	15
Probability	0	$\frac{5}{36}$	$\frac{1}{36}$	0

Ritu observes the above table and remarks that it is correct. Is she right? Explain. **Competency Based Question**

32. Aproov throws two dice once and computes the product of the numbers appearing on the dice. Peehu throws one die and squares the number that appears on it. Who has the better chance of getting the number 36? Why? **NCERT Exemplar**

33. Two different dice are tossed together. Find the probability

(i) that the number on each die is even.

(ii) that the sum of numbers appearing on the two dice is 5.

34. A die has its six faces marked 0, 1, 1, 1, 6, 6. Two such dice are thrown together and the total score is recorded.

(i) How many different scores are possible?

(ii) What is the probability of getting a total of 7? **NCERT Exemplar**

35. Two dice are thrown at the same time and the product of numbers appearing on them is noted. Find the probability that the product is less than 9. **NCERT Exemplar**

36. Two dice are thrown together. Find the probability that the product of the numbers on the top of the dice is

(i) 6

(ii) 12

(iii) 7 **CBSE 2011; NCERT Exemplar**

37. A pair of dice is thrown once. Find the probability of getting

(i) doublet of prime numbers.

(ii) a doublet of odd numbers.

38. Two dice are thrown at the same time. Determine the probability that the difference of the numbers on the two dice is 2. **NCERT Exemplar**

39. A 4-sided fair die is numbered from 1 to 4. Nikhil and Pratik are playing with such a die each. They roll their dice once at the same time. A player wins only if they get a number larger than the other player.

What is the probability of Pratik winning the game? Show your work. **Competency Based Question**

40. Cards marked with numbers 5, 6, 7, ..., 74 are placed in a bag and mixed thoroughly. One card is drawn at random from the bag. Find the probability that the number on the card is a perfect cube.

41. The king, queen and jack of clubs are removed from a deck of 52 playing cards and then well-shuffled. Now, one card is drawn at random from the remaining cards. Find the probability of getting a card of

(i) a heart. (ii) a king. **NCERT Exemplar**

42. There are 80 cards numbered from 1 to 80. One card is drawn at random from them. Find the probability that the number on the selected card is not divisible by 8. **CBSE 2024 (Basic)**

43. A ticket is drawn at random from a bag containing tickets numbered from 1 to 40. Find the probability that the selected ticket has a number,

(i) which is a multiple of 7.

(ii) which is a multiple of 5. **CBSE 2011; NCERT Exemplar**

44. A carton of 24 bulbs contains 6 defective bulbs. One bulb is drawn at random. What is the probability that the bulb is not defective? If the bulb selected is defective and it is not replaced and a second bulb is selected at random from the rest, then what is the probability that the second bulb is defective? **NCERT Exemplar**

45. Box *A* contains 25 slips of which 19 are marked ₹ 1 and other are marked ₹ 5. Box *B* contains 50 slips of which 45 are marked ₹ 1 and others are marked ₹ 13. Slips of both boxes are put into a third box and reshuffled. A slip is drawn at random. What is the probability that it is marked other than ₹ 1? **NCERT Exemplar**

46. A number is selected at random from first 50 natural numbers. Find the probability that it is a multiple of 3 and 4.

47. Rohan has a bag of multiple balls either pink, green or yellow in colour. He randomly picks up one ball. His friend, Farid predicted, 'The probability of Rohan picking a pink ball is definitely $\frac{1}{3}$ as there are 3 colours'. Is Farid's statement true or false. Give a valid reason or a counter example. **Competency Based Question**

48. A bag contains 7 green balls and some red balls. If the probability of drawing a red ball from the bag is thrice that of a green ball, then the number of red balls in the bag are 21 and drawing a red ball is not an equally likely outcomes. Atul at once said that 'It is wrong'. Do you agree with Atul? Justify.

49. A carton consists of 100 shirts of which 88 are good, 8 have minor defect and 4 have major defect. Jimmy, a trader, will only accept the shirts which are good but Sujata, another trader, will only reject the shirts which have major defect. One shirt is drawn at random from the carton. What is the probability that it is acceptable to

(i) Jimmy?

(ii) Sujata? **Competency Based Question**

50. A square of side 5 cm is drawn in the interior of another square of side 10 cm and shaded as shown in the following figure.

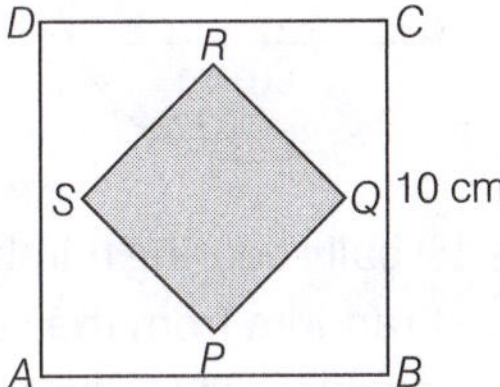

A point is selected at random from the interior of square *ABCD*. What is the probability that the point will be chosen from the shaded part?

Competency Based Question

51. A bag contains 18 balls out of which x balls are red.

(i) If one ball is drawn at random from the bag, then what is the probability that it is a red ball?

(ii) If 2 more red balls are put in the bag, then the probability of drawing a red ball will be 9/8 times that of probability of red ball coming in part (i). Find the value of x. **Competency Based Question**

52. A game of chance consists of an arrow which comes to rest pointing at one of the regions 1, 2 or 3. *O* is the centre of the circle, $OC \perp AB$.

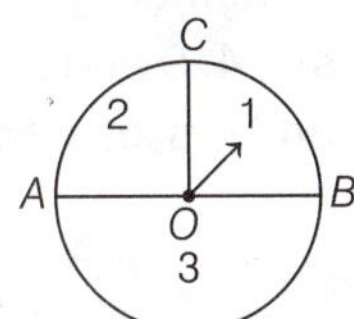

Find the probability that

(i) arrow is resting on 3.

(ii) arrow is resting on 1.

(iii) arrow is not resting on 2.

53. Videocon Electronics has launched two new mobile hands sets: Set I and Set II. Set I is cheaper as compared to Set II. But Set II has built-in device to recharge the battery with an auto-cut power supply when it is fully charged. In a lot, there are 250 pieces of Set I and 100 pieces of Set II. If a mobile is picked at random, then

(i) find the probability of getting Set I.

(ii) find the probability of getting Set II.

Competency Based Question

54. A traffic signal displays green light for 3 minutes to allow passage of traffic on a particular road. If the signal is currently displaying green light, then find the probability that it will turn red within the next half a minute.

55. Anita, Sita, Gita and Rita are four friends having same birthday. What is the probability that (in a non-leap year) **Competency Based Question**

(i) their birthday fall in the month of October?

(ii) their birthdays falls on 10th day of the month?

(iii) their birthday fall in January or February?

56. An integer is chosen at random from 1 and 100. Find the probability that it is

(i) divisible by 8. (ii) not divisible by 8.

57. Two friends were born in the year 2000. What is the probability that they have the same birthday?

58. A box contains 80 discs numbered from 1 to 80. If one disc is drawn at random from the box, find the probability that it bears

(i) a perfect square number.

(ii) a number divisible by 2 and 3.

Competency Based Question

59. A number is selected from the numbers 2, 3, 3, 5, 5, 5, 7, 7, 7, 7, 9, 9, 9, 9, 9 at random. Find the probability that the number selected is

(i) their median.

(ii) their mode.

Long Answer Type Questions

60. A die is numbered in such a way that its faces show the 1, 2, 4, 4, 6, 6. Reema thrown the die two times, total score in two throws noted as the following table given below:

Number in second throw ↓ / +	Number in first throw: 1	2	4	4	6	6
1	2	3	5	5	7	7
2	3	4	6	6	8	8
4	5	6	8	8	10	10
4	5	6	8	8	10	10
6	7	8	10	10	12	12
6	7	8	10	10	12	12

and she get probability that the total score is

(i) odd

(ii) 6

(iii) atleast 8,

are respectively, $\frac{5}{18}, \frac{1}{9}$ and $\frac{5}{9}$. Is she right? Verify.

Competency Based Question

61. A child's game has 8 triangles of which 3 are blue and rest are red and 10 squares of which 6 are blue and rest are red. One piece is lost at random. Find the probability that it is a

(i) triangle.

(ii) square.

(iii) square of blue colour.

(iv) triangle of red colour. **NCERT Exemplar**

62. A bag contains 6 red, 4 black and some white balls.

(i) Find the number of white balls in the bag, if the probability of drawing a white ball is 1/3.

(ii) How many red balls should be removed from the bag for the probability of drawing a white ball to be $\frac{1}{2}$?

CBSE Sample Paper 2023 (Basic)

63. A bag contains white, black and red balls only. A ball is drawn at random from the bag. The probability of getting a white ball is $\frac{3}{10}$ and that of a black ball is $\frac{2}{5}$. If the bag contains 20 black balls, then find the probability of getting a red ball and also find the total number of balls in the bag. **Competency Based Question**

64. A box contains cards bearing numbers from 6 to 70. If one card is drawn at random from the box, then find the probability that it bears

(i) a one-digit number.

(ii) a number divisible by 5.

(iii) an odd number less than 30.

(iv) a composite number between 50 and 70.

Competency Based Question

65. In the given figure, points A, B, C and D are the centres of four circles that each have a radius of length one unit. If a point is selected at random from the interior of square $ABCD$, then what is the probability that the point will be chosen from the shaded region?

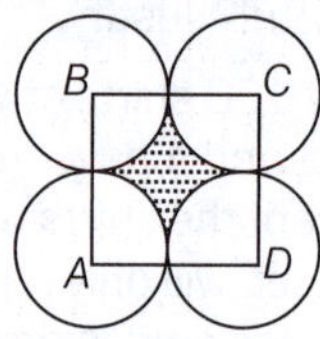

66. In the given figure, a dart is thrown and lands in the interior of the circle. What is the probability that the dart will land in the shaded region?

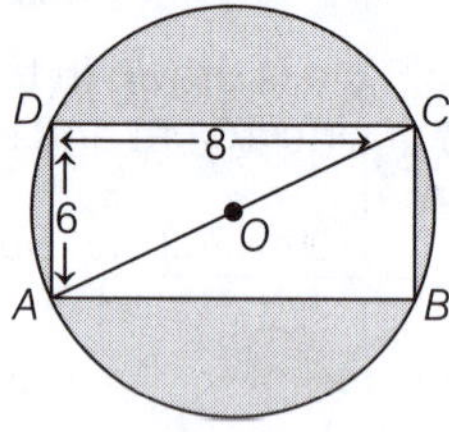

67. A box contains 19 balls bearing numbers 1, 2, 3, ..., 19. A ball is drawn at random from the box. What is the probability that the number on the ball is

(i) a prime number?

(ii) divisible by 3 or 5?

(iii) neither divisible by 5 nor by 10?

(iv) an even number? **Competency Based Question**

68. There are 1000 sealed envelopes in a box, 10 of them contain a cash prize of ₹ 100 each, 100 of them contain a cash prize of ₹ 50 each and 250 of them contain a cash prize of ₹ 10 each and rest do not contain any cash prize. If they are well-shuffled and an envelope is picked up out, what is the probability that it contains no cash prize? **NCERT Exemplar**

69. A number x is selected at random from the numbers 1, 2, 3 and 4. Another number y is selected at random from the numbers 1, 4, 9 and 16. Find the probability that product of x and y is less than 16.

HINTS & SOLUTIONS

Part I

1. (a) Let k be the probability that the player wins a medium prize in his first attempt.
$\because$ The outcomes of one event does not affect the outcome of another, the outcome of the third attempt is independent of the outcomes of the first two attempts.
$\therefore$ The probability of winning a medium prize in the third attempt is k.

2. (d) Since, probability lies between 0 and 1.
$\therefore$ The probability of an event cannot be possible is $\frac{17}{16}$.

3. (b) We know that the probability of an event E is a number $P(E)$ such that $0 \le P(E) \le 1$
$$\frac{7}{0.01} = 7 \times 100 = 700, \text{ not possible}$$

4. (a) $P(A) = P$ (guessing correct answer to a certain test question)
$$= \frac{x}{6}$$
$P(\overline{A}) = P$ (not guessing correct answer to this question)
$$= \frac{2}{3}$$
We know that
$$P(A) = 1 - P(\overline{A})$$
$$\Rightarrow \quad \frac{x}{6} = 1 - \frac{2}{3}$$
$$\Rightarrow \quad \frac{x}{6} = \frac{1}{3} \Rightarrow x = \frac{6}{3} = 2$$

5. (d) Given, probability of winning a game $= p$
$\therefore$ Probability of losing the game $= 1 - p$.

6. (a) Given, $P(E) + P(\overline{E}) = x$ ...(i)
$\because \quad P(E) + P(\overline{E}) = 1$ ...(ii)
From Eqs. (i) and (ii), we get
$$x = 1$$
$$\therefore \quad x^3 - 3 = (1)^3 - 3 = 1 - 3 = -2$$

7. (c) When two coins are tossed, the possible outcomes are HH, HT, TH, TT.
$\therefore$ Number of possible outcomes $= 4$
Let E be an event of getting atmost one tail.
Favourable outcomes are HT, TH, HH.
$\therefore$ Number of favourable outcomes $= 3$
$$P(E) = \frac{\text{Number of favourable outcomes}}{\text{Number of possible outcomes}} = \frac{3}{4}$$

8. (c) Possible outcomes are HH, HT, TH, TT
Favourable outcomes are HT, TH, HH
$$\text{Probability} = \frac{\text{Number of favourable outcomes}}{\text{Total number of outcomes}} = \frac{3}{4}$$

9. (d) Let E be the event of getting an even number less than 4.
Then, outcome favourable to E is 2.
Possible outcomes $= 1, 2, 3, 4, 5, 6$
$$\therefore P(E) = \frac{\text{Number of outcomes favourable to } E}{\text{Total number of possible outcomes}} = \frac{1}{6}$$

10. (d) Do same as Question 24 (i) of NCERT Folder Exercise 14.1

11. (c) Two dice are rolled together.
So, total outcomes are
(1, 1), (1, 2), (1, 3), (1, 4), (1, 5), (1, 6),
(2, 1), (2, 2), (2, 3), (2, 4), (2, 5), (2, 6),
(3, 1), (3, 2), (3, 3), (3, 4), (3, 5), (3, 6),
(4, 1), (4, 2), (4, 3), (4, 4), (4, 5), (4, 6),
(5, 1), (5, 2), (5, 3), (5, 4), (5, 5), (5, 6),
(6, 1), (6, 2,), (6, 3), (6, 4), (6, 5), (6, 6)
Total number of outcomes $= 36$
Now, sample space of getting a sum more than 9 is {(4, 6), (5, 5), (5, 6), (6, 4), (6, 5), (6, 6)}.
Number of favourable outcomes $= 6$
$\therefore$ Probability of getting a sum more than 9 is $\frac{6}{36} = \frac{1}{6}$.

12. (b) Total number of cards left in the pack $= 52 - 6 = 46$
Number of black cards left in the pack $= 26 - 4 = 22$
[$\because$ total number of black cards in a complete pack $= 26$]
$\therefore$ P(getting a black card from the remaining pack) $= \frac{22}{46}$

13. (a) There are 2 black kings in a deck of 52 playing cards.
$\therefore$ Probability of getting a black king $= \frac{2}{52} = \frac{1}{26}$

14. (b) Total number of outcomes $= 7$
Favourable outcome after removing even numbers is 7.
$\therefore$ Number of favourable outcome $= 1$
Total number of outcomes after removing even numbers $= 5$
$\therefore$ Probability of getting a prime number $= \frac{1}{5}$

15. (b) Total number of outcomes $= 52$
Number of favourable outcomes $= 4$
$\therefore$ Probability $= \frac{4}{52} = \frac{1}{13}$

16. (a) Total number of outcomes $= 36$
Favourable outcomes are (1, 1), (1, 2), (2, 1), (2, 3), (3, 2), (1, 4) and (4, 1).
$\therefore$ Number of favourable outcomes $= 7$
$\therefore$ Probability of getting sum of numbers as 2, 3 or 5 $= \frac{7}{36}$.

17. (c) Let there be x blue balls in the bag.

$\therefore$ Total number of balls in the beg $= (8 + x)$

Now, P_1 = Probability of drawing a blue ball $= \frac{x}{8+x}$

and P_2 = Probability of drawing a red ball $= \frac{8}{8+x}$

It is given that, $P_1 = 3P_2$

$$\Rightarrow \quad \frac{x}{8+x} = 3 \times \frac{8}{(8+x)}$$

$$\Rightarrow \quad \frac{x}{8+x} = \frac{24}{8+x} \Rightarrow x = 24$$

Hence, there are 24 blue balls in the bag.

18. (d) Total number of cards $= 50 - 6 + 1 = 45$

Perfect square numbers from 6 to 50 are 9, 16, 25, 36, 49.

$\therefore$ Number of perfect square numbers = 5

$\therefore$ The required probability $= \frac{5}{45} = \frac{1}{9}$

19. (c) Prime numbers less than 23 are 2, 3, 5, 7, 11, 13, 17, 19.

$\therefore$ Number of favourable outcomes = 8

and total number of possible outcomes = 90

$\therefore$ Required probability $= \frac{8}{90} = \frac{4}{45}$

20. (c) When two fair coins are tossed together, the possibility are as follows

HH, HT, TH, TT

$\therefore$ Total number of possible outcomes = 4

The possibility of getting 2 heads is HH

$\therefore$ Number of favourable outcome = 1

Thus, the probability of getting 2 heads

$$= \frac{\text{Number of favourable outcomes}}{\text{Total number of possible outcomes}} = \frac{1}{4}$$

Hence, required probability is $\frac{1}{4}$.

21. (b)

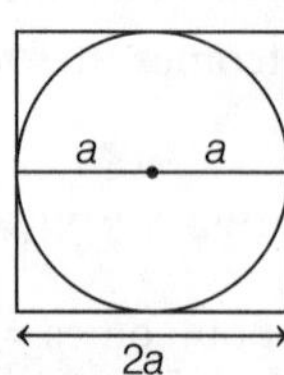

Radius of the circle $= \frac{2a}{2} = a$ units

$\therefore$ Area of the square board $= (2a)^2 = 4a^2$ sq units

$\therefore$ Area of red region = Area of circle $= \pi a^2$ sq. units

$\therefore$ Area of green region = Area of the square board − Area of red region

$= (4a^2 - \pi a^2)$ sq. units

$\therefore$ Probability (keeping the dot on the green region)

$$= \frac{\text{Area of the green region}}{\text{Area of the square board}} = \frac{4a^2 - \pi a^2}{4a^2} = \frac{4 - \pi}{4}$$

22. (a) A bastman hits a boundary 9 times out of 45 balls he plays.

$$P(A) = P\text{ (he hits a boundary)} = \frac{9}{45} = \frac{1}{5}$$

Since, $P(A) + P(\overline{A}) = 1$

$$\Rightarrow \quad P(\overline{A}) = 1 - P(A) = 1 - \frac{1}{5} = \frac{4}{5}$$

$\therefore$ Probability that he does not hit the boundary is $\frac{4}{5}$.

$\therefore$ Both Assertion and Reason are correct and Reason is the correct explanation of Assertion.

23. (b) Possible outcomes $= HH, HT, TH, TT$

Favourable outcomes $= HH$

Total number of outcomes = 4

$\therefore$ Probability $= \frac{\text{Number of favourable outcomes}}{\text{Total number of outcomes}} = \frac{1}{4}$

Both Assertion and Reason are correct but Reason is not the correct explanation of Assertion.

24. (d) When a die is thrown, there are six possible outcomes i.e. 1, 2, 3, 4, 5, 6.

So, sample space, $S = \{1, 2, 3, 4, 5, 6\}$

Here, E_1 = event of getting a number less than 3 $= \{1, 2\}$

and E_2 = event of getting a number greater than 3 $= \{4, 5, 6\}$

Now, $E_1 \cup E_2 = \{1, 2, 4, 5, 6\} \neq S$

$\therefore$ E_1 and E_2 are not complementary events.

Thus, Assertion is false.

Clearly, Reason is true.

25. (b) Number of prizes = 5

Number of blanks in lottery = 20

$\therefore$ Number of tickets in lottery $= 5 + 20 = 25$

$\therefore$ The probability of getting a prize $= \frac{5}{25} = \frac{1}{5}$

and the probability of not getting a prize $= 1 - \frac{1}{5} = \frac{4}{5}$

When a die is tossed once, then possible outcomes are 1, 2, 3, 4, 5, 6.

Favourable outcomes are 1, 2, 3, 4.

$\therefore$ Required probability $= \frac{4}{6} = \frac{2}{3}$

26. (i) Possible outcomes $= RR, RB, RG, GR, GB, GG, YR, YB, YG$

(ii) Total number of outcomes = 9

Favourable outcomes $= RB$

$\therefore$ Probability $= \frac{1}{9}$

(iii) Since, probability of wining the game $= \frac{1}{9}$

and probability of lossing the game $= \frac{8}{9}$

Given, number of participants = 99

$\therefore$ Number of winner students $= 99 \times \frac{1}{9} = 11$

and number of students that losses the game

$= \frac{99 \times 8}{9} = 88$

$\therefore$ Fund collected by school $= 88 \times 5 - 11 \times 10$

$= 440 - 110 =$ ₹ 330

Or

If the same amount of ₹ 5 has been decided for winning or loosing the game.

$\therefore$ Fund collected by school $= 88 \times 5 - 11 \times 5$

$= 77 \times 5 =$ ₹ 385

27. (i) Number of possible outcomes = 15

Number of favourable outcomes = 1

$\therefore P$ (drawn balls bears number 8) $= \frac{1}{15}$

(ii) Favourable outcomes are when balls numbered as 2, 4, 6 and 8.

$\therefore P$ (drawn ball is a solid coloured and bears an even number) $= \frac{4}{15}$

(iii) Favourable outcomes are when balls numbered as 2, 4, 6, 8, 10, 12, 14.

$\therefore P$ (drawn ball bears even number) $= \frac{7}{15}$

Or

Favourable outcomes are when balls numbered as 3, 6, 9, 12 and 15.

$\therefore P$ (drawn ball bears a number which is multiple of 3) $= \frac{5}{15} = \frac{1}{3}$

28. (i) Total angle = 360°

Angle of white = 120°

$\therefore$ Probability $= \frac{120°}{360°} = \frac{1}{3}$

(ii) Total angle = 360°

Angle of blue = 60°

Angle of green = 60°

$\therefore$ Probability $= \frac{60° + 60°}{360°} = \frac{120°}{360°} = \frac{1}{3}$

(iii) Let n students participated in the survey.

$\Rightarrow \frac{90°}{360°} \times n = 15 \Rightarrow n = 15 \times 4 = 60$

$\therefore$ 60 students participated in the survey.

Or

Total angle = 360°

Angle of red = 30°

Angle of blue = 60°

$\therefore$ Probability $= \frac{60° + 30°}{360°} = \frac{90°}{360°} = \frac{1}{4}$

29. (i) Consider, radius of each circle is r, r_1, r_2 and r_3 respectively from innermost circle and to find radius for each ring and thickness of each ring into radius of innermost circle.

Now, radius of innermost circle = 7 cm

$\therefore$ Area of innermost circle $= \pi(r^2) = \pi(7)^2$

$= 49\pi \text{ cm}^2$

and total area of the dart $= \pi(r_3)^2$

$= \pi(28)^2 \text{ cm}^2$

$\therefore$ Probability of Nishant getting a score of 100

$= \frac{\text{Area of required region}}{\text{Total area of dart}}$

$= \frac{49\pi}{(28)^2 \pi}$

$= \frac{7 \times 7}{28 \times 28} = \frac{1}{16}$

(ii) Area of the outermost circular region

= Total area of the dart

− Area of the circular region upto ring 3

$= \pi(r_3)^2 - \pi(r_2)^2$

$= \pi(28)^2 - \pi(21)^2$

$= \pi[784 - 441] = 343\pi \text{ cm}^2$

Total area of dart $= (28)^2 \pi \text{ cm}^2$

$\therefore$ Probability of dart hitting the outermost circular region on the board

$= \frac{\text{Area of required region}}{\text{Total area of the region}}$

$= \frac{343\pi}{784\pi} = \frac{49 \times 7}{28 \times 28} = \frac{7}{16}$

(iii) Area of required region i.e. ring of 75 points

$= \pi(14)^2 - \pi(7)^2$

Probability of getting 75 points

$= \frac{\text{Area of required region}}{\text{Total area of the region}}$

$= \frac{\pi(14)^2 - \pi(7)^2}{\pi(28)^2}$

$= \frac{(14+7)(14-7)}{28 \times 28}$

$= \frac{21 \times 7}{28 \times 28} = \frac{3}{16}$

Or

Kapil gets 25 points each in the first and second throw.

Total number of throw kapil had = 4

Now, two throw are remaining.

Therefore, only two places are left to calculate the probability,

$\frac{25}{\text{1st throw}}, \frac{25}{\text{2nd throw}}, \frac{}{\text{3rd throw}}, \frac{}{\text{4th throw}}$

Now, we make probabilities for 3rd and 4th throw, which are

(25, 25), (25, 50), (25, 75), (25, 100), (50, 25), (75, 25), (100, 25), (50, 75), (75, 50), (50, 100), (100, 50), (75, 100), (100, 75), (50, 50), (75, 75), (100, 100).

Therefore, he can score total points by 3rd and 4th throw in there many ways which are 16.

30. Total number of students = 200

(i) Number of students who do not prefer to walk

$$= 200 - 120 = 80$$

$\therefore$ P (selected students do not prefer to walk)

$$= \frac{80}{200} = \frac{2}{5}$$

(ii) $\because$ 25% of the students preferred to use bicycles.

$\therefore$ Number of students preferred to use bicycles

$$= \frac{200 \times 25}{100} = 50$$

$\therefore$ Total number of students who prefer to walk or use bicycles = 120 + 50 = 170.

P (selected students prefer to walk or use bicycles)

$$= \frac{170}{200} = \frac{17}{20}$$

(iii) (a) 50% of walking students who used bicycles = 60

Number of students who already use bicycles = 50

$$P \text{ (selected students use bicycles)} = \frac{60 + 50}{200}$$

$$= \frac{110}{200} = \frac{11}{20}$$

Or

(b) $\because$ Number of the students preferred to take the bus = 10% of 200

$$= \frac{200 \times 10}{100} = 20$$

$\therefore$ Number of students who preferred to be dropped by car = 200 – (120 + 50 + 20) = 10

$$P \text{ (selected students dropped by car)} = \frac{10}{200} = \frac{1}{20}$$

31. (i) Total number of puppies $= 10 + 20 + 7 + 13 = 50$

Number of puppies prefered red pet food = 13

$\therefore$ Probability that chosen puppies prefer pet food

$$= \frac{\text{Number of outcomes favourable}}{\text{Total number of outcomes}} = \frac{13}{50}$$

(ii) Sixty percent of time, puppies prefer same food at night. Therefore, $P(E) = 0.6$

Now, probability that puppy will not eat egg at night $= 1 - P(E) = 1 - 0.6 = 0.4$

(iii) (a) Probability that chosen puppy neither prefers to have meat nor milk $= \frac{10 + 13}{50} = \frac{23}{50}$

Or

(b) Probability that chosen puppy either prefers to have an egg or milk $= \frac{10 + 7}{50} = \frac{17}{50}$

32. (i) $P(\text{travelling by bus or ship}) = \frac{36° + 33°}{360°} = \frac{69°}{360°} = \frac{23}{120}$

(ii) Car, Number of people who used car $= \frac{177°}{360°} \times 120 = 59$

(iii) (a) P (person used train) $= 1 - \frac{4}{5} = \frac{1}{5}$

$\therefore$ Number of people who used train $= \frac{120}{5} = 24$

Or (b) Number of people who used aeroplane

$$= \frac{7}{60} \times 120 = 14$$

Revenue collected by air company $= 14 \times 5000$

$= ₹ 70000$

Part II

1. 0, an event which is certain to happen has a probability of non-occurrence is zero.

2. Given, $P(E) = 0.07$

$\therefore$ $P(\text{not } E) = P(\bar{E}) = 1 - P(E)$ $[\because P(E) + P(\bar{E}) = 1]$

$= 1 - 0.07 = 0.93$

3. No. e.g. When tossing a fair coin, the probability of getting a head is equal to the probability of getting a tail.

4. False

5. Do same as Q. 19 from NCERT Folder **Ans.** (i) $\frac{1}{2}$ (ii) $\frac{1}{3}$

6. Do same as Example 3 (ii) **Ans.** $\frac{1}{3}$

7. **Hint** There is no such number on a die which is less than 3 and greater than 2.

$\therefore$ Probability will be zero.

8. **Hint** The factors of 36 are 1, 2, 3, 4, 6, 9, 12, 18, 36. Here, we see that 5 is not a factor of 36.

$\therefore$ Number of favourable outcomes = 1 **Ans.** $\frac{1}{6}$

9. Hint Total number of outcomes $= 6 \times 6 = 36$
If E is the event of getting a doublet i.e. event of getting (1, 1), (2, 2), (3, 3) (4,4) (5, 5) (6, 6).
$\therefore$ Number of outcomes favourable to $E = 6$ **Ans.** $\frac{1}{6}$

10. Given, cards marked with the numbers 5 to 75.
$\therefore$ Total number of cards $= 71$
Let E be the event of getting an odd number from 5 to 75
i.e. event of getting $= 5, 7, 9, 11, \ldots, 75$
So, the number of outcomes favourable to $E = 36$
$\therefore$ P (drawn card is of odd number) $= \frac{36}{71}$

11. Hint Total number of outcomes $= 11$
There are 4 vowels namely O, A, I, I.
So, number of favourable outcomes $= 4$ **Ans.** $\frac{4}{11}$

12. If one black card is lost, then total number of remaining cards $= 51$
Number of favourable outcome $= 1$
$\therefore$ Probability of drawing a queen of heart from the remaining 51 cards $= \frac{1}{51}$

13. Total number of possible outcomes $= 26$
Letters in the word 'RAMANUJAN' are R, A, M, N, U, J.
$\therefore$ Number of favourable outcomes $= 6$
Hence, required probability $= \frac{6}{26} = \frac{3}{13}$

14. Total number of possible outcomes $= 23$
Number of students in houses A, B and $C = 4 + 8 + 5 = 17$
$\therefore$ Remaining students $= 23 - 17 = 6$
Thus, number of favourable outcomes $= 6$
So, probability that the selected student is not from houses A, B and $C = \frac{6}{23}$

15. Total number of possible outcomes $= 6 \times 6 = 36$
For a product to be odd, both the numbers should be odd.
Favourable outcomes are (7, 7), (7, 9), (7, 11), (9, 7), (9, 9), (9, 11), (11, 7), (11, 9) and (11, 11).
Number of favourable outcomes $= 9$
$\therefore$ Probability (product is odd)
$$= \frac{\text{Number of favourable outcomes}}{\text{Total number of outcomes}} = \frac{9}{36} = \frac{1}{4}$$

16. Total number of cards in a bag $= 96$
$\therefore$ Number of possible outcomes $= 96$
(i) Let E_1 be the event of getting a card bearing a perfect square.
Here, perfect square numbers are 9, 16, 25, 36, 49, 64, 81 and 100.
$\therefore$ Number of outcomes favourable to $E_1 = 8$
Hence, probability of getting a card bearing perfect square number, $P(E_1) = \frac{8}{96} = \frac{1}{12}$.
(ii) Let E_2 be the event of getting a card bearing a two-digit number.
Here, two-digit numbers are 10, 11, 12,...., 99
$\therefore$ Number of outcomes favourable to $E_2 = 90$
Hence, probability of getting a card bearing a two-digit number, $P(E_2) = \frac{90}{96} = \frac{15}{16}$.

17. In a non-leap year, total number of days is 365.
Out of them, there are 52 weeks and 1 day extra.
Thus, a non-leap year always has 52 Sundays. The remaining 1 day can be Sunday, Monday, Tuesday, Wednesday, Thursday, Friday or Saturday.
Out of these 7 cases, we have Sunday in one case.
$\therefore$ Total number of outcomes $= 7$
Number of favourable outcome $= 1$
Hence, required probability $= \frac{1}{7}$

18. Let E be the event of guessing the correct answer to a certain question.
$\therefore$ Probability (guessing the correct answer),
$$P(E) = \frac{p}{12} \quad \text{[given]}$$
Now, probability (not guessing the correct answer),
$$P(\bar{E}) = \frac{3}{4} \quad \text{[given]}$$
We know that $1 - P(E) = P(\bar{E})$
$$\Rightarrow \quad 1 - \frac{p}{12} = \frac{3}{4} \Rightarrow p = 3$$

19. Given, total number of sold tickets $= 6000$
Let she bought x tickets.
Then, probability of her winning the first prize
$$\frac{x}{6000} = 0.08 \quad \text{[given]}$$
$$\Rightarrow \quad x = 0.08 \times 6000 \Rightarrow x = 480$$

20. Hint No, because the outcomes '1' and 'not 1' are not equally likely.

21. Total number of three-digit numbers $= 900$
Numbers with hundredth digit 8 and unit's digit 5 are 805, 815, 825, ..., 895.
Number of favourable outcomes $= 10$
$\therefore$ Probability (selecting one such number out of all three digit numbers)
$$= \frac{\text{Number of favourable outcomes}}{\text{Total number of outcomes}}$$
$$= \frac{10}{900} = \frac{1}{90}$$

22. False

23. Given, red balls = 4 and white balls = 5

Let there be x yellow balls in the bag.

$\therefore$ Total number of balls $= 4+5+x$

Probability of drawing a red ball $= \frac{1}{5}$

$\Rightarrow \quad \frac{4}{4+5+x} = \frac{1}{5} \Rightarrow x = 11$

$\therefore$ Probability of drawing a yellow ball $= \frac{11}{4+5+11} = \frac{11}{20}$

24. Hint If E is the event of hitting the boundary, then

$$P(E) = \frac{8}{40} = \frac{1}{5} \Rightarrow P(\bar{E}) = 1-P(E)$$

where, $\bar{E}$ denotes the event of not hitting a boundary.

Ans. $\frac{4}{5}$

25. Total number of possible outcomes = 9

Numbers favourable to $|x| < 2$ are -1, 0 and 1.

$\therefore$ Number of favourable outcomes = 3

So, required probability $= \frac{3}{9} = \frac{1}{3}$

26. (i) A coin is tossed, then outcome can be head or tail, so both the outcomes are equally likely.

(ii) The outcomes in this situation are not equally likely because the outcomes depends on many factors such as quality of gun, training of player etc.

(iii) Man can picked either red, blue or green colour lemon candies. Thus, the possibility of red or blue colour lemon candies are not equally likely.

27. The possible outcomes of the experiment of tossing two coins are HH, HT, TH and TT.

(i) Outcomes favourable to Anu are HT and TH.

$P(\text{Anu getting first chance}) = \frac{2}{4} = \frac{1}{2}$

Outcome favourable to Priya is HH.

$\therefore \; P(\text{Priya getting first chance}) = \frac{1}{4}$

Outcome favourable to Jyoti is TT.

$\therefore \; P(\text{Jyoti getting first chance}) = \frac{1}{4}$

(ii) No, the number of cases favourable to each one of them are not equal.

28. When three coins are tossed together, all possible outcomes are HHH, HHT, HTH, HTT, THH, THT, TTH and TTT.

Total number of possible outcomes = 8

(i) Let E_1 be the event of getting exactly 2 tails.

Then, favourable outcomes are HTT, TTH and THT.

Number of outcomes favourable to $E_1 = 3$

$\therefore \; P\text{ (getting exactly 2 tails)} = P(E_1) = \frac{3}{8}$

(ii) Let E_2 be the event of getting atleast two heads i.e. event of getting HHT, HTH, THH or HHH.

$\therefore$ Number of outcomes favourable to $E_2 = 4$

Hence, required probability $= P(E_2) = \frac{4}{8} = \frac{1}{2}$

(iii) **Hint** Do same as part (ii). **Ans.** $\frac{1}{2}$

29. Possible outcomes on tossing a coin 3 times, are

HHH, HHT, HTH, THH, HTT, THT, TTH, TTT

$\therefore$ Total number of outcomes = 8

(i) Let E_1 be the event that Sweta losses the entry fee i.e. she tosses tail three times i.e. TTT.

$\therefore$ Number of outcome favourable to $E_1 = 1$

Hence, required probability $= P(E_1) = \frac{1}{8}$

(ii) Let E_2 be the event that Sweta gets double entry fee i.e. she tosses heads three times i.e. HHH

$\therefore$ Number of outcome favourable to $E_2 = 1$

Hence, required probability $= P(E_2) = \frac{1}{8}$

(iii) Let E_3 be the event that Sweta gets her entry fee back i.e. Sweta gets heads one or two times i.e. event of getting

HTT, THT, TTH, HHT, HTH or THH

$\therefore$ Number of outcomes favourable to $E_3 = 6$

Hence, required probability $= P(E_3) = \frac{6}{8} = \frac{3}{4}$

30. The total number of outcomes of tossing two dice $= 6 \times 6 = 36$

Number of favourable outcomes

$=$ Number of pair of dice, having sum $10 = 3$

[$\because$ (4, 6), (6, 4), (5, 5)]

$\therefore \; P$ (getting a sum 10)

$$= \frac{\text{Number of favourable outcomes}}{\text{Total number of outcomes}} = \frac{3}{36} = \frac{1}{12}$$

31. Yes; since, sum of the two dice as 1 and 15 are impossible events.

Sum of numbers on both dice 6 is (2, 4), (4, 2), (1, 5), (5, 1), (3, 3).

$\therefore$ Required probability $= \frac{5}{36}$

Sum of numbers on both dice 12 is (6, 6).

$\therefore$ Required probability $= \frac{1}{6}$

32. Total number of outcomes for Aproov = 36

Number of outcomes for getting product 36 = 1

[$\because$ only (6, 6) gives product 36]

$\therefore$ Probability for Aproov $= \frac{1}{36}$

Total number of outcomes for Peehu = 6

Number of outcomes for getting 36, which is square of number 6 = 1 [$\because$ only square of 6 gives 36]

So, probability for Peehu = $\frac{1}{6} = \frac{6}{36}$

$\because$ Probability for Aproov < Probability for Peehu

$\therefore$ Peehu has better chance of getting the number 36.

33. **Hint** (i) Favourable outcomes are (2,2) (2,4) (2,6) (4,2) (4,4), (4,6) (6,2), (6,4) and (6,6). **Ans.** $\frac{1}{4}$

(ii) Favourable outcomes are (1,4) (4,1) (2,3) (3,2). **Ans.** $\frac{1}{9}$

34. Two such dice are thrown together, therefore number of all possible outcomes = 36

(i) The different scores which are possible = 6 scores, namely 0, 1, 2, 6, 7 and 12.

(ii) Let E be the event of getting a sum 7

i.e. {(1, 6), (1, 6), (1, 6), (1, 6), (1, 6), (1, 6), (6, 1), (6, 1), (6, 1), (6, 1), (6, 1), (6, 1)}

$\therefore$ Number of outcomes favourable to E = 12

Hence, $P(E) = \frac{12}{36} = \frac{1}{3}$

35. When two dice are thrown simultaneously, then number of possible outcomes = 36

$\because$ Product of numbers is less than 9

i.e. 1, 2, 3, 4, 5, 6, 7, 8 therefore favourable outcomes are (1, 1), (1, 2), (1, 3), (1, 4), (1, 5), (1, 6), (2, 1), (2, 2), (2, 3), (2, 4), (3, 1), (3, 2), (4, 1), (4, 2), (5, 1) and (6, 1) i.e. 16 outcomes.

Hence, P (product < 9) = $\frac{16}{36} = \frac{4}{9}$

36. **Hint** Total number of possible outcomes = 36

(i) Favourable outcomes are (1, 6), (2, 3), (3, 2) and (6, 1). **Ans.** $\frac{1}{9}$

(ii) Favourable outcomes are (2, 6), (3, 4), (4, 3) (6, 2). **Ans.** $\frac{1}{9}$

(iii) Product of the numbers on the top of the dice cannot be 7.

So, its probability is zero.

37. **Hint** Total number of outcomes = $6 \times 6 = 36$

(i) Doublets of prime numbers are (2, 2), (3, 3) and (5, 5).

So, number of favourable outcomes = 3. **Ans.** $\frac{1}{12}$

(ii) Doublets of odd numbers are (1, 1), (3, 3) and (5, 5).

So, number of favourable outcomes = 3. **Ans.** $\frac{1}{12}$

38. **Hint** Favourable outcomes are (1,3) (2,4) (3,5) (4,6) (3,1) (4,2) (5,3) (6,4). **Ans.** $\frac{2}{9}$

39. The total number of outcomes are 16 i.e. {(1, 1), (1, 2), (1, 3), (1, 4), (2, 1), (2, 2), (2, 3), (2, 4), (3, 1), (3, 2), (3, 3), (3, 4), (4, 1), (4, 2), (4, 3), (4, 4)} and the probable outcomes to win the game as 6.

The probability of Pratik winning the game $\frac{6}{16} = \frac{3}{8}$.

40. **Hint** If E is the event of getting a perfect cube

i.e. event of getting $2^3, 3^3, 4^3$.

$\therefore$ Number of outcomes favourable to E = 3 **Ans.** $\frac{3}{70}$

41. Here, king, queen and jack of clubs are removed.

$\therefore$ Remaining cards = $52 - 3 = 49$

$\therefore$ Total number of outcomes = 49

(i) Number of favourable outcomes = 13

$\therefore$ Required probability = $\frac{13}{49}$

(ii) Number of favourable outcomes = $4 - 1 = 3$

$\therefore$ Required probability = $\frac{3}{49}$

42. Total number of possible outcomes = 80

Numbers divisible by 8 are

8, 16, 24, 32, 40, 48, 56, 64, 72, 80.

There are total 10 numbers which are divisible by 8.

Number of numbers (not divisible by 8) = $80 - 10 = 70$

$\therefore$ Number of favourable outcomes = 70

Required probability is

$$P(E) = \frac{\text{Number of favourable outcomes}}{\text{Total number of possible outcomes}} = \frac{70}{80} = \frac{7}{8}$$

Therefore, the probability that the number on the selected card is not divisible by 8 is $\frac{7}{8}$.

43. **Hint** Do same as Example 8 (iv)

Ans. (i) $\frac{1}{8}$ (ii) $\frac{1}{5}$

44. **Hint** Do same as Question 17 of NCERT Folder 14.1.

Ans. $\frac{3}{4}$ and $\frac{5}{23}$

45. Total number of slips in third box = $25 + 50 = 75$

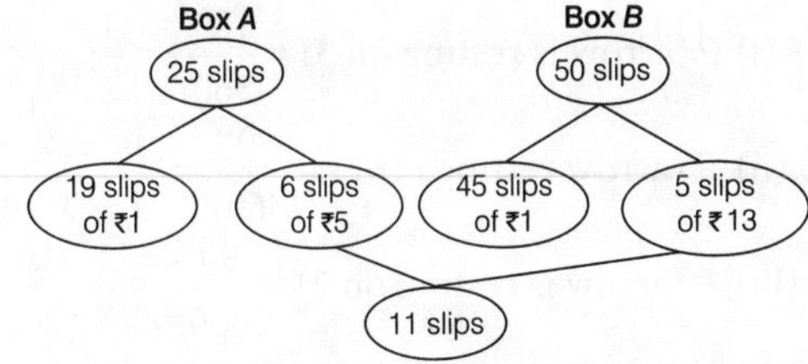

The number of outcomes favourable to event = 11

$\therefore$ Required probability

$$= \frac{\text{Number of favourable outcomes}}{\text{Total number of outcomes}} = \frac{11}{75}$$

46. Total number of possible outcomes = 50

Number of numbers which are multiple of 3 and 4

= 4 [$\because$ multiples of 3 and 4 are 12, 24, 36 and 48]

Probability that the selected number is multiple of 3 and 4 $= \frac{4}{50} = \frac{2}{25}$

47. Farid's statement is false. e.g. If a bag has 1 pink ball, 2 green balls and 2 yellow balls, the probability of randomly picking a pink ball is $\frac{1}{5}$.

48. Hint The probability of an event to be occured is the division of the number of favourable outcomes by the total number of outcomes.

Therefore, it is an equally likely outcome.

Therefore, Atul is wrong.

49. Hint Do same as Example 10. **Ans.** (i) 0.88 (ii) 0.96

50. Area of the square $ABCD = (BC)^2 = 10^2 = 100 \text{ cm}^2$

Now, area of the square $PQRS = (\text{Side})^2 = (5)^2$

[$\because$ side = 5 cm, given]

$= 25\text{cm}^2$

$\therefore$ P (the point will be chosen from the shaded part)

$$= \frac{\text{Area of the square } PQRS}{\text{Area of the square } ABCD} = \frac{25}{100} = 0.25$$

51. Hint (i) Total number of balls in the bag = 18

Total number of red balls in the bag = x

$\therefore$ Probability (red ball) $= \frac{x}{18}$

(ii) Now, 2 red balls are added to the bag.

$\therefore$ Total number of balls in the bag = 18 + 2 = 20

Total number of red balls in the bag = $x + 2$

$\therefore$ Probability of drawing red ball $= \frac{x+2}{20}$

$\therefore$ $\frac{x+2}{20} = \frac{9}{8}\left(\frac{x}{18}\right)$ **Ans.** 8

52. Total angle made by the circle at O is 360°.

Angle subtended by region 1 at O = 90°

Angle subtended by region 2 at O = 90°

Angle subtended by region 3 at O = 180°

(i) P (arrow is resting on 3) $= \frac{180°}{360°} = \frac{1}{2}$

(ii) P (arrow resting on 1) $= \frac{90°}{360°} = \frac{1}{4}$

(iii) P (arrow is resting on 2) $= \frac{90°}{360°} = \frac{1}{4}$

$\therefore$ P (arrow is not resting on 2)

$= 1 - P$ (arrow is resting on 2)

$= 1 - \frac{1}{4} = \frac{3}{4}$

53. Given, total number of handsets = 350

(i) $P(A) = \frac{250}{350} = \frac{5}{7}$ (ii) $P(A) = \frac{100}{350} = \frac{2}{7}$

54. Hint The probability that it will turn red within the next half a minute $= \frac{\frac{1}{2}}{3} = \frac{1}{6}$

55. Hint Do same as Example 11.

Ans. (i) $\frac{31}{365}$ (ii) $\frac{12}{365}$ (iii) $\frac{59}{365}$

56. The total number of outcomes of choosing an integer from 1 to 100 = 100

(i) Number of favourable outcomes

= Number of integers divisible by 8 = 12

[$\because$ numbers divisible by 8 are 8, 16, 24, 32, 40, 48, 56, 64, 72, 80, 88, 96]

$\therefore$ P(getting an integer divisible by 8)

$$= \frac{\text{Number of favourable outcomes}}{\text{Total number of outcomes}}$$

$$= \frac{12}{100} = \frac{3}{25}$$

(ii) We know that,

P (getting an integer divisible by 8)

$+P$ (getting an integer not divisible by 8) = 1

$\Rightarrow$ P (getting an integer not divisible by 8)

$$= 1 - \left(\frac{3}{25}\right) = \frac{25-3}{25} = \frac{22}{25}$$

57. Hint Do same as Example 11 (i) **Ans.** $\frac{1}{366}$

58. Hint (i) Favourable outcomes are

$1^2, 2^2, 3^2, 4^2, 5^2, 6^2, 7^2, 8^2$ i.e. there are 8 favourable outcomes.

Ans. $\frac{1}{10}$

(ii) Do same as Example 8 (iii). **Ans.** $\frac{13}{80}$

59. (i) Median of the numbers is 7.

So, P(Median) $= \frac{4}{15}$

[$\because$ there are four 7's and total numbers are 15]

(ii) Mode = 9

$\therefore$ P(Mode) $= \frac{5}{15} = \frac{1}{3}$ [$\because$ there are five 9's]

60. Yes, Total number of possible outcomes $= 6 \times 6 = 36$

(i) Number of possible outcomes when the sum is odd $= 10$

$\therefore$ Required probability $= \frac{10}{36} = \frac{5}{18}$

(ii) Number of possible outcomes when the sum is $6 = 4$

$\therefore$ Required probability $= \frac{4}{36} = \frac{1}{9}$

(iii) Number of possible outcomes when the sum atleast 8 (greater than 7) $= 20$

$\therefore$ Probability of getting the sum at least $8 = \frac{20}{36} = \frac{5}{9}$

61. Total number of figures $= 8$ triangles $+ 10$ squares $= 18$

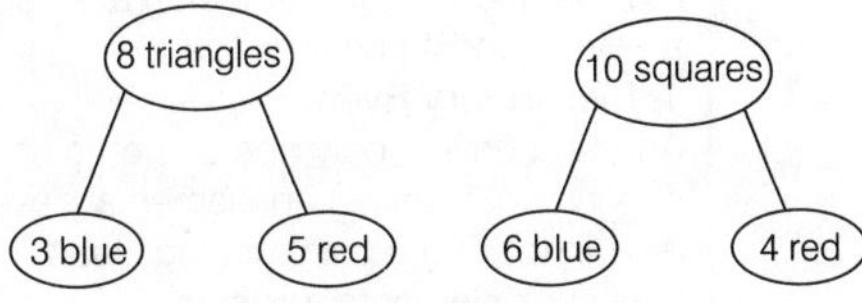

(i) P (lost piece is a triangle) $= \frac{8}{18} = \frac{4}{9}$

(ii) P (lost piece is a square) $= \frac{10}{18} = \frac{5}{9}$

(iii) P (lost piece is square of blue colour) $= \frac{6}{18} = \frac{1}{3}$

(iv) P (lost piece is triangle of red colour) $= \frac{5}{18}$

62. (i) Let number of white balls be n.

Total number of balls $= 6 + 4 + n = 10 + n$

Let E be the event of drawing a white ball.

Given, $P(E) = \frac{1}{3}$

$\Rightarrow \frac{\text{Number of outcomes favourable to } E}{\text{Total number of outcomes}} = \frac{1}{3}$

$\Rightarrow \frac{n}{10+n} = \frac{1}{3} \Rightarrow n = 5$

(ii) Now, total number of balls $= 10 + n = 10 + 5 = 15$

Let x red balls are removed from the bag.

$\therefore$ Total number of balls in the bag $= 15 - x$

Now, $P(E) = \frac{1}{2} \Rightarrow \frac{5}{15-x} = \frac{1}{2} \Rightarrow x = 5$

63. Clearly, probability of getting a red ball

$= 1 - [P(\text{white ball}) + P(\text{black ball})]$

$= 1 - \frac{3}{10} - \frac{2}{5} = \frac{10-3-4}{10} = \frac{3}{10}$

Now, let the number of balls in the bag be x. Since, it is given that the number of black balls in the bag is 20.

$\therefore$ Probability of getting a black ball $= \frac{20}{x}$

$\Rightarrow \frac{2}{5} = \frac{20}{x} \Rightarrow x = 50$

64. **Hint** Do same as Example 8.

Ans. (i) $\frac{4}{65}$ (ii) $\frac{1}{5}$ (iii) $\frac{12}{65}$ (iv) $\frac{3}{13}$

65. Since, radius of each of the given circles is 1 unit.

$\therefore$ Side of square $ABCD = 1 + 1 = 2$ units

Now, area of square $= 2^2 = 4$ sq. units

Clearly, area of shaded region

$= $ Area of square – Area of quadrant (I) – Area of quadrant (II) – Area of quadrant (III) – Area of quadrant (IV)

$= 4 - 4 \times$ Area of a quadrant [$\because$ each quadrant is of equal area]

$= 4 - 4 \times \frac{\pi(1)^2}{4}$

$\left[\because \text{ area of a quadrant of circle with radius } r = \frac{\pi r^2}{4}\right]$

$= (4 - \pi)$ sq. unit

Hence, P (that the point chosen from the shaded region)

$= \frac{\text{Area of shaded region}}{\text{Area of square}} = \frac{4-\pi}{4}$

66. **Hint** Since, ΔADC is right angled at D.

$AC^2 = AD^2 + DC^2 = 6^2 + 8^2$ [by Pythagoras theorem]

$\Rightarrow AC = 10$ [taking positive sqaure root]

Now, radius of circle $= OC = \frac{1}{2} AC = 5$

P (dart will land in the shaded region)

$= \frac{\text{Area of shaded region}}{\text{Area of the circle}}$

$= \frac{\text{Area of the circle} - \text{Area of the rectangle}}{\text{Area of the circle}}$

Ans. $\frac{25\pi - 48}{25\pi}$

67. **Hint** Do same as Example 8.

Ans. (i) $\frac{8}{19}$ (ii) $\frac{8}{19}$ (iii) $\frac{16}{19}$ (iv) $\frac{9}{19}$

68. Total number of envelopes in the box $= 1000$

Number of envelopes containing cash prize

$= 10 + 100 + 250 = 360$

Number of envelopes containing no cash prize

$= 1000 - 360 = 640$

$\therefore$ Required probability $= \frac{640}{1000} = 0.64$

69. **Hint** Two number x and y can be chosen in 16 ways

i.e. (1, 1) (1, 4) (1, 9) (1, 16)(2, 1)(2, 4)(2, 9),(2, 16) (3, 1) (3, 4) (3, 9), (3, 16) (4, 1) (4, 4) (4, 9), (4, 16)

$\therefore$ Total number of possible outcomes $= 16$

Given, product of numbers is less than 16, so favourable outcomes are (1, 1) (1, 4) (1, 9) (2, 1) (2, 4), (3, 1) (3, 4), (4, 1)

i.e. 8 outcomes

Ans. $\frac{1}{2}$

PROBABILITY

Experiment
An operation which produces some well-defined outcomes, is called an experiment.
e.g. Tossing a coin.

Types of Experiment

1. Random Experiment
If an experiment when repeated under identical conditions, do not produce the same outcome every time but the outcome produce in each trial is one of the several possible outcomes, it is called random or probabilistic experiment.

2. Deterministic Experiment
An experiment which when repeated under identical conditions produce the same result or outcome is known as deterministic experiment.

Favourable Outcomes The outcomes which ensure the occurrence of an event are called favourable outcomes to the event.
e.g. The favourable outcomes to the event of getting an even number when a die is thrown are 2, 4 and 6.

Complement of an Event Let E be an event associated with a random experiment. Then, the complement of event E or negation of event E, denoted by $\overline{E}$ as an event which occurs if and only if E does not occur.
e.g. If E is the event of getting an even number in a single throw of a die. Then, its complement is an event of getting an odd number
i.e. $E = 2, 4, 6$
$\therefore \overline{E} = 1, 3$ and 5.

Event An event for an experiment is the collection of some outcomes of the experiment. We generally, denote it by capital letter E.
e.g. Getting an odd number in a single throw of a die is an event and it consists 1, 3, 5.

1. Elementary Event
An event having only one outcome of the random experiment is called an elementary event.
e.g., In tossing a coin, getting Head (H) or Tail (T) are known as elementary events.

Occurrence of an Event
An event E associated to a random experiment is said to be occur in a trial, if the outcome of trial is one of the outcomes that favours E.
e.g. If a die is rolled and outcome of trial is 4, then event of getting an even number has occurred.

Probability of an Event Probability of E denoted by $P(E)$ represents the chance of occurrence of event E.

Probability-An Experimental Approach
The empirical (or experimental) probability of an event E is given by

$$P(E) = \frac{\text{Number of trials in which the event happened}}{\text{Total number of trials}}$$

Probability - A Theoretical Approach
A theoretical approach of probability has some limitation like repetition of experiment is not possible in every situation as it may be unfeasible.

2. Compound Event
A collection of two or more elementary events associated with an experiment is called a compound event.
e.g. In the random experiment of tossing of two coins simultaneously, if we define the event of getting exactly one head, then it is a collection of elementary events i.e. HT and TH.
So, it is a compound event.

Equally Likely Outcomes
The outcomes of a random experiment are said to be equally likely when each outcome is as likely to occur as the other, i.e. when we have no reason to believe that one is more likely to occur than the other.
e.g. When a die is thrown, so the outcomes 1, 2, 3, 4, 5 and 6 are equally likely outcomes.

Some Special Events

1. Impossible Event
An event which is impossible to occur is called an impossible event.
Also, the probability of impossible event is always zero.
e.g. In throwing a die, probability of getting a number 7 is 0 as there are only six possible outcomes.

2. Sure or Certain Event
An event which is sure to occur, is called a sure event and probability of sure event is always 1.
e.g. Probability of getting a number less than 7 in a single throw of a die having numbers 1 to 6 on its six faces.

ACTIVITY 1

To identify arithmetic progressions in some given lists of numbers (patterns).

Prior Knowledge

Concept of Arithmetic Progression (AP).

Materials Required

1. Cardboard
2. White paper
3. Pen/Pencil
4. Scissors
5. Squared paper
6. Adhesive

Theory

1. An arithmetic progression is a list of numbers, in which each term is obtained by adding a fixed number to the preceding term except the first term.

   This fixed number is called the **common difference** *(d)* of the AP and it can be positive, negative or zero.

2. For example, in the list of numbers $a_1, a_2, a_3, a_4, \ldots$ if the differences $a_2 - a_1$, $a_3 - a_2$, $a_4 - a_3$, ... gives the same value, i.e. if $a_{k+1} - a_k$ is same for different values of k, then the given list of numbers are said to make an **arithmetic progression.**

3. The general form of an AP is

   $a, a + d, a + 2d, a + 3d, \ldots$.

   where, a is the **first term** and d is the **common difference.**

   nth term of an AP is

   $$T_n = a + (n - 1)\, d$$

Procedure

1. Take a cardboard of suitable size and paste a white paper on it.
2. Take two squared papers (graph paper) of suitable size and paste them on the cardboard.
3. Let the lists of numbers be

   (i) 1, 2, 5, 9, ...

   (ii) 2, 5, 8, 11, ...

4. Make strips of length 1, 2, 5, 9 units and strips of length 2, 5, 8, 11 and breadth of each strip one unit.
5. Paste the strips of lengths 1, 2, 5, 9 units as shown in Fig. 1.1 and paste the strips of lengths 2, 5, 8,11 units as shown in Fig. 1.2.

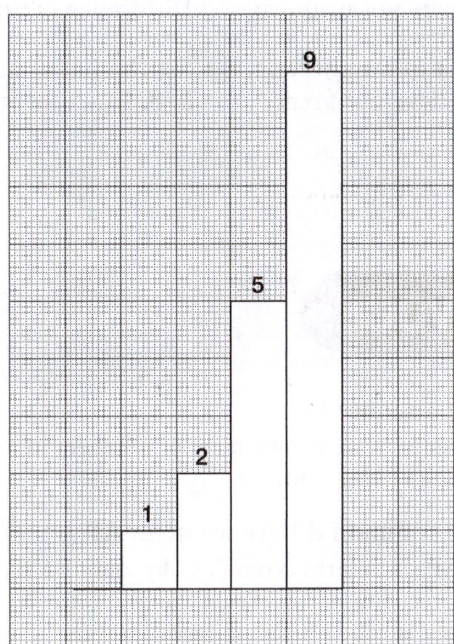

Figure 1.1

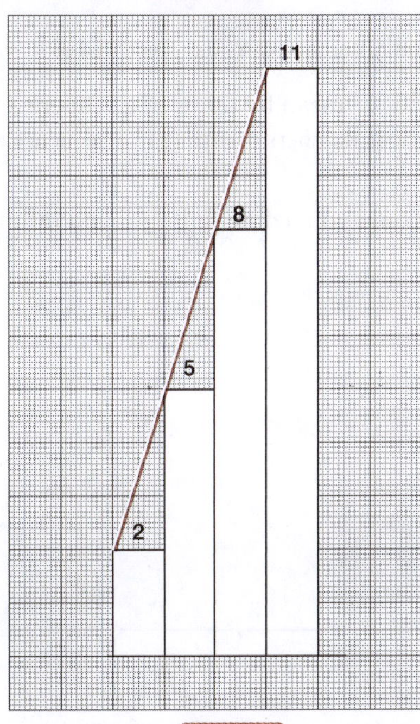

Figure 1.2

Observation

Figure 1.1	Figure 1.2
The difference of heights of first two strips = 1 unit	The difference of heights of first two strips = 3 units
The difference of heights of second and third strips = 3 units	The difference of heights of second and third strips = 3 units
The difference of heights of third and fourth strips = 4 units	The difference of heights of third and fourth strips = 3 units
Difference is not uniform	Difference is uniform.
So, the list of numbers 1, 2, 5, 9, ... does not form an AP .	So, the list of numbers 2, 5, 8, 11, ... forms an AP.

From the above table, it is clear that

1. In Fig. 1.1, the difference of heights (lengths) of two consecutive strips is not same (uniform). So, it is not an AP.
2. In Fig. 1.2, the difference of heights of two consecutive strips is the same (uniform) throughout, so it is an AP.

Result

We have identified arithmetic progressions in some given lists of numbers (patterns).

Application

This activity helps in finding whether the given sequence is an arithmetic sequence or not.

VIVA-VOCE

1 Define a sequence.

Ans. A sequence is an arrangement of numbers in a definite order according to some rule.

2 Define common difference in an AP.

Ans. In an AP, each term is obtained by adding a fixed number 'd' to the preceding term, except the first term 'a'. The fixed number d is called its common difference.

3 How would you represent common difference in an AP?

Ans. Common difference can be represented as $d = a_n - a_{n-1}$.

4 What do we mean by terms of a sequence?

Ans. The various numbers occurring in a sequence are called its terms.

5 How would you define finite AP and infinite AP in one line?

Ans. If number of terms in an AP is finite, then it is called a finite AP, otherwise it is called an infinite AP.

6 What is the condition for a sequence to be an AP?

Ans. There should be equal difference between any two consecutive terms.

7 What is the formula for nth term of an AP?

Ans. The formula for nth term of an AP is $T_n = a + (n-1)d$.

8 Let us consider an AP 1, 3, 5, 7, ... If we add 1 in each term, will the common difference also increased by 1.

Ans. No, the common difference will be remain same.

9 The next term of the AP $\sqrt{3}, \sqrt{12}, \sqrt{27}, \sqrt{48}$, ... is

Ans. $\sqrt{75}$.

ACTIVITY 2

To find the sum of first n natural numbers.

Prior Knowledge

1. Concept of natural numbers.
2. Concept of Arithmetic Progression (AP).
3. Concept of the sum of n terms of an AP.

Materials Required

1. Cardboard
2. Coloured papers
3. White papers
4. Cutter
5. Adhesive

Theory

1. Numbers which are used for counting, i.e. 1, 2, 3, 4, ... are called **natural numbers**. Smallest natural number is 1 but we cannot find the largest natural number as successor of each natural number is again a natural number. The collection of natural numbers is denoted by N.

   $\therefore \quad N = \{1, 2, 3, 4, \ldots\}$

2. For concept of Arithmetic Progression (AP) see Activity 1.
3. For an AP, sum of its n terms is given by

   $$S_n = \frac{n}{2}[2a + (n-1)d]$$

   where, a = first term of an AP, d = common difference and n = number of terms

   Natural numbers $1, 2, 3, 4, \ldots, n$ represents an AP because the difference between two consecutive terms is 1.

   So, to find the sum of all natural numbers upto n or first n natural numbers, we can apply the formula for the sum of n terms of an AP.

   $$\therefore \quad S_n = \frac{n}{2}[2a + (n-1)d] \quad \ldots\text{(i)}$$

   Here, a = first term = 1 ; d = common difference = 1

   $$\therefore \quad S_n = \frac{n}{2}[2 \times 1 + (n-1)1]$$

   $$= \frac{n}{2}[2 + n - 1] = \frac{n}{2}[n+1] \quad \ldots\text{(ii)}$$

Procedure

1. Take a rectangular cardboard of suitable size and paste a coloured paper on it.
2. Let us find the sum of first 10 natural numbers ($n = 10$), i.e. from 1 to 10, so draw a rectangle $ABCD$ of length 10 units (n) and breadth 11 units ($n + 1$).
3. Divide this rectangle into unit squares (square has side 1 unit) as shown in Fig. 2.1.
4. Starting from upper left-most corner, shade one square, 2 squares, 3 squares and so on. (see Fig. 2.1).

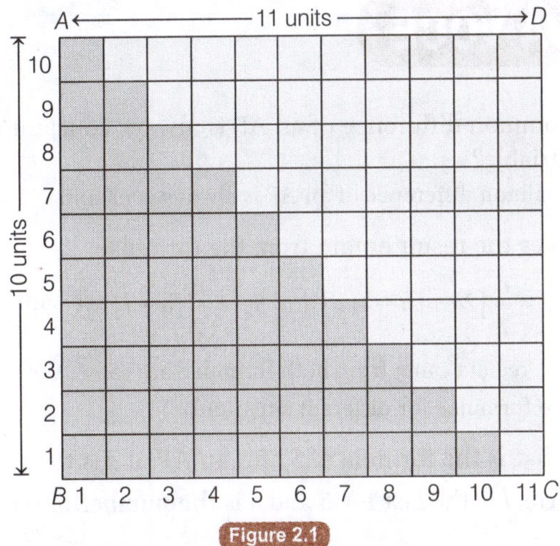

Figure 2.1

Observations

For $n = 4$, in Eq. (ii), we get S_n = ...

For $n = 12$, in Eq. (ii), we get S_n = ...

For $n = 50$, in Eq. (ii), we get S_n = ...

For $n = 100$, in Eq. (ii), we get S_n = ...

1. The shaded colour region looks like a stair case.
2. Length of 1st stair is 1 unit, length of 2nd stair is 2 units, length of 3rd stair is 3 units, and so on, length of 10th stair is 10 units.
3. These lengths give a pattern 1, 2, 3, 4, ..., 10, which is an AP with first term 1 and common difference 1.
4. Sum of first 10 terms $= 1 + 2 + 3 + \ldots + 10 = 55$ ...(iii)

5. We observe that

Area of the shaded region

$$= \frac{1}{2} \times \text{Area of rectangle } ABCD$$

$$= \frac{1}{2} \times \text{Length} \times \text{Breadth}$$

$$= \frac{1}{2} \times 10 \times 11 = 55$$

which is same as obtained in Eq. (iii).

This shows that the sum of the first 10 natural numbers is $\frac{1}{2} \times 10 \times 11 = \frac{1}{2} \times 10\,(10+1)$.

This result can be generalised to find the sum of first n natural numbers, as

$$S_n = \frac{1}{2} n(n+1) \quad \text{...(iv)}$$

Result

We have found the sum of first n natural numbers.

Applications

1. This result can be used to find the sum of given AP of n natural numbers.
2. This result is useful in researches related to larger natural numbers.

VIVA-VOCE

1 Common difference of an AP is always constant or variable?

Ans Common difference of an *AP* is always constant.

2 Does the result obtain from the formulae, $S_n = \frac{n}{2}[2a + (n-1)d]$ and $S_n = \frac{n}{2}[a + l]$ are same?

Ans Yes, results came from both formulae are same. We use these two formulae for different situations.

3 What is the formula of S_n for an AP, if a is the first term, l is the last term and n is the number of terms?

Ans $S_n = \frac{n}{2}(a + l)$

4 What is the formula for a_n in terms of S_n, if S_n is the sum of first n terms of an AP?

Ans $a_n = S_n - S_{n-1}$

5 If we double each of the first n natural numbers, then what will be the sum of first n numbers?

Ans The sum can be calculated by formula, $S_n = n(n+1)$.

$\left[\because S_n = \frac{n(n+1)}{2}\right.$ on doubling the numbers,

$\left.\text{Sum} = 2 \times \frac{n(n+1)}{2} = n(n+1)\right]$

6 If x, y and z are in an AP, then how would you represent y as of x and z?

Ans Given, x, y and z are in AP.

$$\therefore \quad y = \frac{x+z}{2}$$

7 What will be the sum of first 20 natural numbers?

Ans 210

8 What will be the sum of first ten multiples of 3?

Ans 165

ACTIVITY 3

To draw a system of similar triangles, using Y-shaped strips with nails.

Prior Knowledge

1. Concept of similarity of figures.
2. Criterion for similarity of two triangles.

Materials Required

1. Three wooden strips of equal size (approx. 10 cm long and 1 cm wide)
2. Adhesive/Adhesive tape
3. Nails
4. Hammer
5. Thread

Theory

1. Two figures having the same shape but not necessarily the same size, are called **similar figures**. If two figures are similar to each other, then one can be obtained from the other either by shrinking or by stretching without changing its shape.
2. Two triangles are said to be similar, if
   (i) their corresponding angles are equal, **(by AAA similarity criterion)**.
   (ii) two angles of one triangle are respectively equal to the two angles of the other triangle, **(by AA similarity criterion)**.
   (iii) sides of one triangle is proportional to (i.e. in the same ratio of) the sides of the other triangle, **(by SSS similarity criterion)**.
   (iv) one angle of a triangle is equal to one angle of another triangle and the sides including these angles are in the same ratio (proportional), **(by SAS similarity criterion)**.

Procedure

1. Take three wooden strips, say P, Q, R and cut one end of each strip.
2. Join three ends of each strip, by using adhesive/adhesive tape, such that they all lie in different directions. (see Fig. 3.1)

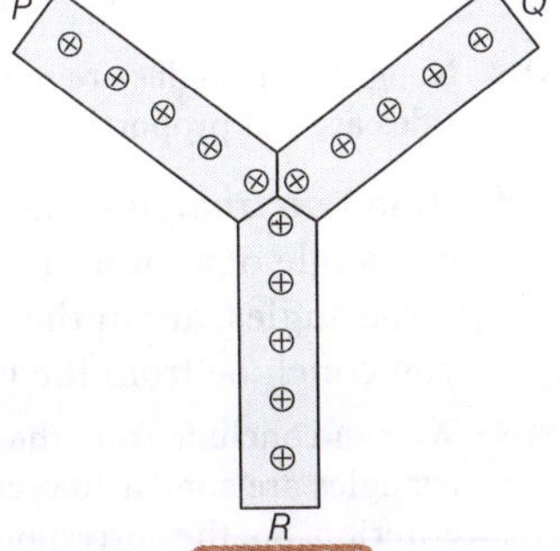

Figure 3.1

3. Fix five nails at same distance on each of the strip and name them $P_1, P_2, \ldots, P_5; Q_1, Q_2, \ldots, Q_5$ and $R_1, R_2, \ldots, R_5$ on strips P, Q and R, respectively. (see Fig. 3.2)

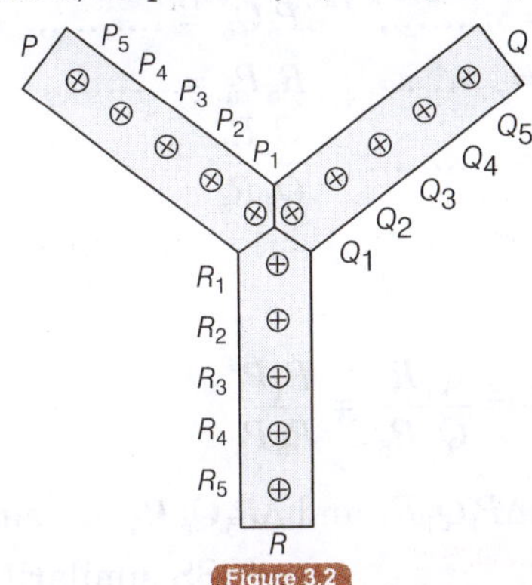

Figure 3.2

4. On three respective strips, tie the thread around the nails of subscript 1 (P_1, Q_1, R_1). (see Fig. 3.3)

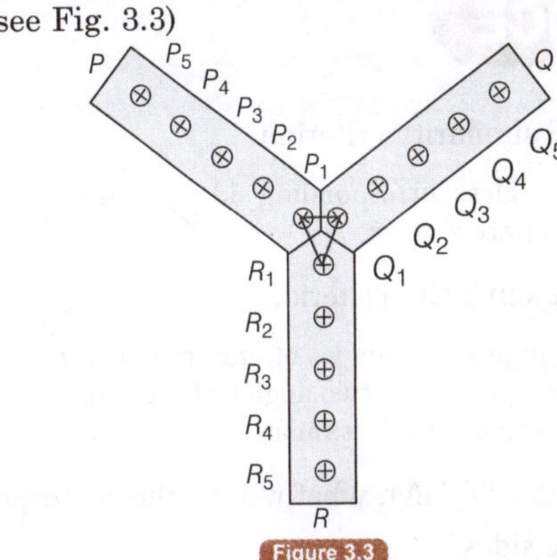

Figure 3.3

5. Tie the thread around the nails of the same subscript on the respective strips for getting more such triangles. Thus, we get triangles $P_1Q_1R_1, P_2Q_2R_2, P_3Q_3R_3, P_4Q_4R_4$ and $P_5Q_5R_5$. (see Fig. 3.4)

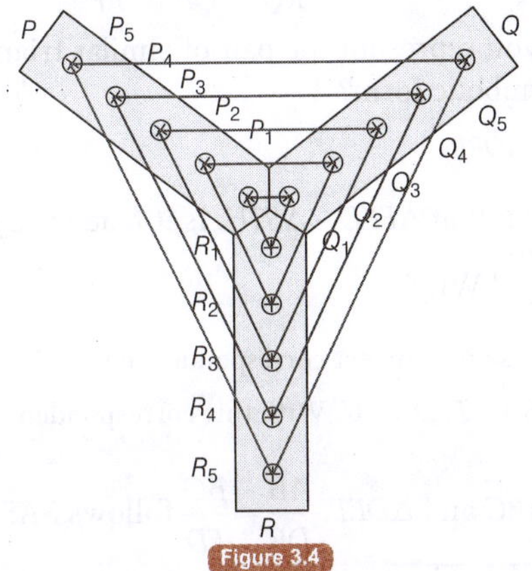

Figure 3.4

Observation

By actual measurement of sides of $\Delta P_1Q_1R_1$ and $\Delta P_5Q_5R_5$ we observe the following results

$P_1Q_1 = \dots\dots\dots,\quad Q_1R_1 = \dots\dots\dots,$

$R_1P_1 = \dots\dots\dots,\quad P_5Q_5 = \dots\dots\dots,$

$Q_5R_5 = \dots\dots\dots,\quad R_5P_5 = \dots\dots\dots,$

$\frac{P_1Q_1}{P_5Q_5} = \dots\dots\dots,\quad \frac{Q_1R_1}{Q_5R_5} = \dots\dots\dots,$

$\frac{R_1P_1}{R_5P_5} = \dots\dots\dots.$

Here, $\frac{P_1Q_1}{P_5Q_5} = \frac{Q_1R_1}{Q_5R_5} = \frac{R_1P_1}{R_5P_5}$

Therefore, $\Delta P_1Q_1R_1$ and $\Delta P_5Q_5R_5$ are similar. [SSS similarity criterion]

Similarly, we can show that any two triangles formed on Y-shaped strips are similar to each other.

Note *By tying a thread at suitable nails, we can obtain non-equilateral similar triangles also.*

Result

We have drawn a system of similar triangles, using Y-shaped strips with nails.

Application

By using this concept, we can find the length of the shadow of pole in sunlight and height of a pole.

VIVA-VOCE

1 Define SSS similarity criterion?

Ans If in two triangles, corresponding sides are in the same ratio, then triangles are similar.

2 Define AA similarity criterion.

Ans If in two triangles, two angles of one triangle are respectively equal to the two angles of the other triangle, then the two triangles are similar.

3 If $\Delta ABC \sim \Delta MLP$, then what will be the corresponding ratio of the sides?

Ans If, $\Delta ABC \sim \Delta MLP$, then $\frac{AB}{ML} = \frac{BC}{LP} = \frac{CA}{PM}$

4 If in ΔABC and ΔPRQ, $\frac{AC}{RQ} = \frac{BA}{QP} = \frac{BC}{RP}$, then how would you represent the pair of similar triangles in their symbolic form?

Ans $\Delta ACB \sim \Delta QRP$

5 It is given that $\Delta FED \sim \Delta STU$. Is it true to say that $\frac{DE}{ST} = \frac{EF}{TU}$? Why?

Ans No, because the correct correspondence is $F \leftrightarrow S$, $E \leftrightarrow T$, $D \leftrightarrow U$. With this correspondence, $\frac{EF}{ST} = \frac{DE}{TU}$.

6 If in ΔABC and ΔDEF, $\frac{AB}{DE} = \frac{BC}{FD}$ follows SAS criterion, then on what basis, we can say that they are similar?

Ans Since, we have $\frac{AB}{DE} = \frac{BC}{FD}$

$\therefore$ On having $\angle B = \angle D$, we can say that they will be similar and will follow SAS criterion.

7 State whether the following triangles are similar or not. Give reason(s).

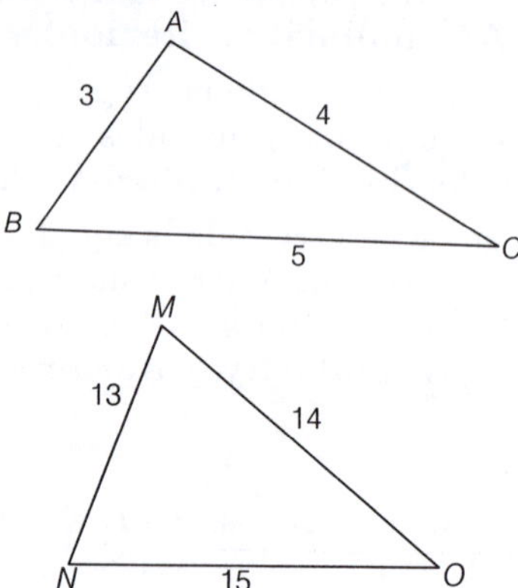

Ans No, given triangles are not similar as their corresponding sides are not proportional.

8 "If in two triangles, one angle of a triangle is equal to one angle of another triangle and the sides including these angles, are in the same proportion." What can you conclude from the given information?

Ans We can conclude from the given information that both the triangles are similar to each other and follows SAS similarity criterion. So, the corresponding angles of both the triangles are equal and their corresponding sides are also in the same proportion.

ACTIVITY 4

To verify Basic Proportionality Theorem (Thales theorem).

Prior Knowledge

Concept of Basic Proportionality Theorem (Thales theorem).

Materials Required

1. Two wooden strips of equal size (approx. 1 cm wide and 30 cm long)
2. Cutter
3. Adhesive
4. Hammer
5. Nails
6. Hardboard
7. White paper
8. Pulleys
9. Thread
10. Scale
11. Screws
12. Coloured glazed papers.

Theory

According to Thales theorem, if a line is drawn parallel to one side of a triangle to intersect the other two sides at distinct points, then the other two sides are divided in the same ratio.

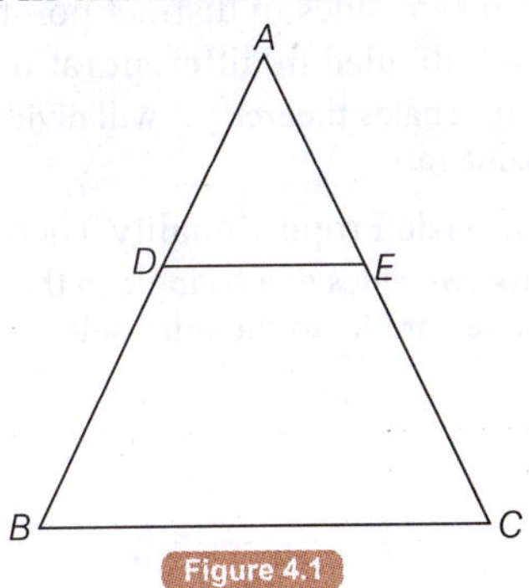

Figure 4.1

In ΔABC, if $DE \parallel BC$, then according to Basic proportionality theorem, $\frac{AD}{DB} = \frac{AE}{EC}$.

Procedure

1. Cut a piece of hardboard of suitable size and paste a white paper on it.
2. Take two thin wooden strips with marking 1, 2, 3, ... at equal distances and fix them vertically on the two ends of the horizontal strip as shown in Fig. 4.2 and name them AC and BD.
3. From hardboard, cut a triangular piece PQR (thickness should be negligible) and paste coloured glazed paper on it and place it between the parallel strips AC and BD such that its base QR is parallel to the horizontal strip AB as shown in Fig. 4.2.

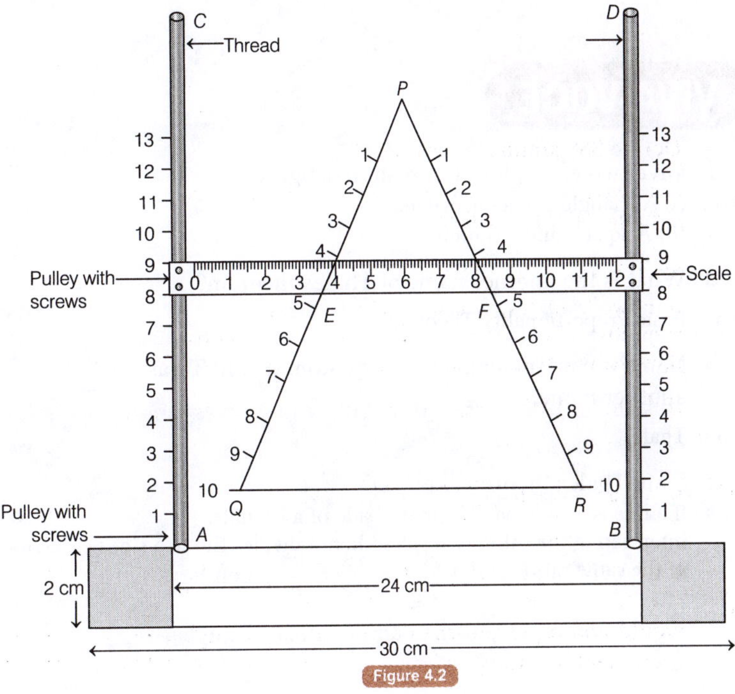

Figure 4.2

4. Graduate the other two sides, PQ and PR of the triangular piece as shown in Fig. 4.2.
5. Put the screws along the horizontal strip and two more screws on the top of the board at the points C and D, such that A, B, D and C become four vertices of a rectangle.

6. Take a ruler (scale) and make four holes on it as shown in the figure and fix four pulleys at these holes with the help of screws.
7. Fix the scale on the board (as shown in figure) by using the thread tied to nails fixed at points A, B, C and D passing through the pulleys, so that the scale slides parallel to the horizontal strip AB and can be moved up and down over the triangular piece freely.

Observation

By actual measurement, we observe the following results

$PE = \text{.........},\quad PF = \text{.........},$

$EQ = \text{.........},\quad FR = \text{.........},$

$\frac{PE}{EQ} = \text{.........},\quad \frac{PF}{FR} = \text{.........}\,.$

Here, $\frac{PE}{EQ} = \frac{PF}{FR}$. So, it verifies the Basic Proportionality Theorem.

Repeat the activity as stated above, slide the scale up and down parallel to the base of the ΔPQR and verify the Thales theorem for different positions of the scale.

Result

Basic Proportionality Theorem (Thales theorem) has been verified.

Applications

1. To establish various criteria of similarity of triangles, we can use this theorem.
2. This theorem can also be used for constructing a polygon similar to a given polygon with a given scale factor.

VIVA-VOCE

1 Give two examples of non-similar figures.

Ans (i) A triangle and a quadrilateral.
(ii) A square and a rhombus.

2 What is the another name of Thales theorem?

Ans Basic Proportionality Theorem

3 Name the mathematician after whom the, BPT has another name.

Ans Thales

4 State Thales theorem.

Ans If a line is drawn parallel to one side of a triangle, intersecting the other two sides, then it divides the two sides in the same ratio.

5 What is the full form of BPT?

Ans Basic Proportionality Theorem

6 If a line divides any two sides of a triangle in the same ratio, then the line is .... to the third side.

Ans Parallel

7 A line is drawn parallel to one side of a triangle to intersect the other two sides in distinct points, does the other two sides are divided in different ratio?

Ans No, according to the Thales theorem, it will divide the other two sides in the same ratio.

8 State converse of Basic Proportionality Theorem.

Ans If a line divides any two sides of a triangle in the same ratio, then the line must be parallel to the third side.

ACTIVITY 5

To find the number of tangents from a point to a circle.

Prior Knowledge

1. Various terms related to a circle like radius, centre, etc.
2. Tangent to a circle.

Materials Required

1. Cardboard
2. Geometry box
3. Cutter
4. Different coloured sheets
5. Adhesive
6. Nails
7. String

Theory

1. A circle is a collection of points which are at a fixed distance from a fixed point. The fixed point is called **centre** of the circle and fixed distance is called the **radius** of circle.

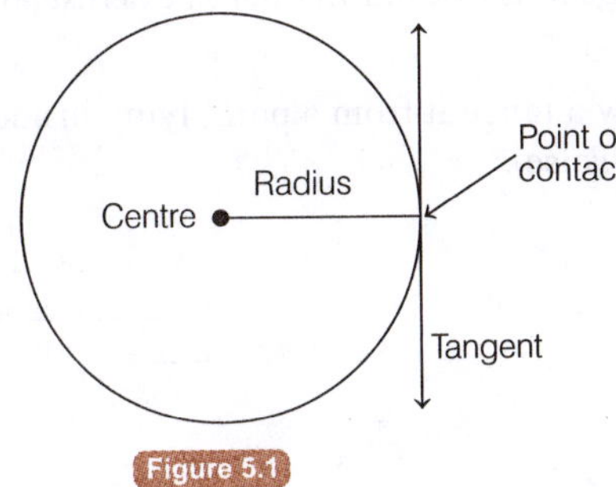

Figure 5.1

2. If any line is drawn in such a way that it touches the circle at only one point, then such straight line is called **tangent** to the circle and the point at which it touches the circle is called **point of contact**. (see Fig. 5.1)

Procedure

1. Take a cardboard of suitable size and paste a coloured sheet on it.
2. Now, draw a circle of suitable radius on another coloured sheet and cut it out.
3. Paste the cut out circle on the cardboard. (see Fig. 5.2)

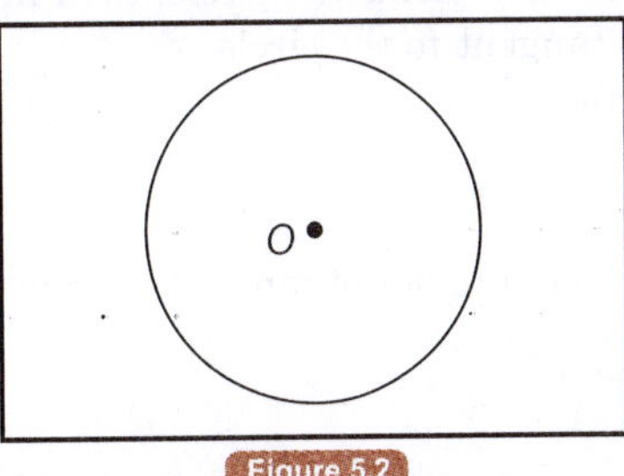

Figure 5.2

4. Now, take any point P outside the circle or on the circle or inside the circle and fix a nail on it. (see Fig. 5.3, Fig. 5.4 and Fig. 5.5).
5. Take a string and tie one end of it at the point P and move the other end towards the centre of the circle. Also, move it up and down from the centre such that it may touch the circle. (see Fig. 5.3, Fig. 5.4 and Fig. 5.5)

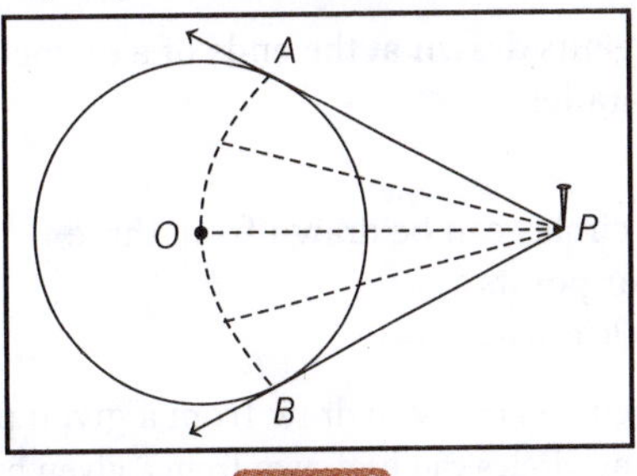

Figure 5.3

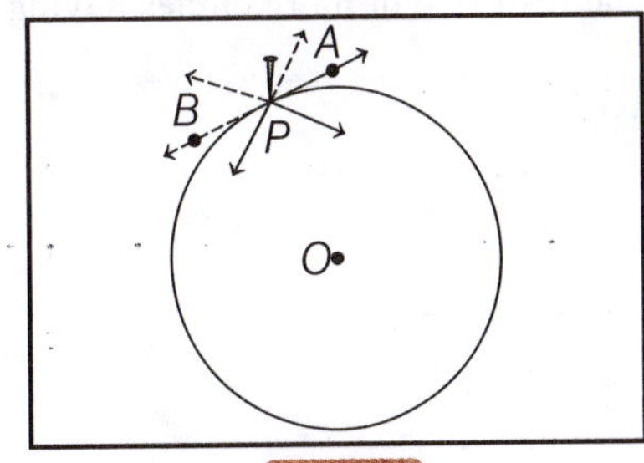

Figure 5.4

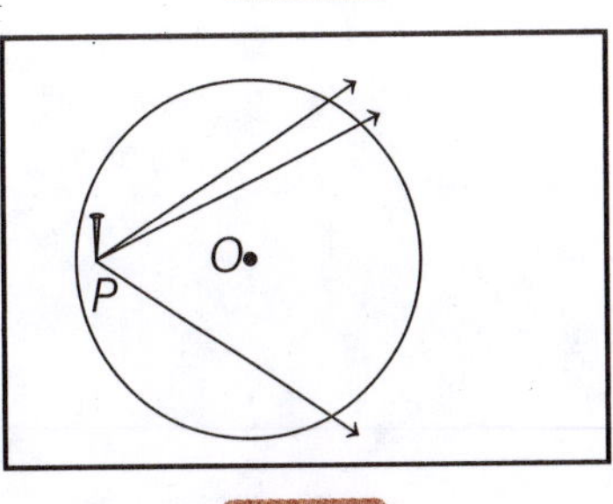

Figure 5.5

Demonstration

1. If the point P lies outside the circle, then there are two tangents AP and BP. (see Fig. 5.3)
2. If the point P is on the circle, then there is only one tangent at P. (see Fig. 5.4)
3. If the point P lies inside the circle, then in this case there is no tangent to the circle. (see Fig. 5.5)

Observations

1. In Fig. 5.3, the number of tangents through P = ...
2. In Fig. 5.4, the number of tangents through P = ...
3. In Fig. 5.5, the number of tangents through P = ...

Result

Number of tangents from a point to a circle has been found.

Application

This activity is useful in verifying the property that the lengths of the two tangents drawn from an external point are equal.

VIVA-VOCE

1 How many tangents can be drawn from a point present on the circle?

Ans One

2 Are the tangents drawn at the ends of a diameter of a circle are parallel?

Ans Yes

3 How many circles can be drawn from three non-collinear points?

Ans Only one circle can be drawn.

4 How many circles can you draw from a given point?

Ans Infinitely many circles can be drawn from a given point.

5 What is the name of two or more circles having the same centre?

Ans Concentric circles

6 Can you draw a tangent to a circle passing through a point lying inside the circle?

Ans No

7 What is the angle between tangent and radius joining the centre to point P, if P lies on the circle?

Ans 90°

8 How many tangents can be drawn from an external point to a circle?

Ans Only two tangents can be drawn from an external point to a circle.

9 We can draw a tangent from a point lying inside the circle (True/False).

Ans False

ACTIVITY 6

To draw a quadrilateral similar to a given quadrilateral as per given scale factor (less than 1).

Prior Knowledge

1. Concept of similarity of figure.
2. Concept of quadrilateral.
3. Concept of similarity of polygons.

Materials Required

1. Coloured chart paper
2. Geometry box
3. Scissors
4. Sketch pen
5. Adhesive

Theory

1. Quadrilaterals is closed figure having four sides.
2. Two polygons having the same number of sides are similar, if
   (i) their corresponding angles are equal.
   (ii) their corresponding sides are in the same ratio.

Procedure

1. From a coloured chart paper, take a cut out of the given quadrilateral *PQRS* and paste it on another chart paper. (see Fig. 6.1)
2. Divide the base (here *PQ*) of the quadrilateral *PQRS* internally in the ratio (given by scale factor) at *A*. (see Fig. 6.2)
3. Join the diagonal *PR* of the quadrilateral *PQRS* with the help of ruler.

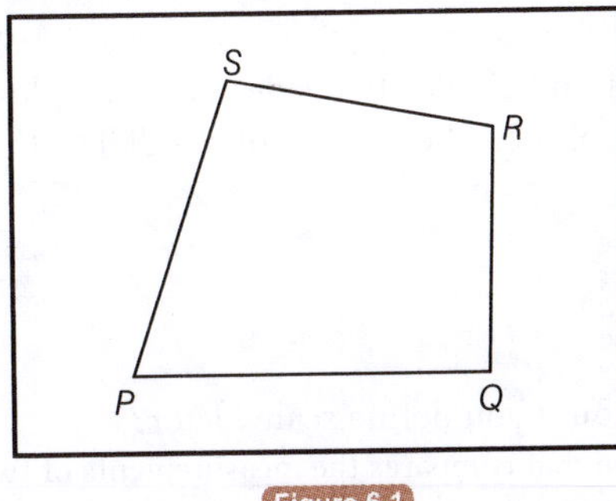

Figure 6.1

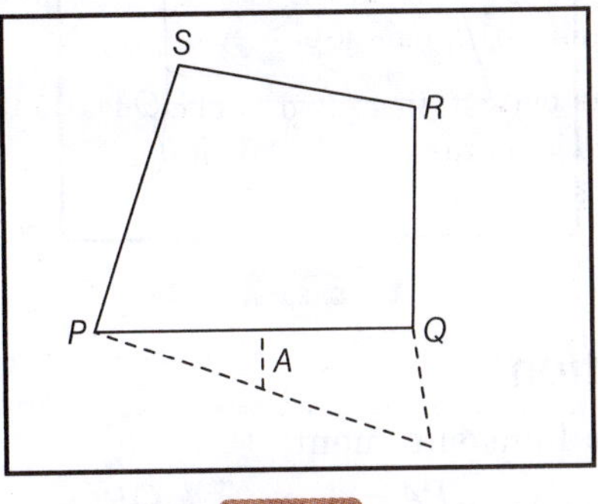

Figure 6.2

4. Draw a line segment *AC* parallel to *QR* with the help of compasses (set squares or paper folding), meeting *PR* at *B*. (see Fig. 6.3)
5. Draw a line segment *BD* parallel to *SR* from *B*, using pair of compasses (set squares/paper folding), meeting *PS* at *D*. (see Fig. 6.4)

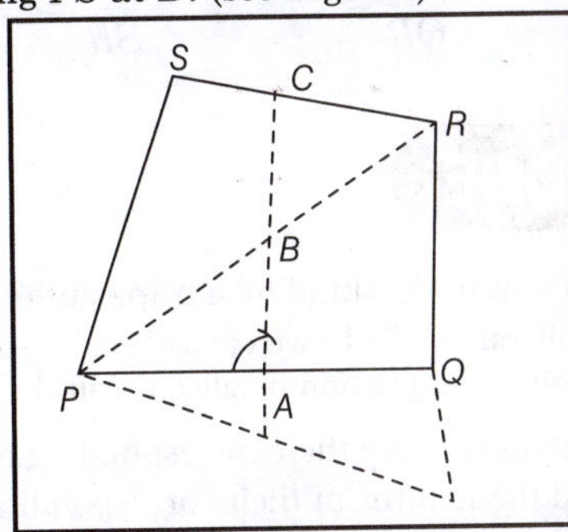

Figure 6.3

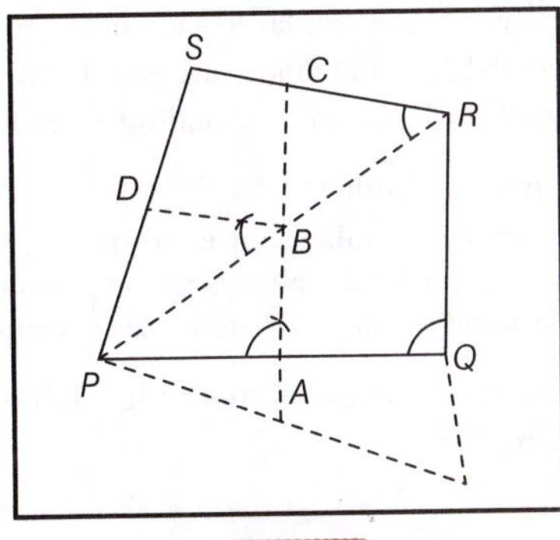

Figure 6.4

6. Colour the quadrilateral *PABD* by using sketch pen. *PABD* is the required quadrilateral, similar to the given quadrilateral *PQRS* for given scale factor. (see Fig. 6.5)

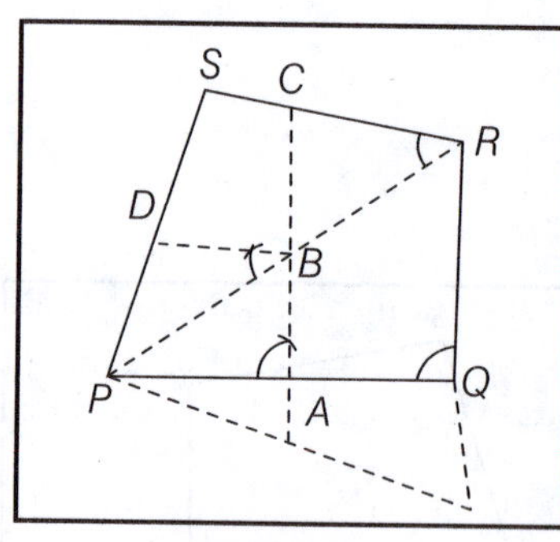

Figure 6.5

Observation

By actual measurement,

$PQ = \dots\dots\dots,\quad PA = \dots\dots\dots,\quad QR = \dots\dots\dots,$

$AB = \dots\dots\dots,\quad RS = \dots\dots\dots,\quad BD = \dots\dots\dots,$

$PS = \dots\dots\dots,\quad PD = \dots\dots\dots,\quad \angle P = \dots\dots\dots,$

$\angle Q = \dots\dots\dots,\quad \angle R = \dots\dots\dots,\quad \angle S = \dots\dots\dots,$

$\angle A = \dots\dots\dots,\quad \angle B = \dots\dots\dots,\quad \angle D = \dots\dots\dots,$

$\frac{PA}{PQ} = \dots\dots\dots,\quad \frac{AB}{QR} = \dots\dots\dots,\quad \frac{BD}{SR} = \dots\dots\dots,$

$\frac{PD}{PS} = \dots\dots\dots,\quad \angle P = \angle \dots\dots\dots,\ \angle A = \angle \dots\dots\dots,$

$\angle B = \angle \dots\dots\dots,\ \angle D = \angle \dots\dots\dots .$

Hence, quadrilaterals $PABD$ and $PQRS$ are ....

1. In ΔPQR, we get $AB \parallel QR$. Therefore, $\Delta PAB \sim \Delta PQR$.
2. In ΔPRS, we get $BD \parallel RS$. Therefore, $\Delta PBD \sim \Delta PRS$.
3. From the above conclusions, (adding the above cases, $\Delta PAB + \Delta PBD$ gives quadrilateral $PABD$ and $\Delta PQR + \Delta PRS$ gives quadrilateral $PQRS$) we see that quadrilateral $PABD \sim$ quadrilateral $PQRS$.

Result

We have drawn a quadrilateral similar to a given quadrilateral as per given scale factor (less than 1).

Application

In day-to-day life, we can use this activity in making pictures (photographs) of same object in different sizes.

VIVA-VOCE

1 What do you understand by a trapezium?

Ans A quadrilateral in which two opposite sides are parallel and two opposite sides are non-parallel, is called a trapezium.

2 If two polygons have their corresponding angles are equal and the lengths of their corresponding sides are not proportional. Does these polygons are similar? Give reason.

Ans No, two polygons are similar to each other, when
(i) their corresponding angles are equal and
(ii) the lengths of their corresponding sides are proportional.

3 Are all squares similar? Why?

Ans Yes, all squares are similar. Since, in squares, their corresponding angles are always 90° and also the lengths of their corresponding sides are in the same proportion.

4 Do diagonals of a trapezium divide each other proportionally?

Ans Yes

5 Any line parallel to the parallel sides of a trapezium divides the non-parallel sides proportionally. Is this statement true?

Ans Yes, this is a true statement.

6 The line joining the mid-points of two sides of a triangle is perpendicular to the third side. Is this statement correct? If not, correct it.

Ans No, the statement is not correct. The line joining the mid-points of two sides of a triangle is parallel to the third side.

7 Identify the statement as True or False.

(i) All congruent figures are similar but the converse is not true.

(ii) Two figures having the same shape but not necessarily the same size, are called congruent figures.

(iii) If a line is drawn parallel to one side of a triangle to intersect the other two sides in distinct points, then the other two sides are divided in the same ratio.

(iv) If a line divides two sides of a triangle in the same ratio, then the line is not parallel to the third side.

Ans (i) True
(ii) False
(iii) True
(iv) False

8 How would you define scale factor?

Ans The ratio that compares the measurements of two similar shapes is called scale factor.

ACTIVITY 7

To determine experimental probability of 1, 2, 3, 4, 5 or 6 by throwing a die 500 times and compare them with their theoretical probabilities.

Prior Knowledge

1. Outcomes of an experiment.
2. Favourable outcome.
3. Concept of probability.
4. Knowledge of a die.

Materials Required

1. A fair die
2. Pen
3. Sheets of white paper

Theory

1. An operation which can produce some well-defined outcomes is called an experiment. e.g. Tossing a coin is an experiment and in this experiment, we get either head or tail as a result, so head and tail are called **outcomes**.
2. The outcomes which ensure the occurrence of an event are called **favourable outcomes** to the event.
3. **Probability** If there are 'n' outcomes associated with a random experiment and m of them are favourable to an event E, then the probability of happening or occurrence of event E is denoted by $P(E)$ and is defined as the ratio $\frac{m}{n}$.

   Thus, probability of an event $E = P(E)$

   $$= \frac{\text{Number of outcomes favourable to event E}}{\text{Total number of outcomes}}$$

   $$\Rightarrow \quad P(E) = \frac{m}{n}$$

   Clearly $\quad 0 \le m \le n$

   $$\therefore 0 \le \frac{m}{n} \le 1 \Rightarrow 0 \le P(E) \le 1$$

4. A die is a small cube having its six faces marked with dots (1 to 6).

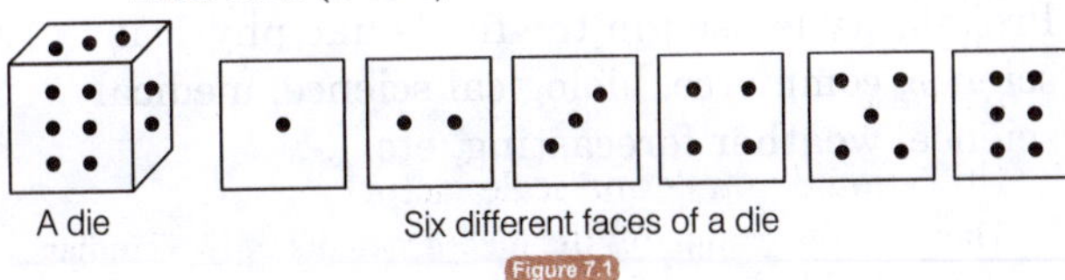

Figure 7.1

On throwing a die, any number from 1 to 6 can come, so total number of outcomes is 6.

On throwing die, the chance of coming of any number from 1 to 6 is 1, so favourable outcome for any number from 1 to 6 will be 1.

$\therefore$ Probability of getting any number (from 1 to 6) on throwing a die

$$= \frac{\text{Number of favourable outcomes}}{\text{Total number of outcomes}} = \frac{1}{6}$$

Procedure

1. Divide the students of the class into ten groups I, II, III, IV, V, VI, VII,VIII, IX and X of suitable size.
2. Each group of students will throw a die 50 times and will observe the occurrence of each 1, 2, 3, 4, 5 and 6.
3. Count the total number of times (frequency) 1 comes up in each group and denote it by $a_1, a_2, a_3, \ldots, a_{10}$, respectively.
4. Calculate the experimental probability of 1 appearing each group as $\frac{a_1}{50}, \frac{a_2}{50}, \frac{a_3}{50}, \ldots, \frac{a_{10}}{50}$.
5. Calculate the experimental probability of 1 based on the data of 1st group, 1st two groups, ..., all the ten groups as

   $$\frac{a_1}{50}, \frac{a_1 + a_2}{100}, \frac{a_1 + a_2 + a_3}{150}, \ldots, \frac{a_1 + a_2 + \ldots + a_{10}}{500},$$

   respectively.
6. Similarly, calculate the experimental probability of 2 based on the data of 1st group, 1st two groups, ..., all the ten groups as

   $$\frac{b_1}{50}, \frac{b_1 + b_2}{100}, \frac{b_1 + b_1 + b_3}{150}, \ldots, \frac{b_1 + b_2 + \ldots + b_{10}}{500},$$

   respectively.
7. Proceed in the same way for getting experimental probabilities for 3, 4, 5 and 6.

Demonstration

1. The probability $\frac{a_1}{50}, \frac{a_1 + a_2}{100}, \frac{a_1 + a_2 + a_3}{150}, \ldots, \frac{a_1 + a_2 + \ldots + a_{10}}{500}$, are coming closer to $\frac{1}{6}$ and the last probability $\frac{a_1 + a_2 + \ldots + a_{10}}{500}$ is closest to $\frac{1}{6}$.

   Same will be the case for $\frac{b_1}{50}, \frac{b_1 + b_2}{100}, \frac{b_1 + b_2 + b_3}{150}, \ldots, \frac{b_1 + b_2 + \ldots + b_{10}}{500}$ and so on.

2. The theoretical probability $P(E)$ of an event E(say 1) = $P(1)$

$$\therefore \quad P(1) = \frac{\text{Number of outcomes favourable to } E}{\text{Number of all possible outcomes of the experiment}} = \frac{1}{6}$$

From steps (1) and (2), it can be seen that the experimental probability of each number 1, 2, 3, 4, 5 and 6 is very close to the theoretical probability $\frac{1}{6}$.

Group number	Number of times a die is thrown in a group	Total number of times a number comes up					
		1	2	3	4	5	6
I	50	$a_1 =$	$b_1 =$	$c_1 =$	$d_1 =$	$e_1 =$	$f_1 =$
II	50	$a_2 =$	$b_2 =$	-----	-----	-----	-----
III	50	-----	-----	-----	-----	-----	-----
—	—	-----	-----	-----	-----	-----	-----
—	—	-----	-----	-----	-----	-----	-----
—	—	-----	-----	-----	-----	-----	-----
—	—	-----	-----	-----	-----	-----	-----
—	—	-----	-----	-----	-----	-----	-----
—	—	-----	-----	-----	-----	-----	-----
X	50	-----	-----	-----	-----	-----	-----
	Total = 500	-----	-----	-----	-----	-----	-----

Observations

1. Each group will complete the following table

$\frac{a_1}{50} = \ldots\ldots$, $\frac{a_1 + a_2}{100} = \frac{\sum_{i=1}^{2} a_i}{100} = \ldots\ldots$, $\frac{\sum_{i=1}^{3} a_i}{150} = \ldots\ldots$,

$\frac{\sum_{i=1}^{4} a_i}{200} = \ldots\ldots$, $\frac{\sum_{i=1}^{5} a_i}{250} = \ldots\ldots$, $\frac{\sum_{i=1}^{6} a_i}{300} = \ldots\ldots$,

$\frac{\sum_{i=1}^{7} a_i}{350} = \ldots\ldots$, $\frac{\sum_{i=1}^{8} a_i}{400} = \ldots\ldots$, $\frac{\sum_{i=1}^{9} a_i}{450} = \ldots\ldots$,

$\frac{\sum_{i=1}^{10} a_i}{500} = \ldots\ldots$.

and same for b_i's, c_i's, ..., f_i's

2. Experimental probability of 1 = $\frac{\cdots\cdot}{500}$

Experimental probability of 2 = $\frac{\cdots\cdot}{500}$

....

....

Experimental probability of 6 = $\frac{\cdots\cdot}{500}$

Experimental probability of 1 is nearly equal to theoretical ... .

Experimental probability of 2 is ...... to theoretical ....

Experimental probability of 6 is ...... to ...... probability.

Result

We have determined experimental probability of 1, 2, 3, 4, 5 and 6 by throwing a die 50 times and compared them with their theoretical probability, therefore the experimental probability of each number 1, 2, 3, 4, 5 and 6 is very closed to the theoretical probability $\frac{1}{6}$.

Application

Probability is used in the fields like physical science, commerce, biological science, medical science, weather forecasting, etc.

VIVA-VOCE

1 What are favourable outcome(s) of an event?

Ans The outcome(s) which ensure(s) the occurrence of an event are called favourable outcome(s) to that event.

2 How would you define the experimental or empirical probability of an event E?

Ans The experimental or empirical probability of an event E is

$$P(E) = \frac{\text{Number of trials in which the event occurred}}{\text{Total number of trials}}$$

3 How would you define the theoretical probability (or classical probability) of an event E?

Ans The theoretical probability (or classical probability) of an event E is

$$P(E) = \frac{\text{Number of outcomes favourable to } E}{\text{Total number of possible outcomes of the experiment}}$$

4 What do you mean by 'NEGATION' of an event?

Ans An event 'not A' occurs if and only if A does not occur. The event 'not A' is called negation of event A and is denoted by $\overline{A}$.

5 What is the probability of a sure event?

Ans The probability of sure event is 1.

6 What is the probability of an impossible event?

Ans The probability of an impossible event is 0.

7 What is the relationship between the probability of an event A and the probability of negation of A?

Ans $P(A) + P(\overline{A}) = 1$

8 If the probability of occurrence of an event is 0.4, then what is the probability that it does not occurs?

Ans $1 - 0.4 = 0.6$

Sample Question Paper 1 (Unsolved)

Mathematics (Basic Level)

Time : 3 hrs | M.M. : 80

General Instructions

1 This question paper has 5 Sections A, B, C, D and E.
2 Section A has 20 Multiple Choice Questions (MCQs) carrying 1 mark each.
3 Section B has 5 Short Answer-I (SA-I) type questions carrying 2 marks each.
4 Section C has 6 Short Answer-II (SA-II) type questions carrying 3 marks each.
5 Section D has 4 Long Answer (LA) type questions carrying 5 marks each.
6 Section E has 3 Case Based integrated units of assessment (4 marks each) with sub-parts of the values of 1, 1 and 2 marks each respectively.
7 All questions are compulsory. However, an internal choice in 2 Qs of 2 marks, 2 Qs of 3 marks and 2 Qs of 5 marks has been provided. An internal choice has been provided in the 2 marks question of Section E.
8 Draw neat figures wherever required. Take $\pi = \frac{22}{7}$ wherever required if not stated.

Section A

Section A consists of 20 MCQs Questions of 1 mark each

1. **The graph of a polynomial $p(x)$ is shown below. The number of zeroes of $p(x)$ is**

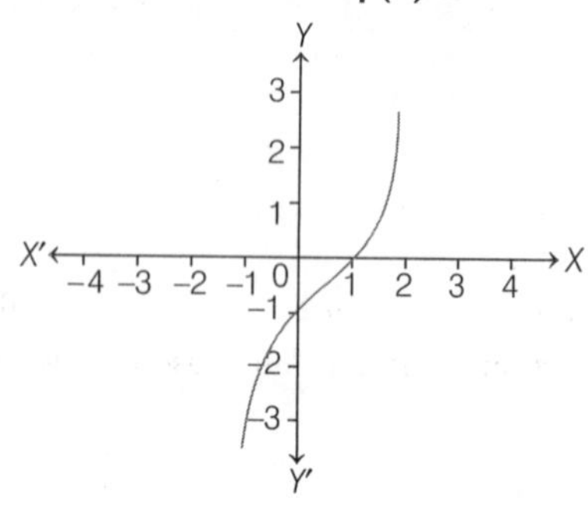

(a) 1 (b) 2
(c) 4 (d) None of these

2. **$7+5\sqrt{8}$ is**

(a) Rational (b) Irrational
(c) can't say (d) None of these

3. **If two tangents inclined at an angle of 60° are drawn to a circle of radius 6 cm, then the length of each tangent is**

(a) $6\sqrt{3}$ cm (b) $3\sqrt{6}$ cm (c) 6 cm (d) 3 cm

4. **If mean $=80$ and median $=110$, then the value of mode is**

(a) 110 (b) 170 (c) 190 (d) 80

5. **The value of $2\sin^2 30° - 3\cos^2 45° + \tan^2 60°$ is**

(a) 0 (b) 2 (c) 1 (d) −1

6. **The positive value of P for which the equations $x^2 + 2Px + 64 = 0$ and $x^2 - 8x + 2P = 0$ will both have real roots**

(a) 10 (b) 9 (c) 8 (d) 11

7. **The mid-point of the line segment joining the points (−7, 9) and (−3, 5) is**

(a) (7, 5) (b) (5, 7)
(c) (7, −5) (d) (−5, 7)

8. **A tangent PQ at a point P of a circle of radius 6 cm meets a line through the centre O at a point Q such that $PQ = 8$ cm, then the length of OQ is**

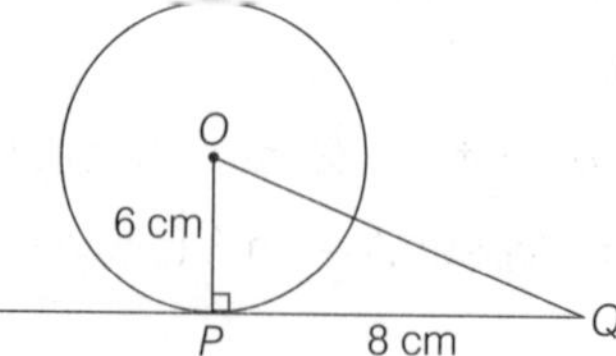

(a) 8 cm (b) 9 cm (c) 6 cm (d) 10 cm

9. **A die is thrown twice, then the probability that 5 will come up atleast once is**

(a) $\frac{11}{36}$ (b) $\frac{5}{36}$ (c) $\frac{1}{6}$ (d) 1

10. Two coins are tossed simultaneously, then probability of getting exactly one head, is

(a) $\frac{1}{3}$ (b) $\frac{2}{6}$ (c) $\frac{1}{2}$ (d) $\frac{1}{8}$

11. The ratio of the length of a rod and its shadow is $1:\sqrt{3}$. Then, the angle of elevation of the Sun is

(a) 0° (b) 60° (c) 30° (d) 90°

12. If 2 is a zero of polynomial

$p(x) = 4x^2 + 2x - 5a$, then the value of a is

(a) 1 (b) 4 (c) −1 (d) 0

13. For what value of k, the equation $kx^2 - 6x - 2 = 0$ has real roots?

(a) $k \le \frac{-9}{2}$ (b) $k \ge \frac{-9}{2}$

(c) $k \le -2$ (d) None of these

14. The point which divide the line segment joining the points $A(0, 4)$ and $B(4, 0)$ internally in the ratio $1:3$ is

(a) (1, 3) (b) (3, 1) (c) (−1, 3) (d) (3, − 1)

15. The distance of the point (20, 15) from the origin is

(a) 15 units (b) 30 units

(d) 25 units (d) 20 units

16. If the lines given by $2x + ky = 1$ and $3x - 5y = 7$ has unique solution, then the value of k is

(a) $-\frac{10}{3}$ (b) $\frac{10}{3}$

(c) Except $-\frac{10}{3}$ (d) None of these

17. The 105th term of the AP $4, 4\frac{1}{2}, 5, 5\frac{1}{2}, 6, \ldots\ldots$ is

(a) 53 (b) 54 (c) 55 (d) 56

18. The prime factorisation of 1350 is

(a) $2 \times 3^3 \times 5^2$ (b) $3^2 \times 5^2$

(c) $2 \times 3^3 \times 5^3$ (d) $2^2 \times 3^2$

Directions (Q.Nos. 19-20) *In question numbers 19 and 20, a statement of Assertion (A) is followed by a statement of Reason (R). Choose the correct option.*

19. **Assertion** (A) The area of a sector of circle of radius 21 cm and central angle 90° is 354 cm^2.

Reason (R) The area of sector of circle is $\frac{\theta}{360°} \times \pi r^2$.

(a) Both Assertion (A) and Reason (R) are true and Reason (R) is the correct explanation of Assertion (A).

(b) Both Assertion (A) and Reason (R) are true but Reason (R) is not the correct explanation of Assertion (A).

(c) Assertion (A) is true but Reason (R) is false.

(d) Assertion (A) is false but Reason (R) is true.

20. **Assertion** (A) If the HCF of 45 and 55 is 5, LCM of 45 and 55 is $99 \times a$, then the value of a is 5.

Reason (R) For any two positive integers a and b. HCF $(a, b) \times$ LCM $(a, b) = a \times b$

(a) Both Assertion (A) and Reason (R) are true and Reason (R) is the correct explanation of Assertion (A).

(b) Both Assertion (A) and Reason (R) are true but Reason (R) is not the correct explanation of Assertion (A).

(c) Assertion (A) is true but Reason (R) is false.

(d) Assertion (A) is false but Reason (R) is true.

Section B

Q. Nos. 21 to 25 are Very Short Answer Type Questions of 2 marks each

21. Prove that

$$\tan^2\theta + \cot^2\theta + 2 = \sec^2\theta \operatorname{cosec}^2\theta.$$

22. Prove that $(\operatorname{cosec} A - \sin A)(\sec A - \cos A) = \sin A \cos A.$

Or

If the area of a semi-circular field is 30800 m^2, then find the perimeter of the field.

23. If the median of the distribution given below is 30, find the values of x and y.

Class interval	0-10	10-20	20-30	30-40	40-50	50-60	**Total**
Number of Students	5	x	20	15	y	5	60

24. A jar contains 24 marbles, some are green and other are blue. If a marble is drawn at random from the jar, the probability that it is green is $\frac{2}{3}$. Find the number of blue marbles in the jar.

Or A box contains 150 apples. If one apple is taken out from the box at random and the probability of its being rotten is 0.06, then find the number of good apples in the box.

25. Find the radius of a circle, if the length of tangent from a point at distance of 13 cm from the centre of the circle is 12 cm.

SECTION C

Q. Nos. 26 to 31 are Short Answer Type Questions of 3 marks each

26. Prove that the line segment joining the points of contact of two parallel tangents of a circle passes through its centre.

27. Find the value of k for which the given system of equations has infinitely many solutions :

$$kx + 3y = k - 3, 12x + ky = k$$

Or

Solve the following pair of equations by substitution method :

$$7x - 15y = 2, x + 2y = 3$$

28. Find the largest positive integer that will divide 444, 486 and 604 leaving remainders 7, 11 and 15 respectively.

29. Find the sum of series

$$7 + 10\frac{1}{2} + 14 + ... + 84.$$

30. A juice seller was serving his customers using glasses as shown in the given figure.

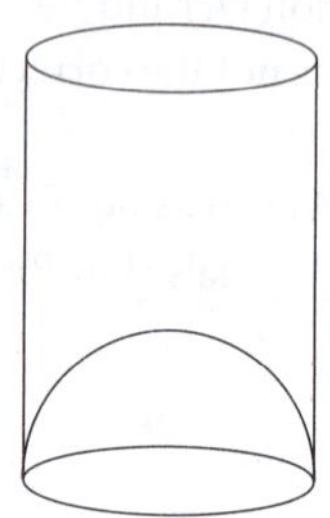

The inner diameter of the cylindrical glass was 5 cm, but the bottom of the glass had a hemispherical portion raised which reduces the capacity of the glass. If the height of a glass was 10 cm. Two friends Love and Vicky went to a juice shop for drink papaya shake.

Juice seller serves juice in the glass which is stated above. After drinking the juice Vicky said that the actual capacity of glass is 163.5 cm^3. Is he right? Explain.

31. PA is tangent to the circle with centre O. If $BC = 6 \text{ cm}$, $AC = 8 \text{ cm}$ and $\Delta ACB \sim \Delta PAO$, then find OA and $\frac{OP}{AP}$.

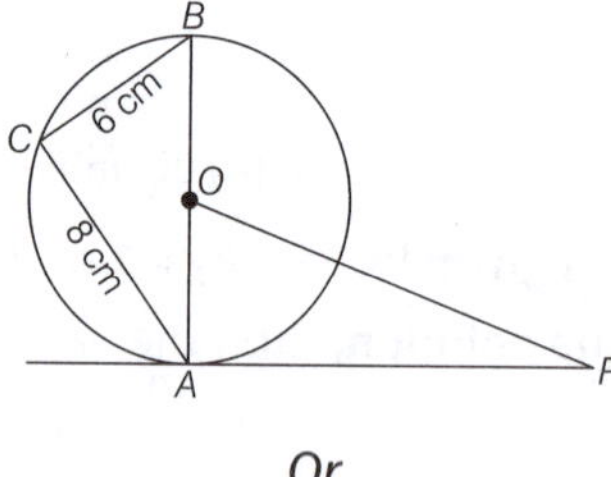

Or

In the given figure, if $\angle ACB = 25°$, then find $\angle ATO$.

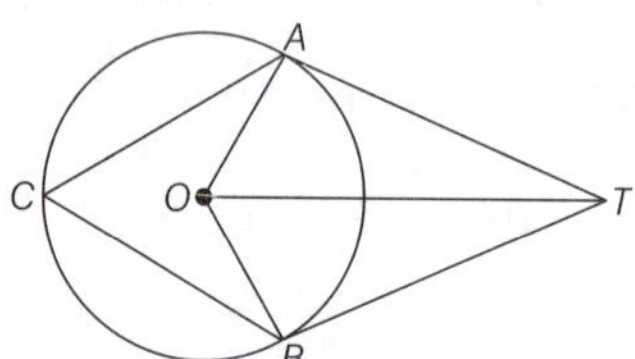

SECTION D

Q. Nos. 32 to 35 are Long Answer Type Questions of 5 marks each

32. ABC is an isosceles triangle with $AB = AC$ and D is a point on AC such that $BC^2 = AC \times DC$.

Prove that $BD = BC$.

33. In a single throw of two die, find the probability of getting

(i) a doublet.

(ii) a number less than 3 on each die.

(iii) an odd number as a sum.

(iv) an odd number on one die and a number less than or equal to 4 on other die.

Or

From a pack of 52 playing cards jacks, queens, kings and aces of red colour are removed. From the remaining, a card is drawn at random.

Find the probability that the card drawn is

(i) a black queen

(ii) a red card

(iii) a ten

(iv) a face card (jacks, queens and kings are face cards)

34. An aeroplane at an altitude of 1500 m find that two ships are sailing towards it in the same direction. The angles of depression as observed from the aeroplane are 45° and 30°, respectively. Find the distance between the two ships.

35. The median of the following data is 525. Find the values of x and y.

Class interval	Frequency
0-100	2
100-200	5
200-300	x
300-400	12
400-500	17
500-600	20
600-700	y
700-800	9
800-900	7
900-1000	4
Total	100

Or

Find the mean, median and mode of the following data.

Class interval	Frequency
0-50	2
50-100	3
100-150	5
150-200	6
200-250	5
250-300	3
300-350	1

SECTION E

Q. Nos. 36 to 38 are Case Study Based Questions of 4 marks each

36. A girl of Class X draw the graph of some polynomial as $y = p(x)$ in her notebook.

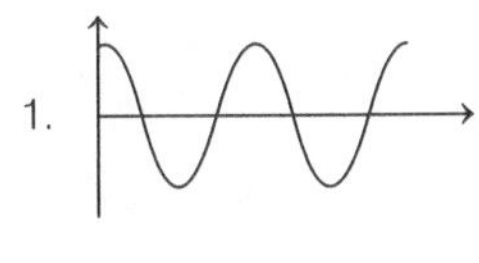
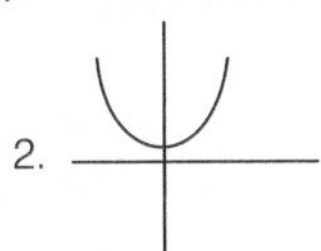
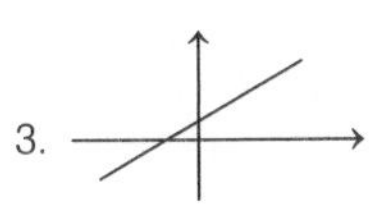
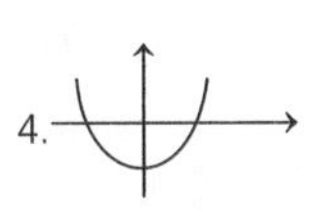
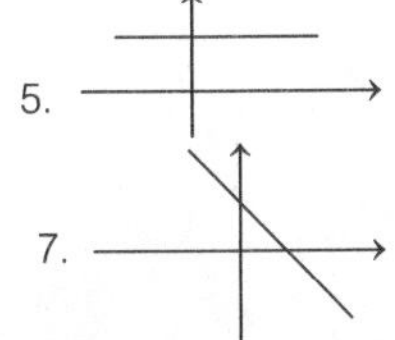
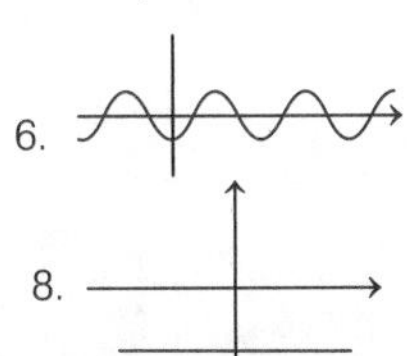

Answer the following questions which are based on graph of polynomial as shown in above figure.

(i) How many polynomials have exactly four zeroes?

(ii) How many polynomials have exactly 1 zero?

(iii) How many polynomials have exactly two zeroes and write an example of a polynomial that have exactly two zeroes?

Or How many polynomials have no zeroes and write an example of a polynomial that have no zeroes?

37. Vishal gets pocket money from his parents everyday. Out of the pocket money, he saves ₹0.50 on first day ₹1.00 on second day ₹1.50 on third day and so on.

Based on the above information, answer the following questions.

(i) What is the total amount saved by Vishal in 10 days?

(ii) What is the total amount saved by Vishal in the month of June if he starts saving from 1st June?

(iii) What is the amount saved by Vishal on 15th day?

Or What is the amount saved by Vishal till 15th day?

38. To conduct sports day activities in your rectangular shaped school ground *ABCD*, lines have been drawn with chalk powder at a distance of 1 m each, 100 flower pots have been placed at a distance of 1 m from each other along *AD*, as shown in figure.

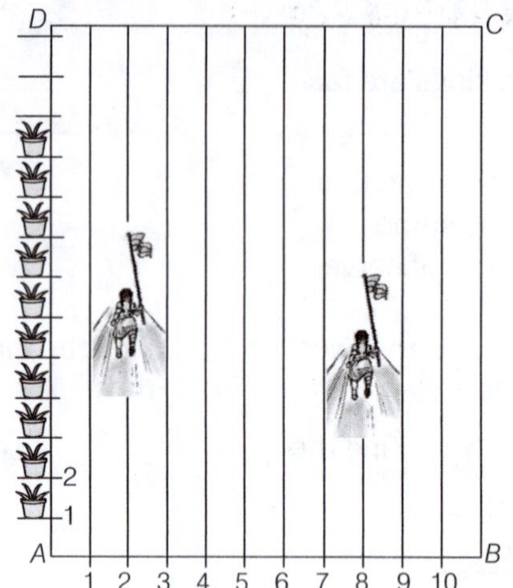

Niharika runs $\frac{1}{4}$th the distance *AD* on the 2nd line and posts a green flag. Preet runs $\frac{1}{5}$th the distance *AD* on the 8th line and posts a red flag.

Answer the following questions which are based on above figure.

(i) Write the coordinates of green flag.

(ii) Write the coordinates of red flag.

(iii) Find the distance between both the flags.

Or If Rashmi has to post a blue flag exactly half way between the line segment joining the flags, then find the coordinates of that point.

Answer Key

1. (a)	**2.** (b)	**3.** (a)	**4.** (b)	**5.** (b)
6. (c)	**7.** (d)	**8.** (d)	**9.** (a)	**10.** (c)
11. (c)	**12.** (b)	**13.** (b)	**14.** (a)	**15.** (c)
16. (c)	**17.** (d)	**18.** (a)	**19.** (d)	**20.** (a)
22. *Or* 720 m	**23.** 5, 10	**24.** 8 *Or* 141	**25.** 5 cm	

27. $k = 6$ or $x = \frac{49}{29}, y = \frac{19}{29}$ **28.** 19 **29.** $1046\frac{1}{2}$

30. Yes **31.** $OA = 5$ cm, $\frac{5}{4}$ *Or* 65°

33. (i) $\frac{1}{6}$ (ii) $\frac{1}{9}$ (iii) $\frac{1}{2}$ (iv) $\frac{5}{9}$ *Or* (i) $\frac{1}{22}$ (ii) $\frac{9}{22}$ (iii) $\frac{1}{11}$ (iv) $\frac{3}{22}$

34. $1500(\sqrt{3}-1)$ m

35. $x = 9, y = 15$ *Or* Mean = 169, Median = 170.83, Mode = 175

36. (i) 1 (ii) 2 (iii) 1 e.g. $f(x) = x^2 - 4$ *Or* 3 e.g. $f(x) = x^2 + 4$

37. (i) ₹ 27.50 (ii) ₹ 232.50 (iii) 7.5 or 60

38. (i) (2, 25) (ii) (8, 20) (iii) $\sqrt{61}$ m *Or* (5, 22.5)

Sample Question Paper 2 (Unsolved)

Mathematics (Basic Level)

Time : 3 hrs	M.M. : 80

General Instructions

See Sample Question Paper 1

Section A

Section A consists of 20 MCQs Questions of 1 mark each

1. If the mean of first n natural number is $\frac{5n}{9}$, then n is equal to

(a) 5 (b) 4 (c) 9 (d) 10

2. In the given circle with centre O, $\angle BAC = 30°$. Find $\angle ACB$.

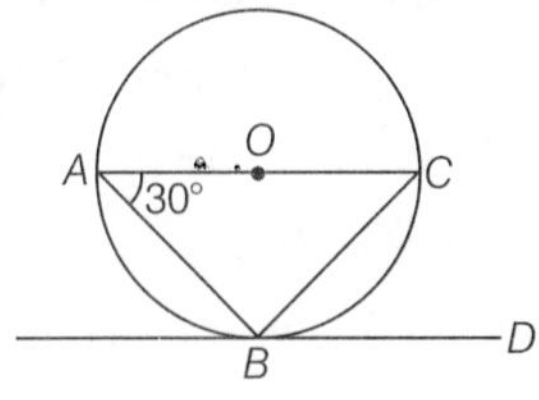

(a) 30° (b) 90° (c) 45° (d) 60°

3. If the product of zeroes of the polynomial $f(x) = ax^3 - 6x^2 + 11x - 6$ is 4, then the value of a is

(a) -11 (b) $\frac{1}{6}$ (c) $\frac{3}{2}$ (d) $\frac{11}{4}$

4. If $0° < \theta < 90°$, then the value of θ that satisfies $\tan 5\theta = 1$ is

(a) 9° (b) 10° (c) 45° (d) 13°

5. In a throw of a die, the probability of getting a prime number is

(a) $\frac{2}{6}$ (b) $\frac{1}{3}$ (c) $\frac{1}{2}$ (d) $\frac{1}{6}$

6. The longest diameter of a cone, which can be fully fitted in a cube edge 8 cm is

(a) 16 cm (b) $8\sqrt{2}$ cm (c) 8 cm (d) 4 cm

7. In the given figure, $\Delta ACB \sim \Delta APQ$. If $AB = 10$ cm, $BC = 15$ cm and $AQ = 8$ cm, then PQ is equal to

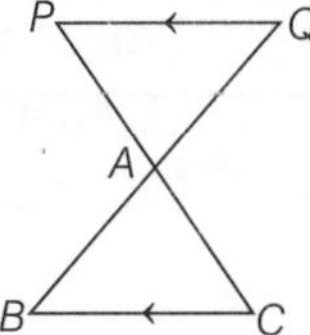

(a) 10 (b) 12

(c) 11 (d) 13

8. The 9th term of the AP whose nth term is given by $3n - 5$ is

(a) 22 (b) 24 (c) 20 (d) 23

9. The angle of elevation of the sun when the shadow of a 10 m long pole is $10\sqrt{3}$ m is

(a) 45° (b) 30° (c) 60° (d) 90°

10. The distance between the points $(b\sin\theta + a\cos\theta, 0)$ and $(0, -a\sin\theta + b\cos\theta)$ is

(a) $a^2 - b^2$ (b) $\sqrt{a^2 + b^2}$ (c) $\sqrt{a^2 - b^2}$ (d) $a^2 + b^2$

11. $\frac{1 - \tan^2 45°}{1 + \tan^2 45°}$ equals

(a) $\tan 90°$ (b) 1 (c) $\sin 45°$ (d) $\sin 0°$

12. The roots of the equation $2x^2 - 3x = 0$ are

(a) $0, -\frac{3}{2}$ (b) $0, \frac{3}{2}$ (c) $-1, \frac{3}{2}$ (d) None of these

13. The LCM of $(2 \times 3^2 \times 5)$ and $(2^2 \times 3 \times 5^3)$ is

(a) 900 (b) 1800 (c) 2500 (d) 4500

14. The median and mode of a frequency distribution are 32 and 38 respectively, then the mean is

(a) 38 (b) 29 (c) 34 (d) None of these

15. A box contain 4 blue, 3 white and 5 red marbles. If a marble is drawn at random from the box. The probability that it will not blue marble is

(a) 1 (b) $\frac{3}{2}$ (c) $\frac{2}{3}$ (d) 0

16. If quadratic equation curve touches the X-axis, then the value of discriminant is

(a) 1 (b) -1 (c) 2 (d) 0

17. The sum of areas of three sectors of radius 'r' formed at the vertices of a triangle is

(a) $2\pi r^2$ (b) πr^2 (c) $\frac{\pi r^2}{2}$ (d) None of these

18. The point of intersection of the lines represented by $4x - 8y = 24$ and the X-axis is

(a) (6, 0) (b) (0, 6) (c) (0, –3) (d) (0, 3)

Directions (Q.Nos. 19-20) *In question numbers 19 and 20, a statement of Assertion (A) is followed by a statement of Reason (R). Choose the correct option.*

19. **Assertion** (A) $\sqrt{a}$ is an irrational number, a is a prime number.

Reason (R) Square root of any prime number is an irrational number.

(a) Both Assertion (A) and Reason (R) are true and Reason (R) is the correct explanation of Assertion (A).
(b) Both Assertion (A) and Reason (R) are true but Reason (R) is not the correct explanation of Assertion (A).
(c) Assertion (A) is true but Reason (R) is false.
(d) Assertion (A) is false but Reason (R) is true.

20. **Assertion** (A) The value of y is 3, for which the distance between the point $P(2, -3)$ and $Q(10, y)$ is 10 units.

Reason (R) Distance between two given points $A(x_1, y_1)$ and $B(x_2, y_2)$ is given $AB = \sqrt{(x_2 - x_1)^2 + (y_2 - y_1)^2}$.

(a) Both Assertion (A) and Reason (R) are true and Reason (R) is the correct explanation of Assertion (A).
(b) Both Assertion (A) and Reason (R) are true but Reason (R) is not the correct explanation of Assertion (A).
(c) Assertion (A) is true but Reason (R) is false.
(d) Assertion (A) is false but Reason (R) is true.

Section B

Q. Nos. 21 to 25 are Very Short Answer Type Questions of 2 marks each

21. Show that $2(\cos^2 45° + \tan^2 60°)$
$$-6(\sin^2 45° - \tan^2 30°) = 6$$

Or

If $\sqrt{3}\sin\theta = \cos\theta$, then find the value of $\dfrac{3\cos^2\theta + 2\cos\theta}{3\cos\theta + 2}$

22. Find the type of triangle formed by the points $P(-5, 6)$, $Q(-4, -2)$ and $R(7, 5)$.

23. Sohan and Rohan are friends. They were both born in 1993. What is the probability that they have the same birthday.

24. A parallelogram has vertices $P(1, 4)$, $Q(7, 11)$, $R(a, 4)$ and $S(1, -3)$. Find the value of a.

25. Show that $\dfrac{2}{5\sqrt{3}}$ is an irrational number.

Or Show that $6 - 2\sqrt{3}$ is irrational.

SECTION C

Q. Nos. 26 to 31 are Short Answer Type Questions of 3 marks each

26. If the 3rd and 9th terms of an AP are 4 and – 8, respectively, then which term of this AP is zero?

27. Calculate the mode for the following frequency distribution

Class	0-10	10-20	20-30	30-40	40-50	50-60	60-70	70-80
Frequency	5	8	7	12	28	20	10	10

Or Solve the following quadratic by factorisation
$$\frac{1}{x+4} - \frac{1}{x-7} = \frac{11}{30},\ x \neq -4, 7$$

28. Find the largest positive integer that will divide 398, 436 and 542 leaving remainders 7, 11 and 15, respectively.

29. Find the value of
$$\frac{\sin 60° + \cot 45° - \operatorname{cosec} 30°}{\sec 60° - \cos 30° + \tan 45°} + \frac{2\cos^2 45°}{33\tan^2 45°}$$

Or

Prove that
$$\frac{(1 + \cot A + \tan A)(\sin A - \cos A)}{\sec^3 A - \operatorname{cosec}^3 A} = \sin^2 A \cdot \cos^2 A$$

30. The New Delhi Municipal Corporation decided to planting trees in between the vacant area of two buildings. If the angle of depression of the top and bottom of 8 m tall building from the top of a multistoried building are $30°$ and $45°$ respectively, then find the height of the multistoried building and the distance between the two buildings.
[given $\sqrt{3} = 1.73$]

31. There are 156, 208 and 260 students in groups A, B and C, respectively. Buses are to be hired to take them for a field trip. Find the minimum number of buses to be hired, if the same number of students should be accommodated in each bus.

SECTION D

Q. Nos. 32 to 35 are Long Answer Type Questions of 5 marks each

32. Calculate the median for the following data.

Class interval	130 -139	140 -149	150 -159	160 -169	170 -179	180 -189	190 -199
Frequency	4	9	18	28	24	10	7

33. A solid toy is in the form of a hemisphere surmounted by a right circular cone. The height of the cone is 4 cm and the diameter of the base is 8 cm. (use $\pi = \frac{22}{7}$)

(i) Determine the volume of the toy.

(ii) If a cube circumscribes the toy, then find the difference of the volumes of cube and the toy.

(iii) Also, find the total surface area of the toy.

Or

A petrol tank is in the form shape of a cylinder surmounted by a conical top. The cylindrical part of the tank has a height of 20 m and a diameter of 10 m and the slant height of the top is 13 m.
$\left[\text{use } \pi = \frac{22}{7}\right]$

(i) Find the cost of petrol which can fill the tank completely at the rate of ₹ 70 per litre.

(ii) Also, find the surface area of the tank.

34. In the given figure, O is the centre of a circle of radius 10 cm. T is a point such that $OT = 26$ cm and OT intersects the circle at E. If AB is the tangent to the circle at E, then find the length of AB.

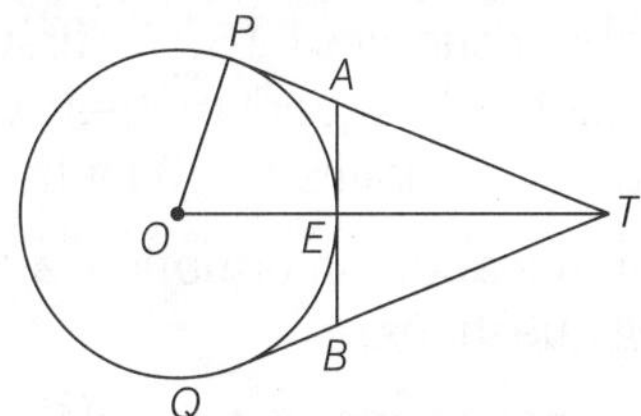

35. Find the length of the median drawn through A on BC of a ΔABC, whose vertices are $A(7, -3)$, $B(5, 3)$ and $C(3, -1)$ and also find the distance of the point $A(7, -3)$ from the origin.

Or Find the centre of a circle passing through the points $(6, -6)$, $(3, -7)$ and $(3, 3)$.

SECTION E

Q. Nos. 36 to 38 are Case Study Based Questions of 4 marks each

36. Mathematics teacher of Class X of a school organized on colouring activity to understand geometrical figure. He interested to make decorative block that shown in the following figure, which is made of two solids, a cube and a hemisphere.

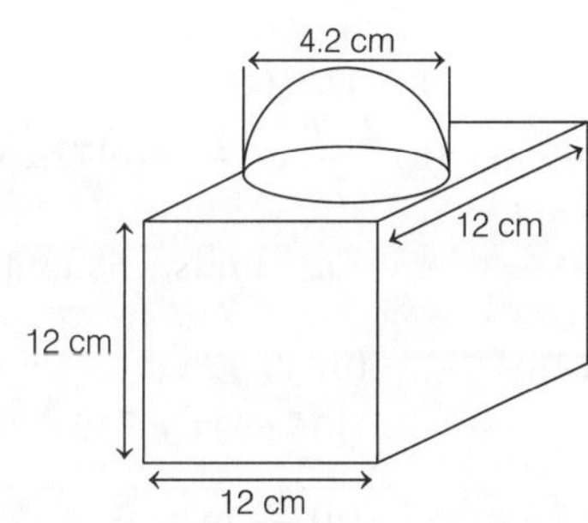

The base of the block is a cube with edge 12 cm and the hemisphere fixed on the top has a diameter of 4.2 cm. $\left[\text{take } \pi = \frac{22}{7}\right]$

Based on the above information, answer the following questions.

(i) Find the total surface area of the cube?

(ii) Find the curved surface area of hemisphere.

(iii) Find the total surface area of the block.

Or

Find the volume of the block.

37. India's literacy rate has increased six times since the end of the British rule in 1947. From 12% to 74% in recent times. Yet India has the world's largest population of illiterate people according to a report of oxfam.

Ram asks the labour to dig a well up to a depth of 10 m. Labour charges ₹ 150 for first metre and ₹ 50 for each subsequent metres. As labour was uneducated, he claims ₹ 550 for the whole work.

Based on the above information, answer the following questions.

(i) What type of series is formed from the given statement?

(ii) What should be the actual amount to be paid to the labour?

Or How much money Ram will save, if he agree with ₹ 550?

(iii) In AP sequence if each term is multiplied by constant k, then the new sequence will be AP or non AP.

38. A group of students of Class X visited India Gate on an education trip. The teacher and students had interest in History as well. The teacher narrated that India Gate, official name Delhi Memorial, originally called All-India War Memorial, monumental sandstone arch in New Delhi dedicated to the troops of British India who died in wars fought between 1914 and 1919. The teacher also said that India Gate, which is located at the eastern end of the Rajpath, is about 138 feet (42 m) in height.

(i) What is the angle of elevation if they are standing at a distance of 42 m away from the monument?

(ii) They want to see the tower at an angle of 60°. So, they want to know the distance where they should stand and hence find the distance?

(iii) If the altitude of the sun is at 60°, then find the height of vertical tower that have a shadow of length 20 m.

Or If the ratio of the length of a rod and its shadow is 1 : 1. What is the angle of elevation of the sun?

Answer Key

1. (c) **2.** (d) **3.** (c) **4.** (a) **5.** (c)
6. (c) **7.** (b) **8.** (a) **9.** (b) **10.** (b)
11. (d) **12.** (b) **13.** (d) **14.** (b) **15.** (c)
16. (d) **17.** (c) **18.** (a) **19.** (a) **20.** (a)
21. $\frac{\sqrt{3}}{2}$ **22.** Scalene triangle **23.** $\frac{1}{365}$ **24.** 7 **26.** 5th term
27. 46.67 *Or* $x = 1, 2$ **28.** 17 **29.** $\frac{4\sqrt{3}-8}{33}$ **30.** 18.92 m, 18.92 m
31. 12 **32.** 166.78
33. (i) $\frac{1408}{7}$ cm^3 (ii) $\frac{2176}{7}$ cm^2 (iii) 172.23 cm^2 *Or* (i) ₹ 132000 (ii) 911.43 m^2
34. $\frac{40}{3}$ cm **35.** 5 units, $\sqrt{58}$ units *Or* $(3, -2)$
36. (i) 864 cm^2 (ii) 27.72 cm^2 (iii) 877.86 cm^2 or 1747.4 cm^3
37. (i) AP (ii) ₹ 600 *Or* ₹ 50 (iii) AP
38. (i) 45° (ii) $\frac{42}{\sqrt{3}}$ m (iii) $20\sqrt{3}$ m *Or* 45°

Sample Question Paper 1 (Unsolved)
Mathematics (Standard Level)

Time : 3 hrs	M.M. : 80

General Instructions

1 This question paper has 5 Sections A, B, C, D and E.
2 Section A has 20 Multiple Choice Questions (MCQs) carrying 1 mark each.
3 Section B has 5 Short Answer-I (SA-I) type questions carrying 2 marks each.
4 Section C has 6 Short Answer-II (SA-II) type questions carrying 3 marks each.
5 Section D has 4 Long Answer (LA) type questions carrying 5 marks each.
6 Section E has 3 Case Based integrated units of assessment (4 marks each) with sub-parts of the values of 1, 1 and 2 marks each respectively.
7 All questions are compulsory. However, an internal choice in 2 Qs of 2 marks, 2 Qs of 3 marks and 2 Qs of 5 marks has been provided. An internal choice has been provided in the 2 marks question of Section E.
8 Draw neat figures wherever required. Take $\pi = 22/7$ wherever required if not stated.

Section A

Section A consists of 20 MCQs Questions of 1 mark each

1. The value of k for which the system of equations $x+3y-3=0$ and $4x+ky+7=0$ has no solution is

(a) 10 (b) 12 (c) 14 (d) 15

2. A box contains 90 discs which are numbered from 1 to 90. If one disc is drawn at random from the box, then find the probability that it bears a two-digits number.

(a) 0.9 (b) 0.8 (c) 1 (d) 2

3. $\sin 45^\circ \cos 60^\circ + \cos 45^\circ \sin 60^\circ$ is equal to

(a) $\frac{1+\sqrt{3}}{2\sqrt{2}}$ (b) $\frac{3+\sqrt{3}}{3\sqrt{3}}$

(c) $\frac{4+\sqrt{3}}{5\sqrt{3}}$ (d) $\frac{6+\sqrt{3}}{2\sqrt{3}}$

4. For grouped data, if $\Sigma f_i = 20$, $\Sigma f_i x_i = 2p + 20$ and mean of distribution is 12, then the value of p is

(a) 100 (b) 120

(c) 110 (d) 210

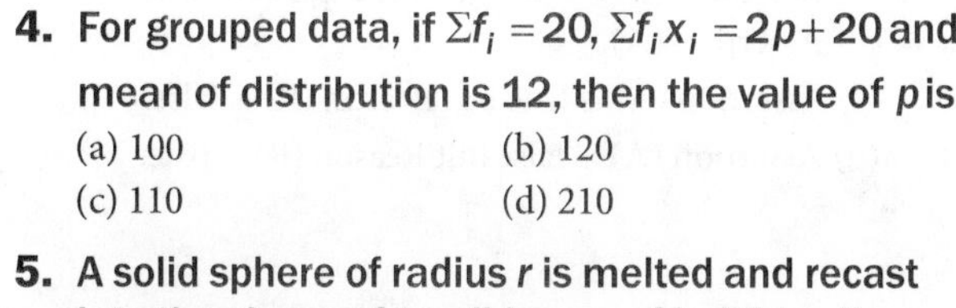

5. A solid sphere of radius r is melted and recast into the shape of a solid cone of height r, then the radius of the cone is

(a) $12r$ (b) $6r$

(c) $4r$ (d) $2r$

6. The value of k, for which one root of the quadratic equation $kx^2 - 14x + 8 = 0$ is six times the other, is

(a) 1 (b) −2 (c) 2 (d) 3

7. The area of a sector of circle of radius 21 cm and central angle 90°, is $\left[\text{take, } \pi = \frac{22}{7}\right]$

(a) 346.5 cm^2 (b) 352 cm^2

(c) 353 cm^2 (d) 216 cm^2

8. If $\tan^2 45^\circ - \cos^2 30^\circ = x \sin 30^\circ \cos 60^\circ$, then value of x is

(a) 4 (b) 3 (c) 1 (d) $\frac{2}{3}$

9. The graph of a polynomial $p(x)$ is shown below. The number of zeroes of $p(x)$ is

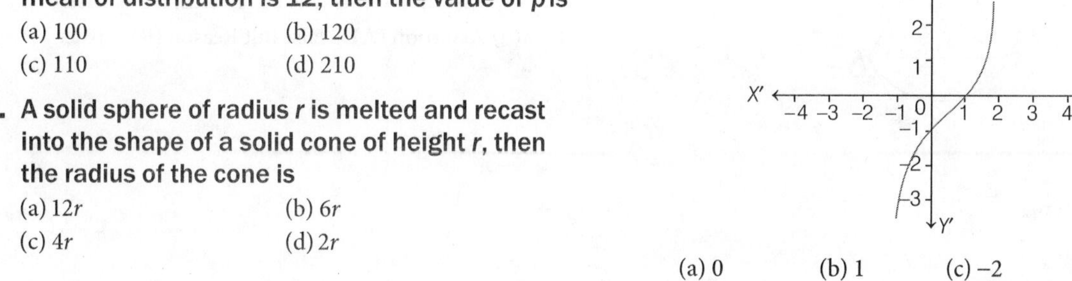

(a) 0 (b) 1 (c) −2 (d) 2

10. If $x = 2$ and $x = 0$, are the zeroes of the polynomials $f(x) = 2x^3 - 5x^2 + ax + b$. The values of a and b is

(a) 2, 0 (b) 2, 3
(c) 3, 0 (d) 7, 0

11. If in a right angled ΔACB, $\tan B = \frac{12}{5}$, then $\sin B$ is

(a) $\frac{12}{13}$ (b) $\frac{5}{13}$
(c) $\frac{7}{13}$ (d) $\frac{9}{13}$

12. A kite is flying at a height of 80 m, above the ground. The string attached to the kite is temporarily tied to a point on the ground. The inclination of the string with ground is $60°$, then the length of the string is

(a) 92.37 m (b) 78 m
(c) 79 m (d) 80 m

13. A toy is the shape of cone over a hemisphere and the radius of the hemisphere is 3.5 cm. If the height of the toy is 15.5 cm, then the total area of the toy is

(a) 214.5 cm^2 (b) 536.5 cm^2
(c) 135 cm^2 (d) 636.2 cm^2

14. In the given figure, $DE \parallel BC$. If $AD = 2.4$ cm, $AB = 8$ cm and $AC = 12$ cm, then AE is equal to

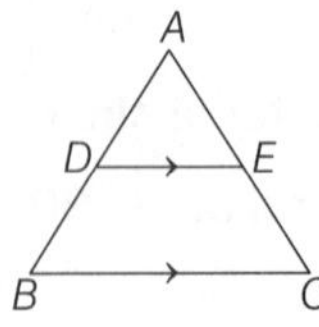

(a) 1.8 cm (b) 3.6 cm
(c) 2.6 cm (d) 5.4 cm

15. In the given figure, AB is a chord of circle, and PQ is a tangent at point B of the circle.

If $\angle AOB = 110°$, then $\angle ABQ$ is

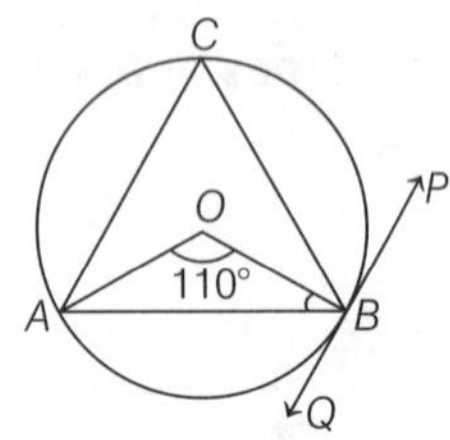

(a) 110° (b) 220°
(c) 55° (d) 70°

16. If the distance between the points $(4, p)$ and $(1, 0)$ is 5 units, then the value of p is

(a) ± 2 (b) ± 6
(c) ± 4 (d) ± 10

17. If the nth term of an AP is $3n - 8$, then its 16th term is

(a) 400 (b) 80
(c) 40 (d) 20

18. The rational form of $0.\overline{254}$ is in the form of $\frac{p}{q}$, then $p + q$ is

(a) 55 (b) 96
(c) 69 (d) 85

Directions (Q.Nos. 19-20) *In question numbers 19 and 20, a statement of Assertion (A) is followed by a statement of Reason (R). Choose the correct option.*

19 **Assertion** (A) For the AP 31, 28, 25, ..., ? 10th term is 4.

Reason (R) The nth term of an AP is defined by $a_n = a + (n - 1)d$.

(a) Both Assertion (A) and Reason (R) are true and Reason (R) is the correct explanation of Assertion (A).
(b) Both Assertion (A) and Reason (R) are true and Reason (R) is not the correct explanation of Assertion (A).
(c) Assertion (A) is true but Reason (R) is false.
(d) Assertion (A) is false but Reason (R) is true.

20. **Assertion** (A) The product of $(3 + \sqrt{5})$ and $(3 - \sqrt{5})$ is a rational number.

Reason (R) The product of two irrational numbers is always rational number.

(a) Both Assertion (A) and Reason (R) are true and Reason (R) is the correct explanation of Assertion (A).
(b) Both Assertion (A) and Reason (R) are true and Reason (R) is not the correct explanation of Assertion (A).
(c) Assertion (A) is true but Reason (R) is false.
(d) Assertion (A) is false but Reason (R) is true.

Section B

Q. Nos. 21 to 25 are Very Short Answer Type Questions of 2 marks each

21. Legs (sides other than the hypotenuse) of a right angled triangle are of length 16 cm and 8 cm. Find the lengths of the side of the largest square that can be inscribed in the triangle.

Or

Prove that $\sqrt{3}+\sqrt{7}$ is irrational.

22. In a right angled ΔABC, right-angled at B, if the ratio of AB to AC is $1:\sqrt{2}$, then find the values of

(i) $\dfrac{2\tan A}{1-\tan^2 A}$ (ii) $\dfrac{2\tan A}{1+\tan^2 A}$

23. Find the sum of the first 20 terms of the AP

190, 167, 144, 121, ...

24. The line segment is of length 10 units. If the coordinates of its one end are (2, –3) and the abscissa of the other end is 10, then find its ordinate.

Or

The line segment joining the points (3, – 4) and (1, 2) is trisected at the points P and Q. If the coordinates of P and Q are $(p, -2)$ and $\left(\dfrac{5}{3}, q\right)$ respectively, find the values of p and q.

25. Poonam saved ₹ 5 in the first week of the year and then increased her weekly savings by ₹ 1.75 each week. In which week will her weekly savings be ₹ 20.75?

Section C

Q. Nos. 26 to 31 are Short Answer Type Questions of 3 marks each

26. If the sum of the deviations of a set of the values $x_1, x_2, x_3, \ldots, x_n$ measured from 50 is (–10) and the sum of deviations of the values from 46 is 70, then find its mean.

27. Represent the following system of linear equations graphically.

$$3x+y-5=0, 2x-y-5=0$$

From the graph, find the points where the lines intersect the Y-axis.

28. Find the value of

$$\frac{5\sin^2 30^\circ+\cos^2 45^\circ-4\tan^2 30^\circ}{2\sin 30^\circ\cos 30^\circ+\tan 45^\circ}.$$

Or

Given $\cos\theta=\dfrac{21}{29}$, determine the value of $\dfrac{\sec\theta}{\tan\theta-\sin\theta}$.

29. For which value of k, will the following pair of linear equations have no solution?

$$3x+y=1, (2k-1)x+(k-1)y=2k+1$$

30. Find the points on the X-axis, which are at a distance of $2\sqrt{5}$ units from the point (7, – 4). How many such points are there?

Or

Consider the following frequency distribution

Class	65-85	85-105	105-125	125-145	145-165	165-185	185-205
Frequency	4	5	13	20	14	7	4

The difference of the upper limit of the median class and the lower limit of the model class is

31 A boy is cycling such that the wheels of the cycle are making 140 revolutions per minute. If the diameter of the wheel is 60 cm, calculate the speed per hour with which the boy is cycling.

Section D

Q. Nos. 32 to 35 are Long Answer Type Questions of 5 marks each

32. The 26th, 11th and the last terms of an AP are 0, 3 and $\frac{-1}{5}$ respectively. Find the common difference and the number of terms.

33. A man sold a chair and a table together for ₹ 1520 thereby making a profit of 25% on the chair and 10% on table. By selling them together for ₹ 1535, he would have made a profit of 10% on the chair and 25% on the table. Find the cost price of each.

34. In the adjoining figure, from an external point P, two tangents PA and PB are drawn to a circle with centre O and radius r. If $OP = 2r$, show that $\angle OAB = \angle OBA = 30^\circ$.

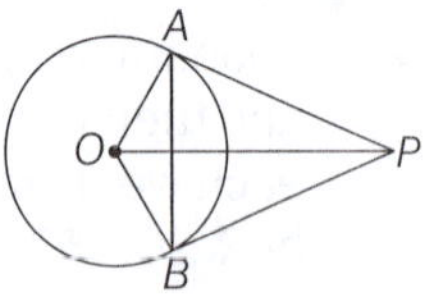

Or

4 Men and 6 boys can finish a piece of work in 5 days, while 3 men and 4 boys can finish it in 7 days. Find the time taken by 1 man alone and 1 boy alone, to finish the piece of work.

35. A right-angled triangle whose sides are 15 cm and 20 cm is made to revolve about its hypotenuse. Find the volume and surface area of the double cone so formed. [take $\pi = 3.14$]

Or

A solid toy is in the form of a hemisphere surmounted by a right circular cone. Height of the cone is 4 cm and the diameter of the base is 8 cm. If a right circular cylinder circumscribes the solid. Find how much more space it will cover?

Section E

Q. Nos. 36 to 38 are Case Study Based Questions of 4 marks each

36. Case Study I

Play Cards

There are three friends and they want to play some interesting game. Firstly, they consider some cards and marked with the numbers 2 to 101 are placed in a box and mixed throughly. One card is drawn from this box.

(i) Find the probability that the drawn on the card is an even number.

(ii) Find the probability that the drawn on the card is a number which is a perfect square.

Or

Find the probability that the drawn on the card is a prime number and it is less than 20.

(iii) Find the probability that the drawn on the card is a number less than 14.

37. Case Study II

Telecasting Tower

A straight highway leads to the foot of a national communication and telecasting tower. A watchman standing at the top of the tower observes a car at an angle of depression of 30° which is approaching the foot of the tower with a uniform speed. Two minutes later, the angle of depression was found to be 60°. The watchman suspects that some terrorist are approaching the tower. It needs half a minute for the watchman to inform the security staff so that it may alert.

(i) The angle of depression from object to the point on the ground is 30°, then find the angle of elevation of the same point on the ground to the same object.

(ii) How much time the car will take to reach the foot of the tower?

Or Suppose a distance between ball and a tree is $10\sqrt{3}$ m and one person is sitting at the top surface of a tree. Find the angle in which the observer see the ball.

(iii) If the angle of elevation of Sun above the tower decrease, then length of shadow of a tower

38. Case Study III

Science Exhibition

For a science exhibition, Vikas presented a diagrammatic representation of rain water harvesting project. Through pipes *AB* and *AC*, each of 12 m long are bringing water from the terrace of a building (as shown in the figure).

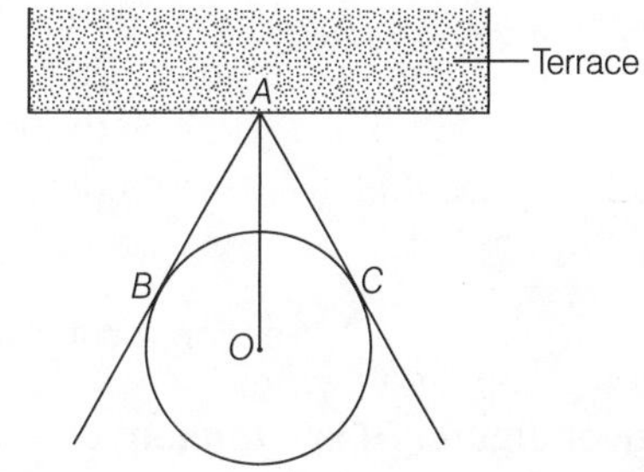

(i) A line drawn from centre of circle to the tangent line is

(ii) If two circles intersect each other at two points, then find the number of common tangents.

Or If the radius of circle is 5 cm, then find the length of *OA*.

(iii) If a line *OA* makes an angle 60° from one of the tangent line, then find the length of *OA*.

Answer Key

1. (b)	**2.** (a)	**3.** (a)	**4.** (c)	**5.** (d)
6. (d)	**7.** (a)	**8.** (c)	**9.** (b)	**10.** (a)
11. (a)	**12.** (a)	**13.** (a)	**14.** (b)	**15.** (c)
16. (c)	**17.** (c)	**18.** (c)	**19.** (a)	**20.** (c)

21. $\frac{16}{3}$ cm **22.** (i) not defined (ii) 1 **23.** -570

24. $-9, 3$ *Or* $p=\frac{7}{3}$ and $q=0$ **25.** 10 **26.** 49.5

27. $(0, 5), (0, -5)$ **28.** $\frac{5}{6(2+\sqrt{3})}$ *Or* $\frac{841}{160}$

29. 2 **30.** $(5, 0), (9, 0)$ or 20 **31.** 15.84 km/h

32. $\frac{-1}{5}, 27$ **33.** ₹600, ₹700 **34.** *Or* 35 days, 70 days

35. 3768 cm^3, 1318.8 cm^2 *Or* $64\pi\text{ cm}^3$

36. (i) $\frac{1}{2}$ (ii) $\frac{9}{100}$ *Or* $\frac{2}{25}$ (iii) $\frac{3}{25}$

37. (i) 30° (ii) 1min *Or* 30° (iii) increase

38. (i) Perpendicular (ii) 2 *Or* 13 cm (iii) 24 cm

Sample Question Paper 2 (Unsolved)

Mathematics (Standard Level)

Time : 3 hrs M.M. : 80

General Instructions

See Sample Question Paper 1

Section A

Section A consists of 20 MCQs Questions of 1 mark each

1. In the given figure, PT is a tangent of a circle, with centre O, at point R. If diameter SQ is produced, it meets with PT at point P with $\angle SPR = x$ and $\angle QSR = y$, then the value of $\angle x + 2\angle y$ is

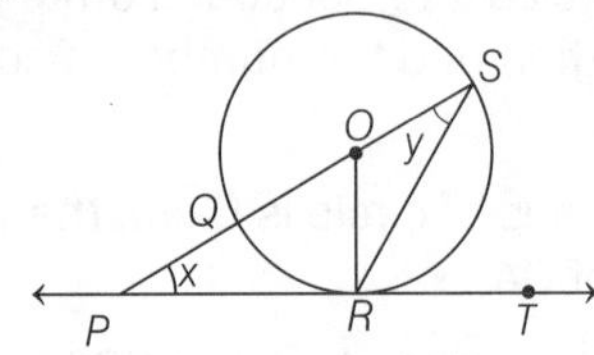

(a) 60° (b) 75° (c) 45° (d) 90°

2. The value of k, for which $2k + 7$, $6k - 2$ and $8k + 4$ are 3 consecutive terms of an AP.

(a) $\frac{15}{2}$ (b) $\frac{13}{2}$ (c) $\frac{17}{2}$ (d) $\frac{11}{2}$

3. If the following pair is similar, then the value of k is

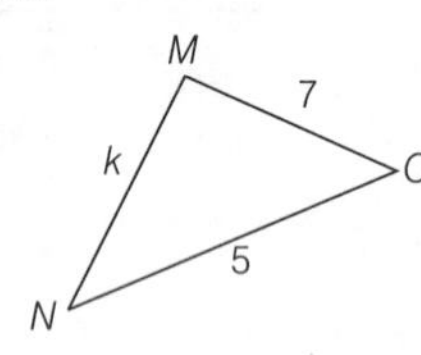

(a) 4 (b) 8 (c) 2 (d) 7

4. The pair of equations $ax + 2y = 7$ and $3x + by = 16$ represent parallel lines if

(a) $ab = 6$ (b) $a = b$

(c) $3a = 4b$ (d) $4b = 5a$

5. Tours of the national capital and the White house begin at 8:30 am from tour agency. Tours for the national capital leave every 15 min. Tours for the White house leave every 20 min. How many minutes after do the tours leave at the same time?

(a) 30 min (b) 60 min

(c) 45 min (d) 75 min

6. If one of the zeroes of the polynomial $f(x) = (k^2 + 8)x^2 + 13x + 6k$ is reciprocal of the other, the value of k is

(a) 4, −2 (b) −4, −2

(c) −4, 2 (d) 4, 2

7. If the sum of zeroes of the polynomial $f(x) = ax^3 - 8x^2 + 7$ is 4, then the value of a is

(a) 3 (b) 4 (c) 8 (d) 2

8. If the difference of mode and median of a data is 24, then the difference of median and mean is

(a) 8 (b) 12 (c) 24 (d) 36

9 If two concentric circles are of radii 10 cm and 8 cm, then the length of the chord of the larger circle which touches the smaller circle is

(a) 6 cm (b) 12 cm (c) 18 cm (d) 9 cm

10. The value of x in the equation $\sin 2x - \sin 45° \cos 45° + \sin 30°$ is

(a) 45° (b) 60° (c) 30° (d) 90°

11. The area of a quadrant of a circle whose circumference is 20 cm is (use $\pi = \frac{22}{7}$)

(a) 12.5 cm^2

(b) 7.95 cm^2

(c) 12 cm^2

(d) 13 cm^2

12. In ΔPQR, $ST \| QR$, $\frac{PS}{SQ} = \frac{3}{5}$ and $PR = 28$ cm, then PT is

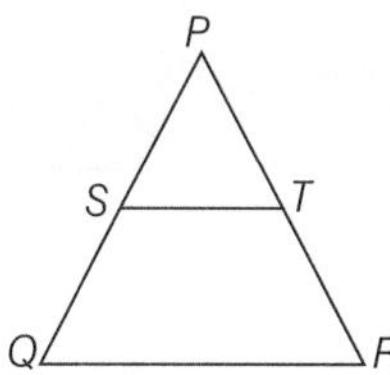

(a) 16.3 cm (b) 11.2 cm (c) 10.5 cm (d) 7 cm

13. The angle of elevation of the top of the tower from a point, which is 40 m away from the base of the tower in the horizontal level, is 45°. Find the height of the tower.

(a) 30 m (b) 40 m (c) 60 m (d) 70 m

14. If points $A(5, P)$, $B(1, 5)$, $C(2, 1)$ and $D(6, 2)$ form a square $ABCD$, then P is

(a) 4 (b) 3 (c) 6 (d) 8

15. The longest diameter of a cone, which can be fully fitted in a cube of edge 8 cm is

(a) $8\sqrt{2}$ cm (b) $6\sqrt{2}$ cm (c) 8 cm (d) 12 cm

16. Find the value of k for which the quadratic equation $3x^2 + kx + 3 = 0$ has real and equal roots.

(a) –6 (b) 6 (c) ± 6 (d) 9

17. If the perimeter of a sector of a circle of radius 6.4 cm is 30 cm, then the area of corresponding sector is (use $\pi = \frac{22}{7}$)

(a) 60 cm^2 (b) 50 cm^2 (c) 55.04 cm^2 (d) 57 cm^2

18. Given that $\sin A = \frac{\sqrt{3}}{2}$ and $\cos B = \frac{\sqrt{3}}{2}$, what is the value of $A + B$?

(a) 90° (b) 120° (c) 60° (d) 150°

Directions (Q.Nos. 19-20) *In question numbers 19 and 20, a statement of Assertion (A) is followed by a statement of Reason (R). Choose the correct option.*

19. Assertion (R) The denominator of a fraction is 4 more than twice the numerator when both the numerator and denominator are decreased by 6, then the denominator becomes 12 times the numerator. The fraction will be $\frac{7}{18}$.

Reason (R) The linear equation used are $x - 2y = 4$ and $12x - y = 66$, whose fraction be $\frac{x}{y}$.

(a) Both Assertion (A) and Reason (R) are true and Reason (R) is the correct explanation of Assertion (A).
(b) Both Assertion (A) and Reason (R) are true and Reason (R) is not the correct explanation of Assertion (A).
(c) Assertion (A) is true but Reason (R) is false.
(d) Assertion (A) is false but Reason (R) is true.

20. Assertion (A) Sum of first 10 even natural number is 120.

Reason (R) If a is the first term, l is the last term and d is the common difference of an AP, then nth term from the end is given by $l - (n - 1)d$.

(a) Both Assertion (A) and Reason (R) are true and Reason (R) is the correct explanation of Assertion (A).
(b) Both Assertion (A) and Reason (R) are true and Reason (R) is not the correct explanation of Assertion (A).
(c) Assertion (A) is true but Reason (R) is false.
(d) Assertion (A) is false but Reason (R) is true.

Section B

Q. Nos. 21 to 25 are Very Short Answer Type Questions of 2 marks each

21. Show that $\frac{2}{5\sqrt{3}}$ is an irrational number.

Or

Show that $6 - 2\sqrt{3}$ is irrational.

22. Prove that $\frac{1 - \sin\theta}{1 + \sin\theta} = (\sec\theta - \tan\theta)^2$, where θ is acute angle.

23. A line segment is of length 15 units. If the coordinate of its one end is (3, 2) and the abscissa of the other end is 15, then find its ordinate.

Or Find the coordinates of the centroid of a triangle whose vertices are (0, 6), (8, 12) and (8, 0). Also, find the length of shortest side of the triangle.

24. Find the value of k, such that the following quadratic equation has equal roots.

$$(k-12)x^2 - 2(k-12)x + 2 = 0$$

25. In the given figure, $ABCD$ is a trapezium with $AB \parallel DC$. If ΔAED is similar to ΔBEC. Prove that $AD = BC$.

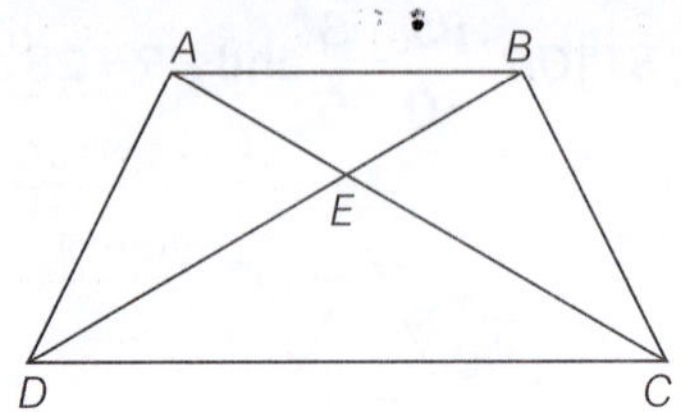

Section C

Q. Nos. 26 to 31 are Short Answer Type Questions of 3 marks each

26. If the 3rd and 9th terms of an AP are 4 and -8 respectively, then which term of this AP is zero?

Or

Find the common difference of an AP, whose first term is 1/2 and the 8th term is 17/6. Also, find the ratio of 4th term and 50th term.

27. A bag contains 18 balls out of which, x balls are red.

(i) If one ball is drawn at random from the bag, then what is the probability that it is red ball?

(ii) If 2 more red balls are put in the bag, then the probability of drawing a red ball will be 9/8 times that of probability of red ball coming in part (i).

Find the value of x.

28. 5 yr hence, the age of Jacob will be 3 times that of his son. 5 yr ago, Jacob's age was 7 times that of his son. What are their present ages?

29. If p is a non-zero rational and $\sqrt{q}$ is irrational, then show that $p\sqrt{q}$ is irrational.

30. Prove that

$$\sqrt{\frac{\sec\theta - 1}{\sec\theta + 1}} + \sqrt{\frac{\sec\theta + 1}{\sec\theta - 1}} = 2\,\mathrm{cosec}\,\theta$$

31. In a ΔABC, $DE \parallel BC$. If $DE = \frac{2}{3}BC$ and area of $\Delta ABC = 81\text{ cm}^2$, then find the area of ΔADE.

Or In ΔABC, points P and Q on sides AB and AC, are such that $\frac{AP}{PB} = \frac{AQ}{QC}$. If PQ is extended to T such that $PT = BC$ and $PB = TC$, then find the value of x.

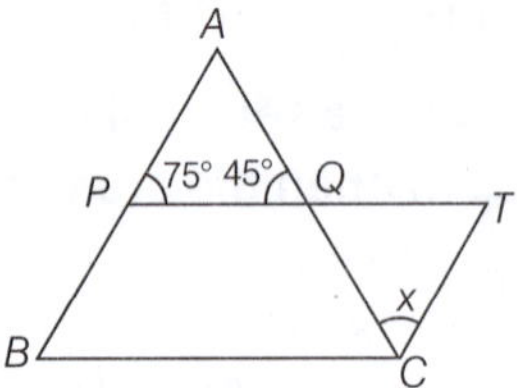

Section D

Q. Nos. 32 to 35 are Long Answer Type Questions of 5 marks each

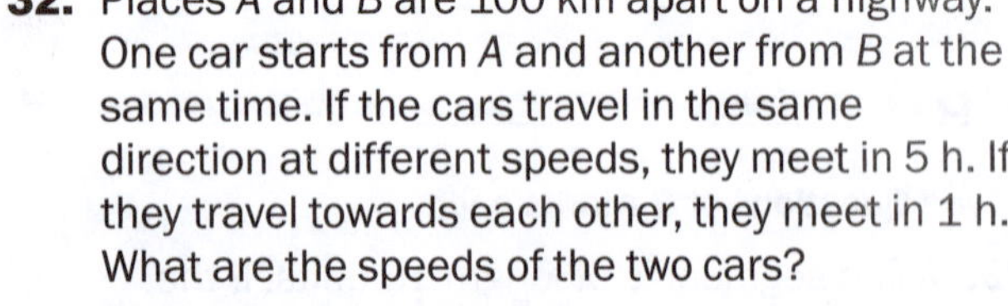

32. Places A and B are 100 km apart on a highway. One car starts from A and another from B at the same time. If the cars travel in the same direction at different speeds, they meet in 5 h. If they travel towards each other, they meet in 1 h. What are the speeds of the two cars?

33. Prove that in two concentric circles, the chord of the larger circle, which touches the smaller circle, is bisected at the point of contact.

34. If α, β are the zeroes of the polynomial $f(x) = 2x^2 + 5x + k$ satisfying the relation $(\alpha+\beta)^2 - \alpha\beta = \frac{21}{4}$, then find the value of k. Also, find the zeroes of the $f(x)$.

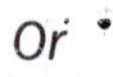

Or

Find the zeroes of the polynomial $p(x) = 4\sqrt{3}x^2 + 5x - 2\sqrt{3}$, and verify the relationship between the zeroes and its coefficients.

35. If the median of the distribution given below is 30, find the values of x and y.

Class interval	0-10	10-20	20-30	30-40	40-50	50-60	Total
Number of students	5	x	20	15	y	5	60

Or If mode of the following series is 54, then find the value of f.

Class interval	0-15	15-30	30-45	45-60	60-75	75-90
Frequency	3	5	f	16	12	7

Section E

Q. Nos. 36 to 38 are Case Study Based Questions of 4 marks each

36. Diwali Celebration

In a Diwali occassion, colourful rangoli is formed by using different colours, diya, candles and light etc. On this occassion, we fire out the crackers and eating sweets etc. (use $\pi = \frac{22}{7}$)

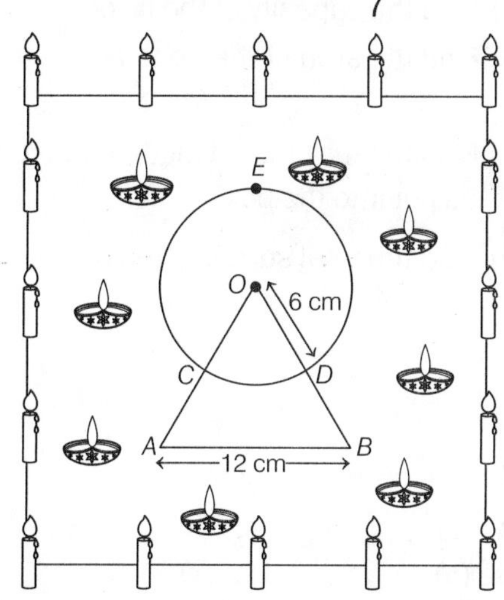

(i) Find the area of circle.

(ii) Find the area of sector OCD.

Or Find the area of the shaded region $OCED$.

(iii) Find the area of an equilateral triangle.

37. A School Boy

Delhi public school society, which has so many schools in different cities of India. One of the branch of Delhi Public School is in Ghaziabad. In that school thousand of students study in the classroom.

Out of them one of the boy is standing in the ground having coordinates (4, 1) facing towards east. He moves 4 units in straight line, then take left and moves 3 units and stop. Now, he is at his home.

The represent of the above situation on the coordinate axes is show below.

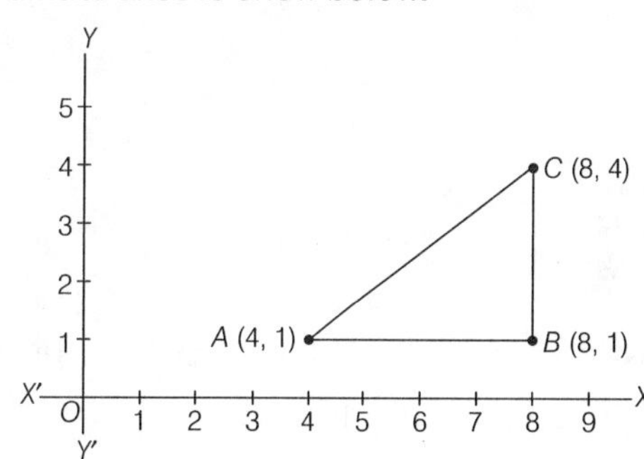

Based on the above information, answer the following questions.

(i) What is the shortest distance between his school and house?

(ii) Suppose point D divide the line segment AB in the ratio 1 : 2, then find the coordinate of D.

Or

If we draw perpendicular lines from points A and B to the X-axis, then find the region covered by these perpendicular lines?

(iii) Find the distance of AB.

38. **The Cuboidal**

In a cuboid, all six faces are rectangles. The opposite faces are identical and hence there are three pairs of identical faces, which are shown in figure.

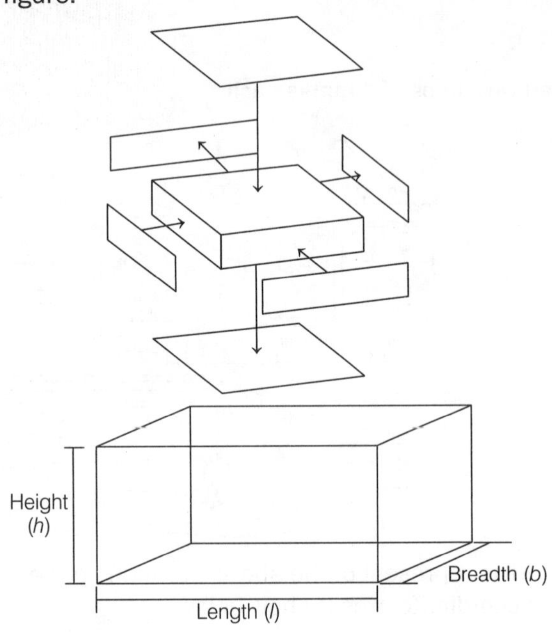

The following formula related to cuboid are given below:

(i) Volume of cuboid $= l \times b \times h$

(ii) Total surface area of cuboid $= 2(lb + bh + hl)$

(iii) Diagonal of the cuboid $= \sqrt{l^2 + b^2 + h^2}$

(iv) Lateral surface area of cuboid $= 2(l + b)h$

Suppose the dimension of the box are $10 \times 8 \times 6 \text{ m}^3$.

Based on the above information, answer the following questions.

(i) Find the capacity of the box.

(ii) Find the area of the front face of the cuboid.

Or

Find the maximum length of the rod that can be put into the box.

(iii) Find the total surface area of the cuboid.

Answer Key

1. (d)	**2.** (a)	**3.** (c)	**4.** (a)	**5.** (b)
6. (d)	**7.** (d)	**8.** (b)	**9.** (b)	**10.** (a)
11. (b)	**12.** (c)	**13.** (b)	**14.** (c)	**15.** (c)
16. (c)	**17.** (c)	**18.** (a)	**19.** (c)	**20.** (d)

23. $-7, 11$ *Or* $\left(\frac{16}{3}, 6\right)$, 10 units

24. $k = 14$

26. 5th term *Or* $\frac{1}{3}, 9:101$

27. (i) $\frac{x}{18}$ (ii) $x = 8$

28. 40 yr and 10 yr

31. 36 cm^2 *Or* 60°

32. 60 km/h and 40 km/h

34. $2, -\frac{1}{2}$ and -2 *Or* $x = \frac{\sqrt{3}}{4}, \frac{-2}{\sqrt{3}}$

35. $x = 5$ and $y = 10$ *Or* $f = 10$

36. (i) $\frac{792}{7} \text{ cm}^2$ (ii) $\frac{132}{7} \text{ cm}^2$ *Or* 94.29 cm^2 (iii) $36\sqrt{3} \text{ m}^2$

37. (i) 5 units (ii) $\left(\frac{16}{3}, 1\right)$ *Or* 4 sq units (iii) 4 units

38. (i) 480 m^3 (ii) 60 m^2 *Or* $10\sqrt{2}$ m (iii) 376 m^2

CBSE
Examination Paper 2025
(Basic Level & Standard Level)

CBSE Examination Paper 2025

Mathematics (Basic Level)

Time : 3 hrs	M.M. : 80

General Instructions

1 This question paper has 5 Sections A, B, C, D and E.
2 Section A has 20 Multiple Choice Questions (MCQs) carrying 1 mark each.
3 Section B has 5 Short Answer-I (SA-I) type questions carrying 2 marks each.
4 Section C has 6 Short Answer-II (SA-II) type questions carrying 3 marks each.
5 Section D has 4 Long Answer (LA) type questions carrying 5 marks each.
6 Section E has 3 Case Based integrated units of assessment (4 marks each) with sub-parts of the values of 1, 1 and 2 marks each respectively.
7 All questions are compulsory. However, an internal choice in 2 Qs of 2 marks, 2 Qs of 3 marks and 2 Qs of 5 marks has been provided. An internal choice has been provided in the 2 marks question of Section E.
8 Draw neat figures wherever required. Take $\pi = \frac{22}{7}$ whenever required if not stated.

Section A

Section A consists of 20 MCQs Questions of 1 mark each

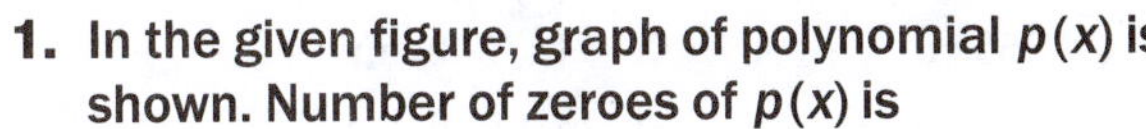

1. **In the given figure, graph of polynomial $p(x)$ is shown. Number of zeroes of $p(x)$ is**

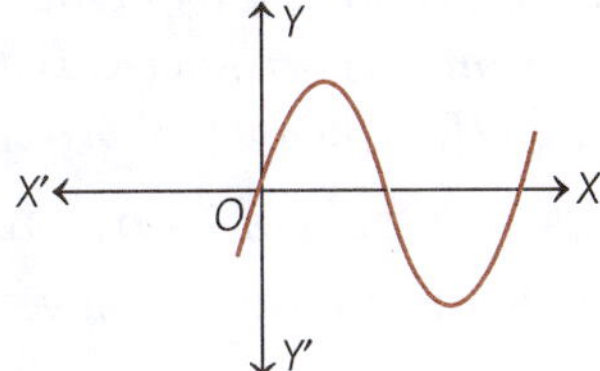

(a) 3 (b) 2 (c) 1 (d) 4

2. **22nd term of the AP $\frac{3}{2}, \frac{1}{2}, \frac{-1}{2}, \frac{-3}{2}, \ldots$ is**

(a) $\frac{45}{2}$ (b) -9 (c) $\frac{-39}{2}$ (d) -21

3. **The line $2x - 3y = 6$ intersects X-axis at**

(a) $(0, -2)$ (b) $(0, 3)$ (c) $(-2, 0)$ (d) $(3, 0)$

4. **Two identical cones are joined as shown in the figure. If radius of base is 4 cm and slant height of the cone is 6 cm then height of the solid is**

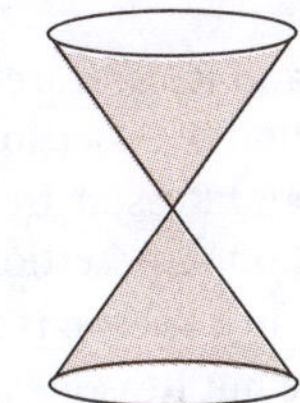

(a) 8 cm (b) $4\sqrt{5}$ cm (c) $2\sqrt{5}$ cm (d) 12 cm

5. **The value of k for which the system of equations $3x - 7y = 1$ and $kx + 14y = 6$ is inconsistent, is**

(a) -6 (b) $\frac{2}{3}$ (c) 6 (d) $\frac{-3}{2}$

6. **Two dice are rolled together. The probability of getting a sum more than 9 is**

(a) $\frac{5}{6}$ (b) $\frac{5}{18}$ (c) $\frac{1}{6}$ (d) $\frac{1}{2}$

7. ***ABCD* is a rectangle with its vertices at (2, −2), (8, 4), (4, 8) and (−2, 2) taken in order. Length of its diagonal is**

(a) $4\sqrt{2}$ (b) $6\sqrt{2}$ (c) $4\sqrt{26}$ (d) $2\sqrt{26}$

8. **In the given figure, *PA* is tangent to a circle with centre *O*. If $\angle APO = 30°$ and $OA = 2.5$ cm then *OP* is equal to**

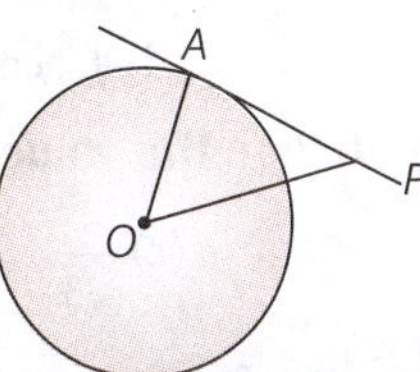

(a) 2.5 cm (b) 5 cm (c) $\frac{5}{\sqrt{3}}$ cm (d) 2 cm

9. **If probability of happening of an event is 57% then probability of non-happening of the event is**

(a) 0.43 (b) 0.57 (c) 53% (d) $\frac{1}{57}$

10. *OAB* is a sector of a circle with centre *O* and radius 7 cm. If length of arc $\widehat{AB} = \frac{22}{3}$ cm then $\angle AOB$ is equal to

(a) $\left(\frac{120}{7}\right)^\circ$ (b) 45° (c) 60° (d) 30°

11. In ΔABC, $DE \parallel BC$. If $AE = (2x+1)$ cm, $EC = 4$ cm, $AD = (x+1)$ cm and $DB = 3$ cm then the value of x is

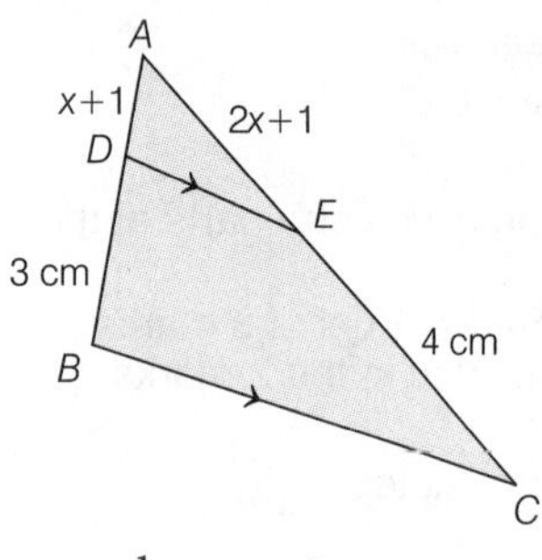

(a) 1 (b) $\frac{1}{2}$ (c) −1 (d) $\frac{1}{3}$

12. Three coins are tossed together. The probability that exactly one coin shows head, is

(a) $\frac{1}{8}$ (b) $\frac{1}{4}$ (c) 1 (d) $\frac{3}{8}$

13. In two concentric circles centred at *O*, a chord *AB* of the larger circle touches the smaller circle at *C*. If $OA = 3.5$ cm, $OC = 2.1$ cm then *AB* is equal to

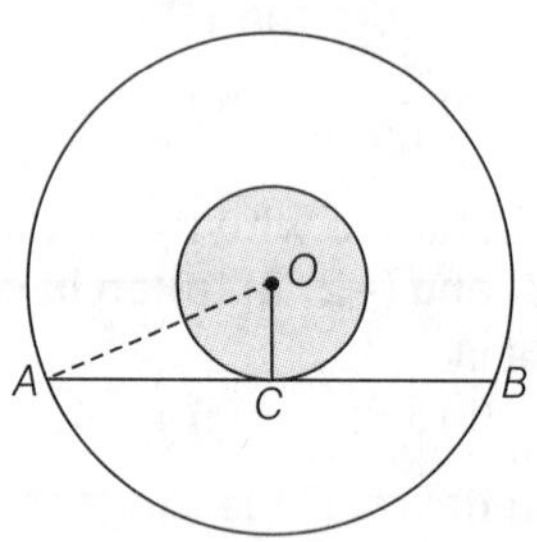

(a) 5.6 cm (b) 2.8 cm
(c) 3.5 cm (d) 4.2 cm

14. If $\sqrt{3}\sin\theta = \cos\theta$ then the value of θ is

(a) $\sqrt{3}$ (b) 60° (c) $\frac{1}{\sqrt{3}}$ (d) 30°

15. To calculate mean of a grouped data, Rahul used assumed mean method. He used $d = (x - A)$, where, *A* is assumed mean. Then, $\bar{x}$ is equal to

(a) $A + \bar{d}$ (b) $A + h\bar{d}$
(c) $h(A + \bar{d})$ (d) $A - h\bar{d}$

16. If the sum of first *n* terms of an AP is given by $S_n = \frac{n}{2}(3n+1)$, then the first term of the AP is

(a) 2 (b) $\frac{3}{2}$ (c) 4 (d) $\frac{5}{2}$

17. In ΔABC, $\angle B = 90°$. If $\frac{AB}{AC} = \frac{1}{2}$ then $\cos C$ is equal to

(a) $\frac{3}{2}$ (b) $\frac{1}{2}$ (c) $\frac{\sqrt{3}}{2}$ (d) $\frac{1}{\sqrt{3}}$

18. The volume of air in a hollow cylinder is 450 cm^3. A cone of same height and radius as that of cylinder is kept inside it. The volume of empty space in the cylinder is

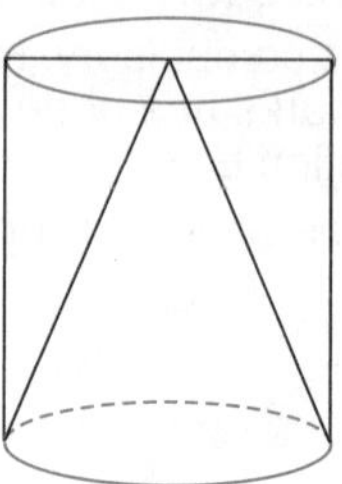

(a) 225 cm^3 (b) 150 cm^3
(c) 250 cm^3 (d) 300 cm^3

Directions (Q.Nos. 19 and 20) *In question numbers 19 and 20, a statement of Assertion (A) is followed by a statement of Reason (R). Choose the correct option.*

19. **Assertion** (A) $(a+\sqrt{b})\cdot(a-\sqrt{b})$ is a rational number, where *a* and *b* are positive integers.

Reason (R) Product of two irrationals is always rational.

(a) Both Assertion and Reason are true and Reason is correct explanation of Assertion.
(b) Both Assertion and Reason are true but Reason is not correct explanation of Assertion.
(c) Assertion is true but Reason is false.
(d) Assertion is false but Reason is true.

20. **Assertion** (A) $\Delta ABC \sim \Delta PQR$ such that $\angle A = 65°$, $\angle C = 60°$. Hence, $\angle Q = 55°$.

Reason (R) Sum of all angles of a triangle is 180°.

(a) Both Assertion and Reason are true and Reason is correct explanation of Assertion.
(b) Both Assertion and Reason are true but Reason is not correct explanation of Assertion.
(c) Assertion is true but Reason is false.
(d) Assertion is false but Reason is true.

Section B

Q. Nos. 21 to 25 are Very Short Answer Type Questions of 2 marks each

21. (a) Solve the equation $4x^2 - 9x + 3 = 0$, using quadratic formula.

Or

(b) Find the nature of roots of the equation $3x^2 - 4\sqrt{3}x + 4 = 0$.

22. In a trapezium *ABCD*, $AB \parallel DC$ and its diagonals intersect at *O*. Prove that $\frac{OA}{OC} = \frac{OB}{OD}$.

23. A box contains 120 discs, which are numbered from 1 to 120. If one disc is drawn at random from the box, find the probability that

(i) it bears a 2-digit number.

(ii) the number is a perfect square.

24. (a) Evaluate $\frac{\cos 45^\circ}{\tan 30^\circ + \sin 60^\circ}$.

Or

(b) Verify that, $\sin 2A = \frac{2\tan A}{1+\tan^2 A}$, for $A = 30^\circ$.

25. Using prime factorisation, find the HCF of 180, 140 and 210.

SECTION C

Q. Nos. 26 to 31 are Short Answer Type Questions of 3 marks each

26. (a) If α and β are zeroes of the polynomial $8x^2 - 5x - 1$ then form a quadratic polynomial in *x* whose zeroes are $\frac{2}{\alpha}$ and $\frac{2}{\beta}$.

Or

(b) Find the zeroes of the polynomial $p(x) = 3x^2 + x - 10$ and verify the relationship between zeroes and its coefficients.

27. Find length and breadth of a rectangular park, whose perimeter is 100 m and area is 600 m^2.

28. Three measuring rods are of lengths 120 cm, 100 cm and 150 cm. Find the least length of a fence that can be measured an exact number of times, using any of the rods. How many times each rod will be used to measure the length of the fence?

29. *AB* and *CD* are diameter of a circle with centre *O* and radius 7 cm. If $\angle BOD = 30^\circ$ then find the area and perimeter of the shaded region.

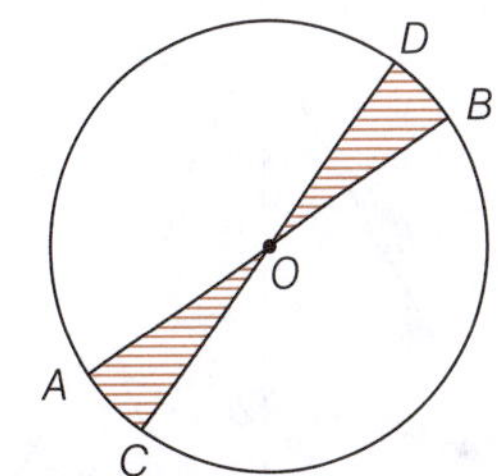

30. Prove that

$$\frac{\tan\theta}{1-\cot\theta} + \frac{\cot\theta}{1-\tan\theta} = \sec\theta \operatorname{cosec}\theta + 1.$$

31. (a) Find the AP whose third term is 16 and seventh term exceeds the fifth term by 12. Also, find the sum of first 29 terms of the AP.

Or

(b) Find the sum of first 20 terms of an AP whose *n*th term is given by $a_n = 5 + 2n$. Can 52 be a term of this AP?

SECTION D

Q. Nos. 32 to 35 are Long Answer Type Questions of 5 marks each

32. (a) Solve the following pair of linear equations by graphical method

$$2x + y = 9$$

and $$x - 2y = 2.$$

Or

(b) Nidhi received simple interest of ₹1200 when invested ₹ x at 6% p.a. and ₹ y at 5% p.a. for 1 year. Had she invested ₹ x at 3% p.a. and ₹ y at 8% p.a. for that year, she would have received simple interest of ₹1260. Find the values of x and y.

33. (a) The given figure shows a circle with centre O and radius 4 cm circumscribed by ΔABC. BC touches the circle at D such that $BD = 6$ cm, $DC = 10$ cm. Find the length of AE.

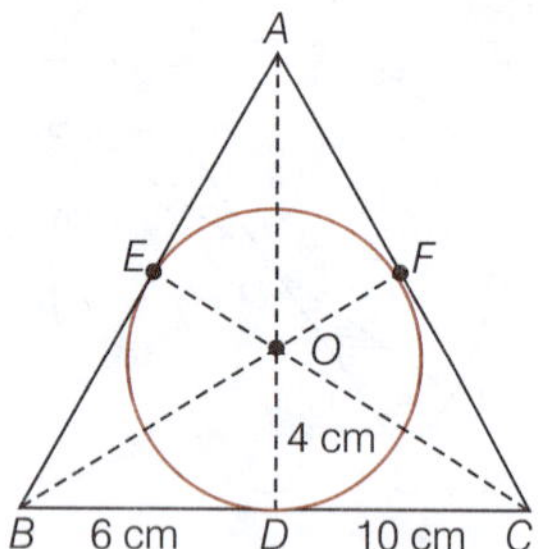

Or

(b) PA and PB are tangents drawn to a circle with centre O.

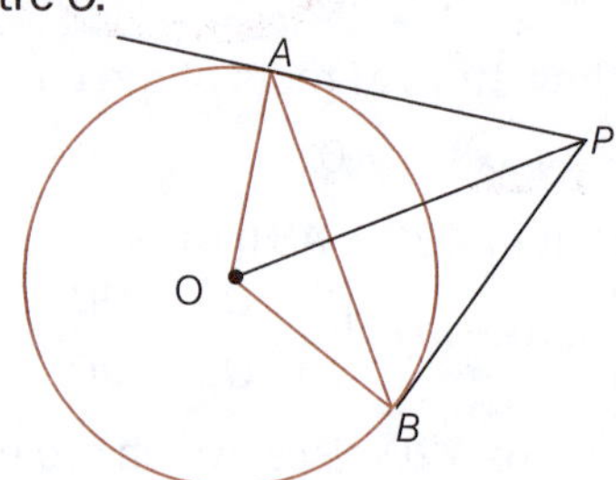

If $\angle AOB = 120^\circ$ and $OA = 10$ cm then

(i) Find $\angle OPA$.

(ii) Find the perimeter of ΔOAP.

(iii) Find the length of chord AB.

34. The angles of depression of the top and the foot of a 9 m tall building from the top of a multi-storeyed building are 30° and 60°, respectively. Find the height of the multi-storeyed building and the distance between the two buildings. [use $\sqrt{3} = 1.73$]

35. Find mean and mode of the following data

Class	15-20	20-25	25-30	30-35	35-40	40-45
Frequency	12	10	15	11	7	5

SECTION E

Q. Nos. 36 to 38 are Case Study Based Questions of 4 marks each

36. A triangular window of a building is shown above. Its diagram represents a ΔABC with $\angle A = 90^\circ$ and $AB = AC$. Points P and R trisect AB and $PQ \| RS \| AC$.

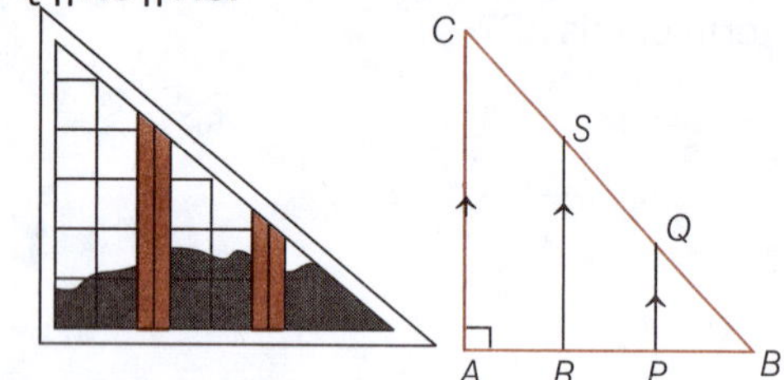

Based on the above information, answer the following questions.

(i) Show that $\Delta BPQ \sim \Delta BAC$.

(ii) Prove that $PQ = \frac{1}{3} AC$.

(iii) (a) If $AB = 3$ m, find the length BQ and BS. Verify that $BQ = \frac{1}{2} BS$.

Or

(b) Prove that $BR^2 + RS^2 = \frac{4}{9} BC^2$.

37. A hemispherical bowl is packed in a cuboidal box. The bowl just fits in the box. Inner radius of the bowl is 10 cm. Outer radius of the bowl is 10.5 cm.

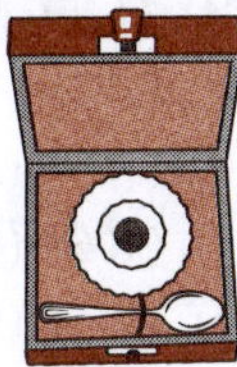
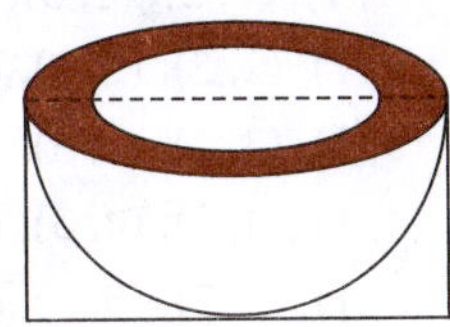

Based on the above information, answer the following questions.

(i) Find the dimensions of the cuboidal box.

(ii) Find the total outer surface area of the box.

(iii) (a) Find the difference between the capacity of the bowl and the volume of the box. [use $\pi = 3.14$]

Or

(b) The inner surface of the bowl and the thickness is to be painted. Find the area to be painted.

38. Gurveer and Arushi built a robot that can paint a path as it moves on a graph paper. Some coordinate of points are marked on it. It starts from (0, 0) moves to the points listed in order (in straight lines) and ends at (0, 0).

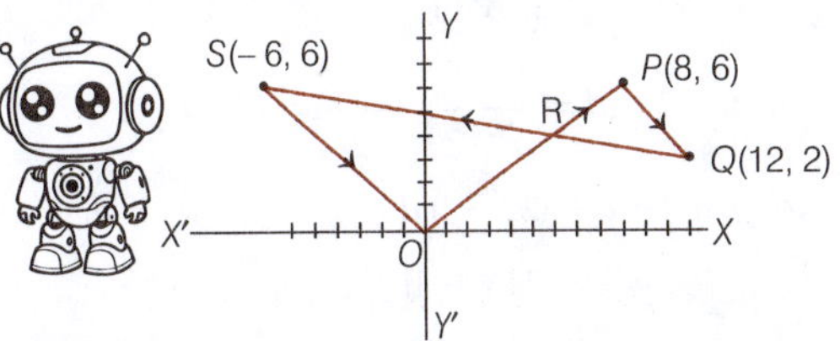

Arushi entered the points $P(8, 6)$, $Q(12, 2)$ and $S(-6, 6)$ in order. The path drawn by robot is shown in the figure.

Based on the above information, answer the following questions.

(i) Determine the distance OP.

(ii) QS is represented by equation $2x + 9y = 42$. Find the coordinates of the point where it intersects Y-axis.

(iii) (a) Point $R(4.8, y)$ divides the line segment OP in a certain ratio, find the ratio. Hence, find the value of y.

Or

(b) Using distance formula, show that $\frac{PQ}{OS} = \frac{2}{3}$.

Solutions

1. (a) $\because$ The graph touches the X-axis at 3 points.

$\therefore$ Number of zeroes of $p(x)$ is 3.

2. (c) Given AP is $\frac{3}{2}, \frac{1}{2}, \frac{-1}{2}, \frac{-3}{2}, \ldots$

$\therefore a = \frac{3}{2}$ and $d = \frac{1}{2} - \frac{3}{2} = \frac{1-3}{2} = \frac{-2}{2} = -1$

Now, $a_{22} = a + (22-1)d$ $\quad [\because a_n = a + (n-1)d]$

$= \frac{3}{2} + 21 \times (-1)$

$= \frac{3}{2} - 21 = \frac{3-42}{2} = -\frac{39}{2}$

3. (d) $\because$ On X-axis, y-coordinate is zero.

Then, options (c) and (d) satisfy this rule.

Now, check points in the given equation.

For (−2, 0),

$2 \times -2 - 3 \times 0 = 6$

$-4 - 0 = 6$

$-4 = 6$ [not satisfy]

For (3, 0),

$2 \times 3 - 3 \times 0 = 6$

$6 - 0 = 6$

$6 = 6$ [satisfied]

4. (b) Given, radius of the base of cone $(r) = 4$ cm and slant height of cone $(l) = 6$ cm

Now, height of one cone,

$h^2 = \sqrt{l^2 - r^2}$

$= \sqrt{(6)^2 - (4)^2}$

$= \sqrt{36-16} = \sqrt{20} = 2\sqrt{5}$ cm

Hence, total height of solid $= 2 \times 2\sqrt{5} = 4\sqrt{5}$ cm

5. (a) The system of equations is inconsistent if

$$\frac{a_1}{a_2} = \frac{b_1}{b_2} \neq \frac{c_1}{c_2}$$

Now, $3x - 7y - 1 = 0$ and $kx + 14y - 6 = 0$

$a_1 = 3, b_1 = -7, c_1 = -1$ and $a_2 = k, b_2 = 14, c_2 = -6$

$\therefore \quad \frac{3}{k} = -\frac{7}{14} \neq \frac{-1}{-6}$

$\Rightarrow \quad 14 \times 3 = -7k$

$\Rightarrow \quad -7k = 42$

$\Rightarrow \quad k = -\frac{42}{7}$

$\therefore \quad k = -6$

Hence, the required value of k is − 6.

6. (c) Two dice are rolled together. So, the sample space of two dice, S

{(1, 1), (1, 2), (1, 3), (1, 4), (1, 5), (1, 6),
(2, 1), (2, 2), (2, 3), (2, 4), (2, 5), (2, 6),
(3, 1), (3, 2), (3, 3), (3, 4), (3, 5), (3, 6),
(4, 1), (4, 2), (4, 3), (4, 4), (4, 5), (4, 6),
(5, 1), (5, 2), (5, 3), (5, 4), (5, 5), (5, 6),
(6, 1), (6, 2), (6, 3), (6, 4), (6, 5), (6, 6)}

$\therefore$ Total sample space $n(S) = 36$

Now, sample space of getting a sum more than 9

= {(4, 6), (5, 5), (5, 6), (6, 4), (6, 5), (6, 6)}

$\therefore$ Probability of getting a sum more than 9 $= \frac{6}{36} = \frac{1}{6}$

7. (d) ABCD is rectangle with its vertices at (2, −2), (8, 4), (4, 8) and (−2, 2).

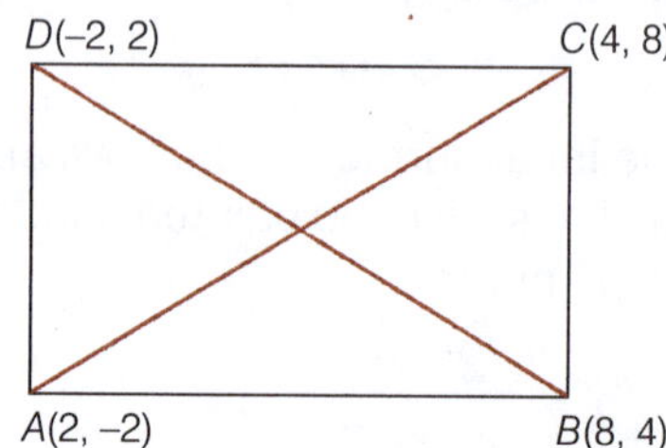

Now, length of diagonal AC by distance formula,

Distance $= \sqrt{(x_2 - x_1)^2 + (y_2 - y_1)^2}$

$[\because x_1 = 2, x_2 = 4, y_1 = -2, y_2 = 8]$

$= \sqrt{(4-2)^2 + (8+2)^2} = \sqrt{(2)^2 + (10)^2}$

$= \sqrt{4 + 100} = \sqrt{104} = 2\sqrt{26}$

8. (b) In the given figure, PA is tangent to a circle with centre O.

$\angle APO = 30°, OA = 2.5$ cm

Now, $\sin 30° = \frac{OA}{OP}$ $\quad \left[\because \sin\theta = \frac{\text{perpendicular}}{\text{hypotenuse}}\right]$

$\Rightarrow \quad \frac{1}{2} = \frac{2.5}{OP}$ $\quad \left[\because \sin 30° = \frac{1}{2}\right]$

$\Rightarrow \quad OP = 2 \times 2.5$

$\Rightarrow \quad OP = 5$ cm

9. (a) The probability of happening of an event is 57%.

Convert the percentage to a decimal

$= \frac{57}{100} = 0.57$

Now, the probability of non-happening

$= 1 - 0.57 = 0.43$

10. (c) Given, radius = 7 cm

and length of arc $= \frac{22}{3}$ cm

Now, length of arc $= \frac{\theta}{360°} \times 2\pi r$

$$\Rightarrow \quad \frac{22}{3} = \frac{\theta}{360°} \times 2 \times \frac{22}{7} \times 7$$

$$\Rightarrow \quad \theta = \frac{22 \times 360}{3 \times 2 \times 22}$$

$$\therefore \quad \theta = 60°$$

11. (b) Given, in $\Delta ABC, DE \parallel BC$

If a line is parallel to one side of a triangle and intersects the other two sides. It divides the two sides in the same ratio.

Since, $DE \parallel BC$, we have

$$\frac{AD}{DB} = \frac{AE}{EC}$$

On substituting the given values, we get

$$\frac{x+1}{3} = \frac{2x+1}{4}$$

$$\Rightarrow \quad 4(x+1) = 3(2x+1)$$

$$\Rightarrow \quad 4x + 4 = 6x + 3$$

$$\Rightarrow \quad 4x - 6x = 3 - 4$$

$$\Rightarrow \quad -2x = -1$$

$$\therefore \quad x = \frac{1}{2}$$

Hence, the required value of x is $\frac{1}{2}$.

12. (d) Given, three coins are tossed together.ss

So, sample space,

$S = \{HHH, HHT, HTT, HTH, TTH, THT, THH, TTT\}$

Now, the space that exactly one coin shows head

$= \{HTT, TTH, THT\}$

$\therefore$ Total sample space = 8

and favourable space = 3

$\therefore$ Probability (getting exactly one head) $= \frac{3}{8}$

13. (a) We know that tangent at a point on a circle is perpendicular to the radius through the point of contact.

$\therefore$ OC is perpendicular to AB.

ΔOCA is a right angled triangle.

$$AC^2 + OC^2 = OA^2$$

[by Pythagoras theorem]

$$\Rightarrow \quad AC^2 + (2.1)^2 = (3.5)^2$$

$$\Rightarrow \quad AC^2 + 4.41 = 12.25$$

$$\Rightarrow \quad AC^2 = 12.25 - 4.41$$

$$\Rightarrow \quad AC^2 = 7.84$$

$$\Rightarrow \quad AC = \sqrt{7.84}$$

$$\Rightarrow \quad AC = 2.8 \text{ cm}$$

Since, OC is perpendicular to chord AB, C is the mid-point of AB.

$$\therefore \quad AB = 2 \cdot AC$$

$$\Rightarrow \quad AB = 2 \cdot 2.8$$

$$\Rightarrow \quad AB = 5.6 \text{ cm}$$

Hence, the length of AB is 5.6 cm.

14. (d) Given, $\sqrt{3} \sin\theta = \cos\theta$

$$\Rightarrow \quad \frac{\sin\theta}{\cos\theta} = \frac{1}{\sqrt{3}} \quad \left[\because \tan\theta = \frac{\sin\theta}{\cos\theta}\right]$$

$$\Rightarrow \quad \tan\theta = \frac{1}{\sqrt{3}}$$

$$\Rightarrow \quad \tan\theta = \tan 30° \quad \left[\because \tan 30° = \frac{1}{\sqrt{3}}\right]$$

$$\Rightarrow \quad \theta = 30°$$

15. (a) The formula for the mean using the assumed mean method is $\overline{x} = A + \overline{d}$

Substitute the given information into the formula for the mean using the assumed mean method.

$$\therefore \quad \overline{x} = A + \overline{d}$$

$$\Rightarrow \quad \overline{x} = A + \frac{\Sigma d_i}{n}$$

Since, $d = x - A$, then $\overline{d} = \frac{\Sigma (x_i - A)}{n}$

$$\Rightarrow \quad \overline{x} = A + \overline{d}$$

16. (a) Given, $S_n = \frac{n}{2}(3n + 1)$

Now, substitute $n = 1$ into S_n,

$$S_1 = \frac{1}{2}[3(1) + 1]$$

$$\Rightarrow \quad S_1 = \frac{1}{2}(3 + 1)$$

$$\Rightarrow \quad S_1 = \frac{1}{2} \times 4$$

$$\Rightarrow \quad S_1 = 2$$

$\because$ S_1 represents the sum of the first term, which is the first term itself.

Therefore, the first term a_1 is 2.

17. (c) In ΔABC, $\angle B = 90°$ and $\frac{AB}{AC} = \frac{1}{2}$

Let $AB = x$ and $\frac{AB}{AC} = \frac{1}{2} \Rightarrow \frac{x}{AC} = \frac{1}{2} \Rightarrow AC = 2x$

By Pythagoras theorem,

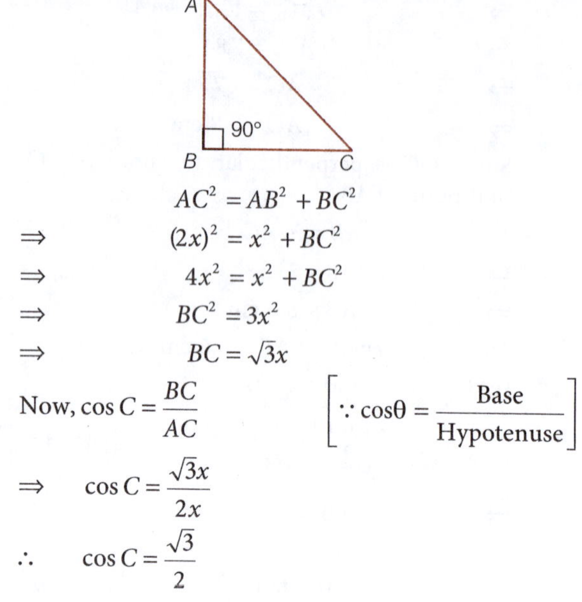

$$AC^2 = AB^2 + BC^2$$

$\Rightarrow \quad (2x)^2 = x^2 + BC^2$

$\Rightarrow \quad 4x^2 = x^2 + BC^2$

$\Rightarrow \quad BC^2 = 3x^2$

$\Rightarrow \quad BC = \sqrt{3}x$

Now, $\cos C = \dfrac{BC}{AC}$ $\quad \left[\because \cos\theta = \dfrac{\text{Base}}{\text{Hypotenuse}}\right]$

$\Rightarrow \quad \cos C = \dfrac{\sqrt{3}x}{2x}$

$\therefore \quad \cos C = \dfrac{\sqrt{3}}{2}$

18. (d) Given, volume of cylinder,

$$V_{\text{cylinder}} = 450 \text{ cm}^3$$

Since, the cone has the same radius and height as the cylinder, its volume is

$$V_{\text{cone}} = \frac{1}{3}\pi r^2 h$$

$\Rightarrow \quad V_{\text{cone}} = \dfrac{1}{3}V_{\text{cylinder}} \quad [\because V_{\text{cylinder}} = \pi r^2 h]$

$\Rightarrow \quad V_{\text{cone}} = \dfrac{1}{3} \times 450 \text{ cm}^3 = 150 \text{ cm}^3$

$\because$ The empty space is the difference between the volume of the cylinder and the volume of cone.

$\therefore \quad V_{\text{empty}} = V_{\text{cylinder}} - V_{\text{cone}}$

$= 450 - 150$

$= 300 \text{ cm}^3$

19. (c) **Assertion** We have, $(a + \sqrt{b})(a - \sqrt{b})$

$$= (a)^2 - (\sqrt{b})^2 = a^2 - b$$

Since, a and b are integers. So, a^2 is also an integer.

The difference between two integers (a^2 and b) is also an integer.

Therefore, $(a^2 - b)$ is an integer and all integers are rational.

So, Assertion is true.

Reason The product of two irrationals is not always rational.

e.g. $\sqrt{2} \cdot \sqrt{3} = \sqrt{6}$, which is irrational.

However, $\sqrt{2} \cdot \sqrt{2} = 2$, which is rational.

So, Reason is false.

Therefore, Assertion is true but Reason is false.

20. (b) **Assertion** Since, $\Delta ABC \sim \Delta PQR$,

$$\angle A = 65° \text{ and } \angle C = 60°$$

We know that the sum of angles in ΔABC is 180°.

$\therefore \quad \angle A + \angle B + \angle C = 180°$

$\Rightarrow \quad 65° + \angle B + 60° = 180°$

$\Rightarrow \quad \angle B = 180° - 65° - 60°$

$\Rightarrow \quad \angle B = 55°$

Since, $\Delta ABC \sim \Delta PQR$, corresponding angles are equal.

$\therefore \quad \angle Q = \angle B$

$\Rightarrow \quad \angle Q = 55°$

So, Assertion is true.

Reason We know that sum of all angles of triangle is 180°.

Reason is true but it does not correctly explain the Assertion.

21. (a) Given, the quadratic equation is $4x^2 - 9x + 3$.

Now, comparing with $ax^2 + bx + c = 0$, we get

$$a = 4, b = -9 \text{ and } c = 3$$

By quadratic formula,

$$x = \frac{-b \pm \sqrt{b^2 - 4ac}}{2a}$$

$$= \frac{-(-9) \pm \sqrt{(-9)^2 - 4 \times 4 \times 3}}{2 \times 4}$$

$$= \frac{9 \pm \sqrt{81 - 48}}{8}$$

$$= \frac{9 \pm \sqrt{33}}{8}$$

$\therefore \quad x = \dfrac{9 + \sqrt{33}}{8}, \dfrac{9 - \sqrt{33}}{8}$

Or

(b) Given, the quadratic equation is $3x^2 - 4\sqrt{3}x + 4$.

Now, comparing with $ax^2 + bx + c = 0$, we get

$$a = 3, b = -4\sqrt{3} \text{ and } c = 4$$

Now, $D = b^2 - 4ac$

$= (-4\sqrt{3})^2 - 4 \times 3 \times 4$

$= 16 \times 3 - 48 = 48 - 48 = 0$

Since, $D = 0$ the equation has two equal real roots.

22. Since, $AB \parallel DC$, $\angle OAB = \angle OCD$ because they are alternate interior angles.

Since, $AB \parallel DC$, $\angle OBA = \angle ODC$, because they are alternate interior angles.

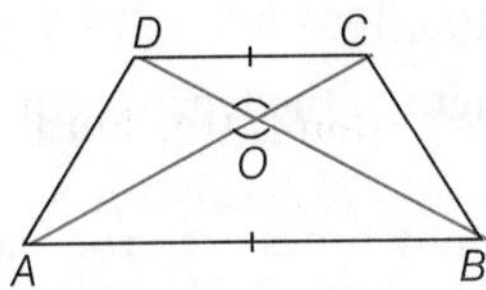

$\angle AOB = \angle COD$

[vertically opposite angles]

In ΔAOB and ΔCOD, we have

$\angle AOB = \angle COD$ [proved above]

and $\angle OAB = \angle OCD$

$\therefore$ $\Delta AOB \sim \Delta COD$ [by AA criterion]

Since, $\Delta AOB \sim \Delta COD$, the corresponding sides are proportional.

Therefore, $\dfrac{OA}{OC} = \dfrac{OB}{OD}$

23. (i) Given, total number of discs = 120

2-digit numbers range from 10 to 99.

The total number of 2-digit numbers

$= 99 - 10 + 1 = 90$

Now, probability of getting 2-digit number,

$\therefore$ P (2-digit number) $= \dfrac{90}{120} = \dfrac{3}{4}$

Perfect square between 1 to 120 are

1, 4, 9, 16, 25, 36, 49, 64, 81, 100.

So, 10 perfect squares between 1 to 120.

$\therefore$ P (perfect square) $= \dfrac{10}{120} = \dfrac{1}{12}$

24. (a) We have, $\dfrac{\cos 45^\circ}{\tan 30^\circ + \sin 60^\circ}$

$$= \frac{\frac{1}{\sqrt{2}}}{\frac{1}{\sqrt{3}} + \frac{\sqrt{3}}{2}} = \frac{\frac{1}{\sqrt{2}}}{\frac{2+3}{2\sqrt{3}}}$$

$$= \frac{2\sqrt{3} \times \sqrt{2}}{5\sqrt{2} \times \sqrt{2}} = \frac{2\sqrt{6}}{10} = \frac{\sqrt{6}}{5}$$

Or

(b) Given, $\sin 2A = \dfrac{2 \tan A}{1 + \tan^2 A}$, for $A = 30^\circ$

LHS $= \sin 2A$

$= \sin 2 \times 30^\circ$

$= \sin 60^\circ$

$= \dfrac{\sqrt{3}}{2}$

RHS $= \dfrac{2 \tan A}{1 + \tan^2 A}$

$$= \frac{2 \tan 30^\circ}{1 + \tan^2 30^\circ} = \frac{2 \times \frac{1}{\sqrt{3}}}{1 + \left(\frac{1}{\sqrt{3}}\right)^2}$$

$$= \frac{\frac{2}{\sqrt{3}}}{1 + \frac{1}{3}} = \frac{\frac{2}{\sqrt{3}}}{\frac{4}{3}} = \frac{6}{4\sqrt{3}}$$

$$= \frac{6 \times \sqrt{3}}{4\sqrt{3} \times \sqrt{3}} = \frac{6\sqrt{3}}{12} = \frac{\sqrt{3}}{2}$$

$\therefore$ LHS = RHS

25. HCF of 180, 140 and 210.

By prime factorisation,

$180 = 2 \times 2 \times 3 \times 3 \times 5,$

$140 = 2 \times 2 \times 5 \times 7$

and $210 = 2 \times 3 \times 5 \times 7$

$\therefore$ HCF of 180, 140 and 210 $= 2 \times 5 = 10$

26. Given, a quadratic polynomial is $8x^2 - 5x - 1$.

α and β are zeroes of the polynomial.

$\therefore$ $\alpha + \beta = \dfrac{-(-5)}{8} = \dfrac{5}{8}$ $\left[\because \alpha + \beta = \dfrac{-b}{a}, \alpha\beta = \dfrac{c}{a}\right]$

and $\alpha \cdot \beta = -\dfrac{1}{8}$

Now, sum of roots $\dfrac{2}{\alpha}$ and $\dfrac{2}{\beta}$.

$$\therefore \quad \frac{2}{\alpha} + \frac{2}{\beta} = 2\left(\frac{1}{\alpha} + \frac{1}{\beta}\right)$$

$$= 2\left(\frac{\alpha + \beta}{\alpha\beta}\right)$$

$$= \frac{2\left(\frac{5}{8}\right)}{-\frac{1}{8}} = 2\left(\frac{5}{8} \times -8\right)$$

$$= -10$$

and product of roots $\dfrac{2}{\alpha}$ and $\dfrac{2}{\beta}$.

$$\frac{2}{\alpha} \cdot \frac{2}{\beta} = \frac{4}{\alpha\beta} = \frac{4}{-\frac{1}{8}} = 4 \times -8 = -32$$

Now, a new quadratic polynomial,

$$x^2 - \left(\frac{2}{\alpha} + \frac{2}{\beta}\right)x + \left(\frac{2}{\alpha} \cdot \frac{2}{\beta}\right)$$

$$= x^2 - (-10)\,x + (-32) = x^2 + 10x - 32$$

Hence, the required quadratic polynomial is $x^2 + 10x - 32$.

Or

(b) Given polynomial is $p(x) = 3x^2 + x - 10$

$$= 3x^2 + x - 10 = 3x^2 + (6-5)x - 10$$
$$= 3x^2 + 6x - 5x - 10 = 3x(x+2) - 5(x+2)$$
$$= (x+2)(3x-5)$$

$\therefore \quad x = -2, \frac{5}{3}$

The zeroes of the polynomial are $\frac{5}{3}$ and -2.

Verification

Sum of zeroes $= \frac{5}{3} + (-2) = \frac{5}{3} - \frac{6}{3} = \frac{-1}{3}$

From polynomial, $-\frac{b}{a} = -\frac{1}{3}$

Product of zeroes $= \frac{5}{3} \times (-2) = -\frac{10}{3}$

From polynomial, $\frac{c}{a} = -\frac{10}{3}$

Hence, the relationship between the zeroes and coefficients is verified.

27. Given, perimeter of rectangle, $P = 100$ m

and area of rectangle, $A = 600 \text{ m}^2$

$\therefore$ Perimeter $= 2(l+b)$

$\Rightarrow \quad 100 = 2(l+b)$

$\Rightarrow \quad 50 = l + b$

$\Rightarrow \quad l = 50 - b \quad \quad \ldots$(i)

Now, Area $= l \times b$

$\Rightarrow \quad 600 = (50-b)\,b \quad$ [from Eq. (i)]

$\Rightarrow \quad 600 = 50b - b^2$

$\Rightarrow \quad b^2 - 50b + 600 = 0$

$\Rightarrow b^2 - (20+30)\,b + 600 = 0$

$\Rightarrow b^2 - 20b - 30b + 600 = 0$

$\Rightarrow b(b-20) - 30(b-20) = 0$

$\Rightarrow \quad (b-20)(b-30) = 0$

$\therefore b - 20 = 0$ or $b - 30 = 0$

So, $b = 20, 30$

If $b = 20$, then $l = 50 - 20 = 30$

If $b = 30$, then $l = 50 - 30 = 20$

Hence, the length and breadth of the rectangular park are 30 m and 20 m, respectively.

28. The prime factorisation of each number

$$120 = 2^3 \times 3 \times 5,\ 100 = 2^2 \times 5^2$$

and $150 = 2 \times 3 \times 5^2$

LCM is the product of highest powers of all prime factors that appear in the factorisation.

LCM (120, 100, 150) $= 2^3 \times 3 \times 5^2 = 600$

The least length of the fence is equal to the LCM that is 600 cm.

Now, how many times each rod measures the fence.

Rod 1 (120 cm) : $\frac{600}{120} = 5$ times

Rod 2 (100 cm) : $\frac{600}{100} = 6$ times

Rod 3 (150 cm) : $\frac{600}{150} = 4$ times

The least length of fence is 600 cm and the 120 cm rod can measure it 5 times, the 100 cm rod 6 times and the 150 cm rod 4 times.

29. Given, AB and CD are diameters of a circle with centre O and radius, $r = 7$ cm and $\angle BOD = 30°$,

$\therefore \quad \angle AOC = \angle BOD = 30°$ [vertically opposite angle]

Now, area of sector $BOD = \frac{30°}{360°} \times \pi r^2$

$$= \frac{1}{12} \times \pi \times 49 = \frac{49}{12}\pi \text{ cm}^2$$

and area of sector $AOC = \frac{30°}{360°} \times \pi r^2$

$$= \frac{1}{12} \times \pi \times 49 = \frac{49}{12}\pi \text{ cm}^2$$

$\therefore$ Total shaded area = Area of sector BOD + Area of sector AOC

$$= \frac{49}{12}\pi + \frac{49}{12}\pi = \frac{98}{12}\pi$$
$$= \frac{49}{6}\pi \text{ cm}^2$$

Now, length of arc $BD = \frac{30°}{360} \times 2\pi r$

$$= \frac{1}{12} \times 2 \times \pi \times 7 = \frac{7}{6}\pi \text{ cm}$$

and length of arc $AC = \frac{30°}{360°} \times 2\pi r$

$$= \frac{1}{12} \times 2 \times \pi \times 7 = \frac{7}{6}\pi \text{ cm}$$

$\therefore$ Total perimeter = Length of arc BD + Length of arc $AC + AB + CD$

$$= \frac{7}{6}\pi + \frac{7}{6}\pi + 14 + 14$$
$$= \frac{14}{6}\pi + 28 = \frac{7}{3}\pi + 28 \text{ cm}$$

30. See Q.4 (iii) on page 233.

31. (a) Let a be the first term and d be the common difference of given AP.

Now, according to given condition,

$$a_3 = 16$$

$\Rightarrow \quad a + (3-1)d = 16 \qquad [\because a_n = a + (n-1)d]$

$\Rightarrow \quad a + 2d = 16 \qquad \ldots(i)$

and $\quad a_7 = a_5 + 12$

$\Rightarrow \quad a_7 - a_5 = 12 \Rightarrow (a+6d) - (a+4d) = 12$

$\Rightarrow \quad 2d = 12 \Rightarrow d = 6$

From Eq. (i), $a + 2 \times 6 = 16 \Rightarrow a = 4$

Therefore, AP is 4, 10, 16, 22, ...

We know that

$$S_n = \frac{n}{2}[2a + (n-1)d]$$

$$\therefore \quad S_{29} = \frac{29}{2}[2 \times 4 + (29-1)\,6]$$

$$= \frac{29}{2}[8 + 28 \times 6] = \frac{29}{2}(8 + 168)$$

$$= \frac{29}{2} \times 176 = 29 \times 88 = 2552$$

Or

(b) We have, $a_n = 5 + 2n$

On putting $n = 1, 2, 3 \ldots$

$\therefore \quad a_1 = 5 + 2 \times 1 = 7$

$a_2 = 5 + 2 \times 2 = 5 + 4 = 9$

$a_3 = 5 + 2 \times 3 = 5 + 6 = 11$

$\vdots \qquad \vdots \qquad \vdots$

So, the list of number becomes 7, 9, 11, ...

Here, $9 - 7 = 11 - 9 = 2$ and so on

So, it forms an AP with common difference, $d = 2$

We have, $n = 20$, $a = 7$ and $d = 2$

$$\therefore \quad S_{20} = \frac{20}{2}[2 \times 7 + (20-1) \times 2]$$

$$\left[\because S_n = \frac{n}{2}[2a + (n-1)\,d]\right]$$

$$= 10\,[14 + 38] = 10 \times 52 = 520$$

So, the sum of first 20 terms of the AP is 520.

Now, we want to know that if there is any n for which

$$a_n = 52$$

If such any n is there, then we have

$7 + (n-1)\,2 = 52 \qquad [\because a_n = a + (n-1)\,d]$

$\Rightarrow \quad 2\,(n-1) = 45$

$\Rightarrow \quad n - 1 = \frac{45}{2} \Rightarrow n = \frac{45}{2} + 1$

$\therefore \quad n = \frac{47}{2} = 23.5$

Hence, 52 is not the term of given AP as 23.5 is not a natural number.

32. (a) Given, $\quad 2x + y = 9 \qquad \ldots(i)$

and $\quad x - 2y = 2 \qquad \ldots(ii)$

Now, from Eq. (i),

$$2x = 9 - y \Rightarrow x = \frac{9-y}{2}$$

When $y = 1$, $x = \frac{9-1}{2} = 4$

$y = 3$, $x = \frac{9-3}{2} = 3$

Table for $2x + y = 9$ is

x	4	3
y	1	3
Points	$A(4, 1)$	$B(3, 3)$

Now, from Eq. (ii),

$x - 2y = 2 \Rightarrow x = 2y + 2$

When $y = 1$, $x = 2 \times 1 + 2 = 2 + 2 = 4$

$y = 2$, $x = 2 \times 2 + 2 = 4 + 2 = 6$

Table for $x - 2y = 2$ is

x	4	6
y	1	2
Points	$A(4, 1)$	$C(6, 2)$

Clearly, lines (i) and (ii) intersect each other at point $A(4, 1)$.

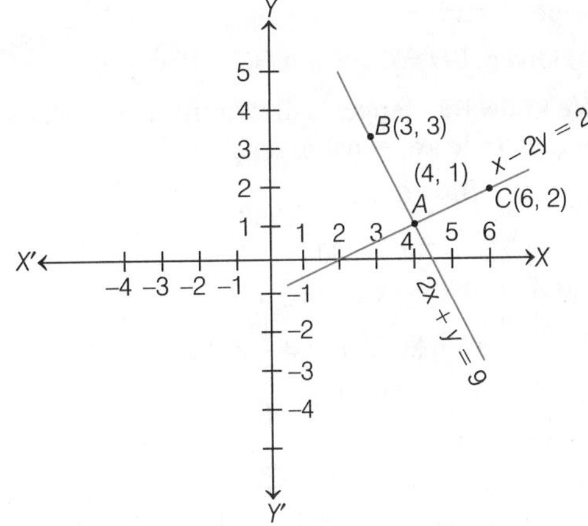

Hence, $x = 4$ and $y = 1$ is the solution of the given system of equations.

Or

(b) Nidhi received ₹1200 when invested ₹x at 6% p.a. and ₹y at 5% p.a. for 1 year.

We know that

$$\text{Simple interest} = \frac{P \times R \times T}{100}$$

The total interest is the sum of the simple interest from x and y.

$$\therefore \quad 1200 = \frac{x \times 6 \times 1}{100} + \frac{y \times 5 \times 1}{100}$$

$$\Rightarrow \quad 1200 = \frac{6x}{100} + \frac{5y}{100}$$

$$\Rightarrow \quad 6x + 5y = 120000 \quad \ldots\text{(i)}$$

Similarly, for second condition, we have

$$1260 = \frac{x \times 3 \times 1}{100} + \frac{y \times 8 \times 1}{100}$$

$$\Rightarrow \quad 1260 = \frac{3x}{100} + \frac{8y}{100}$$

$$\Rightarrow \quad 3x + 8y = 126000 \quad \ldots\text{(ii)}$$

On multiplying Eq. (ii) by 2, we get

$$6x + 16y = 252000 \quad \ldots\text{(iii)}$$

On subtracting Eq. (i) from Eq. (iii), we get

$$(6x + 16y) - (6x + 5y) = 252000 - 120000$$

$$\Rightarrow \quad 11y = 132000$$

$$\Rightarrow \quad y = 12000$$

On substituting $y = 12000$ in Eq. (i), we get

$$6x + 5 \times 12000 = 120000$$

$$\Rightarrow \quad 6x = 120000 - 60000$$

$$\Rightarrow \quad 6x = 60000$$

$$\Rightarrow \quad x = 10000$$

Hence, the values of x and y are 10000 and 12000, respectively.

33. (a) Given, $BD = 6$ cm and $DC = 10$ cm

We know that tangents drawn from an external point to the circle are equal in length.

$\therefore \quad BD = BF = 6$ cm

$CD = CF = 10$ cm

and $AF = AE = x$ cm (say)

Now, area of ΔOBC, $A_1 = \frac{1}{2} \times \text{Base} \times \text{Height}$

$$= \frac{1}{2} \times BC \times OD$$

$$= \frac{1}{2} \times 16 \times 4 = 32 \text{ cm}^2 \quad [\because BC = BD + CD]$$

Area of ΔOBA, $A_2 = \frac{1}{2} \times AB \times OE$

$$= \frac{1}{2} \times (6 + x) \times 4$$

$$= (12 + 2x) \text{ cm}^2$$

and area of ΔOAC, $A_3 = \frac{1}{2} \times AC \times OF$

$$= \frac{1}{2} \times (10 + x) \times 4$$

$$= (20 + 2x) \text{ cm}^2$$

Thus, area of $\Delta ABC = A_1 + A_2 + A_3$

$$= 32 + 12 + 2x + 20 + 2x$$

$$= (64 + 4x) \text{ cm}^2 \quad \ldots\text{(i)}$$

Now, semi-perimeter of

$$\Delta ABC = \frac{1}{2}(AB + BC + CA)$$

$$\Rightarrow \quad S = \frac{1}{2}(x + 6 + 16 + 10 + x)$$

$$\Rightarrow \quad S = \frac{1}{2}(32 + 2x) = (16 + x) \text{ cm}$$

Using Heron's formula,

Area of $\Delta ABC = \sqrt{s(s-a)(s-b)(s-c)}$

$$= \sqrt{(16 + x)(16 + x - 6 - x)(16 + x - 16)(16 + x - 10 - x)}$$

$$= \sqrt{(16 + x)(10)(x)(6)}$$

$$= \sqrt{60x(x + 16)} \quad \ldots\text{(ii)}$$

From Eqs. (i) and (ii), we get

$$\sqrt{60x(x + 16)} = 4x + 64$$

$$\Rightarrow 60x(x + 16) = 16(x + 16)^2 \quad \text{[squaring both sides]}$$

$$\Rightarrow \quad 60x = 16(x + 16)$$

$$\Rightarrow \quad 15x = 4(x + 16)$$

$$\Rightarrow \quad 15x = 4x + 64$$

$$\Rightarrow \quad 11x = 64$$

$$\Rightarrow \quad x = \frac{64}{11}$$

Hence, the length of AE is $\frac{64}{11}$ cm.

Or

(b) Given, $\angle AOB = 120°$ and $OA = 10$ cm

(i) Since, PA is a tangent, so $\angle OAP = 90° = \angle OBP$

In quadrilateral $OAPB$, the sum of angles is 360°.

Here, $\angle OPA = \angle OPB$ because PA and PB are tangents from the same point.

$$\therefore \angle AOB + \angle OAP + \angle OBP + \angle BPA = 360°$$

$$\Rightarrow \quad 120° + 90° + 90° + \angle BPA = 360°$$

$$\Rightarrow \quad \angle BPA = 360° - 300° = 60°$$

Now, $\angle OPA = \frac{1}{2}\angle BPA = \frac{60°}{2} = 30°$

(ii) In right angled triangle OAP, we have

$$\tan(\angle AOP) = \frac{AP}{OA}$$

$$\Rightarrow \quad \tan 60^\circ = \frac{AP}{OA} \quad \left[\because \angle AOP = \frac{1}{2}\angle AOB\right]$$

$$\Rightarrow \quad AP = OA \tan 60^\circ = 10\sqrt{3} \text{ cm}$$

Also, $OP = \dfrac{OA}{\cos 60^\circ} = \dfrac{10}{\frac{1}{2}} = 20$ cm

$$\left[\cos\theta = \frac{\text{Base}}{\text{Hypotenuse}}\right]$$

Now, perimeter of $\Delta OAP = OA + AP + OP$

$$= 10 + 10\sqrt{3} + 20$$

$$= (30 + 10\sqrt{3}) \text{ cm}$$

(iii) Let M be the intersection of OP and AB.

$\therefore$ ΔOMA is a right angled triangle.

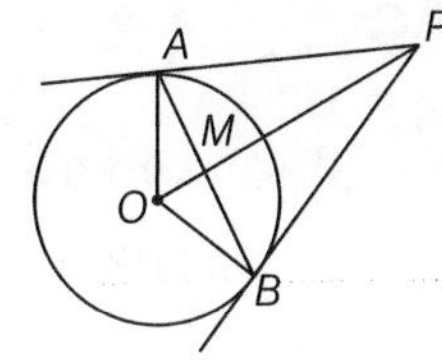

Here, $\angle AOM = \frac{1}{2}\angle AOB = 60^\circ$

Now, $AM = OA \sin 60^\circ = 10 \cdot \dfrac{\sqrt{3}}{2} = 5\sqrt{3}$ cm

and $AB = 2 \cdot AM = 2 \cdot 5\sqrt{3} = 10\sqrt{3}$ cm

34. Let the multi-storied building AB be h m. and distance between the two buildings be d m and CD be the tall building of 10 m.

According to the question,

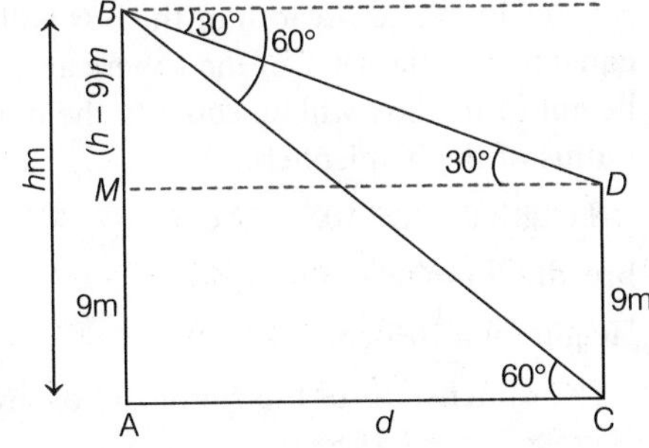

In ΔBMD,

$$\tan 30^\circ = \frac{BM}{MD}$$

$$\Rightarrow \quad \frac{h-9}{d} = \frac{1}{\sqrt{3}} \quad \left[\because \tan 30^\circ = \frac{1}{\sqrt{3}}\right]$$

$$\Rightarrow \quad \sqrt{3}(h-9) = d \qquad \ldots\text{(i)}$$

Now, in ΔBAC,

$$\tan 60^\circ = \frac{AB}{AC} \Rightarrow \frac{h}{d} = \sqrt{3}$$

$$\Rightarrow \quad h = d\sqrt{3} \qquad \ldots\text{(ii)}$$

On putting the value of h from Eq. (ii) in Eq. (i), we get

$$\sqrt{3}(d\sqrt{3} - 9) = d$$

$$\Rightarrow \quad 3d - 9\sqrt{3} = d$$

$$\Rightarrow \quad 3d - d = 9\sqrt{3}$$

$$\Rightarrow \quad d = \frac{9\sqrt{3}}{2} = \frac{9 \times 1.73}{2} = 7.785 \text{ m}$$

$$\therefore \quad h = \frac{9\sqrt{3}}{2} \times \sqrt{3} = \frac{9 \times 3}{2} = \frac{27}{2} = 13.5 \text{ m}$$

So, the height of the multi-storied building is 13.5 m and the distance between the two buildings is 7.785 m.

35. Table for given data is

Class	Class Interval (x_i)	Frequency (f_i)	$f_i x_i$
15-20	17.5	12	210
20-25	22.5	10	225
25-30	27.5	15	412.5
30-35	32.5	11	357.5
35-40	37.5	7	262.5
40-45	42.5	5	212.5
Total		$\Sigma f_i = 60$	$\Sigma f_i x_i = 1680$

Mean, $\bar{x} = \dfrac{\Sigma f_i x_i}{\Sigma f_i} = \dfrac{1680}{60} = 28$

Here, the maximum frequency is 15 and the corresponding class is 25-30. So, this is the modal class.

We have, $l = 25, h = 5, f_1 = 15, f_0 = 10$ and $f_2 = 11$

$$\therefore \text{Mode} = l + \frac{f_1 - f_0}{2f_1 - f_0 - f_2} \times h$$

$$= 25 + \frac{15 - 10}{30 - 10 - 11} \times 5$$

$$= 25 + \frac{25}{9} = \frac{225 + 25}{9} = \frac{250}{9}$$

$$= 27.78$$

Hence, mean and mode of the given data is 28 and 27.78, respectively.

36. Given, ΔABC is a right angled triangle with

$\angle A = 90°$ and $AB = AC$

$\because$ Points P and R trisect AB.

$\therefore \quad AR = RP = PB = \frac{AB}{3}$

Also, $PQ || AC$ and $RS || AC$.

(i) In ΔBPQ and ΔBAC,

since, $PQ || AC$

$\therefore \quad \angle BPQ = \angle BAC$ [corresponding angles]

and $\angle BQP = \angle BCA$ [corresponding angles]

$\therefore \quad \Delta BPQ \sim \Delta BAC$ [by AA similarity criterion]

(ii) Since, $\Delta BPQ \sim \Delta BAC$

$\therefore \quad \frac{PQ}{AC} = \frac{BP}{BA}$ ...(I)

[corresponding sides of similar triangles are proportional]

Since, P is a trisection point of AB.

$\therefore \quad BP = \frac{1}{3}BA$

$\Rightarrow \quad \frac{BP}{BA} = \frac{1}{3}$

Thus, $\frac{PQ}{AC} = \frac{1}{3}$ [$\because$ from Eq. (I)]

$\Rightarrow \quad PQ = \frac{1}{3}AC$ ...(II)

(iii) (a) We have, $AB = AC = 3$ m

Since, points P and R trisect AB.

$\therefore AR = RP = BP = \frac{AB}{3} = \frac{3}{3} = 1$ m

$\therefore$ Also, $PQ = \frac{1}{3}AC$ [from Eq (II)]

$\Rightarrow \quad PQ = \frac{1}{3} \times 3 = 1$ m

Now, in ΔBPQ,

$BQ^2 = BP^2 + PQ^2$ [by Pythagoras theorem]

$= 1^2 + 1^2 = 2$

$\Rightarrow \quad BQ = \sqrt{2}$ m

Now, $AB = AR + BR$

$\Rightarrow \quad 3 = 1 + BR$ [$\because AB = 3$ m, $AR = 1$ m]

$\Rightarrow \quad BR = 3 - 1 = 2$ m

In ΔBRS and ΔBAC,

since, $RS || AC$

$\therefore \quad \angle BRS = \angle BAC$ [corresponding angles]

and $\angle BSR = \angle BCA$ [corresponding angles]

$\therefore \Delta BRS \sim \Delta BAC$ [by AA similarity criterion]

$\therefore \quad \frac{RS}{AC} = \frac{BR}{AB}$

[corresponding sides of similar triangles are proportional]

$\Rightarrow \quad \frac{RS}{3} = \frac{2}{3} \Rightarrow RS = 2$ m

Now, in ΔBRS,

$BS^2 = BR^2 + RS^2$

$= 2^2 + 2^2 = 4 + 4 = 8$

$\Rightarrow \quad BS = 2\sqrt{2}$ m

We have to verify that $BQ = \frac{1}{2}BS$.

$\text{RHS} = \frac{1}{2}BS = \frac{1}{2} \times 2\sqrt{2} = \sqrt{2} = BQ = \text{LHS}$

Hence, $BQ = \frac{1}{2}BS$

Or

(b) In ΔBAC,

$BC^2 = AB^2 + AC^2$

$= 3^2 + 3^2 = 9 + 9 = 18$

We have to prove that $BR^2 + RS^2 = \frac{4}{9}BC^2$.

$\text{LHS} = BR^2 + RS^2$

$= 2^2 + 2^2 = 4 + 4 = 8$

$\text{RHS} = \frac{4}{9}BC^2 = \frac{4}{9} \times 18 = 8$

$\therefore$ LHS = RHS

37. Let r_1 be the inner radius and r_2 be the outer radius.

$\therefore r_1 = 10$ cm and $r_2 = 10.5$ cm

(i) $\because$ The hemispherical bowl fits perfectly inside the cuboidal box.

$\therefore$ The length and breadth of the box will be equal to the diameter of the sphere and the height of the box will be equal to the outer radius of the hemisphere.

$\therefore$ Length $(l) = 2 \times 10.5 = 21$ cm

Breadth $(b) = 2 \times 10.5 = 21$ cm

Height $(h) = 10.5$ cm

$\therefore$ The dimensions of the cuboidal box are $21 \text{ cm} \times 21 \text{ cm} \times 10.5$ cm.

(ii) Total surface area of the cuboidal box

$= 2(lb + bh + hl)$

$= 2(21 \times 21 + 21 \times 10.5 + 10.5 \times 21)$

$= 2(441 + 220.5 + 220.5) = 2 \times 882$

$= 1764 \text{ cm}^2$

(iii) (a) Capacity of the bowl $= \frac{2}{3}\pi r_1^3$

$$= \frac{2}{3} \times 3.14 \times 10^3 = 2093.33 \text{ cm}^3$$

Volume of the box $= l \times b \times h$

$$= 21 \times 21 \times 10.5$$
$$= 4630.50 \text{ cm}^3$$

$\therefore$ Required difference $= 4630.50 - 2093.33$

$$= 2537.17 \text{ cm}^3$$

Or

(b) Inner surface area of the bowl

$$= 2\pi r_1^2 = 2 \times 3.14 \times (10)^2 = 628 \text{ cm}^2$$

Area of the circular ring formed by thickness of the bowl $= \pi r_2^2 - \pi r_1^2$

$$= \pi[(10.5)^2 - (10)^2]$$
$$= 3.14(110.25 - 100)$$
$$= 3.14 \times 10.25$$
$$= 32.185 \text{ cm}^2$$

$\therefore$ Total area to be painted $= 628 + 32.185$

$$= 660.165 \text{ cm}^2$$

38. Given points are $P(8,6)$, $Q(12,2)$ and $S(-6,6)$.

(i) Distance between two points (x_1, y_1) and (x_2, y_2)

$$= \sqrt{(x_2 - x_1)^2 + (y_2 - y_1)^2}$$

$\therefore$ Distance of $OP = \sqrt{(8-0)^2 + (6-0)^2}$

$$[\because x_1 = 8,\ y_1 = 6 \text{ and } x_2 = 0,\ y_2 = 0]$$

$$= \sqrt{64 + 36} = \sqrt{100} = 10 \text{ units}$$

(ii) Given equation is $2x + 9y = 42$ ...(i)

We know that on Y-axis, the x-coordinate is 0.

On putting $x=0$ in Eq. (i), we get

$$2 \times 0 + 9y = 42 \Rightarrow y = \frac{42}{9} = \frac{14}{3}$$

$\therefore$ Required coordinates are $\left(0, \frac{14}{3}\right)$.

(iii) (a) Let point $R(4.8, y)$ divides the line segment OP in the ratio $k:1$.

O(0, 0) —— k —— R(4.8, y) —— 1 —— P(8, 6)

Now, by section formula,

$$(4.8, y) = \left(\frac{k \times 8 + 1 \times 0}{k+1}, \frac{k \times 6 + 1 \times 0}{k+1}\right)$$

$$\Rightarrow \quad (4.8, y) = \left(\frac{8k}{k+1}, \frac{6k}{k+1}\right)$$

On equating x-coordinate, we get

$$4.8 = \frac{8k}{k+1} \Rightarrow 4.8k + 4.8 = 8k$$

$$\Rightarrow \quad 4.8 = 3.2k \Rightarrow k = \frac{4.8}{3.2}$$

$$\Rightarrow \quad k = \frac{3}{2}$$

$\therefore$ So, the required ratio is 3:2.

Also, $y = \frac{6k}{k+1} \Rightarrow y = \frac{6 \times \frac{3}{2}}{\frac{3}{2} + 1}$

$$\Rightarrow \quad y = \frac{9}{\frac{5}{2}} \Rightarrow y = \frac{18}{5}$$

Or

(b) Length of $PQ = \sqrt{(12-8)^2 + (2-6)^2}$

$$= \sqrt{4^2 + (-4)^2}$$
$$= \sqrt{16 + 16} = \sqrt{32} = 4\sqrt{2} \text{ units}$$

and length of $OS = \sqrt{(-6-0)^2 + (6-0)^2}$

$$= \sqrt{36 + 36} = \sqrt{72}$$
$$= 6\sqrt{2} \text{ units}$$

Now, $\frac{PQ}{OS} = \frac{4\sqrt{2}}{6\sqrt{2}} = \frac{2}{3}$ **Hence proved.**

CBSE Examination Paper 2025

Mathematics (Standard Level)

Time : 3 hrs | M.M. : 80

General Instructions

1 This question paper has 5 Sections A, B, C, D and E.
2 Section A has 20 Multiple Choice Questions (MCQs) carrying 1 mark each.
3 Section B has 5 Short Answer-I (SA-I) type questions carrying 2 marks each.
4 Section C has 6 Short Answer-II (SA-II) type questions carrying 3 marks each.
5 Section D has 4 Long Answer (LA) type questions carrying 5 marks each.
6 Section E has 3 Case Based integrated units of assessment (4 marks each) with sub-parts of the values of 1, 1 and 2 marks each respectively.
7 All questions are compulsory. However, an internal choice in 2 Qs of 2 marks, 2 Qs of 3 marks and 2 Qs of 5 marks has been provided. An internal choice has been provided in the 2 marks question of Section E.
8 Draw neat figures wherever required. Take $\pi = 22/7$ wherever required if not stated.

Section A

Section A consists of 20 Questions of 1 mark each

Directions Q. No. 1 to 20 are multiple choice questions of 1 mark each.

1. $\sqrt{0.4}$ **is a/an**

(a) natural number
(b) integer
(c) rational number
(d) irrational number

2. Which of the following cannot be the unit digit of 8^n, where n is a natural number?

(a) 4 (b) 2 (c) 0 (d) 6

3. Which of the following quadratic equations has real and equal roots ?

(a) $(x+1)^2 = 2x+1$ (b) $x^2 + x = 0$
(c) $x^2 - 4 = 0$ (d) $x^2 + x + 1 = 0$

4. If the zeroes of the polynomial $ax^2 + bx + \frac{2a}{b}$ are reciprocal of each other then the value of b is

(a) 2 (b) $\frac{1}{2}$ (c) -2 (d) $-\frac{1}{2}$

5. The distance of the point $A(-3, -4)$ from X-axis is

(a) 3 (b) 4 (c) 5 (d) 7

6. In the given figure, $PQ \| XY \| BC$, $AP = 2$ cm, $PX = 1.5$ cm and $BX = 4$ cm. If $QY = 0.75$ cm then $AQ + CY$ is equal to

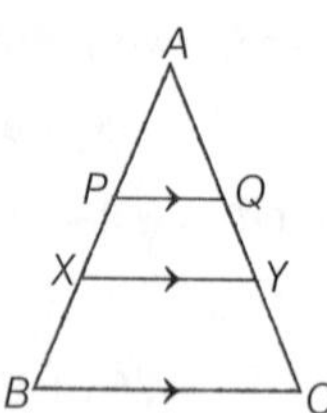

(a) 6 cm (b) 4.5 cm (c) 3 cm (d) 5.25 cm

7. Given, $\triangle ABC \sim \triangle PQR$, $\angle A = 30°$ and $\angle Q = 90°$. The value of $(\angle R + \angle B)$ is

(a) 90° (b) 120° (c) 150° (d) 180°

8. Two coins are tossed simultaneously. The probability of getting atleast one head is

(a) $\frac{1}{4}$ (b) $\frac{1}{2}$ (c) $\frac{3}{4}$ (d) 1

9. In the given figure, PA and PB are tangents to a circle with centre O such that $\angle P = 90°$. If $AB = 3\sqrt{2}$ cm then the diameter of the circle is

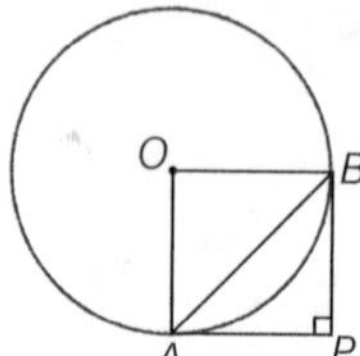

(a) $3\sqrt{2}$ cm (b) $6\sqrt{2}$ cm (c) 3 cm (d) 6 cm

10. For a circle with centre O and radius 5 cm, which of the following statements is true?

P : Distance between every pair of parallel tangents is 5 cm.

Q : Distance between every pair of parallel tangents is 10 cm.

R : Distance between every pair of parallel tangents must be between 5 cm and 10 cm.

S : There does not exist a point outside the circle from where length of tangent is 5 cm.

(a) P (b) Q (c) R (d) S

11. In the given figure, TS is a tangent to a circle with centre O. The value of $2x°$ is

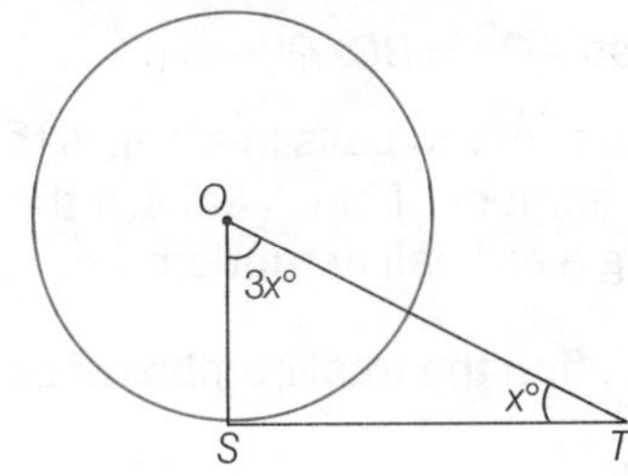

(a) 22.5 (b) 45 (c) 67.5 (d) 90

12. If $x\left(\frac{2\tan 30°}{1+\tan^2 30°}\right)=y\left(\frac{2\tan 30°}{1-\tan^2 30°}\right)$ then $x:y$ is equal to

(a) 1 : 1 (b) 1 : 2 (c) 2 : 1 (d) 4 : 1

13. A peacock sitting on the top of a tree of height 10 m observes a snake moving on the ground. If the snake is $10\sqrt{3}$ m away from the base of the tree then angle of depression of the snake from the eye of the peacock is

(a) 30° (b) 45° (c) 60° (d) 90°

14. If a cone of greatest possible volume is hollowed out from a solid wooden cylinder then the ratio of the volume of remaining wood to the volume of cone hollowed out is

(a) 1 : 1 (b) 1 : 3 (c) 2 : 1 (d) 3 : 1

15. If the mode of some observations is 10 and sum of mean and median is 25 then the mean and median, respectively are

(a) 12 and 13 (b) 13 and 12
(c) 10 and 15 (d) 15 and 10

16. If the maximum number of students has obtained 52 marks out of 80 then

(a) 52 is the mean of the data.
(b) 52 is the median of the data.
(c) 52 is the mode of the data.
(d) 52 is the range of the data.

17. The system of equations $2x+1=0$ and $3y-5=0$ has

(a) unique solution
(b) two solutions
(c) no solution
(d) infinite number of solutions

18. In a right ΔABC, right-angled at A, if $\sin B=\frac{1}{4}$ then the value of $\sec B$ is

(a) 4 (b) $\frac{\sqrt{15}}{4}$ (c) $\sqrt{15}$ (d) $\frac{4}{\sqrt{15}}$

Directions In question number 19 and 20, a statement of Assertion (A) is followed by a statement of Reason (R).

Choose the correct option from the following

(a) Both Assertion and Reason are true and Reason is correct explanation of Assertion.
(b) Both Assertion and Reason are true but Reason is not the correct explanation of Assertion.
(c) Assertion is true but Reason is false.
(d) Assertion is false but Reason is true.

19. Assertion (A) For any two prime numbers p and q, their HCF is 1 and LCM is $p+q$.

Reason (R) For any two natural numbers, HCF x LCM = Product of numbers.

20. In an experiment of throwing a die,

Assertion (A) Event E_1 : getting a number less than 3 and Event E_2 : getting a number greater than 3 are complementary events.

Reason (R) If two events E and F are complementary events then $P(E)+P(F)=1$

Section B

Section B consists of 5 Questions of 2 marks each

Directions This section has 5 very short answer type questions of 2 marks each.

21. (a) Solve the following pair of equations algebraically

$101x + 102y = 304; 102x + 101y = 305$

Or

(b) In a pair of supplementary angles, the greater angle exceeds the smaller by $50°$. Express the given situation as a system of linear equations in two variables and hence obtain the measure of each angle.

22. (a) If $a\sec\theta + b\tan\theta = m$ and $b\sec\theta + a\tan\theta = n$ then prove that

$$a^2 + n^2 = b^2 + m^2$$

Or

(b) Use the identity $\sin^2 A + \cos^2 A = 1$ to prove that $\tan^2 A + 1 = \sec^2 A$.

Hence, find the value of tan *A*, where

$\sec A = \frac{5}{3}$, where *A* is an acute angle.

23. Prove that abscissa of a point *P* which is equidistant from points with coordinates *A*(7, 1) and *B*(3, 5) is 2 more than its ordinate.

24. *P* is a point on the side *BC* of ΔABC such that $\angle APC = \angle BAC$.

Prove that $AC^2 = BC \cdot CP$.

25. The number of red balls in a bag is three more than the number of black balls. If the probability of drawng a red ball at random from the given bag is $\frac{12}{23}$, find the total number of balls in the given bag.

SECTION C

Section C consists of 6 Questions of 3 marks each

Directions This section has 6 short answer type questions of 3 marks each.

26. (a) Prove that $\sqrt{5}$ is an irrational number.

Or

(b) Let *p*, *q* and *r* be three distinct prime numbers.

Check whether $p \cdot q \cdot r + q$ is a composite number or not.

Further, give an example for 3 distinct primes *p*, *q* and *r* such that

(i) $p \cdot q \cdot r + 1$ is a composite number.

(ii) $p \cdot q \cdot r + 1$ is a prime number.

27. Find the zeroes of the polynomial $p(x) = 3x^2 - 4x - 4$. Hence, write a polynomial whose each of the zeroes is 2 more than zeroes of $p(x)$.

28. Check whether the following pair of equations is consistent or not. If consistent, solve graphically.

$$x + 3y = 6$$
$$3y - 2x = -12$$

29. If the points *A* (6, 1), *B* (*p*, 2), *C* (9, 4) and *D* (7, *q*) are the vertices of a parallelogram *ABCD* then find the values of *p* and *q*. Hence, check whether *ABCD* is a rectangle or not.

30. (a) Prove that $\frac{\cos\theta - 2\cos^3\theta}{\sin\theta - 2\sin^3\theta} + \cot\theta = 0$.

Or

(b) Given that $\sin\theta + \cos\theta = x$, prove that

$\sin^4\theta + \cos^4\theta = \frac{2 - (x^2 - 1)^2}{2}$.

31. In the given figure, *TP* and *TQ* are tangents drawn to a circle with centre *O*. If $\angle OPQ = 15°$ and $\angle PTQ = \theta$ then find the value of $\sin 2\theta$.

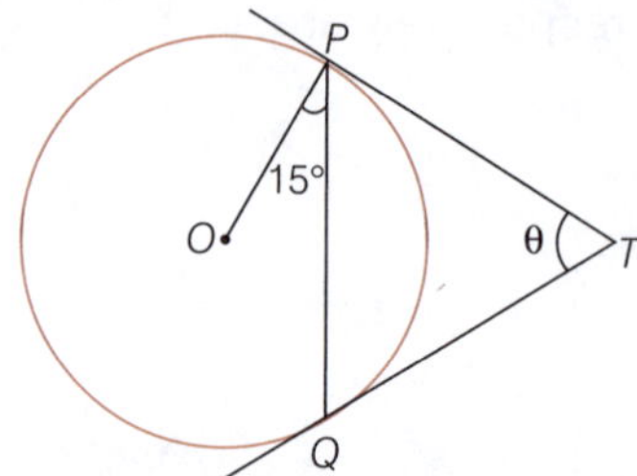

SECTION D

Section D consists of 4 Questions of 5 marks each

Directions This section has 4 long answer questions of 5 marks each.

32. (a) There is a circular park of diameter 65 m as shown in the following figure, where AB is a diameter.

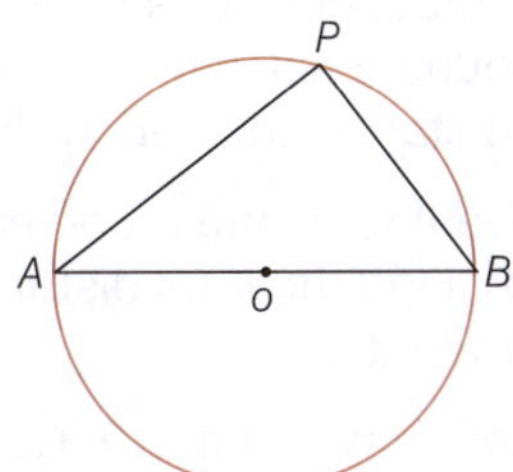

An entry gate is to be constructed at a point P on the boundary of the park such that distance of P from A is 35 m more than the distance of P from B. Find distance of point P from A and B, respectively.

Or

(b) Find the smallest value of p for which the quadratic equation $x^2 - 2(p+1)x + p^2 = 0$ has real roots. Hence, find the roots of the equation so obtained.

33. (a) If a line drawn parallel to one side of triangle intersecting the other two sides in distinct points divides the two sides in the same ratio, then it is parallel to third side.

State and prove the converse of the above statement.

Or

(b) In the given figure, ΔCAB is a right triangle, right angled at A and $AD \perp BC$. Prove that $\Delta ADB \sim \Delta CDA$. Further, if $BC = 10$ cm and $CD = 2$ cm, find the length of AD.

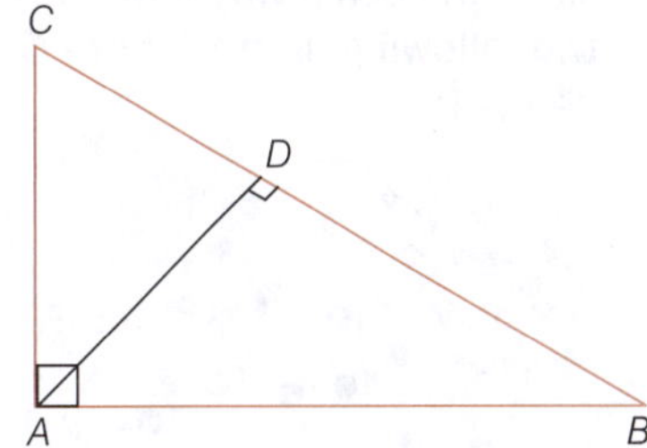

34. From one face of a solid cube ot side 14 cm, the largest possible cone is carved out. Find the volume and surface area of the remaining solid. $\left(\text{Use } \pi = \frac{22}{7}, \sqrt{5} = 2.2\right)$

35. Following distribution shows the marks of 230 students in a particular subject. If the median marks are 46 then find the values of x and y.

Marks	Number of Students
10-20	12
20-30	30
30-40	x
40-50	65
50-60	y
60-70	25
70-80	18

SECTION E

Section E consists of 3 Questions of 4 marks each

Directions This section has 3 case study based questions of 4 marks each.

36. Anurag purchased a farmhouse which is in the form of a semi-circle of diameter 70 m. He divides it into three parts by taking a point P on the semi-circle in such a way that $\angle PAB = 30°$ as shown in the following figure, where O is the centre of semi-circle.

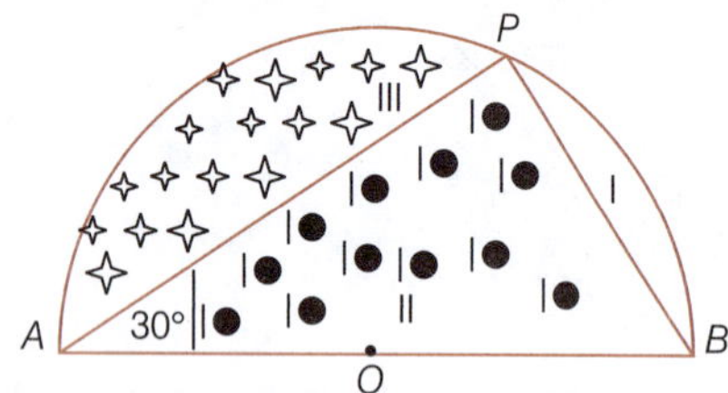

In part I, he planted saplings of Mango tree, in part II, he grew tomatoes and in part III, he grew oranges. Based on given information, answer the following questions.

(i) What is the measure of $\angle POA$?

(ii) Find the length of wire needed to fence entire piece of land.

(iii) (a) Find the area of region in which saplings of mango tree are planted.

Or

(b) Find the length of wire needed to fence the region III.

37. In order to organise, Annual Sports Day, a school prepared an eight lane running track with an integrated football field inside the track area as shown below

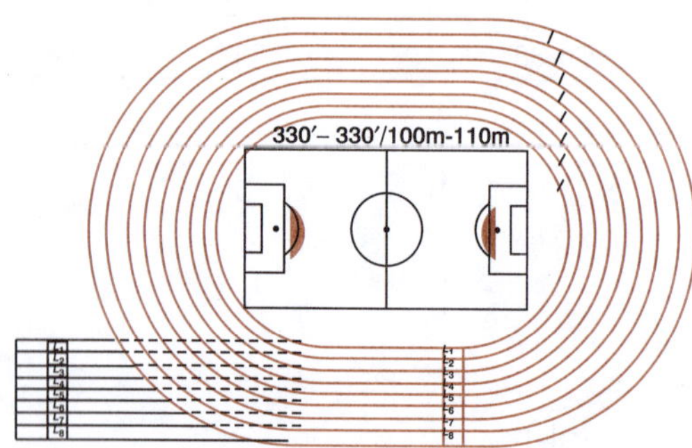

The length of innermost lane of the track is 400 m and each subsequent lane is 7.6 m longer than the preceding lane.

Based on given information, answer the following questions, using concept of Arithmetic Progression.

(i) What is the length of the 6th lane ?

(ii) How long is the 8th lane than that of 4th lane ?

(iii) (a) While practicing for a race, a student took one round each in first six lanes. Find the total distance covered by the student.

Or (b) A student took one round each in lane 4 to lane 8. Find the total distance covered by the student.

38. The Statue of Unity situated in Gujarat is the world's largest Statue which stands over a 58 m high base. As part of the project, a student constructed an inclinometer and wishes to find the height of Statue of Unity using it.

He noted following observations from two places

Situation I The angle of elevation of the top of statue from Place A which is $80\sqrt{3}$ m away from the base of the statue is found to be $60°$.

Situation II The angle of elevation of the top of Statue from a Place B which is 40 m above the ground is found to be $30°$ and entire height of the Statue including the base is found to be 240 m.

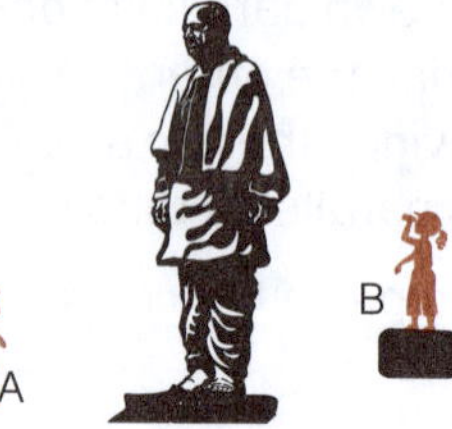

Based on given information, answer the following questions.

(i) Represent the Situation I with the help of a diagram.

(ii) Represent the Situation II with the help of a diagram.

(iii) (a) Calculate the height of statue excluding the base and also find the height including the base with the help of Situation I.

Or (b) Find the horizontal distance of Point B (Situation II) from the statue and the value of $\tan \alpha$, where α is the angle of elevation of top of base of the statue from Point B.

Solutions

1. (d) We have, $\sqrt{0.4} = \sqrt{\frac{4}{10}} = \frac{\sqrt{4}}{\sqrt{10}} = \frac{2}{\sqrt{10}}$

Since, $\sqrt{10}$ is irrational, $\frac{2}{\sqrt{10}}$ is also irrational.

Hence, $\sqrt{0.4}$ is an irrational number.

2. (c) We have, $8^n = (2 \times 2 \times 2)^n = 2^{3n}$

We know that if a number ends with digit 0, then it should be divisible by both 2 and 5.

Here, prime factorisation of 8^n does not contain 5.

Therefore, unit digit of 8^n cannot be zero.

3. (a) We have, $(x+1)^2 = 2x+1$

$\Rightarrow \quad x^2 + 1 + 2x = 2x + 1$

$\Rightarrow \quad x^2 = 0 \quad \ldots \text{(i)}$

On comparing Eq. (i) with $ax^2 + bx + c = 0$, we get

$a = 1,\ b = 0$ and $c = 0$

$\therefore$ Discriminant, $D = b^2 - 4ac = 0 - 4 \times 1 \times 0 = 0$

So, this equation has real and equal roots.

4. (a) Given polynomial is $ax^2 + bx + \frac{2a}{b}$.

Let α and $\frac{1}{\alpha}$ be the zeroes of the given polynomial.

Then, product of zeroes $= \frac{\frac{2a}{b}}{a}$

$\left[\because \text{product of zeroes} = \frac{\text{constant term}}{\text{coefficient of } x^2}\right]$

$\Rightarrow \quad \alpha \times \frac{1}{\alpha} = \frac{2a}{ab} \Rightarrow 1 = \frac{2}{b} \Rightarrow b = 2$

5. (b) Given point is $A(-3, -4)$.

Let the perpendicular from A on the X-axis intersects at B.

Point B lies on the X-axis, so the coordinate of point B is $(-3, 0)$.

Distance of the given point from X-axis $= AB$

Using distance formula,

$$AB = \sqrt{[-3-(-3)]^2 + [0-(-4)]^2}$$
$$= \sqrt{0+16} = \sqrt{16} = 4 \text{ units}$$

6. (c) In ΔAXY, $PQ \parallel XY$

$\therefore \quad \Delta AXY \sim \Delta APQ$

$\therefore \quad \frac{AP}{PX} = \frac{AQ}{QY}$

$\Rightarrow \quad \frac{2}{1.5} = \frac{AQ}{0.75}$

$\Rightarrow \quad AQ = \frac{2 \times 0.75}{1.5} = \frac{1.5}{1.5} = 1$

In ΔABC, $XY \parallel BC$

$\Delta ABC \sim \Delta AXY$

$\therefore \quad \frac{AX}{XB} = \frac{AY}{YC}$

$\Rightarrow \quad \frac{AP+PX}{XB} = \frac{AQ+QY}{YC}$

$\Rightarrow \quad \frac{2+1.5}{4} = \frac{1+0.75}{YC}$

$\Rightarrow \quad \frac{3.5}{4} = \frac{1.75}{YC}$

$\Rightarrow \quad YC = \frac{1.75 \times 4}{3.5} = \frac{7}{3.5} = 2$

Therefore, $AQ + CY = 1 + 2 = 3$

7. (c) Given, $\Delta ABC \sim \Delta PQR$, $\angle A = 30^\circ$ and $\angle Q = 90^\circ$

Here, $\angle B = \angle Q = 90^\circ$

In ΔABC, $\angle A + \angle B + \angle C = 180^\circ$

$\Rightarrow \quad 30^\circ + 90^\circ + \angle C = 180^\circ \Rightarrow \angle C = 60^\circ$

Also, $\angle C = \angle R = 60^\circ$

Now, $\angle R + \angle B = 60^\circ + 90^\circ = 150^\circ$

8. (c) When two coins are tossed simultaneously, then possible outcomes are (H, H), (H, T), (T, H) and (T, T).

$\therefore$ Total number of outcomes = 4

Let E be the event of getting atleast one head i.e. one head or two head. Then, outcomes favourable of E are (H, T), (T, H) and (H, H)

i.e. Number of outcomes favourable of $E = 3$

$$\therefore P(E) = \frac{\text{Number of outcomes favourable to } E}{\text{Total number of outcomes}} = \frac{3}{4}$$

9. (d) Given, PA and PB are tangent to a circle with centre O. Such that $\angle P = 90^\circ$ and $AB = 3\sqrt{2}$ cm.

Since, PA and PB are tangents from the same point P, they are equal in length i.e. $PA = PB \quad \ldots \text{(i)}$

In ΔPAB, $AB^2 = PA^2 + PB^2$

[using Pythagoras theorem]

$\Rightarrow \quad (3\sqrt{2})^2 = PA^2 + PA^2$ [using Eq. (i)]

$\Rightarrow \quad 2PA^2 = 18$

$\Rightarrow \quad PA^2 = 9$

$\Rightarrow \quad PA = 3$ cm

Since $\angle P = 90^\circ$ and $OA \perp PA$, $OB \perp PB$

$\therefore$ Quadrilateral $OPAB$ is a square.

So, $OA = OB = PA = PB = 3$ cm

Now, radius of the circle, $OA = 3$ cm

and diameter of the circle

$= 2OA = 2 \times 3 = 6$ cm

10. (b) Given, a circle with centre O and radius 5 cm.

We know that the distance between two parallel tangents to a circle is equal to diameter of the circle.

Here, radius = 5 cm

$\therefore$ Diameter $= 2\times 5 = 10$ cm

Hence, distance between every pair of parallel tangents is 10 cm.

11. (b) In the given figure, TS is a tangent.

We know that the tangent at any point of a circle is perpendicular to the radius through the point of contact.

$\therefore \; OS \perp TS$

So, $\angle OST = 90°$

Now, in ΔOST, $\angle OST + \angle STO + \angle TOS = 180°$

[angle sum property of a triangle]

$\Rightarrow \quad 90° + x° + 3x° = 180°$

$\Rightarrow \quad 4x° = 90° \Rightarrow x° = 22.5°$

Therefore, $2x° = 2\times 22.5° = 45°$

12. (c) We have, $x\left(\dfrac{2\tan 30°}{1+\tan^2 30°}\right) = y\left(\dfrac{2\tan 30°}{1-\tan^2 30°}\right)$

$$\Rightarrow \quad x\left(\frac{2\times\frac{1}{\sqrt{3}}}{1+\left(\frac{1}{\sqrt{3}}\right)^2}\right) = y\left(\frac{2\times\frac{1}{\sqrt{3}}}{1-\left(\frac{1}{\sqrt{3}}\right)^2}\right)$$

$$\Rightarrow \quad \frac{x}{1+\frac{1}{3}} = \frac{y}{1-\frac{1}{3}} \Rightarrow \frac{x}{4/3} = \frac{y}{2/3}$$

$$\Rightarrow \quad \frac{x}{y} = \frac{4}{3}\times\frac{3}{2} = 2 \Rightarrow x : y = 2 : 1$$

13. (a) Let height of tree, $AB = 10$ m and $BC = 10\sqrt{3}$ m

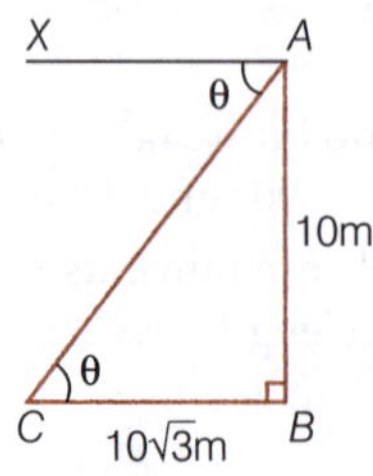

Again, let θ be the angle of depression.

Therefore, $\angle XAC = \angle ACB = \theta$

Now, in ΔACB, $\tan\theta = \dfrac{AB}{BC}$

$\Rightarrow \quad \tan\theta = \dfrac{10}{10\sqrt{3}} = \dfrac{1}{\sqrt{3}}$

$\Rightarrow \quad \tan\theta = \tan 30° \quad \left[\because \tan 30° = \dfrac{1}{\sqrt{3}}\right]$

$\Rightarrow \quad \theta = 30°$

Hence, angle of depression is 30°.

14. (c) Let r and h be the radius and height of the cylinder, respectively.

$\therefore$ Volume of cylinder $= \pi r^2 h$

Since, the cone is hollowed out from the cylinder with greatest possible volume, therefore it has same radius and height as the cylinder.

$\therefore$ Volume of cone $= \dfrac{1}{3}\pi r^2 h$

Volume of remaining wood

= Volume of cylinder − Volume of cone

$= \pi r^2 h - \dfrac{1}{3}\pi r^2 h = \dfrac{2}{3}\pi r^2 h$

Now, $\dfrac{\text{Volume of remaining wood}}{\text{Volume of cone hollowed out}} = \dfrac{\frac{2}{3}\pi r^2 h}{\frac{1}{3}\pi r^2 h} = \dfrac{2}{1}$

Hence, the ratio of volume of remaining wood to the volume of cone hollowed out is 2 : 1.

15. (b) Given, Mode = 10

and Mean + Median = 25

$\Rightarrow$ Mean = 25 − Median

We know that

Mode = 3 Median − 2 Mean

$\Rightarrow$ 10 = 3 Median − 2 (25 − Median)

$\Rightarrow$ 10 = 3 Medain − 50 + 2 Median

$\Rightarrow$ 5 Median = 60

$\Rightarrow$ Median = 12

$\therefore$ Now, Mean = 25 − Median = 25 − 12 = 13

Hence, the mean and median are 13 and 12, respectively.

16. (c) Given, maximum number of students has obtained 52 marks out of 80.

We know that the mode is the value that appears most often in a set of data.

Since, the score 52 is obtained by the maximum number of students, therefore 52 is the mode of the data.

17. (a) Given, pair of equation is

$$2x+1 = 0 \text{ and } 3y-5 = 0$$

On comparing the given equations with standard form of pair of linear equations i.e. $a_1x + b_1y + c_1 = 0$ and $a_2x + b_2y + c_2 = 0$, we get

$$a_1 = 2, b_1 = 0, c_1 = 1$$

and $\quad a_2 = 0, b_2 = 3, c_2 = -5$

Here, $\dfrac{a_1}{a_2} = \dfrac{2}{0} = \infty$ and $\dfrac{b_1}{b_2} = \dfrac{0}{3} = 0$

$\because \quad \dfrac{a_1}{a_2} \neq \dfrac{b_1}{b_2}$

$\therefore$ The system of given equations has unique solution.

18. (d) Given, a ΔABC in which $\angle A = 90°$ and $\sin B = \frac{1}{4}$

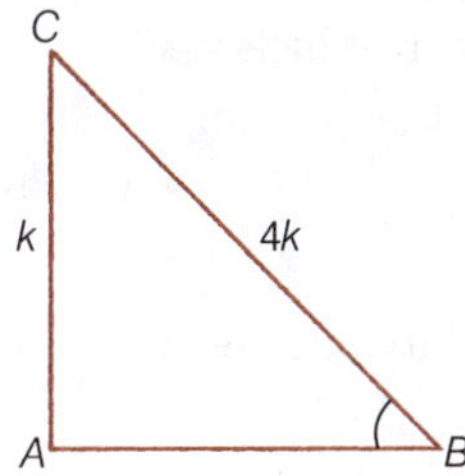

$\therefore$ Now, $\sin B = \frac{1}{4}$

$$\Rightarrow \frac{\text{Perpendicular}}{\text{Hypotenuse}} = \frac{1}{4}$$

$$\Rightarrow \frac{AC}{BC} = \frac{1}{4} = k \quad \text{(say)}$$

Then, $AC = k$ and $BC = 4k$

By Pythagoras theorem, in ΔABC, we get

$$BC^2 = AC^2 + AB^2$$
$$\Rightarrow (4k)^2 = k^2 + AB^2$$
$$\Rightarrow 16k^2 = k^2 + AB^2$$
$$\Rightarrow AB^2 = 15k^2$$
$$\Rightarrow AB = \sqrt{15}\,k$$

[taking positive square root]

Now, $\sec B = \frac{\text{Hypotenuse}}{\text{Base}}$

$$= \frac{BC}{AB} = \frac{4k}{\sqrt{15}k} = \frac{4}{\sqrt{15}}$$

19. (d) We know that HCF of two prime numbers P and Q is 1 and LCM of two prime numbers P and Q is $P \cdot Q$.

Hence, Assertion is false.

Clearly, Reason is true.

20. (d) When a die is thrown, there are six possible outcomes i.e. 1, 2, 3, 4, 5, 6.

So, sample space, $S = \{1, 2, 3, 4, 5, 6\}$

Here, E_1 = Event of getting a number less than 3 = $\{1, 2\}$

and E_2 = Event of getting a number greater than 3 = $\{4, 5, 6\}$

Now, $E_1 \cup E_2 = \{1, 2, 4, 5, 6\} \neq S$

$\therefore$ E_1 and E_2 are not complementary events.

Thus, Assertion is false.

Clearly, Reason is true.

21. (a) Given, pair of linear equation is

$$101x + 102y = 304 \quad \dots \text{(i)}$$

and
$$102x + 101y = 305 \quad \dots \text{(ii)}$$

On adding Eqs. (i) and (ii), we get

$$203x + 203y = 609$$
$$x + y = 3 \quad \dots \text{(iii)}$$

[dividing both sides by 203]

On subtracting Eq. (i) from Eq. (ii), we get

$$x - y = 1 \quad \dots \text{(iv)}$$

Now, adding Eqs. (iii) and (iv), we get

$$2x = 4$$
$$\Rightarrow x = 2$$

On substituting $x = 2$ in Eq. (iii), we get

$$y = 3 - 2 = 1$$

Hence, $x = 2$ and $y = 1$ is the required solution.

(b) Let x and y be the measure of the greater angle and smaller angle, respectively.

We know that the sum of two supplementary angles is equal to 180°.

$$\therefore \quad x + y = 180° \quad \dots \text{(i)}$$

According to the question,

$$x = y + 50 \quad \dots \text{(ii)}$$
$$\Rightarrow x - y = 50 \quad \dots \text{(iii)}$$

On adding Eqs. (i) and (iii), we get

$$2x = 230$$
$$\Rightarrow x = 115$$

On substituting $x = 115$ in Eq. (i), we get

$$y = 180° - 115° = 65°$$

Hence, the measure of the greater angle and smaller angle are 115° and 65°.

22. (a) Given, $a\sec\theta + b\tan\theta = m \quad \dots \text{(i)}$

$$b\sec\theta + a\tan\theta = n \quad \dots \text{(ii)}$$

On squaring and subtracting Eqs. (i) and (ii), we get

$$(a\sec\theta + b\tan\theta)^2 - (b\sec\theta + a\tan\theta)^2 = m^2 - n^2$$

$$\Rightarrow a^2\sec^2\theta + b^2\tan^2\theta + 2ab\sec\theta\cdot\tan\theta - b^2\sec^2\theta - a^2\tan^2\theta - 2ab\sec\theta\cdot\tan\theta = m^2 - n^2$$

$$\Rightarrow a^2(\sec^2\theta - \tan^2\theta) + b^2(\tan^2\theta - \sec^2\theta) = m^2 - n^2$$

$$\Rightarrow a^2 - b^2 = m^2 - n^2 \quad [\because \sec^2\theta - \tan^2\theta = 1]$$

$$\Rightarrow a^2 + n^2 = m^2 + b^2$$ **Hence proved**

Or

(b) Given, $\sin^2 A + \cos^2 A = 1 \quad \dots \text{(i)}$

On dividing Eq. (i) by $\cos^2 A$ both sides, we get

$$\therefore \frac{\sin^2 A}{\cos^2 A} + \frac{\cos^2 A}{\cos^2 A} = \frac{1}{\cos^2 A}$$

$$\Rightarrow \tan^2 A + 1 = \sec^2 A$$

$$\left[\because \tan\theta = \frac{\sin\theta}{\cos\theta} \text{ and } \sec\theta = \frac{1}{\cos\theta}\right]$$

Hence proved.

If $\sec A = \frac{5}{3}$

On squaring both sides, we get

$$\sec^2 A = \left(\frac{5}{3}\right)^2$$

$$\Rightarrow \quad \sec^2 A = \frac{25}{9}$$

Now, we know that $\tan^2 A + 1 = \sec^2 A$

$$\therefore \quad \tan A = \sqrt{\sec^2 A - 1}$$

$$= \sqrt{\frac{25}{9} - 1} = \sqrt{\frac{16}{9}} = \frac{4}{3}$$

$$\therefore \quad \tan A = \frac{4}{3} \quad [\because A \text{ is an acute angle}]$$

23. Let the coordinate of point P be (x, y).

$\because$ Point P is equidistant from points with coordinates $A(7, 1)$ and $B(3, 5)$.

So, by distance formula

$$\sqrt{(7-x)^2 + (1-y)^2} = \sqrt{(3-x)^2 + (5-y)^2}$$

On squaring both sides, we get

$$(7-x)^2 + (1-y)^2 = (3-x)^2 + (5-y)^2$$

$$\Rightarrow 49 + x^2 - 14x + 1 + y^2 - 2y$$

$$= 9 + x^2 - 6x + 25 + y^2 - 10y$$

$$[\because (a-b)^2 = a^2 + b^2 - 2ab]$$

$$\Rightarrow \quad -14x + 6x = 2y - 10y - 50 + 34$$

$$\Rightarrow \quad -8x = -8y - 16$$

$$\therefore \quad x = y + 2$$

[dividing by – 8 on both sides]

Hence proved.

24. Given, $\angle APC = \angle BAC$

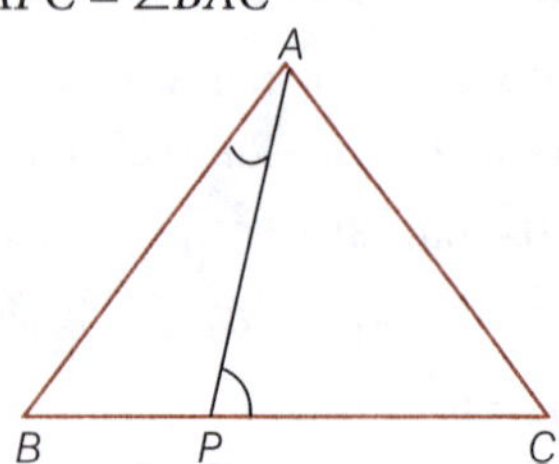

In ΔABC and ΔAPC,

$$\angle BAC = \angle APC \quad \text{[given]}$$

and $$\angle ACB = \angle ACP \quad \text{[common]}$$

$$\therefore \quad \Delta ABC \sim \Delta APC$$

[by AA similarity criterion]

$$\Rightarrow \quad \frac{CA}{CP} = \frac{CB}{CA}$$

[$\because$ corresponding sides of similar triangles are proportional]

$$\Rightarrow \quad CA^2 = CB \cdot CP$$

$$\Rightarrow \quad AC^2 = BC \cdot CP$$ **Hence proved.**

25. Let the number of red and black balls in a bag be x and y, respectively.

$\therefore$ Total number of balls $= x + y$

According to the question

$$x = y + 3$$

$$\Rightarrow \quad x - y = 3 \quad \ldots\text{(i)}$$

If the probability of drawing a red ball is $\frac{12}{23}$.

$$\therefore P \text{ (a red ball)} = \frac{x}{x+y}$$

$$\Rightarrow \quad \frac{12}{23} = \frac{x}{x+y}$$

$$\Rightarrow \quad 12x + 12y = 23x$$

$$\Rightarrow \quad 12y = 11x$$

$$\Rightarrow \quad x = \frac{12}{11}y \quad \ldots\text{(ii)}$$

On putting the value of x in Eq. (i), we get

$$\frac{12}{11}y - y = 3$$

$$\Rightarrow \quad 12y - 11y = 33$$

$$\Rightarrow \quad y = 33$$

On substituting $y = 33$ in Eq. (i), we get

$$x = 3 + 33 = 36$$

Hence, the total number of balls in bag is $33 + 36$ i.e. 69.

26. Let us assume on the contrary that $\sqrt{5}$ is a rational number. Then, there exist positive integers a and b such that $\sqrt{5} = \frac{a}{b}$, where a and b are coprime.

Now, $\sqrt{5} = \frac{a}{b}$

$$\Rightarrow \quad 5 = \frac{a^2}{b^2} = 5b^2 = a^2$$

$\Rightarrow$ 5 divides a^2.

$\Rightarrow$ 5 divides a.

So, 5 is a factor of a. ...(i)

$\Rightarrow \quad a = 5c$ for some integer c.

$\Rightarrow a^2 = 25c^2 = 5b^2 = 25c^2 \quad [\because a^2 = 5b^2]$

$\Rightarrow \; b^2 = 5c^2$

$\Rightarrow$ 5 divides b^2.

$\Rightarrow$ 5 divides b.

So, 5 is a factor of b. ... (ii)

From Eqs. (i) and (ii), we observe that a and b have at least 5 as a common factor. But this contradicts the fact that a and b are coprime. This means that our assumption is not correct.

Hence, $\sqrt{5}$ is an irrational number. **Hence proved.**

(b) We know that a prime number is a number that has only two factors.

Let the values of p, q and r are 2, 3 and 5, respectively.

$\therefore\ p \cdot q \cdot r + q = 2 \times 3 \times 5 + 3 = 33,$

which is a composite number.

[since, a composite number is a natural number or a positive integer which has more than two factors]

(i) Let the values of p, q and r be 3, 5 and 7, respectively.

Then, $p \times q \times r + 1 = 3 \times 5 \times 7 + 1 = 105 + 1 = 106,$

which is a composite number.

(ii) We have, $p \cdot q \cdot r + 1 = 3 \times 5 \times 7 + 1 = 106,$

which is not a prime number.

27. Given the polynomial $p(x) = 3x^2 - 4x - 4$

$= 3x^2 - (6-2)x - 4$ [by middle term splitting]

$= 3x^2 - 6x + 2x - 4$

$= 3x(x-2) + 2(x-2)$

$= (3x+2)(x-2)$

For zeroes, put $p(x) = 0$

$\therefore\quad (3x+2)(x-2) = 0$

$\Rightarrow 3x + 2 = 0$ or $x - 2 = 0$

$\Rightarrow\quad x = \frac{-2}{3}$ or $x = 2$

So, the zeroes of the polynomial are $-\frac{2}{3}$ and 2.

As per given condition, the zeroes of the new polynomial are $\left(\frac{-2}{3}+2\right)$ and $(2+2)$ i.e. $\frac{4}{3}$ and 4.

$\therefore x = \frac{4}{3}$ or $x = 4$

$\Rightarrow\quad \left(x - \frac{4}{3}\right)(x-4) = 0$

$\Rightarrow x^2 - 4x - \frac{4x}{3} + \frac{16}{3} = 0$

$\Rightarrow\quad x^2 - \frac{16x}{3} + \frac{16}{3} = 0$

Hence, the required new polynomial is

$$x^2 - \frac{16x}{3} + \frac{16}{3} = 0$$

28. The given equations can be rewritten as $x + 3y - 6 = 0$ and $-2x + 3y + 12 = 0$.

On comparing with standard form of pair of linear equations, we get

$a_1 = 1, b_1 = 3, c_1 = -6$ and $a_2 = -2, b_2 = 3, c_2 = 12$

Now, $\frac{a_1}{a_2} = \frac{1}{-2}, \frac{b_1}{b_2} = \frac{3}{3} = 1$ and $\frac{c_1}{c_2} = \frac{-6}{12} = -\frac{1}{2}$

Thus, $-\frac{1}{2} \neq 1$ i.e. $\frac{a_1}{a_2} \neq \frac{b_1}{b_2}$

Hence, the pair of linear equations is consistent.

Now, table for linear equation $x + 3y = 6$ is

x	0	6
$y = \frac{6-x}{3}$	2	0

Plot the points A and B and join them to the line AB.

Table for linear equation $-2x + 3y = -12$ is

x	0	6
$y = \frac{-12+2x}{3}$	−4	0

Plot the points C and D, and join them to the line CD.

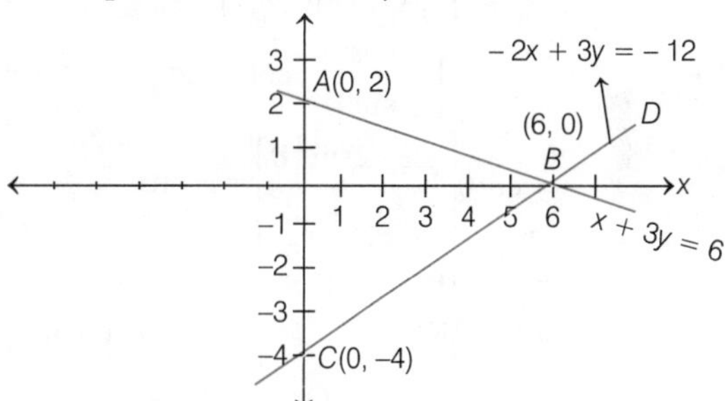

Two lines AB and CD intersect at the point $B(6, 0)$.

Hence, $x = 6$ and $y = 0$ is the required solution of the pair of linear equations.

29. Given, $ABCD$ is a parallelogram in which the coordinates of the vertices are $A(6, 1)$, $B(p, 2)$, $C(9, 4)$ and $D(7, q)$.

$\because ABCD$ is a parallelogram, the diagonals bisect each other.

$\therefore$ The mid-point of the diagonals of the parallelogram will coincide.

$\therefore$ Coordinate of mid-point of AC

= Coordinate of mid-point of BD.

$\Rightarrow \left(\frac{6+9}{2}, \frac{1+4}{2}\right) = \left(\frac{p+7}{2}, \frac{2+q}{2}\right)$

[by mid-point formula]

$\Rightarrow\quad \left(\frac{15}{2}, \frac{5}{2}\right) = \left(\frac{p+7}{2}, \frac{2+q}{2}\right)$

Here, $\frac{p+7}{2} = \frac{15}{2}$ and $\frac{2+q}{2} = \frac{5}{2}$

$\Rightarrow\quad p = 8$

$\Rightarrow\quad q = 3$

Hence, the value of p and q are 8 and 3.

By distance formula,

$$AB = \sqrt{(8-6)^2 + (2-1)^2} = \sqrt{4+1} = \sqrt{5}$$

$$BC=\sqrt{(9-8)^2+(4-2)^2}=\sqrt{1+4}=\sqrt{5}$$
$$CD=\sqrt{(7-9)^2+(3-4)^2}=\sqrt{4+1}=\sqrt{5}$$
$$DA=\sqrt{(6-7)^2+(1-3)^2}=\sqrt{(-1)^2+(-2)^2}=\sqrt{5}$$

Hence, the length of all sides of parallelogram are equal.

$\therefore$ *ABCD* is a square as well as rectangle.

30. (a) LHS $=\dfrac{\cos\theta-2\cos^3\theta}{\sin\theta-2\sin^3\theta}+\cot\theta$

$=\dfrac{\cos\theta[1-2\cos^2\theta]}{\sin\theta[1-2\sin^2\theta]}+\cot\theta$

$=\cot\theta\left[\dfrac{1-2(1-\sin^2\theta)}{1-2\sin^2\theta}\right]+\cos\theta$

$\left[\because \dfrac{\cos\theta}{\sin\theta}=\cot\theta \text{ and } 1-\sin^2\theta=\cos^2\theta\right]$

$=\cot\theta\left[\dfrac{-1+2\sin^2\theta}{1-2\sin^2\theta}\right]+\cot\theta$

$=-\cot\theta+\cot\theta$

$=0=\text{RHS}$ **Hence proved.**

Or

(b) Given, $\sin\theta+\cos\theta=x$

On squaring both sides, we get

$$(\sin\theta+\cos\theta)^2=x^2$$

$\Rightarrow \sin^2\theta+\cos^2\theta+2\sin\theta\cdot\cos\theta=x^2$

$[\because (a+b)^2=a^2+b^2+2ab]$

$\Rightarrow \quad 1+2\sin\theta\cdot\cos\theta=x^2$

$[\because \sin^2\theta+\cos^2\theta=1]$

$\Rightarrow \quad 2\sin\theta\cdot\cos\theta=x^2-1$

$\Rightarrow \quad \sin\theta\cdot\cos\theta=\dfrac{x^2-1}{2}$ ... (i)

Now, LHS $=\sin^4\theta+\cos^4\theta$

$=(\sin^2\theta)^2+(\cos^2\theta)^2+2\sin^2\theta\cdot\cos^2\theta-2\sin^2\theta\cdot\cos^2\theta$

[add and subtract $2\sin^2\theta\cdot\cos^2\theta$]

$=(\sin^2\theta+\cos^2\theta)^2-2\sin^2\theta\cdot\cos^2\theta$

$[\because (a+b)^2=a^2+b^2+2ab]$

$=1-2\dfrac{(x^2-1)^2}{4}$

[from Eq. (i) and $\sin^2\theta+\cos^2\theta=1$]

$=1-\dfrac{(x^2-1)^2}{2}$

$=\dfrac{2-(x^2-1)^2}{2}$ **Hence proved.**

31. Given, $\angle OPQ=15^\circ$ and $\angle PTQ=\theta$

$$TP=TQ$$

[$\because$ length of tangents drawn from an external point are equal]

and $\angle OPT=90^\circ$

[tangent to a circle is perpendicular to radius through the point of contact]

$\therefore \angle QPT=\angle OPT-\angle OPQ$

$=90^\circ-15^\circ=75^\circ$

In ΔPTQ,

By angle sum property,

$PQT+\angle QPT+\angle PTQ=180$

$\angle PQT+\angle QPT+\theta=180^\circ$

Since, $\angle PQT=\angle QPT=75^\circ$

[angle opposite to equal sides are also equal i.e. $TP=TQ$]

$\therefore \quad 75^\circ+75^\circ+\theta=180^\circ$

$\Rightarrow \quad 150^\circ+\theta=180^\circ$

$\Rightarrow \quad \theta=180^\circ-150^\circ=30^\circ$

$\therefore$ The value of $2\theta=2\times30^\circ=60^\circ$

32. (a) Given, the diameter of the circular park = 65 m

According to the question,

Distance of *P* from *A* = Distance of *P* from *B* + 35

$$PA=PB+35$$

We know that angle in a semi-circle is a right angle.

$\therefore \quad \angle APB=90^\circ$

$\therefore$ In ΔAPB, by Pythagoras theorem

$AB^2=PA^2+PB^2$

$\Rightarrow \quad (65)^2=PA^2+PB^2$ $[\because AB=65\text{ m}]$

$\Rightarrow \quad 4225=(PB+35)^2+PB^2$

$\Rightarrow \quad 4225=PB^2+(35)^2+70PB+PB^2$

$\Rightarrow \quad 4225=2PB^2+1225+70PB$

$\Rightarrow 2PB^2+70PB=4225-1225$

$\Rightarrow 2PB^2+70PB=3000$

$\Rightarrow PB^2+35PB=1500$

$\Rightarrow PB^2+35PB-1500=0$

$\Rightarrow PB^2+60PB-25PB-1500=0$

[by middle term splitting]

$\Rightarrow PB(PB+60)-25(PB+60)=0$

$\Rightarrow \quad (PB+60)(PB-25)=0$

$\Rightarrow \quad PB+60=0$ or $PB-25=0$

$PB=-60$ or $PB=25$

Since, distance cannot be negative.

$\therefore \; PB=25$ m

and $PA=25+35=60$ m

Hence, distance of point *P* from *A* and *B* are 60 m and 25 m.

Or

(b) Given the quadratic equation is

$$x^2 - 2(p+1)x + p^2 = 0 \quad \dots \text{(i)}$$

On comparing with $ax^2 + bx + c = 0$, we get

$$a = 1,\ b = -2(p+1) \text{ and } c = p^2$$

Now, discriminant $(D) = b^2 - 4ac$

$$= [-2(p+1)]^2 - 4 \times 1 \times p^2$$
$$= 4(p+1)^2 - 4p^2$$
$$= 4p^2 + 4 + 8p - 4p^2 = 4 + 8p$$

Since, the roots are real.

So, the discriminant must be greater than or equal to zero.

$\therefore \quad 4 + 8p \geq 0$

$\Rightarrow \quad 8p \geq -4 \Rightarrow p \geq -\frac{1}{2}$

So, the smallest value of p for which the equation has real roots is $p = -\frac{1}{2}$.

On substituting $p = -\frac{1}{2}$ in Eq. (i), we get

$$x^2 - 2\left(-\frac{1}{2} + 1\right)x + \left(-\frac{1}{2}\right)^2 = 0$$

$$\Rightarrow x^2 - x + \frac{1}{4} = 0 \Rightarrow \left(x - \frac{1}{2}\right)^2 = 0$$

$$\Rightarrow \quad x - \frac{1}{2} = 0 \Rightarrow x = \frac{1}{2}$$

Hence, the root of the equation is $\frac{1}{2}$.

33. (a) See theorem 1 on page no. 152.

Or

(b) Given, ΔCAB is a right angled triangle at A and $AD \perp BC$

In ΔADB,

$$\angle ADB + \angle BAD + \angle DBA = 180^\circ$$
$$\Rightarrow \quad 90^\circ + \angle BAD + \angle DBA = 180^\circ$$

[since, $AD \perp BC \Rightarrow \angle ADB = 90^\circ$]

$\Rightarrow \quad \angle DBA = 90^\circ - \angle BAD \quad \dots$(i)

Now, $\angle CAB = 90^\circ$ [given]

$\Rightarrow \quad \angle CAD + \angle BAD = 90^\circ$

$\Rightarrow \quad \angle CAD = 90^\circ - \angle BAD \quad \dots$(ii)

In ΔADB and ΔCDA,

$\angle ADB = \angle CDA = 90^\circ$ $[AD \perp BC]$

$\angle DBA = \angle CAD$ [from Eqs. (i) and (ii)]

$\therefore \quad \Delta ADB \sim \Delta CDA$ [by AA similarity criterion]

Now, $\frac{AD}{CD} = \frac{BD}{AD}$

[corresponding sides of similar triangle are proportional]

$$\Rightarrow \quad \frac{AD}{2} = \frac{BC - CD}{AD}$$

$$\Rightarrow \quad AD^2 = 2 \times (10 - 2) = 2 \times 8 = 16 \Rightarrow AD = 4 \text{ cm}$$

Hence, the length of AD is 4 cm.

34. Given, the side of a cube = 14 cm

$\therefore$ The volume of the cube = $(\text{side})^3 = (14)^3$

$$= 2744 \text{ cm}^3$$

$\because$ The largest possible cone is carved out in one face of cube.

$\therefore$ The radius (r) of cone is half the side of the cube i.e. $r = \frac{14}{2} = 7$ cm

and height (h) of the cone is equal to the side of the cube i.e. $h = 14$ cm

$\therefore$ The volume of the cone $= \frac{1}{3} \times \pi r^2 h$

$$= \frac{1}{3} \times \frac{22}{7} \times 7 \times 7 \times 14$$
$$= \frac{2156}{3} \text{ cm}^3$$

So, the volume of remaining solid

$$= \text{Volume of cube} - \text{Volume of cone}$$
$$= 2744 - \frac{2156}{3}$$
$$= \frac{8232 - 2156}{3}$$
$$= \frac{6076}{3} \text{ cm}^3$$

Now, surface area of cube $= 6 \times (\text{side})^2$

$$= 6 \times (14)^2 = 1176 \text{ cm}^2$$

and the curved surface area of the cone

$$= \pi r l$$
$$= \pi r \sqrt{h^2 + r^2} \quad [\because l^2 = h^2 + r^2]$$
$$= \frac{22}{7} \times 7 \times \sqrt{14^2 + 7^2}$$
$$= \frac{22}{7} \times 7 \times \sqrt{245}$$
$$= \frac{22}{7} \times 7 \times 7 \times \sqrt{5}$$
$$= 22 \times 7 \times 2.2 = 338.8 \text{ cm}^2$$

The area of the base of the cone $= \pi r^2$

$$= \frac{22}{7} \times 7^2 = 154 \text{ cm}^2$$

So, the surface area of the remaining solid

= Surface area of cube

+ Curved surface area of cone

− Surface area of base of the cone

$$= 1176 - 154 + 338.8$$
$$= 1360.8 \text{ cm}^2$$

35. Given, median = 46 and $n = \sum f = 230$

$\because$ Sum of frequencies = 230

$\therefore 12+30+x+65+y+25+18 = 230$

$\Rightarrow \quad 150+x+y = 230$

$\Rightarrow \quad x+y = 230-150 = 80$

$\Rightarrow \quad x+y = 80 \quad \ldots \text{(i)}$

Now, the cumulative frequencey table for given distribution is

Marks	Number of Students	Cumulative frequency
10-20	12	12
20-30	30	42
30-40	x	$42+x$
40-50	65	$107+x$
50-60	y	$107+x+y$
60-70	25	$132+x+y$
70-80	18	$150+x+y$

Here, $n = 230$

$\Rightarrow \quad \frac{n}{2} = 115$

Given, median = 46, which belongs to the class 40-50.

So, the median class is 40-50.

Then, $l = 40, h = 10, f = 65$ and $cf = 42+x$

$\because \quad \text{Median} = l + \left\{\frac{\frac{n}{2} - cf}{f}\right\} \times h$

$\therefore \quad 46 = 40 + \left(\frac{115-42-x}{65}\right) \times 10$

$\Rightarrow \quad 6 = \frac{73-x}{65} \times 10 \Rightarrow 73-x = \frac{6 \times 65}{10} = 39$

$\Rightarrow \quad -x = 39-73 \Rightarrow x = 34$

On putting the value of x in Eq. (i), we get

$x+y = 80$

$\Rightarrow \quad y = 80-34 = 46$

Hence, the values of x and y are 34 and 46, respectively.

36. Given, $\angle PAB = 30°$

(i) $\because$ The angle subtended by a diameter on the semi-circle is 90°.

$\therefore \angle APB = 90°$

Now, join P to O.

Here, $OP = OA$ [radii of same semi-circle]

$\therefore \quad \angle OPA = \angle OAP = 30°$

[angles opposite to equal sides are equal]

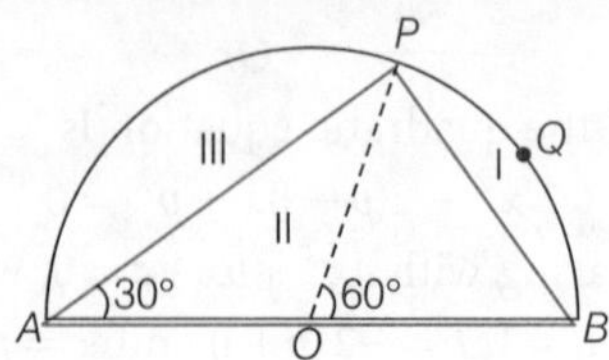

In ΔPOA,

$\angle POA + \angle OPA + \angle OAP = 180°$

[by angle sum property]

$\Rightarrow \quad \angle POA + 30° + 30° = 180°$

$\Rightarrow \quad \angle POA + 60° = 180°$

$\Rightarrow \quad \angle POA = 180° - 60° = 120°$

So, the measure of $\angle POA$ is 120°.

(ii) The length of wire needed to fence entire piece of land = The length of the arc APB + Diameter

$= \frac{1}{2} \times 2\pi r + 70 = \pi \times \frac{70}{2} + 70$

$\left[\because \text{radius} = \frac{\text{diameter}}{2}\right]$

$= (35\pi + 70)$ m

(iii) In ΔAPB, $\cos 30° = \frac{PA}{AB}$ $\left[\because \cos\theta = \frac{\text{base}}{\text{hypotenuse}}\right]$

$\Rightarrow \quad \frac{\sqrt{3}}{2} = \frac{PA}{70}$

$\left[\because AB = 70 \text{ m and } \cos 30° = \frac{\sqrt{3}}{2}\right]$

$\Rightarrow \quad PA = 35\sqrt{3}$ m $\quad \ldots$ (i)

and $\quad \sin 30° = \frac{PB}{AB}$ $\left[\because \sin\theta = \frac{\text{perpendicular}}{\text{hypotenuse}}\right]$

$\Rightarrow \quad \frac{1}{2} = \frac{PB}{70}$ $\left[\because \sin 30° = \frac{1}{2}\right]$

$\Rightarrow \quad PB = 35$ m $\quad \ldots$ (ii)

Now, $OP = OB = 35$ m

[radii of same semi-circle]

Also, $PB = 35$ m

So, ΔPOB is an equilateral triangle.

$\therefore$ Area of an equilateral,

$\Delta OPB = \frac{\sqrt{3}}{4} \times (\text{side})^2$

$= \frac{\sqrt{3}}{4} \times 35 \times 35$

$= 530.42 \text{ m}^2$

So, the area of region I

= Area of sector $OPBQ$

– Area of ΔOPB

[$\because$ each angle of an equilateral triangle is 60°]

$$= \frac{60°}{360°} \times \frac{22}{7} \times 35 \times 35 - 530.42$$

$$= 641.67 - 530.42 = 111.25 \text{ m}^2$$

Hence, the area of region in which saplings of mango tree are planted is 111.25 m^2.

Or

(iii) (b) Now, the length of arc $PB = \frac{\theta}{360°} \times 2\pi r$

$$= \frac{60°}{360°} \times 2 \times \frac{22}{7} \times 35 = 36.66$$

And the perimeter of semi-circle $= \frac{1}{2} \times 2\pi r$

$$= \frac{1}{2} \times 2 \times \frac{22}{7} \times 35 = 110$$

So, length of arc AP = Perimeter of semi-circle − Length of arc PB

$$= 110 - 36.66 = 73.34$$

Hence, the length of wire needed to fence the Region III $= PA +$ Length of arc AP

$$= 35\sqrt{3} + 73.34$$

$$= 60.62 + 73.34 \quad [\because \sqrt{3} = 1.732]$$

$$= 133.96 \text{ m}$$

37. Given, the length of innermost lane i.e. first lane $= 400$ m

And each subsequent lane is 7.6 m longer than the preceding lane.

So, the list of numbers is 400, 407.6, 415.2, …

and its form an AP, where $a = 400$ and $d = 7.6$

(i) 6th lane $= a_6$

$$= a + (6-1)d \quad [\because a_n = a + (n-1)d]$$

$$= 400 + 5 \times 7.6$$

$$= 400 + 38 = 438$$

So, the length of the 6th lane is 438 m.

(ii) 4th lane $= a_4$

$$= a + (4-1)d \quad [\because a_n = a + (n-1)d]$$

$$= 400 + 3 \times 7.6$$

$$= 400 + 22.8 = 422.8$$

So, the length of the 4th lane is 422.8 m.

8th lane $= a_8 = a + (8-1)d$

$$= 400 + 7 \times 7.6 = 400 + 53.2 = 453.2$$

So, the length of the 8th lane is 453.2 m.

Hence, 8th lane is 453.2 m − 422.8 m = 30.4 m longer than 4th lane.

(iii) (a) Total distance covered by the student

= The sum of length of first 6 lanes

$$= S_6 = \frac{6}{2}[2 \times 400 + (6-1)7.6]$$

$[\because$ sum of first n terms of a_n AP is $s_n = \frac{n}{2}[2a + (n-1)d]$]

$$= 3[800 + 38] = 3 \times 838 = 2514$$

So, the distance covered by the student is 2514 m.

Or

(iii) (b) Total distance covered by the student

= The sum of length of first 8 lanes − Sum of length of first 3 lanes

$$= S_8 - S_3 = \frac{8}{2}[2 \times 400 + (8-1)7.6] - \frac{3}{2}[2 \times 400 + (3-1)7.6]$$

$$= 4[800 + 53.2] - \frac{3}{2}[800 + 15.2]$$

$$= 4 \times 853.2 - \frac{3}{2} \times 815.2$$

$$= 3412.8 - 1222.8 = 2190$$

So, the distance covered by the student is 2190 m.

38. Given, the height of base of the statue is 58 m.

(i) Let PQ be the height of base of the statue and PR be the height of statue including base.

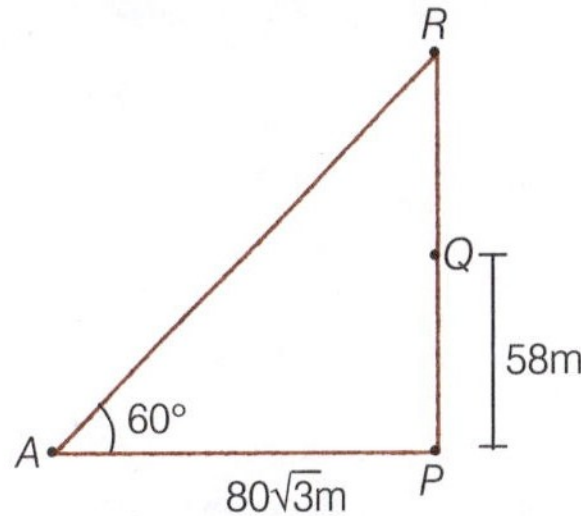

(ii) Let MO be the height of base of the statue and SM be the height of statue including base.

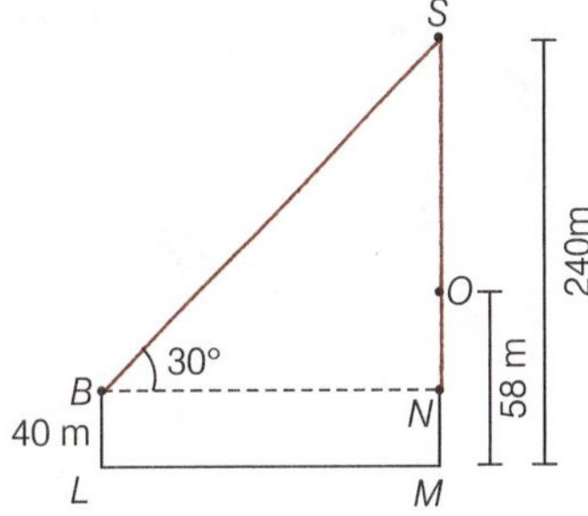

(iii) (a) In ΔAPR,

$$\tan 60° = \frac{PR}{AP}$$

$$\Rightarrow \sqrt{3} = \frac{RQ + PQ}{80\sqrt{3}}$$

$$\Rightarrow \sqrt{3} \times 80\sqrt{3} = RQ + 58$$

$$\Rightarrow 240 = RQ + 58$$

$$\Rightarrow RQ = 240 - 58 = 182 \text{ m}$$

Now, $PR = 182 + 58 = 240$

So, the height of statue excluding base is 182 m, and the height of statue including base is 240 m.

Or

(iii) (b) We have, $MS = 240$ m and $OM = 58$ m

$\therefore \quad OS = MS - OM = 240 - 58 = 182$ m

Also, $BL = 40$ m

$\therefore \quad ON = OM - NM$

$= 58 - 40 \quad [\because NM = BL]$

$= 18$ m

Now, $SN = OS + ON$

$= 182 + 18 = 200$ m

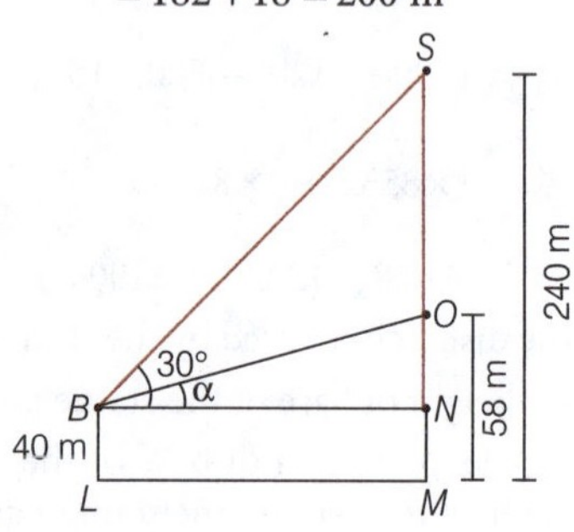

In ΔBNS,

$$\tan 30° = \frac{SN}{BN}$$

$$\Rightarrow \quad \frac{1}{\sqrt{3}} = \frac{200}{BN}$$

$$\Rightarrow \quad BN = 200\sqrt{3} \text{ m}$$

So, the horizontal distance of point B from the statue is $200\sqrt{3}$ m.

Now, in ΔBNO

$$\tan\alpha = \frac{ON}{BN}$$

$$= \frac{18}{200\sqrt{3}}$$

$$\Rightarrow \quad \tan\alpha = \frac{3\sqrt{3}}{100}$$